Adolf Hitler

Adolf Hitler

By JOHN TOLAND

ANCHOR BOOKS
DOUBLEDAY
NEW YORK   LONDON   TORONTO   SYDNEY   AUCKLAND

AN ANCHOR BOOK
PUBLISHED BY DOUBLEDAY
a division of Bantam Doubleday Dell Publishing Group, Inc.
1540 Broadway, New York, New York 10036

ANCHOR BOOKS, DOUBLEDAY, and the portrayal
of an anchor are trademarks of Doubleday, a division of
Bantam Doubleday Dell Publishing Group, Inc.

Adolf Hitler was originally published in hardcover by Doubleday
in 1976. The Anchor Books edition is published
by arrangement with Doubleday.

Grateful acknowledgment is made for permission to quote portions from the following:
The Young Hitler I Knew by August Kubizek. Copyright © 1954 by Paul Popper and
Company. Reprinted by permission of the publisher, Houghton Mifflin Company,
Boston.
Hitler's Secret Conversations, 1941–1944, edited by H. R. Trevor-Roper, translated by
Norman Cameron and R. H. Stevens. Copyright © 1953 by Farrar, Straus and
Young, Inc. Reprinted with the permission of Farrar, Straus & Giroux, Inc., and of
George Weidenfeld & Nicolson Ltd., London.
The Testament of Adolf Hitler: The Hitler-Bormann Documents, February–April 1945,
edited by François Genoud and translated by R. H. Stevens. Copyright © 1959,
Libraire Arthème Fayard; English edition published by Cassell & Co., Ltd. Re-
printed by permission of A. D. Peters & Co., Ltd.
Hitler's Interpreter by Paul Schmidt. Copyright © 1951 by Opera Mundi, Inc. Re-
printed by permission of Opera Mundi, Inc.
Douze ans auprès d'Hitler: Confidences d'une secrétaire particulière d'Hitler, recorded
by Albert Zoller. Copyright © 1949 by Editions René Julliard. Reprinted by permission of Editions René Julliard.

Library of Congress Cataloging-in-Publication Data
Toland, John.
    Adolf Hitler / by John Toland.
        p.   cm.
    Originally published: Garden City, N.Y.: Doubleday, 1976.
    Includes bibliographical references (p.   ) and index.
    1. Hitler, Adolf, 1889–1945.   2. Heads of state—Germany—
Biography.   3. Germany—History—1933–1945.   I. Title.
DD247.H5T56   1992   91-31242
943.086'092—dc20   CIP
[B]
ISBN 0-385-42053-6

Contents

Contents

List of Maps & Tables

Foreword

Adolf Hitler was probably the greatest mover and shaker of the twentieth century. Certainly no other human disrupted so many lives in our times or stirred so much hatred. He also inspired widespread adoration and was the hope and ideal of millions. The passage of more than thirty years since his end has done little to alter the perspective of either enemies or true believers. Today we see the other leaders of his era—Roosevelt, Churchill, Mussolini, Stalin—in a different, more objective light but the image of Hitler has remained essentially the same. To the few who remained his faithful followers he is a hero, a fallen Messiah; to the rest he is still a madman, a political and military bungler, an evil murderer beyond redemption whose successes were reached by criminal means.

As one of those whose life was altered by Hitler, I have done my utmost to subdue my own feelings and to write of him as if he had lived a hundred years ago. I interviewed as many as possible of those who knew Hitler intimately—both worshipers and deriders. Many agreed to talk freely and at length about the unhappy past. Gone was the reluctance of past years to discuss the Führer and his actions for fear their views might be distorted. I conducted more than two hundred and fifty interviews with his adjutants (Puttkamer, Below, Engel, Günsche, Wünsche and Schulze); his secretaries (Traudl Junge and Gerda Christian); his chauffeur (Kempka); his pilot (Baur); his doctors (Giesing and Hasselbach); his favorite warriors (Skorzeny and Rudel); his favorite architects (Speer and Giesler); his first foreign press secretary (Hanfstaengl); his military leaders (Manstein, Milch, Dönitz, Manteuffel and Warlimont); the women he most admired (Leni Riefenstahl, Frau Professor Troost and Helene Hanfstaengl). All but a dozen of these interviews were recorded on tapes which presently are stored in the Library of Congress for safekeeping. All those interviewed whose accounts are included in the book read the passages about themselves and not only made corrections but often added illuminating comments.

Significant new documents, reports and studies have also been utilized to help unravel the mystery of Hitler: the dossiers of the U. S. Army Counter-Intelligence Command, including one agent's interview with Hitler's sister Paula; unpublished documents in the National Archives such as a secret psychiatric report on Hitler in 1918; the unpublished documents from the British Government Archives; the recently discovered Göring-Negrelli correspondence of 1924–25 which sheds new light on Nazi-Fascist relations; the secret speeches of Himmler; and unpublished diaries, notes and memoirs including the revealing recollections of Traudl Junge, Hitler's youngest secretary.

My book has no thesis, and any conclusions to be found in it were reached only during the writing, perhaps the most meaningful being that Hitler was far more complex and contradictory than I had imagined. "The greatest saints," observed one of Graham Greene's characters, "have been men with more than a normal capacity for evil, and the most vicious men have sometimes narrowly evaded sanctity." Deprived of heaven, Adolf Hitler chose hell—if, indeed, he knew the difference between the two. To the end, obsessed by his dream of cleansing Europe of Jews, he remained a Knight of the Hakenkreuz, a warped archangel, a hybrid of Prometheus and Lucifer.

STAB IN THE BACK

1

In mid-October 1918 a hospital train, the sides of its carriages defaced by revolutionary slogans, slowly wended its way through Germany toward the secure eastern marches of the Empire. Among the hundreds of casualties on the train were blinded victims of a recent poison gas attack in Belgium. It had followed a devastating British artillery assault on the night of the thirteenth, one of a relentless series of hammer blows that the German front, retreating, bending but not breaking, had sustained since the battle turned so decisively three months earlier. The 16th Bavarian Reserve Infantry Regiment, which took the brunt of the attack, was dug in on hills and fields, a spectral battleground churned into a morass of craters. The men, physically exhausted, and dispirited as much by ugly rumors of mutinies along the front as by the unceasing Allied attacks, huddled in trenches while British shells tore up the ground around them. The veterans were numbed, the recruits terrified.

Suddenly, thuds mingled with the explosions and a pungent cloud drifted into the trenches. Someone shouted, "Gas!" It was their first experience with mustard gas. To some it smelled sweet, to others acrid; in every case it clung tenaciously to the nostrils. The men slapped on their masks, then hunched, inanimate, against the sides of the trenches. Hours passed. The air inside the masks became dense and stale. One of the recruits, driven half mad by suffocation, wrenched the mask from his face only to gulp in the deadly poison. "It caught him by the throat and flung him back choking, gurgling, suffocating, dying."

It was dawn before the gas began to dissipate and the shelling resumed. The men tore off the masks and gulped in the morning air. "It was still stinking of the stuff," writes one, "and reeked again of high explosives, but to us it was the very breath of heaven." The relief was short-lived. In that cruel and unpredictable pattern calculated to reduce the enemy to madness, gas bombs again mingled with high explosives. Those too slow in putting on their filthy masks keeled over and died as the young recruit had. Those who escaped with their lives were painfully blinded, all but one who still could see faintly. He suggested to the others that they hang on to each other's coattails as he attempted to lead them to safety. Thus they stumbled in goose file, the half blind leading the blind, until they reached a first aid station. Among the men thus rescued from a choking death was a twenty-nine-year-old *Gefreiter* (corporal) named Adolf Hitler.

Still blinded as the train carried him eastward, Hitler was in a state bordering on collapse. Like the other victims, his eyes were swollen, his face puffed up. The voices of these men were ghostlike, without timbre, and they irritably rejected the care of their nurses. They would not allow their inflamed eyes to be treated; they would not eat. In vain the doctors told them that they would soon regain their vision; these men had been deceived too long. They wanted only to lie still and moan and be delivered from pain, even if by death.

This wounded and demoralized corporal who fifteen years later would be the leader of the Reich was not yet aware of the magnitude of Germany's defeat. Four years earlier, as the first great German offensive rolled over Belgian, French and British resistance, Hitler's regiment had first been bloodied in battle in that same area, losing an almost inconceivable eighty per cent of its personnel in less than a week. To the ardent Hitler these losses, far from discouraging, had been proof of the fighting spirit of German troops. He wrote to his Munich landlord, ". . . with pride I can say our regiment handled itself heroically from the very first day on—we lost almost all our officers and our company has only two sergeants now. On the fourth day only 611 were left out of the 3600 men of our regiment."

Many Germans in those early days shared this exultant view of Teutonic heroism. But as the months passed the war degenerated into deadlocked trench warfare, the armies facing each other across a scarred no man's land, clashing as one or the other tried to effect a breakthrough, counting advances in a few miles or even yards with casualties in the millions. The early mood of enthusiasm faded. Defeatism and despair corroded the morale of the men who lived ratlike in their dugouts and trenches. Hunger and misery stalked the homeland as the British blockade cut off the flow of essentials to the German people. As the war extended into its third and then fourth year the soldiers' thoughts turned from victory to survival; they would assail the stupidities of their high command and the futility of further fighting. Hitler was one of those few who scornfully rejected such defeatist talk. Despite repeated acts of heroism he was still a corporal but was not distressed by this lack of recognition. He railed at his comrades, particularly the youthful recruits who brought with them "the poison of the hinterland," and if anyone argued with him he would, according to one comrade, "become furious, and then jam hands into his pockets and pace back and forth with long strides, abusing the pessimists."

And perhaps the pessimists were wrong after all. As 1918 dawned, the Germans, after nearly four years on the defensive, were poised to return to the attack. For the western front was stalemated. On all the other battlefields German arms had conquered. Serbia, Romania and finally Russia had succumbed, the last one as much to revolution as to the German assaults. The peace treaty with the new Soviet regime had put the Germans in command of the vast Ukrainian plain, the breadbasket of Europe. And over a million men released by the collapse of enemy resistance in the East now streamed into France to bring the deadlocked issue of the western front to a decision. The Emperor's Battle—as General Erich Ludendorff, the junior but dominant member of the German high command, called it—was at hand.

Throughout the spring, in four mighty assaults, the Germans forced first the British and then the French to retreat. The British with "backs to the wall" were ordered to fight to the last man. When the final big battle began on July 15 near the city of Rheims both sides were aware that the outcome of the war was at stake. "If my attack on Rheims succeeds," said Ludendorff, "we have won the war." Marshal Foch, commander-in-chief of the Allied forces, concurred. "If the German attack at Rheims succeeds," he was reported to have said, "we have lost the war." The attack failed. No German reserves were left. The Allies on the other hand were fortified not only by fresh American divisions but by supplies and provisions streaming from the United States.

In the German army desertions multiplied. Everywhere there was talk of mutiny and revolt, and when the British launched a surprise attack near Amiens in early August the German lines caved in practically without resistance. The Kaiser's men surrendered en masse at times to a single enemy infantryman. Retreating men shouted to reinforcements coming up to the front, "Strikebreakers!" Yet it was not the end. The Germans retreated but the line held. For every defeatist there still were hundreds of soldiers ready to do their duty. But at home faith was fading. There were numerous strikes and everywhere in the cities radical socialists were talking revolution. To stout spirits like Hitler the secure and unmolested home front, its laggards, its profiteers, its malingerers, its traitors, its Jews who had no love or respect for the German Fatherland, had betrayed the fighting front in its gravest hour. In fact, it was Ludendorff who lost his nerve and pressed the civilian government for an armistice.

Even at this late hour, the ardent spirits like Hitler were convinced that some solution, if not victory, was possible so long as resistance continued. The front had not broken and was retreating in an orderly fashion. It was these profiteers, these malingerers, these Jews who would bring defeat from within.

2

The tragedy to which Hitler was a blinded witness, the collapse of the authority which he held in such unquestioning respect, would eventually open the road for his own astounding rise to power. The world he had known was one ruled by the elite, the descendants of ancient royal houses; high state offices, diplomatic posts, army commissions were all held by men of ancient lineage, aristocrats of superior breeding and education. The war had changed all that. In the trenches men of high and of low births fought side by side; the depleted ranks of noble officers were gradually filled with commoners.

Throughout Europe royalty was clinging to hollow power. From the untitled masses were emerging men like Hitler who would come to wield the substance of power, men of common and often vulgar beginnings, riding the relentless wave of popular revolt against a war which had demanded sacrifices for goals no one could define.

As the train took Hitler to a hospital in the Pomeranian town of Pasewalk, his own pain and despair obliterated any such aspiration, but after several weeks of medical treatment he began to regain his sight. Inflammation of the mucous membrane and swelling of the eyelids had receded; "the piercing in my sockets" began to diminish and "slowly I succeeded in distinguishing the broad outlines of things about me." With sight came an end to depression and the mental instability that had required special treatment from a consulting psychiatrist, Professor Edmund Forster, chief of the Berlin University Nerve Clinic. Little was known about mustard gas and Hitler's inexplicable recovery confirmed Dr. Forster in his diagnosis of the blindness as hysteria. In fact, the patient had experienced the usual symptoms of moderate mustard gas poisoning: burning, swelling, moaning, depression—and recovery in several weeks.

Sight also brought Hitler hope and renewed interest in the events of the day. Berlin itself was in a state of virtual siege as the new Chancellor urged the Kaiser to abdicate so that an armistice could be signed. Hitler had heard stories of rebellion throughout Germany but discounted them as rumor until a delegation of Red German sailors burst into his ward early that November in an attempt to convert the patients to the revolution. Hitler's detestation of Bolshevism was heightened by the fact that three of the leaders were young Jews, none of whom, he was sure, had been at the front. "Now they raised the red rag in the homeland." Indignation was followed by shock. Hitler took to his bed. "I lay there broken with great pains, although I did not let on how I felt; for it was repugnant to me to cry out at a time when you could feel that the collapse was coming." A little later, on November 9, a dignified elderly pastor arrived at Pasewalk hospital to confirm news of the uprisings. Revolution had even broken out in Munich.

The patients were gathered in a little hall and the pastor, so Hitler recalled, "seemed all a-tremble as he informed us that the House of Hohenzollern should no longer bear the German imperial crown; that the Fatherland had become a 'republic.'" As the aged speaker eulogized the services rendered by the Hohenzollerns, he "began to sob gently to himself —in the little hall the deepest dejection settled on all hearts, and I believe not an eye was able to restrain its tears." The pastor went on to say that the war must now be ended, that all was lost and they had to throw themselves upon the mercy of the victorious Allies. To Hitler the revelation was intolerable. "It became impossible for me to sit still one minute more. Again everything went black before my eyes; I tottered and groped my way back to the dormitory, threw myself on my bunk, and dug my burning head into my blankets and pillow."

It was the first time he had wept since standing at his mother's grave eleven years earlier (she had died in agony of cancer), in the churchyard of the Austrian village of Leonding. He had borne the fear of blindness "in dull silence," endured the loss of so many good comrades. "But now I could not help it. Only now did I see how all personal suffering vanished in comparison with the misfortune of the Fatherland." Out of his black despair came a decision. "The great vacillation of my life, whether I should enter politics or remain an architect, came to an end. That night I resolved that, if I recovered my sight, I would enter politics." There was no medical reason for Hitler's second blindness and Dr. Forster was reinforced in his initial conclusion that his patient was definitely "a psychopath with hysterical symptoms." Hitler, however, was convinced that he was permanently blind.

The shame of Germany's surrender on November 11 in the forest of Compiègne overwhelmed him. Life seemed unbearable, but that night, or the next, Hitler was abruptly delivered from his misery, as he lay in despair on his cot, by a "supernatural vision" (perhaps deliberately induced by Dr. Forster).* Like St. Joan, he heard voices summoning him to save

* The possibility that Dr. Forster induced Hitler's hallucination through hypnotic suggestion is given credence by a novel about Hitler and Forster written by the latter's friend, Ernst Weiss, a medical doctor turned playwright and novelist. In this book, *The*

Germany. All at once "a miracle came to pass"—the darkness encompassing Hitler evaporated. He could see again! He solemnly vowed, as promised, that he would "become a politician and devote his energies to carrying out the command he had received."

That night in the lonely ward at Pasewalk the most portentous force
of the twentieth century was born. Politics had come to Hitler, not Hitler
to politics.

Eyewitness, a soldier, "A.H.," arrives at Pasewalk military hospital in 1918 claiming to
have been poisoned by gas. A psychiatrist, the narrator, diagnoses the case as hysterical
blindness and induces an hallucination through hypnosis.

Part 1

I, VISIONARY

Chapter One

DEEP ARE THE ROOTS
1889–1907

1

Hitler rarely talked about his family but to a few confidants he did confess an inability to get along with his father, a dictatorial man. While he revered his mother, a quiet, soft soul, it soon became evident that the former would be the dominating force in his life. Both parents came from the Waldviertel, a rural area of Austria, northwest of Vienna, not far from the present Czechoslovakian border and, according to one member of the family, there was Moravian blood in the line. Hitler was an unusual name for an Austrian and quite possibly it was derived from the Czech names "Hidlar" or "Hidlarček." Variants of these names had appeared in the Waldviertel since 1430 and changed from Hydler to Hytler to Hidler. In 1650 a direct ancestor of Adolf Hitler on his mother's side was called Georg Hiedler. His descendants occasionally spelled their name "Hüttler" and "Hitler." In those days spelling was as unimportant and erratic as in Shakespearian England.

The Waldviertel was a district of modest beauty, hilly and wooded, its graceful slopes covered with orderly forests, broken occasionally by fields cleared by generations of hard-working, frugal peasants. Hitler's father was born on June 7, 1837, in the village of Strones. His mother was a forty-two-year-old unmarried woman, Maria Anna Schicklgruber. Strones was too small to be a parish and so the baby was registered in Döllersheim as Aloys Schicklgruber, "Illegitimate." The space for the father's name was blank, generating a mystery that remains unsolved: he probably was a man from the neighborhood. There is the slight possibility that Hitler's grandfather was a wealthy Jew named Frankenberger or Frankenreither; that Maria Anna had been a domestic in this Jewish household at Graz and the young son had got her pregnant.

When Alois (as his name would be spelled henceforth) was almost five, Johann Georg Hiedler, an itinerant millworker from nearby Spital, married Maria. But her little son continued to have a blighted family life; she died five years later and the stepfather apparently resumed his drifting. Alois consequently was brought up by Hiedler's brother Johann Nepomuk at house number 36 in Spital. This farmhouse and the one next door would play an important role in the life of young Adolf Hitler, for here, in this isolated village, he spent half a dozen pleasant summer holidays.

The situation in Spital became intolerable for Alois and at thirteen he "laced his tiny knapsack and ran away from his home." This is the touching, if accurate, scene later painted by his son Adolf in *Mein Kampf*. "A desperate decision to take to the road with only three gulden for travel money, and plunge into the unknown." He worked his way to the mecca of venturesome youth, Vienna, where he became apprenticed to a shoemaker, but five years later, after learning this trade, he decided to become "something better" so enlisted in the frontier guards. This made him a civil servant, a step above the priesthood. He studied diligently, passed a special examination, and by the time he was twenty-four was promoted to a supervisory rank, an exceptional honor for a boy from the Waldviertel. Promotions came regularly to the ambitious Alois and in 1875 he was made a full inspector of customs at Braunau on the Inn River, just across from Germany.

No one was prouder of Alois' success than the man who had brought him up, Johann Nepomuk Hiedler. No Hiedler had ever risen so high. There was no son to carry on the name of Hiedler and on a late spring day in 1876 Johann decided to do something about it.* On June 6 his son-in-law and two other relatives made the short trip to the town of Weitra where they falsely testified before the local notary that "Hiedler's brother" —they spelled his name "Hitler"—"had several times stated in their presence and before his death [in 1857] as his last and unchangeable will" that he had fathered an illegitimate son, Alois, and wanted him made his legitimate son and heir.

Perhaps the change of name from Hiedler to Hitler was carelessness, but more likely it was a cunning peasant trick to becloud the issue. The next day Johann Nepomuk Hiedler traveled with his three relatives to Döllersheim where the original birth record of Alois was registered. After

* He may have had other motives. There was village gossip that Alois was his natural son. It has also been suggested by Franz Jetzinger, author of a generally accurate book on Hitler's youth, that Hiedler may have wanted to legitimize Alois as insurance for the young man's career, "a strong motive if his father had been a Jew."

examining the document signed by the three witnesses, the elderly parish priest affirmed from the parish marriage book that a man named Georg Hiedler had indeed married a girl named Schicklgruber in 1842. And so he agreed to alter the birth register. But he must have been reluctant or leery. Although he changed the "illegitimate" to "legitimate" and crossed out "Schicklgruber" in the space for the child's name, he failed to write in another name. In the last space, in extremely cramped writing, he penned: "It is confirmed by the undersigned that Georg Hitler whose name is here entered as Father, being well known to the undersigned, did accept paternity of the child Aloys, according to the statement of the child's mother, and did desire his name to be entered in the register of baptisms of this parish." He himself signed the names of the three witnesses and each, in turn, made his mark, a cross.

The amendments on the register were neither dated nor signed. The parish priest had reason to be devious. Not only had he written in the father's name as "Hitler," instead of the "Hiedler" appearing in the marriage book, but he must have known the entire procedure was illegal on two counts: a deceased man could not be recognized as a father except by legal proceedings; moreover, the mother had to corroborate the facts.

There was yet another ambiguity in the matter—the willingness of Alois Schicklgruber to accept the new name. Illegitimacy had been of little embarrassment to him; in lower Austria it was common and in some remote districts ran as high as forty per cent. Children were the lifeblood of any farm community and every healthy worker was welcome. It could even have been more of an embarrassment to change his name once he had achieved a measure of success as a Schicklgruber.

Whatever the motivation, Alois was somehow induced by Johann Nepomuk Hiedler to change his name. (The talk in the village was that he had been persuaded by a promise that the old man would change his will and this gossip was somewhat confirmed six months after Hiedler's death when Alois bought a farm for five thousand florins.) In any case his decision to assume the name of Hitler was momentous. It is difficult to imagine seventy million Germans shouting in all seriousness. "Heil Schicklgruber!"

To the girls of Spital, Alois must have cut a dashing figure in his uniform, close-clipped military haircut, bushy eyebrows, sweeping *Kaiserbart* (handlebar) mustache, and two fiercely jutting tufts of hair on either side of a clean-shaven chin. He too had an eye for the girls. Like his legal father, he had already sired an illegitimate daughter. Nor had marriage to the daughter of an inspector in the imperial tobacco monopoly been much of a restraint to amorous adventures. After all, she was sickly and fourteen years his senior.

One of the most attractive Spital girls was Johann Nepomuk Hiedler's granddaughter, Klara Pölzl, a sweet-faced, quiet sixteen-year-old.

She was slim, almost as tall as stocky Alois, with abundant dark brown hair and even features. Whether it was love at first sight or simply a desire to provide his ailing wife with a willing housemaid, he managed to persuade the family to let Klara follow him to Braunau. She was installed with the Hitlers in an inn where Alois was already carrying on an affair with a kitchen maid, Franziska (Fanni to the customers) Matzelsberger.

This situation was too much for Frau Hitler. She left Alois and was granted a legal separation. Now it was Fanni's turn to enter the Hitler ménage and she established herself more as common-law wife than mistress. She was only too aware of how tempting a pretty maid could be to the susceptible Alois and one of her first acts was to get rid of Klara. Two years later, in 1882, Fanni gave birth to a boy, like his father, illegitimate.

The following year Hitler's estranged wife died of consumption and he married Fanni. The ceremony was timely. Within two months a second child, Angela, was born. At last Alois had a legitimate child, even if conceived illegitimately. He also accepted legal responsibility for the boy, who became Alois Hitler, Jr. Fanni, restored to respectability, was no happier since Alois, Sr., once more showed signs of wandering affections. Like her predecessor, she contracted a serious lung ailment and was forced to leave Braunau for the country air of a nearby village. Since this left Alois alone on the top floor of the Pommer Inn with two infants, it was only logical for him to seek help from his attractive niece. Once more the compliant Klara was installed in the Pommer Inn and this time she became housemaid, nursemaid and mistress. Adolf Hitler's mother-to-be was such a goodhearted girl she also did her best to help restore Fanni to health, visiting her frequently. Curiously, Fanni welcomed the ministrations of her rival.

In the summer of 1884 the wretched life of Fanni ended. Predictably, the next lady in waiting in the Hitler household was already pregnant. Alois wanted to marry Klara; she could care for his two children and he was genuinely fond of her. But the Church forbade their marriage since, by the fake legitimization, his own father and Klara's grandfather were brothers. Alois appealed to the local priests for a special dispensation from Rome. It was granted within the month, undoubtedly because of Klara's pregnancy. And at the first possible moment, on the morning of January 7, 1885, Alois and his niece were married at the Pommer Inn. Present were the two children, Alois, Jr., and Angela, and three witnesses: Klara's younger sister, Johanna, and two customs men. Their new maid had taken care of all the arrangements; in her enthusiasm she overheated the parlor and throughout the ceremony Alois teased her for it. There was no honeymoon and after a simple meal Alois returned to the customs station. Before noon, as Klara later wistfully recalled, "my husband was already on duty again."

Remarkably, the untidy private life of Alois had never interfered with his professional duties. He continued to be an efficient and honest public servant, esteemed by colleagues and superiors alike. He held himself in the same high esteem although his local reputation was not good; extramarital affairs in such a small town inevitably became common gossip. Among the ugly rumors was one that he had bought a coffin for his first wife while she was still alive.

Klara flourished in her new role as *Hausfrau*. She was a model housekeeper and completely devoted to Alois, Jr., and Angela, treating them as if they were her own. Four months after the ceremony she gave birth to a son, and within two years to a girl and another boy. The youngest died within a few days of birth and shortly afterward both of the older children contracted diphtheria and succumbed. The tragedy was hard for Klara to bear. Fortunately she had an outlet for her affections in Alois, Jr., and Angela, but relations with her husband were strained. From the first she had regarded Alois as a superior being and the road from house-maid to mistress to wife was so complicated for a simple girl from Spital that she still addressed her husband as "uncle."

The death of three children apparently affected her regular rate of pregnancy and it was not until April 20, 1889,* that the fourth child was born. He was one quarter Hitler, one quarter Schicklgruber, one quarter Pölzl, and one quarter uncertain. In the baptismal registry he was entered as "Adolfus Hitler." Later Klara claimed that Adolf was a sickly baby and that she always lived in fear of also losing him, but their housemaid remembered Adolf as a "very healthy, lively child who developed very well."

In either case, Frau Hitler lavished love and attention on her boy and, as a result, probably spoiled him. Life went on placidly at the Pommer Inn. The father spent more time with his cronies and his hobby, beekeeping, than he did at home, but he apparently had ceased his sexual wanderings—or at least was becoming more discreet. He was remembered pleasantly by the housemaid, who described him as a "very strict but comfortable man" who treated the help with consideration. One day, for instance, this exalted official actually took off his boots rather than soil the freshly cleaned floor. But to his new customs supervisor Alois Hitler was an unsympathetic figure. "He was very strict, exacting, and pedantic, a most unapproachable person. . . . He took pride in his uniform, and always had himself photographed in it."

When Adolf was three years and four months old his father was promoted and the family moved to Passau, a good-sized city down the Inn on the German side of the river, where the customs inspection office was located. Living in a German city and playing with German children made a lasting mark on the youngster. The distinctive lower Bavarian dialect,

* Crown Prince Rudolf had recently committed suicide at Mayerling.

for instance, would remain his mother tongue. It reminded him, he recalled, "of the days of my childhood."

Frau Hitler had not became pregnant again and it has been suggested that in overcompensating the "sickly" child she was still nursing him. It was not until Adolf was almost five that the next child, Edmund, was born. At last Adolf was freed from his mother's constant surveillance, and almost complete freedom came shortly after when his father was reassigned to Linz. The family, apparently because of the newborn baby, stayed in Passau and the five-year-old Adolf now could play endlessly with the German children or wander at will for hours, his own master.

For a year he reveled in this carefree life. Then in the spring of 1895 the family was reunited in Hafeld, a small farm community some thirty miles southwest of Linz. They lived in a farmhouse situated on nine acres of gently rolling fields. The property established the Hitlers near the top of local society. A month later the six-year-old Adolf was further separated from his possessive mother by entrance into a small *Volksschule* (primary school) several miles away at Fischlam. The regimentation of education was reinforced within a few weeks by rigorous supervision at the hands of his father, who had just retired, after forty years of service, to a life of modest comfort as a minor country gentleman.

It was a pretty house on a slight rise, almost completely hidden by an orchard of fruit and walnut trees and flanked by a brook, artificially straight, churning with clean water. Despite the new restrictions, Adolf must have led a happy life in such pleasant surroundings, for there was no lack of neighboring children for companionship.

It took Adolf and his half sister Angela more than an hour to walk to school, a rigorous trip for a small boy. The building, "shabby and primitive," was separated into two classrooms, one for the boys and one for the girls. The Hitler children made a good impression on the master, who remembered Adolf as "mentally very much alert, obedient, but lively." Moreover both children "kept the contents of their school bags in exemplary order."

"It was at this time that the first ideals took shape in my breast," Hitler wrote in *Mein Kampf*, an account with the usual exaggeration of an autobiography. "All my playing about in the open, the long walk to school, and particularly my association with extremely 'husky' boys, which sometimes caused my mother bitter anguish, made me the very opposite of a stay-at-home." Even at this age he could express himself vocally and before long he became "a little ringleader."

In the months to come his position at home became increasingly difficult. Retirement was proving to be a drudgery for Alois since he had no talent for farming. To add to the aggravation, another child, Paula, was born in the late fall of 1896. With five children, including a crying infant, in the cramped quarters, Alois probably drank more heavily than usual and certainly became quarrelsome and irritable. His main target was Alois, Jr. For some time the father, who demanded absolute obedience, had been at odds with the son, who refused to give it. Later, Alois, Jr., complained bitterly that his father frequently beat him "unmercifully with a hippopotamus whip," but in the Austria of those days severe beatings of children were not uncommon, being considered good for the soul. Once the boy skipped school for three days to finish building a toy boat. The father, who had encouraged such hobbies, whipped young Alois, then held him "against a tree by the back of his neck" until he lost consciousness. There were also stories that Adolf was whipped, if not so often, and that the master of the house "often beat the dog until the dog would cringe and wet the floor." The violence, according to Alois, Jr., extended even to the docile Klara and, if true, must have made an indelible impression on Adolf.

As for young Alois, life at Hafeld had become unbearable. He felt not only mistreated by his father but neglected by his stepmother and out of this deprivation came a deep resentment of his half brother Adolf. "He was imperious and quick to anger from childhood onward and would not listen to anyone," he told an interviewer in 1948, still resentful after fifty-two years. "My stepmother always took his part. He would get the craziest notions and get away with it. If he didn't have his way he got very angry. . . . He had no friends, took to no one and could be very heartless. He could fly into a rage over any triviality."

Feeling abused and rejected, Alois, Jr., followed in the footsteps of Alois, Sr., and ran away from home at the age of fourteen, never to return in his father's lifetime. His vengeful elder retaliated by reducing the boy's inheritance to the legal minimum. The departure of his half brother left Adolf the principal butt of their father's frustrations. The elder Hitler piled additional chores on the youngster's back and carped at him constantly for failing to come up to expectations. A few months later the disgruntled country gentleman sold the burdensome farm for the more enjoyable town life of Lambach half a dozen miles away. For six months the family lived on the third floor of the Gasthof Leingartner just opposite the imposing Benedictine monastery. Freed from farm chores, Adolf's existence also became more palatable and he did well at the modern school. His marks were excellent and in the last quarter of the school year 1897–98 he had twelve 1's, the highest grade. He also had a good natural singing voice and on certain afternoons attended the choir school at the monastery, under the tutelage of Padre Bernhard Gröner. On the way he had to pass by a stone arch in which was carved the monastery's coat of arms—its most prominent feature a swastika.

At this time he became "intoxicated" with that "solemn splendor of brilliant church festivals." The abbot became his idol and he hoped to join the Church himself, one aspiration that curiously met his anti-clerical

HITLER'S FAMILY TREE

Paternal Grandfather UNKNOWN ———— MARIA ANNA SCHICKLGRUBER,
could be Johann Nepomuk Hiedler;   b. Strones 4/15/1795
his brother, Johann Georg Hiedler;   m. in Döllersheim to
or a Jew from Graz named   Johann Georg Hiedler
Frankenberger or Frankenreither.   5/10/1842

FRANZISKA ———— ALOIS SCHICKLGRUBER ————
MATZELSBERGER   b. Strones 6/7/1837
     (illegitimate; legitimized in 1876
     as Alois Hitler)
     d. Leonding 1/3/1903

ALOIS   ANGELA ———— LEO   GUSTAV
HITLER, JR.   HITLER   RAUBAL   HITLER
(illegitimate)   b. 5/17/1885
     d. 12/8/1887.

WILLIAM   ANGELA   LEO
PATRICK   ("GELI")   RAUBAL, JR.
HITLER   RAUBAL

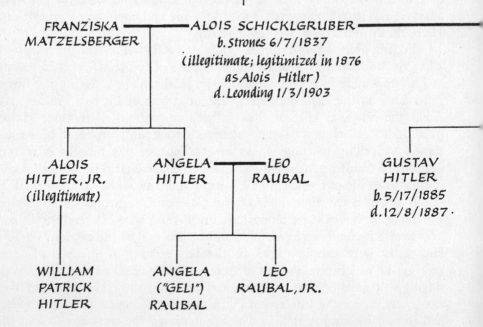

JOHÄNN BAPTIST PÖLZL —————— JOHANNA HIEDLER
b. Spital;   b. Spital 1/19/1830
baptized Spital 5/25/1828   d. Spital 2/8/1906
m. Spital 9/5/1848
d. Spital 1/9/1902

(third marriage)   KLARA
                              PÖLZL
                  b. Spital 8/12/1860
            m. Braunau am Inn 1/7/1885
                  d. 12/21/1907

IDA	OTTO	ADOLF	EDMUND	PAULA
HITLER	HITLER	HITLER	HITLER	HITLER
b. 9/23/1886	b. Autumn 1887	b. 4/20/1889	b. 3/24/1894	b. 1/21/1896
d. 1/2/1888	d. several	d. Berlin	d. 2/2/1900	d. 1950s
	days	4/30/1945		
	later			

father's approval. Adolf later told Frau Helene Hanfstaengl that "as a small boy it was his most ardent wish to become a priest. He often borrowed the large kitchen apron of the maid, draped it about his shoulders in vestment fashion, climbed on a kitchen chair and delivered long and fervent sermons." His devout mother would certainly have welcomed such a career, but Adolf's interest in things priestly ended as quickly as it began. Before long he was caught smoking.

The family was now living in pleasant quarters on the second floor of a spacious house connected to a mill. It was an ideal headquarters for the venturesome boy, providing him with a variety of arenas for his favorite game of cowboys and Indians. To the couple who owned the mill, Adolf was a "little rogue," rarely at home but always "where something was happening," usually as the leader in raids on pear trees and other pranks. When the "wild boy" did come home his trousers were torn, his hands and legs scratched and bruised from his adventures.

Lambach proved to be as dull as the farm to the restless Alois and in 1899 he bought a snug house across from the cemetery wall in Leonding, a village on the outskirts of Linz. The house was no larger than usual but the location was far more to Alois' taste. Leonding had 3000 inhabitants and took on an air of civilization from its proximity to Linz with the latter's theaters, opera house and imposing government buildings. The local companionship was more congenial.

With Alois, Jr., gone from home, it was Adolf who bore the brunt of the father's discipline. It was he, recalled Paula Hitler, "who challenged my father to extreme harshness and who got his sound thrashing every day. He was a scrubby little rogue, and all attempts of his father to thrash him for his rudeness and to cause him to love the profession of an official of the state were in vain. How often on the other hand did my mother caress him and try to obtain with her kindness, where the father could not succeed with harshness!"

In a show of rebellion Adolf decided to run away from home. Somehow Alois learned of these plans and locked the boy upstairs. During the night Adolf tried to squeeze through the barred window. He couldn't quite make it, so took off his clothes. As he was wriggling his way to freedom, he heard his father's footsteps on the stairs and hastily withdrew, draping his nakedness with a tablecloth. This time Alois did not punish with a whipping. Instead he burst into laughter and shouted to Klara to come up and look at the "toga boy." The ridicule hurt Adolf more than any switch and it took him, he confided to Frau Hanfstaengl, "a long time to get over the episode."

Years later he told one of his secretaries that he had read in an adventure novel that it was a proof of courage to show no pain. "I then resolved never again to cry when my father whipped me. A few days later I had the opportunity of putting my will to the test. My mother, frightened, took refuge in front of the door. As for me, I counted silently the blows of the stick which lashed my rear end." From that day on, so Hitler claimed, his father never touched him again.

Even at the age of eleven there was something in the thin-faced youngster's look that set him apart from his fellows. In the class picture that year of the Leonding Volksschule he sits in the center of the top row, several inches taller than his comrades, chin up, arms crossed. With his glint of rebellion, his cocky assuredness, he is patently the top boy. He was breezing through school with little effort and had already discovered another talent. He could draw. A picture of Wallenstein dated March 26 of that year, 1900, indicates a budding talent as an artist. In the classroom he would spend some of his study time surreptitiously sketching. A boy named Weinberger once watched in wonder as Hitler recreated from memory the castle of Schaumberg.

At recess and after school he remained the leader. He had already resided in more places than most of his comrades would visit in their lives and they saw him as a man of the world. In play he was inspired by the adventure stories he was devouring by James Fenimore Cooper and his German imitator, Karl May. The latter had never been to America but his tales of noble Indians and hardy cowboys were accepted as gospel by generations of German and Austrian boys. To Adolf the adventures of old Shatterhand and his comrades were almost an obsession. He tirelessly led his schoolmates into violent re-enactments and when the enthusiasm of the older boys flagged he recruited younger ones and even, on occasion, girls.

It was about this time that he found more significant stimulation in two illustrated magazines devoted to the Franco-Prussian War of 1870. He pored over the words and pictures. "It was not long before the great historic struggle had become my greatest inner experience," he claimed in *Mein Kampf*, which occasionally twisted the truth for political purposes. "From then on I became more and more enthusiastic about everything that was in any way connected with war or, for that matter, with soldiering."

The Boer War, which broke out that same year, also inspired him with Germanic patriotism as well as providing play material. For hours he led his Boers into "hot battle" against those unfortunate ones who had to portray the English. Often he would become so involved that he kept his father waiting an hour or so for the tobacco he was supposed to pick up at the store. The result, recalled Weinberger, was a "hot" reception at home. These adventurous days perhaps helped shape the course of Hitler's career. "Woods and meadows," he once wrote, "were the battlefields on which the 'conflicts' which exist everywhere in life were decided."

That year six-year-old Edmund died of measles. Four deaths were almost too much for Klara to bear, and—with Alois, Jr., gone—there was only one son to carry on the family name. Coming as Adolf was completing his last year at the Volksschule, this latest domestic tragedy height-

ened the conflict between father and son. Alois wanted the boy to follow
his example and tried to inspire him with stories from his own life as a
civil servant. His son yearned to be an artist but for the time kept this revolutionary plan to himself and without argument accepted his father's
plan for the next step in his education. He was eligible to enroll either in a
Gymnasium, which placed emphasis on classical education and prepared a
student for university, or in a *Realschule*, which was more technical and
scientific. The practical Alois decided on the latter and Adolf acquiesced
since such a school also had a course in drawing.

The nearest Realschule was in Linz and on September 17, 1900, he
set out for the first time, green rucksack on his back. It was a long trip,
more than three miles, and halfway there he could see the city lying below
him flanked by the Danube River. It must have been a magic yet formidable sight to a boy raised in villages and small towns. There, on a rise, jut-
ted the famous Kürnberg Castle where the "Nibelungenlieder" were said
to have been composed; below stretched a forest of church spires and clus-
ters of impressive buildings. His road wound down a steep hill to the heart
of the city and the Realschule, a gloomy four-story building on a narrow
street. Utilitarian and forbidding, it looked more like an office building
than a school.

From the beginning Adolf did poorly. No longer the leader, the
brightest, the most talented, he was overwhelmed by his surroundings.
The other students tended to look down on boys from a country suburb;
and the personal interest and attention he had received from teachers in
the smaller schools were not to be found in such a large institution. In
that year's class picture he again was perched on the top row but gone was
the cocky Adolf; in his place sat a lost, forlorn youngster.

Retreating into his shell, he showed increasing lack of interest in
schoolwork. "I thought that once my father saw how little progress I was
making at the Realschule, he would let me devote myself to my dream,
whether he liked it or not." This explanation in *Mein Kampf* could be either an excuse or a reason for his failure to be promoted because of
deficiencies in mathematics and natural history. His detractors claim his
failure was due to inherent laziness but it was just as likely a form of revenge against his father, some emotional problem, or simply unwillingness
to tackle uncongenial subjects.

The next year, however, Adolf changed tactics and showed a marked
improvement in the classroom. Older than his mates, he once more became the leader. "We all liked him, at desk and at play," said Josef
Keplinger. "He had 'guts.' He wasn't a hothead but really more amenable
than a good many. He exhibited two extremes of character which are not
often seen in unison, he was a *quiet* fanatic."

After school the boys, under the leadership of Adolf, who had learned
to throw a lasso, played cowboys and Indians down by the Danube
meadows. Hitler also held sway at recess, lecturing his group on the Boer

War and passing out sketches he made of gallant Boers. He even talked of enlisting in their army. The war helped arouse in young Hitler a yearning for German nationalism, a feeling shared by most of the boys. "Bismarck was for us a national hero," recalled Keplinger. "The Bismarck song and lots more German hymns and songs of the same character, were forbidden to be sung.* It was a crime even to possess a sketch of Bismarck. Although privately our teachers felt well enough that we boys were in the right, they had to punish us severely for singing these songs and brandishing our German loyalties."

For some reason Adolf took his Germanism far more seriously than the others, perhaps as a rebellion against his father, who was a stout advocate of the Habsburg regime. Once Keplinger accompanied him part of the way home, up the steep Kapuzinerstrasse. At the top of the hill Hitler stopped before a small chapel. "You are not a *Germane* [old German]," he bluntly told Keplinger. "You have dark hair and dark eyes." His own eyes, he noted proudly, were blue and his hair (at that time, according to Keplinger) was light brown.

He was already entranced with the heroic figures of German mythology and at the age of twelve attended his first Wagnerian opera, *Lohengrin*, at the Linz Opera House. He was "captivated at once" as much by the Germanic feelings it aroused in him as by the music. Inspirational words—such as those of King Henry to his knights—wakened in him the primal urge of race and nationalism:

> *Let the Reich's enemy now appear.*
> *We're well prepared to see him near.*
> *From his Eastern desert plain*
> *He'll never dare to stir again!*
> *The German sword for German land!*
> *Thus will the Reich in vigor stand!*

This time he finished the school year successfully, passing all subjects and receiving "good" and "very satisfactory" in conduct and diligence. But almost from the beginning of his Second Form he again began slipping; once more mathematics was too much for him and he dropped to a "variable" in diligence. Then, near the end of Christmas vacation, crisis at school was overshadowed by a major family disaster.

On January 3, 1903, Alois left home for his morning visit to the Gasthaus Stiefler. No sooner had he seated himself at the table for regular patrons than he remarked that he wasn't feeling very well. Moments later he died—of pleural hemorrhage.

He was buried two days later in the church cemetery in sight of the Hitler house. On the gravestone was attached an oblong picture of the for-

---

* The Austrian and German anthems had the same music by Haydn and the Pan-Germans would rebelliously sing the lyrics of "Deutschland über Alles." They would also greet each other in secret with the German "*Heil!*"

mer customs official, eyes fixed determinedly ahead. "The sharp word that fell occasionally from his lips could not belie the warm heart that beat beneath the rough exterior," read the commendatory obituary notice in the Linz *Tagespost*. "At all times an energetic champion of law and order and universally well informed, he was able to pronounce authoritatively on any matter that came to his notice."

2

Contrary to popular belief, Alois did not bequeath his family a life of penury. At the time of his death he was receiving a pension of 2420 kronen, a sum considerably more substantial than that received, for example, by the principal of a Volksschule. The widow was granted half of this amount as well as a lump sum equivalent to a quarter of one year's pension. In addition, each child would receive 240 kronen annually "until its 24th birthday or until it becomes self-supporting, whichever shall be the earlier."

The remarkable change in the little house was the absence of tension. Gone was the authoritarian shadow cast by Alois. Adolf, almost fourteen, was the man of the family. Klara attempted to carry out the wishes of her husband concerning the boy, but her only weapon was entreaty. Needless to say, this was no deterrent to Adolf's dream; whenever anyone asked what he was going to be, the answer was invariably, "A great artist."

Even the gentle influence of his mother was diminished at the beginning of the spring term when Adolf was permitted to room in Linz so that he wouldn't have to endure the long daily trip to school. He was installed in the home of an elderly lady, Frau Sekira, with five other schoolboys. Here he became known for his reserve, always using the formal *Sie*, not only with the landlady but with his peers. While this change of locale did little to improve his low standing in school, it did give him more time for drawing and reading. According to Frau Sekira, he used an inordinate amount of candles for night work. Once she found him bent over a map which he was decorating with colored pencils. "Why, Adolf, what on earth do you suppose you are doing?" she asked. The curt answer was: "Studying maps."

The desultory school year ended with a failure in mathematics and Frau Hitler was informed that her son would again have to repeat a year unless he passed a special examination in the fall. This cast only momentary gloom on the household, for that summer they were all invited to Spital for a vacation. With two large, old-fashioned trunks filled with clothes and dishes, the Hitlers set off by train for the country. They were met in Weitra by Klara's brother-in-law, Anton Schmidt, who drove them to the tiny settlement of Spital in his oxcart. It was a pleasant summer. Klara found companionship and sympathy in her family, and Adolf, who contrived to avoid work in the fields, would occasionally play with the

Schmidt children. Once he made them a large dragon kite "with a long colorful tail from different colored paper" which "rose beautifully in the air." But more often he spent his time reading and drawing. The last two pursuits already had marked him as a peculiar youngster; he preferred living in his own dream world. When it rained Adolf was forced to stay in the children's room. "On such occasions," recalled Maria Schmidt, "he often paced up and down or drew or painted and was very angry if he was interrupted. He pushed me out of the room and if I cried outside, he tried to get his mother to give me some tea or something else. We often teased Adolf Hitler and threw something against the window when he was inside, whereupon he quickly jumped out and chased us."

Shortly after the return to Leonding came another change in the family. Angela, "a jolly person who enjoyed life and loved to laugh," married a Linz tax official, Leo Raubal. Adolf intensely disliked Leo and later claimed he drank too much and gambled; but the youngster probably objected more to the fact that his new brother-in-law, a civil servant, heartily disapproved of art as a profession.

Adolf had succeeded in passing his make-up exam and was now involved in the demanding work of the Third Form. His most difficult subject was French, which he would condemn years later as a "complete waste of time." Professor Hümer, the French teacher, had mixed feelings about young Adolf. "He had definite talent, though in a narrow field," he recalled. "But he lacked self-discipline, being notoriously cantankerous, wilful, arrogant and irascible. He had obvious difficulty in fitting in at school. Moreover, he was lazy; otherwise, with his gifts, he would have done much better. In freehand sketching his style was fluent and he did well in scientific subjects. But his enthusiasm for hard work evaporated all too quickly." Dr. Hümer had more than a passing interest in Adolf since he also taught him German and was the class adviser. "He reacted with ill-concealed hostility to advice or reproof; at the same time, he demanded of his fellow-pupils their unqualified subservience, fancying himself in the role of leader, at the same time indulging in many a less innocuous prank of a kind not uncommon amongst immature youths." There was something about the "gaunt, pale-faced youth" that appealed to Hümer, and he did what he could to guide him. But such efforts were fruitless. Young as he was, Adolf had grown set and stubborn in his ways, withdrawing whenever anyone attempted to pry into his private world.

The history professor—Leopold Pötsch—did manage to make an impression on the secretive youngster. Adolf was fascinated by his lectures on the ancient Teutons, which were illustrated by colored slides. "Even today," Hitler wrote in *Mein Kampf*, "I think back with gentle emotion on this gray-haired man, who by the fire of his narratives, sometimes made us forget the present; who, as if by enchantment, carried us into past times and, out of the millennial veils of mist, molded dry historical memories into living reality. On such occasions we sat there, often aflame with enthusiasm, and sometimes even moved to tears."

Outside of this class, however, Adolf was more often moved by tedium and by the spring of 1904 school had become a dull routine. That May he was confirmed on Whitsunday at the Linz Cathedral. This too was a bore to the young artist. Of all the boys Emmanuel Lugert had sponsored "none was so sulky and surly as Adolf Hitler. I had almost to drag the words out of him. . . . It was almost as though the whole business, the whole confirmation was repugnant to him, as though he only went through with it with the greatest reluctance." As soon as the confirmation party got back to Leonding, Adolf ran off to his playmates. "And then," recalled Frau Lugert, "they started charging around the house, playing at Red Indians—a fearful row!"

That year Adolf failed in French. In the autumn his make-up exam was given a passing mark but only on condition that he not return to the Linz school for the Final Form. The nearest Realschule was some twenty-five miles away in Steyr. Once again Adolf would be forced to live away from home. Frau Hitler and the fifteen-year-old journeyed to Steyr where she found a little room for him at the home of the Cichini family. From the beginning Adolf was unhappy. He detested the new town and the view from his room was sinister. "I often used to practice shooting rats from the window." Adolf spent more time shooting rats, reading and drawing than on schoolwork. As a result his grades for the first semester suffered. While he received an "excellent" in gymnastics and "good" in freehand drawing, he was only "adequate" in two favorite subjects, history and geography, and failed mathematics and German. He would go to ridiculous lengths to avoid schoolwork. Upon arriving in class one morning with a huge scarf tied around his neck, he pretended to have lost his voice and got himself sent home.*

* That spring, while visiting in a nearby town, he wrote a revealing poem in a guest book. Four words cannot be deciphered.

> 1. There the people sit in an airy house
>   Refreshing themselves with wine and beer
>   And eat and drink riotously
>   (   ) out then on all fours.
> 2. There they climb up high mountains
>   (   ) with proud faces
>   And tumble down in somersault fashion
>   And cannot find their equilibrium.
> 3. Then they arrive sadly at home
>   And then are forgotten the hours
>   Then comes (   ) his wife (poor?) man
>   And cures his wounds with a beating.

The poem was illustrated by the sketch of a smallish man being beaten with a large stick by a woman with huge breasts. The sketch and poem are remarkable coming from a boy just turned sixteen; it is equally remarkable that he could make such a bizarre entry in a guest book.

Despite all this, his marks gradually improved and he was informed he could graduate if he returned in the fall for a special examination. Adolf brought this relatively good news to his mother on a sultry day in July 1905. She had sold the farm at Leonding, scene of so much turmoil and unhappiness, and now lived in a rented flat in a dour stone-faced building at Humboldtstrasse 31 in the middle of Linz. The year away from his mother's protective care had brought a marked change in Adolf's appearance. He was no longer a boy but a youth with unruly hair, the rudiments of a mustache and the dreamy expression of a romantic young bohemian. One of his classmates in Steyr, named Sturmberger, caught all of this in a pen-and-ink drawing that could have been entitled "Portrait of the Artist as a Young Man."

He was greeted as a hero by the adoring Klara, and mother and son resumed their warm relationship. Shortly they left with Paula for another summer in Spital. Here the youth was stricken by a lung infection (the family had a history of respiratory diseases). This illness brought mother and son even closer together and the summer, despite its problems, must have been a pleasant change for both of them after Adolf's exile in Steyr.

By the time the Hitlers left the country, the youth was well enough to return to Steyr for his make-up examination on September 16. He passed; and that night he and several comrades celebrated with a secret wine party, which left him dead drunk. "I've completely forgotten what happened during the night." He only remembered being wakened at dawn on the highway by a milkwoman. Never again would he suffer such humiliation. It was the first and last time he got drunk.

Despite the certificate, Hitler could not face his *Abitur*, the final examination for a diploma; in fact, the mere thought of additional schooling at an *Oberrealschule* or technical institute was repugnant. Using his lung condition as an excuse—"suddenly an illness came to my help"—he persuaded Klara to let him discontinue his studies. Detractors later charged that Hitler had lied about his ill-health in *Mein Kampf*, but Paula testified that her brother did suffer a hemorrhage; a boyhood friend remembered that "he was plagued by coughs and nasty catarrhs, especially on damp, foggy days," and a neighbor testified that he was "in poor health and had to leave his studies because of a lung problem—as a result of which he was spitting blood."

With no father and no school to deter him, the sixteen-year-old was free to drift, his own master, a despiser of authority. It was an escapist existence. Adolf read voraciously, filled sketchbooks with drawings, went to museums, the opera and the waxworks, once saw a movie near the railroad station that shocked his moral sense ("What a horror of a film!"). No longer did he seek out companionship; no longer was he the leader of childhood games. He wandered the streets of Linz, solitary but not lonesome—his mind churning with dreams of the future. The company of others became tedious. Late in the fall of 1905 he finally met someone he could tolerate. August Kubizek, son of an upholsterer, also had a dream: he would be a world-famous musician. Already he could play the violin, viola, trumpet and trombone and was studying musical theory at Professor Dessauer's School of Music. One evening the two young men met at the opera. Kubizek noted that Hitler was reserved, meticulously dressed. "He was a remarkably pale, skinny youth, about my own age, who was following the performance with glistening eyes." Kubizek himself had a sensitive look and with his high forehead, curly hair and dreamy eyes seemed destined for an artist's life.

Together Adolf and Gustl (Hitler refused to call his new friend "August") began attending almost every opera performance. Other nights they would stroll along the Landstrasse, Adolf twirling his ever present black ivory-handled cane. Once Kubizek got up the nerve to ask his uncommunicative companion if he worked. "Of course not," was the gruff reply; a "bread-and-butter job" was not for him.

Since Hitler did not like talking about himself, their conversation centered on music and art in general. One day, however, Adolf abruptly drew out a black notebook to read a poem he had just written; a little later he showed his new friend several drawings and designs, then confessed he was going to be an artist. Determination at such an age impressed Kubizek ("I was thrilled by the grandeur which I saw here"), and from that moment his admiration for Hitler approached hero-worship. Although his recollections, consequently, are often exaggerated and sometimes even fictionalized, no comrade knew the young Hitler so intimately.

While the two had much in common, they were of conflicting temperaments. Kubizek considered himself "adaptable and therefore always willing to yield," while Hitler was "exceedingly violent and high-strung." These differences only solidified the friendship. Kubizek, a patient listener, relished his own passive role, "for it made me realize how much my friend needed me." Hitler warmed to such a sympathetic audience and would often make speeches "accompanied by vivid gestures, for my benefit alone." These orations, usually delivered when they were walking through the fields or on some deserted woodland path, reminded Kubizek of an erupting volcano. It was like a scene on the stage. "I could only stand gaping and passive, forgetting to applaud." It took some time before Kubizek realized his friend was not acting but was "in dead earnest." He also discovered that all Hitler could stand was approval and Kubizek, enthralled more by Adolf's oratory than by what he said, readily gave it.

On fair days during this seminal period the two young men would occupy a bench on the Turmleitenweg where Adolf read, sketched, and painted water colors, or they would perch themselves on a rock ledge far above the Danube. In such seclusion Hitler poured out hopes and plans, giving his vivid imagination free rein. It was no one-sided relationship.

Adolf seemed to know exactly how Kubizek felt. "He always knew what I needed and what I wanted. Sometimes I had a feeling that he was living my life as well as his own."

While Adolf was enjoying the carefree existence of a young bohemian dandy, he occupied humble quarters. The apartment on the third floor at Humboldtstrasse was rather pleasant if restricted. The kitchen, its single window looking out on the courtyard, was small but homey. Paula and Klara slept in the living room, which was dominated by a portrait of Alois, the personification of the dignified civil servant. The third room, hardly larger than a closet, was occupied by Adolf. Unlike the previous homes, this was a peaceful one, run largely for the young master, whose present each Christmas to his mother was, typically, a theater ticket. To Klara he was a young prince with slumbering talent, obviously destined for fame; and she resisted the practical suggestions of relatives that Adolf learn a respectable trade so he could contribute to the family income.

In the spring of 1906 one of Adolf's dreams was realized; his mother allowed him to visit Vienna, the mecca of art, music and architecture. For a month he roamed the romantic old city (he probably stayed with his godparents, Johann and Johanna Prinz) totally enthralled. He kept Gustl posted. "Tomorrow I go to the opera to see *Tristan*, the day after to *Flying Dutchman*, etc.," he wrote on a three-sectioned postcard on May 7. "Even though I find everything very fine, I am longing for Linz again. To the Stadttheater today." A second postcard, sent the same day, pictured the Royal Opera House. Adolf found the interior uninspiring. "Only when the mighty waves of sound roll through space and the whistling of the wind yields to the frightful rushing billows of sound does one feel nobility and forget the gold and velvet with which the interior is overloaded." These lines were typical of the budding artist—atrocious grammar mixed with poetic imagery, grandiose but sensitive sentiments.

Adolf returned to Linz more dedicated than ever to a life of art and architecture. He insisted that Gustl share this dream, finally persuading him to go into partnership on a ten-kronen state lottery ticket. Hitler talked endlessly of how their winnings should be spent. They would rent the entire second floor of a large house across the Danube and work in the two rooms farthest apart so that Gustl's music should not be a distraction. Adolf himself would furnish every room, create the murals and design the furniture. Their apartment, he daydreamed, would become the headquarters for a circle of dilettantes. "There we would make music, study, read—above all, learn; the field of German art was so wide, said my friend, that there could be no end to the study of it." There was a final delightful and revealing provision: "A lady of exquisite culture would preside over the household as 'chatelaine,' but this educated lady would have to be sedate in temperament and years in order that no expectations or intentions should be aroused of a kind unwelcome to us." This fantasy, like most, was dissolved by reality: their ticket did not win.

After another uneventful summer vacation in Spital, highlighted by his present of a magic lantern to the Schmidt children, Adolf resumed his existence as budding artist and dreamer. In early October he began taking piano lessons from Gustl's teacher. Paula recalled her brother "sitting for hours at the beautiful Heitzmann grand piano my mother had given him." No expense was too great for such a son. It was about this time that Hitler revealed himself to Kubizek in a startling new role. It occurred on the evening they first saw Wagner's *Rienzi*. The story of the hero's rise and fall as tribune of Rome had a curious effect on Adolf. Ordinarily he began criticizing the performers or musicians once the final curtain dropped. This night he not only said nothing but rebuked Kubizek to silence with "a strange, almost hostile glance." Hitler strode into the street, silent, paler than usual, the collar of his black overcoat turned up against the November chill. Looking "almost sinister," he led his puzzled companion to the top of a steep hill. Suddenly he grasped Kubizek's hands tightly. Eyes "feverish with excitement," he began speaking in a hoarse, raucous voice. It seemed to Kubizek as if another being had taken over his friend—"it was a state of complete ecstasy and rapture, in which he transferred the character of Rienzi, without even mentioning him as a model or example, with visionary power to the plane of his own ambitions." Till now Kubizek had been convinced that his friend's true goal was to be an artist or perhaps an architect. This Adolf was a complete stranger, ranting as if possessed of "a special mission which one day would be entrusted to him"—a call from the people to lead them to freedom. This scene may have been one of Kubizek's fictions, but it surely reflected the state of mind of his romantic friend. It was 3 A.M. by the time they descended to Kubizek's house. After the boys solemnly shook hands, Adolf did not head home. Instead he started up the hill again with the explanation: "I want to be alone." His family became the dubious beneficiary of his visionary experience. "Very often," remembered Paula, "he used to give lectures on the themes concerning history and policy to my mother and me in a rhetorical way."

The vision on the hill was followed by a moody period in which he felt as rejected and injured as a Dostoevski hero. He could have stepped out of the pages of *The Adolescent*. The piano lessons stopped within four months. Kubizek felt it was because "those dull, monotonous finger exercises did not suit Adolf at all," but it was more likely occasioned by the ill-health of Klara Hitler. On January 14, 1907, two weeks before Adolf's last piano lesson, his mother called on Dr. Edward Bloch, a Jewish physician known locally as the "poor people's doctor." In a quiet, hushed voice she complained of a pain in her chest; it kept her awake night after night. An examination indicated that Frau Hitler had "an extensive tumor of the breast." Dr. Bloch did not tell the patient she had cancer but the following day he summoned Adolf and Paula. Their mother was "a gravely ill woman," and the only hope, and that but a slight one, was surgery. Bloch was touched by Adolf's reaction. "His long, sallow face was contorted. Tears flowed from his eyes. Did his mother, he asked, have no chance? Only then did I recognize the magnitude of the attachment that existed between mother and son."

The family decided to risk an operation and Klara Hitler entered the hospital of the Sisters of Mercy in Linz on January 17. The next day Dr. Karl Urban removed one of her breasts. By this time Aunt Johanna—a hunchback, irascible but always on hand—had arrived from Spital to keep house for the children. For nineteen days Klara recuperated in a third-class ward at three kronen a day; she could have afforded more comfortable quarters but, typically, economized on herself. The three flights to the apartment on the Humboldtstrasse were too difficult for Klara to climb and late that spring the family moved across the Danube to the suburb of Urfahr into three rooms on the second floor of an attractive stone building at Blütengasse 9. It was a quiet, pleasant neighborhood, a short ride on the streetcar across the long bridge to Adolf's favorite haunts.

The youth had a new preoccupation. He fell in love. Until then his relationship with girls had been trifling. During one vacation in Spital, for example, there had been a brief encounter in a barn with a girl who was milking a cow, but when she showed a willingness to go further, Adolf had rushed off, knocking over a large pot of fresh milk. While strolling the Landstrasse with Kubizek, they had approached a "distinguished looking girl, tall and slim," with thick fair hair swept into a bun, a young Valkyrie. Adolf excitedly gripped his companion's arm. "You must know," he said resolutely, "I'm in love with her." Her name was Stephanie Jansten; and she too lived in Urfahr. He composed numerous love peoms to her, including one entitled *Hymn to the Beloved*, and read them all to his faithful Gustl. Adolf confessed he had never spoken to her but that eventually "everything would be clear without as much as a word being exchanged." Theirs was such an idyllic match, said Hitler, that they communicated by eyes alone. "These things cannot be explained," he said. "What is in me is in Stephanie too." Kubizek urged him simply to introduce himself to Stephanie and her ever present mother. Hitler refused to do this; he would have to mention his profession and he was not yet an academic painter. He was immersed moreover in Norse and German mythology where the women were anything but ordinary, and he probably had a romanticized, knightly concept of all things sexual. No prosaic introduction for this young Siegfried! Fantasy built on fantasy. If all else failed he would kidnap her while Kubizek engaged the mother in conversation.

When Stephanie continued to ignore Hitler's presence he imagined she was angry with him (she was about to become engaged to a lieutenant, and it would come as a complete surprise to learn years later that

Hitler had been her devoted admirer). Despondent, he swore he could bear it no longer. "I will make an end of it!" He decided to jump off the bridge into the Danube. But Stephanie would have to go with him in a suicide pact. He devised a plan complete in every detail, with appropriate dialogue for everyone, including Kubizek, who must witness the tragic event.

It was a convenient love affair for a susceptible youth of imagination. Success would have led to marriage and the end of an artistic career; failure only contributed to another pleasurably painful fantasy. More important matters soon put Stephanie in the background. Adolf's creative drive had made a turn from art to architecture. He was still an indefatigable water colorist, but these paintings, while pleasantly executed with a degree of talent, could not satisfy the ideas and emotions seething inside him. "Adolf never took painting seriously," said Kubizek; "it remained rather a hobby outside his more serious aspirations." His architectural designs, on the other hand, gave expression to an irresistible urge to create as well as a sense of order that was almost obsessive. He was driven to alter the shape of Linz. He would stand in front of the new cathedral, praising some features, criticizing others. He redesigned structure after structure in a passion for improvement. "He gave his whole self to his imaginary building and was completely carried away by it." As he ranged the streets with his one-man captive audience, Hitler pointed out features that must be changed, then explained in detail what had to be done. The town hall was uninspiring and he envisioned in its place a stately modern structure. He would also completely remodel the ugly castle, restoring it to its original grandeur. The new museum did please him and he returned time and again to admire its marble frieze, which depicted historical scenes. But even this had to be changed; he would double the length to make it the longest frieze in Europe.

His plans for a new railroad station showed a flair for city planning: to rid the growing Linz of tracks that were ugly as well as a traffic hindrance, he set his station on the edge of town, running the tracks under the city. The public park would spill over onto the old station site. His imagination was boundless. He planned to run a cog railway to the top of the Lichtenberg where he would place a spacious hotel and a three-hundred-foot steel tower which, in turn, would look down upon a magnificent new high-level bridge spanning the Danube.

His life had become one of isolation. Hitler slept late and stayed in the house most of the day reading, painting and designing. The downstairs neighbor, the wife of the postmaster, would see him leave the house after 6 P.M. and, on his return from his adventures with Kubizek, hear him pace around the living room until early morning. One day her husband suggested Adolf enter the postal service but he replied that he was going to be a great artist someday. "When it was pointed out that he lacked the necessary means and connections for this, he replied briefly: 'Makart and Rubens worked themselves up from poor circumstances.' "

Adolf was restless; and Linz had no more to offer him. He yearned for the world outside, specifically Vienna. He tried to convince his mother that he should be allowed to enter the Academy of Fine Arts. Klara was pressed from the other side by arguments from her son-in-law and Josef Mayrhofer, the children's guardian. Both insisted that it was time the boy selected a respectable profession. Mayrhofer even found a baker who was willing to take Adolf as an apprentice.

But Klara could not resist her son's passionate pleas and that summer he was allowed to withdraw his patrimony, some seven hundred kronen, from the Mortgage Bank of Upper Austria. This was enough for a year in Vienna, including tuition at the academy. Adolf's victory was marred by a deterioration in his mother's health and he probably left home with emotions of guilt, regret and exultation. But examinations for the Academy of Fine Arts were held only in early October and if he didn't go to Vienna now his career would have to be postponed another year. On a late September morning in 1907, Kubizek appeared at Blütengasse 9. Both Klara and Paula were weeping and even Adolf's eyes were wet. His suitcase was so heavy it took both youths to carry it down the stairs and to the streetcar.

During Adolf's first trip to Vienna, he had deluged his friend with postcards. But ten days passed without a word. Kubizek conjured up scenes of illness, accident and even death. He decided to find out what had happened from Frau Hitler. Her first words were: "Have you heard from Adolf?" Her face was more careworn than ever; her eyes were lifeless, her voice listless. With Adolf gone, she seemed to have let herself go and become "an old, sick woman." She began repeating all the laments he had heard so many times: why hadn't Adolf chosen a proper profession? he would never earn a decent living painting or writing stories; why was he wasting his patrimony on "this crazy trip to Vienna?" why did he refuse to take any responsibility for raising little Paula?

Adolf was living near the Westbahnhof on the second floor of Stumpergasse 29 in the flat of a Polish woman named Zakreys. He was depressed. He had taken his exam at the academy with confidence. The verdict was shocking: "Test drawing unsatisfactory."* When the stunned young man asked for an explanation the rector assured him that his drawings "showed my unfitness for painting, and that my ability obviously lay in the field of architecture."

It took the downcast Hitler a few days to realize what Kubizek had already guessed—his painting was only a hobby and his true destiny was as an architect. The road ahead seemed insurmountable; entrance in the

* A contemporary, Marc Chagall, was rejected by the Academy of Art in St. Petersburg.

Academy's School of Architecture depended on a diploma from the building school and to enter this institution he needed a diploma from Realschule. Determined to succeed, yet depressed by the difficulties, he spent the next weeks aimlessly, reading for hours in his little room, attending the opera and wandering the streets to admire the buildings.

In Urfahr, Klara Hitler was dying. The postmaster's wife wrote Hitler and he rushed back. On October 22 he again consulted Dr. Bloch, who revealed that drastic treatment was necessary to save the patient's life. Klara, it seemed, had been operated on too late and "there were already metastases in the pleura." The treatment, continued Dr. Bloch, was not only dangerous—large doses of iodoform on the open wound—but extremely expensive. Money was no object to Adolf and he agreed to remunerate Dr. Bloch for the iodoform in advance, while promising to pay for the treatment itself later.

Kubizek was startled when Adolf unexpectedly turned up at his home, deathly pale, eyes dull. After explaining what had brought him from Vienna, Hitler burst into a diatribe against doctors. How could they say his mother could not be cured? They simply were incapable of curing her. He was staying home, he said, to help take care of his mother since his half sister, Angela, was expecting a second child. Kubizek was surprised that his friend didn't even ask about Stephanie, nor did Adolf mention her for some time, "so deeply engrossed" was he with his mother.

By November 6 she was receiving an almost daily dosage of iodoform. It was an agonizing procedure. Gauze was saturated with iodoform (which had a nauseating, clinging, "hospital" odor) and then folded around the open wound. Not only did the iodoform burn its way into the tissues but once it entered the system the patient could not swallow. Klara's throat burned and yet she could not quench this burning thirst since all liquids tasted like poison.

Hitler devoted himself to his mother, sharing the household duties with the postmaster's wife, Paula and Aunt Johanna. Klara had been installed in the kitchen since it alone was heated all day. The cupboard had been removed and replaced by a couch. Adolf slept here so he could be in constant attendance. During the day he was part-time cook and Frau Hitler confided to Kubizek with pride that her appetite had never been better. At these words her usually pale cheeks colored. "The pleasure of having her son back and his devotion to her had transfigured the serious, worn face."

In the cold, damp days that followed, Kubizek could not believe the change in Hitler. "Not a cross word, not an impatient remark, no violent insistence on having his own way." Adolf "lived only for his mother" and even took over as man of the house. He would scold Paula for doing poorly at school and one day made her swear solemnly to their mother that she would henceforth be a diligent pupil. Kubizek was deeply impressed by this uncharacteristic behavior. "Perhaps Adolf wanted to show his mother by this little scene that he had meanwhile realized his own faults."

Each waking hour was filled with pain for Klara. "She bore her burden well," recalled Dr. Bloch, "unflinchingly and uncomplaining. But it seemed to torture her son. An anguished grimace would come over him when he saw pain contract her face." On the evening of December 20 Kubizek found Frau Hitler, mouth drawn and eyes sunken, sitting up in bed, supported by Adolf to ease the pain. Hitler motioned his friend to leave. As he started out, Klara whispered, "Gustl." Usually she addressed him as Herr Kubizek. "Go on being a good friend to my son when I'm no longer here. He has no one else."

By midnight it was apparent that the end was near but the family decided not to disturb Dr. Bloch. Klara was beyond his help. In the dark early morning hours of December 21—in the glow of a lighted Christmas tree, according to Hitler—she died quietly. After daylight, Angela asked Dr. Bloch to come to the Blütengasse and sign the death certificate. He found Adolf, face wan, at his mother's side. On a sketchbook was a drawing of Klara, a last memory. Dr. Bloch tried to ease Hitler's grief by saying that in this case "death had been a savior." But Adolf could not be comforted. "In all my career," recalled Dr. Bloch, who had witnessed many deathbed scenes, "I never saw anyone so prostrate with grief as Adolf Hitler."

Chapter Two

"THE SCHOOL OF MY LIFE"
DECEMBER 1907–MAY 1913

1

The morning of December 23, 1907, was damp and foggy. Klara was carried out of Blütengasse 9 in a "hard polished wooden coffin with metal corners" and the hearse headed down the slushy street to a church. After a short service the little funeral cortege—hearse and two carriages—proceeded slowly across the Danube and over the hill to Leonding. She was buried, as she wished, beside her husband, with her own name inscribed on his marker. The family, all in black, stood silently in the misty graveyard, within sight of the snug little house they had once occupied. Adolf in a long black overcoat held a black top hat. He seemed even paler than usual to Gustl, his face "stern and composed."

Christmas Eve was lugubrious for the Hitlers. The family made a formal visit to Dr. Bloch to settle the medical bill. The total was 359 kronen, of which 59 kronen had already been paid on account. It was a considerable sum, representing more than ten per cent of Klara's estate, but it was extremely reasonable since it included seventy-seven home and office visits and forty-seven treatments, most of them with iodoform. The balance was paid with profuse thanks. The sisters talked while Adolf, wearing black suit and loosely knotted tie, stared at the floor, a shock of hair tumbling over his forehead. Finally he grasped the doctor's hand and looked directly at him. "I shall be grateful to you forever," he said and bowed. "I wonder if today he recalls this scene," wrote Dr. Bloch thirty-three years later in *Collier's*. "I am quite sure that he does, for in a sparing sense

Adolf Hitler has kept his promise. Favors were granted to me which I feel were accorded no other Jew in all Germany or Austria."

Both Adolf and Paula had been invited to spend the rest of the day with the Raubals and Adolf turned down the invitation. He was becoming increasingly uneasy with brother-in-law Leo, who couldn't resist taking every opportunity to urge him to abandon his foolish dream of becoming an artist. In fact, the youth confided to Kubizek, all his relatives were constantly pestering him and so he was escaping to Vienna. He was bound to become an artist and prove to that narrow-minded clan he was right, not they.

He was equally determined that his friend leave his father's upholstery shop to become a professional musician. The Kubizeks had refused to let Gustl go to Vienna the previous autumn, but Hitler renewed his pleas and arguments, firing the imagination of both Gustl and his mother with tales of Vienna—the operas and concerts, the unlimited opportunities for the study of music. Convincing Herr Kubizek was more difficult. He regarded Adolf as "a young man who had failed at school and thought too highly of himself to learn a trade." But Hitler's power of persuasion even at that age was exceptional and this practical man agreed to let his son go to the capital for a trial period. One of the arguments that had helped sway him was that Gustl would be living with a bona fide art student.

Hitler journeyed again to Leonding to tell his guardian of his decision to return to Vienna for good. This time there was no argument. Herr Mayrhofer readily, if reluctantly, gave his consent—he told his daughter it was his duty to do so—and Adolf spent the next few weeks with Angela and Aunt Johanna, making final family arrangements. By now all bills had been paid to the last groschen, including that for the funeral, which came to the considerable sum of 370 kronen. The neighbors were thanked for their help during Klara's illness. Adolf was so grateful to the postmaster and his wife that he gave them one of his paintings. Even after all obligations were settled, there must have remained at least three thousand kronen from the estate of the economical Klara. Since Angela had assumed responsibility for the eleven-year-old Paula, it is likely she got more than two thirds. Alois Hitler, Jr., later told his elder son that he had persuaded Adolf they should "turn their part of the inheritance over to the girls," since the Raubals were short of funds; Adolf promptly gave his share to Angela, while Alois gave his to Paula. If true, that left Adolf very little with which to start his career in Vienna: an orphan's pension and what was left of his patrimony.

Early in February Adolf received unexpected encouragement from Vienna. A neighbor persuaded Professor Alfred Roller, director of scenery at the Royal Opera, to take a look at young Hitler's paintings and advise him on his career. The offer from Roller helped beat down the family protests, and Adolf made definite plans to leave. On February 10, 1908, he filled out the form for his and Paula's pensions. It was returned three days later with a note that it should have been countersigned by their guardian. Adolf passed on the form to Herr Mayrhofer but was too impatient to wait for an answer from the Pensions Office. He packed his clothes, books and art materials, bade farewell to his family and left Blütengasse 9 for the last time.

Gustl accompanied him to the station—it was probably February 17—and during the wait for his train Adolf spoke of Stephanie. He still had not introduced himself to her but perhaps he would write her. As the train moved out of the station, Adolf called through the open window, "Follow me soon, Gustl." It is doubtful if the young man's reading extended to the inspirational works of Horatio Alger but he certainly would have felt a kinship with Alger's heroes. The third-class fare on the local train was 5.30 kronen and after five hours the eighteen-year-old Adolf Hitler arrived for the third time in the magic city of Vienna. It was only a few minutes' walk from the Westbahnhof to Frau Zakreys' establishment at Stumpergasse 29 but it must have been an arduous one with such bulky luggage. Although the weather was dreary that month, Adolf's spirits were high. On February 18 he wrote an enthusiastic card to Kubizek:

> Dear Friend! Eagerly await news of your coming. Write soon and definitely so that I can get everything ready to receive you in style. All Vienna is waiting. . . . As we said to start with you stay with me. We can see later how we get on. Piano to be had here in the so-called Dorotheum [government pawnshop] for as little as 50–60 florins. Well, many greetings to you also to your esteemed parents from your friend Adolf Hitler. Once again please come soon!

Five days later, on a foggy Sunday, Gustl arrived at the Westbahnhof, a brown canvas bag "overflowing with food." As he stood confused by the bustle of the station waiting room, he saw Adolf coming toward him, already a citizen of Vienna. "In his dark, good-quality overcoat, dark hat and walking stick with the ivory handle, he appeared almost elegant." Hitler was so delighted to see his friend, he kissed him on the cheek. He took one handle of the heavy bag, Kubizek the other, and they emerged into the turmoil of the city. It was already dark but electric arc lights made the station plaza "as bright as day."

They passed through the wide entrance of Stumpergasse 29, an imposing structure, crossed a small courtyard to its humbler annex and struggled up dark stairs to a room on the second floor. Sketches were scattered everywhere. Adolf spread a newspaper over the table and brought out his own sparse food supply—milk, sausage and bread. Kubizek shoved these aside and, like a magician, produced from his canvas bag roast pork, freshly baked buns, cheese, jam and a bottle of coffee. "Yes," Hitler is supposed to have exclaimed, "that's what it is to have a mother!"

After the feast Hitler insisted on conducting his tired friend on a tour of the city. How could Kubizek possibly go to sleep without seeing the Ring? First Adolf introduced him to the grandeur of the Opera House— "I felt as though I had been transplanted to another planet, so overwhelming was the impression"—then came the graceful spire of St. Stephen's, and finally Adolf insisted on "something else special," the delicate St. Maria am Gestade Church. But it was so misty that Kubizek could see little and he was grateful when they finally got home well after midnight and he crawled into the bed the landlady had made up on the floor.

Since the room was too small for two *and* a piano, the persuasive Adolf convinced Frau Zakreys to give up her own large room and move into his. The young men agreed to pay twenty kronen a month, double the original rent. The grand piano took up more space than imagined and, since pacing was a requirement for Adolf, the furniture had to be rearranged to give him a promenade three strides in length.

Within two days Gustl had registered at the Academy of Music and passed the entrance examination. "I had no idea I had such a clever friend," was Hitler's curt comment. Nor was he interested in hearing about Kubizek's progress in the weeks to follow. He made a scene when Gustl was visited by a fellow student, a pretty young girl, and after she left, delivered a tirade, as he paced back and forth, "about the senselessness of women studying." Kubizek had "the impression that Adolf had become unbalanced. He would fly into a temper at the slightest thing." Nothing Gustl did seemed to suit Adolf, "and he made our life together very hard to bear. . . . He was at odds with the world. Wherever he looked he saw injustice, hate and enmity."

The underlying reason was Hitler's own rejection and this came into the open when he suddenly burst into a bitter denunciation of the Academy of Fine Arts. ". . . a lot of old-fashioned fossilized civil servants, bureaucrats, devoid of understanding, stupid lumps of officials. The whole Academy ought to be blown up!" His face was livid; his eyes ("There was something sinister about them") glittered with hatred. Then he finally revealed that he had been thrown out, turned down. "What now?" asked the concerned Kubizek. Hitler sat down at the table and began to read a book. "Never mind," was the calm reply.

Despite his talk of determination to succeed, he had yet to take advantage of Professor Roller's offer of help. Several times, portfolio in hand, he had gone to the studio of the noted stage designer but could never get up the nerve to knock on the door. At last he tore up the letter of introduction "so he would not be tempted again." He could have been afraid his work was not good enough; or been driven by some inner urge for failure; or simply have been overwhelmed by Roller's fame and feared meeting him.

About a week after Hitler left Linz, Herr Mayrhofer was informed by the Pensions Office that the two orphans, Paula and Adolf Hitler, would each be granted three hundred kronen a year until they reached the age of twenty-four. Mayrhofer was authorized to divide the entire six hundred kronen a year as he saw fit and he decided to give each orphan twenty-five kronen a month.

This regular sum, equivalent to some six current American dollars, undoubtedly gave renewed hope to Hitler but, assuming that he still had most of the six hundred and fifty kronen from his patrimony, life would still have been spartan. His roommate later insisted that Hitler often went hungry. "For days on end he could live on milk and bread and butter only." Kubizek never knew how much money Adolf had and assumed he was secretly ashamed of how little it was. "Occasionally, anger got the better of him and he would shout in fury, 'Isn't this a dog's life.'"

The money Hitler saved on food and other economies—he "pressed" his trousers, for example, under the mattress—enabled him to go to the Burgtheater or the Opera several times a week. Nor would Hitler sit in the gallery with girls—"all they were after was flirting." He made Kubizek stand with him in the promenade, where women were not admitted, at the considerable cost of two kronen a ticket. They never saw the end of the longer operas, since they had to leave at 9:45 P.M. in time to get home before the entrance to Stumpergasse 29 was closed. Otherwise they would have to tip the concierge. Back in their own room Hitler would force Kubizek to play on the piano what they had missed.

Hitler never tired of hearing Wagner. Even when Gustl wanted to see a first-class production of Verdi at the Royal Opera, Adolf insisted on dragging his friend to the People's Opera for a second-rate Wagner production. The music would transport him and was "that escape into a mystical world which he needed in order to endure the tensions of his turbulent nature." Together they saw Adolf's favorite opera, *Lohengrin*, ten times. *Die Meistersinger* similarly entranced Hitler, who never tired of quoting the lines from the second act:

> *And still I don't succeed.*
> *I feel it and yet I cannot understand it.*
> *I can't retain it, nor forget it.*
> *And if I grasp it, I cannot measure it.*

Kubizek did manage to inveigle Adolf to several Verdi operas but he only approved of *Aïda*. He objected to the trick theatrical effects. "What would these Italians do if they had no daggers?" One day they heard an organ grinder playing *La donna è mobile* and Hitler exclaimed, "There's your Verdi! Can you imagine Lohengrin's narration on a barrel organ?"

The two young men also spent many evenings at concerts for which Kubizek, as a student at the Academy, got free tickets. Gustl was surprised when Adolf began "developing a taste for symphonic music" and a particular fondness for the Romanticists—Weber, Schubert, Mendelssohn and Schumann. Other favorites included Bruckner, Beethoven and Grieg, whose Piano Concerto in A Minor never failed to move him.

Lack of money did not dim the luster of their Vienna. It was the golden era for opera and music. Gustav Mahler had just quit the Royal Opera for the Metropolitan in New York City but had left behind magnificent productions, many designed by Roller. Particularly notable were their collaborations on *Rienzi* and the first two parts of *The Ring*. The new director, Felix Weingartner, while causing some furor by making cuts in certain Mahler productions, was already carrying out his predecessor's plan to complete *The Ring* with new Roller scenery. Both directors, incidentally, were Jews, as were many Viennese luminaries of literature and the theater, such as Hugo von Hofmannsthal, Arthur Schnitzler, Richard Beer-Hofmann and Hermann Bahr.

Vienna was the capital of an empire in its final years of flowering, a polyglot center with no common tongue and a population gathered from the four corners of Austria-Hungary. It was a brilliant, cosmopolitan city where joy of life ran hand in hand with a sense of impending doom. This seat of the Habsburg dynasty was German in tradition, yet unique among metropolises. It was a capital not only of banking and finance but also of fashion and culture. Unlike Germany, it was a melting pot of incongruous peoples. "Swamped for long centuries by the Slavs, the Magyars, and the Italians," commented one contemporary reporter, "this town, they say, has no longer a drop of German blood." There was a Bohemian theater, an Italian opera, singers from France and clubs for the Polish; and in some cafés there would be Czech, Slav, Polish and Hungarian newspapers but not one in German. You might be "a German of pure breed, but your wife will be a Galician or a Pole, your cook a Bohemian, your nursemaid an Istriote or a Dalmation, your valet a Serb, your coachman a Slav, your barber a Magyar, and your tutor a Frenchman. . . . No, Vienna is not a German town."

Those, like Adolf, who had left the cities and villages of the realm for Vienna fell under its spell despite, perhaps because of, its disturbing contradictions. It was a city of glamor and slums, of cast-iron conventions and radical intellectual experiments, of free thought and violent racial prejudice. Drawn as he had been to this glittering city, "the dubious magic of the national melting pot," as he later described it, began to repel Hitler as the months passed and any kind of success eluded him.

He and Kubizek would leave their room on the Stumpergasse, often with empty stomachs, pass through dingy middle-class streets to the center of the city with its "splendid mansions of the nobility with garishly attired servants in front and the sumptuous hotels." Adolf became increasingly rebellious, railing endlessly at the social injustice of all that unearned wealth. What bothered him more than hunger was the filth of the bug-infested room on the Stumpergasse. Hitler, Kubizek recalled, was "almost pathologically sensitive about anything concerning the body."

His feeling for the city was not unique. "Every outstanding personality brought up in the peculiar intellectual atmosphere of Vienna lived ever after in a dialectical syncretism of love and hatred for the city which offered splendid potentialities for the highest accomplishments, as well as the most stubborn resistance to their realization." So wrote Bruno Walter in his biography of Mahler, whose inspired production of *Tristan*, with its striking orange, purple and gray sets by Roller, Adolf Hitler would see almost monthly for the next five years. Vienna in short was peopled by the *Raunzer* (grumblers) and had a tradition of attacking its most outstanding citizens; it derided Freud's psychoanalysis, hissed at the too modern sounds of Arnold Schönberg and the too bright colors of Oskar Kokoschka, and found much to criticize in the works of Hofmannsthal and Schnitzler.

The youthful Hitler, alternately fascinated and repelled, spent time ferreting out the evils of the gaudy city. According to Kubizek, who saw him as a young Werther with a social conscience, he followed an erratic program of self-education, wandering the Meidling section to "research" the housing conditions of the workers; he haunted the Ringstrasse, inspecting it and adjoining areas by the hour, before returning to his dingy hole of a room to redesign large sections of the capital. The youth was as much city planner as architect and, as he strode up and down the narrow passage between door and piano, he forced Kubizek to listen to endless lectures on "conscientious planning." Once he disappeared for three days, returning with the announcement that the "tenements will be demolished," and proceeded to work all night on designs for a model workers' settlement.

Adolf also would sit at the table until late at night, writing in the uncertain glow of their single source of illumination, a smoky kerosene lamp. Curious, Kubizek finally asked what he was doing and Hitler handed over several scribbled sheets:

> Holy Mountain in the background, before it the mighty sacrificial block surrounded by huge oaks; two powerful warriors hold the black bull, and press the beast's mighty head against the hollow in the sacrificial block. Behind them, erect in light-colored robes, stands the priest. He holds the sword with which he will sacrifice the bull. All around, solemn, bearded men, leaning on their shields, their lances ready, are watching the ceremony intently.

Hitler explained to the puzzled Kubizek that it was a play. Excitedly he described the action which took place at the time Christianity was brought to Bavaria; the mountain men would not accept the new faith and were determined to kill the Christian missionaries. This play was probably never finished and others—such as a drama about the painter Murillo—

were envisaged and occasionally started, their plots usually lifted from Germanic mythology or history. Adolf would write until dawn, then toss the results on Gustl's bed or read aloud a page or two. Each of these dramas required expensive productions with scenes ranging from heaven to hell, and Gustl suggested that Adolf write something simpler—for example, an "unpretentious" comedy. This adjective infuriated Hitler and he put his mind to an even more ambitious project. It was inspired by a casual remark of Kubizek's that the outline of a music drama about Wieland the Smith had been discovered in Wagner's posthumous papers.

The following day Kubizek returned from lunch to find Hitler at the piano. "I'm going to work up Wieland into a musical drama," he said. Adolf's plan was to compose the music and peck it out on the piano to Gustl, who would "put it on paper, adapt where necessary and finally write the score." A few nights later Hitler played the overture on the piano, then anxiously awaited Gustl's opinion. Kubizek thought it was secondhand Wagner, but the basic themes *were* good and he offered to put the music into proper metric form. While Hitler was never satisfied with his friend's changes, he continued to compose day after day as well as to design the scenery and costumes and sketch the hero in charcoal. Adolf would spend his evenings on the libretto, keeping one eye on Kubizek, and when he fell asleep over the orchestration would shake him awake and then read out, in a soft voice—because of the late hour—from his manuscript. After several weeks, however, Adolf put aside the opera. Perhaps some problem or other had come up that demanded his attention. Or perhaps the fire of creation that had possessed him had burned out. He talked less and less about their unfinished project and finally ceased mentioning it.

That spring Kubizek went home for the Easter holidays. He wrote back that he had contracted conjunctivitis, probably from studying so much in the kerosene light, and might arrive at the Westbahnhof wearing glasses. It was a lonely, dreary Easter Sunday for Adolf. That year, 1908, it fell on April 19, the day before his nineteenth birthday. His answer to Gustl on mourning paper was filled with heavy humor: "It filled me with deep sorrow to hear that you are going blind; you will hit more and more wrong notes, misread the music and end up blind while I slowly go deaf. Oweh!"

The room on the Stumpergasse seemed more dismal than ever to Gustl after the countryside of Linz and he persuaded Hitler to go on excursions in the open country. In the mild spring sunshine they spent several Sundays in the Vienna Woods and took steamer rides down the Danube. Although it was the season when a young man's fancy was supposed to turn to love, sex played little overt part in their lives. On promenades, girls and women would often slyly glance at them. At first Kubizek thought their interest was directed to him, but it soon became apparent that the reserved Adolf was the object; he coldly ignored their silent invitations. If the two did nothing about sex, they spent hours at night discussing women, love and marriage, with Adolf as usual dominating the conversation. Over and over he insisted that he must keep "The Flame of Life" pure. That is, he believed—in accordance with his Catholic upbringing—a man and woman should keep themselves chaste in body and soul until marriage and thus be worthy of producing healthy children for the nation.

But the dark side of sex also haunted him and he talked "by the hour" about "depraved [sexual] customs." He railed against prostitution, condemning not only the whores and their customers but society. His condemnation approached obsession and one night after attending a performance of Wedekind's *Spring's Awakening* he took Gustl's arm and said, "We must see the Sink of Iniquity once." They turned down a small dark alley—it was the Spittelberggasse—and walked past a row of small houses, so brightly lit that one could see the girls inside. "In their scanty and slovenly attire they sat there," recalled Kubizek, "making up their faces or combing their hair or looking at themselves in the mirror, without, however, for one moment losing sight of the men strolling by." Occasionally a man would stop in front of a house, converse with a girl—and the light would go out. When the two youths reached the end of the alley Adolf maneuvered them in an about-face and they took another long look at the appalling sight. Back in their room, Adolf went into a lengthy tirade on the evils of prostitution "with a cold objectivity as though it were a question of his attitude towards the fight against tuberculosis, or towards cremation."

Gustl finished his competitive examinations with excellent grades and conducted the end-of-term concert. Three of his songs were sung and two movements of his sextet for strings performed. In the artists' room, a proud Adolf at his side, he was congratulated not only by the head of the Conductors' School but by the director of the Academy of Music.

It was early July, time for Gustl to return to Linz. He was spending the summer with his parents but insisted on paying his half of the rent until his return in the autumn. Adolf himself was silent about his own plans and, when Gustl vowed to get a position as violinist with the Vienna Symphony Orchestra so he could pay more than his half of their expenses, Hitler's reaction was irritable. The compliant Gustl, inured to his friend's dark moods and still glowing with his own success, took no offense. At the Westbahnhof, Adolf assured him "for the hundreth time" how dull it would be living in the Stumpergasse room alone but showed no apparent emotion as they parted ("The more anything touched him, the cooler he became"). Then he did something unusual: grasped both of Kubizek's hands, pressed them firmly and made off hastily without looking back.

Gustl wrote from Linz—a postcard and a letter—and received a picture postcard explaining that Hitler had been "working very hard, often till 2 or even 3 in the morning." Adolf promised to write before he went to Spital for his own vacation, adding testily, "Shan't want to at all if my sister is coming." He probably was referring to Angela, who, along with her husband, remained critical of his way of life. A fortnight passed without word from Adolf. Finally a letter arrived about July 20 which, by the things it said and those it omitted, told much of the curious and lonesome life he was leading:

> Dear Friend. Perhaps you will already have guessed why I have not written for so long. The answer is very simple, I could think of nothing to tell you or what would have interested you particularly. I am still in Vienna, and here I stay. Alone here for Frau Zakreys is at her brother's. Still I am pretty well in my hermit life. There is only one thing I miss. Up till now Frau Zakreys has always drummed me out of bed in the morning. I have been used to getting up very early, in order to work, whereas now I have to look after myself. Is there no news from Linz?

He asked for a guide to Linz and a timetable of the Danube steamer.

> . . . Otherwise I don't know any news, only this morning I caught a murderous stream of bedbugs that soon after was swimming dead in "my" blood, and now my teeth are chattering with "heat." I think such cold days as this year are rare in summer.

Hitler spent the remainder of the month in the stifling, bug-infested room. That his life continued to be dull was indicated in the next letter Kubizek received in August. While replete with Hitler's usual self-pity, mistakes in grammar and spelling, it was "a lovely letter" to the uncritical Gustl—"probably the most revealing letter that he ever sent me." Revealing it was, from its emotional greeting, "Good Friend!" First he asked forgiveness for not writing lately. "There were good reasons, or rather, bad ones; I could not think of any news. That I am suddenly writing to you now after all shows merely that I had to search for a very long time, in order to collect a few items of news for you. So here goes." He passed on their landlady's thanks for the rent money, carelessly calling her "Zakays" and then "Zakrays," although he had correctly spelled her name in a previous letter. He revealed he had just recovered from "a bad attack of bronchial catarrh" and joked heavily about the weather—"It's lovely pleasant weather with us at the moment, i.e. it is raining heavily and in this year of boiling heat that is truly a blessing from heaven." He noted that the Linz authorities, rather than rebuild the theater (one of his own favorite projects), had decided to "patch up the old shack yet again," and charged that they had "as much idea of building a theater as a hippopotamus of playing the violin."

Hitler revealed that he was at last quitting Vienna for Spital and would "probably be leaving on Saturday or Sunday." By the end of August he was enjoying the fresh air of that village. There was little else to enjoy. Increased pressure was being brought to abandon his way of life in Vienna, this time by his aunt Johanna. But, recalled Paula, this "last attempt to persuade him to take up the career of an official was in vain." Even Paula was showing signs of crossing her big brother. Now twelve, she resented his advice, including the reading list he prescribed (one item was *Don Quixote,* which he had sent from Vienna). "Naturally he was a great brother for me, but I submitted to his authority only with inner resistance. In fact we were brother and sister, who did frequently quarrel, but were fond of each other, and yet each spoiled each other's pleasure of living together."

As it had been with Angela and Alois, Jr., so it was now with Paula. There was affection but little understanding or common interest. The unpleasantness of Spital that summer marked the end of Hitler's youth. His refusal to consider a more practical profession cut him off from his family; never again would Spital, the scene of so much pleasure in his boyhood, be a refuge. For the fourth time he set off for Vienna, this time truly on his own.

In mid-September Hitler once more applied for admission to the Academy of Art. But the drawings he submitted, the labor of a year's solitary study, were so lowly regarded that he was not allowed to take the test. Along with the crushing blow of a second rejection, Hitler was faced with the problem of survival. His stay at the Stumpergasse room had probably exhausted his patrimony. Even if he had accepted his share of his mother's inheritance—and this is doubtful—it could have amounted to no more than enough to last another year in Vienna. His first economy was a cheaper room. In mid-November he gave Frau Zakreys notice and paid his share of the rent for the month. Without leaving a note for Kubizek, who was expected momentarily, he moved to the other side of the West-bahnhof to a gloomy building on the Felberstrasse overlooking the railroad yards.

On November 18 he registered his new address with the police (a regulation in both Austria and Germany whenever one moved), listing his occupation as "student" rather than "artist." Several days later Kubizek arrived in Vienna. Adolf had sent him a picture postcard from Spital with a one-line message: "Best wishes for your esteemed Name Day." Though Kubizek had received no word since, he was accustomed to Adolf's long silences and, upon arriving at the Westbahnhof, he expected to see his friend on the platform. There was no Hitler. He checked his heavy case and hurried to Stumpergasse 29. He couldn't understand why Adolf had moved without leaving a message, and gave Frau Zakreys his own present address. Week after week passed without word from Hitler. Kubizek was puzzled. Had he somehow offended Hitler without knowing it? But they had parted the best of friends and Adolf's letters had certainly not been cool.

On his next trip to Linz, Kubizek visited Adolf's older sister. When he asked for Hitler's new address in Vienna, Angela crossly replied that she didn't know; he hadn't written. She began criticizing Kubizek for contributing to her brother's flight from reality. He defended his friend "vigorously," believing she was only mouthing Leo's prejudices and, when the conversation grew unpleasant, left abruptly.

Adolf had cut himself off from Kubizek, from everything that reminded him of Linz and home. His feeling for Kubizek was not as strong as Gustl's for him; as far as Hitler was concerned their relationship had run its course—at least for the time being. Moreover, Gustl had succeeded and he had failed. He celebrated his twentieth birthday alone on April 20, 1909, in the forbidding building on the Felberstrasse. Month after month he endured the cheerless surroundings, continuing the dream life he had led in Linz. He lived a quiet, solitary existence, rarely breaking out of his isolation. His neighbors remembered only that he was polite and distant. The cashier of a nearby restaurant, the Café Kubata, however, was deeply impressed by Hitler "because he was very reserved and quiet, and would read books, and seemed very serious, unlike the rest of the young men." She esteemed him so highly that she always gave "Dolferl" an extra-large portion of *Mehlspeisen*, a meatless, flour-based dish.

By late summer Hitler had to face another crisis. Except for the twenty-five kronen a month pension he had reached the end of his resources. He moved from the Felberstrasse to a smaller building on the south side of the Westbahnhof. The address was Sechshauserstrasse 58 and he occupied another small room, number 21. It was just about as noisy as the last place with the streetcars running down the narrow street. On August 22 Hitler registered his change of address at the police station, this time listing himself as "writer." But in less than a month he left this last refuge of respectability and disappeared into the underworld of poverty. He left behind no word, and on his police form there was a blank for "future address," and "unknown" marked the question: "When moved out." Without funds and unable or unwilling to work, he wandered for the next three months, a tramp. He slept in parks and doorways. For a time his home was a bench in the Prater, the famed amusement center on the other side of the Danube; and in rain he found refuge under the arches of the rotunda, using a jacket as pillow. Winter came early that year and by late October 1909 he was forced to find refuge indoors. He slept in bars, in dingy rooms, in cheap flophouses, in a coffeehouse on the Kaiserstrasse, in the crowded "warming room" on Erdbergstrasse established by a Jewish philanthropist. Once he found a strange shelter in a laborers' barracks, a dirty refuge that had to be shared with other homeless people. He could not sleep for the fetid air and the constant noise of crying children or of some drunk beating his wife.

"Even now I shudder," he later wrote, "when I think of those pitiful dens, the shelters and lodging houses, those sinister pictures of dirt and repugnant filth and worse still." Vienna, which had once been "an enchantment out of 'The Thousand-and-One Nights,'" had been transformed into a jungle of misery and represented, "I am sorry to say, merely the living memory of the saddest period of my life." He turned to the Church for help and would queue up mornings at nine at the convent near his old room on the Stumpergasse for soup. To tramps this was "calling on Kathie" because it was either the name of the Mother Superior or that of St. Katherine's convent itself.

By late fall he had sold most of his clothes, including his black winter overcoat, and so the snow and cold drove him to further humiliation. Huddled in a light jacket late one afternoon just before Christmas, he trudged all the way to Meidling in the outskirts of town. It took two and a half hours to reach his destination, the Asyl für Obdachlose, a shelter for the destitute, and by the time he arrived he was exhausted, his feet sore. Run by a philanthropic society whose principal supporter was the Epstein family, it was originally constructed in 1870 and had been extensively rebuilt and reopened the year before. Here for a modest fee, the homeless —including entire families—were accommodated. Each physically able occupant was expected to help in the housework or tend the grounds. It was a large, modernized structure, sitting alone in a large open field. Its dormitories were spacious and airy with beds lined in military precision, each with its number above a metal clothes rack. The main dining hall, which served a substantial soup with bread, was a model of efficiency yet had a pleasant atmosphere. There were numerous showers, washbowls and toilets—all spotlessly clean.

On that cold December evening Hitler lined up with the other shivering, dejected ones outside the main gate of the Asyl. At last the door opened and the mob of homeless quietly filed in to be segregated by sex, with children accompanying mothers. Hitler got a card entitling him to a week's lodging, and an assignment to one of the large dormitories. To a young man who cherished privacy it must have been a harrowing experience. First he had to endure the humiliation of showering in public and having his bug-ridden clothes disinfected; then his group was trooped like prison inmates to the main dining hall for soup and bread.

It would be difficult for anyone but another recipient of institutionalized charity to understand the shame suffered by a proud young man on his first day within the gates of such an establishment. Entrance into an institution like the Asyl with its efficiency and protectiveness marks an irrevocable enrollment into the bottom rank of the destitute. The inmate has lost the independence of scrounging on his own and becomes, in a sense, a prisoner. The newcomer, overwhelmed by his surrender, is momentarily at a loss. Hitler, too, must have been a picture of dejection that first night in the Asyl, sitting on his neat cot in a large military-like dormitory, surrounded by jabbering comrades, most of whom were veterans of such community living.

A wandering servant in a nearby cot took charge of Hitler. He showed him the ropes: to stay at the Asyl more than the prescribed week, for example, one had only to buy for a few kreuzer the unused portions of admittance cards of those leaving. The servant—his name was Reinhold Hanisch—also had dreams of being an artist and was impressed by Adolf's facile talk. Hitler, in turn, was fascinated by the tales that Hanisch, who had spent several years in Berlin, spun about Germany. Hanisch ("We met every night and kept up our spirits in spite of our troubles") taught his new friend the words to "Watch on the Rhine," noting how Hitler's eyes sparkled at such words as "We Germans fear God but nothing else on this earth."

More important, Hanisch taught his student that to survive a winter in the lower depths not a step must be wasted nor an opportunity lost: on mornings they left the Asyl—Adolf in his threadbare jacket, "blue and frostbitten"—early enough to negotiate the long walk to "Kathie's" in time for soup; then to a warming room or a hospital for several hours' protection from the bitter cold and a little soup, and back to the Asyl at dusk just as the gate opened. In between the major stops they would occasionally earn a few kreuzer by shoveling snow or carrying baggage at the Westbahnhof. But Hitler was too weak for much physical labor; every step on his sore feet was painful. Once there was a call for ditchdiggers and Hitler wondered if he should apply. Hanisch advised him to forget it. "If you begin such hard work it is very difficult to climb up."

Adolf tried his luck at begging. But he had neither the talent nor the gall for panhandling and become a client of a comrade at the Asyl who made a living by selling addresses of those who were "soft touches." Hitler agreed to split the proceeds fifty-fifty and set off with not only the addresses but specific instructions for each customer; for example, he was to greet an old lady on the Schottenring with a "Praised be Jesus Christ," and then say he was an unemployed church painter or a woodcutter of holy figures. Usually she gave two kronen for such a story, but Hitler only got religious platitudes for his trouble. He had similar bad luck with the other prospects and he again turned to the Church, where he got three meat patties and one kronen from the Mother Superior by greeting her with a "Praised be Jesus Christ," along with a reference to the St. Vincent Association.

Hanisch couldn't understand why a man with such education and talent allowed himself to drift so helplessly and asked what Hitler was waiting for. "I don't know myself," was the listless answer. Hanisch had never seen such apathy in the face of distress and decided to do something about it. His interest was not purely altruistic. Seeing a potential meal ticket in the skinny, woebegone Adolf, he encouraged him to make money painting postcards. Hitler protested that he was too shabbily dressed to sell them on the street or door to door. No problem, said Hanisch; he would do it for fifty per cent commission. But they both might get into trouble with the police without a peddler's license. No problem: Hanisch would sell them in taverns disguised as a blind man or consumptive. Hitler's next argument—that he had sold his painting equipment along with his clothes—was again no problem to the resourceful Hanisch. Didn't Adolf have relatives? Nor was Adolf's final protest that he had no writing materials a deterrent to Hanisch. Together with a salesman from Silesia, Hanisch escorted Adolf to the Café Arthaber, opposite the Meidling station. Following the dictation of the two promoters, and using a borrowed pencil, Hitler wrote a card to a member of his family, probably Aunt Johanna, asking her to send some money General Delivery. A few days later Hitler picked up a letter at the post office. In it was a fifty-kronen bank note ("a nice piece of money in those days"). That evening the exuberant Hitler couldn't resist exhibiting the bill as he stood in line at the Asyl. His crafty companion advised him to keep the money hidden; he'd be robbed or, just as bad, "hit" for a loan.

The first priority was a winter coat for the painter, whose cough was getting worse. Hitler rejected the suggestion that he buy a secondhand coat in the Jewish quarter on the grounds that he had been cheated there when he sold his own. Instead they went to the government pawnshop and found a dark coat for twelve kronen. Hanisch wanted Hitler to start painting at once but he insisted on a week's rest. Moreover, there was no suitable place to work in the Asyl. There were better facilities at the Männerheim, the men's hostel where a man had his own room, tiny to be sure, as well as a common room for hobbies.

On February 9, 1910, he made the long trip to the hostel across the center of Vienna to the other side of the Danube. Hanisch did not accompany him; he had decided to get a job as a servant rather than be a nursemaid to Hitler. The XXth District, Brigittenau, was industrial, with a diverse population, including more Jews than any other section except Leopoldstadt. It was a transient area with many of its inhabitants using it as a stopover on the way up the ladder. The Männerheim, about a half mile from the Danube, was a large building at Meldemannstrasse 25–27 taking up most of a block. It could accommodate five hundred men.

A modern structure, not five years old, its facilities were such that some of Vienna's middle-class citizenry were shocked by its "luxuriousness." On the main floor was a large dining room brightly illuminated by arc lights, the lower half of its walls tiled with a warm shade of green. Food could be picked up at counters and paid for by tokens acquired from a marvel of the day, an automatic machine. The food was cheap but good and the portions generous. Roast pork with one vegetable came to nineteen kreuzer and the complete meal cost an additional four kreuzer.

To those who couldn't afford this much, a dozen or so gas stoves were located in an adjacent room. For no charge any guest could cook up his own modest meal "in the most fantastic cooking utensils." The potato was the basic ingredient; scrambled potato pancakes with or without meat filling was a favorite. Combines were formed; those without jobs stayed at home to do the cooking while others worked and paid for the materials.

Just off this kitchen, up three steps, was a reading room, with a dozen tables. There were a number of other reading rooms and game rooms, as well as a library and a "writing" room where a dozen or so men could carry on private business: a Hungarian cut postcards out of cardboard and sold them in the Prater taverns; one old man copied names of betrothed couples from the newspaper and sold them to stores.

There were several dormitories, as neat as those at the Asyl, but most of the occupants enjoyed privacy in tiny cubicles about five feet wide and some seven feet deep. There was just enough space for a small table, a clothes rack, a mirror, a chamber pot and a narrow iron cot, complete with three-sectional mattress, headrest filled with horsehair, double blanket and, miracle of miracles to any sojourner of the lower depths, two clean white sheets that were changed every week. These were not cheerless cells, for each had its own window in addition to adequate artificial lighting. Every floor had an abundance of washbowls, foot bath troughs and toilets; in the basement were a score of tiled showers.* Here too were tailor and barbershops, a shoemaker and a laundry. In addition there were long rows of clean lockers that could be rented by those who needed to store extra clothing or other possessions.

The director was noted as a disciplinarian. He insisted that certain rules be adhered to strictly: the men were to be out of their rooms during the daytime; only chess, checkers and dominoes could be played in the recreational rooms; undue noise, whether argument or enthusiasm, led to expulsion; wine and beer could be consumed on the premises (after all, this was Vienna) but not hard liquor; and city property was to be respected ("There will be no standing on the beds"). There were few disciplinary problems. A few hopeless tramps did a little stealing but most of the men were sincerely trying to work their way back to respectability.

It was to this snuggery for the homeless that Adolf Hitler came on

---

* Several years ago these showers were dismantled since they were not being used. The standards of cleanliness and neatness—despite efforts of the present administration—have deteriorated since Hitler's time. Today's occupants are similar to the frequenters of the Bowery and other American Skid Rows.

that chill February day in 1910. He paid his fee—half a crown a day, cheaper by the week—went through another shower and disinfectant routine and was assigned a cubicle (on the third floor according to its present habitués). Good as the facilities had been at the Asyl, here, where charity was not so institutionalized, he could feel more like an individual.

In less than a week Hanisch appeared at the Männerheim. Four days as a servant had been enough for him. Again he took charge of Hitler and established his protégé with his art materials in the writing room at a long oak table near a window. Before long Hitler was turning out pictures the size of a postcard. He worked slowly, painstakingly copying photographs or paintings of city scenes. Hanisch had little trouble selling these sketches at Prater taverns and pocketing half the proceeds, but he soon realized there was more money in larger works and so Hitler turned to water-color scenes of Vienna, usually double the size of a postcard, completing about one a day.

Within a few weeks the fruits of this partnership, together with the tolerable conditions at the Männerheim, had rescued the two young men from winter and poverty. No longer did they suffer from the cold or go to bed with growling stomachs. Hitler reveled in the cleanliness of the tile showers and, since he had but one shirt, would launder it every few days as he scrubbed himself. Despite his relative prosperity, he still could not afford new clothes and was a disreputable sight in his tattered, disinfectant-streaked clothing, long hair and beard.

Warmth and food inspired an interest in politics and Adolf did much to turn the writing room into a forum for dispute and discourse. Here the intelligentsia of the Männerheim gathered, fifteen or twenty from the upper and middle class, those with some acquaintance with literature, music and art. A scattering of workers were also tolerated if they "behaved decently." Adolf became a leader of this group, holding forth at length on political corruption just as other down-and-outers in Skid Rows throughout the world were doing. These lectures, which occasionally degenerated into shouting matches, were sometimes held during the workday. If a political discussion started in the other end of the room while Hitler was at work he couldn't resist the call of battle and would join in, waving his T-square or brush like a knight bound for combat. If Hanisch returned from his peddling during one of these sessions he would disarm his client and coax him back to his seat. But once Hanisch left, Adolf would be on his feet again, denouncing the villainy of the Social Democrats or praising Karl Lueger, the anti-Semitic Christian Socialist Party leader whose mass appeal impressed Hitler. "When he got excited," Hanisch recalled, "Hitler couldn't restrain himself. He screamed and fidgeted with his hands. But when he was quiet it was quite different; he seemed to have a fair amount of self-control and acted in quite a dignified manner."

Adolf became so interested in politics that he spent hours in the magnificent House of Deputies listening entranced to the colorful debates which often degenerated into a babel of multilingual arguments and even brawls. He would return to the writing room and carry on his own harangues, which involved a hodgepodge of Pan-Germanism, along with denunciations of the Social Democrats for their atheism, their attacks on the state and their efforts to seize total power.

Hanisch never heard his friend rail at the Jews during these tempestuous debates or in private, and he remained convinced that Hitler (most of whose favorite actors and singers were Jewish) was by no means anti-Semitic. On the contrary, Adolf would express gratitude for the Jewish charities of which he had been a beneficiary, along with admiration for Jewish resistance to persecutions, and once denied that Jewish capitalists were usurers. Hanisch remembered only one derogatory comment Hitler made when someone wondered why Jews had remained strangers in the land: his answer was that they were "a different race" with "a different smell."

Two of Hitler's closest friends at the Männerheim were Jewish—a one-eyed locksmith named Robinson who often helped him and a part-time Hungarian art dealer, Josef Neumann, who took pity on Adolf's tattered attire and gave him a long frock coat. Hitler "highly esteemed" the latter and once remarked that he was "a very decent man." He also expressed great regard for the three Jewish art dealers who bought most of his work, and more than once told Hanisch, still his agent, that he preferred doing business with Jews "because only they were willing to take chances."

Hitler himself claimed in *Mein Kampf* that he had become a dedicated anti-Semite in Vienna upon his discovery that the Jew was the "cold-hearted, shameless, and calculating director" of prostitution; that the music and art worlds were controlled by Jews; and, most important, that the Social Democrat press was "directed predominantly by Jews." More likely these revelations came much later and his prejudice was little more than that of the average Viennese. Almost every gentile in the Austrian capital was an anti-Semite. Organized groups worked tirelessly to spread hate against Jews and young Hitler became an avid reader of the trash literature which filled the newsstands.

There is evidence that he was a regular reader of such magazines as *Ostara*, the creation of Lanz von Liebenfels, a mystical theorist who shared many of Hitler's own theories and attitudes. The magazine itself was a concoction of the occult and erotic, its editorial policy "the practical application of anthropological research for the purpose of . . . preserving the European master race from destruction by the maintenance of racial purity." Liebenfels' recurring theme was that Aryans must rule the earth by destroying their dark, racially mixed enemies. The latter were damned as inferiors and yet the pages of *Ostara* abounded in lurid illustrations of Aryan women succumbing to the sexual power and allure of these hairy, apelike creatures.* The magazine appealed simultaneously to superiority and fear, featuring such headlines as:

> ARE YOU BLOND? THEN YOU ARE A CULTURE-CREATOR
> AND A CULTURE-SUPPORTER!
> ARE YOU BLOND? IF SO, DANGERS THREATEN YOU!

Ostara stirred in its readers the primal fear of the limitless power of Jews—their control of money, their ascendancy in the world of art and theater, their strange attraction for women. How the erotic pictures in *Ostara* of blonde beauties embracing dark men must have inflamed Adolf! But as yet all these ideas were unrealized, unfocused—and his anti-Semitism would wane as new ideas and projects pushed it into the background.

Later Hitler would tell Frau Hanfstaengl that his hatred of Jews was a "personal thing"; and his sister Paula that he was convinced his "failure in painting was only due to the fact that trade in works of art was in Jewish hands." One can only guess at the "personal thing" which Hitler claimed motivated his hatred of all things Jewish: perhaps an art dealer or pawnshop operator; perhaps an official at the Academy of Art; perhaps some combination of these things; or even something which lay dormant in the recesses of his mind. There could have been a dawning hatred of Dr. Bloch, even though Hitler sent him cordial New Year's wishes a year after Klara's death and signed it "Your ever grateful Adolf Hitler." It is not at all uncommon for a bereaved son to blame a doctor, consciously or unconsciously, for the death of a beloved parent. How much more reason in a case involving a Jewish doctor and a dangerous treatment already in disrepute. (Bloch himself later eliminated all mention of iodoform in his accounts of Klara Hitler's treatment.)

During this seminal period in Vienna, Hitler wrote a letter to a friend, revealing not only the possible physical effects of such a submerged obsession ("I often grew sick to my stomach from the smell of those caftan-wearers") but a disgust with doctors and a feeling of his own destiny.

> . . . It was probably no more than a little stomach colic and I am trying now to cure myself by a diet (fruit and vegetables) since all the physicians are idiots anyway. I find it absolutely ridiculous to speak of a nervous ailment in my case when I am the healthiest of men otherwise. At any rate, I am again working with brush and palette and have great joy in doing so, even if the oil technique is giving me great difficulties.

* Embittered by the prejudice he was finding in Vienna, Freud would conclude that at the bottom of anti-Semitism lay castration fears because of the Jewish tradition of circumcision.

You know—without exaggeration—I always believe that the world has lost a great deal in that I could not attend the Academy and learn the technical end of the art of painting. Or has fate chosen me for something else?*

By the spring of 1910 Hitler had become so involved with politics and the state of the world that he couldn't fill Hanisch's orders. Reproached, he promised to be more diligent but as soon as Hanisch left the building Adolf would read his newspapers from cover to cover and when he finally sat down to work it wouldn't be long before some discussion lured him from the repetitious painting that was becoming a chore. In desperation, or to get away from Hanisch's nagging, Adolf disappeared on the first day of summer with his Hungarian Jewish friend Neumann. The two had often talked of emigrating together to Germany and so set off in quest of their dream. Somehow they got sidetracked by the wonders of Vienna, particularly Adolf's favorite museums, and never left the city. This spree lasted five days; then, on June 26, with scarcely a kreuzer in his pocket, Hitler returned to the Männerheim. But the brief freedom had its effect. For the next month he worked in spurts, saving only enough to finance another vacation, and before long the partnership with Hanisch ended. Adolf was once more on his own.

In the autumn Hitler made another attempt to enroll in the Academy of Fine Arts. Toting a large portfolio of paintings, he made his way to the office of Professor Ritschel at the Hofmuseum. He requested Ritschel, who was charged with the care and restoration of pictures, to help him get into the Academy. Hitler's work did not impress the professor although he admitted it was executed with remarkable architectural precision. Dejected, Adolf returned to the Männerheim and resumed painting in the writing room. But without Hanisch he found it next to impossible to sell anything. Desperate for money, he appealed to his aunt Johanna, either by mail or on a short trip to Spital. They had parted acrimoniously several summers ago, but Johanna was close to death and apparently had misgivings about her harsh treatment of Adolf. On December 1 she withdrew her entire life savings from the bank. It was a considerable sum, 3800 kronen, and she gave her nephew a substantial part of it.

She died a few months later in early 1911, leaving no will. When Angela Raubal learned that Adolf had received a much larger share of Aunt Johanna's money than anyone else, she immediately applied to the Linz court for her half brother's share of the orphan's pension. It was only fair since she was a recent widow and supported not only her own children

* This letter—along with other equally extraordinary letters and documents pertaining to Hitler that will appear later in this book—comes from the controversial private collection of Dr. Johannes von Müllern-Schönhausen of Vienna, which he has entitled "H.B.H. Privat Archiv."

but Paula. Either through pressure or shame, Adolf agreed to renounce the twenty-five kronen a month that had been keeping his head above water the past few years. He appeared of his own free will at the district court in Linz to state that he was now "able to maintain himself" and was "agreeable that the full amount of the orphan's pension should be put to use for his sister." The court promptly ordered Herr Mayrhofer henceforth to give Adolf's share of the pension to Paula. The children's guardian had already received a letter from Hitler stating that he no longer wanted any part of the money.*

Even without his pension Adolf enjoyed a security undreamed of by a resident of the Männerheim. At the same time he maintained the standards of old, cooking his own meals and continuing to wear the disreputable clothes that kept him in trouble with the management. We will never know if the money from Aunt Johanna had gone into splurges at the opera and theater; or if he had lost it in some plan concocted by one of his comrades—the place seethed with schemes that were legal, slightly shady or downright crooked; or if he had made a foolish display of his money as he had done once before at the Asyl and been robbed; or if he had given some of it to his sisters in atonement. More likely, he had hidden away the money and was doling it back to himself; those who set out to be artists or writers must adopt such shifty stratagems to keep afloat.

Adolf became his own agent and set to work diligently at his corner in the writing room. His comrades respected him because of the artistic air he had acquired. Invariably polite, he never stooped to familiarity though was always ready to help or advise a fellow worker. Yet once politics became a topic, he would toss aside his brush and leap into the fray, shouting and gesturing, his long hair flying. These outbursts made him increasingly unpopular with his fellow lodgers and one day, while preparing his meal in the kitchen, he was roughed up by two big transport workers. He had called them "idiots" for belonging to a Social Democrat labor organization and been rewarded "for his insulting remarks" with a large lump on the head, a bruise on his painting arm and a swollen face.

A new friend, the successor of Kubizek and Hanisch, warned him that he deserved the beating "because you refuse to heed advice and so nobody can help you." Some months previously Josef Greiner had been attracted to the artist as he hunched over a desk in the writing room daubing at a water color of a church. Greiner was a young man of vivid imagination and he and Adolf would sit for hours discussing economics, religion, astrology and the occult. They also talked at length about the gullibility of people. A case in point was an advertisement currently running in the newspapers. Under the picture of a woman whose hair reached the floor was the text: "I, Anna Csillag, with the very long Lorelei-hair, achieved this

---

* Mayrhofer told his daughter Johanna that Hitler had behaved decently in the matter and "he had no complaints about him, or had he heard any."

beautiful hair with the aid of my secret pomade, which I myself invented. Anyone who wants to have such beautiful hair should write to Anna Csillag and receive free a wonderful prospectus with proof and thank-you letters."

"That is what I call advertising," said Hitler, according to Greiner's account. "Propaganda, propaganda as long as the people believe that this crap helps." The concept excited him. Propaganda, he said, could make believers out of doubters. He was convinced he himself could sell the most preposterous item, such as a salve guaranteed to make windows unbreakable. "Propaganda, only propaganda is necessary. There is no end of stupid people."

During the remainder of 1911 and into the following year Hitler settled into a more stabilized routine. He spent less time in fruitless argument and more at painting. The quality of his work improved. His water color of the Minorite Church of Vienna, for example, was so accurate in every aspect that it could have been traced from a photograph. Technically his pictures were quite professional—surprisingly so for a young man without formal art training. While Hitler was blessed with a natural talent for rendering structures, he had virtually none for the human form. When he introduced figures into a composition, they were poorly drawn and badly out of proportion. A number of his pictures were pleasant to the eye even if they lacked the artistry that separates competence from professionalism. Hitler, in short, was more technician than artist; more architect than painter. It was apparent by 1912 that he could draw competently with pencil, paint well with water colors and even better in oils.

He worked steadily and sold almost everything he completed to Jacob Altenberg and other dealers. Yet Hitler himself no longer boasted of his accomplishments. His comrades in the writing room would cluster around a finished picture and admire it, but he would reply "in a disdainful way that he was only a dilettante and had not yet learned how to paint." His real talent, he thought, was in architecture. He later confided to a friend that he only painted to make money and those few pictures that he did cherish were of architectural subjects. With modest financial success came improvement in appearance; his worn clothes were clean, gone was the beard. He had grown so respectable, that the director of the Männerheim would chat with him, "an honor seldom granted to an inmate."

In manner too he had become more circumspect and, while he continued to argue politics, he had received a valuable lesson. "I learned to orate less, but listen more to those with opinions and objections that were boundlessly primitive." He had discovered one does not gain control of other men's minds by antagonizing them.

Nowhere was Hitler's measure of maturity more evident than in the writing room. As a mark of respect, no one thought of occupying his favorite seat at the window. If a newcomer tried to take this place someone would say, "This place is occupied. This is Herr Hitler's place!" One newcomer, Karl Honisch, soon recognized his uniqueness. "We all lived pretty thoughtlessly through the days. . . . I believe that Hitler was the only one among us who had a clear vision of his future way." He told Honisch that although he had been refused admission at the Academy of Fine Arts, he was going to Munich soon to finish his studies there.

Hitler was the nucleus of the intelligentsia in the writing room, recalled Honisch, "because he used to sit in his place day by day with almost no exception and was only absent for a short time when he delivered his work; and because of his peculiar personality. Hitler was, on the whole, a friendly and charming person, who took an interest in the fate of every companion." Friendliness notwithstanding, he kept his distance. "Nobody allowed himself to take liberties with Hitler. But Hitler was not proud or arrogant; on the contrary, he was goodhearted and helpful." If someone needed fifty heller for another night at the hostel he readily contributed his share—"and I saw him several times starting such collections with a hat in his hands."

During ordinary political debates, Hitler kept at work, if occasionally throwing in a phrase or two. But once the key words "Reds" or "Jesuits" came up and someone made a remark that "rubbed him the wrong way," he would leap to his feet and give argument, "not avoiding vulgarisms, in a very impetuous way." Then he would interrupt himself and return to his painting with a gesture of resignation "as if he wanted to say: a pity for every word wasted on you, you won't ever understand."

In a sense Hitler had made peace with Vienna and its lower depths. He had achieved success and recognition. But the city had little to offer him now. For some months his thoughts had been turning toward Germany, the Fatherland. In a frame over his bed hung a slogan:

> *We look free and open*
> *We look steadfastly,*
> *We look joyously across*
> *To the German Fatherland!*
> *Heil!*

He had spent five and a half years loving and hating the glamorous capital of the Habsburgs and would entitle this chapter of his life "Years of Study and Suffering in Vienna." It was a period of "hardship and misery," "the most miserable time of my life," but one that had molded him more than any university could have done. It was, he thought, "the hardest, though most thorough, school of my life."

On May 24, 1913, carrying all his possessions in a single small battered bag, he stepped for the last time through the double doors of the Männerheim. His mates were sorry to see him leave, Honisch recalled.

"We lost a good comrade with him; he understood everyone and helped whenever he could."

Adolf Hitler turned his back on Vienna and looked to Munich for his future. "I had set foot in this town while still half a boy and I left it a man, grown quiet and grave. In it I obtained the foundations for a philosophy in general and a political view in particular which later I only needed to supplement in detail, but which never left me."

The scene of Adolf leaving the hostel that had been home and refuge for three years and three and a half months was indelibly set in the memory of Honisch. With regret he watched Hitler set off on foot with a companion whose name Honisch never could remember. It would have been the wryest irony if it had been his Jewish friend Neumann, who had long shared the dream of emigration to the Reich.

Chapter Three

"OVERCOME WITH RAPTUROUS ENTHUSIASM" MAY 1913–NOVEMBER 1918

1

He stepped off the train from Vienna and climbed the stairs into the hubbub of Munich's Hauptbahnhof. From that first moment almost everything about the capital of Bavaria struck a responsive note. This was home. Even the chatter of the people was pleasing to his ears after the polyglot noise of Vienna. "The city itself was as familiar to me as if I had lived for years within its walls."

It was a pleasant spring day with the sun shining brightly and the air, washed by winds from the nearby Bavarian Alps, seemed much cleaner than that of Vienna. It was a Sunday—May 25—and, except for sightseers, the streets were almost deserted. He gaped at the buildings, the statues, and was seized by a deep love "for this city more than for any other place that I knew, almost from the first hour of my sojourn there. A *German* city!"

After half an hour's enchanted stroll he came to the Schleissheimerstrasse. Very likely he passed by the Königsplatz and was stunned by the grandeur of the great arch, the Propyläen, and the vast square beyond, and then turned down the Briennerstrasse to the imposing, castle-like restaurant-brewery, the Löwenbräuhaus. Here at the edge of Schwabing, the student district, began the Schleissheimerstrasse heading northward.

Within two blocks he came upon number 34, the Popp Tailor Shop. On its window was stuck a handwritten notice: "Furnished rooms to let to respectable men."

It directed him to the third floor where Frau Popp showed him a room containing a bed, table, sofa and chair. On the wall hung two oleographs. "The young man and I soon came to terms," recalled Frau Popp. "He said it would do him all right, and paid a deposit." She asked him to fill out a registration form and he wrote: "Adolf Hitler, Architectural painter from Vienna."

"Next morning my Herr Hitler went out and came back again in no time with an easel he had picked up somewhere. He began his painting straight away and stuck to his work for hours. In a couple of days I saw two lovely pictures finished and lying on the table, one of the cathedral and the other of the Theatinerkirche. After that my lodger used to go out early of a morning with his portfolio under his arm in search of customers."

Hitler had arrived in Munich "full of enthusiasm," intending to study art and architecture for three years, but reality never came up to the dream and he never entered the local Academy of Art. It was even more difficult to make a living as a painter here than in Vienna. The commercial art market was by no means as large and he was forced to undergo the humiliation of peddling his pictures door to door and in beer halls. But he was convinced that despite all obstacles he would in time "achieve the goal I had set myself."

Munich in 1913 with its 600,000 inhabitants was, after Paris, about the liveliest cultural center in Europe, and for some years had been attracting a breed of artists that Hitler himself found decadent: Paul Klee from Switzerland and refugees from the east like Kandinsky, Jawlensky and the Burliuk brothers. All were leaders in the New Artists' Association, which had been founded four years earlier to give its members more freedom. While such a concept repelled the classical-minded Hitler, its exponents brought to Munich an artistic ferment and excitement that must have stimulated the young Austrian. "The nomads, which was how the Munich citizens described those long-haired creatures from the East, from Russia and the Balkans, streamed into Schwabing, the northern district of the city, where the streets seem to run so straight only to insure a perfect light . . . in the countless studios." Despite his distaste for these Eastern refugees, Hitler himself was a bohemian and shared their need for freedom and tradition. Here in Munich his idol had composed *Tristan und Isolde, Die Meistersinger,* and *Das Rheingold,* and here resided Germany's leading poets, Stefan George and Rainer Maria Rilke. Here Richard Strauss was writing his operas, Thomas Mann had recently finished a novella of dissolution, *Death in Venice,* and Oswald Spengler, in a room as barren as Hitler's, was scribbling away at the first volume of *The Decline of the West*. At a nearby Schwabing cabaret, the Eleven Executioners, a disreputable genius of *Henkershumor*, Frank Wedekind, was singing his own shocking songs; throughout the country his plays about sex and depravity disgusted and enthralled audiences.

The spirit of bohemianism, in which even the most outrageous and ridiculous theories of art and politics were welcome, had existed in Munich since before the turn of the century and had attracted unconventional souls from all over the world. Another political extremist had spent more than a year of his exile from Russia several blocks up Schleissheimerstrasse, at number 106; registered as Herr Meyer, his given name was Vladimir Ilyich Ulyanov and in the underground he was called Lenin. Here a dozen years earlier he had been writing tracts based on the theories of Marx.

Now Hitler was haunting the same Schwabing cafés and restaurants and luxuriating in the same easy atmosphere of free thought. His rebellious nature and air of feisty independence were not deterrents. In this milieu he was just another eccentric and he could always find someone to listen to his complaints and dreams. Despite his rapport with Schwabing's bohemianism, and in contrast to his own fiery nature and political radicalism, there had been no change in his painting style. His handling of material continued to be academic rather than experimental, daring or even forceful.

His fascination with Marxism, however, was revived in such fertile ground and he spent hours in the libraries studying whatever he could find about "this doctrine of destruction . . . I again immersed myself in the theoretical literature of this new world, attempting to achieve clarity concerning its possible effects, and then compared it with the actual phenomena and events it brings about in political, cultural, and economic life. Now for the first time I turned my attention to the attempts to master this world plague."

He would return from the libraries to ascend the three flights of stairs to his little room, a book or two under one arm and sausage and white bread for dinner under the other. Herr Popp noticed that he no longer ate at the Löwenbräukeller or smaller restaurants and several times invited him to "sit down and have a bite." But he never did. To Frau Popp he was "an Austrian charmer," a pleasant, helpful young man, if something of a mystery. "You couldn't tell what he was thinking." Often he would remain at home for days. "He just camped in his room like a hermit with his nose stuck in those thick, heavy books and worked and studied from morning to night." Whenever the concerned landlady insisted he spend an evening in their kitchen he always made an excuse. Once she asked him what all the reading had to do with painting. This brought a smile to his dour face. He took her arm and said, "Dear Frau Popp, does anyone know what is and what isn't likely to be of use to him in life?" After these periods of study he would go to a beer hall or café and without any trouble find a receptive ear, and once he started talking someone else would inevitably object, touching off a vociferous political debate. In such arenas and against such antagonists, Hitler sharpened his ideas and theories.

The winter brought Hitler increased hardship since there were fewer customers for his pictures. Even so this period was "the happiest and by far the most contented" in his life. Where Vienna had turned sour under adverse conditions, Munich would never lose its magical allure. "If today I am more attached to this city than to any other spot on earth in this world," he recollected from a prison cell eleven years later, "it is partly due to the fact that it is and remains inseparably bound up with the development of my life; if even then I achieved the happiness of a truly inward contentment, it can be attributed only to the magic which this miraculous residence of the Wittelsbachs exerts on every man who is blessed, not only with a calculating mind but with a feeling soul."

This rewarding if arduous existence was abruptly threatened on a Sunday afternoon early in 1914. At 3:30 P.M. on January 18 he answered a peremptory rap at his door to find a stern-faced officer of the Munich criminal police. The officer—his name was Herle—produced an official document from Austria: a notice for Hitler to "present himself for military service in Linz at Kaiserin Elisabeth Quay 30 on January 20th 1914." If he failed to comply he was liable to prosecution and a fine. More ominous, he was warned that he would be fined heavily and imprisoned up to a year if found guilty of having left Austria "with the object of evading military service."

Adolf was overwhelmed. Three years earlier, while residing at the Männerheim, he had requested permission to report for service in Vienna and had heard nothing since. Officer Herle demanded that Hitler sign a receipt for the induction notice and the young man was so flustered he shakily wrote "Hitler, Adolf." Then Herle arrested him and took him to police headquarters. Next morning he was taken under guard to the Austrian Consulate General. It speaks for Hitler's state that by then the police were sympathetic. The consul general also took pity on the young artist with pinched face, gaunt frame and shabby clothes, and allowed Hitler to send Linz a telegram requesting a postponement until early February. The reply arrived next morning: MUST REPORT ON JANUARY 20. It was already that date and, moved to further compassion by Hitler's alarm, the consul general permitted him to write a letter of explanation to Linz. It was a plea for mercy, replete with grammatical mistakes and misspellings, revealing the fright and desperation of a young man cornered by fate and circumstances. He complained that the summons gave him an "impossible short interval" to settle his affairs, not even enough time to take a bath.

> I am described in the summons as an artist. This title is mine by right, but only in a limited sense is it correct. I do earn a living as a free-lance artist, since I am completely without private means (my father was a civil servant), I do so only to be able to continue my studies. I can devote only a portion of my time to earning a living as I am not yet past the training stage as an architectural painter. Therefore my income is very small, in fact only sufficient to make both ends meet.

His monthly income fluctuated and was presently very low since the art market in Munich was in its "winter sleep about this time and nearly 3 thousand artists live or at least try to live here." He explained how he had applied in 1910 for permission to report for service in Vienna, then painted a pathetic picture of his struggles in that city.

> I was a young, inexperienced person, without financial help and also too proud to seek assistance from anyone or beg. Without any support, depending only on myself, the kronen and heller received for my work were often only enough to provide a place to sleep. For two years my only girl friend was Sorrow and Need, and I had no other companion except constant unsatisfied hunger. I never learned to know the beautiful word "youth." Today, after 5 years, my memories are still in the form of frost-bitten fingers, hands and feet. And yet I cannot recall those days without a certain joy, now that I have come out of the worst of it. Despite great need, amidst my often very questionable surroundings, I kept my name clean, and am not guilty in the face of the law and have a clear conscience except for the omitted military report, of which I did not even know at the time. That is the only thing about which I feel responsible. And for that a modest fine should be sufficient, and I would not protest the payment of same.

His excuses were flimsy but he so successfully played on the sympathies of the consul general that his letter was dispatched along with a note of the consul's own stating that both he and the Munich police were convinced of Hitler's honesty. Since the young man seemed "extremely deserving of considerate treatment," the consul recommended that he be allowed to report to Salzburg rather than go all the way to Linz. The Linz authorities agreed and on February 5, at the expense of the consulate, Hitler journeyed to Salzburg. He was found "unfit for combatant and auxiliary duties, too weak. Unable to bear arms." His generally run-down condition apparently was sufficient to disqualify him.

Adolf returned to his room on the Schleissheimerstrasse where he continued to eke out a living designing posters and selling pictures but his life as a struggling artist and hopeful architect came to an end on June 28. From his room he heard a hubbub in the streets below. As he started down the stairs Frau Popp exclaimed excitedly, "The Austrian heir, Archduke Franz Ferdinand, has been assassinated!" Hitler brushed past her and into the street. He pushed his way through a crowd clustered around a placard to read that the killer of the Archduke and his wife Sophie had been a young Serb terrorist, Gavrilo Princip. Hitler's rooted hatred of all things Slavic, begun at his first visit in Vienna to the House of Deputies, was resurrected.

In Vienna angry mobs were already converging on the Serbian Legation, yet few political experts felt this tragedy would lead to a European crisis. The Kaiser, however, secretly began pressing the Habsburgs to invade Serbia. Germany was ready for war, he told them, and the first country that would rush to Serbia's aid, Russia, was not. Under such pressure Austria declared war on Serbia on July 28. This was followed by a general mobilization of Russia against Austria; whereupon Wilhelm appeared at the balcony of his palace to proclaim "a state of imminent threat of war." An ultimatum was sent to Russia demanding the cessation of mobilization by noon of the following day. There was no answer and at 5 P.M. on the first of August the Kaiser signed the order for Germany's general mobilization against Russia.

The news of war with Russia was received with enthusiasm by a large crowd in front of Munich's Feldherrnhalle, the Hall of Field Marshals. Near the front of the crowd stood Adolf Hitler, hatless, neatly dressed, mustached. No one wanted war more than he: "Even today," he wrote in *Mein Kampf*, "I am not ashamed to say that, overcome with rapturous enthusiasm, I fell to my knees and thanked Heaven from an overflowing heart for granting me the good fortune of being allowed to live at this time." To him it meant the realization of the Greater Germany he had dreamed of since youth.

War fever swept the country. It was generated by emotion rather than logic; with the people in a state close to hysteria, they were eager to seek justice no matter what the cost. War was envisaged as some kind of magical release. Students roamed Munich's streets singing "Die Wacht am Rhein" and shouting for action. One group demolished the Café Fahrig on the Karlsplatz because the band refused to play the national hymn over and over again. Intellectuals too were caught up in the enthusiasm, for it meant an escape from boredom and an end to bourgeois sham. War would be a liberation from social and cultural abuses. Even the socialists, excoriated by Wilhelm a few months earlier as vermin gnawing at the Imperial Oak, accepted the Kaiser's invitation ("We are now brothers") to join the patriotic crusade.

The adherents of Pan-Germanism needed no invitation to follow the parade. "Heil der Kaiser! Heil das Heer!" the leaders of the movement officially proclaimed. "We must gather all men of German tongues into one Reich and one people. An everlasting master race will then direct the progress of mankind!" They could have been speaking for Adolf Hitler. He saw the Hohenzollerns as heirs to the medieval Teutonic Knights who had established German colonies in the Slavic lands to the east, and was therefore convinced that Germany had to fight for her existence, for "freedom and the future."

Two days later, on August 3, the day war against France was declared, Hitler submitted a personal petition to Ludwig III,* requesting permission to enlist in his army, and that afternoon he stood in the crowd outside the Wittelsbach Palace cheering the old monarch. Finally Ludwig appeared and while he was speaking Hitler was thinking: "If only the King has already read my application and approved it!" The following day he received an answer which he opened with "trembling hands." He was accepted as a volunteer. On August 16 he reported to the barracks of his first choice, the Bavarian King's Own Regiment. A poster outside announced that it was filled; but he was accepted by his second choice, the 1st Bavarian Infantry Regiment.

Two of his most pressing problems were solved: he would never have to join the detested Austrian army nor would he have to endure another hard winter on his own. Besides finding a home with sufficient food, clothing and shelter—he had a purpose. There was no more room for doubt; he knew for the first time in his life exactly where he was going and why. Safe in uniform, his only fear was that the war might end before he saw action.

A few days later he was transferred to the 2nd Bavarian Infantry Regiment and began basic training at the large public school on the Elizabeth Platz. It was a short but intensive course of drilling, route marching and bayonet practice that left the recruits fatigued by the end of the day. Within a week Hitler was permanently assigned to the 16th Bavarian Reserve Infantry Regiment. The training continued in Munich at an accelerated pace. One of Adolf's comrades, Hans Mend, noticed that when he first handled a rifle he "looked at it with the delight that a woman looks at her jewelry which made me laugh secretly."

2

On October 7 Hitler told the Popps his unit was leaving Munich. He shook hands with Herr Popp and asked him to write his sister if he died. Perhaps she would like his few possessions. If not, the Popps were to keep them. Frau Popp burst into tears as Hitler hugged the two children, then "turned tail and ran." The next day the regiment was marched to the barracks of the elite King's Own Regiment for a solemn ceremony. In the presence of Ludwig III the men swore allegiance to him as well as to Kaiser Wilhelm. Then Hitler and a few other Austrians were required to swear allegiance to their own monarch, the Emperor Franz Josef. The only record of Hitler's reaction to this memorable occasion was his remark to com-

---

* Bavaria, though a part of the German Empire, retained sovereign independence until 1918.

rades that October 8 would always remain in his memory because on that day they received double rations as well as a special noonday meal of roast pork and potato salad.

Early next morning the regiment marched out of Munich bound for Camp Lechfeld seventy miles to the west. Carrying packs, the men plodded for almost eleven hours, most of it in the teeming rain. "I was put up in a stable," he wrote Frau Popp, "soaked through and through. There was no possibility for sleep." The following day, a Sunday, they marched thirteen hours and bivouacked in the open. But it was so cold they spent another sleepless night. It was midafternoon of Monday by the time they finally reached their destination. They were "deathly tired, ready to drop" but marched proudly into the camp under the staring eyes of a group of French prisoners of war.

The first five days at Lechfeld were the most strenuous in his life with "lengthy practice sessions," as well as extra night marches, in connection with brigade maneuvers. This was all part of the amalgamation of their regiment with another to form the 12th Brigade and the recruits were kept so occupied that it was not until October 20 that Hitler found time to write all this to Frau Popp and inform her that they were moving out that evening for the front. "I'm terribly happy," he concluded. "After arrival at our destination I will write immediately and give you my address. I hope we get to England." That night the recruits were loaded onto trains and Adolf Hitler, the archpatriot from Austria, was at last on his way to do battle for the Fatherland.

A brigade lieutenant, a professional soldier named Fritz Wiedemann, watched with mixed feelings as Hitler and his comrades loaded into the cars. The regimental commander had not been on active service for years, most of the companies were led by reserve officers, and the men had had only perfunctory training. There were few machine guns, the telephone equipment had been originally manufactured by a Nuremberg firm for the British army, and the men didn't even have iron helmets. Instead they were going off to combat in oilcloth caps as did the volunteers of the 1812–13 wars of liberation. What the brigade lacked in equipment and training it made up for in enthusiasm. As each train pulled out, the occupants laughed and sang. It was as if they were bound for a glorious party. There would be a few weeks of gallant and exciting fighting and then victory by the New Year.

At dawn Hitler's train was running along the Rhine, a sight most of the Bavarians had never seen. The sun, drawing up the mist from the river, suddenly revealed the gargantuan statue of Germania looking down from the Niederwald. All along the train the men spontaneously burst into "Die Wacht am Rhein." "I felt as though my heart would burst," recalled Hitler.

Eight days later Hitler's company was thrown into battle near Ypres.

As the recruits started forward in the morning fog to relieve a hard-pressed unit, English and Belgian shells began dropping into the woods ahead. "Now the first shrapnel hisses over us and explodes at the edge of the forest, splintering trees as if they were straws," he wrote an acquaintance in Munich, Assistant Judge Ernst Hepp. "We watch with curiosity. We have no idea as yet of the danger. None of us is afraid. Everyone is waiting impatiently for the command, 'Forward!' . . . We crawl on our stomachs to the edge of the forest. Above us are howls and hisses, splintered branches and trees surround us. Then again shells explode at the edge of the forest and hurl clouds of stones, earth and sand into the air, tear the heaviest trees out by their roots, and choke everything in a yellow-green, terribly stinking steam. We cannot lie here forever, and if we have to fall in battle, it's better to be killed outside." Finally it was the Germans' turn to attack. "Four times we advance and have to go back; from my whole batch only one remains, beside me, finally he also falls. A shot tears off my right coat sleeve, but like a miracle I remain safe and alive. At 2 o'clock we finally go forward for the fifth time, and this time we occupy the edge of the forest and the farms."

The battle went on for three more days. The regimental commander was killed and his deputy, a lieutenant colonel, seriously wounded. Under heavy fire Hitler, now a regimental dispatch carrier, found a medic and the two dragged the deputy back to the dressing station. By mid-November the 16th Regiment, according to Hitler, had but thirty officers and less than seven hundred men. Only one in five recruits remained but still came orders to attack. The new commander, Lieutenant Colonel Engelhardt, accompanied by Hitler and another man, ventured far into the front to observe the enemy lines. They were detected and the area was sprayed with machine-gun fire. The two enlisted men leaped in front of their commander, pushed him into a ditch. Without comment Engelhardt shook hands with the two recruits. He intended recommending them both for the Iron Cross but the next afternoon while he was discussing the citations an English shell smashed into the regimental headquarters tent, killing three men and seriously wounding Engelhardt and the other occupants. Moments earlier Hitler and the three other enlisted men had been forced to leave the tent to make way for four company commanders. It was the first of a series of narrow escapes verging on the miraculous for Adolf Hitler. "It was the most terrible moment of my life," he wrote Judge Hepp. "We all worshiped Lieutenant Colonel Engelhardt."

The unsuccessful attempts to take Ypres ended the German offensive and the battle degenerated into static trench warfare. This meant a relatively quiet existence for those attached to the regimental headquarters, now located in a rest area near the village of Messines. At last Hitler found time to paint. He had brought along some equipment and he finished several water colors, including one of the ruins of a cloister near Messines and another of a trench near the village of Wytschaete. He was called on to do a different kind of painting by Lieutenant Wiedemann, the adjutant of the new regimental commander. The color of the officers' dining room—a small room in a commandeered villa—clashed with a romanticized painting of a dying soldier lying across barbed wire. Wiedemann asked Sergeant Max Amann to find someone on the staff who could repaint the room. Amann brought back Hitler. Wiedemann wondered if the walls should be painted blue or pink. Hitler observed that the sun gave the picture a light violet tone and suggested blue. He fetched a ladder, paints and a brush and, as he worked, conversed with the lieutenant. "What I noticed first," recalled Wiedemann, "was his unmilitary manner and his slight Austrian accent, and most of all, that he was a serious person who obviously had been through quite a lot in life."

Wiedemann and Sergeant Amann now had time to make up the decoration list. They recommended Hitler for the Iron Cross, 1st Class, but since he was on the staff put his name at the bottom of the list. For this reason alone Hitler was turned down and instead given a 2nd Class award. Even so, Hitler was delighted and two days later wrote Herr Popp, "It was the happiest day of my life. Unfortunately, my comrades who also earned it are mostly all dead." He asked Popp to keep the newspapers describing the action. "I want to save them for reminiscences, if the dear Lord spares my life." He was also promoted to corporal, and no longer was called *Kamerad Schnürschuh* (an insulting Bavarian epithet, "Comrade Laced Boots"). He had earned the respect of his comrades and officers. He belonged.

Private Hans Mend hadn't seen Hitler since their recruit days in Munich. There he seemed too slight even to carry a full field pack but now as he slouched around, rifle in hand, helmet askew, mustache drooping, "a lively glow" in his eyes, he was the picture of the front-line fighter. The other messengers respected his apparent fearlessness but couldn't understand why an Austrian should take such risks. "He is just an odd character," one remarked to Mend, "and lives in his own world but otherwise he's a nice fellow."

Despite his lectures on the evils of smoking and drinking, "Adi" was generally liked because of his reliability in a crisis. He never abandoned a wounded comrade or pretended to be sick when it came time for a perilous mission. Moreover, he was a good companion during the long, tedious stretches awaiting action. Being an artist actually drew him closer to his barracks mates. He would draw cartoon sketches on postcards illustrating comical moments of their life. Once, for instance, a man shot a rabbit to take home on leave but left with a parcel containing a brick which someone had exchanged for the animal. Hitler sent the victim of the prank a postcard—with two sketches, one of the soldier unwrapping a brick back home and the other of his friends at the front eating the rabbit.

Unlike the others, Hitler got almost no packages from home and to satisfy his insatiable appetite he was forced to buy extra food from the cooks and kitchen help, thus earning the title of the unit's biggest *Vielfrass* ("glutton"). At the same time he was too proud to share his comrades' packages and would brusquely refuse on the grounds that he couldn't repay the favor. He was almost as brusque in his rejection of Lieutenant Wiedemann's offer at Christmas of ten marks from the mess-hall funds.

The regiment went back to the lines soon after the holidays but there was not enough action for Adolf. "Now we are still in our old position and harass the French and English," he wrote Popp on January 22, 1915. "The weather is miserable. Often for days in water up to our knees under very heavy artillery fire. We are looking forward to a few days of relief. Hopefully there will soon come a general offensive along the whole front. It can't go on like this forever."

It was during this military stalemate that a small white terrier, apparently the mascot of an English soldier, leaped into Hitler's trench and began chasing a rat. Hitler caught the dog, which at first kept trying to escape. "With exemplary patience (he didn't understand a word of German), I gradually got him used to me." Hitler named him Fuchsl (Little Fox) and taught him a variety of circus tricks such as climbing up and down a ladder. Fuchsl never left his new master's side during the day and at night slept beside him.

Late in January Hitler, in another letter to Popp, drew a graphic picture of the static but deadly warfare:

> . . . Because of the constant rain (we do not have winter), the closeness of the ocean, and the low-lying terrain, the meadows and fields are like bottomless morasses, while the streets are covered with slimy mud and through these swamps run the trenches of our infantry, a mass of shelters and trenches with gun emplacements, communication ditches and barbed wire barricades, wolf lairs, land mines, in short, an almost impossible position.

The following month he also wrote Judge Hepp about his battle experiences but then ended the letter, somewhat surprisingly, on a political note:

> I think so often of Munich and each of us has but one wish, that it may soon come to a settling of accounts with the gang, that we'll come to blows, no matter what the cost, and that those among us who have the luck to see our homeland again will find it purer and cleansed from foreign influence, so that by the sacrifice and agony which so many hundreds of thousands of us endure every day, that by the river of blood which flows

here daily, against an international world of enemies, not only will Germany's enemies from the outside be smashed, but also our domestic internationalism will be broken up.

Whenever anyone asked where he came from Hitler would reply that his home was the 16th Regiment—not Austria—and after the war he would live in Munich. But first they had to win! On this point he was fanatic and if one of his mates jokingly remarked that the war would never be won he became incensed and would pace back and forth, asserting that England's coming defeat was as certain as the "Amen in the prayer."

As long as his comrades talked of food or women Hitler kept to his reading or painting, but once the conversation turned to serious subjects he would stop and deliver a lecture. His simple comrades were entranced by his fluency and loved to hear him "spout" on art, architecture and the like. His reputation as an intellectual was enhanced by the fact that he "always had a book spread out in front of him." He carried several in his pack, one by Schopenhauer ("I learned a great deal from him"). This philosopher's recurrent affirmation of the strength of blind will, the triumph of that will, must have struck a responsive chord.

By the end of the summer of 1915 Hitler had become indispensable to regimental headquarters. The telephone lines to battalion and company command posts were often knocked out by artillery and only runners could deliver messages. "We found out very soon," recalled Lieutenant Wiedemann, "which messengers we could rely on the most."* He was admired by fellow runners as much for his craftiness—he could crawl up front like one of the Indians he had read about in his boyhood—as his exceptional courage. Yet there was something in Hitler that disturbed some of the men. He was too different, his sense of duty excessive. "It's more important to bring our messages to their destination," he once lectured a fellow messenger, "than for personal ambition or to satisfy curiosity." He was unnaturally eager to get up front and would often, without being asked, deliver messages for the other runners.

The tempo of fighting increased in June and July and the constant duty began to tell on Hitler. His face became wan and more sallow. In the dark hours of the morning when an English barrage started he would leap out of bed and, rifle in hand, stride rapidly back and forth, "like a race horse at the starting gate," until everyone was awake. He became even more impatient with his neighbors' gripes. If one complained about the smaller meat ration, he sharply retorted that the French ate rats in 1870.

On September 25 the English pressed their attack and by nightfall the position of the entire 16th Regiment was endangered. Phone communication to the front abruptly ceased. Hitler and another man went for-

* Fritz Wiedemann, who became Hitler's adjutant in 1935 only to be dismissed four years later for opposing the Führer's foreign policy, stated in his book, *Der Mann, Der Feldherr werden wollte*, that Hitler's memory of his war experiences was excellent. "I never really caught him lying or exaggerating when he told of his recollections."

ward to find out what had happened and returned "by the skin of their teeth" to report that the lines had been cut. An enemy attack in force was coming. Hitler was sent out to broadcast the warning and somehow survived the deadly barrage once more.

In the past months he had narrowly escaped death an inordinate number of times. It was as if he led a charmed life. "I was eating my dinner in a trench with several comrades," he told an English correspondent, Ward Price, years later. "Suddenly a voice seemed to be saying to me, 'Get up and go over there.' It was so clear and insistent that I obeyed mechanically, as if it had been a military order. I rose at once to my feet and walked twenty yards along the trench, carrying my dinner in its tin-can with me. Then I sat down to go on eating, my mind being once more at rest. Hardly had I done so when a flash and deafening report came from the part of the trench I had just left. A stray shell had burst over the group in which I had been sitting, and every member of it was killed."

Perhaps it was the season of perception. That fall on a night made gray-white with hoarfrost he may have felt the sense of his destiny when he wrote this strange poem:

> I often go on bitter nights
> To Wotan's oak in the quiet glade
> With dark powers to weave a union—
> The runic letters the moon makes with its magic spell
> And all who are full of impudence during the day
> Are made small by the magic formula!
> They draw shining steel—but instead of going into combat
> They solidify into stalagmites.
> So the false ones part from the real ones—
> I reach into a nest of words
> And then give to the good and just
> With my formula blessings and prosperity.

A few weeks later he made a portentous prophecy to his comrades: "You will hear much about me. Just wait until my time comes."

There was no snow that December, only endless rain. Entire sections of the meandering trench lines were flooded. The second Christmas was more dismal than the first. While the others opened parcels and cherished letters from home, Hitler sat on his cot as in a trance. During the three days of holiday he scarcely spoke a word. His comrades tried to cheer him up and offered him the pick of their own parcels. He refused with abrupt thanks, then retreated to his private world. Once the holidays ended, Hitler snapped out of his apathy, becoming so cheerful, in fact, that he could smile at mocking remarks about his "quietly spent holidays."

In the early summer of 1916 Hitler's regiment moved south, just in time to take part in the crucial battle of the Somme. It began with an English attack so relentless that almost 20,000 Allies were killed or fatally wounded on the first day alone. In the Fromelles sector the enemy barrage on the night of July 14 cut all regimental field telephones. Hitler and another runner were sent out "in the face of almost certain death, peppered with shot and shell every meter of the way." They cowered for shelter in watery shell holes and ditches. The other man collapsed from exhaustion and Hitler had to drag him back to their dugout.

By July 20 the Battle of Fromelles was on. It cost both sides many lives—and ended where it had started. For the next two months the struggle lapsed into dull but deadly trench warfare with advances or retreats measured in yards. It was during this time that Hitler lost a close friend; Hans Mend was transferred to the rear to act as interpreter in a prisoner-of-war camp. But he still had two other comrades, Ernst Schmidt and Ignaz Westenkirchner—and, more important, his pet. "How many times at Fromelles, during the First World War, I studied my dog Fuchsl," he reminisced on a winter night twenty-five years later. He told of his fascination with Fuchsl's reaction to a buzzing fly. The dog would quiver as if hypnotized, wrinkle his face like an old man, then suddenly leap forward and bark. "I used to watch as if he'd been a man—the progressive stages of his anger, of the bile that took possession of him." Fuchsl used to sit next to Hitler when he ate, watching each movement. If Hitler gave him nothing after taking five or six mouthfuls, the dog sat up and looked at his master as if to say, What about me? "It was crazy how fond I was of the beast."

After three months the Battle of the Somme still raged. The Allies persistently attacked and, in all, would suffer 614,000 casualties in this one campaign, but it was a useless slaughter, for the German lines did not buckle. For almost a week Hitler continued his charmed life despite a number of dangerous missions. Then on the night of October 7 his luck ended as he slept with the other messengers in sitting position in a narrow tunnel leading to regimental headquarters. A shell exploded near the narrow entrance, knocking the messengers into a heap. Hitler was hit in the thigh but tried to argue Wiedemann into keeping him at the front. "It isn't so bad, Lieutenant, right?" he said anxiously. "I can still stay with you, I mean, stay with the regiment! Can't I?"

3

Hitler was evacuated to a field hospital. His wound, his first, was not serious but in the ward he suffered a curious shock, one that almost made him collapse from "fright." It came as he lay on his cot and suddenly heard the voice of a German woman, a nurse. "For the first time in two years to hear such a sound!" Shortly he was on a hospital train bound for Germany.

"The closer our train which was to bring us home approached the border, the more inwardly restless each of us became." At last he recognized the first German house—"by its high gable and beautiful shutters. The Fatherland!"

At a military hospital just southwest of Berlin the comfortable white beds were such a change after trench life that at first "we hardly dared to lie on them properly." He gradually readjusted to such comfort, but not to the spirit of cynicism he found in some men. As soon as he was ambulatory, Hitler got permission to spend the weekend in Berlin. He found hunger and "dire misery"—and "scoundrels" who were agitating for peace.

After two months he was released from the hospital and transferred to a replacement battalion in Munich. Here, according to *Mein Kampf*, he at last found the answer to the collapse of morale. The Jews! They were behind the front line plotting Germany's downfall. "Nearly every clerk was a Jew and nearly every Jew was a clerk. I was amazed at this plethora of warriors from the chosen people and could not help but compare them with their rare representatives at the front." He was also convinced that "Jewish finance" had seized control of Germany's production. "The spider was slowly beginning to suck the blood out of the people's pores."

His comrades at the front never heard him talk like this; he appeared to be no more anti-Semitic than they were. Occasionally he would make an innocuous remark such as, "If all Jews were no more intelligent than Stein [their telephone operator], then there wouldn't be trouble." And whenever Adolf talked about Vienna and the overriding influence of the Jews, he did so, Westenkirchner recalled, "without spitefulness." Schmidt, in fact, never heard him discuss the subject at all nor did Lieutenant Wiedemann ("It really seems impossible for me to believe that Hitler's hatred for Jews dated back to that time").

Hitler became disgusted with Munich. He found the mood in the replacement battalion despicable. No one honored a front-line soldier. These recruits had no conception of what Hitler had suffered in the trenches. He longed to be back with his own kind and in January 1917 wrote Lieutenant Wiedemann that he was "again fit for service" and wished "to return to my old regiment and old comrades." On March 1 he was back with the 16th Regiment, receiving a warm welcome from officers and comrades alike. Little Fuchsl went into paroxysms of ecstasy—"he hurled himself on me in frenzy." For supper the company cook "turned out an extra special mess in his honor, *Kartoffelpuffer*, bread and jam and cake." At last Hitler was back home where he belonged. That night he wandered around for hours, flashlight in hand, spitting rats on his bayonet —until someone threw a boot at him and he went to bed.

A few days later the regiment entrained for the Arras area to prepare for another spring offensive. But there was leisure time for painting, and

Hitler completed more water colors, scenes of former battles that had meaning to him.* That Easter his art took a popular turn. He painted egg briquettes with calcium and placed them in the garden of the regimental commander, spelling out: "Happy Easter 1917." A few months later there was a new regimental commander, Major Freiherr von Tubeuf, a young, active man who brought discipline back to the unit. He not only made life difficult for both men and officers but criticized his superiors. To work off his frustrations Tubeuf went hunting. Hitler was one of the beaters and he spent two hours crawling around in the brush just behind the front lines flailing away with a long stick and shouting, while his commander (whom he would promote to general in sixteen years) fired away at rabbits.

Despite long and gallant service Hitler was still a corporal. One reason, according to Wiedemann, was that he lacked "the capacity for leadership." Another was his sloppy bearing. He held his head somewhat lopsided toward his left shoulder and slouched around. Although he bathed whenever possible and called a comrade who didn't "a living dunghill," he disliked polishing his boots. Nor would he snap heels at the approach of an officer. More important, there were no authorized spaces as corporal for a messenger. If promoted, Hitler would have had to give up the duty he preferred; and the regiment would have lost one of its best runners.

That summer the regiment returned to its first battlefield in Belgium and participated in the third battle for Ypres. It was as deadly as the first. In mid-July they were bombarded for ten days and nights. When it slackened they could hear under them the ominous sound of digging—the enemy was boring tunnels. Overhead came the drone of planes, then the crash of bombs. In addition there was the constant threat of gas and the men sometimes had to keep their suffocating masks on for twenty-four hours at a stretch. On the last day of July the defenders were confronted with a new terror—tanks. Fortunately, torrential rains turned no man's land into a quagmire and the tanks were bogged down.

In August the shattered 16th Regiment was relieved. They were sent to Alsace for rest and it was at this time that Hitler suffered two grievous losses. A railroad official, captivated by the antics of Fuchsl, offered Hitler two hundred marks for the terrier. "You could give me two hundred thousand, and you wouldn't get him!" was Hitler's indignant reply. But as the troops were disembarking, Hitler couldn't find Fuchsl. His column was already on the move and he had to follow. "I was desperate. The swine who stole my dog doesn't realize what he did to me." At about the same time another "swine" rifled his knapsack and made off with a leather case con-

* In his unpublished diary Gordon Craig, the stage designer, described these wartime paintings as remarkably artistic productions. His praise may have been tempered by gratitude; it was Hitler who literally saved him from starvation in Paris during World War II by buying his sketches.

taining sketches, drawings and water colors. Insulted and injured—first by a civilian slacker and then by one of the new breed of cowardly recruits (no front-line soldier would rob a comrade)—he put aside his paints.

Early that October Schmidt finally persuaded Hitler to take an eighteen-day furlough, his first of the war. Their destination was Dresden, home of Schmidt's sister, but they stopped off at Brussels, Cologne and Leipzig for sightseeing. Hitler particularly enjoyed the last city. It was here that Martin Luther preached his first sermon in St. Thomas' Church—the same church where Bach had played the organ for twenty-seven years and was buried, and where Wagner had been baptized. But what impressed him most was the massive 300-foot monument of the Battle of the Nations, honoring the war dead of 1813, which looked more like a fortress than a shrine. "This has nothing to do with art," he commented, "but it is enormous and beautiful." In Dresden they inspected the famous buildings and visited the art galleries, including the famous Zwinger. He was eager to go to the opera until he examined the program—apparently there was no Wagner—and announced there was nothing worth seeing. Later he visited Berlin by himself and stayed a few days with the family of a front-line comrade. "The city is marvelous," he wrote Schmidt on a postcard. "A real world capital. Traffic is still tremendous. Am gone almost all day. Now finally have opportunity to study the museums a little better. In short: there is nothing lacking."

The unit saw little action for the rest of the year and Hitler had much time for reading. To him novels and magazines were frivolous and he concentrated on history and philosophy. "War forces one to think deeply about human nature," he later told Hans Frank. "Four years of war are equivalent to thirty years university training in regard to life's problems. I hated nothing more than trash literature. When we are concerned with the fate of mankind then one can only read Homer and evangelical works. In the later years of the war I read Schopenhauer and reached for him again and again. [The copy of Schopenhauer's selected works which he kept in his pack was worn out.] Then I was able to do without evangelism—even if Christ was a true fighter. But the turning of both cheeks is not a very good recipe for the front."

Quiet as the western front was, that winter proved the most arduous one yet for the front-line troops. Rations were shorter than ever and the men were forced to eat cats and dogs. Hitler's comrades recalled that he preferred the meat of cat to that of a dog (perhaps because of Fuchsl). His favorite food when he could get it, was toast thickly spread with honey or marmalade. Once he found large crates of zwieback, and to satisfy his hunger he began robbing them systematically, craftily taking packages from the bottom. He shared the loot with his mates and, after getting some sugar on barter, would cook for them the front-line version of an Austrian dessert, *Schmarren*.

At home civilians were also forced to eat dogs and cats ("roof rabbits"); bread was made from sawdust and potato peelings, and there was almost no milk. Germany's allies also suffered. Food supplies were so short in Vienna that the Austrian government was forced to appeal to Berlin for grain. Strikes erupted in Vienna and Budapest, set off not only by hunger but by Germany's failure to make peace with the new Bolshevik government in Russia. They spread to Germany itself, which had been under a virtual military dictatorship for several months, and on Monday, January 28, 1918, workers throughout Germany went out on strike. Peace was their main demand but they also insisted on workers' representation in negotiations with the Allies, increased food rations, the abolition of martial law, and a democratic government throughout Germany. In Munich and Nuremberg only a few thousand workers marched through the streets petitioning for immediate peace without annexation, but in Berlin 400,000 workers walked out of their shops to organize a strike committee. Within a week they were forced back to work but a spirit of rebellion had come alive in the capital and it seemed only a question of time before full-scale revolution would break out.

News of the general strike was received with mixed feelings at the front. Many of the soldiers were as war-weary and disgusted as those back home but almost as many felt they had been betrayed by their own civilians. Hitler called it "the biggest piece of chicanery in the whole war." He was incensed at the slackers and Reds. "What was the army fighting for if the homeland itself no longer wanted victory? For whom the immense sacrifices and privations? The soldier is expected to fight for victory and the homeland goes on strike against it!"

At last Berlin made peace with the Soviets at Brest-Litovsk on March 3 but the terms imposed on the young government were so harsh that leftists in Germany claimed the treaty's real purpose was to crush the Russian Revolution. News of the capitulation of the Bolsheviks exhilarated soldiers like Hitler who remained convinced that Germany must win. Now more than ever total victory seemed in their grasp and the majority of troops responded loyally if not eagerly to the high command's order for a massive offensive. In the next four months Hitler's regiment took part in all phases of the massive Ludendorff spring offensives: on the Somme, on the Aisne and finally on the Marne. Hitler's fighting spirit was higher than ever. On one of his trips out front in June he got a glimpse of something in a trench that looked like a French helmet. He crept forward and saw four *poilus*. Hitler pulled out his pistol—messengers had turned in rifles for side arms by then—and began shouting orders in German as though he had a company of soldiers. He delivered his four prisoners to Colonel von Tubeuf personally and was commended. "There was no circumstance or situation," recalled Tubeuf, "that would have prevented him from volunteering for the most difficult, arduous and dangerous tasks and he was always ready to sacrifice life and tranquillity for his Fatherland and for others." On August 4 Hitler was awarded the Iron Cross, 1st Class, but it was for former achievements and not this outstanding feat and simply read, "For personal bravery and general merit."* It was presented to him by the battalion adjutant who had initiated the award, First Lieutenant Hugo Gutmann, a Jew.

By this time it was evident that the great Ludendorff offensives which had pushed to within sight of the Eiffel Tower had failed miserably. Defeat on the western front came as a shock, particularly after the historic victories in the East where vast areas extending as far as the Caucasus had been conquered. Consequently there was a serious drop in morale even among the older soldiers. Disorders on troop and leave trains approached rebellion. Shots were fired from windows. Men disappeared at every station. Officers attempting to maintain discipline were attacked with stones and grenades. Revolutionary slogans such as "We're not fighting for Germany's honor but for the millionaires," were scrawled in chalk on the cars.

Four days after Hitler received his Iron Cross, an Allied counterattack in the dense fog smashed through the German lines at Amiens. Ludendorff sent a staff officer to the front and immediately moved reserves to the breakthrough area. As these fresh troops moved up, those falling back shouted insults: "Blacklegs! You are prolonging the war!"

It was, Ludendorff wrote, "the black day of the German Army in the history of this war." The Kaiser reacted dejectedly but calmly and remarked, "We must draw only one conclusion: we are at the limit of our capabilities. The war must be ended." A few days later Ludendorff and Hindenburg conferred with Wilhelm at Spa. When the Kaiser ordered his foreign minister to begin peace negotiations, Hindenburg protested that the army still held much enemy territory and Ludendorff excitedly exclaimed that there must be discipline on the home front as well as "more vigorous conscription of the young Jews, hitherto left pretty much alone."

In the face of rebellion at home and impending collapse at the front, Hitler became more argumentative and talked at length of the swindle perpetrated by the Reds. But his voice was lost in the chorus of complaints from replacements. At such times, according to Schmidt, Hitler "became furious and shouted in a terrible voice that the pacifists and shirkers were losing the war." One day he attacked a new non-com who said it was stupid to continue fighting. They fought with their fists, and finally, after taking considerable punishment, Hitler beat his opponent. From that day, Schmidt recalled, "the new ones despised him but we old comrades liked him more than ever."

* In addition to this decoration and the Iron Cross, 2nd Class, he had won in 1914, Hitler received the following awards: September 17, 1917, Military Cross, 3rd Class, with swords; May 9, 1918, the *Regimentsdiplom* for outstanding bravery; May 18, 1918, the *Verwundeterabrechnen* (Medal for Wounded); and on August 25, 1918, the *Dienstauszeichnung* (Service Medal), 3rd Class.

Four years of dehumanizing trench warfare had engendered in Hitler, as in so many other German patriots, an abiding hatred of the pacifists and slackers back home who were "stabbing the Fatherland in the back." He and those like him burned with a zeal to avenge such treachery, and out of all this would come the politics of the future. Hitler was far from the dreamy-eyed volunteer of 1914. Four years in the trenches had given him a sense of belonging along with a degree of self-confidence. Having fought for Germany, he was truly German; and having conducted himself honorably under duress, he had pride in his manhood. He had entered the army a raw youth, remarkably underdeveloped for all his twenty-four years and hardships in Vienna; now he was a man, ready to take a man's place in the world.

Early in September the 16th Regiment was moved back to Flanders. Since they were in reserve, the troops were allowed to take furloughs. With a comrade named Arendt he returned to Berlin where he must have been repelled by the rising spirit of discontent in the capital. He also spent a few days at the family farm in Spital. Several weeks after his return the 16th Regiment marched a third time to the area below Ypres. For the third time they dug into the fields and hills near Comines. Then on the morning of October 14 Hitler was blinded by gas near the village of Werwick. He would recover his eyesight only to lose it again November 9, upon learning that Germany was going to surrender. A few days later he would hear voices and see a vision.

4

It is impossible to know how deep Adolf Hitler's fear and hatred of Jews ran on the day he was gassed in Belgium. Within a year, however, hatred of all things Jewish would become an overt and dominant force in his life. Hitler was only one among millions of other patriots who learned to fear Jews and Reds (almost as a single entity) during this period. For in these months the country was engulfed by a terrifying series of Marxist-inspired uprisings that threatened to destroy the fabric of German existence.

Significantly, the revolutions began while Hitler was suffering the depressing aftereffects of mustard gas. On the day he started east in a hospital train—it was October 16—Prince Max of Baden, the new German Chancellor, received a note from President Woodrow Wilson demanding, in effect, the abdication of Wilhelm before America would agree to an armistice. This quickened the disintegration of the German military and within two weeks open revolt broke out when the fleet was ordered to proceed to sea. The crews of six battleships protested. Mutiny broke out in Kiel as sailors pillaged armories and small arms lockers and took over most of the city. In one barracks a stoker established the Kiel Sailors' Soviet and all but one of the ships still in port ran up the red flag of revolution. The men seized officers, tore off their insignia and escorted them to the prison.

In Munich another insurrection broke out on November 7. It was led by Kurt Eisner, a small elderly Jew wearing a black floppy hat which, large as it was, couldn't contain a shock of wild hair. Epically untidy, he was a living cartoon of the bomb-throwing Red. He had already spent almost nine months in prison for his wartime strike activities. By dusk the revolutionaries, joined by many soldiers, had seized every major military post in Munich and Ludwig III of the House of Wittelsbach had been forced to flee in a car, which ran off the road just south of the city, miring itself in a potato field. It was a fitting end to monarchy in Bavaria.

That evening trucks filled with occupants flourishing red flags rattled through the city. Eisner's men seized the main railroad station and government buildings. No one resisted. Police looked the other way as rebels set up machine guns at strategic corners. The burghers of Munich wakened the next morning to find that their Bavaria had become a republic. Revolution had come, German style, without too much fuss and without a single serious casualty. The people accepted their lot in the same spirit. There was no violent reaction. The Müncheners grumbled and waited.

The flames of orderly revolution were igniting spontaneously throughout Germany. In Friedrichshafen workers at the Zeppelin plant formed a council. The factory workers in the Stuttgart area, including the vast Daimler motor works, struck and, led by socialists with views similar to Eisner's, made similar demands. Sailors engineered revolt in Frankfurt am Main. At Kassel the entire garrison, including a commanding officer, revolted without benefit of bullets. There were a few shots fired in Cologne when the garrison of 45,000 went Red but order quickly settled over the city. A civilian revolt in Hanover succeeded even though authorities ordered troops to use force; instead the soldiers joined the rebels. It was the same in Düsseldorf, Leipzig and Magdeburg.

Government after government throughout Germany collapsed as workers' and soldiers' councils took control. Finally, on November 9, the Kaiser reluctantly abdicated, turning power over to the moderate socialists who were led by a former saddlemaker, Friedrich Ebert. It was the end of the German Empire, begun in France on January 18, 1871, when Wilhelm I, King of Prussia and grandfather of Wilhelm II, was proclaimed the first Emperor of Germany in the Hall of Mirrors at the Versailles Palace.

It was also the end of an era. Forty-eight years earlier Bismarck had achieved his dream of unifying Germany and in so doing had created a new image of Germany and Germans. Overnight the foundation on which rested the security of the Junker landowners in East Prussia and the great industrialists crumbled; and overnight the political philosophy on which the majority of Germans had based their conservative and patriotic way of life had apparently disintegrated with the lowering of the imperial flag.

Perhaps the greatest shock to Germans was to find Ebert sitting in the chancellery. In a single day the Hohenzollern regime had evaporated and a man of the people had taken command. How could it possibly have happened? Ebert himself was uneasy in the seat of power. He realized his presence would be an insult to those raised in imperialism. Moreover, he did not even represent the radical spirit of the streets. In fact, whom did he represent? He was so panicky that when Prince Max appeared at dusk to say farewell Ebert begged him to remain in Berlin as "administrator" for the Hohenzollern monarchy.

At 5 A.M. two days later a representative of the Ebert government, Matthias Erzberger, put his signature to the Allied armistice terms in Marshal Foch's private railroad car. Hostilities would cease at 11 A.M. He had insured peace to a shattered nation at the eleventh hour of the eleventh day of the eleventh month of the year, and in so doing innocently gave birth to the myth of the "November criminals"—that it was the socialists who had sold out the nation. It was the Kaiser and the imperial German generals, of course, who had lost the war but President Wilson had refused to make an armistice with them, insisting he could deal only with democratic elements. And by forcing the socialists to assume the blame for something they had not brought about, Wilson gave Adolf Hitler a political tool that he was destined to wield with devastating force.

5

At the end of November 1918 Hitler was discharged from the Pasewalk hospital as "fit for field service" since the patient "no longer complained of anything but a burning of the membrane." Hitler later testified in court that he could only make out the largest headlines in a newspaper and feared he might never read another book. "The medical records at the hospital," he complained, "were made at a time of revolution. Practically no one got personal attention; we were discharged in hordes. For example, I never even received my soldier's pay-book."

He was ordered to report to the replacement battalion of his regiment. This was located in Munich and on his way he must have passed through Berlin, which was in the hands of the Executive Council of the Workers' and Soldiers' Councils—a coalition not only of soldiers and workers but of Majority and Independent Socialists. This conglomeration had already enacted social reforms which would have seemed impossible a few months earlier. It had established the eight-hour day; granted labor the unrestricted right to organize into unions; increased workers' old-age, sick and unemployment benefits; abolished censorship of the press; and released political prisoners.

While Hitler approved the social reforms, he distrusted the revolutionaries who had effected them: the Executive Council was a tool of the Bolsheviks and the betrayer of the front-line soldiers; and its eventual goal was another Red revolution. When Hitler checked in at the Turkenstrasse barracks of Munich's Schwabing area, he encountered the same spirit of rebellion. This installation had gone over to Eisner earlier in the month and was under the control of a Soldiers' Council. There was no discipline; the place was a pigsty. There was no respect for those who had served in the trenches since the first days of the war. Many were there for food and shelter alone. It was far worse than the Männerheim. What particularly incensed Hitler was the behavior of the council members. "Their whole activity was so repellent to me that I decided at once to leave again as soon as possible."

Fortunately he found an old comrade who experienced the same disgust. "The laziest and most impudent among the men were, naturally, those who had never been anywhere near the trenches," remembered his fellow runner, Ernst Schmidt. "The place was full of laggards and cowards." Some two weeks later, when guards were sought for a prisoner-of-war camp at Traunstein, sixty miles to the east on the road to Salzburg, Hitler suggested to Schmidt that they volunteer. Their group, comprised mostly of so-called "revolution men," was met at the railroad station by an officer. The men treated his order to fall in as a joke: didn't he know drill had been abolished? The next day the contingent, except for a few who had seen service in the trenches, were shipped back to Munich. Hitler and Schmidt remained.

6

In Berlin the Spartacists, a far leftist group named after the slave who led the rebellion against the Romans, had taken to the streets to make revolution with the help of revolting sailors. This was no *gemütlich* Munich uprising. By Christmas Eve the capital was close to anarchy. Other cities followed suit, if not as dramatically, and throughout Germany the structure of the military and police began to crumble.

With their abdication of authority, a new force made an abrupt appearance—a phenomenon known as the Freikorps, bands of idealistic activists from the armed forces who shared Hitler's passion to defend Germania from the Reds. The Free Corps, spawned from the German generation born in Hitler's time, had been prepared for today's action by two previous experiences. First had come the prewar youth movement, the Wandervögel (Birds of Passage). These youngsters tramped around the land, often wearing colorful costumes, in their search for a new way of life.

For the most part from the well-to-do middle class, they despised the liberal bourgeois society they sprang from and were convinced that "parental religion was largely sham, politics boastful and trivial, economics unscrupulous and deceitful, education stereotyped and lifeless, art trashy and sentimental, literature spurious and commercialized, drama tawdry and mechanical." They regarded family life as repressive and insincere. They also were concerned that the relations between the sexes, in and out of marriage, were "shot through with hypocrisy." Their goal was to establish a youth culture for fighting the bourgeois trinity of school, home and church.

They would sit around campfires, under the direction of a Führer, and sing "The Song of the Freebooters," while silently gazing into a campfire in quest of "messages from the forest," or listening to someone read hortatory passages from Nietzsche or Stefan George, who wrote: "The people and supreme wisdom yearn for the Man!—The Deed! . . . Perhaps someone who sat for years among your murderers and slept in your prisons will stand up and *do the deed*." These young people, thriving on mysticism and impelled by idealism, yearned for action—any kind of action.

They found it in the Great War. Perhaps that is why they were as convinced as Hitler of the righteousness of the Fatherland's cause. Life in the trenches brought officers and men closer together in a brotherhood of suffering and blood. The men worshiped the one who led them into desperate hand-to-hand combat. "To them he was not their commanding officer; he was their Führer! And they were his comrades! They trusted him blindly and would have followed him into hell itself if it were necessary." Together they formed a front-line relationship of democracy hitherto unknown in Germany. The miles of trenches were isolated from the rest of the world and became, in effect, a "monastery with walls of flame."

These comrades of the front lines, these former Birds of Passage, shared with Hitler the shame of surrender and distrust of a home front degenerating into Bolshevism. Understandably, these veterans responded with enthusiasm to announcements placed by the military in newspapers and on billboards announcing that the Spartacist danger had not yet been removed and calling for soldiers to rise and join the Free Corps to "prevent Germany from becoming the laughingstock of the earth."

While this illegal army was forming, the Spartacists, with the approval of many Berliners, were taking over the capital. They controlled public utilities, transportation, and munitions factories. In desperation, on January 3, 1919, the Ebert government dismissed the chief of police since he was known to sympathize with the Spartacists and had recently supported the sailors' mutiny. In retaliation, the Spartacists, now openly admitting they were Communists, called for revolution. Berlin workers responded with enthusiasm and by midmorning of the sixth, 200,000 workers, carrying weapons and red flags, massed from Alexanderplatz to the Tiergarten. Nor did the fog and cold dampen the spirit of the crowd. Groups seized the officers of the Social Democrat newspaper, *Vorwärts*, and the Wolff Telegraph Agency. The chancellery itself was surrounded by the angry mob. Inside hid Ebert and his associates.

By the following morning the Communists were ensconced in the statuary on top of the Brandenburg Gate, their rifles covering the Unter den Linden, the Königstrasse and the Charlottenburger Chaussee. In addition to strategic railroad stations, the Government Printing Office and the Bötzow Brewery were occupied. Within twenty-four hours the government held only a few of the city's major buildings.

Berlin—eventually all of Germany—would probably have gone Communist but for the Free Corps. Within a week units from outside the city marched in and crushed the Red centers of resistance. The Spartacist leaders, including the diminutive Rosa Luxemburg, were hunted down and cruelly murdered.

Four days after the death of "Red Rose" the first national election under the new Republic was held. It was a Sunday, clear and cold. For the first time in German history women were allowed to participate and 30,000,000 citizens out of an electorate of 35,000,000 cast their votes for 423 deputies to the National Assembly. The results, while surprising, should have been predictable. The two rightist parties, which wanted a return of the Hohenzollerns yet pretended they didn't, got about fifteen per cent of the Assembly seats; the two centrist parties, which favored the Republic, won almost forty per cent as did Ebert's Majority Socialists; and the far left Independent Socialists took only seven per cent. The result, as much a victory against revolution as it was for a republic, doomed socialization.

Since strife-torn Berlin was not considered safe, Weimar, some hundred and fifty miles southwest of the capital, was made the home of the National Assembly. Its selection was a cultural as well as geographical choice, for Weimar had been the home of Goethe, Schiller and Liszt. The Assembly met on February 6 in the New National Theater but the convocation lacked the pomp and ceremony of a Hohenzollern event. There were no bands, cavalry escorts or dazzling uniforms.

After five days a working government was organized with Ebert named first President of the Reich by a large majority. He appointed a Chancellor who, in turn, selected his own cabinet. The most significant choice was a strong-willed man named Noske (he called himself the "Bloodhound") as Minister of Defense. It meant that the illegal Free Corps would now operate with the blessing of the infant Weimar Republic and continue to defend the nation from Reds and riot.

7

Traditionally Bavarians detested Prussia and all things Prussian, and the events in Weimar were largely ignored in Munich. One of the city's leading intellectuals, as yet unrecognized by the world, was contemptuous of the attempts of the Ebert government to establish democracy throughout Germany. The lonely and impoverished bachelor, Oswald Spengler—misogynous and misanthropic—had finally published the first volume of *The Decline of the West* in the spring of 1918 and, though still unreviewed, the book was making an impact throughout the country. "Like the French in 1793 we must go right through to the end in our misfortune, we need a chastisement compared to which the four years of war are nothing," he wrote a friend, ". . . until finally the Terror has brought to a head such a degree of excitement and despair, that a dictatorship, resembling that of Napoleon, will be regarded universally as a salvation."

Hitler, who considered himself born for and destined to politics, was preparing his return to Munich. The prisoner-of-war camp at Traunstein was about to close and he was being reassigned to the 2nd Infantry Regiment barracks in Schwabing along with his comrade Schmidt. Another young man with similar aspirations was already established in Munich. Alfred Rosenberg, a fanatic anti-Semite and anti-Marxist, had come from his native Estonia by way of Russia to find his true home. Like Hitler, he was artist and architect. Like Hitler, he was more Germanic than a native German, and had left his birthplace "to gain a Fatherland for myself." Moreover, he was determined to warn this Fatherland of the Bolshevik terror that had ravaged the old one, and fight to keep it free from Jewish Communism.

Upon learning that there was a German author named Eckart who shared many of his views, Rosenberg decided to make his acquaintance. Dietrich Eckart—poet, playwright, coffeehouse intellectual—was a tall, bald, burly eccentric who spent much of his time in cafés and beer halls giving equal attention to drink and talk. Son of a Bavarian counselor to the King and former patient at an institution "for nervous diseases," he had entree to aristocratic circles. An original, raffish man with a touch of genius (his brilliant translation of *Peer Gynt* was the standard version), he too was a Pan-German and anti-Semite. With his own money he published a weekly paper that had a circulation of some 30,000.

Rosenberg appeared, without introduction, at Eckart's apartment. The poet was impressed by what he saw in the doorway: an intense, dead-serious young man. Rosenberg's first words were: "Can you use a fighter against Jerusalem?" Eckart laughed. "Certainly!" Had he written anything? Rosenberg produced an article on the destructive forces of Judaism and Bolshevism on Russia. It was the beginning of a relationship that would affect the career of Adolf Hitler. Eckart accepted Rosenberg as a "co-warrior against Jerusalem" and soon his articles on Russia began appearing not only in Eckart's paper but in another Munich weekly, *Deutsche Republik.* The theme of these articles was that the Jew stood behind the world's evils: the Zionists had planned the Great War as well as the Red Revolution and were presently plotting with the Masons to take over the world.

8

To many Bavarians Kurt Eisner was the very model of a revolutionary and it was widely believed that his revolution had been financed by Moscow gold. On the contrary, it had cost him only the eighteen marks in his pocket on that historic day in November, and he was, in fact, the antithesis of the ruthless, pragmatic Russian Bolshevik. He ran the Bavarian Socialist Republic as if he were still installed at the *Stammtisch* of his favorite coffeehouse. What Eisner was attempting to establish was not Communism or even socialism but a unique kind of radical democracy. A poet among politicians whose dream of a reign of beauty, illumination and reason was more in keeping with Shelley than Marx, he was already on the path to oblivion; the January elections had brought a resounding victory for the middle-class parties and an overriding demand for his resignation.

Early in the morning of February 21, realizing his cause was hopeless, he wrote out a statement announcing his resignation, but en route to the Landtag to deliver it, he was assassinated by Count Anton Arco-Valley, a young cavalry officer who had been turned down by an anti-Semitic group since his mother was Jewish. Eisner would have been out of office in an hour, his regime replaced by a middle-of-the-road government. The assassination brought about what Arco-Valley most feared, another surge to the left. Eisner, so recently despised and rejected by almost everyone, became an instant martyr and proletarian saint, and the revolutionary movement was resuscitated. Martial law was declared and a new all-socialist government headed by a former teacher, Adolf Hoffmann, was appointed by the Central Workers' and Soldiers' Council. A general strike was called, a 7 P.M. curfew imposed, and the University of Munich closed since its students were already acclaiming Arco-Valley as their hero.

A fortnight later the first congress of the Third International convened in Moscow and the resolution establishing the Communist International (Comintern) was unanimously adopted. In the ensuing victory celebration Lenin called on workers of all countries to force their leaders to withdraw troops from Russia, resume diplomatic and commercial relations, and help rebuild the fledgling nation with an army of engineers and instructors.

Berlin was already responding to the call for world revolution. The previous day, workers, ignoring orders from the Communist Party, had converged on the center of the city to demonstrate and loot. Joined by the Red Soldiers' League and other radical military groups, they seized more than thirty local police stations. Sailors besieged the main police headquarters on the Alexanderplatz which was defended by several companies of Free Corps infantry. The following day 1500 delegates of the Workers' Councils voted overwhelmingly to call a general strike. The capital was immobilized: no electricity, no transportation.

The revolutionaries concentrated on the eastern part of the city, setting up machine guns at key points. To counter them, Defense Minister Noske, using dictatorial powers recently bestowed on him, brought more than 30,000 Free Corps troops into the city on March 5. The rebels were driven back block by block while Berlin's bars, dance halls and cabarets remained open for business as usual.

After four more days of bitter house-to-house fighting with cannon, machine guns and strafing airplanes pitted against rifles and grenades, Noske announced that anyone "who bears arms against government troops will be shot on the spot." Scores of workers were lined up against walls and executed without trial. It was all over by the thirteenth. More than 1500 revolutionaries were dead and at least 10,000 wounded. The spirit of revolt, however, continued to spread throughout the country. Radicals were in power in Saxony and a state of siege existed in the Ruhr basin. Ben Hecht of the Chicago *Daily News* syndicate cabled: GERMANY IS HAVING A NERVOUS BREAKDOWN. THERE IS NOTHING SANE TO REPORT.

Munich too was on the verge of another revolution, this one inspired by a coup d'état in Budapest. On March 22 news arrived that a popular front of Socialists and Communists had seized control of Hungary in the name of the councils of workers, soldiers and peasants. A Hungarian Soviet Republic was announced under the leadership of an unknown, Béla Kun. A Jew himself, twenty-five of his thirty-two commissars were also Jews, provoking the London *Times* to characterize the regime as "the Jewish Mafia." The triumph of Béla Kun emboldened the leftists in Munich. Early on the evening of April 4 delegates from the councils trudged through streets piled with twenty inches of snow, the heaviest downfall in years. Their destination was the Löwenbräuhaus, only two blocks from Hitler's prewar rooming house. Here a resolution was read aloud: "Elimination of the parties, union of the entire proletariat, proclamation of a Soviet Republic and brotherhood with the Russian and Hungarian proletariat. And then no power on earth will be able to prevent the immediate execution of full socialization."

It was a coffeehouse revolution, an innocent version of the bloody reality. Its spiritual leader was Ernst Toller, the poet, and his platform included a demand for new art forms in drama, painting and architecture so the spirit of mankind could be set free. The Cabinet was a congeries of engaging eccentrics: the Commissar for Housing, for instance, ordered that henceforth the living room in all homes must be above the kitchen and bedroom. But the jewel in this crown of originals was Franz Lipp, selected as Commissar for Foreign Affairs (even though he had spent some time in a mental institution) on the grounds that he was the picture of a diplomat with his neat beard and gray frock coat. Lipp sent an indignant telegram to Moscow charging that Eisner's successor had stolen the keys to the ministry toilet, and declared war on Württemberg and Switzerland "because these dogs have not at once loaned me sixty locomotives."

The end came abruptly on Palm Sunday, April 13, when the former Minister President, the socialist schoolteacher Hoffmann, attempted to seize Munich by force. His *Putsch* never had a chance despite the exploits of soldiers like Adolf Hitler. He, for one, prevented the men at his barracks of the 2nd Infantry Regiment from going over to the Reds by climbing onto a chair and shouting, "Those who say we should remain neutral are right! After all, we're no pack of Revolutionary Guards for a gang of vagrant Jews!" Although Hitler and others held the Munich garrison to neutrality, the Hoffmann Putsch was crushed by nightfall and this time the Red professionals—led by Eugen Leviné, a native of St. Petersburg and the son of a Jewish merchant—took over the government. They had been sent to Munich by the Communist Party to organize revolution and, after arresting the poet Toller, promptly converted it into a genuine Soviet. But they proceeded to violate strict party orders to avoid any armed action, "even when a local or momentary success might be possible," by dispatching, in the name of the Bavarian Soviet Republic, a considerable force to confront an army of 8000 men that Hoffmann had hastily gathered to retake Munich. The Hoffmann army was approaching Dachau, a city ten miles above Munich.

The Red commander-in-chief was the man just arrested by the Communists, Ernst Toller. After release from a cellar he went forth to battle on a borrowed horse, as a knight of old, determined that "the revolution must be cleanly fought." On April 18 this Red knight directed the attack against the Hoffmann forces but, being a humanist and individualist, he persistently ignored orders from Munich. First he refused to shell Dachau and instead attempted to avoid conflict by negotiation. When firing erupted and the issue was forced he led his men to an almost bloodless triumph. The Hoffmann forces retreated in panic. The Soviet leaders ordered Toller to shoot the officers he had captured. Naturally he released them and once more he was imprisoned.

After the debacle at Dachau, Hoffmann was forced to accept help from War Minister Noske's Free Corps units. A tactical plan for the conquest of Munich was drawn up with amazing promptness and executed so effectively that the city was completely encircled by April 27. In vengeful retribution the surrounded Reds hunted down enemies of the Soviet Republic throughout Munich. Sailors captured seven members of the anti-Semitic Thule Society, including its attractive secretary. In all a hundred hostages were imprisoned in the Luitpold high school.

By April 29 the ring around Munich tightened and the revolutionaries were in a panic. A false alarm that the Whites had occupied the main railroad station emptied Red headquarters, except for Toller (who had been released to set up a last-ditch defense) and the commander of the Red Army. He decided to wreak final vengeance on the Whites, whose Free Corps troops had recently executed fifty-two Russian prisoners of war in a stone quarry and shot a dozen unarmed workers; he ordered the execution of the hostages in the high school. The horrified Toller rushed to stop the massacre but by the time he arrived at least twenty people had been slaughtered.

Students slipped through what was left of the Red lines and reported these atrocities to Free Corps commanders who issued orders to march into the city at dawn. The first of May was clear and warm as Free Corps units converged on the city from several directions. They had little difficulty routing scattered revolutionaries despite some opposition in the area surrounding the Hauptbahnhof and in the Schwabing section. On all sides the Free Corps men were cheered by the relieved citizenry. In the Marienplatz an open-air mass for the troops was held as red flags were hauled down and replaced by the blue and white of Bavaria.

While Lenin was boasting to a huge May Day crowd in Red Square of the triumphs of Communism ("The liberated working class is celebrating its anniversary freely and openly not only in Soviet Russia, but in Soviet Hungary and Soviet Bavaria"), Free Corps troops were ranging through Munich extinguishing nests of resistance and arresting Red leaders. The streets of Munich belonged to the Free Corps and soon they were marching down the Ludwigstrasse, goose-stepping as they passed the Feldherrnhalle, with one unit, the Ehrhardt Brigade, wearing swastika-decorated helmets and singing, "Swastika on helmet, Black-white-red band . . ."

By May 3 Munich was secured but at the cost of sixty-eight Free Corps lives. These, of course, had to be avenged. Thirty Catholic workers of the St. Joseph Society were seized at a tavern while making plans to put on a play. They were brought to the cellar of the Wittelsbach Palace where twenty-one of them were shot or bayoneted to death as dangerous Reds. Hundreds were shot under similar circumstances and thousands were "chastised" by cruising Free Corps squads. The repression continued with issuance of a series of harsh edicts, some almost impossible to obey, such as the one to surrender all arms immediately or be shot. In the name of law and order citizens were routed out, insulted, beaten and murdered.

The Free Corps had saved Munich from the iron heel of the Soviet Republic and its excesses but these seemed pale compared to the cure.

"It would require a volume to narrate all the atrocities committed by the Whites," reported the French military attaché in Munich; ". . . organized barbarism was given free rein . . . a savage debauchery, an indescribable orgy. . . ." But the British officials saw none of this or else they approved of what they observed. "The result of the Soviet episode at Munich, so far as at present can be seen," reported the Political Intelligence Department of the British Foreign Office, "is to strengthen the cause of law and order throughout Germany, and to discredit Spartacism and Bolshevism with the masses." In all more than a thousand so-called "Reds" were executed by the Free Corps. So many bodies littered Munich in so short a time that they became a health menace and unidentified corpses had to be dumped into shallow ditches.

9

The idealistic youth of the Wandervögel had brought their high hopes into the trenches and now, as Free Corps men, onto the streets of Germany. "This is the New Man, the storm soldier, the elite of Mitteleuropa," wrote their poet laureate, Ernst Jünger. "A completely new race, cunning, strong, and purposeful." These would be soldiers of the battle for German salvation. "New forms must be molded with blood, and power must be seized with a hard fist."

Jünger could have been speaking for Adolf Hitler, whose slumbering antipathies had been reawakened by the Red regimes in Munich, and shortly after the liberation of Munich came the event that would change his life and turn the course of world history. On June 28, 1919, the victorious Allies signed the Treaty of Versailles. With little delay the German government ratified its terms. These were harsh. Germany was forced to accept sole responsibility for causing the war and required to pay *all* civilian damage caused by the conflict. Great chunks of territory were wrested from the Reich: Alsace-Lorraine went to France, the Malmédy area to Belgium, most of Posen and West Prussia to Poland. Germany also lost her colonies. Danzig was to be a free state; and plebiscites would be held in the Saar, Schleswig and East Prussia. Further, the Allies would occupy the Rhineland for at least fifteen years and a belt thirty miles wide on the right bank of the Rhine was to be demilitarized. The humiliation was made complete by a regulation forbidding the Germans to have submarines or military aircraft and limiting her army to 100,000 men.

This new force, the Reichswehr, almost immediately exercised a power far beyond its size. To keep the ranks free from Bolshevik influence, a bureau was organized to investigate subversive political activities among the troops and to infiltrate workers' organizations. Among the recruits selected by Captain Karl Mayr, the officer in charge of this unit, was Hitler. He was particularly qualified for such a task but Mayr picked him because of his "exemplary" war record and, perhaps, out of pity. "When I first met him he was like a tired stray dog looking for a master." Mayr got the impression that Hitler "was ready to throw in his lot with anyone who would show him kindness" and that he was "totally unconcerned about the German people and their destinies."

In truth, Hitler was in a state of ferment and turmoil because of the epidemic of revolution. Never had he been so concerned for the state of his adopted country. Recently he had been handed a racist pamphlet—perhaps one of Eckart's—and it brought to mind similar pamphlets he had read in Vienna. "Involuntarily I saw thus my own development come to life again before my eyes." His simmering hatred of Jews had been activated by what he himself had witnessed on the streets of Munich. Everywhere Jews in power: first Eisner, then anarchists like Toller, and finally Russian Reds like Leviné. In Berlin it had been Rosa Luxemburg; in Budapest Béla Kun, in Moscow Trotsky, Zinoviev and Kamenev. The conspiracy Hitler had previously suspected was turning into reality.

Before embarking on their duties, he and his fellow political agents were ordered to attend a special indoctrination course at the University of Munich with instructors such as Professor Karl Alexander von Müller, a conservative with right radical leanings. "For me," wrote Hitler, "the value of the whole affair was that I now obtained an opportunity of meeting a few like-minded comrades with whom I could thoroughly discuss the situation of the moment. All of us were more or less firmly convinced that Germany could no longer be saved from the impending collapse by the parties of the November crime, the Center and the Social Democracy, and that the so-called 'bourgeois-national' formations, even with the best of intentions, could never repair what had happened."

During the war Hitler had told Westenkirchner that in peacetime he would become either an artist or go into politics and when his comrade asked him which party he preferred the answer was, "None." His circle at the indoctrination course had also come to the conclusion that only an entirely new movement could answer their needs. They decided to call it the Social Revolutionary Party "because the social views of the new organization did indeed mean a revolution."

Added impetus was given such a movement by one of the lecturers, Gottfried Feder, Professor von Müller's brother-in-law. Founder of the German Fighting League for the Breaking of Interest Slavery, he was an engineer by profession but an economist at heart. He spoke to the political agents about the speculation and economic character of stock exchanges and loan capital. This was a stimulating revelation to Hitler. "Right after listening to Feder's first lecture, the thought ran through my head that I had now found the way to one of the most essential premises for the foundation of a new party." Inspired by Feder's demand to end interest slavery, he restudied Marxism, "and now for the first time really achieved an understanding of the content of the Jew Karl Marx's life effort." At last his *Kapital* was intelligible.

After one of his lectures Professor von Müller noticed a small group in lively discussion. "The men seemed spellbound by one of their number who was haranguing them with increasing vehemence in a strange guttural voice. I had the odd feeling that their excitement was his work. I saw a pale, small face under an unsoldierly flowing lock of hair, with close-cropped mustache, and remarkable large light blue eyes that shone fanatically."

"Do you know you have a natural orator among your students?" Müller told Captain Mayr, indicating the pale-faced soldier. Mayr called out, "You, Hitler, come up here." Hitler approached "awkwardly, with a kind of defiant embarrassment." His talent for oratory led to an assignment in a Munich regiment as a lecturer. "I started out with the greatest enthusiasm and love. For all at once I was offered an opportunity of speaking before a larger audience; and the thing that I had always presumed from pure feeling without knowing it was now corroborated: I could 'speak.'" With each speech Hitler grew more confident and his voice developed to such an extent that his words could be understood in every corner of the squad rooms.

His social life was by no means as successful since many of those to whom he made friendly overtures regarded him as a spy. A small man named Thiele publicly snubbed his advances and, when Hitler insisted on following him down the street and expounding on the true mission of the German artist, suddenly interrupted. "Tell me," said Thiele, "did they shit into your brain and forget to flush it?" According to a witness, "the astonished long-distance speaker made calf's eyes and departed without a word."

Hitler could not even get along with two fellow agents who shared his room at the barracks. They complained to Captain Mayr about his "physical habits." Moreover, he "talked and walked in his sleep and made himself generally a nuisance." He was moved to a private room, a small one on the second floor. Formerly a storeroom, its windows were barred but Hitler "seemed to be happy in his cubicle."

Despite Hitler's social shortcomings, Captain Mayr was impressed enough by his abilities as a speaker to send him on a special mission outside Munich; returning German prisoners of war at the Lechfeld transit camp were evidencing Spartacist leanings, and an Enlightenment Detachment was assigned to transform these men into anti-socialist patriots.

The propaganda team left Munich on July 22 and within five days Hitler himself received an education in practical politics. The returnees were bitter and resentful. Cheated of their youth and hope, forced to live like animals in the trenches, they had come home to chaos and hunger. Hitler offered them targets for their hatred as he spoke eloquently of the "Versailles disgrace," the "November criminals" and the "Jewish-Marxist World Plot." His flair for such work was duly noted in a series of commendatory reports. "Herr Hitler, if I might put it this way," commented one observer, "is the born people's speaker, and by his fanaticism and his crowd appeal he clearly compels the attention of his listeners, and makes them think his way."

He returned to Munich and speeches in the squad room. Another duty was to help investigate the fifty or so radical organizations that had recently sprung up in Munich. These included racists, Communists, rabid nationalists, anarchists, and superpatriots, covering the political spectrum from the Bloc of Revolutionary Students and the Society of Communistic Socialists to the Ostara Bund and the New Fatherland.

Early that autumn Hitler was ordered to attend a meeting of a tiny political group calling itself the German Workers' Party. The evening made so little impression on him that he did not mention it in *Mein Kampf*, even though, according to one of the twenty-three participants present, he addressed the gathering in the discussion period and, indeed, "spoke very well." It is doubtful if he took the trouble to find out that the party had been founded earlier that year by a toolmaker in the Munich railroad works, Anton Drexler. Its program was a bizarre combination of socialism, nationalism and anti-Semitism. Its background was shrouded in mystery, seeded as it was by a small group called the Political Workers' Circle, the brain child of Rudolf Freiherr von Sebottendorff, himself a man of mystery. He was a short, corpulent man with slightly protruding eyes, who was "an artist rather than a pedant, a sybarite rather than a Platonist" and had "a certain predilection for firearms but did not openly exhibit it."

Like Hitler, he believed in the Germanic wave of the future and so threw his considerable energies into the formation of a Bavarian branch of the Teutonic Order. Membership was restricted to Germans who could establish the "purity of their blood" for three generations; and every candidate had to pledge he would join energetically in "the struggle against internationalism and Jewry." The revolutions throughout the country forced Sebottendorff to give his organization the innocent title of Thule Society as a cover. By this time he had decided to implement an idea he had long entertained: to win workers to his *völkisch* cause,* he instructed one of the members of Thule, a down-at-the-heels sports writer, to form a Political Workers' Circle. This man sought out Anton Drexler (he had already organized a small ineffectual group of workers called the Free Labor Com-

---

* Völkisch is impossible to translate in a single word. Literally meaning "folkish," it had overtones of racism; but to translate it simply as "racist" is to ignore its folk-nationalistic implications. Throughout the book it will remain völkisch.

mittee for a Good Peace) and they joined forces to found a new political organization. The preliminary meeting of the German Workers' Party was held at a little restaurant, the Fürstenfelder Hof, early that January. Some two dozen workers, most of them railwaymen of Drexler's shop, were on hand to hear Drexler outline the dual purpose of the party: to liberate the workers from Marxist internationalism by ending the divisive class warfare and to make the upper classes aware of their responsibility to the workers. All they really wanted, said Drexler, was "to be ruled by Germans." Drexler suggested calling their group the German National Socialist Party (the same name of a similarly motivated party founded a year earlier in Bohemia, whose emblem, incidentally, was the swastika), but there was objection that the word "socialist" might be misinterpreted.

Painstakingly Drexler penned out notes for a program. The skilled worker should not consider himself to be a proletariat but a middle-class citizen. And the middle class itself had to be enlarged and strengthened "at the cost of big capitalism." The program also included a cautiously anti-Semitic declaration that "religious teachings contrary to the moral and ethical laws of Germany should not be supported by the state" or, in fact, even tolerated. Within two weeks a foundation meeting was held in the Thule headquarters. The seedy sports writer, Karl Harrer, was elected chairman with Drexler as his deputy.

It could hardly be called a party since it consisted of little more than a six-man committee. "Our meetings were private because of this Red threat," recalled Drexler, a serious, undistinguished, sickly man. "We could do little but discuss and study. I embodied my own ideas in a slight brochure called *My Political Awakening. From the diary of a working-man.*" His dream was to find someone with energy and nerve who could make something out of his pamphlet "and contrive a real driving force behind us. It would need to be an outstanding personality, anyhow, who could even attempt to do such a thing, a man of intense conviction, single-eyed, and absolutely fearless."

On September 12 Hitler was ordered by a Major Hierl to attend another meeting of the little Workers' Party. A "single-eyed" man of conviction if ever there was one, he walked into the Sterneckerbräu, a little beer hall on the Herrenstrasse, early that evening to find forty or so workers. The main speaker was supposed to be the poet Eckart but he was sick and had been replaced by the economist Feder, whose subject was "How and by what means is capitalism to be eliminated?"

Hitler had heard Feder's lecture at his indoctrination course and so could concentrate on the membership. His impression was neither good nor bad. This was apparently another of those groups which "sprang out of the ground, only to vanish silently after a time." Obviously its founders had no conception of how to make their club into a genuine party. The evening was a bore and he was relieved when Feder finished talking. Hitler started to leave at the announcement of a free discussion period, but something "moved" him to remain. A few minutes later he was on his feet belaboring a professor who had just advocated the separation of Bavaria from Prussia. Hitler talked for fifteen minutes so ably and cuttingly that the professor ". . . left the hall like a wet poodle, even before I was finished."

Drexler was so impressed by Hitler's delivery and logic that he whispered to his secretary, "This one has what it takes, we could use him!" He introduced himself but Hitler didn't get the name of the unprepossessing man with glasses. Like a religious fanatic, Drexler pressed a copy of his booklet, a forty-page pamphlet with a pink cover, into Hitler's hand and mumbled that he must read it and please come again.

Hitler returned to his little room on the upper floor of the barracks. As usual he had trouble sleeping and set out crusts of bread and leftovers on the floor for the mice. He had gotten into the habit of passing the hours before dawn "watching the droll little beasts chasing around after these choice morsels. I had known so much poverty in my life that I was well able to imagine the hunger, and hence also the pleasure, of the little creatures."

At about five that morning he was still awake on his cot following the antics of the mice when he remembered the pamphlet that Drexler had forced upon him. Hitler was surprised to find himself enthralled from the first page. "Involuntarily I saw my own development come to life before my eyes." The ideas and phrases of the little book kept intruding into his thoughts the following day. He was struck by the phrases "National Socialism" and "new world order," as well as the prediction that a new political party would capture the disillusioned and disinherited among not only the workers but civil servants and the solid lower middle class.

But his interest waned quickly and he was surprised to receive a postcard informing him that he had been accepted as a member of the German Workers' Party. He was requested to attend a committee meeting the following Wednesday. He had no intention of joining a ready-made party since he wanted to found his own and he was about to send off an indignant refusal when "curiosity won out" and he decided to have another look at the queer little group.

This meeting took place in another run-down restaurant on the Herrenstrasse, the Altes Rosenbad. Hitler walked through a dim, deserted dining room to the back where four people sat around a table. He recognized the too eager author of the pamphlet, who enthusiastically welcomed him as a new member of the Deutsche Arbeiterpartie. ("Now we have an Austrian with a big mouth!" he had told a fellow committeeman.) Drexler explained that they were waiting for the chairman of the national organization, Harrer.

At last the sports writer arrived. He was clubfooted, ungainly and shabby. The minutes of the previous meeting were read and the treasurer reported there were seven marks fifty pfennig on hand. Letters were read and discussed at intolerable length. It was worse than Hitler had imagined. "Terrible, terrible! This was club life of the worst manner and sort. Was I to join this organization?" When they began to discuss new membership, Hitler asked a number of questions about the practical aspects of organization. He learned there was no program, not a leaflet, not even a rubber stamp, only good intentions. He quickly glanced through their few directives. They were unclear or vague.

He left depressed by what he had seen but still undecided whether to join or not. It was the "hardest question" of his life and he debated with himself for the next two days. Reason told him to decline but his feeling argued for acceptance. He had vowed to enter politics and this absurd little club had one transcendent advantage—it had not "frozen into an 'organization,' but left the individual an opportunity for real personal activity." Being so small, it could also be more easily shaped to his needs.

Hitler had already reported his findings to Captain Mayr, who passed them on to a group of high-ranking officers and capitalists who met once a week at the Hotel Four Seasons to discuss means of rebuilding Germany's military power. They had come to the conclusion that this could only be achieved with the support of the workers. The little German Workers' Party could be a start and, according to Mayr, General Ludendorff himself appeared at Mayr's office one day with a request that Hitler be allowed to join the organization and build it up.

It was illegal for members of the new army to join political parties but "to please Ludendorff, whose wishes were still respected in the army, I ordered Hitler to join the Workers' Party and help foster its growth. He was allowed at first the equivalent of twenty gold marks in the current inflation money weekly for this purpose." So, in a sense, Hitler was ordered to do what he had already decided to do. He registered as a member of the DAP and was given a membership card.

Hitler's plunge into practical politics was accompanied by an equally important ideological development which also came to fruition as the result of an order of Captain Mayr. Hitler was instructed to answer a letter from a fellow trainee in the education unit requesting information on the Jewish menace. His lengthy answer, four days after the meeting at the Sterneckerbräu, revealed a surprising progression in his own solution of the Jewish question. It was replete with denunciations of Jews that would become all too familiar: "He burrows into the democracies sucking the good will of the masses, crawls before the majesty of the people but knows only the majesty of money. . . . His activities result in racial tuberculosis of the people." The anti-Semitic program, he concluded, should start with legal attempts to deprive Jews of certain privileges on the grounds that they were a foreign race. "But the final aim must unquestionably be the irrevocable *Entfernung* of the Jews." This word could be translated as "removal" and merely mean expulsion from Germany but it is more likely he meant "amputation," that is, liquidation of Jewry.

This was Hitler's first known political document and for the first time he had succeeded in transforming his hatred of the Jews into a positive political program.

Part 2

IN THE BEGINNING WAS
THE WORD

Chapter Four

BIRTH OF A PARTY
1919–1922

1

"When I entered the circle of these few men, there could be no question of a party or a movement." But what the German Workers' Party did give Hitler that autumn was a platform for his own ideas. Just as the writing room in the Männerheim first released his pent-up hatreds and hopes, so this insignificant group of malcontents gave him needed impetus.

His first task was to turn what was essentially a debating society into a political organization. "Our small committee which in reality consisted of seven heads and represented the entire party was nothing more than the head of a small skat club," recalled an amused Hitler in a serialized newspaper story of those first days. "1919 in Munich was a sad time. Little light, lots of dirt, unrest, poorly dressed people, impoverished soldiers, in short, the picture resulting from four years of war and the scandal of the revolution."

The light at their meeting in the back room of the Rosenbad was a single gas flame that burned poorly. "When we were assembled . . . how did we look? Forbidding. Military pants, dyed coats, hats of undefinable shapes but shiny from wear, our feet in remodeled war boots, and a thick cudgel in our hands as a 'walking stick.'" In those days it was a sign of distinction, a proof that one belonged to the people.

"We were always the same faces. . . . First we received the brotherly greetings, and we were informed that the 'seeds' had been planted in respective places, or even established and we were asked if we could make such a report also, and the necessity was stressed to act as a unit." The treasury was usually about five marks and once it reached the high point of seventeen.

Hitler finally persuaded the committee to increase membership by holding larger meetings. At the barracks he personally typed out on the company typewriter some of the invitations to the first public meeting, others he wrote by hand. On the night of the first meeting the committee of seven waited "for the masses who were expected to appear." An hour passed but no one came. "We were again seven men, the old seven." Hitler changed his tactics. The next invitations were mimeographed and this time a few came. The number rose slowly from eleven to thirteen and finally to thirty-four.

The pittance collected from these meetings was invested in an advertisement in the *Münchener Beobachter*, a völkisch, anti-Semitic newspaper, for a mass meeting in the cellar room of the Hofbräuhaus on October 16.

If only the usual number turned up, the expenses would bankrupt the party. Hitler had insisted in the face of Harrer's pessimism that a crowd would come and by 7 P.M. seventy people had collected in the smoky room. There is no record of the reception given the main speaker but almost from the moment Adolf Hitler stepped behind the crude lectern placed atop the head table the audience was "electrified." He was supposed to speak for twenty minutes but went on for half an hour, spilling out a stream of denunciations, threats and promises. Abandoning all restraint, he let emotion take over and by the time he sat down to loud applause sweat covered his face. He was exhausted but elated "and what before I had simply felt deep down in my heart, without being able to put it to the test, proved to be true; I could speak!"

It was a turning point not only in his career but in that of the German Workers' Party. Three hundred marks had been donated by the enthusiastic listeners, now the organization had funds to advertise more extensively and print slogans and leaflets. On November 13 a second mass meeting was held, this time in another beer hall, the Eberlbräu. More than 130 men (mostly students, shopkeepers and army officers) paid an admission fee of fifty pfennigs, something new in local politics, to hear four speakers. The main attraction was Hitler. In the middle of his speech hecklers began to shout out but he had alerted his military friends and within minutes the agitators "flew down the stairs with gashed heads." The interruption only spurred Hitler to greater rhetorical heights as he closed with an exhortation to stand up and resist. "The misery of Germany must be broken by Germany's steel. That time must come."

Once more he carried the audience with him. He spoke with a primitive force and unabashed emotion that set him apart from the intellectuals who appealed to reason. A police observer, after describing Hitler as a merchant, reported that he had "held forth in an outstanding manner" and was destined to become "a professional propaganda speaker." His appeals were visceral—love of country and hatred of Jews for bringing about the defeat of 1918. By his manner and use of the language of the streets and the trenches, war veterans recognized that he had shared the democracy of the machine gun, barbed wire and muck and thus represented the sacred comradeship of the front lines.

In two weeks another enthusiastic meeting was held with an audience of more than 170, and on December 10 a larger hall, the Deutsches Reich, was used. When the attendance fell off despite an announcement (which spelled Hitler with two *t*'s) that the place was heated, several committee members protested that the meetings were too frequent. There was violent debate in which Hitler argued that a city of 700,000 inhabitants could stand not one meeting every two weeks but ten every week. The road they had taken, he said, was the right one; sooner or later success was bound to come. His persistence was rewarded. The new hall on the Dachaustrasse was near an army barracks and the influx of soldiers raised the attendance to over two hundred.

Hitler's ascendancy deeply concerned some of the other members, who objected to his volcanic, mercurial style. Moreover, he was changing the entire face of the organization with the influx of his rough-mannered army friends, and they feared it would all end in ruin. While Drexler was equally distressed, he was so convinced that Hitler was the hope of the party that he supported the move to make him the new chief of propaganda. Promotion only made Hitler more critical of the inefficiency of the party's business procedures. How could one administer properly without an office and equipment? On his own he found an office at the Sterneckerbräu, scene of his introduction to the party. It was small and had once been a taproom. The rent was so little, fifty marks a month, that the committee didn't even complain when the landlord removed the wood paneling and left the room looking more like "a funeral vault than an office." Using funds he got from Captain Mayr as well as those from the party treasury, he had an electric light installed along with a telephone, a table, a few borrowed chairs, an open bookcase and two cupboards. Hitler's next step was to insist on a paid business manager who would work full time. He found one in his barracks, a sergeant "upright and absolutely honest," who also brought along his small Adler typewriter.

That December Hitler called for a complete reform of the party's organization from a debating society to a genuine political party. A majority of committee members, content to remain just another extreme rightist group, opposed these changes. They could not see, as Hitler clearly did, that propaganda was not an end in itself, only a means to overthrow the Weimar Republic. Once again the plodding Drexler supported Hitler and the two spent hours in the Drexler apartment discussing plans and programs. Their chief bond was a common distrust and hatred of Jewry. Having lost several jobs, so he said, because of Jews and trade unionists, Drexler had become "a radical anti-Semite and anti-Marxist." He lived in the pleasant Nymphenburg district and Hitler would travel there by trolley car. They would become so involved in work that Frau Drexler usually had to call them to supper several times. "My little girl used to climb on Hitler's knee," remembered Drexler, "she knew she was always welcome." He was Uncle Adolf to her.

One evening in the last days of 1919 Hitler arrived at the Drexlers' "armed with a sheaf of manuscript" on which he had roughly sketched out the official party program. They worked for hours "boiling it down" to make it as pithy as possible. "We cracked our brains over it, I can tell you!" recalled Drexler. By the time they finished it was morning. Then Hitler sprang up and banged his fist on the table. "These points of ours," he exclaimed, "are going to rival Luther's placard on the doors of Wittenberg!"

There were twenty-five points to the program and Hitler wanted to present them to the public at a mass meeting. Predictably there were objections from the committee, not only to a number of the points but to an open meeting. At first dubious, Drexler was finally carried away by the idea and at the next meeting gave Hitler his full support. Those who objected were overruled and a date was set: February 24, 1920.

Leaflets and posters printed in bright red were plastered all over Munich but by this time Hitler himself began to fear he might be speaking to "a yawning hall." The meeting was to start at 7:30 P.M. and when Hitler entered the great Festsaal of the Hofbräuhaus at seven-fifteen he found it jammed with almost 2000 people. His heart "burst with joy." What particularly pleased him was that more than half the crowd appeared to be Communists or Independent Socialists. He was confident that the true idealists among this hostile group would swing over to his side and he welcomed any disturbance they might provoke.

The meeting opened quietly with the main address by an experienced völkisch speaker named Dingfelder. He attacked Jews but did so obliquely. He quoted Shakespeare and Schiller and was so bland that even the Communists weren't offended by anything he had to say. Then Hitler got to his feet. There were no catcalls. He looked anything but an orator in his worn, old-fashioned blue suit. He opened quietly, without emphasis, outlining the history of the past ten years. But as he told of the postwar revolutions that swept through Germany, passion crept into his voice; he began to gesture, his eyes flashed. Angry shouts came from all parts of the large hall. Beer mugs flew though the air. Hitler's army supporters—"swift as greyhounds, tough as leather, and hard as Krupp steel"—eagerly went into battle armed with rubber truncheons and riding whips. Troublemakers were hustled outside. At last some degree of order was restored and

Hitler resumed speaking, undismayed by the continuing chorus of derisive shouts. His experiences at the Männerheim had accustomed him to such disturbances and he seemed to draw energy from them. The audience warmed to his spirit as well as his words and applause began to drown out the heckling.

He spoke scathingly of the tons of paper money being printed and how the corrupt Social Democrat government only prosecuted petty hoarders. "What can such a hoarder do if his name is Hummelberger and not Isidor Bach?" This anti-Semitic jibe was followed by as much protest as approval but once he directed his attack at the Jews from the East applause drowned out the hecklers. There were shouts of "Down with the Jewish press!"

Unaccustomed to speaking to such a large audience, his voice would be loud one moment, weak the next. But even his inexperience was appealing. A twenty-year-old law student named Hans Frank was struck by his obvious sincerity. "The first thing you felt was that there was a man who spoke honestly about how he felt and was not trying to put something across of which he himself was not absolutely convinced." After the polished phrases of the first speaker his words had an explosive effect. They were often crude, always expressive. And even those who had come to hoot him were compelled to listen. He spoke simply and so clearly that those at the farthest tables could hear. What particularly impressed young Frank was that he "made things understandable even to the foggiest brain . . . and went to the core of things."

Finally he submitted to the audience the twenty-five theses of the program, asking them to "pronounce judgment" on them point by point. There was something for almost everyone but Jews. For the patriotic, union of all Germans in a Greater Reich; colonies for excess population; equality for Germany among nations; revocation of the Versailles Treaty; creation of a people's army; and a "ruthless battle" against criminals to ensure law and order. For the workers, abolition of all income unearned by work; confiscation of war profits; expropriation of land without compensation for communal purposes; and profit sharing in large industrial enterprises. For the middle class, the immediate socialization of the great department stores and their lease, at low rates, to small tradesmen; "generous development" of old-age national health standards. For the völkisch-minded, the demand that Jews be treated as aliens, denied the right to hold any public office, deported if the state found it impossible to feed its entire population, and expelled immediately if they had emigrated after August 2, 1914.

After each point Hitler would pause to ask if everyone understood and agreed. The majority shouted out raucous approval but there were organized cries of derision and some protesters jumped up on chairs and tables. Again and again the truncheon and whip brigade went into action and by the end of Hitler's two-and-a-half-hour tirade there was almost unanimous support for every word he uttered. The final applause was tumultuous and young Frank was fully convinced that "if anyone could master the fate of Germany, Hitler was that man."

To Hitler the evening, including its riotous objections, had been an unalloyed triumph, and as the crowd filed out he felt that the door to his future had at last opened. "When I closed the meeting, I was not alone in thinking that now a wolf had been born, destined to burst in upon the herd of seducers of the people." He was living up to his own name, for Adolf was derived from the Teutonic word meaning "fortunate wolf." And from that day on "wolf" would have a special meaning for him—as nickname among close friends; as a pseudonym for himself and his sister Paula; and as a name for most of his military headquarters.

There was little notice of Hitler's emergence in the Munich newspapers, but the meeting meant the first major step forward for the German Workers' Party. A hundred new members were enrolled. At Hitler's insistence a list of members had already been drawn up and proper membership cards issued. To give the impression of size the first card was numbered 501, with the members listed in alphabetical order. Hitler, painter, was number 555.

2

He began a new life, mixing with an enlarged circle of colorful characters whose common denominator was a love of things German and a fear of Marxism. There was a Munich physician, a believer in the sidereal pendulum, who claimed this gave him the power to detect the presence of a Jew in any group of people. Of far more importance was a former company commander, Captain Ernst Röhm, a homosexual. Röhm was an exemplary officer, a comrade to be trusted in peril. He was short and stocky with closely cropped hair and an engaging smile. He was a walking monument to the war; the upper part of his nose had been shot away and a bullet had left a deep scar in one cheek. An officer in the new Reichswehr, he once remarked, "Since I am a wicked and immature man, war and unrest appeal to me more than the orderly life of your respectable burgher." From the moment the two met at a secret meeting of a nationalist group called the Iron Fist, Röhm was convinced that the dedicated corporal was just the man to head the German Workers' Party. Röhm had already changed the working-class character of the Drexler-Harrer organization by bringing in so many soldiers. They were the ones who kept order at rowdy meetings. Between Hitler and Röhm were bonds of blood and suffering since both belonged to the brotherhood of the front-line fighter, and though Röhm had recently replaced Captain Mayr as Hitler's commander he insisted that his subordinate use the familiar *du*, a familiarity which was leading to Hitler's acceptance by other officers.

An even closer acquaintance was the writer Dietrich Eckart, who had once remarked that the new breed of political leader must be able to stand the noise of a machine gun. "I prefer a vain monkey who is able to give the Reds a salty reply, and doesn't run away when people begin swinging table legs, to a dozen learned professors." Moreover their man had to be a bachelor. "Then we'll get the women!" They had become friends, not merely political acquaintances, despite differences in age (twenty-one years) and background (Eckart was a university man of culture). Both were bohemians, both could speak the language of the gutter, both were nationalists and hated Jews. Eckart believed Jews who married German women should be jailed for three years and, if they repeated the crime, executed.

Eckart, a born romantic revolutionary, was a master of coffeehouse polemics. A sentimental cynic, a sincere charlatan, constantly on stage, lecturing brilliantly if given the slightest opportunity be it at his own apartment, on the street or in a café. A drug addict and drunkard, his vulgarity was tempered by vestiges of his social background. Hitler reveled in the company of this warm and voluble intellectual buccaneer who was playing Falstaff to Hitler's Prince Hal in Munich's ribald night world. Eckart became the younger man's mentor. He gave Hitler a trench coat, corrected his grammar, took him to better-class restaurants and cafés and introduced him to influential citizens ("This is the man who will one day liberate Germany"). The two spent hours discussing music, art and literature as well as politics and the association with the tempestuous writer left a lasting mark on Hitler.

Several weeks after the Hofbräuhaus meeting the two men set off together on an adventure in Berlin. Elite Free Corps troops under General Walther von Lüttwitz, ordered to disband by the socialist Weimar government, had instead marched on the capital where they seized control of the city and installed their own Chancellor, a minor civil servant named Kapp. Both Hitler and Eckart saw the potentialities of the right-wing Kapp Putsch and volunteered to go to Berlin and determine whether there was any possibility for joint revolutionary action in Bavaria. Captain Röhm approved the project and they were sent off in an open sports plane. It was Hitler's first flight and the pilot—a young war ace, Lieutenant Robert Ritter von Greim, winner of the Pour le Mérite—would become the last Luftwaffe commander. The weather was so turbulent that despite Greim's skill Hitler kept vomiting. For a time it appeared as if the mission was aborted since the airport at their interim stop was occupied by striking workers, but Hitler snapped on a fake goatee and Eckart posed as a paper dealer, and the party was permitted to proceed to Berlin. When they touched down at Berlin the wan Hitler vowed that he would never, never fly again.

Although Berlin had surrendered to the Free Corps on March 13 without a shot being fired, theirs was a hollow victory. No one of stature would accept a position in "Chancellor" Kapp's cabinet. From the beginning his hastily planned Putsch was a fiasco and what brought it down was not a counterattack or acts of sabotage. Berliners, joining the rest of the nation in a wave of anti-militarist feeling, had apparently concluded that another revolution was too much, and when a general strike was called by the Ebert government the workers responded so wholeheartedly that it was impossible for the Kapp regime to function. Electricity was shut off; trolley cars and subways stopped. There was no water; garbage rotted in the streets; shops and offices were closed.

Only Berlin's night life went on unimpeded, in darkness or candlelight. It was corruption out of an overdone movie with heavily rouged girl prostitutes of eleven competing with whip-toting Amazons in high lacquered boots. There were cafés for every taste and perversion— homosexuals, lesbians, exhibitionists, sadists, masochists. Nudity had become boring and art itself was plumbing the nadir of obscenity, disillusionment and cynicism. Berlin was the center of the Dadaist movement and one of its poets, Walter Mehring, was giving Berliners a frightening look into the future in the form of a slangy, satirical verse:

> C'mon, boys, let's all go
> Off to the pogrom with a ho-ho-ho.
> Pull in your bellies and throw out the Jews.
> With swastika and poison gas
> Let's have a go at murder in the mass.

The general strike of the Ebert government turned into a Frankenstein monster. By crushing the Kapp forces so successfully, it opened the way for another wave of leftist revolt. The Communists stirred up disorders throughout Germany to such a degree that President Ebert was forced to beg General von Seeckt, who had walked out on the government a few days earlier, to accept command of all military forces and crush the Red revolt. His first act was to recommission all the Free Corps troops which had just been disbanded. In a wry turn of events, the mutineers of yesterday were called on to enforce law and order today, and in a stroke of black comedy worthy of a Dadaist playwright Ebert paid the Free Corps troops the bonus that the Kapp regime had promised them to overthrow his government.

The task facing the reorganized Free Corps was formidable. In Saxony a Soviet republic had already seized power and by March 20 a Red Army of 50,000 workers had already occupied most of the Ruhr. That same day the Communist *Ruhr Echo* announced that the red flag must wave victoriously over the entire nation. "Germany must become a Republic of Soviets and, in union with Russia, the springboard for the coming victory of the World Revolution and World Socialism."

On April 3 the Free Corps troops swept through the Ruhr, wiping out Red strongholds and dealing ruthlessly with any survivors. "If I were to tell you everything," a youthful volunteer of one Free Corps unit wrote his family, "you would say I was lying to you. No pardon is given. . . . We even shot 10 Red Cross nurses on sight because they were carrying pistols. We shot these little ladies with pleasure—how they cried and pleaded with us to save their lives. Nothing doing! Anybody with a gun is our enemy."

By the time Hitler and Eckart arrived in Berlin after their sickening plane ride from Munich, the Kapp Putsch was nearing its end. From the airport they proceeded to the Reich Chancellery where they talked with Kapp's press representative, Trebitsch-Lincoln, a Hungarian Jew. An adventurer and something of a rascal—he was arrested in New York as a spy for the Kaiser—he informed them that Kapp had already fled and they had better stay under cover lest they be arrested. Eckart, unhappy at finding a Jew in charge, reputedly seized Hitler's arm and said, "Come on, Adolf, we have no further business here."

But the two stayed on in the capital to meet their hero, General Ludendorff, who was preparing to flee south in disguise, and to confer with a number of North Germans who shared their dreams: members of the Stahlhelm (Steel Helmet), a supernationalist group of veterans; and with leaders of völkisch organizations who were getting substantial financial backing from industrialists. Eckart also introduced his pupil to the salon of Helene Bechstein, wife of the piano manufacturer. She was instantly enthralled by "Germany's young Messiah" and promised to present him to others in her influential circle.

Hitler returned to Munich on March 31. That same day he became a private citizen, perhaps of his own accord, more likely because he was ordered to do so. He packed his belongings, received his demobilization pay of fifty marks along with a coat, cap, jacket, pants, a suit of underwear, a shirt, socks and shoes. He sublet a small back room at Thierschstrasse 41, a middle-class district near the Isar River dominated by three- and four-story buildings with shops and offices on the ground floor and small apartments and rooms above. Hitler's was a tiny cell, eight by fifteen feet, not much bigger than his cubicle at the Männerheim. It was the coldest room in the house and, according to the landlord, Herr Erlanger, "Some lodgers who've rented it since got ill. Now we only use it as a storeroom; nobody will have it any more."

It was no accident that Hitler had chosen a room a few doors from the offices of the *Münchener Beobachter*. It had a new name, the

Völkischer Beobachter; and continued to be the mouthpiece for anti-Semitic and anti-Marxist sentiments. Hitler's opinion of Jews was largely reflected in this newspaper. Recently, for instance, a story on page one had carried this headline: "Do a Real Job on the Jews!" The author recommended that Germany be cleared of all Jews, no matter how ruthless the measures. From such articles, most of them written by refugees from Russia, Hitler absorbed new information concerning the rising peril of Communism.

His own chief targets were Jews and the peace treaties. Next on his list was the fight against Marxism; both he and Eckart had a grudging admiration for the dedication of German Communists and did their best to win them over. In an article entitled "German and Jewish Bolshevism" Eckart had even recommended what he called "German Bolshevism." And once, with Hitler on the platform beside him, he told a party meeting that the German Communists were idealistic men unconsciously working for Germany's salvation.

The Russian exiles resisted such a compromise and their articles and conversations on the peril of Bolshevism were having an increasing effect on Hitler. The most persuasive of these apostles of doom from the East was Alfred Rosenberg, the young architect-artist from Estonia. At their first meeting, neither was much impressed by the other. "I would be lying if I said I was overwhelmed by him," recalled Rosenberg. It was only when he heard Hitler speak in public that he became enthralled. "Here I saw a German front-line soldier embarking on this struggle in a manner as clear as it was convincing, counting on himself alone with the courage of a free man. That was what drew me to Adolf Hitler after the first fifteen minutes."

The attraction and admiration became mutual in the next few months with the appearance of Rosenberg's articles in Eckart's weekly paper and other nationalist-racist publications. What particularly impressed Hitler was Rosenberg's revelations that Bolshevism was but the first step in a vast global Jewish plot to conquer the world. Final "proof" of this was revealed the day after the historic Hofbräuhaus meeting with publication in the *Völkischer Beobachter* of "the Protocols of the Elders of Zion." This purported to be the verbatim report of twenty-four secret sessions of the Elders of Zion in Basel, Switzerland, in a conspiracy to conquer the world.* This book was supporting evidence of Hitler's own prejudice and fears. It was also a turning point in his relations with Rosenberg. Hitler began taking his warnings of Bolshevism to heart; and the

* The "Protocols" was written in France, a hotbed of anti-Semitism, by agents of the Czar and published a few years later in Russia, at the end of the nineteenth century; its first publication in Germany had come a year after the armistice in a Russian émigré magazine but had caused little stir. An amateurish forgery, it had been accepted as gospel by both Wilhelm II and Nicholas II. A copy was found, along with the Bible and *War and Peace*, in the Czar's house in Ekaterinburg, after the murder of the imperial family.

Communist issue, till now subsidiary, gradually took on more import in the party credo.

Hitler was not alone in acceptance of the "Protocols." That May a long article appeared in the London *Times* asserting that it should be taken seriously and seemed to be a bona fide document written by Jews for Jews. The "Protocols"—spreading throughout Europe and into the Americas—spurred a virulent anti-Semitism which had been inaugurated by the advocates of Christianity. For centuries Catholics had been instructed that the Jews had killed Christ and the first Protestant, Martin Luther, had charged that the Jew had not only transformed God into the devil but was "a plague, pestilence, pure misfortune"—a blight on Christianity and the world which had to be dealt with peremptorily.

Hitler's hatred of Jews had come primarily from his own observation in the last days of the war and during the revolutions that followed.* What he learned from Rosenberg, the Thule Society, or from Gobineau, Luther and other famous anti-Semites merely buttressed his own conclusions. He borrowed only what he wanted from such sources. He probably had been much more influenced by pamphlets and freakish right-wing newspapers that breathed venomous anti-Semitism. Since his early days in Vienna he had devoured such gutter literature and its seed came to fruition on Friday the thirteenth of August 1920, at a mass meeting in Munich's famous Hofbräuhaus.

For two hours he expounded on the subject of "Why We Are Against the Jews," and from the beginning made it clear that his party alone "will free you from the power of the Jew!" In great detail he told how the Jews had polluted society since medieval days. While distinguished by neither originality nor rhetoric, his speech was a marvel of propaganda. Although his own anti-Semitism was personal rather than historical, Hitler demonstrated a genius for amalgamating facts with events of the day in a manner calculated to inspire resentment and hate. He was often interrupted by shouts of approval and laughter. Eighteen times the audience burst into loud applause and the reaction was particularly boisterous when he referred to the Jew as a nomad involved in "highway robbery."

His earlier attacks on Jews had been low key in comparison to this carefully prepared denunciation. For the first time in public he charged that the Jewish conspiracy was international and that their advocacy of equality of all peoples and international solidarity was only a scheme to denationalize other races. Previously he had called the Jew despicable, immoral and parasitic; tonight the Jew was a destroyer, a robber, a pest with the power to "undermine entire nations." Hitler called for an all-out

---

* It was ironic that Erlanger, the landlord of the house where Hitler presently resided, was a Jew who had only pleasant memories: "I often encountered him on the stairway and at the door—he was generally scribbling something in a notebook. . . . He never made me feel that he regarded me differently from other people."

struggle to the death. There was no difference between the East and West Jews, the good or bad ones, the rich or poor ones, it was a battle against the entire Jewish race. The slogan "Proletarians of the world, unite" no longer applied. "The battle cry must be 'Anti-Semites of the world, unite.' People of Europe, free yourselves!" Hitler demanded, in short, a "thorough" solution which he vaguely but ominously described as "the removal of Jews from the midst of our people." He had taken a long step forward on the road of anti-Semitism. Earlier in the year the *Münchener Post* had been amused by his comic impersonations of Jews. "Adolf Hitler behaved like a comedian, and his speech was like a vaudeville turn." But this present speech brought a more sober recognition from the same newspaper of his platform magic. "One thing Hitler has, you must give him credit, he is the most cunning rabble rouser in Munich practising such mischief."

Yet he was far more than a mischief maker whose appeal was merely to racists. His call for active anti-Semitism was also being heeded by those whose ultimate dream was a greater Reich—respectable, middle-class, middle-aged burghers who had subscribed to the words of Heinrich Class, president of the Pan-German League, back in 1913. "The Jewish race is the source of all dangers. The Jew and the German are like fire and water." In time, preached Class, a man would arise to lead them in this fight against Jewry. "We await the Führer! Patience, patience, he will come. Persevere, work and unite!"

Scribbled outlines of other speeches delivered by Hitler during this period indicate the depth of his obsession: "The bloody Jew. Butchering of spiritual leadership of people The Russian funeral parlor." "The Jew as dictator and today's Germany? Battle between democracy and Dictatorship—No. Between Jew and Germanic. Who understands this?" "Hunger in peace (inflation) through stock market and speculation? Need for luxuries etc. who profits? The Jews . . . Genocide Preparation for this mass insanity—can be proven through mass need—hunger—Hunger as a weapon at all times. Hunger to serve the Jews." "The world revolution means subjugation of the entire world under the dictatorship of the world exchange and its Masters, Judai."

As can be seen from these excerpts, Hitler's obsessive hatred was developing into an encompassing political philosophy. At the same time his hitherto obscure concept of foreign policy was taking shape. By September of that year he had reached the point where he told one audience, "We are tied and gagged. But even though we are defenseless, we do not fear a war with France." In addition he was considering the possibility of a foreign ally and recently had declared, "For us the enemy sits on the other side of the Rhine, not in Italy or elsewhere." Also for the first time— perhaps inspired by Rosenberg and the "Protocols"—Hitler publicly assailed the Jews for their internationalism. His equation of Jews and internationalism and his selection of Italy as an ally against France were still tentative concepts but did indicate his striving for a logical and practical foreign policy. He had come out of the war with the conventional beliefs and prejudices of the front-line soldier, and emerged from the traumatic series of Red revolutions with many of the conventional beliefs and prejudices of the man in the street. At last he was putting his own system in order. But his primary goal, hatred of Jews, which had been surfacing and submerging erratically since the days of struggle in Vienna, was not at all conventional.

Adolf Hitler was advancing faster in the field of practical politics. Almost singlehandedly he had broadened the base of the party which now bore the name of *Nationalsozialistische Deutsche Arbeiterpartei* (NSDAP)—the National Socialist German Workers' Party. It was a name he hoped would inspire and incite, that would scare off the timid and attract those willing to bleed for their dreams.

In this same spirit, Hitler insisted upon a party flag that could compete with the flaming red Communist banner. "We wanted something red enough to out-Herod Herod," recalled Drexler, something to outdo the Reds but "quite different." Finally a dentist from Starnberg submitted a flag which had been used at the founding meeting of his own party local: a swastika against a black-white-red background. The swastika—originally a Sanskrit word meaning "all is all"—long a symbol of the Teutonic Knights, had been used by Lanz von Liebenfels, the Thule Society and a number of Free Corps units. For centuries it had represented not only for Europeans but also for certain North American Indian tribes the wheel of the sun or the cycle of life. From now on, and perhaps forevermore, the swastika would have a sinister connotation.

3

The Kapp Putsch and the annihilation of Communist regimes in central Germany had left the cause of socialism in disarray. Ebert and his Majority Socialists had widened the breach between themselves and the left-wing Independent Socialists by the opportunistic use of Free Corps units against the workers of the Ruhr. In early autumn of 1920 the dissidents—who themselves were divided almost equally between pro-Communists and anti-Communists—met for five days in Halle to determine the future course of the Independent Socialist Party and its relationship to the Third International. The most inspiring speaker at the congress—Grigori Zinoviev, president of the Third International—came from Moscow. The Soviets had sent him to swing the almost 900,000 German socialists to the far left. He spoke for hours "in a somewhat broken German which only heightened the effect of his talk." It was received tumultuously by the pro-Communists.

Bitter debates between right and left ensued and some observers felt

the former had the better argument, but the idea of world revolution was
too exhilarating to resist. Two hundred and thirty-seven voted to join the
Third International under the conditions laid down by Lenin. A hundred
and fifty-six voted no—and then walked out of the hall in a body. But of
those who remained most became Communists.

One delegate who left Halle alarmed as well as disillusioned was Otto
Strasser. He had listened to Zinoviev with mounting annoyance and concern. What he said "sounded like a new Messiah-doctrine" with Moscow
dominating Germany. Strasser and an elder brother, Gregor, had long followed the socialist dream. Both were prepared to face drastic reforms but
not those directed by a foreign power. What they sought was a German-
oriented socialism and Otto had thought he would find it among the revolutionary Independent Socialists.

After Halle he was a man without a party. Disgusted, he journeyed to
Landshut to consult his brother, who had organized a Free Corps-type private army of his own with infantry and artillery batteries and a machine-
gun company. Gregor admitted that nothing was more dangerous than the
Russians and that there wasn't a single political party that could successfully oppose them. "Nothing can be done with talking," he said, "only action." Two important guests, he said, were coming to discuss the problem.

The next morning, according to Otto Strasser's account, a large car
drew up in front of his brother's chemist shop. Two men stepped out.
Otto recognized the first: General Ludendorff, a hero to all nationalists.
Behind at a respectful distance, "like a battalion orderly," was a pale-faced
young man with a stubby mustache, clad in an ill-fitting blue suit. It was
Hitler. "We must unite all nationalist groups," announced the general.
The political training was up to Herr Hitler. Ludendorff himself would
take over the military leadership of these nationalist organizations. He
asked Gregor to subordinate himself and his storm battalions "under my
military leadership and also to join Herr Hitler's party."

Otto was not at all impressed with Hitler although he promised to
make Gregor the first national *Gauleiter* (party district leader) and give
him the *Gau* of Lower Bavaria. The younger Strasser interrupted. What,
he asked, was the NSDAP program? "The program isn't the question,"
said Hitler. The only question was power. Otto objected. Power was only
the means of accomplishing the program. "These are the opinions of the
intellectuals," said Hitler curtly. "We need power!" It was obvious he did
not like Otto and a moment later he accused him of fighting with the
Reds against the Kapp regime.

Otto retorted with his own accusation. How could someone calling
himself a National Socialist support a reactionary like Kapp? He explained
that he had fought as a socialist in Berlin just as he had earlier marched in
Munich against the Soviet regime. Each course seemed to be the right
one; *he* was truly a National Socialist.

Ludendorff interrupted. "The politics of the nationalist opposition can't be communistic," he said, "but it also can't be capitalistic." When he was quartermaster general he had fewer problems with workers than with capitalists. This surprising statement cleared the air and the meeting ended amicably but without a definite decision from the elder Strasser. He wanted to think over the proposition. That evening Gregor told his brother that he had made up his mind to join forces with Ludendorff and Hitler, even though he also had not been too impressed with the latter. "The general will use him at the right place," he said. "I trust Ludendorff in this regard."

Hitler's refusal to reveal his political program to Otto Strasser was not because he had none or could not express it but probably because he was too stubborn to discuss it with a "traitor" who had fought against the Kapp forces. Moreover, Hitler had come to win over Gregor and his battalions and he had the definite feeling at parting that both would eventually be in his camp. Gregor Strasser was his kind of man: a front-line junior officer who, like himself, had won the Iron Cross, 1st Class; he was obviously a man of conviction: an ardent nationalist, opposed to both Marxism and capitalism, who recognized that the Jews were "the backbone and the brains" of both.

The winning of Gregor Strasser was but one of Hitler's accomplishments since he had joined the little German Workers' Party. In less than a year he had not only transformed the character of the organization but raised its membership to almost three thousand. All his time was devoted to the NSDAP and he had traveled widely, making himself and the party fairly well known. He had been the main speaker at some eighty mass meetings, traveled to Berlin with Eckart during the Kapp Putsch and addressed an international congress of National Socialists at Salzburg.

Success on the platform had not turned Hitler's head. In fact he would pace up and down in his little room complaining to his personal bodyguard, Ulrich Graf, a former butcher, of his inability to "go out there and tell the people what he knew, and what he wanted to do. 'If I could only speak! If I could only speak!' he used to shout." Dissatisfied not only with his delivery but with the conduct of the mass meetings, he determinedly set about improving both. He attended rival rallies and invariably found that the main speaker delivered his address "in the style of a witty newspaper article or of a scientific treatise, avoided all strong words, and here and there threw in some feeble professional joke." Such tedious meetings taught him what not to do. He made his own lively and rousing. The atmosphere was down-to-earth and genial with free beer, sausages and pretzels, and even, when party funds permitted, concertina music and folk singing. Then at the psychological moment Hitler himself would make a dramatic appearance with band playing and swastika banners flying. Usually he began quietly. Then, feeling out each audience as an actor would,

he adapted his manner and speech to its needs, finally rousing it to a pitch
of almost uncontrollable enthusiasm.

The success of the mass meetings did not satisfy Hitler. He wanted a
wider forum and for that he needed his own newspaper. The *Völkischer
Beobachter* was on the brink of bankruptcy because of numerous libel actions. This was the paper Hitler wanted. A financial crisis was the opportunity he had been waiting for. At 2 A.M. on the morning of December 17
Hitler burst into Eckart's apartment excitedly announcing that the
Beobachter had to be sold because of debts and was "in danger" of falling
into the wrong hands. A separatist leader intended buying it as a platform
for his program. The party must get it instead. The asking price was
reasonable—only 180,000 marks; and Hitler was positive Eckart could raise
this from wealthy friends.

At eight the next morning Drexler was at Eckart's door. It was an unspeakable hour for a man of the latter's habits and "at first," recalled
Drexler, "he was bad-tempered. Then we started off." By noon they had
collected 60,000 marks from General von Epp whose Free Corps unit
helped overthrow Munich's soviet government in 1919, and 30,000 more
from other contributors including an anti-Semitic doctor. Drexler himself
signed a note for the paper's debts of more than 100,000 marks and at four
that afternoon the purchase of the *Beobachter* was properly registered.
Now Hitler and the NSDAP—thanks primarily to an eccentric author and
a toolmaker—were prepared for the next leap forward.

4

A month later, on January 22, 1921, the first national congress of the
NSDAP was held in Munich. In little more than a year the party had become a respected force in Bavarian right-wing politics largely because of
Hitler's magnetic personality and obsessive drive. His abilities as an orator,
moreover, had turned the original organization from discussion to action.
Most of the founders, including Drexler, viewed this transformation with
growing concern. While they appreciated the vitality Hitler brought to
their lethargic group, they were beginning to wonder if it was worth it. In
a remarkably short period of time Hitler had become the dominant force,
backed by his fervently faithful entourage. These followers—Röhm, the
Strassers, Rosenberg—brought with them the undeniable aura of violence.
Many of Hitler's private friends and associates were just as repugnant to
the old guard, who felt he had too many bohemian comrades. And what
genuine socialist would have intimate connections with bankers, industrialists and socialites such as the Bechsteins?

The first congress would seem to have been the logical place for
Hitler to stage a revolt and openly seize power that seemed his for the asking. But he restrained himself since only 411 members answered the call

to Munich. Nor was the widening split in policy and tactics yet well enough known to rank-and-file members. On the surface there was unity at the congress, obvious as it was to insiders that a confrontation was in the offing, and everyone joined in the effort to make Hitler's first appearance twelve days later at the Zirkus Krone a success.

The winter had been a severe one with food riots rampant throughout Germany. These public disorders were heightened by a demand of the Allied Supreme War Council in Paris for exorbitant war reparations. Germany, close to bankruptcy, was expected to pay 134 billion gold marks. A large segment of the population already lived with little or no heat and went to bed hungry, and the annual payment was believed to hold out a bare subsistence for the workers as well as hardships for the middle class.

The spirit of indignation was so general that all the major political parties considered holding a common protest demonstration on the Königsplatz. This was canceled lest it be broken up by the Reds. On February 1 Hitler demanded a final decision. The inappropriately named action committee put him off until the following day, and he was informed they "intended" to hold the meeting in a week. "With this the cord of my patience snapped and I decided to carry through the protest demonstration alone." That noon Hitler reserved the Zirkus Krone for the following evening—the manager was a party member and he reportedly charged Hitler little or nothing—and then dictated copy for a flashy poster. Many of the party faithful had qualms. The circus arena could accommodate an audience of 6000 and it seemed impossible that even a moderate number could be induced to attend at such short notice.

The posters were not put up until Thursday morning. Moreover, a cold rain mixed with snow was falling. Hitler himself was so concerned that he hastily dictated leaflets and sent them off to the printer. That afternoon two hired trucks covered with red festoons and flying large swastika flags cruised the city. Each vehicle was manned by a score of party members who tossed out the leaflets and shouted slogans. It was the first time that propaganda trucks had been used by non-Marxists in Munich streets and in some working-class sections they were greeted with raised fists and angry shouts.

By seven that night Hitler got a depressing telephone report from the Zirkus Krone: the auditorium was far from filled. Ten minutes later came a more favorable report and at seven forty-five he was informed that three quarters of the seats were occupied with long lines queuing at the box office windows. As he entered the building "the same joy" seized him as it had a year before at the Hofbräuhaus. "Like a giant shell this hall lay before me, filled with thousands and thousands of people." The ring itself was black with humanity.

"Future or Ruin" was his theme, and his heart rejoiced in the conviction that down there before him lay his own future. After the first half hour he had the feeling that contact had been established and the audience was his. Applause began to interrupt him "in greater and greater spontaneous outbursts." This was finally succeeded by a remarkable hush, a solemn stillness. "Then you could hardly hear more than the breathing of this gigantic multitude, and only when the last word had been spoken did the applause suddenly roar forth to find its release and conclusion in the *Deutschland* song, sung with the highest fervor." The man who had released this flood of emotion was himself intoxicated, and he remained on the platform for twenty minutes watching the arena empty. Then, "overjoyed," he went out into the sleet to his dingy, unheated little room on the Thierschstrasse.

Hitler's performance at the Zirkus Krone was pilloried and praised in the Munich press and he was as pleased by the vituperation as by the approbation. It was not only that he thrived on opposition but that the violence of the attacks against him showed he was rousing visceral feelings. Despite the turbulence he generated, Hitler was becoming the darling of the respectable nationalist forces then making Munich their capital and receiving considerable secret support from the police president and his subordinate, who headed the department's Political Division. These two officials did their best to suppress complaints to the police against party breaches of peace and to protect Nazis when police action could not be forestalled. "We recognized that this movement, the National Socialist Party . . . should not be suppressed," they would testify three years later at Hitler's trial. "We did do that, and we refrained deliberately because we saw in the party the seeds of Germany's renewal, because we were convinced from the start that this movement was the one most likely to take root among workers infected with the Marxist plague and win them back into the nationalist camp. That is why we held our protecting hands over the National Socialist Party and Herr Hitler."*

The Bavarian government also gave him a measure of official recognition. Hitler and other party leaders were received by Gustav Ritter von Kahr, the right-wing Minister President, who was devoted to the preservation of Bavaria's peculiar status against encroachment by the Weimar regime. Bavaria still retained much of its autonomy, such as its own postal service, and its citizens continued to resent any directives from benighted northerners. Upon this issue Hitler and Kahr found common ground and although the Minister President disagreed with the "raging Austrian" on many points he felt the leader of the NSDAP could be useful as a propagandist in his own battle with Weimar.

---

* Nor were these the only protectors of the radical right. Even those judges, police, state and local officials, and military who wished to curb Hitler exhibited considerable partiality toward nationalists involved in violence. Out of 376 political assassinations in Germany between January 1919 and June 1922, 22 were committed by leftists and 354 by rightists. Leftists received, on an average, 180 months' imprisonment while rightists got only four months. Ten leftists were sentenced to death; no rightists.

Kahr's friendly reception gave public notice that Hitler was now a political force. Such recognition was welcome since his differences with the old guard in the party were coming to a head. Hitler's transformation into a personality because of his magnetism and crowd appeal indicated that he had not only altered the original purposes of the party but intended to seize complete control. His adversaries, therefore, took advantage of his absence in Berlin (where he was consolidating ties in that area with conservatives, nationalists and right-wing radicals) to engineer an alliance with a group of socialists from Augsburg. It seemed innocent but Hitler realized this was a sly tactical move to weaken his influence. He hastened back home and launched a startling counterattack. On July 11 he announced his resignation from the party. Three days later he put his cause before the general membership in an ultimatum. He would not return to the party unless he was made first chairman and given dictatorial powers. "I make these demands," he said, "not because I am power hungry, but because recent events have more than convinced me that without an iron leadership the party . . . will within a short time cease to be what it was supposed to be: a national socialist German Workers' Party and not a western association." It was the first manifest appearance of the concept Adolf Hitler had brought from the war—the *Führerprinzip*, the leadership principle, absolute obedience to the commander.

Hitler gave the committee eight days to act but Drexler was so incensed that he refused to compromise. The situation was exacerbated by distribution of an anonymous pamphlet to party members. Entitled "Adolf Hitler—Traitor?" it was a libelous concoction of fact and fancy but most charges—such as the ones that Hitler called himself "The King of Munich" and wasted large sums of money on women; and that he was in the pay of the Jews—were so ridiculous that it is difficult to believe the author himself took them seriously.

The eight-day deadline passed. Still Drexler and the committee refused to act. It looked as if Hitler's bluff had failed but in a last-hour secret session Eckart persuaded Drexler to compromise. He, in turn, brought around the rest of the executive committee on the grounds that they would still be a minor group but for Hitler. The latter was presented with a formal, flowery notice granting him the dictatorial powers he demanded and offering to make him chairman in recognition of "your exceptional knowledge, your unusual sacrifice and honorable accomplishments for the growth of the movement, and your unusual oratorical abilities."

A special congress was convened for July 29 to formalize Hitler's selection as new chairman. The meeting was opened by a left-wing Bavarian named Hermann Esser, who had become one of the Führer's closest advisers despite his youth. Widely known as a lady's man, Hitler described him as "a greyhound you must keep on a leash." He introduced Hitler, who proceeded to declare that he had fought repeatedly to keep the organization from turning into a tea club. "We do not wish to unite with other organizations," he said, "but insist that they annex themselves to us so that we can retain the leadership. Anyone who cannot accept this can leave." This went for the Augsburg group and any other out-of-towners. "Our movement came from Munich and stays in Munich." In closing, he reaffirmed his friendship for Drexler and said he was prepared to take on the position of chairman. A poll was taken. There were 543 votes for Hitler and one against.

With Hitler and his "armed Bohemians" now in absolute control of the NSDAP, all the traditions of the German Workers' Party were dumped overboard, since the elitists were dedicated to the proposition that a new order could not be built on old foundations. There would be no more parliamentary debate and democratic procedures. Henceforth, they would follow the Führer principle.

At the same time Hitler did his best to placate the old guard by making no display of power. He issued no general orders and refrained from enforcing the strict discipline he might have. Instead he spent the summer consolidating inner-party support in Munich and quietly expanding the rough-and-ready group which kept order at political meetings into a cohesive uniformed, paramilitary unit. It was established early in August under the innocent name of Gymnastic and Sports Division and, according to a party proclamation, was "intended to serve as a means for bringing our youthful members together into a powerful organization for the purpose of utilizing their strength as an offensive force at the disposal of the movement." Two months later it was given a more descriptive name: *Sturmabteilung* (Storm Detachment). To Hitler the SA was merely a political weapon to keep order and to march around in uniform to impress the discipline-loving burghers. But its leader, Captain Röhm, regarded it as a genuine armed force, his private army. The nucleus came from Free Corps units and one of their early battle songs was revised:

> *Swastika on helmet,*
> *Armband black-white-red,*
> *Storm Detachment Hitler*
> *Is our name.*

With the establishment of a private army and the party apparatus under his complete control, Adolf Hitler was now ready to set the NSDAP on a new, more revolutionary course. In the next months he instigated a series of public provocations. The campaign opened with apparently random acts: the assault of a Jew in the street, illegal display of flags and distribution of pamphlets, and a number of minor public brawls. These petty disturbances of the peace were succeeded, on the evening of September 14, 1921, by one of significance. The occasion was a meeting at the Löwenbräukeller of the Bavarian League, a federalist organization which accepted the social program of the Weimar Constitution while deploring its centralism. Its leader, an engineer named Ballerstedt, was preparing to address the crowd just as Hitler, who regarded him as "my most dangerous opponent," marched in. Scores of SA troops sans uniform had been planted in the audience near the podium and they leaped to their feet to give Hitler a raucous demonstration. Hundreds of other party adherents planted throughout the audience joined in. Then Hermann Esser climbed on a chair, shouting that Bavaria was in its present low state because of the Jews. This brought a chorus of demands that Ballerstedt "give the floor" to Hitler. Someone threw the light switches in an effort to prevent a brawl. It only created tumult. When the lights went on again the SA flooded onto the stage, engulfing Ballerstedt. After beating him up, the SA group shoved him off the stage into the audience.

At an examination by the police commission investigating the fracas, Hitler expressed no regrets. "It's all right," was his dogged comment. "We got what we wanted. Ballerstedt did not speak." The matter did not end with an inquiry. Hitler and Esser were both informed they would be tried for violating the peace. The impending trial only inspired violence which erupted on the evening of November 4, during a Hitler speech at Munich's Hofbräuhaus. By the time he entered the vestibule at 7:45 P.M. the hall was overflowing with more than eight hundred occupants. The women were told to take seats near the front, as far from the doors as possible. The warning didn't faze Frau Magdalena Schweyer, proprietor of a vegetable and fruit shop opposite Hitler's dwelling and his faithful adherent. "I was too excited really to be frightened. It was plain there'd be some trouble: half the people in the place belonged to the Reds." In fact, hostile workers from the Maffei factory, the Isaria Meter Works and other shops far outnumbered Hitler's followers. Moreover the party no longer enjoyed the secret protection of the Bavarian government since Minister President von Kahr had been forced to resign in favor of a more moderate man.

When Hitler saw that the Social Democrats had come early and taken most of the places, he ordered the doors closed. He told the SA bodyguard—there were less than fifty on hand—that this was their chance to show loyalty to the movement "and that not a man of us must leave the hall unless we were carried out dead." They were to attack at the first sign of violence on the theory that the best defense was a good offense. "The answer was a threefold *Heil* that sounded rougher and hoarser than usual." This romanticized account by Hitler was mirrored in the recollections of his followers who saw him as he undoubtedly saw himself: the pure man of iron will from the trenches come to lead the Fatherland back to honor and glory.

As Hitler started toward the speaker's platform, workers shouted threats. Hitler ignored them and pushed forward. Hermann Esser was now standing on the front table, calling the meeting to order. He jumped down and Hitler took his place. At first there were boos but even those who had come to jeer listened to his arguments and he was able to talk for more than an hour without interruption. But his opponents were only biding their time as they downed numerous mugs of beer, storing the empty ones under the tables for ammunition.

All at once someone interrupted Hitler and he shouted a retort. There were isolated angry shouts throughout the room. A man jumped on his chair and yelled, "*Freiheit* [Freedom]!" A beer stein hurtled at Hitler's head. Then half a dozen more. "Duck down!" the young monitors up front shouted to the women. Frau Schweyer obeyed. "One heard nothing but yells, crashing beer mugs, stamping and struggling, the overturning of heavy oaken tables, and the smashing of wooden chairs. A regular battle raged in the room." Curious, she looked up to see Hitler still standing atop a table despite the barrage of heavy mugs flying past his head. The outnumbered SA fought so ferociously that within half an hour the enemy had been driven down the stairs. It looked as if a shell had exploded in the hall demolishing chairs, tables and beer mugs. Finally above the din came the voice of Hermann Esser: "The meeting goes on. The speaker has the floor."

Hitler resumed his speech even as his storm troopers were bandaged or carried out of the room. He finished to an outburst of applause, moments before an excited police officer entered and shouted, "The meeting is dismissed!"

5

The brawl at the Hofbräuhaus was evidence to Hitler that success comes to one unafraid to use force. Victory that night brought him and the NSDAP a spate of publicity. But with the rise in membership came a demand among more solid citizens to put an end to such uncivilized behavior. The new Bavarian government was also eager to curb Hitler but wanted more definite provocation and in a display of fair play gave him a pistol permit.

His show of force was a symptom of the rising nationalist and völkisch resentment throughout Germany. Earlier in the year, after Germany rejected the Allied demand for increased war reparations, French and Belgian troops had occupied Duisburg and Düsseldorf as sanctions. Two months later the Allies issued an ultimatum for payment of two billions annually along with twenty-five per cent of the value of all German exports. This was accompanied by a threat to occupy the entire Ruhr.

The moderate conservative cabinet answered with resignations but the Center Party, which now controlled the government, bowed to the Allied demands. This capitulation infuriated nationalists such as Hitler and

set off a series of violent acts, including assassination of Matthias Erzberger, who was not only a leader of the Center Party but the "criminal"
who had signed the armistice. The assassins were hailed as heroes by many
of those Germans calling for law and order.

Before the end of 1921 nationalists had new cause for wrath when the
League of Nations announced that Poland was to receive that part of
Upper Silesia where four fifths of the mines and heavy industries were lo-
cated. Winter and the steady deflation of the mark with its attendant
hardships aggravated German discontent. On Easter Sunday, 1922, the atmosphere of violence was heightened by Foreign Minister Walther
Rathenau's startling turn to the East; he signed a treaty with the Soviet
Union at Rapallo. Anti-Bolshevists like Hitler were incensed, not realizing
the benefits of such an alliance to their own cause of a resurgent Reich.
They ignored the fact that this emergence of Germany from political isolation was a severe blow to the Western Allies.

Germany and Russia agreed to resume diplomatic relations, to
renounce all claims for reparations on each other, and to resume trade.
Neither was to enter into an economic agreement affecting the other without prior consultation. Russia was in need of modern technology; Germany was determined to circumvent the restrictive military clauses of the
Versailles Treaty without arousing the suspicions of the International
Control Commission operating on its territory. Lenin had already
requested German assistance in reorganizing the Red Army; General Hans
von Seeckt, head of the Reichswehr, readily complied, and the military of
the two powers came into close contact. Small German military units
began training Russians while gaining expertise in the use of special weapons.

The full extent and impact of this co-operation could not be
calculated by Rathenau's critics and, even though German rearmament
was given tremendous impetus by his pact, the very Germans who wanted
a strong army labeled him a Red for consorting with the Soviets. This was
only one more black mark against a man who had undeservedly become
the symbol of subservience to the West since he felt obliged to carry out
with determination the onerous economic promises of the Versailles
Treaty. Moreover, he was a wealthy Jew, accused by the Nazis of secretly
plotting for Jewish domination of the world. On the fourth of June this
gifted patriot was murdered, gangster style, by two former members of the
Free Corps.

By a quirk of fate the most feared activist in Bavaria was imprisoned
that same day. Hitler—after telling his followers: "Two thousand years
ago the mob of Jerusalem dragged a man to execution in just this
way"—was placed in Stadelheim prison for inciting a riot. The warder led
him to a cell with a private toilet, "amiably" pointing out that other
celebrities had shared these quarters, including Ludwig Thomas, the

Bavarian dramatist, and fellow revolutionary Kurt Eisner. Hitler was not particularly pleased by news of Rathenau's murder. Such isolated acts of vengeance seemed petty to him and this one was primarily a lesson in security. Henceforth he would install a searchlight in the back of his car "to blind the driver" of any pursuing vehicle.

As a result of the assassination, the Weimar government hastily passed a Law for the Protection of the Republic, a Draconian decree designed to halt radical right terrorism. Violent opposition came from Bavarian nationalists of all shadings. At the height of this controversy Hitler was released from Stadelheim. Isolation from the turbulent arena of politics had forced him to reassess his churning ideas. His almost five-week term in jail with nothing to do but read or think had helped mold his obsessive hatred and fear of Jews into a more connected and purposeful polemic. He wasted no time joining the assault of the Law for the Protection of the Republic and on the day of his release he made one of the most trenchant speeches of his career. Entitled "Free State or Slavery," its apparent target was the new law but in fact was a lethal denunciation of Jews and their insidious plans to conquer the world. Never before had he marshaled his material with more dramatic effect or given such a "reasonable" explanation of *how* and *why* the Jews had gained such power.

All over Europe, he told a receptive audience in the Bürgerbräukeller, a great conflict was raging between the ideals of nationalist-völkisch forces and those of international Jewry. It was the Jew who founded Social Democracy and Communism; it was the Jew who controlled the stock exchange and the workers' movement. At this point Hitler made a shrugging gesture in imitation of the stage Jew and drew an appreciative laugh. He went on to claim that the Jew was a destroyer, a robber, an exploiter. Moreover, Bolshevist Judaism was preparing for the decisive battle and had two great aims: "To make the nation defenseless in arms and to make the people defenseless in spirit."* To do so the Jew had to muzzle those who spoke out in protest. This at last, after more than an hour's denunciation of the Jewish menace, was the lead to Hitler's main theme. "We know that the so-called 'Law for the Protection of the Republic' which

---

* The depth and virulence of Hitler's anti-Semitism in 1922 were revealed during a conversation he had that year with an acquaintance, Josef Hell. When Hell asked what Hitler intended doing if he ever had full freedom of action against the Jews, the latter suddenly lost his poise. "He no longer looked at me," recalled Hell, "but beyond me into emptiness and made his next statement in a rising voice; he was seized by a sort of paroxysm and wound up shouting at me as if I were a large audience: 'If I am ever really in power, the destruction of the Jews will be my first and most important job. As soon as I have the power, I shall have gallows after gallows erected, for example, in Munich on the Marienplatz—as many of them as the traffic allows. Then the Jews will be hanged one after another, and they will stay hanging until they stink. They will stay hanging as long as hygienically possible. As soon as they are untied, then the next group will follow and that will continue until the last Jew in Munich is exterminated. Exactly the same procedure will be followed in other cities until Germany is cleansed of the last Jew!' "

comes from Berlin today is nothing else than a means for reducing all criticism to silence." But the National Socialists could not be silenced and he
was calling directly for physical violence. "So as I come to the end of my
speech I want to ask something of those among you who are young. And
for that there is a very special reason. The old parties train their youth in
the gift of gab, we prefer to train them to use their bodily strength. For I
tell you: the young man who does not find his way to the place where in
the last resort the destiny of his people is most truly represented, only
studies philosophy and in a time like this buries himself behind his books
or sits at home by the fire, he is no German youth! I call upon you! Join
our storm troops!"

He warned that their lot would be hard, with nothing to win and everything to lose. "He who today fights on our side cannot win great
laurels, far less can he win great material goods—it is more likely that he
will end up in jail. He who today is leader must be an idealist, if only for
the reason that he leads those against whom it would seem that everything
has conspired." His call to sacrifice and idealism sent the audience into ecstasy.

In the following two weeks Hitler continued to assail the new law
and on August 16 he was the star performer at a mass demonstration on
the Königsplatz. It had been called by the United Fatherland Leagues and
every patriotic society in Munich was expected to join in a combined protest against Weimar's decree. Before the arrival of Hitler and his group
there was little excitement. Then came the sound of a stirring march from
two brass bands, and finally the sight of marching men all wearing
swastika armbands. There were six columns of them carrying fifteen National Socialist flags. In minutes the square became jammed with about
fifty thousand excited, expectant people.

As Adolf Hitler stepped up to the platform there was little applause.
He stood silent for a moment. "Then he began to speak, quietly and
ingratiatingly at first," recalled Kurt Lüdecke, an ardent nationalist who
was seeing Hitler for the first time. "Before long his voice had risen to a
hoarse shriek that gave an extraordinary effect of an intensity of feeling."
He seemed to be only one more fanatic—a threatening, beseeching figure
with small hands and intense, steel-blue eyes but, before he knew it,
Lüdecke fell under Hitler's spell. As if hypnotized, he suddenly saw the
"fanatic" turn into a patriot hero, another Luther. "His appeal to German
manhood was like a call to arms, the gospel he preached a sacred truth."
Hitler had gained another uncritical convert.

That evening Lüdecke heard Hitler again, this time at the Zirkus
Krone. Once more Lüdecke was transfixed. After the speech he was introduced to the speaker, who was disheveled and perspiring. A dirty trench
coat was flung carelessly over his shoulders. But all Lüdecke saw was a

man of character and courage and the next day he offered himself to Hitler and his cause "without reservation." They talked for more than four hours, then solemnly clasped hands. "I had given him my soul."

6

Out of the controversy over the Law for the Protection of the Republic and the widening split between Weimar and Bavaria came plans for another coup d'état. Its instigator was an obscure Munich public health official, Dr. Otto Pittinger, who planned to overthrow the Bavarian government with the support of the NSDAP and other nationalist organizations and replace it with a dictatorship under former Minister President von Kahr.

Hitler's new convert, Kurt Lüdecke, was given the task of relaying final instructions to possible co-conspirators in the Berlin area. He ranged through North Germany, envisaging himself as the "German Paul Revere" rousing nationalists from bed, until he learned that nothing at all was happening in Bavaria itself. He took the train back to Munich—it was late September 1922—and drove at once to Pittinger's headquarters where the doctor was just emerging. "Is this the coup d'état?" said Lüdecke accusingly. But Pittinger, looking "very haughty in his goggles," ignored him and sped off in a Mercedes for a vacation in the Alps. His uprising had fizzled out. Only the National Socialists were ready to march, and their leader had been forced to go into hiding.

Lüdecke found Hitler in a shabby attic room, his only companions a large dog and Graf, his bodyguard. "I was ready—my men were ready!" he angrily told Lüdecke. "From now on I go my way alone." Even if not a soul followed he would go it alone. "No more Pittingers, no more Fatherland societies! One party. One single party. These *gentlemen*, these counts and generals—they won't do anything. *I* shall. *I alone.*"

Earlier that year Hitler had confessed to Arthur Möller van den Bruck, who was writing a book called *The Third Reich:* "You have everything I lack. You create the spiritual framework for Germany's reconstruction. I am but a drummer and an assembler. Let us work together." Envisaging a nationalistic, socialist corporate state, Möller refused Hitler's offer, then told a colleague, "That fellow will never grasp it. I would rather commit suicide than see such a man in office."

The lesson learned in the ignominious Pittinger Putsch convinced Hitler that he must act alone as Führer. It was a concept that excited Lüdecke and he suggested the party copy the technique of Benito Mussolini, who was striving to be the leader of Italy. His Fascist movement was nationalistic, socialistic and anti-Bolshevik; his Blackshirts had recently occupied Ravenna and other Italian cities. Lüdecke volunteered to go to Italy as Hitler's representative to see if Mussolini might prove to be a valuable ally.

In Milan Il Duce received Lüdecke graciously even though he had never heard of Hitler. He agreed with Hitler's views on the Versailles Treaty and international finance but was evasive about the measures that should be used against Jews. What impressed Lüdecke most was Mussolini's supreme assurance when asked if he would resort to force in case the Italian government did not yield to his demands. "We shall *be* the State," he said as if he were royalty, "because it is our will."

Lüdecke's report to Hitler was enthusiastic. Mussolini, he said, would probably seize control of Italy within months. He also confirmed that there were remarkable similarities between Fascism and National Socialism. Both were ardently nationalistic, anti-Marxist and anti-parliamentarian, both were dedicated to a radical new order. In addition, the two leaders were alike. Both came from the people and were war veterans.

Hitler was particularly interested in Mussolini's use of brute force to gain political power. "His eyes grew thoughtful," recalled Lüdecke, "when he heard how the Blackshirts marched into Bolshevized towns and took possession, while the garrisons kept benevolently neutral or, in some cases, even quartered the Fascisti." It only proved what could be achieved by nerve.

Inspired by Mussolini's success and reassured by his own growing support throughout Bavaria, Hitler decided to make his show of force that autumn. He selected Coburg, a town in Upper Bavaria more than a hundred and sixty miles north of Munich. The occasion was a "German Day" celebration which had been organized by a group of völkisch societies. The guests of honor were to be the Grand Duke and Duchess of Coburg. Both were openly nationalistic and she was a relative of the late Czar.

Hitler was invited to attend and to "bring some escort." Choosing to interpret this invitation broadly, he left Munich in a special train on Saturday morning, October 14, 1922, with some 600 SA men, many of whom were paying their own expenses. There was a festive air as the storm troopers, equipped with rations for two days, piled into the special train to the music of their forty-two piece brass band.

It was a rollicking party more like an excursion tour and even in Hitler's compartment there was a holiday air. With him were seven men, the brains and brawn of the inner circle: a former sergeant (Max Amann), a wrestler (Graf), a horse trader and ex-barroom bouncer (Christian Weber), a pamphleteer and ex-Communist (Esser), an architect (Rosenberg), an author (Eckart) and a self-styled sophisticate (Lüdecke). To the last-mentioned, the two most interesting were the ebullient Eckart, who "outshone all the others with his wit and common sense," and Rosenberg, a "block of ice!" who gazed toward him with pale lackluster eyes as though he weren't there.

The train stopped for half an hour in Nuremberg to pick up more adherents. The band struck up again and the men shouted as they waved swastika flags from the windows. Curious bystanders gathered to see what kind of a circus train it was. Jews in another halted train jeered at the swastika flags until Julius Schreck, who would later become Hitler's chauffeur, "leapt into the midst of them and started laying about him."

By the time the train pulled into the Coburg station there were 800 storm troopers. Grim-faced, Hitler stepped out to the platform. He had chosen Coburg as a battleground because of its preponderance of socialists and Communists. He would emulate Mussolini and drive them from their own stronghold. The people of Coburg, Bavarians for only two years, were taken aback by the noisy group that piled out behind Hitler onto the platform with their large band and red banners. The brass band struck up a march and then, with military precision, the SA paraded into town. In the van were eight husky Bavarians in leather shorts carrying alpenstocks. Just behind a row of men carrying large red and black flags came Hitler and his entourage of seven, followed by 800 men armed with rubber bludgeons or knives. Some wore faded and mended field-gray uniforms, some their Sunday best; their only common distinction was a swastika band on the left arm. Hitler himself was the epitome of the common man in his belted trench coat, slouch hat and ridiculous calf-high boots.

A mob of workers pressed from both sides shouting "Murderers! Bandits! Robbers! Criminals!" The National Socialists ignored the epithets, never breaking step. Local police guided the line of march to the Hofbräuhauskeller in the very center of town, then locked the gates, but Hitler insisted on quartering his men in a shooting gallery. To the beat of drums the storm troopers marched back through the hostile mob toward the outskirts of town. As cobblestones began to fly at the columns, Hitler signaled with a wave of his whip, and his men turned on the attackers with their bludgeons. The crowd fell back and the storm troopers continued their march, strutting like soldiers after their first battle. One of the proudest was the bon vivant Lüdecke, who felt as if he had been finally accepted by the rank and file. "Seeing that one brawls as well in an English suit as in shoddy clothes, they forgave me my tailor."

The following morning, Sunday, the leftists called a mass demonstration "to throw out the Nazis." Ten thousand protesters were expected to collect at the square but the size of the opposition only spurred Hitler to defiance. Resolved "to dispose of the Red terror for good," he ordered the SA, whose ranks had grown to almost 1500, to march on the Fortress of Coburg by way of the square. At noon the storm troopers with Hitler in the lead paraded into the center of the city but there were only a few hundred demonstrators at the square. Yesterday the citizens had stood on the sidewalks watching the SA pass by with silent disapproval. Today hundreds of imperial flags hung from the windows and friendly crowds lined the way, cheering the National Socialists with their strange emblem. Today they were heroes. They had ended Red domination of the Coburg alleys and streets. "That's typical of your bourgeois world," Hitler remarked to the men marching at his side. "Cowards at the moment of danger, boasters afterwards."

Coburg proved to Hitler that he and his SA could emulate Mussolini. In little more than two weeks the latter set another example. On October 28 Il Duce's Blackshirts marched into Rome (he took the train) and seized control of Italy.

Four days later Esser, in his usual role as introducer of the Führer, dramatically announced at the banquet hall of the Hofbräuhaus: "Germany's Mussolini is called Hitler!"

Chapter Five

"SUCH A LOGICAL AND FANATICAL MAN" 1922–1923

1

By 1922 Adolf Hitler had surrounded himself with a diverse group from every class which embraced a wide spectrum of cultures and occupations. All shared, to varying degrees, his nationalism and fear of Marxism. Two aviators were among them: Hermann Göring, a fighter ace and last commander of the famed Richthofen Flying Circus; and Rudolf Hess, who had started the war as an infantry officer in Hitler's regiment and ended it as a pilot. Although both were convinced Hitler was the answer to Germany's future and both came from well-to-do families, they differed strikingly in appearance, character and temperament.

Göring was buoyant, theatrical, an extrovert, who made friends easily and nearly always dominated them. His father had been a district judge before accepting an appointment from Bismarck as Reichs Commissar for Southwest Africa. He was married twice and had eight children. Hermann, the next to youngest, was an indifferent scholar whose dream was to serve his country in battle. Through the offices of his godfather he was admitted to the Royal Prussian Cadet Corps. He distinguished himself in the war and, after his twentieth air victory, was awarded the highest military decoration, the Pour le Mérite order. After the armistice he became a pilot for the Swedish airline and got engaged to a married woman, Carin von Kantzow, whose father was a member of the Swedish nobility and whose mother came from a family of Irish brewers. They were to get married as soon as her divorce was final.

Göring could have enjoyed a life of comparative ease in Sweden but he felt the urge to return to Germany and help "wipe out the disgrace of Versailles—the shame of defeat, the corridor right through the heart of Prussia." He enrolled at the University of Munich to study history and political science but was more interested in practical politics and once tried to form his own revolutionary party among officer veterans. "I remember a meeting at which they were discussing getting meals and beds for veteran officers. 'You damn fools!' I told them. 'Do you think that an officer who is worth his salt can't find a bed to sleep in, even if it happens to be the bed of a pretty blonde? Damn it, there are more important things at stake!' Somebody got fresh and I banged him over the head. Well, of course, the meeting broke up in an uproar." That ended his attempt to head a revolution and it wasn't until the fall of 1922 at a mass meeting that he found someone worth following. It was a meeting at the Königsplatz protesting Allied demands to hand over alleged war criminals. A series of speakers from various parties took the platform. Then the crowd began calling out, "Hitler!" By chance he was standing near Göring and Carin, who had been married early that year, and they overheard him remark that he wouldn't think of addressing "these tame bourgeois pirates." Something about the man in the belted trench coat impressed Göring so much that he went to a party meeting at the Café Neumann. "I just sat unobtrusively in the background. I remember Rosenberg was there. Hitler explained why he hadn't spoken. No Frenchman is going to lose sleep over that kind of harmless talk, he said. You've got to have bayonets to back up your threats. Well, *that* was what I wanted to hear. He wanted to build up a party that would make Germany strong and smash the Treaty of Versailles. 'Well,' I said to myself, '*that's* the party for me! *Down with the Treaty of Versailles*, God damn it! That's my meat!'"

At party headquarters he filled out a membership application. The appearance of such a war hero in the shabby office must have caused a stir. "Anyway," he recalled, "somebody tells me that Hitler would like to see me immediately." One look at the imposing Göring was enough for Hitler. Here was the ideal Nordic: luminous blue eyes, straight features and pink and white complexion. "He told me that it was a stroke of fate that I should come to him just as he was looking for somebody to take charge of the SA." They agreed to postpone the announcement a month, but Göring immediately began training the SA as a military organization. "Military! I'll tell the world it was military!"

He may have looked the perfect Germanic type but he was no racist by Hitler's standards and, in fact, had a number of Jewish friends. Göring had joined the NSDAP "precisely because it *was* revolutionary, not because of the ideological stuff. Other parties had made revolution, so I figured I could get in on one too!" A man of action, he was drawn to an organization dedicated to action and he was just the man Hitler needed at that moment. He had invaluable connections with Junker officers and members of society, and was a display piece for parades and meetings. Nor was he squeamish about bashing in a few heads if necessary.

Compared to Göring, Rudolf Hess was colorless. Born in Alexandria, Egypt, he was sired by a well-to-do wholesaler and exporter who persuaded him to enter the family business, although he would have preferred to become a scholar. He attended boarding school in Bad Godesberg before enrolling at the École Supérieure du Commerce in Switzerland. His studies were interrupted by the war, and when it ended he could not bring himself to continue a business career. Like Göring, he entered the University of Munich, reading history, economics and geopolitics. He too felt betrayed by the "November criminals" but, instead of trying to make a revolution of his own, joined the Thule Society. He took part in demonstrations, spoke on street corners (despite his painful self-consciousness), and as a member of a Free Corps unit helped overthrow the Bavarian Soviet regime.

He too was searching for a leader and had won a prize at the university for writing an essay on the theme "How must the man be constituted who will lead Germany back to her old heights?" The man, he wrote, should be a dictator not averse to the use of slogans, street parades and demagoguery. He must be a man of the people yet have nothing in common with the mass. Like every great man, he must be "all personality," and one who "does not shrink from bloodshed. Great questions are always decided by blood and iron." To reach his goal, he must be prepared "to trample on his closest friends," dispense law "with terrible hardness" and deal with people and nations "with cautious and sensitive fingers" or if need be "trample on them with the boots of a grenadier."

Hess found his ideal in Hitler and for more than a year had served as his trusted lieutenant and confidant. At the same time he also gave allegiance to a man married to a Jew. General Karl Haushofer returned to Germany in 1911 after three years in Tokyo as military attaché, speaking fluent Japanese. He brought back an abiding interest in Asian affairs along with a conviction that a nation's existence depended on the space it controlled. The war was proof to him of this theory. An encircled and suffocated Germany had gone down to humiliating defeat because she lacked *Lebensraum* (living space). After the armistice he became professor of geopolitics at the University of Munich, teaching his students that national salvation lay in self-sufficiency and for this Germany must have not only autarchy (national economic independence) but Lebensraum. Hess was almost as enthralled by Professor Haushofer as he was by Hitler and his hope was to bring the two together. One impediment was Frau Haushofer, whose father was a Jewish merchant. And while

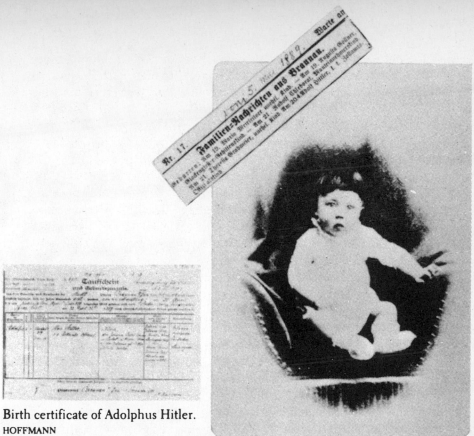

Baby Adolf. BUNDESARCHIV

Birth certificate of Adolphus Hitler.
HOFFMANN

Hitler's mother. LIBRARY OF CONGRESS

Hitler's father. LIBRARY OF CONGRESS

Alois Hitler with son Alois, Jr. HANS HITLER   Angela (Hitler) Raubal and son Leo.
                                                 HANS HITLER

Angela, Hitler's half sister, and Alois, his half
brother, with Granny. HANS HITLER

Top picture, choir school at Lambach monastery about 1899, Hitler top row, second from right. HARRY SCHULZE-WILDE

Above, Hitler, the leader of his class in a village school. Leonding, 1900. HARRY SCHULZE-WILDE

Right, Hitler, the failure in a city school. Linz, 1901. LIBRARY OF CONGRESS

Paula, Hitler's younger sister, studying family album about 1950. HANS HITLER

Alois Hitler, Jr., about 1950. HANS HITLER

Hitler's best boyhood friend, August Kubizek. HARRY SCHULZE-WILDE

Kubizek about 1960. His doctor is on the right. HARRY SCHULZE-WILDE

Above, Hitler at sixteen as sketched by F. Sturmberger, a schoolmate from Steyr who presently resides in Linz. LIBRARY OF CONGRESS

Below, Dr. Bloch, who treated Hitler's mother for cancer, in his office at Linz. This picture was taken in 1938 by order of Bormann for the Führer's "personal film cassette." The inscription read: "The Führer often sat on the chair beside the desk." BUNDESARCHIV

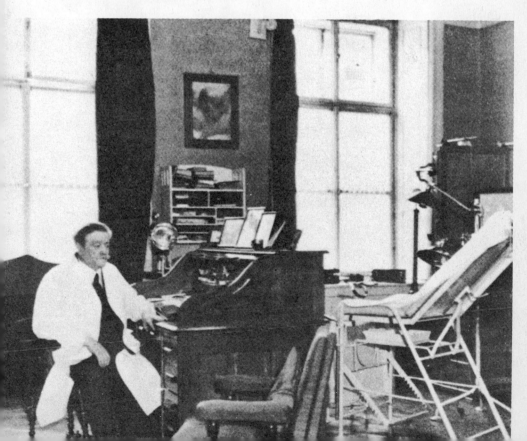

Water color of old Vienna by Hitler in 1911–12.

Auersberg Palace, Vienna, 1911–12. Architecturally
accurate but the figures are far out of proportion.

Ruins of Becelaere, Belgium. 1917.

Above, Hitler, extreme left, in trenches. HOFFMANN

Below, l. to r., two World War I comrades— Ernst Schmidt and Sergeant Max Amann—with Hitler and his dog Fuchsl. HARRY SCHULZE-WILDE

Above, Hitler decorated
with the Iron Cross.
U. S. ARMY

Below, Dr. Edmund
Forster, the first
psychiatrist to treat Hitler,
October–November 1918.
FESTSCHRIFT ZUR 500-
JAHRFEIER DER UNIVERSITAT
GRIEFSWALD 17. 10. 1956, II. 411.

Hess followed the letter of racist doctrine, he was a man of sentiment as devoted to her as he was to the Herr Professor.

Hess was a retiring man, modest and unassertive. Although he had fought well on the battlefield and in the streets and his prize-winning essay breathed blood and iron, he was far from bloodthirsty. Yet while he preferred books and music to brawling, he was never found wanting in beer-hall battles and had won Hitler's affection by his action in the bloody fracas at the Hofbräuhaus. With his solid square face, bushy black eyebrows, intense and clenched lips, he was the picture of a man "prepared to trample on his closest friends." Only when he broke into a smile was the true Hess revealed—an ingenuous, bucktoothed young idealist. Ilse Hess, then Ilse Pröhl, recalls that "he rarely smiled, did not smoke, despised alcohol and had no patience with young people enjoying dancing and social life after a war had been lost." An enigma, except to those who knew him intimately, Hess was the ideal disciple. Too bashful and unaspiring to strive for power, he was prepared to follow Hitler wherever he led.

Another blind follower was Julius Streicher. Where Hess and Göring lagged far behind their leader in anti-Semitism, Streicher surpassed Hitler in the virulence of his language. A stocky, primitive man with bald head and gross features, he gave off an aura of raw energy. He had excessive appetites alike at table and in bed. He could be bluffly jovial or blatantly brutal, shifting effortlessly from maudlin sentimentality to ruthlessness. Like Hitler, he was rarely seen in public without a whip but where the former draped his from the wrist like a dog leash, Streicher flaunted his as a weapon. In younger days he had "restlessly wandered from place to place with a rucksack full of anti-Semitic books and pamphlets." His speech was glutted with sadistic imagery and he relished attacking personal enemies in the foulest terms. Convinced that the Jew was plotting against the Aryan world, he had an endless catalogue of abuse at the tip of his tongue.

He was made for the NSDAP and, soon after founding the Nuremberg branch of the party in 1922, he spawned a newspaper dedicated to the damnation of Jews. *Der Stürmer* went a long step beyond *Ostara*, the Viennese magazine that exercised such influence on the youthful Hitler, in filth and virulence and was already a source of dismay to many of those close to Hitler. The Führer himself was repelled by pornography, disapproved of Streicher's sexual activities, and was concerned by the incessant intraparty quarrels this erratic disciple instigated. Yet at the same time he admired Streicher's boundless energy and fanatic loyalty. "More than once Dietrich Eckart told me that Streicher was a schoolteacher, and a lunatic to boot, from many points of view. He always added that one could not hope for a triumph of National Socialism without giving one's support to men like Streicher." Hitler had an unexpected answer for those who reproached Streicher for his gross exaggerations in *Der Stürmer*: "The truth is the opposite of what people say: he *idealized* the Jew. The Jew is baser, fiercer, more diabolical than Streicher depicted him."

Such were the men close to Hitler. His movement cut across all social classes and so all types were drawn to him—the intellectual, the street fighter, the fanatic, the idealist, the hooligan, the condottiere, the principled and the unprincipled, laborers and noblemen. There were gentle souls and the ruthless, rascals and men of good will; writers, painters, day laborers, storekeepers, dentists, students, soldiers and priests. His appeal was broad and he was broad-minded enough to accept a drug addict like Eckart or a homosexual like Captain Röhm. He was all things to many while he himself was ready to accept anyone who offered fealty in the battle for Germany's resurrection against the machinations of Jewish Marxism.

"My happiest memories are of this time," he recalled in a sentimental flood of recollections on a winter evening nineteen years later. He talked fondly of his early supporters. "Today, when I happen to meet one of them, it moves me extraordinarily. They showed a truly touching attachment towards me. Small stallkeepers of the markets used to come running to see me 'to bring a couple of eggs to Herr Hitler.' . . . I'm so fond of these unpretentious fellows."

Never one to underrate a follower no matter how humble, and perhaps remembering the miserable days in Vienna, Hitler opened up the new, more spacious party headquarters on Corneliusstrasse to those down-at-heels followers who needed refuge from the cold. "In the winter time," recalled Philipp Bouhler, "the anteroom was a place to warm up for unemployed party members and supporters who, loud and freezing, played cards there. You often couldn't hear yourself speak, and from time to time Christian Weber, who was in charge, appeared with a long horse whip to clear out the room."

2

In the fall of 1922 the activities of Adolf Hitler began to interest the Allies. At the suggestion of the American ambassador, Captain Truman Smith—Yale man, West Pointer, and now assistant military attaché in Berlin—was dispatched to Munich "to assess the reported developing strength of the National Socialist movement." Smith was instructed to meet Hitler and "form an estimate of his character, personality, abilities, and weaknesses." He was also to investigate the NSDAP's strength and potentialities. Specifically Smith was to find the answer to these questions: "Was there danger that Bavaria would declare itself independent of Germany? Did there exist in Munich danger of a renewed Communist revolt? Did the possibility exist that Hitler's National Socialists were strong enough to seize power in Bavaria? Was the 7th division of the Reichswehr, which was garrisoned in Bavaria, loyal to the Reich or was its loyalty divided between Berlin and Munich? Could it be depended upon to put down disorders or revolts whether staged by the right or left?"

Captain Smith arrived in Munich just before noon on November 15. After settling at the Marienbad Hotel he called on the acting United States consul, Robert Murphy, at the consulate on Ledererstrasse. The twenty-eight-year-old Murphy (later ambassador to Belgium), informed Smith that the new Bavarian Minister President was "not a strong character, being merely a tool" of former Minister President Kahr. The National Socialists, he said, were rapidly increasing in strength and their leader, while "a pure and simple adventurer," was nevertheless "a real character and is exploiting all latent discontent." Hitler understood the Bavarian psychology but it was questionable if he was "big enough to take the lead in a German national movement."

In the next few days Smith talked with generals, civil officials, Crown Prince Rupprecht ("certainly no genius, but still seems to possess considerable political ability"), a liberal newspaper editor, and Max Erwin von Scheubner-Richter, a refugee of German origin from a Baltic state, who had borrowed his wife's title. The last, a close friend of Rosenberg's, was beginning to exert considerable influence on Hitler. Scheubner-Richter assured Smith that the party's anti-Semitism was "purely for propaganda," and then invited him to attend a review of storm troopers before the new National Socialist headquarters.

"A remarkable sight indeed," Smith noted down in his hotel room that evening. "Twelve hundred of the toughest roughnecks I have ever seen in my life pass in review before Hitler at the goosestep under the old Reichflag wearing red arm bands with Hakenkreuzen. Hitler, following the review, makes a speech . . . then shouts, 'Death to the Jews' etc. and etc. There was frantic cheering. I never saw such a sight in my life."

The next day, Saturday, Smith spoke with Ludendorff at his home. The general confessed that he had "formerly believed that Bolshevism had first to be stamped out in Russia before it could be crushed in Germany. He has now changed his mind, and thinks that Bolshevism must first be crushed in Germany." He asserted that the Allies "*must* support a strong German government capable of combatting Marxism" and that such a government will never "develop out of the existing chaotic parliamentary conditions" but "can only be formed by patriotic men." He was convinced that the "Fascist movement was the beginning of a reactionary awakening in Europe," and that Mussolini had "real sympathy for the national cause in Germany."

At 4 P.M. the following Monday, Smith met Hitler where he had interviewed Scheubner-Richter. The room was "drab and dreary beyond belief; akin to a back bedroom in a decaying New York tenement." The first words Smith wrote down in his notebook after the meeting were: "A marvelous demagogue. I have rarely listened to such a logical and fanatical man. His power over the mob must be immense." Hitler described his movement as a "union of Hand and Brain workers to oppose Marxism," and said that the "present abuses of capital must be done away with, if Bolshevism is to be put down." The parliamentary system had to be replaced. "Only a dictatorship can bring Germany to its feet." He stated that it was "much better for America and England that the decisive struggle between our civilization and Marxism be fought out on German soil rather than on American and English soil. If we (America) do not help German Nationalism, Bolshevism will conquer Germany. Then there will be no more reparations and Russia and German Bolshevism, out of motives of self preservation must attack the western nations."

He discoursed on other subjects but did not even mention Jews until Smith queried him point-blank about anti-Semitism; and then Hitler replied disarmingly that he merely "favored the withdrawal of citizenship and their exclusion from public affairs." By the time Smith left the dingy room he was convinced Hitler would be an important factor in German politics. He accepted a ticket for Hitler's next speech on November 22 and, upon being unexpectedly summoned back to Berlin, passed it on to Ernst Hanfstaengl, a towering lantern-jawed eccentric who had graduated from Harvard. Would Hanfstaengl be kind enough to take a look at this fellow Hitler and pass on his conclusions? "I have the impression he's going to play a big part," said Smith, "and whether you like him or not he certainly knows what he wants."

He was relying on Hanfstaengl's judgment because of the latter's unusual background. His mother came from a well-known New England family, the Sedgwicks; two of his ancestors were Civil War generals, one of whom helped carry Lincoln's coffin. Two generations of Hanfstaengls had served as privy councilors to the Dukes of Saxe-Coburg-Gotha and were connoisseurs and patrons of the arts. The family owned an art publishing house in Munich well known for its excellent reproductions. Hanfstaengl had been brought up in an atmosphere of art and music, the home a rendezvous for Lilli Lehmann, Wilhelm Busch, Sarasate, Richard Strauss, Felix Weingartner, Wilhelm Backhaus, Fridtjof Nansen and Mark Twain. He himself played the piano with verve and his six-foot-four frame hunched over the keyboard like an impish bear was a common sight in the best Bavarian salons. His nickname was Putzi (little fellow).

On the twenty-second Hanfstaengl took a streetcar to the Kindlkeller, a large L-shaped beer hall filled with a conglomerate audience. There were a few ex-officers and minor civil servants, some small shopkeepers and numerous young people and workers. Many wore the Bavarian national costume. From the press table Hanfstaengl searched in vain for someone he knew. He wondered where Hitler was and a journalist pointed to a trio on the platform. The short one was Max Amann, the one with the glasses was Anton Drexler, and the third was Hitler. He wore clumsy ankle-high shoes, a dark suit. His white collar was starched and he reminded Hanfstaengl of a waiter in a railway station restaurant. But after Drexler introduced him to the audience and Hitler strode swiftly and confidently past the press table he was "the unmistakable soldier in mufti."

The applause was deafening. Hitler stood like a sentry, legs firmly stretched, hands folded behind his back, as he began reviewing the events of the past few years in a quiet, reserved voice. Methodically he built up his case against the government, never stooping to histrionics or vulgarisms. He spoke carefully in literary High German, occasionally allowing a Viennese accent to creep in. Hanfstaengl, not a dozen feet away, was particularly impressed with the speaker's clear blue, guileless eyes. "There was honesty, there was sincerity, there was suffering and the dignity of mute entreaty." After about ten minutes Hitler had the audience's complete attention. Now he relaxed his position and used his hands and arms like a trained actor. He began to insinuate with sly malice in Viennese coffeehouse style, and Hanfstaengl noticed that the women nearby were enjoying the performance enormously. Finally one of them called out, "That's right, bravo!" and, as if in acknowledgment, Hitler raised his voice and with a sweeping gesture began condemning war profiteers. There was a roar of applause.

Hitler wiped the sweat from his brow and took a mug of beer from a man with a dark mustache. It was a telling touch of theater for the beer-drinking Müncheners. When he resumed speaking his gestures became more sweeping. Every so often someone would shout out an insult and he would calmly raise his right hand slightly as if catching a ball or fold his arms and spit out a brief rejoinder that would crush the heckler. "His technique resembled the thrusts and parries of a fencer, or the perfect balance of a tightrope-walker. Sometimes he reminded me of a skilled violinist, who, never coming to the end of his bow, always left just the faint anticipation of a tone—a thought spared the indelicacy of utterance." Gone was all caution as he stormed at his favorite enemies—the Jews and Reds. "Our motto shall be—if you will not be a German, I will bash your skull in. For we are convinced that we cannot succeed without a struggle. We have to fight with ideas, but, if necessary, also with our fists."

As Hanfstaengl emerged from his fascination, he looked around and noted with astonishment how the audience's behavior had changed. "The muffled restlessness of the masses who, an hour ago, had shoved against me and uttered all manner of nasty remarks, had become a deeply moved community. People were sitting listening breathlessly, who had long since forgotten to reach for their beer mugs and instead were drinking in the speaker's every word." Nearby a young woman was staring at Hitler "as though in some devotional ecstasy, she had ceased to be herself and was completely under the spell of Hitler's despotic faith in Germany's future greatness." The speech built to a climax that was "an orgasm of words." Suddenly it was over. The audience cheered frenziedly, clapped and pounded the tables. Hitler's exhaustion reminded Hanfstaengl of "a great artist at the end of a gruelling concert." His face and hair were soaked and his starched collar had wilted ("Whenever I make a speech of great importance I am always soaking wet at the end, and I find I have lost four or six pounds in weight.")

On the spur of the moment, Hanfstaengl approached the committee table where Hitler was receiving compliments with a self-assured smile free of any arrogance. "Captain Truman Smith asked me to give you his best wishes," said Hanfstaengl. Smith's name piqued Hitler's interest and he asked how Hanfstaengl liked the speech. "Well, I agree with you," he said careful not to hurt Hitler's feelings. "About ninety-five per cent of what you said I can set my name to, and five per cent we will have to talk about that." What he particularly objected to was Hitler's blatant anti-Semitism.

"I am sure we shall not have to quarrel about the odd five per cent," said Hitler affably. He seemed modest and friendly as he stood dabbing at his face with a crumpled handkerchief. He cleared his throat, coughed, then held out a hand. It felt "hardboned, rough," like the "grip of a front-line soldier."

That night Hanfstaengl could not fall asleep. "My mind still raced with the impressions of the evening. Where all our conservative politicians and speakers were failing abysmally to establish any contact with the ordinary people, this self-made man, Hitler, was clearly succeeding in presenting a non-Communist program to exactly those people whose support we needed." Hanfstaengl decided to help him.

In Berlin Captain Smith turned in a long detailed report on his visit to Munich and, on December 5, Embassy Counselor Robbins dispatched a personal message to the Under Secretary of State: "My own prognostication on the general attitude of the Bavarian outfit is that sooner or later a serious break is going to come from here. Hitler, the young Austrian Sergeant, who fought in the German army during the war, and who is now leading a Fascist movement, known as the 'Grey shirts', is working very slowly and I should say efficiently along the same lines as Mussolini. I am told by some of our men who have been down there, that he is an extraordinary orator and though not of the highest moral standing, a great leader of men. He is obtaining a great deal of money from the manufacturers just as Mussolini did and is going very slowly. He told Truman Smith, our Assistant Military Attaché, who was down there, that he had no intention of starting any big movement for the next month or so, and probably not before two months, that he is collecting funds and equipment, and that all was going well."

The report caused little stir in the State Department, which was concerned with more pressing matters, and was filed away. But in Germany there was growing concern over the increase in membership in the NSDAP and its private army. In mid-December a police official of the Bavarian State Ministry of the Interior filed a disturbing report charging that the Hitler movement was "without a doubt dangerous to the government, not only for the present form of government, but for any political system at all, because if they really achieve their dark ideas in regard to the Jews, Social Democrats, and Bank-capitalists, then there will be much blood and disorder."

Another urgent warning was received almost simultaneously by the new Reich Chancellor, Wilhelm Cuno. It came from a curious source, the Bulgarian consul in Munich, and concerned a frank conversation the Bulgarian had recently had with Hitler. Parliamentary government in Germany, said the latter, was about to collapse since the parliamentary leaders had no mass support. Dictatorship was inevitable from either the right or the left. The big cities of North Germany were controlled largely by the left but in Bavaria his NSDAP was certain of victory. Thousands were joining every week. Moreover, seventy-five per cent of the secret police in Munich were National Socialists and there was an even higher percentage among rank-and-file city police. Hitler predicted that Bolsheviks would gain control of North Germany. To save the nation, Bavarians would have to organize a counterrevolution and, to do so, they would need an iron-fisted dictator, a man "ready, if necessary, to march across fields of blood and corpses."

It was a terrifying forecast of things to come, particularly its ominous assertion that Hitler's plan for crushing Bolshevism and resisting French occupation of the Ruhr would win applause from most patriotic nationalists in Bavaria. They had endured a few terrifying days of Red rule and were prepared to act ruthlessly against anyone preaching leftist doctrine.

3

In the first days of 1923 a quarrel between the French and British at the Reparations Commission resulted in the withdrawal of the latter's delegation. This gave France the opportunity to solve the reparations problem by force. On January 11 French and Belgian troops marched into the Ruhr on the excuse that Germany had failed to fulfill her obligations. This act not only inflamed nationalist spirit throughout Germany but quickened the descent of the mark, which plunged from 6750 to the dollar to 50,000 within two weeks (on Armistice Day, 1918, it was 7.45 to the dollar). The last payment of railway expenses by the Weimar government to the Committee of Guarantees for a trip to Berlin had "required seven office boys with huge waste-paper baskets full of [twenty-mark] notes to carry the full sum from the office down to the railway station." Now it would take forty-nine office boys.

The invasion of the Ruhr, along with inflation and increased unemployment, broadened the base of nationalism and brought Hitler more adherents. Disdaining co-operation with other groups, including the Majority Socialists, he organized protest meetings of his own and announced that twelve public rallies would be held on January 27, the First Party Day of the NSDAP.

Although the Bavarian police president informed Hitler that these demonstrations were banned, he defiantly shouted that the police could shoot if they wished but he himself would be in the first row. He was as good as his word and on the assigned day hurried from one rally to another by car. "Neither during the war nor during the revolution have I experienced such hypnotic mass-excitement," recalled historian Karl Alexander von Müller, who attended the rally at the Löwenbräukeller. The audience rose as one man, with shouts of "Heil!" as Hitler strode down the aisle. "I was very close when he marched through and I saw that this was different from the man I had met here and there in private houses: his small pale face expressed an inner fanaticism. His eyes glanced from right to left as if looking for enemies to conquer. Was it the mass which gave him this strange power? Did it flow from him to the mass? I noted down, 'Fanatically hysteric romanticism with a brutal will.' "

The following day, again flaunting a police ban, the trooping of SA colors took place on the Marsfeld with 6000 storm troopers shivering in the snow. Some wore a uniform of ski cap, brown jacket and leggings while others were in business suits. There was a varied array of flags with swastikas of various sizes. It was a motley group but, once called to attention, the men stood as rigidly as if they were elite troops of the Kaiser. Although the police were ready for trouble there were no disorders. In fact the two-day affair turned out to be anticlimax. There was no Putsch, no public disturbance. Only its repercussions were of import. Hitler's defiance of the police brought a number of middle-of-the-road leaders to his side and drove the University of Munich students down a much more radical path. More significantly, it lowered the prestige of the Bavarian government itself. In his first serious confrontation with the establishment Hitler had come out the victor.

"He is an extraordinary person," reported an American writer, Ludwell Denny, after attending a Hitler rally a few days later. "His speech was intense and brief; he constantly clenched and unclenched his hands. When I was alone with him for a few moments, he seemed hardly normal; queer eyes, nervous hands, and a strange movement of the head." His personal life was certainly not normal. He still lived in the dingy building on the Thierschstrasse but had sublet a larger room, not as cold as the first, if as scantily furnished. It was ten feet wide at most and the head of the bed projected above the single narrow window. The floor was covered with cheap, worn linoleum. On the wall opposite the bed there was a makeshift bookshelf. Illustrations and drawings hung on the walls. The upper shelves of the bookcase overflowed with volumes on the World War, German histories, an illustrated encyclopedia, *Vom Kriege* by Clausewitz, a history of Frederick the Great, Houston Stewart Chamberlain's biography of Wagner, the memoirs of Sven Hedin, a collection of heroic myths, von Wartenburg's world history and something entitled *Geographical Character Pictures*. The bottom shelf, according to Hanfstaengl, was devoted to novels, a collection of semi-pornographic works by Eduard Fuchs (a Jew), and A *History of Erotic Art*.

Frau Reichert who sublet to Hitler, found her tenant extraordinarily moody. "Sometimes weeks go by when he seems to be sulking and does not say a word to us. He looks through us as if we were not there." Though he paid his rent punctually and in advance, he was "a real Bohemian type." She forgave him this, since he was so nice, and let him use her hallway, which boasted a small upright piano. He lived in spartan simplicity, his almost constant companion a large dog named Wolf. Ever since his relationship with Fuchsl in the war he had need for the faithfulness he found in dogs, and had a unique understanding of them. "There are stupid dogs and others who are so intelligent that it's agonizing." In this dingy room he must have thought of his mother and her tragic death, for he wrote about it that year in a poem entitled "Think of It!" Stripped of its amateurish sentimentality, it probed revealingly.

> *When your mother has grown older.*
> *And you have grown older,*
> *When what was formerly easy and effortless*
> *Now becomes a burden,*
> *When her dear loyal eyes*
> *Do not look out into life as before,*
> *When her legs have grown tired*
> *And do not want to carry her any more—*
> *Then give her your arm for support,*
> *Accompany her with gladness and joy.*
> *The hour will come when, weeping, you*
> *Will accompany her on her last journey!*
> *And if she asks you, answer her.*
> *And if she asks again, speak also.*
> *And if she asks another time, speak to her*
> *Not stormily, but in gentle peace!*
> *And if she cannot understand you well,*
> *Explain everything joyfully;*
> *The hour will come, the bitter hour*
> *When her mouth will ask no more!*

By his own admission, Hitler was a recluse in his youth and had little need of society, but after the war he confessed that he could no "longer bear solitude." Though his room was a lonely refuge and prison, he lived a second existence in the cafés, salons, coffeehouses, and beer halls of Munich. He became a habitué of the Café Weichard (next to the Volkstheater), the Carlton Tea Room (an elite rendezvous on the Briennerstrasse) and the Café Heck (on the Galerienstrasse). He would sit for hours in a secluded corner of the latter at his reserved table where he would observe the life flowing around him.

Every Monday he would meet with intimates at the Café Neumaier, an old-fashioned coffeehouse at the corner of the Peterplatz and the Viktualien Markt. It was a long room with paneled walls and built-in benches. Here at the table reserved for regular customers he would try out his latest ideas on his adherents, many of them middle-aged couples. Here also they would gossip and joke while eating a frugal supper, some of which they had brought with them.

Other evenings were spent at Dietrich Eckart's apartment on the Franz Josef Strasse. "What a wonderful atmosphere in his home! How he took care of his little Anna." This was his housekeeper, Annerl, with whom he had been living since separating from his wife. Perhaps Hitler's most constant companion these days was his new acolyte, Hanfstaengl, who introduced him to important people such as William Bayard Hale, classmate of President Wilson at Princeton and leading European correspondent for the Hearst papers, and Wilhelm Funk, whose salon attracted wealthy nationalist businessmen. Together Hitler and Hanfstaengl often attended the soirées of Frau Elsa Bruckmann, the wife of a publisher and born a Hungarian noblewoman, who was greatly impressed by the new political leader. Hitler was dazzled by life at this level. After one visit to the Bechstein suite in a Munich hotel he told Hanfstaengl that he had felt embarrassed in his blue suit. Herr Bechstein had worn a dinner jacket, the servants were in livery and nothing but champagne was served before the meal. "And you should have seen the bathroom, you can even regulate the heat of the water."

Hanfstaengl became a frequent visitor to the little room on the Thierschstrasse and one day Hitler asked him to play something on the piano in the hallway "to calm him." Hanfstaengl found the old upright badly out of tune but played a Bach fugue. Nodding, Hitler listened absently. Then Hanfstaengl began the prelude to *Die Meistersinger*, hoping the old piano wouldn't fall to pieces under his assault. He played "with plenty of Lisztian *fioriture* and a fine romantic swing," and Hitler became so excited that he strode up and down the narrow hallway gesticulating as if conducting an orchestra. "This music affected him physically and by the time I had crashed through the finale he was in splendid spirits, all his worries gone."

Hanfstaengl found that Hitler knew *Die Meistersinger* "absolutely by heart and could whistle every note of it in a curious penetrating vibrato, but completely in tune." Almost daily musical sessions took place in the hallway. Hitler had little liking for Bach and Mozart, preferring Schumann, Chopin and some works of Richard Strauss. His favorites were Beethoven and Wagner. He had "a genuine knowledge and appreciation" for the latter and never tired of hearing Hanfstaengl's colorful versions of *Tristan* and *Lohengrin*.

Infatuated with Hanfstaengl's style, Hitler would introduce him to all his social circles as a showpiece. "Whereas he otherwise kept the different groups in watertight compartments and told no one where he was going or whom he had been talking to," recalled Hanfstaengl in his unpublished memoirs, "he dragged me around from house to house as his resident musician, and had me sit down at the piano to perform." Once at the home of the photographer Heinrich Hoffmann he began playing Harvard football marches. When he explained how cheerleaders and marching bands would stir up the crowd to almost hysterial mass shouting Hitler's interest quickened. Whereupon Hanfstaengl demonstrated on the piano how German marches could be adapted to the buoyant American beat. "That is it," exclaimed Hitler, and paraded up and down like a drum major, "that is what we need for the movement, marvelous." Hanfstaengl wrote several marches in this style for the SA band but his most significant contribution was the transference of the Harvard "Fight, Fight, Fight" to "Sieg Heil, Sieg Heil!"

Hitler often visited the small Hanfstaengl apartment in Schwabing across from the large school where he had done his basic training in 1914. Probably the greatest attraction was Hanfstaengl's wife, Helene, an American of German descent who was tall, brunette and strikingly attractive. He came in his best suit, the shiny blue serge. "He was respectful, even diffident," recalled Hanfstaengl, "and very careful to adhere to the forms of address still *de rigueur* in Germany between people of lower rank when speaking to those of better education, title, or academic attainment." From the first it was obvious he was physically attracted to Helene, as much by her warm, quiet charm as by her looks, and he treated her with a respect bordering on worship. In her unpublished memoirs written ten years later, she describes their first meeting on a Munich street in early 1923: "He was at the time a slim, shy young man, with a far-away look in his very blue eyes. He was dressed almost shabbily—a cheap white shirt, black tie, a worn dark blue suit, with which he wore an incongruous dark brown leather vest, a beige-colored trench coat, much the worse for wear, cheap black shoes and a soft, old greyish hat. His appearance was quite pathetic."

She invited the shabby Hitler to come for dinner "and from that day he was a constant visitor, enjoying the quiet, cozy home atmosphere, playing with my son, and talking over his plans and hopes for the renaissance of the German Reich. It seemed he enjoyed our home above all others to which he was invited, for with us he was not constantly bothered with curious questions and introduced to other guests as the 'coming savior,' but could if he wished sit quietly in a corner, reading or making notes. We didn't 'lionize' him." She saw Hitler as a warm man and was moved by his feeling for her two-year-old son, Egon. "Evidently he liked children, or he was a good actor." One day the youngster ran to meet Hitler at the door, bumped his head sharply against a heavy chair, and began crying. "Hitler with a dramatic gesture beat the chair severely, reprimanding it for hurting 'good little Egon.' This was a surprise and delight to the youngster and from that day, each time Hitler came he would have to repeat this act; Egon urging him 'Please, Uncle Dolf, spank the naughty chair.'"

By spring Hitler felt so at ease with the Hanfstaengls that he would amuse them with imitations of other followers (such as the affectionate Görings) and play on the floor with Egon. For hours he could idly gossip as he consumed a cup of coffee sweetened with squares of chocolate or, on occasion, sip a glass of the best dry Johannisberger wine after improving it with "a heaping spoonful of castor-sugar." Often they went out together in public and one evening saw the second part of the movie *Fredericus Rex*. The scene Hitler liked above all was that in which the monarch threatened to behead the Crown Prince. "It is imposing to think the old King would have beheaded his own son to enforce discipline," he remarked on the way home. "That is the way German justice should be handled. Either acquittal or beheading."

The lightning change from sentiment to ruthlessness was disconcerting to the Hanfstaengls and they discussed Hitler's private life at length. What, for example, was his true relationship with women? One day he told them, "The mass, the people, to me is a woman," and likened his audiences to a woman. "Someone who does not understand the intrinsically feminine character of the mass will never be an effective speaker. Ask yourself what does a woman expect from a man? Clearness, decision, power, action. . . . If she is talked to properly she will be proud to sacrifice, because no woman will ever feel that her life's sacrifices have received their due fulfillment." Another time he asserted that he would never marry. "My only bride is my Motherland," he said, referring to a nation commonly known as the Fatherland. In that case, Hanfstaengl jokingly replied, why not take a mistress? "Politics is a woman," replied Hitler. "Love her unhappily and she will bite off your head."

Some of Hitler's associates felt sure that Jenny Haug, sister of one of his drivers, was his mistress. She was devoted to him and reportedly carried a small pistol in an armpit holster in her role as voluntary bodyguard. Helene Hanfstaengl could not take this story seriously. "Putzi," she said, "I tell you he is a neuter."

One of Hitler's closest companions during these days disagreed. "We chased girls together and I used to follow him like a shadow," recalled Emil Maurice, who also served as Hitler's chauffeur. The two would spend time at the art academy and in artists' studios admiring models posing in the nude. Calling himself "Herr Wolf," Hitler would occasionally pass an evening with Maurice roaming the night spots and streets for girls. Since the latter was attractive to women, he would act as go-between. Every so often, according to Maurice, Hitler would entertain one of these conquests-by-proxy in his little room. "He always offered flowers, even when he was penniless. And we used to go and admire the ballet dancers."

The NSDAP became practically a full-time occupation for Hanfstaengl and he freely gave out advice ranging from enlarging Hitler's tiny mustache to a more fashionable style ("If it is not the fashion now, it will be later because I wear it!") to disparaging his adviser Rosenberg for his "humbug philosophy." While Hitler usually rejected advice he did not hesitate to borrow a thousand dollars, interest-free, from Hanfstaengl, who had just received part of his share of the sale of the family art shop in New York City. Converted into depreciated marks, this was a tremendous sum and enabled Hitler to purchase two American rotary presses and turn the weekly *Völkischer Beobachter* into a daily.

Hanfstaengl's generosity turned out to be a stroke of luck for someone he detested. Hitler made Rosenberg editor of the daily *Beobachter*, replacing Eckart, who was often absent from his desk for weeks. This position not only intrenched Rosenberg's position as the party's expert on the East but reinforced the influence of fellow refugees from Russia such as Scheubner-Richter, a mystery man connected with German industrialists, generals and high society who, besides serving as intermediary with Ludendorff, was becoming one of Hitler's leading advisers. All of the Russian émigrés were fanatically dedicated to the destruction of Bolshevism and most of them were imbued with the czarist solution to the Jewish conspiracy—terror and brute force. To such zealots social and economic anti-Semitism were effete and ineffective methods. Only the pogrom worked.

4

The spring of 1923 was a busy season for Hitler. The most pressing need was money and he set out on a series of tours to raise funds for the party. In early April he and Hanfstaengl headed for Berlin in Hitler's rickety Selve with Maurice at the wheel. They drove through Saxony even though much of that area was under the control of the Communists. At the outskirts of a town just north of Leipzig they were stopped at a road block manned by Red militia. The imposing Hanfstaengl flourished his

Swiss passport, then announced in a broad German-American accent that he was a paper manufacturer from abroad come to visit the Leipzig fair. The others in the car were his chauffeur and his valet. The ruse worked. Although Hitler said, "They would have had my head," as they drove away, it was apparent that he resented being taken for a valet.

In Berlin they not only begged money but spent a Sunday visiting the War Museum and the National Gallery. At the latter Hitler stopped in front of Rembrandt's "Man in a Golden Helmet" and drew attention to the heroic, soldierlike expression. It proved, he said, that the great painter, "in spite of the many pictures he painted in Amsterdam's Jewish quarter, was at heart a true Aryan and German!" Afterward they watched the women boxers in Luna Park. Hitler looked on without expression but insisted on staying for several matches, remarking that "at least it was better than this duelling with sabres that goes on in Germany."

Next day they left home, making a long detour around Saxony. Hitler beguiled the tediousness of the way by whistling long passages from the Wagner operas and entertaining his fellow passengers with impersonations. He would even mock himself by reciting a poem written in his honor that consisted of a long series of ill-scanning couplets of words ending with "itler." "When he was in a good mood," recalled Hanfstaengl, "Hitler would repeat this with embellishments of his own and have us in tears of laughter."

They stopped in Bayreuth, home of Richard Wagner, and were admitted into the festival theater, by the caretaker. The stage was still set for *The Flying Dutchman*, which had been playing when war was declared in 1914, and this gave Hanfstaengl the opportunity to point out that the original stage scenery had been designed by his own great-grandfather, Ferdinand Heine. Hitler was entranced by everything, particularly Wagner's study where his instructions to the artists and staff still hung on the wall.

On the last day of the trip, during a picnic lunch, Hitler mentioned the monument they had seen outside Leipzig commemorating the Battle of the Nations against Napoleon, and then made a comment that disturbed Hanfstaengl: "The most important thing in the next war will be to make sure that we control the grain and food supplies of Western Russia." This indicated that Rosenberg and his Russian friends had been propagandizing Hitler again, and Hanfstaengl retorted that a war with Russia would be futile. The country to reckon with was America with its tremendous industrial potential. "If you have them on the other side you will lose any future war before you start it." Hitler grunted and made no reply but it was obvious that the argument "had not really sunk in."

Upon return to Munich, he embarked on a campaign attacking France's occupation of the Ruhr but often did so obliquely, as if more interested in rousing his audiences against Jews. On April 13, for instance, he blamed them directly for the Ruhr takeover as well as the loss of the war and inflation. He charged that "so-called World Pacifism" was a Jewish invention; that the leaders of the proletariat were Jews ("Jews again!"); that the Freemasons were tools of the Jews ("Once more the Jews!"); and that, in fact, the Jews were conspiring to conquer the world! "So," he shouted, "Russia and Germany had to be overthrown in order that the ancient prophecy might be fulfilled! So the whole world was lashed into fury! So every lie and propaganda agency was brutally set in action against the State of the last—the German—idealists! And thus it was that Judah won the World War. Or would you wish to maintain that the French, the English, or the American people won the war?" He concluded in a burst of emotion demanding justice for the two million Germans who had died in the World War and the millions of orphans, crippled and widows who remained. "We owe it to these millions to build a new Germany!"

In his obsessive hatred of Jews, Hitler had gone over the edge of reality. His anti-Semitism, though expressed in logical terms, had passed all boundaries of logic. He had turned the world upside down: France, England and America had really lost the war. Germany was the eventual winner since she was freeing herself from the Jews. If Hitler was deceiving himself, he also had succeeded in deceiving his listeners. Hitler skillfully appealed to primitive emotions and when audiences left meetings they remembered few details, only that they must join Hitler's crusade to save Germany; that France must be driven out of the Ruhr and, most important, that the Jews must be put in their place.

In the past year Hitler's platform technique had improved markedly. His gestures had become as varied and flexible as his arguments. Hanfstaengl was particularly impressed by a soaring upward movement of the arm. "It had something of the quality of a really great orchestral conductor who instead of just hammering out the downward beat, suggests the existence of hidden rhythms and meaning with the upward flick of his baton." Utilizing his knowledge and feeling for music, Hitler's speeches became musical in tempo. The first two thirds were "in march time," quickening until the last third became "primarily rhapsodic." His power of mimicry was also put to adroit use. He would impersonate an imaginary opponent, "often interrupting himself with a counter-argument and then returning to his original line of thought after completely annihilating his supposed adversary."

Despite the complicated structure of his speeches, they were easy to follow, being designed primarily for emotional appeal. Thus he could switch from subject to subject without losing his listeners because the bridge between topics was an appeal to some emotion—indignation, fear, love or hate. Despite twistings and turnings, he drew along the listeners as an accomplished actor will guide his audience through some complicated progression in a play.

Hitler also had the rare ability to involve his listeners in the proceedings. "When I talk to people," he told Hanfstaengl, "especially those who are not yet Party members, or who are about to break away for some reason or other, I always talk as if the fate of the nation was bound up in their decision. That they are in a position to give an example for the many to follow. Certainly it means appealing to their vanity and ambition, but once I have got them to that point, the rest is easy." All men, rich or poor, he said, had an inner sense of unfulfillment. "Slumbering somewhere is the readiness to risk some final sacrifice, some adventure, in order to give a new shape to their lives. They will spend their last money on a lottery ticket. It is my business to channel that urge for political purposes. In essence, every political movement is based on the desire of its supporters, men or women, to better things not only for themselves but for their children and others . . . The humbler people are, the greater the craving to identify themselves with a cause bigger than themselves, and if I can persuade them that the fate of the German nation is at stake, then they will become part of an irresistible movement, embracing all classes."

Audiences were always properly prepared for his virtuoso displays by pagan-military pageantry. In addition to stirring music and flying banners, new features had been added—Roman-type standards that Hitler had designed himself and a Roman-style salute. Perhaps he had borrowed both from Caesar by way of Mussolini but he claimed that the stiff-arm salute at least was German. "I'd read the description of the sitting of the Diet of Worms, in the course of which Luther was greeted with the German salute. It was to show him that he was not being confronted with arms, but with peaceful intentions. . . . It was in the Rathskeller at Bremen, about the year 1921, that I first saw this style of salute." Whatever source, the salute, the vibrant "Heils!" together with the music and banners did much to assure the audience that the man they were about to hear was the true voice of Germany.

On the same day that Hitler spoke out against France and the Jews he staged another confrontation with the Bavarian government. He called upon the Minister President and brought along with him a former military officer who was the commander of a private army of the *Arbeitsgemeinschaft der Kampfverbände* (Working Group of Combat Organizations), a conglomeration of radical right-wing groups. The two delivered an ultimatum, demanding that the Bavarian government itself demand nullification of the Law for the Defense of the Republic. If Weimar refused to comply, then Bavaria must defy the law.

This was Friday the thirteenth, and Hitler wanted the answer by Saturday. It did not come and the radical right military group held a "military exercise" on Sunday. It was Easter and Hitler stood in an open car, arm outstretched as the storm troopers and other followers paraded past.

From the Görings' car Helene Hanfstaengl noticed in Hitler's eyes "a glow of triumph and satisfaction." After the review he brought "a gorgeous bouquet of roses" to the Hanfstaengl apartment as her birthday gift. They all had "a jolly tea hour together," marked by Hitler's vivacity and wit. A week later on his own birthday he was glumly paranoiac. He warned Hanfstaengl not to eat any of the swastika-decorated cakes which, along with other gifts, almost filled his little room. "Don't forget," he said, "this building belongs to a Jew and it is child's play to let poison trickle down the walls in order to dispose of an enemy."

On Monday the Minister President finally gave his answer to Hitler: he personally objected to the edict for the Defense of the Republic but since it was the law of the land he was obliged to enforce it. In protest Hitler called for a mass demonstration on May 1. The possibilities were explosive since the day was not only a sacred holiday to labor and Marxists but the anniversary of Munich's liberation from the Soviet Republic. On the evening of April 30 the forces of the radical right wing began converging on the Oberwiesenfeld, a military training area several miles north of Munich's main railroad station. By dawn there were 1000 men on hand. Guards were mounted in expectation of leftist attacks but hour after hour passed without action. "At six o'clock," recalled Hitler, "gangs of Reds gathered to meet us. I sent some men to provoke them but they didn't react."

By nine all detachments from outside the city had arrived, swelling the Hitler forces to some 1300. They stood in the warm sun leaning on rifles, waiting with mixed boredom and anxiety, while a disgusted Hitler strode around carrying a steel helmet by its chin straps and asking, "Where are the Reds?" Just before noon a detachment of army troops and green-uniformed police appeared and rapidly surrounded the armed demonstrators. With them was a chagrined Captain Röhm. He told Hitler that he had just come from the commanding general of the area who demanded that the arms be turned over immediately or Hitler would have to take the consequences.

Hitler was incensed but still withstood the pleas of Gregor Strasser and others to defy the government and charge the troops. The decision to turn over arms must have been a bitter one. But if Hitler had attacked, his forces would certainly have been repelled and the fruitless carnage might have meant his end as a political leader, perhaps even as a man. He did achieve a success of sorts in the retreat from the Oberwiesenfeld. In Schwabing his troops came upon a detachment of Communists, put them to flight and set fire to their flags and banners. This was Hitler's moment and he boomed out a short speech: this fire, symbolic of Bolshevist world pestilence, he said, was only a modest prologue to the day in which the National Socialists would seize power! It was a rousing address that lifted the spirits of his men and appeared to change a blundering enterprise into a triumph. But their elation was fleeting. By evening it was apparent that Hitler's first revolutionary move was a fiasco. By that failure he lost many adherents of stature. "I reject Hitler completely!" exclaimed one former Free Corps commander. "He failed miserably on the first day of May and he will always fail."

He was not the only loser at the Oberwiesenfeld. It was even more of a defeat and embarrassment for the Bavarian government. When Hitler was called to answer official charges of having endangered public security he replied with an insolent confidence that put the prosecutor general on the defensive. By refusing to be cowed, Hitler made political capital out of disaster. Rebounding from defeat was becoming a pattern.

A number of foreign observers, however, predicted it was the beginning of his end. Robert Murphy, for one, reported that the Nazi movement was now "on the wane." The people, he wrote, "are wearied of Hitler's inflammatory agitation which yields no results and offers nothing constructive; his anti-Semitic campaign made many enemies; the rowdy-like conduct of his youthful following has antagonized order-loving members of the community."

5

Murphy was only reflecting the impressions of local officials throughout Bavaria who misread the resultant political lull after May Day as a definite turn away from Hitler and his movement. This inertia continued except for a brief flurry caused by the execution of a German nationalist, Albert Leon Schlageter, who had blown up railroad tracks near Duisburg as a protest against French occupation of the Ruhr. He was tried for sabotage by the French and shot on May 26.

When Hanfstaengl heard that a number of patriotic organizations were going to stage a protest demonstration in the Königsplatz the following week, he felt that Hitler should return from his holiday in the mountains and participate. He took the train to Berchtesgaden, a beautiful resort town on the border of Germany and Austria near Salzburg where he found Hitler ("I had fallen in love with the landscape") registered under the name of Herr Wolf at the Pension Moritz on a steep hill known as the Obersalzberg. At first Hitler was not enthusiastic about addressing a demonstration with so many diverse speakers, but Hanfstaengl persisted and the two began blocking out a speech.

That night Eckart, who shared Hanfstaengl's bedroom, complained that Hitler would parade around swinging his rhinoceros-hide whip in a swashbuckling manner to impress the wife of the pension manager. "The way Adolf is carrying on now goes beyond me," he said. "The man is plain crazy." He told of overhearing Hitler show off to the lady in question by denouncing Berlin in extravagant terms: ". . . the luxury, the perversion, the iniquity, the wanton display and the Jewish materialism disgusted me so thoroughly that I was almost beside myself. I nearly imagined myself to be Jesus Christ when he came to his Father's Temple and found the money changers." Whereupon, claimed Eckart, Hitler brandished his whip and exclaimed that it was his mission to descend upon the capital like a Christ and scourge the corrupt.

The following day Hitler accompanied Hanfstaengl to the station and, as they descended the Obersalzberg, remarked that Eckart, whom he had recently replaced as editor of the party newspaper, had become "an old pessimist, a senile weakling." Schopenhauer had only turned him into a doubting Thomas. "Where would I get if I listened to all his transcendental talk? A nice ultimate wisdom that! To reduce oneself to a minimum of desire and will. Once will is gone, all is gone. This life is war." He began whistling the Swan Song from *Lohengrin* in "a curious soft tremolo."

Anton Drexler and his wife also disapproved of Hitler's play-acting on the Obersalzberg. They were equally disconcerted by his growing enthusiasm for revolutionary action. Their alarm was shared by others who objected to his associating with industrialists, wealthy socialites and bankers rather than building a solid base of genuine socialists from the working class. Hitler must have been aware that he faced another revolt within the party, one born of discontent and dismay among those who first held highest hopes for him as leader of Germany's renaissance.

Early that September Hitler attempted to bolster his slipping prestige by a public appearance. The occasion was the German Day celebration in Nuremberg which took place the first two days of September, the anniversary of the Battle of Sedan. More than 100,000 nationalists swarmed into the ancient city, parading through the streets and, according to a state police report, generating "such enthusiasm as had not been seen in Nuremberg since 1914." The streets were a sea of Nazi and Bavarian flags as the crowd roared "Heil!" waved handkerchiefs and tossed flowers and wreaths at Ludendorff and the marching units. "It was the unbridled expression of that multitude of defeated, miserable, displaced, and shattered people, who now saw a ray of hope, of freedom from slavery and need. Many women and men cried, so overcome were they by emotion."

The largest number of marchers came from the NSDAP and after the opening parade Hitler spoke at one of the meetings. He looked more groomed than he had at Coburg, with pressed suit, low-cut shoes and neatly slicked-down hair. "In a few weeks the dice will roll," he declared prophetically. "What is in the making today will be greater than the World War. It will be fought out on German soil for the whole world."

On the second day the German Battle League was formed. Outwardly an association of nationalists, it was a creature of the NSDAP: its secretary-general was Scheubner-Richter, its military leader was another

Hitler man, one of its main organizations (the *Reichsflagge*) was dominated by Röhm; and its initial proclamation (written by Feder) sounded as if it came out of Hitler's mouth. It declared opposition to parliamentarianism, international capital, the class struggle, pacifism, Marxism and the Jews.

German Day at Nuremberg and the founding of the German Battle League marked Hitler's public return to revolutionary tactics. This became more apparent a month later when he was officially made political leader of the new organization. Its "action program" called openly for seizure of power in Bavaria and the rumor spread that Hitler was preparing a revolution. He did, in fact, announce openly that h' intended to act rather than allow the Reds to seize power again. "The task of our movement, as always is . . . to prepare for the coming collapse of the Reich, so that when the old trunk falls the young fir tree may be already standing."

Although the Minister President of Bavaria, Eugen von Knilling, shared some of Hitler's beliefs, he had been pushed to the edge of patience by his rabble-rousing tactics. On September 26 Knilling told his Cabinet that the emergency was so grave that a state commissar general should be appointed who, while subordinate to the Cabinet, "would have a free hand in the exercise of the executive power." He proposed former Minister President von Kahr, who had the support of several nationalist groups and was held in esteem by both conservative monarchists and the Catholic Church.

In the name of law and order Kahr accepted this onerous position and his first act was to ban fourteen mass meetings the Nazis had planned for the morrow. This action was both a threat and an opportunity for Adolf Hitler, who had just returned from a trip to Switzerland to solicit funds. If he submitted it could mean ruin. If he successfully resisted, he could become a politician of national importance. He was cautioned to retreat and fight another day; the movement was not yet strong enough for action. But those close to the rank and file urged him to act. "If nothing happens now the men will sneak away," said the head of the SA Regiment Munich. "In order to keep the men together," said Scheubner-Richter, "one must finally undertake something. Otherwise they will become left radicals."

These were the urgings Hitler heeded. This impulse for action set him on the road to revolution and he began searching Munich and its environs for activist allies. His days were filled with interviews and visits to a variety of influential men: military figures, politicians, industrialists and officials. He talked to the party faithful as well as those who wavered—promising, threatening and cajoling. The one sentence he continuously used was "We must compromise these people so that they have to march with us."

"Absolutely no one could ever persuade him to change his mind, once it was made up," recalled Helene Hanfstaengl. "On a number of occasions when his followers tried to coerce him I noticed the faraway, unheeding expression in his eyes; it was as though he had closed his mind to all ideas but his own." That autumn the faraway, unheeding expression in his eyes had a specific meaning. He saw himself emulating Mussolini—and his march would be to Berlin. Nor was this a vision he revealed only to intimates. In a conference with right-wing military men he called for an attack on Berlin with all Bavaria's forces. "Hitler now had definite Napoleonic and Messianic ideas," recalled one of those present. "He declared that he felt the call within himself to save Germany and that this role would fall to him, if not now then later. He then drew a number of parallels with Napoleon, especially with the return of Napoleon from Elba to Paris."

Chapter Six

THE BEER HALL PUTSCH
1923

1

On the last day of September 1923 Hitler received an unsettling letter from "an old member and fanatic member of your movement," who pointed out a startling prediction in the current yearbook of the well-known astrologer, Frau Elsbeth Ebertin. "A man of action born on 20 April 1889," it said, "can expose himself to personal danger by excessively uncautious action and very likely trigger off an uncontrollable crisis." The stars showed that this man was "to be taken very seriously indeed; he is destined to play a 'Führer-role' in future battles." He was destined to "*sacrifice himself for the German nation.*"

Although no name was mentioned, it was apparent that Frau Ebertin was referring to Hitler, and while she did not specify any particular date, she warned that acting rashly in the near future would endanger his life. Another astrologer, Wilhelm Wulff (years later he would advise Himmler's SS on astrological matters), also cast Hitler's horoscope late that summer and *was* definite about a date. His prediction was also ominous: "violence with a disastrous outcome" for the subject during the period of November 8–9, 1923.

Such prophecies were seriously regarded in many quarters. Several German psychiatrists and psychologists were already considering the idea of "psychological astrology." Dr. O. A. H. Schmitz—an ardent disciple of the Swiss psychiatrist, C. G. Jung—had recently suggested that astrology might be exactly what psychology needed. But Hitler's comment on Frau Ebertin's prediction was: "What on earth have women and stars got to do with me?"

Whether he believed in astrology or not, Hitler was convinced that his own destiny would eventually lead him to success; and, as Helene Hanfstaengl had noticed, he tuned out all but affirmative voices. By coincidence he found one of them the same day he received Frau Ebertin's astrological warning. It came in Bayreuth at the Villa Wahnfried, Wagner's home, where he was paying homage to Cosima, the eighty-six-year-old widow of the master. Winifred Wagner, the English wife of Wagner's son Siegfried, was already entranced by Hitler and his movement. She welcomed him warmly; her six-year-old daughter Friedelind thought he looked funny in his Bavarian leather shorts, thick woolen socks, red and blue checked shirt and baggy short blue jacket. "His sharp cheekbones stuck out over hollow pasty cheeks and above them were a pair of unnaturally bright blue eyes. There was a half-starved look about him but something else too, a fanatical glow."

Ill at ease, Hitler walked shyly, awkwardly around the music room and library, tiptoeing as if he were in a cathedral. But later in the garden, as he told the Wagners of his plans for the near future, "his voice took on tone and color and grew deeper and deeper until we sat like a circle of little charmed birds listening to the music although we didn't pay any attention to a word he said." After he left, Frau Wagner said, "Don't you feel that he is destined to be the savior of Germany?" Siegfried laughed indulgently. So far as he was concerned, Hitler was an obvious "fraud" as well as an upstart.

Hitler was across the street, making a pilgrimage to the home of the aged Houston Stewart Chamberlain, paralyzed in his wheel chair. This son of an English admiral had been drawn to Germany, seeing in her people the master race. He was talented and neurotic, and widely regarded as one of the leading men of culture of his day. A worshiper of Wagner, he had married his daughter Eva. The English prophet of racism was so taken by Hitler that he had a "longer and more refreshing sleep" that night than any since he had seen stricken in August 1914. He wrote Hitler a few days later: "With one blow you have transformed the state of my soul. That Germany, in the hour of her greatest need, brings forth a Hitler —that is proof of her vitality."

Chamberlain's words must have helped solidify the growing sense within Hitler that he was a man of fate. A week or so later, while motoring in his new car through the Bavarian hills with Rosenberg and the Hanfstaengls, fog unexpectedly enshrouded the highway and the open red Mercedes lurched into a ditch. No one spoke on the way back to Munich, then he turned to Helene. "I noticed you were not at all frightened by our mishap. *I* knew we would not be injured. This will not be the only accident which will leave me unharmed. I shall pass through them all and succeed in my plans."

2

Another aspect of fate, in the guise of the inflation, also appeared to be working in favor of Hitler and his march on Berlin. By the beginning of October it took 6,014,300 marks to equal a single prewar mark. The price of one egg equaled that of 30,000,000 in 1913. Many municipalities and industrial firms took to printing their own "emergency money" to meet expenses. The Reichsbank could not refuse to accept this emergency money or to treat it as of equal value with their own notes. The printing of government money itself became farcical: a thousand-mark note issued in Berlin the previous December was now stamped over in red: *Ein Milliarde Mark*; and a 500,000,000-mark note printed by the Bavarian State Bank a few weeks earlier was stamped: *Zwanzig Milliarden Mark*. This 20-billion-mark note presumably could be exchanged for more than $800 but by the time the holder of the modest-looking little note with the astronomical figure got to the cashier it would be worth a fraction of that —providing any cashier was willing to surrender hard foreign currency for it. People were frantic. They dared not hold currency for an hour. A missed trolley car to the bank could mean a man's monthly salary was reduced to a quarter or less. A waiter in Baden told a young American reporter, Ernest Hemingway, that he had saved up enough money for a *Gasthaus*. Now the money wouldn't buy four bottles of champagne. "Germany debases her money to cheat the Allies," said the waiter. "But what do I get out of it?"

The burden of inflation naturally fell on those who could not pay with notes—the workers and the elderly. The first were reduced to a near starvation diet and the latter were brought to poverty level overnight. Pensioners and those who lived on interest from bonds and life insurance found themselves destitute. Securities bought with gold marks were paid off in paper money that deteriorated in value in one's hand. In America only Southerners, whose families had suffered a similar fate after the Civil War days, would have understood.

About the sole ones who rejoiced were those deeply in debt who could pay off their obligations with worthless paper. But the greatest beneficiaries were the exchange barons, the profiteers and opportunistic foreigners who bought up jewelry and real estate at ridiculously low prices. Large estates and buildings went to these vultures for a few hundred dollars. Family heirlooms were exchanged for enough to feed a family a few weeks. There were scenes beyond belief: a woman who had left a basketfull of money on the street, returning a moment later to find the money dumped in the gutter and the basket stolen; a worker with a salary of two billion marks a week able to buy his family only potatoes. And when distribution of the most basic food broke down, raids on potato fields in law-abiding Germany became commonplace.*

By mid-October Hitler, after drawing almost 35,000 new members into the party since January, was more than ever convinced that the people were ready for revolution. "I can only take action," he told a Nuremberg audience, "where my fanatical belief and love for the entire German people lead me." Never had his speeches been delivered with more passion. "You cannot imagine how silent it becomes as soon as this man speaks," one ardent follower wrote her family that October. It was as if the entire audience was no longer able to breathe. "Sometimes it almost seems to me as if Hitler used a magic charm in order to win the unconditional confidence of old and young alike." Another fascinated listener got so close he could see the spit fly under his mustache. "For us this man was a whirling dervish. But he knew how to fire up the people, not with arguments, which are never possible in hate speeches, but with the fanaticism of his whole manner, screaming and yelling, and above all by his deafening repetition, and a certain contagious rhythm. This he has learned to do and it has a fearfully exciting primitive and barbaric effect."

In Bavaria the pressure exerted by such rousing, hypnotic speeches made Commissar von Kahr's task, despite his dictatorial power, an impossible one. Called upon to restrain Hitler violence, he was under pressure from a large segment of the Bavarian leadership to go easy on him. The temper of Bavaria was conservative and nationalistic and, while many regretted Hitler's crude tactics and violent language, they shared his dream of a strong, rejuvenated Germany. "There are decent emotions which lead misguided people to the Nazis," commented a liberal member of the Bavarian Democratic Party, "men who honorably desire to serve their people and their state." Because of this attitude Bavarian police authorities, aggravated as they were, did little to restrain Hitlerian violence. The head of the army in Bavaria, General Otto von Lossow, was also resisting demands from Berlin to curb Hitler and to ban his newspaper. In the face of Lossow's continued defiance, he was dismissed, an act so infuriating to the Bavarian government that it assumed command of all Reichswehr units in the state.

---

* The most poignant movie of these days was made not by a German but by D. W. Griffith. This was *Isn't Life Wonderful*, with Neil Hamilton and Carol Dempster as a German couple whose future depends on a tiny patch of potatoes. The climax comes when they secretly gather the potatoes at night, then, hitching themselves like horses to their cart, start through the woods. They are set upon by marauders who steal their crop. The best German film was Pabst's *Die freudlose Gasse* (*Street Without Joy*) in which Greta Garbo, in her first major role, portrays the daughter of a bourgeois family in Vienna brought to starvation by wicked stock manipulators. There are realistic scenes of shoppers waiting all night in front of a butcher store. In the finale the frenzied mob attacks the repulsive butcher who has grown rich on their suffering.

This defiance, tantamount to revolt, was repeated the next day by army men stationed throughout Bavaria. They renounced the Weimar Republic by taking an oath to the Bavarian government "until an adjustment between Bavaria and the Reich has been arrived at, and I renew my obligation to obey my superior officers." It was mutiny, executed legalistically, formally and without violence—but mutiny nonetheless. "There will be no civil war," a Bavarian cabinet member confided to Robert Murphy. "The ship of state had merely listed too far to the left, and it was and is Bavaria's duty to right it."

Commissar von Kahr himself attacked the federal government in print. In the *Münchener Zeitung* he justified Bavarian defiance and called for an overthrow of the new government of Chancellor Gustav Stresemann, a self-made man with liberal faith in freedom and political rights. Stresemann himself was a nationalist; he charged that 33,000 Marxists held official posts in Prussia and that "as a result domestic politics are purely Marxist; that is to say they are directed against the natural order of things and are oriented towards compulsion, agitation, demagoguery and street fighting. Foreign policy is becoming internationalized and those who control it are careful to ensure that Germany never becomes powerful again." Here again were thoughts and words that could have come from Hitler.

A few days later General von Lossow—still in command of his troops despite dismissal by the Weimar Republic—was reported to have made a speech declaring that there were only three possibilities: going on as usual "in the old jogtrot way," seceding Bavaria from the Reich, or marching on Berlin to proclaim a national dictatorship. Hitler was dedicated to the last proposal. The secession of Bavaria from the federal government was as distasteful to him as doing nothing since an independent Bavaria would probably mean a return to a monarchist government with Crown Prince Rupprecht, the pretender, as King.* Yet could he force Commissar von Kahr and General von Lossow to join him in a march on Berlin without declaring Bavarian independence? The answer was supplied by Rosenberg and Scheubner-Richter. Their plan was to kidnap Prince Rupprecht and Kahr at the ceremony on November 4 celebrating German Memorial Day. Several hundred storm troopers would seal off the alley near the Feldherrnhalle where the dignitaries would assemble. Hitler would then politely inform the prisoners that he had seized the government to prevent

* To illustrate the cross-purposes within Hitler's inner circle, Captain Röhm had already made two attempts to enlist Prince Rupprecht's co-operation. On the first occasion he fell to his knees and, with clasped hands, begged Rupprecht to work with Hitler; he was summarily dismissed in a "not too friendly fashion." On the second, Röhm suggested that Hitler, Ludendorff and the Crown Prince jointly rule Bavaria, using this state as a base to win over North Germany with an armed invasion consisting of the various patriotic organizations. "I told him that was nonsense," recalled Rupprecht's political adviser.

a Red takeover and prevent the separation of Bavaria from the Reich. The Putsch would be, according to Rosenberg, "both short and painless," since Kahr and Rupprecht would be impelled to co-operate.

Hanfstaengl thought it was a "crazy plan," arguing that any attack on the Crown Prince would surely force the army to retaliate. Emphasizing the impracticability and senselessness of the operation, Hanfstaengl turned his warning into a personal attack on Rosenberg. If Hitler kept listening to these Baltic plotters, he said, it would mean the ruin of the movement. Hitler agreed to veto the kidnaping but would make no immediate promises concerning Rosenberg.* "We must think first of a march on Berlin," Hanfstaengl remembered him saying. "Once we have dealt with the immediate situation then we can look around and I can find Rosenberg another job."

3

By now the Bavarian government was run, under the supervision of Minister President von Knilling, by a triumvirate of "vons": Kahr, Lossow and Colonel Hans Ritter von Seisser, chief of the Bavarian state police, who had gathered together a group of bright staff officers too young to challenge his position. The triumvirate resembled a dictatorship in the old Roman caretaker sense and, though the three men represented a variety of ultraconservative and right radical values, they agreed that Hitler's revolutionary tactics were not pro bono publico and should either be channeled properly or outlawed. The breaking point was reached on October 30 when Hitler made it clear to a wildly receptive audience at the Zirkus Krone that he was ready to march on Berlin. "The German problem will be solved for me only after the black-white-red swastika banner floats on the Berlin Palace!" he shouted. "We all feel that the hour has come and, like the soldier in the field, we will not shirk our duty as Germans. We will follow the order to keep in step, and march forward!"

In an effort to split the triumvirate, Hitler requested an interview with Colonel von Seisser. They met privately on November 1 at the home of a veterinary who headed the Bund Oberland, a nationalistic paramilitary organization. Hitler tried to persuade Seisser that Kahr was unfit and only a pawn of the Bavarian government, then proposed, as he had a week

---

* Hitler often told differing stories to his confederates. He may have dismissed the kidnap plot out of hand as his remark to Hanfstaengl implied. Rosenberg, however, was convinced the Putsch was on until he discovered on German Memorial Day that there were strong police units in the alley and informed Hitler that the coup de main had to be abandoned.

Helene Hanfstaengl repeatedly noticed Hitler's habit of keeping his advisers at odds with each other and in the dark—"he never confided a single plan, visit or the fact that he made new acquaintances, to more than one or two followers at a time. This often led to uncomfortable situations when different party members suddenly discovered they were not completely in the picture—H's idea of complete personal control of all plans."

earlier, that Seisser and Lossow align themselves with himself and Ludendorff. But Seisser again declared he would have nothing to do with the
World War idol, nor would the top officers in the army. Hitler admitted
that, while the generals would be against Ludendorff, majors and lower-
grade officers would support him in defiance of their own commanders. It
was "high time" to take action, warned Hitler. "Our people are under
such economic pressure that we must either act or they will swing to the
Communists."

While Seisser privately agreed with Kahr that the Nazis were "trash,"
both did act. On November 6 the triumvirate conferred with representatives of the nationalist organizations. Their most urgent task, said
Kahr, was the establishment of a new national regime. They all agreed
that the Weimar government had to be overthrown but it must be done
in concert and not independently as certain nationalist organizations were
planning. He didn't mention any name but everyone knew he was referring to Hitler. It was questionable, said Kahr, if Chancellor Stresemann
could be ousted in the normal way. "The atypical way must be prepared.
Preparations have already been made. But if the atypical way must be
taken, then everyone must cooperate. It must be accomplished according
to a united, sufficiently prepared and thought-out plan."

The next speaker, Lossow, supported Kahr and his determination to
crush any Putsch by force of arms. "I am ready to support a rightist dictatorship if the affair is likely to succeed," said the general. He would participate if there was a fifty-one per cent chance for success. "But if we are
merely to be harassed into a Putsch, which will come to a sorry end in five
or six days, I will not cooperate." In conclusion, both he and Colonel von
Seisser underlined their warnings to members of the Battle League to co-
operate—or else.

That evening Hitler met with his advisers in the apartment of
Scheubner-Richter to draft their own plan of action. They agreed to stage
a full-fledged Putsch on the following Sunday, November 11. There were
two reasons for this date, one historical, one practical. This would be the
fifth anniversary of Germany's surrender. It would also be a holiday with
all offices deserted and police and military at low strength. The streets
would be relatively free of traffic and the storm troopers could march
unimpeded.

The next morning the conspirators met again, this time with the senior leader of the Battle League. Probably Ludendorff was present though
he later denied it, but Hitler certainly was there and so were Göring and
Scheubner-Richter. Final arrangements for the Putsch were adopted: the
major towns and cities of Bavaria would be controlled with the seizure of
railroad stations, telegraph offices, telephone offices, radio stations, public
utilities, town halls and police headquarters; Communist and socialist
leaders along with trade union heads and shop stewards were to be

arrested. Numerically Hitler's forces in Munich would have superiority with 4000 armed Putschists facing perhaps 2600 state police and army troops.

Early that same evening Hitler called a second meeting, this time with two additional members, ex-Police President Pöhner, and his former assistant, Wilhelm Frick, who had remained with the police and was still protecting Hitler and his followers. The conspirators discussed a development that called for a drastic change in plan. Commissar von Kahr had unexpectedly announced he was holding a mass "patriotic demonstration" at the Bürgerbräukeller the next night. The outward purpose was to outline the aims of his regime but it was probably an attempt to forestall any display of unified action by the National Socialists among leading government officials, military leaders and prestigious civilians. Hitler was asked to attend but it seemed obvious that the invitation was a trap. Perhaps the triumvirate was going to announce Bavaria's break with Berlin and the restoration of the Wittelsbach monarchy.

Hitler argued that it was a heaven-sent opportunity. The triumvirate as well as Minister President von Knilling and other government officials would be on the same platform. Why not simply escort them to a private room and either convince them to go along with a coup d'état or, if they were adamant, imprison them? Hitler was undoubtedly talking for effect. He knew very well that he could not mount a successful Putsch without the full co-operation of the triumvirate. He had no real intention of seizing the government of Bavaria, only of attempting to arouse the Bavarians by dramatics and thus successfully defy Berlin. He actually had no long-range program and was willing to trust to luck and fate.

His co-conspirators were not and the argument went on for hours. But Hitler refused to budge and finally, at 3 A.M. on November 8, everyone accepted, if reluctantly, his proposal: the Putsch would be launched that night at the Bürgerbräukeller. As soon as the guests filed out into the cold early morning air Scheubner-Richter handed his servant a packet of letters addressed to influential publishers—to be delivered as soon as their offices opened.

It dawned bitter and windy. The cold had come early to Bavaria that year and snow was already falling in the hills south of the city. On the most important day of Hitler's life he had a headache and a throbbing toothache. His colleagues had urged him to see a dentist but he said he "didn't have time, and that there was going to be a revolution which would change everything." He must follow his star. When Hanfstaengl asked what would happen to their project if he fell seriously ill, Hitler replied, "If that should be the case or if I should die it would only be a sign that my star has run its course and my mission is fulfilled."

Late that morning orders were issued to SA leaders by phone, letter

or in person to alert their men for action. There were no details, no explanations. Moreover, many of those closest to Hitler still had no idea there
was a change in plans. Just before noon, in his little whitewashed office,
Rosenberg (sporting a violet shirt and scarlet tie) was discussing the
morning's *Völkischer Beobachter* with Hanfstaengl. On the front page
was a picture of the general who had brought the Prussian army to the
Russian side against Napoleon at Tauroggen. The caption was: "Shall we
find a second General Yorck in our hour of need?" While these two, who
detested each other, were weighing the possible effects of the picture, they
heard stamping outside and a hoarse voice: "Where is Captain Göring?"
The door was flung open and Hitler, wearing his tightly belted trench coat
and gripping his whip, burst in "pallid with excitement."

"Swear you will not mention this to a living soul," he said with
suppressed urgency. "The hour has come. Tonight we act!" He asked
them both to be part of his personal escort. They were to bring pistols and
rendezvous outside the beer hall at seven o'clock. Hanfstaengl hurried
home to tell his wife to take their son Egon to the villa they had just built
in the country, then informed a number of international journalists, including H. R. Knickerbocker, that they "must under no circumstances"
miss the meeting that evening.

By afternoon Hitler had controlled his excitement and was gossiping
at the Café Heck with Heinrich Hoffmann, his photographer crony, as
though this was just another ordinary day. Suddenly Hitler suggested they
visit Esser, who was laid up with jaundice. While Hoffmann waited outside, Hitler revealed to Esser that he was going to announce the national
revolution that evening. He needed help. At exactly 9:30 P.M. Esser, carrying a flag, was to rush up to the podium of the Löwenbräukeller, where a
nationalist meeting was to be held, and announce the National Socialist
revolution.

Hitler emerged to tell Hoffmann that Esser felt much better and the
two strolled aimlessly along the Schellingstrasse. Moments later Göring
approached and Hitler took him off for a private talk only to return with
the announcement that he had a terrible headache and must leave. By
now Hoffmann was completely bewildered. What on earth, he asked, was
Hitler doing that evening? He answered mysteriously that he would be
"very busy on a very important job," then set off for party headquarters.

By now the SA men were getting out of their work clothes and putting on uniforms which consisted of field-gray windbreakers with swastika
armbands, field-gray ski cap, and revolver belt. They were bound for various rendezvous. Karl Kessler of the 2nd Company, was instructed to report to the Arzbergerkeller while shoemaker Josef Richter was sent to the
Hofbräuhaus. Members of the Bund Oberland were also on the move. Instead of a swastika they wore a sprig of edelweiss and were equipped with
steel helmets. One of the key units, the Führer's special hundred-man body-

guard, gathered at the Torbräu. Their leader, a tobacconist, was haranguing them. "Any one of you who isn't going into this heart and soul had better get out right now." It was their task, he said, to bear the brunt of whatever happened that night at the Bürgerbräukeller. "We're going to run the government out."

It was dark when a car stopped in front of Scheubner-Richter's apartment house and General Ludendorff got out. He talked a few minutes with Scheubner-Richter, then left. Moments later Scheubner-Richter and his servant also drove off at top speed. "Hansl," Scheubner-Richter said, "if things don't go right today, we will all be in jail tomorrow." At party headquarters they met Hitler and other leaders. After some discussion the group headed for the Bürgerbräukeller in two cars. It was almost 8 P.M. The beer hall was about half a mile from the center of Munich on the other side of the Isar River. It was a large rambling building, flanked by gardens and containing a number of dining rooms and bars. The main hall, the largest in the city, except for the Zirkus Krone, could hold 3000 at its sturdy round wooden tables. Officials knew there might be trouble and there were on hand 125 municipal policemen to control the crowd. In addition there was a mounted detachment as well as a number of officers scattered in the audience. In case of an emergency, a company of green-uniformed state police had been installed in a barracks only a quarter of a mile away.

By the time the Hitler caravan crossed the Isar River the hall was closed to all but important personages. Every seat was taken and Hanfstaengl wasn't able to bring in his little group of international journalists. A few minutes past eight Hitler's red Mercedes, followed by Scheubner-Richter's car, approached the beer hall. Hitler was disturbed by the milling crowds. Would his trucks be able to get through this mob? The two cars slowly pushed their way to the front entrance, which was blocked by a phalanx of policemen. Hitler persuaded the police to leave and make room for his troops, which were expected shortly, then led the way through the beer-hall door which Hess held open. There was such a crush that the door shut in the face of Hanfstaengl, who was bringing up the rear with an American woman journalist. He warned the police that there would be a scandal if the foreign press was excluded, but what opened the way was the fact that his companion was smoking an American cigarette, a luxury in Germany. At the edge of the anteroom Hitler stood near a large pillar peering into the jammed hall at the platform where Kahr was speaking in a droning voice. He denounced Marxism and called for a resurgent Germany. His manner was pedantic, as if he were lecturing, and the audience listened politely, relieving the boredom with beer.

Hanfstaengl figured that Hitler would fit more naturally into the scene if he too had a beer and so bought three at the serving counter for three billion marks. Hitler occasionally sipped his as he waited impatiently for the special Brownshirt bodyguard unit. Trucks filled with other storm troopers were already outside but they stayed in place until a few minutes after 8:30 P.M. when his helmeted bodyguard finally arrived. This was the signal for action. The trucks emptied and the armed Nazis surrounded the building. Bewildered and outnumbered the municipal police—unprepared for a political battle—did nothing.

Captain Göring and the bodyguard unit, armed with machine pistols, streamed into the building. Ulrich Graf, Hitler's personal protector, was waiting in the cloakroom for their arrival and hurried up to his chief, who had removed his trench coat to reveal a black long-tailed morning coat cut in Bavarian provincial style. Graf whispered into Hitler's ear and it reminded one onlooker of a patron petitioning the headwaiter for a good table. More than twenty police blocked the invaders but the leader of the bodyguard unit shouted, "Out of the way—you there!" and the police obediently did an about-face, like Keystone Cops, and marched in step right out the front door.

Hitler set aside the beer he had been nursing, pulled out his Browning pistol and, as the storm troopers shouted, "Heil Hitler!" he started into the hall with ex-butcher Graf, Scheubner-Richter (who was squinting myopically in the smoke-filled room) and his faithful servant, Harvard-graduate Hanfstaengl, an ex-police spy, business manager Max Amann, and the idealist-activist student of geopolitics, Rudolf Hess. Brandishing weapons, this motley band began pushing its way through the packed humanity toward the platform. By this time one group of Brownshirts had blocked the exit while another group set up a machine gun positioned to rake the audience. Tables overturned in the uproar. A cabinet member scrambled for cover under his table. Some made for the exits in consternation but were warned back and, if they resisted, were beaten or kicked.

The Hitler phalanx was blocked and, amidst the uproar, he climbed onto a chair waving his pistol. "Quiet!" he shouted and when the tumult continued he fired a round into the ceiling. In the shocked silence Hitler said, "The national revolution has broken out! The hall is surrounded!" No one was to leave the hall. Sweat poured down his pale face. He looked insane or drunk to some but a few were struck by the ridiculous sight of a pistol-brandishing revolutionary in such a badly cut morning suit. Comic as he looked, Hitler was dead serious. He ordered the triumvirate to follow him into an adjoining room, guaranteeing their security. But the three men did not move. Finally Kahr took a backward step as Hitler began clambering over a table toward the speakers' platform. Seisser's aide, a major, came forward, hand in pocket as if about to draw his pistol. Hitler jammed his own pistol against the major's forehead and said, "Take your hand out."

Hitler assured the triumvirate and the audience that everything could be settled in ten minutes. This time the three men and two aides followed Hitler to the side room. "*Komödie spielen* [Put on an act]," whispered Lossow to his colleagues. In the private room Hitler was more agitated than ever. "Please forgive me for proceeding in this manner," he said, "but I had no other means." He answered Seisser's accusations of breaking his word not to make a Putsch with an apology: he did it for the good of Germany. He told them that ex-Police President Pöhner was going to be the new Bavarian Minister President and Ludendorff would assume command of the new national army based on the radical right Battle League, and lead the march on Berlin. After the Putschists seized power, Hitler promised, the triumvirate would have even greater powers: Kahr would be made Regent of Bavaria; Lossow Reich Army Minister; and Seisser Reich Police Minister.

When the three failed to respond Hitler drew out his pistol (all in jest, he later testified). "There are five rounds in it," he said hoarsely, "four for the traitors, and if it fails one for me." He handed over the weapon to Graf, who already was armed with a machine pistol. Under such circumstances to die or not to die was meaningless, replied Kahr coolly. What interested him was General Ludendorff's position in the matter. Hitler didn't seem to know what to do. He took several quick swallows of beer, apologized to Kahr, then charged out of the room. The audience outside was getting out of hand. Someone shouted, "Theater!" Another that this was a Mexican revolution. There was a cacophony of whistles and jeers until Göring, emulating his chief, fired a pistol shot into the ceiling. He bellowed out that this display was not directed against Kahr, the Reichswehr or the state police. When argument failed, he tried humor. "You've got your beer," he shouted. "What are you worrying about?"

The uproar did not faze Hitler. He pushed his way up to the platform ignoring the catcalls and insults. He raised his pistol. The din continued and he shouted angrily, "If silence is not restored, I will order a machine gun placed in the gallery!" All of a sudden he was no longer the figure of fun. "What followed then," recalled Professor von Müller, the conservative historian, "was an oratorical masterpiece, which any actor might well envy. He began quietly, without any pathos." He made it appear as if the triumvirate was about to come around as he assured the audience that Kahr had his full trust and would be Regent of Bavaria. He promised that Ludendorff would assume leadership of the army; that Lossow would be Army Minister and Seisser Police Minister. "The task of the provisional German National Government is to organize the march on that sinful Babel, Berlin, and save the German people!"

From the first words, recalled Hanfstaengl, the insignificant man in the comical cutaway, who resembled a nervous "provincial bridegroom" on display in the dusty window of a Bavarian village photographer, became a superman. "It was like the difference between a Stradivarius lying in its case, just a few bits of wood and length of catgut, and the same violin being played by a master." Professor von Müller couldn't remember in his entire life "such a change of attitude of a crowd in a few minutes, almost a few seconds. There were certainly many who were not yet converted. But the sense of the majority had fully reversed itself. Hitler had turned them inside out, as one turns a glove inside out, with a few sentences. It had almost something of hocus-pocus, or magic about it. Loud approval roared forth, no further opposition was to be heard."

"Outside are Kahr, Lossow and Seisser," Hitler said earnestly. "They are struggling hard to reach a decision. May I say to them that you will stand behind them?"

"Ja! Ja!" roared the crowd.

"In a free Germany," shouted the impassioned Hitler, "there is also room for an autonomous Bavaria! I can say this to you: either the German revolution begins tonight or we will all be dead by dawn!" The crowd his, he headed back for the private room to bring the triumvirate to heel.

The man who could decide the matter was already approaching the Bürgerbräukeller in Hitler's Mercedes. General Ludendorff was in the back seat with his stepson (an ardent Putschist) and Scheubner-Richter. Despite the fog, their car careened across the bridge from the inner city at reckless speed. The sight of the general at the entrance of the beer hall brought a chorus of Heils! But Ludendorff, seeing how far things had gone, was "amazed and far from pleased." Hitler hurried out of the anteroom to shake hands with him. They conversed briefly and the scowling Ludendorff agreed to help convince the triumvirate. They disappeared into the side room.

Irritated as he was by Hitler's unilateral action, Ludendorff applied the force of his rank and personality on his two fellow officers. "All right, gentlemen," he told them, "come along with us, and give me your hand on it." It was the general who responded first. Lossow extended his hand and said, "Good." Then the colonel gave his hand to Ludendorff. The civilian, Kahr, was the last to submit but the first to speak once the entire group returned to the platform. Ramrod stiff, his face a mask, the commissar declared that he would serve Bavaria as Regent for the monarchy. The applause that interrupted this sober announcement was "fanatic," according to one police official.

As he surveyed the enthusiastic audience, Hitler was in a state of ecstasy. "I am going," he said emotionally, "to fulfill the vow I made to myself five years ago when I was a blind cripple in the military hospital: to know neither rest nor peace until the November criminals had been overthrown, until on the ruins of the wretched Germany of today there should have arisen once more a Germany of power and greatness, of freedom and splendor."

Then Ludendorff, pale and somber, spoke briefly and earnestly, giving Müller the impression that here was a man who realized "this was a matter of life and death, probably more death than life." In complete control of the situation, Hitler went down the line shaking hands to the accompaniment of wave after wave of cheers. Overcome by mass excitement and beer, the audience could hardly contain its delight. Forgotten were earlier derision and even anger. The crowd stood and roared out "Deutschland über Alles." Tears streamed down many a cheek and some people were so emotionally wrought they could not even sing. But someone next to a state police official turned and said, "The only thing missing is the psychiatrist."

4

There was also high emotion across the Isar at the Löwenbräukeller. The main hall, resounding with the blast of two brass bands, was jammed with more than 2000 members of the Battle League and SA. Only a small part of the audience was made up of the scar-faced Captain Röhm's fanatic followers, but he was the main attraction. He called "for revenge and retaliation against the traitors and the despoilers of our people. . . ."

Then Esser, who had dragged himself from a sickbed, mounted the podium. The plan had been changed somewhat and he did not charge up the aisle carrying a flag or immediately announce the revolution. He was to wait for word that Hitler's coup had succeeded. In the middle of his speech, at 8:40 P.M., a cryptic telephone message was received from the Bürgerbräukeller: "Safely delivered!" Röhm purposefully strode up to the platform and interrupted Esser. The Kahr government, he shouted, had been deposed and Adolf Hitler had declared a national revolution. Reichswehr soldiers tore off the Republic cockades from their hats, leaped onto tables and chairs shouting. Storm troopers embraced each other. The band blared out the national anthem. When the pandemonium subsided Röhm shouted for everyone to march on the Bürgerbräukeller. The men piled out of the Löwenbräukeller as if it were on fire and formed up. With shouting and cheers the raucous army started down the street toward the Isar River. A motorcycle courier stopped the procession with new marching orders from Hitler: Röhm's men were to turn toward the university and occupy General von Lossow's headquarters on the Schönfeldstrasse; the storm troopers were to proceed to St. Annaplatz, pick up a cache of 3000 rifles in the basement of the monastery, then take up positions at Giessing. Only the Bund Oberland was to continue on to the Bürgerbräukeller.

As Röhm's force marched down the Briennerstrasse followed by one of the brass bands, gathering crowds cheered them on. Near the head of the column, proudly holding an imperial war flag, was a fervent young nationalist, there because of allegiance to Röhm and Strasser, not Hitler. His name was Heinrich Himmler. The enthusiasm of jubilant onlookers was heady and the men continued like conquerors up the broad Ludwigstrasse to the entrance of the military district building. Röhm halted his troops outside the gates and strode into the building where he had worked for so many years. The guards threatened to shoot but Röhm outfaced them. He marched up to the second floor to the office of the duty officer, who declared that he was bowing only to force, and then gave the order to open the gates to the rioters. Röhm posted guards, emplaced machine guns at windows and strung barbed wire around the building. He did just about everything except take over the telephone switchboard. This, incredibly, he left in charge of the duty officer, who had no revolutionary leanings.

At the beer hall Hess was rounding up "enemies of the people" as hostages. He stood on a chair in the great hall calling out names of officials and officers, including Minister President Knilling, Police President Mantel and Prince Rupprecht's political adviser. They dutifully stepped forward as if they were unruly schoolboys—all except Justice Minister Gürtner, who made a break for freedom but was caught. At first they were incarcerated in a small room upstairs but then it was decided that Hess should transfer them for safekeeping to a house near the Tegernsee, a lake south of Munich.

Others in Hitler's inner circle were off on assignments: Max Amann, the squat but formidable street fighter, led a group to a bank which he seized for the new government's central offices, while Scheubner-Richter, Esser and Hanfstaengl were reconnoitering the city streets to check on the progress of the revolution. They found a city of confusion. Many citizens were enthusiastic, others perplexed, and some indignant. Few knew what was going on, including those involved in the action since conflicting orders kept emanating from the Bürgerbräu.

The man principally responsible for the first successes of the Putschists was Frick of the Munich Police Presidium. He persuaded his colleagues on duty not to launch any counterattack against the Putschists, then hovered near a phone to calm bewildered police officials who called in for information. His advice always was to wait and do nothing. Because of this state of inaction, his former chief, the deposed Police President Pöhner, was able to walk into police headquarters and, without any show of force, take charge. His first act was to make arrangements for a press conference with the leading non-Marxist newspapers.

At the Bürgerbräukeller Hitler was in a state of euphoria with the police under control and district headquarters occupied by Röhm. Then came a report from the engineer barracks: the Putschists were having an argument with the engineers. Hitler made a snap decision to leave his command post to straighten out the matter in person. It was a grave tactical error, followed by a second: placing General Ludendorff in charge. No sooner had Hitler left the building than General von Lossow said he had to go to his office and issue orders. This seemed reasonable to Ludendorff, who allowed Lossow to march out of the beer hall with Kahr and Seisser not far behind. Hitler did no good at the engineer barracks, being turned away at the gate. He returned half an hour later and was appalled to find that the triumvirate had been allowed to escape. He assailed Ludendorff. How could he have done such a thing? Now Lossow could sabotage the revolution! The general looked frostily down his nose at the former corporal. A German officer, he said, would never break an oath!

Hitler's spirits were raised at 11 P.M. by the arrival of a thousand-man military unit. It was almost the entire complement of the Infantry School, an elite group of cadets. Except for a handful of dissidents, they had been persuaded to join the uprising en masse by Lieutenant Gerhard Rossbach, a veteran of the Free Corps movement. The cadets had placed their own commander under house arrest and accepted the flamboyant Rossbach (like Röhm, a homosexual and gallant fighter) as their new leader. To the blare of a brass band the cadets marched smartly up to the beer hall, wearing swastika armbands and carrying National Socialist flags. Standing at attention, former Quartermaster General Ludendorff and ex-Corporal Hitler reviewed them. Then the cadets marched off to occupy the offices of Commissar von Kahr while the leaders of the Putsch set off in their cars for military district headquarters. At Röhm's command post—the office of General von Lossow—the group began discussing the future course of the revolution. Ensconcing himself in an easy chair, Ludendorff demanded that someone get hold of Lossow or Seisser on the phone. A number of calls were made but neither could be reached. Scheubner-Richter expressed the feeling that something was wrong. Lossow had said he was coming here to his own office. Where was he? And where were Kahr and Seisser? Ludendorff again protested that these three gentlemen had given their oath in full view and sound of thousands. They could not possibly have changed their minds.

Major Max Schwandner, an officer on the staff of the commander of army units in Bavaria, was just entering the building. He had heard rumors of a Putsch and sought out the duty officer, who could only say that "the affair was extremely unclean and fishy." "While we spoke," recalled Schwandner, "Captain Röhm stormed into [the room] in full uniform of the old army with all [his] medals and asked for General von Lossow. I immediately told Röhm that this Putsch was in clear violation of yesterday's understanding with von Lossow. Röhm replied in a voice vibrant with sincerity that everything was all right. Von Lossow, Kahr and von Seisser had all declared themselves in accord with everything and would soon come to Hitler in the military district headquarters. I said only that that was something different."

After Röhm left, the duty officer motioned to Schwandner and whispered, "The affair is crooked." Lossow, he said, was with Seisser and the commandant of the Bavarian army at the 19th Infantry barracks and would "definitely not come here." A little later a call came through the still unmonitored switchboard. It was from Lossow at his new command post, safe in the center of the regimental barracks complex. He ordered a counterattack on the Putschists he had recently pledged to support; loyal army battalions in Augsburg, Ingolstadt, Regensburg, Landshut and other surrounding localities were to be transported to Munich by rail. Schwandner promptly called the transport officer, passed on Lossow's orders and agreed to phone instructions to half of the battalions himself. The Putsch was being planned in one room and sabotaged in the one next to it. Finally just before midnight it occurred to the plotters to limit the switchboard to Putschist traffic but by then all of Lossow's counterorders had been transmitted.

Despite the marching troops, the bands and the excitement, most Müncheners had no idea revolution once more had come to their city. One of the Führer's closest friends, Heinrich Hoffmann, spent the evening in the Fledermausbar without learning that anything out of the ordinary had taken place, and only at midnight did he discover that the revolution was on. By that time jubilant gangs of young people were keeping guests in downtown hotels awake with their songs and cries of triumph.

At the American Consulate Robert Murphy, the acting consul, was composing a telegram to the Secretary of State:

. . . ACCORDING TO HITLER TASK OF THIS GOVERNMENT IS
TO MARCH ON BERLIN, WAGE TWELFTH HOUR FIGHT;
ASSERTED THAT THE DAWN WOULD SEE EITHER NEW
NATIONAL GOVERNMENT OR THE DEATH OF THE SPEAKER. . . .*

It was a night of terror for those opponents of the coup who were dragged from their homes and held hostage; and for some picked out of the phone book if their names sounded Jewish, who were corraled by the Brownshirts. One unit descended on the socialist Munich *Post*, but while it was smashing the presses, orders came from an irate Hitler to desist since he wanted the plant for his own purposes.

At military district headquarters it was becoming increasingly evident that the triumvirate had broken their word (no one seemed to recall that it had been made under duress) and that events were getting out of hand. Scheubner-Richter and his servant Aigner left to bring back Seisser but

* When Murphy was not permitted to send this telegram in code, he indignantly demanded an interview with Hitler himself. "After hours of argument, I finally did get in to see him at 3 A.M., only to be told rather mildly that I could not send my telegram. My protest was only a formality by that time, since I had already sent my colleague, Halstead, in a car to file the telegram from Stuttgart."

could not locate him. On their return they found a "somewhat depressed" Hitler.

Aigner was ordered to take Rosenberg to a printing shop to make copies of the announcement of the new government signed by the principal partners. This done, Rosenberg proceeded to the offices of the *Völkischer Beobachter* to write an editorial for the morning edition. Entitled "Call to the German People," it exhorted the public to hand over President Ebert and other Social Democrats "dead or alive to the People's National Government."

Aigner was already back at military district headquarters where he was instructed by his employer to go home for champagne and food, and to tell Frau Scheubner-Richter that "everything was in order and she should not worry." The situation was deteriorating. Röhm had finally become suspicious of what was going on in the next room and arrested the duty officer. He also issued orders to seize all other army officers in the building but not in time to catch the enterprising Major Schwandner, who had accomplished his mission of summoning troops to Munich. Warned by a civilian employee, he slipped out just before the cordon was drawn.

Things were also not going well for the Putschists at the headquarters of Commissar von Kahr. He had gone there after his escape from the beer hall to find that machinery had already been set in motion to crush the Putsch. Understandably, he did nothing to stop these measures (he had just received an indignant message from Prince Rupprecht: "Crush this movement at any cost. Use troops if necessary") and was helping direct the defense of his building against the lively threat of Lieutenant Rossbach and his thousand cadets from the Infantry School. It should have been easy for the revolutionists to carry out Ludendorff's order to take the building "whatever the cost," and it would have been an important victory but it turned into a standoff with cadets and police facing each other at bayonet point, each group waiting for the other to fire the first shot. No one wanted bloodshed. The cadets had no wish to fire at men in uniform and many of the police shared the young men's faith in Hitler. Negotiations went on interminably until the man of action, Rossbach, became impatient and shouted to his cadets: "What? Still negotiating here? You know General Ludendorff's orders. Why the hesitation? Order your men to fire!"

At last the cadets moved into position with skirmishers advancing in a semicircle followed by machine-gun crews. The police countered by inviting three rebels inside to discuss the matter. They accepted the invitation but with the understanding that if they did not appear in ten minutes the attack would begin. The minutes passed and just as the cadets prepared themselves for action a command rang out, "Companies withdraw!"

The cadets pulled back. The siege was over. The battle that might have swung the decision was lost by default, primarily because the Hitler forces were reluctant to fire upon men they wanted as allies. All the cadets had done was keep Commissar von Kahr bottled up for several crucial hours. Now he left the building and joined Lossow and Seisser at 19th Infantry barracks.

The faint hope held at military district headquarters that the triumvirate would not act overtly against the Putsch faded when it was learned that General von Lossow had sent out this message "to all German wireless stations" at 2:55 A.M.:

> State Commissar General v. Kahr, Col. v. Seisser and General v. Lossow repudiate the Hitler Putsch. Expressions of support extracted by gunpoint invalid. Caution is urged against misuse of the above names.
>
> *v. Lossow*

At the 19th Infantry Regiment, Kahr, hunched and brooding on a settee, was being called upon to write a proclamation to be posted throughout the city. He finally composed one that satisfied everyone. Deception, he said, had turned a demonstration for Germany's awakening into sickening violence. "Had the senseless and purposeless attempt at revolt succeeded, Germany would have been plunged into the abyss and Bavaria with it." He dissolved the NSDAP and other right-wing organizations, declaring that those responsible for the Putsch would "ruthlessly be made to suffer the punishment they deserve." It had been a long and bitter evening for the commissar.

It was not until 5 A.M. that confirmation of the repudiation of the Putsch by the triumvirate reached military district headquarters. The informant was the deposed commandant of the Infantry School. He regretfully informed Hitler that the triumvirate did not feel honor bound to their oaths since they were made at pistol point. General von Lossow was going to put down the Putsch with force. If Hitler was stunned, he did not show it. He made a long speech to his fellow conspirators, ending with the declaration that, if need be, he was determined to fight and die for his cause. With Ludendorff's concurrence, he ordered Scheubner-Richter and his servant (who had returned with the champagne and refreshments) to find their own newly designated Minister President and order him to seize the police headquarters with an Oberland unit. Pöhner set off on his mission with gusto and was so confident that he walked into the Police Directory with a single companion. He was escorted to the office of the major in charge and, to his consternation ("It came like a blow from a club"), was arrested. His former assistant, Frick, was already in custody.

By this time Hitler, Ludendorff and the staff were on their way back to the beer hall, leaving Röhm and his followers to hold the military district building. Dismayed as he was, Hitler had not yet given up. "If we get through, very well," he remarked grimly, "if not, we'll have to hang ourselves." It was still dark as word went out to those Putschists not manning strongholds to assemble at the beer hall. A wet, chilling snow was falling as units converged on the Bürgerbräu. The men had the impression that something had gone wrong but knew no details. Even so they proceeded through the empty streets, flags flying, with at least one group of SA men lustily singing Eckart's "Sturmlied": "Germany, awake! Break your chains in two!"

5

It was a dull, overcast dawn with a biting damp chill. The cold wet snow continued to fall spasmodically. The rank and file of Putschists were gathered glumly in the smoke-filled, dank main hall of the Bürgerbräukeller. Unshaven and unwashed, they were eating a breakfast of coffee, cheese and bread. The excitement and exaltation of last night had evaporated. Then someone announced that the triumvirate had publicly denounced the revolution and the army would not participate. Someone else mounted the speakers' platform, recent scene of such high drama, and began raging against all the traitors—the bourgeois and the generals. "March to Berlin!" he shouted. There was some applause but the suggestion struck Hitler's lawyer, Hans Frank, as "highly romantic and very unpolitical."

The leaders were in a private room upstairs where Ludendorff sat "stony-faced and frightening in his unperturbed calm," as he sipped red wine for breakfast. In his old tweed shooting jacket he was still an impressive figure. But his show of confidence cracked upon getting the information that Lossow had publicly denounced the new government. "I will never again trust the word of a German officer," he exclaimed and retreated into glum silence.

The coup which had seemed so successful at midnight was unraveling in the cold light of day and Hitler's next step revealed his desperation. He ordered a Battle League unit to seize the police station and rescue the incarcerated Pöhner. Continuing to act as if there was still hope, he then sent a detachment of storm troopers to the Jewish printing firm of Parcus to confiscate stacks of freshly printed inflation money. (This being Germany, each revolutionist had to be paid his stipend.) The sum was 14,605 trillion marks and, in true German fashion, the Parcus brothers demanded and got a receipt.

By this time more Putschist units were arriving in trucks from outside localities. Wet, freezing and weary, they knew nothing of the turn of events and were in good spirits. The largest contingent came from Landshut and halfway to Munich they had been overtaken by a truckload of state police who exchanged Heils with them. Their leader was the druggist, Gregor Strasser. He sat in the cab of the lead vehicle and as it

rumbled along the peaceful but busy streets someone observed that everyone was going to work as usual. "This is no revolution. Something is
wrong."

"We'll see," said Strasser. At the beer hall he was informed by Captain Göring that "those fellows" had broken their word to the Führer but
the people were still with him. "We're going to try the whole thing over
again." Then a short, stocky man with a shining bald pate—it was Julius
Streicher—burst into the main hall to harangue the gathering on behalf of
Hitler. Gesturing with his whip, he spoke raucously and obscenely in an
effort to work up enthusiasm. Arms were passed out to those who had
none and the men were reloaded into trucks and taken to their posts.

By this time the Battle League unit ordered by Hitler to occupy
police headquarters was back at the military district building—mission
unaccomplished. They had argued with the police for a few minutes before leaving to avoid a fight. Hitler turned the task of rescuing Pöhner
over to his faithful bodyguard unit. This hardy group reached the Police
Directory at 9:30 A.M., set up machine guns to cover the building and
made as if to attack. But again the rebels had no stomach for shedding
blood. They returned to the beer hall—mission still unaccomplished—
only to be dispatched minutes later on an easier task: arrest of the Marxist
city councilors who had refused to fly the swastika flag over the City Hall.

They forced their way into the old Rathaus. Their commander,
the tobacconist, flung open the door of the council room. Cocking his
weapon, he shouted that all Social Democrats and Communists were
under arrest. Outside in the Marienplatz, according to his account, a large
crowd "greeted the appearance of the councillors with jeers and insults. As
a matter of fact it was we troopers who had to defend them from the onslaught of the people. Otherwise actual fatalities might have occurred. It
was quite a job getting them safely loaded into the lorries."

As these trucks started for the beer hall, Putschist speakers began haranguing a crowd which grew so dense that the number 6 trolley cars
bound for Sendling were unable to move. The main speaker was Streicher,
who proved to be a greater attraction than the famous revolving figures of
the Rathaus clock. By now the Platz was festooned with swastika banners
and the party flag waved from the top of the City Hall.

The Putsch was marked by confusion and hesitation on both sides. In
some parts of the city the municipal police were pulling down Putschist
posters and arresting rebels while in the inner city rebels were arresting
police for attempting to put up government posters repudiating the
Putsch and dissolving the NSDAP. Hitler's men held most of the major
downtown bridges over the Isar River, including the most important, the
Ludwigsbrücke, connecting the beer hall with the center of the city. At
the Museum bridge citizens were chiding the youthful Putschists. "Do
you have your mother's permission to play with such dangerous things in

the street?" called out one worker. The little ten-man detachment returned sheepishly to the beer hall.

At another Isar bridge rumors were spreading among the men from Landshut that "something had gone wrong and that betrayal was in the cards." Their fears were justified; at 10 A.M. trucks loaded with men in green uniforms arrived. These were the state troopers, who hurriedly set up two heavy machine guns. The Putschists did nothing since their orders were to hold fire. The state police also had orders to stand in place and the two sides simply stared at each other.

At the beer hall the rebel leaders were in dispute. Colonel Hermann Kriebel, who had served in the war on Ludendorff's staff, wanted to withdraw to Rosenheim on the Austrian border where they might win over the local right radicals. Göring seconded this. It was his home town and he assured everyone it was strongly pro-Hitler. Here they could assemble reinforcements and regroup. "The movement cannot end in the ditch of some obscure country lane," was Ludendorff's sarcastic retort. It was up to Hitler. He hesitated briefly but he was a born gambler and the prospect of a lengthy guerrilla campaign was not appealing. He wanted to win or lose on one throw of the dice and he vetoed the Kriebel plan.

The discussion dragged on until late morning while the situation on the streets deteriorated. At military district headquarters Captain Röhm and his men were under siege by army and state police troops. While the older members of the Battle League were not all eager to face such overwhelming odds, the 150 men of Röhm's own group were ready for combat.

Word of the government attack against Röhm brought arguments at the Bürgerbräukeller to a halt. It was evident that the Putschists had to act now or surrender ignominiously. According to Ludendorff, it was he who first thought of marching in force into the heart of Munich to rescue Röhm. "We march!" he said. If it was Ludendorff's idea, it was carried out in Hitler fashion—as a propaganda parade, a display of power designed to arouse support for the Putsch from the citizenry. "We would go to the city," Hitler later testified, "to win the people to our side, to see how public opinion would react, and then to see how Kahr, Lossow and Seisser would react to public opinion. After all, those gentlemen would hardly be foolish enough to use machine guns against a general uprising of the people. That's how the march into the city was decided on."

Ludendorff was convinced that army troops would not impede the march, and recently had assured a friend: "The heavens will fall before the Bavarian Reichswehr turns against me." Hitler was just as confident that neither army nor state police would fire on a war hero like Ludendorff, who would be in the front row. Hitler's decision ("the most desperately daring decision of my life") was made and orders were hurriedly dispatched to units manning the bridges. Outside the beer hall Colonel

Kriebel, the professional soldier, began setting up the line of march. Hitler was just leaving the conference room about 11:30 A.M. as Eckart sauntered in. Once they had been the closest friends. Now Hitler "looked very dark and said, 'Good day,' in a hard voice." Outside the affronted author received another rebuff when he greeted Ludendorff respectfully. The general gave him "an indifferent tip of the hat."

The parade formed quickly. There was no band to lead off since the musicians who had reported to the beer hall that morning got neither breakfast nor pay and marched off after playing a dutiful chorus of the "Badenweiler," the march of Hitler's regiment in the war. In the van were picked skirmishers and eight men carrying the swastika and the black-white-red flags. Next came the leaders: Hitler with Scheubner-Richter on his right and Ludendorff on his left. Alongside were Colonel Kriebel, personal bodyguard Graf, the commander of the Munich storm troopers, and Captain Hermann Göring romantically militant with steel helmet decorated with a large white swastika and wearing a smart black leather coat open enough so that his Pour le Mérite could be seen. He was somewhat ruffled because his idea to bring along the captured councilors as hostages had been vetoed. But the Führer had curtly rejected the scheme; he wanted no martyrs.

Behind the leaders were three units marching abreast in columns of four. On the left was Hitler's hundred-man bodyguard, steel-helmeted and armed with carbines and potato masher grenades; on the right the Bund Oberland; and in the middle the battle-seasoned Munich SA Regiment. There followed a motley collection of men, some in uniform or parts of tattered World War uniforms, some wearing work clothes or business suits. The cadets from Infantry School, smart and ultramilitary, were sandwiched between students, shopkeepers, middle-aged businessmen and hard-faced freebooters. The only common mark was a swastika brassard on the left arm. Most of them had rifles and many had fixed bayonets. Others, particularly the SA, held pistols in chilled hands.

Scheubner-Richter, wearing a pince-nez, grasped Rosenberg's hand and said, "Things look ugly," then gloomily prophesied to Hitler that this would be their last walk together. The Führer himself was pale and grave. Against the bitter cold he wore his familiar trench coat and carried his slouch hat. Ludendorff, overcoat over hunting jacket, was impassive, but he turned and ordered his servant to go home so he wouldn't get hurt.

It was almost noon when the straggling column moved off. In fifteen minutes the 2000 men reached the Ludwig bridge and a small force of state police. The police commander stepped forward as the Putschist skirmishers slowly advanced, called out to halt or be fired upon, then turned to his men and told them to load with live ammunition. As he spoke a bugle blasted, and selected Putschists suddenly converged on the police with bayonets leveled, shouting, "Don't shoot at your comrades!"

The police hesitated and before a shout could be fired were overrun. The column continued across the bridge and marched straight ahead. The Zweibrückenstrasse was lined with people, many cheering enthusiastically and waving swastika flags. Bystanders began joining the parade. This enthusiasm inspired the marchers to song and, without band accompaniment, they broke into their favorite, "Storm Song." As they approached the Isartor where its author Eckart, who had gone on ahead, stood in the crowd near the ancient gate, he located a grim-faced Hitler in the first row. Their eyes met and "he stared at me as if to imply, 'So where are you?'"

The chilled men, their exhalations visible in the cold, continued unimpeded and in another fifteen minutes flowed into the Marienplatz, still festooned with swastika banners from the rallies. The Nazi flag still waved atop the City Hall and a large crowd was singing patriotic songs. At this point there was confusion among the marchers. Some were under the impression they were to turn around and return to the beer hall, while others assumed they would continue into the city and rescue Röhm. Colonel Kriebel was surprised when Ludendorff led the way to the right into the Weinstrasse and toward the Odeonsplatz but said to himself, "If Ludendorff is marching that way, naturally we'll go with him." The general himself had not planned this move. "At certain moments in life one acts instinctively and doesn't know why. . . . We just wanted to get to Röhm and bring him back."

The impulsive turn to the right by the heavy-set man in the dark brown overcoat was bringing the Putschists face to face with government forces. In moments the column approached one of Munich's most revered landmarks, the Feldherrnhalle. Here a line of city police blocked the way. But the Putschists surged forward singing, "*O Deutschland hoch in Ehren* [O, Germany high in honor]."

Looking down from her hotel room, Frau Winifred Wagner was amazed to see her idol, Hitler, marching down the narrow Residenzstrasse next to Ludendorff. Just ahead in the Odeonsplatz small groups of green-uniformed men were scrambling into a blocking position. There was only room enough in the street for eight abreast. Hitler locked arms with Scheubner-Richter in preparation for trouble but Ludendorff touched no one, still supremely confident that no one would fire on him. Directly ahead was a cordon of state police under First Lieutenant Michael Freiherr von Godin. Faced with an oncoming mob, Godin called out, "Second Company, double time, march." The state police jogged forward but the Putschists did not break, standing off the enemy with leveled bayonets and pistols. Godin used his rifle to parry two bayonet thrusts, "overturning the men behind them with rifle at high port." All at once a shot exploded. Godin heard it zing past his head; it killed a sergeant. "For a fraction of a second my company stood frozen. Then, before I could give an order, my people opened fire, with the effect of a salvo."

The Putschists returned the fire and panic broke out as marchers and bystanders scrambled for safety. One of the first to fall was Scheubner-Richter—shot in the lungs. Another was Graf, who had leaped in front of Hitler to take the half dozen bullets meant for him. In falling, the personal bodyguard clutched Hitler, yanking him down so sharply that his left arm was dislocated. On the other side Scheubner-Richter also helped drag Hitler to the pavement. Ludendorff's faithful servant, who had been ordered to go home, was bleeding on the asphalt. His friend Aigner, the servant of the dying Scheubner-Richter, crawled to him. He was dead. Someone stepped over Aigner. It was General Ludendorff marching erectly, left hand in coat pocket, into the line of fire.*

As Hitler sprawled on the ground thinking he had been shot in the left side, comrades tried to shield him. Eighteen men lay dead in the street: fourteen followers of Hitler and four state police, all, incidentally, more or less sympathetic with National Socialism. Those in the front of the marching column alone knew what had happened. The crowd jammed up behind only heard firecracker explosions ahead, then a rumor that both Hitler and Ludendorff were killed. The Putschists scrambled to the rear.

Ludendorff marched through the police cordon and into the arms of a lieutenant who placed him under arrest and escorted him to the Residenz. Once inside, the man who moments before had acted like a hero in fiction began behaving like a spoiled child. He petulantly refused an offer by a police colonel to inform his family of his safety and forbade the colonel to call him "Excellency." From now on he was "Herr Ludendorff" and he would never don uniform as long as the offending police officer wore one.

Hitler painfully struggled to his feet, cradling his injured arm. He was in agony as he slowly moved away from the battleground, face pale, hair falling over his face. He was accompanied by Dr. Walter Schultze, chief of the Munich SA medical corps, a towering young man. They came upon a small boy lying at the curb, bleeding profusely. Hitler wanted to carry him off but Schultze called to his wife's cousin (a botany student named Schuster) to take the boy. At Max Joseph Platz they finally reached Hitler's old gray Selve, which had been loaded with medical supplies. An elderly first

* Most accounts picture Ludendorff as courageous for staying on his feet and Hitler as ignoble for dropping to the street even though Hitler's arm dislocation indicates he was dragged down. Undoubtedly Hitler would have hit the ground on his own since he was a seasoned front-line soldier. Robert Murphy testified that "both Ludendorff and Hitler behaved in identical manner, like the battle-hardened soldiers they were. Both fell flat to escape the hail of bullets." Another eyewitness, a watchman, also saw Ludendorff throw himself to the ground and then find cover "behind a corpse or wounded man." A second watchman corroborated the fact that no one was standing after the volley.

aid man named Frankel got in the front seat with the driver while Hitler and the doctor got into the rear seat. Schuster stood on the running board holding the wounded boy. Hitler told the driver to head for the Bürgerbräu-keller so he could find out what was going on. But at the Marienplatz they came under heavy machine-gun fire and had to change directions several times. They found the Ludwig bridge blocked and turned back. By this time the boy had regained consciousness and Schuster dismounted so he could take the youngster home. The car continued toward the Sendlinger-torplatz. Here they encountered another burst of fire near the old southern cemetery. Since it was impossible to get back to the beer hall, there was nothing to do but keep driving south toward Salzburg.

Göring's display of his Pour le Mérite decoration had not saved him and he lay on the pavement with a bullet in his upper thigh. Frau Ilse Ballin, who had rushed from her home to help the wounded, found him bleeding profusely. With the help of her sister, she dragged the heavy burden indoors. The sisters dressed Göring's wound and were about to summon an ambulance when he weakly asked them to help him get to a private clinic. He could not bear the indignity of arrest. Frau Ballin, the wife of a Jewish merchant, had pity on him and thus he escaped prison.

6

What had started as a battle ended in a frenzied scramble for refuge as if some natural disaster had struck the Marienplatz. One group of Putschists got inside a young ladies' academy and were allowed to hide under beds and in closets. Others burst into a *Konditorei* and hid their arms under ovens, in flour sacks and coffee machines. The state police rounded up hundreds, disarming them on the street. Those left behind at the beer hall to hold the command post were so unstrung by the catastrophe they surrendered without resistance to green and blue police. They stacked arms and went home to brood. At military district headquarters Captain Röhm also surrendered, realizing there was nothing to be gained by further resistance. The Putsch was over but victorious state police marching away from the beer hall were abused by indignant citizens with cries of: "Pfui! Jew defenders! Betrayers of the Fatherland! Bloodhounds! Heil Hitler—Down with Kahr!"

The SA troops from Landshut were still at their post when word came of the debacle at the Feldherrnhalle. Rumor spread that Ludendorff was dead and Hitler seriously wounded. Gregor Strasser assembled his men and they marched off "filled with bitterness and disappointment at Kahr's betrayal." At a forest they found an SA group from Munich smashing rifles against trees. Strasser ordered them to stop such nonsense. The rifles could come in handy in the future. In closed ranks the Landshut unit paraded defiantly to the Hauptbahnhof singing new words to "Swastika and Steel Helmet." They had been betrayed, they sang, but remained true to the Fatherland.

Another group of SA men was on the highway in cars and a truck loaded with the captured Munich councilors. At a woods on the road to Rosenheim the convoy halted and their commander led the pale prisoners into the woods. They thought that their "last hour had struck" but were only subjected to the indignity of changing clothes with the SA so the latter could return to Munich as civilians. Minister President von Knilling and the other principal hostages were also free. Hess had successfully transported them out of the city to a villa on the Tegernsee but while he was out telephoning Munich to find out what was happening the young man he had placed in charge of the prisoners was persuaded to drive them home. Hess had lost not only his hostages but his transportation.

After hiding his weapons, Scheubner-Richter's servant returned to the scene of carnage in a borrowed civilian coat to find out what had happened to his master. The Feldherrnhalle was barred and Aigner told a police official who he was. "After much pleading he accompanied me inside where, near the entrance, all the dead were lying side by side. I was close to madness when I had to look for him among the bodies." Aigner found his master lying next to his own best friend, Ludendorff's servant. "Sick in my soul and totally shattered I returned to our residence in Widenmayerstrasse." Frau Scheubner-Richter asked where her husband was. Aigner lied but she insisted on the truth. "I can still remember her words: 'That's terrible but that is why one is an officer's wife.'"

Hanfstaengl missed all the action. He was at his apartment when his sister phoned to say that Putschists were marching into the center of Munich. In the street he encountered an SA acquaintance in a state of collapse who told him that Hitler, Ludendorff and Göring were dead and it was the end of Germany. As Hanfstaengl headed back home to prepare for flight an open car screeched to a halt beside him. Inside were Amann, Esser, Eckart and Hoffmann. He went with them to the photographer's apartment where it was agreed to escape singly to Austria.

Hanfstaengl never thought of hiding in his country home at Uffing but a mishap would force Hitler to do so. His car was some ten miles from Munich when he broke a long silence to announce abruptly that he must have been shot in the arm. "Is it warm?" asked Dr. Schultze. It was not. Perhaps a bullet was there or something was broken. They parked in the woods and with difficulty the doctor began removing Hitler's leather jacket, two sweaters, necktie and shirt. Schultze discovered that the left arm was severely dislocated but it would be impossible to set it properly in a car without assistance. He fastened Hitler's injured arm to his body with a kerchief, then suggested they flee to Austria. Hitler vetoed this and they kept driving south. On nearing Murnau Hitler remembered

"In the Beginning Was the Word," a painting by H. O. Hoyer. BUNDESARCHIV

Hitler making a street talk. IMPERIAL WAR MUSEUM

Sterneckerbräu in Munich where NSDAP was founded in 1920. HOFFMANN

Early picture of Hitler in full SA (Brownshirt) uniform. LIBRARY OF CONGRESS

Early party meeting at Hofbräuhaus in Munich. Gregor Strasser is at Hitler's right. To his left, Franz Xavier Schwarz, party treasurer, Max Amann, the party's publisher and the Führer's former sergeant; and Ulrich Graf, the bodyguard. The Beer Hall Putsch would start here in 1923. STADTARCHIV, MUNICH

Leaving party meeting, circa 1922. IMPERIAL WAR MUSEUM

The Beer Hall Putsch, November 9, 1923. LIBRARY OF CONGRESS

The Beer Hall Putsch, November 9, 1923. HAUPTSTAADTARCHIV, MUNICH

Julius Streicher addresses crowd in the Marienplatz, November 9, 1923.
HAUPTSTAADTARCHIV, MUNICH

Left, Hitler's cell at Landsberg prison. STADTARCHIV, MUNICH. Right, Hitler returns
fifteen years later and tells Max Wünsche, his ordnance officer (who took picture),
that his time in prison gave him the opportunity to write *Mein Kampf*. Over the
cell door was a large plaque: "In this room lived Adolf Hitler from 11 November
1923 to 20 December 1924." MAX WÜNSCHE

Two previously unpublished letters. Left, Winifred Wagner encloses a book of poetry which she hopes will help Hitler over the long hours. "The poetry is to be interpreted in the frame of reference of Richard Wagner as a drama that can only be understood in connection with the music." EDWARD WHALEN.

Below, Hitler's half sister Angela writes their brother about her visit to Adolf in prison and ends the myth that his family did not enthusiastically support his political career. "His spirit and soul were again at a high level.... The goal and victory is only a question of time. God grant it be soon." HANS HITLER

Common room of Nazi prisoners at Landsberg. Behind Hitler, Emil Maurice, early companion and chauffeur. To left, Colonel Hermann Kriebel, military leader of the Putsch. Ilse Pröhl, later Frau Hess, smuggled in the camera that took this and other prison pictures. LIBRARY OF CONGRESS

Hitler in prison with Maurice, Kriebel, Hess and Dr. Friedrich Weber of Bund Oberland. IMPERIAL WAR MUSEUM

Release from prison, 1924. LIBRARY OF CONGRESS

Hitler and two friends outside Haus Wachenfeld, the modest villa he bought on the Obersalzberg which grew into the Berghof. HANS HITLER

that the Hanfstaengl villa in Uffing was only a few miles away. He ordered the driver to hide the Selve, then started on foot with the doctor and first aid man toward Uffing.

They arrived at the Hanfstaengl villa, a small stone structure near the village church, about 4 P.M. Without comment Helene led the three exhausted men up to her sitting room. Hitler began to lament the death of Ludendorff and his faithful Graf, both of whom he had seen drop. He became more and more excited. It was Ludendorff's trustfulness, he said, which had cost him his life, and Graf's faithfulness which had robbed Hitler of a perfect adjutant. He began criticizing and condemning the triumvirate for their treachery "and swore he would go on fighting for his ideals as long as breath was in him."

Helene suggested that he get some sleep. He would probably be discovered soon and would need all his strength to face capture. Dr. Schultze and the aid man helped Hitler to a bedroom one floor up where they tried to set his dislocated arm. But the first attempt failed since the arm was so swollen. Hitler grimaced as they tried again, this time successfully. Then the aid man began to bind the arm and shoulder. Helene could hear Hitler's moans of pain through the door.

Foreign newspapers were running garbled stories of the Munich Putsch. In New York City it was described as a militarist uprising with Hitler playing a secondary role. In Rome, where Kurt Lüdecke was again conferring with Mussolini on behalf of Hitler, the noon editions declared that Crown Prince Rupprecht had joined the revolutionists.

By the morning of November 10 the Putschists were either in captivity or flight. Hess, stranded in Tegernsee without a car, was finally able to reach his fiancée, Ilse Pröhl, by phone and tell of the fiasco with the hostages. Could she find some transportation and take him to Professor Haushofer's apartment? Ilse set off from Munich on her bicycle. It was a trip of more than thirty miles and the return with Hess was arduous. One would ride the bicycle for some distance, then rest it against a tree and continue on foot; the other would pick up the bike and repeat the process. (It was his idea.) At last they reached Haushofer's home in the Bavarian capital. He agreed to hide the fugitive even though he thought the Putsch was "a ridiculous matter," for he was fond of Hess despite his limitations—"his strong side was not intelligence but heart and character." Hess was despondent; the Putsch might not have failed if he had not lost the hostages. He talked of suicide. But Haushofer argued him out of this, advising him to surrender instead. This was counsel Hess could not take and, after several days, he left the Haushofer home to hide with friends outside the city. Before long he was risking arrest by bicycling back to Munich every so often to look after Ilse, who had fallen sick.

7

It had been a restless, anxious night at Uffing. Hanfstaengl had not come home and Hitler, rolled up tightly in his host's English traveling rug to ease the pain, had been unable to sleep. Hitler sent for Helene Hanfstaengl and told her the aid man was being dispatched to Munich in hopes of persuading the Bechsteins to send out their closed car to take him to Austria. Dr. Schultze was also going to the city. To make sure everything possible had been done for Hitler's arm, he was bringing back a discreet colleague, an assistant to the eminent Dr. Sauerbruch.

The morning seemed interminable, even the maids were too excited to eat. Only Egon, not quite three years old, was normal and had to be kept under strict supervision lest he call over the wall that Uncle Dolf was there. Just before noon Dr. Schultze returned with Sauerbruch's assistant. Together they explored the shoulder. It was all right and they changed the bandage. Then Dr. Schultze was instructed to tell Drexler that he should represent Hitler in his absence. This information was also to be passed on to Hess, several other party leaders, and Ludendorff, if he was alive.

After the departure of the two doctors Hitler tried to reassure his hostess that her husband was safe, then fretted about what might have happened to his comrades. If he got any sleep that night it was shattered early the next morning by the deafening tintinnabulation of bells from the nearby church. It was Sunday the eleventh. Hitler did not appear until lunch. Because of the sling, he could not wear his coat and had draped Hanfstaengl's huge dark blue terry cloth bathrobe around him. It brought a smile to his gaunt face. He felt like a pseudo-Roman senator, he said, and he told Helene the story of how his father had ridiculed him as the "toga boy."

As the afternoon wore on Hitler grew restless and began pacing up and down the sitting room. He became increasingly impatient concerning the Bechstein car. Why the delay? It was only a matter of hours, perhaps minutes, he fretted, before he would be traced to Uffing. At dusk he asked Helene to close the shutters and draw the curtains, then resumed his moody pacing. Just after 5 P.M. the phone rang. It was Helene's mother-in-law, who had a villa nearby, and as the elder Frau Hanfstaengl began to relate that her house was being searched by police, she was abruptly interrupted by some official who firmly but courteously forbade her to speak. Then he spoke directly to Helene: he and his men would soon be at her villa.

She walked slowly upstairs. Hitler, still in his host's outsized bathrobe, was standing expectantly in the doorway. She quietly told him the police were coming. "He completely lost his nerve for the moment and exclaimed 'Now all is lost—no use going on!'" He snatched his revolver from a cabinet.

"What do you think you're doing?" said Helene. She grasped his hand and took the weapon from him without a struggle. "How can you give up at the first reverses?" she scolded. "Think of all your followers who believe in you, and who will lose all faith if you desert them now." She spoke calmly. "How can you leave all the people you have gotten interested in your idea of saving your country—and then take your own life?" He sank into a chair, burying head in hands. She slipped up to the next floor to hide the revolver. The first thing she saw was a large bin where she had been hoarding flour. She thrust the gun down into the snowy substance and hurried back to find Hitler in the same dejected position.

She told him that the party had to know what to do while he was in prison and offered to write down instructions to each of his closest followers. All he had to do was sign a number of blank sheets which she could fill in later and deliver to his lawyer. Hitler thanked her for helping him remember his duty and began dictating instructions. First he requested that Amann keep business matters and finances in order, then Rosenberg was to "watch over" the party newspaper and—countermanding earlier instructions to Dr. Schultze—"lead the movement from now on." Hanfstaengl was to help build up the *Völkischer Beobachter* through his foreign connections. Esser and others were to carry on the political end. After all instructions were written and signed, Helene hid the papers in the flour bin.

Moments later came the sound of cars, followed by crisp commands and, most startling of all, the yelp of police dogs. After a wait of several moments there was a knock. It was a diffident young state police lieutenant accompanied by two other officers. The lieutenant politely introduced himself and apologetically wondered if he might search the house. Helene led the officers up the stairs and opened the door to the sitting room. There stood Hitler still in pajamas and bathrobe. The unexpected apparition startled the officers and they stopped. She beckoned them on and once everyone was in the room Hitler not only regained his composure but "broke forth in a tirade against the government, its officials, raising his voice more and more." Completely shattered a moment ago, Hitler now was master of himself. Abruptly he cut himself off and curtly asked the lieutenant to waste no time. He shook hands with the young man and said he was prepared to leave.

It was bitterly cold and he had no overcoat but he refused to put on one of Hanfstaengl's outsize garments, instead draped his trench coat over the blue bathrobe. He was allowed to pin his Iron Cross on the coat. As the group started down the stairs Egon scampered into the hall. "What are you bad, bad men doing to my Uncle Dolf?" he demanded. Deeply moved, Hitler patted the little boy's cheek, silently shook hands with

Helene and the maids, then turned quickly and strode out the door. Peering out a window, Helene caught a last glimpse of him as the police vehicle turned toward Weilheim, the district seat. His face was deathly pale.

He arrived there about 9:45 P.M. and was formally arraigned at the district office before being hustled to the prison at Landsberg, some forty miles west of Munich. By this time it was raining hard and gusts of wind occasionally rocked the car. Throughout the tiring trip over winding, deserted roads Hitler was depressed and sullen. Except for a single question concerning the fate of Ludendorff (who in fact was now free after assuring authorities he was little more than an innocent bystander), he remained silent.

At Landsberg prison the chief warden was preparing for a possible attempt by Putschists to free Hitler. An army detachment was on its way to stand guard but had not arrived by the time the great nail-studded, iron entrance gate creaked open to admit Hitler. He was brought to the fortress section of the prison and put into Cell 7, the only one with an anteroom large enough for a military guard. Its former occupant, Count Arco-Valley, the assassin of Eisner, had just been transferred to another.

Hitler was left in the charge of Franz Hemmrich, who helped him undress. "He refused a bite or soup, but lay down on the cot. I went away after securely locking him in." From one lonely bunk in northern Germany where he had lain blind until a vision restored his sight, Hitler had come full circle to another in the south, with only the bare walls and ceiling for company.

When Arthur Möller van den Bruck, who had recently published *The Third Reich*, learned of the abortive Putsch he said, "There are many things that can be said against Hitler. But one thing one will always be able to say: he was a fanatic for Germany. . . . Hitler was wrecked by his proletarian primitivism. He did not understand how to give his National Socialism any intellectual basis. He was passion incarnate, but entirely without measure or sense of proportion."

Hitler was already being talked of in the past tense and it was generally agreed that he could no longer be taken seriously as a political force in Germany. He had cast the dice, lost everything. "Our history has gone astray," wrote Möller. "Nothing of ours is succeeding in the world. Nothing today; nothing yesterday. Nothing—if we think back—nothing for the last generation. . . . Our cause was still-born from the start. . . . Something has gone wrong with everything. And when we try to set anything aright, it breaks to pieces. . . . An evil spell hangs over the Reich."

But in Munich a defiant underground order of the day was already being issued to Nazis: "The first period of the national revolution is over. It has brought the desired clearing [of the air]. Our highly revered Führer, Adolf Hitler, has again bled for the German people. The most shameful treachery that the world has ever seen has victimized him and the German people. Through Hitler's blood and the steel directed against our comrades in Munich by the hands of traitors the patriotic Battle Leagues are welded together for better or worse. The second phase of the national revolution begins."

In his youth Hitler suffered two major depressions: rejection by the Vienna Academy of Art and the death of his mother. Later he underwent two more crises: the surrender of Germany while he lay gassed and the catastrophe at the Feldherrnhalle. It would take a man of extraordinary will to rise above this last shock and, profiting by his own mistakes, resume his ordained path. In the past few months Hitler, the drummer, had given way to Hitler, the Führer.

Part 3

A MIND IN THE MAKING

Chapter Seven

IN LANDSBERG PRISON
1923–1924

1

Early on the morning after Hitler's arrest, Helene Hanfstaengl received a phone call from an American correspondent, Hubert Knickerbocker. Might he come to Uffing for an interview and bring along his wife and Dorothy Thompson? Helene reluctantly agreed, then phoned her mother-in-law, whose father had been a general in the American Civil War.

> She loves, and always has loved, excitement of all sorts, and this opportunity of participation in current events was too good to let slip by. . . . So Mama had a thrillingly interesting time, asking questions, and giving her impressions of the situation. By my silence, Dorothy Thompson was probably erroneously led to believe I was the typical "German *Hausfrau*," as she described me in an article soon after.*

Afterward the party returned to the Hanfstaengl villa and, while Knickerbocker was photographing the rooms, Helene surreptitiously retrieved Hitler's revolver and papers. She stowed them in a briefcase and accompanied Knickerbocker back to Munich, where she went to see Hitler's lawyer. "These are the papers," she told him. "Pass them on and let's see what happens."

The small town of Landsberg had not changed outwardly in five hundred years. Nestling in the valley of the Lech River, it was hemmed on

---

* Helene Hanfstaengl's reticence, combined with the volubility of her mother-in-law and her sister-in-law, Erna, resulted in a distortion by several historians, who wrote that Hitler was nursed at Uffing by Hanfstaengl's mother and sister.

both sides by steep and wooded heights. A bulwark against Swabian invasion since the Middle Ages, it was surrounded by ancient walls pierced by watchtowers. To get to the prison from the Munich side, one crossed an old wooden bridge over the Lech, which was scarcely more than a gushing stream. On the hill ahead was the Gefangenenanstalt und Festungshaftanstalt Landsberg, a complex of grayish-white buildings encircled by high stone walls. The prison was divided into two sections, one for ordinary criminals and one for political prisoners.

In the Festung section the man in Cell 7 refused to eat. Hitler brooded in his room but not because of its smallness and discomfort. His room at the Männerheim had been only half the size and the room on the Thierschstrasse was far gloomier. The narrow white iron bed was comfortable by his monkish standards, and the double barred window not only flooded the room with daylight but looked out on trees and shrubbery to a far pleasanter prospect than that in Munich.

The pain in Hitler's arm was so excruciating he could get little sleep. The house doctor, Brinsteiner, had discovered that he "suffered from a dislocation of the left shoulder with a break in the upper arm and, as a result, a very painful traumatic neurosis." He remained under constant medical treatment and would, in Dr. Brinsteiner's opinion, "most likely suffer permanently a partial rigidity and pain in the left shoulder."

But it was not pain alone that accounted for his utter dejection, or even the realization that his hopes for a march on Berlin had ended in disaster. What hurt as much was the feeling that he had been betrayed—by the triumvirate, by the army, by Fate itself. Moreover, the debacle at the Feldherrnhalle was being ridiculed in the newspapers as a "miniature beer hall revolution" and a Redskin raid schoolboy-style. Foreign correspondents were describing him as "Ludendorff's noisy lieutenant," a pawn in a royalist coup d'état, and the New York *Times* printed his political obituary on the front page: "The Munich putsch definitely eliminates Hitler and his National Socialist followers." Ridicule had always cut Adolf Hitler deeply. Beatings and hunger could be endured but not derision.

Visitors were shocked by his appearance. He was thin and pale, almost unrecognizable. "I found him sitting like a frozen thing at the barred window of his cell," recalled Anton Drexler. Hitler had not tasted food for almost two weeks and the doctor warned Drexler that the prisoner would die if the fast continued. Drexler returned to Cell 7, determined to save someone he had once tried to strip of party leadership. "I said he'd no right to give up all for lost, however bad things seemed. The party would look to him to start it all up again someday. But I couldn't make any impression. He was utterly in despair. So I nearly fell into despair myself, but at last I said how we'd all rather die than go on without him." Drexler talked for an hour and forty-five minutes until finally convinced he had "won him around."

Perhaps Hitler had a relapse since several others also claimed credit for saving him from starvation. One, Hans Knirsch, the founder of the National Socialist Workers' Party in Czechoslovakia, was greeted by an emaciated and despondent Hitler. Knirsch too accused him of deserting the cause to which he had won many adherents. Without him the cause was lost and the party would disband. At first Hitler kept shaking his head but finally he "timidly asked who would continue to follow a man with such a fiasco behind him." Knirsch replied that the Putsch had, in fact, raised everyone's enthusiasm. Hitler must not lose faith in himself; most great leaders reached success over their failures. This, said Knirsch, convinced Hitler and on advice from the prison doctor he was served a bowl of rice. He ate it greedily, "then promised that he would remember Knirsch's admonitions."

It could have been Knirsch who saved Hitler, or Drexler or (so said Lüdecke) Frau Bechstein. There is even the possibility it was Helene Hanfstaengl, who wrote Hitler that she had not prevented him from committing suicide in Uffing only to let him starve himself to death in Landsberg; that this was exactly what his worst enemies prayed he was going to do. "Her advice turned the scale," according to her husband, who was hiding out in Austria. "Hitler had a great admiration for her and his whole appearance at Uffing after the Putsch must have been part of some subconscious urge to turn for succor to this woman, who corresponded so closely to his repressed yearnings. Also, amidst the annihilation of all that he had organized, the Uffing house must have acquired the aura of an extra-territorial asylum." There can be no doubt that Helene's words had a telling effect on Hitler as did the visit of Frau Bechstein, who had done so much for him. Thus he was in a mood to be moved by the words uttered by the simple Drexler, and finally convinced by the arguments of Knirsch. In any event, before Hitler agreed to take the first bite of food he was prepared to be saved, if not ready to do so on his own initiative.

Even after Hitler broke his fast he would not give evidence for his trial. At first he insisted on being questioned but as soon as interrogators arrived he refused to say a word. In desperation, the chief prosecutor dispatched his assistant, Hans Ehard, to Landsberg to "see if he would get anything out of Hitler." Ehard's efforts were as fruitless as his predecessors' but he patiently continued speaking across a table in a "friendly voice as if to a sick horse." Hitler sat in sullen silence "staring blankly like a sheep," then abruptly indicated a pile of reports on the table and sarcastically said that all those official records would certainly not "hinder my future political work!"

"Well, Herr Hitler," replied Ehard after some thought, "you're probably annoyed by the presence of a stenographer." He ordered the secretary, a prison employee, to leave and take with him the offending papers. Once they were alone, Ehard tried a new tack, pointing out that he was only doing his job. Wouldn't Hitler please discuss the matter? Taken off guard by Ehard's unofficial approach, Hitler suddenly poured out words in a torrent. He not only gave details of how the Putsch was planned and executed but why he had been forced to take such drastic action. His voice rose and his face turned bluish. It was, thought Ehard, as if he were addressing a vast audience. Occasionally the assistant prosecutor would insert a question. If it was an embarrassing one, Hitler would subside into sullen silence, almost immediately broken by another eruption of words. Ehard returned to Munich and turned over his report to his superior and to Georg Neithardt, who would be the presiding judge at the trial. The former was impressed by what he read but the latter said, "Hitler hasn't told you everything and he'll probably want to do it just at the trial." But Ehard didn't believe Hitler was saving his best arguments. He doubted that the man in Cell 7 could possibly reveal anything more than he had and then, recalling Hitler's volubility, warned the judge that such a man could not be "stifled."

The resurrection of Adolf Hitler was confirmed early the following month by his half sister Angela. She came to the prison "on a cloudy foggy December evening" expecting to find him despondent. "Never in my life will I forget this hour," she wrote their brother, Alois Hitler, Jr. "I spoke with him for half an hour. His spirit and soul were again at a high level. Physically he is quite well. His arm still gives him trouble, but they think it is almost healed. How moving is the loyalty he is accorded these days. Just before me, for example, a count visited him and brought a Christmas package from the Villa Wahnfried from B. That which he has accomplished is as solid as a rock. The goal and the victory is only a question of time. God grant it be soon." The package had come from the Wagner home in Bayreuth and several days later Winifred Wagner sent another containing a book of poetry. Frau Wagner had lost none of her faith in Hitler. "Believe me," she reportedly told one audience, "Hitler is the coming man in spite of everything, and for all that he will pull the sword out of the German oak."

His racist allies remained confident of eventual triumph and were reforming their ranks under such innocuous titles as "Völkischer Singing Club," "Völkischer Pathfinder Detachment," "League of True German Women," and "German Rifle and Hiking League." The old Battle League was also resuscitated under a new name, Frontring, by Captain Röhm, who was in Stadelheim prison with another group of Putschists; it was designed as an "umbrella organization" for all paramilitary groups recognizing the leadership of both Hitler and Ludendorff in the racist movement. Hitler disliked the idea but Röhm, still regarding himself as Corporal Hitler's superior officer, ignored his protests.

Hitler's party, although disbanded by law, began covert political operations. The underground center was Munich where Rosenberg set up a committee to continue the NSDAP. But progress was impeded by personal squabbles and ideological feuds. While Rosenberg considered himself Hitler's temporary political heir, an exiled group in Salzburg—Esser, Streicher, Amann and Hanfstaengl—regarded him as an impostor. They neither liked nor respected Rosenberg. But perhaps that was exactly why he was chosen. He was not the type to attempt to take permanent control of the party, nor did he have followers. Moreover no one else was available. Göring was also hiding in Austria, slowly recuperating from his painful wound; Scheubner-Richter was dead; Eckart, released from Landsberg, was dying in Berchtesgaden; and Drexler disapproved of the direction in which Hitler was taking the party. Of one thing Hitler could be sure: Rosenberg was loyal.

He managed to steal into Austria one night "through a forest deep with snow" to confer with the Salzburg group. "I talked to one after the other of our comrades, trying to give renewed courage and to dispel all senseless rumors." He left a few days later, skiing across the border, under the assumption that he had reassured the dissidents. They were only reinforced in the conviction that he was an incompetent and continued to make separate plans which ranged from building up the party treasury by counterfeiting or armed holdups, to crossing the border with machine guns for a raid on Landsberg prison. Nothing worked, including the dispatch of Lüdecke to the United States to get money for Hitler. "I was howled down in derision," he reported, "every time I spoke of him as a coming power."

In Munich Hitler was still taken seriously. That Christmas a group of Schwabing artists in the movement celebrated the holiday season in the Blute Café with a living tableau, "Adolf Hitler in Prison." The curtain rose on a cell. Snowflakes were falling outside a small barred window. A man sat at a desk, face buried in hands, and an invisible male chorus was singing "Silent Night, Holy Night." Then an angel placed an illuminated Christmas tree on the table. Slowly the man turned and revealed his face. "Many thought it was indeed Hitler himself," remembered Heinrich Hoffmann, who had provided the *Doppelgänger*, "and a half-sob went through the hall." When the lights went up the photographers noticed moist-eyed men and women hurriedly putting away handkerchiefs.

On New Year's Day, 1924, the financial fate of Germany was settled in London at a meeting between Hjalmar Schacht, the new Reich Commissioner for National Currency, and Montagu Norman, governor of the Bank of England. Schacht, who had already abolished emergency money, began with a frank disclosure of Germany's desperate financial situation. Once the Ruhr crisis was settled, he said, it would be "necessary to set German industry going again," and this could only be done with the assistance of foreign credit and the founding of "a second credit bank in addition to the Reichsbank, a bank based entirely on gold." He thought he could raise half of the capital for this *Golddiskontbank* in foreign currency within Germany itself. "The remaining half I should like to borrow from the Bank of England."

Norman, so wrote Schacht in a memoir characteristically entitled *The Old Wizard,* was not impressed until Schacht announced that the new bank would issue bank notes based on its gold capital of two hundred million marks. "I intend," he said, "to issue those notes in pound sterling." While Norman was silently pondering this extraordinary idea, Schacht continued: "And just think, Mr. Governor, what prospects such a measure would afford for economic collaboration between Great Britain's World Empire and Germany. If we desire to establish European peace we must free ourselves from the limitations imposed by mere conference resolutions and Declarations of Congress. Economically, the European countries must be more closely linked."

Within forty-eight hours Norman not only formally approved the loan at the exceptionally low interest of a flat five per cent but convinced a group of London bankers to accept bills far exceeding the loan, "provided they are endorsed by the Golddiskontbank." With a few bold strokes, the self-styled Old Wizard had deprived Adolf Hitler of one of his most potent political weapons—economic disaster.

2

That Hitler was physically able to stand trial was attested by the prison physician, Dr. Brinsteiner, who also stated categorically in a special report to the warden on January 8 that his patient had no symptoms of psychic disorders or psychopathic tendencies. The doctor, who seems to have had some psychiatric training, concluded that "Hitler was at all times in control of himself, and his will and his mental capacity were not impaired by any illness even if the aims and purposes of the Putsch are interpreted as being faulty."

Hitler had profited by brief imprisonment in Stadelheim prison two years earlier. Similarly the enforced confinement at Landsberg obliged him to re-evaluate his past. In the quiet of his little cell he had come to recognize some of his own mistakes. He had intended the Putsch, for example, to be the beginning of a march on Berlin and the abrupt seizure of power after Mussolini's example. "From its failure I learned the lesson that each country must evolve its own type and methods of national regeneration."

He was able to convince himself that Fate had come to his rescue in the guise of crushing defeat. "It was the greatest good fortune for us National Socialists that this Putsch collapsed," he later wrote and listed three reasons: it would have been "absolutely impossible" to co-operate with Ludendorff; the abrupt takeover of power throughout Germany would have led to the "greatest difficulties" since the party had not begun to make the proper preparations; and the "blood sacrifice" of fourteen comrades at the Feldherrnhalle eventually proved to be "the most effective propaganda for National Socialism."

In the past weeks he had done more than face facts. He had leafed through almost everything in print he could lay his hands on: Nietzsche, Chamberlain, Ranke, Trcitschke and Marx. He raced through Bismarck's memoirs and a number of recollections of the World War. "Landsberg was my college education at state expense," he told Frank—and without the "pretentious intellectualizing" of professors. "Anyway, will-power is greater than knowledge. If God had only 'known' the world and not 'willed' it, there would still be chaos today."

Hitler entered prison convinced his own destiny had turned on him but now through rationalization he had persuaded himself that it had saved him. Reaffirmation of his own and Germany's destiny came, according to Hanfstaengl, who had found it safe to return to Bavaria, that January with the death of Lenin. He went into raptures and told Hanfstaengl that history was repeating itself. In 1762 Frederick the Great (whom he hoped to emulate) had also been transported by news of Czarina Elizabeth's death. "Now is the time," he said, "when everything will be golden sunshine." The Soviet Union would succumb and the whole structure of Communism tumble down.

In ten weeks Hitler had raised himself from the depths of despair. Confident that he would be the leader of Germany, he spent long hours worrying over the nation's economic problems and even evolved (so he confided to Frank) a clever way of putting many unemployed back to work: he would construct a system of highways binding the nation closer together and would then mass-manufacture a small economical car that the little man could afford. On February 22, when he and his companions were escorted through the prison gates and driven to detention quarters in Munich, he was mentally and physically prepared for the trial that would determine his future. It would begin in four days.

By chance Frau Ebertin, who had predicted failure of his Putsch, was also in Munich writing an astrological tract. She had a new prophecy for Hitler: he would not be crushed by his humiliating defeat but rise as a phoenix. "It will turn out that recent events will not only give this [Hitler] movement inner strength, but external strength as well, so that it will give a mighty impetus to the pendulum of world history."

All Germany, if not the world, was watching Munich on the morning of February 26, for the political significance of the treason charges against Hitler, Ludendorff and eight co-defendants went far beyond their personal fate. The new republic and democracy were as much on trial as one of Germany's most respected war heroes and a fanatic from Austria.

Carin Göring wrote her mother from Innsbruck, ". . . at this very moment the trial is beginning in Munich. . . . Oh, may God help him that all may go well." The object of her concern, dressed in his best suit and wearing the Iron Cross, was seated serenely in a large classroom of an old red brick structure, the abandoned Infantry School. Hitler was prepared to do battle with spirit and determination. He wanted to be Goethe's "anvil or hammer."

General Ludendorff was the first defendant named in the accusation but it was obvious from the beginning that Hitler was to be the center of attention. He was first to be called to the stand and his opening words made it obvious that he intended to be the hammer. He had come not as defendant but as accuser. In a strong baritone voice he described to the court, much as he had to Ehard in prison, what impelled him to launch the Putsch. He spoke of the march, the bloody assault, his escape to Uffing and his admittance to Landsberg prison. He had but one regret—that he too had not suffered the same fate as his dear slaughtered comrades.

He assumed all responsibility for what had happened ("The other gentlemen have only co-operated with me") and then denied that he was a criminal. How could he be treated as one when his mission in life was to lead Germany back to honor, to its proper position in the world? The effect of his words, delivered with the conviction of the true believer, could be seen on the faces of the little presiding judge and the chief prosecutor. Neither protested Hitler's accusatory manner or attempted in any way to control his rhetoric. Nor had Assistant Prosecutor Ehard much hope that either would keep Hitler in check: Judge Neithardt, an ardent nationalist, convinced as he was that the Putsch was a "national deed," was determined to find Ludendorff innocent; and the chief prosecutor, prodded by student attacks for daring to accept his assignment, felt compelled to proceed cautiously.

If these officers of the court were under Hitler's influence, Oswald Spengler was not. In a lecture that day he ridiculed the Nazis' love of flags, parades and slogans. "These things undoubtedly satisfy feelings, but politics are something else," he said, and described the trial as that "wretched Hitler case." It only confirmed his view that Hitler was a potential Caesar.

Much of the second day was spent in tedious examinations of other defendants, but Hitler once more dominated the proceedings on February 28. In a closed session he described in extravagant terms how both Munich and Berlin had been corrupted by the Red regime. "You have one classic example here in Munich. We should never have freed ourselves from the Red era if recovery had not emanated from the healthy section of the people." His words generated a heated response and he, in turn, vociferously defended his proposed march on Berlin.

As the trial proceeded Hitler continued to dominate the judges and the courtroom with his oratory and shrewd tactics. At the same time Ludendorff had become a minor character in the drama. Moreover his resentment against the principal co-defendant was becoming obvious. "Hitler misled me," he complained to Hans Frank after the trial. "He lied to me. He told me on the evening of his mad Putsch that the army was behind it to a man. . . . He is only a speech maker and an adventurer." Perhaps he resented that the speech maker and adventurer, the despised corporal, was acting more like the traditional officer of honor than the general. While Hitler accepted responsibility Ludendorff consistently avoided it. He conducted himself with arrogance, snapping at the attorneys and judges as if it were a court-martial and he the presiding officer. He would "bark at the court in *Kommandostimme*, the tone of the parade ground," recalled an English correspondent, G. Ward Price, "every syllable clipped harsh, and when his imperious voice rose, the little Chief Justice in the middle of the Bench would quiver until his white goatee flickered so badly he had to seize it to keep it quiet."

Newspaper objections to the meek judge were growing and some foreign observers found it difficult to believe they were at a trial. On March 4 a chorus of criticism directed at Neithardt was heard in the Bavarian State Ministers' Council. State Minister Schweyer charged that the public insults heaped on the army and state police by the defendants endangered the safety of the state police itself. Another minister expressed doubts of Neithardt's ability to conduct the trial. At this point a third minister declared that the manner in which the trial was being conducted was viewed with concern in responsible circles, especially in Berlin, while a fourth revealed that he had personally censured the presiding judge for allowing Hitler to orate four hours at a stretch—and Neithardt's only reply was, "It is impossible to keep Hitler from talking."

After each day's session he would be escorted back to a cell in the same building. Here it was that two antagonists—Rosenberg and Hanfstaengl—visited him. The first brought Hitler unwelcome news: a strong segment of the party's underground movement was bent on participating in the spring elections as part of a united block of völkisch organizations. It was an attractive idea to those like Gregor Strasser, the druggist from Landshut, since it appeared to offer the party the chance to extend activities into North Germany. Strasser had convinced Rosenberg that the party should participate in national politics but Hitler derided the idea. Unification struck him as particularly dangerous at a time when the NSDAP was illegal and at the point of dissolution. Moreover, Hitler would have to delegate authority from prison and he was shrewd enough to realize that what one delegated could easily be lost. His safest course was to keep the party in a state of suspended animation until his release. Hitler's opposition took the form of sarcasm: what a comedown for the party to enter the election under the name of *Der völkischer Block!* "I told him," recalled Rosenberg, "that under the name of NSDAP preparations could not have been made in time. We simply had to wait until we could reorganize our party on a legal basis." Rosenberg left assuming he had Hitler's reluctant approval, and began paving the way for a dangerous split in the party.

Hanfstaengl's visit was social and he brought along his three-year-old son. "Now pay close attention, boy," he lectured Egon on their way to the former Infantry School building. They were going to visit Onkel Dolf in prison but someday he would be the leader of the nation and free it from its present misery. The boy envisioned Hitler sleeping on a bare earthen floor with only rats for company. But the reality was disappointing. Overlooking a garden-like back yard, Hitler's cell was very ordinary. The boy was placed on a chair in front of a table while the two men talked, but all he could remember of their spirited conversation was that Onkel Dolf's voice was so resonant that the little table vibrated. Hitler then gave the visitors tea after climbing onto a chair and fishing around on top of a huge brown wardrobe for a box of cookies.

Despite official and unofficial protests the trial continued to be a sounding board for Hitler, and he surpassed himself at the closed sessions of March 11 and 14. These were the days when the defendant was allowed by the law, unlike the English adversary system, to go on at length and freely interrogate the witnesses. And so Hitler treated the triumvirate as if they were the guilty parties. When General von Lossow took the stand Hitler jumped to his feet, shouting out questions. The towering, shaven-headed general bellowed back and pointed a long forefinger at the ex-corporal as if it were a pistol. Hitler sank back into his seat, momentarily subdued, but in a minute was on his feet again attacking the three men who had promised to join him.

General von Lossow's contemptuous declaration that Hitler was only fit to play the role of a political drummer brought such rowdy insults that the defendant was cautioned by the judge to lower his voice. He did so, but only until Lossow described him as part sentimental, part brutal. This time Hitler sprang out of his chair like a jack-in-the-box. "And where is your word of honor! Was this the sentimental and brutal Hitler?"

No, replied Lossow coolly, staring down his nose at the defendant, it was Hitler with the bad conscience. This brought a fresh barrage of insults and Lossow turned to the presiding judge. When no rebuke to Hitler was forthcoming, the general bowed and left the courtroom. Only then did Judge Neithardt tardily announce that Hitler's behavior was a personal insult not to be tolerated. "I accept the reprimand," was Hitler's ironic retort.

"I never can think without melancholy and bitterness about this monstrous trial," recalled one German journalist. "What went on there reminded me of a Munich political carnival. A court which time after time gave the accused the opportunity to make lengthy propaganda speeches; a lay judge who, after Hitler's first speech, declared (I heard it myself): 'But he's a colossal fellow, this man Hitler'; a presiding judge who let one man [Hitler] ridicule the highest officials in the Reich, as 'His Highness, Herr Fritz Ebert': . . . an officer who shouted to an American journalist who was chatting in English with a colleague, 'Speak German in my presence!'; a presiding judge who banished a newspaper cartoonist from the courtroom because one of the accused felt he had been the subject of a cartoon—doesn't all this belong in the Munich picture book of a great political carnival?"

The *Fasching* spirit continued to the end with Hitler's oratory reaching its peak in his final speech. One part lecture, another part exhortation, and a third part invective, it was always compelling and particularly effective since, under German law, the defendant had the last word. Hitler stoutly denied that he was only fit to be the drummer of the nationalist movement and that he was motivated by ambition alone. The charge that he wanted to be a minister was ridiculous. "I aimed from the first at something a thousand times higher than a minister. I wanted to become the destroyer of Marxism. I am going to achieve this task, and if I do, the title of minister will be an absurdity." Moments later Hitler revealed his innermost intention. "The man who is born to be a dictator is not compelled; he wills; he is not driven forward; he drives himself forward; there is nothing immodest about this. . . . The man who feels called upon to govern a people has no right to say: If you want me or summon me, I will cooperate. No, it is his duty to step forward."

He told the members of the court that, despite the failure of the November Putsch, they must honor him as the future power in Germany. For it was destined that the army and those who supported the ideals of the Putschists would be reconciled. "I believe that the hour will have come when the masses, who today stand on the street with our swastika banner, will unite with those who fired upon them. I believe that this blood will not always separate us. When I learned that it was the municipal police which fired, I had the happy feeling that at least it was not the Reichswehr; the army stands as untarnished as before. One day the hour will come when the army will stand at our side, officers and men."

"Herr Hitler," protested Judge Neithardt, "you say that the municipal police was stained. I cannot permit that."

Hitler ignored the gentle rebuke and without breaking his rhythm boomed out his final words: "The army which we have formed grows from day to day; from hour to hour it grows more rapidly. Even now I have the proud hope that one day the hour is coming when these raw recruits will become battalions, when the battalions will become regiments and the regiments divisions, when the old cockade will be raised from the mire, when the old banners will once again wave before us; and then reconciliation will come in that eternal last Court of Judgment—the Court of God—before which we are ready to take our stand. Then from our bones, from our graves will sound the voice of that tribunal which alone has the right to sit in judgment upon us. For, gentlemen, it is not you who pronounce judgment upon us, it is the eternal court of history which will make its pronouncement upon the charge which is brought against us."

Hitler won the battle of words and when the court retired to consider the verdict a number of observers were convinced he would be found not guilty. Judge Neithardt was bent on acquitting Ludendorff regardless of the testimony and the three lay judges, including one who had peered grimly at Hitler throughout the trial, were also unanimously for freeing the chief defendant. "On the evidence of my defense," Hitler commented long after the trial, "they were convinced that Kahr, Lossow and Seisser must have been equally guilty. They were informed of the objection that an acquittal might entail the risk of having the affair referred to the court at Leipzig. This made the jury reflect. They decided it was more prudent to have me found guilty, the more so as they had been promised a remission of the sentence after six months."

When Assistant Prosecutor Ehard arrived on April 1 for the sentence announcement he found the room crowded with women bearing flowers for their idol. He ordered the flowers removed. Other female adherents asked permission to take a bath in Hitler's tub. He denied the request. Just after 10 A.M. the defendants posed for a picture in front of the building. Ludendorff, in full military dress complete with pointed helmet, scowled. To his left stood Hitler in unbelted trench coat so neatly cleaned and pressed it looked new, clutching a velours hat in right hand. His mustache was neatly clipped, his hair slicked down, and he looked as calm, assured and well fed as a successful businessman. For the first time in his life he was on the paunchy side—170 pounds.

By the time the accused were escorted to the courtroom, a large crowd clustered outside the building. It took almost an hour to read out the sentence and there was no outburst when Hitler (along with Pöhner, Kriebel and Weber) was sentenced to five years in Landsberg prison. Six months were deducted because of the pretrial detention. As predicted, Ludendorff was set free. Once more he answered the consideration shown his rank by petulance. "I look upon this acquittal as a disgrace which my dress of honor and my decorations have not earned," said the man who had denied responsibility for the Putsch. His heated protest annoyed and embarrassed presiding Judge Neithardt, who was most responsible for the acquittal.

Even in guilt Hitler was honored by the court. It refused to deport him to Austria as an undesirable alien. "Hitler is German-Austrian. In the opinion of the court a man who thinks and feels as German as Hitler, a man who voluntarily served 4½ years in the German army during the war, who earned high war decorations for bravery in the face of the enemy, who was wounded and whose health was impaired . . . should not be subjected to the Republic Protection Law." The court saved its scorn for Hitler's three enemies, declaring that the tragedy could have been prevented if Kahr, Lossow and Seisser "had clearly said 'no' to Hitler's demands for participation [in the Putsch] or if the repeated attempts by the accused on the night of November 8 to clarify the situation had met with a measure of cooperation."

Hitler's sentence was the first announced. While the others were being read out, he was hurried outside to a waiting car to prevent any demonstration. By late afternoon Hitler was back in Cell 7. It had been refurnished in his absence and looked much more inviting. But his earlier confidence was gone and jailer Franz Hemmrich noticed that he "looked more wretched than ever." This depression soon passed. Before long he opened his leather briefcase and brought out an empty diary. On the frontispiece in the upper right-hand corner he wrote: "Motto: When a world comes to an end, then entire parts of the earth can be convulsed, but not the belief in a just cause." Below this he inscribed these words:

The trial of common narrow-mindedness and personal spite is over—and today starts

MY STRUGGLE (Mein Kampf)

Landsberg on 1 April
1924

The trial that only the Putschists wanted was over and, although Hitler had won the battle of propaganda, he was back in prison. For all he knew, he would remain there four and a half years. To a large segment of the German public and to the Western world in general, the sentence was ridiculously mild for treason and armed uprising. "The trial," commented the London *Times*, "has at any rate proved that a plot against the Constitution of the Reich is not considered a serious crime in Bavaria."

3

Hitler had two comrades on the upper floor of the Festung. Colonel Kriebel was in Cell 8 and the leader of the Bund Oberland, Dr. Weber the veterinary, was in number 9. Although Hitler complained daily about the barred windows, life at the fortress was passable. At 6 A.M. the two night warders went off duty and the cell doors would be opened. Invariably Hitler was dressed, washed and waiting ("He took a good deal of care of his teeth and mouth. That came of his having been gassed in the war"). An hour later convict trustees served the political prisoners a breakfast of coffee and bread or porridge in their common room. At eight the doors to the court and garden were opened and the men were allowed to wrestle, box or exercise on the parallel bars and vaulting horse. Because of his injured arm Hitler "had to content himself with the job of referee."

After half an hour the prisoners strolled in the long narrow garden, bordered on one side by the prison building and the other by a twenty-foot wall. A gravel path was Hitler's favorite promenade and here he would stroll back and forth, usually with Emil Maurice, his chauffeur, voicing the political theorems he had jotted down in his diary. "Sometimes," recalled Hemmrich, "those who had formerly belonged to the Storm Troops would start singing party songs as they stamped along. At first we took no notice, or at least we raised no objection to this, but when the convicts on their side took to yelling in unison and disturbed the peace of the whole neighborhood, we put a stop to it."

At about 10 A.M. the men were brought in from their exercise and mail was distributed. Numerous food packages arrived from nationalist organizations and private admirers. Hitler particularly looked forward to poppy seed strudel, an Austrian specialty, which a group of National Socialist women brought every Friday. But, recalled Dr. Weber, the Chief gave the bacon, sausage and ham to his companions, preferably those on the ground floor. "Upstairs with him were the elite. Yes, even behind the wall there existed a class system. They were not equal before the law, nor were they equal as prisoners."

Just before noon the political prisoners were served dinner—usually a one-pot meal—in the common room. The others waited behind their chairs until Hitler strode in, then someone called out, "Attention!" He stood at the head of the table "until every man in turn came forward with his table-greeting." Politics was rarely discussed. Hitler usually chatted about theater, art or automobiles. After the meal they would smoke and gossip for a quarter of an hour while the table was cleared, and then the Chief would retreat to his cell on the top floor to read, write in his diary or try to catch up on his correspondence. This period was interrupted at about four o'clock for tea or coffee, which was brewed in the common room. At four forty-five the gates to the garden were unlocked again and Hitler would walk alone, or with Maurice, for more than an hour. At six each man had supper in his own cell—a herring or sausage and salad. Those who wanted could buy half a liter of beer or wine. After another hour of sport or exercise the men assembled in the common room before returning to their cells. At ten lights went out.

Occasionally Hitler varied his schedule, retreating to his cell as soon as breakfast was over to study or receive visitors. According to Hemmrich, who soon became his enthusiastic admirer, he exercised a great influence over his comrades. Because of his "sense of soldierly discipline," there were none of the usual outbursts of temper of men penned up together. "He was always at their command to be of help or service."

Usually he was "singularly cheerful" but bad news made him "a trifle thoughtful and anxious." He was particularly disturbed by the rancor of party feuds. It was becoming increasingly obvious that the NSDAP was being split in two and that the schism was due in large part to his own vague instructions to his proxy. Rosenberg had joined with Strasser and others to support the völkisch bloc in the Bavarian state elections; more significant, these two, with the help of Ludendorff, had not only formed the National Socialist Freedom Movement but entered a slate of thirty-four candidates in the national elections.

The Bavarian election came first, in April, and the ill-assorted völkisch bloc scored an unexpected triumph, winning 191,862 votes, and finished second to the Bavarian People's Party. The Görings were delighted with the triumph. "Also," Carin wrote her father from Austria, "it means pardon for all of us living in foreign countries. I really can't believe it I'm so happy. It has been a very bad time. In North Germany we are counting on even more votes for Hitler and his movement, and then Hitler can at last come into power. You see, dear Father, I believe so much in him! He is a wonderful man, a genius, such a one, I am convinced, as God seldom gives to the world."

The national election a month later proved to be as successful as predicted, with the newly formed National Socialist Freedom Movement polling almost two million votes. Thirty-two of the thirty-four candidates —including Strasser, Röhm, Feder, Frick and Ludendorff—were elected. It was ironic that Hitler, who had opposed the basic idea, was responsible in large part for their victory. His oratory at the trial had introduced National Socialism to many voters who were impressed by its leader's forceful manner and his effectively enunciated ideas. But other more profound and lasting forces also contributed to the triumph. The tandem appeal of patriotism and racism was growing throughout the nation. Moreover, even though inflation had been ended by the drastic national currency reform, those in the middle class who had lost homes and property were expressing displeasure at the polls along with those in the working class who were still unemployed.

Understandably, Hitler was not overjoyed by the elections. Ludendorff was claiming credit for the victory and, being free, was in a position to capitalize on his claim. Hitler was forced to join in the applause while fearing that the new group might swallow up his outlawed party. Nor was his apprehension groundless. The threat to his political power was illustrated by circulation of a pamphlet to völkisch groups which admitted that the National Socialists were "pioneers and forerunners" of the völkisch movement, then sarcastically declared that "they are not [its] savior." The whole affair was a painful but valuable lesson to Hitler. Never again, he vowed, would he take a stand unless he was sure he had the power to enforce it.

Hitler was being attacked from his own stronghold. At the offices of the *Völkischer Beobachter*, which had been closed down after the Putsch, Drexler and Feder were conducting a campaign against him. "They called Hitler a dictator and a prima donna and proclaimed that he must be brought under greater control if the party was ever to be built up again," recalled Hanfstaengl. One day Drexler cornered Hans Frank in a small Munich park and poured out a stream of complaints against their imprisoned leader. "He intrigued against me and broke all his promises, pushed me out, and now has wrecked the party for all time with this crazy Putsch!" Once Hitler was free the rowdy Brownshirts would take to the streets again. "There are terrible times ahead for Germany. Hitler betrayed me and that is why I oppose him wherever I can."

That May Kurt Lüdecke returned from his money-raising trip abroad to find confusion in the ranks of the underground NSDAP. "The various groups quarreled internally and with each other. Nor were their antagonisms private scandals—enemies clawed each other in public regardless both of the spectacle they were giving the shocked onlookers and of the damage they were doing to themselves." From Hanfstaengl, Amann and Esser he learned that Rosenberg was the cause of party deterioration. But Rosenberg told him a different story. "They attack me," he said, "because I represent Hitler, whom they dare not attack, helpless though he is. If they eliminate me, they move one step nearer the top."

Lüdecke decided to travel to Landsberg to find out from Hitler how the danger could best be dispelled. According to Lüdecke's account, Hitler declared that the party must pursue a new line of action. Its future lay not in armed coups but the ballot box. "I am convinced this is our best line of action, now that conditions in the country have changed so radically." Hitler appeared to be not at all downcast by the party squabbles. "Indeed, he was so confident of final victory that my own misgivings were dispelled, for his mood was contagious." But the party split continued to widen. A few weeks later Strasser joined with Ludendorff in proposing the foundation of the National Socialist Freedom Party, thus creating a single völkisch party of which the NSDAP would be but a part. This raised the intensity of interparty rancor which, in turn, forced Hitler into making a radical decision. On July 7 *Der Völkische Kurier* announced that he had "laid down the leadership of the National Socialist movement, and that he will refrain from all political activity during his term of detention. He requested his adherents not to visit him in prison since he had so much work and was also engaged in writing a book."

In some circles it was deduced that Hitler was pretending to write as an excuse to avoid the internecine political battle. But even before his arrest he had been seriously thinking of composing a history of the Jews. Now he had a better idea, which obsessed him to such a degree that he welcomed a vacation from politics so he could get it down on paper. In addition to jotting down ideas in his diary, he dictated to Maurice. Then, in the privacy of his cell, he would laboriously type out the manuscript with two fingers on the typewriter loaned to him by the warden.

Guard Hemmrich recalled: "As he finished one section of the book after another he would read it aloud to the others in their evening assemblies." The book was not always written under favorable conditions. The window, for instance, leaked during a heavy rain. One day while mopping the floor Hitler burst into laughter. There was the prison cat "perched on top of a stool in the middle of the mess and puddle and licking at it after her own finicky fashion." His most helpful assistant was a newcomer to the top floor. After Hitler's sentence Rudolf Hess had taken Professor Haushofer's advice to surrender. Hess helped Hitler formulate ideas, took dictation and relieved him of typing chores. Frau Wagner also helped by providing quantities of bond paper, carbon paper, pencils, ink and erasers.

At first the book was to have been a general history but the first volume—under the ponderous working title *Four and a Half Years of Struggle Against Lies, Stupidity and Cowardice*—now included an autobiographical account of Hitler's childhood, his years in Vienna, the war, the Red revolution and the beginnings of the party in Munich. It turned out to be the story of a poor boy's political education and gave him the opportunity to discourse not only on his three favorite subjects—Jews, Marxism and racism—but the futility of parliamentary government, syphilis, the decline of the theater, the monarchy, and responsibility for loss of the war.

Writing down his political theories was in itself a process of self-education. "During my imprisonment I had time to provide my philosophy with a natural, historical foundation." The authorities had made a mistake by imprisoning him. "They would have been far wiser to let me make speeches all the time, without giving me respite!"

It was remarkable how Hitler had gained ascendancy over his jailers. He had already converted a majority of the staff to National Socialism and even the warden became so impressed that he permitted Hitler's lights to stay on until midnight. Surveillance was so lax that the prisoners established their own underground newspaper, which was typed and then hectographed. One section was comic, the other serious. Hitler usually wrote the leading article and would often contribute caricatures. The existence of the paper was not discovered until one man thoughtlessly wrote home about it but by the time Hemmrich raided the editorial office in Cell 1 nothing could be found.

It was also Hemmrich's duty to spy on the evening get-togethers in the common room to make sure no revolution was being plotted. But the eavesdropper became propagandized by Hitler's words and soon fell almost completely under his spell. He and his assistants would gather outside the door "all ears, alert for what he was saying about things that concerned our own interests. We were immensely struck by his speaking."

Hitler would close these meetings with a Sieg Heil! and the group would burst out into a revised version of the song composed by Gregor Strasser's group on the day of the Putsch.

> *Even if they betrayed us*
> *Or herded us like mistreated animals,*
> *We knew what we were doing,*
> *And remained true to the Fatherland.*
> *Hitler's spirit in our hearts*
> *Cannot sink,*
> *Cannot sink.*
> *Storm Troop Hitler*
> *Will someday rise again.*

As Hitler became more involved in his book he left his men to their own devices. Out of boredom one evening a dozen of them subjected him to an old-fashioned peasant hazing. They smeared their faces with oven rust and black, wrapped themselves in sheets and marched to Cell 7 armed with pokers and brooms. Brandishing their weapons, they demanded that he subject himself to their tribunal. What followed was a parody of the Munich trial, Bavarian comedy style. Hitler, so wrote Hemmrich, joined in the fun and solemnly accepted his sentence, an auto tour of Germany, then "laughing still but shaking his head, went back to work."

Hanfstaengl, one of the less reverent visitors, noticed that Hitler was gaining weight and advised him to take part in prison sports and cut down on sweets. Hitler had an answer for each admonition: "A leader cannot afford to be beaten at games" and "I shall always be able to get the extra pounds off by speaking." Hanfstaengl brought him several art books but it was a recent copy of the satirical weekly *Simplicissimus* that did most to cheer him up. On the front page was a cartoon showing Hitler in armor entering Berlin on a white horse as if he were Sir Galahad. "There you are," he said, "they can laugh but I shall get there yet!"

He received many ladies, including a monthly visit from eighty-three-year-old Frau Carola Hoffmann (no relation to the photographer), whom he called "my beloved and devoted *Mütterchen*." Still pretty and petite, she was a retired schoolteacher who had taken it upon herself the past few years to do his laundry and see that he was properly dressed. She fed him on cakes and cream and, like a good mother, made him pay for the sweets with lectures on how to behave in polite society. Once Carin Göring came for financial assistance but had to be satisfied with a picture of the Führer inscribed "To the honored wife of my SA Commander."

Ilse Pröhl, the fiancée of Hess, was a regular visitor. Every Saturday she bicycled to Landsberg from Munich and one time managed to smuggle in a camera. Hitler and Hess would be waiting for her on top of the Festung staircase and the former invariably kissed her hand in his gallant Viennese manner before leading her to the common room for lunch. Once she came by train with her mother, who was not too fond of Hess, particularly now that he was a prisoner. But a kiss from Hitler changed all that. "My mother was totally unpolitical but as soon as she got back to Munich she joined the party—all because of that hand-kiss."

Professor Haushofer also visited Hess to bring him books and articles on political science and geopolitics, including works by Sir Halford Mackinder. He sometimes saw Hitler but never alone. "I avoided it," he later testified. "I always had the feeling that he felt the distrust of a semi-educated person towards a scientifically educated person." Perhaps it sprang from Haushofer's expressed hope that Hess would continue his academic career and not enter political life, or the fact that the professor openly described the Putsch as a tragic mistake. He was aware that Hitler was writing his political autobiography and that he had discussed Lebensraum and geopolitics with Hess "but I received the impression, and I am utterly convinced, that Hitler never understood these things and did not have the right outlook for understanding them." Realizing that neither Hess nor Hitler understood political geography, Haushofer tried to explain the basis, for example, of the second edition of Ratzel's work. But it was useless. Hitler took from geopolitics only what he wanted.

While Hess still revered the professor, he had already decided to become Hitler's personal secretary and devote his life to National Socialism. By now he was the Chief's closest confidant and, from this position of trust, he confirmed not only Hitler's genuine disgust with the wrangles disrupting the party but his preoccupation with the book. On July 16 Hess wrote a university friend that Herr Hitler wanted to know nothing of present-day politics. "For the time being he has withdrawn himself publicly from the leadership [of the party]. The reason is that he does not want to assume the responsibility for what happens outside without his knowledge, and possibly against his better judgment. Nor is he able to smooth out the constant quarrels, at least not from here. He considers it unnecessary to bother with such petty disagreements. On the other hand, he is convinced that once he obtains his freedom, he can steer everything back on the right track."

Determined opposition to the völkisch merger came from left-wing Nazis in North Germany who denounced the racists as "enemies" of the working class. Collaboration with them, warned one student leader, would force "the true National Socialists, especially the workers," to leave the NSDAP. While these northern leftists agreed with Esser on the impossibility of merger, they wanted no part of him and, two days after the Weimar meeting, one of them wrote a letter obviously intended for the Führer's eyes. It expressed a desire for Hitler to come to the north once he left prison but to leave Hermann Esser behind. Such men would not be tolerated in the north. "We will not build a Chinese Wall around Hitler as was done in Munich in 1923. Here live men of northern blood who refute spiritual servitude, who are not cowardly. We are not speakers and mercenaries . . . but only men who ask for contact with the Führer . . . men who want to serve the cause."

The rising crescendo of disagreement among these in basic agreement reinforced Hitler's decision to stay out of politics and on July 29 he sent another appeal for privacy to *Der Völkische Kurier*. "Since I am presently engaged in a work which must not be disturbed" he would from now on refuse all interviews not confirmed in writing. Wearied as he was of politics and visitors, he did take time that day to see a German-Bohemian party member, N. S. Kugler, who asked a crucial question: "Has your position on the Jewish question been somewhat changed?" This was one subject near his heart. "Yes, yes," he told Kugler, "it is quite correct that I have changed my opinion concerning the methods of fighting Jewry. I have come to the realization that I have been far too soft up to now! While working on my book, I have finally come to realize that the harshest methods of fighting must be employed in the future if we are to win. I am convinced that this is not only a matter of life and death for our people but for all peoples. The Jew is a world pest."

4

Throughout the summer Hitler luxuriated in his pleasant quarters, preparing himself for the battle to come. He confined most of his efforts to the book, secure in the expectation of an early parole. It seemed to be assured on September 18 when Warden Leybold dispatched an extremely favorable report to the Bavarian Ministry of Justice. It declared that during his months of imprisonment Hitler had "proved himself to be a man of strict discipline and order," who was "at all times co-operative, modest and courteous to everyone, particularly to the officials of the institution." Leybold concluded with a prediction that Hitler, upon release, would not resort to any violence or illegality. "There is no doubt that he has become a much more quiet, more mature and thoughtful individual during his imprisonment than he was before and does not contemplate acting against existing authority."

At first it seemed certain that Leybold's strong recommendation would bring about Hitler's release in early fall, but on September 22 the Bavarian state police sent a confidential report to the Ministry of the Interior recommending that Hitler not be released on October 1; and if this came about "unexpectedly" he should be deported as a security measure. The moment he was set free, Hitler would generate riots "because of his energy." Penal Chamber I ignored this recommendation and declared Hitler eligible for parole but an appeal from the Minister of Justice on the grounds that the prisoner had flagrantly violated visiting privileges was upheld. Parole was denied.

Hitler's frustration was complete but, as he had done before, he lifted himself out of this depression and returned to work on his book. "All day long," recalled Hemmrich, "and late into the night one could hear the typewriter going in his room, and his voice dictating to Hess." Nor did he neglect his duty as Führer. On the first anniversary of the Munich Putsch he spoke "with deep emotion" to the political prisoners gathered in the common room. While charging himself "with the entire responsibility for the whole affair," he demonstrated how it had failed for historical reasons. "His hearers were profoundly impressed with the Leader's sincerity and deep morality."

November passed and though there was still no indication that parole was at hand, he remained stoic.

In the meantime one of his most prestigious followers, Göring, was in a Venice hotel attempting to negotiate a badly needed loan from Benito Mussolini. Although still recuperating from his painful wound, which required heavy drug dosage, the former war ace was exerting himself in the Führer's service. He was involved in a frustrating correspondence with Leo Negrelli, an agent of Mussolini, in hopes of getting two million lire from the Fascists as well as a promise from Il Duce to see Hitler once he was out of prison. In return the National Socialists would publicly support Italy's claim to the South Tyrol—an action that would lose numerous supporters, particularly in Bavaria.

But apparently the Fascists doubted they would get their money's worth from a party whose attempt to emulate the March on Rome had ended so disastrously, and Göring's pleading became shrill. "The Fascists were at one time small and laughed at," he argued.* "One should not believe that National Socialists have no future." In a few years they would be in power. He enlarged upon the embarrassment the NSDAP would

---

* The 1924–25 correspondence between Göring and Negrelli was recently discovered and translated by Ben E. Swearingen. It sheds new light on this hitherto obscure period of Göring's career, as well as giving new information on the early Nazi-Fascist relationship.

face because of its support of such an unpopular cause as the South Tyrol; and pointed out what a bargain Mussolini was getting for a mere two million lire. "For this you would have in our press an important speaking-trumpet. Besides you will get your two million back at the *latest* in five years."

A few days later Göring became more insistent. "It would really be good if the greatest national movements would have more understanding of each other. . . . Anti-Semitism must in a certain sense be international. The Jew must be fought in all countries."

But the month of November slipped by with Mussolini still refusing to commit himself (nor is it likely that he ever did loan the two million lire) and the Führer still in prison. A few of his comrades were released by mid-December. "Hitler bore these repeated disappointments about his own return to freedom with equanimity and philosophy," remembered Hemmrich. "The remainder prepared to celebrate the season at Landsberg as best as they could." They put up holiday decorations and set up a Christmas tree in the common room. But before they could decorate it the efforts of the state cabinet to prevent Hitler's parole finally ended. On December 19 the Bavarian Supreme Court—perhaps influenced by a threat from the three lay judges of the Hitler trial to make a public appeal —ordered his immediate release.

Warden Leybold himself brought the news to Hitler, and early the following afternoon, after spending more than a year in prison, Hitler bade farewell to his comrades, gave them all his money (282 marks), then shook hands with Hemmrich and thanked him for all he had done. There followed a tearful parting with Leybold. "When I left Landsberg," recalled Hitler, "everyone wept (the warden and the other members of the prison staff)—but not I! We'd won them all to our cause."

It was a raw, gray day. Hitler tersely greeted the two who had come to take him home, his printer, Adolf Müller, and Hoffmann, the photographer, before stepping briskly into the touring car, its canvas top raised as protection against the cold. He turned to Hoffmann, who had not been allowed to take photographs in the prison, and told him to get his picture. After one was taken at the ancient city gate, which had a fortress atmosphere, Hoffmann wanted to know what Hitler intended to do now. "I shall start again, from the beginning," he said. As they sped toward Munich Hitler reveled in the experience. ("What a joy it was for me to be in a car again!") He asked Müller to go faster. "No," was the reply. "It's my firm intention to go on living for another twenty-five years."

At Pasing they were met by a group of Nazi motorcyclists who accompanied them into the city. Party faithfuls were waiting outside his apartment house. At the top of the stairs, Hitler was almost bowled over by his exuberant dog. He found his room filled with flowers and laurel wreaths. Neighbors had covered the table with food and drink, including a bottle of wine. Prison had not marked him with self-pity. Far from regretting his months in Landsberg, he professed they had been essential for his development. "That period gave me the chance of deepening various notions for which I then had only an instinctive feeling. It was during this incarceration, too, that I acquired that fearless faith, that optimism, that confidence in our destiny, which nothing could shake thereafter."

Hitler left Landsberg hardened by adversity, more settled in his own convictions. Unabashed by the party feuds and the apparent blighting of his political ambitions, he had returned to Munich determined to take a new political road. Never again would he make the old mistakes. He had been a Führer in name only, serving a party that had been founded by others. From now on he would be a true Führer, shaping his own program in his own way toward long-range goals.

His first task was to assess the political situation. The National Socialist bloc had lost more than half its seats in the December elections with the popular vote slipping from 1,918,300 to 907,300. Moreover the NSDAP itself was still illegal and he would have to operate underground. On the positive side, he was not only free but deportation proceedings against him had been quashed by the man who had recently fought his parole; Justice Minister Gürtner had undoubtedly been influenced by Austrian refusal to take Hitler back. He had come out of prison as a martyred saint to all völkisch groups, and this racist movement, despite the evidence of the December elections, was burgeoning. This growth, ironically, had been unleashed by the Putsch; many people who had wavered between the moderate and radical wings of the patriotic movement swung to extremism as a result of their emotional involvement in the abortive uprising.

In a sense the NSDAP had a stronger base than ever and, while its two warring groups were wide apart, Hitler was confident he could somehow induce both factions to place loyalty to him above their differences. He was to be the program and his followers would have to equate völkisch aims with his personal political success. The image of Adolf Hitler, the national martyr, would become the personalization of flag, freedom and racial purity.

What had been thought out carefully in the peace and solitude of his cell was quite another thing in the unaccustomed freedom of Munich. On that first evening of liberty he didn't know what to do with himself. "I had the impression that any moment a hand would be laid on my shoulder, and I remained obsessed by the idea that I'd have to ask leave for anything I wanted to do!" Shrewd enough to realize that only time would enable him to regain "contact with reality," he decided to remain quiet for several weeks before embarking on the task of "reconciling the enemy brothers."

One of the first steps in his project to regain civilian composure was a visit to the Hanfstaengls on a snowy Christmas Eve. They had moved from their cramped apartment to a spacious house across the Isar River, a pleasant sector near Herzog Park boasting such prestigious neighbors as Thomas Mann. As Hitler entered the studio he looked around nervously, then said, almost pleadingly, "Hanfstaengl, play me the 'Liebestod.'" After Hanfstaengl "hammered out this tremendous thing from *Tristan and Isolde,* with Lisztian embellishments," Hitler began to relax. Helene brought in her new daughter, Herta. Hitler crooned over the baby and apologized for what had happened at Uffing. "You are the most feudal acquaintances I have," he finally said, surveying the studio. Suddenly, in mid-sentence, he darted a glance over his shoulder. "I'm sorry," he explained, "that's what jail does to you. There is always some damn jailer standing behind watching you." In Landsberg, he explained, someone was constantly observing him through the observation hole in the door. "A horrible feeling, that! I am certain they were seeking for some pretext to have me transferred to an insane asylum. You know I went on a hunger strike for two weeks and they tried to make that grounds for an insanity charge." (Perhaps that was why he ended his fast.)

After dinner and the presentation of gifts that lay under the candlelit Christmas tree, Helene, Hitler and four-year-old Egon settled around the piano while Hanfstaengl played piece after piece on the Steinway. A military march seemed to inspire Hitler to stride up and down the room like a soldier, hands clasped behind his back, recalling scenes from the Great War. For the benefit of Egon, he began imitating a battle, reproducing the noise of howitzers, 75s and machine guns, separately and all at once.

This was followed by a lecture on politics which evolved into a tirade against the Jews. His anti-Semitism, thought Hanfstaengl, seemed to have acquired more specific racial undertones; he had become convinced that Wall Street and, in fact, all America was controlled by the Jews. Then his thoughts—and words—abruptly turned to his dearest friend in Landsberg. "*Ach, mein Rudi, mein Hesserl,*" Hitler exclaimed emotionally. "Isn't it appalling to think he's still there!"

Before he left, Hitler managed to have a few moments of privacy with Helene in the studio. She was seated on a large sofa and all at once he dropped to his knees and put his head in her lap. "If only I had someone to take care of me," he said.

"Look, this won't do," said Helene and asked him why he didn't get married. "I can never marry because my life is dedicated to my country." She thought he was acting like a little boy, and perhaps he was. Seventeen years ago, almost to the day, his mother had died. "It would have been awful if someone had come in," recalled Helene. "Humiliating to him. He was taking a chance, he really was. That was the end of it and I passed it off as if it simply had not happened."

Chapter Eight

HITLER'S SECRET BOOK
1925–1928

1

Hitler was invited to spend New Year's Eve at Hoffmann's home. He refused but when the party was under way a girl urged the photographer to phone the Führer and try again. To Hoffmann's surprise Hitler said he would come "but only for half an hour." His arrival was eagerly awaited, particularly by the ladies, none of whom had met him. Nor were they disappointed. "In his cutaway coat he looked very smart," wrote Hoffmann. "He had not yet started to wear the lock of hair hanging from his forehead, and his air of modest reserve only served to enhance his charm." The women were particularly entranced by his little mustache.

One pretty girl maneuvered Hitler under the mistletoe and kissed him. "I shall never forget the look of astonishment and horror on Hitler's face! The wicked siren, too, felt that she had committed a faux pas, and an uncomfortable silence reigned. Bewildered and helpless as a child, Hitler stood there, biting his lip in an effort to master his anger. The atmosphere, which after his arrival had shown a tendency to become more formal, now became almost glacial." Hoffmann tried to laugh it off. "I'm glad that it didn't happen to one of the more elderly among my guests. But then, you've always had luck with the ladies, Herr Hitler!" Not amused, the Führer bade everyone a polite, cool farewell.

Ever since release from Landsberg, he had lived in semisolitude. He was finding it difficult to adjust politically as well as socially. Determined to confine his activities to behind-the-scenes discussions with Esser and

Pöhner, he refused to reveal his new plans and put off worshipful delegations who sought his advice and blessing. At the same time he did not make the mistake of discouraging the adulation of rank-and-file followers, and his silence made them more eager than ever to hear his first speech.

Hitler needed this concentrated solitude to become familiar with recent drastic political and economic developments. The regime in France which had been demanding occupation of the Ruhr had been replaced by a more conciliatory group, and a more equitable payment by Germany of war reparations had been recently instituted by the Allies. On the economic front the establishment of a stable mark had stemmed the toboggan slide to economic chaos. The dual prospect of a peaceable settlement with France and economic recovery meant that Hitler had been deprived of political assets.

On the other hand, a social change had come about which now offered him the chance to re-enter politics on a national scale. Rapid technical developments, urbanization, dispersal of the population and the industrialization of the past decade had upended the middle class. The small merchant, the independent businessman and the farmer were in a state of uncertainty and fear. It was the middle class that had suffered most during the inflation. The margin of affluence which had set these people above the working class had been wiped out along with their savings and capital. Many blamed their misfortunes on the Reds and Jews and their bitterness was already turning into hatred, making them receptive to Hitler's message of anti-Semitism.

The new year presented as many opportunities as difficulties and his political future would depend on ability to cope with both. He made his first move on the fourth day of 1925 in the form of a gesture of truce to the new Minister President of Bavaria, Heinrich Held. He spent half an hour alone with Held, pledging his loyalty and offering to co-operate in the fight against the Reds. He promised to confine himself to legal means in his future political struggles and made such a favorable impression that Held reportedly remarked that evening, "This wild beast is checked. We can afford to loosen the chain."

Alfred Rosenberg was not one of the few admitted to Hitler's company in these days of seclusion and preparation. He knew that Hitler was driving around the countryside with Esser, Amann, Hoffmann and Hanfstaengl and he was irked at being excluded from this select company. "He valued me very much, but he did not like me," Rosenberg later complained. Piqued as well as concerned about the party split, Rosenberg persuaded his friend Lüdecke to write an article warning that the party was doomed unless its members stopped sniping at each other.

After sending a copy of this article to Hitler, Lüdecke requested an interview. It took place at the little room on the Thierschstrasse and, after attacking Ludendorff and delivering a lecture on the Jews, Hitler finally got around to the article. Lüdecke, he said, could not possibly know the real facts of the Putsch or the trial since he'd been out of the country. He derided Rosenberg's attempt to separate him from Esser ("That fellow has more political sense in his fingertips than the whole bunch of his accusers in their buttocks"), then sarcastically advised Lüdecke to see that Rosenberg "comes to his senses and stops playing the offended innocent."

Although Hitler seemed to be rejecting Lüdecke's counsel to end party squabbles, he took it—intending to effect it in his own way. This decision to heal party wounds, combined with his promises to Minister President Held, soon bore fruit. On February 16 the Bavarian government canceled the state of emergency and removed its restrictions on the NSDAP. Ten days later the *Völkischer Beobachter* was back on the stands with a lengthy editorial by Hitler entitled "A New Beginning." He promised to confine himself henceforth to organization and policy, not personal and religious differences, and called for peace among all völkisch elements within the party. They must unite, he said, to defeat the common enemy, Jewish Marxism. It was the new Adolf Hitler in action, determined to operate legally and willing to compromise for the sake of a party unity. At the same time he was going to run the party *his* way, and despite a pledge to work within the governmental framework, he had not tempered his attack on his primal enemy—the Jew.

On the following day, February 27, Hitler made his eagerly awaited return to public life at a party convention in the Bürgerbräukeller where he had launched the Putsch. His speech was scheduled to begin at 8 P.M. but at midafternoon lines were already forming in front of the beer hall. By the time the police closed the doors at 6 P.M. the large hall was jammed with 4000 people. Another thousand were turned away. National Socialists from all over the nation were on hand—with three important exceptions: Röhm, Strasser and Rosenberg. "I won't take part in that comedy," the latter told Lüdecke that afternoon. "I know the sort of brother-kissing Hitler intends to call for." Rosenberg was proud and refused to shake hands with a man he felt had forsaken him.

There was almost as much excitement in the hall as there had been on the night of the Putsch, and as Hitler marched down the aisle wildly enthusiastic adherents waved beer mugs, cheered and hugged each other. Lifting his eyes above the party leaders, he appealed to the multitude beyond. While his words were fervent, they were not designed to antagonize either faction. He didn't make the mistake of going into the details of the squabbles of 1924; he ignored them. He called Ludendorff "the most loyal and selfless friend" of the movement and urged all those who "in their hearts remained old National Socialists" to join together behind the swastika flag and crush their two greatest enemies: Marxism and Jews. The first was an appeal to revolutionaries like Esser, the second to Drexler and his more conservative völkisch followers.

After an inspirational appeal for national regeneration ("It is madness to believe that a great people of sixty or seventy million cannot be destroyed. It perishes as soon as it loses its drive for self-preservation") he turned his attention to the party officials at the front tables. He neither asked for their loyalty and support nor offered any compromise. He ordered them to join the crusade or get out. "If anyone comes and puts conditions to me, then I say to him: 'My friend, wait and see what conditions I will put to you.' I am not out to get the great masses. After a year you can judge, my party comrades, if I have acted correctly and that it is good; if I have not acted correctly, then I will place my office back in your hands. Until that moment, however, I alone lead the movement and no one makes conditions for me so long as I personally assume all responsibility. And I unconditionally assume responsibility for everything that happens in the movement."

The frenzy in his manner was communicated to the audience. Cries of "Heil!" rang out. Women wept as the crowd pressed from the rear, climbing onto chairs and tables. Men who had been bitter enemies surged to the platform and shook hands, some of them unable to restrain tears. Then Max Amann shouted, "The wrangling must stop! Everyone for Hitler!" Rudolf Buttmann of the German Nationalist Party came forward to make an emotional announcement that all his doubts had suddenly "melted away within me as the Führer spoke." Buttmann's use of this title, hitherto uttered only in private, underlined Hitler's overwhelming success. From now on he would be the Führer in public. He had not only unified the NSDAP but established the leadership principle, the unquestioned rule of one man.

Drained emotionally as well as physically, Hitler left Munich that evening with Winifred Wagner. He and a few aides stayed overnight at her home in Bayreuth, but their presence was such a secret that the younger children of the family would not learn about it for years.

The resurrection of Hitler was followed the very next day by a political development of significance. In the national elections occasioned by the death of Ebert, seventy-eight-year-old Field Marshal von Hindenburg became the second President of the Republic. It was obvious that the sympathies of this hero of the right did not lie with the Republic and, while he attempted to remain neutral, he did little to strengthen the republican forces. There continued to be frequent cabinet crises, often over trivial issues such as the conservative proposition to award a large financial indemnity to the Hohenzollerns. When this was carried over vigorous socialist protest, a new bill was introduced to indemnify all dispossessed princes. This, too, was passed despite a socialist referendum to override it. Even the question of the colors of the German flag produced a cabinet crisis and Chancellor Hans Luther was forced to resign over it.

It seemed inevitable that this change in national politics should add impetus to Hitler's rise in power. But his return to the politics of the beer hall had been too sudden and triumphant to suit the Bavarian government. It only proved how dangerous his gift of oratory was to the state. He had injected new life into the party too fast, too excessively and the police forbade him to address five mass meetings set for early March on the grounds that he had inflamed the Bürgerbräu audience with such violent phrases as "Fight Marxism and Judaism not according to middle-class standards but over corpses!"

Hitler protested the ban in person. "Those who want to have a fight with us can have one," he told police officials. "Whoever attacks us will be stabbed from all sides. I will successfully lead the German people in their fight for freedom, if not peacefully, then with force. This sentence I repeat emphatically for the benefit of police spies so that no erroneous reports will be circulated." These were strong words for a man on parole and the end result was a ban on speaking in public throughout Bavaria. Open NSDAP meetings could be held, but not if their Führer spoke. Before long the proscription extended to almost every German state; Hitler had been deprived of his major political weapon. He was forced to transfer his platform to the homes of his wealthy supporters. He spoke—recalled Heinz Haushofer, whose father took him to a Munich salon—as if he were at the Zirkus Krone, except that he remained seated. "It was terrible . . . shouting and arm waving. He was not interrupted. He just spoke and spoke, like a record running in a groove, for an hour or an hour and a half until he became absolutely exhausted . . . and when he was finished and breathless, he just sat down once more a simple and nice man. . . . It was just as if he switched into another gear. And there was no in-between."

The ban obliged Hitler to confine himself to rebuilding the party and he tirelessly went from one closed meeting to another in Munich, exhorting audiences much as he had done in the Bürgerbräukeller. By grass-roots technique—shaking hands with men, kissing the hands of women and holding innumerable intimate conversations—he came into contact with the entire metropolitan membership. He succeeded not only in solidifying his magnetic attractions to the commonalty but in winning complete organizational control of the city party. At the same time Esser and Streicher roamed Bavaria duplicating Hitler's tactics as they rallied local organizations behind the Führer.

By the end of March Hitler controlled almost all Bavarian locals but he was forced to turn over the fate of the party in North Germany to Gregor and Otto Strasser. The first was a good organizer and a gifted speaker and could, as a delegate to the Reichstag, travel free on railroads. After the inspiring speech in the Bürgerbräu, he pledged his allegiance to Hitler but Otto, already a clever journalist despite his youth, had reservations. How long, he wondered, would the honeymoon with Hitler last?

Hitler accepted his enforced retirement from public life much as he had his imprisonment and took advantage of its opportunities. He utilized his free time to establish a solid party apparatus with the help of two colorless but efficient bureaucrats: Philipp Bouhler and Franz Xaver Schwarz. The first became executive secretary of the party. An owlish-looking individual who invariably bowed to Hitler before addressing him, he was obsessed with details. Schwarz, formerly an accountant at the Munich City Hall, was party treasurer. He brought to his job the talents of an adding machine and the spirit of a miser. Together the two men, by subordinating themselves completely to the Führer, became indispensable to the party machinery.

The efficient depersonalization of the party's internal organization by Bouhler and Schwarz enabled Hitler to concentrate on long-range political strategy, write articles and travel extensively in the north to make personal appearances at closed party meetings. He also had the leisure to repair broken friendships, chastise recalcitrants, bring opponents together and attend to personal problems. He reinstated Rosenberg as editor of the refounded *Völkischer Beobachter*, then wrote him a letter praising his integrity and calling him "a most valuable collaborator."

A few days later Hitler wrote another letter and solved a nagging personal problem—deportation to Austria—by facing it directly. He requested the city officials in Linz to cancel his Austrian citizenship since he intended to become a citizen of Germany. Three days later the provincial government of Upper Austria issued an emigration permit absolving him "from allegiance to the Austrian State." For a fee of 7.5 schillings Hitler was freed of the threat of deportation. And though he was not yet a German citizen, and consequently unable to vote or hold elective office, he was confident that this matter could be resolved when it became necessary.

Of more immediate concern were the rebellious actions of the contumacious and egocentric Captain Röhm. From the beginning he had attempted to make the SA his private army rather than Hitler's political instrument, and while the Führer was in prison he had formed a new organization from storm troop remnants under the name of Frontbann. Convinced that everything he had been working for since the Putsch would be lost if he subordinated the Frontbann to the party, Röhm presented Hitler with a memorandum on April 16 that the 30,000 men of the Frontbann could be the foundation of a national political organization but it must be under Röhm's absolute authority. His request was accompanied by appeals to their past friendship and a vow of personal loyalty.

Hitler had learned how disastrous it was to be dependent on an organization he did not control. Determined to make the new SA solely his instrument, he demanded that the Frontbann accept his personal authority at once. In an apparent effort to apply pressure, Röhm tendered his resignation from the Frontbann and requested a written acknowledgment of this action from the Führer. After waiting for an answer in vain he again wrote Hitler on the last day of April. "I take this opportunity," he concluded, "in memory of the fine and difficult days we have lived through together, to thank you [he used the familiar *Dir*] for your comradeship and to beg you not to exclude me from your personal friendship." There was still no reply and the following day Röhm announced formal resignation of his offices and withdrawal from politics. By maintaining silence, Hitler had forced Röhm to become a man without party or a Frontbann, and was himself free to set up a revitalized SA tailored for his own purposes.

Röhm was shocked and hurt. He complained bitterly, according to Lüdecke: "Though he often does what we advise, he laughs in our faces at the moment, and later does the very thing as if it were all his own idea and creation. I've never seen a man so magnificently unaware that he is adorning himself with borrowed plumage. Usually he solves suddenly, at the very last minute, a situation that has become intolerable and dangerous only because he vacillates and procrastinates. And that's because he can't act as clearly and logically as he can think and talk. . . . Hitler wants things his own way and gets mad when he strikes firm opposition on solid ground. And he doesn't realize how he can wear on one's nerves, doesn't know that he fools only himself and those worms around him with his fits and heroics. But nobody is perfect, and he has his great qualities. Apparently there's nobody else who would do better than he." Röhm, who had so freely bestowed upon the humble corporal the gift of his "*Du*," was caught between admiration and contempt.

2

That spring at least two of Hitler's personal dreams were realized. First, he managed somehow to acquire a new red Mercedes in which he spent many pleasant hours touring the Bavarian countryside with his bosom companions. He also established an auxiliary headquarters in the mountain village of Berchtesgaden. In this breath-taking scenic area he always found refreshment and mental stimulation. He reveled in the simple life and would wander the hills wearing *Lederhosen*. "Having to change into long trousers was always a misery to me. Even with a temperature of ten below zero I used to go about in leather shorts. The feeling of freedom they give is wonderful."

At first he stayed at the Pension Moritz on the Obersalzberg in a small cottage above the main building. Here in privacy he finished writing the first volume of his book. His principal sounding board was Hess, who had become private secretary at three hundred marks a month, but he also sought editorial advice from Father Bernhard Stempfle, the former editor of an anti-Semitic newspaper, and Hanfstaengl, who set to work crossing out superlatives. Hitler almost always reinstated what the latter eliminated as well as his efforts to "wean him away" from the provincial views of men like Hess and Rosenberg. "You cannot have a *Weltanschauung*," said Hanfstaengl, "unless you have viewed the world." He suggested Hitler travel abroad during the lull enforced by the speaking ban. In three or four months he could visit America, Japan and India as well as France and England.

"What would happen to the movement if I did that?" The party structure had fallen apart while he was in prison and had to be rebuilt. Hanfstaengl's observation that he would return "full of new plans for the future" nettled Hitler. "What curious ideas you have," he said. "What do you think I can learn from them? And why should I try to learn anyone else's language? I am too old and have no interest and no time."

Hanfstaengl offered to teach him English so he could read British and American newspapers and understand something of the broader world outside Germany. While never refusing the offer, Hitler could never make up his mind to accept it. And even the influence of Helene Hanfstaengl was waning. In hopes of instilling in him some of the social graces, she suggested he learn to waltz. He refused on the grounds that it was an unworthy preoccupation for a statesman and, after her husband noted that Washington, Napoleon and Frederick the Great all enjoyed dancing, retorted that it was "a stupid waste of time and these Viennese waltzes are too effeminate for a man to dance. This craze is by no means the least factor in the decline of their Empire. That is what I hate about Vienna."

Perhaps this rejection of Helene had something to do with her rejection of him the previous Christmas Eve. He was turning to other women for solace. Just across the street from his new rooming house in the town of Berchtesgaden (where he lived, in his own words, "like a fighting cock") was a boutique run by the Reiter girls, Anni and Mitzi. If one can believe Maurice, Mitzi caught the Führer's eye while he was walking his Alsatian in the Kurpark. A friendship between Prinz and Mitzi's police dog led to a flirtation between the owners. Hitler invited Mitzi to a concert, but her older sister protested on the grounds that Hitler was twenty years older than her sixteen-year-old sister. Hitler left in mortification but soon returned with an invitation to both sisters to attend a party meeting. Years later Mitzi claimed that Hitler went beyond flirtation: he called her Mitzerl, compared her beautiful eyes to his mother's and asked for a kiss. When she refused the Führer declared that they must not see each other again. But before long he was walking her around the lake. At a secluded spot he put his hands on her shoulders and suddenly kissed her. "He said, 'I want to crush you.' He was full of wild passion." Before long they were lovers; and while she had visions of marriage, he only talked of renting an apartment in Munich where they could live together.

Hitler found feminine stimulation of a different nature from

Winifred Wagner, who accepted him uncritically. He became a hero in the household and delighted in playing the role of the mysterious figure fleeing from enemies bent on assassinating him. In the dead of night he would steal into the Villa Wahnfried. "Late as it was," recalled Friedelind Wagner, "he never failed to come into the nursery and tell us gruesome tales of his adventures. We . . . listened while he made our flesh creep, showing us his pistol which, of course, he carried illegally—a small one that he could hide in his palm, but it held twenty bullets." Then it was that he told the children that the bags under his eyes had been caused by poison gas in the war.

At Wahnfried he was called Wolf. Everybody liked him, even the new schnauzer, which snarled at strangers, but the children were particularly attracted to him. "He drew them quite effortlessly with his hypnotic power. . . . His life was fascinating to us, because it was completely unlike ours—it all had a story-book quality."

On July 18 the first volume of his book was published in Munich by Eher. At Amann's suggestion the title had been changed to *Mein Kampf*, the name he had given his diary. Sales were good, a little under 10,000 by the end of 1925, but it was criticized then and later as abominably written, pompous and turgid. It read like a Horatio Alger novel grafted onto a political tract. Even its subtitle, *A Reckoning*, was novelistic. Even so, the detailed subjective portrayal (self-serving as it was) of the development of a young man's personal and political convictions gave insight into the nationalistic völkisch wave sweeping across Germany.

Since his release from prison Hitler's anti-Semitic diatribes had been overshadowed by preoccupation with party politics. The book was the channel for these feelings and here he developed the theme to new heights. He made it clear that his hatred and fear of Jews was the center of his private life as well as his political career. At the end of the chapter describing his blindness at Pasewalk he flung down the gauntlet: "We can not bargain with the Jews, only present them with a hard 'either-or.' But I was now resolved to become a politician." And in his role as politician it would be his mission to solve the Jewish question with radically harsh methods—and in the name of God. "Therefore, I am now convinced that I am acting as the agent of our Creator by fighting off the Jews, I am doing the Lord's work." To the growing army of racists in Germany, the pages of *Mein Kampf* were an inspiration and their author the personification of their struggle against all enemies at home and abroad.

3

Hitler must have known that giving Gregor Strasser full power to reorganize the NSDAP in North Germany would be risky and the more successful he became the more dangerous he would be as a political rival.

While anti-Semitic, Strasser was no reactionary. His political philosophy could be traced to Spengler and the front-line socialism of the war, based on the elitist principle that leadership of the proletarians must come from the military. He was a typical left-wing National Socialist and this made him particularly useful in bringing party revolutionaries back into line. A husky, outgoing man, he would move crowds as well as individuals and by late summer helped bring more prosperity to the cause than Hitler had expected. The number of cells in some sections doubled and even tripled. This increase came largely through Strasser's appeal to the working class and his freedom from the autocratic control of the Munich leadership.

In early September the struggle against the south became an open issue at a party conference in Hagen. Gregor Strasser had called the meeting to form a coalition against Munich bureaucracy. The conferees naïvely hoped to pry the Führer from his reactionary Bavarian advisers so he could lead Germany toward a revolutionary völkisch millennium. Strasser's program was endorsed. The delegates voted to unite for greater efficiency in organization and propaganda, and approved publication of a series of articles expressing programmatic policies that included economic reforms verging on national Bolshevism. Their editor was to be a brilliant twenty-nine-year-old who had replaced the methodical Himmler as Strasser's secretary. Josef Goebbels was just over five feet tall and weighed not much more than a hundred pounds. Moreover, his small frame had been wracked by infantile paralysis, leaving him with a deformed foot. Goebbels was compensated by a variety of talents: he was a facile writer and, despite an appearance of frailty, was a commanding figure on a platform with his magnetic baritone voice, expressive hands and appealing dark eyes.

Son of a Rhenish petty bourgeois Catholic family, he was molded by academia rather than home or church. His character was most significantly shaped by the University of Munich to which hundreds of disillusioned soldiers had flocked after the armistice. He had been exempted from service because of his clubfoot, but his hero was a tall, strikingly handsome veteran named Richard Flisges—pacifist and anarchist—who instilled in him ideals that would color the rest of his life. Flisges also introduced him to Dostoevski, whose emotional mysticism inspired young Goebbels.

He transferred to Heidelberg and left in 1921 with a Ph.D. in literature. The next few years he spent writing a romantic autobiographical novel entitled *Michael*, several plays and numerous lyric poems. To support himself he worked at a bank, as floorman of the Cologne stock exchange, as tutor, as part-time bookkeeper. It was during this frustrating period that he split with Flisges, for he had come to loathe the internationalism of Marxism. He moved to a völkisch socialism and in Hitler ("the incarnation of our faith and idea") he found a second Flisges to worship. At the same time he was bound to Gregor Strasser. It was this split fealty and its inevitable denouement that helped determine the course of the NSDAP.

This struggle was complicated by an ideological dilemma. In many respects Goebbels was still a Marxist and he persistently attempted to convert Communists to National Socialism. He was determined to evolve a theory which would erect "the bridge from left to right over which those willing to sacrifice came together." He, along with Gregor Strasser, believed that the party should champion the cause of workers in general and trade unionism in particular. This was one of the main points of difference between Hitler and Goebbels. He hoped to influence Hitler on his next trip north; then he could prove that the only thing separating the Communists and Nazis was the Reds' dedication to internationalism.

At last on November 4 the two met in Braunschweig, and when Hitler shook his hand Goebbels was in ecstasy. "Like an old friend," he wrote in his diary. "And those big blue eyes. Like stars. He is glad to see me. I am in heaven." The personal encounter was the beginning of Goebbels' enchantment with the Führer, an enthrallment intensified at a second meeting several weeks later in Plauen. "Great joy! He greets me like an old friend. And looks after me. How I love him!"

Yet within twenty-four hours Goebbels was participating in an open revolt against the central party organization at a meeting of northern Gauleiters. He had been delegated to help Strasser draft a new party program aimed at liberating the Führer from the "reactionary" Munich group and turning him to the left. This program called for state ownership of all land, division of large agricultural estates among landless farmers and nationalization of corporations. It was presented to the Gauleiters at a two-day conference in Hannover on January 24–25, 1926. The sessions were stormy, largely due to the surprise appearance of Gottfried Feder, Hitler's proxy. To Goebbels he was "the servant of capital and interest, the revaluation shit and principal program drafter of the movement." According to Strasser's younger brother, the Gauleiters, with the lone exception of Robert Ley, voted for the new program point by point. Finally Feder, who had objected to almost everything, said, "Neither Hitler nor I will accept this program." He was reminded that he was only a guest but he persisted. As he was announcing that Hitler opposed the Marxists' request for confiscation of crown property as a "Jewish swindle," he was shouted down. Goebbels leaped to his feet, furiously attacking the Munich leadership. He demanded Hitler's expulsion from the party unless he freed himself from their influence. This ultimatum seemed strange coming from someone who had recently written, "How I love him!" but it could have been a product of that adoration, since he was convinced that the Munich bureaucrats were leading Hitler to ruin.

Whatever the case, Feder's report of the fractious meeting finally roused Hitler to action. He summoned all party leaders to Bamberg on Sunday, February 14. There was an uneasiness among the northerners as they took their seats for the secret meeting. They were far outnumbered by the southerners and from the moment Hitler stepped to the rostrum he dominated the proceedings. He had come to Bamberg aware of the problem that faced the party and the threat to his leadership, but his first ringing words made it clear that he was the Führer and the nucleus of the movement. There were to be no more parliamentarian debates, no more democratic procedures in the NSDAP. He would tolerate no splinter groups. Each Gauleiter, each member, was to pledge allegiance to the Führer, and to the Führer alone.

He did not make the mistake of assaulting either Strasser or Goebbels. Perhaps his intuition told him the truth—that both really were loyal to him and merely wanted to guide him away from the likes of Streicher and Esser. He had come to Bamberg not to humiliate the northerners but to bring them back into the fold. He launched his oblique attack on the leftists in purely leftist rhetoric, then offered as an alternative to the two conflicting views a new concept. He took the party out of politics and into the mythology of the leader. The original party program, he said, "was the foundation of our religion, our ideology. To tamper with it would [constitute] treason to those who died believing in our idea." In other words, National Socialism was a religion and Hitler was its Christ. Crucified at the Feldherrnhalle and risen after Landsberg, he had returned to lead the movement and the nation to salvation.

The unexpected thrust of his speech took the northerners completely by surprise. Goebbels had come to Bamberg confident that Hitler could be wooed to the left yet he neither endorsed their position nor debated the issues. Rather he faced the party leadership with a choice: to reject or accept him as the Führer. To have denied him would have meant the end of the party. Strasser replied briefly and nervously. He was a beaten man. And Goebbels, except for shouting out several slogans, remained silent, except in his diary: "My heart aches!"

Convinced it was only a matter of time before the wounds of Bamberg healed and the party arose stronger and more united than ever, Hitler took to the road for financial support. On the last day of February he was allowed to speak to the National Club of 1919 at Hamburg's prestigious Atlantic Hotel since it was not a public rally. His words, which indicated how much he had learned in Landsberg prison, were directed not to the lunatic fringe but to the solid German citizen. He abandoned the style of the Zirkus Krone, opening the address with calm persuasiveness. He told how Germany had lost the war because of Marxism, how the Reds had attempted to take over the country and how they continued to dominate the politics of Germany. Within an hour he had won the audience, not by pyrotechnics or emotion but by logic, not by appeals to racism but to patriotism, property and prosperity.

Once he began to talk of Marxism, however, his style became more forceful. "In a struggle, one side must succumb—either Marxism will be abolished or we shall be abolished." He called for a mass movement dedicated to a relentless attack on the Reds. "Such a movement can only rely upon men's fists just as one can only eradicate poison with a poisonous antidote. This movement must act in exactly that resolute manner. Victory will be decided solely by the stronger skull, greater resolution and greater idealism." This was strong meat for an upper-class audience but it brought forth "stormy applause."

To win, he said, this movement had to be as intolerant as Marxism. "There should be no doubts about it: we recognize clearly that if Marxism wins, we shall be destroyed; we cannot expect a different end. But if we win, we shall destroy Marxism, and down to the roots, without any tolerance. We shall not rest until the last newspaper is destroyed, the last organization dissolved, the last training center closed and the last Marxist converted or eradicated. A middle course does not exist for us!"

It was a remarkable speech, one indicating that he was at last looking for the broadest base of support in a vigorous but legal campaign to gain control of the nation. Nor had he forgotten that he had not yet gained complete control of his own party despite Bamberg. He began directing his charm on the two leaders of the opposition—Gregor Strasser and Goebbels. By early March the first capitulated, despite serious reservations, and sent out a letter to his adherents recalling all copies of his own program.

It took a special trip to Munich early in April to win the second but by the end of Goebbels' second day as the Führer's personal guest he was so excited he had difficulty getting to sleep. The next day Hitler gave him a conducted tour of party headquarters followed by a three-hour monologue ("Brilliant"), rehashing the Bamberg arguments. Captivated, Goebbels came over to Hitler's beliefs one by one, and finally surrendered in a gush of hyperbole.

We ask. He gives brilliant replies. I love him. Social question. Quite new perspectives. He has thought it all out. . . . He sets my mind at rest on all points. He is a man in every way, in every respect. Such a firebrand, he can be my leader. I bow to the greater man, the political genius!

He left Munich in a state of ecstasy ("Farewell Munich! I love you very much!"), not only forgiven for his past sins but confirmed as co-Gauleiter of the Ruhr area.

With Goebbels and Strasser apparently converted, Hitler once more headed north to get financial support and also to solidify his position with leftist party members. On May Day he addressed an enthusiastic closed meeting at the City Hall in Schwerin, some sixty miles east of Hamburg. By 2 P.M. the large hall was packed with National Socialists from Altona, Hamburg, Bremen, Lübeck and Lüneburg. Hundreds were turned away. The *Hamburger Nachrichten* reported that Hitler's arrival was preceded by "wall-shattering" music.

He had developed body gestures which were, according to Müllern-Schönhausen, the result of lessons from one of the most renowned seers and astrologists in Europe, Erik Jan Hanussen. The two reportedly met that year in Berlin at the home of a wealthy socialite and Hanussen's first words were: "If you are serious about entering politics, Herr Hitler, why don't you learn how to speak?" A master of body language, Hanussen explained that Hitler was not taking advantage of movements to emphasize his words. In the next few years, so Müllern-Schönhausen claimed, they continued to meet briefly and Hanussen not only taught him the tricks of elocution but also advised him on the selection of his associates. Not until the end of 1932, however, would he cast Hitler's horoscope—and seal his own doom.

4

By mid-spring of 1926 Hitler had gained complete control of the NSDAP with establishment of the principle that the Munich local was the hub of the entire movement and should provide the leadership of the national party. This was confirmed at a general membership meeting at the Bürgerbräu on May 22. Here, as supreme Führer, Hitler was invested with the power to select and dismiss any Gauleiter or subleader. This meant termination of all democratic procedures and complete subservience to the Führer principle. As a final precaution, Hitler insisted that the twenty-five points of the original party program be declared unalterable. He got his way—and was now in sole charge of the party's ideology.

In his heart Goebbels had already gone completely over to Hitler but he kept up the façade of loyalty to Strasser, who still had doubts about the Führer. On June 10 Goebbels assured his diary that he would only go to Berlin as Hitler's representative if he could remain "absolutely independent" but two days later was eager to accept any invitation. "Then I would be away from all the muck. Now all depends on his decision. Does he want me?" By the time they met again Goebbels had worked himself into a state of exultant hero-worship.

Hitler is the same dear comrade. You cannot help liking him as a man. And on top of it that overriding mind. You always discover something new in that self-willed head. As a speaker he has developed a wonderful harmony of gesture, histrionics and spoken word. The born whipper-up! Together with him you can conquer the world. Give him his head and he will shake the corrupt Republic to its foundations. His best epigram yesterday: "For our struggle God gave us His abundant blessing. His most beautiful gift was the hate of our enemies whom we too hate with all our heart."

Early the next month Hitler all but conciliated the warring factions at the party congress in Weimar. The site had been chosen because Thuringia was one of the few states where Hitler was allowed to speak in public. His major address on the last day of the congress, July 4, was more emotional than political. "Deep and mystical," wrote Goebbels. "Almost like the Gospels. Shuddering we pass together with him along the edge of life's abyss. Everything is being said. I thank providence for having given us this man!" As Hitler walked off the stage the audience exploded into applause and the cheers continued for several minutes. Later Hitler, wearing an ill-fitting field jacket and puttees, stood in the back seat of an open car to review 3500 (the enthusiastic Goebbels put the number at 15,000) storm troopers who marched past, a bit out of step, with right arms raised in salute.

It was an impressive end to a memorable congress despite complaints that there were still fewer than 40,000 members in the NSDAP. Numbers did not concern Hitler at the moment. The party was one of the smallest in Germany but it was an iron fist, his iron fist. He returned to Berchtesgaden to complete the second volume of *Mein Kampf* and to recharge himself for the final task in the reconstruction of the party: conversion of the spell he had cast at Weimar into bureaucratic control of all party locals.

One man he intended to use in this endeavor was Josef Goebbels, who came to visit Hitler's mountain retreat and fell deeper under his spell. "He is like a child: kind, good, merciful. Like a cat: cunning, clever, agile. Like a lion: roaring and great and gigantic. A fellow, a man." And on July 25, his last full day in Berchtesgaden, came the ultimate conversion. "Farewell, my Obersalzberg!" Goebbels wrote that night. "These days have signposted my road! A star shines leading me from deep misery! I am his to the end. My last doubts have vanished. Germany will live. Heil Hitler!"

Hitler kept him in suspense for several months and when Goebbels finally received confirmation that he was going to Berlin he excitedly scribbled: "Berlin signed and sealed. Hurray!" It was more of a victory for Adolf Hitler. Outwardly he had made his peace with Gregor Strasser by admitting him to the party hierarchy but Strasser's talents and energy remained a slumbering threat to the Führer principle. By sending Goebbels to Berlin, where Strasser also had his headquarters, Hitler converted Strasser's former private secretary into his rival.

On November 7 Goebbels set off for Berlin and access to the corridors of power. He was heading for a new life, personally as well as politically, for he had broken his engagement with a girl named Else with whom he had been carrying on a tempestuous affair. How could a rising star in the National Socialist constellation be married to, or even sleep with, a half Jew?

There were almost 50,000 party members by the end of the year, as well as an efficient party directorate with Hess as secretary, Schwarz as treasurer and Bouhler as secretary-general.* The directorate had started with three automobiles and a staff of twenty-five but was growing rapidly. It was a quasi state within a state with departments for foreign policy, labor, industry, agriculture, economy, interior, justice, science and press. Party auxiliaries were either formed or envisioned: a Hitler Youth and leagues for women, teachers, law officers and physicians.

The most important arm of the party was the SA. Eight new units had been installed at the Weimar party congress as demonstrable proof that they were an integral part of the NSDAP. At the same time local and regional storm troop units were co-ordinated with the Führer in direct control. To fit in with his new policy of legality, Hitler chose Franz Pfeffer von Salomon, "a born organizer" and disciplinarian, to preside over a legitimate, non-military organization. "In order to prevent the SA from taking on any sort of secret character from the start," Hitler wrote Pfeffer, "it should not be hidden and should march under a bright sky to destroy all myths that it is a 'secret organization.' . . . Thus the fight against today's state will not take on the atmosphere of a society out for vengeance but a great world-wide movement and war against Marxism, its structure and its wire-pullers. We do not need a hundred or two hundred dedicated conspirators but hundreds of thousands of fanatic fighters for our *Weltanschauung*. . . . We must show the Marxists that the future boss of the streets is National Socialism, just as one day National Socialism will be boss of the state." The official SA uniform was brown shirt with brown tie. The color was purely accidental; a large consignment of brown shirts, originally intended for German troops in East Africa, was available at wholesale.

The end of 1926 was also marked by publication of the second volume of *Mein Kampf*. Subtitled *The National Socialist Movement*, it was based on the history of the party from the day the twenty-five points of the program were presented to the Munich Putsch. History of a sort had replaced autobiography. Since Machiavelli there had rarely appeared such pragmatic instructions on politics, and Hitler's precepts on propaganda and organization were practical for those operating on street level. His analysis of crowd psychology indicated he had read Freud's *Group Psy-*

* The official membership figures for this period are unreliable. Schwarz deliberately numbered all members consecutively to obscure losses caused by resignations or expulsion. Moreover, Gauleiters and local leaders consistently turned in misleading reports so they wouldn't have to send headquarters its full share of the dues.

chology and the Analysis of the Ego, published a few years earlier in Germany. "A group is extraordinarily credulous," wrote Freud, "and open to influence; it has no critical faculty, and the improbable does not exist for it. The feelings of a group are always very simple and very exaggerated, so that it knows neither doubt nor uncertainty." Similar principles had been expressed by William McDougall and Gustave Le Bon but their works had not yet been translated into German. Ironically it took a Viennese Jew to instruct Hitler that the orator who wished to sway a crowd "must exaggerate, and he must repeat the same thing again and again." And it was Freud too who pointed out that the mass was "intolerant but obedient to authority. . . . What it demands of its heroes is strength or even violence. It wants to be ruled and oppressed and to fear its masters." Typically Hitler took what he wanted from his compatriot, combining Freudian theory with his own ideas to forge a formidable weapon.

The book also indicated that Hitler had drastically altered his foreign policy. He had come out of the war convinced that France was Germany's chief foe and in a speech in July 1920 even considered the possibility of an alliance with the Soviet Union once their Jews were expelled. Now, six years later, in the next to the last chapter of this second volume, he admitted it had been a mistake to look upon France as the main enemy, and completely rejected a war of revision. National Socialist foreign policy must be altered, he said, namely (and the stress is his), "*to secure for the German people the land and soil to which they are entitled on this earth.*" Several pages later he was more explicit. "*We take up where we broke off six hundred years ago. We stop the endless German movement to the south and west, and turn our gaze upward toward the land in the east.*" And by the east he meant primarily Russia which, he charged, had fallen under "the yoke of the Jew." And Fate had chosen Germany to help bring about conquest of this vast Jew-ridden territory.

Expansionism had long been a German dream. In 1906 Klaus Wagner wrote that "every great people needs new territory. It must expand over foreign soil. It must expel the foreigners by the power of the sword." Combining it with anti-Semitism was Hitler's contribution. No longer were the borders of nations decided by royalty, he said. Today it was "*the inexorable Jew who struggles for his domination over the nations. No nation can remove this hand from its throat except by the sword.*" And so by the sword he would eliminate the Jewish menace, France, Russia and Marxism, while thrusting Germany and the Germanic ideal to the fore. This conclusion, the result of seven years of probing, had come to him since his vision at the hospital in Pasewalk, by his individual, unsystematic, almost inspirational method.

Hess took a copy of the book to Professor Haushofer. Would he review it in his periodical? Haushofer was "quite unhappy" with what he read, particularly (since his wife was Jewish) with Hitler's racial diatribes.

He also saw no relationship between his own theory of Lebensraum and Hitler's conquest of the East. He refused to write a review. "For me at that time," he later recalled, "it seemed to be one of the many ephemeral publications for purposes of agitation. It is self-evident that I had no part in its origin."

Hitler himself had second thoughts about the entire book and later admitted to Frank that he was no author. "Thoughts run away from me when I write." *Mein Kampf,* he admitted, was merely a collection of lead articles for the *Völkischer Beobachter.* "Of one thing I am sure, if I had known in 1924 that I would become Chancellor, I would not have written the book."

A few days after publication of the second volume Hitler turned a Nazi Christmas celebration at the Hofbräuhaus into another virulent attack on Jews. "Christ," he said, "was the greatest early fighter in the battle against the world enemy, the Jews."* He was not the apostle of peace. His life's purpose and life's teaching was the battle against the power of capitalism, and for this he was crucified on the cross by his archenemy, the Jews. "The work that Christ started but could not finish, I—Adolf Hitler—will conclude."

A few months later the self-proclaimed Messiah's greatest political weapon was restored. The public-speaking ban in Bavaria was lifted on March 5, 1927. Four nights later he addressed a large, excited throng at the Zirkus Krone. At 8:30 P.M. there was a shout from outside of "Heil Hitler!" and the band struck up a rousing march. Hitler entered, wrapped in trench coat, followed by his entourage. He quickly strode down the aisle as the audience cheered, feet stamped. Once Hitler reached the platform there was abrupt silence. Then 200 Brownshirts marched in preceded by two drummers and the flag. The audience broke into thundering Heils and held out arms in Fascist salute. On the stage, Hitler stood stern-faced, his right arm out. The music mounted, flags passed by the stage, glittering standards with swastikas in wreaths with eagles, patterned after the banners of the Roman legions. The SA men took position below the stage except for flag- and standard-bearers riveted at attention behind the speakers.

At first Hitler spoke slowly, deliberately, then the words began tumbling out in a torrent. According to one police reporter, his gesticulations as he jumped excitedly back and forth fascinated "the spell-bound thousand-headed audience. When he is interrupted by applause, he extends his hands theatrically. The word 'no,' which appears repeatedly in the latter part of the speech, is deliberately and theatrically emphasized." This was oration Hanussen-style. For two and a half hours Adolf Hitler

---

* Hitler did not consider Jesus a Jew but a *Mischling* (a half Jew who did not adhere to the Jewish religion and therefore was free of the Jewish virus) on the grounds that, with immaculate conception, he only had two Jewish grandparents.

talked of Germany's crisis, concluding that in such chaos the Jews alone were winners. It was an inspirational exhibition, notable not for what he said but how he said it. Of one thing alone he was certain. He planned to attain his goal this time, legally and by utilizing to the utmost the magnetic forces within himself.

During a major speech such as this Hitler would drink as many as twenty small bottles of mineral water and his shirt would be wringing wet. Sometimes, especially in warm weather, he also insisted on having a piece of ice on the rostrum so he could keep his hands cool. After a speech he would leave at once for a nearby room—provided by the sponsors of the meeting—and take a bath.

5

In this and subsequent orations Hitler seemed to be following the socialist line of Gregor Strasser; he even used the terminology of the leftists in attacks on capitalism and the decadent bourgeoisie. But the brunt of the battle to win urban workers over to National Socialism he left to someone more qualified. Josef Goebbels had set off for Berlin in a third-class railroad compartment with a worn satchel containing two suits, several shirts, a few books and a pile of manuscripts. He arrived to find the Berlin Gau in complete disarray and later would write that "what went as the party in Berlin in those days in no way deserved that description. It was a widely mixed collection of a few hundred people with National Socialist ideas." Although much of his account was more fictional than his diaries, this was no exaggeration. Meetings in the capital often degenerated into shouting matches and slaps in the face were commonplace. One quarrel between Gregor Strasser and a man named Hagemann became so acrimonious that it ended in a challenge to a duel.

Goebbels was faced with an apparently impossible task. Besides being at odds with one another, the thousand party members under his jurisdiction were opposed on the streets by overwhelming numbers of Communists and Social Democrats. Gau headquarters were located in a "filthy basement" of a building in the Potsdamerstrasse. "There was complete confusion. The finances were a mess. The Berlin Gau then possessed nothing but debts." This state of affairs inspired rather than depressed Goebbels. He moved his headquarters to a better area, set up regular office hours and established a sound accounting system under his personal control. By February 1927 the Gau owed nothing while owning almost 10,000 marks' worth of office equipment as well as a used car.

Goebbels decided it was now time to broaden the base of membership and to do that he had to attract the attention of a jaded public. "Berlin needs its sensations as a fish needs water," he wrote, "this city lives on it, and any political propaganda not recognizing this will miss the mark." His speeches and articles took on a crisp, graphic style attuned to the Berliner; his SA troops deliberately sought physical combat with the Reds—preferably when the odds were in their own favor—on his theory that "He who can conquer the streets can also conquer the masses; and he who has conquered the masses has thereby conquered the state."

He rehearsed his speeches before a full-length mirror and, according to his landlady, would practice body movements by the hour. Once on the podium he was a brilliant improviser, and soon perfected a variety of styles. Before a meeting he would ask what audience he would face. "What record must I use—the national, the social or the sentimental? Of course, I have them all in my suitcase."

He appealed directly to the masses in graphic, aggressive language. A consummate actor, he could switch from humor to sentiment and then to invective. Often he deliberately provoked the Reds into vocal protests which he would twist to his own advantage. "Making noise," he once said, "is an effective means of opposition." To him propaganda was an art and he was, by all accounts, including his own, a genius at it—and he sold National Socialism with American-style showmanship as if it were the best soap in the world.

He entered the lists of battle in the working-class district of Wedding by announcing in glaring red posters that "The Bourgeois State Is Approaching Its End," and inviting workers to a mass meeting on February 11, 1927, at the Pharus Hall, a center commonly used for Communist Party gatherings. It was an open declaration of war. No sooner did the chairman open the meeting than a Marxist worker shouted out that he wanted to clarify a point in the agenda. The chairman ignored him and when the worker repeated his request he was thrown out by storm troopers. This touched off a brawl in which eighty-three Reds were beaten up. A dozen Nazis were also injured and Goebbels showed his talent as propagandist by bringing these men on stage where their moaning was more effective. The Battle of Pharus Hall brought the party to the front pages of the newspapers, and Berliners who knew little or nothing about Hitler and his movement were made aware of a new political force in town. The publicity was meant to be derogatory but in the next few days 2600 applications for membership were received, and 500 of these applicants also wanted to join the SA.

With every meeting the size of the audience increased and by the time Hitler appeared at the Clou restaurant center there were 5000 present. The occasion was a closed celebration of the Marxist holiday, May Day, and the Führer began like a Lenin: "We are socialists, we are enemies of today's capitalistic economic system for the exploitation of the economically weak, with its unfair salaries, with its unseemly evaluation of a human being according to wealth and property instead of responsibility and performance, and we are determined to destroy this system under all conditions." This was followed by a long dissertation on Lebensraum, in Hitler's continuing effort to pound this concept into the membership. Sixty-two million Germans, he said, were crowded into an area only 450,000 kilometers square. "This is a ridiculous figure when one considers the size of other nations in the world today." There were two solutions: either decrease the population by "chasing our best human material out of Germany" or "bring the soil into consonance with the population, even if it must be done by war. This is the natural way which Providence has prescribed."

Goebbels had hoped for another Red disturbance but all was peaceful and the speech wasn't even reported in the major newspapers. Determined to keep the party in the public eye, Goebbels organized another meeting, three days later, in the Veterans Association Hall. He made up a provocatively anti-Semitic poster ("A people in distress! Who will save us? Jakob Goldschmidt?") and had thousands of copies plastered throughout Berlin. Goldschmidt, a leading German banker, was invited to attend the meeting but at the last minute his board of directors persuaded him to send his private secretary instead.

Goebbels was in good form, delighting his audience with his irony. "Welcome, workers of Berlin!" he began. "Welcome also to a charming young lady, the secretary of Jakob Goldschmidt. And please don't bother to take down every word I say. Your boss will read it all in tomorrow's papers." He went on to speak scornfully of "Jew journals" and "press synagogues" until a heckler called out, "You don't look so good yourself." The man, an elderly pastor, kept interrupting until Goebbels finally signaled his Brownshirts to evict him. In the process the minister was so badly beaten he had to be taken to a hospital. The newspapers described the victim as a "white-haired and respectable" pastor of the Reformed Church (he was, in fact, an alcoholic who had been removed from the pulpit and was destined to become an active member of the NSDAP), and this aroused such public indignation that the police commissioner declared the Berlin party illegal.

The ban came as an unpleasant surprise to Goebbels and he did his best to alleviate the situation with slogans such as "Banned but not Dead." With the party forced underground, he had to rely on cover organizations with innocent names such as "The Quiet Lake," "The Beautiful Acorn" and "Hikers of 1927." The Police Department countered with still another ban, this one on Nazi speechmaking throughout Prussia.

Goebbels still had his wit and he was inspired to publish a weekly paper. He gave it an appropriate name, *Der Angriff* (*The Assault*), and brought it out on the day dedicated to American independence. But the reality fell far below his dream and he was shocked by the first issue. The venture seemed doomed to failure. "What a miserable provincial sheet!" he admitted. "Baloney in print!" Only several hundred party members subscribed and few copies were sold at the stands. But Goebbels was convinced that the basic idea was good and gradually transformed it into a going concern by copying the make-up and content of the Communist Party paper.

The problem of Berlin, aggravated by the bitter feud between Goebbels and Strasser, created an atmosphere of sober realism at the annual party meeting in Munich late that July. The expected rate of growth in the urban areas was disappointing. Rather than address the meeting on this crisis, Hitler spoke only in generalities, his heat directed at a target no one in the Bürgerbräu would defend—the Jew.

It was almost as if he were not concerned with the party doldrums and had more important things on his mind. His speeches of the last few months indicated that he was obsessed with his personal ideology, his Weltanschauung. Again and again he hammered at race and the fact that Germany's future lay in conquest of eastern territories. Over and over he preached his pseudo-Darwinist sermon of nature's way: conquest of the weak by the strong.

This program was carried a step forward at the third Party Day in Nuremberg. Almost 20,000 members, 8500 of them in uniform, flooded into the ancient city and there was the usual pageantry—a march with flags and standards to the strains of rousing military airs. It was on the last day of the celebration, Sunday, August 21, that Hitler connected the concept of Lebensraum with anti-Semitism but few realized the significance of this misbegotten marriage, for his terms were too vague. He reiterated his demand for more living space for the German people, then pointed out that power and power alone was the basis for acquisition of new territory. But, he said, Germany had been robbed of her power factors by three abominations: internationalism, democracy and pacifism. Hitler then linked this evil trinity with racism. Were not internationalism, democracy and pacifism all creations of the Jew? Surely if obscurely Hitler had joined Lebensraum with anti-Semitism. His unsystematic search for a Weltanschauung was close to realization.

Hitler was still living at his little room on the Thierschstrasse, and although he was received as a hero in some of the best homes in Germany, his standard of living remained monastic. It was common talk in the neighborhood that he even shared some of his short supply of shirts and socks with the needy. In his modest room he received admirers rich and poor, from all over Germany, exhibiting a willingness and aptitude for making himself agreeable. Many a hand-kiss insured lifelong devotion from women; men were reassured by his firm handshake, his down-to-earth, man-to-man approach.

His speeches also became models of political acumen. During one in Hamburg that autumn Gauleiter Albert Krebs noted that he was conforming strictly to the outline on which there were written a number of catchwords. "Even entire sentences and phrases, which seemed spontaneous and improvised, had been written down. Hitler was not an intuitive speaker as many people, particularly his opponents, believed; he built his speeches systematically and he knew exactly what effect he wanted and how to get it. While Krebs did not realize that Hitler was going through the process of testing his personal world view in public, he did get an insight into the momentous development taking place in the mind of the Führer. "It was clear to him that he could only win the attention of the mass by avoiding the usual terminology and working with new words and new conceptions. His train of thought was of such generally compelling nature that people of different political directions could agree with it. So during his first public appearance in Hamburg, he was able within a single hour, to persuade a suspicious and reserved audience to applaud, and this applause increased until it became, at the conclusion, an enthusiastic ovation. Later the most level-headed listeners declared that, though they were still against the speaker and his party, Hitler himself was obviously much more reasonable then they had imagined."

He was learning how to appeal to the basic needs of the average German. No longer was he the völkisch fanatic, the frightening revolutionary of the Munich Putsch, but a reasonable man who sought only the welfare of the Fatherland. His "basic values and aims" were as reassuring as they were acceptable. His listeners could not possibly know that the "reasonable" words were a mask for one of the most radical programs in the history of mankind, a program that would alter the map of Europe and affect the lives, in one way or another, of most of the people on earth.

That fall Hitler stopped off in Berlin to settle the Goebbels-Strasser feud in person. According to Otto Strasser's account, Hitler appeared at his office with a demand to end the quarrel. "Then tell it to Goebbels," was the feisty answer. "He is the aggressor." Otto Strasser's show of independence by no means reflected his older brother's attitude toward Hitler. The Führer had gone out of his way to demonstrate his trust in Gregor. In addition to bringing him into the party hierarchy, he was grooming him for even higher positions. It was Gregor who had appeared on the same platform with Hitler in his first public appearance in Bavaria; it was Gregor who chaired the last annual party meeting. He would not listen to his brother's warnings that Hitler was becoming dangerously powerful. "Look," he argued, "you know as well as I do that Hitler is no leader but only a popular tribune of the people. He is manageable." Hitler was like a stubborn horse. "We shouldn't let him throw us off but must try to break him in and lead him in the right direction."

Hitler was no horse, said Otto, but a tiger, "and once he throws you off, he'll get rid of you for good." Gregor protested. He could manage the Führer, who was, after all, "a weak, good-natured and honest person. You don't know how much weight he gives to my words and how often he has said to me, 'Gregor, you're right once more. What would I be without you?' Do you think he says such things to Streicher?"

6

By the end of 1927 Hitler had demonstrated that he could handle people as individuals and in groups. It was also evident that his interest in rebuilding the party was long-range. Further, he realized something his advisers did not: before launching an all-out campaign to broaden the base of the movement he must have a burning public issue on which he could mobilize support from worker and burgher alike. Just as important, he would need a clearly defined world outlook to give him direction. This Weltanschauung would come in a year but the issue would not arise for two years and would originate in New York City's Wall Street.

The spring of the new year brought a revocation of the ban against the party in Berlin, followed by a burst of political energy on the part of Goebbels in an effort to win substantial gains in the Reichstag during the coming elections. While his appeal was directed largely at the worker, he called on nationalists and socialists to bury their differences. "Socialism and nationalism are things which supplement, not contradict, each other. Against each other they are destructive; with each other they are revolutionary and progressive."

The national elections of May 20 were a personal triumph for Goebbels, who was sent to the Reichstag, but defeat for the Führer since the party elected only eleven other delegates. The Nazis had lost 100,000 votes and two seats over the past two years. The loss could be laid neither to Hitler nor to poor organization but to the healthy state of the economy and the absence of a crucial issue. No longer could mere mention of the Versailles Treaty and the "November criminals" win a voter. Politicians are often the last to sense a new trend and the Nazi elite who had gathered at party headquarters in Munich that evening to celebrate a major political breakthrough were deep in gloom at the succession of dismal returns brought in by messengers on bicycles.

Hitler arrived about midnight. Ignoring the atmosphere of dejection, he surprised his followers with a philosophical, almost detached speech. The old politicians expected the usual remarks of a defeated leader. But Hitler dwelt mostly on the healthy gains made by the two working-class parties—the Social Democratic and the Communist. He neither minimized their victory nor treated it as a National Socialist defeat and, in fact, seemed curiously pleased that the two "enemy" parties had defeated the German moderate middle and rightist parties. Unlike his comrades, the Führer felt that a bright political future lay ahead.

After the election Hitler returned to Berchtesgaden, his fount of inspiration. At last he had a place of his own, the Haus Wachenfeld on the Obersalzberg. It was a simple country house in Upper Bavarian mountain style, surrounded by a wooden veranda, with heavy rocks on the pitched roof to prevent the shingles from being ripped off in a storm. The first time he looked through the villa he had been "completely captivated." Luckily for him the owner, the widow of an industrialist, was a party member and she rented it to him for a hundred marks a month. "I immediately rang up my sister in Vienna with the news and begged her to be so good as to take over the part of mistress of the house." Angela brought along her two daughters, Friedl and Angela Maria. The latter, usually called Geli, was a twenty-year-old vivacious girl with light brown hair. "It was not that she was so very pretty," recalled Ilse Pröhl, who had recently married Hess, "as that she had the famous Viennese charm." There were a few critics, including Hanfstaengl, who characterized her as "an empty-headed little slut, with the coarse bloom of a servant-girl, without either brains or character," but most people liked Geli, including Helene Hanfstaengl, who considered her "a nice, rather serious girl," by no means a flirt. And the photographer Hoffmann described her as "a lovely young woman who, with her artless and carefree manner, captivated everybody." On the other hand, his daughter Henriette considered her "coarse, provocative and a little quarrelsome." At the same time, Henriette was convinced that the "irresistibly charming" Geli was the Führer's only true love. "If Geli wanted to go swimming . . . it was more important to Hitler than the most important conference. Picnic baskets were packed, and we drove to the lake." Not even Geli could get the Führer into the water. No politician, he argued, should ever allow himself to be photographed in swimming trunks.

Their difference in age, nineteen years, was about the same as that between Hitler and Mitzi Reiter, the former object of his affection. By her own account, Mitzi in a fit of jealousy had tried to commit suicide the previous summer. In a bizarre attempt to choke herself, she tied one end of a clothesline on a door, the other around her neck, but her brother-in-law freed her after she lost consciousness.

In the discreet love affair with Geli (which most likely was never consummated), it was Hitler who was the jealous partner. One day, recalled Frau Hess, Geli sketched the costume she wanted to wear at the next Fasching carnival and showed it to him. "You might as well go naked if you want something like that," he said indignantly and sketched his idea of a proper costume. "Then she got angrier, much angrier than he had been. She picked up her drawing and ran out the door, slamming it shut. And Hitler was so contrite that within half an hour he was looking for her."

His frustrated love life was overshadowed by a new book which embodied a philosophy of life, a unification of his political and personal convictions. While outwardly unsystematic, his intuition had its own relentless symmetry; and for the past four years, as seen from his speeches and private conversations, he had been methodically chopping a path through the jungle of his mind in search of the idea.

From the first words he dictated to Max Amann ("Politics is history in the making") it was obvious that he was embarked on a venture of significance. An essential of Hitler's conclusions in this book was the conviction drawn from Darwin that might makes right. It led to a vital link between self-preservation and Lebensraum. "The compulsion to engage in the struggle for existence lies in the limitation of the living space; but in the life-struggle for this living space lies also the basis for evolution." The consequence was an eternal battle between nations which could only be won by a people dedicated to strict racial, folk and blood values. Once standards were lowered and pure blood was mixed with inferior blood the end was in sight. "Then the Jew can make his entry in any form, and this master of international poisoning and race corruption will not rest until he has thoroughly uprooted and thereby corrupted such a people." This was the first time Hitler not only defined his terms but interwove race, folk and blood values with his hatred of Jews.

In *Mein Kampf* he had simply drawn up charges against Jews as enemies of the world and effectively stated the case for a drive to the East to attain living space. Now at last he was ready to bring all the threads of his political and personal convictions together into a consistent (if twisted and paranoid) Weltanschauung, and he waited until the last few pages of his new book to do it. "It is not my task here to enter into a discussion of the Jewish question as such," he began tentatively. Jewry had "special intrinsic characteristics which separate it from all other peoples living on the globe"; it was not a religious community with a "territorially bounded state"; and it was parasitical rather than productive. He had stated all this many times before in far stronger terms but at this point he abruptly explored a new idea. "Just as every people as a basic tendency of all its earthly actions possesses a mania for self-preservation as its driving force, likewise is it exactly so with Jewry too."

Hitler's continued use of non-polemic language was surprising. The Jew, he wrote, was merely impelled by the same motives as everyone else in this deadly struggle for life; the only difference was a different purpose. But then Hitler abruptly turned shrill. "His ultimate goal is the denationalization, the promiscuous bastardization of other peoples, the lowering of the racial level of the highest peoples as well as the domination of his racial mishmash through the extirpation of the folkish intelligentsia and its replacement by the members of his own people." This different goal, expressed in such comparatively calm terms, was what made the Jews the threat of mankind. And since their ultimate aim was conquest of the entire world, Hitler's battle against the Jews was for the good not only of Germany but of the entire world.

By the end of the summer of 1928 Hitler had finally come to the realization that his two most urgent convictions—danger from Jews and Germany's need for sufficient living space—were entwined. If the Reich failed to acquire essential living space it would perish. If the Jewish menace were not stemmed there could be no struggle for Lebensraum, no culture, and the nation would decay.

This, in all likelihood, marked Hitler's point of no return and was the essence of his Weltanschauung. Now a dual task lay before him: to conquer new living space in the East and to annihilate the Jews. What had seemed to be two separate if parallel courses was a single road. It was as if for months he had been observing the twin mountain peaks from his villa on the Obersalzberg, both of which he wanted to climb—and only now realized that the *same* trail led to both. He had seen the light. Martin Luther and all the other anti-Semites before Hitler merely talked of eliminating the Jews but with his new blueprint for the future he hoped to materialize their dream—and become Haman II.

He himself forbade publication of what became known as *Hitler's Secret Book* and appeared for the first time thirty-two years later. Perhaps he feared it was too philosophically heavy for his adherents, too flimsily transparent for the more sophisticated; perhaps he did not want to reveal the ultimate mass-murder plan that hid behind its terminology. Within the pages also lay clues to his motivation for genocide. They were replete with revealing references: the Jew was a "master of international poisoning and race corruption," as well as the instigator of the "evil pacifist liquid manure [which] poisons the mentality favoring bold self-preservation." He referred to the flood of "disease bacilli" now breeding in Russia; and called the crowded working-class districts of Germany (the result of inadequate Lebensraum) "abscesses in the national body" as well as "breeding grounds of blood mixing and bastardization, and of race lowering, thus resulting in those purulent infection centers in which the international Jewish racial-maggots thrive and finally effect further destruction."

This obsession with Jewish poisoning and corruption twice took on a startling personal nature in the book. He referred to the hated Erzberger, who signed the 1918 armistice, as "the bastard son of a servant-girl and a Jewish employer." He could have been talking of his own father. And then he must have been thinking of his mother when he wrote: "If a man appears to have cancer and is unconditionally doomed to die, it would be senseless to refuse an operation, because the percentage of the possibility of success is slight."

Fear that his father may have been part Jewish (which could be a substantial part of why he wanted no children); anguish, anger and guilt at his mother's painful death from cancer along with mixed feelings about the Jewish doctor who, with Hitler's consent, treated her *drastically* with iodoform—all this would seem to permeate *Hitler's Secret Book*. And perhaps it was no coincidence that shortly after finishing this work he made a voluntary visit to a psychiatrist. He sought help from a party member in Munich, Dr. Alfred Schwenninger, to allay a "fear of cancer." There is no record of the treatment but it was soon evident that the psychiatrist missed a golden opportunity to turn Hitler from his awful goal; Dr. Schwenninger also failed to remove his patient's fear of cancer which, along with the obsession to eliminate all Jews, would persist to the last day of his life.

Chapter Nine

A DEATH IN THE FAMILY
1928–1931

1

Hitler's first efforts to implement his Weltanschauung were made by proxy. In Berlin Josef Goebbels was doing his utmost to rejuvenate the party after defeat at the recent elections. During the summer of 1928 he wrote three articles for *Der Angriff* in an attempt to woo those workers who had voted leftist. In language that could have come from a Communist, he charged that the worker in the capitalist state was "no longer a living human being, not an originator, not a creator. He is changed into a machine. A number, a robot in a factory without sensibility or goal." Only National Socialism would bring him dignity and make his life meaningful. In a surprisingly short period Goebbels had replaced Strasser as the chief recruiter of workers in the north, and in so doing apparently removed him as a political rival to the Führer. That Hitler was pleased with Goebbels and approved his socialist line became clear when he permitted *Der Angriff* to become a biweekly and made its editor propaganda chief of the party.

In politics Hitler could be forgiving. If a former opponent was contrite the Führer was likely to reward him. It was his way of turning a liability into an asset. After crushing Gregor Strasser's attempt to change the direction of National Socialism, he had put him in charge of reorganizing the party; and Strasser had so successfully centralized administration that he was becoming one of the most powerful men in the NSDAP. Due primarily to his and Goebbels' efforts party membership rose to some 100,000 by the end of the year.

To solidify his gains in the north, Hitler came to Berlin on November 16, 1928, to speak at the huge Sportpalast on racial and national regeneration. Since it was likely Reds would try to break up the meeting, Hitler's personal bodyguard was present in force. This was a small select group of young men, ranging in age from eighteen to twenty, pledged to protect the Führer with their own lives. They called themselves *Schutzstaffel* (guard detachment) or SS for short. Most of the audience of more than 10,000 had never before heard Hitler and his first words made little impact. The problem was the new loudspeaker system. Standing at the back of the hall, the British journalist Sefton Delmer had trouble making out what Hitler was saying. Delmer did hear him urge Germans not to eat oranges and, putting him down as a "crackpot," left the hall. The cacophony was such that Hitler himself turned off the microphones and shouted. In a few minutes he quieted the Red hecklers and completely dominated the vast audience. "Whoever shows his fist to the German people, we will force to be our brother," he said and then raised the bogy of racial degeneration. "The bastardization of great states has begun. The negroization of culture, of customs—not only of blood—strides forward. The world becomes democratized. The value of the individual declines. The masses apparently are gaining the victory over the idea of the great leader. Numbers are chosen as the new God."

Hitler felt a strain in his throat. For over an hour he had been forcing his voice and, realizing he was "about to fall down from exhaustion," he brought the speech to a close. "We fight against the idea of numbers and the delirium of the masses. We want to see those who are superior take the reins of government in their hands. There are 100,000 among us for whom voting is of no consequence—only the authority of the leader. And these 100,000 know that democracy in itself is a deception." It was a triumph of magnetism over matter. "When Hitler speaks," commented Goebbels about this address, "all resistance collapses before the magic effect of his words. One can only be his friend or his enemy . . . this is the secret of his strength: his fanatical faith in the movement, and with it in Germany."

An American journalist, Louis Lochner, witnessed the same phenomenon a month later at a talk to the students of Berlin University. "My first impression of him was that of a consummate showman. As movie cameras were turned upon him, he pretended not to notice them, spoke earnestly to his shadow, Rudolf Hess, and, as the cameras continued to click, began to write as though he were drawing up an outline of his remarks. It was good acting." Lochner noticed that Hitler's young adherents were hypnotized. "I came away from that meeting wondering how a man whose diction was by no means faultless, who ranted and fumed and stamped, could so impress young intellectuals. Of all people, I thought, they should have detected the palpable flaws in his logic."

One of these fascinated young intellectuals was Albert Speer, an assistant at the Institute of Technology. He had come with some reluctance at the urging of his students and expected to see Hitler in military tunic with swastika armband. "But here he was wearing a well-fitted blue suit and looking markedly respectable. Everything about him bore out the note of reasonable modesty." What struck Speer was that he spoke hesitatingly and somewhat shyly as if he were delivering a historical lecture. "To me there was something engaging about it—all the more so since it ran counter to everything the propaganda of his opponents had led me to expect: a hysterical demagogue, a shrieking and gesticulating fanatic in uniform. He did not allow the bursts of applause to tempt him away from his sober tone." As Hitler's shyness disappeared, he began orating with hypnotic persuasiveness and, along with the rest of the audience, Speer was carried on a wave of enthusiasm which he could almost feel physically. "It swept away any skepticism, any reservations."

2

Hitler's personal approach would have been ineffective without an efficient party organization, and while the 1929 party congress in Nuremberg was outwardly a rally, an emotional testimony of dedication to the Führer and his ideals, the organization of the party was being buttressed in the working sessions. By the end of that summer Hitler had succeeded in setting up a functionary corps in line with an appeal to the German middle class by admitting university graduates and other representatives of the bourgeoisie into the party bureaucracy. While allowing Goebbels and Strasser to win over the workers, he directed his opening campaign primarily to militant veterans and capitalistic businessmen, for he realized he would never get into power without them. He dramatized his new thrust by publicly joining with the Stahlhelm, rabidly nationalistic veterans, and Alfred Hugenberg, the nation's leading film and press lord and head of the völkisch right-wing German National People's Party, in a fight against acceptance of the new American liberalized formula (the Young Plan) for reparations payment. On the surface it seemed a suicidal move that would lose all the new adherents from the left. But Hitler was convinced that he could keep both sides in line and he was counting on success in the forthcoming national plebiscite on the Young Plan to reaffirm his judgment.

In the meantime he and the party were enjoying the financial benefits of their *mariage de convenance* with industry. Hitler bought the Barlow Palace, a three-story building on the Briennerstrasse, as national party headquarters; then early that September moved from his monastic room to one of the most fashionable sections of Munich across the Isar, where he took a nine-room apartment covering the entire second floor of 16

Prinzregentenplatz. He brought along Frau Reichert, his landlady from the Thierschstrasse, and her mother, Frau Dachs.

His sister Angela remained in charge of the Berchtesgaden villa (now his property), but she allowed her daughter Geli, now twenty-one, to take a room in Uncle Alf's new apartment while pursuing her medical studies in Munich. His feelings for her had not altered but their relationship changed. While maintaining the role of uncle, Hitler began overtly, if discreetly, to act more like a suitor. They were occasionally seen together in public at the theater or at his favorite table in the garden of the Café Heck where he often held court late in the afternoon.

Hitler was so enthralled, according to Hanfstaengl, that "he hovered at her elbow with a moon-calf look in his eyes in a very plausible imitation of adolescent infatuation." She inveigled him into going shopping even though he confessed to Hoffmann "how he hated it when Geli tried on hats or shoes, or inspected bale after bale of material, engaging the shopgirl in earnest conversation for half an hour or more, and then, finding nothing that suited her, walked out of the shop." Hitler knew that this would happen on every shopping expedition—yet "always followed her like a faithful lamb."

At the same time Hitler remained the stern uncle, restricting the high-spirited girl's social life to restaurants, cafés and an occasional visit to the theater. Even when she nagged him into letting her go to a Shrovetide ball it was under rigid conditions: her escorts were Max Amann and Hoffmann and they were instructed to bring her back at 11 P.M. Hoffmann warned that these restraints were making her extremely unhappy but the Führer replied that he felt bound to watch over his niece. "I love Geli, and I could marry her." At the same time he was determined to remain a bachelor. What Geli regarded as restraint, he said, was wisdom. "I am quite determined to see that she does not fall into the hands of some unworthy adventurer or swindler."

That Hitler was sexually frustrated seems borne out by an inept attempt to kiss the seventeen-year-old daughter of Heinrich Hoffmann. One day he found Henriette alone at home. "Won't you kiss me?" he said quite seriously, according to her account. Usually he addressed her with the familiar "thou." Today it was "you." ("I liked him because he always was considerate, he always helped me when I wanted something from Father, money for tennis lessons, for instance, or for skiing expeditions. . . . But kissing him?") She politely refused and after a moment's silence Hitler struck the palm of his hand with his whip and slowly walked away.

Of more significance was his meeting with another pretty seventeen-year-old who worked in Hoffmann's photo shop. Eva Braun, the daughter of a teacher and the product of a convent, was—like Geli—a modern girl, athletic and lively. She preferred jazz to opera and American musical comedies to the dramas of Kaiser and Wedekind. Unlike Geli, she was on the plump side and had fair hair. "She was a terror, it's true, the trouble-maker of the class," recalled a teacher, Fräulein von Heidenaber, "but she was intelligent and quick to seize the essential aspects of a subject, and she was capable of independent thought."

They met late on a Friday afternoon in early October. Eva had stayed in the shop to catch up on filing and was on a ladder reaching for the files on the top of a cupboard. "At that moment," she later told her sister, "the boss came in accompanied by a man with a funny mustache, a light-colored English-style overcoat and a big felt hat in his hand. They both sat down on the other side of the room, opposite me." She sensed that the newcomer was examining her legs. "That very day I had shortened my skirt and I felt slightly embarrassed because I wasn't sure I'd got the hem even."

After she climbed down Hoffmann introduced her to the stranger. "Herr Wolf. Our good little Fräulein Eva." A few minutes later they were all sitting down to beer and sausages. "I was starving. I gobbled my sausage and had a sip of beer for politeness' sake. The elderly gentleman was paying me compliments. We talked about music and a play at the Staatstheater, as I remember, with him devouring me with his eyes all the time. Then, as it was getting late, I rushed off. I refused his offer of a lift in his Mercedes. Just think what Papa's reaction would have been!" But before she left, Hoffmann took her aside and asked, "Haven't you guessed who that gentleman is? It's Hitler! Adolf Hitler!" "Oh?" replied Eva.

In the days to come Hitler would quite often drop in at the studio with flowers and candy for "my lovely siren from Hoffmann's." On the rare times he took her out, he avoided his usual haunts for tea in an obscure corner of the Carlton Café or a movie in Schwabing. But by the end of the year his visits to Hoffmann's studio had become a rarity. Perhaps it was because of Eva's boast to several fellow employees that she was Hitler's mistress and he was going to marry her. Hoffmann, who was sure she had never even visited Hitler's apartment, summoned her to his office. Eva broke into tears, confessing she had lied and he threatened to fire her if she repeated the story.

3

The Young Plan plebiscite late in 1929 turned out to be a triumph for Chancellor Stresemann and his liberal program, although he died before the vote was counted. The uneasy alliance of Hitler and Hugenberg's National People's Party needed 21,000,000 votes to defeat the measure and got less than 6,000,000. While this was a crushing defeat for Hugenberg, Hitler cleverly turned it into a victory of sorts. Never one to espouse a lost cause, he turned on Hugenberg with a vengeance, breaking their alliance as unpredictably as he had made it. He was already confidently preparing his forces, enlarged by the publicity of the plebiscite issue, for the coming national elections even though it was a rare observer who now rated the Nazis highly. In his memoirs the former English ambassador to Berlin, Lord D'Abernon, mentioned the Führer once in a footnote. Hitler, he wrote, had been "fading into oblivion" ever since 1924. Both Dr. Arnold Wolfers, director of studies at the Berlin Hochschule für Politik, and the historian Arnold Toynbee concurred with this obituary.

Hitler was thinking of victory and felt it was possible if he could win new workers to his cause. To do this, there must be a dramatic new propaganda ploy. The opportunity came early in 1930, with the death of a law student in Berlin. Horst Wessel, the twenty-one-year-old son of a preacher and a Freemason, had rebelled against his bourgeois upbringing to become a dedicated Brownshirt in the bloody street battles against the Reds. He wrote a poem, "Raise High the Flag!" immortalizing comrades who had sacrificed their lives—"shot dead by Red Front and Reaction," which was published in *Der Angriff* and later set to music.* Wessel fell in love with a onetime prostitute named Erna and moved in with her. In an effort to eject the couple her landlady sought help from the Communists. A Red gang burst into the lovers' room. Their leader, an intimate of Erna's, reportedly shouted, "You know what that's for!" and shot Wessel. In an attempt to make political capital out of the sorry affair, the Communists called Wessel a pimp, which he was not. On his part Goebbels publicly transfigured the lover into a working-class Jesus, which he was not. "Leaving home and mother," wrote Goebbels, the novelist manqué, "he took to living among those who scorned and spit on him. Out there, in a proletarian section, in a tenement attic he proceeded to build his youthful, modest life. A socialist Christ! One who appealed to others through his deeds."

While Wessel lay dying in a hospital, Goebbels turned a private feud into political assassination by having Wessel's song sung at the conclusion of a meeting in the Sportpalast: "The banners flutter, the drums roll, the fifes rejoice, and from millions of throats resounds the hymn of the German revolution, Raise high the flag!" At last, on February 23, Wessel died. "His spirit has risen in order to live on in all of us," wrote Goebbels. He is "marching within our ranks." To cap the propaganda campaign Goebbels decided to stage an extravagant funeral with Hitler delivering the final oration. But the Führer had reservations about such show-

* Hanfstaengl wrote that the melody was "exactly that of a Vienna cabaret song of the turn of the century," to which the words originally ran more or less like this:

And as your eye met mine
And as my lips kissed yours
Then did love enshroud us.

Wessel merely "hotted up the tune to march time."

manship. So did Göring, who had returned from Sweden after a cure for drug addiction to win election to the Reichstag. The situation in Berlin, he argued, was already tense enough and the Führer's safety could not be guaranteed. "If anything goes wrong," he said, according to Hanfstaengl's recollection, "it would be a catastrophe. After all, there are only twelve of us in the Reichstag, and we simply haven't enough strength to make capital out of this. If Hitler comes to Berlin it will be a red rag to the Communist bulls and we cannot afford to take the consequences."

Hitler pleaded illness and the funeral had to proceed without him. Göring was right. The procession turned into a battle march with the Reds assaulting the mourners, and even as Goebbels stood at the graveside and dramatically called the roll: "Horst Wessel?" and the storm troopers shouted back "Present!" stones flew over the cemetery wall into the grave. Nothing could have pleased propagandist Goebbels more. "As the coffin came to rest in the cool ground," he wrote, "there went up outside the gates the depraved cry of the subhuman. . . . The departed, still with us, raised his weary hand and beckoned into the shimmering distance: Forward over the graves! At the end of the road lies Germany!"

From such words one would never guess at the true relationship between ordinary Reds and Nazis. While they fought each other relentlessly, they felt a unique comradeship, and it was no rarity for them to unite if one of their brawls in a bar or beer hall was interrupted by the police. Both groups were driven by fervor for a cause, both believed that the end justified the means. They shared similar socialist goals and had the same contempt for parliamentary procedures. On the previous May Day they had paraded down the streets of Berlin arm in arm, in joint protest against suppression of marching demonstrations, shouting their common slogan: "Freedom, Work and Bread." Moreover, they both hated the Jewish police commissioner, Bernhard Weiss (renamed "Isidor" by Goebbels), and alike regarded the police as "Isidor's" army, a brutal enemy of all revolutionaries.

Two months after Goebbels had squeezed the last drop of propaganda out of Horst Wessel, the Hitler-Otto Strasser feud came out in the open. Since his brother's departure for Munich and party eminence, Otto had become the leading editorial writer of the three newspapers Gregor had founded. While they still carried the National Socialist emblem on their mastheads, they had become a platform for Otto's iconoclastic views, which often ran contrary to those of Hitler. Their differences were brought to a head that April by Otto Strasser's full support of the Saxon metalworkers' strike. Industrialists such as Fritz Thyssen of the United Steel Works insisted that Hitler repudiate Strasser if he wanted more subsidies.

At first Hitler tried threats but these failed and he came to Berlin to exert the force of his personality. The two men met twice at the Hotel

Sanssouci. For almost seven hours Hitler flattered, cajoled, promised and threatened but the two meetings only revealed their differences. Neither made a single concession and Otto Strasser rejected a tempting offer to be party propaganda chief. Despite their inability to come to terms, Strasser and his circle did not break at once with the party "because there was still hope that Hitler had been impressed by the discussions" and might even abandon the "Rosenberg line." They were also unwilling to make a public issue of the break, which might hurt the party's chances in the forthcoming provincial elections in Saxony. Otto Strasser, however, realized that he and his socialist followers could not remain in the NSDAP; not after Hitler had professed his intention to follow Mussolini's Fascist principles and deal with industrialists. The talks also revealed Hitler's determination to keep his Weltanschauung so vague and "infinitely interpretable" that he could exercise complete control by means of absolute authority. He knew instinctively that the moment National Socialism was pledged to a concrete program the Führer principle would be compromised.

Hitler must have felt humiliated that young Strasser had contradicted him so flagrantly and openly, but he drove back to Munich without much comment and upon arrival made no public attack. Nor did he carry out a threat to proceed against Otto "with all the means at my disposal." He did nothing except proclaim in the press, as did Gregor Strasser, that no dispute had taken place in Berlin and he and Otto were in agreement. Rather than punish the rebel openly, Hitler began expelling from the party those who contributed to his papers; and at the end of June he finally gave Goebbels veiled instructions to purge Otto Strasser and his followers. "The National Socialist Party, as long as I lead it," he wrote, "will not be a debating club for rootless men of letters and chaotic salon Bolshevists, but will remain what it is today, an organization of discipline created not for doctrinaire foolishness or political Wandervögel but dedicated to fight for the future of Germany in which class distinction will be broken and a new German people will decide its own destiny!" Goebbels consequently was instructed to *"ruthlessly clean up* the party of all those elements in Berlin." He did so within a few weeks, and Strasser's subsequent call for a general exodus of socialists from the party brought only twenty-four followers. Otto's own brother rejected him, signing a declaration with two other left-wing party members that "they were united behind the leadership of Adolf Hitler and submitted themselves to the strict discipline of the party organization." To a mutual friend, Gregor characterized his brother as the eternal dissident. "The departure of my brother and his fight against the party is pure madness."

While Otto Strasser's split with Hitler caused a sensation in the newspapers, it had little effect within the party. During the long bitter factional struggle between north and south, Hitler had done his best to act as arbiter. He was intent only on conciliation and compromise, and in victory he had been magnanimous. He had rewarded Gregor Strasser with a high party post; and even when Otto embarrassed him in front of witnesses he had done his best to minimize their differences. He made it appear that it was Otto himself who forced his own explusion from the party. Now at last the internecine battle was over and Hitler could concentrate all his energies on the national elections in September.

4

Hitler offered something to almost every German voter in 1930—the farmer, the worker, the student, the patriot, the racist and the middle-class burgher. The common denominator of his wide appeal was the world depression which had followed the Wall Street crash of 1929 and abruptly ended Germany's remarkable recovery. By late summer there were almost three million unemployed in the nation and Chancellor Brüning's policy of economic retrenchment was making matters worse. Here at last was the burning issue that could bring him political control of Germany, thought Hitler. His appeal to workers was couched in Communist terminology. "Working Germany, awake! Break your chains in two!" proclaimed Goebbels' *Der Angriff*. To farmers, whose recent profits were being wiped out by the world-wide decline of agricultural prices, Hitler offered tax adjustments and import duties. The lower middle class, with no trade unions to fight for them, were offered hope; to those just above them in the social hierarchy to whom poverty was a stigma—self-respect; and to the young idealists in and out of universities—an idealistic new world.

This last group was not large but it provided Hitler with a militant, dedicated cadre for the future. They listened entranced as he preached against materialism and selfishness, promised to establish social harmony and a front rank in his crusade for social justice and a revitalized Germany. Convinced that Hitler would create a genuine socialist regime, these young people roamed the streets of the large cities chanting the slogan they shared with their Communist adversaries, "Freedom, Work and Bread!" The rising generation "felt something was moving and the terrible stagnation was over," recalled one follower. "You had to live through it to really understand it." It was a chance to serve that attracted most of these young idealists and Hitler was the only politician of his day who understood the power of such an appeal.

A number of intellectuals, the social elite and royalty itself were also drawn to him. That spring the Kaiser's young son, August Wilhelm ("Auwi"), wrote his dear battle comrade Hitler that it was his "heart's desire" to inform him personally that he had just been admitted to the party. "It was for me a very emotional moment and my thoughts turned to you in loyalty." The Prince feared the spread of Communism and his conversion influenced Prince Philip von Hessen, a nephew of the Kaiser and grandson of Queen Victoria, to join in support of Hitler.

In 1930 he was offering Germans something new—a feeling of unity. He welcomed everyone to join in the crusade. There was no class distinction; the only requirement was willingness to follow Hitler without hesitation in his fight to the death against the Jews and the Reds, in his struggle for Lebensraum and the glory and the good of Germany. "What we felt," wrote an early party member, "what our hearts compelled us to think, was this—Hitler, you're our man. You talk like a human being who's been at the front, who's been through the same mess we were, and not in some soft berth, but like us an unknown soldier." It was these transcendental appeals which roused the emotions of such divergent voters. Nor did Hitler press his anti-Semitism—particularly the "removal" of Jews—except with völkisch groups and the workers. To the more educated and the idealistic this issue was discussed either in whispers or an offhand manner.

That summer Hitler campaigned tirelessly with his omnibus program, delivering twenty major speeches in the final six weeks. A born politician, he found it not only natural but inspiring to mix with crowds, shaking hands, kissing babies and bowing to women. He would eat with the working-class and middle-class adherents more often than with the elite, and his man-to-man approach appealed to the clerk and small businessman as well as the laborer.

Although he approached each group with a separate message, Hitler never forgot the lesson he had learned in Landsberg: that he must win the masses. Consequently he never allowed himself to take an aggressive stand on minor issues. Over and over he hammered at the money barons, the Reds, the Marxists and the "system" that had brought unemployment, lowered farm prices and wiped out the savings of the middle class. He did not pit class against class. He could embrace them all.

Never had Germany—or the world for that matter—been subjected to such persuasion. Goebbels organized six thousand meetings—in large halls, in tents that could hold ten thousand, in the open air. There were torchlight parades; towns, cities and villages were plastered with glaring red posters. The entire Nazi press blanketed the country with special campaign editions that ran into millions of copies; and those that couldn't be sold were given away.

In a final admonition to party workers on the morning of the election Goebbels gave them cynical but practical advice on how to electioneer. "Do it jokingly, do it seriously! Treat your dear fellow creatures as they are used to being treated. Stimulate their rage and their fury, direct them to the proper course." That day long lines queued up at polling places throughout the country. A record 35,000,000 ballots were cast, 4,000,000 more than in 1928. Hitler arrived at the election center in Munich just after midnight to be greeted by an excited Adolf Müller, the party printer: "I think we've won. We may get sixty-six seats!" This would have meant an amazing increase of fifty-four seats since 1928 but Hitler replied that if the German people could think correctly the figure would be higher. "Within myself I was saying: 'If it could be a hundred!'" A hundred and seven seats were won. "How to express what I felt at that moment? We'd gone up from twelve seats to a hundred and seven!"

What surprised the National Socialists came as a sickening shock to their opponents. Officials checked and rechecked for errors before announcing that the Nazis had won 6,371,000 votes, more than eighteen per cent of the total vote. In two years the Hitler movement had risen from 810,000 votes to become the second largest party in the Reich. After pronouncing Hitler dead politically, the Social Democrats had made the mistake of concentrating their attacks on the Reds.

The Communists also made a substantial gain of 1,326,000 votes and the Social Democrats lost fewer than 60,000 votes, an indication that Hitler's gains had come mainly at the expense of the middle-class parties. The most sensational Nazi increase was among the farmers and lower middle class in the rural and Protestant areas in the northern half of the country, but considerable gains were also made among Catholics. In the days before the Beer Hall Putsch Hitler had sought almost exclusively for the dissident, disenchanted, desperation vote. Now he had received support from people who expected him to bring them better lives. It was Hitler's elastic appeal and forceful oratory which had attracted the new voters but it was the tireless work of thousands of cell leaders and cell foremen in the party's efficient vertical organization that got them to the polls.

For the past year or so Hanfstaengl's acid remarks had alienated Hitler but astonishing election victory brought him back to favor. Hess phoned that the Führer was most anxious to see him. Half an hour later Hitler was at the Hanfstaengl home with a proposition: would he take over the post of foreign press chief of the party? "Great things are before us. In a few months, or at the most in a couple of years, we must irresistibly sweep to power. You have all the connections and could render us a great service."

Hanfstaengl accepted and a few days later accompanied Hitler to Leipzig for the trial of three young officers accused of spreading Nazi propaganda in the army. Hitler himself took the stand on September 25 and made a clever, paradoxical speech which managed to appeal to almost everyone. After assurances that he would come to power peacefully through the ballot box, he pledged allegiance to the army and promised to fight against the shameful Treaty of Versailles even if he had to do so "with illegal means." He ended with a vow to the revolutionaries in his party that once he came to power there would be a National Socialist

Court of Justice. "Then the November 1918 revolution will be avenged and heads will roll!" Once again Hitler had demonstrated his political agility by satisfying both burgher and revolutionary almost simultaneously, reassuring the first of his peaceful intentions and promising the second bloody vengeance. The effect of his words went far beyond Germany, for he was spokesman of the second largest party in the land and his inflammatory remarks about treaties were no longer the meaningless polemics of a minor politician.

Hanfstaengl was besieged by foreign correspondents who wanted interviews with Germany's new phenomenon. Hitler hurriedly composed an article for the London *Sunday Express*. "The election, so to speak," he wrote, "took the temperature of the German people. The world was shocked to discover Germany in a fever—a high fever. That fever is bound to continue—to rise against existing conditions and unbearable burdens." He demanded not only the revision of the Versailles Treaty and the Young Plan but "the return of the Polish Corridor, which is like a strip of flesh cut from our body." He denied, however, the accusation that Germany was guilty of causing the war, and accused President Wilson of betraying solemn promises to the Reich. "If the German people must suffer as they are suffering today and will be suffering tomorrow," he warned in conclusion, "then let us have suffering that may come from saying 'No' rather than that laid on us by saying our 'yes.' "

A few days later Hitler changed his pace by assuring a reporter for the London *Times* that he would operate in a strictly legal manner. "Don't condemn us, therefore, if we should act as yourselves would act in our place. I hope that England will never find herself in a position like that of Germany, but if she were in such a position and if, in her darkest hour, she was stabbed in the back, what would be the attitude of England when on her feet once more? What would be the attitude of English patriots towards those among their own nation who had sought to destroy their country?"

Two weeks later, on October 13, the 107 Nazi deputies marched into the Reichstag for the opening session clad in brown shirts, each one answering the roll call with a resounding "Present, Heil Hitler!" Socialist member Toni Sender was appalled. "This was the élite of the 'Aryan' race! —this noisy, shouting, uniformed gang. I looked at their faces carefully. The more I studied them, the more I was terrified by what I saw: so many men with the faces of criminals and degenerates. What a degradation to sit in the same place with such a gang!"

The words of delegate Gregor Strasser to the Reichstag were relatively reassuring—"Let us leave it at that and go along with the old system as long as democracy still exists . . . we are now for the democratic Weimar Republic as long as it suits us"—but action on the streets of the capital cast an ominous shadow of things to come. Hundreds of SA men in civilian clothes were already smashing the windows of Jewish shops, cafés and department stores.

5

The international publicity which followed the September elections was a mixed blessing to Hitler. Along with the prestige came an unwelcome visit from his nephew, William Patrick Hitler, who lived in England with his mother. In 1910 Alois Hitler, Jr., then working as a waiter in Dublin, had married an Irish girl, Brigid Elizabeth Dowling. Their life was hectic because Alois kept changing his way of earning a living. He opened a small restaurant in Liverpool, sold it to buy a boardinghouse, turned hotel owner, went bankrupt, and finally became a razor blade salesman. It was an unhappy existence for Brigid and several times she left home. Their quarrels intensified after the birth of William Patrick because Alois shared his father's doctrine that children should be disciplined at an early age; several times while Brigid was out of the house Alois beat the baby, and by the time William Patrick was three the family broke up. According to Brigid Alois deserted them and returned to Germany but Alois told his relatives that his wife had run away with an engineer, taking the boy with her.

When Brigid and her son read about Hitler's electoral success they saw it as "an opportunity of making some money by giving an interview to the Hearst press." After all, Alois had never sent them anything for support. Negotiations were started with a Hearst representative in London and early that October pictures of William Patrick began appearing in the American press under the caption: "This young London office worker, William Patrick Hitler, is a nephew of Adolf Hitler, Germany's new political leader. He was born in Liverpool and knows little of his uncle's aims." He knew so little, in fact, that he wrote his father asking for further details about the life of the new political wonder. "The reply," William Patrick told an OSS interviewer years later, "came in the form of a demand from Adolf for a conference, tickets for the passage were enclosed." Upon arrival in Munich, mother and son found Hitler "in a perfect rage." At a family meeting, also attended by Angela Raubal and Alois, Hitler said he was "gaining some importance and the family need not think they could climb on his back and get a free ride to fame." Release of family information to the Hearst newspapers, he claimed, would destroy his chances of political success in view of his half brother's remarriage without bothering to divorce Brigid. "How carefully I always kept my personal affairs out of the press!" he said according to an article William Patrick wrote nine years later in *Paris Soir*. "These people must not know who I am. They must not know where I come from and from what family . . . even in my

book I did not say a word about such things, not a word, and now accidentally my nephew is discovered. Investigations are made, and spies are sent
to dig up our past." At this point, in the *Paris Soir* account, Hitler angrily
declared that William Patrick was not even a relation, since his father,
Alois, Jr. (who was listening to all this without comment), had been
adopted by Alois Hitler, Sr. He and his mother (according to the OSS interview) should go back to London and tell the Hearst people that they
had discovered the leader of the Nazi Party was another Adolf Hitler and
no kin of theirs. This solution "pleased" Hitler and, after urging the two
to get back to England "as quickly as possible and disclaim all relationship
in the present and in the future," he handed over to Alois two thousand
dollars to cover the expenses of mother and son in Munich as well as passage home. Alois paid the expenses, bought the tickets and promised to
send the rest by mail because it would be "much safer." William Patrick
swore it never arrived. (Curiously, a story about Adolf Hitler soon appeared in the New York *American,* a Hearst publication, under the by-line
of Alois Hitler, Jr. In it Alois described his younger brother as a very lika-
ble and generous boy, a dreamer as far removed from reality as the sun
from the moon. On his mother's death Adolf took his younger sister Paula
to Vienna where they endured a grim struggle against pitiless poverty.
Adolf, so Alois wrote, had to sweep streets and perform other menial jobs
to get food for Paula and himself. Then he went to Munich where he got
work as a house painter and decorator.)

   Not long after William Patrick and his mother returned to England
Hitler summoned his lawyer to the apartment on Prinzregentenplatz.
Hitler pointed to a letter before him and said "it concerned a 'disgusting
blackmail' plot in connection with one of his most loathsome relatives
with respect to his own ancestry." As Hans Frank recalled it, Hitler was
referring to William Patrick Hitler, who had "hinted" that the press was
very interested in a certain aspect of Hitler's ancestry, namely that he was
part Jewish. The Führer, consequently, ordered Frank to investigate the
matter confidentially.

   His report, gathered from "all possible sources," was most disconcerting: Hitler's father, it seemed, was "the illegitimate child of a cook
named Schicklgruber from Leonding, near Linz, employed in a household
in Graz." This cook "was working for a Jewish family named Frankenberger
when she gave birth to her son. And Frankenberger—this happened in the
late 1830s—paid a paternity allowance on behalf of his nineteen-year-old
son from the birth of the Schicklgruber woman's son until he was 14."
There was also a long correspondence between the Frankenbergers and
the cook (Hitler's grandmother), "the general trend of which was the
unexpressed common understanding of the participants that the
Schicklgruber woman's child had been conceived in circumstances which
rendered the Frankenbergers liable for the paternity allowance." Frank's

report concluded regretfully that the possibility could not be dismissed that Hitler's father was half Jewish.

The Führer heatedly challenged Frank's deduction with the embarrassed explanation that his grandfather, who was impoverished, had successfully blackmailed the Frankenbergers on the false charge of paternity. Hitler swore that this information came directly to him from both his father and grandmother. He must have been truly shaken by Frank's evidence to tell such a patent lie: his grandmother had died forty years before his own birth. More important was the admission that his grandmother *had* received money from a Jew, for this allowed the terrible possibility that his own blood might be tainted. The chance that Adolf Hitler was part Jewish was minimal.* The important point was that he *feared* so and he would instigate at least two subsequent investigations to reassure himself. A physician named Schuh, who had known Hitler since 1917, recalled he "suffered all his life from painful doubts: did he or did he not have Jewish blood? And he often told us this." Hitler's inability to produce the documentary proof of his own Aryan background, something he demanded from others, could explain why he told William Patrick Hitler: "These people must not know from where and from what family I come."

Despite this distressing personal matter, 1931 augured well for Adolf Hitler. He had suddenly become a best-selling author. *Mein Kampf* had sold an average of little more than 6000 copies annually until the last year when the amount rose to 54,086. This got him a respectable personal income which promised to continue indefinitely. Furthermore, the Brown House, the new party headquarters, was opened on the first of the year. Purchased and renovated by special contributions, profits from Hitler rallies, gifts and dues, it represented the substance and reliability of the NSDAP as a party. On the second floor were the offices of Hitler, Hess, Goebbels, Strasser and the SA. The Führer's office was large and attractively decorated in reddish brown. Ceiling-high windows overlooked the Königsplatz. There was a large bust of Mussolini, and among the pictures on the wall were a painting of Frederick the Great and another of the first attack of the Führer's old regiment in Flanders. "Hitler was not often there," recalled Frank. His method of working was totally unsystematic. He would "breeze in" but before he could be pinned down "just breeze out again." Once cornered, he would hastily finish the business, then launch into "an hour-long monologue."

He preferred to spend his time downstairs in the small refreshment

---

* The research of Nikolaus Preradovic, University of Graz, casts some doubt on Frank's evidence. He found no record of either a Frankenberger or a Frankenreither in the books of the Jewish congregation in Graz, Austria. These books, it is true, begin in 1856, nineteen years after Hitler's father was born, but that was because Jews had been driven out of the Steiermark in 1496 and were only allowed to return in 1856. Before that time, according to Preradovic, there was "not one single Jew" in Graz.

room where he would sit in a corner at the "Führer" table over which hung a picture of Dietrich Eckart. But even this soon palled. The sedentary existence of the Brown House was not for him. He was driven by an urge to move, to win mass support for himself and the party among the people, or to hold high-level conversations with those who could give him either political or financial assistance. The problems he faced at the beginning of 1931 were truly formidable, largely due to the NSDAP's phenomenal membership growth which, in turn, brought an expansion of bureaucracy in every department of the party with the resultant frictions and jealousies.

Most troublesome was the SA, many of whose members refused to take Hitler's avowals of legality seriously. The storm troopers had always boasted of their tradition of violence and saw no reason why they should knuckle under to the civilian leaders in Munich. These men were among the most idealistic and many were socialists at heart, sharing with their Communist rivals a revolutionary zeal that was becoming an embarrassment to the Führer. From the first he had trouble with its leaders, who wanted to make the SA the military arm of the party, whereas he had insisted that its main function was to protect rallies and mobilize political loyalty. First had been Captain Röhm, whose violent disagreement with Hitler led to voluntary exile in South America; then came Pfeffer von Salomon, whose similar demands for a stronger SA had led to his recent resignation.

The dissatisfaction of the leaders was shared by their men. Recently dissident Brownshirts in Berlin had revolted on the grounds that they were hungry, overworked and constantly exposed to injuries as well as arrest in their battles with the police and Reds. They refused to act as mere bodyguards for party rallies and, after their seven demands, including a reasonable one for more funds, were turned down by Goebbels, one troop went berserk and raided a local party headquarters guarded by the SS. It took Hitler's personal intervention to put down the revolt. He toured the various SA meeting places, accompanied by armed SS troops, calling for reconciliation. Like a patient and forbearing father, he pleaded, promised and scolded. He spoke little about the seven Brownshirt demands but kept the matter on a personal level, calling for allegiance to himself. Then he announced that he himself would become the new commander of the SA. The wild cheers that followed signaled an end to the brief rebellion and Hitler could return to the election trail.

His promise to head the SA personally was an empty one. He had neither the time nor the inclination to take on such an assignment and by the beginning of 1931 the Brownshirts were still without effective leadership. Then on January 4 it was announced that Captain Röhm (recently recalled from Bolivia where he had helped the Republic fight one of its wars with Paraguay) would become the new chief of staff of the SA.

What attracted Röhm back to Germany was Hitler's willingness to give him a fairly free hand in the internal structure of the 60,000-man organization. Resigned to keeping the storm troopers as a disciplined marching unit for the time being, this capable organizer and inspiring leader began reshaping the SA in his own image.

But efficiency was no cure for the deep-seated complaints within the organization, and it soon became evident that another serious revolt was brewing in the capital. The basic grievances of the Berlin Brownshirts remained. Their leader, Captain Walter Stennes, was incensed by the inequities within the organization and once more demanded a system based on "what you know," not "who you know." He openly complained that Hitler "changed his mind every few months with new orders" and that it was impossible to operate under such conditions. Stennes' men were perplexed and perturbed. While agreeing with him, they felt irresistibly drawn to the Führer.

The issue surfaced on February 20, 1931, after Hitler issued orders to both the SA and SS to cease fighting the Reds and Jews in the streets. "I understand your distress and rage," he told the Brownshirts, "but you must not bear arms." They grumbled but did nothing until late the following month when the Führer bowed to a Weimar government decree requiring all potential rallies to be approved by the police. The indignant Stennes denounced this capitulation to the establishment, then called a secret conference of SA leaders at midnight of March 31. All those present declared themselves in favor of Stennes and against Hitler.

In an attempt to settle the matter without bloodshed and publicity, the Führer ordered Stennes to report to Munich for a desk job at the Brown House. Stennes refused and Hitler loosed the SS on the rebels. Open resistance ended within twenty-four hours. It had been a puny rebellion. All Stennes wanted was to bring about pure National Socialism, to serve a party, not an individual. "Whoever goes with me has a hard road," he told his men in a farewell speech. "I recommend, however, that you stay with Hitler for the sake of the National Socialist idea which we do not want to destroy."

On April 4 both *Der Angriff* and the *Völkischer Beobachter* printed articles by Hitler condemning the Stennes "Putsch." He reaffirmed that socialism had always been a major part of the NSDAP but criticized "the buffoons of salon-bolshevism and salon-socialism" who had drifted into the party. He claimed that Stennes was one of these and that he had tried "to introduce into the SA a series of concepts that, accurately, belong to the continuously seditious requisites of the Communists."

These articles only created more furor among the dissident Berlin Brownshirts and Hitler once more rushed to the capital in his role as conciliator and middle-of-the-road revolutionary. This time he took along Hanfstaengl, who wrote: "Hitler had to go around from suburb to suburb and beseech them with tears in his eyes to rely on him to see that their interests were protected." He managed to restore order and spent the next day in a commercial travelers' hotel with Stennes. The latter impressed Hanfstaengl as more the victim than the leader of the revolt. "I found him a very decent fellow, a nephew of Cardinal Schulte of Cologne, and he took me over to one of the open windows, where our conversation was drowned by the noise of traffic, and said: 'Does Hitler realize that the real instigator of this revolt is standing by him?'—and that was Goebbels. 'He has been egging them on to demonstrate in the streets in spite of Hitler's orders that we were not to get into fights, and now they blame it all on me.'"

As usual the appearance of Hitler (backed up by his faithful SS force) brought unity to the SA and this time it was lasting. The dismissal of Stennes and a handful of followers caused no reverberations. Goebbels managed to emerge safely from the farrago, even though many besides Stennes felt he had played an insidious part in the revolt. The Führer himself had suspicions and at an informal gathering of Gauleiters a little later made allusion to them. "When a mother has many children and one of them goes astray," he said, "it is the wise mother who takes the child by the hand and holds on to him."

Hitler also realized that it had taken the force of the SS to bring his straying children back into the fold and, recognizing this, he replaced Stennes as leader of the Berlin-run SA with an SS man. The SS was exultant with its expanded role as protector of the Führer principle. "We were not loved everywhere," their chief, Heinrich Himmler, told a conference of SS leaders a few weeks later. "When we have done our duty we may be stood in the corner; we should expect no thanks. But our Führer knows the value of the SS. We are his favorite and most valuable organization because we have never let him down."

At the same time Hitler the mediator was ready to welcome back into the fold all those storm troopers who had strayed or hesitated—with the exception of those too independent spirits who had to be purged and replaced by loyal adherents. The response to Hitler's gesture of amnesty was almost unanimous. While many Brownshirts were disappointed in Hitler and his insistence on legality, such logic dissolved before his nearly Christlike declaration: "I am the SA and SS and you are members of the SA and SS as I am within you in the SA and SS."

No sooner had the SA been brought into line than their leader, Captain Röhm, came under heavy attack for alleged homosexuality. Earlier Hitler had brushed aside similar charges, "The SA is a collection of men for a particular political goal. It is not a moral institution for raising young girls, but an association of rough fighters." A man's private life, he added, was his own so long as it did not interfere with the National Socialist mission.

The scandal was already becoming a party issue. There were whispers that many of the officers purged in the Stennes Putsch had been replaced by Röhm's homosexual friends. Röhm appeared to act as unconcerned about such accusations as he was about those that his storm troopers committed atrocities. "I know the SA people have been a rough and ready lot in the past, my dear Herr Delmer," he told the correspondent of the London *Daily Express* late in April at the Reichs Restaurant in Berlin. "But from now on, you just watch! My men will be quiet and disciplined and orderly. My job is to prevent the millions of German unemployed from coming under Communist influence as they easily might. I want to turn them, instead, into an orderly citizen force for the defense of Germany against the internal and external Bolshevik enemy." Delmer protested that the rowdy shouts of "Germany, awake!" and "Perish, Judah!" didn't sound much like discipline and good order.

"Oh, don't take those slogans at their face value. That is all only half as serious as it sounds." Then he said something that roused the newsman's interest. "I am removing the rowdy undisciplined from the SA. A little cleansing is good for all such armies." That was why he was presently in Berlin. He explained that there had been a mutiny in the capital under Captain Stennes, a "madman" who had challenged his and Hitler's authority. But Röhm assured Delmer that the mutineers had been quelled and all was in order.

A week later, at Röhm's suggestion, Delmer journeyed to the Brown House to interview the Führer. Hitler admitted he had two demands: cancellation of the war reparations debt and a "free hand in the East." While he was not interested in restoration of the old frontiers or even the return of lost colonies, he demanded that the surplus millions of Germans must be allowed to expand into the Soviet Union. How, asked Delmer, could Hitler get into Russia without violating Polish territory? Hitler's only answer was a cryptic "A way can be found for everything."

Just then Prince August Wilhelm burst into the room with the dramatic announcement that 2400 Brownshirts had been wounded or killed in fights with the Marxists in the first four months of 1931. "*Mein Führer*," he exclaimed, "this is civil war!" "Yes," said Hitler offhandedly. "Undoubtedly this is civil war." Convinced Hitler was a completely ruthless man, Delmer began his article, which was published on May 3, with a prediction: "Germany is marching with giant strides to join the Fascist nations of Europe."

6

Hitler spent the summer of 1931 in consolidating the party and revamping the SA in light of the weaknesses made evident by the Stennes revolt. At the same time he was profoundly disturbed by a personal crisis.

He learned that his chauffeur and companion, Maurice, had become secretly engaged to his niece Geli, who had been living a restricted life in the Prinzregentenplatz apartment. Ironically it was the Führer himself, the perpetual matchmaker, who had given the idea to Maurice. "I'll come and have supper with you every evening when you are married," he urged the young man. "Following his advice," Maurice told an interviewer, "I decided to become engaged to Geli, with whom I was madly in love, like everybody else. She gladly accepted my proposal." For some time the inner circle had known they were lovers; Maurice had openly lamented about "his unhappy love" to Goebbels. Finally he steeled himself to confess. Hitler flew into a rage, accused Maurice of disloyalty and dismissed him as chauffeur.

Some of those close to the Führer were convinced he was only a concerned relative. "His affection was that of a father," Frau Anny Winter, the housekeeper, insisted years later. "He was concerned only with her welfare. Geli was a flighty girl who tried to seduce everybody, including Hitler, and he merely wanted to protect her." In a sense Geli had become a captive. Hitler gave her everything she wanted except freedom and insisted that she have an escort he trusted even when she went to her singing lessons. She complained to a relative that "her life was very hard; that Hitler insisted that she accompany him wherever he went and it was very embarrassing for her, particularly since she knew that Gregor Strasser was opposed to Hitler's being seen with her and furthermore, because it prevented her from meeting any other young people."

One evening the Hanfstaengls met the couple at the Residenz Theater and they all had late supper at the Schwarzwälder Café. Hanfstaengl noticed that Geli "seemed bored, looking over her shoulder at the other tables, and could not help feeling that her share in the relationship was under compulsion." Frau Hanfstaengl also got the feeling that the girl was repressed, as if "she couldn't do with her life what she wanted." But Frau Winter persisted in her belief that it was Geli who was the chaser. "Naturally she wanted to become Gnädige Frau Hitler. He was highly eligible . . . but she flirted with everybody, she was not a serious girl."

There was no doubt that Geli was impressed by her uncle's fame. Every time they had tea at the Café Heck their table would be besieged by admirers, many of them women who kissed his hand and begged for souvenirs. It was equally evident that the Führer's fondness for her went far beyond that of an uncle. "He loved her," averred Maurice, "but it was a strange affection that did not dare to show itself, for he was too proud to admit to the weaknesses of an infatuation."

There were others who claimed that the two were having a love affair, and Otto Strasser publicized a sensational hearsay story of their aberrant sexual relations that was given credence only by those who wanted to believe the worst of Hitler. He deeply loved his niece but it was unlikely that they had sexual relations. He was too reserved to openly court any woman and too cautious to ruin his political career by taking a mistress into his own apartment—particularly the daughter of a half sister.

By September Geli was involved with another young man, an artist from Austria who had become so enamored on first sight, according to Christa Schröder (Hitler's secretary), that he proposed to her. Once she started to tell Frau Hoffmann of the unhappy romance but, after admitting she was in love with an artist from Vienna and was miserable, cut herself off with: "Well, that's that! And there's nothing you or I can do about it. So let's talk about something else." As soon as Hitler learned of the liaison he forced her to break with the artist, apparently with the connivance of his half sister Angela.

In mid-September Geli phoned her voice teacher that she was taking no more lessons and was leaving for Vienna, then set out for Berchtesgaden to see her mother. No sooner had she arrived than she got a phone call from Uncle Alf urgently requesting her to return to Munich at once. She felt obliged to do so but, upon learning that he was about to leave Munich to attend a meeting of Gauleiters and major SA leaders, she "reproached him for having made her come for nothing." Her indignation turned to fury when he forbade her to leave for Vienna during his absence. The argument continued at a spaghetti lunch for two on September 17. From the kitchen Frau Winter heard their voices loudly raised in argument and, as Geli rushed out of the dining room, the cook noticed her face was flushed.

Geli stayed in her room until she heard her uncle start down the stairs to join Hoffmann, who was accompanying him on the trip, then she followed Hitler to the hallway. She held something in her left hand but Frau Reichert couldn't see what it was. "*Servus*, Uncle Alf!" she called down. "*Servus*, Herr Hoffmann!"

At the outside door Hitler stopped, looked back, and mounted the stairs. He fondly stroked Geli's cheek and whispered something. But Geli remained stiff, resentful. "Really," she told the housekeeper moments later, "I have nothing at all in common with my uncle."

As the new chauffeur, Julius Schreck, drove the Mercedes along Prinzregentenstrasse, Hitler was silent. Suddenly he turned to Hoffmann. "I don't know why," he said, "but I have a most uneasy feeling." Hoffmann, whose unofficial duty was to amuse and cheer up the Führer, told him it was probably just the *Föhn*, a south wind peculiar to the Alps which caused a strange depression. Hitler didn't answer and they drove on toward Nuremberg.

From the kitchen of the apartment, Frau Reichert heard something smash and remarked to her mother, "Geli must have picked up a perfume bottle from her dressing table and broken it." This may have been when she rummaged in the pockets of Hitler's jacket and found a letter written

on blue paper. It was from Eva Braun. Hitler had renewed his liaison with
her some months previously but so discreetly that Geli had not known
about it. Later in the day Anny Winter saw Geli angrily tear this letter in
four parts. The prying housekeeper pieced them together and read something like this:

> Dear Herr Hitler,
>   Thank you again for the wonderful invitation to the theater. It was a
> memorable evening. I am most grateful to you for your kindness. I am
> counting the hours until I may have the joy of another meeting.
>
>   Yours,
>   Eva

Geli locked herself in her room with instructions not to be disturbed.
But her show of temper did not disturb Frau Winter and so the
housekeeper left the apartment as usual that evening and went home.
Frau Reichert and her daughter slept in and they both heard a dull sound
during the night but thought nothing of it. They too were used to the
"capricious" girl.

But next morning Frau Reichert became alarmed when she found
Geli's door still locked. She phoned Max Amann and Franz Schwarz.
These two summoned a locksmith. Geli was lying on the floor next to a
couch, a 6.34-caliber pistol beside her. She was shot in the heart.

That morning Hitler and Hoffmann left the Deutscher Hof Hotel in
Nuremberg to continue their journey to Hamburg. As the Mercedes left
the city Hitler noticed a car was following them. Fearing this might be an
attack, he was about to tell Schreck to speed up. Then he realized the
other vehicle was a taxi and a pageboy from the Deutscher Hof, who sat
next to the driver, was gesticulating to stop. Upon learning from the boy
that Herr Hess had telephoned from Munich and was holding the line,
Hitler rushed back to the hotel, flung hat and whip onto a chair and went
into a phone booth. He left the door open and Hoffmann could hear him
say, "Hitler here. Has something happened?" After a short pause he cried
out, "Oh, God, how awful!" Then his voice rose almost to a scream.
"Hess, answer me—yes or no—is she still alive?" Apparently the line was
cut or Hess had hung up.

"Hitler's frenzy was contagious," recalled Hoffmann. "With its accelerator jammed to the floor boards the great car screamed its way back to
Munich. In the driving mirror I could see the reflection of Hitler's face.
He sat with compressed lips, staring with unseeing eyes through the
windscreen." By the time they reached the apartment Geli's body had
been removed. Since it was Saturday the newspapers didn't carry the story
until the following Monday. There were innuendoes that the Führer himself had done away with his niece and allegations that Minister of Justice
Gürtner had destroyed the evidence. The Munich *Post*, a socialist daily,

gave a long account filled with circumstantial detail about the frequent arguments between Geli and Hitler. It also alleged that the bridge of her nose had been broken and there were other signs of maltreatment.*

Depressed and humiliated, Hitler told Frank that "he could not look at a paper any more since the terrible smear campaign would kill him. He wanted to step out of politics altogether and not appear in public any more." In desperation, he fled with Hoffmann to the empty country house of his printer, Adolf Müller, on the Tegernsee. Upon arrival their driver, Schreck, whispered to Hoffmann that he had hidden the Führer's gun, fearing he might use it on himself. The moment Hitler got to his room he clasped hands behind his back and began pacing. Hoffmann asked what he would like to eat. Hitler shook his head. Hour after hour he paced without pause. It went on all night. At dawn Hoffmann knocked softly at the door. There was no answer. He entered but Hitler continued pacing, hands still clasped behind his back, staring into the distance.

Hoffmann phoned home and got a recipe for spaghetti, a favorite dish of Hitler's. But he still refused to eat. He paced relentlessly two more days without food. Once he came to the phone to hear that Frank had taken the necessary legal steps to stop the scurrilous press campaign. In a tired and weak voice he said, "I thank you. I will get myself back together again. I will never forget you for this."

At last word reached the Müller villa that Geli had been buried in Vienna; present at the ceremony in the Central Cemetery were Röhm, Müller, Himmler and young Alfred Frauenfeld, the self-appointed National Socialist Gauleiter of Vienna. Although Hitler was banned from entering his homeland because of his politics, he decided to risk arrest and that night he got into the front seat of the Mercedes next to Schreck. Hoffmann sat alone in the back as they drove silently to the Austrian border, followed by bodyguards in another large car. By the time they arrived it was dawn.

Outside of Vienna Frauenfeld was waiting for Hitler in a small car since the Mercedes would have been too noticeable. They drove without a word to the Central Cemetery. Hitler placed flowers on the grave. On the marble slab was this inscription:

---

* Hitler could not have killed Geli since he was in Nuremberg nor is it likely that he or one of his associates ordered her done away with to prevent scandal. If that had been the case, murder would certainly have been committed somewhere else than in the Führer's own apartment. Some of Hitler's adherents claimed that the death was accidental: she was probably frightened by some noise and shot herself in fright. There was also the theory that she was playing theater with the gun and it went off. From the evidence, however, the most logical conclusion is that she shot herself—perhaps in desperation, perhaps in jealousy, perhaps for an unknown reason. William Patrick Hitler's mother told Hanfstaengl that the "immediate family know very well that the cause of Geli's suicide was the fact that she was pregnant by a Jewish art teacher in Linz." In a 1971 interview Hans Hitler, a second cousin of the Führer, speaking for the family, denied this categorically.

Here Sleeps Our Beloved Child
Geli
She was Our Ray of Sunshine
Born 4 June 1908—died 18 September 1931
The Raubal Family

While en route to Frauenfeld's apartment, Hitler suddenly broke his long silence. He asked if, by chance, they passed the Opera. Frauenfeld said it would take a slight detour. "Ach, please do so," said Hitler. "At least drive by even though I cannot go in." At Frauenfeld's Hitler ate a good breakfast, then began speaking quietly, not of the tragedy, but of the political future of Germany and himself. His voice was firm and confident as he assured Frauenfeld that he would take over power in Germany by 1933 at the latest, before the Poles seized Danzig. Once back in his own car, Hitler gazed fixedly ahead. Finally he said, as if thinking aloud, "So. Now let the struggle begin—the struggle which must and shall be crowned with success."

A day or two later he drove north to attend the Gauleiter conference. The party stopped at an inn overnight and at breakfast the following morning he refused to eat a piece of ham. "It is like eating a corpse!" he told Göring. Nothing on earth would make him eat meat again.*

In Hamburg he addressed a large, sympathetic audience. He spoke as forcefully and brilliantly as ever. Twice before—at the hospital in Pasewalk and in Landsberg prison—he had emerged from suicidal depressions. Perhaps these were a form of regeneration, for each time he had bounced back from the depths with renewed vigor and a new sense of direction. This was his third resurrection.

* He had made such remarks before and had toyed with the idea of vegetarianism but this time, according to Frau Hess, he meant it. From that moment on, she said, Hitler never ate another piece of meat except for liver dumplings. "Suddenly! He ate meat before that. It is very difficult to understand or explain."

Part 4

THE BROWN REVOLUTION

Chapter Ten

"IT IS ALMOST LIKE
A DREAM"
1931–JANUARY 30, 1933

1

Hitler recovered sufficiently from the death of Geli to attend the leadership meeting in the north that was already in session. It was of such import that only Gauleiters and major SA leaders were present and so successful that it marked the end of the party's reorganization. "The movement," he said a few days later, "is today so united that the Gauleiters and political leaders instinctively make the right decisions." As a result, there followed purges of "all lazy, rotten, useless" elements and a thinning of ranks that strengthened the party structure and buttressed Hitler's personal control.

With his own house in order, Hitler felt free to re-enter national politics. On October 14, 1931, an interview was arranged with President von Hindenburg through General Kurt von Schleicher, who had been one of the Old Gentleman's closest advisers. Hitler was visibly ill at ease in the presence of Hindenburg, an overwhelming figure with his six-foot-five-inch height and deep, booming voice. Hitler's lengthy remarks irritated the field marshal, who later reportedly complained to Schleicher that Hitler was a queer fellow who would never become Chancellor; the best he could hope for was to head the Postal Department. Disappointing as the meeting was, Schleicher still had hopes for Hitler; he had been impressed not only by the Führer's success at the last elections but by his nationalistic program. "An interesting man with exceptional speaking abilities," was his judgment. "In his plans he soars in the clouds. You then have to hold him by the coattails in order to keep him on the ground." Schleicher, whose name in German meant "intriguer," was a brilliant improviser but impetuosity tended to lead him into dangerous waters. Privately he felt quite able to handle any former corporal.

Hitler was used to being underestimated. For the next few months he contented himself with building a base of mass support among those Germans who had become disillusioned with the government's failure to cope with rising unemployment. He also made an unprecedented attempt to win foreign approval by talking directly to the American people. He was scheduled to make a radio broadcast on Friday night, December 11, over CBS to explain the "course, meaning and aims" of his party. The German government canceled the speech at the last moment but a translation was published in the Hearst newspapers which were noted for their extreme anti-Communist policy. In it Hitler expressed the hope that Americans, out of an inner impulse for self-preservation, would join him in the "struggle against this world pest" known as Bolshevism.

On the first day of 1932 Hitler told a Munich audience that God was on his side in the battle for a better world. Didn't the Bible say that the lukewarm was condemned to be spewed out? A victory of sorts seemed to offer itself almost immediately in the form of an invitation to Berlin from Hindenburg's advisers. They urged him to help prolong the field marshal's presidency but this went against Hitler's scruples, he said, since it would more or less force him to support Chancellor Brüning's policies. The refusal indicated that Hitler might be prepared to risk his entire political future in a presidential election even though an open contest with Hindenburg was a gamble. The Old Gentleman was a legend. His conservatism would draw many votes from the right and his defense of the Weimar Republic against an extremist like Hitler was sure to attract moderates and democrats alike.

Goebbels wrote in his diary, ". . . the chess game for power begins," and urged Hitler to take the chance. His chief concern was getting enough money to run a campaign. Hitler helped solve this particular problem with a single speech at the Park Hotel in Düsseldorf, center of the German steel industry. In line with a recent decision "to work systematically on the influential personalities of business," and under the auspices of Fritz Thyssen, he addressed an influential group at the Industry Club on January 17.

In confidential conversations prior to the Düsseldorf speech, Hitler had already drastically revised his economic program. He was now for elimination of unions and for managerial freedom as well as a program of public works and rearmament to be directed by the leaders of big business in the interest of economic recovery. Within an hour he had the rapt attention of his audience, for he spoke of matters that directly concerned these hardheaded businessmen. He asserted, for example, that private property was justified and then drew a frightening picture of the growth of Communism. "Bolshevism, if unchecked, will change the world as completely as Christianity once did. . . . If this movement continues to develop, three hundred years from now Lenin will be regarded not only as one of the revolutionaries of 1917, but as the founder of a new world doctrine and he will be worshiped as much perhaps as Buddha." Millions of unemployed and deprived Germans made desperate by the depression, he said, were already looking to Communism for the answer to their distress. That was Germany's most pressing problem of the day and it could be solved not by economic decrees but by political power. The NSDAP alone was prepared and willing to stem the Red tide. Without National Socialism there would no longer be a middle class in Germany, and only with it could the nation be united and revitalized.

Rarely had Hitler spoken so effectively, alternating between emotion and logic. In one moment he shook his listeners with terrible visions of Bolshevism and the end of the system that had brought them security; in the next he appealed to their selfishness: if they wanted their industrial complex to survive and expand they would need a dictator at the helm of government, one who would eventually lead Germany back to its position as a world power. His listeners could visualize fifty years of accomplishment and wealth dissipating and many went home prepared to contribute considerable sums to the man who promised to save them.

2

In mid-February Hindenburg announced he would stand again for President. This forced Hitler to make his own decision. It was apparent that the NSDAP had to run a presidential candidate and no one but Hitler had a realistic chance. Even so he hesitated. "I know that I shall come to power, all others will fail," he once told Frank. "I see myself as Chancellor and I will be Chancellor. I do not see myself as President, and I know I will never be President." His reluctance was genuine and he wavered for almost two weeks before Goebbels finally persuaded him to run. Then he acted with dispatch to make himself eligible. He hastily became a citizen of Germany through the machinations of the Nazi Minister of Interior in Braunschweig, who made him a councilor of that state. The following day, February 27, Hitler formally announced his candidacy for elections to take place in fifteen days.

The economic depression and political rancor had already turned Germany into a quasi battlefield. "Berlin was in a state of civil war," wrote Christopher Isherwood. "Hate exploded suddenly without warning, out of nowhere; at street corners, in restaurants, cinemas, dance halls, swimming-baths; at midnight, after breakfast, in the middle of the afternoon. Knives were whipped out, blows were dealt with spiked rings, beer-mugs, chair-legs or leaded clubs; bullets slashed the advertisements on the poster-columns, rebounded from the iron roofs of latrines."

Hate scourged the land as the victims of the depression turned on those more fortunate than themselves. Shopkeepers driven out of business cursed the great department stores; the millions of unemployed envied those with jobs and hated the "bosses"; thousands of university graduates found the future barred to them and turned their despair on the establishment. The depression had hit almost every level. Peasants, burdened with taxes and faced with low prices, despised city people while the masses of white-collar unemployed envied the peasants their crops. Those without work camped in hordes on the outskirts of the larger cities. Beggars haunted every street corner and by the time of the election campaign there were six million registered unemployed in the land—with millions of others working only part time or too proud to register as jobless.

To multitudes of these casualties of economic collapse Adolf Hitler was the answer. They cared little about the rumors of his deals with industrialists since he had never compromised with the Weimar government and had remained outspoken in his opposition to the Versailles Treaty and the Red menace. His call was simple: "For Freedom and Bread." Amid the confusion of the nation he seemed to stand like a rock, insisting only on what was best for Germany. Hindenburg countered with posters urging voters to remember his past services: "He hath kept faith with you; be ye faithful unto him." Goebbels answered with: "Honor Hindenburg: Vote for Hitler."

The Führer's appeal was to both the defeated middle-aged and the idealistic youth, and as he toured the country speaking tirelessly he called upon both to join him in his battle against the establishment. The campaign, masterminded by Goebbels, was a marvel of inventiveness. It was the rare wall in the nation that wasn't plastered with glaring red Nazi posters; leaflets were showered on the populace from planes. Fifty thousand small propaganda records were mailed to those well enough off to own a phonograph; "talking pictures" of speeches by Hitler and Goebbels were projected at night in public squares. The heart of the program, however, was a backbreaking speaking schedule. In the first eleven days of March Hitler and Goebbels each made at least one major speech daily and usually two or three.

In the meantime the Hindenburg camp was disordered. Split from the beginning, it was staggered by a whispering campaign alleging that the President's son Oskar had secretly become both a Catholic and a member of the Social Democratic Party. Even more ridiculous was the charge that Hindenburg's two middle-aged daughters were leaders in the Socialist Students League. More time was spent in denying rumors than in attacking Hitler's policies and each denial helped give the fiction more of an appearance of fact. Hindenburg's supporters began arguing and he did little himself to get votes. He made but one public appearance, three days before the election, when he asserted that he had consented to run only because so many Germans of all political hues urged him to stay in office to prevent a takeover by either left or right.

By early evening of election day, March 13, the results showed that Hindenburg was pulling ahead of Hitler. The party militants like Goebbels had been confident that he would sweep into the presidency and, as the returns widened the margin, they grew despondent. An hour after midnight there was no doubt that Hindenburg was winning by more than 7,000,000 votes and was only about 350,000 votes short of the necessary majority. Though there would have to be a runoff election between the two leaders, Goebbels for one was sure that "the dream of power was temporarily over."

Not so Hitler, who had waited stoically at the Café Heck with intimates. He hurried to the Brown House and dictated a statement exhorting the party to begin the battle for the runoff without delay. "The first election is over, the second begins today. I will also lead this one personally!" In the space of a week he and Goebbels, roused from his depression, addressed meetings of Gauleiters, Reichstag deputies and party editors so inspirationally that those present were convinced that Hitler would win next time.

Success in the runoff election was suddenly threatened by publication in the Social Democratic *Münchener Post* of incriminating letters between Röhm and a doctor specializing in psychology. It seemed they shared two interests—homosexuality and astrology. When Hans Frank, after reviewing the evidence, refused to handle a libel suit against the paper, Röhm—with much embarrassed twisting and turning—confessed he was a "bisexual." Hitler's lawyer was flabbergasted, for he had always thought homosexuals were effeminate thrill seekers. "And here," recalled Frank, "was actually the prototype of a brave, aggressive soldier, who gave the impression outwardly, with his scarred face, his upright soldierly posture, that he was very much the whole man."

Hitler had long tolerated Röhm's homosexuality—a remarkable attitude for those days—but his first reaction upon reading the documentary evidence was to lose his temper. Finally he calmed down. "This is a terrible blow," he told Frank. "Such a horrible mess! It's not human, it's bestial, worse, even animals would not do such a thing." He asked if Röhm had "abused" young men or boys. There was nothing in the records to indicate this, said the lawyer, and Hitler became calmer. "That would be utterly intolerable. As long as it is between grown men—what Röhm does. Children are not his victims?" Frank assured him that there was not a single instance. "Well, then we can at least consider whether to keep him or not, but God help him if he abuses young boys! Then he must go!"

If the Röhm scandal distracted Hitler, he certainly had put it behind him by the time the runoff campaign began. He was full of his usual vigor and optimism. This time there was only a week to campaign and Hitler decided to use an airplane so he could make three to four speeches daily.

He invited Sefton Delmer to accompany him on the tour and the British correspondent was impressed that the rigorous schedule was maintained despite bad weather. In almost every city Hitler was besieged by adoring women. In Coblenz two girls cornered him in the corridor of his railway car. From the Führer's compartment, Delmer could hear a series of sobs and hysterical cries from the girls but not a sound from Hitler. He seemed to be in a trance as the correspondent entered the compartment. Ignoring Delmer, he flung aside the window curtain and gazed out at the people on the platform "with his mesmeric stare turning in an arc like a searchlight from left to right, exposing everyone within sight to the emotion the two girls had inspired in him and which he was now throwing back into the crowd."

Only rarely in the rigorous campaign did Hitler's spirits noticeably flag. One of these moments was witnessed by Albert Krebs, Gauleiter of Hamburg. Upon arrival at Hitler's suite in the Hotel Atlantic with a printed copy of a speech made by the Führer the night before, Krebs was greeted with a rhythmic call of *"Mei Supp! Mei Supp!"* (Bavarian for *Meine Suppe*), first from Hitler and then, rather disrespectfully, from his entourage. By the time Krebs was admitted to the Führer's presence the breakfast soup had arrived. Hitler hunched over it, looking tired and melancholy. He glanced up at Krebs and "in a tone of undisguised alarm" asked what he thought about vegetarian diets, then, without waiting for an answer, began a long impassioned lecture which revealed "hypochondriacal fears for his health."

It was the first time Hitler had ever revealed himself as a human being to Krebs—his name in German meant cancer—and the Gauleiter was shaken to hear him explain in detail the reasons for his reformed living habits; outbreaks of perspiration, states of extreme excitement, trembling of limbs and stomach cramps. The last, Hitler insisted, were the forerunner of cancer and this gave him only a few years to finish his work. "I do not have the time to wait," he announced over his plate of soup. "If I had time I wouldn't have become a candidate. The Old Gentleman [Hindenburg] won't last much longer. But I cannot lose even a year. I must come to power quickly in order to solve the gigantic problems in the little time remaining to me. I must! I must!" All at once Hitler ended the discussion. "One can say," commented Krebs, "that he pulled himself together and it was immediately noticeable in his physical bearing, facial expression and voice. The depression was over; the human being Hitler once more became the Führer."

While he gave the public a picture of youthful energy, the Hindenburg forces ran another desultory campaign. This time Hindenburg did not make a single speech, spurring rumors that he was dying. There were also whispers that pensions and salaries would be cut and unemployment relief would be ended if he won re-election. By election eve it appeared that Hitler would win. Even Spengler, who had been deriding him, decided to vote National Socialist on the grounds that "Hitler is a fool but one must support the movement." On Sunday, April 10, Hitler got an additional 2,000,000 votes, raising his total to 13,418,051. The old field marshal increased his total by less than 700,000, yet this gave him a solid majority, fifty-three per cent. The Communist vote had slipped badly. More than a quarter of their voters had either listened to Goebbels' appeals or gone over to Hindenburg to keep Hitler out of the presidential palace.

In London, the *Daily Telegraph* predicted the end of Adolf Hitler while in Munich the iconoclastic Spengler and his sister hung swastika flags out of their windows. "When one has a chance to annoy people," he said, "one should do so."

3

A few days after the election Brüning was persuaded to enact a decree outlawing the SA and SS. The effect of this act was to ruin the politically naïve Chancellor, for it was not only ineffective but brought a concerted storm of protest from the right. This was the opportunity that the politically ambitious General von Schleicher had been waiting for. His dream was to establish a government of the right that would include the Nazis but not give them control. After all, Corporal Hitler and his people were, in Schleicher's words, "merely little children who had to be led by the hand."

He met secretly with the Führer that May and promised to remove the ban on the SA and SS if Hitler agreed not to attack the new rightist government. The deal was made and late that month Schleicher chose as figurehead Chancellor for his regime a wealthy, polished gentleman jockey, Franz von Papen. An ex-General Staff officer, he was also a member of the Prussian Landtag. The astounded Papen's first reaction was "I very much doubt if I am the right man," but it took only a few minutes to persuade him that he might be. Before Papen knew it he was standing, somewhat dazed, before Hindenburg.

"Well, my dear Papen," said the field marshal with paternal kindliness, "I hope you are going to help me out of this difficult situation." He knew only that Papen was a former cavalry officer, financially independent, well known on the racecourses, and had some experience in foreign affairs. But he was pleased with his military bearing and gentlemanly appearance. Again Papen protested that he was not the right man but this time was persuaded in even shorter order by Hindenburg's words: "You have been a soldier and done your duty in the war. When the Fatherland calls, Prussia knows only one response—obedience."

Hitler was spending the weekend at Mecklenburg when Goebbels phoned that Hindenburg wanted to see him that same afternoon. The Führer hastened back to the capital where he was informed by the President that he was going to appoint Papen (no news to the Führer thanks to Schleicher) and asked if Hitler was going to support him. "Yes," was the answer and the brief interview was over.

Undoubtedly Schleicher thought he was acting in the best interest of the people. Convinced that Brüning was too weak to handle Hitler, he was confident, like so many other military men, that the army itself could deal properly with such a radical—and utilize him to help establish a strong nationalist Germany. Schleicher had at last achieved his first aim but as so often happens with those attempting to outdo Machiavelli he was too clever for his own good. He soon learned that Hitler's pledge to support the new government was provisional. He could not consider the matter, he said, until Papen showed his good faith by dissolving the Reichstag and abolishing the repressive measures against the National Socialist movement. Papen did so but Hitler still withheld his support. Instead he sanctioned resumption of street battles with the Reds. A new wave of violence swept over Germany. In July alone eighty-six died in the fighting, including thirty Reds and thirty-eight Nazis. Both sides were equally belligerent. Skirmishes turned into battles in the summer heat. On Sunday, July 10, eighteen police were killed and the following Sunday a Nazi march under police escort through the working-class district of Altona was broken up by a volley of shots from roofs and windows. The marchers fired back. Nineteen people were reported killed and 285 wounded.

Three days later Papen invoked the President's emergency powers—Article 48 of the Weimar constitution. This article had already been invoked a number of times, by Ebert in the economic crisis of 1923 to abolish the eight-hour day, and several times by Brüning to suspend newspapers. Using the argument that the Prussian government could no longer deal with the Reds, Papen made himself Reichs Commissioner of Prussia. This meant the end of parliamentary government in that state and foreshadowed what could be done in every state by a man resolute enough to use the emergency authority granted by the constitution.

4

Elections for the Reichstag were set for the last day of July. It was another whirlwind campaign and Hitler's second "Flight over Germany."

Once more Hitler chartered a plane and the same pilot. Hans Baur had proved so competent in all kinds of weather—several times they had made forced landings in storms and fog—that Hitler now refused to fly with anyone else. He also had a second private chauffeur, twenty-one-year-old Erich Kempka. He would meet Hitler's plane in the western part of Germany while Schreck would be on hand in the east. In this election the two drivers covered more than fifty thousand kilometers, most of it over unpaved highways. Hitler treated Kempka as a member of the family. He was equally familiar with Baur. While resting in Weimar after a week of strenuous campaigning, Hitler took him on a tour of the park near their hotel, the Belvedere. For an hour Hitler queried Baur about his World War experiences as a fighter pilot while the rest of the entourage lagged behind. Then Hitler turned and told Gauleiter Sauckel to drive into town and get fifteen young ladies for partners at afternoon coffee. By this time word had gone out that Hitler was at the Belvedere dining room and women began to appear singly and in couples for a look at him. The Führer excitedly poked Baur, who sat at his right. "Just look, Baur, there is a beautiful little lady, a beauty!" Baur sympathized that it was too bad the Führer could only see women at a distance, not at close range. "You're right, Baur," said the amused Hitler. "Now if you make a little side trip, no rooster will crow about it, but with me the ladies advertise and I can't afford that. Women can't keep their mouths shut. So I like them all."

Finally the fifteen girls from town arrived and they were so entranced by Hitler that they ignored their own partners and kept staring worshipfully at him. Embarrassed, he suggested they all move to the Artists' Café. The group piled into cars with everyone but the Führer having at least one girl on his lap. In moments almost every woman in this restaurant was crowding around Hitler. Harassed, he told Hanfstaengl to play the piano but after listening to two pieces he excused himself on the ground that he had to prepare for tomorrow's speeches.

Hitler appeared in some fifty cities in the last two weeks of the campaign, generating rabid enthusiasm wherever he went. Once he kept an open-air crowd of 10,000 in Stralsund waiting in the rain for six hours while Baur was looking in vain for a place to make a forced landing in the dark. An economic paralysis extended throughout the nation and that was one reason Hitler's audiences listened to his lengthy speeches as if hypnotized. Eleven-year-old Egon Hanfstaengl heard him address a large crowd in a vast tent on the outskirts of Munich. "He ran the gamut of emotions, and a wave of frenzied enthusiasm swept the mass." There were rich and poor in the audience, professors and workers. At the beginning they were uneasy in one another's presence but soon all were shouting and applauding wildly as a single entity. Egon noticed one incongruous couple—a professor and a charwoman—leaving the tent "amid the tumultuous acclamation, talking together excitedly, fraternizing in fact. Such was the power of

Adolf Hitler." Afterward Egon was taken by his father to the Brown
House. "All right, boy," said Hanfstaengl, "sit down somewhere, keep
quiet and learn something." A messenger handed a ream of typed pages to
Goebbels. "It was the transcript of Hitler's speech, which had apparently
just been completed. The Führer left the group and sat down behind his
desk, with Goebbels standing behind him, looking over his shoulder. They
seemed to run through the speech to groom it for publication. Hitler appeared to be talking to himself as he marked things with a pencil. 'That
was good . . . this was effective . . . this must be cut . . .' Not more than
an hour ago he had finished one of the most emotional speeches of his career. He had preached, entreated, thundered, and shrieked. Yet, here he
was, as cool and rational as any man I've seen."

During the campaign anti-Semitism never was an issue. It was well
known that Hitler detested Jews but many voters were ready to overlook
this as long as he kept his prejudice on a sensible level. The majority of
Germans agreed that there were too many Jewish lawyers and objected to
their monopoly of department stores and the entertainment industry.
Many Jews themselves deplored the postwar flood of Jews from the East
who brought with them the costumes and customs of the ghettos. Two
well-known Jewish bankers, in fact, had already requested the new
Minister of Labor, Friedrich Syrup, to stop further immigration of these
Eastern Jews since their presence increased latent anti-Semitism. Jews
regarded themselves as Germans first and then Jews. They had become so
integrated into the German economy that they were willing to overlook
the social prejudice that remained. After all, even in enlightened Britain
and America Jews were excluded from the best clubs and hotels. Nor was
toleration of National Socialism confined to German Jews. A group of
Palestinian extremists had recently announced that, except for Hitler's
anti-Semitism, the NSDAP movement was acceptable and would save
Germany.

On July 31 (despite a special edition of a Vienna newspaper revealing
Hitler's antecedents under the banner headline HEIL SCHICKLGRUBER) * the
Nazis won 13,732,779 votes, half a million more than the combined
total of their closest rivals—the Social Democrats and Communists. Encouraged by a victory giving him 37.3 per cent of all the votes, Hitler
proposed to his own party that he run for Chancellor.

Göring protested. So did Strasser, for it wrecked his entire policy of
seizing power by a coalition with other right-wing parties. But Hitler was
too impatient for power to be dissuaded. A messenger immediately was
dispatched to Berlin informing Schleicher of Hitler's demand. The general

* Early in 1932 Austrian Chancellor Dollfuss urged the owner-editor of the *Wiener
Sonn-und-Montags Zeitung* to investigate Hitler's ancestry. Documents revealing the illegitimate birth of Hitler's father were found and the above-mentioned special edition
was brought out in hopes of influencing the German elections.

could not take it seriously, so sure was he that Hindenburg would balk at bestowing such an honor on an ex-Gefreiter. He invited Hitler to a meeting in Mecklenburg under the illusion that he could "talk him out of his plans." The two met on August 5 at the Fürstenberg barracks near the capital, and Hitler demanded not only the chancellorship but passage of an enabling bill which would give him power to govern the nation by decree—in effect, to establish a dictatorship. The meeting went so well that Hitler was convinced Hindenburg would also be brought around and, in elation, he proposed that a tablet be fastened to the wall in commemoration of such a historic conference.

Although he brought his euphoria back to the Obersalzberg it was not shared by Goebbels, who doubted they would gain power so easily. He was all for action, not dubious compromises, and his zeal permeated the Nazi ranks. "The whole party is ready to take over power," he wrote in his diary on August 8. "The SA men are leaving their places of work in order to make themselves ready." By August 10, when Hindenburg left his own country home for Berlin, the capital was in a state of semi-siege. To end the crisis Papen offered to resign but Hindenburg was enraged at the thought of making Hitler Chancellor. The upstart Austrian had already broken his promises to Schleicher; besides, Hitler had no governmental experience and couldn't even control the hotheads in his own party. The President even refused to invite him to a meeting.

The next morning, August 13, Hitler checked in at the Hotel Kaiserhof, which had become his Berlin headquarters. It was more like a military command post with the telephone in the anteroom ringing almost constantly. The revolving doors of the Kaiserhof itself never seemed to stop and the lobby seethed with activity. On the main floor, in the emergency office set up for the Führer's adjutants and staff officers, portable typewriters clattered without interruption as representatives of the native and foreign press besieged Otto Dietrich, Hitler's press chief, and Hanfstaengl for the latest pronouncements from the man of the hour.

At noon Hitler saw Schleicher, who informed him that Hindenburg could only offer him the vice-chancellorship. Understandably irate, Hitler attacked the general for breaking his promise and stormed out. Moments later he was in Chancellor Papen's office berating the administration for its leniency with the old system. Papen was taken aback by his caller's aggressive attitude. "The President is not prepared to offer you the post of Chancellor," he said, "as he feels he does not yet know you well enough." Hitler was in no mood for half a loaf. He had dedicated himself to wiping out the Marxist parties, he said, and this could not be done unless he took over the government and ran things his own way. One could not shy away from bloodshed, he added ominously. That was a lesson of history. Had the King of Italy offered Mussolini a vice-chancellorship after the march on Rome?

He left the chancellery in a black mood, driving directly to Goebbels' apartment. Here he waited, irritated and frustrated, for a summons from Hindenburg. At last, at three in the afternoon, Papen's state secretary phoned. Hitler was interested in but one thing: was Hindenburg making him Chancellor? The state secretary would only reply that the President wished to speak with the Führer. The meeting in the study of the presidential palace was short and formal. Hindenburg had made up his mind not to appoint a man like Hitler to such a responsible post but would "make one more appeal to his patriotism" to co-operate with Papen. He opened cautiously by stating that he welcomed the participation of the National Socialists in the government. Hitler just as politely replied that this was out of the question; as head of the largest party in the nation, he would have to insist on a new cabinet with himself as Chancellor.

"*Nein!*" exclaimed Hindenburg. Never could he "before God, his conscience, and the Fatherland bear the responsibility of entrusting all governmental authority to a single party." Hitler regretted that he could accept no other alternative. "You are going into opposition, then?" "I have no other choice," said the Führer.

With some feeling, Hindenburg complained of the recent clashes between the Nazis and the police. Such incidents, he said, strengthened his conviction that there were wild uncontrollable elements in the NSDAP. He was ready, however, to accept Hitler in a coalition government. The invitation was followed by a lofty rebuke, from field marshal to corporal. "Then I must warn you to carry on your opposition in a chivalrous manner and to remain conscious of your responsibility and duty toward the Fatherland. I do not doubt at all your love for the Fatherland. But I am going to proceed very harshly against any acts of terror or force, such as have been regrettably perpetrated by members of the SA."

The severity of this lecture was somewhat mitigated by Hindenburg's closing words: "We are both old fellow soldiers and want to remain so since our paths may be crossing again. Thus I extend my hand to you as a comrade-in-arms." Hitler emerged from the study overwhelmed by the personality of the marshal but, once the door closed, he turned on Papen for maneuvering him into such a humiliating scene. Out of all this, warned Hitler, would possibly come the downfall of the President. He would not be responsible for what happened next.

When Hitler entered the Goebbels apartment Hanfstaengl noted that he was "as white as a sheet. He said practically nothing and was very moody for a time." Then, curiously, he abruptly brightened up and began to speculate on accepting the vice-chancellorship. "I can imagine that to work with Papen would, in a way, be quite good fun. Somehow you feel that he was a soldier during the war and quite a reckless fellow." The Chancellor, he mused, looked as though he would act like a true comrade.

"Mind you, if it amuses his vanity to go on living with his wife in the Chancellor's palace and they confide the real power to me, I would not mind."

Newsboys in the street were shouting out headlines from extras: SHOCKING PRETENSION—HITLER'S BREACH OF FAITH—HITLER REPRIMANDED BY THE REICH PRESIDENT." The stories, which stated that Hitler had demanded complete power, were based on a government communiqué issued so soon after the interview that it must have been prepared ahead of time. This infuriated Hitler and broke the spell Hindenburg had cast over him. He felt he had been "deceived" by the military and the politicians. A hostile biographer agreed. "Now that the National Socialists had reached the ante-chamber of power," wrote Rudolf Olden, "and were taking part in political parleys, they encountered a measure of haughtiness, contempt and trickery which, if they had not come out victorious, would have earned their just indignation. For all the doors that were thrown open to them, for all the hands that shook theirs, there was not one of the 'respectable people' who received them, who did not want to exploit them, and usually to trick them."

Schleicher was almost as dismayed by the Papen communiqué as Hitler, since he was still convinced that the best solution was to get the Nazis into the government. He hastily sent word to the Führer that there was still a chance to work out an agreement and asked for a meeting. Hitler's brusque refusal to see him sent the ordinarily self-possessed general into a state of shock. That evening a friend found Schleicher pale and frightened, incoherently muttering to himself. Finally his words could be made out: "The decision was right, one could not have given the power to Adolf Hitler."

Throughout the city embittered Brownshirts, long held in check by party leadership, were clamoring for action. By this time Hitler had regained his composure. He summoned SA commanders to the Goebbels apartment and such were his powers of persuasion that they accepted his argument that it was not yet time to seize power, and that a Putsch at this time would be disastrous. All units were sent on a two-week furlough.

Later that night Hitler started south for his retreat on the Obersalzberg. As Schreck wound his way along the dark roads there was silence in the car. Finally Hanfstaengl heard the Führer muttering to himself "in a sleepy and fatalistic baritone from which the metal was almost gone, '*Wir werden ja sehen. Es ist vielleicht besser so* [We shall see. Perhaps it is better so].'" The Führer was more philosophical than his followers and he began to encourage them with words like "Only we ourselves can finish what we have begun," "I would rather besiege a fortress than be a prisoner of it," and "Later on we will say that everything had to happen this way." Perhaps it was because the others could see only the present and he had eyes only for the future. The gamble to outbluff Hindenburg had failed but he was convinced that his fate would see him through.

5

Within a few days Hitler had made another of his remarkable recoveries from adversity but each of those who saw him at Berchtesgaden in those critical hours had a different impression. Joachim von Ribbentrop, a friend of Papen's, had arrived to patch up matters between Chancellor and Führer, and within an hour became a disciple of the latter. "There was room for neither discussion nor contradiction," he recalled. "He simply stated facts that his listeners were expected to accept. He was clearly monomaniacal; a man hard to influence and not given to compromise." Ribbentrop, come on a mission of persuasion, left so convinced that Hitler alone could save Germany from Communism that he joined the NSDAP.

Three American correspondents saw the Führer several days later, on August 17. Louis Lochner, H. V. Kaltenborn and Karl von Wiegand were scheduled for a joint interview but the last, who represented the Hearst press, insisted on seeing him alone. After fifteen minutes Wiegand returned in an angry mood to the little hotel, which stood just above the Haus Wachenfeld. "That man is hopeless," he told his two colleagues. "He gets worse every time I see him. I got nothing out of him. Ask him a question and he makes a speech. This whole trip has been a waste of time."

Hitler came out the front door of his villa just as Kaltenborn and Lochner were climbing up to the open porch. Kaltenborn began with an embarrassing question: "In your attitude of antagonism towards the Jews, do you differentiate between German Jews and the Jews who have come into Germany from other countries?"

Hitler's clear blue eyes seemed to bore into Kaltenborn. "We believe in a Monroe Doctrine for Germany," he exclaimed. "You exclude any would-be immigrants you do not care to admit. You regulate their number. You demand that they come up to a certain physical standard." He had no concern with the Jews of other lands, only any anti-German elements in his own country. "And we demand the right to deal with them as we see fit."

Lochner brought the subject back to the immediate political situation. Was it true that Herr Hitler had asked Hindenburg for the creation of a National Socialist government with power equivalent to that of Mussolini? Hitler heatedly denied making any such deal, then asserted that he did have "the right to complete control." He began talking as if he were already at the helm and gave a candid preview of the kind of rule he would bring to Germany. It had to be some kind of authoritarian government. Parliamentarianism was not native to continental Europeans, nor did it belong to their tradition. "Yet we cannot substitute brute force." A government must have the support of the masses. "You cannot establish a dictatorship in a vacuum. A government that does not derive its strength from the people will fail in a foreign crisis."

At the opening session of the new Reichstag the National Socialist delegates behaved correctly, sitting in silence during opponents' speeches and co-operating in the election of parliamentary officers. Such exemplary conduct was rewarded by support of the Center Party for Göring as president of the Reichstag. Several days passed in peaceful and constructive activity. Political stability had at last returned to Germany—thanks to Adolf Hitler. But within a week he abruptly changed course, apparently on the spur of the moment. He ordered his delegates to make no objections to a Communist motion of no confidence in the Papen government.

The session erupted into a wild shouting match and when Papen, who had rushed out to get Hindenburg's signature on a document to dissolve parliament, tried to get the floor, President Göring pretended not to see him. Ignoring the decree which the infuriated Papen had flung onto the presidential desk, Göring called for a vote. It was an overwhelming defeat for Papen—512 to 42.

Hitler was elated by the success of his unexpected coup and prepared for the national election with confidence. On the platform he exercised his usual magic. One witness to this was an enemy—the son of the last Emperor of Austria-Hungary. At a large open-air meeting in Berlin, Otto von Habsburg stood on the fringe of the crowd with a group of Communists who had been abusing Hitler. Then the Führer made his appearance and before he opened his mouth those who had just been berating him all at once were enthralled. "He had them before he even spoke. He had some sort of magnetic gift." By the end of the speech, to young Habsburg's amazement, the Reds around him were cheering along with the rest of the enraptured crowd.

Despite Hitler's crowd appeal, his campaign was sluggish since the financial and physical resources of the party had been severely strained to the breaking point. Too, Germany had been emotionally drained by the seemingly endless elections. Goebbels could not stir up the enthusiasm of the previous campaign and attendance at rallies and meetings slacked off. Spengler, for example, was so exasperated by the continual elections that his halfhearted support of Hitler turned to sarcasm. There was no real Caesar in Germany, he wrote that fall, and a true Führer must be "a hero, not a heroic tenor."

In the midst of Hitler's attempts to generate life in the campaign he was once more beset by personal misfortune. On the first of November Eva Braun, his mistress of some months, shot herself with a pistol as Geli

Raubal had done. While she had fallen desperately in love, he had become so involved with elections that he could spend little time with her. He would send her brief messages and even these became less frequent as the political situation intensified. To add to her misery, at least one malicious rival for the Fuhrer's affections showed her photographs of the electioneering Hitler posing with beautiful women.

A little after midnight on All Saints' Day she wrote a letter of farewell to Hitler, then shot herself in the neck, severing an artery. She got to the phone and gasped out to a surgeon, Dr. Plate, that she had shot herself through the heart.

Hitler left the campaign trail and, carrying a bunch of flowers, hastened to the private clinic where she was recovering. "Do you think," he asked Dr. Plate, "that Fräulein Braun shot herself simply with the object of becoming an interesting patient and of drawing my attention to herself?" The surgeon assured the Führer that it appeared to be a genuine case of attempted suicide. She had felt so neglected that she wanted to end it all. When the doctor left, Hitler turned to his companion, Hoffmann. "You hear," he said, "the girl did it for love of me. But I have given her no cause which could possibly justify such a deed." As he paced in agitation he muttered, "Obviously I must now look after the girl." Hoffmann objected. Who could possibly blame him for what happened? "And who, do you think, would believe that?" said Hitler, who knew more about human nature. Nor was there any guarantee that she might not try again.

This incident distracted Hitler from a campaign that was showing signs of deteriorating, and two days later he was presented with another embarrassing problem. On his own, Goebbels joined the Reds in a wildcat strike of Berlin transport workers asking for a pfennig or so an hour increase in pay. It was not the first time that the two parties, with many goals in common, had fought together; and for the next few wet, raw days the Communists and the National Socialists ate communally on the picket line. Side by side they pelted rocks at strikebreakers, tore up streetcar tracks and built barricades.

Hitler could not publicly disavow the actions of his impetuous disciple but he was privately angry at alienating so many middle-class voters and sent orders to end the strike. "The entire press is furious with us and calls it Bolshevism, but as a matter of fact we have no option," explained Geobbels in his diary. "If we had held ourselves aloof from this strike our position among the working classes would have been shaken."

Goebbels' impetuous act also put a crimp in the flow of bourgeois money for the campaign and on Sunday, November 6, Hitler lost more than two million votes along with thirty-four seats in the Reichstag. No longer could a simple alignment with the Center Party give him a majority. More significant, it indicated that the Hitler flood tide had ebbed and the strategy of gaining power through the ballot box had reached a dead end.

There was talk that Hitler once more threatened to commit suicide and it is quite possible that he said as much in his despair. But the pattern of defeat followed by renewed vigor was repeated and in a few days he began to emerge from depression. By the time he granted another interview to Sefton Delmer he seemed to have completely regained his confidence. During their talk in the back room of the Hotel Zum Elefanten in Weimar he surprised the Briton by changing the subject from politics to a rumor that the British government wished to re-establish monarchy in Germany. Delmer said it was the first he had heard of such a story. "The British government is interested only in such measures as are consonant with order and stability in Germany."

"Quite right. Quite right," exclaimed Hitler. "Germany would go up in flames, if anyone tried to put the Hohenzollerns back. Nor have I the slightest intention of becoming a race horse for a royal jockey to jump on my back just as I am about to pass the winning post." This bitter remark may have been prompted by a recent insult from the Crown Princess Cecilie at their meeting in Potsdam; as he was leaving, a member of his entourage heard the Crown Princess exclaim, "Open the windows quickly, it smells here!" The Führer's uncontrollable flatulence would continue to embarrass him.

6

His defeat was of little consolation to Papen, who was still badly outnumbered in the Reichstag. Putting personal distaste aside, he wrote Hitler that the recent elections provided a new opportunity for uniting the country. "We must endeavor to put aside the bitterness of the election campaign and place the good of the country, which we both seek to serve, above all considerations." The memory of their August meetings was too bitter and the response was a letter of accusation. The Führer refused the Chancellor's invitation to a conference on the grounds that discussions led to misconceptions. After their last conference hadn't Papen publicly announced that Hitler demanded total power when he had only requested leadership? Moreover, he was not ready "under any circumstances to repeat the proceedings of August 13" when Papen had insisted on sharing responsibility with Hindenburg. "Unfortunately you could not be persuaded to assume your part of this responsibility. I assumed mine. Instead your chancellery, through trickery—against my wishes and my explanations—successfully lured me into a colloquy with the Reich president. . . . I do not want to have a repetition of this game."

Thwarted, Papen reported to Hindenburg on the afternoon of November 17 that he was unable to negotiate with other parties and that any coalition under his leadership was impossible. The President accepted his resignation and the following day asked Hugenberg what he thought of Hitler as Chancellor. The latter no longer trusted the Führer. "His entire manner of handling political affairs makes it very difficult, in my opinion, to give him leadership. At any rate, I have grave doubts." The marshal then turned to his adviser, Meissner, and wondered if it was true that Hitler had been a house painter in Munich. Without waiting for an answer he turned back to the gray-haired Hugenberg. "My dear young friend, you have spoken out of my own heart!" he said and proceeded to help perpetuate the myth that persists to this day. "One can't put a house painter in Bismarck's chair."

The next morning, at Hitler's insistence, the two men had a private talk. It began poorly with Hindenburg reproaching his visitor for the rude behavior of youthful Nazis in East Prussia. "Not long ago, at Tannenberg, they shouted out so that I could hear: 'Wake up, wake up!' And yet I'm not asleep!" Hitler explained that his followers had not meant to be offensive; they were merely chanting the National Socialist slogan, "Germany, awake!"

After about an hour Meissner entered and the talk became more pointed. Hitler refused to join a non-partisan cabinet unless he was made Chancellor. "In the interest of the Fatherland," he said, "my movement must be preserved and this means that I must have the leadership." Why then did the Nazis join the Reds in the recent transportation strike? "If I had tried to restrain my people," explained Hitler frankly, "the strike would have taken place nonetheless, but I would have lost my following among the workers; this would not have been in Germany's interest."

Much as he distrusted the "house painter," Hindenburg did his utmost to gain his co-operation. "I can only repeat my request: Give me your help." It was an open call for personal allegiance. "I do appreciate the great idea which inspires you and your movement, and I would like to see you and your movement join the government." At the same time he could not give Hitler the chancellorship. Of course, Hitler was free to form a National Socialist government once he had a majority.

With clenched fists on knees, Hitler exclaimed, "Herr Feldmarschall! In order to negotiate with other parties it is only logical, Herr Feldmarschall, that I first have a mandate from you!" He could not conceal his irritation.

Hindenburg smiled ironically.

There was an awkward pause. "Herr Feldmarschall," Hitler finally said, "I have no intention of ruling as dictatorially as the Feldmarschall seems to assume. If you insist that I produce a Reichstag majority, then I cannot desist from putting before the Reichstag a kind of enabling act for special and urgent matters." He alone could get passage of such a decree and that would solve the problem.

This was unacceptable to Hindenburg and once more he tried the personal approach, appealing to Hitler's sense of duty as a soldier. It invoked the "old comradeship-in-arms" which had brought them together in the war. "Meet me half-way in this matter so that we can work together." Hitler departed, intransigent as ever, but Hindenburg must have thought he had made an impression on the ex-corporal when he remarked to Meissner, "Well, well, it seems as if this Hitler is getting sensible little by little."

Petitions for Hitler's appointment as Chancellor deluged Hindenburg and two days later he felt compelled to see him once more. This time Hitler brought with him a carefully prepared statement. Parliamentary government, it read, had failed and was not an expression of the will of the people. The National Socialists alone could prevent Communism and he requested Hindenburg to appoint him leader of a presidential cabinet.

Hindenburg would only repeat his suggestion that Hitler find a majority in the Reichstag to support his chancellorship. Hitler's response was visibly cool but the President ended the ten-minute talk with another offer of friendship.

In the next few days Hitler and Meissner exchanged long letters but the endeavor to reach agreement was fruitless since the former kept insisting on being made a presidential Chancellor with the same sweeping powers as those granted Papen. This impasse so concerned an influential group of business leaders that they decided to apply direct pressure on the field marshal. They had been contributing to the NSDAP under the impression that once the party came to power they would be able to influence its economic policy. Hitler, for example, had assured I. G. Farben that his government would definitely support production of synthetic gasoline; and in a private speech to a group known as the Circle of Friends at the Kaiserhof earlier in the year he had promised to abolish all trade unions along with all other political parties.

Late that November, thirty-nine prominent businessmen (including Hjalmar Schacht, former Chancellor Cuno, and tycoons like Krupp, Siemens, Thyssen, Bosch, Wörmann and Vögler) signed a letter petitioning Hindenburg to appoint Hitler Chancellor of Germany. These pragmatic men were placing a bet on the NSDAP. They were confident Hitler's socialism was a fraud and that, once in power, he would be the tool of capitalism.*

The machinery of parliamentary government had brought Germany to a political standstill. Hindenburg was finding it impossible to form a new cabinet which could operate with a deadlocked Reichstag. "I am

---

* Hitler was not as yet a major beneficiary of German industry. "After weighing all the facts," writes H. A. Turner, "we must recognize that the financial subsidies from industry were overwhelmingly directed *against* the Nazis." The bulk of the funds in the party treasury came from membership dues.

ready to leave at any time," he complained to the chairman of the Center Party, who was urging him to drop Papen, whose style pleased him. "If I don't have the confidence at home or abroad which I must have, I don't want to force myself on the country; for this I am too proud." Frustrated on all sides, Hindenburg summoned Papen and Schleicher, the new Minister of Defense, to his office on the first day of December. They arrived about 6 P.M. and, along with Meissner and Oskar von Hindenburg, ranged themselves in a semicircle around the President's desk. Papen pointed out that Hitler would accept responsibility only as head of another presidential cabinet, and suggested that his government remain in office for the time being. He realized he would not get the support of the Reichstag and that body would have to be suspended for a short period. This procedure involved a breach of the constitution by the President but the situation was grave enough to warrant such action. Then if the police could not keep order the army could step in.

"You can do a lot with bayonets," cut in Schleicher sarcastically, "but one thing you cannot do—sit on them for a long time." Papen's plan would not work, said the Minister of Defense, and suggested one that would: replacement of Papen as Chancellor by himself. This would split the Nazis into two factions and he would get a majority in the Reichstag. He would simply offer Gregor Strasser and one or two of his close supporters posts in the new government and thereby get the votes of sixty Nazi delegates. Other support would come from the Social Democrats and bourgeois parties.

For weeks Papen had noticed that Schleicher was "no longer as frank and open" as previously and their "relationship had become distinctly cool." Even so the Chancellor was amazed that the general who had helped him into office was now proposing to get rid of him. Schleicher had always seemed to support Papen's policies and had even initiated some of them. Resentfully, Papen argued that his Minister of Defense's scheme meant the abandonment of the President's long-range policy of striving for a more satisfactory relationship between administration and parliament.

Exhausted by almost uninterrupted discussions since early morning, Hindenburg sat in silence until the argument finally ended. Then he rose and turned to Papen. "Herr Reichskanzler," he said, "I desire you to undertake immediately the necessary discussions to form a government, to which I shall entrust the carrying out of your plan."

Schleicher was dumfounded. As he left the office with Papen the latter suggested staying in office for a few months until the constitution was amended and parliamentary peace restored. "Then I can resign and you will be able to take over the government with every hope of a good start."

Schleicher's icy retort was that made to Luther as he was leaving the Diet of Worms: " 'Little monk, little monk, you have chosen a difficult path.' "

This was painfully apparent the next morning at a cabinet meeting. After Papen had given an account of the previous night's conference with the President he called upon Schleicher, who got to his feet and declared that any attempt to form a new government under Papen would reduce the country to chaos. Nor could the police and the armed services ensure law and order in the event of civil war. After a study of the matter, he said, the General Staff had concluded that local units such as the police and the technical emergency service were so infiltrated with Nazis that the army could not control a Hitler Putsch.

When no minister challenged the army study, Papen hastened to the President's office. Hindenburg, drained by the events of the past day, listened to his complaints in silence. "My dear Papen," he said in a voice that had lost its confident ring, "you'll consider me a cad if I change my mind now. But I am now too old, at the end of my life, to take the responsibility for a civil war. We'll have to let Herr von Schleicher try his luck in God's name."

Rising with the help of his cane, Hindenburg slowly approached Papen and shook his hand. Papen was moved to see "two great tears" roll down the Old Gentleman's cheeks. A few hours later he sent a photograph of himself to Papen as a parting gift. On it was written: "I had a comrade!" the title of a famous soldier song.

When Schleicher appeared before the President and was requested to form a government he made a show of protest: "I am the last horse in your stable and ought to be kept in reserve." Only the threat of resignation by Hindenburg brought Schleicher to accept the appointment. So he said and perhaps he was truly reluctant. He greeted congratulations with a thin smile and another quotation, this one in Latin: "We who are about to die salute you."

And so on December, 2, 1932, Kurt von Schleicher became the first general to be appointed Chancellor since the man who replaced Bismarck in 1890. One of his first acts was to invite Gregor Strasser to his home (they had met previously in a dentist's residence) and offer to make him Vice-Chancellor and Minister President of Prussia. The proposition appealed to Strasser but he was loyal to Hitler and said he must first check with his chief. What he didn't add was that the problem was getting through the protective circle of sycophants and adulators which had formed around the Führer and seemed to control him. "Along comes Hindenburg," Strasser had recently complained to Frank, "a man of honor, who honestly and decently offers him a place in the government, and there stands the '*wahnfriedische*' Lohengrin-Hitler with his darkly menacing boys. Frank, I see black: Göring is a brutal egotist who cares nothing for Germany as long as he becomes something. Goebbels is a limping devil and basically two-faced, Röhm is a pig. This is the Old Guard of the Führer. It is terrible!"

Someone in Papen's office learned about the secret Schleicher-Strasser meeting and told a correspondent, who informed Hanfstaengl, who in turn passed the story on to Hitler. Thus Papen—or a Papen associate— paid back Schleicher in his own coin. The immediate victim, however, was Strasser, who had been dealing with Schleicher in good faith on the Führer's behalf, with the conviction that the best way to keep the party from disintegrating was to get into power at once—even at the price of co-alition.

While Hitler, whose suspicions of Strasser had been inflamed by Goebbels, understandably took it as a betrayal, more moderate advisers were inclined to consider Schleicher's latest offer—this time of the vice-chancellorship to the Führer. At a stormy conference of party leaders at the Kaiserhof on December 5 Strasser begged Hitler to accept. But Goebbels and Göring vehemently opposed such a deal and Hitler went along with them. Strasser gave warning that Schleicher would merely dissolve the Reichstag if NSDAP support was not forthcoming. But Hitler, still rankled by Strasser's "betrayal," refused to discuss the matter further.

Two days later Strasser again saw the Führer at the Kaiserhof. This time Hitler openly accused him of treason. Reportedly Strasser replied, "Herr Hitler, I am no more a traitor than any other willing messenger. My plan is to prevent a further deterioration of the party, not to bring it about." Too angry to find the right phrase, Strasser turned, slammed the door and took a taxi to the Hotel Excelsior. Alone in his room he fumed with indignation but he waited until the next morning, December 8, to pen a letter resigning his party offices on the grounds that the Führer no longer trusted him. No call for open revolt, it urged all party officials to remain in their posts. Strasser could not bring himself to deliver the mes-sage to Hitler in person but sent it by mail, then waited next to the tele-phone for a call.

The letter landed at the Kaiserhof, in Goebbels' words, "like a bombshell." Hitler went into such shock that he was momentarily unable to make any decisions. Nor could he pick up the phone and plead with Strasser, who had certainly left the door open for discussion by neither sur-rendering his seat in the Reichstag nor revoking his party membership. When no message came from the Kaiserhof, Strasser packed his bags and set off for the railroad station. After drinking beer with a friend he took the night train to Munich.

Hitler spent the evening in the Goebbels apartment. "It is difficult to be cheerful," Goebbels noted in his diary. "We are all depressed, above all because of the danger of the whole party falling apart, and all our work having been in vain." At 2 A.M. Robert Ley phoned to report that there was a marked feeling of uncertainty and agitation in party circles. He urged the Führer to return to the Kaiserhof at once. Hitler did so but the arrival of the early morning paper with headlines on Strasser's resignation, set off a tempestuous scene. Hitler was convinced that Strasser had leaked the story to the "Jewish newspapers." He stammered that Gregor had "stabbed him in the back five minutes before the final victory," then was silenced by his own tears.

"Such contemptible behaviour eludes the understanding of us all," wrote Goebbels. "Treason! Treason! Treason! . . . For hours the Führer paces anxiously up and down the hotel room. . . . Once he stops and says: 'If the party should ever break up, I will make an end of things in three minutes with a pistol.' "

Finally someone suggested that the most sensible course was to summon Strasser and patch up the quarrel. Whereupon Hitler ordered his chauffeur, Schreck, to find Strasser "at any price." But he was already at his apartment in Munich, hastily packing to leave for a holiday in Italy. To a friend, who happened to drop by, Strasser said in a resigned voice: "I am a man marked by death." He warned his friend to stay away from the apartment. "Whatever happens, mark what I say: From now on Germany is in the hands of an Austrian, who is a congenital liar, a former officer, who is a pervert, and a clubfoot. And I tell you the last is the worst of them all. This is Satan in human form." Although it was at least the second time Strasser had used such words to damn the Hitler inner circle, he still revered the Führer. Only recently he had told Rosenberg, "I fought as one of Hitler's men and as one of Hitler's men I want someday to go to my grave."

That same day party leaders and Gauleiters assembled in the palace of the president of the Reichstag to hear a declaration attacking Strasser. Still in an emotional state, Hitler stammered with a sob that he had been shocked by Strasser's treachery. According to Goebbels, the assemblage "burst into a spontaneous ovation for the leader. All shake hands with him, promising to carry on until the very end and not to renounce the great Idea, come what may. Strasser now is completely isolated, a dead man."

Strasser's drastic action was no revolt, only a personal attempt to save the Führer from men such as Goebbels. He represented no faction and no important party member followed him into oblivion. Nor was any purge necessary. Hitler merely announced that Strasser had started an authorized three-week sick leave, and once it was known that the Führer had withdrawn his confidence in the traitor the general membership withdrew theirs.

Even so Hitler remained shaken by the desertion of one of his paladins and did his utmost to wipe out the memory of Strasser. In mid-December he issued two long memoranda designed to decentralize the latter's administrative empire. Never again would he allow one man to hold such power in the party. Most of Strasser's political functions went to Hess since he was "most familiar with [Hitler's] basic ideas . . . and his intentions."

While the Führer had regained control of the party, the membership remained uneasy and demoralized. Their political future was bleak. "It is hard to hold the SA and the party officials to a clear course," Goebbels confided to his diary on December 15, and on the twenty-fourth, "I sit here all alone and worry about many things. The past is difficult and the future is cloudy and dark. The terrible loneliness overwhelms me with hopelessness. All possibilities and hopes have disappeared."

Hitler too had fallen into a depression that was undoubtedly intensified by his usual Christmas season despondency. (Later Hitler confided to his valet that he could not abide Yuletide decorations. His mother, he explained, had died near a lighted Christmas tree.) "I have given up all hope," he wrote to Frau Wagner after thanking her for a present. "Nothing will ever come of my dreams." He had no hope left, his opponents were too powerful. "As soon as I am sure that everything is lost you know what I'll do. I was always determined to do it. I cannot accept defeat. I will stick to my word and end my life with a bullet."

Enemies were already celebrating his political demise on the assumption that he had at last overreached himself. "Hitler is finished—not as an agitator or as a leader of an aggressive minority, but as a possible dictator." So wrote William Bullitt in an eleven-page report to President-elect Franklin Roosevelt. "Hitler's influence is waning so fast that the Government is no longer afraid of the growth of the Nazi movement."

At the same time, according to Müllern-Schönhausen, Hitler once more sought help from Hanussen. The famous seer cast a concise horoscope indicating that, although Hitler's constellation was favorable for the near future, there were still a few hindrances to his rise to power. Only one thing, Hanussen reportedly told Hitler, would remove these hindrances—a mandrake (a root in the shape of a man) found in a butcher's yard in the town of Hitler's birthplace by the light of the full moon. Hanussen himself volunteered for this bizarre mission and is said to have reported back to the Haus Wachenfeld in Obersalzberg on New Year's Day, 1933. With appropriate ceremony he presented the mandrake to the Führer that morning along with a rhymed prediction that Hitler's rise to power would begin on January 30:

The way to the goal is still blocked,
The right helpers not yet gathered,
But in three days—from three countries,
Through the bank everything will change!
And then on the day before the end of the month,
You stand at your goal and a turning point!
No eagle could carry you on your path,
The termites had to gnaw your way!
To the ground falls what was rotten and withered.
It already creaks in the beams!

If Hitler gave credence to this prediction—which was publicized and ridiculed—he would not have been the first famous European to take such matters seriously. The astrologer Louis Gauric had informed Pope Leo X that he would succeed to the pontificate; Nostradamus correctly predicted the death of Henri I; and Pierre Le Clerc reportedly convinced Napoleon that he would be emperor. In any case, the Führer must surely have been startled by the third and fourth lines in the Hanussen poem—for he had recently accepted an invitation to meet secretly in three days with former Chancellor von Papen, at the home of a banker, Baron Kurt von Schröder, one of those wealthy men who had earlier petitioned Hindenburg to appoint him Chancellor. A logical explanation of this explicit forecast is that Hanussen (as his more cynical contemporaries believed) was a clever fraud who based his predictions on information from reliable sources. It should be noted that "through the bank" is a literal translation of *Durch die Bank*, which is also an idiom, meaning "across the board," and the line could be read: "Everything will change radically." Perhaps the wary Hanussen was using this ambiguous term deliberately, to cover several possibilities.

That evening Hitler attended a performance in Munich of *Die Meistersinger* with the Hesses and Eva Braun. Later they all had coffee at the Hanfstaengl home. "Hitler was in his most benign mood," wrote Hanfstaengl. "It took us right back to the twenties when we had first met him. The conductor that evening had been Hans Knappertsbusch and Hitler had not liked his *tempi* and interpretation and was expatiating on the subject. He could really do so with good sense and would hum or whistle many of the passages, the words of which he knew by heart, in order to show what they meant." The Führer continued to reminisce about the old days in a charming manner and then, before leaving, signed his name in the guest book, pointedly adding the date. Then he looked up to Hanfstaengl and, with suppressed excitement, said, "This year belongs to us. I will guarantee you that in writing."

7

Hitler's meeting with Papen at Baron von Schröder's home in Cologne took place as scheduled on January 4. It was supposed to be secret but despite elaborate precautions by all parties a reporter from a Berlin newspaper (he had bribed a member of Hitler's bodyguard) was on hand to take pictures of Hitler and Papen separately entering the Schröder mansion. At the outset of the two-hour conference the latter suggested that the Schleicher regime be replaced by a Hitler-Papen government in which both would be equal. Hitler replied to this startling proposition at length: If he were made Chancellor he would have to be the actual head of government; he would accept some Papen men as ministers but only if they agreed to his policy of eliminating Social Democrats, Communists and Jews from leading positions in the nation. The two men, according to Schröder, "reached agreement in principle" and while leaving the house cordially shook hands.

When Schleicher was shown a picture of this handclasp he stormed to the presidential palace to charge Papen with treachery. He asked Hindenburg never to receive the former Chancellor again except in his presence. But the Old Gentleman was too fond of the dashing ex-cavalryman to believe him capable of deceit. Instead he authorized Papen to continue to meet with Hitler informally while instructing his secretary to keep these negotiations secret from Chancellor von Schleicher.

A few days later Hindenburg further reduced Schleicher in stature. Instead of supporting his proposed confiscation of bankrupt estates in eastern Germany, the President backed his own fellow Junkers. While it is true that Schleicher had been treated like a subordinate, he committed a grievous political mistake by overreacting. He refused to have any more dealings with the rebellious Junkers and in declaring open war on them not only filled Hindenburg's anterooms with angry representatives of the Junker families demanding dissolution of the Schleicher government but brought upon himself the ire of the military caste. The general should have kept in mind that the Junkers and the officer corps had been bound in common cause for two hundred years.

The beneficiary of his ineptitude was Adolf Hitler and he used the rising tide of discontent to good advantage in his appeals to the voters of Lippe. He was throwing all the weight of the party into this minor campaign as though it were another national election. His purpose was to win a victory of such proportions that he could negotiate with Hindenburg and Papen from strength. Gambling that he could come back from the November defeat and regain his mass popularity, Hitler spoke in practically every Lippe village and town. Wherever he went he was greeted with enthusiasm and on January 15 the power of his personal appeal was evident when he won 39.6 per cent of the popular vote, a gain of 17 per cent. Hitler was in Weimar on election day, "his face beaming like that of a small boy," and he termed the victory "a success whose importance it is not possible to overestimate." He felt so confident that the following day he brought the conflict with Strasser (who had returned from vacation in Italy) into the open. In a three-hour speech to his Gauleiters he charged Strasser with treason and wanted it known publicly that he was not only through with him but was now prepared to "break the necks of all party defeatists." The audience responded with "delirious ovations." Although a group of party dissidents were prepared to follow Strasser in a showdown with the Führer, he himself had no relish for a fight. Broken, Strasser resigned his seat in the Reichstag and drove back to Munich.

With Strasser's final exit from the political scene, Hitler felt so secure that he was in a mood to compromise when he saw Papen again on the evening of January 18. This time they met at the home of Joachim von Ribbentrop in the fashionable Berlin suburb of Dahlem. To ensure secrecy Papen was brought to the meeting by the Ribbentrop chauffeur and Hitler's car was driven into the garage so he, Röhm and Himmler could surreptitiously enter the house through the garden.

"Hitler insists on being Chancellor," wrote Frau von Ribbentrop in her notes of this conference. "Papen again considers this impossible. His influence with Hindenburg was not strong enough to effect this. Hitler makes no further arrangements for talks. Joachim tentatively suggests a meeting between Hitler and Hindenburg's son." The discussion ended inconclusively and if Papen was disconcerted by Hitler's inflexible manner, their hostess was not. She was by now as impressed with him as her husband and thought he was "a marvelous man, a true gentleman."

8

With each day Schleicher's position was becoming more untenable and by January 20 he had succeeded in antagonizing almost every party from right to left. His extremity was Papen's opportunity. Ever since his resignation the ex-Chancellor had regularly visited his neighbors—Hindenburg and son—bringing gaiety and frivolity into their dour household. But today he took the short walk through the snowy gardens of the chancellery for a definite purpose. Instead of amusing the President he informed him in detail of the meetings with Hitler and the possible amalgamation of conservative parties. Why not, he suggested persuasively, make Hitler Chancellor—so long as policies were dictated by himself?

The greatest obstacle to this was not the President but his son, who openly disliked the Führer. But Oskar's feelings were apparently based more on snobbery than ideology and he accepted an invitation to discuss their differences at the luxurious Ribbentrop villa on Sunday evening, January 22.

It was decided that Oskar should bring along his father's state secretary, Meissner, and to keep the parley secret from Chancellor von Schleicher, these two started the evening in a box at the Prussian State Opera House where an early work of Wagner's, *Das Liebesverbot*, was being performed. An icy wind was blowing down the Unter den Linden as the party arrived at the theater. One of the main topics of conversation before the curtain went up was the Nazi demonstration held a few hours earlier in front of Communist headquarters. Schleicher had permitted a parade of 20,000 Brownshirts while banning a counterdemonstration by the Reds, and then was forced to send out police to protect the marchers with armored cars and machine guns.

During the intermission Oskar and his wife made themselves conspicuous by greeting many acquaintances. But when the lights went down for the final act Hindenburg and Meissner left by a side entrance, leaving their wives behind. They hailed a taxi, giving their destination only when inside. They saw no car following them and assumed they had tricked Schleicher's spies but to be on the safe side they got out some distance from the Ribbentrop home and trudged through the snow. After some difficulty they located the Ribbentrop gate.

In the salon they found Papen, Hitler, Göring and Frick. The atmosphere was stiff and, after some awkward small talk, Hitler abruptly suggested to Oskar that they retire into the next room. Before Meissner could say anything the two were out of the room and Ribbentrop had closed the door behind them. According to young Hindenburg, Hitler dominated the conversation: he alone could save Germany from the Reds; he alone could be a strong Chancellor since no other government could operate without National Socialist support.

After an hour the two men returned, solemn-faced and the entire company moved into the dining room where a simple one-pot meal of peas and bacon was served from a silver bowl by a gloved servant. Hitler drank mineral water, the others champagne. Hindenburg and Meissner, the last to come, were the first to go and as their taxi plunged into the swirling snow Meissner noticed that his companion was "extremely silent, and the only remark which he made was that it could not be helped—the Nazis had to be taken into the government. My impression was that Hitler succeeded in getting him under his spell." It may have been simpler than that. Hitler could have threatened to make a public scandal of an open secret in high places: the Eastern Aid Fund had been put into effect six years earlier to help the Junkers retain their properties. President von Hindenburg had not only profited handsomely by this act (one reported figure was 620,000 marks) but had already turned over his estate to Oskar to avoid death duties. Nor had conveyance fees been paid. These were grounds for impeachment, and even if no conviction ensued, the name of Hindenburg would be besmirched.

Papen had noticed the impression Hitler had made on Oskar and after the latter's departure pledged his allegiance to the Führer. He promised to support him for Chancellor, vowing he would under no circumstances accept the appointment himself. The clandestine meeting ended with the Hitler party furtively disappearing into the garage. But Schleicher's spies had not been fooled. The next morning the Chancellor phoned Meissner with a sarcastic question: how had he liked last night's one-pot supper? Being a master of intrigue, the general knew he must act quickly. He told Hindenburg that he needed a "military dictatorship" to control the Nazis and tried to persuade him to dissolve the Reichstag and suspend elections. But Hindenburg, weary of Schleicher's interminable schemes, refused to authorize any such emergency measures.

When word of the proposed military dictatorship leaked out, both the Social Democrat and Center parties branded Schleicher as an enemy of the people. His plan was not only unconstitutional but "open high treason." In a futile attempt to placate these dissidents he made another blunder by stating publicly that he had no intention of violating the constitution. This only succeeded in incensing Hugenberg and his Nationalist Party, who promptly abandoned Schleicher.

The sudden turn of events in Hitler's favor brought him back to Berlin on January 27, but then almost immediately he became so frustrated by the intrigues in the capital that he told Ribbentrop he was going to leave. "Joachim proposes link-up with Hugenberg for a national front," Frau von Ribbentrop noted. "Hitler declares that he has said all there is to say to the field marshal, and does not know what to add. Joachim persuades Hitler that this last attempt should be made, and that the situation is by no means hopeless."

Hitler reluctantly agreed to talk with Papen that evening but, as soon as the meeting was arranged, changed his mind on the grounds that he was in no position to talk freely. He announced testily that this time he was really leaving the capital but did agree to let Ribbentrop see the ex-Chancellor on his behalf. That evening Ribbentrop somehow convinced Papen that a Hitler chancellorship was the only solution; and the next morning Papen passed on this conviction to Hindenburg. The field marshal wavered. For months he had been inundated with requests to appoint Hitler, and lately his own son had come to the same conclusion. Though his own distaste for the "Czech corporal," as he persisted in calling him, was as strong as ever, it was apparent that the Old Gentleman was at last in the mood to accept Hitler.

At the moment Schleicher was convening with his cabinet members: he told them that he proposed asking Hindenburg once more for an order to dissolve the Reichstag and if this failed he would be forced to resign. He temporarily adjourned the meeting to see the President. It was a short interview. Would Hindenburg grant a dissolution decree? "Nein!" In that case, said Schleicher, the only alternative was a Hitler government. Hindenburg muttered that the Schleicher government hadn't been able to win a majority but perhaps he himself could find one that could stabilize Germany. He accepted the resignation of the cabinet and, in an exasperated aside, muttered that he didn't want to argue any more about it.

Hindenburg's mind seemed to be wandering. "Whether what I am going to do now is right, my dear Schleicher," he said, "I don't know; but I shall know soon enough when I am up there." He pointed heavenward. "I already have one foot in the grave and I am not sure that I shall not regret this action in heaven later on."

"After this breach of trust, sir," was the bitter answer, "I am not sure that you will go to heaven."

Before the day was out, Papen was back in the presidential office along
with Oskar and Meissner. Once again the elder Hindenburg suggested
Papen take the chancellorship but all three advisers reiterated that Hitler
was the only possible choice. "It is my unpleasant duty then to appoint
this fellow Hitler as Chancellor?" grumbled the Old Gentleman. But he
insisted that the new government include General Werner von Blomberg
(whom he described as a "nonpolitical passionate soldier with pleasant
manners") as Minister of Defense and Papen as Vice-Chancellor. The
problem was to get Hitler to accept these appointments.

The next morning, a Sunday, Papen saw Hitler. He was agreeable—
but had his own demands: new general elections and an enabling law
which would give him as Chancellor authority exceeding that of a former
Kaiser. It was early afternoon by the time Papen finally reported to Hindenburg that all parties were agreed on the new government. Only then
did he mention Hitler's demand for new elections and he made it sound
reasonable. He clinched the point with Hitler's promise that these would
indeed be the *last elections*. Out of relief that the constitutional crisis was
at last ending, neither the President nor his protégé was at all struck by
the implications of this promise.

When Göring got the good news he rushed off to be the first to bring
it to the Führer, who was having coffee at the Goebbels apartment. For a
long time, according to the Goebbels diary, the three men were in such ecstasy that they said nothing. Then they rose and shook hands emotionally.
A homey touch was added by Magda Goebbels, who entered with a tray
of freshly baked nut cakes just as the three men formed a circle by grasping hands. The celebration was brought to an abrupt end by the appearance of a messenger from Schleicher who warned of a possible military uprising if Hindenburg named the Führer. Hitler and Göring reacted with
alarm. Neither thought of checking with trusted adherents at the Potsdam
and Berlin barracks to find out if the troops were actually on alert. Instead,
Hitler telephoned the commander of the Berlin SA, ordering him to alert
all local Brownshirts. Who else had to be warned? asked Hitler and gave
the answer himself: Papen, Oskar von Hindenburg and Meissner. While
Goebbels and Göring tumbled out of the apartment to carry out these
missions, Hitler phoned a Nazi police major, instructing him "to prepare
for a sudden seizure of the Wilhelmstrasse by six police battalions." Finally he sent word to the Defense Minister-elect, General von Blomberg,
who was taking the night train from Geneva, to proceed at once from the
Berlin railroad station to the presidential palace to be sworn in—and thus
be prepared to suppress any Putsch.

The rumor of a military coup spread rapidly through government circles, causing considerable panic in the capital throughout the night. The
next morning—Monday, January 30—panic was succeeded by a monumental argument in Papen's residence. Hugenberg, the Nationalist Party

leader, violently objected to Hitler's demand for new elections and it appeared as if the new government was already doomed. Hugenberg wrangled on at such length that Papen finally exclaimed in desperation, "If the new government is not formed by eleven o'clock, the army is going to march. Schleicher may establish a military dictatorship." And to the query where he got this intelligence, Papen impatiently shouted, "From Hindenburg, Jr.!"

Just then there was a loud cry of "Heil!" from the crowd outside the Papen villa and Hitler entered with Göring. It was 10:35 A.M. and Papen suggested they all follow him to the chancellery. They paraded through the snow-covered chancellery garden and up to Meissner's office. Here they met other ministerial candidates and while they all were waiting to be brought into the President's office Papen raised the question of elections.

"Elections?" Hugenberg testily declared that he thought the question had been settled. Hitler drew him aside but the Führer's considerable powers of persuasion only provoked Hugenberg to vociferous objections. Hitler tried to pacify the old man by seizing his hand and promising to make no changes in the cabinet no matter how the elections came out. The answer was still no.

At that moment Meissner appeared. "Gentlemen, it is five minutes past the appointed time," he said. "The President likes punctuality." Papen saw his coalition breaking up at the threshold of success. "Herr Geheimrat," he begged, "do you want to risk the national unity which has finally been achieved after so many difficult negotiations? You cannot possibly doubt the solemn word of a German man!"

Hugenberg continued to argue bitterly until the harried Meissner rushed out again, watch in hand. "The President requests you not to keep him waiting any longer," he announced. "It is now eleven-fifteen. The Old Gentleman may retire at any moment!"

Once more Hitler seized Hugenberg's hand and this time promised to consult the Center and Bavarian People's parties to ensure the widest possible basis for parliamentary majority. The threat of Meissner's watch probably helped induce Hugenberg to say that he would leave the decision to Hindenburg. Hitler hastily agreed to this and Göring boomed out, "Now, everything is in order!" and they all filed into the President's office.

Hindenburg was so irked he didn't personally offer the post of Chancellor to Hitler—the only Chancellor so slighted. Nor did he greet the new cabinet with a welcoming speech or even outline what tasks lay before them. The swearing-in ceremony was finished rapidly in the style of a shotgun wedding. But Hitler could not let such a historical moment pass in silence and, to everyone's surprise, began a speech. After solemnly vowing he would observe the Weimar constitution, he promised to find a majority in the parliament so that the President would no longer have to sign emergency decrees. Further, he would solve the economic crisis and unite a Germany torn by bitterness and debate. There was a pause for an appropriate response from Hindenburg but the field marshal would only say, as if dismissing the troops, "And now, gentlemen, forward with God!"

Hanussen's prediction, if it was one, had come true. The man who had failed to graduate from high school, who had been refused admission to the Academy of Fine Arts and who had lived as a tramp on the streets of Vienna was Chancellor of Germany on the thirtieth day of January 1933. As he left the room in a daze, Hitler caught sight of Hoffmann, whom he had brought along to take pictures of the ceremony. Clapping his head, he exclaimed, "Good God, I forgot all about you, Hoffmann! And now, I'm afraid, it's too late!" In his haste to get back to the Kaiserhof, Hitler left his new governmental colleagues with scarcely a word. He stood up in his car as it crept slowly through the mass of delirious adherents who were shouting themselves hoarse.

"We've done it!" he announced triumphantly to the party faithful waiting for him at the hotel. All crowded around and he shook the hands of maids and waiters as well as those of rank and wealth.

The news was received throughout Germany with mixed feelings. The liberals were horrified but to the average German anything was better than the parliamentary shambles of the past year. And for many young idealists, the dispossessed, the embittered patriots and the racists there was unrestrained joy. Their dreams were coming true. In Munich Egon Hanfstaengl rushed into his classroom, bursting with the news. "Kurt!" he shouted to a friend. "We've done it! We're in power!" Then he remembered that Kurt was a Jew. Kurt smiled a little thinly before replying: "I'm glad for you. I wish I could be one of you."

No group was more surprised at the sudden ascension of Adolf Hitler than the Berlin Brownshirts. They had been living in poverty for years, risking their lives on the streets of the capital, often in opposition to their Führer's wishes. Now at one stroke their dream was realized but it was only through the newspapers that most of them learned there would be a torchlight parade that evening.

Every able-bodied SA and SS man was out in uniform. Those who expected the usual trouble with the police were surprised by smiles from their old enemies, some of whom now wore swastikas. Carrying torches, the storm troopers started from the Tiergarten at dusk, joined by thousands of Stahlhelm men, and passed under the Brandenburg Gate in disciplined columns to the blare of martial music. Hour after hour they marched down the Wilhelmstrasse shouting the "Horst Wessel Lied" and other fighting songs. First they paid homage to Hindenburg, who stood at a window of the presidential palace and, moments later, to Hitler, who looked down fondly from a window of the chancellery.

Young men perched in trees along the Wilhelmstrasse; boys clung to the iron fences like "bunches of grapes." The excitement was intensified by the winter darkness as the stream of flares glowed hypnotically and the drums beat thunderously. It had all been staged by the master showman, Goebbels, and Hitler himself was so impressed that he turned and asked, "How on earth did he conjure up all these thousands of torches in the space of a few hours?" The little doctor had also managed to take over the radio stations and the country was being treated to a running eyewitness account of the procession.

Papen watched the marchers over Hitler's shoulder. He noticed that as they approached Hindenburg there were respectful shouts but the sight of Hitler brought frantic acclaim. "The contrast was most marked and seemed to emphasize the transition from a moribund regime to the new revolutionary forces. . . . It was an extraordinary experience, and the endless repetition of the triumphal cry: 'Heil, Heil, Sieg Heil!' rang in my ears like a tocsin." As Hitler turned to speak to Papen, his voice was choked. "What an immense task we have set ourselves, Herr von Papen—we must never part until our work is accomplished."

Hans Frank, the lawyer, also stood behind Hitler on that intoxicating night. "God knows our hearts were pure that day," he stated not long before he was hanged, "and if anyone had told us of the events to come, no one would have believed it, least of all I. It was a day of glory and happiness." Tears of joy ran down the cheeks of the celebrants down below. "Everyone felt the same—that things will get better," remembered one Brownshirt who had revolted with Stennes. "Although realistically there was no reason for them to believe things would improve, they believed it. They had hope again. It was remarkable. I don't think that Germany will ever again find another man who could inspire as much hope, trust and love as Hitler did at that moment."

"Some of the uncanny feeling of that night remains with me even today," wrote Melita Maschmann, who had been taken to the parade by her parents. "The crashing tread of the feet, the sombre pomp of the red and black flags, the flickering light from the torches on the faces and the songs with melodies that were at once aggressive and sentimental." To most foreign observers it was an ominous sight. "The river of fire flowed past the French Embassy," wrote Ambassador François-Poncet, "whence, with heavy heart and filled with foreboding, I watched its luminous wake."

Hitler had a late supper with Hess, Göring, Goebbels, Röhm and Frank in a small private room. Compulsively he talked on and on. "Some foreign source today called me 'anti-Christ,'" he said. "The only kind of anti I am is anti-Lenin." According to Frank, Hitler went on to say he hoped Hindenburg could be won over to his side. "The Old Gentleman liked it very much when I said to him today that I would serve him as Chancellor as loyally as in the days as a soldier when he was my hero."

Without respite the talk switched to Communism. "This evening marks the end of the so-called 'Red Berlin.' People are only Red when they have no other way. Those who count on the so-called intelligence of a people are always caught short with the masses. The emotions of a people are like those of a woman, more or less, I would say." Hitler was still talking as they strolled through the garden. "This chancellery," he said, "is like a cigar box. A very unimpressive place for a reception. We will change all that."

That night an exultant Goebbels wrote in his diary: "It is almost like a dream . . . a fairy tale. . . . The new Reich has been born. Fourteen years of work have been crowned with victory. The German revolution has begun!" Few Germans that evening realized this, and perhaps none recalled the prophetic words written by Heinrich Heine, a Jew, not quite a century earlier: "German thunder is truly German; it takes its time. But it will come, and when it crashes it will crash as nothing in history crashed before. The hour will come. . . . A drama will be performed which will make the French Revolution seem like a pretty idyll. . . . Never doubt it; the hour will come."

Chapter Eleven

AN UNGUARDED HOUR
1933–JUNE 1934

"Neither a nation nor a woman is forgiven for *an unguarded hour* in which the first adventurer who comes along can sweep them off their feet and possess them."

KARL MARX

1

The next morning Frau Goebbels brought flowers to Hitler. He was looking out the window of his room in the Kaiserhof. Slowly he turned and, "with an almost solemn gesture," took the bouquet. "These are the first flowers, and you are the first woman to congratulate me," he murmured, according to her reverent account. After moments of silence he said as if continuing a monologue, "Now the world must realize why I couldn't be Vice-Chancellor. How long my own party members did not understand me!" After another long silence she started for the door. "Yes," she heard him softly exclaim, "now I must remain by myself for some time."

He regarded what had happened as fate, another step on a path long since mapped out. But those who had put him in power were convinced he was merely their dupe. Papen, for one, boasted to his circle: "We have hired him for ourselves," and then reassured a critical friend: "What do you want? I have Hindenburg's confidence. Within two months we will have pushed Hitler so far in the corner that he'll squeak."

The junkers, as embodied by Papen, thought they had bought a restitution of authoritarian rule but Hitler had no intention of being their puppet and at once began laying the foundation for a dictatorship. First he dismissed out of hand a list of questions and demands submitted by the Center Party with the comment that, since negotiations with that party had failed, new elections were necessary. Then, through Papen, he persuaded Hindenburg to dissolve the parliament.

Few realized the import of these first steps. Editorials in the liberal bourgeois papers foresaw no revolutionary changes. After all there were only two other Nazis in Hitler's cabinet—Göring and Frick. "The make-up of the cabinet shows that Herr Hitler had to accept significant restrictions," pontificated the *Frankfurter Zeitung* that day—and forty-eight hours later remarked that "it has become all too evident that the government revolves around Hugenberg, not the Chancellor." Even the Social Democrats were not alarmed since it was widely believed that Hitler could never get the two-thirds majority to change the Weimar constitution.

A similar view was held by the New York *Times:* "The composition of the Cabinet leaves Herr Hitler no scope for the gratification of his dictatorial ambition." And the British ambassador reported: "On the whole the press has taken the appointment of Herr Hitler to the chancellorship with almost philosophic calm," and the "populace took the news phlegmatically."

While all these observers were assuring the world of Hitler's impotence, he was hiding his revolutionary intentions behind a flow of inspirational but conservative phrases in a radio address to the voters on the first of February. He made it clear that he wanted only a return to the old virtues of the past. He said nothing of his plans for the Jews, said nothing, in fact, that offended or alarmed the average citizen.

During the speech the American chargé d'affaires in Berlin was dining with one of those kingmakers who had helped put Hitler in power. Hjalmar Schacht, president of the Reichsbank, revealed that he was the Führer's court financial and economic adviser, and then assured the American that the Nazis would "make no attempt to carry out their well-known demagogic reforms" and that consequently "all big business viewed the new regime with sympathy."

While the last remark was an exaggeration, Hitler would not have been Chancellor without the support of industrialists and the military. The majority in the officer corps agreed with Karl Dönitz, a rising man in the navy, who felt it was simply a choice between Hitler and the Reds.

The support of the military was as self-serving as that of the industrialists, and Hitler knew it. His opinion of generals was not high. "Before I became Chancellor," he admitted years later, "I thought the General Staff was like a mastiff which had to be held tight by the collar because it threatened all and sundry." His experiences with generals to date had not been happy ones: Lossow had "betrayed" him in Munich and Schleicher had tried to keep him out of the chancellery. But now that he was in power he was determined to make his peace with the military and enlist them in the regeneration of Germany.

He took the first step on the evening of his fourth day as Chancellor by accepting an invitation to dine at the home of General von Hammerstein, who had been outspoken in his contempt for the Nazis. The party had been arranged by the new Minister of Defense, General von Blomberg, and its purpose was to introduce the Führer to leaders in the armed forces. After dinner he rose to speak. At first he was stiff before such company, as he told of the disastrous economic problems facing the nation. The answer was not a renewed export drive since production exceeded demand throughout the world and Germany's former customers had developed their own markets. Unemployment and depression, he concluded, would continue until Germany recovered her former position in the world.

Interest in the room was aroused. It was a solution most of them cherished. Hitler went on to say that pacifism, Marxism and that "cancerous growth, democracy," must be eradicated. Rearmament was the first requirement for a resurgent Germany and once the Fatherland had regained its power there would come "the conquest of the land in the East and its ruthless Germanization." Lest this revelation of his blueprint for the future cause apprehension, Hitler promised that his listeners need not concern themselves over the domestic or foreign policy. The army would not be used to deal with unrest at home and should devote itself for the next few years "to the operation of its main objective, training for the defense of the Fatherland in the case of aggression." As reassurance regarding the SA, he added that the army would be "the sole bearer of arms, and its structure would remain unaltered."

Admiral Erich Raeder was favorably impressed and assumed everyone else present shared his feeling. But Generals Werner von Fritsch and Friedrich Fromm were apprehensive of the talk of aggression and General Ritter von Leeb had the impression Hitler was trying to bribe them. "A businessman whose wares are any good," he later observed sarcastically, "does not need to boost them in the loudest tones of a market crier."

The response was mixed, but Hitler had won over a number of new adherents. Those who hoped to transform the new government into a military dictatorship as the first step to a restored monarchy were ready to sanction the National Socialist reforms and many of those with qualms were inclined to go along out of respect for Field Marshal von Hindenburg.

Using the emergency powers of the constitution that had once felt his scorn, Hitler next pushed through a decree, "for the protection of the German people," controlling political meetings and restricting the press. Neither Papen nor any of his colleagues in the cabinet protested regulations that enabled Hitler to paralyze rival parties and to control public opinion. Faced by such unanimity, Hindenburg also succumbed and signed the decree. This was followed shortly by an emergency decree replacing the political regime in Prussia with one of his own choice. The first protests were answered by reason—Papen as the newly appointed Prussian Minister President could surely control the new Minister of the Interior, Göring—but the fact remained that Hitler had accomplished his second step toward dictatorship.

There was a new elite in Germany. The borough president of Hamburg came from a notions shop, one of hundreds who had risen overnight from the lower middle class. Teachers, lawyers and businessmen were also among the leaders. Never before had so many men of modest means been thrust into political prominence. These were the old Nazi fighters whose dedication to the movement and Hitler was now drawing dividends.

Perhaps no other German Chancellor had been so well prepared for assumption of leadership as Hitler, who had regarded himself as Führer for some time. The same could not be said for the party. It had been held together by his magnetism and the dream of power and jobs. This new elite did manage to carry out a National Socialist revolution on the local level but only because of the complacency of the conservatives and the confusion among liberal and leftist opponents.

While the rank and file were clumsily organizing the villages, towns and provinces, their Führer was establishing authority over his disarrayed opponents. At first many misread his diffident, somewhat embarrassed manner with strangers as a sign of weakness. But in short order he gained the upper hand over those who underrated him. "In cabinet meetings," recalled Finance Minister Count Lutz Schwerin von Krosigk, who had been a Rhodes scholar, "one could not but recognize and admire the qualities which gave him mastery of all discussions: his infallible memory, which enabled him to answer with the utmost precision questions on the remotest problems under consideration; his presence of mind in discussions; the clarity with which he could reduce the most intricate question to a simple—sometimes too simple—formula; his skill in summing up concisely the results of a long debate; and his cleverness in approaching a well-known and long-discussed problem from a new angle."

Schwerin von Krosigk and other governmental officials had never before been subjected to such a dynamic personality and it was no wonder they succumbed. His ascendancy over these men of substance was portrayed by a picture in the *Illustrierte Beobachter* that month. No longer was he clad in an ill-fitting suit, no longer did he slouch in wrinkled trench coat, whip in hand. Now smiling and confident, clad in a soft overcoat of good cut and quality, he was the picture of radiant confidence.

2

Despite his personal success, the fate of the Brown Revolution was still in doubt at the end of the first six weeks of power. The emergency deposition of the Prussian government was causing grave concern in other states. By the middle of February Göring had drastically purged the Prussian police of men he could not rely on and issued an order instructing his police force "to avoid at all costs anything suggestive of hostility to the SA, SS and Stahlhelm, as these organizations contain the most constructive national elements. . . . It is the business of the police to abet every form of national propaganda." This was followed by an ominous note to the effect that the police should act decisively against "organizations hostile to the state" and should not hesitate to use their firearms. On the contrary, they would be punished if they failed "in their duty." He was declaring open season on Communists, Marxists and their sympathizers.

Seven of the smaller states were already as hamstrung politically as Prussia, but the larger states—including Bavaria, the home of National Socialism—refused to bow to the Hitler government. This rebellion was accompanied by a Communist campaign calling for resistance to the Nazis. On February 21 the Union of Red Fighters exhorted the Young Proletarians to disarm the SA and SS. "Every comrade a commander in the coming Red Army! This is our oath to the Red soldiers of the Soviet Union. Our fight cannot be broken by machine guns or pistol-barrels or prison. We are the masters of tomorrow!" A few days later the official Communist organ, *Red Sailor*, openly called for violence: "Workers, to the barricades! Forward to victory! Fresh bullets in your guns! Draw the pins of the hand-grenades!"

These revolutionary appeals may have been mere verbiage but Göring took them at face value—or professed to—and raided the Karl Liebknecht House in Berlin on February 24. An official announcement proclaimed that the police had discovered plans for a Communist uprising. On the evening of February 26 Hanussen predicted that this revolution would soon literally burst into flames. At a séance attended by some of the most influential people in the capital he claimed to see smoke . . . an eagle rising from flames . . . and then a large Berlin building engulfed in fire. Those of his listeners who were aware that there had been three attempts the previous day to set fire to governmental buildings must have been particularly impressed.

The arsonist, a twenty-four-year-old native of Holland, Marinus van der Lubbe, had in fact also made up his mind to burn down the Reichstag. A strong, lumpish young man, his protest against capitalism was setting buildings on fire. Four years earlier he had resigned in disgust from the Communist Party to join International Communists, a tiny splinter group which opposed Moscow policies. He had come to Berlin a week earlier under the impression that great things were about to happen there. But attendance at Social Democratic and Communist demonstrations convinced him that the German workers would start a revolution only under the impetus of some startling event. He hoped the sight of governmental strongholds going up in flames would inspire the lethargic German masses to revolt.

Not discouraged by the three abortive fires, on Monday noon—it was February 27—he bought four packages of fire lighters at a shop on the Müllerstrasse and then set off on foot for the Reichstag. Shabbily dressed in pitifully short trousers and peaked cap, he kept circling the ornate gilt- and glass-domed building until he found the best way to enter was from the west—the door least often used. It was a freezing day, heightened by a sharp wind. To warm up he stayed in the post office for half an hour, then walked some more and at about nine that evening was back at the Reichstag. The western approach was deserted and in moments he had scaled the wall and was on the balcony of the first floor.

At 9:30 P.M. a theology student on his way home heard breaking glass inside the parliament building. He saw a figure with a burning object in his hand and ran to alert a police sergeant at the northwestern corner of the Reichstag. The sergeant found the broken window and a glow behind it but watched in astonishment and it was some minutes before he summoned the fire brigade. The first engines arrived just before ten and by then the Session Chamber was in flames.

At his Berlin quarters opposite the Reichstag, Hanfstaengl was awakened from a sickbed by the screams of the housekeeper. He looked out the window at the fire and telephoned the Goebbels apartment where a party for the Führer was in mid-career. When Goebbels heard the news he thought it was a joke. "If you think that, come down here and see for yourself," retorted Hanfstaengl and hung up. A moment later his phone rang. It was Goebbels. "I have just talked to the Führer and he wants to know what's really happening. No more of your jokes now." The annoyance and suspicion in Goebbels' voice seemed genuine and Hanfstaengl lost his temper. He said the place was in flames and the fire brigades were already there. He was going back to bed to nurse his fever.

After Hitler saw the red sky above the Tiergarten he shouted. "It's the Communists!" and set off with Goebbels for the scene of the fire. They found Göring inside the burning building, brown hat turned up in front and looking immense in a camel-hair coat. He had been one of the first to reach the conflagration, and his first order was characteristic: "Save the tapestries!" He told Hitler that it was the work of the Reds. "A number of Communist deputies were present here in the Reichstag twenty minutes before the fire broke out. We have succeeded in arresting one of the incendiaries." And to Goebbels' excited question, "Who was it?" Göring replied complacently, "We don't know yet, but we shall squeeze it out of him, have no fear, Doctor."

"Are the other public buildings safe?" asked Hitler.

"I've taken every possible precaution. I've mobilized all the police.

Every public building has been given a special guard. We are ready for anything."

The party began a tour of the destroyed area across pools of water and charred debris. As they entered a lobby filled with foul-smelling smoke a policeman held up his arms to warn Hitler that a candelabrum might crash at any moment. The Chancellor (after remarking contemptuously, "Good riddance to that trashy old shack") fell back to join Sefton Delmer, who had arrived to cover the fire. "God grant that this be the work of Communists," he said—a sign to the correspondent that he was not yet absolutely certain it was a Red plot but only hoped so. "You are now witnessing the beginning of a great epoch in German history, Herr Delmer. This fire is the beginning." He tripped over a fire hose but lost neither his balance nor the thread of his speech. "If the Communists got ahold of Europe and had control of it six months—what am I saying!— two months—the whole continent would be aflame like this building."

After they had climbed the stairs to the next floor they were approached by Papen, who had rushed from a dinner at the Herrenklub in honor of Hindenburg and was immaculate in gray tweed overcoat and black Homburg. "This is a God-given signal, Herr Vice-Chancellor!" Hitler exclaimed. "If this fire, as I believe, is the work of the Communists, then we must crush out this murderous pest with an iron fist!" Papen was relieved that the Gobelin tapestries had been saved and the library was untouched and, when Hitler invited him to attend a conference in Göring's office to decide on what should be done, politely but pointedly declined. He thought he should first report to Hindenburg.

The fire seemed to fascinate Hitler and after arrival at the office of the Reichstag president he leaned over the stone parapet overlooking the holocaust as if magnetized by the flames. By this time the conference room was filling with cabinet ministers as well as other officials and dignitaries including Prince Auwi, the Lord Mayor of Berlin, the police president and the British ambassador. Then the man who had undertaken the initial investigation entered. Rudolf Diels, chief of the political police in the Prussian Ministry of Interior, had come to inform the Führer and Göring that the arsonist, a Dutch national named van der Lubbe, had been found, bare to the waist, inside the Reichstag. When an enraged interrogator yelled, "Why did you do it?" the young radical had replied, "As a protest."

Göring began shouting slogans and orders. "This is the beginning of a Communist uprising. Not a moment must be lost. . . ." He was cut off by Hitler: "Now we'll show them! Anyone who stands in our way will be mown down!" His face was scarlet from excitement and heat. "The German people have been soft too long. Every Communist official must be shot. All Communist deputies must be hanged this very night. All friends of the Communists must be locked up. And that goes for the Social Democrats and the Reichsbanner as well!"

Diels finally managed to tell Hitler that the arsonist denied any connection with the Communist Party and swore he alone had set all the fires inside the Reichstag. Diels added that the confession rang true and that the fire was undoubtedly the work of a single madman.

"This is a cunning and well-prepared plot," scoffed Hitler and resumed his irrational diatribe. "The only thing is that they have reckoned without us and without the German people. In their ratholes, from which they are now trying to crawl out, they cannot hear the jubilation of the masses."

Diels tried to say that it was ridiculous to think the Communists were about to stage a Putsch. Countless Red turncoats had told him it was all talk. But Hitler would not listen. He flew into another outburst, vilifying these "subhumans" and shouting that he needed no more proof to be convinced that the Communists, by "shamefully setting fire to a German palladium," had wished to give the signal for their loudly heralded mass action."

The tempestuous conference ended about 11 P.M. and, after another meeting at the Prussian Ministry of Interior to discuss security measures, Hitler set out for the local offices of the *Völkischer Beobachter* to see how the paper was covering the fire. "It took half an hour before I could find anyone to let me in. Inside there were a few compositors sitting around, and eventually some sub-editor appeared very heavy with sleep." Hitler sent for Goebbels and the two worked until dawn preparing the next edition, which would accuse the Reds of a plot to seize power amid the "general panic."

In the meantime Göring was raging at the man who had been assigned to draw up the report for the official Prussian press service. After a glance at a twenty-line draft which mentioned one arsonist, Göring shouted, "That's sheer rubbish! It may be a good police report but it's not at all the kind of communiqué I have in mind!" Grabbing a blue pencil, he changed one hundredweight of incendiary material to one thousand and, when the author protested that it would be impossible for a single man to carry such a load, retorted: "Nothing is impossible. Why mention a single man? There were ten or even twenty men! Don't you understand what is happening? The whole thing was a signal for a Communist uprising!" After Göring wrote an entirely new communiqué, indicating that van der Lubbe's accomplices were two Communist members of the Reichstag, the original author asked him to sign it, since it was not an official report but a political document. "The news agencies," he explained, "will only accept it from me if you sign it officially." Grudgingly Göring scrawled a large "G." By this time all police radio stations were issuing calls for the arrest of Communist members of the Reichstag, the provincial diets and town councils. Communist functionaries were also to be apprehended and all Red newspapers suppressed.

The stimulation of that night emboldened Hitler to throw off his last inhibitions, for late the next morning he flung himself into an open battle for power. It started incongruously at a cabinet meeting as the Chancellor politely greeted each minister according to rank. After this traditional beginning he took over in dictatorial fashion. The crisis was such, he said, as to warrant "a ruthless settling of accounts" with the Communists which "must not be dependent on legal considerations." He proposed, therefore, an emergency decree to protect the nation from the Reds but made it sound purely defensive and innocuous, referring almost casually to a "special measure to safeguard all the cultural documents of the German people." But when Frick read off his draft it should have been obvious that the decree canceled most rights expected by a democratic society. First it suspended the civil liberties granted by the Weimar constitution—free speech, free press, sanctity of the home, secrecy of mail and telephone conversations, freedom to assemble or form organizations and inviolability of private property. Next it authorized the Reich Minister of Interior to seize control temporarily of any state government unable to maintain order. Not a single minister opposed the deprivation of civil rights but Papen did protest that the threat to intervene with states would be deeply resented, particularly in Bavaria. Papen's dissent was short-lived; he approved a minor change that was a modification in name only. That evening Hitler and he reported to Hindenburg. The Führer argued that the decree was necessary to put down the Red revolution and, when neither Papen nor Meissner expressed disapproval, the President signed without comment.

A civil state of emergency had been substituted for the military measure sought by the conservatives, with the cabinet holding those powers usually bestowed on the commander-in-chief in a military dictatorship. On the surface such power was not so ominous since the cabinet was still overwhelmingly non-National Socialist. The decree was passed so hastily and under such emotional circumstances that no one was sure exactly who had originated the idea to abolish civil rights rather than curtail them as previous chancellors had done. Possibly it was not an underhanded plot of Hitler's in his avowed move toward dictatorship but an accident of history. The fire had obviously brought Hitler to the edge of hysteria and he truly feared a Red revolution. Certainly his erratic actions as well as those of Göring and others close to him were not those of conspirators with a levelheaded plan. Nor did Hitler react so much in panic as in utter faith in his mission. So far as he was concerned the fire was proof of all he had been saying about Reds and Jews for years.

The emergency measures that followed, designed primarily to put down a non-existent revolt, turned out to be a leap forward in Hitler's drive for total power. Truckloads of SA and SS men hastily sworn in as auxiliaries were helping the police enforce the decree. They descended on the rooms and taverns of known Reds and carted them off to prison or interrogation cellars. More than three thousand Communists and Social Democrats were taken into protective custody by the regular police. Airdromes and ports were under strict surveillance while trains were searched at frontiers.

Göring was in his glory and the following day, as Prussian Minister of Interior, he spoke to the nation by radio about the insidious plans of the Reds, groups of whom planned to don Brownshirt and Stahlhelm uniforms and carry out terrorist acts in an effort to destroy the unity of the nation. The burning of the Reichstag, he predicted, was only the first of many other fires that would distract the police and leave the people at the mercy of the revolutionaries. But, he concluded, the nation need not fear. "I may say to the Communists that my nerves have not yet collapsed, and I feel myself strong enough to give the knockout blow to their criminal plans!"

While his explanation was widely accepted in Germany, the outside world was not so gullible. "The assertion that German Communists had any association with the fire is simply a piece of stupidity," stated the London *News Chronicle* and this view was generally shared in diplomatic and foreign press circles. There was a growing feeling that it was the Nazis themselves who had burned the Reichstag as a pretext for crushing the Communists.

Next day, March 2, Sefton Delmer went to Hitler for the answer. He railed at foreigners for making such accusations when they should be grateful for his courageous acts against the common Red foe. Delmer finally broke in to say that the mass arrests were spreading the fear that Hitler planned a bloody reprisal upon his enemies. "I need no St. Bartholomew's night," retorted Hitler. Tribunals had been set up to try enemies of the state and put an end to conspiracies. Delmer took this to mean that he was going to slaughter his foes legally and wondered if the suspension of civil rights would be permanent.

"No," said Hitler. "When the Communist menace is stamped out the normal order of things shall return. Our laws are too liberal for me to deal effectively and swiftly with this Bolshevik underworld. But I myself am only too anxious for the normal state of affairs to be restored as quickly as possible. First, however, we must crush Communism out of existence."

With each day the belief grew throughout Europe that the Nazis were responsible for the Reichstag fire. This theory was strengthened by the startling revelation that there was a tunnel running from Göring's palace to the Reichstag, and the resultant outcry from abroad helped spur Hitler to insist on a trial of van der Lubbe and his purported Red associates despite an objective police report that there was "no doubt" that he had "committed the crime entirely by himself." It was a foolish decision, for it soon became obvious that the quick trial Hitler hoped to clear the air would drag on for months and provide considerable fuel for his enemies both home and abroad.

3

The short-term advantages of the fire did work to the Führer's advantage. Coming so close to the elections, it played on the fears of revolution shared by most Germans. Few objected when squads of Brownshirts ripped down the Red election posters and replaced them with their own. Hitler did not make the political mistake of outlawing the Communist Party but decided to wait until after the elections lest the working-class vote swing over to the Social Democrats. Instead the Nazis inundated the country with terrifying stories of the bloodbath that the Reds had planned to follow the harsh methods that would have to be installed and called on the voters to give the NSDAP a mandate. Göring was blunter: "Fellow Germans, my measures will not be crippled by any judicial thinking," he told a Frankfurt audience on March 3, just two days before the elections. "My measures will not be crippled by any bureaucracy. I won't have to worry about justice, my mission is only to destroy and exterminate. This struggle will be a struggle against chaos, and I shall not conduct it with police power. A bourgeois state might have done that. Certainly I shall use the power of the state and the police to the utmost, my dear Communists, so don't draw any false conclusions; but I shall lead the Brownshirts in this struggle to the death and my claws will grasp your necks!"

It was a confession that brute force would be applied outside the law, and it could have been made only in the charged atmosphere of the Reichstag fire. Fortunately for the Nazis, the Papens, Hindenburgs and industrialists were not at all concerned by alarming words and gave substantial, if occasionally tacit, support to the Hitler campaign. As the Prussian Minister of Finance assured a visiting Austrian, there was no possibility of Nazi excesses so long as "pragmatic, decent" men like Schwerin von Krosigk were in the cabinet. The violent words of buffoons like Göring and Goebbels should not be taken seriously, for "the conservative element would actually run things and Hitler would just be on the sidelines."

The industrialists were so sure of their ability to handle him that some twenty-five of them had decided at a recent meeting to underwrite the election financially. After Krupp von Bohlen expressed the unanimous feeling of the industrialists in support of Hitler, Göring made an appeal for funds: "The sacrifice we ask is easier to bear if you realize that the elections will certainly be the last for the next ten years, probably for the next hundred years." This threat of an end to democratic procedures was taken as a promise by banker Schacht, who said: "And now, gentlemen, cash on the counter." The industrialists conferred in whispers. The elder Krupp pledged 1,000,000 marks (about $250,000) for the Ruhr combine and the representative of I. G. Farben promised 400,000 marks. Other contributions brought the total up to 3,000,000.

With all this money at their disposal, the National Socialists and their two coalition partners were able to blanket the nation with publicity. All major party speeches were broadcast and, to those without radios, loudspeakers on streets and squares blared out the promises and threats of the new government. Hitler made frequent use of Hindenburg's name as proof of his own legitimacy. Months earlier the same speakers had pictured the old man as a senile fool; now he was transformed into a heroic figure of towering strength.

With the prospect of consolidating power after an overwhelming victory, the party members threw themselves enthusiastically into a campaign that had governmental blessing. No longer were the SA and SS repressed by the police, who now looked upon them as auxiliaries and turned their backs on excesses committed in the name of patriotism.

In his speeches Hitler criticized opponents for having no program yet presented none of his own. All he wanted was four years in office to prove himself. Election eve was turned into a semi-holiday by Goebbels, who labeled it "Day of the Awakening Nation." It seemed that almost everyone was for Hitler. He was the hope of the young idealists and carried the same banner as the patriots. Those who feared a Moscow-inspired revolution saw only two alternatives, a Red or Brown Germany, and the latter seemed more palatable. Many of his former critics, like Theodor Heuss, who would become the first President of the German Federal Republic, claimed to see signs of moderation in Hitler. "He rants much less. He has stopped breathing fire at the Jews and can make a speech nowadays lasting for four hours without mentioning the word 'Jew.'" Hitler even had some Jewish support; the Jewish National Union not only advocated the Führer's ban on entry of Eastern "peddler Jews" but supported his new government.

Despite outer appearances and the vast amounts of money and energy expended on the campaign, the National Socialists received only 43.9 per cent of the votes, and it took those of his nationalist allies to give him a bare majority in the parliament. Narrow as was the margin of victory, it was enough for Hitler to claim a clear mandate from the people and resume his attempt to take control of those states not under his rule. Assured of support from Berlin, the Nazis in Bavaria decided to force the issue. The SA in Munich was mobilized and at noon, March 9, Gauleiter Adolf Wagner, accompanied by Captain Röhm in full SA regalia, appeared at the office of Minister President Held. They demanded that Held immediately appoint a general state commissar, General Ritter von Epp, who had helped crush the Soviet Republic of 1919.

Held wired protests to Berlin but received the answer that Epp had been appointed commissar. Another protest to Hindenburg brought a definitive reply indicating how powerless the Old Gentleman had become: he requested Held to address all further complaints directly to Adolf Hitler. Bavaria was at last legally in the hands of the National Socialists. The same procedure—threats of violence from below and telegraphic intervention from Berlin—summarily brought all the remaining free states into subjection.

On the day of the takeover in Bavaria Hitler flew to Munich where he was greeted tumultuously. He was euphoric. "Munich is *the* city of Germany closest to my heart," he said. "Here as a young man, as a soldier and as a politician I made my start. The city is also baptized in the blood of those who died in 1923." He instructed the local party leaders to set up a stable Bavarian government even at the expense of admitting non-party members. "Your assignment, gentlemen," he said, "is difficult. But it is important for the political stability of the nation that the power of the Reich no longer be disturbed by special movements or even separatist disturbances in Bavaria. I must finish the work of Bismarck: states are states only as long as they are useful for the good of the Reich."

Later someone asked what should be done with Dr. Ehard, the only effective state prosecutor at the Hitler trial of 1924. "He was severe but he also was objective and polite," said Hitler. "Leave him in the Ministry of Justice."

Many foreigners erroneously believed that Hitler had already consolidated control throughout Germany. Consummate politician that he was, he was assuming power gradually and with the people's consent. "Authority," he remarked to Frank, "is only a springboard, a step to the next step," consequently conciliation with all levels of German society was his present byword. Out of respect for both the Hohenzollerns and Hindenburg, he selected the Potsdam garrison church for the opening of the new Reichstag on March 21. The ancient town, founded by Frederick Wilhelm I and containing the grave of Frederick the Great, was also steeped in Prussian military tradition. It was gaily decorated with swastika banners and the black-white-red flags of the former empire. Guns boomed. Army, Stahlhelm and SA troops formed ranks. Bells pealed out as the official motor caravan headed down the road to the little church in the bright spring sunlight.

Once the towering form of Hindenburg appeared in the field-gray uniform of a Prussian field marshal, the audience rose. Leaning with one hand on his cane and carrying his field marshal's baton in the other, he advanced slowly with dignity. At the imperial gallery he turned, raised his

baton and saluted the empty seat of the Kaiser and the royalty lined up
behind it. The marshal completely dominated the much smaller man beside him. Ill at ease in his cutaway, Hitler looked to Ambassador François-
Poncet "like a timid newcomer being introduced by an important protector into a company to which he does not belong."

The two sat down facing each other. Then Hindenburg took out a
pair of tortoise-shell glasses and began to read his speech. The tasks facing
the new government, he said, were varied and difficult and he called for a
revival of the disciplined and patriotic spirit of old Prussia.

Hitler's speech was directed to those in the crowded church rather
than to the people at home listening to their radios. The war had been
forced on the Kaiser and Germany, he said and summarized the legacy of
economic depression and unemployment he had inherited. After outlining
a program for the future he turned to Hindenburg as if he were still his
commander and paid him extravagant homage as military and civilian
leader. "We consider it a blessing to have your consent to the work of the
German rising."

Hitler walked to Hindenburg's chair, bent low to grasp his hand. The
old man, visibly moved, slowly descended into the crypt of Frederick the
Great and Frederick Wilhelm I, followed by his son and an adjutant who
laid wreaths on the two tombs, to the well-timed accompaniment of cannon salutes.

The ceremony, stage-managed by Goebbels made its expected impression. All those present—the military, the Junkers and the monarchists—
were convinced Hitler was subservient to Hindenburg and would follow the
Prussian ideal. But two days later Hitler made it clear to any objective observer that he was subservient to no man. The setting was different—
Berlin's Kroll Opera House, temporary site of the Reichstag—and so was
the atmosphere: SA and SS men patrolled the corridors and behind the
stage hung a huge swastika flag as a reminder of who was going to be
master of Germany. At 2:05 P.M. President Göring opened the session.
After a brief speech, including recitation of the song "Germany, Awake!,"
he turned over the floor to Hitler, who had entered in the simple uniform
of a Brownshirt.

There was a momentary silence, followed by a single shout of "Sieg
Heil! Sieg Heil!" This set off wild applause as the Führer strode up to the
podium through a forest of raised arms. It was his first appearance before
parliament and he began reading off a speech that was remarkable for its
prudence and moderation. He vowed to respect private property and individual initiative; promised aid to peasants and middle class alike. He
would end unemployment and promote peace with France, Britain and
even the Soviet Union. But to do all this he needed enactment of the Law
for Alleviating the Distress of People and Reich. This so-called enabling
act gave him overriding if temporary authority in the land but he made

it sound moderate and promised to use its emergency powers "only in so far as they are essential for carrying out vitally necessary measures."

After giving reassurance to parliament, President, the states and the Church that none of their rights would be infringed, Hitler concluded on a firm note that should have canceled out these reassurances. If the Reichstag refused this "opportunity for friendly co-operation," the new regime was prepared to fight for its principles. "It is for you, gentlemen of the Reichstag, to decide between war and peace."

During the recess the foes of the measure mobilized and when the session was resumed the leader of the Social Democrats made a courageous if poorly delivered protest despite chanting in the corridors from the Brownshirts: "We want the bill—or fire and murder!" Hitler himself responded, even though Papen tried to restrain him, in a style reminiscent of the early beer-hall days in Munich, by attacking the Social Democrats with sarcasm and invective. "I do not want your votes. Germany will be free, but not through you. Do not mistake us for the bourgeoisie. The star of Germany is in the ascendant, yours is about to disappear, your death knell has sounded."

Hitler's assault not only crushed the futile revolt of the Social Democrats but intimidated the Center Party. The vote was taken and when Göring announced the results—far beyond the required two-thirds majority with 441 for the bill, 94 against—the National Socialists leaped to their feet cheering as if their team had scored a winning goal in the final seconds of play. Then with hands outstretched they sang the "Horst Wessel Song":

> *Raise high the flags! Stand rank and rank together,*
> *Storm troopers march with steady, quiet tread. . . .*

Democracy was expunged from the German parliament with scarcely a protest. Only the Social Democrats voted against the bill. The other parties handed over to Hitler powers that he privately vowed never to relinquish. And powers surrendered to a man who has use for them are seldom relinquished.

The Center leader got a letter from Hindenburg commending his support of Hitler. "I wish to assure you that the Chancellor has expressed his willingness, even without formal constitutional obligations, to take measures based on the Enabling Act only after consultations with me." These words, honestly meant, momentarily reassured the betrayed Centrists. The majority of Germans were eager to be reassured and many of them were rushing to join the NSDAP. Others gave their support in less overt ways. Civil servants and bureaucrats (no different from civil servants and bureaucrats in other lands) stayed at their posts to keep the machinery of government running as smoothly as if the most conservative party had won.

The victory in the Reichstag also brought into the open a number of industrialists who had secretly supported Hitler. The steel magnate Krupp openly heiled acquaintances on the street. He wrote Hitler a letter of congratulations stating that he and his colleagues were convinced that Germany at last had "the basis for a stable government." He was rewarded by being chosen as czar of German industry, thus sanctifying the marriage between big business and National Socialism. It was also no accident that Hitler chose Hjalmar Schacht as president of the Reichsbank. This brilliant financier had helped bring Hitler into industrial circles and shared his detestation of democracy and parliamentarianism. (Hitler's Finance Minister approved the choice since he regarded Schacht as a genius in his field. "At the same time he was one of the most apt liars I ever knew," recalled Schwerin von Krosigk. "He stretched the truth until he was right.")

Before his selection Hitler asked Schacht how much the banks could contribute to his public works and armament program. Schacht refused to mention a specific sum but declared the Reichsbank should furnish whatever money was needed "to take the last unemployed off the streets." He got the job and his first act in office was to invent the system of "Mefo" bills—so called after Metall-Forschungsgesellschaft A.G., a dummy corporation formed by four armament firms, the state assuming liability for its debts. The Mefo bills were drawn chiefly by government contractors and were, in effect, not unlike promissory notes that could be extended to five years as a sort of short-term credit. The original feature of Schacht's scheme was to give unlimited credit to the regime and thus allow Hitler to rearm Germany on a large scale.

It was not only bureaucrats and industrialists who were finding it possible to serve the Führer. A number of intellectual and literary figures were espousing the regeneration of Germany. These included the philosophers Krieck and Bäumler, the poets Bluck and Binding, and Germany's most distinguished dramatist, Gerhart Hauptmann, who refused to renounce his honors no matter what government was in power. "I am delighted that Hauptmann should agree with me," wrote Rudolf Binding early that spring, "that we serve the nation to which we belong and have no reason to leave the Academy when the regime changes. The Academy has to safeguard the freedom of artistic creation, not the freedom of political observations." In this spirit of co-operation, Hauptmann several weeks later hung a swastika flag out his window; and some months later assured Harold Nicolson that Germany would "liberate itself" as Italy had done.

4

A revolution was going on but since it was almost bloodless on the surface many Germans did not—or chose not to—realize it. This preliminary stage of the Brown Revolution was given an innocuous name, *Gleichschaltung* (co-ordination). It appeared to be an efficient process of unifying the nation and was received with little alarm. What it did was bring the political, economical and social life of the nation under the control of the NSDAP and plant the seeds of a faceless dictatorship. There was little resistance primarily because Hitler kept within the law. Consequently his opponents believed he wanted a government similar to the Weimar Republic. A set of instructions issued to Social Democratic locals on the day of the enabling law enactment illustrates that party's obtuseness. It was filled with advice on filling out questionnaires and other mundane matters and but one paragraph mentioned the Nazi revolution in progress. While their leaders were being searched at night for weapons, while thousands of Communists and suspected Communists were being jailed, the Social Democratic Party, which should have been the bulwark of democracy, was exhorting its followers to stop making bookkeeping errors.

"The whole city lay under an epidemic of discreet, infectious fear," Isherwood wrote of Berlin that spring. "I could feel it, like influenza, in my bones." The city was "full of whispers. They told of illegal midnight arrests, of prisoners tortured in the S.A. barracks, made to spit on Lenin's picture, swallow castor-oil, eat old socks. They were drowned by the loud, angry voice of the Government, contradicting through its thousand mouths."

Outside the capital, particularly in the smaller towns and cities, a series of mass meetings, parades and pageantry distracted the people. Voluntary organizations were "co-ordinated" into the National Socialist fabric. Gradually every citizen found himself involved with the regime. Old familiar street names were changed. In Herne, for example, Rathausplatz was now Adolf Hitler Platz and Bebelstrasse became Hermann Göring Strasse. Almost every week there was some new organization: the Country School for Mothers, the Mother and Child Welfare Organization, Childrensland Camps, the Food-Supply Welfare Organization.

A month after Hitler had failed to persuade a majority of the electorate to vote for him, he had won the temporary confidence of most Germans by his gradual process of co-ordination. Isherwood watched these solid citizens smile approvingly at the young storm troopers "in their big, swaggering boots who were going to upset the Treaty of Versailles. They were pleased because it would soon be summer, because Hitler had promised to protect the small tradesmen, because their newspapers told them that the good times were coming . . . And they thrilled with a furtive sensual pleasure, like schoolboys, because the Jews, their business rivals, and the Marxists, a vaguely defined minority of people who didn't concern them, had been satisfactorily found guilty of the defeat and the inflation, and were going to catch it."

Jews and Marxists had been systematically persecuted since the take-over. Albert Einstein's bank deposits were seized when a bread knife—categorically a lethal weapon—was found in his house. In Germany such stories were branded as foreign propaganda while in the United States Secretary of State Cordell Hull was assuring leaders of American Jewry that the physical mistreatment of German Jews had "virtually terminated." Even so the outcry of liberals from abroad increased to Hitler's annoyance and he announced that Jewish business in Germany would suffer until the Jews in England and America ceased their atrocity propaganda.

They did not and on April 1 Hitler instituted a boycott with these words: "I believe that I act today in unison with the Almighty Creator's intention: by fighting the Jews I do battle for the Lord." It was only a tentative step, almost as if Hitler were testing to see how far his countrymen would let him go. On the eve of the boycott Italian Ambassador Cerruti had urged him in the name of Mussolini to soften his attitude toward the Jews. Hitler replied that there were few Jews in Italy and Il Duce did not understand the Jewish question which he himself had studied "for long years, from every angle, like no one else." He predicted "with absolute certainty" that in five or six hundred years the name of Hitler would be honored in all lands "as the man who once and for all exterminated the Jewish pest from the world."

Brownshirts were posted before the doors of most Jewish stores and offices. There was little violence and the young SA men were, for the most part, polite when reminding shoppers that they were about to patronize a Jewish business. "Little knots of passers-by collected to watch the performance—interested, amused or merely apathetic." In fact a good number went into the department store Isherwood was watching. He too entered, bought the first thing he saw, a nutmeg grater, and walked out twirling his parcel. This act of defiance was greeted by a wink from one of the young SA monitors. Although the boycotters got support from organizations which called upon farmers to support them, it was ineffective against the large department stores and banks and ended after three days.

Hindenburg himself protested further anti-Semitic measures and wrote the Chancellor a strong letter condemning discrimination against Jewish war veterans. "If they were worthy of fighting and bleeding for Germany, they must be considered worthy of continuing to serve the Fatherland in their profession." But the Old Gentleman was no match for a man whose secret goal in life was Jewish extinction. Hitler replied that the Jews, who monopolized up to eighty per cent of the professions of law and medicine, were now pushing their way into government posts. "One of the major reasons why the old Prussian state was such a clean one was that the Jews were granted only a very limited access to the civil service. The officer corps kept itself almost entirely pure." It was an argument that could not fail to impress the field marshal. This, coupled with a vague promise to give some consideration to Jewish veterans, was enough to permit enactment of decrees on April 7 removing all Jews from civil service posts and restricting the freedom of the legal profession. That same day Hitler told the Doctors' Union that he was aware of their present distress, especially among the young members, and in so doing subtly revealed his two-pronged Weltanschauung. "It is precisely for these young Germans that a Lebensraum and possibilities for the exercise of their profession must be created by a vigorous repression of an alien race. . . . This work of cleansing through racial hygiene now being undertaken will perhaps take centuries. The important thing is to lay a firm foundation today for future political development."

Several weeks later, under the Law Against Overcrowding of German Schools, the number of Jews in higher institutions was reduced. Hitler defended his action in a talk with Bishop Berning and Monsignor Steinmann. After reminding the priests that the Church had banished Jews into ghettos and forbidden Christians to work with them, Hitler explained that he regarded the Jews as "nothing but pernicious enemies of the State and Church, and therefore he wanted to drive the Jews out more and more, especially from academic life and public professions." He was only going to do more effectively what the Church of Rome had been attempting for so many centuries.

Many Jews did leave the country but others did not feel the anti-Semitic program was directed against them personally. For centuries the Jews had survived similar decrees by swimming with the current. What could happen to them in a nation that had produced Goethe and Beethoven? Besides, Hitler's real target was the Eastern Jew.

With all its outward appearance of success, the NSDAP was neither unified nor organized. It had come to power with a weak cadre structure and too many inept "old fighters" in key positions. The party grew rapidly and there were already more than a million and a half members with another million applications awaiting approval. But Hitler was not pleased to see the party become so unwieldy and ordered Schwarz to halt applications on the first of May.

This also marked the beginning of his attack on labor unions. He declared a Day of National Labor and treated it as a celebration of unity between workers and government. The main rally was held that evening at Tempelhof airfield where several hundred thousand workers and their leaders gathered to hear the Führer expound on the dignity of labor and the need for national unity. All lights were extinguished except those beating on the orator and the vast crowd listened in awed silence. He spoke in generalities but with such passion that when he finished the workers cheered as if he had promised them the world, and before they could emerge from the magic of his words they were singing the national hymn and the "Horst Wessel Lied." And as the last strains died down the sky exploded with fireworks. "It was indeed a brave, a magnificent fete," recalled the French ambassador. "The German participants and the foreign guests left with the conviction that a wave of reconciliation and of concord had swept over the Third Reich."

The next morning the SA and SS, with the help of police, seized union offices throughout the nation. Labor leaders who had yesterday pledged allegiance to the government were arrested in their homes; union files and bank accounts were confiscated and labor newspapers shut down. Before nightfall organized labor in Germany was obliterated. But Hitler promised the workers they would be better off than ever in the new German Labor Front and their rights would be fully protected. There was no uprising, no organized protest, and by the end of the month the vast army of workers was marching obediently behind the swastika. They had changed from red to brown without breaking step.

Success did not turn Hitler to excess. To the dismay of the party radicals he became cautious and prudent, as illustrated by his answer to Franklin Delano Roosevelt's plea for world peace in mid-May. Germany, Hitler replied, would welcome the possibility suggested in the President's proposal of bringing the United States into European relations as a guarantor of peace. Absent were the bellicose demands of the first days of office. "The German government wishes to come to a peaceful agreement with other nations and all difficult questions. Germany knows that in any military action in Europe, even if completely successful, the sacrifice would be out of all proportion to any possible gains."*

Only a man completely in control of his party could have changed course so radically. "The speech was the best thing I have heard Hitler do," Lochner wrote his children. "I often wonder how the Nazis would have mobbed their opponent—like Stresemann or Brüning—if he had dared hold such a conciliatory speech! That's the interesting thing about dictatorship, anyway: when it comes to foreign policy, they are tame as lambs (witness Mussolini, Hitler, Stalin, Pilsudski), for they know they have so much trouble consolidating their power at home that they want to avoid everything possible that might look like trouble with foreign nations. It is quite obvious that Hitler doesn't want war."

The speech not only placated the West but was further proof to Hindenburg that the new Chancellor could be trusted. By this time Hitler had succeeded in ingratiating himself with the Old Gentleman. Always

* Hitler had genuine admiration for the decisive manner in which the President had taken over the reins of government. "I have sympathy for Mr. Roosevelt," he told a correspondent of the New York *Times* two months later, "because he marches straight toward his objectives over Congress, lobbies and bureaucracy." Hitler went on to note that he was the sole leader in Europe who expressed "understanding of the methods and motives of President Roosevelt."

polite and deferential, the force and apparent logic of his arguments had torn down the last vestige of the President's distrust. "Within three weeks," Hitler recalled, "we had progressed so far that his attitude toward me became affectionate and paternal."

With Hindenburg under his influence, there was little to impede the gradual assumption of total power and by early summer a series of new decrees entrenched the NSDAP as the ruling force in Germany. First came the subjugation of agrarian organizations under the Entailed Farm Laws "for the preservation of the insoluble bonds of blood and soil." Combined with a settlement policy "based on race," this gave Hitler the foundation for settlement of the Eastern regions by pure Germans after the conquest of that area. While governmental control of the land was being solidified by the political organization of peasants under local, district and state National Socialist leadership (incongruously named Reich Nutrition Estate), Hitler was applying himself to the subjection of Germany's economy. On May 3 the Reich Estates of Trade and Handicraft was established and within a month it had assumed the functions of the German Chamber of Industry and Commerce. More significantly, the Adolf Hitler Foundation of German Business was set up on the first of June to the mutual benefit of both the industrialists and the NSDAP. Thus organizational supervision, together with control of market and price policies, put German industry on the road to complete subservience to the government.

Hitler was now prepared to make the next and perhaps most important step: the elimination of political opposition. The Communists had already been eliminated and on June 22 the Social Democratic Party was outlawed as "hostile to the nation and state." Its members were expelled from the Reichstag and many of its leaders joined other dissidents in the newly formed concentration camps. Within a few days the State Party voluntarily disbanded; and two weeks later—while Hitler was telling his Reich governors, "We must now eliminate the last remnants of democracy" —the German People's Party also disbanded.

By this time Hitler had added five more Nazis to his cabinet and so there was little opposition when he proposed that Germany become a one-party state. The new proposal ignored not only the constitution but the enabling law itself, for it stripped the Reichstag of all its powers and made a travesty of the parliamentary system. "When we discussed the measure in the cabinet, there was practically no opposition," recalled Papen, and by the time Hitler called for a vote it passed without dissent. It became the law of the land on Bastille Day, July 14.

Germany, like the Soviet Union, was controlled by a single party and that party was controlled by a single man who, in turn, was possessed by a dream.

5

In every German village and town the red and black swastika waved side by side with the black-white-red flags of the old Reich. Hitler's concept of revolution by absorption was working in a nation that wanted its uprisings orderly and legal. The Führer's storm troopers were now accepted almost as an arm of government; and nearly every important post was held by Nazis or someone controlled by the party. In the classroom and the church, the Brown Revolution was receiving commendation and blessing.

Hitler continued to say that the upheaval was temporary. "The revolution is not a permanent state of affairs," he told the state governors just before the nation was declared a one-party state. "The stream of revolution released must be guided into the safe channel of evolution." Ability must be the only authoritative standard, not membership in the party.

Hitler wanted no bloody uprising, no sweeping reforms to repel the average citizen or industrialist, and he laid down guidelines to his own Gauleiters. "To gain political power we had to conquer rapidly with a single blow; in the economic sphere other principles of development must determine our action. Here progress must be made step by step without any radical breaking up of the existing conditions which would endanger the foundations of our life." Such words deliberately courted physical defiance from his strongest supporters, the Brownshirts, who had waited long years to enjoy the fruits of the spoils system. But he carried off the extraordinary feat of dampening the revolution from below by the sheer force of his personality.

He proclaimed the end of the economic revolution and replaced the party's economic specialist with a representative of big business. Hitler's socialism was his own and subordinate to his secret aims. His concept of organized economy was close to genuine socialism but he would be a socialist only so long as it served the greater goal. He had the bohemian's rather than the revolutionary's disdain for private property and wanted only enough capital to rebuild the army and restore the economy so that he could lead Germany to its proper destiny. He was a Caesar rather than a Lenin, using socialism to get the masses moving. If he had believed they could have been propelled by capitalism it is likely he would have carried that banner. To Hitler, saving Germany justified any means.

It appeared as though he was creating a society of workers. To them he was the soldier-laborer, and they helped propagate this image. Thus millions of Germans humiliated by defeat in war and brought to the edge of economic disaster in peace readily identified with the warrior-worker hero. In ever increasing numbers Communists, whose leaders were in concentration camps, found a home in National Socialism. It was not at all difficult to accept Hitler's definition of the difference between socialism and Marxism: "German socialism is directed by Germans; international socialism is an instrument of the Jews."

By mid-1933 the majority of Germans supported Hitler. The bourgeoisie and the workers, the military and the civil service, the racists and some of the best brains in the country swelled the Nazi ranks. It has long been a political principle that power corrupts. It can also sanctify. Hitler the street ruffian a year earlier had been made respectable by the power of his office. Some Germans were seduced by expediency but more by a wave of idealism. Reform seemed to be sweeping the Reich. Moreover, the economy had taken a turn for the better, and the streets of the large cities were no longer filled with beggars.

An increasing number of intellectuals and artists followed the lead of playwright Gerhart Hauptmann in paying homage, if in varying degrees, to the Führer. Spengler spent an hour and a half with him that July; they agreed about German policy toward France and shared the same disdain for the mediocre leadership in the Evangelical Church. On parting, Hitler assured the author that he "considered it of great importance for people outside the party to be won over to a German policy." Spengler agreed and left with a feeling that the Führer, while insignificant, was a "very decent fellow." Richard Strauss, scarcely Hitler's favorite composer, was even more forthcoming and announced that he was quite satisfied with the change in Germany and, when the Führer attended a new performance of *Der Rosenkavalier* in Berlin, was happy to be received in his box during the intermission.

The princes of the Church were more eager to curry his favor. "Hitler knows how to guide the ship," announced Monsignor Ludwig Kaas, leader of the recently outlawed Catholic Party after an audience with the Pope. "Even before he became Chancellor I met him frequently and was greatly impressed by his clear thinking, by his way of facing realities while upholding his ideals, which are noble. . . . It matters little who rules so long as order is maintained." Pius XI subscribed to the same principles, as was proved on July 20 when a concordat between the Vatican and Hitler was signed. The Church agreed to keep priests and religion out of politics while Hitler, among other things, granted complete freedom to confessional schools throughout the country, a notable victory for German Catholics. His Holiness welcomed Hitler's representative, Franz von Papen, "most graciously and remarked how pleased he was that the German Government now had at its head a man uncompromisingly opposed to Communism and Russian nihilism in all its forms."

The Vatican was so appreciative of being recognized as a full partner that it asked God to bless the Reich. On a more practical level, it ordered

German bishops to swear allegiance to the National Socialist regime. The new oath concluded with these significant words: "In the performance of my spiritual office and in my solicitude for the welfare and the interest of the German Reich, I will endeavor to avoid all detrimental acts which might endanger it."

On every level of society Germans were finding a reason to support the new government. The Führer's fantastic popular appeal was evident from the crowds that flocked to Spital to honor the birthplace of his mother. They descended on the farmhouse where the boy Hitler had spent his summers. They climbed on the roof to take pictures, found their way into the courtyard to wash at the wooden trough as if it contained holy water, chipped pieces from the large stones supporting the barn, and carried off everything portable as souvenirs. When the present owners of the farm returned from the fields they would be engulfed by tourists. "It was like a country fair," recalled Johann Stütz. "They painted swastikas on the cows and would parade around singing Hitler songs. Before long the place looked like a ruin."

Late in July 1933 Hitler took time off to make another pilgrimage to Bayreuth. He laid wreaths on the graves of Richard and Cosima Wagner and their son Siegfried. He also attended the annual festival. It was the first time he had seen the Wagner family since becoming Chancellor and he wandered around the library at Wahnfried with undisguised satisfaction. "It was right here that you received me ten years ago," he told Winifred Wagner and then became dejected. "If the Putsch hadn't failed everything would have been different; I would have been the right age. Now I am too old. I have lost too much time and must work with double speed." The moment of depression passed as quickly as it had come and he predicted he would stay in power for twenty-two years. "Then I'll be able to retire, but first I must get more power into my hands so I won't have to bother with the cabinet. Just now they think they have a perfect right to meddle in things that are none of their business." During a vegetarian lunch he confided that once he had full power he would dissolve the monasteries and confiscate their property.

That summer Hitler spent much of his time at his mountain villa on the Obersalzberg. He invited the Hanfstaengls for a holiday at Haus Wachenfeld. Hanfstaengl was busy but sent Helene and Egon, who was twelve. Hitler offered them a ride from Munich and sat in the front seat with the chauffeur. At a lonely stretch of road near Rosenheim their car spluttered and came to a stop. In moments seven bodyguards, automatics in hand, surrounded the car. Kempka examined the motor as Hitler held a flashlight. "It's the old trouble again, my Führer," explained the chauffeur. "Some Reds must have dumped sugar lumps in the gas tank." Hitler warned the bodyguards to keep a sharp lookout, then watched with interest as Kempka unscrewed part of the mechanism, sucked and blew through it, spitting gas and sugar on the road.

Like any other proud householder, Hitler showed Helene and Egon through Haus Wachenfeld. His room on the first floor, which faced directly toward Salzburg, was modest, in keeping with the rest of the villa. "He had a small writing table, and a number of simple bookshelves," recalled Egon. "I especially looked to see what kind of literature the Führer had chosen for relaxation." Surprisingly, the majority of the books were the wild West novels of Karl May, more suitable for Egon himself than a Chancellor.

The Hanfstaengls were the only house guests but other party members who were staying at nearby boardinghouses and inns would visit. "Göring was constantly around. He and Hitler used to walk on the narrow tile paths in the garden, talking confidentially. Round and round the same plot of grass. If you sat on the veranda in front of the house you could catch bits of conversation as they went by. Göring did most of the talking: 'I have just signed twenty death warrants. . . .' That's about the only utterance I remember for sure. Mother heard it too and both of us were surprised at this grim glimpse behind the scenes of glorious statecraft."

They all had meals together in the pleasant but modest dining room downstairs. Egon couldn't stand the Austrian cooking that was prepared by Angela Raubal, particularly string beans served in a sauce made of milk, flour and quantities of sugar, but he was fascinated by the free and easy table conversation. "They talked about music, and politics, and Chinese art—in fact, about anything. Hitler was rather gracious, for his standards. I mean he didn't make you remember all the time that he was the Führer. As a rule, Hitler never converses, he either listens, or—more commonly—preaches, making his utterances as though they were endowed with the authority of revealed religion. But here, in his '*Landhaus*' he frequently appeared wholly in the becoming guise of an ordinary host, an average man. He talked a lot about motorcars, engines, the size and performance of different ships, and technical things of that sort."

By this time it had become known that the Führer was at Haus Wachenfeld and tourists from all over Germany began congregating on the Obersalzberg. He stayed indoors to avoid being seen and one day the crowd called Egon over and asked whether Hitler was likely to appear. The twelve-year-old went to the Führer and said in stilted German: "Herr Hitler, a devoted multitude is eagerly awaiting your appearance at the gateway."

Hitler burst into laughter and followed Egon outside to greet his admirers. "They nearly swooned. After he went back in, they thanked me profusely, and one hysterical woman picked up some pebbles on which

Hitler had stepped and put them in a little vial which she crushed ecstatically against her breast." Later, after another crowd had gathered, Egon collected a stack of postcards, photos and pieces of paper from the group, then wordlessly placed the stack in front of Hitler along with a pen. "My God, boy," he exclaimed with a smile, "you don't give up either, do you!"

By the time Hitler came down from his mountain and returned to Berlin he had decided to present a similarly affable face to the world. That August he allowed Egon's father to publish a book of anti-Hitler caricatures from German and foreign magazines and newspapers. Entitled *Fact vs. Ink,* the jacket showed a good-natured Führer laughing indulgently at his critics. Hanfstaengl cannily picked excellent cartoons, some satirical, some savage, covering the past ten years. In his foreword, prefaced by a quotation from Hitler's hero, Frederick the Great ("Pamphlets are to be hung lower"), Hanfstaengl explained that the book was an attempt to differentiate between the real and the fictional Adolf Hitler.

This kind of propaganda appalled Goebbels but Hitler was swayed by Hanfstaengl's reasoning that British and Americans would be impressed. There was already a feeling among many foreign observers that Hitler was an object more of fun than fear. "While the myth of the leader is growing by leaps and bounds in Germany," observed the *Literary Digest,* "certain independent European dailies and weeklies are stressing the comic aspects of Germany's dictator. They picture Hitler as a comedian, all the more laughable because of his seriousness." The traditional English compassion for the underdog was also working to Hitler's advantage in his dealings with France over reparations and boundaries. Lord Lothian argued that National Socialist brutality at home was "largely the reflex of the external persecution to which Germans have been subjected since the war." British attacks on the Treaty of Versailles were second only to those in Germany.

With this good will Hitler set about revising his nation's foreign policy. It was dominated by his dual doctrines of race and space and, though he occasionally made a detour, he always returned to Germany's Lebensraum in the East. Hitler's hope was to inveigle England to join him as a silent partner in the crusade against Communism. To do that he must convince the English that the Reich had renounced world trade and global naval ambitions. Briefly, Germany would control the continent of Europe and be a bulwark against Communism while England ruled the seas. To further strengthen himself before launching his drive to the East, Hitler sought support from Italy, which was sympathetic to Nazi principles and shared a common hostility toward France because of Mussolini's ambitions in the Mediterranean.

The diplomats Hitler had inherited from the Weimar Republic came from a different class and abhorred his methods, but the majority agreed with most of his basic aims—for entirely different reasons—and persuaded themselves that they could use him and his brand of socialism for their own purposes. "It was generally believed and hoped," recalled career diplomat Herbert von Dirksen, "that the incurable revolutionaries would be eliminated in time and that their successors, after having tasted the wine of power and the comforts which it brought, would turn to productive work, and to a more conservative mentality." And so Dirksen and like-minded colleagues "felt it to be our duty to assist in this process of normalization."

Hitler was as astute in his manipulation of the diplomatic service as he was with the industrialists and militarists. He allowed all the leading officials to remain at their posts, including one Jew and one married to a Jew. He also declared that the Reich desired to establish friendly relations with the Soviets so long as they did not intervene in German internal affairs. His campaign against home-grown Reds did not represent any hostility to Russia and to show his good faith he secretly allowed the Soviet Union to postpone payments on a long-term credit agreement negotiated before his takeover.

By the fall of 1933 Hitler felt the cautious international game had been played to the end. He decided to walk out on the League of Nations, which, among other things, had a confused policy toward rearmament. "We must make a break," he told Papen in a state approaching exaltation. "All other considerations are completely irrelevant." When Hindenburg questioned the wisdom of leaving the League, Hitler argued that it had to be done to affirm Germany's full equality. Against his better judgment, the Old Gentleman gave grudging consent. A gift of two large properties—along with Hitler's and Göring's oral promises to contribute 400,000 marks apiece from Reich and Prussian funds for their improvement—may have influenced him.

On October 14 Hitler formally announced to the world by radio that Germany was withdrawing from the conference and the League. "To be written down as a member of such an institution possessing no such equality of rights is, for an honor-loving nation of sixty-five million folk and for a government which loves honor, an intolerable humiliation."

There was justification in this charge and, in a sense, his withdrawal from a body that discriminated against the losers was more of a symbolic rejection of the Treaty of Versailles than a challenge to the West. He went out of his way to reassure the French of his peaceful intents by including a hope for German-French reconciliation.

Hitler's shock tactic was a gamble—and yet, with its protestations of peace, a fairly safe one. The British predictably felt more sympathy than condemnation. Lord Allen of Hurtwood told the House of Lords: ". . . we are compelled to admit that we and other nations during the last fifteen years have not handed out to Germany that full measure of wise and fair play which the country merited when it threw out from its own land the regime which made the war."

Hitler characteristically faced the problem of gaining wide approval at home by announcing that he was submitting his decision to a plebiscite to take place by month's end. Within hours his office was flooded with congratulatory messages, including a telegram from Catholic Action "unanimously" supporting their Führer. "It is not ambition which made the Führer leave the League of Nations," Martin Heidegger, one of Germany's greatest living philosophers, told his students, "nor a passion, nor blind obstinacy, nor a desire for violence; it is nothing but the clear wish to be unconditionally responsible for assuming the mastery of the destiny of our people." (Heidegger, then a Nazi, left the party a few months later.)

Hitler had by no means abandoned his two-faced foreign policy. On October 18 he spoke reasonably and temperately to *Daily Mail* correspondent Ward Price. Although the Germans would "put up with no more of this persistent discrimination" against their country, they certainly wanted no second World War.

Reassuring words to a reporter mean little in the world of diplomacy. The German ambassador in Italy wired his foreign office that Mussolini was "very much upset over our step and deplored it extremely." Il Duce not only regarded withdrawal from the League as a severe blow to his own prestige but "saw no way out of the situation and did not know how Germany intended to make any further progress."

Concerned as he was by Mussolini's irritation, Hitler concentrated his attention on winning a convincing mandate in the forthcoming plebiscite. He campaigned as if for an election, utilizing the resources of the party to convince the people to back his withdrawal from the League of Nations. The Church again gave enthusiastic support. Every bishop in Bavaria approved a statement by Cardinal Faulhaber requesting a Ja vote: "In this way the Catholics will profess anew their loyalty to people and Fatherland and their agreement with the farsighted and forceful efforts of the Führer to spare the German people the terror of war and the horrors of Bolshevism, to secure public order and create work for the unemployed." It reflected public resentment at the lost war and the repressive Treaty of Versailles. That was why Hitler had set the date of the plebiscite for November 12, the day after the anniversary of the armistice.

He appealed to all classes as if they were a unified group. "You cannot afford internal conflict in the fight to regain your position among nations," he told the workers at the Siemens plant. "If Germany does not wish to remain as an outcast, it must insist on equal rights, and that can only be accomplished if all Germans hold together as one man. Accept me as your Führer. I have shown that I can lead, and I do not belong to any class or group, only to you."

On election eve Hindenburg identified himself with Hitler, from whom he had accepted such liberal gratuities. "Tomorrow show your national honor and identify yourself with the Reich government," he advised the nation in a broadcast. "Speak up with me and the Chancellor for the principle of equality and for peace with honor and show to the world that we have restored German unity and with God's help shall preserve it."

It was an invocation that few patriots could resist. When the votes were counted the next day 95.1 per cent approved Hitler's foreign policy; and in the Reichstag election 92.2 per cent voted National Socialist, the only party on the ticket. Although some foreign observers scoffed at these results (2154 out of 2242 inmates at the Dachau concentration camp voted for the Führer), the results were a true barometer of German feeling. Adolf Hitler had won his gamble on foreign policy while solidifying his position at home. His mandate was so overwhelming that he was able, within weeks, to pass a law unifying party and state. It stated that the NSDAP was to be "the representative of the German state idea and indissolubly linked to the state."

With the entire population of Germany incorporated into the new regime, Hitler's policy of Gleichschaltung was officially completed. While the Führer had gained considerable power by consent (and threat), he was not yet a true dictator since resistance was still possible from the military and even from the failing Hindenburg. Hitler had led Germany onto the road to dictatorship. They needed no whip to follow a Siegfried who was bringing them out of economic depression and wiping out the dishonor of Versailles.

This could not have been accomplished, of course, without repression. The concentration camp (a term borrowed from the British of Boer War days) had become an accepted part of the national scene and was as much a threat to those on the outside as punishment for those inside. Nor was there any serious protest in the press after confiscation of Marxist and Social Democratic newspapers and publishing houses. Editors and publishers were brought under control and the last vestiges of independence were obliterated with establishment of the Reich Press Chamber. Along with freedom of the press also went that of literature, radio, theater, music, films and fine arts.

By December of 1933 Germany stood on the threshold of totalitarianism, brought there more by the needs of the time and the wish to conform than by terror. Nor was the spirit of conventionality a matter of class. It existed among scientists as well as workers. "We wish thus to conform to the spirit of the total state and to co-operate loyally and honestly," the president of the German Mathematical Association told his colleagues. "Unconditionally and joyfully we place ourselves—as is a matter of course for every German—at the service of the National Socialist movement and behind its leader, our Chancellor Adolf Hitler."

And so came totalitarianism and conformity to every profession on every level of society. Although other nations and races were congratulating themselves that such compliance was peculiarly Germanic and the repressiveness of this regime was typically Teutonic, both were a result of the intolerable demands of economics, geography and the times. These Germans marching to the tune of National Socialism were not unique in their love of order and militarism, or in their cruelty and arrogance.

6

One sour note among Hitler's successes was the delay in the Reichstag fire trial. It did not get under way until the first day of autumn and by that time the German Communists had convinced most of the world that the conflagration had been started by the accusers. First they published in Paris a book purporting to be an exposé of the Hitler terror and the burning of the Reichstag, which was based on fancy. "We had no direct proof, no access to witnesses, only underground communications to Germany," Arthur Koestler later confessed. "We had, in fact, not the faintest idea of the concrete circumstances."

The expatriate Communists followed this success with their own trial. It began in London on September 14, 1933, and was presided over by an international committee of jurists including D. N. Pritt of England and Arthur Garfield Hays of the United States. The illustrious audience included George Bernard Shaw, whose work, particularly *St. Joan*, was admired by Hitler. Shaw had declined a place on the jury and was present in his usual role as dissenter: "Whenever a prisoner is used as a stick with which to beat a Government," he said, "his fate is sealed in advance." After six days the kangaroo court published its predictable findings: "grave grounds exist for suspecting that the Reichstag was set on fire by, or on behalf of, leading personalities of the National Socialist Party."

The next day the German trial opened in Leipzig. Göring took a personal hand in the prosecution and was made to look like a fool by the four Communist defendants. Finally Göring lost his temper and shouted at Georgi Dimitrov (later Prime Minister of Bulgaria), "You wait until we get you outside this court, you scoundrel!" Göring had the last word but the victory went to the Communists, all of whom were acquitted by the court. Van der Lubbe, who had testified over and over that he and he alone was guilty, was sentenced to death and executed.

The outside world preferred to believe that the Dutchman was only a tool of the Nazis who had set fire to the Reichstag as an excuse to crush the Reds. So did many historians, including Bullock and Shirer, but their judgment was reached before publication of a detailed book by Fritz Tobias which concluded that neither the Nazis nor the Communists were involved in the fire and that van der Lubbe *was* the sole arsonist. While the Tobias book was questioned by some historians, including Bracher, its findings have been corroborated by Hans Mommsen in an authoritative article published by the Institut für Zeitgeschichte, a body not at all likely to favor any Nazi interpretation. Further, examination of van der Lubbe's history and the trial transcripts indicated he was of above-average intelligence and that his action was a lone-wolf attack on the establishment.

While the verdict of the judges of Leipzig was obviously swayed by foreign opinion, it was also an indication that the court system still maintained a measure of independence. Hitler's reply to a Göring complaint that the judges behaved disgracefully ("You would think we were on trial, not the Communists") was revealing: *"Mein lieber* Göring, it is only a question of time. We shall soon have those old fellows talking our language. They are all ripe for retirement anyway, and we will put in our own people. But while the Old Gentleman is alive, there is not much we can do about it."

Hanfstaengl claimed he overheard this pronouncement at a chancellery luncheon, and that autumn he made another attempt to turn Hitler on a course more acceptable to the West. He phoned Martha Dodd, the attractive daughter of the American ambassador, and announced: "Hitler should have an American woman—a lovely lady could change the whole destiny of Europe. Martha, you are the woman!" (Like so many others in the Führer's intimate circle, Hanfstaengl was unaware that Hitler already had a mistress, Eva Braun, if a neglected one.)

Martha Dodd was "rather excited by the opportunity that presented itself" and agreed to meet the Führer and attempt "to change the history of Europe." At the Kaiserhof tearoom Hitler kissed her hand and murmured a few embarrassed words. She found it difficult to imagine that she was face to face with one of the most powerful men in Europe. "He seemed modest, middle class, rather dull and self-conscious—yet with this strange tenderness and appealing helplessness." When she described her impressions at dinner her father was "greatly amused at my impressionableness" and advised her not to wash the hand that had been kissed by the great man.

If Ambassador Dodd was unimpressed by Hitler, his British colleagues were taking him most seriously. They were willing to make considerable concessions to his rearmament demands and their eagerness to secure some sort of agreement was revealed by a visit to Berlin early in 1934 of the Lord Privy Seal, Anthony Eden. Hitler impressed Eden as much more than a demagogue. "He knew what he was speaking about and, as the long interviews proceeded, showed himself completely master of his subject." All Germany asked as a precondition to any international guarantee was the possibility of self-defense. If such a convention were concluded, Hitler promised to guarantee that the SS and SA would be deprived of arms. As if to underline his desire for conciliation, Hitler made an exceptional gesture the following day, February 21, by coming to the British Embassy for lunch. It was the first time the Führer had ever entered a foreign embassy. He showed little interest in food or drink but "thawed materially" once they began discussing their personal experiences in the war. When Eden remarked that ex-soldiers should be the last ever to wish for another war Hitler "assented heartily."

After lunch Hitler was prepared to make more detailed proposals. He asked for 30 per cent of the combined number of military aircraft possessed by his neighbors and was prepared to agree that the number of German aircraft should never exceed 60 per cent of those in the French air force. He also pleasantly surprised Eden by offering to trim down the SA and SS, adding "that his own common sense and political instinct would never allow him to sanction the creation of a second army in the state. Never, never!"

It was a season for concessions and Hitler made another gesture of amity, this time to the United States, on March 14. Foreign Minister von Neurath cabled his consul general in New York to communicate orally the following note to Ambassador Dodd, who would soon arrive there on the S.S. *Manhattan:*

THE REICH CHANCELLOR REQUESTS MR. DODD TO PRESENT HIS GREETINGS TO PRESIDENT ROOSEVELT. HE CONGRATULATES THE PRESIDENT UPON HIS HEROIC EFFORT IN THE INTEREST OF THE AMERICAN PEOPLE. THE PRESIDENT'S SUCCESSFUL STRUGGLE AGAINST ECONOMIC DISTRESS IS BEING FOLLOWED BY THE ENTIRE GERMAN PEOPLE WITH INTEREST AND ADMIRATION. THE REICH CHANCELLOR IS IN ACCORD WITH THE PRESIDENT THAT THE VIRTUES OF SENSE OF DUTY, READINESS FOR SACRIFICE, AND DISCIPLINE MUST BE THE SUPREME RULE OF THE WHOLE NATION. THIS MORAL DEMAND, WHICH THE PRESIDENT IS ADDRESSING TO EVERY SINGLE CITIZEN, IS ONLY THE QUINTESSENCE OF GERMAN PHILOSOPHY OF THE STATE, EXPRESSED IN ITS MOTTO "THE PUBLIC WEAL BEFORE PRIVATE GAIN."

The message fell far short of its purpose, being not only offensive in wording but ill timed. A week earlier the American Jewish Congress had held an effective mock trial at Madison Square Garden entitled "Civilization against Hitlerism, a presentation of factual record of laws and acts of the Hitler regime." Samuel Seabury, a well-known attorney, acted as counsel for Civilization and the witnesses included Mayor Fiorello

LaGuardia, Al Smith and Raymond Moley. Civilization was unanimously pronounced the winner.

7

Hitler's promise to hold in check the SS and SA reassured France to a certain extent but their leaders could not be persuaded that Hitler's rearmament program was designed for defense alone. "The British were eager to get it all over with," recalled Ambassador François-Poncet. "They sent us note upon note urging us to state what guarantees seemed to us to strengthen security sufficiently to gain our consent to a relative rearmament of the Reich." The British themselves were privately concerned, particularly by the rapid growth of the German air force, but there was still considerable public sympathy for the plight of the new Reich, with many ridiculing the notion that Hitler was driving toward war.

Ambassador François-Poncet shared the view that concessions should be made to Germany. "Better a limited and controlled armament than unlimited, uncontrolled and unrepressed armament of the Reich!" He felt any agreement, even a mediocre one, was better than none and did his utmost to win over his superiors. Early that April he journeyed to Paris to present his views in person but, in an interview with Premier Doumergue, "was not permitted to breathe one word" and was cut short every time he attempted to broach the subject. The French decision was to check German ambitions by setting up an anti-Nazi bloc in the East: Poland, the U.S.S.R. and Czechoslovakia would be the links in this security chain under the aegis of Mother France.

When France and the Soviet Union approached agreement that spring, Hitler understandably feared that this was the beginning of an encirclement of the Reich. To counter the proposed bloc, Hitler needed a strong ally. The best prospect was Italy, whose leader had shown little desire for such a union since 1924 when he refused to lend the Nazis a few million lire. It grated on Hitler to be a supplicant but pride gave way to necessity and he made another effort. Controlling his resentment, he wrote Mussolini, ". . . admiration for the historic efforts of Your Excellency is linked with the desire for co-operation in a spirit of true friendship for our two ideologically related nations which can contribute immeasurably to the tranquilization of Europe through suitable attention to identical interests." He argued that since Germany had disarmed it had the right to demand the disarmament of other states, then listed in detail all the usual arguments. To accent the import of the message, Hitler had the letter delivered by Hermann Göring.

Several weeks later Hitler's foreign press secretary and unofficial court jester, Hanfstaengl, also visited Mussolini and suggested that he meet the

Führer. "You are both admirers of Wagner and that will give a common starting point," Hanfstaengl remembered saying. "Think what it would mean if you invited him to the Palazzo Vendramin in Venice where Richard Wagner died. He would gain the benefit of your long experience and obtain much-needed insight into the problems of Europe as seen from outside Germany." Mussolini was not averse to the idea and in his good time sent an invitation which, after a show of reluctance, was accepted.

The historic meeting was doomed from the start. According to Filippo Bojano, Italian press representative in Berlin, Mussolini was motivated primarily by curiosity to see the politician all Europe was talking about. "Hitler is simply a muddleheaded fool," he confided to Bojano. "His head is stuffed with philosophical and political tags that are utterly incoherent. I can't make out why he waited so long to take over power, and why he played the buffoon, with his ridiculous electoral contests, in order to take legal possession of the reins of power. Either he is a revolutionary or he is not. Fascist Italy would never have come into being without a march on Rome. We are dynamic, and Signor Hitler is just a prater."

This contemptuous attitude was so publicized that the Italian press turned out en masse, directors and all, "to see this strange freak, Hitler." When he stepped out of his Junkers at Lido airfield on June 14 he looked like a struggling salesman in his worn trench coat over a blue serge suit. He was met by a Duce wearing black shirt, jack boots and glittering gold braid, backed up by Italian troops in full dress. Mussolini flung his arm out in Roman salute so vigorously that correspondent H. R. Knickerbocker thought "he might lose his hand."

Hitler sidled forward uncertainly, his hand almost apologetically responding with a feeble Nazi salute. He was obviously embarrassed by the show Mussolini had staged and, after blinking in the sunlight, awkwardly descended the steps to shake hands with his *beau idéal*. "They were not over three yards from me," wrote Knickerbocker, "and I was fascinated to watch the expressions on their faces. Beneath the obligatory cordiality I found I could see an expression of amusement in Mussolini's eyes and of resentment in Hitler's." Nor did the Führer's embarrassment ease when his host led him down the line of troops. He acted like a schoolboy at his first formal party. He didn't know what to do with his new fedora. First he took it off to salute the Italian flag, then started to put it back on but stopped himself and clutched it in his right hand. Then as he walked alongside Mussolini, who was chatting away in his voluble but eccentric German, he kept shifting the hat from hand to hand as if it were a hot potato.

There was another bit of comedy when the flustered Hitler tried to get Mussolini to precede him in boarding the launch which was to carry them to Venice. But Mussolini, the perfect host, maneuvered himself behind the Führer and waved him down the gangplank as if he were shooing a chicken into a coop. At the hotel landing, Hitler leaped out and jogged forward with bent head. "Mussolini stepped forth superbly. He was aware of being the cynosure of all eyes. His glances flashed, his figure was upright; he was—histrionically—the Duce."

Once inside his suite, Hitler began loudly abusing his advisers for allowing him to arrive in civilian clothes when Mussolini was so effectively attired. He was so upset that the first conversation with his host, despite a glowing official report, was another disaster. Il Duce dominated the talk, which centered on Austria, speaking in a bravura German which was sometimes incomprehensible to Hitler, while Mussolini in turn misunderstood much of Hitler's Austrian German.

The next morning the two men reviewed a parade of Fascist troops in the Piazza San Marco. At one point two columns had an argument about right of way directly in front of the rostrum. Neither unit would give in and when both plunged straight ahead the musicians began caterwauling. Later Hitler asked his new personal adjutant, Lieutenant Fritz Wiedemann, what he thought of the military value of such troops. Wiedemann, adjutant of Hitler's regiment during the war, replied that fighting ability had nothing to do with parading. "This remark, however, made no impression at all on Hitler, especially since, at the very moment, he glanced out the window at an Italian warship and saw to his amazement an array of sailors' shirts and underwear flying from the masts instead of the usual fleet flags."

Only a fool or a master of comedy would have staged the concluding and most important meeting of the dictators at the Lido golf course. "I noticed," recalled Bojano, "that Hitler was speaking all the time in a very excited way, while Mussolini listened, silent and with a scowl on his face." During the two-hour talk Bojano rarely saw Il Duce open his mouth. "He was so bored by Hitler's drivel that that very evening, in the middle of the official reception, he decamped in a hurry, and left the lagoon, stating that he did not want to see anybody."

Hitler left Venice stung by the realization that he had been not only snubbed by Mussolini but outmaneuvered diplomatically. The Führer had agreed to the full recognition of the independence of Austria which he felt belonged within the Reich, while receiving in turn no definite promise of support on the disarmament question. It was thus with amusement that those diplomatic officials who had been present read Foreign Minister von Neurath's circular to foreign missions:

. . . THE REICH CHANCELLOR'S VISIT TO VENICE WENT OFF WITH EXCEPTIONAL CORDIALITY AND MOST HARMONIOUSLY, AND MADE A GREAT IMPRESSION ON THE PUBLIC AS WELL. . . .

HITLER AND MUSSOLINI GOT ON EXTREMELY WELL TOGETHER AND

CONCEIVED FEELINGS OF PERSONAL FELLOWSHIP OVER AND ABOVE THEIR
MUTUAL ESTEEM.

THE CONVERSATIONS, WHICH WERE DETAILED AND WERE HELD IN AN
ATMOSPHERE OF INTIMACY, RANGED OVER ALL THE QUESTIONS ARISING
FROM THE AFFINITY BETWEEN THE TWO CONCEPTS OF THE STATE, AND
FAR-REACHING AGREEMENT WAS ESTABLISHED. FORMAL AGREEMENTS HAD
NOT BEEN ENVISAGED AND WERE, IN CONSEQUENCE, NOT CONCLUDED. . . .

State Secretary Ernst von Weizsäcker of the Foreign Office confided
to a Swiss official that he "could not foresee any closer collaboration between the two men."

Chapter Twelve

THE SECOND REVOLUTION—
"ALL REVOLUTIONS
DEVOUR THEIR OWN CHILDREN"
FEBRUARY–AUGUST 1934

1

Hitler's promise to reduce the number of storm troopers was sincere. For years the SA had shown an independence that troubled him and for months its commander, Captain Röhm, had been demanding a military role for his men. The army, naturally, opposed it.

Hitler knew that his best chance for survival was to back the military leaders since he could never achieve his ultimate aims without their full support, and so had announced: "The Reichswehr is the sole bearer of arms of the nation; the SA is responsible for the political education of the people." These words stirred up old resentments among the four million Brownshirts, who recalled the long struggle between the northern and southern factions of the party. While remaining loyal to Hitler as their spiritual leader, many felt he had betrayed the Brown Revolution and was selling out to the right. They regarded themselves as the symbol of party radicalism and were not at all satisfied with the reforms of the first year of power. For months Röhm ("Only he who is without pessimism has ideals") had been calling for a Second Revolution that would bring them the social and material benefits they had fought for. "Anyone who thinks that the tasks of the SA have been accomplished," he told eighty thou-

sand Brownshirts at Tempelhof airfield, "will have to get used to the idea
that we are here and intend to stay here, come what may." While the majority of party members shared this anti-capitalistic, anti-conservative sentiment, it was the SA that was most radical and ardent. Over and over
Röhm let it be known that he and his men were the true guardians of the
National Socialist idea ("We are the incorruptible guarantors of the
fulfillment of the German revolution").

Hitler sympathized with the radicals but his head told him that further revolution was not feasible until Germany had recovered from economic disaster and rebuilt her armed forces; and this could not be done
without the full support of industry and the military. At the same time, in
his continuing role as conciliator, he made Röhm minister without portfolio in his cabinet, promised to appoint him Minister of Defense and sent
him a rare commendation on the first day of 1934, remarkable for its use
throughout of the familiar second person singular. Hitler meant to praise
Röhm while subtly warning him to leave the defense of the country to the
military, but Röhm missed the point. Emboldened, he dispatched a
memorandum to the Defense Ministry claiming that national security was
a prerogative of the SA.

This brought the conflict to a head and General von Blomberg asked
Hitler to make a definite ruling. It was thus with regret that the Führer invited SA and Reichswehr leaders to a conference in the marble-pillared
lecture hall of the ministry on the last day of February 1934. In a "moving, gripping" speech Hitler urged both sides to compromise. The party,
he said, had solved unemployment but within eight years an economic re-
cession would ensue and the only remedy was creation of living space for
the surplus population. This might necessitate short, decisive military action in the West and then in the East. But a civilian militia, as suggested
by Röhm, would not be the "least bit suitable for national defense." The
solution was a people's army, rigorously trained and equipped with the
most modern weapons. The SA must confine itself to internal political
matters.

At this point Hitler forced Blomberg and Röhm to sign an agreement
in his presence. The SA was granted two paramilitary functions: certain
units were to operate as a police force along the nation's borders; the
premilitary training of youths age eighteen to twenty-one was to be undertaken by the SA while those from twenty-one to twenty-six not serving in
the armed forces were to be trained in "SA sport," a code name for organized military training.

It was a blow to Röhm but afterward he invited everyone to a luncheon of reconciliation in his home, formerly a millionaire's mansion.
"Hitler did not take part," recalled General von Weichs. "The food was
good—the atmosphere frosty. At any rate it seemed as if peace was re-

stored. One certainly believed that the authority of Hitler in the party was so great that his decision would remain binding on the SA."

Once the army men left, Röhm's true feelings, liberated perhaps by drink, exploded. "What that ridiculous corporal says means nothing to us," he told his followers. "I have not the slightest intention of keeping this agreement. Hitler is a traitor and at the very least must go on leave. . . . If we can't get there with him, we'll get there without him." At least one listener was shocked. It sounded to SA Obergruppenführer Viktor Lutze like treason and he reported it to Hess. When the Führer's deputy hesitated to act, Lutze took it upon himself to travel to the Obersalzberg and inform Hitler himself of the dangerous discontent within the highest ranks of the SA. Here again he met with an apparent lack of interest. "We must let the matter develop," said the Führer and closed the discussion as if unwilling to admit that his beloved Brownshirts were in a state of discontent approaching revolt. A few weeks later, however, he flatly refuted Röhm's comment, "The grey [army] rock must be submerged by the brown flood," with the statement that "the new army would be a grey one not a brown one."

Röhm countered by calling a press conference in Berlin that April for the diplomatic corps and foreign journalists. He was an imposing figure, squat, powerful, intense, and he spoke in the flat but authoritative tones of someone who expects to be obeyed. "The SA is the heroic incarnation of the will and thought of the German revolution," he told the foreigners but his next words were obviously intended for Hitler. Those in the party who opposed the Brownshirts, he said, were reactionaries and bourgeois conformists. "The SA *is* the National Socialist Revolution!"

Secretly enemies of Röhm in the SS were already deeply involved in a plot to destroy him. At first it seemed curious that the prime mover was Reinhard Heydrich, head of the SD (*Sicherheitsdienst*, Security Service), and not the SS chief himself. For some time Himmler was reluctant to support the intrigue, perhaps out of fear that an open conflict with the SA would cause a fatal breach within the party. But he was tempted to forget this upon learning that Göring had also joined the conspirators. Göring was not only one of the Führer's closest associates but could give Himmler a post he coveted, chief of the Prussian Secret State Police Office (*Geheimes Staatspolizeiamt*).* No sooner had Himmler allied himself with the cabal than he was made head of the Gestapo and he reciprocated by dropping hints to all the SS units that an open struggle with the Brownshirts was on the horizon. This seemed a certainty when Heydrich reported he had collected evidence that Röhm was plotting treason. The truth was that Röhm had not the slightest intention of launching a

---

* Some post office officials made up an abbreviated stamp for the new organization— Gestapa. Colloquial usage soon turned this into Gestapo, a name that would soon be a synonym for terrorism.

Putsch. He wanted only to force Hitler to give the SA its proper position in the Reich, by setting the Führer "in a golden cage" as it were, to isolate him from evil advisers. He was waging a war of nerves, not treason, but his threatening words were cause for alarm. On June 4 Hitler summoned Röhm to the chancellery and, according to the former's account, their conversation lasted almost five hours. "I implored him for the last time to oppose this madness of his own accord—let him at the same time use his authority so as to stop a development which in any event could end only in catastrophe. . . . The Chief of Staff left this interview after assuring me that the reports were partly untrue and partly exaggerated, and that moreover he would for the future do everything in his power to set things to rights."

Although one witness in the anteroom, Papen's adjutant, swore he heard them "bellowing at each other," there was no indication in Hitler's account that this discussion was a stormy one. It is probable that Röhm left at midnight with the impression that the Führer was sympathetic but under pressure from the military to curtail SA activities. It was also likely that Hitler himself imagined he had just made a genuine truce with Röhm since the SD was almost immediately informed that the Führer had come to agreement with the SA chief on several points.

It was agreed that a monthlong leave for the entire SA would start as scheduled. This was announced by the *Deutsches Nachrichtenbüro* (German News Bureau) on June 7. The following day the DNB published an intriguing "Order of Chief of Staff Röhm," stating: "I have decided to follow the advice of my physicians and take the cure, in order to fully restore my health which has been severely impaired the last few weeks by a painful nervous complaint."

The two announcements reassured the military leaders, who felt that it signaled Röhm's decline, but appalled Heydrich, who had only three weeks to complete his dossier against the SA and thus force Hitler to act decisively. Röhm's sister-in-law, among others, warned him about rumors of a Göring-Goebbels-Himmler plot against him. "He had some feeling that there was something wrong," she recalled, "but still did not take it seriously. He never had any doubts whatsoever about Hitler."

2

Discontent from an entirely different quarter descended on Hitler hours after his return from the humiliating visit with Mussolini in Venice. On June 17, a pleasant Sunday, Franz von Papen was preparing to make an address at the University of Marburg. There was considerable interest in what the Vice-Chancellor would say since he had delivered a controversial speech six months earlier at the Bremen Club warning of the growing unrest in Germany over the new regime's assaults on the principles of law and the restrictions placed on the Church. As Papen entered the great auditorium, which was packed with students, professors and a scattering of uniformed party members, there was an air of expectancy. He began with a direct attack on the controlled press in general and Goebbels in particular.

The audience was stunned by such words coming from the official who held the second highest position in the government but this was only the beginning. After criticizing Nazi bigots and doctrinaires along with the single-party system, he urged Hitler to break with those calling for Röhm's Second Revolution. "Have we gone through the anti-Marxist revolution in order to carry out the Marxist program? . . . No people can afford to indulge in a permanent revolt from below if it would endure in history. At some time the movement must come to a stop and a solid social structure arise."

The few shouts of protest from party members were drowned out in tumultuous applause. Only the *Frankfurter Zeitung* managed to print a few extracts from the speech in its afternoon edition. Goebbels ordered all copies of this paper impounded and forbade a scheduled replaying of the speech over the radio. But the text was smuggled out of the country and published, causing a sensation not only abroad but throughout Germany, and when the Vice-Chancellor appeared at a Hamburg race track he was greeted by shouts, "Heil Marburg!"

For the first few days Hitler made no public comment. It was Papen who forced the issue by threatening to resign unless Goebbels' ban on his speech was lifted. Hitler tried to calm his Vice-Chancellor. He admitted Goebbels had blundered, then berated the insubordination of the SA as if he approved that part of the speech. He promised to lift the ban and requested Papen to withhold his resignation until the two of them went to Neudeck to see Hindenburg.

Papen agreed to wait but Hitler broke his word. The next day, June 21, he hastily set out for Neudeck alone and without removing the ban on the speech. His announced purpose was to report to the President on the recent meeting with Mussolini, but it is more likely he wished to see the Old Gentleman without the inhibiting presence of Papen. He may also have wanted to check on Hindenburg's health and find out how much time he had left to make arrangements to be his successor. To accomplish this he would need the support of the military and it was significant that the first person he met on the steps of the Hindenburg estate was Defense Minister von Blomberg in full uniform despite the sweltering heat.

The President had his own reasons for seeing the Führer. He wanted to be enlightened on the turmoil caused by Papen's speech, but he left most of the talking to Blomberg, acting stiff and Prussian, who made it clear that internal peace was the first priority. If Hitler could not remove the present intolerable tension, he said, the President would declare martial law and turn over the job to the army. No mention was made of Röhm and the Second Revolution, nor was any necessary. The Old Gentleman, who had left Berlin in a wheel chair—purchased over his protest that it was too expensive—rallied himself and in a somewhat shaky voice reaffirmed Blomberg's words. It was all over in four minutes and soon Hitler was in his plane winging back to Berlin. During that silent journey his thoughts probably centered on Röhm. "If during these months I hesitated time and again before making a final decision," Hitler would explain to the Reichstag in several weeks, "it was due to two considerations: First I could not easily convince myself that a relationship which I thought to be founded on loyalty could be a lie; second, I still cherished the secret hope that I might be able to spare the movement and my SA the shame of such a disagreement and that it might be possible to remove the mischief without serious conflicts."

Sometime that night Hitler made up his mind to take action. In the morning he phoned Viktor Lutze, who months earlier had warned him against Röhm, and instructed him to report to the chancellery at once. "He led me into his study," wrote Lutze in his diary, "and, taking me by the hand, swore me to secrecy until the whole matter was settled." The Führer revealed with some emotion that Röhm had to be removed because of a determination to arm the SA and set it against the army. "The Führer said that he had always known I would be no party to such matters. Henceforth I was to accept no orders from Munich and take instructions only from him."

In the meantime Heydrich and Himmler were doing their utmost to entrap Röhm and that same day the latter summoned one of his SS commanders, Freiherr von Eberstein, and told him that Röhm was plotting a Putsch. Eberstein was to pass the word on to the military district commanders and put his own troops on "unobtrusive alert," confining them to barracks for emergency action. Within hours the warning was passed through army channels: the chief of the General Army Office informed his officers that an SA coup d'état was imminent and that the SS, which supported the army, should be given any weapons they needed.

By now Hitler had become so convinced that Röhm was plotting an uprising that he told Defense Minister von Blomberg he was summoning all SA commanders to Bad Wiessee, a spa on the Tegernsee where Röhm was taking his rest cure. When they had assembled, continued Hitler, he would personally arrest them and "square accounts." The army was prepared for action. First, Colonel General Freiherr Werner von Fritsch, commander-in-chief of the Reichswehr, passed on the order to place all troops in a state of alert. Leaves were canceled and the men confined to barracks.

Almost simultaneously Hess broadcast a remarkable speech over a nationwide radio hookup that was both a warning and a plea to Röhm: "Woe to him who breaks the faith, and thinks to serve the revolution through rebellion!" he said and then referred to such plotters as "credulous idealists." The entire speech could have been spoken by Hitler himself, for it urged Röhm to abandon his Second Revolution and return to the fold. The following day a blunter warning came from Hermann Göring: Anyone who eroded confidence in Hitler would "pay with his head." Secluded as he was at Bad Wiessee, Ernst Röhm should have been aware of these portents. Another came on June 28 when the German Officers League formally expelled him from its ranks.

Rumors of an imminent showdown were circulating in Berlin and that same day Sefton Delmer got firsthand information about the dilemma Hitler faced from the assistant to Papen's press counselor. "Now we are in the middle of the war for Hindenburg's succession," he explained, with Hitler on one side and the Vice-Chancellor and his fellow conservatives on the other. The showdown, he predicted, would take place at the next cabinet meeting when Papen would force Hitler "to suppress the terrorist anarchy" of Röhm and his Second Revolution gangsters. If the Führer refused the Papen group would resign and Hindenburg would dismiss Hitler and hand over executive power to the army. "Whichever way things go, my boss reckons he has got Hitler by the short hairs. If he accepts, he is shorn of power. If he refuses the army takes over. I only hope Hitler refuses. Even though that might mean a shooting war!"

At the moment the Führer was in Essen, visibly enjoying a vacation as a guest at the wedding of the local Gauleiter. Another guest, Lutze, was concerned. "I had a feeling," he wrote in his diary, "that it suited certain circles to aggravate and accelerate 'the affair' just at this moment when the Führer was absent from Berlin and could therefore neither see nor hear things himself, but was dependent on the telephone."

It was the telephone, indeed, which played a major role in the developing intrigue. No sooner had Hitler arrived with Göring at the wedding breakfast than he was interrupted by a call from Himmler in Berlin, who read off a series of alarming reports. Göring nodded his head in confirmation as he learned of the supposed SA machinations and Hitler became so wrought up that he returned at once to his local quarters. "Here in the hotel room," according to Lutze, who was one of those hastily summoned, "the telephone was going almost uninterruptedly. The Führer was deep in thought but it was apparently clear that he would now have to take action."

The conference was enlivened by the arrival of Göring's secretary with further information from Himmler of an imminent Brownshirt revolt. This report, along with another from an agent of Heydrich that Röhm's Brownshirts had just insulted a foreign diplomat, was too much for Hitler. "I've had enough," he said. "I shall make an example of them." He ordered Göring to return to the capital and be prepared to act upon receiving the code word (it was *Kolibri,* hummingbird), then made a call of his own. He phoned Röhm in Bad Wiessee and complained about the alleged molesting of foreigners. This could not be tolerated, he said with some heat, and told Röhm he wanted to speak to the top SA leaders gathering at the Tegernsee two days later at 11 A.M.

The conversation either did not perturb Röhm or he pretended it didn't, for when he returned to the dinner table he seemed "very well pleased." He informed his guests, one of whom was General von Epp, that Hitler was going to attend the congress of SA leaders on June 30, adding with relish that this would give him the opportunity to "tear the mask from Goebbels." He knew that he could count on his SA and the army. Such an unrealistic comment meant Röhm either was fantasizing or was unaware of the extent of the intrigues swirling around him.

These gathered momentum with Göring's return to Berlin. The following morning, Friday, June 29, he alerted the Prussian police unit along with the Führer's faithful SS bodyguard unit, recently christened *Leibstandarte-SS Adolf Hitler.* More significant, he gave himself plenary powers in Prussia based on Hitler's declaration of a state of emergency, and then delegated authority in Silesia to the commander of the SS Southeast Region with orders to arrest a number of Brownshirt leaders, disarm all SA headquarters guards and seize the Breslau police headquarters.

By this time the general army alert was in effect even though many of its senior officers were still not convinced that Röhm intended to stage a revolt, and that morning one of them flew to Berlin to express such doubts to Army Commander-in-Chief von Fritsch. This skeptic was General Ewald von Kleist, head of the army in Silesia, and he told Fritsch, in the presence of General Ludwig Beck, that he had been assured by the SA leader in Silesia (a close friend of Röhm's) that Brownshirt preparations for action were only a reaction to army alerts aimed against them. Kleist was convinced that a third party—he mentioned Himmler—was attempting to set the SA and army against each other. Concerned, Fritsch summoned General von Reichenau, head of the Army Office and a loyal Nazi even before 1933. This urbane officer, the very model of a Prussian general with his ever present monocle and imperturbable manner, listened to Kleist repeat his story before commenting: "That may be true, but it's too late now."

A flood of new evidence—consisting of rumors, fake reports and doctored documents—was already being directed into army channels to convince the doubting Thomases that after the Putsch Röhm would execute or dismiss all senior army officers beginning with Fritsch. Fictitious death lists were passed around from so many sources that they began to seem real. An article in the day's *Völkischer Beobachter* by Defense Minister von Blomberg appeared to reinforce this illusion. He proclaimed that the army stood loyally behind the Chancellor.

If Röhm read this article he apparently didn't take it as a personal warning. Enjoying the beauty of Bad Wiessee, he calmly greeted arriving SA dignitaries at his pension and expressed satisfaction at the morrow's meeting with the Führer. Nor was he at all perturbed when a general, a comrade of the war, warned him that he was "making a fatal error" if he believed that the army would not open fire on revolting SA troops. Röhm's actions that evening were hardly those of a man planning an uprising. After a leisurely session of *Tarok*, the three-handed Bavarian card game, he received an injection for neuralgia from his doctor, then turned in for a peaceful sleep.

Not so Hitler. His suite at the Hotel Dreesen in Bad Godesberg was like a military headquarters on the eve of battle and he acted like an irresolute general with his first command. Just before midnight he ordered Gruppenführer Josef (Sepp) Dietrich, commander of his SS bodyguard, to descend on Bad Wiessee with two companies, but a few moments later two phone calls, one from Berlin and another from Munich, forced a drastic change in plans. The first, from Himmler (who had just told the Ribbentrops, "Röhm is as good as dead"), was that the Berlin SA was planning a Putsch which would start at 5 P.M. with the occupation of the government buildings. During the conversation Hitler answered only in monosyllables but once he put the receiver down he shouted, "It's a Putsch!" It seemed that Karl Ernst, head of the Berlin storm troopers, instead of going to Bad Wiessee as planned, had remained in Berlin to direct treasonous operations! (He was in Bremen preparing to take a honeymoon cruise.)

The Führer's stream of denunciations was interrupted by the second call, this from Adolf Wagner, the Gauleiter of Bavaria, who reported that rowdy Brownshirts were already in the streets of Munich shouting, "The Reichswehr is against us!" (Certain units had been alerted by a pamphlet of mysterious origin: "SA, take to the streets, the Führer is no longer for us!")

Hitler's rage turned to panic. Here was proof positive that Röhm was mutinying. "It was at last clear to me," he later said, "that only one man could oppose and must oppose the Chief of Staff [Röhm]. It was to me that he had pledged his loyalty and broken that pledge, and for that I alone must call him to account."

He made a sudden decision, which caught his comrades by surprise: he was going to Bad Wiessee and personally face the "nest of traitors." He ordered his private plane to be prepared for take-off, then paced between terraces and hall pouring out his feelings. How could Röhm have done such a thing? How could he have betrayed his Führer?

3

It was a shaken Hitler who climbed into the three-motored Junkers 52, a replacement for the regular plane, which had engine trouble. It was about 2 A.M. He slumped into his seat, stared fixedly ahead into the darkness. Otto Dietrich, his press chief, "had no idea what was up," until an adjutant instructed everyone to release the safety catch on his gun.

Lutze, who knew, was thinking of Röhm. He hummed to himself:

> Red of the morning, red of the morning,
> Thou lightest us to early death.
> Yesterday mounted on a proud street,
> Today a bullet through the breast.

It was a cloudy night with spits of rain. In the gray light preceding dawn Baur landed the plane on the drenched runway at Oberwiesenfeld, the military exercise field where Hitler had had his first humiliating confrontation with police and army twelve years earlier. The airport director was distressed. He had been instructed by Chief of Staff Röhm to alert the entire SA leadership as soon as the Führer's plane, D-2600, approached. But with the last-minute change in aircraft there was only a small group—party personages and several army officers—on hand to greet Hitler. "This is the blackest day in my life," he told them. "But I shall go to Bad Wiessee and pass severe judgment."

Hitler was driven to the Bavarian Ministry of the Interior where he leaped out of the car, followed by a rattled Gauleiter Wagner, who was also Minister of Interior. The Führer strode into the building, the skirt of his leather coat flying, and up the stairs toward Wagner's office. As he burst into the anteroom the head of the Upper Bavarian SA started to salute but Hitler rushed at him, shouting, "Lock him up!" He began cursing all traitors in general and the SA leaders whose men had been lured to the streets of Munich by pamphlets in particular. "You," he yelled, "are under arrest and will be shot!"

It was 6 A.M. when the Führer, still in "a terrifying state of excitement," emerged from the building. A second plane with armed reinforcements had not yet landed but he was too impatient to wait. He got into Kempka's car, taking his usual place beside the chauffeur, and instructed him to head for Bad Wiessee. They started off, followed by another car driven by Schreck. In the entire party there were only eight or nine men and the Führer's secretary, Fräulein Schröder. From the back seat Goebbels talked incessantly of the Brownshirt plot but Hitler only stared ahead. The sun was just breaking through clouds on the horizon. It was going to be "Hitler weather."

In less than an hour they reached the Tegernsee, nestling at the gateway to the Alps, its pure waters steaming with early morning mist. "We are now going to the Pension Hanselbauer," Hitler told Kempka. There was "some dirty work afoot" and they had to surprise the Hanselbauer's occupants. It was almost seven and church bells were calling the faithful to early morning mass when Kempka slowly, cautiously pulled up at the pension. Kempka noticed that some of the windows were closed, others open; there was no guard at the door. Hitler was first to enter. The ground floor appeared to be deserted; there was no one in the dining room, which was set for the midday banquet. Then the landlady appeared, understandably shocked to find herself face to face with the Führer. She started to express the honor she felt but he brusquely asked to be taken up to Röhm.

While the others in the party took positions in front of other rooms, a plainclothes detective knocked on Röhm's door. Then Hitler, revolver in hand, went in. Kempka, peering from behind his Führer, glimpsed a sleep-drugged Röhm blinking with genuine amazement and shock. He was in bed alone.

"Ernst," said Hitler, and then used the familiar *Du,* "you are under arrest." There was none of the fury Hitler had shown at the Ministry of the Interior. He was "somewhat tense but not visibly excited." Briefly and curtly he accused Röhm of being a traitor and told him to get dressed. Protesting vigorously, the SA chief began pulling on civilian clothes but Hitler had already gone and Röhm's words were wasted on the detectives left behind.

The Führer was banging at the opposite door. It opened and an Obergruppenführer named Heines stared out drowsily. Behind him stood his bed partner—an attractive young man who doubled as his chauffeur. "A disgusting scene, which made me feel like vomiting," wrote Goebbels.

Hitler went immediately to the next door, leaving Lutze behind to search for weapons. "Lutze, I've done nothing!" exclaimed Heines. "Can't you help me?"

"I can do nothing," said Lutze, more in embarrassment than self-righteousness, and repeated the phrase. Either from indignation or shock Heines refused to get dressed and would not do so until Hitler returned and told him to obey or be shot on the spot. Heines obeyed and was locked in the laundry with Röhm and his colleagues. With them were ten or so SA guards who had slept through the break-in, as well as Heines' chauffeur and several other good-looking youths taken in *flagrante delicto.*

While Hitler was discussing what should be done next, Kempka was sent to a nearby pension to apprehend Max Vogel, Röhm's cousin, who also served as his chauffeur. Vogel was in bed with a girl—the only such case that morning. Kempka, a good friend of his fellow chauffeur, apologetically announced he was under arrest. As they went to the garage for the Röhm car, Vogel made a curious last request: could he drive it just once more? Kempka understood and let him make a few slow turns in the driveway as he himself stood on the running board.

Just as Kempka and his prisoner got back to the Hanselbauer a truck filled with about forty armed Brownshirts of Röhm's "Headquarters Guard" arrived from Munich. Their commander was still locked up in the laundry and they were unhappy about it. One of Hitler's adjutants, Wilhelm Brückner, shouted an order to return to Munich at once. They did nothing except stare back sullenly, and a pitched battle seemed likely.

Then Hitler strode forward. "Didn't you hear what Brückner said?" In a tone of command that managed to be charming, he ordered the guardsmen to return to Munich. "On the way you will meet SS troops and they will disarm you." His manner more than his words took all the fight out of them and the truck drove off.

The prisoners were loaded into two commandeered buses and the caravan started off. Hitler's Mercedes led the way and SA men bound for the lunch banquet at the Hanselbauer would be stopped and interrogated by Hitler. Those whose names appeared on a list hastily drawn up by Goebbels were disarmed and instructed to sandwich their own cars in the cavalcade.

It was about 9:30 A.M. by the time the growing procession reached the Brown House. It had been cordoned off by army troops and Hitler took time to thank them for coming to his aid and give assurances that he had never intended using them against the SA. Once inside party headquarters, Hitler told Goebbels to telephone the code word to Göring. The purge was on. "I gave the order to shoot those who were the ringleaders in this treason and I further gave the order to *burn out down to the raw flesh the ulcers of this poisoning of the wells* in our domestic life and of the poisoning of the outside." The use of words dredging up memories of his mother's cancer and Dr. Bloch revealed the depth of his emotional upheaval.

The cells of Stadelheim were already filled with SA leaders put there by the SS. Those still in the Brown House, such as Röhm, demanded to see the Führer and when he refused asked for Goebbels. He was too occupied with the phone conversation with Göring and, before he finished, the last prisoners were on their way to Stadelheim in an armored car. Their leader was put in a solitary cell, not far from the one he had occupied after the Beer Hall Putsch.

At the Brown House, General von Epp was demanding a court-martial for Röhm. This upset Hitler's equilibrium and he reverted to his early morning rage. Röhm, he exclaimed, was a proven traitor and deserved to die. The general was so taken aback by this outburst that he could not reply but, as he walked away, muttered to his aide, "Crazy!"

A little later, at 11:30 A.M., a conference of SA leaders began in the spacious council chamber. Hitler had not yet regained his composure and

Hitler confers with Captain Pfeffer von Salomon, head of the Brownshirts, prior to his replacement by Röhm in 1930. Alfred Rosenberg, who introduced "The Protocols of Zion" to the Führer, on right. LIBRARY OF CONGRESS

The depression. One-man demonstration in Berlin, August 1930. BUNDESARCHIV

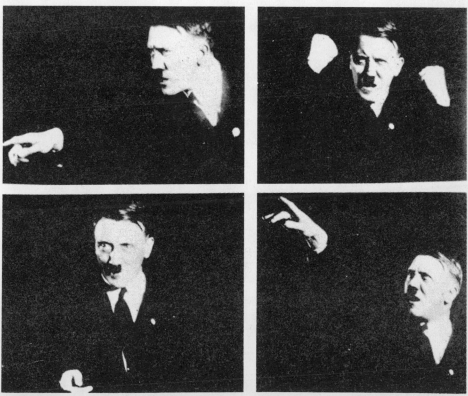

Hitler learns to use his hands; his teacher, reportedly, was the famous seer Hanussen. BUNDESARCHIV

Geli Raubal, the only true love of Hitler, commits suicide in his Munich apartment during the 1931 presidential campaign. HANS HITLER

Geli with mother, left, and Paula Hitler. TOLAND COLLECTION

Hitler in February 1932, autographed to Egon Hanfstaengl. EGON HANFSTAENGL

Tenant strike in Berlin. Reds join Nazis. BUNDESARCHIV

Chancellor Hitler with President von Hindenburg
and his son Oskar. BUNDESARCHIV

Propaganda poster. The grandparents:
"That we should live to see this!" The
grandchildren: "When will I see the
Führer?" BUNDESARCHIV

Hitler campaigns for electoral approval
of his policies in 1933. Ernst Hanfstaengl,
his foreign press officer, is at the extreme
right, mostly obscured. BUNDESARCHIV

Above, a Brownshirt points to
the Führer's pistol shot in
the ceiling. STADTARCHIV, MUNICH

Right, re-enactment of the
march, November 9, 1933.
Göring to Hitler's right.
Dr. Schultze, who treated
Hitler's injury in 1923,
second row left. DR. SCHULTZE

Above, ceremony for those who
died in the Putsch. Memorial
designed by Troost. In row
behind Hitler, extreme left,
Göring and Keitel;
extreme right, Dr. Schultze.
DR. SCHULTZE

Left, Brownshirt Chief Ernst
Röhm. SCHULZE-WILDE

Above, Party Day, Nuremberg,
1934. Dramatized by Leni
Riefenstahl's documentary film,
Triumph of the Will.
BUNDESARCHIV

Right, Leni Riefenstahl.
LENI RIEFENSTAHL

his address to his apprehensive audience was a series of disconnected complaints about the SA. Throughout the hourlong tirade Hitler's listeners stood in discomfort. One was fascinated by the foam that kept spewing from his mouth. "In a voice frequently choked with emotion," he accused Röhm of planning to kill him in order to hand Germany over to her enemies. Röhm and his conspirators, he promised, would be shot.

The killings had not yet started since Hitler was waiting for Sepp Dietrich, commander of the elite Leibstandarte, to do the job. He appeared shortly and explained to the exasperated Führer what had kept him so long: his trucks, for one reason, could not travel fast over wet roads on worn tires. For all his show of annoyance at the delay, Hitler had no orders to give. He told Dietrich to wait while he and his advisers argued the fate of the accused. Three hours passed without a decision.

While the Führer vacillated, his associates in Berlin were already carrying out executions. The Himmler-Heydrich-Göring triumvirate needed only the code word Kolibri to set their long-laid plot into action. When Papen reported to Göring's office he was annoyed to see the area "full of SS guards armed with machine-guns." The next surprise was to learn that Hitler had given Göring power to deal with the insurgents in the capital. Papen protested on the grounds that he was the Chancellor's deputy and in his absence such authority could be granted only to him. He insisted that Hindenburg declare a state of emergency and bring in the Reichswehr to restore law and order. Göring refused. He and Himmler's SS had complete control of the situation. He cut short Papen's protests and ordered the Vice-Chancellor to return home immediately for his own safety. Before Papen got there police cars were careening through the streets of Berlin rounding up enemies of the regime. One unit surrounded Papen's office, shot to death his press officer and arrested other members of his staff. The Vice-Chancellor might as well have been incarcerated; for as soon as he entered his own house it became a prison. Papen found his telephone wire cut and a police captain in the reception room who informed him that he was to have no contact with the outside world.

Few Berliners noticed that anything at all unusual was going on that hot Saturday morning. To the many strollers in the Tiergarten and on the Unter den Linden the greatest concern was the increasing heat as the sun climbed. Correspondent Delmer, however, had such a nagging worry that he interrupted his morning sculling session and drove back to his office. "I have stuck my neck right out on that 'Hitler dictatorship in peril' report," he kept saying to himself. What if nothing happened? But when his taxi was held up by a cordon of municipal police his fears were allayed. "Something *had* happened." The police, wearing steel helmets and armed with rifles and submachine guns, were surrounding Röhm's opulent Berlin residence on a corner of the Tiergartenstrasse.

In a suburb, two Gestapo agents were being ushered into General von

Schleicher's study by his cook and when one of the visitors asked if that was Schleicher at the desk the former Chancellor looked up and said, "Ja." The men opened fire. Frau von Schleicher, in a corner listening to the radio, rushed toward her stricken husband and was cut down by bullets. He died instantly and she succumbed shortly at the hospital.

In Munich, Hitler still hesitated about passing final judgment on Röhm and his colleagues. The discussion in the meeting room grew so loud that Sepp Dietrich, waiting in the outer office, could hear voices through the double doors of the meeting room. At last this portal opened about 5 P.M. and Martin Bormann, Hess's assistant, emerged. He escorted Dietrich back to Hitler. "Return to the barracks," instructed the Führer, and gave an order that Dietrich felt was wrung out of him: "Select an officer and six men and have the SA leaders shot for treason."

Dietrich examined a list handed over by Bormann. It contained the names of all those taken to Stadelheim but Hitler had checked off only a dozen. They included Heines and the chief of the Upper Bavarian SA—but not Ernst Röhm. Hitler could still not bring himself to make that decision.

When Hans Frank, the Bavarian Minister of Justice, learned that many SA leaders were jailed at Stadelheim he decided to go there in person and take charge. Upon arrival, he ordered the SA prisoners placed in the custody of a detachment of state police, then had himself admitted to Röhm's little cell.

"What does it all mean?" asked Röhm. "What is going on?"

Frank could give little information or assurance. He hoped that everything would proceed legally. Röhm replied that he was prepared for the worst. "I am not concerned about my own life but please take care of my relatives, they are women totally dependent on me." As Frank opened the cell door Röhm pressed his hand. "All revolutions," he said, "devour their own children."

No sooner had Frank returned to his own office than Sepp Dietrich entered with a colleague to announce that he had orders to shoot a number of SA leaders. He produced a list checked personally by Hitler. Stunned, Frank said the executions could not take place under any circumstances. Dietrich insisted that the Führer himself had ordered it but was persuaded to telephone the Brown House. First he talked to Hess. After a pause Dietrich extended the receiver to Frank. "Hitler wants to speak with you."

Hitler began shouting: "You refuse to carry out an order from me? Are you in sympathy with that criminal scum? I'm going to destroy those boys, roots and all!"

Frank protested that there was no written authorization, just a list of six names. "I marked that list myself," said Hitler in more controlled language. "These gentlemen are criminals against the Reich. I am the Reich Chancellor. It is a matter of the Reich, which is never under your jurisdiction."

At Stadelheim the first six victims were led out into the courtyard, each guarded by two policemen. "The Führer and Reich Chancellor has condemned you to death," an SS officer droned out. "The sentence will be carried out forthwith." When the head of the Upper Bavarian Brownshirts, August Schneidhuber, realized the chief executioner was Dietrich, he cried out: "Sepp, my friend, what on earth's happening? We are completely innocent!" With set face Dietrich clicked his heels. "You have been condemned to death by the Führer," he said. "Heil Hitler!"

The first man was placed before the firing squad. He refused to have his eyes covered. Shots reverberated in the courtyard walls. The next victim and the next also disdained blindfolds. Dietrich witnessed the first few shootings but before it was Schneidhuber's turn he had to walk off. "I had had enough."

It was dark by the time Hitler's car started for the airfield. "I have pardoned Röhm," he promised General von Epp, who was seeing him off, "because of his services." Hitler took his place in the front of the plane and he sat silently as Baur headed the Junkers 52 toward Berlin.

For the average Berliner there was little on the surface to indicate that the nation was undergoing an upheaval. True, sinister rumors were beginning to circulate and there were traffic tie-ups on the Charlottenburger Chaussee, what with police barriers and the stream of army trucks. It was also known that house arrests were taking place but the violence was under cover. Few citizens knew that General von Schleicher and his wife had been murdered or that Gregor Strasser had been seized at his lunch table and put into Cell 16 of the Gestapo prison. There he was peppered with shots by unseen assailants from the cell window while he dodged around like a rat in a cage until wounded. Then one of the gunmen entered to finish the job. Thus the enemy of Goebbels and Göring perished, still faithful in his own fashion to the Führer.

The ringmaster of the purge in Berlin was Göring, who briefed foreign correspondents in the Ministry of Propaganda late that afternoon. "Göring arrived in one of his full-dress uniforms," wrote a Gestapo official. "Once again he did not walk; he strutted up to the platform with slow, mincing steps. He began the session with a long, impressive pause, leaning forward slightly, his chin propped in his hand, and rolling his eyes as if he feared his own revelations." When he mentioned Schleicher in connection with the Röhm-Strasser plot, someone asked what had happened to the former Chancellor. "He was foolish enough to resist," said Göring with what one chronicler described as a wolfish smile. "He is dead."

Later in the day DNB published another excuse for the purge in the form of a telegram the Führer had sent to Viktor Lutze appointing him Röhm's successor. In it he listed a dozen "tasks" for the new SA commander and his leaders and the first was: "I demand from the leader of the SA just as he demands from each SA man, blind obedience and absolute discipline." He also condemned "official journeys in costly limousines or cabriolets," sumptuous feasts, intoxication and brawling in public. "It is my special desire that every mother can give her son to the SA, to the party, or to the Hitler Youth, without fear that he might be morally injured there." In the future, therefore, all Brownshirt leaders who misbehaved would be immediately drummed out of the SA and the party. "I want my SA leaders to be men, not ridiculous apes." Such words, coming at such a time, were received with derision by most foreign observers, but the average German read them with approbation, relieved to know that the Führer shared their own revulsion of the Brownshirt rowdies.

He further called on every SA chief to show "completely honest, loyal and true fealty to the Reichswehr" and "prove himself a real leader, friend and comrade." Finally, after praising the old SA fighters—"the ones who have conquered Germany and not the clever latecomers of the year 1933, and subsequently"—he made the first mention of his personal bodyguard troops: "I desire that the SS man shall be educated mentally and bodily to be the most highly-trained National Socialist."

By evening the death toll was appalling. General von Bredow, a friend of Schleicher, was gunned down at his front door. The acting police president of Breslau was disemboweled by a shotgun and an SS cavalry leader murdered in his own smoking room. The ghost writer of the recent controversial Papen speech lay lifeless in an underground cell of the Gestapo prison in the Prinz Albrechtstrasse. Other executions were taking place, under the supervision of the SS, at the Lichterfeld Barracks. Here died an official of the Ministry of Transport, the president of Catholic Action as well as Karl Ernst, who had been brought back from his honeymoon. His last words were: "Heil Hitler!"

The Brownshirts were in a state of confusion. Some units were alerted, issued revolvers and ordered to catch traitors—only to be rounded up themselves by SS troops and carted off for detention. Others were beaten up in the streets by roving Himmler men and some shot out of hand. Still others were marked for arrest or death but spared by friends in the SS. For thousands, who felt they had sacrificed everything for the party, it was a night of terror and disillusionment.

It was not until 10 P.M. that the Hitler plane finally touched down at Tempelhof airfield. Waiting was a tight little group—Göring, Himmler, Frick, a few Gestapo officials and a police escort. The first to step out of the plane was the Führer, clad in brown shirt, black bow tie, leather jacket and black army boots. "He wore no hat; his face was pale, unshaven, sleepless, at once gaunt and puffed," recalled a Gestapo official. After shaking hands, Hitler drew Göring and Himmler aside and listened attentively to their reports. While Hitler perused a list given him by Himmler, a finger slowly moving down the page, his two companions whispered to each other. As the trio slowly headed for the car followed by an escort at a discreet interval, Hitler revealed that Röhm himself was not to be executed. He had given his word to General von Epp. Göring and Himmler were vexed. If the leader of the revolt was spared it would make a mockery of the day's massacre. The argument continued as they drove away.

4

President von Hindenburg took the executions calmly. His first reaction was a cranky "I told you so" to Meissner. "For months I have been telling the Chancellor to lock up this immoral and dangerous Röhm; unfortunately he did not listen to me; now see how much blood has been spilled!"

The next morning, the first of July, was pleasantly warm and Berliners were strolling the streets with their children as if it were any ordinary Sunday. Few realized the import of the curt announcement of half a dozen executions for treason or the continued transport of SS troops. Those who were privileged to see the Führer knew that he was going through one of the most traumatic crises of his turbulent career. It reached a climax that afternoon when he finally was forced to approve the execution of Röhm. Even Hitler's sentence of death was marked by affection. He instructed Brigadeführer Theodor Eicke to give Röhm the chance to commit suicide.

It was still light by the time Eicke and two subordinates arrived at Stadelheim with Hitler's verbal order. At first the prison governor refused to hand over the prisoner without something in writing but he wilted under Eicke's shouts and ordered a warder to escort the three SS men to Cell 474 in the new prison block. There slumped Röhm on an iron cot, bare to the waist and sweating heavily in the sweltering heat.

"You have forfeited your life," said Eicke. "The Führer gives you one more chance to draw the right conclusions." He placed a pistol loaded with a single bullet on a table, then left the cell. Eicke waited in the passage for almost fifteen minutes, then he and his deputies drew their own revolvers and pushed back into the cell. "Chief of Staff, prepare yourself!" shouted Eicke. And, when he saw his deputy's gun quivering, said, "Aim slowly and calmly." Two shots reverberated deafeningly in the little cell. Röhm collapsed. "My Führer!" he gasped. "My Führer!"

"You should have thought of that earlier; it's too late now," said Eicke. It was 6 P.M. The man who should logically have been the first to die was among the last to perish. With his demise those who remained on the death list in the Berlin area—at Lichterfeld Barracks and Columbia House, a former prison converted into an SS torture chamber—were prepared for execution.

Papen was still alive because influential friends and foreigners would drive slowly past his house every so often. That Sunday Ambassador Dodd left a card at the door with a handwritten message: "I hope we may call on you soon." Dodd considered Papen a devious coward but he couldn't help liking him personally and his card had been left "as a protest against the brutality of the Nazis."

The people still knew little of what was happening, nor was the truth well served by Göring's long version of the killings issued later in the day. "The purge will now be carried on ruthlessly," said Göring after assuring the citizenry that the nation was now at peace and the Führer in complete control. The unruly elements of the SA would be eliminated. "The people must know that we are in earnest to do everything for them." Like most communiqués from any nation, it was a hodgepodge of truth and fiction, and gave the public the opportunity to believe what it was eager to believe: that there was nothing to worry about and a nasty but necessary job had been done in the most honorable way for the good of the state.

This announcement was followed almost immediately by publication of an order issued to the Reichswehr by General von Blomberg expressing complete loyalty to the Führer. Despite protestations about remaining "outside the inner political struggle," it was graphic proof that the army was irrevocably bound in blood to Adolf Hitler.

Even as Blomberg was assuring the populace that the crisis was over, the killings continued into the early morning hours of July 2. At Columbia House Gruppenführer Karl Schreyer was called out of his cell by a non-com who said, "You will be shot on the Führer's orders." Schreyer had seen three comrades precede him to execution at half-hour intervals. "Put your head under the tap like the others, so that you'll look fresh and make a good impression." Schreyer was then led down the stairs to a small sports car which would take him to Lichterfeld for execution. A Mercedes roared up and an officer of the Leibstandarte leaped out, signaling violently. "Stop! Stop!" he shouted. "Nothing more is to happen; the Führer has given Hindenburg his word that the shooting is now finally over."

It was 4 A.M. A hundred men, perhaps two hundred—the exact number will never be known—had been murdered without trial.

Throughout the Reich that hot Monday the average German was congratulating himself with grim satisfaction that the roughneck Brownshirts were at last under control. "No one loved Röhm and his parvenu officers," recalled correspondent Delmer, "the ex-waiters, ex-hotel porters and ex-plumbers, who had been bossing the common people more arrogantly than any Prussian Guards Officers in the days of the Kaiser. They and their brand-new, elegant motorcars, roaring ruthlessly about the streets, were feared and hated by the German little man." By eliminating these ruffians Hitler had become his hero.

Hindenburg was having second thoughts. The brutal murder of General von Schleicher and his wife upset him deeply enough to demand an investigation. He simply could not accept the official version that the couple had been shot resisting arrest. At the same time he was incapable of putting his indignation into effect and he dutifully signed a congratulatory telegram to Hitler drafted by the Nazis. It read:

> FROM THE REPORTS PLACED BEFORE ME, I LEARN THAT YOU BY YOUR DETERMINED ACTION AND GALLANT PERSONAL INTERVENTION, HAVE NIPPED TREASON IN THE BUD. YOU HAVE SAVED THE GERMAN NATION FROM SERIOUS DANGER. FOR THIS I EXPRESS TO YOU MY MOST PROFOUND THANKS AND SINCERE APPRECIATION.

With this certificate of support, Hitler now had the uneasy sanction of almost the entire nation.

5

Approval of the purge did not extend beyond Germany's borders and scathing articles and editorials flourished abroad. Much as he flinched from foreign attack, Hitler's primary concern was a faint but growing suspicion among his own people that they might have been deceived. These misgivings were fostered by whispered revelations: for example, that one of the victims was Hitler's old nemesis, Bavarian State Commissar von Kahr, of the triumvirate which had "broken its word" in the Beer Hall Putsch; and that Dr. Willi Schmid, a music critic, was arrested in his apartment while playing the cello, then murdered under the impression that he was Wilhelm Schmid, the local Brownshirt leader.

Tiny as was this seed of doubt, it aggravated Hitler's own distressed state of mind. Genuinely shaken by the liquidation of old friends and comrades, he hid from the public. Privately he commissioned Hess, now his closest friend and associate, to embark on a number of missions of mercy (occasioned by remorse) to widows and relatives of the victims. Hess did his best to comfort the widow of the music critic by counseling her to look upon her husband's death as that of a martyr for a great cause. He also assured her a pension from the Reich. Frau Strasser and Röhm's mother were also offered pensions. The latter, still unable to believe that her son could be a homosexual (to this day his older brother and sister-in-law vehemently deny it), curtly turned down the offer. She would not take a pfennig from the murderer of her son.

Hitler also attempted to make amends to Papen, inviting him to attend an emergency session of the cabinet on July 3 just as if he had never been held in custody. All affability, Hitler invited the Vice-Chancellor to take his usual place at the table. Nettled, Papen said that was out of the question and demanded to see Hitler alone. The two moved into the next room where Papen told about his own house arrest and the murder of his press officer. He requested an immediate judicial inquiry into the matter, then insisted that his resignation be announced immediately. Hitler's polite refusal sent Papen directly to the Bendlerstrasse to see his old friend General von Fritsch. The army commander-in-chief stared as if facing a ghost. "As you can see, I am alive," said Papen. "But this *Schweinerei* has got to be stopped." Why, he asked, hadn't Fritsch prevented the purge in the first place? The army chief sheepishly explained that it had been impossible to act "without explicit orders from Blomberg or Hindenburg." The former had "rigidly opposed any intervention" and the latter could not be reached.

In the cabinet meeting General von Blomberg was congratulating the Führer on behalf of the armed forces for acting so expeditiously against traitors. This gave Hitler a felicitous opportunity to justify such harsh actions. "When a mutiny takes place," Schwerin von Krosigk recalls his saying, "then the captain of a ship cannot wait until the ship reaches shore to take court action. He must take things in hand at the time and place it happens."

Not a single member of the cabinet protested (including the Minister of Justice, a number of whose right-wing friends had perished), and this group then proceeded to do what it had been brought together to do: promulgate a law legalizing the "measures taken on June 30 and on July 1 and 2" as an "emergency defense of the state."

Papen was not the only official who wanted to resign. Bavarian Minister of Justice Frank also offered to step down. "Does one desert a ship in the middle of the ocean?" said Hitler caustically. "I have quarrels with many but I must hold everything together. We are a troop in battle." Justice and revolution, he argued, were incompatible. "Don't forget that every revolution has its victims!" Hitler could understand Frank's feelings of revulsion at the purge but nothing could be done about that now. "I have too many deadly enemies. Everything now hinges on my authority." When Frank protested that the police were assuming too much power and that too many party members were taking the law into their own hands, Hitler replied: "Justice and jurists serve the community best when they leave all political necessities to other organs."

He even had an answer for the growing number of concentration camps. "If I had a spacious Siberia at my disposal as Moscow has, then I wouldn't need any concentration camps. . . . Who in the world talks about the millions of victims of Bolshevism? The Jewish press of the world pursues me because I am an anti-Semite. Herr Stalin is their darling." Frank tore up his resignation.

Papen was not so easy to bring around. He insisted on getting the remains of his press officer—ashes in an urn—and arranging a proper burial at Schönberg cemetery despite warnings from Himmler against provoking any public demonstration. Papen not only delivered a moving oration at the funeral but kept bombarding the Führer with letters protesting against the continued imprisonment of four of his subordinates and pressing for a public inquiry into his press officer's death. A model of patience himself for a change, Hitler urged Papen to be patient. A special meeting of the Reichstag to explain the purge fully was to be held in forty-eight hours. At the time he, as Führer, would take full responsibility for everything that had happened, including those unfortunate events committed "in an excess of zeal."

The thirteenth of July was a Friday. Security measures at the Kroll Opera House were such that one veteran diplomat commented: "I have often seen governments in other countries in hot water, but even in the most dangerous period under the Czars I never saw anything like this." Hitler's path from the chancellery to the stage was flanked on both sides by heavily armed police and SS troops, and there were repeated searches of the opera's anterooms. Detectives were planted throughout the auditorium while soldiers in steel helmets and armed with swords guarded entrances. "No one present—and the American, French, and Russian Ambassadors made a point of not attending—could fail to recognize that a period of wild, hostile fear had begun among the men who wield power."

At 8 P.M. a grim-faced Führer stepped to the podium clutching the lectern as if for balance. Extending an arm in stiff salute, he began speaking in a voice harsher than usual, as if giving assurance that he was once more in control of events. He gave a lengthy, emotional account of the purge which, he explained, was necessitated by the treasonous actions of various groups which he described as "destructive elements" and "pathological enemies of the state." He could have been describing himself in earlier days—as well as his present role in world politics. With the skill of a born storyteller he gave his version of the events leading up to the dramatic decision to put down the rebellion in person. Except for the foreign observers, almost everyone in the opera house was spellbound by his performance, and throughout Germany enthralled crowds clustered around radios. At the American Embassy Ambassador Dodd, who had vowed never again to attend an address of the Chancellor or seek an interview except upon official grounds ("I have a sense of horror when I look at the man"), was listening with disbelief to Hitler's claim that only seventy-four plotters—including a few civilians and party members—had died for their infamy; and that he had executed three SS men who had "scandalously illtreated" those taken into protective custody. The last was an apparent attempt to convince Papen that the murders of innocent victims like his press chief had been punished. And this spirit of conciliation was extended with an emotional offer of amnesty to those not yet punished who had shared in the guilt of treason. "May we all feel responsible for the most precious treasure that there can be for the German people: internal order, internal and external peace, just as I am ready to undertake responsibility at the bar of history for the twenty-four hours in which the bitterest decisions of my life were made, in which fate once again taught me in the midst of anxious care with every thought to hold fast to the dearest thing which has been given us in this world—the German people and the German Reich!"

The hand-picked audience rose as one to applaud enthusiastically. Almost as an anticlimax, the main purpose of the meeting was promptly accomplished: the Reichstag unanimously approved the bill legalizing the executions as "emergency defense measures of the state." Hitler had been given, ex post facto, a license to murder. There was not a single word of protest. The legislators had enshrined the Führer as the sole source of law.

Minister of Defense von Blomberg was not alone among the military in his endorsement of Hitler's ruthless cleansing of the SA and the liquidation of Generals von Schleicher and von Bredow. The officer corps accepted the death of two comrades with surprising equanimity, shutting their eyes to Hitler's methods on the grounds that suppression of the Putsch was a guarantee of internal peace. "Our verdict on the affair," recalled Karl Dönitz, "was decisively influenced by the cabinet resolution, which, by citing a state of national emergency, gave legal sanction to all the measures taken."

The sentiments of the officers drifted down to the enlisted men, who greeted Hitler with cheers when his open car drove past an infantry column on maneuvers a few days later. "This type of spontaneous demonstration," reported the French military attaché, "is not usual in the German army."

Only a handful of officers were bold enough to speak out in protest and their leader was almost as old as Hindenburg. Field Marshal August von Mackensen, an officer of distinction, had tried to reach the President by telephone in hopes of stopping the purge but he was always told the Old Gentleman was too sick to talk. Balked, Mackensen finally went directly to the Führer and made a plea for the re-establishment of common decency in public life. His words moved Hitler to such an extent that it took a moment before he could say: "It may be as you say, Herr Feldmarschall, but I cannot help myself. I cannot go back."

Determined to inform Hindenburg of the truth, Mackensen helped compose a memorandum outlining the details of the Schleicher-Bredow assassinations and demanding punishment for those responsible. It also urged the President to drop Blomberg, Goebbels, Ley, Neurath and two other Nazis from the cabinet and hand over control of the nation to a small directorate. Hitler was not named; presumably he was to remain as Chancellor under a military dictatorship.

The memorandum concluded on an emotional note: "Your Excellency has thrice before saved Germany from foundering: at Tannenberg, at the end of the war and at the moment of your election as President of the Reich. Excellency, save Germany for the fourth time! The undersigned generals and senior officers swear to preserve to their last breath their loyalty to you and to the Fatherland." Mackensen had persuaded twenty-eight other senior officers of the General Staff, many of whom were members of the regiment to which both Hindenburg and Schleicher belonged, to affix their signatures. It was dated July 18 and arrived in Neudeck on the twentieth. But this gallant effort was of no avail. If the ailing field marshal ever read the memorandum, which was probably kept from him by his entourage, he took no action.

It appeared as if all influential segments of German society had either been intimidated or won over, and what could have been a personal disaster for Hitler turned out to be a victory of sorts; the purge had at least brought a sweeping conclusion to the factionalism which had long wracked his party. With a stroke the SA was castrated.

The SA's loss was Himmler's gain. On the same day Mackensen's memorandum arrived in Neudeck, Hitler promoted the SS to the status of an independent organization and permitted it to form armed units. It was a body blow to the military, which had compromised its honor to approve of the bloody elimination of the Brownshirts, only to be faced with an even more formidable rival.

The cost to the party was considerable, with the loss of many of its most ardent members, the idealists of the SA. "You have to realize that we sacrificed everything," said Hein Ruck, who later became a trusted lieutenant of Hitler's favorite commando, Otto Skorzeny. "We slept on a mattress in the kitchen and in the morning three of us would buy a bouillon cube for ten pfennig; that was our breakfast." Ruck himself was arrested twenty times during the struggle for power and his experience was not exceptional. "Then, to put it bluntly, we were betrayed. We wanted a new society and we suddenly had to face the fact that reaction was with us. Hurray, patriotism! No more revolution. And June 30 was the logical consequence of the movement which was now being destroyed by Hitler." Men like Ruck were convinced that Röhm had merely attempted to bring Hitler back to the old road of revolution—and socialism. "And here it was that Hitler really made his first true enemies, enemies in his own camp. For me and my friends, Hitler as a human being was finished."

Another young SA leader, Werner Naumann, was also disillusioned and angry. Although he would become Goebbels' private secretary, he too could never forget. "The Röhm affair," he recently said, "was important to the development of the Third Reich because here for the first time we had an unlawful, illegal action, one sanctioned by the Reichswehr, as well as the entire bureaucracy and legal body of the nation. It was totally unlawful and illegal, and nobody stood up to say, 'So far and no further.' Not even the Church. And none of these groups could say they knew nothing about the matter. Everyone knew what happened. And, in my opinion, this was the beginning of the end, because from now on the move was from the lawful and legal to the illegal and unlawful, and from now on there could be no turning back the clock."

And so, while Hitler appeared to be at the crest of his popularity, there remained a deep and bitter schism within his own movement. Thousands of the most motivated Nazis would never forget the weekend of shame. A state of underground war was declared by those SA leaders who felt betrayed by Hitler. Their resentment against his elite SS erupted into the open several weeks later in the restaurant of Stettin's Preussenhof Hotel where Viktor Lutze was drinking beer with about twenty fellow Brownshirts and three SS commanders. "One of these days," declaimed the new commander of the SA, his tongue loosened by beer, "the unjust and arbitrary action of 30 June will be avenged." Lutze openly intimated that it was Himmler and his SS who had egged on Röhm. "Who is up to their necks in what Röhm was supposed to have done? Was it the SA? These bestialities were not the SA's work or, at least, not the SA alone; the other side was much worse. Shall I give you names? I can produce names straight away!" One of the SS men tried to quiet tipsy Lutze but he had the last word. "I shall go on saying this, even if I am dismissed tomorrow and sent to a concentration camp!"

6

A month earlier, during his frustrating excursion to Italy, the Führer had promised Mussolini to respect Austrian independence. It was a considerable concession since *Anschluss,* incorporation of his homeland into a Greater Germany, had been one of Hitler's first goals. Despite this promise his own SS did not cease sending considerable financial and moral support to Austrian Nazis, who carried on a compaign of terrorism, blowing up railways and power stations with German dynamite and murdering supporters of Chancellor Engelbert Dollfuss with German weapons. Ironically the diminutive Dollfuss was a nationalistic, authoritarian reactionary who was countering the threats of both Nazism and socialism with suspension of parliamentary government. Earlier in the year Dollfuss had put down revolt from the left by bombarding socialists entrenched in a huge housing development until they surrendered. Since then he had concentrated on wiping out the local Nazis, reinforced by assurance from Mussolini that he would restrain Hitler from retaliation.

Perhaps the Austrian Nazis were inspired by the hubbub following the Röhm affair to take direct action. More likely, though there is no proof, Hitler approved it. At any rate, on July 25 they suddenly launched their own Putsch, under the code name Operation Summer Festival. At noon a secret striking force of 150 local Nazis in the uniforms of the Austrian army broke into the chancellery on the Ballhausplatz to seize Dollfuss and his advisers. The plot had already been discovered and all but two of the cabinet had fled, but the plucky Dollfuss had remained. He was shot in the throat from a range of six inches. As he lay on the floor, ignored and bleeding profusely, other rebels were broadcasting the lie that the Chancellor had resigned.

In Berlin the news of the uprising was welcomed in official circles and DNB prepared a statement to the effect that the people had revolted in righteousness. "The inevitable has happened. The German people in Austria have risen against their oppressors, jailers, and torturers." Hitler—in Bayreuth attending the Wagner festival—pretended indifference at first but as the afternoon wore on he became concerned over the possible repercussions of the revolt. Would Mussolini assume he had broken his word and bring his own superior military force into play? (Il Duce, in fact, was furious, not only because the word given in Venice had been broken but for personal reasons: Frau Dollfuss and her children were his house guests and it had been his painful duty to inform them Dollfuss was dying.) Hitler appeared in his box with the Wagner family that evening for the performance of *Das Rheingold*, but it was doubtful if he enjoyed it since he was often interrupted by whispered communiqués from Schaub or Brückner who were getting telephoned reports in the anteroom. These included a disturbing one that Mussolini had ordered a concentration of troops and aircraft on the Austrian border in line with his promise to aid Austria. By the time the curtain fell it seemed obvious that the Vienna Putsch was headed for failure, and when Hitler arrived at the Wagner home young Friedelind noted that he was "extremely" nervous and somewhat incoherent. His chief aim seemed to be to rush to a nearby actors' restaurant so he could mingle with the celebrities and create the impression he had nothing to do with the Austrian Nazi fiasco.

Later in the evening word arrived from Berlin that Chancellor Dollfuss had died at 6 P.M. but the Putsch had been quelled. Hitler telephoned the Wilhelmstrasse and asked State Secretary von Bülow for more details. When Bülow replied that Minister Rieth, German representative in Austria, was bargaining for the safe conduct of the arrested assassins to the German border, Hitler shouted that Reith had no business at all playing the part of mediator. At 11 P.M. the Führer rang up Bülow again for further information on the captured Putschists. "The Reich

Chancellor," so Bülow noted in his official memorandum, "replied that he would have the expelled conspirators taken into protective custody and transferred to a concentration camp."

In his extremity, Hitler turned to Papen, whom he had recently humiliated with house arrest, and requested him to replace Rieth. Papen was in no mood to comply but Hitler persisted, appealing in the name of patriotism. The least Papen could do was to talk over the matter in person. Why not fly in the Führer's personal plane to Bayreuth? Papen could not resist such insistence and early the next morning took off from Tempelhof with his son. On the trip south his mind was in a turmoil. Why had Hitler turned to him of all people? Was it because he had protested against the terrorist methods of the Nazi underground in Austria and was a personal friend of Dollfuss? Papen found the Führer in "a state of hysterical agitation, denouncing feverishly the rashness and stupidity of the Austrian Nazi Party for having involved him in such an appalling situation." At first Hitler refused Papen's terms for acceptance: the dismissal of his own appointee as inspector of the Austrian Nazi Party. But when Papen said it was a choice "between him and me," Hitler finally acceded and Papen accepted the post.

In the waiting room he met an old friend, Hjalmar Schacht, president of the Reichsbank, who was next in line to see the Führer. He too was offered an important assignment, as head of the Ministry of Economic Affairs. Schacht was unhappy with the course of the Nazi Reich, particularly the excesses of the recent purge, but, like Papen, he convinced himself—so he later wrote—that he must help the country by acceptance. "There remained the one and only possibility of working from within outward, of making use of those very governmental activities in an attempt to combat the excesses of the system and direct its policies along decent lines." Like Papen, he too claimed to have accepted his post provisionally. His condition was put in the form of a question: "Before I take office I should like to know how you wish me to deal with the Jewish question."

"In economic matters," said Hitler, a master at handling opportunists, "the Jews can carry on exactly as they have done up to now."

Assured of Papen's help on the diplomatic front and with Schacht as master mind of accelerated rearmament, Hitler felt prepared to weather the criticism from abroad raised by the Dollfuss murder. The most scathing attacks were coming from Mussolini. He had not only wired Austrian Vice-Chancellor Prince Ernst Rüdiger von Starhemberg that Italy would fight for Austrian independence but traveled to Vienna to express his feelings in person. "It would mean the end of European civilization if this country of murderers and pederasts were to overrun Europe," he told Starhemberg, then charged Hitler with instigation of the revolt in Vienna. He became so emotional, according to Starhemberg, that his eyes rolled. "Hitler is the murderer of Dollfuss, Hitler is the guilty man, he is responsible for this." He called the Führer "a horrible sexual degenerate, a dangerous fool," and described Nazism as a "revolution of the old Germanic tribes in the primeval forest against the Latin civilization of Rome." Nor could one compare Nazism to Fascism. "Certainly there are outward similarities. Both are authoritarian systems, both are collectivist, socialistic. Both systems oppose liberalism. But Fascism is a regime that is rooted in the great cultural tradition of the Italian people; Fascism recognizes the right of the individual, it recognizes religion and family. National Socialism, on the other hand, is savage barbarism; in common with barbarian hordes it allows no rights to the individual; the chieftain is lord over life and death of his people. Murder and killing, loot and pillage and blackmail are all it can produce." He began to shout. "This abominable and repulsive spectacle that Hitler showed the world on the thirtieth of June would not have been tolerated in any other country in the world. Only these primitive Germans, prepared even for murder, will put up with such things." Hopefully, he added, the assassination of Dollfuss might do some good. Perhaps the Great Powers would recognize the German danger and organize a grand coalition against Hitler. A common front was the only answer, he said. "Hitler will arm the Germans and make war—perhaps even in two or three years. I cannot stand up to him alone. We must do something, we must do something quickly."

Mussolini's disgust at Hitler and Germany was such that he began expressing similar feelings in public. "Thirty centuries of history allow us to regard with supreme indulgence certain doctrines taught beyond the Alps by the descendants of people who were wholly illiterate in the days when Caesar, Virgil and Augustus flourished in Rome," he announced from the top of a tank at the inauguration of the fifth *Fiere del Levante*. His private epithets, such as the one describing Germans as pederasts and murderers, also began to be echoed in the Italian press.

7

The shock of the purge, followed so quickly by that of the Dollfuss murder, had a perceptible effect on Hindenburg. He declined rapidly and was confined to his bed. It was a spartan iron bed but he refused to get a more comfortable one on the grounds that he had always slept on a field cot. Nor would he buy a robe despite his chills. Soldiers don't have robes, he grumbled. He had no money for such things and besides he was about to die.

The Führer was still at Bayreuth when he learned that the Old Gentleman was sinking fast. He rushed to Neudeck on the first day of August with a small party including two public relations experts. The group was coolly received. Oskar von Hindenburg led the Führer into the President's bedroom. "Father," he said, "the Reich Chancellor is here." Hindenburg, lying with eyes closed, did not react and Oskar repeated the words. Without opening his eyes, the marshal said, "Why did you not come earlier?"

"What does the President mean?" Hitler whispered to the son.

"The Reich Chancellor could not get here until now," Oskar told his father, who only muttered, "Oh, I see." After a silence Oskar said, "Father, Reich Chancellor Hitler has one or two matters to discuss."

This time the Old Gentleman opened his eyes with a start, stared at Hitler, then shut them again and clamped his mouth shut. Perhaps the President had expected to see *his* Reich Chancellor, his Franzchen— Papen.

Hitler emerged "tight-lipped" and would not discuss the scene. That night his party stopped at the Finckenstein estate where Napoleon had carried on a romance with Countess Walewska. The host suggested Hitler sleep in the Little Corporal's bed but he curtly declined the honor.

The next morning, even while Hindenburg was expiring, Hitler's cabinet passed a law combining the offices of President and Chancellor. The vote was unanimous, with the absent Papen's signature affixed by proxy. The measure was to be effective with the death of Hindenburg and this occurred within minutes. The Old Gentleman died with the words: "My Kaiser . . . my Fatherland" on his lips. He was laid out on the iron cot with a Bible in his hands.

Thanks to a legal coup, Hitler now carried the title of Führer and Reich Chancellor. This meant he was also supreme commander of the armed forces and his first act was to summon General von Blomberg and the three commanders-in-chief of the three armed forces. "We were in his study," Admiral Erich Raeder later testified, "and Hitler asked us to come to his desk without ceremony or staging. There we took the oath which he, as Chief of State and Supreme Commander of the Armed Forces, read to us."

The four men repeated this oath: "I swear before God to give my unconditional obedience to Adolf Hitler, Führer of the Reich and its people, Supreme Commander of the Armed Forces, and I pledge my word as a brave soldier to observe this oath always even at the risk of my life."

It was unprecedented. The previous oath had demanded loyalty and obedience to the constitution and the President. This one to a specific individual established a personal link between Führer and every soldier, sailor and airman. Yet not one officer made the slightest protest or even questioned the unique wording, and before the end of the day every serviceman in the land had taken the same oath of personal fealty.

The first stage of Hindenburg's funeral ceremonies took place at the Kroll Opera House on August 6, where his coffin was carried past the ranks of army field gray and brown and black of the SA and SS. These diverse groups were at last united by similar oaths of loyalty to the Führer.

It was symbolic that the music for the occasion was the funeral march from *Götterdämmerung*.

Burial took place the next noon not, where Hindenburg had wished, at Neudeck but, on Hitler's insistence, at the scene of the marshal's greatest triumph, Tannenberg. The body was placed on a catafalque in the center of the monument to the battle, an impressive structure with eight square towers some sixty feet high with fires flaming at the top of each. It reminded Ambassador François-Poncet of a castle built by the Teutonic Knights.

Hitler strode forward to face the coffin. At the podium he discovered that an adjutant had laid out the wrong speech and there was an embarrassing pause that must have puzzled radio listeners all over Europe. But he quickly collected himself and began extemporizing one of the shortest speeches correspondent Lochner, for one, had ever heard him deliver. Hitler ended with fulsome praise of Hindenburg's military and political achievements in words befitting a Wagnerian hero, not an orthodox fundamental Lutheran: "And now enter thou upon Valhalla!"

At the end of the services, Hitler kissed the hands of Hindenburg's daughters. Moved by the solemnity of the moment, if not by opportunism, General von Blomberg impulsively suggested that the armed forces should henceforth address him not with the customary "Herr Hitler" but as "Mein Führer." Hitler accepted the proposal and returned to Berlin. Here he sought further consolidation of his power by phoning Papen and asking if the Old Gentleman had left a political testament. Papen replied that he would ask young Hindenburg. "I should be obliged," said Hitler, "if you would ensure that this document comes into my possession as soon as possible." Papen promptly sent his private secretary to Neudeck. He returned with two sealed envelopes which Papen turned over to the Führer. It was obvious to Papen that Hitler was displeased with the contents of the envelope addressed to him when he said frostily, "These recommendations of the late President are given to me personally. Later I shall decide if and when I shall permit their publication." Rumors that Hitler intended to suppress the testament became so insistent among foreign correspondents that Hanfstaengl brought up the subject at teatime. "Tell your foreign friends to wait until the document is published officially," retorted Hitler irritably. "I don't care what that pack of liars thinks."

Finally on August 15 the testament was released for publication. It praised the achievements of Hitler and his government while stressing the importance of the army as the "symbol of, and firm support for," the new state. There was talk in the capital that the document had been doctored by the editor of Hindenburg's memoirs and that Oskar von Hindenburg and his father's adviser, Meissner, were co-conspirators in the deception. A measure of credence was given this rumor when Oskar swore in a radio speech to the nation that his father had always supported Hitler. The cynics notwithstanding, the son was not lying. Despite Hindenburg's repugnance for some aspects of the Hitler regime, he *had* seen the Führer as his direct successor.

Oskar's words were not necessary, for Hitler already had massive support on all levels of German society. Even the Association of National German Jews issued an appeal in his favor. And so, on August 19, almost 90 per cent of the German people freely voted their approval of Adolf Hitler as Hindenburg's successor. In doing so, they also sanctioned his program and leadership, and propelled him another step closer to dictatorship.

Chapter Thirteen

TRIUMPH OF THE WILL
1934–1935

1

After victory in the plebiscite Hitler retreated to Berchtesgaden for a late summer holiday. He spent hours strolling around his beloved Obersalzberg, engaging in one of his favorite pastimes, conversation. But he was also making preparations for the impending Party Day Congress in Nuremburg, which could be blighted by bitter memories of the Röhm purge. He was determined to prevent this through his usually reliable combination of threat, promise and conciliation. The nation was still in a state of unrest and a number of intellectuals like Spengler, who had given grudging approval of National Socialism, were now enemies.

He was also concerned by foreign journalists eager for material that would damn or ridicule his regime. Dorothy Thompson had found such a story for an article in *Harper's Bazaar*. "This is not a revolution," an American visitor at the Passion play in Oberammergau (which blamed the Jews for the death of Jesus*) reportedly told her, "It's a revival. They think Hitler is God. Believe it or not, a German woman sat next to me at the Passion play, and when they hoisted Jesus on the cross, she said, 'There he is. That is our Führer, our Hitler!' And when they paid out the thirty pieces of silver to Judas, she said: 'That is Röhm, who betrayed the Leader.'" Thompson's story was almost identical to the August 23 entry in Ambassador Dodd's diary describing the same drama: "When Jesus was tried before the angry Jewish court, a well-dressed German, looking

---

* Only in 1975 was the text revised to place the blame instead on Lucifer, the fallen angel of evil.

very solemn, said to me: *'Es ist unser Hitler* [He is our Hitler].' Ida
Horne, a distant kinswoman of mine, sitting in another part of the hall,
told me as we came out together: 'A woman near me said, as Judas received his thirty pieces of silver, *'Es ist Röhm!'* I suspect half the audience, the German part, considers Hitler as Germany's Messiah."

A contrary opinion, that Hitler was more Judas than Messiah, ran
deep among many Brownshirts who had remained, if reluctantly, in the
party. One such, Max Jüttner, Röhm's former subordinate, could not help
praising his dead chief while discussing the coming Party Day with the
Führer. Hitler lost his temper. "Why are you bringing up that subject?"
he shouted. "This matter is closed. Röhm has been adjudged." Alarmed,
Jüttner protested that the Führer would not have made Röhm chief of
staff if he had lacked good qualities. With one of his lightning changes,
Hitler patted Jüttner on the shoulder. "You are right," he said, "but you
couldn't possibly know the whole story. Röhm and Schleicher intended to
make a Putsch against me and it had to be averted. I wanted to have these
matters examined before a regular court, but events overwhelmed me and
many SA leaders were shot without my consent. Because of all the world
publicity I took the blame."

Hitler chose young Alfred Speer as stage manager of the pageant at
Nuremberg that was to consolidate his gains and bring back unity to the
party. Speer tore down the temporary bleachers on Zeppelin Field and, inspired by the Pergamum altars, erected a stone structure 1300 feet long
and 80 feet high. Crowning the stadium was a giant eagle with a 100-foot
wingspread and on all sides were hung thousands of swastika banners.
Positioned around the field at 40-foot intervals were 130 anti-aircraft
searchlights with a range of 25,000 feet. Göring had resisted loaning these
since they were the greater part of his strategic reserve but Hitler backed
Speer. "If we use them in such large numbers for a thing like this," he
reasoned, "other countries will think we're swimming in searchlights."

His imagination went beyond propaganda of the moment. Envisaging
a permanent record that could be exported, he asked Leni Riefenstahl, the
noted actress and director, to produce a commemorative film. He admired
her work, particularly *The Blue Light*, and assured her she would have
complete co-operation if she made a feature-length film of the 1934 Party
Day. She yielded despite qualms, but once out of his sight decided she was
not qualified to do a documentary. She turned over the direction to an associate and left for Spain to work on a film of her own. By the time she
returned the Nuremberg Rally was only two weeks off. Awaiting her was a
letter from Hess: the Führer was shocked to find she had delegated the assignment to someone else and wanted to see her at once.

Hitler was not angry, only persuasive. "You'll only have to give up six
days of your life," he argued and, when she retorted that with cutting that
meant six months, said, "Ah, but you are so young!" She insisted that she

was the last person in the world to do such a film. "I'm not a member of the party and I don't even know the difference between SA and SS."

"That is why I want you to do it," said Hitler. "That will give it a fresh approach." She took over the difficult task herself and, to bring additional interest to the six-day program, devised shots from planes, cranes, roller skates and a tiny elevator platform attached to the tallest flagpole. Upon arrival in Nuremberg a week before the opening day, with a crew of 120, including sixteen cameramen, she got all the assistance Hitler had promised. The city's fire-fighting equipment as well as public utilities were turned over to her.

The participants were already flooding into Nuremberg. Carefully selected months in advance, each had a number, a designated truck, a designated seat in the truck, and a designated cot in the vast tent city near Nuremberg. By the time the ceremonies began on September 4 the thousands of party members had been rehearsed to perfection. That evening the Führer made a short welcoming speech at the old Rathaus, followed by Hanfstaengl's long one urging the foreign press to "report on affairs in Germany without attempting to interpret them." Afterward at least ten thousand enthusiasts crowded around Hitler's hotel, the Deutscher Hof, repeating the chant "We want our Führer!" until he at last came out on the balcony. Their fanatical faces reminded William L. Shirer (then with Universal Service) of the crazed expressions on Holy Rollers in Louisiana.

The next morning Hitler appeared at the Luitpold arena, more as an object of reverence than as an orator. He entered dramatically, followed by Göring, Goebbels, Hess, Himmler and several aides, to the strains of the "Badenweiler March." After a stirring rendition of the *Egmont* Overture, Hess came forward and slowly read the names of those who had died in the 1923 Putsch. To the audience of 30,000, if not to the foreign correspondents, it was a moving experience. The most important words were spoken by Gauleiter Wagner, who read a proclamation of Hitler's in a voice so similar to the Führer's that some correspondents listening on the radio thought it was he. "The German form of life is definitely determined for the next thousand years," read out Wagner. "For us, the unsettled nineteenth century has finally ended. There will be no revolution in Germany for the next thousand years."

Intoxicated as he was by the almost constant ovation from admirers, Hitler was nevertheless nagged by anxiety. Many Brownshirts had brought their resentment and disillusionment to the festivities, and the possibility of an embarrassing or even dangerous episode made him so tense that occasionally his own resentment flared up. During one meal at the restaurant frequented by party officials he suddenly turned on Hans Frank. "You certainly annoyed me by delaying things on the thirtieth of June in Munich!" he exclaimed and, when Frank again offered to resign, cut him off impatiently. "In a few weeks this whole joke of state justice will end."

The Reich would command and Bavaria and the other states would obey, he said, then, after an uncomfortable silence, walked out.

In the rising excitement of the rally Hitler regained his mood of exultation. This was particularly evident on the evening of the seventh when 200,000 party faithful with more than 20,000 unfurled flags crowded into Zeppelin Field and lined up with military precision. The effect of Speer's 130 giant searchlights was more breath-taking than imagined. "The floodlit stadium gave the impression of a giant hall ringed by titanic gleaming white pillars," Speer recalled, "with an occasional cloud floating surrealistically through the majestic wall of light, like a translucent anemone drifting through the sea." In the awesome silence, Hitler's voice came across the field from loudspeakers with eerie effect. "We are strong and will get stronger!" he said, and made it as much a threat as a promise.

Leni Riefenstahl and her cameramen were filming the scene from a dozen angles, despite interference from officious Brownshirts who, at Goebbels' instigation and unbeknown to the Führer, kept harassing her cameramen, pushing them from the best vantage points and even dismantling several of their camera stations.

Hitler himself was threatened by possible SA reaction and was prepared to meet it when he faced 50,000 storm troopers en masse two days later. "There was considerable tension in the stadium," recalled Shirer, "and I noticed that Hitler's own S.S. bodyguard was drawn up in force in front of him, separating him from the mass of the brown-shirts." He wondered if one in the huge crowd would draw a revolver throughout the Führer's "carrot and club" harangue in which he finally absolved them all of complicity in Röhm's plot.

The session ended without incident, insuring the success of the concluding event on the following day, September 10. This was designated as Army Day and mobile units with the most modern equipment maneuvered flawlessly on the great meadow. It was the first public display of military might in Germany since the war and the audience of 300,000 was raised to a state of almost uncontrollable excitement at the sight of a realistic sham battle. Militarism, wrote Shirer in his diary, was not just a product of the Hohenzollerns. "It is rather something deeply ingrained in all Germans. They acted today like children playing with tin soldiers."

Hitler appeared to be as intoxicated as the crowd and after his final speech the cheering could not be quelled for some time. At last Hess could make himself heard and he bade farewell to the Führer on behalf of the NSDAP. "The party is Hitler," he said. "Hitler, however, is Germany just as Germany is Hitler. Heil Hitler! Sieg Heil! Sieg Heil! Sieg Heil Hitler!" The frenzied crowd joined in the chant of "Hail Victory!" It was exhilarating, inspiring, thrilling, but to those not under Hitler's spell it was bone-chilling, an animal roar, a shriek from the cave.

Nothing could have better symbolized the wedding of the Führer and the army and he decided to make a conciliatory gesture to the senior generals. After a tattoo held by massed bands in front of his hotel that evening, he invited them to dinner. "I know that you accuse me of many wrong things which exist in the party," he said, according to General von Weichs, who was taking word-by-word notes. "I admit that you are 100% correct, but you must remember that in the time of struggle, the intelligentsia deserted me, so that I still have to work primarily with personnel of low quality. I am constantly endeavoring to rectify this defect. But just as the construction of the officer corps for the new Armed Forces will take years to complete, so will the creation of a good corps of leaders for the party require even longer time." His words were effective for, as Weichs noted, "he knew how to fit his speech to his audience with masterful skill."

Later Hitler visited the soldiers' bivouac where he, the veteran corporal, mingled familiarly with the men, joking and reminiscing about old times. He returned to the hotel in a relaxed mood and, during a late snack with intimates, described the reunion in detail. It was a fitting end to the eventful week.

Hitler's high spirits were in evidence two days later at the reception in his honor at the presidential palace. All those diplomats who had been avoiding him were forced to be on hand to pay formal respects to the new president. Never had Ambassador Dodd seen him "quite so happy-looking as while he went down the line greeting the representatives of all foreign countries." Despite some annoyances and a few anxious moments, he had succeeded in accomplishing at Nuremberg what he had set out to do. The party was reunited, and the people and the armed forces were with him.

Nor had the memorial to the party been blighted by Goebbels' interference. Leni Riefenstahl and her cameramen came away with thousands of feet of extraordinary material. While the film was being edited she was deluged by protests from party leaders who had not been included or others who complained that there wasn't enough propaganda. When she refused to make any changes Hitler suggested a compromise: fit into the film pictures of the disgruntled leaders. This was an offense to Riefenstahl's artistic principles and she refused. Hitler just as heatedly persisted. According to her version, she stamped her foot and shouted, "I won't do it!" "Are you forgetting whom you are talking to?" he replied but such was her conviction and such was Hitler's appreciation of her talent that she completed the film without any changes. She did allow it to be called *Triumph of the Will* because she had no better title. At the premiere she was greeted coolly by party officials but even Goebbels, her greatest critic, realized it was an outstanding achievement and, in its way, far more effective propaganda for the Führer and National Socialism than any other film yet made. It was awarded the May Day "cultural achievement" award for best film of the year and was later recognized universally as one of the most important documentary films ever made, eventually winning a gold medal at the 1937 World Exhibition in Paris, for its artistry, if not its message.

2

There was gossip that Leni Riefenstahl was Hitler's mistress. This charge was as unfounded as those that he was sleeping with other famous actresses such as Olga Tschechowa, Lil Dagover and Pola Negri. It was not sex that Hitler sought from such charming women but the stimulation that his suppressed bohemian nature craved.

Unity Mitford, daughter of Lord Redesdale, had just come out in England. She was in Munich attending art classes and was caught in the excitement of the new Germany. From the moment Hitler kissed her hand she became a dedicated advocate of National Socialism. Hitler had never met anyone like this gay, irrepressible, golden-haired girl who would make the bluntest and most surprising remarks. Her freedom of expression, original outlook on life and lively humor, which she shared with her five sisters, was a new and refreshing experience to Hitler and his delight in her company soon generated a rumor—as unfounded as the others— that she was his mistress.

With Hitler's rise to power, he found an increasing number of women eager for his company. Perhaps it was his widening range of interest which soured his long-standing relationship with Frau Bechstein. She began to criticize him openly and upbraid him for some of his reforms. According to Friedelind Wagner, she would usually begin by asking the Führer if he were crazy and then shower him with such a deluge of abuse that he was unable to defend himself. "During these violent scoldings, Hitler would stand there like an abashed schoolboy who had committed a misdemeanor."

Eva Braun was even more distressed at Hitler's broadening horizon. A few days after he came to power he had given her a matching ring, earrings and bracelet of tourmalines for her twenty-first birthday. But this was no indication that he planned to marry his mistress. She saw less of him than before. Occasionally he would phone her from Berlin—usually from a public booth. To prevent her parents from finding out how intimate were her relations with the Führer, she had persuaded them to let her have a private phone in her bedroom. Whenever he came to Munich he would invite Eva to his apartment but in Berchtesgaden she stayed at some hotel for appearance's sake.

By the autumn of 1934 Eva was stricken with long spells of melancholy. She had no hope that Hitler would marry her. As head of the Third Reich, he told her, he must devote himself to the nation with no family distractions. He was, in fact, like the Pope. His excuse to Captain Wiedemann was more blunt. Yes, he confided one evening, he did miss family life but if he got married he would lose many female votes. "So," he concluded, "I have a girl at my disposal in Munich." Hitler was even more revealing to his secretary, Christa Schröder. "Eva is very nice," he said, "but, in my life, only Geli could have inspired in me genuine passion. I can never think of marrying Eva. The only woman I could have tied myself to for life would have been Geli."

Hitler's relationship with his sister-in-law from England was also becoming an embarrassment. Brigid Hitler, former wife of his half brother Alois, was in desperate financial straits and made a second effort to get some aid from her famous relative. She returned to Germany with her son William Patrick and approached Hitler in hopes he "might be willing to pay something to keep her quiet." Hitler invited mother and son to Berchtesgaden where the latter was astounded (so he told the OSS years later) to be "roundly upbraided" by the Führer's sister Angela, who repeated the fiction that Hitler "was not even his uncle."*

In the meantime Hitler was devoting much of his time to foreign policy. Since success in this field almost always depends on power, Hitler was doing his best to rearm the Reich overnight. Behind the smoke screen of the disarmament negotiations at Geneva he was hastily building up Germany's armed forces on every level. Heartened by public reaction to the impressive military display at Nuremberg, Hitler issued a secret order three weeks later trebling the size of the 100,000-man army. That same day 70,000 recruits were enrolled. The defense budget rose to 654 million marks.

The sudden activation of nine corps headquarters, fourteen infantry divisions and seven motorized combat battalions even under tight security generated alarming rumors of infringements of the Versailles Treaty. These, combined with a deterioration in Anglo-German relations, were a real concern to Hitler. It was becoming obvious, moreover, that Britain and France were moving closer to military unity in view of German expansion. On the other hand, there were indications that England was not ready to take any great risks. "No country, and especially not England," the private secretary to the British Foreign Secretary confided to Otto, Prince von Bismarck, that autumn, "would ever go to war for the interests of other nations outside its own territory." And since Hitler had no designs on the British Empire and his entire foreign policy was based on

* William Patrick Hitler eventually moved to America with his mother and served in the U. S. Navy during World War II. At present he lives in the New York metropolitan area under a different name and has a son, Adolf.

Britain's forbearance if not friendship, his campaign to win back their sympathy was straightforward.

One step in this courtship was a formal party on December 19. Of the twenty-five guests there were four from Britain—a well-known member of the Anglo-German Fellowship, Lord Rothermere and his son, and Ward Price, the editor of the *Daily Mail*, the most influential Rothermere newspaper. For the occasion Hitler wore full evening dress rather than the party uniform. As the guests sat down to a simple meal of roast chicken he said, "It is ten years today since I was released from prison at Landsberg." He told how almost the entire staff of the prison, including the chief warder, had been converted to National Socialism. "The Bavarian Government was furious, and sent most of the warders to the Police School as punishment. Before they had been there six months the place had become a National Socialist recruiting center, and had to be closed."

After dinner Hitler invited the non-smokers to accompany him to a special room. Lord Rothermere, along with Ribbentrop and some of the ladies, joined Hitler. He had been introduced to the newspaper magnate by the Princess Stephanie von Hohenlohe, a half Jew. What attracted Rothermere to Hitler was a common hatred of Bolshevism and several weeks later the *Daily Mail* roundly applauded when more than 90 per cent of the Saar electorate (at the urging of the Catholic Church) voted for union with Germany. Late in January 1935 Hitler received two more friendly guests from England: Lord Allen of Hurtwood, who brought a message of good will from Prime Minister Ramsay MacDonald; and the Marquess of Lothian, a left-wing liberal who became so impressed by Hitler's assurances of peaceful intentions that he helped persuade Foreign Secretary Sir John Simon of the Führer's sincerity.

Even France was relieved by the peaceful return of the Saar to Germany and formally presented to Germany a joint proposal for a general settlement which included equality of armaments and an Eastern Locarno.* Hitler replied cautiously on February 14 that he welcomed the armament negotiations but wouldn't it be better if Germany and England had preliminary discussions before the general talks?

Sir John Simon agreed to come to Berlin early the following month. The prospect of his visit at first generated an aura of optimism in the Berlin foreign community but on March 5 Shirer noted in his diary: "Something has gone wrong with the drive for a general settlement. Simon was supposed to arrive here day after tomorrow for his talks with the Germans, but this morning von Neurath told the British that Hitler had a cold and asked Simon to postpone his trip. A little investigation in the Wilhelmstrasse this afternoon revealed it's a *'cold diplomatique.'*"

* The crux of the agreements made at Locarno ten years earlier was a treaty of mutual guarantee binding the signatories to respect the frontiers between Germany, France and Belgium—including the demilitarized Rhineland.

The Führer had been provoked by publication of a British White Paper decrying the acceleration of the German arms program. What had particularly alarmed the English was the unbridled enthusiasm shown by the inhabitants of the Saar upon Hitler's arrival to help celebrate formal occupation of that contested territory.

Hitler made the next move in this diplomatic chess game on March 10 and did it by revealing exclusively to Price of the *Daily Mail* that the Luftwaffe had recently become an official branch of the armed forces. As Hitler hoped, there was no official outburst of condemnation from either England or France. Instead, Sir John Simon, who probably already had this information, informed Commons that he still planned to go to Berlin once the Führer recovered from his cold; the French reaction was merely a proposal from the War Ministry to extend the period of military service.

Hitler trumped this feeble rejoinder without benefit of counsel from his own generals. On the morning of March 15 he ordered his chief adjutant to meet him in Munich at the Four Seasons, the hotel which once had been the headquarters of Sebottendorf's anti-Semitic activities. He instructed the adjutant to announce the reintroduction of conscription and another enlargement of the armed forces. That evening the Reich Defense Council convened to discuss Hitler's disconcerting conscription plan. General von Blomberg's expressions of concern over possible reaction from the major powers were minimized by Ribbentrop: There was nothing at all to worry about. "What you say is all stuff and nonsense!" retorted Blomberg irritably, and continued throughout the night to attack the measure. But by the time he and Fritsch reported to Hitler next morning his objections had been stilled.

That afternoon, a Saturday, some hundred foreign correspondents crowded into the conference room of the Propaganda Ministry. Nobody knew why they had been called so suddenly and there was an air of excitement. At last Goebbels entered, "looking very important and grave," and read out in a loud voice the text of a new decree proclaiming universal military service and raising the peacetime army to 300,000 men. Although everyone had expected as much, it came as a shock. Lochner and several other correspondents raced for the telephones in the hall even while Goebbels was answering questions.

At that moment the French ambassador was getting the news first hand from the Führer in his study at the chancellery. François-Poncet protested that this notification was a flagrant violation of the Treaty of Versailles, and he expressed regret that Germany had presented France with a fait accompli without previous contact or discussion.

Hitler's confident, solemn retort was that his intentions were purely defensive. France had nothing to fear. His main enemy was Communism, he said, and launched into such a diatribe against the Russians that

François-Poncet left feeling almost confident that Hitler had no desire to wage war against either France or Britain—only the determination to destroy the Soviet regime.

The French answer to Germany's new show of power was a meaningless appeal to the League of Nations and on the morning of March 25 the official British delegation met Hitler in an atmosphere of amiability. Paul Schmidt, acting as the Führer's interpreter for the first time, noticed his smile was "especially friendly" when he greeted Sir John Simon, Anthony Eden and Ambassador Sir Eric Phipps. They grouped themselves around a low table at the Reich chancellery together with Neurath and Ribbentrop.

Simon announced that both the government and people of Britain wanted peace above all and earnestly wished Germany could co-operate with other European nations toward that objective. The British public, the decisive factor in England, he said, "was very disturbed" by such events as German "withdrawal from the League of Nations, Austria and certain unilateral announcements." England as a whole "was not at all anti-German, but she was strongly opposed to anything which was liable to disturb the peace."

"Hitler's reply," recalled Eden, who understood enough German to realize that Schmidt was interpreting ably, "was a skillful piece of special pleading which was none the less threatening in its undertones." In his second encounter, Eden was "most unfavorably impressed," by the Führer's personality. He seemed "negative to me, certainly not compelling," and was, moreover, "rather shifty." At the same time Eden admired the way Hitler conducted the meeting, "without hesitation and without notes, as befitted the man who knew where he wanted to go."

He explained each of his acts credibly without being convincing. He brushed off the accusation of violating the Versailles Treaty, for example, with the argument that he had never signed it. Fixing Sir John with his blue eyes, he added that he would rather have died than do so. Nor was Germany a violator of treaties—except at the time the Prussian army arrived to help the English during Waterloo. And on that occasion Wellington had made no protest. "This must have been the nearest to humour Hitler ever approached," observed Eden. "I thought it a good thrust, delivered without a flicker of a smile."

During the morning session Hitler astonished not only the British but his own interpreter by arguing calmly and politely. But after lunch he lost his poise when the subject of the proposed Eastern Pact, which involved Lithuania, arose. "We will have nothing whatever to do with Lithuania!" Hitler exclaimed. A conspiracy trial of minority Germans was presently in session there. His eyes blazed, his voice became hoarse and he rolled his r's. "In no circumstances shall we make a pact with a state which stamps upon the German minority in Memel!" he raged. In a moment the storm subsided and once more he was the polished negotiator. This time he argued against the pact on ideological grounds. "Between National Socialism and Bolshevism," he said quietly but with force, "any association is out of the question."

That evening at a banquet a relaxed Hitler engaged Eden in a lively discussion of their wartime experiences. They had fought opposite each other on the river Oise and together they drew a map of the battle lines on the back of a dinner card.* Some of the conversation was overheard by François-Poncet and after the meal he asked Eden if it was true he had fought Hitler. When Eden replied it seemed so, the French ambassador wryly remarked, "And you missed him? You ought to be shot." That night Eden wrote in his diary, "Results bad; whole tone and temper very different to a year ago, rearmed and rearming with the old Prussian spirit very much in evidence. Russia is now the bogey."

At ten the next morning Sir John proposed that they take up the key question of armaments. Britain, he said, had recently been engaged in separate discussions with other powers in preparation for a great naval armaments conference which would revise existing naval treaties. He invited Germany to take part in similar informal discussions in London. Hitler readily accepted. He repeated a previous offer to Ambassador Phipps to limit German tonnage to 35 per cent of that of the British fleet. At the same time he did not see "any heavenly or earthly authority" which could force him "to recognize the superiority of the French or Italian fleets."

At this point Hitler dramatically produced a telegram and began reading it with impassioned indignation. Again the abrupt change from moderate statesman to fanatic was startling. The message announced the guilty verdict on those minority Germans accused of treason in Lithuania. What would Britain do, asked Hitler angrily, if the Treaty of Versailles had ripped off part of her territory and turned it over to a country like Lithuania; what if Englishmen were then tortured and imprisoned merely because they acted like Englishmen?

His rage soon ran its course and he resumed his role as man of moderation, asking only for military parity with England and France. Refreshments were served at the British Embassy at noon. It was the second time the Führer had entered a foreign embassy. Afterward the conferees returned to the chancellery where Hitler complained about Soviet attempts to push westward and in this connection he scathingly referred to Czechoslovakia as "Russia's thrust-out arm." He also reiterated his demand for German equality of rights in armaments and Schmidt was impressed that Simon and Eden listened patiently and placidly. "Only two years ago the skies would have fallen if German representatives had put forward such demands as Hitler was now doing as though they were

* Winston Churchill fought nearby as a lieutenant colonel in the 6th Royal Scots Fusiliers from November 1915 to June 1916.

the most natural thing in the world. Nor could I help wondering whether Hitler had not got further with his method of the *fait accompli* than would have been possible with the Foreign Office method of negotiation."

That evening Hitler was host at a dinner in the chancellery. From his simple brown tunic and red swastika armband he had changed into tails. To his interpreter he was "a charming host, moving amongst his guests as easily as if he had grown up in the atmosphere of the great house." Afterward Hitler exulted over his diplomatic success to a party of friends, including Winifred Wagner. He slapped his knee and clapped hands like a schoolboy, she recalled. "Great fellows, the English," he said. "Even when they lie they do it on a magnificent scale, not a bit like the niggardly French."

The day after the talks Hitler told Chief of Naval Command Raeder about the 35 per cent ratio with England and instructed him to build up the navy according to plan—but with "no big public announcements, so as to avoid complicating England's difficult situation vis-à-vis the other Great Powers." Hitler was determined to work in harmony with the British and continued his courtship of those influential citizens who showed sympathy for Germany's plight. In April he gave a luncheon in his Munich apartment for Sir Oswald Mosley, who had resigned from the Labour Party to become leader of the British Union of Fascists. Mosley observed that Hitler's "hypnotic manner was entirely absent; perhaps I was an unsuitable subject; in any case, he made no attempt whatever to produce any effect of that kind. He was simple, and treated me throughout the occasion with a gentle, almost feminine charm."

In London a far more important adherent to the German cause was reaffirming earlier sympathies. The occasion was a long conversation between Ambassador Hoesch and the Prince of Wales, during which the heir to the throne "once again showed his complete understanding of Germany's position and aspirations."

3

In Berlin, preoccupation with the international scene was briefly overshadowed by preparation for the wedding of Hermann Göring and Emmy Sonnemann, an actress. (His first wife, Carin, had died after a long illness in 1931.) They were inundated with presents donated by organizations and individuals seeking favor. Museums sent paintings on permanent loan, the most valuable being two priceless oils by Cranach. In addition to oriental rugs, tapestries, silver candelabra and jewels were pepper cake from Saxony, Kirsch from the Black Forest, cheese and cattle. The smaller items were on display in the Berlin residence, the bulkier transported by truck to Karinhall, the country estate near the capital named after his first wife but misspelled.

The wedding on April 10 could have been produced in Hollywood, and a play-by-play account was given by radio to the nation. The pomposity of the ceremony—performed by a bishop and witnessed by the Führer himself—was relieved when two storks were observed circling around the Evangelical Cathedral. An irreverent flying comrade had swooped down and released them over the *Dom*. As the bride and groom left the church a military band thundered out the march from *Lohengrin*. Passing under a long arch of extended swords, they were greeted outside by ecstatic cheers and a mass Roman salute.

The next day Göring invited Lochner and five other correspondents to see the presents at the Minister President's palace. "Gentlemen," he told them, "I have asked you to come here in order that I may show you the gifts which *mein Volk* have given me. Just like Majesty, *nicht wahr?*" "Anyway," Lochner wrote to his daughter, "Göring need not starve. If he ever gets in a pinch, the hocking of all the gifts will bring in a million or more."

The Göring circus was relegated to the background that same day when the British, French and Italians opened their conference at Stresa. Contrary to Hitler's expectations that French suggestions would not win the support of the other two powers, the meeting led to the issuance of a joint communiqué condemning Germany's illegal rearmament and reaffirming loyalty to the principles of Locarno. The presence of Laval, MacDonald and Mussolini gave force to the announcement. Hitler, hoping to isolate the French, found himself in danger of being isolated himself. This was emphasized several weeks later by a Franco-Soviet pact of mutual assistance, which was so unsettling to the Führer's basic strategy that he made new efforts to reassure his friend Lord Rothermere that England had no reason at all to fear the Reich. From the earliest days of the party, Hitler wrote on May 3, he had envisaged co-operation with Great Britain. "Such an agreement between England and Germany would represent the weighty influence for peace and common sense of 120,000,-000 of the most valuable people in the world. The historically unique colonial aptitude and the naval power of Britain would be combined with that of one of the first military nations of the world."

While Rothermere needed no convincing and continued to present a picture of a benign Germany in his papers, the general reaction in England was one of apprehension. When the MacDonald government leaders learned that Hitler would make a major political announcement after mid-May, they became concerned enough to schedule a Commons debate on rearmament to follow it.

The dreaded speech was delivered on May 21 and once more Hitler surprised the world. Earlier in the day he had promulgated a secret defense law which placed Schacht in charge of war economy and reorganized the armed forces: The Reichswehr officially became the Wehrmacht

(Armed Forces) and Hitler was named its supreme commander; Blomberg's title was changed from Minister of Defense to Minister of War and he was given the title of commander-in-chief of the armed forces; and Beck's unrevealing title of *Chef des Truppenamtes* was changed to Chief of the General Staff. In private at least, a spade was being called a spade but when Hitler faced the microphone that evening, relaxed and confident, he was the model of moderation. His chief aim was peace nor had he any dream of conquest. All war ever did, he proclaimed, was destroy the flower of the nation.

After reiterating that "Germany needs peace and desires peace," he offered to make bilateral non-aggression pacts with all his neighbors (perfidious Lithuania excepted, of course!) and promised to observe the Locarno Treaty. All he wanted was a fleet 35 per cent the size of Britain's navy. That, he promised, would be the end of his demands. "For Germany," he vowed, "this demand is final and abiding."

In many influential quarters abroad his words were taken at face value, the London *Times* calling his address "reasonable, straightforward and comprehensive." In a stroke Hitler had reversed the trend of isolation and prepared the way for a sympathetic reception of German demands at the forthcoming naval conference. It opened exactly two weeks later at the British Foreign Office with Joachim von Ribbentrop as head of the German delegation. He seated himself at the conference table armed with good advice from the Japanese naval attaché in London. Captain Arata Oka informed his German counterpart that the Japanese had come to the Washington Conference in 1921 under the false impression that one could make "a deal" with the English. "Consequently we were unprepared when the English quickly drove a wedge between our diplomats and our naval experts, separating them into almost hostile groups." He recommended that the Germans concentrate on one clear demand—such as the 35 per cent ratio—and hold to it tenaciously even if it threatened to wreck the conference. Once the English realized the Germans were firm they would slowly give in—and have greater respect for their antagonists.

Simon opened the session at 10 A.M. with his usual amiability, pointing out that it was the task of the conferees to prepare the ground for the forthcoming conference of all major naval powers; otherwise the armaments race would continue at a greater pace. It was not enough to limit tonnage; certain types of dangerous vessels, for example, should be eliminated.

Following Oka's advice, Ribbentrop refused to discuss anything but Germany's demand for a 35 per cent ratio. "If the British government does not immediately accept this condition," he said, "there is no point at all in continuing these negotiations. We must insist upon an immediate decision." Once the British accepted this ratio, he promised, the technical details regarding the program of naval construction could be settled promptly.

Schmidt was interpreting, though Ribbentrop spoke good English, and was startled that his principal had immediately brought up—and so undiplomatically!—the most difficult question on the agenda. Schmidt wondered if it was Ribbentrop's lack of experience or blind obedience to instructions. What Ribbentrop was doing, besides following Oka's shrewd advice, was to implement the disconcerting tactic that Hitler had been using so successfully for years. The speech a fortnight ago was the carrot, this was the club.

As Schmidt translated Ribbentrop's words, he could see Simon flush. It was not usual, he replied stiffly, to make such conditions at the beginning of negotiations and he could, of course, make no statement on the subject. So saying, he bowed frigidly and left the room. After a moment's embarrassment Sir Robert Craigie took Simon's place and firmly presented Britain's objections. But the dogged Ribbentrop could not be moved. They met again in the afternoon without progress and Schmidt was sure the talks had been torpedoed. He had begun to wonder what the weather would be like on the flight to Berlin when, to his surprise, the British suggested they meet again next morning, this time in the historic board room of the Admiralty.

It was a large paneled chamber dominated by a long table surrounded by red leather chairs. Schmidt's surprise at the friendly atmosphere was raised to astonishment ("I scarcely believed my own ears") when the redoubtable Craigie opened the proceedings with the announcement that the British were prepared to meet Herr von Ribbentrop's demands. Complete victory was achieved the next day, June 6, when Sir John returned, beaming as if nothing had happened. Full agreement was reached so amicably that Ribbentrop, dropping his "rather awkward manner," became outright sociable. The British not only allowed Germany to fix her naval tonnage at 35 per cent of their own fleet but conceded a 45 per cent ratio for submarines. Ribbentrop returned to Germany as a conquering hero. The attainment of all of Germany's secret naval aims by negotiation had transformed Hitler from a man of force to a statesman. France, stunned at such unilateral action (made incidentally on the anniversary of Waterloo) by a so-called ally, sent an angry note to London but British public opinion was almost universally favorable and (except for Winston Churchill, who damned the agreement as damaging British security) even those politicians generally hostile to Hitler supported the agreement.

The Prince of Wales, predictably, was pleased by the pact and on the day of its signing reported to Ambassador Hoesch (the occasion was a luncheon with the Queen at Ascot) that his own enthusiastic approval of contact between German and British veterans, made recently in a controversial speech, had been done "entirely on his own initiative." (He didn't mention that his father had reprimanded him for it. "How often have I told you, my dear boy, never to mix in politics, especially where foreign matters are concerned. The views you expressed yesterday, however sensible, are, I happen to know, contrary to those of the Foreign Office." Never must he again speak on such controversial matters without consulting the government. The royal rebuke, while disturbing, had not inhibited the Prince, who promptly made another controversial speech attacking the London County Council for banning the use of weapons, including wooden guns, in the Cadet Corps of the schools within their jurisdiction.) The Prince of Wales added that "the timidity and hesitation which, as is well known, were characteristic of politicians, were much slower in achieving results than a frank word spoken at the right moment, even though it might exceed the bounds of reserve normally maintained." His remarks were sent by airgram to the Wilhelmstrasse where they gave impetus to the exaggerated views of pro-German feelings in England and contributed to the Führer's unwarranted assumption that from now on there would be no limit to British concessions.

The Soviet Union reacted almost as violently to the London pact as the French. It confirmed suspicions that elements of Britain's ruling class, including the heir to the throne, were helping Germany strengthen its navy in the Baltic Sea for an attack on the U.S.S.R. while supporting Japanese ambitions in the Far East. Despite such apprehensions the Soviets signed a new trade treaty with Hitler, who advanced their credit to 200 million marks and was preparing to boost that figure to 500 million over a ten-year period. This was no abandonment of his dream of Lebensraum but another devious move in the international game of diplomacy. For, while he talked peace with the West and did business with the East, rearmament in Germany continued as secretly as possible at a rate exceeding the estimates of most foreign observers.

4

As the political life of Adolf Hitler expanded so did his personal life. Two inner circles had formed around him—one composed of top associates like Goebbels, Göring, Hess (and their wives) and another on a more personal level: the chauffeurs, secretaries, servants and other intimates. This innermost circle, which included such disparate members as an architect, Speer, and a pilot, Baur, was also taking in some of the younger military adjutants, like Navy Lieutenant von Puttkamer and the representative of the Luftwaffe, Nikolaus von Below. A few belonged to both circles. The most notable was Martin Bormann, who had been working for Hess since the early days and now, as his representative in Berlin, was given the opportunity of assiduously devoting himself to the daily needs of the Führer. Although unknown to most Germans, the indefatigible Bormann had become Hitler's shadow, remaining at his shoulder most of the day ready to jot down on cuff or notebook his slightest whim.

Hitler himself moved easily between the two circles as well as among a constellation of top military and civilian circles. What he could not do was conduct the affairs of high office in a businesslike manner. A night person, he usually arrived at his desk shortly before noon. He would glance through the press dispatches that Otto Dietrich had selected for him and then rush off to lunch. Upon returning, he would postpone matters that bored him to retire in privacy and consider those that did not. For hours he would discuss the rebuilding of Berlin, Munich and Linz with architects Speer and Giesler, while State Secretary Hans Lammers and Otto Meissner, whom the Führer had inherited from Hindenburg, impatiently waited for decisions that only the head of state could make.

His working methods were a constant concern to Captain Wiedemann. Rarely could his personal adjutant get him to read a file before making an important decision. "He was of the opinion," wrote Wiedemann, "that many matters took care of themselves as long as one didn't stir them up. And he was not often wrong about this. The question was merely how such matters took care of themselves." He was similarly bohemian in his selection of visitors. Some officials would wait for days in the anteroom but if an acquaintance of the old days showed up he was as likely as not to be invited at once to lunch where he could voice problems which were often solved on the spot.

Preoccupation with the international scene disrupted Hitler's already erratic schedule and consequently he found almost no time for his mistress. The love of Adolf Hitler had become Eva Braun's whole life, even though he had made it plain that they could never marry while he was Führer of the Reich. "For me marriage would have been a disaster," he explained to his inner circle seven years later. "There's a point at which misunderstanding is bound to arise between man and wife; it's when the husband cannot give his wife all the time she feels entitled to demand." A woman lived only for her husband's sake and expected him to live for hers. Whereas the man, a slave to his thoughts, was ruled by duty. "I'd have had nothing of marriage but the sullen face of a neglected wife, or else I'd have skimped my duties. . . . The bad side of marriage is that it creates rights. In that case, it's far better to have a mistress. The burden is lightened, and everything is placed on the level of a gift." Noting the crestfallen expressions on the faces of his two middle-aged spinster secretaries, Johanna Wolf and Christa Schröder, he hastily added, "What I've said applies only to men of a higher type of course!"

Eva had sunk into a deep depression that was momentarily relieved by one of her lover's rare visits. "Yesterday he came quite unexpectedly," she wrote in her diary on February 18, "and it was a delightful evening. . . . I am so endlessly happy that he loves me so much, and pray that it will always be so." Within two weeks she wrote: "I am again deathly unhappy. Since I cannot write him, this diary has to be the depository of all my tales of woe." He came on Saturday but after spending "a few wonderful hours" with her he left and sent no word when he would return. "I am sitting on hot coals thinking every moment he might come."

A week later she wrote disjointedly as if in great haste or under emotional stress:

> I wish that I were very sick since I have not heard from him for 8 days. Why doesn't something happen to me, why do I have to go through all this. I wish I had never seen him. I am desperate. Now I am buying sleeping pills, at least I will be half dazed and don't think about it so much any more. . . . Why does he torment me like this and not just put an end to the whole thing.

A few days later she made excuses for him: he had "so much to do politically." But her resolve to "wait patiently" dissolved even though he invited her to the Four Seasons Hotel.

> I had to sit next to him for 3 hours without being able to say a word. At parting he handed me, as he did once before an envelope with money. How nice it would have been if he had written a greeting or a nice word with it, it would have made me so happy. But he does not think of such things.

By the end of the month loneliness turned to bitter jealousy upon hearing gossip that Hitler had found another woman, nicknamed the Walküre.

> . . . I think it is unconscionable for him not to tell me. He should know me well enough to realize that I would never get in his way if he suddenly discovered his heart belonged to another.

In desperation she sent him a letter late that May which was an entreaty of sorts. Then she wrote in her diary:

> . . . If I don't have an answer by 10 tonight, I will simply take my 25 pills and gently slumber to the other side.
> Is this the enormous love he so often promised me when he doesn't send me a comforting word in three months?
> Granted that he has had his head full these days with political problems, but there must be time for some relaxation. What about last year? Didn't Röhm and Italy give him a lot to handle and still he found time for me. . . .
> I am afraid there is something else behind it.
> I am not to blame. Certainly not.
> Maybe it is another woman—but not the Walküre girl, that is not plausible; but there are so many others.
> What other grounds could there be? Can't find any.

A few hours later she made a final pitiful entry:

Dear God, I am so afraid he won't answer today.* If only someone would help me, everything is so terribly hopeless. Perhaps my letter reached him at an inopportune time. Perhaps I shouldn't have written at all.

Whatever the case, this uncertainty is harder to bear than a sudden end.

Dear God, please help me so that I can speak to him today. Tomorrow will be too late.

What Eva Braun did not know was that at the time Hitler received her letter of desperation he was undergoing an operation. For some months he had been troubled by a sore throat. His voice, abused by numerous speeches of interminable length delivered in all kinds of weather, had become hoarse and discovery of a growth on his larynx revived an old fear; for months, according to Speer, he had been talking of Emperor Frederick III, who died of throat cancer. The throat irritation was accompanied by stomach pains—perhaps similar to those he suffered as a youth in Vienna—for which he took Neo-Balestol. Apparently he took excessive amounts of the drug, which contained fusel oil, and at least once he was so stricken with a form of intoxication that he summoned Dr. Grawitz to complain of headache, vertigo, buzzing in the ears and seeing double. On May 23, two days after his important foreign policy speech, Professor Karl van Eicken, head of Berlin University's otolaryngology department, removed a one-centimeter polyp from the Führer's vocal cord. It was an easy operation which took place in Hitler's chancellery apartment, requiring only a small amount of morphine as a sedative. Even so Hitler slept deeply for fourteen hours. "I was quite concerned," Eicken later revealed. After the operation Eicken warned him to speak softly for a few days, and in the future not to let his emotions "lead him to shout and scream loudly. . . . He admitted he had been told that before, but forgot himself during a speech.†

Eicken assured his patient that what he had removed was a "simple polyp," that is, a small benign growth. But Hitler still worried that he might have cancer like his mother. Perhaps his absorption by morbid doubts (and the affairs of state) might explain why he had not bothered to answer Eva's letter of desperation or instructed an aide to phone a few words of consolation.

Feeling hopeless and abandoned, she swallowed twenty tablets of Vanoform, a narcotic, in the early hours of May 29. She was found in a coma by her sister Ilse. After administering first-aid treatment, learned while working as a receptionist for a surgeon, she phoned her employer, Dr. Martin Marx, whose discretion she trusted. While he was treating Eva

* The translation of the diary in the National Archives is crude: *"Mein Gott"* in this sentence, for example, emerges as "Goddammit."

† From November 14, 1938, issue of *Time*, which also reported that Hitler had previously requested Professor Heinrich von Neumann of Vienna, the world's foremost otolaryngologist, to examine his larynx. Neumann, an Orthodox Jew, refused.

she found the notebook containing the diary. Determined to keep the second suicide attempt a secret, she ripped out the incriminating pages so as not to involve Dr. Marx, a Jew. Ilse also feared her father might react violently and the Führer might question the mental stability of his mistress; she suggested the suicide was part theater. After all, Eva had only taken twenty pills of a type milder than Veronal—aware that one of her sisters would say good night to her after returning home.

Dr. Marx obligingly recorded the case as excessive fatigue resulting in an overdose of narcotics. Hitler accepted this explanation (although Ilse Braun remains convinced that he had guessed the truth). In any case the "accident" accomplished what words of entreaty had not. That summer he found Eva a place of her own. On August 9, 1935, she and her younger sister, Gretl, moved into a three-room apartment in the quiet residential Bogenhausen section—a short walk from the Führer's Munich apartment. He paid the rent indirectly through Hoffmann and furnished the place with furniture bought on sale.

The master of the establishment was seldom there, and when he did come it was after the neighbors were asleep. Even then his trysts with Eva were scarcely private since secret police kept watch on the stairs and outside the building. Moreover, his larynx was still bothering him and he was continually clearing his throat loudly. He consulted a doctor at Berchtesgaden the day before Eva moved into her new flat and complained that some foreign body was in his throat. While accepting a bouquet from an admirer, a thorn had impaled itself under a fingernail, and he feared he'd swallowed the thorn inadvertently after withdrawing it with his teeth. The doctor found nothing and simply brushed Hitler's pharynx with a 2½ per cent solution of silver nitrate but the patient expressed renewed concern about cancer to Professor van Eicken, who submitted a series of preparations (calling his patient Adolf Müller) to a colleague at the university. Finally on August 21 came confirmation that "Adolf Müller" had nothing to fear; the polyp *was* benign.

Hitler's anxiety was eased—at least for the moment—but he still found little time to visit Eva, involved as he was in preparations for the forthcoming Nuremberg Party Day of 1935. Moreover, his nocturnal visits to Eva's apartment were occasioning rumors that could damage him politically. Eva's new-found freedom had raised another problem. Her father felt disgraced at an illicit relationship, even one with the Führer of all Germany. On September 7 Fritz Braun nerved himself and sent a letter urging Hitler to return his Eva "to the bosom of her family." Braun was prudent enough to have Hoffmann deliver the letter in person, and the photographer with even more prudence turned it over to Eva. She tore it up but gave her father the impression that the Führer had read it without deigning to reply. A similar letter was written by Frau Braun, unbeknownst to her husband, and sent directly to Hitler. It was never answered.

Hitler's first major speech at Nuremberg came on September 11. It turned from a plea for cultural development into another attack on Jews. He charged that they had never produced an art that was characteristically their own and never would. It was such a mild rebuke that foreign observers wondered if it was true that his anti-Semitic program was being muted as reassurance to the other Great Powers. On the contrary, the growing agitation in the West for a boycott of German goods had convinced him that the time had come to enact some of those legal measures against Jews which had been suggested in his first recorded anti-Semitic declaration almost exactly sixteen years earlier. On September 13 he ordered that a decree be drafted within forty-eight hours under the title "The Law for the Protection of German Blood and Honor."

No sooner had those assigned this task completed a draft prohibiting marriages and extramarital intercourse between Jews and citizens of "German or related blood" than a messenger arrived with new orders from Hitler. They were also to write up a Reich citizenship law. The harried authors soon ran out of paper and were reduced to using old menu cards. It was 2:30 A.M., September 15, by the time it was agreed that only those of "German or related blood" could be citizens.

The other provisions were acceptable and at 9 P.M. Hitler addressed an extraordinary session of the Reichstag in Nuremberg. Passage of these laws, he said, was actually to the advantage of the Jews. It might possibly "create a level ground on which the German people may find a tolerable relation towards the Jewish people." These moderate words were immediately followed by threatening ones: "Should this hope not be fulfilled and the Jewish agitation both within Germany and abroad continue, then the position must be examined afresh."

5

Fortunately for Hitler, the attention of the world was suddenly turned from this new assault on the rights of Jews as well as his illegal expansion of the Wehrmacht by a foolish act of Benito Mussolini, his onetime model. On the third of October Italy invaded Ethiopia. Moral indignation was almost universal. How could a civilized nation attack a weak foe forced to battle planes and tanks with tribesmen on horseback? Britain and America, with conveniently short memories of their own pacification programs, were particularly abusive, and the former led the campaign in the League of Nations to invoke limited economic sanctions against Italy. Despite numerous anti-Italian and pro-Ethiopian sympathizers in Germany, Hitler publicly refused to help Emperor Haile Selassie, while secretly sending him some military aid. At the same time Hitler gave Mussolini raw materials so as to embroil Italy (and, hopefully, England) in a debilitating campaign that would leave Germany more freedom of action. His public support of Il Duce was also a test case to see how Britain would react to German defiance of the League of Nations. It was soon evident that the English would do nothing in reprisal and this must have strengthened his conviction that they were going to come to an agreement with him.

Hitler went into seclusion to regain control of the situation and himself. He was not seen in public during the last four weeks of autumn; Rosenberg assumed that the Führer was ill but it was just as likely that he was suffering one of his pre-Christmas moods of despondency. What is more, he was faced with another crucial, and unpleasant, decision that involved the future of the NSDAP and the course of National Socialism itself. Hitler had reached his Rubicon. While he and the party had gained control over all aspects of public life in Germany, the Brown Revolution remained at a standstill. He had let everything in the domestic scene slide at the expense of foreign policy and was reacting rather than initiating. Public interest in the party as a consequence was at a low level. There were fewer applications for membership and the members themselves were showing less devotion to party activities.

On the third day of January 1936 Hitler summoned his Gauleiters and Reichsleiters to a conference in hopes this group could reconcile the issues that had arisen. He opened his talk with the full revelation of the plans to rearm the nation, hinted at the grand future he envisioned for Germany and then, with an air of desperation reminiscent of the black days of late 1932 when the party seemed about to split apart, begged his listeners to realize that all this could not be achieved unless the party leadership "formed a single community, loyal to him." This plea was followed by an emotional demand for absolute devotion, which was succeeded—as in 1932—by a threat to kill himself. The audience was stunned and Chairman Hess promptly assured Hitler that everyone in the room would follow him wherever he went with unquestioning loyalty.

The Führer's spirits were abruptly revitalized and by mid-January he was prepared to take his next step forward—seizure of the demilitarized Rhineland zone which encompassed all German territory west of the Rhine as well as a thirty-mile strip east of the river that included Cologne, Düsseldorf and Bonn. He was heartened in this ambition by the death of a monarch. On the evening of January 20 King George V died and was succeeded by Edward VIII, a man of individuality and independence who had made no secret of his sympathies with many of Germany's aspirations. In his first broadcast as King he made it clear that he would not change. Confirmation came the following day from Washington when Ambassador Hans Luther cabled the Wilhelmstrasse that the chief of the Western European Affairs Division of the U. S. State Department had recently been informed by the new King in an "extremely frank" conversation that he "disapproved of France's efforts to revive the *entente cordiale* and to hitch Britain to the French wagon. . . . He further deprecated the French desire to force Germany to her knees and declared that he had much sympathy for Germany's difficult position." In three talks with the King during his first month of reign the Duke of Coburg got personal reassurance from Edward. "To my question whether a discussion between [Prime Minister] Baldwin and Adolf Hitler would be desirable for future German-British relations," reported the duke, "he replied in the following words: 'Who is King here? Baldwin or I? I myself wish to talk to Hitler, and will do so here or in Germany. Tell him that please.'"

Such encouraging words from England, together with the weak half measures of the League of Nations against Italian aggression, strengthened the Führer's resolve to reoccupy the Rhineland. If England could not even bring herself to make an all-out effort to check Mussolini, surely she would never do more than formally protest if he followed in Il Duce's footsteps. On February 12 he summoned his chargé d'affaires in Paris for a conference regarding possible French reactions to remilitarization of the Rhineland. That same afternoon he spoke to General von Fritsch about military action. The army chief of staff was not at all enthusiastic. Why not negotiate? Hitler argued that a conference would take weeks and explained that he was only thinking of a symbolic operation. How long would it take to put nine battalions of infantry and some artillery into the Rhineland? Two days, said Fritsch, but warned that it should not be undertaken if there was the slightest risk of war.

Hitler agreed in principle but recalled his ambassador to Italy, Ulrich von Hassell, and said he was "at present considering an extremely far-reaching question." Should Germany take the Paris ratification of the Franco-Russian pact as grounds for denouncing the Locarno Treaty and stationing troops in the Rhineland? At that point, according to Hassell's official memorandum, the Führer revealed that until then he had always envisaged the spring of 1937 as the right moment to seize the Rhineland but political developments made him wonder whether the psychological moment had not already arrived. "He was now asking himself whether he should not approach Mussolini with the suggestion that he, for his part, should make use of the violation of the Locarno obligations, which the inclusion of Russia represented, as a pretext for denouncing the Pact, whereupon Germany would follow suit."

In any case Hitler had just about made up his mind to act in the near future even while assuring the French of his peaceful intentions. "Is it not plainly to the advantage of both our countries to keep on good terms?" he told journalist Bertrand de Jouvenel on February 21. "I wish to succeed in making a *détente* with France . . . It is extraordinary that you should still consider German aggression possible." Those Frenchmen who were tranquilized by such words should have heeded the significance of the Führer's subsequent answer to Jouvenel's criticism of certain Francophobic passages in *Mein Kampf:* "You want me to revise my book as if I were a writer preparing a new edition. But I am not a writer. I am a politician. . . . I enter my revision into the great book of history!"

It was not until the following day that Ambassador von Hassell informed Mussolini of the Führer's grave concern about possible ratification of the Franco-Soviet pact. Mussolini replied that, while he disapproved of this treaty, it did not concern Italy directly. At least it was an indication that Mussolini would stand aloof if Germany denounced the Locarno Treaty, and so the Führer gave the word to set in motion Operation Winter Exercise. On March 2 Blomberg issued preparatory orders to the chiefs of the three services to transfer units on Z-Day (D-Day) into the demilitarized Rhineland zone. Three days later Blomberg fixed Z-Day as the seventh of March, a Saturday. The stage was set but for some reason Hitler lost his nerve and asked his Wehrmacht adjutant, Colonel Friedrich Hossbach, if the operation could still be stopped. The answer was yes. Hitler's next words were even more revealing: Find out the very latest moment Winter Exercise can be called off.

By that afternoon Foreign Secretary Eden had returned to London. He reported to the cabinet in the evening that the French wished to invoke their authority over the Rhineland. "To the British people this was a much more doubtful cause," he observed in his memoirs. "There was not one man in a thousand in the country at the time prepared to take physical action with France against a German occupation of the Rhineland."

It was indeed France, not England, that concerned the Führer, and he was unable to "sleep a wink" that night. "Again and again," he later confided to Hoffmann, "I asked myself the same question: What will France do? Will she oppose the advance of my handful of battalions? I know what I would have done, if I'd been the French: I should have struck and I would not have allowed a single German soldier to cross the Rhine."

On Friday, Z-Day minus one, it was announced that the Reichstag would meet the following noon and the diplomatic community in Berlin guessed something momentous was afoot. That evening reporters and photographers of the leading German newspapers were invited to a conference in the Ministry of Propaganda. The mystified journalists were informed by Goebbels that they were to be taken on a journey next morning so secret that they were being held in custody until then. For the second straight night the Führer tossed sleeplessly on his simple white iron bed, fretting over the possible course of France. England did not worry him; he had selected Saturday to move since no English officials would be in their offices. "They will only be back on Monday," he told Wiedemann, "and by then the excitement will be over!"

Early on Saturday morning the special press group was driven to Tempelhof where a Junkers transport was waiting. When the plane took off the reporters still had no idea where they were going. The pilot himself did not know his destination; at a specified time he was to open a sealed envelope that would direct him to the Rhineland.

At 10 A.M. the German ambassador called on Eden. After some discussion regarding another Anglo-German naval agreement, Hoesch abruptly said: "I have a communication of very great importance to make. I am afraid that the first part of it will not be to your taste, but the later portions contain an offer of greater importance than has been made at any time in recent history." He began to read a memorandum charging that the Franco-Soviet pact violated the Treaty of Locarno. Consequently Germany was taking back the demilitarized zone of the Rhineland. Hoesch hurriedly read on that Hitler offered to sign separate non-aggression pacts with Eastern countries as well as those in the West. He also was willing to re-enter the League of Nations.

Eden expressed deep regret over the Rhineland move but said he would give careful consideration to the German proposals. Her attitude toward the League, he added, was most important. At this point Hoesch said he must make it clear that there were no conditions attached to his country's return to the League, then added casually that as for the Rhineland only a few small German detachments would move into that zone. Once Hoesch left, Eden summoned the French ambassador to express his deep regret at Germany's action. The denunciation of Locarno was "deplorable," said Eden, but it would require consideration by the British cabinet. This could not be done until Monday since most of its members were at their country homes.

After short interviews with the Italian and Belgian representatives, Eden telephoned Prime Minister Baldwin and then set off at once for Chequers to brief him. "Though personally friendly to France," recalled Eden, "he was clear in his mind that there would be no support in Britain for any military action by the French. I could only agree. I told him of the earnestness with which Hitler had spoken to me of Locarno. I could not believe him anymore." Neither did Baldwin but he agreed all they could do was await the French reaction.

At about 11:30 A.M. the Junkers carrying the German press landed at Cologne and half an hour later the reporters were standing with thousands of other patriotic Germans at the Hohenzollern Bridge which stretched across the Rhine. Here eighteen years earlier dejected German soldiers had retreated from France, leaving their guns behind. Suddenly the crowd could hear the tramp of feet, the rumble of iron-clad wheels and the clop of horses' hoofs. There was fervent cheering as the first soldiers moved onto the bridge. Other units were crossing at least five other bridges as a handful of fighter planes flew cover overhead. Only three of the nineteen infantry battalions in Operation Winter Exercise crossed the Rhine but the fervor (for Germans) and fear (for French) inspired by this handful of troops was momentous.

At the Kroll Opera House Hitler was addressing the Reichstag. He had been greeted with tremendous applause, except from the diplomatic section, and his words were received with rapt attention. The UP correspondent, Richard Helms, a recent graduate of Williams College, was watching Hitler "like a hawk." After a long preamble on the inequities of the Treaty of Versailles and the dire need for Lebensraum, the Führer's delivery seemed to slow down. He began nervously passing a handkerchief from hand to hand behind the lectern. He was unnaturally pale and seemed under a strain. Then in a low, controlled voice he announced, "At this moment, German troops are marching."

The opera house went berserk.

The three battalions were, in fact, across the Rhine—with orders to stage a fighting withdrawal if challenged by French troops.

Part 5

WAR IN MASQUERADE

"Such subtle covenants shall be made
Till peace itself is war in masquerade."

Dryden

Chapter Fourteen

"WITH THE ASSURANCE OF A SLEEPWALKER" MARCH 1936–JANUARY 1937

1

London never seriously considered taking action when German soldiers marched into the Rhineland on that Saturday morning, March 7, 1936. From Berlin François-Poncet urged "energetic reaction." Perhaps this sparked a spirit of resistance in the French government, which called on its General Staff to act. Like most such groups, it was conservative to the point of timidity. General Gamelin warned that "a war operation, however limited, entailed unpredictable risks and could not be undertaken without decreeing a general mobilization." He did agree to rush thirteen divisions to the Maginot Line.

A pusillanimous gesture, it panicked Gamelin's opposite number in Berlin. On Sunday morning General von Blomberg begged Hitler to at least withdraw troops from Aachen, Trier and Saarbrücken. If the French attacked, he said, the Germans would have to pull back without a battle, thus suffering a moral and military defeat of the first order. Hitler remained resolute despite misgivings. He told Blomberg to wait. If necessary they could retreat tomorrow. Nor did he waver when the French Premier broadcast a message of stern defiance: Never would France negotiate while Strasbourg was threatened by German guns.

By Monday more than 25,000 German troops, greeted by censer-swinging priests conferring blessings on them, were established in the

Rhine zone. While there were still only words from the French, Hitler was consumed by anxiety. He couldn't, he later confessed, endure another such strain for ten years. "The forty-eight hours after the march into the Rhineland," he told his interpreter, "were the most nerve-racking in my life." If the French had retaliated "we would have had to withdraw with our tails between our legs, for the military resources at our disposal would have been wholly inadequate for even a moderate resistance." He made a triumphal tour of the reoccupied area without incident and on the trip back home in his special train relaxed. "Good Lord, am I relieved how smoothly everything went!" he said and turned boastful from relief. "Yes, the world belongs to the courageous. God helps him." He asked that a record of Wagner's *Parsifal* be played and, as he listened, remarked that he had built his religion out of that opera. "You can serve God only as a hero," he said.

In Paris the Locarno powers convened with results so inconclusive that French Foreign Minister Flandin flew to London for help. The attitude there was typified by Lord Lothian's remark: "The Germans, after all, are only going into their own back garden." Neville Chamberlain, being groomed to succeed Baldwin as Prime Minister, emphasized to Flandin that public opinion was against enforcing any sanctions and then wrote in his diary, "His view is that, if a firm front is maintained by France and England, Germany will yield without war. We cannot accept this as a reliable estimate of a mad dictator's reaction."

Surprisingly, this general feeling of helplessness was overridden the very next day, March 12, when the Council of the League of Nations met in London and unanimously passed a resolution condemning Germany as a treaty-breaker. This occasioned an alarmist telegram to Berlin from the three Wehrmacht attachés. Blomberg rushed with it to the Führer, who jammed the message into his pocket without reading it. He refused to consider Blomberg's pleas to make concessions and gruffly told him to refrain in the future from attempting to influence political matters. Policy, he said, was made in the Reich chancellery and not in the War Ministry. His Foreign Minister was far more bellicose than the generals. Neurath opposed any concessions at all, advising the Führer to await official reactions abroad before pulling out of the Rhineland.

This was the advice taken by Hitler, who then told an audience in Munich, "I go the way that Providence dictates with the assurance of a sleepwalker." Within hours word came from Ribbentrop in London that the crisis was over and Eden seemed interested only in negotiations.

The Führer was ecstatic. What would have happened if anybody else had been Germany's leader at that time? he later boasted to his inner circle. "Anyone you care to mention would have lost his nerve. I was obliged to lie, and what saved us was my unshakable aplomb. I threatened unless the situation eased in twenty-four hours to send six extra divisions into the Rhineland. In fact, I only had four brigades."

Holding the weakest hand in the game, Hitler had bluffed England and France, proof that words of condemnation from international bodies were futile without force behind them. At the same time he had learned that his own political instincts were sounder than those of his generals. It was a victory of far-reaching import, reinforcing faith in his own destiny. He had discovered how far a resolute man, unafraid of using force, could go against adversaries terrified by the thought of another world war.

He was also shrewd enough to capitalize on the Rhineland to further solidify his power at home. He dissolved the Reichstag and submitted this policy to plebiscite. Rather than an election campaign, it was a triumphal parade from city to city with the majestic new dirigible, *Hindenburg*, painted all over with swastikas, flying escort overhead. "I have not usurped this office," he told the people of Karlsruhe. "What I have done, I did according to my conscience, and to the best of my knowledge, filled with concern for my people, realizing the necessity of protecting its honor, in order to lead it again to a position of honor in this world. And should unnecessary sorrow or suffering ever come to my people because of my actions, then I beseech the Almighty God to punish me."

On March 29, without benefit of guns, 98.8 per cent of the electorate voted for Hitler.

No head of state in the world enjoyed such popularity. Moreover, he had maneuvered his country in little more than three years from supplicant to challenger. Nowhere was this rise of status more recognized than in England, and Thomas Jones, a Welsh Liberal with important connections, came to Germany as an unofficial ambassador. His first stop was at Dahlem where Ribbentrop, knowing of his intimate relationship with Baldwin, urged him to act as go-between with the Prime Minister.

"I want Mr. Baldwin to meet Hitler," said Ribbentrop according to Jones's diary. "He is not the dictator in conversation. He is like Mr. Baldwin. The issues we have to discuss will decide the fate of generations . . . Baldwin should hear Hitler's view straight from the Chancellor with no intermediary. Hitler would speak with him with complete candor." Ribbentrop did his utmost to make the Führer appealing: he was conservative at heart, lived the life of an artist and was devoted to music and painting. "In foreign policy," added Ribbentrop, "only Hitler counts and von Ribbentrop's advice."

"What about the General Staff?" asked Jones.

"The Junkers as an influence have ceased in the government of the Reich," replied the Foreign Minister. "The reintroduction of conscription was not an army decision, but Hitler's own. The fundamental idea of Na-

tional Socialism is not to conquer and dominate others but to be ourselves."

The following morning, May 17, they flew to Munich to see the
Führer and took with them Schmidt, the interpreter. These four met that
Sunday just after noon in the spacious sitting room of Hitler's apartment,
which struck Jones as solid and Victorian. "We might have been in Park
Terrace, Glasgow, in a shipowner's drawing-room in 1880." Jones said that
Baldwin hoped to co-operate with Germany but "there was a long way to
go." Although the recent victory of Italy in Ethiopia had shocked supporters of the League of Nations, there remained a deep and widespread
faith among Englishmen in this organization.

It was apparent, Hitler replied, that the British were divided between
strengthening the League as presently constituted and transforming it into
a consultative body. He himself favored the latter policy and opposed undertaking vast undefined commitments which were unrealizable. The
Ethiopian affair had taught that there would have been a better solution
without an international organization. "The effect of the League," he said,
"had been to raise the hope of the Ethiopians, to delude the other nations
into imagining something effective was being done at Geneva, and to let
Italy 'get away with it.' " He could have been talking about his own gamble in the Rhineland, but if Jones perceived this he did not note it in his
diary. The hour-and-a-half interview ended on an exchange of personal
confidences. "I pointed out that Mr. Baldwin was a shy and modest statesman who had never entirely got over his astonishment at finding himself
Prime Minister and when this was translated, the Führer smiled and inter-
jected: 'And I also.' "

It was a particularly trying time for Hitler. His chauffeur Schreck had
recently been killed in a crash and he himself was having trouble sleeping.
Several days after the Jones interview he complained to Dr. Brandt of a
high, metallic buzz in the left ear. Brandt advised him to stroll before retiring, then have a hot and cold foot bath and several mild sleeping pills.
The Führer did take the pills, and he settled into a more regimented
schedule at the new Reich chancellery which had been rebuilt according
to his own design. At night he would invariably lock himself in his spartan
bedroom. The only decoration was an oil portrait of his mother copied
from an old photograph. On the right of the bed was a night table; Karl
Krause, one of his valets, had strict instructions to have a similar table in
the same position wherever he slept. In the morning the Führer insisted
on shaving himself and getting dressed without help. Only when he was
putting on his jacket would he emerge from his room, greet Krause and
proceed to the library for a breakfast of two cups of milk, up to ten pieces
of zwieback and several pieces of semi-sweet chocolate. He would eat erect

while examining reports from DNB. Breakfast was over in five minutes and, without pause, he set off for the office.

About his only recreation in these busy days was an almost nightly movie in the enormous drawing room. Krause would give him a list of five or six films and he would select several. If one bored him, he would exclaim, "Trash!" and call for another. "His favorite actress was Greta Garbo," according to Sir Ivone Kirkpatrick, "and one of his favorite films *Lives of a Bengal Lancer*, which he saw three times. He liked this film because it depicted a handful of Britons holding a continent in thrall. That was how a superior race must behave and the film was compulsory viewing for the SS." He preferred French productions since, he said, they recorded the life of the petite bourgeoisie so faithfully. "I'm sorry they can't be shown to the public," he told Friedelind Wagner, although it was he who had taken over the responsibility of censoring films not cleared by the Goebbels office.

When Hitler's health showed no improvement, Dr. Brandt advised him to go on vacation, preferably to Berchtesgaden, where he always slept better. He took this advice and spent as much time as possible the next few months at Haus Wachenfeld. That summer he again attended the Wagner festival. Since Unity Mitford and her sister Diana were also on hand, Frau Wagner suggested inviting them to luncheon. Hitler was delighted. "You know Unity lives on little more than a mark a month," he said, according to Friedelind Wagner. "Her parents have cut off her allowance to force her back to England. She has returned once or twice but always runs away again."

The idyl at Bayreuth was disturbed on the night of July 22 when he was visited by two Germans residing in Morocco who belonged to the foreign organization of the NSDAP. They brought a letter from a Spanish general named Franco, leader of a military revolt against the republican government. He desperately needed planes to ferry troops from Africa for action against the "Reds." Hitler immediately summoned Göring, who happened to be at the festival. He urged Hitler to support Franco for two reasons: to prevent the further spread of Communism and "to test my young Luftwaffe." Hitler approved sending part of the transport fleet along with a number of experimental fighter units, bombers and antiaircraft guns—but no more. It was to Germany's advantage to prolong the Civil War in Spain and keep Mussolini, who was already giving extensive aid to Franco, from establishing better relations with France and England. An isolated Mussolini would have to turn to Germany.

Ribbentrop advised Hitler to keep out of the Spanish affair. No laurels were to be won there and he feared "fresh complications with Britain, which would undoubtedly dislike German intervention." But Hitler argued that it was his duty as a National Socialist to support Franco. If Spain went Communist, France (already governed by a leftist regime) would also be Bolshevized. "Wedged between the powerful Soviet bloc in the east and a strong Franco-Spanish bloc in the west, we could do hardly anything if Moscow chose to attack us."

2

That summer the Olympics were staged in Berlin despite efforts by liberals in Great Britain, the United States and France to boycott them, largely because of Germany's anti-Semitic policies. In his eagerness to turn the Olympics into a showcase for Nazi achievements, Hitler made a number of concessions. Token Jews—notably Helene Mayer, the fencer, and Rudi Ball, the hockey star—were allowed to represent the Reich, and Captain Wolfgang Fürstner, another Jew, was charged with erecting and organizing the Olympic Village. More important, anti-Semitic posters along the highways as well as notices barring Jews from resorts were removed. In Berlin, Streicher's *Der Stürmer* disappeared from the newsstands. The entire anti-Semitic campaign, in fact, was muted. These marks of conciliation were given such international publicity that foreigners thronged to Berlin, where they were greeted enthusiastically.

The opening ceremonies on August 1 were blessed by a clear blue sky. That afternoon Hitler led the parade to the stadium down the Via Triumphalis. His car, followed by a long caravan, proceeded slowly down the ten-mile boulevard, protected from the crowds by 40,000 Brownshirts and other guards. When the procession reached the stadium Hitler, in the simplest uniform, and the two Olympic officials strode forward, followed by the King of Bulgaria, crown princes from Sweden, Greece and Italy, and Mussolini's sons. They marched through the tunnel into the world's largest stadium to be greeted by a brassy voluntary from thirty trumpets. The orchestra, led by Richard Strauss and assisted by a chorus of 3000, broke into "Deutschland über Alles" followed by the "Horst Wessel Lied" and the "Olympic Hymn," composed by Strauss for the occasion. The crowd of 110,000 cheered as Hitler took his place in the official stand. Some of the delegations used the Olympic salutation, a stiff right arm extended to the side but, to the delight of the audience, Austrians modified this to the Nazi salute. The Bulgarians outdid them by adding a smart goose step. The greatest applause came for the 250-member French team, whose salute was more Roman than Olympian. They were followed by the British in straw hats who, by merely executing an "eyes right," offended numerous onlookers. The Americans got the least applause, and some derogatory stamping of feet, as they passed the Tribune of Honor, eyes right, without even dipping their flag.

The next day Hitler was present to congratulate Hans Wölke, a German, for breaking the Olympic record for the shot-put. He also congratulated the three Finns who swept the 10,000-meter run as well as the German women who placed first and second in the javelin throw. By the time the German entrants in the high jump were eliminated it was dark and so he was not there to shake hands with the three American winners, two of whom were black.

This led the President of the International Olympic Committee to inform the Führer that, as guest of honor, he should henceforth congratulate all victors or none. Hitler chose the latter course and so did not meet Jesse Owens, who won four gold medals. That the Führer publicly turned his back on the great black athlete was denied by Owens himself, who further claimed that Hitler did pay him a tribute. "When I passed the Chancellor he arose, waved his hand at me, and I waved back at him. I think the writers showed bad taste in criticizing the man of the hour in Germany."

To the surprise of his entourage, the Führer attended almost every track and field event. Face contorted, he would watch the Germans perform with the passionate interest of a boy. (During the hockey game at the Winter Olympics in Garmisch-Partenkirchen he had been too nervous to stay till the end and had to have someone give him a brief account later.) The games ended on August 16 with Hitler on hand for the final ceremonies. As the orchestra played "The Games Are Ended," the crowd joined in the emotional farewell of the athletes, who rocked in time to the music. There were isolated shouts of "Sieg Heil!" for Hitler, who had been given no role at all in the final exercises. Others took up the cry and soon the stadium reverberated with the chant, "Sieg Heil! Unser Führer, Adolf Hitler, Sieg Heil!"

The games had been an almost unqualified Nazi triumph. Germans had won the most gold medals (33), as well as the most silver and bronze; and, surprisingly, defeated the second-place Americans by 57 points. More important, many of the visitors left Germany pleased by their hosts' cordiality and impressed by what they had seen of Hitler's Reich. The success of the games was further enhanced by a two-part documentary filmed by Leni Riefenstahl that won world-wide acclaim, despite Goebbels' attempted sabotage. He even tried to keep her from setting foot in the stadium.

In the paeans of self-congratulation that followed there was a tragic note. Captain Fürstner, replaced at the last moment as commandant of the Olympic Village because he was Jewish, attended the banquet honoring his successor, then shot himself.

3

After the Rhineland coup the Führer became ever more engrossed in the problems and opportunities of foreign policy at the expense of domestic matters. Content to leave things as they were, he forced party and state to accept an uneasy coexistence. He also began to isolate himself from old party comrades. "He became markedly less ready to receive political visitors unless he had expressly sent for them," recalled Otto Dietrich. "At the same time he contrived to erect barriers between himself and his associates. . . . Hitler could no longer tolerate objections to his ideas, or in fact anything which cast doubt on his infallibility."

When Ignatius Phayre, a writer for *Current History*, came to Haus Wachenfeld for an interview that summer, he found the Führer had aged perceptibly the past year. While he talked at length of music and painting, of his days in Vienna and even of the Röhm purge, he refused to answer questions about his future in politics. Instead he rhapsodized at length on the beauties of the Obersalzberg. Here and here alone he could "breathe and think—and live! . . . I remember what I was, and what I have yet to do—if only my strength lasts, and God and Fortune remain with me to the end!"

He mused in the same melancholy vein to his sister Angela as they sat on the porch looking out toward Salzburg. He was upset over a story that he had cheated a neighboring farmer of a thousand marks on the sale of a piece of property. "Look, Adolf, it is not that bad," she said. "A thousand marks more or less won't seem so important when you become 'The Old Man of the Obersalzberg' in a few decades!" Hitler was silent, then put an arm around her shoulder. "First of all, a thousand marks more or less *is* the point and secondly, dear Angela, I shall never become the Old Man of the Obersalzberg. I have so little time."

Their close relationship changed later that summer, largely because of her growing disapproval of his liaison with Eva Braun, whom she privately referred to as *die blöde Kuh* (the stupid cow). But her attempts to turn Hitler against his mistress failed. Since Eva's second suicide attempt he had been more attentive and had recently bought her a snug two-story house near the apartment she shared with her sister. Hoffmann had paid 30,000 marks for the villa, turning it over to Eva and Gretl ostensibly as payment for photographs the two sisters had taken. Hitler also brought Eva to Obersalzberg so often that Angela now refused to shake hands with her and frigidly addressed her as "Fräulein" rather than the more polite "Gnädiges Fräulein." Angela usually saw to it that there was no room at Haus Wachenfeld so that Eva had to seek lodging at the Platterhof.

The relations between Angela and her half brother had become so strained by autumn that she decided to give up her post as housekeeper. It was rumored that she had been dismissed by Hitler over Eva, but according to the family their principal argument concerned her plans to remarry. Hitler wanted Angela to stay on as chatelaine of Haus Wachenfeld but she was as stubborn as he and left to wed Professor Martin Hammitzsch, director of the State School of Building Construction in Dresden.* The Führer was "too busy," according to the official news release, to attend the wedding.

So Eva became the undisputed mistress of Haus Wachenfeld, which was already undergoing total reconstruction. As official summer residence it had to be enlarged to accommodate high-level diplomatic negotiations —and provide Eva with a bedroom, boudoir and bath adjoining his own room and studio. The construction of this show place, which was renamed the Berghof, as well as an expansive complex on the mountainside was turned over to Martin Bormann, who was doing his utmost to make himself absolutely indispensable in small as well as large matters to the point of absurdity. Once at lunch Hitler seasoned his food with sauce, then wondered what was in it. Bormann left the table and several hours later, after several hectic phone calls to Berlin, announced to a bemused Hitler: "Mein Führer, the ingredients of Maggi are as follows . . ." Less amusing was his treatment of subordinates. One day while dictating to Hildegard Fath, Hess's private secretary, he ordered her to take off her glasses. When she protested, he simply snapped them in two and said: "You're far prettier without them."

As Bormann rose, others were dropping out of favor. Esser was transferred to a minor position as a glorified travel agent, Rosenberg was shoved into the background and Hanfstaengl was treated with marked coolness. The latter's uninhibited comments were making him suspect in party circles and there were rumors that he was on a black list. Moreover, one of his last links to Hitler was broken in 1936 when Helene was granted a divorce. Informed of this, Hitler blurted out, "Well, I'll have to send her a telegram right away and wish her luck." But he quickly added, "No, that wouldn't do after all," and concluded, "Frau Hanfstaengl is one of the few real ladies in Germany." He continued to send her flowers on her birthday.

Hanfstaengl conveyed his concern to Egon—now fifteen—late that

---

* Another bone of contention, according to Hans Hitler, the Führer's second cousin, was Angela's insistence on making public appearances. "She liked to make herself important . . . and Hitler could not tolerate that." Another relative on his mother's side, Fritz Pauli, was much more of an embarrassment. He not only married a Jewess but, having a peculiar sense of humor, delighted in publicizing it. He printed up postcards of the Hitler family tree with his wife's maiden name (Rosenthal) as the bottom branch, then passed them out with the remark that this was the Jewish side of Adolf Hitler.

The story that Hitler treated his younger sister badly was denied after the war by Paula herself. When Hitler's notoriety spread to Vienna she changed her name to Wolf. Even so, she was dismissed from her job. "I went to Munich and described my difficult position in life to my brother. With full understanding he assured me that he would provide for me in future." He gave her 250 marks a month, raising that figure to 500 in 1938. In addition he gave her a present of 3000 marks every Christmas and helped her buy a villa. She would occasionally visit him in the Obersalzberg but rarely for more than two weeks.

summer when their yawl lay becalmed in Lake Starnberg. "Boy, listen to what I have to say, and don't forget a word of it. Things are not well. We all believed in the movement, didn't we? I'm still trying to believe in it." He said he had found much corruption and that Hitler was listening to a number of despicable criminals and perverts. "At the rate we're going, we'll have a war—a war in which England and America will be against us. It's dangerous for Germany, and for the world." The country was in a foul state internally because of the blackguards sitting behind official desks. "I've tried, God knows, to get at Hitler and warn him." But he would not listen. "It's no use saying that he just doesn't know what goes on. He must know. And if he knows, he must be held responsible." Hanfstaengl revealed that his own enemies had tried to frame him for embezzlement. "Well, they failed and I cleared myself completely. But they are not through. I expect to be fighting for life itself before long. They're almost certain to get around to liquidating me sooner or later."

The youth was not surprised, for he too had felt the change in Hitler and wondered why his father didn't flee at once. Hanfstaengl replied it wasn't as easy as that. He had helped bring the party into power and saved the Führer several times from physical and political danger. "We're all responsible," he said. "The foundation, 95 per cent of the original aims are good. There is still a chance."

In the meantime they made contingency plans for escape, agreeing on a code word, the name of the little yawl. A message beginning with "Perhaps" would be the signal for Egon to board a train for Switzerland. He should leave without talking to anyone, not even his mother. Nor need he worry about reprisals against her now that she was divorced. Hitler undoubtedly was fonder of her than ever. "Pretend you notice nothing, but quietly walk out of the picture, and keep walking without delay."

The crisis came within six months. Hanfstaengl was ordered to fly at once to Spain, purportedly to protect the interests of German correspondents in that country, but once in the air, the pilot informed him that he was to parachute over the Red lines between Barcelona and Madrid. Hanfstaengl shouted that it was a death sentence. The sympathetic pilot explained he had been given orders signed by Göring, just before take-off, but before long one of the engines clattered and he called back that there was something wrong. He added with a meaningful look at Hanfstaengl that he had to land at a small airfield. Once on the ground, Hanfstaengl pretended to call Berlin for instructions, then came out of the phone booth and informed the pilot that the Führer had ordered him to return to Uffing. He took the night train to Munich and the following morning took another to Zurich, from where he sent his son a message with the code word. Egon packed a few clothes and an autographed picture of the Führer, slipped an automatic into an overcoat pocket, then boarded the Zurich train and hid in a toilet for several hours. Just before midnight he was reunited with his father.*

4

Distracted as he was by personal problems, Hitler did not break stride in his drive for German supremacy. In the summer of 1936 he composed a long memorandum on war economy written in foreboding language and typed in triplicate with one copy each for Göring and Blomberg and a third for his personal file. In it he stated that military strength must be raised to the limits of Germany's potential. Nor did the urgency of the task permit any "gentle scruples." Germany not only lacked raw material but was overpopulated and could not feed itself from its own soil. "To keep on saying these things is absolutely pointless. We must now put measures into effect which can bring the future a final solution, and for the interim a temporary relaxation. The final solution lies in expanding the living space or the raw material and food resources of our people." It was the problem of the government, he continued, to eventually resolve the shortages of raw materials. "It is better to consider and solve these problems in peace than to wait until the next war before attempting to carry out these economic investigations and experiments in the midst of other demands." Autarchy (a self-sufficient economy) must be established as rapidly as possible with the following aims: "I. The German army must be ready for war in four years' time. II. The German economy must be ready for war in four years."

At the same time he was attempting to solidify connections with the British. They, in turn, were demonstrating persistent ineptitude in coping with a leader of such determination and cunning. They were convinced that Hitler could be brought into line with understanding and concessions; and he had kept this misinterpretation alive the past year with conciliatory talk and vague offers of treaties. The parade of dignitaries from England bearing messages of hope and good will continued. Historian Arnold Toynbee returned from Germany convinced of Hitler's peaceful intentions. He was followed by one of the authors of the Versailles Treaty, David Lloyd George, the wartime Prime Minister who had campaigned with the slogan, "Hang the Kaiser!" On the afternoon of September 4 Hitler greeted him warmly on the steps of the Berghof. "I have always been interested in promoting good relations between our two countries," said Lloyd George, "and I renewed my efforts after the close of the Great

* Until recently it was generally believed that the plane incident was simply a cruel practical joke to punish Hanfstaengl for making adverse remarks about the fighting spirit of Germans fighting in Spain. But in Hanfstaengl's book *Zwischen Weissem und Braunem Haus*, published in 1970, the author has included a letter from Luftwaffe General von Schoenbeck which indicates that it may indeed have been a murder plot.

War." Action must be taken, he said, to bring about agreement within the next few months, otherwise the two nations would drift apart.

"I agree with all my heart," replied Hitler. He also had dreamed of such an alliance as a young man. Both nations came from common racial stock and mutual understanding was essential. The menace to the future of civilization was Bolshevism. This was no fanatical obsession, he hastened to elaborate, but a real danger and Western Europe must stand together as a bloc against it. He was also concerned about the Spanish Civil War and the extraordinary extent of the hold which Bolshevism had on that country. "Why have I so much anxiety? It is not that I fear an attack from Russia. But if all the countries around me go Bolshevik, what is to become of my country from an economic point of view? All here is on the razor's edge."

After the guest left, Hitler confided to Heinz Linge, his other valet, that the former Prime Minister had told him there was a considerable period during the Great War when England was on the point of surrendering. "I told Lloyd George I believed this and that the disaster for Germany was that we surrendered at 'five minutes to 12.'" His guest agreed that Germany had surrendered too soon. "But I told him that if ever there is another war between Germany and England, Germany will fight until 5 minutes after 12, so long as I am the Führer."

Schmidt accompanied the Prime Minister back to his hotel. At the entrance they were greeted by Lloyd George's daughter, who laughingly called out, with mocking salute, "Heil Hitler!" The old man did not smile. "Certainly, Heil Hitler!" he said in all seriousness. "I say it too, for he is really a great man."

Lloyd George was predictably impressed by the 1936 Party Day at Nuremberg. More spectacular than ever, it was marked by the launching of two new campaigns: the Four-Year Plan for economic self-sufficiency and an anti-Bolshevik crusade against "the powers of disorder." On a bright Sunday morning, Hitler spoke of the Bolshevik menace to 160,000 massed Brownshirts and SS men in the huge Nuremberg stadium, then drove back to the city in an open Mercedes acknowledging the plaudits of the multitude who jammed the narrow streets and hung from the dormer windows. In the car behind rode Richard Helms of UP, along with half a dozen other foreign correspondents who had been invited to have lunch with the Führer at the storied Nuremberg Castle. "By the time we got there," remembered Helms, "I was suffering from megalomania too. I decided I must be ten feet tall, even if the cheering wasn't for me."

The guests were taken to the parapet of the castle where they met a far less impressive Hitler. What struck Helms was his commonplace manner. Ill at ease, displaying none of the pyrotechnics he had shown earlier that morning, his knees would sway back and forth. It was difficult to believe this was the person who shortly before had thrown back his arms, proclaiming to an army of roaring, hypnotized storm troopers, "The wonder of this age is that you have found me—an unknown man among millions." Yet when someone mentioned Bolshevism the words began gushing out and Hitler was once more the orator. Moscow, he charged, was seeking to dominate Europe and Germany would not permit it. "People wonder why we are fanatics against Bolshevism. It is because we— Italy too—have lived through the same sort of thing which is happening in Spain." From the street down below came such an insistent chant of "We want to see our Führer" that he stepped to the parapet to acknowledge his admirers.

Helms left, more impressed by what he had observed at the castle than at the stadium. Here, he thought, was a very "rational man with what to him was a very rational program."

On the last day of the rally the crowd was treated to an impressive military display. After a mock aerial fight and a demonstration of the efficiency of late-model anti-aircraft guns, a mechanized battle was fought in the arena with frightening reality. So ended the Party Day with assurance of peace, proclamations of new aims and a threatening display of military strength. Not only the faithful left convinced of their Führer's infallibility. Lloyd George had been overwhelmed by almost everything he saw and heard in Germany. In an article for the *Daily Express* he wrote that Hitler had singlehandedly raised Germany from the depths. He was a born leader of men, a dynamic personality with resolute will and dauntless heart who was trusted by the old and idolized by the young.

Before he could resume the course that would make a fool of Lloyd George, Hitler sought an understanding with Italy. He sent Hans Frank to Rome with an invitation to Mussolini to visit Germany not only as dictator of Italy but as leader of the original Fascist revolution. Now Il Duce showed genuine interest in liaison with Germany, and on October 21 his Foreign Minister and son-in-law, Count Galeazzo Ciano, arrived in Berlin to make preliminary arrangements. First Ciano talked to his opposite number, Neurath, who (so reported the Italian) ridiculed Ribbentrop's illusions of a meaningful Anglo-German friendship. Ciano was equally skeptical of a new Locarno and suggested Italy remain in the League of Nations to perform "a work of sabotage useful for our common ends." Three days later Ciano met Hitler at the Berghof. In a mood to captivate, Hitler began by saying, "Mussolini is the first statesman of the world with whom no one else has the right even remotely to compare himself." The Germans and Latins, he continued, complemented each other. Together they could unite in an invincible coalition against Bolshevism and the Western democracies.

Having charged his son-in-law with the task of driving a wedge between England and Germany, Il Duce had given him a document fallen into Italian hands: a telegram from the British ambassador in Berlin to London referring to the Hitler government as one of dangerous adventurers. Upon reading this, the Führer angrily exclaimed, "According to the English there are two countries in the world today which are led by adventurers: Germany and Italy. But England too was led by adventurers when she built her Empire. Today she is governed merely by incompetents." He assured Ciano that there was no need to be concerned about England since rearmament was proceeding at a far more rapid rate in both Germany and Italy. By 1939 Germany would be ready for war, in four or five years much more than ready.

Their new relationship, providing for co-operation over a wide range, was sealed in a secret agreement and signed in Berlin by Ciano and Neurath. A few days later Mussolini referred to it in a speech delivered in the Piazza del Duomo in Milan, using a term that would come to have an ominous ring in Western ears: ". . . this Berlin-Rome line is not a diaphragm but rather an *axis*, around which can revolve all those European states with a will to collaboration and peace."

For the remainder of the autumn of 1936 one of Hitler's concerns was Spain. Small but significant quantities of German supplies and personnel had already been delivered to Franco, and the Führer considered giving more substantial aid. A special air unit capable of providing vital tactical air support for the insurgents, was operational by November, and on the eighteenth Hitler, in concert with Mussolini, finally recognized the Franco regime as the legal government of Spain.

While the Foreign Ministry urged Hitler to proceed with caution, Göring, now in charge of the Four-Year Plan, regarded the Spanish conflict as a prelude to a genuine conflict. "We are already in a state of war," he told a conference of air officials on December 2—though not an official shot had yet been fired. Even so, beginning with the new year, "all factories for aircraft production shall run as if mobilization had been ordered." A few days later he was as frank with a group of industrialists and high officials in Berlin. He revealed that war was in sight and Germany was on the threshold of mobilization. "The battle we are now approaching," he said, "demands a colossal measure of production capacity. No limit on rearmament can be visualized. The only alternatives are victory or destruction."

Göring's announcement was followed by a disturbing report from General Wilhelm Faupel, the new representative to Franco: unless at least one German division was sent without delay to Spain along with a cadre of training officers, the war might be lost, and when this suggestion was ignored by the Wilhelmstrasse, he returned home to present his case to the Führer in person. They met in the chancellery on December 21 along with Göring, Blomberg, Hossbach, Fritsch and Lieutenant Colonel Walter Warlimont, who had just returned from his post as military representative at Franco's headquarters. After Faupel requested three divisions to avert a prolonged encounter, Hitler turned to Warlimont. It was a civil war, Warlimont pointed out, and had to be won with Franco's men alone. Successful co-operation between Spanish and German troops was impossible. The aid already given was sufficient to save the insurgents from defeat. Moreover, Franco was the right man in the right place and would make the best of the situation. The other military men backed Warlimont.

Hitler liked what he heard. Germany would *not* send troops on a large scale, he concluded; his reason was not military but political and he proceeded frankly to reveal that the last thing he wanted was a quick Franco victory. A bitter, lengthy war in Spain would divert world attention from Germany's ambitious rearmament program. He did promise to continue sending the anti-Communists help and if a military disaster seemed likely aid would be increased. His last words were a lesson in cunning; he would leave the honor of sending troops in force to Mussolini. The deeper Il Duce became involved in Spain the closer he would be driven to Germany, and if the conflict continued long enough he would be committed in fact as well as in words to the Axis.

Diplomatically 1936 was a successful year for Hitler and at minimal cost. England had been charmed and Italy brought to the threshold of an unequal partnership. He also had persuaded Japan to sign an Anti-Comintern Pact with Germany which contained secret agreements (vague to be sure) that each should help the other against the Soviet Union. Admittedly spineless, the agreement was important as a propaganda ploy to justify German rearmament.

The only setback of the season was the constitutional crisis in England caused by the King's determination to marry Mrs. Wallis Warfield Simpson. He told Prime Minister Baldwin, "If I can marry her as King well and good," but if the government opposed the marriage, as Baldwin had given Edward to believe it would, *"then I was prepared to go."* A large segment of the public sympathized with Edward VIII but the Church and the Prime Minister remained adamant.

Ribbentrop was driven to distraction by the crisis since the Führer was counting on the King's support in the coming negotiations. "He's our greatest hope!" Ribbentrop told Fritz Hesse, a representative of DNB who doubled as press agent in the German Embassy. Considered an expert in British affairs, he also had a covert mission as special representative of the Foreign Office to deal unofficially with British officials, particularly Sir Horace Wilson, the industrial adviser to the Prime Minister. "Don't you think the whole affair is an intrigue of our enemies to rob us of one of the last big positions in this country?" Shortly Ribbentrop again sent for Hesse. He had just spoken on the telephone to the Führer, who refused to take the talk of abdication seriously. It was a piece of make-believe and he had ordered the German press not even to mention the matter. Hitler's confidence gave Ribbentrop assurance. "You'll see," he predicted, "the Führer will be proved right, the whole affair will go up in smoke and the King will be grateful to us for having treated the crisis with such tactful reticence."

On the evening of December 9 Edward signed the Instrument of Abdication to become the first monarch in British history to give up the throne voluntarily. That evening he told his subjects and the world in a moving broadcast that he was unable to "carry the heavy burden of responsibility and to discharge my duties as King, as I wish to do, without the help and support of the woman I love."

Hitler could not understand how any man could give up rule for romance. He telephoned Ribbentrop and (according to Hesse) dejectedly informed his ambassador he might as well pack his trunks and give up the game for lost. "Now that the King has been dethroned, there is certainly no other person in England who is ready to play with us. Report to me on what you've been able to do. I shan't blame you if it amounts to nothing."

5

This disappointment notwithstanding, 1936 had brought Hitler such success that the Yuletide season was his first happy one "in long years," so he told Frau Göring. "It was, I believe, my most beautiful Christmas." This despite severe stomach cramps, insomnia and eczema. On December 25 he selected a personal physician recommended by Hoffmann, the photographer. Dr. Theo Morell was a skin specialist with a lucrative practice in Berlin's Kurfürstendamm, his patients including the leading film and stage personalities. He was fat, swarthy, with a full round face and peered nearsightedly through thick glasses. His hands were large, hairy, his nails often dirty. In practice too he was occasionally careless. He was known to have wrapped a patient's arm with a bandage he had just used to wipe a table; and to inject the same needle without sterilization into two patients.

For some reason, perhaps out of the friendship that had sprung up between Frau Morell and Eva Braun, Hitler chose him from among all the doctors in Germany. And for the first time since his army days Hitler removed all of his clothes for a complete physical examination. Morell diagnosed the pains and cramps in the epigastric region as gastroduodenitis, for which he prescribed Mutaflor and Gallestol. Hitler also suffered from meteorism, uncontrollable farting, a condition aggravated by his vegetarianism for which Morell prescribed Dr. Köster's Antigas pills. These contained nux vomica but Morell, unaware that this was a seed containing strychnine, instructed his patient to take two to four at every meal. In addition, Morell supplemented Hitler's vegetarian diet with large doses of vitamins, often administering them intravenously together with glucose for energy.

The most prestigious specialists in the country—including Dr. Grawitz, head of the German Red Cross, and Professor Dr. Bergmann of the Berlin Charity Hospital—had failed to cure Hitler's stomach cramps or clear up eczema so painful he couldn't wear boots. The skin specialist from the Kurfürstendamm promised to do both within a year. It took him little more than a month and Hitler jubilantly announced that the miracle doctor had saved his life. "Both Grawitz and Bergmann let me go hungry. I was only allowed tea and zwieback. . . . I was so weak I could hardly work at my desk. Then came Morell and made me well." The Führer insisted all his new-found health came from Morell, claiming that improved gum conditions had come through Mutaflor injections, not the conscientious massaging and brushing prescribed by his dentist, Dr. Hugo Blaschke.

By the time Hitler addressed the Reichstag on January 30, 1937, to commemorate his first four years in office, he was in good spirits and looking younger than his age. He reasserted his divine mission. "Today I must humbly thank Providence whose grace has enabled me, once an unknown soldier in the war, to bring to a successful issue the struggle for our honor and rights as a nation." It was a speech of promise rather than of threat and made an impact because its boasts had a basis in reality. Hitler's achievements in the first four years had truly been considerable and impressive. Like Roosevelt, he had paved the way to social security and old-age benefits. And, like Roosevelt, he had intuitively divined that the professional economists, whose thinking was hobbled by accepted theory, had little understanding of the depression. Both leaders, consequently, had defied tradition to expand production and curb unemployment.* Hitler also was changing the face of the land with a network of *Autobahnen* that would help unite the nation in peace and mobilize it in war. To put the population on wheels, he was developing a "People's Car" so compact and inexpensive that the average German could afford it. He asked Ferdinand Porsche to design a vehicle that would get some forty miles per gallon, accommodate four passengers and have an air-cooled engine that would not freeze up in winter. He envisaged other innovations for the future. In large cities there would be automated underground parking, traffic-free centers, numerous parks and green areas, and strict pollution control. In line with his personal obsession with cleanliness (perhaps

* "Hitler also anticipated modern economic policy," commented economist J. Kenneth Galbraith in 1973, ". . . by recognizing that a rapid approach to full employment was only possible if it was combined with wage and price controls. That a nation oppressed by economic fear would respond to Hitler as Americans did to F.D.R. is not surprising." Perhaps he understood economics too little to know what he was doing. "But in economics it is a great thing not to understand what causes you to insist on the right course."

in connection with his recurring poison-cancer phobia), the problem of pollution so concerned him that he encouraged industry to work toward the complete elimination of noxious gases. Anti-pollution contrivances were already installed in some factories in the Ruhr basin, and new plants were required to construct preventive devices to avoid pollution of the waters.

His interest in city planning extended to towns and villages. Space (another obsession) was essential, he told intimates, "and I am delighted to see our architects planning on broad and spacious lines. Only thus shall we avoid the springing up of more towns in which the houses are cluttered up almost on top of each other, as one sees in Zwickau, Gelsenkirchen and so on. If I were banished to a town of this kind, devoid of all beauty, I should lose heart and happiness just as surely as if I had been banished from my Fatherland. I am therefore determined that some measure of culture and beauty shall penetrate even into the humblest of our towns, that, step by step, the amenities of all our towns will reach a higher level."

The welfare and training of the youth of the nation were also given priority. Drastic changes had already been made in the educational system, with high schools specializing in natural science and non-classical curriculum placed on the same level as the humanistic Gymnasia. With five hours a day for physical training, compulsory courses in racial biology and emphasis on German history and literature, subjects such as ancient languages and science suffered. "The goal of our education is formation of character," wrote one Nazi pedagogue. "We don't intend to educate our children into becoming miniature scholars. . . . Therefore, I say: Let us have, rather, ten pounds less knowledge and ten calories more character."

The character-building process was accompanied by semi-deification of Hitler. Before lunch the children of Cologne were required to recite this invocation:

> *Führer, my Führer, bequeathed to me by the Lord,*
> *Protect and preserve me as long as I live!*
> *Thou hast rescued Germany from deepest distress,*
> *I thank thee today for my daily bread.*
> *Abide thou long with me, forsake me not,*
> *Führer, my Führer, my faith and my light!*
> *Heil, my Führer!*

British Ambassador Phipps reported back to London: ". . . the German schoolboy is being methodically educated, mentally and physically to defend his country . . . but I fear that, if this or a later German government ever requires it of him, he will be found to be equally well-fitted and ready to march or die on foreign soil." This ominous development began in the training of the *Jungvolk*, the organization preparing boys of ten to fourteen to become Hitler Youth. "The Young Folk is the newly won element of eternity in inexorable truth," wrote the author of a booklet on the subject. "For us an order and an imperative are the most sacred duties. For every order comes from the responsible personage, and that personage we trust—the Führer. . . . So we stand before you, German Father, German Mother, we, the young leaders of the German Youth, we train and educate your son, and mould him into a man of action, a man of victory. He has been taken into a hard school, so that his fists may be steeled, his courage strengthened, and that he may be given a faith, a faith in Germany."

Upon graduation into the Hitler Youth each boy was given a dagger on which was engraved "Blood and Honor" and informed that now he could not only wear the brown shirt but defend it by force of arms. "We took this to mean that we were not to put up with anything from anybody," commented one member of the Hitler Jugend, recently escaped to England, "that we were superior to all civilians and could beat them up if they gave themselves airs."

Before 1933 the aim of Hitler Youth was to bring together young people from all walks of life, to break their ties with Communist organizations by persuasion and propaganda, and to indoctrinate them in the Fight for Power. Afterward, the mission was to build them physically, educate them politically and train them to work for Führer and nation. Contrary to popular belief, however, they were not given formal military training and the uniform, according to Hartmann Lauterbacher, Schirach's deputy, "was more in the nature of a national costume which was worn by members of youth organizations before the existence of the Hitler Jugend, not only in Germany but in other countries as well."

While preparing the nation mentally and physically for the future, Hitler had managed in four years to raise the standards of health to such a degree that many foreigners were impressed. "Infant mortality has been greatly reduced and is considerably inferior to that in Great Britain," wrote Sir Arnold Wilson, M.P., a seven-time visitor since the take-over. "Tuberculosis and other diseases have noticeably diminished. The criminal courts have never had so little to do and the prisons have never had so few occupants. It is a pleasure to observe the physical aptitude of the German youth. Even the poorest persons are better clothed than was formerly the case, and their cheerful faces testify to the psychological improvement that has been wrought within them."

Working conditions were improved with more windows, less crowding and better washrooms. Under the slogan "Beautification in Every Place," all offices and workrooms were kept clean and neat; there were abundant flowers so that those who labored could also enjoy their surroundings. Such gains were not illusory. Never before had the worker enjoyed such privileges. The *Kraft durch Freude* (Strength through Joy) program initiated by Robert Ley's Labor Front provided subsidized concerts, theater performances, exhibitions, dances, films and adult education courses for the workers. The most revolutionary project was subsidized tourism. The humblest laborer and his family could now travel aboard luxury liners for undreamed-of holidays.

"The worker sees that we are serious about raising his social position," said Ley. "He sees that it is not the so-called 'educated classes' whom we send out as representatives of the new Germany, but himself, the German worker, whom we show to the world." Single-class ships were constructed with employers and white-collar personnel placed on an equal basis with the workers. This spirit of social democracy was what Hitler meant when he told the Reichstag on January 30, "A radical transformation has taken place and has produced results which are democratic in the highest sense of the word, if democracy has any meaning at all."

He strove to unite people of all social levels—except, of course, the Jews—and his brand of socialism excluded neither the wealthy nor the middle class. "The bourgeois must no longer feel himself a kind of pensioner of either tradition or capital, separated from the worker by the Marxist idea of property," he told one interviewer, "but must aim to accommodate himself as a worker to the welfare of the community." In practice, this concept glorified the worker while underlining Hitler's theory of social equality. He himself was publicized as construction worker, artist and student; as a man of the people who sat next to his chauffeur and ate simple meals. He refused to accept any honorary doctorates and would address workers in plants with the intimate plural form *Ihr*, boasting that he too was without estates or stocks—but neglecting to note that *Mein Kampf* had made him a millionaire.

The spirit of equality was even felt in the armed forces. There was far more camaraderie than formerly between officers and enlisted men in the regular service and the elite SS units were models of democracy. Here there was no differentiation between ranks but a brotherly spirit of all for one and one for all that would have been frowned upon by most British and American officers. Nowhere was egalitarianism more evident than in the Youth Labor Service where young men and women of all classes between the ages of seventeen and twenty-five were obliged to work for a period as farm hands and laborers for *Volk und Vaterland*. This service had been instituted to alleviate unemployment but went far beyond Roosevelt's Civilian Conservation Corps, which had a similar aim, to become the manifestation of socialism. The walls of the labor camp barracks were hung with flags, pictures of the Führer and other leaders and inspirational slogans such as: "Germany needs you, as you need Germany," "Thy people is everything; thou art nothing," and "Labor service is honor service of the German youth." An American visitor, G. S. Cox, found a pair of remarkable slogans in one camp, a quotation from Hitler: "The Jew is not a German but merely a trader; not a citizen but an exterminator," side by side with another from Kant, "Have the courage to use your reason." Cox found the trainees a cheerful lot. "They were in splendid health, with plenty to eat—a luxury some of them had not experienced for years—and they were kept too busy to have time to criticize."

Of all of the achievements of Hitler's first four years, perhaps the most consequential was his unification of the nation. Hitler had not set the clock back, diplomat George Kennan warned a superior. "Germany has simply been unified and thoroughly so. What Bonaparte and Napoleon III left undone in this direction, Versailles completed, and Hitler is now stamping out the last vestiges of particularism and class differences. That he is doing this by reducing everything to the lowest and most ugly common denominator is neither here nor there. German unity is a fact. Hitler may go but the unity will remain, and with it, barring outside interference, will remain—must remain—the jealousy, the uncertainty, the feeling of inferiority, the consequent lust to dominate Europe which are all that most Germans really have in common."

No objective observer of the German scene could deny Hitler's considerable exploits and, while labor had lost its unions, so had management lost its right to organize politically. Every individual, in fact, had lost his rights, his liberty, while the nation was gaining in equality and prosperity. But loss of civil liberties was not the only price paid for Hitler's program: although he had lifted the country out of depression and ended unemployment by original means, his insistence on speeding up rearmament at all costs was forcing the nation into a potentially disastrous economic crisis. The brilliant Schacht had done his best to oppose the efforts of Hitler and the military to make Germany economically independent, first, by vetoing plans of the War Ministry and I. G. Farben to produce artificial rubber, and then by refusing Blomberg's request for expansion of fuel oil production for fear it would upset the peacetime balance of the economy. But by early 1936 Schacht's influence had waned and the economy had been thrown off balance by Hitler's order to increase the army to thirty-six divisions. There were two primary reasons: import prices had risen 9 per cent while export prices were falling 9 per cent; and with two successive bad harvests, German agriculture was unable to supply the needs of the nation. Existing raw material stocks were shrinking. There was already a disturbing shortage of food and fuel. This latter crisis was precipitated by a Russian embargo on German exports combined with a Romanian demand for higher prices. Heating, light, lubricating and diesel oil supplies were at a dangerously low level and could not be replaced by home production.

It was this emergency which had occasioned Hitler's aforementioned memorandum in the midsummer of 1936 on war economy. His answer to

the oil crisis had been one repeated years later in the United States—
autarchy. He knew, of course, that Germany could not possibly produce
enough raw materials within her present borders to attain complete self-
sufficiency yet insisted that the nation do its best. He held out the assurance that absolute autarchy *was* possible once Germany expanded to the
east. Against Schacht's advice, he demanded increases in the production of
synthetic rubber, iron ore, fats, textiles and light metals and then called for
a solution of the fuel crisis within eighteen months.

He ignored the warnings of experts that the production costs of such
a program were exorbitant, nor did he heed the cries of outrage from industrialists when he maintained the production of arms rather than stock-
piling raw materials. Instead he counterattacked by threatening big business with state intervention if it refused to join in the battle for autarchy.
He declared that "finance and economics and all theories are there to
serve the struggle of a people to assert itself." To Hitler it was simply a
question of will power and he demanded an economic mobilization "com-
parable to the military and political mobilization." Nor did he care how it
was achieved so long as the Wehrmacht was operational in four years.

This was the Four-Year Plan he had announced at the 1936 Nuremberg rally. The following month he chose Göring to administer it and,
significantly, his choice of collaborators included but one old party
member, the top posts going to co-operative civil servants, representatives
of industry and General Staff officers. This meant that the NSDAP, except for Göring, whose loyalty was to himself and Hitler, had been virtually excluded from the decision-making process in the nation's economic
life.

In a speech calling for national mobilization, Göring declared that
workers and peasants must apply their full strength, inventors must place
themselves at the disposal of the state, and business must "think not
of profit, but of a strong, independent national German economy." In
words that would be paraphrased a generation later by an American President, he adjured all Germans to serve their nation. "Each one of us should
ask himself every day what he can do, how he can contribute to the success of the common effort."

Two months later Hitler himself made a pressing appeal to an important group of industrialists to trust Göring as executor of this urgent mission: "He is the best man for this job, a man of iron will and determination. Therefore march in serried ranks behind him." At the same
meeting Göring told the industrialists it was no longer a question of producing economically but of producing. He was not at all concerned how
foreign exchange was brought in. Only those who broke the law *without
success* would be prosecuted.

"It was incumbent on me to denounce this economic nonsense," wrote Schacht, "and to oppose this irresponsible and wanton flouting of the law, as openly as possible." He did so in a speech to the Chamber of Commerce on his sixtieth birthday, and his audience was almost the same as Göring's. He also decried Göring's claim that the only important thing was to produce. "If I sow a hundred-weight of grain on a certain area of land and harvest only three-quarters of a hundred-weight, then that is the most utter economic nonsense imaginable." It was a declaration of war by an official already out of favor and within a few months Schacht was forced to resign as Minister of Economics. This left Göring free to carry out his Führer's plan to transform the German economy into a barefaced instrument for rearmament—and war.

If Hitler had died in 1937 on the fourth anniversary of his coming to power—the great economic crisis notwithstanding—he would undoubtedly have gone down as one of the greatest figures in German history. Throughout Europe he had millions of admirers. Gertrude Stein (who found Roosevelt boring) thought Hitler should get the Nobel Peace Prize. In magazine and newspaper articles George Bernard Shaw defended Hitler and other dictators; Shaw's speeches on Fascism infuriated fellow Fabians and brought a spate of passionate letters from anti-Fascist exiles. Another outspoken adherent was Sven Hedin, the renowned Swedish explorer, who wrote that Hitler was endowed with an indomitable passion for justice, breadth of political vision, unerring foresight and "a genuine solicitude for the welfare of his fellow citizens." Hedin, himself one sixteenth Jew and proud of it, defended Hitler's anti-Semitism while disapproving of its harsh methods. An impartial investigation of the conduct of the Jews in the years after the armistice, he said, showed why Germans loathed Jews. "Wherever the policy of subservience and defeatism was preached, its leading protagonists were Jews. And as a rule they were the same Jews who formed the vanguard of Communism and Bolshevism." His summary of Hitler's accomplishments could have been written by Goebbels: "A man who within the space of four years has raised his people from the very lowest depths to self-consciousness, pride, discipline and power deserves the gratitude of his fellow citizens and the admiration of all mankind."

Beyond inspiring individual foreigners, Hitler, by example, stimulated the growth of similar movements throughout Europe. The most important was the British Union of Fascists, the Blackshirts, and Hitler had recently honored their leader, Sir Oswald Mosley, by attending the luncheon reception following his wedding to Diana Mitford. In France—where anti-Semitism had long been an aspect of nationalism, royalism and, at times, Catholicism—the Action Française under Charles Maurras flourished and was influencing such gifted authors as André Malraux. There was also the Croix de Feu, an extreme right-wing veterans' organization, under the leadership of Colonel François de la Rocque, and half a dozen similar groups. While Fascism in practice was repugnant to such non-conformists, the accomplishments and words of both Hitler and Mussolini had mobilized them against the liberal state, democracy and parliamentarianism.

In Belgium young Léon Degrelle, who would come to regard himself as the spiritual son of Hitler, founded his Rexist movement as a bulwark against Communism. "Our movement," he commented years later, "was more Falangist than Fascist, more spiritual than political." Rexism to him was a reaction against the corruption of the times; a movement of political renovation and political justice; a battle against disorder, incompetence, irresponsibility, uncertainty and, above all, Bolshevism.

The Fascist influence extended to the United States where the German-American Bund members openly wore a Nazi uniform of white shirt, black tie, jack boots and swastika emblems; and to China, where Chiang Kai-shek had secretly organized an elite group known as the Blue Shirts. "Fascism is now thought to be backward," one of its members remarked many years later. "But then it seemed to be a very progressive means of resurrecting the country." Its primary goal apparently was preservation of the nation. "Fascism is the only tool of self-salvation of nations on the brink of destruction," stated a contemporary editorial in the Blue Shirt publication, *She-hui hsin-wen.* "It saved Italy and Germany. . . . Therefore there is no other road than imitating the Fascist spirit of violent struggle as in Italy and Germany." Chiang Kai-shek was equally enthusiastic. "Can Fascism save China?" he asked a group of Blue Shirts and provided the answer: "Yes! Fascism is what China now most needs." Despite public disclaimers to Westerners, he too loathed democracy. ("In the last several decades we have in vain become drunk with democracy and the advocacy of free thought") and subscribed to Hitler's Führer principle. "The most important part of Fascism," he told a group of party cadres eight months after Hitler took power, "is absolute trust in a sagely able leader." Unless the nation completely trusted this one man, it could not be reconstructed. "Therefore, the leader will naturally be a great person and possess a revolutionary spirit, so that he serves as a model for all party members. Furthermore, each member must sacrifice everything, acting directly for the leader and the group, and indirectly for society, the nation, and the revolution. From the day we joined this revolutionary group, we completely entrusted our rights, life, liberty, and happiness to the group, and pledged them to the leader. . . . Thus for the first time we can truly be called Fascist."

The accomplishments of Hitler in his first four years of power had done much to encourage others of a like mind. The appeal of Fascism was not only to the disgruntled and disenfranchised but to responsible men of good will. It drew unto itself youthful elements as well as intellectuals who found it a refreshing alternative to bourgeois liberalism. And while each country had its own particular brand of Fascism, all its adherents (including Hitler and Mussolini) believed that, come what may, the spiritual unity of their nation would solve all problems. This end, they believed, justified the means.

Chapter Fifteen

"SUCH A LITTLE HUMAN WORM"
1937–FEBRUARY 1938

1

Hitler followed the speech of January 30, 1937, with another, three months later, that was far more revealing. This address to 800 district leaders at the dedication of the elitist political education school in Vogelsang was a private, frank, often repetitious monologue. His purpose was twofold: to instruct these leaders, the cream of the movement, in their duties, and to memorialize the beginning of the political instruction of 3000 carefully selected young men, one of whom hopefully would follow in his footsteps.

He was like some Metternich or Machiavelli instructing his sons in political and diplomatic tricks and dispensing practical and cynical advice on how to manipulate the masses. "An organization only has a future if it subdues in a natural manner the freedom of the individual so that the whole benefits." That was why they could never tolerate any authority above that of nationhood: "No matter what it is, not even the Church." He compared their totalitarianism with democracy, describing the latter as an anthill with everyone scurrying off in different directions. These democrats had freedom to do what they wanted and consequently were worthless as individuals. "They are soft, they are not worth anything, they have no resistance." How ridiculous it would be to concern the average man with problems that gave headaches to better heads. Imagine burdening "such a little human worm" with the final decision, for example, of the Rhineland crisis! What if the Four-Year Plan had to be first presented to a democratic parliament? "Only the Jew could have thought up and introduced such idiocy."

He then turned to the problem of finding the leaders of tomorrow, and when he declared that rank and wealth were of no consequence he might have been talking of his own boyhood. "It is only necessary to have ability. It matters not who their fathers are, what their mothers were. They only must have the stuff of leadership in them. Pure abstract thinking is of no value. The Führer must be able to lead. He must be able to say, 'This has to be done. I recognize it.' He must consult with those men responsible for carrying out his plan but in the final analysis it is he who must stand up for his ideas and decisions. He must make the decision." What more beautiful kind of genuine democracy was there?

After giving practical advice on a variety of subjects, he abruptly turned to the Jewish menace, talking in the private, obscure terms everyone in the hall understood. "The question to me is never to take a step that might have to be retracted and bring harm to us. You know, I always go to the very brink of boldness but not beyond. One has to smell out: 'What can I get away with and what can't I?'" There was laughter and applause, and he responded by immediately turning emotional. "I am not going to challenge my opponent immediately to a fight. I don't say, 'Fight,' just for the pleasure of fighting. Instead I say, 'I will destroy you. And now cleverness helps me to maneuver you into such a corner that not a blow will be struck until you get a thrust into your heart! That is it!'" His last words, leaving no doubt that he meant to solve the problem by killing the Jews, were drowned out by a spontaneous mass scream of blood lust. This flesh-creeping roar was preserved on tape, a reminder to posterity of man's primal brutality and how like the shrieks of the mob in the Roman Colosseum for the death of a fallen gladiator it must have been!

When the uproar died Hitler reverted to his quiet, reasonable catalogue of pragmatic advice as if what he had just said was to be filed in secrecy. He concluded with a call for all-out national rearmament: "I want the German people to emerge as the strongest people in Europe, not the second or third!" Exultant waves of applause swept the hall. "And even if this sacrifice fails, it will not be, in my eyes, the last chapter of German history, but the next to last chapter. We shall write the last chapter!"

Except to his closest adherents, Hitler had never been so candid. The very informality of the speech, its almost total absence of emotional appeal—except for the brief, terrifying revelation of his plan for the Jews— were themselves fearsome. Stripped of pretense, this was a cold and calculated soliloquy by a man enjoying almost absolute power.

2

On the brink of total dictatorship, Hitler remained the artist. Art and politics to him were inseparable. One of his first steps to inaugurate Nazi art and architecture was to disband the Bauhaus, an institution founded immediately after the World War by architect Walter Gropius to create a functional experimental architecture by utilizing the resources of painting, sculpture and industrial design as well as architecture. This school had drawn to it some of Europe's most talented architects and painters— Klee, Kandinsky, Feininger and Mondrian—and was the epitome of modernity. Consequently it was anathema to the classically and romantically minded Hitler.

The architect he admired above all was Professor Paul Ludwig Troost. "I could no longer bear the things I had drawn up to then," Hitler later confessed to Speer. "What a piece of luck that I met this man!" He was so impressed, in fact, that he confided to Troost's young wife "that once he came to power and became the leader of the German people," he would call on her husband, whose work had "clarity, strength and nobility."*

Perhaps his most memorable project for Hitler was a modern art museum for Munich, the Haus der Deutschen Kunst, to be built from voluntary public contributions. The Führer himself had participated in laying the cornerstone in the fall of 1933. Prior to the ceremony thousands of Brownshirts, SS and Hitler Youth paraded along the Prinzregentenstrasse to the building site. The Führer was greeted by the mason's foreman and other workmen in medieval costumes. After an orchestra played the prelude to *Die Meistersinger*, Hitler once more proclaimed his theory of Germany's cultural mission, then bestowed on Munich the title of "the capital city of German art." Moments later, however, a chill came over the proceedings when he struck the cornerstone with a silver hammer so energetically that it broke. There was an awkward silence because of a superstition that the architect would die if the hammer broke. Goebbels tried to make light of it: "When the Führer strikes, he strikes mightily." But it was no joke to Hitler, who was convinced that it was a bad omen. So feared Troost and within a few days he was hospitalized by angina pectoris. He died a few months later of pneumonia.

Frau Troost carried on her husband's work and Hitler would visit her studio every time he came to Munich. Their relationship extended beyond architecture. A lady with a mind of her own, she expressed it forthrightly. When someone asked one day what she thought of Speer, she turned to the Führer and said that if Herr Hitler had asked her husband to design a building of 100 meters, Professor Troost would have thought it over and reported back next day that the building could only be 96 meters for structural and aesthetic reasons. "But if you said to Speer, 'I need a building of 100 meters,' he would immediately reply, 'Mein Führer, 200

* In his memoirs Speer claims he often accompanied Hitler to the Troost studio and considered the professor his "second teacher." Theirs, he asserted, was a "close relationship." Frau Troost denies this. Speer, she said in a 1971 interview, never met her husband and was brought to the Munich atelier only after Troost's death.

meters!' and you would say, 'You are my man.'" Not at all offended, Hitler joined in the laughter. "He always liked to laugh," she recalled. "Hitler really had a good sense of humor—from the heart and not, as Speer says, sarcastic."

To the surprise of his aides, Hitler did not resent Frau Troost's candor. Argument with her only stimulated him—except on one memorable occasion. For the grand opening of the Haus der Deutschen Kunst in the summer of 1937 an ambitious exhibition of German art was scheduled. The judges, including Frau Troost, made their selection according to artistic standards and therefore a good many modern paintings were chosen. Since Hitler considered such art degenerate, he and Frau Troost had a violent argument at the museum just before the opening day. She argued that the selection was good since it embraced a representative cross section. Pointing to a pile of rejected paintings, she said, "These are gray. They have already been refused by our grandmothers." The colors had all faded into a dull brown. Hitler pointed to a huge painting of a man on a hill playing a violin. Why was that refused? "It's impossible," she retorted. "Too sweet for our exhibition." She asked Hitler why he accepted an artist only after his second stroke. As the quarrel grew more acrimonious the group following them hung back. Hitler never raised his voice but his manner became coldly formal. Ignoring the storm signals, she said she could not betray her artistic convictions. "And since you can't approve our selection and have a completely different opinion, I resign this moment as a member of the jury." The Führer bade her farewell with cool formality, delegating to Hoffmann, the photographer, the chore of selecting the best entries, but a few weeks later Hitler was back at the Troost studio as if nothing had happened.

The exhibition opened on July 18 with parades through the streets of Munich depicting two thousand years of German culture. Teutonic Knights with large swastikas on their chests hauled a huge sun while others carried aloft tinfoil-covered replicas of the cosmic ash tree Yggdrasill which, according to legend, held earth, heaven and hell together. The exhibition was not so much an evocation of the past as old-fashioned. The most modern paintings were those by artists such as Adolf Ziegler. Although there were good works, particularly in the field of sculpture, most of the paintings were soulful or heroic, idyllically pastoral or rhapsodies of rustic family life. Little of the stress and strain of life in postwar Germany was portrayed.

In his speech that day Hitler declared that this House of German Art had been designed for the art of the German people, not for an international art. It was not the function of artists, he said, to retreat into the past or to distort or make ugly. "The new age of today is at work on a new human type. Men and women are to be more healthy, stronger: there is a new feeling of life, a new joy of life." And what did the decadent moderns manufacture? "Misformed cripples and cretins, women who inspire only disgust, men who are more like wild beasts, children who, were they alive, must be regarded as cursed of God." If these "artists" really saw things this way, "then one has but to ask how the defect of vision arose, and if it is hereditary the Minister of the Interior will have to see to it that so ghastly a defect of vision shall not be allowed to perpetuate itself—or if they do not believe in the reality of such impressions but seek on other grounds to impose this humbug upon the nation, then it is a matter for a criminal court." Nothing could have more clearly outlined his conviction of the import of art than this threat to sterilize modern artists with defective vision and treat the others as dangerous criminals. He put the most prestigious German artists in this category—even Emil Nolde, a crusty genius of the Expressionist school who sympathized with National Socialism—and had already started the campaign to suppress such painters. Thousands of works by Nolde, Barlach, Feininger, Corinth and Grosz had been confiscated along with a number by foreign artists, including Picasso, Matisse, Van Gogh, Braque and Cézanne. Some 730 of these paintings were being concurrently exhibited in Munich as "Degenerate Art." They were hung haphazardly without frames with such crude comments as "Thus did sick minds view Nature" or "German peasants looked at in the Yiddish manner." There was one section illustrating the influence of Negro art, another that of Marxist ideology, and a large one devoted to Jewish artists.

The exhibit also included paintings by the insane to prove that the creations of the modernists were even more disordered. Two portrait sketches by Kokoschka were placed next to an impressionistic head created by a lunatic. "The artists ought to be tied to their pictures so that every German can spit in their faces," exclaimed one outraged visitor. While such virulence was not uncommon, this exhibition, which later toured throughout the nation, attracted two million paying visitors, five times as many as those filing into the Haus der Deutschen Kunst to see Hitler's concept of the best in German art. Admittedly many of the two million had been drawn by the advertised lure of obscenity, but many of them had undoubtedly come to see for the last time the forbidden fruits of great art.

3

That year's Party Congress opened on September 6. Hitler arrived in Nuremberg that Monday afternoon and, after inspecting his personal bodyguard, drove through the beflagged city to the ringing of church bells and the cheering of crowds. The following day he made his usual dramatic appearance at Congress Hall to the accompaniment of the "Badenweiler March." Once more it was his *alter vox*, Wagner, who read out the Führer's proclamation. After contrasting Bolshevik violence and bloodshed with the moderate National Socialist revolution, it charged that there had been a concerted attempt the past year to spread the Communist chaos to East and West. There was one comforting certainty: "The whole world may begin to burn about us but the National Socialist state will emerge from the Bolshevist conflagration like platinum." Germany had solved her social problems peacefully and equitably while other countries staggered under strikes and terrorism brought about by Jewish-Bolshevik agitators.

It was a speech designed to keep the populace complacent rather than inflame its warlike spirit, while he himself was preparing to woo an ally for the conflict he knew was inevitable. Benito Mussolini had agreed to come to Germany on two conditions: that he bring no civilian evening clothes and that he have the opportunity of meeting *mit der grossen Menge* (with the great multitude). He left Rome on September 23, attired in a chic new Fascist Militia uniform specifically designed for the occasion, and accompanied by a retinue of one hundred. He was met two mornings later at Munich's main station by a host dressed in simple party uniform. Hitler held out his arms in welcome as the drums rolled and the crowd shouted "Heil!" and "Duce!"

The party made its exit along a red carpet extending through the station and drove in state to the Führer's apartment on Prinzregentenplatz. Here they had their first conversation and, since Mussolini spoke German, interpreter Schmidt had the opportunity of comparing them. With his unruly lock of hair, Hitler had an untidy bohemian appearance. "His voice was rough and often hoarse as he flung out sentences full of rolling *r*'s either at me or at Mussolini. Sometimes his eyes blazed suddenly, and then equally suddenly became dull as if in a fit of absent-mindedness." Il Duce was completely different. "Firmly erect, swaying from the hips as he talked, his Caesarian head might have been modeled from the old Romans, with its powerful forehead and broad, square chin thrust forward under a wide mouth. He had much more vivacious expression than Hitler when his turn came to thunder against the Bolshevists or the League of Nations. Indignation, contempt, determination and cunning alternately lit up his mobile face, and he had the histrionic sense native to Latins." Yet he never seemed to say a word too much. Schmidt was also struck by the difference in their laughs. Hitler's was marked by derision and sarcasm whereas Mussolini's was free and wholehearted.

In an hourlong talk they agreed in general to show friendliness to Japan, support Franco and thwart the ambitions of France and Britain. This, their only political discussion of the visit, was evidence that Hitler was beginning to realize there was little hope he would inveigle England into underwriting, even covertly, his program of expansion. From that moment on Mussolini was rushed through a series of ceremonies and appearances, including an impressive parade of goose-stepping SS men that he would never forget, army maneuvers in Mecklenburg and inspection of the vast Krupp works in Essen. The culmination of the tour came on the afternoon of September 28. As the separate trains of the two dictators approached their destination, the railway station near the Olympic Stadium, Hitler's pulled up alongside Il Duce's on an adjacent track and for the next fifteen minutes the two trains ran side by side. The operation, practiced by the engine drivers for days, was so smoothly executed that the Italians and Germans could carry on easy conversations through the open window. Then Hitler's train began to gain almost imperceptibly so that it reached the station platform a few seconds ahead of the other, giving him time to walk across the platform and greet Mussolini with outstretched hand just as his train pulled to a stop. It was a marvel of efficiency and, along with the goose-stepping troops and maneuvers, had the impressive effect Hitler hoped for.

There was more to come. Almost a million spectators, many brought in from the provinces by special trains, lined the triumphal avenue from the station to the center of Berlin, which had been decorated with Fascist and National Socialist flags. Long banners hung from rooftops to the street and at every square there were huge pylons displaying alternately the German and the fasces emblems. Work had been shut down at 4 P.M. so that the local population could swell the ranks. The enthusiastic crowd was held back by 60,000 SS men, recruited from all over Germany. Never before had there been such stringent security measures, numerous plainclothes men mixing with the crowd while armed launches patrolled the Spree.

The spontaneous cheers at the sight of the two dictators standing side by side in an open car delighted Il Duce. The reception was even warmer the following day when the two men drove back to the Olympic Stadium so that Mussolini could have his promised meeting with the masses. This time Hitler let Mussolini enter first to have a moment of private adulation. Then Hitler made a brief introductory speech broadcast to the "115 million citizens of our two countries who are sharing with deep emotion in this historic event." Theirs, he asserted, was a "community, not only of opinion, but also action. Germany is once again a world power. The strength of our two nations constitutes . . . the strongest guarantees for the preservation of a civilized Europe, true to her cultural mission, and armed against disruptive forces."

Il Duce strode to the microphones. Since he had insisted on speaking in German and became so excited by the spectacle that he talked faster and faster, his listeners could catch only a few words. "The Berlin-Rome Axis," he shouted, "was formed in the autumn of 1935, and during the last two years it has worked splendidly for the ever closer association of our two peoples and for European peace." His visit, he said, was not an ordinary diplomatic or political episode but a demonstration of unity between two revolutions with a common purpose.

All at once the skies dumped a torrent on the stadium and Mussolini's script began to disintegrate. "The greatest and most genuine democracies that the world knows today are Germany and Italy," he said in a voice distorted by the rain-soaked microphones and loudspeakers. He continued manfully and the audience sat stolidly to the end. "I have a friend, I go with him through thick and thin to the very end." What followed was even more chaotic. He was forced to make the slow trip back to the capital alone in an open car just so the population could take another look at him. He had no raincoat and arrived soaked and bedraggled at his quarters where there was no hot water for a bath.

While he did not catch cold, Mussolini slept poorly and awakened next morning exhausted and depressed. But by the time his train departed for home he had regained his spirits. He had come to Germany with a feeling of disdain for Hitler. How could you trust a man who was unmarried, childless and without even a mistress? He left deeply impressed by what he had seen. If he had not found out about Eva Braun, he had seen power far beyond what even he had dreamed; and from that moment on the role of the two dictators was reversed; it was Mussolini who was under the influence of his junior. Dr. Carl Gustav Jung, the Swiss psychiatrist, had personally observed the two dictators and noted startling differences. In contrast to Il Duce, Hitler was like a robot. "He seemed as if he might be a double of a real person, and that Hitler the man might perhaps be hiding inside like an appendix, and deliberately so hiding in order not to disturb the mechanism."

No specific agreements were signed in Berlin nor was a final communiqué issued, but the German Foreign Office informed all its missions that the two leaders had agreed that neither should draw closer to England without the other's approval and that Italy would henceforth have a free hand in the Mediterranean while Germany enjoyed the same privilege in Austria.

Hitler was as pleased with the arrangement as Mussolini, for he still held Il Duce in high regard. Their toasts at the chancellery banquet had been more meaningful than any communiqué, with Hitler reasserting that the two countries had been drawn together in sincere friendship by a common political purpose, and his guest replying that German-Italian solidarity was a living and active one and the two nations were "immune against any attempt to separate them." With the Axis a reality, Hitler was now in position to make his next move.

4

Late in October he confided to a group of Gau propaganda chiefs that people in his family did not live to a great age. Hence the great problems, particularly that of Lebensraum, must be solved as soon as possible. Those who followed him would no longer be able to do this since he alone was capable of it. "Now," he said, "I feel as fresh as a foal in the meadow."

A week later, on November 5, 1937, he summoned his military chiefs, his Wehrmacht adjutant, Hossbach, and Foreign Minister von Neurath. The ostensible reason was to resolve the growing competition between Blomberg and Göring for raw materials. The Minister of War deeply resented the latter's use of his position as chief of the Four-Year Plan to favor the Luftwaffe and had been pressing the Führer to forbid it.

Just before this conference Hitler privately told Göring that the main reason for calling the meeting, so the latter testified, was "to put pressure on General von Fritsch, since he was dissatisfied with the rearmament of the army. He said it would not do any harm if Herr von Blomberg would also exercise a certain amount of pressure on von Fritsch." When Göring questioned Neurath's presence, the Führer replied that he "did not want to make the thing look too military," and merely hoped "to make it very clear to Commander-in-Chief Fritsch that the political situation required a forced speed in armament."

It is probable Hitler did say something like this, for it was characteristic of him to avoid taking sides or offending either party in a dispute, and when everyone was assembled at 4 P.M. he began talking of foreign policy rather than of the quarrel. It was apparent from his sober mien that this was no ordinary conference and, once he swore them to secrecy, his listeners (with the possible exception of Göring) prepared themselves for a shock. It came a moment later when he requested "in the interest of a long-term German policy, that his exposition be regarded, in the event of his death, as his last will and testament." So read the detailed notes drafted a little later by Colonel Hossbach. Hitler went on to say that the aim of German policy was to make secure, preserve and enlarge the racial community. In fact Germany's future depended on acquiring sufficient Lebensraum and this living space could only be found in Europe. "There had never been spaces without a master, and there were none today: the attacker always comes up against a possessor. The question for Germany ran: where could she achieve the greatest gain at the lowest cost." Germany's problem, he informed his startled audience, "could only be solved by means of force and this was never without attendant risk." The question was *when* and *how*.

German power, he said, would attain its peak within six years or so. Thereafter her military equipment would be obsolete and the other powers would have rearmed. They must take the offensive while the rest of the world was still preparing its defenses. "If the Führer was still living it was his unalterable resolve to solve Germany's problem of space at the latest by 1943–45."

Hitler scarcely glanced at his notes, facts and figures rolling out in a startling display of photographic memory, a gift reportedly shared by Caesar,

Napoleon and Lenin. Baron von Neurath sat stiffly, and the military leaders fidgeted uncomfortably as Hossbach, no stenographer, feverishly scribbled down what Hitler was saying. Germany's first objective, he continued, was to secure its eastern and southern flanks by seizing Czechoslovakia and Austria. Undoubtedly both England and France had "already tacitly written off the Czechs," and the former was having too many problems of its own to wage war against Germany. He warned that the defense measures of the Czechs were growing from year to year and the Austrian army was also getting stronger. At the same time he held out the promise of large quantities of food for the Reich from both these countries once they were annexed. It would also mean "shorter and better frontiers, the freeing of forces for other purposes," and the possibility of creating new units up to a level of about twelve divisions, that is, one new division per million inhabitants. Italy certainly would not object to the elimination of the Czechs but he could not honestly estimate what her attitude would be to Austria; that depended essentially upon whether Il Duce was still alive. "The degree of surprise and swiftness of our action were decisive factors for Poland's attitude. [Significantly he had signed a minorities treaty with this neighbor earlier in the day.] Poland—with Russia at her rear—will have little inclination to engage in war against a victorious Germany." Similarly, Russian intervention would have to be countered by lightning operations.

It was growing dark by the time Hitler finished. He asked for comments. Both Blomberg and Fritsch opposed the Führer's blueprint for conquest; they urged him not to cast France and England in the role of enemies. The French army would certainly not be too distracted by war with Italy to be a formidable opponent on the western front. Blomberg also protested that it would be extremely difficult to break through the Czech defenses, which were as strong as the Maginot Line, then joined with Fritsch to elucidate all these points once more. The latter was so concerned that he offered to cancel his leave—he was planning to go to Egypt to recuperate from an attack of bronchial catarrh—but the Führer told him that was not necessary; possibility of conflict was not *that* imminent.

Hitler left most of the rebuttal to Göring, sitting back to listen attentively. The discussion became so heated that Hossbach was finding it almost impossible to jot down what was being said. "However," he recalled, "I do remember exactly that the sharpness of the opposition both in content and form did not fail to make its impression on Hitler, as I could see from his changing expression. Every detail of the conduct of Blomberg and Fritsch must have made plain to Hitler that his policies had met with only plain impersonal contradiction, instead of applause and agreement." Equally unenthusiastic, Neurath warned that a conflict between Italy and France was not as likely as the Führer seemed to think, and while Admiral Raeder did not join the argument, it was apparent that he too was skeptical.

The meeting finally ended at 8:15 P.M. After Hitler left, Göring took Raeder aside to allay his concerns. Surprisingly, Blomberg, who had so recently registered objections, also begged the admiral not to take the Führer seriously; his oration was intended only to spur Fritsch into accelerating the rearmament program. Nor was there the slightest danger of any naval conflict with the English. Raeder left the chancellery relieved that Hitler did not really mean to wage war. After all the navy did not have a single battleship in service and the army and air force were equally unprepared. "In no way were we armed for war, and a war against England," he recalled, "would have been sheer madness."

On the other hand, Neurath took the Führer at his word but it was not until reaching his office that the Foreign Minister really fathomed what he had heard. He became physically sick and had to summon a doctor. Within forty hours Neurath (who was to suffer several heart attacks over the matter) was so driven by conscience that he ignored his oath of secrecy. He met with Generals Beck and Fritsch at the Bendlerstrasse to discuss ways of inveigling Hitler to abandon his plans for war. These two promised to do what they could; they had no desire to fight without a better than even chance of victory. It was agreed that Fritsch would re-emphasize to the Führer the military folly of waging war, after which Neurath would argue the political case.

Fritsch did interview the Führer at the Berghof on November 9. While he left no record of the result, he wrote his good friend, the Baroness von Schutzbar, that day: "Again and again new difficult matters were brought before me which must be attended to before my departure. I am really very tired and exhausted, far more than you can tell from my appearance." Hours later he left for his holiday in Egypt, but his arguments must have made no impression. Hitler would not even see Neurath.

Did Hitler mean what he said at the momentous conference? Was it theater, as Göring suggested and both Blomberg and Raeder had come to believe? Or was it a rare glimpse into his mind? The Führer's unpublished book and the numerous speeches and observations made on Lebensraum and the Jews strongly indicate he was dead serious. So would a speech he made two weeks later warning the political cadets at Sonthofen that Germany could not survive without adequate living space and that war must be risked to attain this goal.

While his words at the fateful conference did not constitute a blueprint for war, they did suggest what he might do if diplomatic threats failed. He was resolved to wage diplomatic war even at the risk of a general conflict. Time was working against him. By 1943 he had to liquidate minor, preliminary obstacles one by one either by diplomatic blackmail or by a series of Blitzkriegs: first Czechoslovakia, then Poland and France. Hopefully England would be won over to neutrality but if not she too had to be taught a military lesson that would forcibly disinterest her in continental affairs. Thus by 1943 the way would be cleared to wage major warfare—and to knock out the primary enemy, Russia. In any case, he was seriously dedicated to a warlike course and, with a gambler's instinct for timing, he was prepared to embark on the ultimate course envisaged in 1928.

5

In England there was a new Prime Minister, set on a more conciliatory posture toward Germany. "Our objective," wrote Neville Chamberlain just before accepting the appointment, "should be to set out the political guarantees which we want as a general settlement; and if the discussions have to break down, we want the breakdown to be due to Germany's refusal to accept our reasonable requirements in the political field." Energetic, strong-willed and self-confident, Chamberlain promptly began moderating the foreign policy of his predecessor, Baldwin. "I believe the double policy of rearmament and better relations with Germany and Italy will carry us safely through the danger period," he wrote in a private letter, "if only the Foreign Office will play up." And since he ran his cabinet like a managing director, there was no doubt that he would override Foreign Secretary Eden, who doubted the possibility of agreement with Hitler on acceptable terms.

Chamberlain's announced willingness to work with Hitler was given a test that autumn when the Lord President of the Council, Lord Halifax, received a gilded card inviting him to attend a hunting exhibition in Berlin sponsored by Reich Master Huntsman Hermann Göring. As Master of the Middleton Hounds, Halifax was tempted to accept, and Chamberlain thoroughly approved since the promise was held out that Halifax would be able to see Hitler.

He left England intending to sound out the Führer on a possible understanding but as an envoy he was an unfortunate choice. Upright, religious and conventional, he knew little of German history and character, nor had he even read *Mein Kampf*. He found Göring "frankly attractive: like a great schoolboy, full of life and pride in what he was doing. . . . A modern Robin Hood: producing on me a composite impression of film-star, gangster, great land-owner interested in his property, Prime Minister, Party manager, head gamekeeper at Chatsworth." He had expected to dislike Goebbels intensely—but didn't. "I suppose it must be some moral defect in me, but the fact remains."

These impressions, along with his friendly reception by Berliners, who nicknamed him Lord Halalifax (Halali was the German equivalent of Tallyho!), favorably prepared him for a meeting with the Führer at the Berghof on the morning of November 19. As he looked out the car window Halifax saw a pair of black-trousered legs and assumed this was a footman descending to help him up the snow-swept steps, until he heard someone hoarsely whisper in his ear, "Der Führer, der Führer."

The tall, gaunt Briton hastily jackknifed out of the car to be met with a friendly smile from Hitler, who insisted on showing Halifax and Sir Ivone Kirkpatrick of the Berlin Embassy around the house before they settled themselves at an inconveniently low table in the study. "I have brought no new proposals from London," said Halifax, "I have chiefly come to ascertain the German government's views on the existing political situation, and to see what possibilities of a solution there might be."

At these words the Führer frowned so angrily that the interpreter Schmidt thought he would lapse into a silent sulk. Instead he launched into a series of "highly categorial demands." He railed at the British press, which he charged had tried to wreck the Halifax visit by publishing so-called German demands, and became overtly annoyed when Halifax stiffly defended the freedom of the press in England.

With gentle, stately courtesy Halifax tried to conciliate the peevish Hitler. He praised his host for keeping Communism out of Germany and expressed the hope that their two nations, along with France and Italy, could lay a very solid foundation for peace. Then he made a diplomatic blunder. Eden had warned him not to mention the situation in central and eastern Europe yet, in an effort to be conciliatory, he brought up the subject. Once he had naïvely revealed British intentions, Hitler began to list Germany's desiderata: a close union with Austria, end of suppression of Sudeten Germans in Czechoslovakia, and freedom to extend economic relations with southeastern and eastern Europe inasmuch as Germany was the principal importer of the products of those countries. His argument was consistent without being credible, so he abruptly changed to diatribe. "Obstacles are repeatedly being put in my way in southeast Europe by the Western powers," he shouted, "and political ambitions which I have never entertained are attributed to me!"

Halifax tactfully reiterated that England was always open to any solution not based on force, then added with no tact at all, "That also applies to Austria." It was as if he had touched an alarm button. Hitler excitedly retorted that force had never been considered in the case of Austria since it was the population itself that had demanded Anschluss with Germany.

By the time they adjourned for lunch Schmidt felt that a battle for peace had been lost. "Hitler was still in a bad temper," recalled Kirkpatrick. "Neurath was ill at ease and Lord Halifax could only talk through the interpreter. I made ineffective efforts to get a conversation going, but they all collapsed pitifully under Hitler's determination not to play." When he did talk his sarcastic comments approached rudeness. "I can't see what there is in shooting," he observed when the subject which had brought Halifax to Germany arose; "you go out armed with a highly perfected modern weapon and without risk to yourself kill a defenseless animal." He sardonically suggested that they spare all the bother of the hunt and kill a cow in the slaughterhouse. "In short," recalled Kirkpatrick, "he behaved throughout like a spoiled, sulky child."

They went downstairs where the Führer was served a large cup of chocolate topped by a huge island of whipped cream, while the others had coffee. The mood became more relaxed, particularly when several SS men demonstrated how the huge leaded picture window could be lowered noiselessly into the floor, turning the room into a covered terrace.

On the night train back to Berlin, Neurath had tea with the two Britons. It was a pity, he said, that the Führer had been tired and out of sorts but it had been an excellent thing for him to meet foreigners. When they were alone, Halifax confided to Kirkpatrick that Hitler had bewildered him and "it was doubtful whether the conversation had done more than might have been achieved by a talk between two men of different nations neither of whom could understand the language of the other." For an envoy who had been so credulous, the day's entry in Halifax's diary displayed surprising insight. "He gave me the impression of feeling that, whilst he had attained to power only after a hard struggle with present-day realities, the British government was still living comfortably in a world of its own making, a fairyland of strange, if respectable, illusions. It clung to shibboleths—'collective security,' 'general settlement,' 'disarmament,' 'non-aggression pacts'—which offered no practical prospect of a solution of Europe's difficulties."

But by the time he returned to London (after another interview with Göring, who assured him, "Under no circumstances shall we use force") Halifax was convinced he *did* understand Germany—and fell into the appeasement camp. He assured his colleagues that the Führer was "very sincere," and then reported to the cabinet that "the Germans had no policy of immediate adventure. They were too busy building up their country, which was still in a state of revolution."

His private secretary was dismayed. "I am amazed," he wrote, "that Halifax with all his High Church principles is not more shocked at Hitler's proceedings, but he is always trying to understand Germans. He easily blinds himself to unpleasant facts and is ingenious and even jesuitical in rounding awkward corners in his mind."

Hitler's reasoning for bringing round Halifax was far different and peculiarly his own: "I have always said that the English will get under the same eiderdown with me; in their politics they follow the same guidelines as I do, namely, the overriding necessity to annihilate Bolshevism."

That Yuletide, like the previous, was not a period of depression for Hitler. He was positively jovial on Christmas Eve, according to valet Krause. While the two of them knelt on the floor of the Munich apartment wrapping gifts, Krause accidentally tied a knot on top of his master's thumb. Hitler laughed, clapped Krause on the back of the neck and then asked for his dinner jacket. He was bent on celebrating the night before Christmas in style and commandeered his valet as a companion. Avoiding SS guards, the two sneaked down the stairs like conspirators to a waiting taxi. "No one saw us and Hitler was quite relieved. I wanted to sit next to the driver but Hitler grabbed my arm and I got in the back with him." For the next two hours the taxi toured around Munich, constantly changing directions. Finally Hitler gave his destination: the Luitpold Café.

The driver, having no idea who his passengers were, seemed relieved to get rid of them and drove off rapidly once he had his fare. "He probably thought we were a couple of nuts," recalled Krause, "probably not too unjustifiably so; the whole thing struck me as pretty peculiar too." Instead of going into the café Hitler set off for the Königsplatz. Noticing that Krause kept looking around nervously, he said, "Don't be afraid. No one would believe that Adolf Hitler would be walking here alone in Munich." Even so he lowered his own head when someone approached. It began to hail and the Führer linked arms with his valet since his patent leather shoes were slippery. On and on they walked until they came back to the apartment. The Führer seemed as delighted as a boy that he had not only eluded his guards but managed to walk around the city unnoticed. But the next day Himmler reprimanded Krause for participating in such an escapade. Thereafter, he ordered, such plans must be reported even if the Führer forbade it.

6

By the end of the year Prime Minister Chamberlain had confirmed his conviction that only a policy of appeasement would bring lasting peace to Europe. Even Foreign Secretary Eden, despite qualms, expressed qualified hopes in his own recommendations for "The Next Steps Towards a General Settlement with Germany," which he submitted on New Year's Day, 1938. "The conversations between Lord Halifax and Herr Hitler showed that, if we wish for a general settlement with Germany, it will be for us, and not for the German Government, to take the next step by putting forward some concrete proposals. . . . The next step, therefore, lies with us. It is important, if we are really anxious to prevent the hopes created by the recent conversations from evaporating, that we should keep moving, that there should be no long delay. We must keep moving."

The "concrete proposals" Eden was referring to were such bribes as the offer to Hitler of what didn't even belong to England—a large section of Africa owned by Belgium and Portugal—and concessions to Sudeten Germans in Czechoslovakia. Hitler could not be bought so cheaply. His talk with Halifax had confirmed that the British would acquiesce in any expansion to the east and southeast as long as it was done with a show of legality. At the same time it was apparent that Fritsch, Blomberg and other senior military leaders feared his adventurous policy would lead to disaster. They blanched at the thought of using the threat of war as a diplomatic weapon, and a confrontation with their Führer seemed inevitable.

The crisis was precipitated by a onetime prostitute, Fräulein Erna Gruen, presently working in the office of Blomberg as a typist-secretary. After a brief acquaintance the field marshal, a widower of six years, decided to make her his wife even though marriage with a woman whose mother worked in a laundry was a violation of the officers' code.

On January 12 the field marshal and typist were married in a room of the War Ministry with Göring and Hitler as witnesses. But no sooner had the couple left on a honeymoon than rumors spread about the past of the young Frau Blomberg. From their dossiers the Berlin police found that she not only had a record as a prostitute but had posed for pornographic pictures. These revelations confounded Hitler and shock was followed by indignation. Convinced that Blomberg had inveigled him into being a witness at the wedding so he would be compelled to quash any rumors that might arise, Hitler ordered Göring to inform the field marshal of Erna's past. If he agreed to dissolve the marriage some way would be found to avoid a public scandal. If not Blomberg would have to be fired.

His logical successor was Fritsch, who was far more opposed to the Führer's policy. Göring had come to the chancellery prepared for this possibility with another dossier given him by Himmler and Heydrich. It purported to prove that Fritsch had committed criminal homosexual acts with two Hitler Youth and a male prostitute known as Bavarian Joe. Here was a timely excuse to rid himself of a most unco-operative commander-in-chief and Hitler readily availed himself of it.

When Göring left the room he must have been elated. In a single stroke Minister of War Blomberg and the best candidate to supplant him had apparently been eliminated, leaving Göring the most likely successor. The next morning he informed Blomberg of the Führer's ultimatum but the field marshal stonily refused to annul the marriage.

At the Bendlerstrasse generals were receiving roguish telephone calls from prostitutes delighted by the success of one of their number. The officer corps, which had winked at the murders of Generals von Schleicher and von Bredow, could not excuse this insult to their honor. The consensus was that Blomberg must resign at once and, unless he wished to be stricken from the officer list, divorce his wife. Fritsch was delegated to carry this demand to Hitler, who had about decided to do so on his own. Still the affair dejected him. "He walked up and down the room," recalled his personal adjutant, Wiedemann, "hand behind back—a brokenhearted man—while mumbling over and over, 'If a German field marshal marries a whore, then anything in this world is possible!'"

He called in Hossbach and they discussed a successor. His chief adjutant could see no objection to Fritsch; the evidence of homosexuality must have been manufactured. The two argued until late that evening and as Hossbach was leaving he asked permission to let Fritsch know of the charges against him. Absolutely not, said Hitler, and gave his adjutant a direct order not to do so. Hossback went directly to General von Fritsch's apartment. The general indignantly denounced the charges. "If Hitler wants to get rid of me," he exclaimed, "then he has only to say the word and I will resign!"

"What an influence a woman can exert on the history of a country, and thereby the world, without even knowing it," wrote Colonel Jodl in his diary the following day, January 26. That morning Hossbach had the grit to tell Hitler he had disregarded orders and seen Fritsch. Surprisingly the Führer did not lose his temper. He seemed to accept Fritsch's claim of innocence, remarking that there was now no reason why he shouldn't be named Minister of War. He went out of his way to praise the general and swear he had no desire to get rid of him. A few hours later, however, Hitler summoned Hossbach and began angrily assailing Fritsch. The adjutant begged him not to act until he had confronted the general in person. Reluctantly the Führer agreed to an interview that evening.

During the day Wiedemann also approached Hitler with another unwelcome proposal. Göring had persuaded Wiedemann to recommend him as Minister of War but Hitler said, "By no means! Göring doesn't even know how to hold an inspection. I know more about it than he does!"

Hitler heard the same proposition later in the day when he regretfully informed Blomberg of his dismissal and, out of courtesy, asked him to recommend a successor. Blomberg suggested the man who had helped ruin him. This time Hitler was even blunter: Göring was too impotent and lazy. In that case, said Blomberg, why didn't the Führer take over the post of Minister of War himself? Apparently Blomberg out of malice was willing to cripple the officer corps which had betrayed him by placing Hitler in charge of the armed forces.

Hitler neither accepted nor rejected this recommendation, only asked who could then take charge of the OKW Staff. When Blomberg offered no candidate Hitler asked who was in charge of *his* staff. General Wilhelm Keitel, replied Blomberg, hastily adding that the prospective father-in-law of his own daughter would not be suitable for such an important position. "He's nothing but the man who runs my office."

"That's exactly the man I am looking for!"

Blomberg returned to his office that noon and, appearing to be "absolutely shattered and near collapse," told Keitel what had happened. He confessed knowing all along of his wife's disreputable past, "but that was no reason for casting a woman out forever." He had parted from Hitler amicably, he said, with the assurance that if war should come he would once again be at the Führer's side. When Keitel suggested a divorce, "for their children's sake," Blomberg protested that it had been a love match on both sides and he would "rather put a bullet in his head than that." He rushed out of the office with tears in his eyes.

At 5 P.M. Keitel was shown into Hitler's study. The Führer complained of loneliness; Keitel would have to stand by him. With some agitation he spoke of his admiration for Blomberg and how much he owed him, then complained at being tricked into acting as a witness for the wedding. Would the officer corps ever have accepted such an impossible marriage? Keitel was forced to agree that they would not. The next question was on the succession. Whom did Keitel propose? Like Blomberg, he proposed Göring and Hitler again objected. Keitel's next choice was Fritsch. The Führer stepped to his writing desk and came back with an indictment signed by the Minister of Justice charging that officer with a criminal homosexual offense. Hitler admitted suppressing an earlier similar indictment since he could not bring himself to believe the charge, but the question of succession to the most important military post in the land made it necessary to clear up the matter once and for all. He was going to have a private conversation with Fritsch and ask him point-blank if he was guilty—then watch for his reaction.

This confrontation came late that evening in the Führer's library. Fritsch knew none of the details concerning the alleged homosexual acts with two Hitler Youth and Bavarian Joe. He thought he was being queried about a silly matter involving two other Hitler Jugend and was indignant that such an innocent affair was being taken seriously. He explained that occasionally he had invited the two boys to dinner and later given them lessons in map reading, and if one was not attentive he would administer a light tap on the rear with a ruler.

Hitler had never heard about *these* two youngsters, and fired Fritsch peremptorily. Before the dazed Fritsch was out of the chancellery Hitler was giving his personal adjutant an excited version of the scene. "Imagine, Wiedemann, all of a sudden it was not only two boys but *four* he was mixed up with! The case cannot be kept secret any longer."

Hitler was still agitated when Keitel reported to him the following afternoon and learned that Fritsch was confined to his apartment. The conversation again turned to a successor. This time Hitler said that he had decided to take over the supreme command himself. Keitel was to remain as his chief of staff. Along with the post went an unpleasant chore. He was to fire Hossbach for going behind Hitler's back to warn Fritsch. The Führer never wanted to see him again.

Wiedemann was almost as perplexed and angry as Hossbach at this dismissal. He approached the Führer, who was nervously pacing the floor of the winter garden. "Mein Führer," he impulsively exclaimed, "you have wronged someone grievously today." What did Wiedemann mean?

"Colonel Hossbach!" "Yes, Wiedemann," said Hitler at last, "you are right. But it was only today that I saw the 'human being' Hossbach behind the General Staff 'machinery.' Tell him that I am sorry but I cannot reverse his dismissal now. He should take a trip to the Mediterranean and then join me for dinner in the future. I will also give him a letter of recommendation specifying his excellent qualifications." This mood of forgiveness soon passed, and he never sent the letter of recommendation. "That fellow did nothing but lie to me," he would say, "and I will make sure he never gets on the General Staff again!"*

In the following week the Führer addressed himself to the problems left in the wake of the Blomberg-Fritsch scandals. First he ordered a full Gestapo investigation of the latter, then concentrated on selection of a new army commander-in-chief. He settled on General Walther von Brauchitsch, an admirer though not a party member, but pretended that his first choice was Reichenau. General Gerd von Rundstedt, as representative of the army, indignantly disapproved. To the officer corps Reichenau was not only a rabid Nazi but a military radical not fit to hold any important command. Rundstedt in turn nominated Beck. Hitler would not accept him. His next choice, of course, was Brauchitsch. It had developed into a horse trade and this time Rundstedt said the Führer's candidate would be acceptable to the army.

This was not yet the end of the affair. Brauchitsch revealed that he could not accept the post unless a pressing personal problem was settled. He was in the midst of divorce proceedings but his wife was demanding a considerable settlement and he was already in debt. Hitler not only gave the general 80,000 marks but persuaded Frau von Brauchitsch to accept the terms. It was a good bargain for the Führer. He now had an army commander-in-chief indebted to him. Furthermore, the woman Brauchitsch planned to marry, Frau Charlotte Schmidt, was, according to Ulrich von Hassell, "a two hundred per cent rabid Nazi." Because of Hitler's manipulations and determination along with the vacillation of the most senior generals, the crisis was finally resolved.

Surprisingly, the abortive mutiny of the army hierarchy did not permeate to the field. Except for Fritsch's close friends, few officers knew of the scandals or that both he and Blomberg had been dismissed. And so it was with some mystification that many of the commanding generals of the Wehrmacht arrived in Berlin for a conference on February 4, 1938, and learned what had occurred from the morning newspapers. They were summoned to a large hall in the chancellery where Hitler informed them of the criminal charges against Fritsch and the need to dismiss Blomberg because of his unfortunate marriage. "We were flabbergasted," recalled

* Hitler did approve Hossbach's subsequent appointment as commanding general of an army.

Heinz Guderian. "These serious allegations against our most senior officers, whom we knew to be men of spotless honor, cut us to the quick. They were quite incredible, and yet our immediate reaction was that the first magistrate of the German state could not simply have invented these stories out of thin air."

The astounded officers meekly accepted Hitler's announcement of the reorganization of the Wehrmacht, and that evening Hitler legalized his takeover of the armed forces at a cabinet meeting. After presenting Keitel and Brauchitsch, he announced that he himself was now in command of the armed forces. It was the last time the cabinet would ever meet and it was fitting that its members merely sat and approved.

Just before midnight the people of Germany were informed by radio of the Führer's momentous decree. They also learned that Blomberg and Fritsch had resigned, sixteen high-ranking generals had been dismissed and forty-four more transferred to other posts. Finally, Hermann Göring was granted the baton of a Luftwaffe field marshal as a consolation for not being named Minister of War. The house cleaning also extended to the diplomatic service. Foreign Minister von Neurath was replaced by Ribbentrop, who believed that every hour not spent in preparing for war against England was an hour lost to Germany. There was no longer any possibility of an agreement with the British, he had recently told Hitler, since they would not tolerate a powerful Germany. "On that point they will fight."

It was a day to remember in German history. The most powerful dissidents in the Wehrmacht had been eliminated or curbed and the two leading military men in the land, Keitel and Brauchitsch, were both in Hitler's debt and little more than uneasy deputies.

Once he had delivered his monologue to the cabinet, Hitler set off for Berchtesgaden with Major Rudolf Schmundt, who had replaced Hossbach as chief military adjutant, and a new army adjutant, Gerhard Engel. Next morning he must have read the headlines of the *Völkischer Beobachter* with supreme satisfaction:

STRONGEST CONCENTRATION OF ALL POWERS IN THE
FÜHRER'S HANDS!

At last he was the supreme dictator of the German Reich. He was ready to embark on his final course.

Chapter Sixteen

THE RETURN OF THE NATIVE
FEBRUARY–APRIL 1938

1

The repercussions of Hitler's bloodless purge were felt almost immediately in Vienna. At the German Legation, Franz von Papen—once Chancellor and now merely a minister to a small country—was called on the telephone. It was Lammers, secretary of the chancellery. "The Führer wished to inform you," he said, "that your mission in Vienna has ended. I wanted to tell you before you read about it in the newspapers." Papen was almost speechless. He had been persuaded by Hitler to take the minor post to restore the dangerous situation created by the Dollfuss murder. "I had served my purpose, it seemed, and could now go," he recalled with some bitterness. To "obtain some picture of what was going on" he decided to go at once to Berchtesgaden where he found Hitler exhausted and disturbed. "His eyes seemed unable to focus on anything and his thoughts seemed elsewhere. He sought to explain my dismissal with empty excuses." The distracted Führer paid little attention to the conversation until Papen remarked that only a face-to-face meeting between Hitler and Austrian Chancellor Kurt von Schuschnigg could solve the numerous problems dividing the two countries.

"That is an excellent idea," said Hitler and told Papen to return to Vienna and arrange a meeting for the near future. "I should be very pleased to invite Herr Schuschnigg here and talk everything over with him."

Schuschnigg accepted Papen's invitation with some uneasiness, then

confessed to his Foreign Minister, Guido Schmidt, that he did so "to forestall a coup and to gain time until the international situation should improve in Austria's favor." He added ironically that he only wished his
place opposite Hitler at the conference table could be filled by a psychiatrist. Schuschnigg was, indeed, ill suited to face such a ruthless opponent.
A devout Catholic, an intellectual, a decent man with little vanity or driving ambition, he would enter the contest at a disadvantage.

On the evening of February 11, accompanied by Guido Schmidt, he
boarded the night express for Salzburg. Once the train reached the
birthplace of Mozart the sleeping car was detached. The next morning the
two men drove through the ancient city, past the airport and across the
Salzach River to the German border. Papen was waiting with a Hitler salute. The German customs officials also smartly raised their arms, as did
their Austrian counterparts in violation of the law. It was an alarming
omen and moments later came another. Papen trusted the guests wouldn't
mind that three generals had "quite accidentally" arrived at the Berghof.
If he had been a Dollfuss, Schuschnigg might have protested, but he
disliked scenes and had no desire to provoke Hitler. "No," he said, "I
don't mind but it's strange."

On the outskirts of Berchtesgaden they turned sharply to the left, at
the foot of the Obersalzberg where half-tracks were waiting to take them
up the steep, icy road to the Berghof. They passed neat snowbound farmhouses and an old church, then came upon SS barracks, some still under
construction. All at once there was a sharp turn and the tracked vehicle
stopped below the large terrace of the Berghof.

Hitler advanced with outstretched hand, the genial host. After intro-
ducing the three generals behind him, he led the Austrian Chancellor into
his study on the second floor. Here the Führer abruptly shed his affability,
bluntly accusing Austria of following anything but neighborly policy. Was
it friendly to stay complacently in the League of Nations after Germany
withdrew? In fact, Austria had never done anything to help Germany.
The whole history of Austria was one uninterrupted act of high treason.
"And I can tell you right now, Herr Schuschnigg, that I am absolutely determined to make an end of all this. The German Reich is one of the
Great Powers and nobody will raise his voice if it settles its border problems."

Determined not to lose his temper, Schuschnigg retorted that Austria's entire history had been an essential and inseparable part of German
history. "Austria's contribution in this respect is considerable."

"Absolutely zero, I'm telling you, absolutely zero!" exclaimed Hitler,
sounding like anything but a man born and raised in Austria himself,
and, when Schuschnigg brought up Beethoven, reminded him that the
composer came from the Lower Rhineland. "I am telling you once more
that things cannot go on this way. I have a historic mission; and this mis-

sion I will fulfill because Providence has destined me to do so. I thoroughly believe in this mission; it is my life. . . . Look around you in Germany today, Herr Schuschnigg, and you will find that there is but one will." He had chosen the most difficult road that any German ever took and made the greatest achievement in the history of Germany, greater than any other German. And not by force! "I am carried along by the love of my people. I can go about freely and without guard at any time in Germany. And that because I am borne by the love and trust of my people."

He accused Austria of fortifying the German border and making ridiculous efforts to mine the bridge and roads leading to the Reich. "You don't seriously believe you can stop me or even delay me for half an hour, do you? Perhaps you will wake up one morning in Vienna to find us there —just like a spring storm. And then you'll see something! I would very much like to save Austria from such a fate, because such an action would mean blood."

When Schuschnigg replied that Austria was not alone in the world and an invasion of his country would probably mean war, Hitler scoffed. Nobody would move a finger for Austria—not Italy, nor England, nor France. "Think it over, Herr Schuschnigg," he said, lowering his voice. "Think it over well. I can only wait until this afternoon. If I tell you that, you will do well to take my words literally. I don't believe in bluffing. All my past is proof of that."

His tactics were getting on Schuschnigg's nerves. He longed for a cigarette but had been warned earlier not to light up in the Führer's presence. He asked Hitler exactly what he wanted. "That," replied Hitler, ending the session with dramatic abruptness, "we can discuss this afternoon." He rang a bell and the doors opened silently from the outside. They ate in the dining room, served by handsome young SS men in snow-white uniforms. In front of the others Hitler treated his guest politely; the conversation was relaxing and inconsequential.

Coffee was served in an adjoining walled-in winter garden. Suddenly the host excused himself and returned to his study with Ribbentrop. His departure was a relief to Schuschnigg, who began chain-smoking. It also gave him the opportunity of chatting with the three generals, none of whom knew why they had been summoned to the Berghof. It was almost 4 P.M. before the Austrian was led to a small room for a meeting with Ribbentrop, who handed over a two-page typewritten draft of an agreement that was essentially an ultimatum: Germany would renew its full support of Austria's sovereignty if all imprisoned Austrian National Socialists, including the assassins of Dollfuss, were set free within three days and all dismissed National Socialist officials and officers were reinstated in their former positions. In addition, Artur Seyss-Inquart, the leader of the moderate Pan-German faction, was to be appointed Minister of Interior with full, unlimited control of the nation's police forces; a "moderate" Austrian

Nazi was to be Minister of Defense, and the incumbent propaganda chiefs were to be removed as part of "the smooth execution of a press truce."

To Schuschnigg these concessions amounted to the end of Austrian independence and, suppressing indignation, he began to contest the various points like a dispassionate lawyer. He had just managed to squeeze a few minor concessions from Ribbentrop when word came that the Führer was ready to see him upstairs.

Hitler was excitedly pacing up and down the study. "Herr Schuschnigg," he said, continuing to omit the *von*, "I have decided to make one last attempt." He pushed another copy of the draft agreements at the Austrian. "There is nothing to be discussed about it. I will not change one single iota. You will either sign it as it stands or else our meeting has been useless. In that case I shall decide during the night what will be done next."

Schuschnigg refused to sign. Even if he did, he said, it would be valueless since by constitution President Miklas alone could appoint cabinet members and grant amnesty. Nor could he in any way guarantee that the time limits stipulated in the document would be observed.

"You must guarantee that!"

"I could not possibly, Herr Reichskanzler."

Schuschnigg's studied, courtroom rejoinders infuriated Hitler. He rushed to the door and shouted, "General Keitel!" He turned back to Schuschnigg. "I shall have you called later." The bellow was heard in the winter garden and Keitel trotted upstairs like an obedient dog, entering the study just as Schuschnigg was about to leave. Out of breath, Keitel asked what commands the Führer had. "None at all! Just sit down." Puzzled, the head of OKW perched in the corner dutifully and from now on fellow officers would nickname him *Lakeitel*, for *Lakai* (lackey).

Unaware that Hitler was bluffing, Schuschnigg was badly shaken by the time he reached the winter garden. He related what had happened to Foreign Minister Schmidt, who said he would not be surprised if they were arrested "within the next five minutes."

Upstairs, another Austrian, a moderate Nazi, an art critic, was assuring the Führer that Schuschnigg was a scrupulous man who would honor his promises. Impressed, Hitler made one of his lightning tactical shifts and the next time Schuschnigg walked into the study he found a magnanimous Führer. "I have decided," he said, "to change my mind—for the first time in my entire life. But I warn you—this is your very last chance. I have given you three more days before the agreement goes into effect."

After the shock of the first two conversations, the minor concessions wrung out of Hitler seemed more important than they were and Schuschnigg agreed to sign the compact. Once the revised document was sent out to be retyped, Hitler again became the genial host—one who has just sold the guest an objet d'art for an exorbitant price and is assuring him it is a bargain. "Believe me, Herr Bundeskanzler, it is for the best. Now we can abide by this agreement for the next five years."

It was evening by the time the two copies of the agreements were signed. Hitler asked Schuschnigg and Schmidt to stay for dinner but they were anxious to get back to Salzburg. Accompanied by Papen, they proceeded in silence through the foggy night toward Salzburg. Finally Papen said, "Now you have some idea, Herr Bundeskanzler, how difficult it is to deal with such an unstable person." He quickly added that he was sure it would be different the next time. "You know the Führer can be absolutely charming." Schuschnigg wondered if there would be a next time.

At the Berghof Hitler was already engaged in another bluff. He instructed his generals to sham invasion maneuvers near the Austrian border for the next few days. Hopefully, the threat of attack would induce Austrian President Miklas to ratify the agreement. If Schuschnigg was having second thoughts, so was Hitler. "This Schuschnigg was a harder bone than I first thought," he jotted down in his notebook. "The appearance of Keitel seemed to impress him but I don't believe that his signature means a capitulation. One must be hellishly careful to see that no change of mood occurs. His Jesuit brothers are by no means to be trusted."

2

Schuschnigg had three days to get their agreement approved by his colleagues and President Miklas. It was Sunday when the Chancellor arrived back in Vienna and time would run out on Tuesday the fifteenth. He conferred at once with Miklas, who was willing to grant amnesty to those Austrian Nazis still in prison while vigorously objecting to the appointment of Seyss-Inquart. "I would give him any other post," he said, "but I refuse to give him the police and the army."

News of the secret meeting in Berchtesgaden soon spread to the coffeehouses, the unofficial parliament of Austria, and an uneasy spirit pervaded the nation. Bitter arguments sprang up among the cabinet members with one group complaining that Schuschnigg should publicly proclaim Hitler's brutal tactics at the Berghof and the other commending the Chancellor's policy of caution. Twenty-four hours before Hitler's ultimatum was to run out so much disagreement remained that an emergency conference was held in the office of the President. Present, besides the two principals, were the mayor of Vienna, the president of the National Bank and a former Chancellor. After reviewing the situation Schuschnigg presented three possible courses: select a new Chancellor who would be under no obligation to the commitments at the Berghof; carry out the agreements under a new Chancellor; or carry it out under Schuschnigg.

An atmosphere of desperation settled over the room due to more reports of German invasion maneuvers at the border, and the argument that followed was not only heated but digressive. The most unlikely proposals were made, including one that Braunau, Hitler's birthplace, be ceded to Germany. Schuschnigg felt sure that Hitler would invade Austria if a single one of his demands was turned down and at last Miklas bowed to pressure, reluctantly agreeing to the Chancellor's third proposal: to leave Schuschnigg in office and accept the Berchtesgaden pact.

The Führer's charade at the Berghof, along with his sham invasion, had intimidated the Austrians into capitulation. That evening a new cabinet was sworn in and the following day, February 15, some of the truth was transmitted secretly to Austrian representatives abroad. They were informed by ciphered telegram that there had been "sharp disagreements" at Berchtesgaden, owing to increased German demands and personal pressure from Hitler; only after hours of negotiations had a basis of agreement at last been found. Fearing even this language was too strong, the government hastily dispatched another telegram which ordered the recipients to "regard references in the previous telegram to difficulties connected with the Berchtesgaden conversations as for your personal information only."

In Vienna there was a rising demand that Schuschnigg reveal exactly what had happened in Berchtesgaden but, having promised to keep silent until after Hitler addressed the Reichstag on Sunday, he kept his word as a man of honor.

The German Legation phoned Berlin that there was "considerable agitation in Vienna because of the political and economic consequences" of the agreement, that the city "resembled an anthill," and that "quite a few Jews were preparing to emigrate." Secret SD reports confirmed this, one agent informing Heydrich on February 18 that the Chancellor was under heavy attack from both Jews and Catholics. "The Jews were attacking mainly through the stock exchange, to exert pressure on the currency. Since February 17, 1938 there has been an extraordinarily heavy flight of capital, which led to a substantial drop in Austrian securities in Switzerland and London, as well as in other foreign countries. Schilling notes are being taken over the border illegally in large quantities, so that they have not been quoted since last night."

On February 20 Hitler made his eagerly awaited speech to the Reichstag, which was also broadcast throughout Austria. After announcing that he and Schuschnigg had "made a contribution to the cause of European peace," he accused Austria of mistreating its "German minority." It was, he added, "intolerable for a self-conscious world power to know that at its side are co-racials who are subjected to continuous suffering because of their sympathy and unity with the whole German race and its ideology."

On and on he orated and, though quoting facts and figures at length, he managed to entrance most of the audience at the Kroll Opera House. "During the rhetorical passages his voice mounted to the pitch of delirium: he was a man transformed and possessed. We were in the presence of a miracle." These words came not from a German but from an English observer, Major Francis Yeats-Brown.

In Vienna journalist G. E. R. Gedye roamed the streets during the "interminable hours of that speech" to see how the populace was reacting. It was a city of the dead. He found only ten people at one of the busiest corners, all listening tensely under a loudspeaker. The local Nazis were delighted that Hitler was at last coming out into the open and, not long after he finished, began congregating and shouting over and over: "Sieg Heil! Sieg Heil! Heil Hitler! Heil Hitler!"

Gedye took a taxi to the German Legation, a focal point of activity. As he drew near another chant of "Sieg Heil!" could be heard. "As one first caught it in the distance it was just a rhythmic throb, like the beating of a feverish pulse, which as one approached seemed to change into the in-articulate but disciplined cawing of some militarised rookery—a-a-a-ah—Aaaah—Aah-A-a-a-ah—Aah! and finally into audible words. The dam of four years had been pierced by the Hitler speech and the Brown flood was beginning to trickle into the streets of Vienna."

While the oration was greeted in Rome with some sympathy and understanding, there was underlying concern since it did not confirm Austria's independence. The German chargé in Rome reported that the Italians were unhappy that Hitler, in violation of their 1936 pact, had not previously consulted them and if Berlin "should continue to use this method" it might mean the end of the Axis.

Schuschnigg's reply to Hitler came four days later at the opening session of the Federal Diet in a speech broadcast throughout both countries. The stage of the parliament was decorated with a mass of tulips in the Austrian colors of red-white-red. Near the rostrum was a bust of the martyred Dollfuss. Although the Chancellor walked erectly to the podium his restrained manner was that of a Jesuit scholar. He was greeted with shouts of "Schuschnigg! Schuschnigg!" for the word had gone out that he was going to make a fighting speech. "The one and only point on the order of the day," he said in a tired voice, "is: Austria." This brought renewed shouts. Inspired, he began to speak movingly of those who had fought for Austrian independence from the Empress Maria Theresa to Dollfuss. Never before had his delivery been so effective, so fervent. Gone were the restraints of the self-effacing intellectual who had allowed himself to be bullied at the Berghof. His tone hardened when he finally mentioned the Berchtesgaden agreements. "We have gone to the very limit of concessions, where we must call a halt and say, 'Thus far and no further.'" He went on to declare that "neither Nationalism nor Socialism is the watchword of Austria, but patriotism!" The nation would remain free and for this Austrians would have to fight to the end. He ended with a fighting

motto: *"Rot-Weiss-Rot! Bis in den Tod!* [Red-White-Red! Until Death!]
Austria!"

The members of the House stood to applaud frenziedly. Their shouts
were picked up by the crowds outside. Someone started singing *"Gott
Erhalte* [God preserve]" and it became a roaring chorus. They sang
"Andreas Hofer," the anthem of revolt that came from the Tyrol, Schuschnigg's birthplace. The enthusiasm in the streets carried over to a general
feeling of hope throughout the land and as far as Paris. In a debate on foreign affairs the next day at the Chamber of Deputies the French Foreign
Minister declared that Austrian independence was "an indispensable element of the European balance," while one deputy went so far as to predict that "France's fate would be decided on the banks of the Danube."

Throughout Austria local Nazis began demonstrating. The center of
the agitation was Graz where the swastika had been raised on the roof of
the town hall during Schuschnigg's speech. Defying the government's ban
on political meetings, the local Nazis subsequently announced a rally of
65,000 party members from all over Austria for the weekend. Schuschnigg
reacted immediately by dispatching troops, bombers and an armored train
to Graz. The Nazis backed down and canceled the meeting but it was little consolation to the Chancellor. The disturbance should have been
quelled by Seyss-Inquart and his police, not by the army.

3

French indignation at Hitler's threat to Austria took the form of a
proposal to London that the two big powers send a joint note of protest to
Berlin. It arrived at an inauspicious time. Anthony Eden had just resigned
and the Foreign Ministry was momentarily without leadership. The English public had not yet been aroused by the events in Austria and their
Prime Minister remained devoted to the policy of appeasing Germany.
Furthermore, Chamberlain was supported by the London *Times,* which
consistently played down the importance of the events in Austria. "Fundamentally," it editorialized, "a close understanding between the two German states is the most natural thing possible." Goebbels could not have
put it more convincingly. "Austria can never be anti-Germanic."

Not even Franklin D. Roosevelt's condemnation of all aggressors
the previous autumn had affected Chamberlain's policy. Nor had he been
moved by the President's practical suggestion, which followed his call to
"quarantine" the Japanese, Nazis and Fascists from the community of nations. Roosevelt dispatched Captain Royal Ingersoll, chief of the navy's
War Plans Division, to London with instructions to explore the implementation of a long-range naval blockade of Japan. The proposition found
such approval in the British Admiralty that its members told Ingersoll
they were "prepared to stop all Japanese traffic crossing a line roughly

from Singapore through the Dutch East Indies, New Guinea, New Hebrides and around to the east of Australia and New Zealand." But Prime Minister Chamberlain put an end to the plan for mutual blockade early in 1938 by rejecting another proposal of Roosevelt's calling for Britain to join an international conference to discuss essential principles of international law that would, incidentally, awaken America to the true nature of the "bandit nations," as Roosevelt was privately calling them. At first the President did not grasp the full implication of Chamberlain's unexpected rejection, but it soon became clear that his refusal to join an international conference meant that the British government would take no part in any quarantine, either in the Orient or in Europe. Chamberlain's rebuff was such a blow to Roosevelt that it led him to abandon a vigorous foreign policy that might have stemmed further aggression all around the world—and so changed the course of history. Instead he allowed the United States to revert to isolation.

By the beginning of March, therefore, Great Britain was irrevocably bound to appeasement. On the third of the month the Ambassador to Germany, Sir Nevile Henderson, called at the chancellery to inform Hitler that His Majesty's Government was ready, in principle, to discuss all outstanding questions. Despite Henderson's obvious effort to be friendly and absolutely correct, "his general bearing, which was that of the perfect English gentleman," recalled interpreter Schmidt, "always somehow irritated both Ribbentrop and Hitler, who could not endure 'fine people.'"

It took Henderson ten minutes to state the object of his visit: a genuine desire to improve mutual relations between their two countries. Britain, he said, was prepared to make certain concessions to settle the grave problems of limitation of armaments and restrictions of bombing as well as a peaceful solution to the Czech and Austrian problems. What contribution to general security and peace in Europe was Hitler ready to make?

During this lengthy exposition the Führer crouched in his armchair scowling and when Henderson finally stopped he angrily replied that only a small percentage of Austrians supported Schuschnigg. Why did England persist in opposing a just settlement and interfering in "German family matters"? He abruptly went on the offensive, charging that the Franco-Soviet and Czecho-Soviet pacts were definite threats to Germany. That was why Germany had to be so heavily armed. In consequence any limitation of arms depended on the Russians. And this was a problem complicated "by the fact that one could place as much confidence in the faith in treaties of a barbarous creature like the Soviet Union as in the comprehension of mathematical formulae by a savage. Any agreement with the U.S.S.R. was quite worthless and Russia should never be allowed into Europe."

Theirs was a rambling conversation that, after two hours, left the case of Austria in limbo by begging the question "with a vague reply." The fol-

lowing
Austria
the Fü
delete
sinc
he
tir

ent his chief economic adviser, Wilhelm Keppler, to
imself to Schuschnigg as a personal representative of
bearing fresh demands which included everything
en. But Keppler's main interest was economic and,
luss as a financial imperative for both countries,
efactor than a predator. "The Führer's wish at the
igg, "was for an evolutionary development; in
oll up Austria from within, if possible without
lvement." The time, concluded the amiable
ate this process.

ro.
teers
!" The
radios w
"This means
stria told his
never allow

rply to Keppler's new demands, such as the
Nazi as Minister of Economics, cancellation
Beobachter and formal legalization of Na-
he incredulous Schuschnigg, could Hitler
this fresh set of impositions? His govern-
ian Nazis only on the basis of long-term
ce. Schuschnigg recalled that the inter-
eppler reported that it "began tempes-
ely conciliatory manner," and that he
nigg will by no means submit to force
come along to a great extent, if this is
of prestige. We can rely on his loyalty
ements." He further reported that the
ent progress, particularly in Graz where
rofessed National Socialism. "At present
kes to the movement, in order to wring
Schuschnigg."

and. A vote
ome—meant
with Austria
scite threat-
d not toler-
neral Keitel
ake appro-
lan, Opera-
tempted to

the Nazis only incited new disturbances,
of undeclared civil war. In Vienna storm
would cross the Danube Canal to the Jew-
uting, "Sieg Heil! Sieg Heil!" one night
They would be confronted by opponents
and "Red-White-Red to the Death!"
usually brought to an end by truncheon-
s the patriots who got beat up, for the loy-
re to Minister of the Interior Seyss-Inquart

e where he
tical study.
neral Beck
stria. "We
one, noth-
two corps
ustria, he
rch across
ch an op-
nal. Beck
us forma-
amateur

igg dispatched an appeal to Mussolini on
ht have to hold a plebiscite to save the situa-
ds of reassurance. Professing to believe the
any would not use force, he urged Schusch-
. The message was cold comfort to a Chan-
on from abroad while under attack at home

ith logis-
he wrote,
. "In my

by workers for being too lenient and by Nazis for being too *Hitler*
decided to ignore Mussolini's advice.

On March 9 he announced the plebiscite in a *fe*
Innsbruck. He stepped onto the podium in the town squa
traditional Austrian gray jacket and green waistcoat and an
tionally that the nation would go to the polls in four days
question: "Are you in favor of a free and German, independe
a Christian and united Austria?" For the second time he s̨
rather than scholar. "Tyrolians and Austrians, say 'Yes' to T̨
to Austria!" he declared and then ended his speech in Ty̨
with the famous words of Andreas Hofer, calling for volun̨
Napoleon: "*Marde, 's ischt Zut* [Men, the time has come]
ence of 20,000 shouted defiance. Most of those listening a̧
equally inspired. Prince Starhemberg, however, was dismayed.
the end of Schuschnigg," the former Vice-Chancellor of Au̧
wife. "Let us hope it is not the end of Austria. Hitler can̨
this."

As he feared, the announcement did force the Führer's h̨
for a free and united Austria—and this was the likely outc̨
the delay, if not the end, of Anschluss. And since the union
was a necessary preliminary to eastward expansion, the plebi̧
ened to wreck Hitler's entire program of Lebensraum. He cou̧
ate such a challenge and on the morning of March 10 told Gȩ
that the Austrian problem was so "acute" that he should r̨
priate preparations. Keitel remembered that a General Staff p̨
tion Otto, had been drawn up in case Otto von Habsburg at̨
regain the throne of Austria. "Prepare it," ordered the Führer.

Keitel rushed to OKW headquarters in the Bendlerstrass̨
found to his dismay that Operation Otto was simply a theorȩ
Regretting his haste to please the Führer, he turned over to Gȩ
the task of submitting a report on the possible invasion of Au̧
have prepared nothing," complained Beck, "nothing has been ̧
ing at all." When Beck reported to Hitler and suggested using
and the 2nd Panzer Division for the military occupation of ̧
was appalled to learn that these troops should be prepared to m̨
the border by Saturday the twelfth. The thought of preparing s̨
eration within forty-eight hours was inconceivable to a professi̧
protested that it meant orders would have to go out to the vari̧
tions at 6 P.M. that same evening. Then do it, said Hitler th̨
strategist.

More concerned with Italian reaction to an invasion than ̧
tics, the Führer hastily dictated a letter to Mussolini. Austria,
was approaching a state of anarchy and he could not stand idly b̨

responsibility as Führer and Chancellor of the German Reich and likewise as a son of this soil . . . I am now determined to restore law and order in my homeland and enable the people to decide their own fate according to their judgment in an unmistakable, clear and open manner." He reminded Il Duce of Germany's help in Italy's critical hour, the Abyssinian war, and promised to repay Italian support by recognizing the boundary between Italy and the Reich as the Brenner Pass. "This decision will never be questioned or changed." It was noon by the time he handed over the sealed letter to Prince Philip von Hessen with instructions to deliver it personally to Il Duce. As the prince boarded the special plane carrying a basket of plants for his garden in Rome, he had no idea how important his mission was.

Throughout Austria posters were being plastered on billboards announcing the plebiscite. Sound trucks circulated through towns and cities urging all Austrians to vote *"Ja"* on Sunday. In Vienna patriots were at last making more noise than the Nazis as groups ranged the streets shouting "Heil Schuschnigg!" "Heil Liberty!" and "Sunday is polling day; we vote *Ja!*"

Heartened by public enthusiasm, Schuschnigg continued to act resolute. "I am neither able nor prepared to play the role of puppet," he wrote Seyss-Inquart in reply to the Minister of the Interior's charge that the plebiscite was contrary to the Berchtesgaden agreements. "I cannot be expected to look on with folded hands while the country is ruined economically and politically." He concluded with an urgent request to Seyss-Inquart, as the minister responsible for security, to take measures to bring terrorism to an end. Otherwise he would not be able to hold the opposing forces in check.

Although Seyss-Inquart was generally regarded as Hitler's cat's-paw, he too was concerned for his country's independence, and while he sympathized with some of the policies of the Austrian Nazis, they did not regard him as one of their number. He was much closer in ideology and nature to Schuschnigg. Both considered themselves patriots; both were devout Catholics; both were intellectuals, shy men of culture with a deep love of music. Seyss-Inquart proved he was more patriot than Nazi by promising to appeal to his followers over the radio to vote affirmative on Sunday.

Schuschnigg went to bed that evening "fully satisfied" that the Nazi threat to the plebiscite had been scotched—unaware that Seyss-Inquart by now had little influence in his own party. The hard-core Austrian Nazis were already on the streets marching in columns of four toward the center of disorder, the official German Tourist Bureau which boasted a hastily painted larger-than-life oil portrait of Hitler. Their shouts of *"Ein Volk, ein Reich, ein Führer!"* were greeted at first with amusement by the patriots, who outnumbered them three to one. Then windows were smashed and the police, who had been standing by, formed cordons to prevent further damage. Making no move to subdue the howling mob of Nazis, they concentrated on the patriots to such an extent that eventually the outnumbered wearers of the swastika dominated the streets.

4

At 2 A.M. on March 11 the improvised invasion plan, still bearing the code name Operation Otto, was issued. In it, Hitler took personal control. "If other measures prove unsuccessful," it read, "I intend to invade Austria with armed forces in order to establish constitutional conditions and to prevent further outrages against the pro-German population." The units involved were to be prepared by noon of March 12. "I reserve the right to decide the actual moment of invasion. The behavior of the troops must give the impression that we do not want to wage war against our Austrian brothers."

At 5:30 A.M. Schuschnigg's bedside phone rang. It was his chief of police reporting that the German border at Salzburg had just been closed and all railroad traffic stopped. He hurried to the chancellery on Ballhausplatz where he learned that German divisions in the Munich area had been mobilized, destination presumably Austria. Equally alarming were the telegraphed texts of German newspapers alleging, for instance, that Communist flags flew in Vienna while mobs shouted "Heil Moskau! Heil Schuschnigg!"

At about 10 A.M. Glaise-Horstenau, Schuschnigg's minister without portfolio, a Nazi, arrived at the Ballhausplatz with written instructions from Hitler and Göring. He was accompanied by Seyss-Inquart, who had met him at the Aspern airport. Badly shaken, Seyss-Inquart reported the demands from Berlin: Schuschnigg must resign and the plebiscite was to be postponed for two weeks so that a "legal poll," similar to the Saar plebiscite, could be set up. If Göring did not get a telephone answer by noon he would assume that Seyss-Inquart was prevented from making the call and would "act accordingly." It was already eleven-thirty and Seyss-Inquart, a reasonable man, extended the deadline until 2 P.M. in the Führer's name.

Schuschnigg used this time to assess possibilities of resistance. He telephoned the chief of police, who informed him that Vienna remained quiet. He had thrown a cordon—"in as far as that is possible"—around the inner city but so many Nazi policemen had been restored to their jobs that the government could no longer count on its police force. In this extremity Schuschnigg summoned the "inner cabinet," his closest advisers, to discuss the emergency. He presented three alternatives: rejection of the ultimatum followed by an appeal to world opinion; acceptance followed by his own resignation; and a compromise, accepting Hitler's demands for technical changes in the plebiscite but resisting all other demands. They decided upon compromise.

It was almost 2 P.M. and moments later the two reluctant messengers of doom, Seyss-Inquart and Glaise-Horstenau, were back. They could not accept the proffered compromise and Schuschnigg was faced with the unpleasant choice between complete submission or defiance. He hurriedly conferred with President Miklas and it was decided to call off the plebiscite. Returning to his office, he informed the inner cabinet members of the decision. They were momentarily struck dumb and in the silence could hear a sound truck announcing the plebiscite, then blasting out "*Oh, Du Mein Österreich* [Oh, You, my Austria]!"

Moments later the Chancellor was telling Seyss-Inquart and Glaise-Horstenau that Berlin's demands for postponement of the plebiscite had been granted. At the same time extensive security measures, such as an 8 P.M. curfew, would have to be taken. Concerned, the two men excused themselves to transmit this information to Göring by telephone.*

"These measures of Chancellor Schuschnigg are in no way satisfactory," replied Göring, who then hung up to think things over. He should have conferred with Hitler who, according to Papen, was currently "in a state bordering on hysteria," but instead acted on his own. A few minutes past 3 P.M. he was back on the phone with Seyss-Inquart. "Berlin cannot agree in any way to the decision taken by Chancellor Schuschnigg," he said, ruthless beneath a veneer of joviality. He demanded that Schuschnigg and his cabinet resign. He also repeated the demand to send Berlin a telegram asking for German help.

The two ministers solemnly marched back to the large room where their cabinet colleagues were assembled. Seyss-Inquart, "white in the face and agitated," read from his notebook Göring's ultimatum, and then quailed under a bombardment of questions. "Don't ask me," he replied bitterly, "I'm nothing more than an historic telephone girl." If he himself were not appointed Chancellor within two hours, he added, the German armies would move on Austria.

Life in Vienna was continuing as if nothing had happened. Planes circled overhead dropping clouds of leaflets urging the citizens to vote "Ja" on Sunday. On the streets truck columns of the "Fatherland Front" were greeted with patriotic shouts and waving handkerchiefs; strangers would welcome each other with: "*Österreich!*" For once the nation appeared to be united. All at once the gay waltzes and patriotic marches that had been coming from every radio station were abruptly changed by an announcement ordering all unmarried reservists of the 1915 class to report immediately for duty. Before long a stream of army trucks loaded with steel-helmeted troops headed for the German border.

* This and other telephone conversations between Berlin and various capitals during the next few days are from official transcripts found by Allied authorities in the Reich chancellery.

In desperation Schuschnigg sought help from London. He told how he had given way to Hitler's demands rather than risk bloodshed and asked "for immediate advice of His Majesty's Government as to what he should do." This telegram ironically reached Prime Minister Chamberlain during a lunch at 10 Downing Street in honor of the Ribbentrops. Chamberlain frostily invited Ribbentrop into his study "for a private word" with himself and Lord Halifax, the new Foreign Secretary. "The discussion," as Ribbentrop reported it to Hitler, "took place in a tense atmosphere and the usually calm Lord Halifax was more excited than Chamberlain, who outwardly at least appeared calm and cool-headed." After the Prime Minister read out the telegram from Vienna, Ribbentrop "professed to be ignorant of the whole situation" and, in fact, expressed doubts about the truth of the reports. If it were true, he added, it might be the best way of achieving a "peaceful solution."

These words were enough to placate a man already determined to keep on good terms with Hitler; Chamberlain agreed with Ribbentrop that there was no proof of violent German action even when his own Foreign Secretary angrily charged that Schuschnigg had been "threatened with invasion." Then Chamberlain asked Lord Halifax to send off a reply to the Austrian government that must have made him wince: "His Majesty's Government cannot take responsibility of advising the Chancellor to take any course of action which might expose his country to dangers against which His Majesty's Government are unable to guarantee protection."

Schuschnigg had no illusion about getting any help from either England or Italy and about 4 P.M. tendered his resignation. President Miklas reluctantly accepted it but flatly refused to follow Göring's order to appoint Seyss-Inquart. Instead he selected the chief of police but he declined. So did the inspector general of the armed forces as well as the leader of a former Christian Social government. No one wanted the position and Miklas appealed to Schuschnigg to reconsider. He refused to take part "directly or indirectly—in the preparations for Cain once more to slay his brother Abel," but when Miklas replied in dismay: "I see that everyone deserts me," he reluctantly agreed to continue in office as ex-Chancellor until a new head of government was appointed. So saying, Schuschnigg returned to his own office and began clearing his desk.

As the afternoon wore on the emotional strain in the chancellery became almost unbearable. Pressure from Berlin, and particularly from Göring, who was in his element, was growing. At 5 P.M. the field marshal was shouting over the phone at a Nazi underground leader named Odilo Globocnik that a new cabinet must be formed by 7:30 P.M. At that time Seyss-Inquart was to telephone the Führer that it had been done, said Göring and dictated a list of the ministers that included his own brother-in-law. A few minutes later Seyss-Inquart himself was on the phone informing Göring that Miklas had accepted Schuschnigg's resignation but was insisting on replacing him with a former Chancellor. Göring roared out to tell Miklas to accept German demands. If not, "then the troops which are already poised all along the borders will march and Austria will have ceased to exist. . . . Tell him that we are not joking! If we are in possession of the report that you have been appointed Chancellor by 7:30 P.M., the marching orders will be stopped, and the troops will remain on our side of the border." In the meantime Seyss-Inquart was to send all National Socialists to the streets throughout the country. "If Miklas could not understand the situation in four hours," he concluded ominously, "he'll understand it in four minutes."

"Well, all right," said Seyss-Inquart dubiously.

Göring did not have to wait until seven-thirty for a report. In less than an hour he was informed that Miklas still refused to make the appointment. "Now listen here," Göring shouted at Seyss-Inquart, "I am willing to wait for another few minutes. I expect you to call me then immediately on the priority wire here in the Reichskanzlei. But you have to make it snappy. I cannot take the responsibility, in fact, I am not supposed to wait another minute." He gave the impression that he was under orders but more likely acted under his own authority since Hitler was not yet ready to press the issue. "If things don't happen within that time you will have to take over by force, all right?"

Nazis were already taking over the streets of Vienna in response to orders from Berlin. One mob sweeping toward the inner city shouted, "Heil Hitler! Sieg Heil! Hang Schuschnigg!" In the chancellery Schuschnigg heard the shouts and the tramp of feet. Convinced that this was a prelude to invasion, he went to the President's office to make a final appeal but Miklas remained adamant, stubbornly refusing to appoint a Nazi as Chancellor, and when Schuschnigg insisted, said, "You will desert me now, all of you." Still Schuschnigg saw no other possibility than Seyss-Inquart, a practicing Catholic with a reputation as an honest man, and suggested that he himself speak immediately on the radio to the Austrian people.

Shortly Schuschnigg entered the Corner Room on the first floor of the chancellery adjoining the grand staircase. Here in the middle of the room stood a microphone, barely five paces from the place Dollfuss had been murdered by the Nazis. There was a hush as Schuschnigg stepped to the microphone at 7:50 P.M. and told of the German ultimatum. Throughout Austria people were engrossed by a broadcast which William Shirer described as the most moving he had ever heard. "President Miklas asks me to tell the people of Austria that we have yielded to force. Because under no circumstances, not even in this supreme hour, do we intend that German blood shall be spilt, we have instructed our army to retreat without offering any resistance in the event of an invasion and to await further decisions." Shirer thought Schuschnigg's voice would break into sobs but he controlled himself. "Thus," he concluded, "I take leave of the Austrian nation with a German farewell which also expresses my heartfelt wish: God save Austria!"

There was not a sound in the Corner Room until the commissioner for cultural propaganda, who bore the old aristocratic German name of Hammerstein-Equord, lurched forward on crutches to shout into the microphone: "Long live Austria! Today I am ashamed to be a German." Hurriedly some technicians turned on a recorded version of the national anthem, composed by Haydn, and almost identical to "Deutschland über Alles."

Seyss-Inquart must have run from the Corner Room to a telephone because it was only 7:57 P.M. by the time he had Göring on the line. "The government has just put itself out of office," he reported. Austrian troops were being withdrawn from the German border. "The gentlemen here have decided to sit and wait for the invasion."

When Göring learned that Seyss-Inquart had not been nominated as Chancellor he lost his temper. "All right then. I am going to give marching orders now to the troops. And it is up to you to see that you will be in charge. Inform all leading personalities of what I tell you now: everybody who resists our troops or organizes resistance will be summarily dealt with by our tribunals." Seyss-Inquart's halfhearted protests were shouted down. "All right, now. You have got your official orders."

The crowd outside the Austrian chancellery, swollen to an estimated 100,000, was getting rowdy as Nazi supporters of both sexes chanted the name of the Führer and cavorted in the glow of smoking torches. Even more unruly groups ranged through the inner city singing Nazi songs and shouting, "Down with the Jews! Heil Hitler! Sieg Heil! Kill the Jews! Hang Schuschnigg! Heil Seyss-Inquart!"

Between delivering ultimatums to Vienna in an effort to force the situation, Göring had been urging Hitler to invade Austria come what may. The Führer hesitated until about 8:15 P.M. Then as he was reflectively strolling with Göring a police official saw him abruptly slap his thigh. "Now, get moving!" he cried. Half an hour later Hitler signed Instruction Order Number Two for Operation Otto which declared that German troops would march into Austria at dawn the next morning "to prevent further bloodshed in Austrian towns."

Three minutes after Hitler signed the order Göring was at a phone in the winter garden giving further orders to Keppler, the economic expert. Seyss-Inquart was to send a telegram in the name of the provisional Austrian government, urgently requesting that Germany help them restore law and order by dispatching troops to Austria. Seyss-Inquart was to take care of the matter at once. "He does not really have to send the telegram. He only has to say that he did. You get me?"

Neurath chanced to overhear this and brought the information to those in the anteroom. "For heaven's sake," exclaimed Papen, "see that it does not turn out to be a second Ems telegram. The request must be genuine and in black and white!"* Concerned, Papen turned to Captain Wiedemann. "What will this military march into Austria prove?" he said. "It will only get the whole world against us. A police action would have been sufficient." Wiedemann agreed but Neurath chided them both for taking the matter so tragically. Hitler, he said, had been dreaming for years of getting his best divisions into Austria. "Why don't you let him have that pleasure!"

His pleasure of the moment was the arrival of the telegram from the provisional government of Austria requesting the immediate aid of German troops in the exact words dictated by Göring, another case of legality after the fact. It gave Hitler the opportunity to masquerade his troops as liberators and, in high spirits, he ordered them to march in with bands playing and regimental colors flying. One thing was lacking, reassurance from Mussolini. And this arrived at 10:25 P.M. in the form of a long-distance call from Prince Philip von Hessen. "I have just returned from the Palazzo Venezia," he told Hitler, whose heart must have been pounding. "Il Duce took the news very well indeed. He sends his very best regards to you." The Austrian question no longer interested him.

Elated, Hitler exclaimed, "Then please tell Mussolini that I shall never forget this." Words of gratitude spilled out. "Never, never, never! Come what may!" He could not restrain himself. "And listen—sign *any* agreement he would like. I feel no longer in that terrible position which we faced only a short while ago, militarily, I mean, in case I might have got into a conflict. You can tell him again: I thank him most heartily. I will never forget him!" He couldn't stop talking. "Whenever he should be in need or in danger, he can be sure that I will stick with him, rain or shine—come what may—even if the whole world would rise against him— I will, I shall—"

In Vienna, the new Chancellor's first significant act was to request Keppler to urge the Führer to cancel the invasion order. Then Seyss-Inquart turned his attention to Schuschnigg. He thanked his predecessor for services to Austria and, since the streets were still dominated by celebrating Nazis, offered to drive him home. "Or would you like to go to one of the embassies? Perhaps the Hungarian Embassy, which is just across the street?"

Schuschnigg preferred retiring to his own apartment. As he approached the grand staircase Schuschnigg noticed two lines of civilians wearing swastika armbands. Realizing for the first time that the chancellery had been occupied, he pointedly ignored their outstretched Nazi sa-

* The peremptory telegram sent in 1870 by the French Foreign Office to King Wilhelm of Prussia, who was taking the waters at Ems, was published in shortened form by Bismarck. The deletions made the French demands seem insulting and helped precipitate the Franco-Prussian War.

lutes and continued downstairs where the military guard saluted him properly. After a few words to them of thanks and farewell, he climbed into Seyss-Inquart's car. As it slowly drove off, young Nazis leaped on the running boards to protect the former Chancellor from the raucous crowd.

In Berlin, Seyss-Inquart's plea to restrain the German troops was just being relayed by telephone to the German Foreign Office. Then Keppler added a similar appeal. His petition was passed on to military headquarters and the chancellery. A three-way telephone argument ensued. Was this unexpected request from Vienna to stop the invasion based on reality? Should it be turned over to Hitler, who had retired two hours earlier in a state of euphoria after the call from Rome?

At 2:30 A.M. Hitler was awakened. After a moment's reflection he rejected the proposal and went back to bed. But his military leaders, deeply disturbed by the specter of invasion, kept mulling the question. About 4 A.M. the chief of the OKW Operations Staff, General von Viebahn, implored General Keitel by phone to "work on Hitler to give up the move into Austria." Keitel promised and called back shortly without having done so to say Hitler had again refused. "The Führer never knew anything about all this," Keitel later confessed. "If he had, his opinion of the Army Chiefs would have been shattering and I wanted to save both sides that experience."

The insistent telephone appeals from the army General Staff, Brauchitsch and finally Viebahn had turned that night into sheer "hell" for Keitel. Brauchitsch himself was most dejected, and Viebahn became so distraught that before long he was alternately praying out loud and predicting dire disaster before sinking into moody silence. When Jodl told him to get a grip on himself the general locked himself in a room, threw an inkwell against the door and threatened to shoot anyone who tried to come in.

5

Early that Saturday morning Hitler flew to Munich with Keitel to take part in the triumphal entry into his homeland. Before leaving, he signed a proclamation describing his version of the events that led to the crisis. "Since early this morning soldiers of the German armed forces have been marching across the Austro-German frontiers. Mechanized troops and infantry, German airplanes in the blue sky, summoned by the new National Socialist government in Vienna, are the guarantors the Austrian nation shall at an early date be given the opportunity to decide their own future by a genuine plebiscite." This was followed by a personal note, "I, myself, as Führer and Chancellor will be happy to walk on the soil of the country which is my home as a free German citizen."

At 8 A.M. his troops had begun streaming into Austria and at some points frontier barriers were dismantled by the inhabitants themselves. It was more like an improvised maneuver than an invasion. The 2nd Panzer Division, for instance, was advancing with the help of a Baedeker's guide and refueling at local gas stations. As the troops marched in they were bombarded with flowers by ecstatic women and children. Nazi tanks flew flags of both nations and were gaily decorated with greenery. "The populace saw that we came as friends," recalled General Heinz Guderian, "and we were everywhere joyfully received." Almost every village and town, houses decorated with swastika flags, greeted the Germans with jubilation. "Their hands were shaken, they were kissed, and there were tears of joy." All that delayed a rapid march to Vienna were the numerous mishaps that littered the roads with disabled tanks and trucks.

Hitler arrived in Munich about noon and led his cavalcade of cars to Mühldorf, less than an hour's drive from Braunau, where the commander of the invasion force, General von Bock, reported that his troops were meeting no resistance. The road to the Inn River was so clogged with cars and onlookers that Hitler's caravan did not cross it until midafternoon. His car inched its way into Braunau through a jubilant crowd struggling to touch the vehicle as if it were some religious relic. It slowly passed through the ancient town gate to the Pommer Inn where he had been born not quite forty-nine years earlier. The procession into familiar territory continued to the accompaniment of cheering crowds. At Lambach Hitler ordered the driver to stop in front of the old cloister (whose coat of arms was the swastika) where he had once taken singing lessons.

In London the cabinet was meeting in emergency session. Chamberlain's glum judgment was that the Anschluss had been inevitable, ". . . unless the Powers had been able to say: 'If you make war on Austria, you will have to deal with us.'" And that had never been a possibility. "At any rate," he concluded, "that question is now out of the way." He dismissed the fait accompli as a matter of little consequence.

It was dark when the first stage of Hitler's sentimental journey ended at Linz, whose streets he had wandered in solitude so many evenings. The crowd of 100,000 waiting in the market square engulfed the caravan in a display of joyous hysteria which amazed Hitler's aides and adjutants. When the Führer appeared on the balcony of the City Hall with the new Chancellor of Austria the people were in a frenzy. "The atmosphere of the whole demonstration was electric and excited beyond belief," recalled Keitel. Tears ran down Hitler's cheeks, and Guderian, standing next to him, was sure "this was certainly not play-acting."

After a brief, nostalgic speech Hitler returned to the Hotel Weinzinger. The proprietor had given up his own suite, whose main room was filled with stuffed animals. Hitler, who detested hunting, several times stumbled over the head of a polar bear, nor was the large double bed, over which hung a gaudily framed picture of Josephine Baker, to his taste. In this unlikely setting he and Seyss-Inquart conferred without even discussing Anschluss.

Hitler had not entered his homeland considering Anschluss in the fullest sense of the term, envisioning rather a loose union such as Austria had once had with Hungary. But the enthusiasm of the day was altering his concept and he confided to his valet: "It is fate, Linge. I am destined to be the Führer who will bring all Germans into the Greater German Reich."

Seyss-Inquart returned to the capital that evening to find Viennese Nazis gathered to greet the Führer. A torchlight procession awaited in place and the demonstrators had grown weary from cheering. General Guderian's tanks had left Linz before dusk but it was snowing and the road, under repair, was torn up for miles. At least fifty tanks broke down and the advance guard did not reach Vienna until after midnight. Even at that hour Guderian found the streets filled with excited citizens who broke into "frantic rejoicing" on sighting the first German soldiers. Preceded by an Austrian military band, the invaders marched past the opera house. They were greeted with flowers and raucous friendliness. Enthusiasts tore off the buttons of Guderian's overcoat for souvenirs before hoisting him to their shoulders and carrying him to his quarters. What puzzled the citizens was the convergence at sunup of German officers on food stores where they bought up large quantities of butter, sausage and other food.

On Sunday morning Göring phoned Ribbentrop in London to tell of the wild reception Hitler had received. It was also a lie, he said, that Germany had issued an ultimatum to Austria or to President Miklas. Ribbentrop swallowed all this and replied that the average Englishman didn't really care what happened in Austria. Still a note of concern moderated Ribbentrop's own jubilation. *If* there should be any sort of threat or trouble, he asked, would the Führer stand firm?

Göring had already sent a courier by plane to urge Hitler to press beyond their original plan. "If the enthusiasm is so great," he suggested, "why don't we go the whole hog?" Perhaps Hitler was unaware of all Göring had been doing the past few days but it was just as likely that he was letting his field marshal proceed as if on his own so that he would have to take the blame if something went wrong. In either case, their minds ran in the same channel and Hitler himself had already ordered an official of the Ministry of the Interior to draft a law for the reunification of Austria and Germany. By noon it was ready, approved and dispatched in final form to Seyss-Inquart in Vienna with orders to have it passed within the day.

Shocked at first, the more the new Chancellor thought about the proposed legislation the better he liked it. Moreover, Hitler promised that a free and secret vote would be held within a month to confirm the law.

After convincing himself that the decree was not only inevitable but "valuable and useful," Seyss-Inquart urged his cabinet to approve it on the grounds that Anschluss was "the will of the people." The cabinet unanimously agreed to turn over the country to Hitler but once more President Miklas showed his intransigence by refusing to sign the document and declared himself "hindered in the exercise of his office," thus giving him the constitutional right to turn over his functions to the Chancellor.

While Hitler was confident that Anschluss would be enacted, there remained one concern. Ever since the telephone call from Prince von Hessen, he had fretfully awaited Mussolini's formal approval. Almost two days had passed without a word from Rome. Mussolini, in fact, had been "floored" by the news of the Anschluss, exclaiming, "That damned German!" At last he regained his composure and that Sunday sent off a brief telegram:

I CONGRATULATE YOU ON THE WAY YOU HAVE SOLVED THE AUSTRIAN PROBLEM. I HAD ALREADY WARNED SCHUSCHNIGG.

The Führer's joy was complete. In gratitude he sent an even briefer reply:

MUSSOLINI, I SHALL NEVER FORGET THIS.

Feeling a need to share his triumph with Eva Braun, he phoned her to join him in Vienna.

Earlier in the day he had treated himself to a visit to nearby Leonding. Together he and Linge walked to his parents' grave in the churchyard across from the old homestead. Hitler took a wreath from his valet, told him to retire with the rest of the staff so he could meditate. After placing the wreath against the marker he stood silently for several moments. Afterward, still quiet and thoughtful, he revisited the scenes of his childhood, concealing his emotions even from intimates. He recognized an old schoolmate named Hagemüller and they chatted briefly. Later he held a reunion in Linz at the hotel for other friends, including a watchmaker and his former history professor, Dr. Hümer.

That evening Seyss-Inquart, more lackey than head of state, returned to Hitler's suite. The Führer was so deeply moved upon learning that the law making Austria a province of Germany was passed that he wept. "Yes," he finally managed to say, "a good political action saves blood." So ended Austria's independence and so ended Sunday, March 13, the day on which Schuschnigg had hoped his nation would affirm its independence by plebiscite.

6

Sigmund Freud had promised his family to leave Austria once the Nazis took over. Now he told an English colleague, Dr. Ernest Jones, "This is my post and I can never leave it." This reminded Jones of the officer on the *Titanic* who, when asked why he abandoned ship, replied:

"I never left the ship, she left me." Freud got the point. He admitted Austria no longer existed and agreed to depart for England, "the land of his early dreams." He escaped none too soon. The restructuring of Austria in line with the NSDAP's notion of relationship between party and state was already in process under the personal supervision of Rudolf Hess. More sinister was Himmler's administration of the purge of the police and the neutralization of political opposition. Gestapo Chief Heydrich was installed on the Morzinplatz where his agents were examining statute books and records seized from the chief of the Austrian Secret Service. At least one political murder had already been perpetrated, that of Papen's closest adviser, the German Embassy councilor.

Local storm troopers began the persecution of Jews, dragging them from their homes and offices and forcing them to scrub Schuschnigg's propaganda slogans from walls and pavements with acid. Others were rounded up to wash toilets in the SS barracks and sweep the streets. Such bullying was distasteful to many of the Wehrmacht officers, and journalist Gedye watched two of them "kick over the bucket of two very old Jews who were scrubbing the pavements and tell them they could go, cursing the Nazi stormtroopers who were supervising."

Such scenes did not dampen the fervor of most Viennese, intoxicated as they were by the events of the past forty-eight hours. "It is impossible to deny enthusiasm with which both the new regime and last night's announcement of incorporation in the Reich have been received here," telegraphed the British ambassador to Viscount Halifax on Monday. "Herr Hitler is certainly justified in claiming that his action has been welcome by the Austrian population." There was good reason. Anschluss would probably end unemployment. There were 600,000 Austrians out of work, and particularly hard hit were professional men; some doctors were seen begging from door to door.

Later than morning Hitler set out for Vienna. He could average only twenty miles an hour, impeded partly by the crowds, partly by the stalled trucks and tanks. It was almost 5 P.M. by the time his cavalcade reached the outskirts of the capital. Every building, including churches, flew the Austrian and German flags. Masses lined the streets, shouting themselves hoarse at the sight of Hitler in his open car, erect with arm outstretched. The ovation was frantic, spontaneous. His car stopped before the Hotel Imperial and, upon entering, it was another dream come true. As a youth he had always longed to go inside. Now it was bedecked in long red banners, bearing his mark, the swastika.

The crowds kept shouting a variation of an old German drinking song: "We won't go home, we won't go home till the Führer talks!" until he stepped out onto the balcony of the royal suite. After acknowledging their frenzied yells with a salute and wave, he withdrew. But the mob tirelessly kept up its chant hour after hour, forcing him to show himself again and again.

At first he was quiet as if numbed by the endless ovation, but as the evening wore on (so intimates of the Führer told Pierre Huss of INS), he began reminiscing of the nights he used to walk past the Imperial Hotel. "I could see the glittering lights and chandeliers in the lobby but I knew it was impossible for me to set foot inside. One night, after a bad blizzard which piled up several feet of snow, I had a chance to make some money for food by shoveling snow. Ironically enough, the five or six of us in my group were sent to clean the street and sidewalk in front of the Imperial Hotel." On that particular evening the Habsburgs happened to be entertaining inside. "I saw Karl and Zita step out of their imperial coach and grandly walk into this hotel over the red carpet. We poor devils shovelled the snow away on all sides and took our hats off every time the aristocrats arrived. They didn't even look at us, although I still smell the perfume that came to our noses. We were about as important to them, or for that matter to Vienna, as the snow that kept coming down all night, and this hotel did not even have the decency to send a cup of hot coffee to us." The cheerful music inside not only made him wish to cry but made him boil with the injustice of life. "I resolved that night that someday I would come back to the Imperial Hotel and walk over the red carpet in that glittering interior where the Habsburgs danced. I didn't know how or when, but I have waited for this day and tonight I am here."

He awoke Tuesday morning without the stomach cramps he had felt in Linz. He made a spirited address to the huge crowd of 200,000 which gathered in the Heldenplatz to honor him. Now, he said, they had a new mission and their country a new name, *Ostmark*. But both mission and name came from their own history since assaults from the east had been broken on the frontiers of the old East Mark. Neither the new mission nor the new name cooled the ardor of his listeners, who shouted as enthusiastically as any Munich audience. At the end of his speech Hitler turned to the radio announcer and said in an undertone, "Announce that *Reichsstadthalter* [keeper of the Reich's city] Seyss-Inquart will now speak." No one was more surprised than the Chancellor to discover he had been transformed into a sort of provincial viceroy. He accepted the demotion in good grace as the crowd cheered. At that hour Adolf Hitler could do no wrong.

Then came the parade, past the Winter Palace and its tall spearlike iron fencing with Austrian generals trailing General von Bock on horseback; the Austrian army had just been absorbed into the Wehrmacht. During the pause in the impressive procession the good Catholic Papen turned to Hitler with a warning that the Anschluss would evaporate if he subjected the Church here to the attacks it had suffered in Germany.

"Have no fear," said Hitler, "I know that better than anyone."

Later in the day Cardinal Innitzer greeted him with the sign of the cross and gave assurance that so long as the Church retained its liberties Austrian Catholics would become "the truest sons of the great Reich into whose arms they had been brought back on this momentous day." According to Papen, Hitler was delighted with the cardinal's patriotic words, shook his hand warmly and "promised him everything."

Eva Braun also experienced the exultation of the moment and wrote on a postcard to her sister Ilse *"Ich bin verrückt* [I am crazy]." She had come to the city chaperoned by her mother and her best friend, Herta Schneider. She was lodged in a separate room just across the corridor from her lover's suite and their private meetings were so discreet that none of the Führer's aides or adjutants was aware of her presence. Late that afternoon the Führer flew back to Munich without her.

The next day he was greeted in Berlin as a conquering hero. "The city seemed simply delirious with joy," Lochner wrote his family. "The kids and girls are especially hysterical." Hitler spoke triumphantly of the Anschluss. "Germany has now become Greater Germany and will so remain." He was happy, he said, that he had been chosen by Providence to bring about this great union with Austria—"the land which had been the unhappiest is now the happiest."

But all was not well at home. The court-martial of General von Fritsch, abruptly postponed when Schuschnigg announced his plebiscite, was finally convened and in short order Fritsch was found innocent. The incident was an embarrassment to Hitler but he had discovered the political trick that would never go out of fashion—he drew attention from it with boasts of victory. He hurriedly assembled the Reichstag so he could report on the great events in Austria. Within three days, he said, the entire population of Austria had welcomed him "without a single shot having been fired." For the first time in history, he said, the entire German nation, the Greater Reich, would go to the polling booth on April 10 to testify to its allegiance. All he wanted was another four years to consolidate internally an Anschluss which had just been accomplished externally. The immediate response throughout Germany was almost total approval for everything the Führer had done or was about to do, and it was with the utmost confidence that he began the election-plebiscite campaign in Königsberg on March 25. "This National Socialist idea," he said, "goes far beyond the bounds of a small Germany."

He spent the last ten days of electioneering in his homeland where Himmler and Heydrich had almost completely reorganized the Austrian security system.* The wave of his popularity had not subsided. A declara-

---

* The latter was also involved in discreet but assiduous research for any personal information concerning the Führer. Dollfuss and Schuschnigg had reportedly collected numerous documents indicating that Hitler's grandfather might have been Jewish, that Geli Raubal might have been murdered, and that his service in the war was nowhere as heroic as party propagandists said. The revelation of such material, even if based only on

tion signed by Cardinal Innitzer and five other prelates had been sent to the newly appointed commissioner of Austria instructing Austrian Catholics how to vote: "On the day of the plebiscite, it is the obvious national duty of us bishops to declare ourselves as Germans for the German Reich, and we expect all faithful Christians to recognize where their duty to the people lies."

Wherever Hitler went he was greeted as savior and Führer. His return to Linz on April 8 was greeted with renewed frenzy. The lobby of the Weinzinger was jammed with citizens who clamored to see him. One was the best friend of his youth, Gustl Kubizek. He was told by Hitler's "office manager," Albert Bormann, that the Führer was not well enough to receive anyone that day. Would he come tomorrow for lunch? Hitler greeted Kubizek on the ninth with the joyful cry: "Gustl!" then took his outstretched right hand and held it firmly. Hitler said he no longer had a private life as in the old days. He gazed out a window at the Danube and the iron bridge that had offended him as a boy. "That ugly thing, still there! But not much longer, you can be sure of that, Kubizek!" He began to enlarge on the ambitious plans he had for Linz. There would be a great new bridge as well as a new opera house along with a modern concert hall worthy of Bruckner. Talk of the new symphony orchestra he would establish in Linz reminded Hitler of Kubizek's ambitions. What had he become? The embarrassing answer was: town clerk of Eferding. The war, explained Kubizek, had forced him to abandon his musical ambitions or starve. But he did direct an amateur orchestra and his three sons were musically gifted. This brought a spontaneous offer from Hitler to assume responsibility for the training of the three boys. "I don't want gifted young people to have such a hard time of it as we had. You know best what we had to go through in Vienna."

They had been talking for an hour when the Führer rose. Kubizek assumed the interview was over but Hitler was only summoning an adjutant so he could give instructions for the musical education of the three Kubizek boys at the Bruckner Conservatory. Nor was this the end. After examining all the drawings, letters and postcards Kubizek had brought along, Hitler suggested his old friend write a book about him. Finally he gripped Kubizek's hand and said they should meet more often.

Later in the day Hitler proceeded to Vienna, the city of their youth-

rumor, could seriously damage the Führer's reputation at one of the most critical periods of his career. Some postwar charges against Hitler are equally unfounded. It is widely believed, for example, that he turned the village of Döllersheim into an artillery range soon after taking over Austria for the purpose of obliterating the birthplace of his father and the grave of his grandmother along with any incriminating records. It is true that Döllersheim today is a decaying mass of rubble. It was destroyed, however, not by Hitler but by the Russians after the war. A German military training area was established in and around the village in 1941 but its farms and houses were practically intact by the time the Russians arrived.

ful dreams, where he made the final speech of the campaign. He was proud, he said, to have been born in Austria. "I believe that it was God's will to send a boy from here into the Reich, to let him grow up, to raise him to be the leader of the nation so as to enable him to lead back his homeland into the Reich."

The elections the following day exceeded his hopes. In Austria 99.73 per cent of the voters approved Anschluss. In Germany 99.02 per cent voted in favor of union, while 99.8 per cent approved his list of candidates for the new Reichstag. Hitler's bold action (the result of considerable pressure from Göring) had been confirmed almost unanimously by the peoples of Austria and Germany. "For me," he said, "this is the proudest hour of my life." It also confirmed the conviction that his was the correct path and that he should continue along it to the next station— Czechoslovakia.

Chapter Seventeen

"ON THE RAZOR'S EDGE"
MAY–OCTOBER 1938

1

Even before Hitler marched into Austria he had suggested that he would no longer suffer the "severe persecution" of the German minority in Czechoslovakia. While this was in line with a vow to return lost people and land to the Reich, his main concern was Czechoslovakia's threatening geographical and political position. Here, he reasoned, was an artificial country created by the Allies after the war, a peninsula thrust into what remained of the Reich as a perpetual threat from the east.

Hitler was not alone in regarding it as a dagger aimed at the heart of Germany. The specter of simultaneous drives from east and west into the waist of the Reich inspired a counter German military plan known as Case Green: a surprise attack on Czechoslovakia. For about two years, however, Case Green was little more than a staff study; the easy seizure of Austria changed all that. Overnight Hitler had been given the opportunity to upset the balance of power in Europe; a thrust into Czechoslovakia, neutralizing her formidable defense system, would position his army for a drive against Poland or the U.S.S.R. All he needed was an excuse to invade and he had a ready-made one: three and a half million Sudeten Germans, inspired by the absorption of Austria, were now demanding a similar Anschluss, on the debatable grounds that they were a cruelly repressed minority. Their grievances, along with a traditional hostility to all things Czech, had plagued the tiny republic since its foundation. For the past three years Hitler had been covertly subsidizing the Nazi Sudeten Party led by Konrad Henlein and it now controlled the entire German minority movement. In late March 1938 German support took a more ominous character when the Führer named Henlein as his personal representative with instructions to make demands that could not possibly be accepted by the Czech government. This strategy, he hoped, would create a constant state of unrest that would finally "necessitate" German armed intervention to prevent civil war and protect the lives of its nationals in the Sudeten.

With an excuse at hand, Hitler was still restrained by apprehension that France, England and perhaps Russia would resist any effort to seize Czechoslovakia. Before facing such odds he needed the blessing of his sole ally. And so on May 2, 1938, he set out for Rome to get it, accompanied by a retinue of five hundred, consisting of diplomats, generals, security agents, party leaders and journalists, all wearing uniforms of one type or another.

It was with mixed feelings that Hitler left Berlin. Elation over the bloodless conquests of the Rhineland and Austria was tempered by recurrence of the gastrointestinal pains "miraculously" cured by Dr. Morell's Mutaflor. Concern over his health spurred him to spend several hours on the train bound for Rome writing out a will; from *Mein Kampf* alone he had amassed a fortune.*

The five trains of the Führer's party were met at the Brenner Pass by flowers, banners and formations of Italian soldiers and Fascist troops. A band played the national anthems of both countries as the Duke of Pistoia welcomed the Germans in the name of the King. The German railway cavalcade proceeded into Italy past guards of honor posted on both sides of the tracks. Houses were decorated with placards and banners acclaiming the Führer and Italian-German friendship. As the delegation neared Rome, Hitler summoned an adjutant and—within hearing of Linge —ordered him to go through the train informing everyone that a very little man would greet them in Rome but they were to behave themselves and not laugh. "That is an order. The little man is the King of Italy."

It was dark when they arrived at the beflagged San Paolo station specially constructed for the occasion. It annoyed Hitler that he was met by King Victor Emmanuel, not Mussolini, and he annoyed His Majesty by seating himself first in the state carriage. Drawn by four horses, it proceeded past illuminated fountains along the old Roman triumphal way. A profusion of searchlights and torches turned night into day; the gaudily lit

---

* By 1943 his accumulated royalties with Eher Verlag would amount to 5,525,811 R.M. To the party he left all his personal possessions, the Berghof, his furniture and his pictures. To Eva Braun and his two sisters he left the same amount, 12,000 marks a year for life. Alois was granted a lump sum of 60,000 marks and there were further bequests to relatives in Spital, Frau Winter and his valets. He also ordered the party to "worthily take care of my adjutants Brückner and Wiedemann for life."

Colosseum seemed on fire. Cheering crowds lined the route and at one point African cavalry charged down the avenue at the guest of honor like something out of *The Desert Song*. But Hitler felt demeaned by riding in such an ancient vehicle. Hadn't the House of Savoy ever heard of the automobile? Nor did he find his accommodations in the Quirinal at all to his taste. The palace was uncomfortable as well as gloomy and reminded him of a museum.

From the very beginning he and Victor Emmanuel were on bad terms. Hitler resented the sovereign's open coolness and kept complaining that Mussolini himself should have served as host. The reception banquet at the Quirinal did nothing to ease the situation. Hitler, eyes moving nervously, slowly led the Queen, a majestic figure taller than himself, on his arm. Behind came the diminutive King leading the governor's tall wife. The foursome made a comical sight and Hitler knew it. As the Queen entered the great reception hall the Italians either bent very low or kneeled down. Several kissed the hem of her gown. After the ordeal, Hitler confided to his pilot that it had been "a frightful hour. Such ceremonies are terrible for me. I shall never get used to such things."

During the meal he and the Queen did not exchange a word. Hitler was particularly annoyed by the huge crucifix the Queen wore around her neck. She had done it deliberately, he thought, to annoy him. The royal family was going beyond the bounds of being ungracious. The King was spreading malicious stories about his guest, including one that the Führer demanded a woman on his first night at the Quirinal. "Boundless amazement," wrote Ciano in his diary. "The explanation: it seems he cannot go to sleep unless a woman turns down the bed before his eyes. It was difficult to find one, but the problem was solved by recruiting a chambermaid from a hotel. If this were really true it would be weird and interesting, but is it? Isn't it just a piece of spite on the part of the King, who also alleges that Hitler has himself injected with stimulants and narcotics?" Part of the last charge was only too true and there was reason to believe the bed-turning routine was also accurate. But it was still malice on the King's part and it continued a few days later at a performance of *Aïda* in Naples. After the first act the audience politely held applause, looking toward the distinguished guest in the royal box to give him the opportunity of starting it. In embarrassment Hitler turned to the King for his cue. "The monarch, with a disdainful sneer," wrote Louis Lochner, "professed not to notice his guest's discomfort."

After the opera Hitler was scheduled to review a formation of Nazis from the German colony. Since he wore tails, he had instructed Linge to bring along a military cap and coat for the occasion but the King's adjutant warned him that the train back to Rome was due to leave in a few minutes. Rather than disappoint the waiting party members, Hitler hurried to the street as he was and trooped the line of civilians as military commander with right hand raised in salute. Normally he hooked left thumb in belt but these trousers had no belt and he pressed hand against hip. It was a comical sight as he raced along, bareheaded, like a Teutonic Groucho Marx, the long tails of his coat fluttering. "The German Führer and Reich Chancellor," wrote the amused Wiedemann, "looked like a head waiter at the peak of business in a restaurant and he himself must have realized what a ridiculous figure he made." Once on the train he vented his rage on Ribbentrop, who loudly charged the chief of protocol with disloyalty to the government and the Führer.

By the time Hitler returned to Rome he had regained his composure and, at the Palazzo Venezia banquet on May 7, he made an effective speech that, according to Count Ciano, "was extremely successful in melting the ice around him." In effect, he offered the South Tyrol as a present to his host, a most generous gift since it would infuriate his own countrymen, particularly those from Bavaria. He had made the same offer through Göring back in 1924 while in Landsberg prison. In that case he had agreed to support Italy's claim to this hotly contested area for two million lire and to his chagrin got not one lire for his pains. Perhaps tonight's offer was some sort of signal to Il Duce that *this time* a substantial quid pro quo must be forthcoming.

This speech was the first event of political significance since Hitler's arrival. Satisfied to stay in the background and let the King play host, Il Duce had cleverly evaded any serious discussion by submitting his guests to a program that kept them busy day and night. Ribbentrop did eventually manage to present to Ciano a draft treaty of an alliance which he scanned without comment. Mussolini's son-in-law, in fact, had already written in his diary: "The Duce intends to make the pact. We shall make it, because he has a thousand and one reasons for not trusting the Western democracies."

More important, Hitler eventually succeeded in broaching the question that most concerned him—Czechoslovakia. Almost offhandedly, Mussolini gave the impression that this little country was not at all important to him and he would look the other way. This assurance was worth all the real and imagined insults Hitler had been subjected to and he now felt free to take the next step in his program.

President Beneš and other Czech leaders were under the illusion that Hitler would never risk an attack on their country for fear of setting off a general war. And if he did, wouldn't France, England and Russia somehow manage to restrain him? But these three were in no mood to act as protectors. "You only have to look at the map," Chamberlain had recently written his sister, "to see that nothing that France or we could do, could possibly save Czechoslovakia from being overrun by the Germans if they wanted to do it. . . . Therefore, we would not help Czechoslovakia—she would simply be a pretext for going to war with Germany. That we could not do, unless we had a reasonable prospect of being able to beat her to her knees in a reasonable time and of that I see no sign. I have therefore abandoned any idea of giving guarantees to Czechoslovakia or the French in connection with her obligations to that country." The Prime Minister's continuing lack of resolve disturbed the French leaders and, though they continued to make bold statements, perceptive observers were convinced that France, whose foreign policy had been in tow of the British since the Rhineland seizure, would not spring to the Czechs' defense. The third potential defender was publicly taking every opportunity to urge England and France to stand up to the Germans, while privately doing nothing. Stalin wanted Hitler controlled by the West, not himself, and on May 6 the Soviet chargé d'affaires in Prague admitted to the American ambassador that his country definitely would not supply Czechoslovakia any military aid unless France did so. Besides, how could they get the troops there? Poland and Romania stood between them and both these countries had understandably refused to allow passage of the Red Army. At the same time Stalin was assuring Beneš in private that the Soviet Union was ready to assist him militarily "even if France does not do so and even if Poland and Romania refuse to permit Soviet troops to pass in transit to Czechoslovakia."

This was all part of the attempt to convince liberals of the world that the Soviets were the true defenders of a brave little beleaguered nation when, in fact, they were no more willing to fly to its aid than England or France. Hitler had guessed as much and now that he had Mussolini's tacit approval of a march into Czechoslovakia he ordered Goebbels to intensify the press campaign against that hapless country. Activity among the Sudetenland Germans increased with assurance that *Der Tag* was at hand. This rumor was given credence by alarming reports on May 19 and 20 that Hitler's troops were mobilizing on the Czech borders: eleven infantry and four armored divisions were already converging on the Bohemian frontier while German and Austrian troops were poised for attack in southern Silesia and northern Austria.

On the afternoon of Friday, the twentieth, Beneš called an emergency meeting of the cabinet and the Supreme Defense Council. Shortly after 9 P.M.—without consulting their French allies—a "partial mobilization" was ordered. By dawn of Saturday, Czech troops occupied the border fortifications and the Sudeten territories—and Europe was swept by a crisis fever not experienced since 1914. A small power had taken the initiative against a powerful one, making known that she would not be a pawn in the game of European power politics. In so doing, Czechoslovakia was also forcing her reluctant sponsors, France and England, to back her up.

As a consequence, French Premier Daladier summoned the German ambassador and showed him a mobilization order lying on his desk. "It depends upon you, Excellency," he said, "whether I sign this document or not." And in Berlin British Ambassador Henderson warned Foreign Minister von Ribbentrop that "France had definite obligations to Czechoslovakia and that, if these had to be fulfilled, His Majesty's Government would not guarantee that they would not be forced by events to become themselves involved." Convinced that England was the prime enemy, Ribbentrop decelerated from outright rage to righteous indignation, stoutly denying that German troops threatened the Czech borders. If France and Britain were "crazy enough" to use armed force against Germany, "then once again we should have to fight to the death."

Ribbentrop left Berlin by special plane that evening to meet Hitler in Berchtesgaden. He was as incensed as his Foreign Minister, for not a single major military movement or concentration aimed at Czechoslovakia had taken place. Who then had started the rumor? It could have been the Communists, the Czechs or the anti-Hitler group which included such disparate elements as Schacht, the self-styled financial wizard, and Admiral Canaris, chief of the German intelligence service. More likely, panic itself was the villain.

The Western press spread the story that the Führer had been forced by foreign pressure to call off his invasion and by so doing made the mistake of humiliating him. "Hitler had embarked on no military enterprise," wrote Weizsäcker, "and could not therefore withdraw from one. But unfortunate provocation by the foreign press now really set Hitler going. From then on he was emphatically in favor of settling the Czech question by force of arms."

Before the week was out Hitler acted with dramatic suddenness. On May 28 he summoned his top military leaders, officials of the Foreign Office and other important functionaries to a special conference. As this unusually large group was gathering outside the chancellery winter garden, the general assumption was that Hitler was about to call for new military measures. An agitated Göring drew Captain Wiedemann aside. "Doesn't the Führer realize what he is doing? This will mean war with France!" The army was not combat-ready, he said, and promised to tell this to the Chief.

Hitler began speaking calmly but his words were explosive: "It is my unshakable will to wipe Czechoslovakia off the map. . . . We shall have to use methods which, perhaps, will not find the immediate approval of you old officers." This attack, he explained, was but part of a much broader strategy to acquire living space. When Germany made its inevitable drive to the east for Lebensraum, Czechoslovakia would be a threat to the rear. Consequently, she had to be eliminated and this was the propitious moment since neither Britain nor France wanted war, Russia would not intervene and Italy was uninterested.

When Hitler finished, Göring pushed forward, eyes agleam, and grasped his hand. "Mein Führer," exclaimed the man who had vowed to stop him an hour earlier, "let me congratulate you wholeheartedly on your unique concept!"

There were no protests, not even discussion. Hitler walked over to Keitel, Brauchitsch and Beck, who were standing together in one corner. "So," he said, "we shall just tackle the situation in the east [Czechoslovakia]. Then I will give you three or four years' time, and then we will tackle the situation in the west."

The three generals said nothing but the following day Beck wrote another critical memorandum. Germany, he claimed, was no stronger than in 1914 and far more vulnerable to air attack. She was confronted, furthermore, by a coalition comprising Czechoslovakia, France, Britain and America. "Germany's opponents," he concluded, "have time and space at their disposal and their resources of men and materials are superior to those of Germany and her allies."

On May 30 Beck delivered this grim appraisal to Brauchitsch, who asked Keitel how best to bring it to the Führer's attention. He was advised to delete the political section lest Hitler toss aside without reading it the part discussing the balance of military strength in case France intervened. Brauchitsch followed this counsel and the same day a truncated version was presented during a conference in the School of Artillery at Jüterbog. The Führer objected strenuously: the report was not objective and overrated French military strength. "It was another disaster for the army," wrote Keitel, "and resulted in a further lack of confidence in Brauchitsch, which I bitterly regretted, although the Führer did not hold Brauchitsch responsible as much as Beck and the General Staff."

Brushing aside all objections, Hitler concluded that Czechoslovakia must be dealt with by force and gave the army until October 1 to do it. Thus the fourth version of Case Green was put into motion. Work on the Westwall, the defense system on the French border, was accelerated under the direction of Fritz Todt, who had built the Autobahn complex. Within weeks more than a half million men were working on fortifications designed to hold off France with a minimum of troops while forces in the east seized Czechoslovakia in a lightning stroke. At the same time an intensive program of propaganda warfare was inaugurated, its purpose, in the Führer's own words, "to intimidate the Czechs by means of threats and wear down their power of resistance; and on the other hand it must give the national racial groups indications as to how to support our military operations and influence the neutrals in our favor."

Hitler's determination to drive forward was solidified by a dispatch from his ambassador in Moscow, sent on the day of the Jüterbog conference. Count von der Schulenburg reported that Czechoslovakia, intent on avoiding a conflict, was ready to make concessions within the bounds of reason. "Here the view prevails that the Soviet will for the present avoid being drawn into the war at all costs. The reasons for this attitude are to be found in strained internal conditions and in fear of a war on two fronts."

The stage was set for a European crisis that would make the events in May seem inconsequential.

2

Although Hitler had put Case Green in motion, his intent was primarily to use it for bargaining. The question was how close to the precipice of war he would go, and early that summer he himself probably did not know. Relying on intuition as he had in the Rhineland and Austrian crises, he allowed his personal adjutant, Wiedemann, to go to London in July for an informal talk with Lord Halifax. It was an extraordinary mission of exploration privately arranged by Wiedemann's close friend, Princess Hohenlohe, half Jewish by birth, which completely circumvented Ribbentrop. Wiedemann's official commission was to explore the possibilities of a state visit to England by Göring, but Hitler had also personally instructed him to inform Halifax that the crucial question of the moment was the mistreatment of the Sudeten Germans. "If there is no satisfactory solution in the near future, I will simply have to solve it by force. Tell this to Lord Halifax!"

Wiedemann repeated his warning in mid-July and Halifax replied cordially that much could be settled before that deadline. He also agreed in principle to a visit by Göring and extended a vague invitation to the Führer himself as a guest of the King. Wiedemann flew back to Germany in high spirits. He was kept waiting at the Berghof for several hours while the Führer strolled outside with Unity Mitford, and upon his return Hitler impatiently interrupted Wiedemann's report of British approval of the Göring visit to London. "By no means, no longer!" he exclaimed and refused to hear another word about Halifax. "I do not know," recalled Wiedemann, "whether this change in Hitler had come from something Unity Mitford had told him or whether he feared the possibility of Göring gaining too much political power by such a step. In any case, there was no opportunity for me to inform him of something he did not want to hear about."

Several weeks later Fritz Hesse, the covert representative of the Wilhelmstrasse, was recalled from London and chastised by Ribbentrop for sending a report indicating that Chamberlain was prepared to consider the cession of the Sudeten territories to Germany. "What's the good of sending me this kind of stuff?" said the Foreign Minister according to Hesse's account. The Führer, it seemed, was convinced the English planned to smash Germany to pieces once they had completed their own rearmament and had recently told Ribbentrop: "There is no international morality left, everybody snatches whatever booty he can. I shall take this as a lesson." Before he allowed the English to encircle him, he would strike first.

Hesse explained that Chamberlain's personal adviser had asked him to inform Hitler unofficially that a London *Times* editorial suggesting Britain was prepared to accept a solution favorable to Germany had been planted by the Prime Minister himself. With this in mind, wasn't it likely that Hitler could obtain autonomy for the Sudeten Germans without even a threat of military action? "Autonomy!" exclaimed Ribbentrop. "There can be no question of autonomy any longer." Before the lying reports of German troop movements, he said, Hitler might have been satisfied with autonomy. But now that was not enough. Hesse "went cold all over" when he heard this. For the first time he realized how real the danger of war was. He begged the Foreign Minister to assure Hitler that he could obtain the cession of the Sudetenland peacefully. Impressed, Ribbentrop promised to talk to Hitler but the following day he summoned Hesse to report that the Führer had ridiculed the idea of the Czechs surrendering their military bastion. "I simply don't believe it," he said. "They can't be that stupid!"

While Hitler's position hardened, his generals continued to resist his policy of expansion. Beck began openly to circulate gloomy predictions: the question of guilt in a new war would be a greater factor than it had been in the World War; and the aftermath of defeat would be far more disastrous than in 1918. That July he composed a third long memorandum for Brauchitsch declaring that he was positive an attack on Czechoslovakia would bring about another great conflict. "The outcome of such a war would be a general catastrophe for Germany, not only a military defeat." The people, he went on, did not want this war, nor was the Wehrmacht prepared for it.

When Beck presented this document on July 16 he spoke even more courageously, urging Brauchitsch to organize resistance among military leaders. "History will burden these leaders with blood-guilt," read his notes for this discussion, "If they do not act in accord with their specialized political knowledge and conscience. . . . If they all act with resolution, the execution of a policy of war is impossible. . . . Extraordinary times demand extraordinary measures."

In early August Brauchitsch was persuaded to convene the senior army commanders. It was he, in fact, who read a memorandum prophesying that a Czech invasion would lead to a general war that Germany was doomed to lose. Was the Sudetenland worth risking the existence of the nation? The consensus was that citizens and soldiers alike were against war. The generals also agreed that the training and equipment of their troops might be up to defeating the Czechs but certainly not the combined powers of Europe. There were only two objections and these rather mild ones. General Busch repeated the cliché that soldiers should not interfere with politicians and Reichenau, the first general to go Nazi, warned his colleagues to confront Hitler singly rather than en masse. Brauchitsch decided to take his advice and faced the Führer alone. It is doubtful if he stated the case as forcefully as he had done to his peers, but even in milder form it brought a verbal explosion that promptly brought him back in line.

Discouraged by the commanders' negative attitude, Hitler invited their chiefs of staff to dinner at the Berghof on August 10. He regaled them for three hours with his political theories, but they too were not impressed. Universal opposition only made the Führer more determined and five days later, after witnessing artillery exercises near Jüterbog, he gathered his senior officers in a mess hall to announce that he had decided to solve the Czech problem by force that fall. He assured his listeners that so long as Chamberlain and Daladier were in power there would be no widespread war, and concluded with a reminder of his own prophetic powers.

Two days later Soviet Ambassador Maisky told Halifax that German policy was "at least 50 per cent bluff," and that the irresolute stance of the French and British "constituted a real danger for peace," since it gave an exaggerated impression of Germany's strength both at home and abroad. Additional pressure was brought to bear upon the British the following afternoon by a gentleman farmer from Pomerania. Ewald von Kleist-Schmenzin, a descendant of the great poet and a monarchist, had long been an enemy of Hitler. Using a passport provided by Admiral Canaris, he was in England as a representative of the moderates in the German General Staff who hoped to stop Hitler's aggression. Late that afternoon he was in private conversation with Sir Robert Vansittart, chief diplomatic adviser to Halifax. Kleist began with the sober announcement that war was a certainty unless the British stopped it. There was only one real extremist in Germany, he said. "Hitler has made up his mind for himself. All the generals in the German army who are my friends know it and they *alone* know it for a certainty and know the date at which the mine is to be exploded."

"Do you mean that such people as Goebbels and Himmler are not pushing Hitler in that direction as well?" asked Vansittart.

"I repeat that I discount them. Hitler has taken this decision by himself." All the generals were "dead against war but they will not have the power to stop it unless they get encouragement and help from outside. As I have already told you, they know the date and will be obliged to march at that date."

When asked the date, Kleist laughed. "Why, of course you know it," and it took some time to convince him that the British leaders did not have this information. "After the twenty-seventh of September it will be too late," he said, and the latest time to stop the operation was the middle of September. Hitler must be made to understand that England and France were not bluffing. A leading British statesman should make a speech aimed at the German public emphasizing the horrors of war.

Vansittart immediately wrote a detailed account of the meeting for Chamberlain. But he was too dedicated to appeasement to take Kleist seriously, and his position was reinforced the next day by a telegram from Henderson in Berlin. In the ambassador's opinion the chief danger of war lay not in Hitler himself, who stood to lose most, "but in the forces working for war, namely German and Czech extremists, communists, and other influences and the universal hatred abroad of Nazism." He advised London "not to drive Herr Hitler into a situation where his prestige being at stake he would feel himself obliged to yield to his extremists."

Kleist had come much closer to the truth. At home Hitler was surrounded by disapproval. The generals were still unconvinced by his arguments. The prime mover, Beck, once more offered his resignation and, when Brauchitsch continued to decline it, refused to serve any longer. Hitler solved the problem by accepting the resignation and ordering Beck to keep it secret from the public "for reasons of foreign policy." As a loyal German, Beck agreed but continued to support the anti-Hitler group which was secretly plotting to arrest the Führer once he gave the final order for execution of Case Green. Rarely in history had so many leading military and civilian leaders plotted to overthrow a government by force. Among the conspirators were General Erwin von Witzleben, commander of the Berlin area military district, Admiral Canaris, who had provided the passport for Kleist, former Commander-in-Chief of the Army Kurt von Hammerstein-Equord, and Beck's replacement as chief of staff, Franz Halder. It was the last who sent a second secret negotiator to London to repeat Kleist's warnings—again to no avail. The plot also involved Hjalmar Schacht and many other civilians, including Professor Haushofer's oldest son and other key Foreign Office officials such as Theodor Kordt who was spreading false stories about Ribbentrop to foreign diplomats.

At the same time open pressure on the Führer intensified. Late in August Weizsäcker took Hess aside after a private dinner and cautioned that if the Führer attempted to solve the Sudeten problem by force war between Germany and the West would inevitably follow. Hess passed on this warning to Hitler. Another came a few days later from his Minister of Finance, Schwerin von Krosigk. "After many years' acquaintance with England and the Englishman," wrote the Oxford graduate, "I am of the opinion that their repeatedly announced attitude, that is expressed in the cautious English manner, makes it crystal clear that their resolution to intervene does *not represent a bluff*. Even if Halifax and Chamberlain should not want war, behind them stand as their eventual successors the warmongers Churchill/Eden."

He urged Hitler to be patient. Time, he said, was working for Germany. Her rearmament and economic progress were steadily outdistancing those of the Allies. Further, France was showing an increasing willingness to break with Czechoslovakia and in America there were also signs of a reaction to the Jewish propaganda directed against the Reich. "That means we can only win by waiting. And that is why the Communists, Jews and Czechs are making such frantic efforts to push us into a war *now*."

All these admonitions had little effect on the Führer. He seemed set on war. After watching infantry maneuvers late that summer, he slapped a thigh with his gloves and remarked to two adjutants that war was the father of everything. "Every generation must experience war once," he said.

On September 3 he summoned Brauchitsch and Keitel to the Berghof to discuss the latest version of Case Green and learned to his dismay that the main thrust was to be made into the center of the Czech defense system by the Second Army. An attack on such a strongly fortified area, he complained, would mean bleeding to death uselessly. Another Verdun. Such an assault corresponded to Czech expectations. One should be launched instead by the Tenth Army into Bohemia. Brauchitsch protested somewhat mildly, citing the poor state of the motorized divisions, the paucity of reinforcements and the inadequate training of leaders, but Hitler brushed aside these objections as defeatist and ordered motorized and armored divisions added to the Tenth.

It was Hitler, the former corporal, who was the warrior, not his generals and observers feared that Hitler would declare himself openly at the impending Nuremberg Rally. "The anxiety is no less great in Germany than elsewhere," Henderson wrote in a personal letter. "And dictators can and must speak more clearly than the leaders of a democracy."

The Party Congress at Nuremberg that year served as a dramatic prelude to the developing political crisis by its impressive display of Nazi power and discipline. The title of the 1938 festivities was appropriate: "First Party Rally of Greater Germany," as were the trappings. Hitler had brought from Vienna, after a hundred and forty years, the insignia of the First Reich—the Imperial crown, the Orb of Empire, the Scepter and the Imperial Sword. At the presentation of these symbols of imperialism he solemnly vowed that they would remain in Nuremberg forever. But he made no mention of war during his opening address or the following afternoon when he received the entire diplomatic corps. He was graciously thanked by the spokesman, François-Poncet, who concluded with the observation that the greatest glory of a statesman was to attain his goal without making one mother weep. According to Wiedemann, Hitler responded with "a malicious smile."

Hitler's refusal to discuss international politics at Nuremberg inspired conjectures and rumors, including one directed to Henderson, that Hitler had become "quite mad" and was bent on war at all costs. In the next twenty-four hours Henderson spoke to a number of Hitler's close advisers, urging Anglo-German co-operation in a Sudeten settlement. Göring said he planned to go hunting the end of the month and "hoped to goodness the Czechs wouldn't upset his shooting plans by starting trouble in the middle of them," and Goebbels expressed the pious hope that the Führer would refer to co-operation with the English in his final speech. "He appeared to me anxious," reported a suspicious Henderson, "and I begin to doubt whether he is egging Hitler on to extremes."

In the midst of these interviews, Henderson received instructions to deliver a personal warning to Hitler that England "could not stand aside" in the event of a general conflict. Henderson protested: the Führer was on the borderline of madness and a second crisis could push him over the edge. The matter consequently was dropped.

Since Hitler was already convinced England had no intention of risking war over Czechoslovakia, he was going ahead with his invasion plans come what might. It was a decision combining shrewd calculation, intuition and an irresistible impulse. "You know I am like a wanderer who must cross an abyss on the razor's edge," Hitler told Frank. "But I must, I simply must cross." A few hours after the British decided not to transmit a warning, he summoned Keitel, Brauchitsch and Halder to Nuremberg. They met in the Deutscher Hof just before midnight of September 9, and it was the new chief of staff who outlined the revised version of Case Green. Surprisingly, it still entrusted the main thrust to the Second Army but did involve a pincer movement that had not been mentioned in the previous discussion. Hitler admitted that it was a clever idea. "But its success is nevertheless too uncertain for it to be depended on. Especially as a rapid success is necessary from a political point of view. The first week is politically decisive, within which a far-reaching territorial gain must be achieved." German howitzers, he pointed out, could not smash the Czech fortifications. More important, this plan ruled out the element of surprise.

Hitler kept lecturing Halder and Brauchitsch to the dismay of Keitel, who already agreed with everything the Führer proposed. By three o'clock Hitler had lost his patience, and he categorically ordered his generals to do as he proposed, then coldly and sullenly dismissed them. As the three men stopped in the vestibule for a drink, Halder indignantly asked, "What is he really after?"

"If you haven't found out," replied the irritated Keitel, "then you have my sympathy."

Brauchitsch intervened before another argument started and the trio set about to meet Hitler's demands. While Halder was busy writing out the new orders, Keitel took Brauchitsch aside. "Why do you fight with him [Hitler] when you know that the battle is lost before it's begun? Nobody thinks there is going to be a war over this, so the whole thing wasn't worth all that rear-guard action." It was the kind of practical advice that gave increasing currency to his nickname "Lakeitel." Afterward Keitel expressed his bitter disappointment in Brauchitsch to his own chief of operations. Jodl seconded the motion and wrote in his diary: "There is only one undisciplined element in the army—the generals, and in the last analysis this comes from the fact that they are arrogant. They have neither confidence nor discipline because they cannot recognize the Führer's genius." They still looked upon him as a corporal of the Great War "instead of the greatest statesman since Bismarck."

It was not Hitler but Göring who made the first public announcement on Czechoslovakia the following day. "A trifling piece of Europe," he said, "is making life unbearable for mankind. The Czechs, the vile race of dwarfs without any culture—nobody even knows where they came from—are oppressing a civilized race; and behind them, together with Moscow, there can be seen the everlasting face of the Jewish fiend!"

If such words had been uttered by Hitler, Europe would have trembled but even President Beneš ignored Göring's diatribe. "I firmly believe that nothing other than moral force, good will, and mutual trust will be needed," he broadcast in both Czech and German. Afterward William Shirer encountered the President in the hall of Broadcasting House. The American correspondent wanted to warn Beneš he was dealing with gangsters but didn't have the nerve. He observed that Beneš's face was "grave, not nearly so optimistic as his words, and I doubt not he knows the terrible position he is in."

Publicly Chamberlain did not. On September 11 the Prime Minister told a group of journalists: "Herr Hitler has repeatedly expressed his own desire for peace and it would be a mistake to assume that those declarations were insincere." At the same time he was expressing apprehension in a private letter: "I fully realise that if eventually things go wrong and the aggression takes place, there will be many, including Winston, who will say that the British government must bear the responsibility and that if only they had had the courage to tell Hitler now that, if he used force, we would at once declare war, that would have stopped him." But it was wrong, he felt, to let the vital decision of war and peace "pass out of our hands into those of the ruler of another country, and a lunatic at that."

The final ceremony of the Nuremberg Rally came on September 12. It was the last chance for Hitler to deliver the speech the world dreaded he might make. He arrived at the huge outdoor stadium just before 7 P.M. to the concerted roar of "Sieg Heil!" and slowly walked toward the rostrum in the glare of a spotlight, looking to neither side, right hand raised in salute. He spoke at first only of the party's struggles and at such length that some foreign observers began to hope he was not going to bring up the question of the day. Suddenly he began to condemn the Czechs. "I am in no way willing that here in the heart of Germany a second Palestine should be permitted to arise. The poor Arabs are defenseless and deserted.

The Germans in Czechoslovakia are neither defenseless nor are they deserted, and people should take notice of that fact."

The audience roared, "Sieg Heil! Sieg Heil!" This was the moment the world had been waiting for all week, but instead of following such stridency with an ultimatum, he merely demanded justice for the Sudeten Germans, then concluded with bluster rather than threat: "We should be sorry if this were to disturb or damage our relations with other European states, but the blame does not lie with us!"

The French, English and Czechs had feared so much that such words were reassuring; it was generally believed that the sound and fury were for the benefit of German extremists and that Hitler was ready to work for a peaceful solution. Mussolini shared this belief, for he observed as he turned away from his radio, "I had expected a more threatening speech. . . . Nothing is lost."

3

This sense of well-being was brief. Hitler's oratorical condemnation of injustice inspired scenes of protest among the Sudeten Germans. By morning Eger was blanketed with swastika flags. Ten thousand protesters jammed the streets shouting, "We want self-determination!" State police opened fire, killing one demonstrator and wounding a score more. Within twenty-four hours bloody disorders spread through the Sudetenland and the death toll rose to twenty-one. Aroused by Henlein's call for freedom, the Sudeten Germans went on strike and refused to pay taxes. Prague declared a state of siege. Martial law was proclaimed in the border districts and more Sudeten Germans were shot down. Throughout Europe there were renewed rumors of an ultimatum by Hitler—or an outright invasion. Paris and London panicked. That evening Daladier sent an urgent message to Chamberlain. An invasion of Czechoslovakia, he said, had to be avoided at all costs or France would be forced to fulfill the obligations of her treaty. He proposed that they immediately invite Hitler to meet with them and work out a reasonable settlement.

The cryptic reply he got from Chamberlain kept Daladier perplexed for hours: "Some time ago I came to a resolution. I believe it to be useful. . . . I cannot tell you anything yet, but I will let you know about it a little later." That same evening Chamberlain telegraphed Hitler suggesting a man-to-man conference. Hitler was delightfully taken by surprise and described his feeling with a colorful idiom that would have perplexed Milton: "I fell from Heaven!" That afternoon he sent a reply placing himself at Chamberlain's proposal and suggesting that they meet the next noon at Berchtesgaden.

In England the first reaction of relief was followed by enthusiasm that their Prime Minister was making such an original move to keep peace. In Prague newsboys shouted out: "Extra! Read how the mighty head of the British Empire goes begging to Hitler!" The Czech citizens spontaneously massed in the streets to demonstrate that they stood behind their President's efforts to resist. In Rome Mussolini remarked to his son-in-law, Count Ciano, "There will be no war. But this is the liquidation of English prestige."

Early that morning, September 15, Chamberlain left 10 Downing Street to the cheers of an extraordinarily large crowd for that hour. Before boarding his plane at Croydon, in the presence of Halifax and other dignitaries, he paused to speak into the BBC microphones. "My policy has always been to ensure peace. The prompt acceptance of my suggestion encourages me to hope that my visit today will not be without results."

At about 8 A.M. the Lockheed Electra took off. It was the first long flight for the sixty-nine-year-old Prime Minister and he was as excited as a boy. But it would be wrong to assume he was an aging innocent proceeding to the slaughter. Chamberlain was a hard bargainer. "My method is to try and make up my own mind first on the proper course, and then try and put others through the same course of reasoning." Like his father, a successful businessman who became an outstanding statesman, he was a devout Unitarian, the very embodiment of Victorian virtues. His spare, ascetic figure, his chilling manner and his sardonic smile reminded many of a headmaster. Only his intimates knew that this austere exterior emanated from painful shyness and that beneath the armor lay warmth and sensibility.

The question was whether such an individual, convinced as he was that the Führer was half mad and needed to be handled cautiously, could cope with the situation. As he flew over London Chamberlain himself experienced "some slight sinkings," yet was buoyed by the thought that he too held strong cards and that, as long as he could keep negotiating with the Führer, Czechoslovakia would be safe.

He sat through the flight to Munich, according to one fellow passenger, "as always, aloof, reserved, imperturbable, unshakeably self-reliant." Henderson greeted him as he descended from the plane at 12:30 P.M. and was surprised how remarkably fresh he looked for a man of his age. "I'm tough and wiry," explained Chamberlain.

Despite the drizzle, enthusiastic crowds were waiting all along the route to the Munich railroad station shouting "Heil!" and lifting arms in salute. It was after four o'clock by the time the Chamberlain party started up the steep, winding road to the Berghof. The sky was dark and clouds hid the mountains as rain began to pelt down. Hitler, the polite host, waited at the head of the long flight of steps to the terrace. After exchanging stilted pleasantries over tea, Hitler abruptly asked what procedure his guest proposed for the meeting. Chamberlain said he preferred a tête-à-tête. Hitler led the Prime Minister and interpreter Schmidt upstairs to his study, leaving behind a patently annoyed Ribbentrop.

In this simple, wood-paneled room, almost bare of ornament, Hitler began quietly listing complaints against his neighbors as he presented a history of events leading up to the present crisis. Chamberlain listened attentively, answered questions with a friendly smile, then looked the Führer full in the face and said he was prepared to discuss the possibility of righting any German grievances so long as force was not used.

"Force!" said Hitler, excited for the first time. "Who speaks of force?" Wasn't it Beneš who was applying force against the Germans in the Sudetenland? As the mountain wind howled, rain slashed against the window, and he himself poured out such a torrent of words that Chamberlain asked him to stop so he might have a chance to understand what he was talking about. "I shall not put up with this any longer," exclaimed Hitler. "I shall settle the question in one way or another." It was the first time the alarmed Schmidt had heard him use such a phrase with a foreign statesman. "I shall take matters into my own hands."

Chamberlain was startled but answered resolutely, "If I have understood you right, you are determined to proceed against Czechoslovakia. If that is so, why did you let me come to Berchtesgaden?" This trip was a waste of time, and under the circumstances, he said, it was best to return to England at once. "Anything else seems pointless."

Hitler hesitated before this unexpected counterattack. Now, thought Schmidt, was the moment if he really wants to come to war. The interpreter stared at the Führer in agonized suspense: the question of peace was poised on the razor's edge. To Schmidt's astonishment, Hitler backed down. "If, in considering the Sudeten question," he said calmly, "you are prepared to recognize the principle of the right of peoples to self-determination, then we can continue the discussion in order to see how the principle can be applied in practice."

Then came a second surprise. Chamberlain did not immediately assent, objecting that a plebiscite in the Sudentenland held immense practical difficulties. Amazingly, Hitler did not flare up at this rebuff. Perhaps, thought Schmidt, the Führer had been frightened by Chamberlain's threat to go home. The Prime Minister said that he could not give Hitler an answer on the question of self-determination without first consulting his colleagues. "I therefore suggest that we break off our conversation at this point, and that I return to England immediately for consultation, and then meet you again."

Hitler looked uneasy as Schmidt translated the first words but, once he realized that Chamberlain would see him again, could not hide his relief. He expressed immediate agreement and, when Chamberlain asked "how the situation was to be held in the meantime," unhesitatingly promised that he would not give the order to march unless some "particularly atrocious incident occurred."

This ended the three-hour talk. They chatted cordially on the way downstairs, Hitler hoping that his guest would see some of the scenic beauties before he left. But Chamberlain could not spare the time "since lives were being lost." He left the Berghof pleased with the talk. "I had established a certain confidence, which was my aim," he wrote his sister, "and on my side, in spite of the hardness and ruthlessness I thought I saw in his face, I got the impression that here was a man who could be relied upon when he had given his word." At home he was greeted with encomiums of praise, including a poem composed in his honor by England's poet laureate, John Masefield:

> As Priam to Achilles for his son,
> So you, into the night, divinely led,
> To ask that young men's bodies, not yet dead,
> Be given from the battle not begun.

In Washington, Roosevelt was concerned. Fearing that such talks would only postpone the inevitable conflict, he lamented at a cabinet meeting that the Prime Minister was for "peace at any price," and bitterly observed to Harold Ickes that apparently England and France were going to leave the Czechs in the lurch, then "wash the blood from their Judas Iscariot hands." Before the weekend was over, further opposition to Chamberlain began to appear within his own cabinet but he stood firm. American Ambassador Joseph Kennedy had sent the Prime Minister an ominous report by the noted aviator, Charles Lindbergh, of overwhelming German air power based on a recent inspection of the Luftwaffe. Chamberlain had been as impressed as Kennedy and so England, which was poorly prepared for war, remained committed to appeasement.

On September 18 Chamberlain told the French delegation headed by Daladier which had come to England to discuss the problem: "There must be some cession of territorial area to the Reich. But it would be very difficult for us to carve up Czechoslovakia, unless the Czechoslovakian Government themselves were prepared to admit the necessity for frontier rectifications."

Daladier agreed that a little "friendly pressure" might persuade the Czechs to cede "some portions of Sudeten territory." At the same time, they had to be assured "of some sort of international guarantee of what remained." And Germany must participate in such a guarantee. Chamberlain hesitated but after a break in the proceedings agreed. If the French returned home still apprehensive, he was quite pleased with himself. "I have still many anxious days before me," he wrote his sister, "but the most gnawing anxiety is gone, for I feel that I have nothing to reproach myself with, and that on the contrary up to now things are going the way I want."

At the same time there remained the unpleasant job of telling the Czechs that they must give up the Sudetenland, and when Beneš was informed the next day after lunch by the British minister, he was so agitated he refused to discuss the matter at first. The embarrassed Sir Basil Newton stressed that a quick ratification must be forthcoming since Chamberlain hoped to resume talks with Hitler within forty-eight hours. Beneš bitterly charged that his country had been abandoned. The guarantees he already possessed, he said, had proven valueless. He feared the proposed solution would not be final, only a stage in the eventual domination of his country by Hitler. These words notwithstanding, Newton reported that he believed Beneš was "more likely to accept than refuse and is receptive to any reason which will help him justify acceptance to his people."

While Chamberlain anxiously waited all that Monday for an answer, Beneš was desperately searching for help from another quarter. On Tuesday he summoned the Soviet minister and asked two questions: Would the U.S.S.R. fulfill her treaty obligations if France did likewise? In the event of a Hitler attack would the Soviets support Czechoslovakia in an appeal to the League of Nations even if France refused to do so? Affirmative answers finally arrived from Moscow at 7 P.M. and forty-five minutes later Czech Foreign Minister Krofta was telling Newton that his government must reject the British-French proposal.

A little later, however, Newton's French counterpart, Victor de Lacroix, was hastily summoned to see Czech Prime Minister Hodža. He begged Lacroix to get a telegram from Paris stating that France would back out of the treaty if it came to fighting. "It was the only way of saving the peace," he said and assured Lacroix that he was acting with the consent of Beneš—which was a lie.

Lacroix transmitted this information to Paris while Newton was doing the same to London. In his message, Newton concluded with the suggestion that Halifax send Beneš an ultimatum to accept the proposal "without reserve and without further delay failing which His Majesty's Government will take no further interest in the fate of the country."

Despite the late hour, Halifax rushed to 10 Downing Street. He returned to the Foreign Office after midnight and instructed Newton to urge the Czechs to reconsider, otherwise Chamberlain would be forced to postpone or cancel his second meeting with Hitler.

It was two o'clock in the morning by the time Newton, accompanied by his French colleague, arrived at Hradschin Castle to see the President. Wakened from a fitful sleep, Beneš collapsed at Lacroix's first words "as if he had hit him with a club," and burst into tears. Shaken, the betrayed Beneš promised to give a final reply by midday.

The first word of acceptance came from the devious Hodža, who in-

formed Newton that the Czech reply was affirmative and an official answer to that effect would be delivered as soon as possible. But the argument continued until late afternoon when Newton and Lacroix were
summoned to the Ministry of Foreign Affairs. Each minister was handed a
note stating that the Czechoslovakian government "sadly" accepted the
Franco-British proposal.

That evening the Beneš government publicly announced its surrender
in a communiqué that brought shame to many Westerners.

> We relied upon the help that our friends might have given us; but when
> the question of reducing us by force arose, it became evident that the Eu-
> ropean crisis was taking on too serious a character. Our friends therefore
> advised us to buy freedom and peace by our sacrifice, and this in propor-
> tion to their own inability to help us . . . The President of the Republic
> and our government had no other choice, for we found ourselves alone.

Hitler had won a victory by proxy.

4

The next morning, September 21, just before boarding a plane for his
second flight, Chamberlain told newsmen: "A perfect solution of the
Czechoslovakian problem is an essential preliminary to a better understanding between the British and German peoples; and that, in turn, is
the indisputable foundation of European peace. European peace is what I
am aiming at, and I hope this journey may open the way to it."

This time the two leaders would meet at Bad Godesberg on the
Rhine. When the Prime Minister's plane landed at Cologne he was
greeted by dignitaries and a guard of honor while an SS band played "God
Save the King." The British were driven to quarters in the Petersberg
Hotel located on the heights across the river from Godesberg. Hitler
greatly admired the view from the restaurant—he often came up at coffee
time—and he wanted to impress the visitors with the vista of the spectacular country of the Drachenfels; less than fifty miles up the Rhine was the
fabled rock of the Lorelei.

From his balcony Chamberlain could look across the river at the
Dreesen Hotel where the first meeting would take place at 5 P.M. Late in
the afternoon he was driven down the steep road to the river and onto a
ferry. Thousands of onlookers lined both banks, intent on the progress of
the little vessel as it plowed across the river in a scene reminding Henderson of the varsity boat-race day.

It was a short trip from the landing to the Dreesen on the west bank.
Always the affable host, Hitler first inquired about the accommodations at
the Petersberg. But it was all business once they adjourned to a conference
room and seated themselves at the end of a long baize-covered table.
Chamberlain began with a recital of the concessions he and the French

had wrung out of the Czechs. After outlining the comprehensive and complicated plan to carry out the turnover of territory, he mentioned the guarantee the British and French had given the Czechs, then leaned back with an expression of satisfaction as if to say, thought Schmidt: "Haven't I worked splendidly during these five days."

To the interpreter's surprise, Hitler quietly, almost regretfully replied, "I am exceedingly sorry, Mr. Chamberlain, but I can no longer discuss these matters. This solution, after the developments of the last few days, is no longer practicable."

The Prime Minister bolted upright. Schmidt noticed that his kindly eyes gleamed angrily under bushy brows. Chamberlain indignantly exclaimed he could not understand. This solution answered the very demands the Führer had made at Berchtesgaden. After hedging on the grounds that it was impossible to make a non-aggression pact with the Czechs before the claims of Poland and Hungary were satisfied, Hitler retaliated by criticizing the British-French proposal point by point, then peremptorily demanded that the Sudetenland be occupied by the Germans "forthwith."

Chamberlain replied that he was both disappointed and puzzled at such an attitude. This was a brand-new demand, going far beyond what Hitler had proposed at Berchtesgaden. He had returned to Germany with a plan that gave the Führer everything he wanted, doing so at the risk of his political career. At this point Sir Ivone Kirkpatrick handed the Prime Minister a note that German troop formations had just crossed the frontier at Eger. Chamberlain seized on this. There were bound to be such incidents, on both sides, he said and urged the Führer to join him in an effort to do "all that was humanly possible to settle matters in an orderly, peaceful way, and not to allow the work for peace to be disturbed by shootings and incidents." What proposal, he asked, could Hitler make so they could reach agreement in principle?

The answer chilled Chamberlain: immediate occupation of the Sudetenland by German troops with the frontier to be determined later by a plebiscite. Since this amounted to almost complete capitulation by the Czechs, an acrimonious, tedious debate followed which was spiced by the arrival of another message from Eger, this one to Hitler that twelve German hostages had been shot. The result, of course, was a dissertation by the Führer on the iniquity of the Czechs, followed by an avowal that, "if Prague fell under Bolshevik influence, or if hostages continued to be shot, he would intervene militarily at once."

After three hours the first conversation ended in complete discord but with the understanding that they would meet again on the morrow.

Despite a calm visage, the Prime Minister was still angry and indignant as he recrossed the Rhine and was driven up the mountain to his own hotel. Only then did he wonder if he had made a mistake by not breaking off the talks and going home. Was Hitler actually on the edge of madness, or a sort of Dr. Jekyll and Mr. Hyde? If so, it was Chamberlain's responsibility to break through the deadlock. The question was how to do it.

He was not the only one at the conference who doubted Hitler's sanity. At the Dreesen several newsmen were circulating a story that the Führer was so distraught over the Czech crisis that he would fling himself to the floor and chew the edge of the carpet. This report had been inspired by a remark of one Hitler aide that the Chief had become so furious that he was "eating the carpet." This slang expression was taken literally by some American correspondents, who should have translated it into "climbing the walls." Such naïveté amused Hitler's adjutants, who had seldom seen the Führer lose his temper. When he did, he occasionally went into a tirade for half an hour but usually his outbursts were brief. "I was present at quite a few such 'fits,' " wrote Wiedemann, "and all I can say is that they were no different from the displays of others with a hot temper and little self-control."

Some intimates believed the Führer displayed anger for effect. If so, his outbursts that afternoon had surely placed his opponent on the defensive. Chamberlain was already writing him a conciliatory letter. In it he suggested that he himself ask the Czechs whether they thought there could be an arrangement by which the Sudeten Germans themselves could maintain law and order.

After breakfast on the twenty-third this letter was sent across the river. In no mood for reconciliation, Hitler took it as a flat rejection of his ideas and, after long and "feverish" discussions with Ribbentrop and other advisers, composed an unfriendly reply which was a repetition of what he had said at the conference table. It was too long for a written translation and Hitler instructed Schmidt to deliver it in person and translate it verbally. The interpreter left the Dreesen about 3 P.M., a large brown envelope under his arm. On approaching the Petersberg Hotel, Schmidt noticed newsmen crowding around the entrance. One called out: "Do you bring peace or war?" Schmidt was careful to give no hint, not even a shrug of his shoulders. He was taken immediately to Chamberlain, who was waiting on the balcony. Moments earlier he and Henderson had been worriedly pacing but, in a remarkable exhibition of self-control, the Prime Minister greeted Schmidt as if it were only a casual occasion.

Upon the interpreter's return, Hitler's first words were anxious ones: "What did he say? How did he take my letter?" But he visibly relaxed upon learning that Chamberlain had shown no excitement or anger. Within the hour the ferry brought two emissaries from Chamberlain who solemnly delivered the Prime Minister's answer. It was a model of diplomacy, being simultaneously conciliatory and ominous. First Chamberlain promised to put Hitler's proposals before the Czechs and therefore requested a memorandum detailing Hitler's demands. Upon receipt of this document, he proposed returning to England.

The threat of departure must have spurred a second meeting. It was agreed that Chamberlain should return to the Dreesen that evening not only to pick up the memorandum but to listen to Hitler's explanation of it. Their conversation started about 10 P.M. and, since more participants were on hand, took place in a small dining room. Henderson, Kirkpatrick, Ribbentrop and Weizsäcker sat informally in a semicircle around Hitler and Chamberlain while Schmidt translated the memorandum. Hitler demanded withdrawal of all Czech armed forces from an area shown on an accompanying map. Evacuation would start on September 26 and the territory would be formally ceded to Germany on the twenty-eighth.

"But that's an ultimatum!" exclaimed Chamberlain, lifting his hands in protest.

"*Ein Diktat!*" chorused Henderson, who liked to display his German. Chamberlain refused to transmit such a document to the Czechs. Its tone, not to mention its content, would cause indignation among neutrals, he said, and began to scold Hitler as if he were a recalcitrant member of his own cabinet. It was one of the rare occasions when Hitler was placed on the defensive, and was followed by a concerted attack by the three British statesmen on the timetable of the proposal, which allowed the Czechs an impossibly short period to evacuate and turn over the Sudetenland. Impracticable and dangerous, it could lead to a European war.

During the ensuing deadlock an adjutant entered with a message for the Führer. After glancing at it he handed it to Schmidt, who translated it out loud in English: "Beneš has just announced over the wireless general mobilization of the Czechoslovak forces."

It was Hitler who finally broke the silence. "Despite this unheard-of provocation," he said in a barely audible voice, "I shall of course keep my promise not to proceed against Czechoslovakia during the course of negotiations—at any rate, Mr. Chamberlain, so long as you remain on German soil." This remark, misleading by being softly spoken, was followed by a statement that could not be misinterpreted. The Czech mobilization, he said tersely, settled the whole affair. Chamberlain hastily pointed out that mobilization was a precaution, not necessarily an offensive measure, but the Führer replied that so far as he was concerned mobilization was a clear indication that the Czechs did not intend to cede any territory. Again Chamberlain dissented. The Czechs, he argued, had agreed to the principle of self-determination in the Sudetenland and would not go back on their word.

Then why mobilize? persisted Hitler

Germany mobilized first, said the Prime Minister.

You call that mobilization? retorted the Führer sarcastically and made another threat: the crisis could not drag on very much longer. He quoted an old German proverb: "An end, even with terror, is better than terror without end." The memorandum, he said, represented his last word.

In that event, said Chamberlain, there was no purpose in further negotiations. "He would go home with a heavy heart, since he saw the final wreck of all his hopes for the peace of Europe. But his conscience was clear; he had done everything possible for peace. Unfortunately, he had not found an echo in Herr Hitler."

A walkout was the last thing Hitler wanted and he hastily reassured the British that he would not invade Czechoslovakia during the negotiations. It was as if a thunderstorm had cleared the atmosphere. "To please you, Mr. Chamberlain," he said after a short recess, "I will make a concession over the matter of the timetable. You are one of the few men for whom I have ever done such a thing. I will agree to October 1 as the date for evacuation."

After negotiating a number of other minor alterations, Chamberlain agreed to transmit the memorandum to the Czechs. It was one-thirty in the morning and the meeting adjourned. The Führer thanked the Prime Minister for his work on behalf of peace, assuring him that "the Czech problem was the last territorial demand which he had to make in Europe."

Chamberlain left with a hearty "Auf Wiedersehen!" and those who watched him stride out of the hotel could not discern the slightest strain of displeasure on his face.

5

After a few hours of needed sleep, Chamberlain flew back to England and the following day met with the full cabinet. It was necessary, he explained, to appreciate people's motives and see how their minds worked if one would understand their actions. Herr Hitler "would not deliberately deceive a man whom he respected and with whom he had been in negotiation." Consequently it would be a great tragedy if they "lost this opportunity of reaching an understanding with Germany on all points of difference between the two countries."

He told of his apprehension as he was flying home up the Thames, imagining a German bomber taking the same course: "I asked myself what degree of protection we could afford to the thousands of homes which I saw stretched out below me. And I felt that we are in no position to justify waging a war today in order to prevent a war hereafter."

Never had there been such opposition from the cabinet. First Lord of the Admiralty Duff Cooper could place no confidence in the Führer's promises and proposed an immediate general mobilization. Chamberlain urged his colleagues to postpone any such decision and it was agreed to first consult the French, who had already ordered a partial mobilization.

When the cabinet met again Sunday morning there was opposition from a new source. "I cannot rid my mind of the fact," confessed Foreign Secretary Halifax, "that Herr Hitler has given us nothing and that he is dictating terms, just as though he had won a war but without having had to fight." So long as Nazism lasted, peace was uncertain.

Lord Hailsham, an earlier supporter of Chamberlain, agreed with Halifax. An argument ensued. Lords Stanhope and Maugham wanted pressure put on the Czechs to accept the Hitler memorandum while Lord Winterton urged rejection of the proposals on the grounds of morality. In an effort to restore order in his deeply split cabinet, Chamberlain argued that it was wrong to talk of accepting or rejecting Hitler's terms, or even of feeling humiliated. It was up to the Czechs to accept or reject.

No sooner had this meeting ended in discord than Chamberlain was subjected to another harrowing experience. Jan Masaryk, the Czech ambassador, arrived with a bitter protest. His government, he said, was "amazed" at the contents of Hitler's memorandum. It was a de facto ultimatum which deprived Czechoslovakia of every safeguard for its national existence. "Against these new and cruel demands my government feels bound to make their utmost resistance and we shall do so, God helping."

That evening the French delegation was back in London to discuss the situation. Its leader, Daladier, declared that France could not recognize Hitler's right to seize the Sudetenland but would give only a vague response to Chamberlain's question: would France declare war if Hitler simply imposed on Czechoslovakia a frontier based on strategic considerations? When Chamberlain pressed for a more specific answer Daladier replied that France might "try a land offensive, after a period of concentration."

This meeting was adjourned for half an hour so that Chamberlain could consult with his cabinet. "I am unwilling to leave unexplored any possible chance of avoiding war," he told his colleagues. "Therefore I suggest that, basing myself on the personal conversations I have had with Herr Hitler, I should write a personal letter." It would be delivered to the Führer by Chamberlain's closest adviser, Sir Horace Wilson, and would contain a last appeal suggesting a joint commission to determine how to put into effect the proposals already accepted by the Czechs. "If the letter fails to secure any response from Herr Hitler, Sir Horace Wilson should be authorized to give a personal message from me to the effect that if this appeal was refused, France would go to war and if that happened, it seemed certain that we should be drawn in."

The following morning, September 26, Wilson, who shared some of Hitler's apprehension about Jews, set off for Berlin with the letter.* The Führer listened quietly but with growing restlessness until he heard how

* In 1968 Wilson told journalist Colin Cross that "he could understand Hitler's feelings on the Jews and put the question: 'Have you ever met a Jew you liked?'"

shocked the British public had been by the terms of his Godesberg memorandum, then he burst out, "It is no use talking any more!"

This did not stop Sir Horace, who—despite "gestures and exclamations of disgust and impatience" from Hitler—insisted that Schmidt continue reading the Chamberlain letter. When the interpreter came to the words "the Czechoslovakian government . . . regard as wholly unacceptable the proposal," Hitler leaped to his feet and started for the door, muttering again that it was useless to keep talking.

"It was an exceptional scene," recalled the interpreter, "especially as Hitler seemed to realize when he reached the door how impossible his behavior was, and returned to his seat like a defiant boy." He barely controlled himself so that Schmidt was able to finish the letter but then let himself go more violently than the interpreter had ever witnessed during a diplomatic interview. Hitler shouted that Germans were being treated like niggers. One wouldn't even treat Turks like that. "On 1 October I shall have Czechoslovakia where I want her!" he exclaimed, and if France and England decided to strike, let them. He didn't care a pfennig. Finally calm was restored and Hitler agreed to negotiate with the Czechs. He insisted, however, that they agree to accept the Godesberg memorandum within forty-eight hours. Come what may, he added, German troops would occupy the Sudetenland on the first of October.

The fury of the afternoon carried over that evening to the Sportpalast. Rarely if ever had Hitler spoken with such abandon or venom. His principal target was Beneš. "It is not so much a question of Czechoslovakia, it is a question of Herr Beneš!" It was he who was set on destroying the German minority; it was he who was putting his nation at the service of the Bolsheviks. "He now holds the decision in his hand. Peace or war! Either he will now accept this offer and at last give Germans their freedom, or we will take this freedom for ourselves!" All Germany—"a people vastly different from that of 1918!"—stood united with him. "We are determined! Let Herr Beneš choose!"

Hitler sat down. Up sprang Goebbels shouting, "One thing is sure: 1918 will never be repeated!" This brought the Führer to his feet again. Slamming right hand on the rostrum, he roared, "Ja!" then slumped to his seat, hair plastered to his forehead with sweat, exhausted.

The speech brought despair to those hoping for peace. In London workmen dug trenches near Buckingham Palace; air raid posters were pasted up. From Paris, Ambassador Bullitt, a personal friend of Roosevelt's, phoned Washington: "I believe the chances are about ninety-five in a hundred of war beginning midnight Friday." The President, who had also been getting words of appeasement from his ambassador in London, Joseph Kennedy, cabled Hitler an appeal (his second in two days) to continue the negotiations.

Chamberlain too issued another appeal to the Führer in the form of a

"Heil Hitler!" Berlin.
BIBLIO. FÜR ZEIT.

The Berghof. Hitler's official residence at Berchtesgaden. The famed picture window could be lowered into the floor. Erich Kempka, Hitler's chauffeur, took this and the following three candid photographs of a typical pilgrimage to the Obersalzberg in the first years of Hitler's regime. KEMPKA

Hitler greets admirer Viennese style. The two colorfully dressed youths are *Wandervögel* (wandering birds), hippies of the day. KEMPKA

Above, in center, Bormann, face partially covered, appears in most unofficial pictures and yet was almost unknown to the German public. KEMPKA

Right, "Mein Führer!" KEMPKA

The Führer laughs at his critics. His first foreign press secretary, Ernst Hanfstaengl (Harvard graduate and acquaintance of Roosevelt), was allowed to publish two books of anti-Hitler cartoons under the title *Facts vs. Ink*. Hanfstaengl, against Goebbels' violent protests, persuaded Hitler that this kind of propaganda would impress Westerners, particularly Americans. HANFSTAENGL

Der Häuptling vom Stamm der wilden Kopfjäger nach der Schlacht von Leipzig — in vollem Kriegsschmuck

Right, Professor Gerdy Troost, widow of Hitler's favorite architect, objects to the exclusion of the best modern works at the first art exhibition in Munich's Haus der Kunst. One of the few who dared speak frankly to the Führer, she resigned moments later as judge. This is one of seventeen photographs in this book, most of them published for the first time, taken by Hitler's movie cameraman, Walter Frentz. He formerly worked for Leni Riefenstahl. FRENTZ

Below, March 1938. Hitler receives Reichstag ovation after announcing *Anschluss* of Austria. IMPERIAL WAR MUSEUM

Candid shot of Hitler on the veranda of the Berghof in 1938. WÜNSCHE

Hitler standing in limousine outside the Rheinhotel Dreesen in Bad Godesberg, where he was to meet with British Prime Minister Neville Chamberlain. September 1938. IMPERIAL WAR MUSEUM

Hitler, Chamberlain and Ribbentrop talk peace in Munich one week later. BUNDESARCHIV

Left, General von Fritsch, shortly before his death in Poland. IMPERIAL WAR MUSEUM.
Right, General Halder, wearing rimless glasses, and Field Marshal von Brauchitsch
pose over map. July 3, 1939. IMPERIAL WAR MUSEUM

Left, two months after invading Poland in 1939 Hitler narrowly escapes death at
Hofbräuhaus in Munich. A bomb hidden in a column behind Hitler exploded a few
minutes after he unexpectedly ended his speech and rushed to the railroad station.
That afternoon Frau Troost had warned him of possible assassination and he decided
to take earlier train. The ordnance officer in charge of scheduling, Max Wünsche,
stares intently at his chief from the front row. BIBLIO. FÜR ZEIT. Right, Polish Jews
humiliated by Nazis. IMPERIAL WAR MUSEUM

Rare pictures of Hitler planning invasion of the West in early 1940 in the old Reich Chancellery. Left, Göring and Captain von Puttkamer, the Führer's naval adjutant, watch Hitler explain how to skirt the Maginot Line. Almost all his commanders opposed the unorthodox plan—which worked. PUTTKAMER. Right, Keitel, Jodl, Hitler, Schmundt (chief adjutant) and Puttkamer. PUTTKAMER

Hitler's military inner circle, May 1940. Front row, l. to r., Brückner (personal adjutant), Otto Dietrich (press chief), Keitel, Hitler, Jodl, Bormann, Below (Hitler's Luftwaffe adjutant), Hoffmann the photographer. Middle row, Bodenschatz (Göring's chief of staff), Schmundt, Wolf, Dr. Morell (Hitler's chief physician), Hansgeorg Schulze (Hitler's ordnance officer, killed in battle and replaced by his brother Richard). Back row, Engel (Hitler's army adjutant), Dr. Brandt (Hitler's surgeon), Puttkamer, Lorenz (DNB), Walther Hewel (Foreign Office), unknown, Schaub (Hitler's personal adjutant), Wünsche. BIBLIO. FÜR ZEIT.

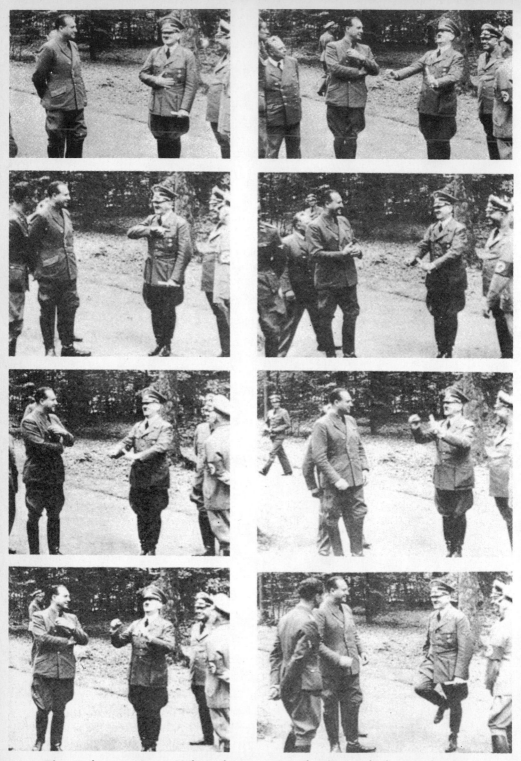

The jig that never was. Hitler's elation at news that France had surrendered was briefly filmed by Walter Frentz at Brûly-de-Pesche, not, as generally believed, in Compiegne. The above frames (and there were no others, Frentz revealed to the author) were cleverly "looped" (repeated) by a Canadian film expert, making it appear that Hitler was executing a dance. The same technique was later used in cat food commercials. TRANSIT FILM, MUNICH statement to the press. The British, he said, would guarantee that the Czechs kept their promise to evacuate the Sudetenland so long as the Germans abstained from force. His envoy, Wilson, was back in the Reich chancellery late the next morning with this new proposal, but Hitler refused to discuss it. There were only two possibilities open to the Czechs: accept or refuse the German proposal. "And if they choose to refuse I shall smash Czechoslovakia!" He threatened to march into the Sudetenland if Beneš did not capitulate by 2 P.M. the next day.

Sir Horace suddenly rose and read out a short message which Schmidt translated as slowly and emphatically as possible so that Hitler could mark its purport: "If France, in fulfillment of her treaty obligations, should become actively involved in hostilities against Germany, the United Kingdom would deem itself obliged to support France."

Hitler was furious. "If France and England strike, let them do so. It's a matter of complete indifference to me. I am prepared for every eventuality. It is Tuesday today and by next Monday we shall all be at war."

Wilson wanted to continue the conversation but Henderson signaled him against doing so. Sir Horace did get one moment alone with the Führer before leaving and reiterated that a catastrophe must be avoided at all costs. "I will still try to make those Czechs sensible," he promised.

"I would welcome that," said Hitler and repeated emphatically that England could wish for no better friend than he.

Despite the fervor of last evening's crowd at the Sportpalast, William Shirer (broadcasting from the balcony) had noted in his diary that there was no war fever. "The crowd was *good-natured*, as if it didn't realize what his words meant." This was illustrated again late Wednesday afternoon when a motorized division rolled through Berlin. Rather than cheer, most of those leaving their offices ducked into subways and the few that remained at the curb watched in silence.

Captain Wiedemann also noticed this lack of public enthusiasm and when he walked into the chancellery loudly remarked: "It looks like a funeral march out there!" "Shh!" whispered an adjutant. "He is sitting right here by the window." Hitler pensively watched the procession. Finally someone heard him mutter: "I can't wage war with this nation yet." Perhaps it was with this in mind that he sent off a message to Chamberlain, one that, for him, was conciliatory.

In England, which was far less ready for war than Germany, the Prime Minister was preparing himself for a broadcast to the nation. Criticism of appeasement was on the rise and he too was assailed with doubts. "I am wobbling about all over the place," he remarked just before he walked up to the microphone at 8 P.M.—the same moment the order for mobilization of the British fleet was issued—and bared some of his apprehension to the public. "How horrible," he said, "how fantastic, how incredible it is that we should be trying on gas-masks here because of a quarrel in a faraway country between people of whom we know nothing! It seems all the more impossible that a quarrel which has already been settled in principle should be the subject of war." He proceeded to prepare the people for more concessions. "I am myself a man of peace to the depths of my soul. Armed conflict between nations is a nightmare to me; but if I were convinced that any nation had made up its mind to dominate the world by force, I should feel that it must be resisted. Under such a domination, life for people who believe in liberty would not be worth living: but war is a fearful thing, and we must be very clear, before we embark on it, that it is really the great issues that are at stake."

Two hours later the Prime Minister's hopes were raised by the latest letter from Hitler. After opening with the usual diatribe against the Czechs, it concluded with an oblique suggestion that Chamberlain continue his efforts to "bring the government in Prague to reason at the very last hour." To the despairing Chamberlain it seemed the gap was narrowing and he hastily scribbled a draft reply inviting himself to another rendezvous. "I feel convinced that we could reach agreement in a week. . . . I cannot believe that you will take the responsibility of starting a world war, which may end civilization, for the sake of a few days' delay in settling this long-standing problem."

He then composed a personal message to Mussolini telling of this last appeal to the Führer. "I trust Your Excellency will inform the German Chancellor that you are willing to be represented and urge him to agree to my proposal, which will keep all our peoples out of war." And so, with reborn hope, he worked till long after midnight preparing the speech he was to make to Parliament in the morning, the day on which Herr Hitler's ultimatum would expire.

That dreaded day, Wednesday, September 28, started in frenzy at the core of the crisis, Berlin. At 8 A.M. French Ambassador François-Poncet phoned Weizsäcker urgently requesting an audience with the Führer so that he could present new suggestions. Weizsäcker hastened to the Kaiserhof Hotel where his own chief was staying. But Ribbentrop was so annoyed "at the prospect of his game being upset, this time from Paris," that a violent scene resulted.

"It is a monstrous thing," said the subordinate, according to his account, "that you should want to start a war when the real differences between the two sides are so small and are concerned only with the method by which the Sudetenland should be incorporated."

"You should leave that to the Führer!" exclaimed Ribbentrop, and in this mood the two set off for the chancellery.

At 10 A.M., four hours before Hitler's ultimatum would end, François-Poncet telephoned Henderson to report that he feared the worst. His request to see Hitler was still unanswered; apparently the Führer was not receiving ambassadors today. Henderson promised to do what he could. First he phoned Göring to inform him of Hitler's refusal to see François-Poncet, who had fresh proposals on which war or peace depended. Göring cut him short. So recently the aggressor in Vienna, he was now playing the role of peacemaker. "You need not say a word more," he said, "I am going immediately to the Führer."

Never had Schmidt seen such hectic activity at the chancellery. "Ministers and Generals, with their train of Party members, aides-de-camp, officers and heads of departments, who had hurried round to consult Hitler, were sitting or standing everywhere." Hitler wandered from group to group expounding his views at length but not listening to a word of advice. He had retired to the winter garden for privacy when Göring finally arrived to make his appeal for reason. Noticing Neurath in the anteroom, the Reichsmarschall persuaded the former Foreign Minister to join him, but once in the conference room it was Neurath who carried the burden of argument. "Mein Führer," he began, "do you wish to start a war under any circumstances? Of course not!"

Ribbentrop was hovering outside the winter garden, hoping to be invited in. Then Göring came out and belligerently strode over to him shouting, "Herr von Ribbentrop, if war should break out, I will be the first one to tell the German people that you pushed things to this end!" To the edification of the adjutants and aides, these two high officials began exchanging threats and insults. At one point Ribbentrop accused his opponent of fearing combat and Göring roared back that as soon as the Führer said "March!" he would take off in the leading airplane—on condition that Ribbentrop sat beside him! "If the situation had not been so serious," recalled Wiedemann, "it would have been comical to see the two insulted 'primadonnas' clawing at each other as often happens on stage before the final rehearsal."

A little after 11 A.M. Ribbentrop was finally admitted into the winter garden so that he could be present during the delayed interview with François-Poncet. Flourishing a map, the French ambassador prophesied that an attack on Czechoslovakia would spread throughout Europe. "You are naturally confident of winning the war just as we believe that we can defeat you. But why should you take the risk when your essential demands can be met without war?"

It was apparent that François-Poncet's arguments were gradually tilting the balance in favor of peace. No longer did Hitler flare up nor could he answer the Frenchman's logic. All at once an adjutant interrupted. Ambassador Attolico was outside with an urgent message from Rome.

As soon as Attolico saw the Führer emerge from the winter garden he shouted unceremoniously from a distance that he had an urgent message from Mussolini! "Il Duce informs you that, whatever you decide, Führer, Fascist Italy stands behind you." Catching his breath, he added,

"Il Duce is, however, of the opinion that it would be wise to accept the British proposal, and begs you to refrain from mobilization."

"Tell Il Duce that I accept his proposal," said Hitler, then returned to the winter garden to inform François-Poncet that Mussolini had just asked whether he would accept his counsel—failing, however, to add that he had agreed to do so. The two continued their conversation but Hitler's attention kept wavering. It was obvious that he was still pondering Il Duce's message and before long he got to his feet, indicating the interview was over. François-Poncet asked whether he should advise his government that the Führer was inflexible. Distractedly Hitler replied that he would give an answer early in the afternoon.

The parade to the winter garden continued. A few minutes past noon Henderson made his way through the crowd in the reception room. "It is going better," a German friend whispered to him. "Only stick to it." In the conference room Hitler listened patiently while Schmidt translated Chamberlain's offer to come to Berlin at once for a conference; he then replied that he must first communicate with Mussolini.

Il Duce seconded the idea. He suggested that they all meet in Munich. Hitler agreed and invitations were hastily dispatched to Daladier and Chamberlain. The one to the latter arrived while he was addressing the House of Commons and Queen Mary, who was in the gallery with Halifax, Baldwin and other notables. Chamberlain had just announced Hitler's acceptance of Mussolini's suggestion to delay mobilization and during the resultant mutter of approval the Chancellor of the Exchequer passed him a slip of paper. The Prime Minister's face was transformed. In a broken voice he continued: "That is not all. I have something further to say to the House yet. I have now been informed by Herr Hitler that he invites me to meet him at Munich tomorrow morning. He has also invited Signor Mussolini and M. Daladier." Some unidentified member shouted: "Thank God for the Prime Minister!" thereby touching off an unprecedented demonstration of hysterical shouting. Queen Mary, a symbol of self-control, wept without restraint as did the Duchess of Kent and Mrs. Chamberlain. "From all sides," wrote Sir John Simon in his memoirs, "there was impetuous cheering, in which few failed to join, and we adjourned almost at once by common consent. I saw men, some of whom have since spoken slightingly of what Chamberlain was trying to do, cross the floor in tears and with unrestrained emotion grasp him by the hand." One of the few members of Commons not overcome by the moment was Winston Churchill. "And what about Czechoslovakia?" he was heard to mutter bitterly. "Does no one think of asking their opinion?"

With few exceptions the people of the democracies shared the relief. In the streets of Paris, London and New York jubilant crowds read the extras proclaiming the end of the crisis. From Paris, Ambassador Bullitt wrote his friend Roosevelt, "I am so relieved this evening that I feel like embracing everyone and wish I were in the White House to give you a large kiss on your bald spot." And from Washington the President dispatched a two-word cable to Chamberlain: GOOD MAN.

From another President, Beneš, the Prime Minister received a longer message, this a plea: "I ask Mr. Chamberlain very earnestly for help because it is our real desire to contribute to peace. I beg therefore that nothing may be done in Munich without Czechoslovakia being heard."

While most Germans were equally relieved, the anti-Hitler group was dismayed. The news scotched their latest scheme to seize Hitler by force and set up a military regime. When Halder learned of the Munich meeting he could "no longer see his way clear to set the Putsch apparatus in operation under such circumstances."

At 6 P.M. Il Duce's luxurious train left Rome to enthusiastic cheers. He was in an expansive mood, for he was not only being hailed around the world as the savior of peace but had managed to win Hitler's gratitude by supporting him through the crisis. Mussolini also felt he had scored a diplomatic victory over the British and ridiculed them good-naturedly at dinner with Ciano. "In a country where animals are adored to the point of making cemeteries and hospitals and houses for them, and legacies are bequeathed to parrots, you can be sure that decadence has set in. Besides, other reasons apart, it is also a consequence of the composition of the English people. Four million surplus women. Four million women sexually unsatisfied, artificially creating a host of problems in order to excite or appease their senses. Not being able to embrace one man, they embrace humanity."

6

Early the following morning, September 29, the Führer met Mussolini between Munich and the border. Beyond being a mark of courtesy to an ally, it gave Hitler an opportunity to bring Il Duce up to date on the latest developments. As the two dictators headed for the Bavarian capital in the Führer's train, Hitler revealed that, with the Westwall completed, he feared no attack from that quarter. If England and France were foolish enough to make an assault, the war would be over before the enemy could complete mobilization. "I have no need to mobilize. The German army stands ready and asks only to be allowed to realize my aims."

The other two conferees were Munich-bound by air. Chamberlain left Heston in a slight rain after telling journalists, "When I was a little boy, I used to repeat, 'If at first you don't succeed, try, try again!' This is what I am doing. When I come back I hope I may be able to say, as Hotspur says in *Henry IV*, 'out of this nettle, danger, we pluck this flower, safety.'"

To the shouts of "Long live Daladier!" and "Long live peace!" the French Premier boarded his plane at Le Bourget. It took off in a milky fog. At 11:15 A.M. the twin-motored plane set down at Munich's airport. François-Poncet watched Daladier descend, brow deeply furrowed with wrinkles. He had left a tense, fearful city and was surprised to find the Germans exuberant. They greeted him as a hero with enthusiastic hails.

Chamberlain landed a few minutes before noon and he too got a joyous reception on his trip to the Regina Palace Hotel. He was there only for minutes before taking off in an open car for the newly built Führerbau where the conference would take place. In the complex of National Socialist buildings clustered around the Königsplatz, it was a compact but monumental stone structure with a spacious central hall, sixty-five feet high and a hundred feet wide, from which two impressive stone staircases curved up to the conference room.

Chamberlain and his two colleagues, all in black suits, arrived first. Next came Mussolini, advancing with lively step, his chest thrown out, completely at ease, and patronizing, as if he were the host. The last to arrive was the Führer. The hard, strange look in his eyes impressed Daladier. The conferees and their aides congregated around a buffet set up in a salon, shaking hands courteously but coldly as they surveyed each other. Hitler did his best to be affable but his brows were furrowed with concern since most of his guests spoke no German and he was unable to communicate with them freely. At last the stilted buffet was over and Hitler led the way into a large rectangular room overlooking the Königsplatz. It was an impressive room with leather-covered walls, a profusion of green plants and paintings and a huge marble fireplace over which hung the imposing portrait of Bismarck by Lenbach.

Hastily prepared and poorly organized, the conference began in confusion and became increasingly muddled. With no chairman, no agenda or agreed procedure, it splintered into a series of involved individual discussions. At one point Hitler became so restive at Chamberlain's nagging concern over the matter of compensating the Czechs for property in the Sudetenland that he shouted, "Our time is too valuable to be wasted on such trivialities!"

Mussolini brought some degree of order into the proceedings by submitting a written proposal for the solution of the Sudeten question which he presented as his own even though the Germans had drafted it. By then it was 3 P.M. and there was a recess for lunch. The proceedings were even more chaotic after the bolted meal. Often three or four would talk at once, making Schmidt's task almost impossible. He would have to insist that the preceding translation be heard first and, to friends watching in amusement through glassed doors, he looked like a schoolmaster trying to keep an unruly class in order. To complicate matters, outsiders began to invade the room. One by one Göring, François-Poncet, Henderson, Attolico and

Weizsäcker wandered in with legal clerks, secretaries and adjutants. They all crowded around the principals, who were grouped in a semicircle before the huge fireplace, until it looked like a high-stake game of chance.

Il Duce had taken command of the proceedings. The other three principals could speak only their own language, while he held forth in all four. Although his English was laborious, his French Italianate, and his German questionable, he took over as interpreter-general, a dictatorial but amiable director of an undisciplined chorus. He would ask Hitler a question in German, get the answer and then summarize the meaning rather than the exact words for the French and English delegations. "That was my great day," he later told SS Captain Eugen Dollmann, whom he had brought along as an interpreter. "All eyes were on me, not on Mr. Daladier or Mr. Chamberlain. It was an occasion worthy of the Caesars—do you remember?"

As the evening approached the atmosphere in the room grew thicker. Finally the British introduced their own proposal, generally acceptable except on the plebiscite in the Sudetenland and an international guarantee of Czechoslovakia's new borders. At the height of this prolonged but not particularly caustic discussion Dollmann was summoned from the room: a mysterious veiled woman demanded his presence. In the guardroom he found the wife of Ambassador Attolico, who demanded that he "immediately and without delay" ask Herr Hitler how the conference was going. She explained that she had promised the Madonna in the Pilgrim's Church at Loreto to bring back a fat golden candle if the conference went well and world peace was preserved. Her train was leaving in half an hour. Dollmann said he could not possibly accost the Führer but would ask Il Duce or Ciano. They would not do; she instructed him to find out from Himmler, who knew everything. Left with no alternative, Dollmann finally located the Reichsführer. "His initial surprise gave way to amusement. He authorized me to announce that peace was assured."

Agreement did seem assured but there were still a number of points to clarify. It was already 8 p.m. and Hitler was becoming impatient. He had arranged an elaborate banquet to conclude the conference and the food was getting cold. He suggested they adjourn for dinner since the discussion would probably go on for several hours more. The British and French turned down the invitation on the grounds that they had to telephone their governments but Schmidt felt it was because they were in no mood to attend a banquet. "They had secured peace, but at the price of a serious loss of prestige." The British hurried off to the Hotel Regina, while the French returned to the Four Seasons where they had food sent up to their rooms. In the meantime the Germans and Italians were celebrating a victory at the Führerbau with champagne and a variety of delicacies.

It was a few minutes past ten by the time the four principals and their advisers were again seated at the fireplace. After extensive redrafting and tedious delays that continued until past midnight, agreement was finally reached. "Actually the whole thing was a cut-and-dried affair," Göring later told an American psychologist. "Neither Chamberlain nor Daladier was the least bit interested in sacrificing or risking anything to save Czechoslovakia. That was clear as day to me. The fate of Czechoslovakia was essentially sealed in three hours. Then they argued for hours more about the word 'guarantee.' Chamberlain kept hedging. Daladier hardly paid any attention at all. He just sat there like this." (Göring slumped down and assumed a bored expression.) "All he did was nod approval from time to time. Not the slightest objection to anything. I was simply amazed at how easily the thing was managed by Hitler. After all, they knew that Skoda, etc., had munition plants in the Sudetenland, and Czechoslovakia would be at our mercy. . . . When he suggested that certain armaments which were across the Sudeten border should be brought into the Sudeten territory as soon as we take it over, I thought there would be an explosion. But no—not a peep. We got everything we wanted; just like that." (He snapped his fingers.)

At 1:30 A.M. an acceptable document was ceremoniously placed on a mahogany table next to a huge, elaborate inkwell. The pact provided for a four-stage evacuation of the Sudetenland to begin on October 1. An international commission would determine which districts were to hold plebiscites and make final determination of the borders.

Hitler appeared satisfied. The first to sign, he found the pretentious inkwell empty and a substitute had to be hastily provided. The last to arrive, the Führer was the first to leave and William Shirer was struck by "the light of victory in Hitler's eyes as he strutted down the broad steps" of the Führerbau.

It was some time before Chamberlain and Daladier left and it was their painful duty to inform the two Czech representatives, anxiously waiting off stage throughout the long day, of the fate of their country. They were brought to Chamberlain's room at the Regina about 2:15 A.M. The atmosphere was oppressive as the Czechs waited for sentence to be passed. Chamberlain made a long introductory speech, then, as Daladier was handing over a copy of the agreement, he began yawning. One of the Czechs was in tears. "Believe me," François-Poncet consoled him, "all this is not final. It is but one moment in a story which has just begun and which will soon bring up the issue again."

Daladier wakened to the cheers of a delirious and vocal crowd outside his hotel. They sang songs and called for "dear little Daladier" until he came out to the balcony.

Later in the morning Chamberlain was given an ovation by the Müncheners as he drove in an open car to Hitler's apartment for a final informal talk. The Prime Minister had come on a personal mission of vital import. He had composed a short statement hopefully to be signed by himself and Hitler. It went far beyond the documents promulgated at the Führerbau and expressed a determination never to go to war with one another again. "If he signs it," he told his Parliamentary Secretary at breakfast, "and sticks to it that will be fine, but if he breaks it that will convince the Americans of the kind of man he is."

When Hitler heard a translation of the memorandum, he exclaimed, "Ja! Ja!" and without ado the two affixed their signatures. Chamberlain handed over one copy and kept another, convinced that Hitler was as enthusiastic as he. But Schmidt had the feeling that he had agreed to the wording with a certain reluctance and signed it only to please Chamberlain. Hitler, it seemed, made a practice of spreading conflicting impressions. Once alone with his valet, he exulted that the Prime Minister, an old man, had traveled all the way just to see him. "I gave him a noseful. He won't be visiting me again soon." Yet a moment later he gave Major Gerhard Engel, his army adjutant, the impression that he "liked the old gentleman and wanted to continue negotiations with him." Hitler assured Engel that he himself was "not considering taking any steps that would be potentially dangerous. First gains had to be digested. The solution to the Polish question would not run away."

It was 5:38 P.M. when Chamberlain's plane touched down at Heston. He stood in the open doorway, smiling as he waved the document he and Hitler had signed. "I've got it!" he shouted at Halifax. "I've got it!" With the roar of the crowd in his ears, Chamberlain read a letter from the King asking him to "come straight to Buckingham Palace, so that I can express to you personally my most heartfelt congratulations on the success of your visit to Munich."

On the trip from airport to palace he was given a hero's welcome, rare in the history of England. The streets, as he described in a private letter, "were lined from one end to the other with people of every class, shouting themselves hoarse, leaping on the running board, banging on the windows, and thrusting their hands into the car to be shaken." It seemed that all England wanted to congratulate and thank him. "No conqueror returning from a victory on the battlefield," commented the London *Times*, "had come adorned with nobler laurels."

He was engulfed in front of 10 Downing Street and when the screaming throng refused to disperse he came to an open window. The cheering intensified, finally turning into a raucous rendition of "For he's a jolly good fellow!" Chamberlain stood beaming at the window, the same one at which Disraeli had announced "peace with honour" on returning from the Berlin Congress of 1878. "This is the second time in our history," he said, "that there has come back from Germany to Downing Street peace with honour. I believe it is peace for our time."

The weeks of crisis were at last over and the English, with few exceptions, were unrestrained in their joy but there was no celebration in

Prague when the new premier, General Jan Syrovy, announced over the radio that his government had been forced to accept the Munich Diktat since they had been deserted and stood alone. It was a choice, he said, "between a reduction of our territory and the death of the nation."

7

Mussolini also received an ovation, perhaps the greatest, in his own opinion, of the entire twenty years of Fascism. At every station and grade crossing multitudes awaited his train, many on their knees, to acclaim him. He was given a Caesar's welcome in Rome as his open car traveled down the Via Nazionale, passing under a triumphal arch of leaves and branches. Upon entering the Palazzo Venezia the mob in the piazza began chanting "Du-ce! Du-ce!" The spontaneous roar, when he at last appeared on the balcony, indicated that perhaps never before had he enjoyed such popularity.

Still, through the world Chamberlain was the most honored of those who met at Munich. His lean figure and hawk nose had become a household symbol of peace. Former Crown Prince Wilhelm sent him a secret letter of thanks "for saving the peace," and the ex-Kaiser wrote Queen Mary with indelible pencil that he had not the slightest doubt that the Prime Minister "was inspired by heaven and guided by God" in averting "a most fearful catastrophe." Most Germans shared the sentiment and awoke on the first of October with the prayer that no incident impede the march of their troops into the Sudetenland. The Führer's train arrived at the Czech border before dawn and Reichenau, the first of the generals to pledge allegiance to Hitler, reported with words that astounded Wiedemann: "Mein Führer, the army today is making the greatest sacrifice that soldiers can make to their supreme commander, namely to march into enemy territory without firing a shot."

Wiedemann could not believe that a German general could make such a ridiculous remark. Then another general chimed in: "Yes, mein Führer, I was with my old regiment this morning. The men were weeping for being forbidden to attack the Czech bunkers!"

"And all along," said Hitler, "those defeatists tried to tell me that my politics would lead to war!" This, delivered in a sharp tone, alarmed Wiedemann, who stood directly behind him. Whom did he mean by defeatists?

At Chequers the tension and exhaustion of the past hours were just catching up with Chamberlain. "I came nearer there to a nervous breakdown than I have ever been in my life," he confessed in a letter. "I have pulled myself together, for there is a fresh ordeal to go through in the House." It came on Monday, October 3. By then the high emotion had worn off for many and relief at deliverance from war was being replaced by humiliation. Duff Cooper opened the debate over Munich in the Commons by tendering his resignation from the cabinet. A European war would follow the invasion of Czechoslovakia, he said. "The Prime Minister has believed in addressing Herr Hitler through the language of sweet reasonableness. I have believed that he was more open to the language of the mailed fist."

Obviously tired and irritable, Chamberlain rose to reply that the agreement he had signed with Hitler in the Führer's flat was extremely significant. There was sincerity and good will on both sides and it would be extremely difficult for Hitler to take back the emphatic declarations he had made. He was applauded but without enthusiasm, for a feeling of guilt pervaded the House. The debate continued for three days with the denunciations climaxed by an eloquent damnation from Churchill. "All is over," he said. "Silent, mournful, abandoned, broken Czechoslovakia recedes into the darkness." He did not begrudge the loyal, brave people of Britain their natural and spontaneous outburst of joy and relief on learning of the pact. "But they should know the truth. They should know that there has been gross neglect and deficiency in our defences. They should know that we have sustained a great defeat without a war, the consequences of which will travel far with us. . . . And do not suppose that this is the end. This is only the beginning of the reckoning."

Chamberlain and his co-appeasers had sought a new revisionist settlement in East Central Europe which Hitler would underwrite. But now it was obvious that the Führer's program ran counter to this and no accommodation had ever been possible. Already Chamberlain and his umbrella were becoming the symbol of pusillanimity, and such was his concern that he sought help from Adolf Hitler. He dispatched a secret message wondering if the Führer, who was to make a speech at the Sportpalast that evening, "could give the Prime Minister some support in forming public opinion in Britain." Hitler obliged, launching a blistering attack on Chamberlain's detractors in the House. But aid and comfort from such a dubious source were not necessary. The following day, October 6, the House of Commons hastily approved Chamberlain's policy "by which war was averted in the recent crisis." The vote was 366 to 144 with some 35 dissidents—including Cooper, Eden and Churchill—abstaining.

The attack of those three had far greater effect in Berlin where every word launched at Chamberlain was taken as a personal insult by Hitler. He had come out of the Führerbau after signing the pact pleased—so agreed his adjutants and aides—convinced that the Czech problem was solved once and for all, and he intended to keep his part of the bargain.

The chorus of condemnation in England changed all that. There were already whispers in the Wilhelmstrasse that Ribbentrop and Himmler were taking advantage of Hitler's annoyance to persuade him that Germany had not fully exploited the Western democracies' fear of war at Munich and that England only negotiated to gain time so she could strike later when better armed.

Aware of this discontent, François-Poncet did his best "to calm Hitler down" by suggesting he sign an agreement with France similar to the one concluded with Chamberlain. "I wished to flash before his eyes the possibility of further agreements, economic and financial, which might lead to a future organization in Europe; I hoped to direct his mind toward prospects and in directions other than those of violence."

But Hitler was convinced, or allowed himself to be convinced, that he had been deceived by perfidious Albion. On October 9 he publicly displayed these feelings in a bitter speech at Saarbrücken comparing the British attitude to that of a governess. He went on to attack that malevolent trio of Churchill, Cooper and Eden, far surpassing the acidity of the Sportpalast speech.

The effects of his diatribe were felt three days later when the International Commission selected to implement the Munich agreement voted unanimously to dispense with plebiscites. Its members had already bowed to German demands that the 1910 census be used in determining those districts to be ceded to the Reich and it was becoming increasingly obvious that the original pact was being contorted to strip Czechoslovakia of her last defensive line of fortifications.

François-Poncet made a final appeal for reason to Hitler in mid-October. The occasion was his farewell to the Führer, he was being transferred to Rome. Hitler had always liked him and showed his appreciation for seven years' service in Berlin by inviting the French ambassador to his mile-high mountain tea house atop the Kehlstein. Built under the direction of the indefatigable Bormann at a reported cost of thirty million marks, it was a remarkable engineering feat. Equally so was the five-mile winding asphalt road from the Berghof which had been blasted out of the side of the mountain at the cost of several lives. François-Poncet was driven up this road to an undergound passage dug into the peak. At the end of the corridor he was escorted into a copper-lined elevator, its shaft hacked out of solid rock. After a ride of about four hundred feet, François-Poncet found himself in a gallery of Roman pillars. Beyond was an immense glassed-in circular hall. Great logs were burning in a huge open fireplace. On all sides extended such an immense panorama of mountains that it gave the Frenchman a sensation of being suspended in space. The entire view, bathed in the autumn twilight, was grandiose, almost hallucinating.

In this fantastic setting—which was already palling on Hitler after several visits because of its grandiosity—ambassador and Führer held their last interview. Pale and drawn, the latter confirmed his disappointment with the aftermath of the Munich agreement. The crisis was far from over; in fact, threatened to worsen if the situation did not improve. Great Britain, he complained, was "sonorous with threats and calls to arms."

The ambassador pointed out that a reaction was inevitable after the excess of joy following the preservation of peace. Furthermore, Hitler's own harsh speech at Saarbrücken had spread the impression that the sacrifice of Czechoslovakia had only increased Germany's appetite and thereby strengthened the position of the adversaries of the Munich pact.

Hitler protested. It was the British who had started the present trouble. Nor had he uttered a word against France. As he went on to defend his treatment of the Czechs, François-Poncet interrupted, urging him not to linger over the past. The future was more important. The democracies and the totalitarian states must now demonstrate that they could live side by side in peace "and gradually lead Europe towards more normal and enduring conditions." Hitler objected neither to the interruption nor to the concept. He was quite prepared, he said, to do this.

As they descended the mountain François-Poncet reviewed the conversation. "I know that he is changeable, dissembling, full of contradictions, uncertain," he reported to Paris. "The same man with the debonair aspect, with a real fondness for the beauties of nature, who discussed reasonable ideas on European politics around the tea table, is also capable of the worst frenzies, of the wildest exaltations, and the most delirious ambitions. There are days when, standing before the globe of the world, he will overthrow nations, continents, geography and history, like a demiurge stricken with madness. At other moments, he dreams of being the hero of an everlasting peace, in which he would devote himself to the erection of the most magnificent monuments."

These apparent conflicts within the Führer were leading many foreigners to conclude that he was simply insane. One was Sigmund Freud, now safely established in London. "You cannot tell what a madman will do," he told an American admirer. "You know he is an Austrian and lived for years in great misery." When Hitler took over that country it seemed to go to his head.

A former disciple had a far different theory and that October in Zurich expounded it to H. R. Knickerbocker, who had just come from Prague. "Hitler belongs in the category of the truly mystic medicine man," said Dr. Carl Gustav Jung, who had spent hours discussing the Führer with Ernst Hanfstaengl immediately after the latter's escape from Germany. "His body does not suggest strength. The outstanding characteristic of his physiognomy is its dreamy look. I was especially struck by that when I saw pictures taken of him in the Czechoslovakian crisis; there was in his eyes the look of a seer." This prompted Knickerbocker to ask why Hitler made nearly every German fall down and worship him, yet made little impression on foreigners. "He is the first man to tell every German what he has been thinking and feeling all along in his unconscious about German fate, especially since the defeat in the World War, and the one characteristic which colors every German soul is the typically German inferiority complex, the complex of the younger brother, of the one who is always a bit late to the feast. Hitler's power is not political; it is *magic*." Hitler's secret was that he allowed himself to be moved by his own unconscious. He was like a man who listens intently to whispered suggestions from a mysterious voice and "then *acts upon them*. In our case, even if occasionally our unconscious does reach us through dreams, we have too much rationality, too much cerebrum to obey it—but Hitler listens and obeys. The true leader is always *led*." Hitler sang a purely Teutonic song which rang true to Germans and they chose him as their representative. He was the demagogue appealing to the primitive, an echo from their own tribal past.

Jung predicted that England and France would not honor their new guarantee to the Czechs. "No nation keeps its word. A nation is a big, blind worm, following what? Fate perhaps. A nation has no honor, it has no word to keep." Therefore, why expect Hitler to keep his word? "Because Hitler is the nation."

Part 6

"TO THE VERY BRINK OF BOLDNESS"

Chapter Eighteen

CRYSTAL NIGHT
NOVEMBER 1938–MARCH 1939

1

The path of anti-Semitism in Hitler's Germany was tortuous. The first Jewish restrictions in 1933 were so inconclusive that it seemed as if the Führer were deliberately compromising his principles. Could this be an attempt to solve the Jewish question by rational means acceptable to those Germans who wanted Jews controlled but not persecuted? There followed a period of struggle between the racial radicals in the party and moderates in the government and civil service which came to a climax during the summer of 1935. At this time the latter took the offensive, objecting openly to the continuing mistreatment of Jews on the grounds that it was bad for business. The "unlawful" activity against Jews must end, Reich Bank President Schacht told a small, influential group including Interior Minister Frick, Finance Minister Schwerin von Krosigk, Justice Minister Gürtner and Education Minister Rust. Otherwise, he warned, he could not complete his task of economic rearmament. For example, the Jewish agent of Alliance Insurance in Egypt had been so harried that he resigned, leaving the market to the English. Many Jewish importers were canceling large orders and it was ridiculous to imagine that it was possible for a nation to succeed economically without Jewish business. Schacht had no objection to the public display of signs such as "Jews not wanted," since these could even be found in the United States, but he bitterly opposed those put up by Streicher proclaiming, "Whoever buys from a Jew is a traitor to the people." It was unanimously agreed by the group that "wild single actions" must cease so that the Jewish question could be solved legally.

The first steps in the direction of legalization were taken a few weeks later at Nuremberg by the Führer himself, when he proclaimed the Law for the Protection of German Blood and Honor, legalizing a number of repressive measures which were promptly justified by the official Catholic *Klervsblatt* as "indisputable safeguards for the qualitative make-up of the German people." Even Streicher seemed to be satisfied now that the matter was being solved "piece by piece" in the best German legal tradition. "We don't smash any windows and we don't smash Jews," he boasted. "Whoever engages in a single action of that kind is an enemy of the State, a provocateur, or even a Jew."

Were the Nuremberg laws an attempt by Hitler to solve the Jewish question by less harsh "acceptable" methods? Or was he merely biding his time before effecting his dream of extermination? In either case solution of the problem, for the time being at least, had been taken from the party and turned over to the law. This resulted in growing resentment among the more radical Nazi racists. Held in restraint during Hitler's ensuing expansion program, they finally broke out three years later, in 1938, with the destruction of synagogues in Munich, Nuremberg and Dortmund. A wave of Jew-baiting swept the nation. "The entire Kurfürstendamm," wrote Bella Fromm, a diplomatic correspondent from Berlin, "was plastered with scrawls and cartoons. 'Jew' was smeared all over the doors, windows, and walls in waterproof colors. It grew worse as we came to the part of town where poor little Jewish retail shops were to be found. The SA had created havoc. Everywhere were revolting and bloodthirsty pictures of Jews beheaded, hanged, tortured, and maimed, accompanied by obscene inscriptions. Windows were smashed, and loot from the miserable little shops was strewn over the pavement and floating in the gutter."

The tide of anti-Semitism was given impetus on November 7, 1938, when a young Jew, Herschel Grynszpan, shot a minor German Foreign Office official in Paris. Grynszpan, whose parents had been deported from Germany to Poland, had gone to the embassy to assassinate the ambassador only to be sidetracked by Counselor Ernst vom Rath. Himself an enemy of anti-Semitism, Rath was being investigated by the Gestapo but it was he who took the bullets intended for his superior.

"Being a Jew is not a crime," sobbed Grynszpan to the police. "I am not a dog. I have a right to live and the Jewish people have a right to exist on this earth. Wherever I have been I have been chased like an animal."

On the afternoon of November 9 Rath died. The news reached Hitler at the Munich town hall where he was attending a meeting of party leaders. He left the room with his escort, conferred briefly with Goebbels before boarding his special train. Goebbels returned to the meeting to announce that Rath's murder had inspired anti-Jewish riots in the districts of Kurhessen and Magdeburg-Anhalt. The Führer, he said, had decided that if the riots spread spontaneously throughout Germany they were not to be discouraged.

The party leaders took this to mean that they were to organize demonstrations while making it appear that they had nothing to do with them. But SA Chief Lutze either misunderstood Goebbels or refused to believe Hitler had given such a command. After assembling all Gruppenführer present, he ordered them not to participate in any actions against the Jews. While these SA officials were transmitting Lutze's instructions (which in some cases were ignored), the party leaders were telephoning conflicting orders to the provinces.

At first the SS did not participate in the ransacking of shops and burning of synagogues. Upon learning that Goebbels had ordered a pogrom, Himmler directed his men to prevent excessive looting, then dictated a file memorandum: "The order was given by the Propaganda Directorate, and I suspect that Goebbels, in his craving for power, which I noticed a long time ago, and also in his empty-headedness started this action just at the time when the foreign political situation is very grave." His castigation may have been only for the record. Hours earlier Himmler himself had violently attacked the Jews in a secret speech to his SS generals. The Jews, he said, were bent on destroying Germany and so had to be driven from the Reich "with unexampled ruthlessness." If Germany did not win this all-out battle against Jewry, "there won't be a single refuge for a true Teuton left, everybody will be starved and butchered."

If Himmler objected to the terrorism sweeping the country, his chief assistant did everything he could to capitalize on it. Soon after midnight Heydrich sent urgent teletypes to all headquarters and stations of the SD and police, enjoining them to co-operate with the party and SS leaders in "organizing the demonstrations." Finally, as many Jews, particularly rich ones, were to be arrested "as can be accommodated in existing prisons. For the time being, only healthy men, not too old, are to be arrested. Upon their arrest, the appropriate concentration camps should be contacted immediately in order to confine them in these camps as fast as possible."

It was a night of despair for the Jews in Germany, with the police standing by as witnesses of the destruction and beatings. One policeman was found by the deputy police chief of Berlin weeping in front of a looted shoe shop. It had been his duty to enforce order and yet, in violation of all his ideals, he had done nothing. By official count 814 shops, 171 homes were destroyed, and 191 synagogues put to the torch; 36 Jews were killed and another 36 seriously injured. But the figures, Heydrich himself admitted, "must have been exceeded considerably."

Otto Tolischus cabled the New York *Times* that he had just witnessed a wave of destruction unparalleled in Germany since the Thirty Years' War. "Beginning systematically in the early morning hours in almost every town and city in the country, the wrecking, looting and burning continued all day. Huge but mostly silent crowds looked on and the police confined themselves to regulating traffic and making wholesale arrests of Jews 'for their own protection.' "

The reaction from abroad was immediate and the acts of brutality were given an unforgettable name—inspired by the multitude of smashed windows—Crystal Night. On all sides Germany was assailed as a barbarous nation. Many Germans agreed and other party officials beside Himmler joined in the condemnation of Goebbels. Frau Funk, wife of the Minister of Economics, overheard her husband cursing him over the phone: "Are you crazy, Goebbels? To make such a mess of things! One has to be ashamed to be a German. We are losing our whole prestige abroad. I am trying, day and night, to conserve the national wealth, and you throw it willy-nilly out of the window. If this thing does not stop immediately, you can have the whole filthy mess."

Göring complained directly to the Führer that such events made it impossible for him to carry out his mission. "I was making every effort, in connection with the Four-Year Plan," he later testified, "to concentrate the entire economic field to the utmost. I had, in the course of speeches to the nation, been asking for every old toothpaste tube, every rusty nail, every bit of scrap material to be collected and utilized. It would not be tolerated that a man who was not responsible for these things should upset my difficult economic tasks by destroying so many things of economic value on the one hand and by causing so much disturbance in economic life on the other hand." Then Hitler, according to Göring's account, "made some apologies for Goebbels, but on the whole he agreed that such events were not to take place and must not be allowed to take place."

Hitler was already giving the impression that he knew nothing of Crystal Night and added his own complaints. "It is terrible," he told Frau Troost. "They have destroyed everything for me like elephants in a china shop . . . and much worse. I had the great hope that I was about to come to an understanding with France. And now that!" But Fritz Hesse, summoned to Munich from London for a special press conference, claimed he overheard otherwise from Hitler's own lips the very night Crystal Night was set into motion. At dinner the Führer was boasting how he had bluffed the English and French at Munich when an adjutant whispered something to Goebbels. He turned and muttered to Hitler. At first Hesse couldn't hear what was said, but when the others at the table lapsed into silence it became clear that the Propaganda Minister was explaining a mass attack which he and the SA were going to launch against the Jewish shops and synagogues in a few hours. There was no doubting the Führer's approval, recalled Hesse. "Hitler squealed with delight and slapped his thigh in his enthusiasm."*

The following day Hesse called on Ribbentrop, who was still irritated at not being invited to the previous day's press conference. First, he labeled the Munich Conference a piece of first-class stupidity. All it meant was that it postponed hostility for a year, when the English would be much stronger. "Believe me, it would have been much better if war had come now. We hold all the military trumps. Who knows what will happen in a year?" But the worst was that the Führer imagined he had called the English bluff. "For years I've tried to make it clear to him that he must be careful of the English because they are dangerous. But he won't believe it. . . . Instead he fools about and makes bombastic speeches. You heard him yourself yesterday! As for that little beast, Goebbels, have you heard what his gangs have done everywhere? These imbeciles have smashed up the Jewish shops—which have long been Aryan property anyhow. They've spoiled my game for me."†

Despite Hitler's protestations to moderates, the pogrom continued and by November 12 an estimated 20,000 Jews had been shipped to concentration camps. That day Göring, who had objected to the destruction of property on economic grounds, called a meeting of the Council of Ministers to determine who would have to pay for it. He began by announcing that this conference was of decisive importance and his next words had a significance his listeners could not fathom at the time. "I have received a letter from Bormann sent me by order of the Führer, asking that the Jewish question be now, once and for all, treated in its entirety and settled in some way. Yesterday the Führer telephoned me to point out again that decisive measures must be undertaken in a coordinated manner." Inspired by this directive, the conferees agreed that the Jews themselves would have to pay for the damage in the form of a billion-mark fine.

"I certainly would not like to be a Jew in Germany!" remarked Göring and brought the four-hour meeting to a close with a grim forecast: "If in the near future the German Reich should come into conflict with foreign powers, it goes without saying that we in Germany should first come to a showdown with the Jews." Furthermore, the Führer was about

* Johannes Popitz, the Prussian Minister of Finance, got a similar account from Göring. When Popitz remarked that those responsible for Crystal Night should be punished, the Reichsmarschall replied blandly: "My dear Popitz, do you wish to punish the Führer?"

† In reply to postwar claims that Goebbels had nothing to do with Crystal Night, his personal adviser, Leopold Gutterer, signed an affidavit to the effect that Goebbels admitted his involvement at a small party in 1942. "Influential circles of the National Socialist economic leadership," Goebbels reportedly said, "took the emphatic standpoint that one could not remove the Jews from the economic life of Germany to any greater extent than had been done to date. Therefore, *we* decided: 'Good, then we will mobilize the streets and in that way solve the problem within twenty-four hours.'"

to suggest to those foreign powers so concerned over the plight of German Jews that they be deported to the island of Madagascar. "He explained it to me November 9," concluded Göring. "He wants to say to the other countries: 'Why are you always talking about the Jews? Take them!'"

While this plan for the complete elimination of Jews from the Reich economy was getting under way, other Germans, including many party leaders, were privately expressing deep concern at the excesses of Crystal Night. The bureaucrats and party leaders, aware that such violent actions always get out of hand, protested that a pogrom was too costly and accomplished almost nothing in the battle against Jews. Others were repelled by the inhumanity of such actions but did little more than grumble cautiously. Gerhart Hauptmann, for instance, complained to a friend that Hitler had ruined Germany. "This scum will bring war to the whole world, this miserable brown comedian, this Nazi hangman is rushing us into a world of war, into destruction!" Then why didn't Hauptmann emigrate in protest like Mann and Zweig? "Because I'm a coward," replied the famous playwright, "do you understand? I'm a coward."

Those safe from reprisals were heaping abuse on Hitler. Almost every newspaper and radio commentator in the United States responded to Crystal Night with outrage. From Washington, Ambassador Dieckhoff wrote the Foreign Office that he hoped "the storm at present sweeping across the United States will subside again in the foreseeable future and we shall be able to work again." Until Crystal Night, he reported, most Americans ignored the anti-German propaganda but now even German-Americans were incensed. "What particularly strikes me is the fact that, with few exceptions, the respectable patriotic circles, which are thoroughly anti-Communist and, for the greater part, anti-Semitic in their outlook, also begin to turn away from us. The fact that the Jewish newspapers write still more excitedly than before is not surprising; but that men like Dewey, Hoover, Hearst, and many others who have hitherto maintained a cooperative reserve and have even, to some extent, expressd sympathy toward Germany, are now publicly adopting so violent and bitter an attitude against her is a serious matter. . . . In the general atmosphere of hate, the idea of boycotting German goods has received new fuel, and trade negotiations cannot be considered at the moment."

National outrage was climaxed by a rare denunciation from President Roosevelt. At a news conference on November 15 he read a prepared statement to the reporters. The news from Germany, he said, had deeply shocked American public opinion. "I myself could scarcely believe that such things could occur in twentieth century civilization. With a view to gaining a firsthand picture of the situation in Germany I have asked the Secretary of State to order our Ambassador in Berlin to return at once for report and consultation." But official condemnation did not extend beyond the verbal and the United States continued its trade relations with the Third Reich.

Perhaps the protests from abroad had some effect on Hitler. A week after Crystal Night he supported the civil service, which sought to protect in the part-Jew "that part which is German," rather than the party which looked on the part-Jew as a carrier of the "Jewish influence." His support came in the form of the First Regulation to the Reich Citizenship Law which separated so-called non-Aryans into definite categories. A Jew was defined as anyone descended from at least three Jewish grandparents, or an individual with two Jewish grandparents who also belonged to the Jewish religious community or was married to a Jew.

Then came a curious category: the *Mischlinge* (half-breeds), those descended from only one Jewish grandparent, or those with two Jewish grandparents who neither practiced the Jewish religion nor were married to a Jew. In practice this split non-Aryans into two distinct groups with the Mischlinge no longer subject to repressive measures. With one bureaucratic stroke Hitler made it possible for a substantial portion of the hated enemy to escape his wrath. Was his resolve to exterminate Jews truly weakening or, again, was he merely waiting for a more suitable time to act decisively? Or was this a conscious or even unconscious attempt to save himself, since there was still the possibility that one of his own grandfathers was Jewish? The Mischlinge regulation also saved Jesus, who by Hitler's argument, being the son of God, had but two Jewish grandparents; neither did he practice the Jewish religion, nor was he married to a Jew.

2

From his youth Hitler had held cynical views of the democracies and their leaders' ability to speak one way while acting another. Consequently he was not as concerned about the vocal protests from the West throughout the latter part of 1938 as were many of his most faithful followers. Rudolf Hess, for one, was extremely downcast. On December 23 he spent two hours with the Bruckmanns, early supporters of the Führer, and told how he had implored Hitler in vain to stop the pogrom.

While Hitler must have been aware of the defection of these old adherents, he remained in such good spirits that he let himself be persuaded to wear tails for the New Year's Eve celebration at the Berghof. "My sister," Ilse Braun wrote in her diary, "had been at great pains to persuade him to dress with a minimum of good taste. 'Look at Mussolini,' she would say, 'he has a new uniform. And you, with those postman's caps.'" He kissed Ilse's hand, remarking that the Braun sisters were all beauties. "When he looked at me, beads of sweat formed between my breasts, and I did not have the courage to say *Danke schön*, though I had promised myself to make a great speech."

After accepting formal congratulations from the guests and his staff, the Führer participated in an ancient Teutonic ceremony. Molten lead was poured into a small basin of water and the shape it assumed supposedly determined the future. "Hitler did not seem satisfied with his results, for afterwards he sat down in an armchair, gazing dejectedly at the fire, and hardly spoke for the rest of the evening. Eva was extremely worried about him."

His dark mood was intensified a few days later by a revolt of bankers against his vast rearmament program. "The reckless expenditures of the Reich," read a memorandum composed by Hjalmar Schacht, president of the Reichsbank, and signed by every governor of the bank, "represents a most serious threat to the currency. The tremendous increase in such expenditures foils every attempt to draw up a regular budget; it is driving the finances of the country to the brink of ruin despite a great tightening of the tax screw, and by the same token it undermines the Reichsbank and the currency." The stability of the currency, warned Schacht, could not be stabilized in the face of such an inflationary expenditure policy and the "time has come now to call a halt."

Schacht knew that Hitler would be infuriated because the declaration in effect called for the end of military adventures. He told Schwerin von Krosigk what he had done, adding that he expected to be fired. (He had already lost his post as Minister of Economics to Walther Funk, whose powers were promptly annexed by Göring as chief of the Four-Year Plan.) The Finance Minister said that if Schacht went he would ask for his own dismissal, then composed a similar memorandum and sent it to the Führer.

Days passed but nothing happened. Finally at midnight of January 19, 1939, Schacht's phone rang. He was ordered to report to the Führer the following morning at nine. It was an unusual hour for an interview since Hitler rarely went to bed before three in the morning. According to Schacht, the Führer said, without preamble, "I have called you in order to hand you your dismissal as president of the Reichsbank." Schacht took the piece of paper extended to him. "You don't fit into the National Socialist picture," continued Hitler, then waited for some comment. Schacht remained silent until Hitler reprimanded him for condemning Crystal Night at a Christmas party of bank office boys. "If I had known that you approved of those happenings," Schacht finally said, "I might have kept silent."

This reply seemed to take Hitler's breath away. "In any case," he said indignantly, "I'm too much upset to talk to you any more now." Both men agreed that Schacht should take a long trip abroad and he left for India soon thereafter. Hitler was relieved to be rid of him. "When it is a question of a bit of sharp practice," Hitler later told his inner circle, "Schacht is a pearl beyond all price." But whenever he was called upon to show strength of character, he always failed.

Soon after Schacht's dismissal Captain Wiedemann was summoned to the winter garden. For the past months Hitler had been treating him with increasing coolness and Wiedemann guessed he too was going to be fired. Ever since Crystal Night the Führer had seemed to inhabit an imaginary world which had nothing in common with reality and whenever Wiedemann attempted to discuss any defect in the system Hitler ignored him.

"I have no use for people in high places and in my closest circle who do not agree with my politics," Hitler curtly told Wiedemann. "I hereby discharge you as my personal adjutant and appoint you consul general in San Francisco. You can accept or refuse this new position." Without hesitation Wiedemann accepted, adding that he hoped he wouldn't have to take a cut in salary. At this, Hitler's tone became milder. "I will always keep an open ear for your financial welfare." Thus, after four years' close association, the two war comrades parted without bitterness.

The exit of Schacht and Wiedemann signaled the return to grace of Josef Goebbels, who had fallen from favor due to his sexual adventures. "Every woman inflames my very blood," he wrote in his twenties. "I pace back and forth like a wolf." Nor had marriage to Magda restrained him. At the same time he kept his numerous affairs under control, never compromising himself publicly. That is, until he fell in love with Czech actress Lida Baarova in the summer of the Olympics. Magda imagined it was one of his usual flirtations but finally lost her patience in 1938 and demanded a divorce. Hitler had shown remarkable tolerance to homosexuality but was distressed by the party leaders who abandoned mates who had helped in the rise to power. He demanded that Goebbels give up the actress. At first he refused, offering to resign from his ministry and become an ambassador to Japan or some such distant country. Finally he succumbed to pressure and renounced his great love. No sooner had Baarova returned to Czechoslovakia under "advice" from the police than Hitler summoned the entire Goebbels family to the Berghof. Pictures of the couple and three of their children at the entrance to the Kehlstein tea house were published as public proof that all was well with the household.

This stage reconciliation took place only a few weeks before Crystal Night and the anguish of losing Lida Baarova—along with a desire to rehabilitate himself with people like Himmler and Rosenberg who felt that the scandal had dealt "the severest kind of blow to the moral status of the party"—might have caused him to act so recklessly that November night.

The reinstatement of Goebbels coincided with Hitler's new approach to the Jewish question. On his most recent trip to her atelier in Munich, Frau Troost had urged Hitler to reinstate a Jewish composer, Arthur

Piechler, to the school of music in Augsburg. Why shouldn't Jews be judged individually? she argued. The few she knew were not only experts in their field but valuable human beings.

"Those are your personal experiences," said Hitler after some thought. "If I'd had similar ones, then I never would have taken my path. But I had much different experiences—like those in Vienna." He must place the fate of the German people above all else. "The Jew lives and serves his own law but never that of the people or the nation where he has become a citizen. He does not belong to the German people and can therefore be among us only as a guest but not as it was during the period between 1918–1933 when he took all the top positions in art, culture, and the press, as well as in trade and the banks. It is my responsibility to see that our nation's future once more has a healthy and strong foundation based on national characteristics. I have made it my life work to build a safe existence and future for the German people and especially the German worker." This was all a prelude to refusing her request "on principle." Curiously, on his next visit to Munich he reversed himself and agreed to reinstate Professor Piechler.

Just as the false accusations of troop movements on the Czech borders early in 1938 had roused Hitler to premature action, so the storm of protests from abroad over Crystal Night may have hardened his resentment toward Jews and prompted him to look for new ways of dealing with them. An indication of this complete loss of objectivity came on January 21, 1939, when he told Czech Foreign Minister Chvalkovsky that no German guarantee would be given to a state which did not eliminate its Jews. "Our own kindness was nothing but weakness and we regret it," he said. "This vermin must be destroyed. The Jews are our sworn enemies and at the end of this year there will not be a Jew left in Germany." They were not going to get away with what they had done in November 1918. "The day of reckoning has come."

A few days later a Foreign Ministry circular on the Jewish question as a factor in foreign policy was dispatched to all diplomatic missions and consulates. "The ultimate aim of Germany's Jewish policy," it said, "is the emigration of all Jews living on German territories." Since the advent of National Socialism only slightly more than 100,000 Jews had legally or illegally left Germany to find homes in new host countries. Even this modest influx of Jews from Germany had already aroused the resistance of the native populations of America, France, Holland and Norway. Despite the moral denunciation of Germany, the Western nations were hermetically sealing their own boundaries against Hitler's Jews. This ground swell of anti-Semitism confirmed the validity of shipping out Jews en masse, and the goal of the new German policy, concluded the circular, "will be an international solution of the Jewish question in the future, not dictated by false sympathy for the 'Jewish religious minority which has been expelled,' but by the mature realization by all peoples of the danger which the Jews represent for the racial preservation of the nations."

On January 29 Hitler proclaimed his abrupt change in tactics even more explicitly. In a speech to the Reichstag on the sixth anniversary of the Nazi rise to power he declared war on world Jewry. Significantly, hours earlier he had ordered the navy to begin building a mighty submarine fleet to be completed within five years. England, America and France, he charged, were "continually being stirred up to hatred of Germany and the German people by Jewish and non-Jewish agitators," when all he wanted was peace and quiet. These lying attempts to bring about a war could not in the slightest influence Germany's manner of settling her Jewish problem, he said, and for the first time since his rise to power he publicly lifted the veil on his ultimate plan: "In the course of my life I have often been a prophet, and have usually been ridiculed for it. . . . I will once more be a prophet: If the international Jewish financiers in and outside Europe should succeed in plunging the nations once more into a world war, then the result will not be the Bolshevization of the earth, and thus the victory of Jewry, but the annihilation of the Jewish race in Europe!" He was crying out to the Jews the paranoiac warning: "Stop, before you force me to kill you!"

3

In the past year Hitler had destroyed one sovereign state, reduced and paralyzed another and, in the process, humbled the West. Nineteen thirty-nine promised even greater political conquests. On January 1 Mussolini finally made up his mind to accept the German offer of the past autumn and transform the Anti-Comintern Pact from a propaganda front to a full-fledged military alliance. "During this month," wrote Ciano in his diary, "he plans to prepare the acceptance of his views by public opinion, about which he doesn't give a damn." The reason: Mussolini feared war with the West was now inevitable.

In his New Year's message Hitler announced that the German government had but one wish: ". . . that in the coming year, too, we may succeed in contributing to the German pacification of the world." The next step in his "peaceful" program of pacification was the complete control of Czechoslovakia. For some time he had regretted the Munich Pact since it had become apparent he could have annexed the entire country without reprisals. Now he would have to find some acceptable excuse to march in and liquidate what was left.

In February he ordered Goebbels to launch a massive propaganda campaign against the Czech government: it was still terrorizing its ethnic German citizens, concentrating troops along the Sudeten borders, conspiring with the Soviets and grossly mistreating its Slovak population. The last accusation proved to be the most fruitful, for radical Slovak nationalists eagerly rose to the bait and began increasing their demands for complete independence. It was an explosive situation that needed but a single misstep from some inexperienced Czech in high places to set off another crisis —and give Hitler the excuse he needed.

In London the spirit of anti-appeasement was reinforced by a fallacious report from Erich Kordt of the German Foreign Office. He secretly informed a British official that Hitler was planning to bomb London in the near future. (It was a deliberate attempt by the anti-Hitler group in Germany to push England into a war with the Reich and was only the first of other false alarms to be planted by Kordt and other Foreign Office men in the plot.) Chamberlain took the bombing scare seriously enough to call a special cabinet meeting and, although no Nazi planes appeared, the temperature of suspicion was raised. Ambassador Henderson was brought from Berlin to report on possible Hitler military action and he did his utmost to convince Permanent Under Secretary of State for Foreign Affairs Cadogan that the Germans were not even "contemplating any immediate wild adventure and that their compass is pointing towards peace." The astute Cadogan was not so sanguine. He suggested that Hitler's intentions were "strictly dishonorable" yet he too was hesitant to believe reports that Hitler was about to engulf Czechoslovakia.

Henderson returned to his post in Berlin where he continued to send back optimistic assessments. Rumors of Nazi adventures in the Ukraine or in Holland were dying down, he reported. "Although it is suggested in some quarters that this calm may only be a prelude to another storm, I am not inclined to take that pessimistic view at present."

Yet the very next night even he was concerned by Hitler's actions at the annual banquet for the diplomatic corps. "The apparent friendliness which he had shown at the motor exhibition was notably absent at this dinner," Henderson wrote in his memoirs. "He kept his eyes fixed over my right shoulder and confined his remarks to general subjects, while stressing the point that it was not Britain's business to interfere with Germany in Central Europe." Although the Führer's attitude left Henderson "with a feeling of vague uneasiness," he did not bother to mention it in his next report to London.

Evidence of German intrigue was soon forthcoming. On March 6 British Ambassador Newton reported from Prague that relations between the Czechs and Slovaks "seem to be heading for a crisis." Matters had come to a head over a demand for financial assistance on the part of the Slovaks. What role, if any, "Germany is playing in the dispute is a matter for conjecture but it may be noted that the Slovak Minister of Commerce and Minister of Transport visited Berlin last week accompanied by experts."

For some reason this telegram was delayed forty-eight hours and by that time Henderson had recovered from his "vague uneasiness." On March 9 he wrote Halifax a long letter, expressing conviction that both Hitler and the German people longed for peace. "Hitler himself fought in the World War and his dislike of bloodshed, or anyway of dead Germans, is intense." Although Nazi extremists might be tempted to urge continued aggression, Hitler's inclination as a demagogue would be to please the majority rather than the fanatical minority. "That is one reason why, since I can find no justification for the theory that he is mad or even verging on madness, I am of the opinion that he is not thinking to-day in terms of war."

4

That evening the President of Czechoslovakia, Emil Hacha—who once admitted he understood very little about politics—finally committed the blunder Hitler was waiting for: he dismissed the Slovak government from office and ordered troops to prepare to move into the Slovakian district. The next day, Friday, Hacha declared martial law.

Hitler reacted with rapidity. He canceled his trip to Vienna to take part in the celebration of the Anschluss so that he could prepare for his next invasion. The slight but nagging fear that the Soviets might rush to Prague's aid was relieved almost immediately. Even as Hacha was resorting to martial law, Stalin told the Eighteenth Party Congress that they must be cautious and not allow the West to use the U.S.S.R. to pull its own chestnuts out of the fire. It was in line with Soviet policy to proclaim publicly that they were Czechoslovakia's only faithful ally while risking nothing. The excuse for inaction was that their pact with the Czechs required them to provide aid only *after* France had acted.

On Saturday, his favorite day for a coup, Hitler went into action, improvising with customary agility. First he instructed General Keitel to draft an ultimatum demanding that the Czechs submit to the military occupation of Moravia and Bohemia without resistance, then issued disruptive orders to agents in Czech and Slovak territory. At the same time Henderson was telephoning Halifax to proceed circumspectly. He doubted "whether Herr Hitler has yet taken any decision and I consider it therefore highly desirable that nothing should be said or published abroad during the weekend which will excite him to precipitate action."

Nothing was needed. That evening Hitler's two puppet leaders in Austria, accompanied by five German generals, drove across the Danube to break into a meeting of the new Slovak cabinet at their seat of government, Bratislava. The members were told to proclaim the independence of

Slovakia but the new Prime Minister stalled for time by announcing that he would first have to discuss the situation with the Prague government. His predecessor, Josef Tiso—a Roman Catholic priest who was a Friar Tuck in the flesh—had been placed in a monastery under house arrest, but he now dramatically re-entered the scene. The corpulent Monsignor Tiso ("When I get worked up I eat half a pound of ham, and that soothes my nerves") escaped from his prison and demanded that a meeting of the new Slovak cabinet be held early Sunday morning, March 12.

At this secret convocation Tiso revealed that he had received an "invitation" to see Hitler in Berlin. He had accepted, he said, under threat of occupation by German and Hungarian troops. At exactly 7:40 P.M., March 13, Tiso was ushered into Hitler's office by Ribbentrop. The Führer, looking stern and implacable, was flanked by his two top military men, Brauchitsch and Keitel; orders had already been issued to the army and air force to stand by for a possible invasion of Czechoslovakia at six o'clock on the morning of the fifteenth.

"Czechoslovakia," said Hitler accusingly, "owes it only to Germany that she has not been mutilated further." Nor did the Czechs appreciate the great self-control exhibited by the Germans. He raised his voice, either in anger or a show of it, and asked what kind of a game they were playing. He assumed the Slovaks wanted independence and that was why he had prevented Hungary from seizing their territory. He wanted one question cleared up *"in a very short time."* He accented each of these words, then put the question directly to Tiso: did Slovakia want to lead an independent existence or not? "Tomorrow at midday," he said, "I shall begin military action against the Czechs, which will be carried out by General von Brauchitsch." He pointed to his commander-in-chief. "Germany does not intend to take Slovakia into her Lebensraum, and that is why you must either immediately proclaim the independence of Slovakia or I will disinterest myself in her fate. To make your choice I give you until tomorrow midday, when the Czechs will be crushed by the German steamroller."

Tiso hesitated briefly, then telephoned the Slovak cabinet in Bratislava and said in German that he was speaking from the Führer's office. He requested them to convene the Slovak parliament for the following morning. Once he was sure his stupefied listeners understood the message, Tiso rang off. He arrived in Bratislava in time to read to the assembled deputies a Slovak declaration of independence drafted by Ribbentrop. Opposition to the proclamation collapsed and a new Slovakia, independent in name only, was born.

That afternoon in London, Chamberlain stoutly parried angry questions in the House of Commons over the government's failure to stand up to Hitler. What about Britain's guarantee to Czechoslovakia? asked one critic. That guarantee, he retorted, referred only to unprovoked attack. "No such aggression," he said, "has taken place."

While Chamberlain was making excuses in Parliament, Hitler acted and, as usual, made it appear as if he were only reacting. His tool in the final step of the drama was President Hacha of Czechoslovakia. Harried and confused by the events of the past few days, Hacha now urgently requested an interview with the Führer—a case of the fly seeking an invitation to the spider's net.

After keeping Hacha in suspense for hours, Hitler finally agreed to see him. Already psychologically crushed, the President of Czechoslovakia, accompanied by his daughter and his Foreign Minister, boarded a train for Berlin. He could not fly because of a weak heart.

As he was leaving Prague a British newsman who had often seen Hitler at close quarters arrived. Sefton Delmer noticed that the habitués of cafés on Wenceslas Square were stolidly sipping their coffee unaware of what was going on. Suddenly, at dusk, troops of white-stockinged Sudeten Germans, six abreast, marched through the square, carrying Nazi banners and shouting: "Sieg Heil! Sieg Heil!" They were followed by Fascist collaborators waving the Czech tricolor. At first the crowds obeyed the demands to salute the Nazi banners. But once the factories closed and the workers flooded into the square there was a different spirit. They refused to make way for the marchers and fighting erupted. The police supported the demonstrators, who continued to march about shouting: "Ein Reich, ein Volk, ein Führer!" If Prague was symbolically German, the important Czech industrial town of Moravska Ostrava on the Polish border was already that in fact. Elite troops of Hitler's own bodyguard division occupied this area soon after dark to safeguard its modern steel mill from Polish seizure.

In Berlin Hitler and his guests were assembling in the drawing room of the chancellery to see a movie, *A Hopeless Case*. Next to the Führer sat General Keitel, on hand to issue, if necessary, executive orders to begin the invasion. At 10:40 P.M. the train from Prague pulled into Anhalt Station but it was not until an hour after midnight that Hacha was summoned by the Führer. He had waited that long, so he told Keitel, to give the old gentleman a chance to rest and recover from the tiring trip but the delay only increased Hacha's anxiety and by the time he and Foreign Minister Chvalkovsky passed by an SS guard of honor and entered Hitler's study his face was "flushed with agitation."

Hacha made a personal appeal by assuring the Führer that he had never mixed in politics. In a sad exhibition of abasement, he threw himself on Hitler's mercy. "He was convinced that the destiny of Czechoslovakia lay in the Führer's hands," read the official German minutes of the meeting, "and he believed it was in safekeeping in such hands."

Even this servility could not stem the vitriol stored up in Hitler. After repeating the alleged wrongs perpetrated by Masaryk and Beneš, he charged that "under the surface the Beneš spirit lived in the new Czechoslovakia." Frail little Hacha was a pitiable figure as he cringed under this attack. Abruptly Hitler—either from compassion or a need to change tactics—hastened to add that he did not mean to imply any distrust of Hacha, and he had "come to the conclusion that this journey by the President, despite his advanced years, might be of great benefit to this country because it was only a matter of hours now before Germany intervened."

Both Hacha and his Foreign Minister sat as if turned to stone until Hitler again gave them a glimmer of hope by insisting that he harbored no enmity against any nation and remained convinced of Hacha's loyalty. But this was extinguished by a declaration that the Beneš tendencies still flourished. The die had been cast on Sunday, said Hitler. The order for the invasion by the German troops and for the incorporation of Czechoslovakia into the German Reich had already been given.

The two Czechs sat stupefied. Hitler announced that his army would enter their country from all sides at 6 A.M. while the Luftwaffe occupied all Czech airfields.

Threat was again followed by promise. Hacha could serve Czechoslovakia by a simple decision. He would have to act quickly—or at six o'clock German troops and planes would go into action. "I would have irremediably lost face if I'd had to put this threat into execution," Hitler recalled several years later, "for at the hour mentioned fog was so thick over our airfields that none of our aircraft could have made its sortie."

He suggested that Hacha and his Foreign Minister withdraw to discuss privately what should be done, but to Hitler's relief Hacha said, "The position is quite clear." He admitted that resistance would be folly yet how could he possibly restrain the nation in less than four hours? Hitler replied that it had to be done somehow, then added hopefully that he saw dawning "the possibility of a long period of peace between the two peoples." If the decision was to resist, he concluded sharply, he saw "the annihilation of Czechoslovakia."

With these ominous words, Hitler ended the interview. As the two dejected Czechs were escorted to an adjoining room, Ribbentrop attempted to place a telephone call to Prague. The line was out of order and Schmidt was asked to try again. As the interpreter was dialing he heard Göring exclaim from the adjoining room that Hacha had fainted. A call went out for Dr. Morell, who had been kept on duty in case the ailing Czech President needed him. If anything happens to Hacha, thought Schmidt, the whole world will say tomorrow that he was murdered in the chancellery. Just then the line to Prague was opened. Schmidt went for

Hacha and to his surprise found him recovered, thanks to Dr. Morell's vitamin injection. Hacha came to the phone and, after informing his cabinet what had happened, advised capitulation.

In the meantime Schmidt was making a fair copy of a brief official communiqué which had been composed beforehand. It stated that the President of Czechoslovakia confidently laid the fate of the Czech people and country in the hands of the Führer of the German Reich. It was, in reality, a document of surrender, and Hacha asked for another of Morell's injections. This revived him so much that he refused to sign it despite urgings of Ribbentrop and Göring. These two, according to the official French report, then proceeded to hound the two Czechs pitilessly. "They literally hunted Dr. Hacha and Mr. Chvalkovsky round the table on which the documents were lying, thrusting them continually before them, pushing pens into their hands, incessantly repeating that if they continued in their refusal, half of Prague would lie in ruins from bombing within two hours, and this would only be the beginning. Hundreds of bombers were waiting the order to take off, and they would receive that order at six in the morning if the signatures were not forthcoming."*

At last Hacha gave in and, face still flushed, signed the document at 3:55 A.M. with trembling hand. He turned to Dr. Morell and thanked him for his ministrations. The moment the pen dropped from Hacha's nerveless fingers the Führer rushed from the conference room to his office where his two middle-aged secretaries were waiting. His face was transfigured, recalled Christa Schröder, as he exclaimed, "Children, quickly, give me a kiss! Quickly!" Schröder and Wolf bussed him on both cheeks. "Hacha has just signed," he said in exultation. "It is the greatest triumph of my life! I shall go down in history as the great German!"

Late as it was, Hitler stayed up to savor the triumph. "I was sorry for the old gentleman," he confided to Hoffmann, and other intimates. "But sentimentality, in the circumstances, would have been out of place and might well have jeopardized success."

Dr. Morell interrupted to remark that but for him the communiqué might not have been signed. "Thank God," he said, "that I was on the spot and in time with my injections!"

"You go to hell with your damn injections!" exclaimed Hitler. "You made the old gentleman so lively that for a moment I feared he would refuse to sign!" The celebration was briefly interrupted by Keitel, who reported that executive orders for the invasion of Czechoslovakia had been issued with the proviso not to open fire unless there were signs of resistance, and even then there would be attempts to negotiate before resorting

* Göring admitted at Nuremberg that he had told Hacha, "I should be sorry if I had to bomb beautiful Prague." But he hadn't intended doing it since "resistance could always be broken more easily without such bombing. But a point like that might, I thought, serve as an argument and accelerate the whole matter."

to force of arms. He asked Hitler's permission to retire and was instructed to report back in a few hours so he could accompany the Führer to the special train which would take them to the Czech border.

5

At dawn on March 15 two disheveled men, "ashy-pale with fear," appeared at the American Legation in Prague to ask for asylum. They revealed they had been Czech spies in Germany and were known to the local Gestapo. "Their faces were twitching and their lips trembling when I sent them away," recalled George Kennan. A little later he had to follow instructions and turn two German fugitives from Hitler into the snow-swept street "where they were no more than hunted animals." Next came a Jewish acquaintance who had to be told he could stay only until he could calm his nerves. "He paced wretchedly up and down in the ante-room, through the long morning hours."

In London, Lord Halifax first learned of the invasion from his ambassador in Prague. Several hours later Henderson phoned from Berlin advising his chief to postpone the visit of the president of the Board of Trade to Germany. "It does not appear to me possible to prevent Germany from 'restoring order' but I would nevertheless deprecate visits at this juncture of any British Cabinet Minister."

Within the hour Henderson was on the phone again reading off the agreement signed by Hitler and Hacha, and at 11 A.M. he was dictating the text of a Hitler proclamation just issued to the German people: since Sunday, it read, "wild excesses" against Germans had taken place in many Czech villages, and from hour to hour the appeals from victims and persecuted had increased.

The shell-shocked Henderson at least realized that it was "the final shipwreck" of his mission to Berlin. "Do you wonder that I regard Berlin as a soul-scarifying job?" he hurriedly scrawled to Halifax in an informal letter. "Hitler has gone straight off the deep end again."

Hitler slept during most of the train trip from Berlin, not wakening until about noon on that memorable Ides of March. "I must be the first in Prague," he told his valet as he dressed. The closer they came to the frontier the more excited he became. At midafternoon his party disembarked near the frontier and transferred to a ten-vehicle motor convoy. Hitler sat in the first car next to the driver, Kempka, as the column set off slowly in the blinding snowstorm. They passed through the open barriers of both customs stations and before long came upon German marching columns struggling in the drifts and ice. Kempka turned off the main road onto winding lanes and muddy byroads and it was dusk before they reached Prague. No one took notice of the convoy as it approached Hradschin Palace. The party was billeted in the castle and someone was sent into town to get cold Prague ham, rolls, butter, cheese, fruit and Pilsner beer. It was the first time Keitel ever saw Hitler drink beer.

The reaction to Germany's latest aggression was immediate and vehement. In response to public indignation, both the French and British governments gave military guarantees to Poland, Romania, Greece and Turkey and at the same time inaugurated political and military talks with the Soviets. Outrage extended to Hitler's own ally and that evening Ciano caustically wrote in his diary that the invasion of Czechoslovakia had destroyed the state established at Munich.

The Führer had already sent Prince Philip von Hesse to Rome with a letter of explanation. He hoped that Mussolini would understand and look at the latest move in the right light. Although Il Duce grumbled to Ciano, "The Italians will laugh at me; every time Hitler takes another state, he sends me a message," he decided that now, more than ever, it was essential to ally himself with a winner. "We cannot change our policy now," he said, "after all, we are not political whores." At the same time submission to his junior partner was humiliating; never before had Ciano seen his father-in-law in such distress.

Hitler was oblivious to criticism from home or abroad and his complacency seemed justified on March 16. As he surveyed his latest conquest from the walls of the castle of the Kings of Bohemia, the swastika flying from its battlements, he savored the pleasure of possessing an ancient city with so many historical memories to Teutons. In front of the City Hall twenty-seven leaders of the Protestant uprising against the Habsburgs had been beheaded in 1621; and in the Republikplatz Kaiser Wilhelm, Bismarck and Moltke had resided during the Prussian-Austrian War at the famous Hotel Zum blauen Stern. The magnificent structures of Prague, a number designed by German architects, owed much in his opinion to Teutonic culture. Only Germans built such bridges, towers and buildings!

An aide interrupted Hitler's revery to inform him that neither France nor Britain had mobilized. "I knew it," he said and made a prediction: "In fourteen days no one will talk about it any more." Of more interest to him was the report that pro-Nazi Czechs were already coursing through Prague's streets marking Jewish shops in large colored letters: "JID" or "JUDE."

The factual dissolution of Czechoslovakia came later in the day when Monsignor Tiso sent a telegram to Berlin asserting Slovak independence and requesting German protection. Without delay Hitler's troops moved into Slovakia. The provinces of Ruthenia also asked to be absorbed into his orbit, but Hitler was more interested in appeasing the Hungarians, whose troops he allowed to swarm over the border and seize Ruthenian territory all the way to the Polish frontier. After a mere twenty years of independence all of Czechoslovakia was again in bondage.

Although they had stopped short of mobilization, the British were infuriated. "I can well understand Herr Hitler's taste for bloodless victories," Halifax warned the German ambassador, "but one of these days he will find himself up against something that will not be bloodless."

For some time he as well as the outspoken Cadogan had objected to aspects of Chamberlain's appeasement policy yet had supported him out of loyalty. But the moment had come to take a stand. The Foreign Secretary went to Chamberlain and made it clear that the nation, the party and the House of Commons demanded that Hitler's aggressions be condemned publicly and positively.

Chamberlain heeded this advice. On the eighteenth Ambassador Henderson was temporarily recalled from Berlin and that night, the eve of his seventieth birthday, the Prime Minister made a speech at Birmingham which changed the course of British foreign policy. He warned that it would be a great mistake to suppose that Great Britain, despite its detestation of war, "has so lost its fibre that it will not take part to the uttermost of its power in resisting such a challenge if it were made." It was hardly an inspiring call to arms but, coming from this symbol of conciliation, it aroused the audience to enthusiasm, for it did mean the virtual end of appeasement.

It also revealed that Hitler had made his first serious miscalculation. Czechoslovakia was his by threat of force but in time it would inevitably have fallen peaceably into his orbit; and by breaking an international agreement, freely entered into by his own government, he had completely reversed official and public opinion in both France and England. No longer would Chamberlain and his followers take Hitler at his word. He had broken the rules of the game—and not for a good enough cause.

How, then, had the Führer come to make such an obvious blunder? First, he had not expected his move to provoke such a violent reaction. Hadn't the West accepted the same excuses for restoring law and order in Austria? Hadn't they been satisfied with just as specious arguments at Munich? He had been convinced he must seize the territory Germany needed to guarantee the future of the Teutonic race while he still had his physical vigor and Germany's military strength was still superior to that of its enemies.

When he marched into Czechoslovakia he was not certain where he would strike next or against whom, only that he must have Bohemia and Moravia before launching (or threatening to launch) any further military action. And so in Hitler's eyes he had committed no blunder, only sustained a public relations setback. What concerned him was the next step.

Chapter Nineteen

THE FOX AND THE BEAR
JANUARY–AUGUST 24, 1939

1

On the day Hitler announced the protectorate of Bohemia and Moravia from Hradschin Castle, the British Foreign Office was warned by the Romanian ambassador that secret sources indicated Hitler would take over Romania and Hungary within the next few months. Those hastily reconstructing foreign policy in London were led further astray by an alarming note from their own ambassador in Paris. It was filled with errors since Sir Eric Phipps typed it himself for the sake of secrecy. "Hitler's personal wish," he wrote, "backed by Goering, Himmler, Ribbentrop, Goebbels and Reichenau, is to make war on Great Britain before June or July." The information had probably been planted by the German anti-Hitler faction in their continuing effort to start a shooting conflict. The Führer, in fact, had no desire to fight England, and the proposed domination of both Romania and Hungary was still only in the economic sphere. His sights were set on a solution of Germany's festering differences with Poland, which had been created after the World War by the Allies primarily to contain German aggression. Not only had the Reich lost most of the provinces of West Prussia and Posen but a corridor was cut to the Baltic along the Vistula River to give landlocked Poland an outlet to the sea. Danzig, at the end of this corridor, was made a free city so it could serve Poland as a seaport. Nothing aroused patriotic Germans more than this so-called Polish Corridor which isolated their province of East Prussia from the rest of the Fatherland. And the focal point of resentment lay in Danzig, which was populated almost exclusively by Germans.

Surprisingly, the most nationalistic of Germans devoted little space to the Polish question in *Mein Kampf* and his early speeches. It was not that Hitler entertained friendly feelings for the Poles—a non-Aryan inferior people according to his standards—but that he was obsessed by the Soviet Union, the only country large enough to meet Germany's needs for living space. From the beginning of his regime Hitler had minimized the Polish question and in 1934 signed a ten-year non-aggression pact with Warsaw. Publicly he made a show of German-Polish friendship and at Munich, it will be remembered, graciously invited the Poles to join in the dismemberment of Czechoslovakia. This they did with relish, not realizing that the guests at such banquets usually pay the bill in the end. It was presented a month after Munich when Ambassador Josef Lipski was invited to have lunch with Ribbentrop at the Grand Hotel in Berchtesgaden. At last the time had come, said Ribbentrop, to settle their differences. He proposed—and his manner was friendly—that Poland return Danzig and allow Germany to construct its own corridor linking East Prussia with the rest of the Reich. In return Germany would let Poland use Danzig as a free port, guarantee her existing borders and extend their pact. Ribbentrop further suggested that the two countries co-operate on the emigration of Jews from Poland and establish "a joint policy towards Russia on the basis of the Anti-Comintern Pact."

Since many influential Poles shared Hitler's fear of Red Russia and hatred of Jews, the prospects of a peaceful settlement seemed hopeful. But the Polish Foreign Minister, Colonel Josef Beck, kept avoiding Hitler's invitations to Germany while doing his best to strengthen links with Russia. Late in 1938 a joint statement of Russo-Polish friendship was issued and trade talks were initiated.

This double game could not be played indefinitely with a man such as Hitler and at last Beck was forced to accept his hospitality. Early in January 1939 he came to the Berghof. If he feared being browbeaten like Schuschnigg, Tiso and Hacha, he was pleasantly surprised. There were no threats, only inducements as Hitler hinted of possible liquidation of Czechoslovakia with further benefits to Poland. This approach failed. As diplomatically as possible Beck refused even to consider the return of Danzig.

Several weeks later Ribbentrop journeyed to Warsaw so he could repeat the German offer. He was treated to a round of dancing, theater and hunting along with an endless supply of caviar and green vodka but at the conference table he got nothing but more Polish charm. It was rumored at the Wilhelmstrasse that Hitler, offended at Beck's continued refusal to accept what he considered a most generous offer, shouted that the only way to deal with the Poles was by threat. This tactic, used so successfully against Austria and Czechoslovakia, was implemented that March. Ribbentrop warned Warsaw that Polish outrages against the German minority were becoming intolerable. This pronouncement was followed by a press campaign with Göring's newspaper, *Die Zeitung*, charging that German women and children were being molested in Polish streets while German houses and shops were smeared with tar. Far from intimidated, Beck summoned the German ambassador on Tuesday and made his own threat: any attempt to change the status quo of Danzig would be regarded as an act of aggression against Poland.

"You want to negotiate at the point of a bayonet!" exclaimed the German ambassador.

"That is your own method," said Beck.

This and other indications of Polish pluck were rewarded by a startling offer of military assistance from London in case of Nazi aggression. Beck accepted "without hesitation" and on the last day of March Chamberlain, "looking gaunt and ill," walked into the House of Commons and dropped wearily into his chair. A few minutes later he rose and began reading a statement slowly and quietly, head lowered as if he could barely make out the words. "In the event of any action, which clearly threatens Polish independence," he said, "and which the Polish Government accordingly considers it vital to resist with their national forces, His Majesty's Government would feel themselves bound at once to lend the Polish Government all support in their power." The Poles, he added, had been assured to this effect, and the French had authorized him to announce that they joined Britain in these assurances. As he sat down there was spontaneous cheering, the first genuine display of approval since his return from Munich. The unconditional offer was the first material proof that Chamberlain had indeed abandoned appeasement. At last England was united and committed.

The following day, April 1, the Führer responded to this unanimity with a satirical speech. What right, he asked, had the English to interfere with Germany's right to live? "If today a British statesman demands that every problem in the realm of vital German rights must first be discussed in England, then I could demand just as well that every British problem must first be discussed with us. Certainly, this Englishman might give me the answer that Palestine is no affair of the Germans. We do not want to have anything to do with Palestine. However, just as we Germans have no business in Palestine, so England has no business in Germany's living space." And if England maintained that the Germans had no right to do this or that, what right had the English to shoot down Arabs in Palestine who were only standing up for their homeland?

He turned from sarcasm to threat. "The German Reich," he said, "is in no sense prepared to tolerate intimidation permanently, or even a policy of encirclement." This was relatively mild and it must have taken will power to control his feelings so well. Privately he seethed, and, upon receiving confirmation of the British guarantee to the Poles that afternoon from Admiral Canaris, he flared up. Features distorted by rage, he stormed about the room, hammering his fists on the marble table and spewing curses. "I'll cook them a stew they'll choke on!" Could he have been thinking of a pact with Stalin?

Perhaps Hitler's remarkable poise during the speech that evening came from the conviction that he was speaking from strength. Madrid had fallen to Franco, and the Civil War in Spain had just officially ended. In addition, England's attention was being diverted that very day by "fresh rumors of Italian pressure" on Albania, a diversion that fitted neatly into Hitler's plan. He summoned Keitel and told him the Polish problem imperatively demanded a solution. What a tragedy it was, he said, that sly old Marshal Pilsudski, with whom he had signed the non-aggression pact, had died so prematurely. But the same might happen to himself at any time. "That was why he would have to try as soon as possible to resolve this intolerable position for Germany's future whereby East Prussia was geographically cut off from the rest of the Reich; he could not postpone this job until later, or bequeath it to his successor." He was sure, he added, that Britain would turn her back on Poland once she saw Germany's determination.

And so, as a result of his failure to realize that Britain had jettisoned appeasement in fact as well as in words, Hitler issued a war directive on April 3 marked "Most Secret" and delivered by hand to senior commanders only. "Since the situation on Germany's eastern frontier has become intolerable, and all political possibilities of peaceful settlement have been exhausted," it began, "I have decided upon a solution by force." The attack on Poland, Operation White, would begin on the first of September.

The responsibility for opening hostilities on the western front would be left to England and France. If these nations attacked Germany in retaliation, the Wehrmacht was to conserve its strength in this quarter as much as possible. "The right to order offensive operations is reserved absolutely in me." So was decision regarding any air attack on London.

This indicated that he did not take seriously the Anglo-French pledge to support Poland. The Allies might, at worst, declare war but it would only be to save face and if the Germans restrained themselves from responding offensively a deal could be worked out. On such miscalculations are the fates of nations decided. This directive was countersigned by Keitel who, together with all the commanders he consulted, opposed any conflict with Poland. All agreed that Germany was not yet ready for war.

Hitler's charge that political possibilities of a peaceful settlement with Poland had been exhausted was not without foundation. Not only was Colonel Beck avoiding discussions with Hitler but he had just arrived in Dover to consummate the pact with the British. He was welcomed warmly by officials and public alike. Beck enjoyed the lavish entertainment, particularly an intimate lunch with the King and Queen, but being aloof, secretive and suspicious, he embarked on the formal talks in a less receptive mood. He objected strenuously when Chamberlain, having swallowed his own suspicions of Russia, suggested that they both join the Soviets in an anti-Hitler front. Fearing a Russian attack far more than one from the Nazis, Beck refused to do anything to precipitate a war with Hitler. On this point he would not budge and the temporary mutual assistance pact with the British which he signed April 6 excluded any Soviet participation.

Most nations operate their foreign policy on the pragmatic proposition that at least two irons in the fire are better than one. The Soviet Union, no exception, was negotiating simultaneously with England and Germany. This urgent need for allies stemmed in part from the dangerous weakening of the Red Army brought about two years earlier by Stalin's bloody purge (inspired, incidentally, by Hitler's elimination of the Röhm circle) of Marshal Tukhachevsky and other top military leaders.* Although it was not generally known, Germany had been secretly strengthening the Red Army for almost two decades. Both Germany and the Soviet Union had been excluded from the negotiations leading to the Versailles Treaty and, since outcast nations are often drawn together by shared grievances, they covertly began an extensive military collaboration. Its chief architect was the commander of the tiny postwar German army, General Hans von Seeckt. Late in 1920 he created an administrative organization within the Defense Ministry with offices in Berlin and Moscow. Before long the Junkers Corporation was granted concessions for the manufacture of airplane motors in a suburb of Moscow while Bersol, a joint stock company, began manufacturing poison gases in Samara Province. More significantly, German technical experts were helping the Russians establish three ammunition plants while a staff of sixty German military and civilian instructors trained a squadron of the Red Air Force composed solely of Germans. Similarly, German tank officers were being trained by German experts at a so-called "heavy vehicle experimental and test station" near Kazan.

This mutually profitable secret arrangement developed, it will be

---

* Afterward Heydrich boasted that this emasculation of the Red Army was his work. Upon receiving information that the Tukhachevsky clique was plotting to eliminate Stalin, Heydrich fed it back to Stalin, through President Beneš, along with forged supportive papers. Before long a Soviet representative was in Berlin negotiating with Heydrich for the incriminating papers. He was paid three million rubles in bills that must have been marked; whenever a German agent tried to spend one in Russia he was arrested. Marked money was not the only piece of Russian trickery. It was Stalin himself who had leaked the original material to the unsuspecting Heydrich; Tukhachevsky had become too powerful and was a threat to Stalin's dictatorship.

recalled, into a political rapprochement which was formalized on Easter Sunday, 1922, by the Treaty of Rapallo. It was an effective alliance against the Versailles powers, giving assurance to the Soviets that Germany would not join in any international consortium to exploit their economy while freeing the Germans from threat of complete encirclement. But the rise of Hitler marked a turning point in Soviet-German relations which, by 1938, were practically at an end. The tide again changed dramatically when the Munich Pact was signed by France and England without consulting the Soviets.

Ignored by the West, the Soviet Union once more looked to Germany. Early in 1939 it accepted a Hitler overture to discuss a new trade treaty by inviting one of Ribbentrop's aides to Moscow; and a few days later Stalin gave credence to a sensational story in the London *News Chronicle* that he was signing a non-aggression pact with the Nazis. In a speech to the eighteenth congress of the Communist Party he declared that the Soviet Union was not going to be drawn by the West into any war with Germany. "We are in favor of peace and consolidation of our business relations with all countries." German newspapers seized upon the *all* as a further overture to the Reich, and Soviet newspapers responded by congratulating them for their discernment.

Within a month Peter Kleist, Ribbentrop's expert for Poland and the Baltic states, was instructed to improve his personal relations with the people at the Soviet Embassy in Berlin. Kleist wondered if this was a prelude to another dramatic change in foreign policy and it was with mixed feelings, a few days later, that he accompanied a German specialist in East European economic affairs to the Soviet Embassy in its stately quarters on Unter den Linden. They had been invited to tea by Georgi Astakhov, the mild, ascetic-looking Soviet chargé d'affaires. It was obviously an unusual occasion; no other Russian was present. After chatting about French Impressionism, Astakhov suggested they get down to business. It was absurd, he said, for Germany and the Soviet Union to fight each other over ideological subtleties. Why not establish a common policy? Kleist remarked that ideological subtleties had become important realities but Astakhov waved this aside with a movement of his hand. Stalin and Hitler, he said, were men who created those realities and never let themselves be dominated by them.

Kleist left the embassy in a thoughtful mood. Obviously Astakhov was passing along a signal from the Kremlin to Ribbentrop. But to Kleist's surprise Ribbentrop, who had ordered him to make the initial overture, now told him to avoid further contact with Astakhov. "I do not think the Führer would wish that conversation to be continued."

Stalin took the next step. On April 17 Soviet Ambassador Alexei Merekalov called on Ribbentrop's chief subordinate, Baron von Weizsäcker. It was the Russian's first visit in ten months and the excuse for coming was a matter ordinarily handled at a lower echelon. Toward the end of their conversation Merekalov asked what Weizsäcker thought of Russian-German relations. His reply was: Germany always desired mutually satisfactory commercial relations with Russia. Ambassador Merekalov's answer was an unmistakable signal for rapprochement: there existed for Russia no reason why she should not live with Germany on a normal footing. "And from normal, the relations might become better and better."

In the meantime the Soviets continued to woo the other side. But Chamberlain did not want to be rushed into closer diplomatic relations with Russia. He could not believe that she had the same aims and objects as Britain had, let alone any sympathy with democracy. The Prime Minister was convinced that a Russian alliance would divide Balkan resistance to Germany. And so, while playing "hard to get" with the Soviets, he buttressed the guarantee of assistance to Poland by offering another to Romania.

On April 19 Romania's Foreign Minister, Grégoire Gafencu, called at the Reich chancellery and received a firsthand impression of Hitler's reaction to this proposed guarantee. At first mention of England, he sprang from his chair and paced the room. Why, he shouted, couldn't the English see that he only wished to reach an agreement with them? If England wanted war she could have it! "And it will be a war of unimaginable destructiveness," he warned. "How can the English picture a modern war when they can't even put two fully equipped divisions in the field?"

The next day, April 20, was Hitler's fiftieth birthday and perhaps his recent show of anger was an indication of impatience. Time was fleeting and he believed he had only a few more years of good health to accomplish his mission. The 1939 birthday was celebrated as usual by a major military parade. This magnificent spectacle—with all three branches of the Wehrmacht as well as the *Waffen* (armed) SS represented—was designed as a warning to enemies. At Hitler's express request the latest medium artillery, heavy tank guns, anti-aircraft guns and air force searchlight units were displayed. Overhead roared a menacing cloud of fighter and bomber squadrons. The attending foreign diplomats were suitably impressed by this greatest military display in German history, nor did they miss the significance of the guest of honor at Hitler's side, President Hacha of Czechoslovakia.

Although numerous Germans were appalled by the demonstration, the majority felt a surge of pride to see such armed might. The fiftieth birthday was also an excuse to subject the public to another flood of propaganda in praise of Hitler.

For a multitude of worshipers he was Germany's savior: "The Führer is the only man in our century who has possessed the strength to take into his hand the thunderbolt of God and fashion it anew for mankind." For others he was more than Messiah—God himself: "My children look upon the Führer as He who gives orders for everything, arranges everything. To them the Führer is the Creator of the world."

School children were taught to give homage in song:

> *Adolf Hitler is our savior, our hero,*
> *He is the noblest being in the whole wide world.*
> *For Hitler we live,*
> *For Hitler we die.*
> *Our Hitler is our Lord,*
> *Who rules a brave new world.*

Hitler himself even forbade the use of the term Third Reich and complained to his inner circle of the growth of this cult worship, which in some instances went to ludicrous lengths. During a recent study course arranged by the party, a lady lecturer had told in all seriousness of her experience with a talking dog. When asked "Who is Adolf Hitler?" the dog replied, "Mein Führer." The lecturer was interrupted by an indignant Nazi who shouted that it was abominable taste to relate such a ridiculous story. The lecturer, on the verge of tears, replied, "This clever animal knows that Adolf Hitler has caused laws to be passed against vivisection and the Jews' ritual slaughter of animals, and out of gratitude this small canine brain recognized Adolf Hitler as his Führer."

If the Church looked upon Hitler as neither the Messiah nor God, it nevertheless honored him on his fiftieth anniversary. Special votive masses were celebrated in every German church "to implore God's blessing upon Führer and people," and the Bishop of Mainz called upon Catholics in his diocese to pray specifically for "the Führer and Chancellor, the inspirer, enlarger and protector of the Reich." The Pope did not fail to send his congratulations.

These honors did nothing to temper the anger Hitler had revealed to the Romanian ambassador nor was his resentment solely directed at England. Hitler was outraged by the recent appearance in the United States of an unauthorized condensed version of *Mein Kampf* which included passages omitted from the authorized American edition as well as editorial comments by Alan Cranston calling attention to Hitler's distortions. Printed in tabloid form and priced at ten cents, half a million copies were sold in ten days. On the cover was printed: "Not one cent of royalty to Adolf Hitler."* This affront was followed by another from President

---

* The Führer's agents promptly sued on the grounds that his copyright had been violated. The court decided in favor of Hitler, ordering the publishers to cease and desist from printing and distributing any more copies of the Cranston version. "It was a beautiful example of democracy in action," said Cranston, now United States senator from California, in 1974. He admitted that legally Hitler was right and he was wrong. "But those 500,000 copies we sold helped awaken a great many Americans to how wrong Hitler was in those monstrous policies of his that were soon to plunge us into World War."

Roosevelt in the form of a joint message to Hitler and Mussolini (who had just invaded Albania) appealing for assurances against further aggressions. "You have repeatedly asserted that you and the German people have no desire for war," Roosevelt told Hitler. "If this is true there need be no war."

Ruffled, Hitler delivered his answer on April 28. Never before had a speech such a large audience, for it was broadcast not only throughout Germany and parts of Europe but carried by the major networks in the United States, an incredible contrast to the days in Vienna when Hitler would lecture to whoever would listen—if only the trees. Then his auditors often ignored or ridiculed him. Now the world trembled.

The immense audience inspired him. William Shirer, for one, never had heard the Führer speak so eloquently. He opened with a brilliant defense of his foreign policy that turned into a denunciation of Britain's new foreign policy which, he charged, thereby removed the basis for their naval treaty of 1935. This unexpected abrogation of a treaty he himself had so eagerly sought was followed by an equally devastating attack on Poland and cancellation of the Polish-German non-aggression pact since it had been "unilaterally infringed" by the Poles. Having torn up two treaties, Hitler proceeded to welcome new negotiations so long as they were on equal terms. "No one," he said, "would be happier than I at the prospect."

It was a remarkable display of mental gymnastics soon surpassed by an assault on Roosevelt which—for the German audience, at least—was a masterpiece of irony and sarcasm. This was the Hitler of the early years, the beer-hall entertainer and debater. He took up the President's message point by point, demolishing each one like a schoolmaster. His heavy sarcasm fell upon delighted ears in the Reichstag and with each riposte the laughter and applause grew louder. The presiding officer, Göring, led the uproar, his sides shaking.* When the Führer at last came to the President's request for assurance that Germany would launch no more aggression, his answer was a sardonic counterattack that brought still heartier laughs—yet failed to respond to the question: Was he going to invade Poland?

The speech was designed more to satisfy Hitler's people than to persuade his enemies. What he needed was time to bring the Polish question to a favorable conclusion and, feeling that his address had accomplished its purpose, he went into virtual seclusion at his semi-official vacation residence, the Berghof. He refused to make a single attempt to approach Poland during the ensuing hot summer but to Russia he was readily available. The tentative offer of friendship so slyly advanced to Kleist over teacups was developing into true romance. Shortly after the explosive Reichstag

* When Göring was shown a movie of this speech at the Nuremberg Trials he again laughed uncontrollably.

speech a seemingly innocuous item appeared on a back page of Soviet newspapers: Maxim Litvinov had been succeeded by V. M. Molotov. It was sensational news and nowhere was it more appreciated than in the German Embassy. That evening the German chargé telegraphed the Wilhelmstrasse that the Foreign Commissariat was giving no explanations but the dismissal appeared to be the result of differences of opinion between Stalin and Litvinov, whose wife, Ivy, was English. He himself symbolized collective security against the Axis, and his exit meant that Stalin was abandoning this line. The replacement of the Jewish Litvinov by a gentile further indicated that Stalin, already distrustful of Britain's tentative overtures, was opening the door wider to his fellow anti-Semite in Berlin. The embarrassing fact that Molotov had a Jewish wife was kept from Hitler, not only by the Russians but by his own diplomats.

The news of Litvinov's replacement by Molotov struck the Führer "like a cannon ball." Beyond their common violent hatred and fear of Jews, he had long grudgingly admired Stalin's ruthless methods. Even so Hitler was not yet convinced that collaboration with the Soviets was wise. On May 10 he summoned an expert on Russian affairs to Berchtesgaden to determine whether Stalin was prepared for a genuine understanding with Germany. Gustav Hilger, economic attaché at the German Embassy in Moscow, with two decades' experience in Russia, was somewhat taken aback by such a query. He was "tempted to give Hitler a résumé of German-Soviet relations since 1933, and to remind him how often the Soviet government, during the first years of his rule, had expressed the desire of maintaining the old friendly relationship" but restrained himself, merely reminding Hitler of Stalin's declaration to the party congress exactly two months ago that there was no reason for war with Germany. To Hilger's surprise neither Hitler nor Ribbentrop could remember the substance of Stalin's remarks.

Hitler listened to Hilger's lengthy thesis that the Soviet Union was no military threat since she needed peace to build up her economy, but remarked as soon as Hilger left that he was "a bit of a Russian himself now" and might have succumbed to Soviet propaganda. "But if he is right then I must not fall in with Stalin's peace overtures. I must interrupt the internal consolidation of that giant as quickly as possible." He ordered Ribbentrop to mark time with the Soviets.

On his part, Stalin ordered Astakhov to resume trade talks with the Germans. On May 20 Molotov inserted himself into the negotiations by inviting Ambassador von der Schulenburg to the Kremlin. The usually dour Molotov was a genial host but beneath the veneer of amiability lay a flintlike obduracy and once serious discussion got under way he complained that Hitler's apparent reluctance to conclude a new economic agreement gave the Soviets the impression that the Germans were not in earnest and were only playing at negotiating for political reasons.

For the present, at least, the Führer was more concerned with strengthening his ties with Mussolini. Upset as he was by Il Duce's surprise invasion of Albania (Hitler had wanted a diversion, not the real thing), he had been negotiating ever since then for a more binding Axis treaty. This was signed with considerable ceremony in Berlin on May 22. Dubbed the Pact of Steel, it bound Italy's destiny inextricably to Germany's. To Hitler the agreement was a diplomatic triumph, pledging as it did each party to support the other in case of war "with all its military forces on land, on sea, and in the air." Incredibly Mussolini had been so anxious to please Hitler that he had not had his cabinet or his political and legal experts check the text, which did not even include a clause specifying that it was in effect only in case of attack by an enemy. Il Duce had carelessly placed the fate of Italy in his partner's hands.

It was almost as if Hitler had received a license to risk war and the next day a confident Führer gathered the senior Wehrmacht officers in his study at the chancellery. The solution of Germany's economic problems, he explained, had somehow become inextricably tied to her differences with Poland. "Danzig is not the subject of the dispute at all. It is a question of expanding our Lebensraum in the East and of securing our food supplies, of the settlement of the Baltic problems."

Therefore Poland (which would always side with Germany's enemies despite treaties of friendship) must be destroyed. "We cannot expect a repetition of the Czech affair," he warned. "There will be war. Our task is to isolate Poland." He reserved to himself the right to give the final order to attack since battle with Poland would be successful only if the West stayed on the sidelines. "If this is impossible, then it will be better to attack in the West and settle Poland at the same time."

The contradiction puzzled his listeners and, while most were staggered by Hitler's words, faithful Keitel convinced himself that the Führer was only trying to show his commanders that their misgivings were unfounded and that war would not really break out. This despite Hitler's next words: a bald prediction of a "life and death" war against England and France. "The idea that we can get off cheaply is dangerous; there is no such possibility. We must burn our boats, and it is no longer a question of justice or injustice, but of life or death for eighty million human beings." The basic aim was to force England to her knees. "We shall not be forced into a war," he said, "but we shall not be able to avoid one."

This was not the irrational ranting of a man possessed by the will to conquer but an admission that Germany could not continue as a great nation without war. Only the limitless resources of the East could save the Reich; and the alternative, accommodation with the West, entailed unacceptable risks. If he exposed to the world that he had been bluffing and shirked the test of war, German prestige and power would deflate like a leaky balloon.

With the possible exception of Keitel and Raeder, the other listeners filed out of the winter garden in shock. As for the Führer, he set out for his refuge on the Obersalzberg in high spirits, stopping off at Augsburg to see a local production of *Lohengrin*. Even as he relaxed at the Berghof, Hitler kept exploring the possibilities of a deal in the East. Although he had ordered Schulenburg to "sit tight" he began fretting about the English negotiations in Moscow. What if they concluded a treaty with the Bolsheviks before he did? If so, what would Stalin do if Germany invaded Poland? He had to know and on May 26 Ribbentrop dictated instructions for Schulenburg to inform Molotov that Germany's former policy of hostility to the Comintern was to be abandoned if Hitler could be assured that the Soviets had, in fact, renounced their aggressive struggle against Germany as indicated by Stalin's recent speech. If so, then the time had come "to envisage the tranquilization and normalization of German-Russian foreign political relations."

Hitler was willing to postpone the dream of Lebensraum. He instructed Schulenburg to convince Molotov that the Germans had no intention at all of expanding into the Ukraine. The Russians also should not fear the recent Pact of Steel, which was aimed exclusively at the Anglo-French combination. Schulenburg was further enjoined to assure Molotov that, should Hitler find it necessary to use military force against Poland, the Soviet Union would not suffer. Furthermore, a pact with Germany was far more practical than one with perfidious Albion, which only wanted someone else to do her dirty work—as usual. The offer was tempting, for behind the diplomatic language was an obvious invitation to divide up Poland. And the argument that England and France could not, or would not, come to Poland's aid in time was one to appeal to a pragmatist like Stalin.

This offer was made so spontaneously that the Wilhelmstrasse was thrown into a mild panic. First Ribbentrop hastily informed the Japanese ambassador of Hitler's proposal, then urged him to wire Tokyo for concurrence. While General Oshima's critics at home looked upon him as Hitler's toady, he could, if the occasion demanded, be extremely intransigent. He refused even to send such a telegram, arguing that any Axis accord with the Soviet Union (whose troops and tanks were battling the Japanese on the Manchurian-Outer Mongolian border in a bitter if undeclared war) would destroy all chances of bringing Japan into the three-power pact with Germany and Italy that Hitler desired and the Japanese had kept side-stepping.

Disconcerted, Ribbentrop telephoned Ambassador Attolico for his opinion—not, he said, as ambassador but as expert on Russian affairs. Attolico agreed with Oshima that any Axis approach to the Kremlin would only make it easier for the Russians to "sell more dearly its own goods" in Paris and London. The harried Ribbentrop must have discussed

SENTIMENTAL JOURNEY, JUNE 1940.
HITLER REVISITS HIS BATTLEFIELDS OF 1914–18.

Hitler tells a joke. Extreme right, Below. FRENTZ

"Never again trench warfare," he assures entourage. PUTTKAMER

Bormann, Himmler, Keitel, Hitler and Puttkamer. PUTTKAMER

Fun on the auto tour. Arno Breker, the sculptor, threatened with a dagger by his wife if he ever should be disloyal. Left, Gerda Daranowsky Christian, Hitler's secretary and former employee of Elizabeth Arden. FRENTZ

GERMANY
BETWEEN WARS

NORTH
SEA

GREAT
BRITAIN

HOLLAND

Amsterdam

Rotterdam

Hambu

Bremen

Hanover

London

Southampton

Dover

GER

Essen
RUHR
Düsseldorf

Cologne

ENGLISH CHANNEL

Ypres

Fromelles

Werwick
Lille

Antwerp

Brussels

BELGIUM

Le Havre

SOMME R.

Arras

Cambrai

LUXEMBOURG

Coblenz

RHINE

Frankfurt
am Main

Compiegne

OISE R.

AISNE R.

RHINELAND

MAIN R.

Versailles

Paris

SEINE R.

MARNE R.

Rheims

Verdun

Saarbrücken
SAAR

Heidelberg

Stuttgart

Montoire

FRANCE

ALSACE-LORRAINE

Strasbourg

Augsb

SAÔNE R.

SWITZERLAND

Lausanne

Vichy

Geneva

Lyon

RHÔNE R.

Milan

Turin

ITALY

N

Genoa

0   Miles   100
palacios

Marseille

Toulon

MEDITERRANEAN SEA

DENMARK

Copenhagen

SWEDEN

BALTIC SEA

Memel

LITHUANIA

FREE CITY OF DANZIG

Königsberg

EAST PRUSSIA

Lübeck

Pasewalk

POLISH CORRIDOR

VISTULA R.

Berlin

ODER R.

Frankfurt an der Oder

Poznan

Warsaw

Brest-Litovsk

braunschweig

Beelitz

POLAND

ELBE R.

NY

Leipzig

Dresden

Weimar

Breslau

UPPER SILESIA

ODER R.

Cracow

SUDETEN

Eger

Prague

Nuremberg

Pilsen

Brno

CZECHOSLOVAKIA

DANUBE R.

Spital

Braunau

Urfahr

Munich

Leonding

Linz

Bratislava

Lambach

Vienna

Tegernsee

Salzburg

Budapest

Berchtesgaden

Innsbruck

AUSTRIA

HUNGARY

RENNER PASS

Trieste

Zagreb

Venice

Fiume

DANUBE R.

Belgrade

ADRIATIC

YUGOSLAVIA

SEA

Sarajevo

EUROPE
UNDER HITLER

0   Miles   300

N

▨	Hitler's Third Reich
▧	German Conquests & Satellites
◩	Italy & Vassals
▨	Vichy France & Colonies
♟	Hitler's Headquarters
▲ CONCENTRATION CAMPS	✦ KILLING CENTERS

WEDEN

FINLAND

Helsinki

Volkhov

Tikhvin

Vologda

Leningrad

Novgorod

Tallinn

Stockholm

ESTONIA

Pskov

Kalinin

Yaroslavl

VOLGA R.

Kazan

Gorki

Novgorod

LATVIA

Velikiye Luki

Rzhev

Moscow

BALTIC SEA

Riga

Polotsk

Smolensk

Vyazma

Kaluga

Ryazan

Penza

LITHUANIA

Kaunas

Mogilev

Tula

U.S.S.R.

Gdynia

Wolf's Lair

E. PRUSSIA

Bryansk

Orel

Voronezh

Saratov

Danzig

TREBLINKA

Gomel

Kursk

DON R.

POLAND

Poznan

Brest-Litovsk

Belgorod

Stalingrad

KULMHOF

Warsaw

SOBIBOR

LUBLIN (MAIDANEK)

Kharkov

Kamensk

Cracow

BELZEC

L'vov

Zhitomir

Kiev

DNIEPER R.

Dnepropetrovsk

Rostov

AUSCHWITZ

Werewolf

Cherkassy

Zhdanov

CZECHOSLOVAKIA

SLOVAKIA

Vinnitsa

Krivoy Rog

Bratislava

Cernauti

Nikolayevsk

Kerch

Krasnodar

Budapest

Odessa

CRIMEA

Maikop

HUNGARY

ROMANIA

Novorossisk

zreb

Ploesti

Sevastopol

Yalta

YUGOSLAVIA

Belgrade

Bucharest

Constanza

BLACK SEA

Batum

BULGARIA

Sofia

Istanbul

Bari

Tirana

Salonika

Ankara

TURKEY

ALBANIA

aranto

GREECE

Athens

Smyrna

SYRIA

RHODES

CYPRUS

CRETE

palacios

Hitler in Paris with Speer and Breker.
U. S. ARMY

Hitler in Paris, l. to r., Architect Giesler, Breker, Keitel, Hitler, Bodenschatz, Engel, Bormann, Schaub and Speer. FRENTZ

Two faces of Adolf Hitler. PUTTKAMER

Generalissimo Franco leans forward from train car to speak with Hitler and the German interpreter. October 1940. Part Jewish, Franco refused Hitler's offer to join the Axis.
U. S. ARMY

Hitler talks peace with Soviet Foreign Minister Molotov, November 1940. The man in the center is Stalin's interpreter. After this meeting Hitler decides definitely to invade Russia. IMPERIAL WAR MUSEUM

Hitler and Papen on the Berghof veranda. FRENTZ

Hitler celebrates Christmas 1940 with young Luftwaffe officers. FRENTZ

The same day. Engel is promoted to major. Puttkamer affixes the new insignia. FRENTZ

Bormann at wheel with Frau Hess. Hess in jump seat; in back Professor Haushofer, the geopolitician, and Hildegard Fath, Hess's secretary. FATH

Hess with his wife on a skiing holiday in the mid-thirties. He usually kept a stiff upper lip—to cover his buck teeth. FATH

Athlete Hess takes off. FATH

Just before his flight to England in May 1941, Hess and his son. The girl is Bormann's daughter. FATH

the matter by phone with Hitler in Berchtesgaden and received new instructions. That evening another telegram went to Moscow canceling the offer to the Russiàns. Ambassador von der Schulenburg should make no move without further orders.

Concluding that he had approached the Russians on too high a level, Hitler ordered Weizsäcker to sound out Astakhov. He did so on the last day of May and the tone and content of their talk was so reassuring that the Führer authorized a message to Schulenburg later that same day instructing him to "undertake definite negotiations with the Soviet Union." On the heels of this message came another suggesting that economic talks with the Russians also be resumed. But Stalin's suspicions exceeded Hitler's and when nothing substantive had been achieved by the end of June the latter reluctantly ordered suspension of negotiations. The honeymoon that each side seemed so eager to consummate was off.

2

Stalin's Western suitors were no nearer to a treaty than Hitler. In London Lord Halifax was reaching the end of his patience with the Kremlin's reluctance to get down to business. Saying no to everything, he complained to Ambassador Maisky, was not his idea of negotiation since it had "a striking resemblance to Nazi methods of dealing with international questions." The Soviet answer was a tart article in *Pravda* on June 29 with this headline: BRITISH AND FRENCH GOVERNMENTS DO NOT WANT A TREATY ON THE BASIS OF EQUALITY FOR THE USSR. What actually lay behind Soviet hesitation was a lively suspicion that the British aimed to get Russia embroiled in a war with Hitler while reducing their own military contribution to a minimum. The Japanese ambassador in London, equally skeptical, reported to Tokyo his impression that the English were playing their usual double game: using the Soviet treaty negotiations as a threat against Hitler while utilizing a German-oriented peace plan against Stalin.

In the meantime Hitler remained at the Berghof much of the summer, removing himself from the diplomatic scene and making no important announcements. Perhaps this silence was born of his own uncertainty, perhaps it was in line with his conviction that most problems solved themselves if left alone. In any case, he could have done nothing more calculated to confuse his opponents. It was a season for passivity. He listened patiently to a written warning from Mussolini delivered in person by one of his generals. War was inevitable, said Il Duce, but added that their two countries needed peace. "It is from 1943 onwards that a war effort will have the greatest prospects of victory." Hitler did not deign to argue as the general read on of Mussolini's reluctance to anticipate a European war. The Führer's own intent was to localize the war by isolating Poland and he needed no advice from an Italian about how to do it.

To his adjutants he appeared markedly relaxed. He left his mountain fastness in mid-July for a brief stay in Munich where he attended a special performance of *Tannhäuser* at the State Opera House. This production boasted a new feature added for the personal benefit of the artist-bohemian Hitler: two nude girls, one posing as Europa astride a bull and the other depicting Leda with her swan.

A week later he was at Bayreuth enjoying the year's Wagner festival which, besides *The Ring*, included stirring performances of *Tristan* and *Parsifal*. He had invited his old school friend Kubizek to attend every performance but did not see him until August 3, the day after the final performance of *Götterdämmerung*. That afternoon an SS officer escorted Kubizek to Haus Wahnfried. Hitler grasped his old friend's right hand in both of his, and Kubizek could hardly speak.

Kubizek hesitatingly brought out a large bundle of postcards with the Führer's picture and wondered if they could be autographed for friends back in Austria. Hitler put on his reading glasses—he was careful to remove them for photographers—and obligingly began signing cards as Kubizek methodically blotted each signature. Afterward Hitler led him into the garden to Wagner's tomb. "I am happy," he said, "that we have met once more on this spot which always was the most venerable spot for us both."

This episode was one of the rare evidences of Hitler's private life, which had become overshadowed by his responsibilities as Führer. He had little time for Eva Braun, and it was not until the beginning of 1939 that she was moved into quarters in the chancellery. She slept in Hindenburg's former bedroom, whose main decoration was a large picture of Bismarck, and there were standing orders from the Führer never to open the window curtains. This bleak room, along with an adjoining boudoir, led directly to Hitler's library, but she was required to enter his suite through the servants' entrance.

Although they lived as husband and wife, the two went through an elaborate charade to persuade the staff that they were merely good friends. In the morning she would address him as "Mein Führer," and this form of address became such a habit that she used it, so she confessed to her best friend, even in private. The circle privy to their secret was beginning to widen, however, because of at least one ridiculous slip in security. Just before his dismissal, Captain Wiedemann went to the Führer's room one morning to deliver an emergency message and to his surprise saw outside the door Eva's petite Viennese shoes next to Hitler's boots—left to be shined as if it were a hotel. "I could not help recalling La Fontaine's fable," he wrote in his memoirs, "and I burst out laughing as I went downstairs."

When important guests arrived at either the chancellery or at Berchtesgaden, where Eva's pleasant apartment adjoined the Führer's, she was confined to quarters and this was hard to endure. She longed to meet Admiral Horthy, President Hoover, King Carol of Romania, the Aga Khan and other notables and yet was forced to stay in her room like a child. She was particularly disturbed, she confided to friends, when Hitler refused her pleas to meet the Duchess of Windsor since the two women, she thought, had so much in common. She did console herself with the thrill of knowing that the great of the world were coming from all over the world to honor her lover. This knowledge made her "Back Street" existence endurable. Moreover, anything was better than the earlier days of loneliness and doubt which had led to two attempted suicides.

On the political front Ribbentrop authorized resumption of talks with Astakhov on the day Hitler was enjoying *Tristan* at Bayreuth. Although the results delighted the Foreign Minister, Peter Kleist warned him not to let Stalin see that Germany was in a hurry and, above all, not to negotiate any special offers merely to conclude a pact. They should wait and probably within six months reach an agreement that would satisfy both parties. Ribbentrop laughed. They could sign a pact within a fortnight! He ignored Kleist's advice to be patient and, in his eagerness to complete a treaty that would checkmate England, instructed Schulenburg to meet Molotov again and propose serious political talks. At this meeting on August 3, the German ambassador got the impression, so he reported, that the Soviets were determined to sign with England and France "if they fulfill all Soviet wishes." This was certainly the impression Molotov hoped to make. Both he and Stalin had noted the eagerness in the Wilhelmstrasse and were tempting the Germans while leading on the British.

By this time Hitler had become even more impatient than Ribbentrop. His campaign deadline against Poland was less than a month off and he needed assurance from Stalin that the Red Army would not intervene. At this point he either forced the issue or was blessed by luck. The day after Schulenburg's inconclusive talk with Molotov a crisis in Poland arose. Danzig Nazis informed the Polish customs officials that they could no longer carry out their normal duties. Poland responded with an irate demand to withdraw the order, whereupon the president of the Senate of the Free City of Danzig indignantly denied that any such order had been issued and charged that Poland was only looking for a pretext to threaten Danzig.

If it was indeed a case of the tail wagging the dog, the latter quickly took command on August 9. Berlin warned Warsaw that any repetition of the ultimatum to Danzig "would lead to greater tension in the relationship between Germany and Poland." The tempest in the teapot grew into a serious crisis with Poland's retort that she would consider any possible German intervention an aggression.

The controlled German press was already in full cry. POLAND! LOOK
OUT! warned one headline. WARSAW THREATENS BOMBARDMENT OF DAN-
ZIG—UNBELIEVABLE AGITATION OF POLISH MEGALOMANIA! blared another.
While Goebbels shouted, the Foreign Office waged its campaign in a
lower key with Julius Schnurre, Ribbentrop's economic expert, assuring
Astakhov that German interests in Poland were really quite limited.
"They do not at all need to collide with Soviet interests of any kind," he
said, "but we must know those interests."

From his mountain retreat Hitler became personally involved by
sending his private plane to Danzig for Carl Burckhardt, the League of
Nations' high commissioner for the Free City. Burckhardt arrived at the
Obersalzberg on August 11 and was driven up to the tea house on the
Kehlstein.

Hitler was occupied by a different matter. "Perhaps something enormously important will happen soon," he remarked to Speer as they rode
up in the elevator to the main room. Almost as though speaking to himself, he mentioned something about sending Göring on a mission. "But if
need be I would even go myself. I am staking everything on this card." He
was referring to a treaty with Stalin but by the time Burckhardt walked in
he had worked himself into an excess of rage over Poland. "If the slightest
thing happens without warning," he exclaimed, "I will pounce on the
Poles like lightning with all the power of mechanized forces which they
don't even dream of!" He shouted at the top of his voice, "Do you understand me?"

"Very well, Monsieur Chancellor, I quite realize that means a general
war."

A look of pain and fury came over Hitler's face. "Very well," he said,
"if I am forced into this conflict, I prefer to do it today rather than tomorrow. I will not conduct it like Wilhelm II, who always had scruples of
conscience before waging total warfare. I will fight relentlessly to the bitter end."

He calmed down as if he had let off sufficient steam and quietly assured his guest that he had no desire to fight Britain and France. "I have
no romantic aspiration," he said pleasantly, "no appetite for domination.
Above all I seek nothing in the West. Neither today nor tomorrow." But
he had to have a free hand in the East. "I must obtain a sufficient quantity of wheat for my country." He also needed a colony outside of Europe
for timber. That was as far as his ambitions extended. "Once and for all,"
he said somberly, "it is necessary that you realize that I am ready to negotiate and discuss all these matters."

He reaffirmed that, given freedom in the East, he would happily conclude a pact with the British and guarantee all their possessions. This
promise was obviously meant to be transmitted to London, as was the
threat that followed. "Everything that I have in mind is directed against

Russia; if the West is too stupid and blind to understand this then I will
be forced to come to terms with the Russians, to crush the West and then
after its defeat, turn with all my forces against the Soviet Union. I need
the Ukraine so they can't starve us out as in the last war."

3

What Burckhardt did not know was that the British had recently
made a secret offer to Hitler through one of Chamberlain's top advisers.
In a private conversation at his house in West Kensington, Sir Horace
Wilson assured Fritz Hesse, Ribbentrop's undercover representative, that
the Prime Minister would be prepared to offer the Führer a defensive alliance for twenty-five years that could include economic advantages for the
Reich and the return of German colonies by stages "in due course." In return Hitler must promise to take no more aggressive action in Europe.

Hesse was not sure he had heard right and asked Sir Horace to explain again in detail. He did. "If I were Hitler," said the astounded Hesse,
"I would accept your proposition. But whether he will do so, no one can
tell." Hesse transmitted the offer to the Foreign Office and before long
was on a special plane bound for the Reich with a typewritten sheet provided by Wilson summarizing the proposals. While impressed, Ribbentrop wondered how he could convince Hitler that they should be taken
seriously. Did Hesse really think the British would go to war on Hitler's
side in case the Soviets attacked Germany? Would they break off their
conversations in Moscow before negotiating with Germany? Hesse believed they would.

When Hitler first heard the proposals, so an eyewitness informed
Hesse, he was transported with joy. "It's the greatest news I've had for a
long time!" he exclaimed and began romancing like a child. The dream of
his life, an alliance with mighty England, was coming true! But almost immediately he had misgivings and accused Wilson of laying a trap to save
the Poles from a well-deserved thrashing. "What does Hitler want?" Hesse
asked his informant—Walther Hewel, Ribbentrop's liaison man at the
chancellery. The answer was: the Führer had his heart set on forcing the
Poles to capitulate.

That week Ribbentrop asked Hesse if he was "completely convinced"
that England would go to war over Danzig. All of his sources, he answered, indicated that Chamberlain could not act otherwise. Any invasion
of Polish territory would result in war. "The Führer doesn't believe this at
all!" exclaimed Ribbentrop. "Some donkeys told him that the English
would only bluff and a German counterbluff would drive them to their
knees." Puzzled by the contradiction between Ribbentrop's personal convictions and his public posture, Hesse asked if he really thought the English were bluffing. The Foreign Minister asserted that he *had* warned the

Führer that the English were not soft and degenerate and would fight if they believed the balance of power in Europe depended on it or their empire was seriously threatened.

Two days later Ribbentrop told Hesse that he had transmitted all of the latter's arguments to Hitler. But he remained convinced that if the English were really ready to plunge into war over such a trivial matter as Danzig, then war with England was absolutely inevitable.

Ribbentrop promised to speak again to Hitler and marveled at the "surprisingly calm way" the Führer considered Hesse's alternatives. Still, Hitler was consumed by fear that it was merely a maneuver to trick him. What guarantee was there that the English would keep their word? "The Führer," Ribbentrop reported, "would only consider solid guarantees." This hardened attitude was reflected in Ribbentrop's own diplomatic posture upon meeting Mussolini's son-in-law on August 11 in Salzburg. Ciano had come with emphatic instructions from Mussolini to insist upon postponement of any invasion of Poland. The matter must be solved by conference.

Ribbentrop, as well as his Führer, had resented Il Duce's sending an emissary instead of coming himself. Besides both despised Ciano for the drinking bouts and sexual escapades he reportedly indulged in whenever he visited the Reich. Ribbentrop dutifully mouthed his master's thoughts at the meeting with Ciano. Perhaps the Foreign Minister had even come to share them. At any rate, he acted like a carbon copy of Hitler as he peremptorily brushed aside all of Ciano's eloquent pleas for a peaceful solution. Finally Ciano asked what Ribbentrop wanted: the Corridor or Danzig? "Not that any more," was the answer. "We want war."

The coolness between Ciano and Ribbentrop spread to their secretaries and scarcely a word was exchanged during lunch. At one point Ciano, pale and shaken, whispered to a compatriot, "We are almost at blows."

Surprisingly Ciano, who had allowed himself to be bullied by Ribbentrop, stood up to the Führer the following day at the Berghof. During lunch Ciano poked fun at the floral decorations, which interpreter Dollmann guessed had been arranged by Eva Braun; and once serious discussions began, he countered Hitler's arguments with energy and wit. He warned that a war with Poland could not be confined to that country since this time the West would surely declare war. In the most explicit terms, Ciano pointed out that Italy was not prepared for a general war, in fact, didn't have sufficient matériel to remain in combat for more than a few months. All affability, Hitler suggested they postpone further talk until morning and drive up to his retreat on Kehlstein mountain while there was still good light. Ciano complied with obvious lack of enthusiasm and, as Hitler drew him to a window and expatiated on the scenic grandeur that lay outside, shivered uncomfortably. He then proceeded to drink cup after cup of hot tea, which he disliked. The trip to the mountaintop left Ciano disconsolate and that evening he telephoned his father-in-law: "The position is serious."

By morning Ciano was a beaten man. At the second talk with Hitler he said not a word of Italy's inability to take part in the war. His brilliant debating power had suddenly deserted him, and to Schmidt's amazement, "he folded up like a jackknife." Gone was the cool decisiveness and statesmanship of yesterday as he listened apathetically to the Führer's assurance that England and France would never go to war on Poland's account. "You have been proved right so often before when we others held the opposite view," said Ciano, "that I think it very possible that this time, too, you see things more clearly than we do."

A few hours later a dispirited Ciano was airbound for home. "I return to Rome," he wrote in his diary, "completely disgusted with the Germans, with their leader, and their way of doing things. Now they have dragged us into an adventure which we have not wanted and which might compromise the regime and the country as a whole."

Soon after Ciano's departure Hesse was ordered to meet Ribbentrop at a hotel in Salzburg. After staring silently at a writing table for ten minutes the Foreign Minister finally looked up somberly at Hesse. "I have just come from the Führer," he said. "He is, unfortunately, not in a position to discuss Chamberlain's offer." He was referring to Wilson's proposals. "He has quite different intentions. Chamberlain's offer will not be discarded. We shall return to it when the time has come." He instructed Hesse to fly back to London at once and keep his ears open. "The Führer means to play a very dangerous game. I do not know whether it will succeed or not. In any case, we don't want a war with England. Give us a signal in good time if the danger becomes acute."

The supreme confidence exuded by Hitler to Ciano was largely playacting. He was deeply concerned at Stalin's reluctance to come to an agreement. This anxiety was aggravated by a report that a British-French delegation had recently arrived in Moscow and was about to conclude successful negotiations with the Soviets. In truth, the Russians were in no mood to negotiate, concerned as they were that the Allies were toying with them. First the Anglo-French delegation had taken six days to arrive by slow cargo-passenger ship and train when they could have made it in a single day. Next the British senior officer had come without proper credentials, and when the talks finally got under way it seemed that the British were not at all serious: a Soviet offer to provide 136 divisions for a common defense against the Nazis was matched by a British proposal to provide one mechanized and five infantry divisions.

Not knowing all this, the Führer ordered Ribbentrop to put more pressure on the Kremlin, and a conference between Molotov and Schulenburg was hastily arranged. On the evening of August 15 the Foreign

Commissar listened attentively to everything the German ambassador had to say but could give no quick answer. First, he said, an understanding must be reached on several points. Would the Germans, for example, be willing to influence Japan to take a different attitude toward the Soviets? Would the Germans conclude a pact of non-aggression? If so, under what conditions?

Hitler was too impatient for deliberations. He ordered Ribbentrop to reach an understanding at once with Molotov; and thereby let his adversary set the pace of events. Stalin took immediate advantage. Through Molotov he replied that before any political pacts could be signed their economic agreements must be concluded. Ribbentrop responded with a further plea to Schulenburg for haste, pointing out that the first stage of the economic agreements had just been completed. His instructions became almost hysterical. The next conversation with Molotov, he said, should be conducted "by pressing emphatically . . . for a rapid realization of my trip and by opposing appropriately any possible new Russian objections. In this connection you must keep in mind the decisive fact that an early outbreak of open German-Polish conflict is probable and that we therefore have the greatest interest in my having my visit to Moscow take place immediately."

Stalin realized that every hour of delay was painful to Hitler (perhaps his agents had learned of Hitler's September 1 deadline) and so ordered Molotov to procrastinate as usual at his next meeting with Schulenburg on August 19. The Foreign Commissar consequently argued tediously over every point despite his guest's repeated and emphatic pleas for action. But half an hour after Schulenburg departed the Soviets surprisingly reversed their tactics. Molotov invited the German back to the Kremlin. He arrived late that afternoon and it was immediately apparent that Molotov had good news. After apologizing for inconveniencing Schulenburg, the Foreign Commissar said he had just been authorized to hand over a draft of a non-aggression pact and to receive Herr von Ribbentrop in Moscow. He did not explain, naturally, that the Anglo-French-Soviet military talks in Moscow had reached such an impasse that Stalin had lost all patience with the West. Perhaps he had intended to join with Hitler all along and only used the Anglo-French talks as a maneuver to get better conditions from Hitler.

Even so the Russians proceeded deliberately. Molotov told Schulenburg he could not receive Ribbentrop until a week *after* the signing of their economic agreement. If that took place today, the date would be August 26, if tomorrow, the twenty-seventh. Hitler must have read Schulenburg's report with mixed feelings—delight at the probability of concluding the treaty and exasperation at Stalin's insistence on first signing their economic agreement. It was little better than blackmail but Hitler felt there was no alternative. The trade agreement was rushed through and signed in

Berlin two hours after midnight. It granted the Soviet Union a merchandise credit of 200 million Reichsmarks, at the reasonable interest of five per cent, to be used to finance Soviet orders of machine tools and industrial installations. Armaments "in the broader sense," such as optical supplies and armor plate, were to be supplied in proportionately smaller amounts. The credit would be liquidated by Soviet raw materials.

Outmaneuvered by Stalin, just as he had outmaneuvered the Austrians and Czechs, Hitler could not possibly wait the week that Molotov proposed. He composed a personal message to Stalin which was dispatched from Berlin at 4:35 P.M., August 20. In it Hitler sincerely welcomed the signing of the new German-Soviet commercial agreement as a first step in the reordering of German-Soviet relations. He also accepted the Soviet draft of the non-aggression pact although there were a few questions connected with it which should be clarified as soon as possible. Then he got down to the crux of the matter: speed in concluding this pact, he said, was of the utmost importance since tension between Germany and Poland was becoming intolerable. A crisis might arise "any day."

Two hours after Schulenburg delivered the message to the Kremlin, he was summoned back for a personal reply from Stalin himself: "I thank you for the letter," it began. He hoped the pact would mark a decided turn in their political relations. "The people of our countries need peaceful relations with each other." He agreed to see Ribbentrop on August 23.

Throughout the twentieth Hitler had been silently pacing up and down the great hall in the Berghof waiting anxiously for news from Moscow; the expression on his face kept anyone from disturbing him. In expectation he had already sent the pocket battleship *Graf Spee* to a waiting position in the Atlantic; twenty-one U-boats were in offensive positions around the British Isles.

At dinner (according to Speer) Hitler was handed a telegram. After reading it, his face flushed a deep red and he stared vacantly out the window. All at once he slammed both fists on the table, making the glasses rattle. "I have them!" he exclaimed in a voice choked with emotion. "I have them!" He slumped back and, since no one dared to ask any questions, the meal resumed in silence.

After coffee a euphoric Hitler told his guests that Germany was concluding a non-aggression pact with Russia. "Here, read this," he said. "A telegram from Stalin." Hoffmann recalled that the Führer was so delighted he slapped his knee, something the photographer had never seen him do before. There was great ado as Kannenberg, the major-domo, brought out champagne. Glasses were clinked and the entourage drank a toast to the great diplomatic coup. Presently Hitler led everyone to the little movie theater in the basement to see a film of Stalin reviewing a massive Red Army parade. How lucky, remarked the Führer, that such military might was now neutralized.

Hoffmann worried about repercussions among the faithful National Socialists who had been fighting the Reds for decades. "The party will be just as astounded as the rest of the world," Hitler purportedly replied, "but my party members know and trust me; they know I will never depart from my basic principles, and they will realize that the ultimate aim of this last gamble is to remove the Eastern danger and thus to facilitate, under my leadership, of course, a swifter unification of Europe."

On the face of it, Stalin and Hitler *were* most unlikely allies. What could they possibly have in common? In fact, there were a number of similarities. One admired Peter the Great while the other saw himself as the heir of Frederick the Great. Both were advocates of ruthless force and operated under ideologies that were not essentially different. Communists and Nazis alike were self-righteous and dogmatic; both were totalitarian and both believed that the end justified the means, sanctifying injustice, as it were, in the name of the state and progress.

Hitler had long admired Stalin, regarding him as "one of the extraordinary figures in world history," and once shocked a group of intimates by asserting that he and the Soviet leader had much in common since both had risen from the lower classes, and when one listener protested comparison with a former bank robber, he replied, "If Stalin did commit a bank robbery, it was not to fill his own pockets but to help his party and movement. You cannot consider that bank robbery."

Nor did the Führer look upon Stalin as a true Communist. "In actual fact, he identifies himself with the Russia of the Czars, and he has merely resurrected the tradition of Pan-Slavism. [Perhaps Hitler was unconsciously speaking of himself and Germany.] For him Bolshevism is only a means, a disguise designed to trick the Germanic and Latin peoples."

Both Stalin and Hitler felt sure they could use each other. Both dictators were wrong but in that hectic summer of 1939 there was not a major nation in the world which was not operating under some misconception. Europe was a cauldron of distrusts, deceit and double-dealing. Even as Ribbentrop prepared to leave for Moscow, Stalin had not completely abandoned the hope of an Anglo-French-Soviet military alliance against Hitler. And while the English were doing their halfhearted best to consummate this agreement, they were secretly inviting Göring to England. On all sides nation was dealing behind the back of nation, each mouthing platitudes of sincerity or uttering threats.

4

The apparent winner was Hitler. He wakened on the morning of August 22 full of confidence. After Ribbentrop had left the Berghof with final instructions for his mission to Moscow, the Führer summoned his senior commanders and their chiefs of staff for a special meeting in the spacious reception hall. It was a lecture, not a conference, with Hitler sitting behind a large desk doing all the talking. "I have called you together to give you a picture of the political situation, in order that you may have insight into the various elements on which I have based my decision to act, and in order to strengthen your confidence." The conflict with Poland, he said, was bound to come sooner or later and there were a number of reasons why it was best to act promptly. "First of all two personal factors: my own personality and that of Mussolini. Essentially all depends on me, on my existence, because of my political talents. Probably no one will ever again have the confidence of the German people as I have. There will probably never again be a man with more authority than I have. My life is, therefore, a factor of great value. But I can be eliminated at any time by a criminal or an idiot." The second personal factor was Il Duce. If something happened to him, Italy's loyalty to their alliance would be questionable.

On the other hand there was no outstanding personality in either England or France. "Our enemies have men who are below average. No personalities. No master, no men of action . . ." Furthermore, the political situation was favorable, with rivalry in the Mediterranean and tension in the Orient. All these fortunate circumstances would no longer prevail in two or three years. "No one knows how long I shall live. Therefore conflict is better now."

Then he became specific. Relations with Poland, he said, had become unbearable. "We are facing the alternative to strike or to be destroyed with certainty sooner or later." What could the West do? Either attack from the Maginot Line or blockade the Reich. The first was improbable and the second would be ineffective since now the Soviets would supply Germany with grain, cattle, coal, lead and zinc. "I am only afraid that in the last minute some *Schweinehund* will produce a plan of mediation!"

The commanders, led by Göring, clapped enthusiastically.* "Mein Führer," said the Reichsmarschall "the Wehrmacht will do its duty!" Despite their applause, Göring and the other military commanders were unanimously against war since all were convinced that Germany was not yet properly prepared to wage one. There was only a six weeks' supply of ammunition, as well as alarming shortages of steel, oil and other important materials.

Hitler was as aware of all this as his generals but envisaged a different type of warfare: the *Blitzkrieg*, a sudden all-out attack of such force and intensity that victory would be assured quickly. The concept was strategic as well as tactical. The dehumanizing years of trench combat in the Great War, not to mention the deprivations of those on the home front, were

---

* According to one colorful account which stretches all credulity, Göring jumped on the table and danced around triumphantly like a savage, which would indeed have been a sight to behold.

still searing memories to Hitler. He had vowed that the misery of a long conflict would never again be visited on Germany. That is why he geared the Wehrmacht to armament in breadth rather than in depth. He had purposely organized Germany's economy for a relatively high production of ready armaments but not to wage long-range war with mass-productive powers. His goal was to produce armaments quickly, not to increase Germany's armament-producing plant or to retool her armament-producing machinery.

A series of Blitzkrieg attacks—sustained by short, intensive bursts of production—would permit Hitler to act as if Germany were stronger than she actually was by avoiding the massive production for conventional war that would have meant economic ruin. His was a poor man's philosophy that could only succeed with audacity. Already he had achieved a series of cheap victories by risking a conflict that his more affluent enemies were eager to avoid at almost any cost.

Blitzkrieg not only appealed to his gambling instinct but was perfectly suited to his position of dictator. A democracy could hardly have sustained the necessary bursts of economic effort, the concentration on turning out tanks, for instance, followed by an abrupt concentration on civilian items. What would have brought down a democracy did not apply to the National Socialist state with the peculiar weaknesses and strengths of its economy.

By choosing Blitzkrieg, Hitler confounded some of his own generals, whose theories were still rooted in the past. They did not realize, as he did, that Germany was far readier for combat than England and France. It was a gamble but he figured he could achieve victory over Poland so rapidly that he would never even have to cross swords with England or France. The odds were that they would then see the futility of retaliation. Somehow he had to neutralize the West—whether by threat or force of arms—so that by 1943 he could achieve his true aim, conquest of Russia. With eyes open, Adolf Hitler was prepared to meet his destiny.

On the morning of August 22 not one of the military men listening to Hitler's blueprint for invasion uttered a word of criticism, nor was there any protest from the field commanders, who were brought in after lunch for their inspirational message. The Führer exhorted them to have no mercy. "Might is right," he said and announced that the invasion would likely begin at dawn on Saturday, August 26.

Early that evening Ribbentrop and his party took off for Moscow in two Condors. There was a general feeling of extreme tension. "Nobody," recalled Peter Kleist, "could guarantee that the Soviets would not spring on us an Anglo-French agreement, all neatly tied up, when we arrived in Moscow." Nor could anyone predict whether Ribbentrop would be forced into the "long, soul-destroying negotiations" habitually conducted by the Russians.

The news of Ribbentrop's trip took Japanese Ambassador Oshima by complete surprise and that midnight he made a special trip to Weiz-säcker's home in Berlin to express his displeasure. Ordinarily a man of poise, Oshima's face was rigid and gray. How, he asked, could such a turn-about be explained to Tokyo?

Early the next afternoon, August 23, Henderson handed over Chamberlain's letter to the Führer. It declared categorically that Britain was determined to fulfill its promises to Poland. At the same time Chamberlain made another plea for peace. Why couldn't there be a truce so that Germany and Poland could discuss their problems directly? "At this moment," he concluded, "I confess I can see no other way to avoid a catastrophe that will involve Europe in war."

Hitler replied excitably in violent language; and Henderson expressed the hope that a solution might be found if their two nations co-operated. Hitler curtly retorted that this should have been done before. This brought a protest that the British government had given guarantees and must honor them. "Then honor them," snapped the Führer. "If you have given a blank check you must also meet it."

Henderson stoutly defended the British position but insisted on doing it in German, a language whose subtleties he had not yet mastered. Hitler brushed aside his arguments and began to threaten. The slightest attempt by Poland to make any further move against the Germans or Danzig, he said, would mean immediate intervention. Furthermore, mobilization in the West would be answered by German mobilization.

"Is that a threat?" asked Henderson.

"No, a protective measure!" In vain Henderson tried to assure Hitler that Chamberlain had always championed Germany. "I too believed that until this spring," said Hitler almost sadly. Thereupon Henderson blurted out that he personally had never believed in an Anglo-French-Russian pact. He preferred that Germany rather than England should have a treaty with Russia. Hitler's answer was ominous. "Make no mistake," he said, "it will be a long treaty." Henderson was not content to let this subject alone. He argued that the Führer knew as well as he did that the Russians always made difficulties. In any case he was convinced that Chamberlain had not changed in his attitude to Germany.

"I must judge by deeds in this matter," said Hitler and resumed recriminations. This brought a threat from Henderson that any direct action by Germany would mean war, which in turn touched off another display of almost hysterical violence. In such a war, exclaimed Hitler, Germany had nothing to lose and Great Britain much. He had no desire for war but would not shrink from it and his people were much more behind him than last September. He abruptly ended the conversation by stating that a written reply to Chamberlain would be handed over to Henderson in the afternoon.

Weizsäcker, a silent witness to this uneven duel, was as convinced as Henderson of Hitler's genuine agitation. But no sooner had the door closed behind the Englishman than the Führer slapped himself on the thigh (it was becoming a habit) and laughed. "Chamberlain won't survive that conversation," he said triumphantly. "His cabinet will fall this evening."

While waiting for the Führer's written answer, Henderson returned to Salzburg where he telephoned his subordinates in Berlin instructing them to inform London that Hitler was "entirely uncompromising and unsatisfactory but I cannot say anything further until I have received his written reply." A little later came a summons to return to the Berghof. This time Hitler, according to Henderson's report, had recovered his calm and "never raised his voice once." But he was no less obdurate, charging that "England was determined to destroy and exterminate Germany."

Henderson protested that war between their two countries would only benefit the lesser races of the world. To this Hitler replied that it was England who was fighting for the lesser races whereas he was only fighting for Germany and this time the Germans would battle to the last man. It would have been different in 1914 if he had been Chancellor then! "At the next instance of Polish provocation," he continued, "I shall act." He repeated his threat of the morning but this time without histrionics. "The questions of Danzig and the Corridor will be settled one way or another. Please take note of this. Believe me, last year—on October 2—I would have marched either way. I give you my word of honor on that!"

That afternoon the two German Condors landed at Moscow airport where Ribbentrop was pleased to see the swastika flying side by side with the hammer and sickle. After the Foreign Minister reviewed an honor guard of the Soviet air force, he was driven to his quarters, the former Austrian Embassy. (Was this Tartar irony?) Count von der Schulenburg informed him that he was expected in the Kremlin at 6 P.M. but couldn't say whether it would be Molotov or Stalin who would negotiate with him. "Odd Moscow customs," thought Ribbentrop to himself.

After Schulenburg and Hilger had made their reports, both advised Ribbentrop to allow himself plenty of time and not give the impression of being in a hurry. Interrupting with an impatient movement of the hand, he enjoined the ambassador to inform the Russians that he had to be back in Berlin within twenty-four hours. So saying, he hastily had a snack before heading for the Kremlin.

At 6 P.M. Ribbentrop was facing Stalin. He was affable, good-natured.

Molotov was impassive. Ribbentrop spoke first, expressing his nation's desire to establish German-Soviet relations on a new footing. He understood from Stalin's March speech that he felt the same. Stalin turned to Molotov. Did he want to speak first? The Foreign Commissar dutifully replied that it was Stalin's prerogative to reply.

He did in a manner which Ribbentrop had never encountered before. "For years," said Stalin concisely, "we have poured pails of manure at one another. That should not stop us from coming to an understanding. This was the drift of my speech in March, the meaning of which you have understood perfectly." With a notebook opened in front of him for reference, he continued without pause to practical matters: the spheres of influence in the countries between Germany and the U.S.S.R. were defined, with Finland, most of the Baltic States and Bessarabia in the Russian orbit; in the event of war between Germany and Poland they would meet at a definite "line of demarcation."

It was obvious that Stalin had come to the room to do business, not dally, and by the end of three hours he and Ribbentrop had agreed upon everything except two Baltic ports which Stalin insisted on having in his sphere. Ribbentrop said he would have to check with the Führer first and the talks were adjourned so he could do so.

Hitler was as eager to do business as Stalin. Within an hour a phone call from the Wilhelmstrasse brought this laconic reply: "Answer is yes. Agreed." In the meantime Ribbentrop sat down to another quick meal at his quarters, bubbling over with enthusiasm for Stalin and Molotov.

The Foreign Minister was in high spirits as he drove back to the Kremlin with the favorable answer from Hitler, this time with a larger retinue, which included two photographers. Secret police rushed out of the darkness as the German cars slowly moved into the mysterious inner city and proceeded past the largest cannon of its time, so huge that no one had ever dared fire it, past little wooden houses and cathedrals. Finally the procession reached a modern administration building where Stalin was waiting. In short order, final agreement on the non-aggression pact was reached. It was a concise, clear contract. Each party was to desist from any aggressive action against the other and lend no support to any power attacking the other. The treaty was to last for ten years and continue for another five unless renounced by either party a year prior to its expiration.

It was a conventional agreement, but not so its secret protocol, which carved up Eastern Europe. Equally extraordinary was Stalin's willingness to be photographed at the signing of the documents. He entered into the spirit and stage-managed the best-known picture of the signing. He beckoned to Ribbentrop's SS adjutant, Richard Schulze, to join the group but this young man couldn't imagine Stalin meant him. Finally Stalin took the extremely tall Schulze by the arm and placed him next to Ribbentrop. Perhaps Stalin wanted to add youthful appeal to the picture; perhaps he knew that Schulze's younger brother was Hitler's SS ordnance officer.

Toast followed toast but the most noteworthy was one from Stalin that was never revealed to the Russian people: "I know how much the German nation loves its Führer," he said. "I should therefore like to drink to his health." One of the most important treaties in world history had been completed and signed without argument in a few hours, proof that both Hitler and Stalin wanted the agreement, that both knew exactly what they would give to get what they wanted, and that both wished the deed done swiftly.

To Hitler the pact was *his* triumph, not Stalin's. He had apparently forgotten his own prediction in *Mein Kampf* that any German-Russian alliance would inevitably bring a war which would cause "the end of Germany." He had since changed his mind, so he confided to Bormann several years later, and hoped an entente with the Soviets would be "honestly sincere if not unreservedly friendly." He imagined after so many years of power that Stalin, the realist, would have shed the nebulous Marxist ideology, retaining it only as a poison for external use. The brutal manner in which he treated the Jewish intelligentsia encouraged such a belief. "In a spirit of implacable realism on both sides we could have created a situation in which a durable entente would have been possible. . . . An entente, in short, watched over by an eagle eye and with a finger on the trigger!"

Upon learning the treaty was signed, Hitler jumped up from the dinner table, exclaiming, "We've won!" Although he had waived the opportunity to seize all of Poland, the argument had neutralized Russia. Now he was free to proceed against Poland. Without the Soviet Union on their side, neither England nor France would do more than mouth threats. In addition he was assured of getting from the East all those raw materials he might be deprived of by a possible British blockade.

He was paying Stalin to do exactly what he would undoubtedly have done without a pact. The economy of the Soviet Union as well as its military efficiency was still in such disarray after the purges that Stalin could not even think of fighting the Reich. In fact he had never seriously sought a protective alliance against Hitler. What he and his associates in the Kremlin desired above all was neutrality; the pact with Germany not only gave this but fulfilled their aim of provoking war among the capitalist powers. To Stalin, Nazi Germany was just another capitalist enemy.

At about 3 A.M., August 24, Hitler led his entourage onto the Berghof terrace. The sky on the north and northwestern horizon blazed with the colors of the rainbow. Across the valley, a startling red glow from these Northern Lights was cast on the Unterberg, a mountain of legend. "The last act of *Götterdämmerung*," recalled Speer, "could not have been more effectively staged. The same red light bathed our faces and our hands."

Hitler abruptly turned to his Luftwaffe adjutant, Below. "Looks like a great deal of blood," he said. "This time we won't bring it off without violence."

Chapter Twenty

"A CALAMITY WITHOUT PARALLEL IN HISTORY" AUGUST 24–SEPTEMBER 3, 1939

1

The world awakened Thursday morning, August 24, to headlines proclaiming a treaty that was a traumatic shock not only to ordinary citizens but to diplomats. "I anticipate an ultimatum to Poland," Henderson reported from Berlin. "Whether eleventh hour attempt of Polish Government to re-establish contact will avail, I much doubt. But I regard it as *last* hope, if any, of peace: if there is a last hope."

The Polish people were extremely upset by the German-Soviet pact despite attempts by their newspapers to belittle it as a sign of German weakness. The government itself expressed supreme confidence that British and French assistance would turn the tide in case of war with Hitler. French Communists seemed to be torn between loyalty to their own country and Mother Russia. Confusion was even greater among their American colleagues. At first the *Daily Worker* ignored the treaty as if waiting for instructions from Moscow. Finally Earl Browder, the party leader, announced that it had weakened Hitler. With nary a qualm most extreme left-wing "progressives" obediently accepted a new party line: the agreement with Hitler had been consummated so that Russia could prepare herself for the eventual battle against Fascism. President Roosevelt's response was to send another of his moral telegrams to Hitler urging him "to refrain from any positive act of hostility for a reasonable and stipulated period" but, like its predecessor, it was filed and forgotten.

In Moscow Stalin was congratulating himself. Convinced that the British would compromise in the face of political reality, he imagined that the spheres of influence he had been granted would fall to him bloodlessly, by negotiation. Hitler's other allies were not so sanguine. The Italians, while admitting that Hitler had "struck a master blow," were uneasy and the Japanese feared that the alliance would encourage Stalin to increase pressure on Manchuria. Prime Minister Hiranuma, whose cabinet had already held more than seventy meetings in a futile effort to reach agreement on a concordat with Germany and Italy, was so embarrassed and dismayed that he announced, "The cabinet herewith resigns because of complicated and inscrutable situations recently arising in Europe."

The German public was generally pleased and relieved: the threat of encirclement, a war on two fronts, had miraculously evaporated thanks to the Führer. Those who found the pact the hardest to swallow were his staunchest followers but most of them quickly convinced themselves that the Chief knew exactly what he was doing.

Hitler flew up to Berlin to greet the returning hero, Ribbentrop, and he spent the evening in the chancellery listening to his Foreign Minister rhapsodize over the masters of the Kremlin, who made him feel "as if he were among old party comrades." Further, a picture of Czar Nicholas in the Winter Palace had convinced Ribbentrop that they could do business with Russia since it indicated that the Communists themselves revered a Czar who worked for the people. While Hitler took all this in with some interest, he was much more enthralled by the pictures Hoffmann had taken. Hitler, it seemed, had requested a close-up of the Soviet leader to see if his earlobes were "ingrown and Jewish, or separate and Aryan." One profile view in particular was most reassuring. His new brother-in-arms, according to the earlobe test, was no Jew.

But Hitler shook his head disapprovingly at the photographs of the final ceremonies. Every one showed Stalin with a cigarette. "The signing of the pact is a solemn act which one does not approach with a cigarette dangling from one's lips," he said and instructed the photographer to paint out the cigarettes before releasing the pictures to the press.

The Führer also interrogated at length the ordnance officer who had accompanied Ribbentrop. He reported that Stalin, before inviting his guests to sit down at the celebration dinner, had carefully inspected the table to see that everything was in order. This reminded Fräulein Schröder of the Führer himself and the secretary imprudently remarked on the similarity. Hitler did not appreciate the analogy. "*My* servants and *my* house," he said with some irritation, "are always perfect!"

The following day, Friday, August 25, was a crucial and crowded one. It began with a letter to Mussolini, explaining with some embarrassment what had taken place in Moscow. After giving assurances that the treaty only strengthened the Axis, Hitler trusted that Il Duce would understand why he had been forced to take such a drastic step. Hitler's next act was to ask Schmidt to translate the key passages of the speech Chamberlain had made in Commons the previous day. He listened intently to the Prime Minister's admission that the Moscow Pact had come as "a surprise of a very unpleasant character," but that the Germans were laboring under a "dangerous illusion" if they believed that the British and French would no longer fulfill their obligations to Poland.

"These words," recalled Schmidt, "made Hitler pensive, but he said nothing." Perhaps this confirmed a nagging uncertainty. The assault on Poland was scheduled to start early next morning but he was in such doubt that just before noon he instructed the high command to postpone the issuance of the executive order to attack for one hour—until three that afternoon. Then he summoned the British ambassador to the chancellery. Henderson arrived at 1:30 P.M. to find the Führer in a conciliatory mood. He was now prepared "to make a move toward England which should be as decisive as the move towards Russia which had led to the recent agreement." His conscience, Hitler said, compelled him to make this final effort to secure good relations. But this was his last attempt.

To Henderson he appeared to be calm and normal. But he did lose his temper as soon as he began enumerating the charges against the Poles, such as firing on civilian aircraft. These conditions, he shouted, "must cease!" The Danzig problem and the Corridor must be solved without further delay. The only result of Chamberlain's last speech could be "a bloody and unpredictable war between Germany and England." But this time Germany would not have to fight on two fronts. "Russia and Germany will never again take up arms against each other."

When Henderson kept repeating stolidly that England could not go back on her word to Poland, Hitler's threatening posture reverted to one of reasonableness. Once the Polish question was solved, he was prepared and determined to approach Britain again with a large comprehensive offer: he would, for instance, accept the British Empire and pledge himself personally to its continued existence. But if the British rejected his proposal, he concluded ominously, "there will be war." And this was his last offer.

Half an hour later, at exactly 3:02 P.M., he confirmed the order to attack Poland at dawn. On the surface his gamble appeared to have been motivated by mere opportunism. Admittedly a cunning virtuoso of day-to-day politics, his foreign policy did have a basic thrust: a step-by-step play to gain domination over continental Europe that was closely allied to his radical anti-Semitic program. In Rome his ambassador, accompanied by Ciano, was just entering the Palazzo Venezia with the text of the unusual letter written earlier in the day. At three-twenty Ambassador Hans Georg von Mackensen handed over the document to Il Duce. The pact had mightily impressed Mussolini, who, like all politicians, appreciated a brilliant coup. Yet he was realistic enough to face the fact that his own army, which had performed so feebly in Albania, was not endowed with sufficient morale, training or skill to wage a genuine war. He did not say so to Mackensen, only mouthed protestations of agreeability: he was in complete accord with the Moscow Pact while remaining an "unswerving anti-Communist," and stood behind the Führer come what may (this he emphasized expressly), "unconditionally and with all his resources."

No sooner had Mackensen left the room than Il Duce either changed his mind or had it changed for him. According to Ciano, it was he who convinced Mussolini to compose an answer to Hitler, admitting frankly that Italy was not ready for war and could only participate if Germany immediately delivered sufficient "military supplies and raw materials to resist the attack which the French and English would predominantly direct against us."

At the same time the Italian ambassador in Berlin was explaining to the Führer that Il Duce's answer was on its way. While Hitler was waiting for the next visitor, French Ambassador Coulondre, an aide brought in a news report from England which Schmidt glimpsed over his employer's shoulder. England and Poland had just concluded a pact of mutual assistance in London. Visibly concerned, the Führer brooded in silence. For months the signing of this agreement had been delayed for one reason or another. That it should take place on this of all days, a few hours after he had made his "last" offer to England, was no coincidence. This guarantee of military aid (even though it could never be implemented) might give the Poles such a false sense of security that they would refuse to negotiate with Germany.

At 5:30 P.M. Coulondre was finally escorted into the office. After exhibiting rage over Polish provocations, Hitler expressed regret over a possible war between Germany and France. "I had the impression at times," recalled Schmidt, "that he was mechanically repeating what he said to Henderson, and that his thoughts were elsewhere. It was obvious that he was in a hurry to bring the interview to an end." He half rose to his feet in a gesture of dismissal but the elegant Coulondre would not be put off without a retort. He spoke with forcible words that Schmidt would never forget: "In a situation as critical as this, Herr Reichskanzler, misunderstandings are the most dangerous things of all. Therefore, to make the matter quite clear, I give you my word of honor as a French officer that the French army will fight by the side of Poland if that country should be attacked." Then he assured Hitler that his government was prepared to do everything for the maintenance of peace right up to the last.

"Why then," exclaimed Hitler angrily, "did you give Poland a blank check to act as she pleased?" Before the Frenchman could reply, the Führer leaped to his feet for another tirade against the Poles. "It is painful for me to have to go to war against France; but the decision does not depend on me." With a wave of the hand he dismissed the ambassador.

A minute later, at 6 P.M., Attolico entered. He bore with him the text of Mussolini's letter, which had been dictated over the phone by Ciano. The announcement that Italy was not prepared for war, on the heels of the British-Polish pact and Coulondre's crystal-clear declaration of France's intentions, hit the Führer like "a bombshell." To him it was the completely unexpected defection "of an ally." But he controlled himself, dismissing Il Duce's envoy with the curt comment that he would send an immediate reply. As Attolico went out the door Schmidt heard Hitler mutter, "The Italians are behaving just as they did in 1914."

The waiting room was a pit of rumor and counterrumor as scraps of information were passed around. War seemed inevitable. Weizsäcker, for instance, saw only a two per cent possibility of preventing a world war in which Italy would leave Germany in the lurch. Inside his office Hitler was telling General Keitel: "Stop everything at once. Get Brauchitsch immediately. I need time for negotiations."

Keitel rushed out into the anteroom. "The order to advance must be delayed again," he excitedly told his aide. The news spread that the threat of war had been averted at the last minute. The Führer was returning to negotiation! There was general relief except from Hitler's chief adjutant, Rudolf Schmundt, who was glum. "Don't celebrate too soon," he told Warlimont. "This is only a postponement." Major Engel shared Schmundt's deep concern. Never before had the army adjutant seen the Chancellor in such "total confusion." The Führer was even arguing bitterly with Hewel, whose opinion he usually respected. Hitler bet that if war started with Poland the English would surely not join in. "Mein Führer," asserted Hewel, "do not underestimate the British. When they see there is no other alternative, they stubbornly go their own way." Hitler was too angry to argue and turned away.

Göring was also convinced that the English were not merely mouthing words of warning and was surreptitiously negotiating for peace. A man of action, he had already initiated discussions with England without consulting Ribbentrop, whom he distrusted. It was not as daring as it appeared, for he intended keeping his Führer informed of any developments. His desire for peace was hardly altruistic. Being a freebooter with the touch of the gangster, his prime aim in life was to enjoy the fruits of the plunder he was amassing thanks to his privileged position. War could bring an end to his sybaritic existence. On the other hand, Hitler was driven by principle, warped though it was, and could not be bribed. He might compromise but only if it brought him closer to his long-range goal. Realizing all this, Göring carried on his devious policy of peace with caution. As unofficial go-between in this intrigue he selected a wealthy

Swedish businessman named Birger Dahlerus. He had a German wife as well as interests in the Reich and so shared Göring's desire to prevent war between Germany and England. Furthermore, he was in a position to do something about it, for he had influential English friends who were willing to work clandestinely on the project.

Earlier that month Dahlerus had arranged a secret meeting between Göring and seven Englishmen in a house conveniently close to the Danish border. Here it was that the Reichsmarschall first expounded his views and hopes for peace to the foreign businessmen. Little was done except talk until the historic military conference at the Berghof two weeks later. This spurred Göring to telephone Dahlerus in Stockholm and urge him to come as soon as possible. The situation, he guardedly revealed, had worsened and the chances of a peaceful solution were rapidly diminishing. Göring persuaded Dahlerus to fly at once to England with an unofficial message to the Chamberlain government, urging that negotiations between Germany and England take place as soon as possible.

And so on that eventful morning of August 25 Dahlerus had flown to London by ordinary passenger plane but it was not until early evening that he was ushered into the office of Lord Halifax. The Foreign Secretary was in an optimistic mood and—since Hitler, it will be recalled, had just called off the invasion—it did not appear that the services of a neutral would be of further use. Dahlerus was not so optimistic and telephoned Göring for his opinion. The Reichsmarschall's reply was alarming. He feared that "war might break out at any moment."

Dahlerus repeated these words to Halifax the next morning and offered to deliver to Göring—the only German in his opinion who could prevent war—a personal message from Halifax confirming England's genuine desire to reach a peaceful settlement. Lord Halifax excused himself so he could discuss the matter with Chamberlain. In half an hour he returned with the Prime Minister's approval. The letter was written and Dahlerus was rushed to Croydon airdrome.

In Berlin Ambassador Attolico was on his way to the chancellery with another message from Mussolini. It contained an imposing list of the material Italy would need if she participated in a war: six million tons of coal; seven million tons of petroleum, two million tons of steel and a million tons of lumber. Since Attolico was opposed to war, he deliberately made Mussolini's terms impossible to fulfill. To Ribbentrop's icy query as to when this vast amount of material was to be delivered, Attolico answered, "Why, at once, before hostilities begin."

It was an unreasonable demand. Surprising, considering the strain he must have been under, was Hitler's calm reply, which was relayed to Mussolini by telephone at 3:08 P.M. He could meet Italy's requirements in most areas, he said, but regretted it was impossible to deliver before the outbreak of war for technical reasons. "In these circumstances, Duce, I understand your position, and would only ask you to try to achieve the pinning down of Anglo-French forces by active propaganda and suitable military demonstrations such as you have already proposed to me." In the light of his pact with Stalin, he concluded, he did not "shrink from solving the Eastern question even at the risk of complications in the West."

It was no idle threat. The Wehrmacht was now prepared to attack on September 1 and was only waiting for the Führer's final confirmation. An oppressive heat lay over Berlin that Saturday afternoon. Despite the headlines in the papers—IN CORRIDOR MANY GERMAN FARMHOUSES IN FLAMES! POLISH SOLDIERS PUSH TO EDGE OF GERMAN BORDER!—many Berliners were enjoying themselves at the surrounding lakes. The less fortunate were more concerned by the temperature than by politics.

At 6:42 P.M. Attolico got another call from Rome. It was Ciano with another urgent message for the Führer. In it Mussolini apologetically explained that Attolico had misunderstood the delivery date. He didn't expect the raw materials for a year. He regretted not being more helpful at such a crucial time and then, unexpectedly, made a plea for peace. A satisfactory political solution, he said, was still possible. When Hitler read these words he concluded that his ally was abandoning him. Somehow he controlled his feelings and sent off another conciliatory reply. "I respect the reasons and motives which led you to take this decision," he said and tried to infuse his partner with his own optimism.

Disappointed and exhausted, the Führer retired earlier than usual, only to be awakened soon after midnight. Göring had to see him at once on urgent business: the Swedish go-between he had mentioned the other day was back with an interesting letter from Lord Halifax. It was about 12:30 A.M. August 27, when Dahlerus was ushered into the Führer's study. Hitler waited solemnly, staring fixedly at the neutral who was striving for peace. Göring stood beside him, looking pleased with himself. After a brief friendly greeting, Hitler launched into a lecture on Germany's desire to reach an understanding with the English, which degenerated into an excited diatribe. After describing his latest proposals to Henderson, he exclaimed, "This is my last magnanimous offer to England." His face stiffened and his gesticulations became "very peculiar" as he boasted of the Reich's superior armed might.

Dahlerus pointed out that England and France also had greatly improved their armed forces and were in good position to blockade Germany. Without answering, Hitler paced up and down, then suddenly stopped in his tracks, stared and began talking again (Dahlerus recalled), this time as if in a trance. "If there should be a war, then I will build U-boats, build U-boats, build U-boats, build U-boats, U-boats, U-boats." It was like a stuck record. His voice became more and more indistinct.

Abruptly he was orating as if to a huge audience, but still repeating himself. "I will build airplanes, build airplanes, airplanes and I will destroy my enemies!" In consternation, Dahlerus turned to see how Göring was reacting. But the Reichsmarschall appeared not at all perturbed. Dahlerus was horrified: so this was the man whose actions could influence the entire world!

"War doesn't frighten me," continued Hitler, "encirclement of Germany is an impossibility, my people admire and follow me faithfully." He would spur them to superhuman efforts. His eyes went glassy. "If there should be no butter, I shall be the first to stop eating butter, eating butter." There was a pause. "If the enemy can hold out for several years," he finally said, "I, with my power over the German people, can hold out one year longer. Thereby I know that I am superior to all the others." All at once he asked why it was that the English continually refused to come to an agreement with him.

Dahlerus hesitated to answer honestly but finally said that the trouble was founded on England's lack of confidence in Hitler. At this the Führer struck his breast. "Idiots!" he exclaimed. "Have I ever told a lie in my life?" He continued to pace, again stopped. Dahlerus, he said, had heard his side. He must return to England at once and tell it to the Chamberlain government. "I do not think Henderson understood me, and I really want to bring about an understanding."

Dahlerus protested that he was a private citizen and could go only if the British government requested it. First he must have a clear definition of the vital points on which agreement could be reached. For example, what exactly was Hitler's proposed corridor to Danzig? Hitler smiled. "Well," he said, turning to Göring, "Henderson never asked about *that*." The Reichsmarschall tore a page out of an atlas and began outlining with a red pencil the territory Germany wanted.

This led to a clarifying discussion of the main points in Hitler's offer to Henderson: Germany wanted a treaty with Britain that would eliminate all disputes of a political or economic nature; England was to help Germany get Danzig and the Corridor; in return Germany would guarantee Poland's boundaries and let her have a corridor to Gdynia; the German minority in Poland would be protected; and, finally, Germany would give military aid whenever the British Empire came under attack.

Dahlerus ingenuously took Göring at face value and was inclined to think the best of Hitler. Moreover, he had no training in diplomacy. In his favor were a sincere desire for peace, courage and admirable persistence. As soon as he returned to his hotel he put in a long-distance call to an English friend. Before long he had assurance that the British government would welcome him as a messenger. At eight that peaceful Sunday morning he boarded a German plane at Tempelhof. As it headed at low level for London he wondered if he was merely a pawn in a game of intrigue. He was fairly sure that Göring was honestly working for a peaceful settlement. But was Hitler?

Hitler treated that Sabbath as a weekday. Having canceled the imminent celebration in Nuremberg which bore the inappropriate title "Party Day of Peace," he introduced a wartime measure of food and clothes rationing. Then the armed forces were placed on a semi-emergency basis with all naval, army and air attachés ordered to remain in Berlin until further notice.

Under the pall of this martial atmosphere Peter Kleist of Ribbentrop's office was secretly approached by two important Polish diplomats with a mediation proposal. They hinted that Foreign Minister Beck was being forced to act belligerently toward Germany only to satisfy a rabid group of Polish patriots. What Beck needed was time to calm things down. Kleist dutifully reported this to Ribbentrop and was soon explaining the details to Hitler himself. He listened with barely concealed impatience and then announced peremptorily that if Beck could not even assert himself in Poland there was no help for him. Furthermore, Kleist was to cease making any more semi-official contacts with the Poles. He gave this order with some acrimony, adding that Herr von Ribbentrop should have issued such an order long ago. As Kleist walked thoughtfully out of the chancellery he was certain that the decision had at last been reached—and it was war!

That sultry Sunday Hitler also took time to answer a plea for peace from Premier Daladier, doing so as one veteran to another. "As an old front-line soldier," he wrote, "I know, as you do, the horrors of war." There was no longer any need for dispute since the return of the Saar had ended all further German claims on France. The mischief-maker was England, which had unleashed "a savage press campaign against Germany" instead of persuading the Poles to be reasonable. He begged Daladier, a patriotic Frenchman, to put himself in Hitler's place. What if some French city—say Marseilles—were prevented from professing allegiance to France as a result of defeat in battle? What if Frenchmen living in that area were persecuted, beaten, bestially murdered? "I cannot in any circumstances imagine, Monsieur Daladier, that Germany would fight against you on these grounds." Hitler agreed with everything Daladier had written in his letter and again called on their common experiences as front-line soldiers to understand that it was impossible for a nation of honor to renounce nearly two million of its people and see them ill-treated on its own frontiers. Danzig and the Corridor must, in all honor, return to Germany.

A little after noon a German plane landed at Croydon. Birger Dahlerus stepped out. The place seemed dead since civilian air traffic between England and the Continent had come to a standstill. He was driven to the Foreign Office past air raid wardens patrolling streets where shopwindows were pasted over with strips of paper, then taken through back alleys to 10 Downing Street. Chamberlain, Halifax and Cadogan were waiting. They were grave but "perfectly calm." As Dahlerus told about the long meeting with Hitler he sensed an air of skepticism. His report differed from that of Henderson on several points and Chamberlain asked if he was absolutely certain he'd understood what Hitler said. Dahlerus, whose command of German was superior to Henderson's, replied that any misinterpretation was out of the question.

Throughout this conversation Chamberlain's remarks were colored by distrust of Hitler; he asked what impression the Führer had made on Dahlerus. The answer ("I shouldn't like to have him as a partner in my business") brought the only smile of the day from the Prime Minister. Since the British doubted his interpretation of Hitler's demands, Dahlerus suggested that they allow him to return to Berlin with their reactions. Chamberlain hesitated. Ambassador Henderson, presently in London, was scheduled to fly back to Berlin that day with their answer to Hitler's proposals. Dahlerus suggested that the ambassador wait a day. Then he could let the British know exactly how Hitler felt *before* they made an official reply based only on Henderson's assessment.

He suggested phoning Göring so he could ask point-blank if the German government would agree to Henderson waiting a full day. "Do you intend to phone from the Foreign Office?" asked Chamberlain. Dahlerus did and Chamberlain agreed. In a few minutes the go-between was in Cadogan's room hearing Göring say that he could not possibly give an immediate answer without conferring with the Führer. Half an hour later Dahlerus again phoned. This time Göring announced that Hitler accepted the plan "on the condition that it was genuine." Cadogan insisted that Dahlerus fly back to Berlin secretly, so the plane which had brought him to England was transferred from Croydon to a smaller field, Heston.

It was 11 P.M. by the time Dahlerus arrived at Göring's Berlin residence. After assuring the Reichsmarschall of his personal conviction that both the English government and her people truly wanted peace and were acting in good faith, Dahlerus outlined the British response to the Hitler proposals. Göring rubbed his nose. The British reply, he said, was hardly satisfactory and the whole situation was highly precarious. He would have to confer with Hitler alone. Dahlerus nervously paced the floor of his hotel room as he waited for the answer. Finally at 1:30 A.M. Göring telephoned. Hitler, he said in a robust voice, *did* respect England's views and welcomed her desire to reach a peaceful agreement. He also respected England's decision to honor her guarantee of Poland's boundaries as well as her insistence on an international guarantee in this matter of five great powers. Dahlerus was particularly relieved by his last concession since it surely meant that Hitler had shelved any other plans he might have had for Poland.

2

Often amateur diplomats merely confuse matters, but this time Dahlerus had succeeded in breaking a log jam. By 9 P.M. when Henderson's plane landed at the Berlin airport matters had progressed substantially. The ambassador had returned to his post armed with an official version of the offer Dahlerus had delivered unofficially. It also contained a clause stating that Beck had just agreed to enter at once into direct discussions with Germany.

The streets of the capital were pitch-dark from the blackout and the few people abroad reminded Henderson of apparitions. The exertions of the past months had left the ambassador exhausted. He had recently undergone an operation for cancer only to discover his was a terminal case. But he kept his condition private and never complained about the pressure of work. No sooner had Henderson begun a hurried meal at the embassy than word came from the chancellery: Hitler wanted to see him without delay. Fortified by half a bottle of champagne, Henderson drove out of the embassy driveway. A considerable crowd was waiting at the gate in absolute silence but, as far as he could see, with no hostility.

As Hitler read the German translation of the British note he registered no emotion even though it ended with the mixed expression of promise and threat that had become the Führer's own trademark: a just settlement of the questions between Germany and Poland could open the way to world peace; failure to reach it would bring Germany and Great Britain "into conflict and might well plunge the whole world into war. Such an outcome would be a calamity without parallel in history."

Hitler passed the note to Ribbentrop without comment, amazing Schmidt with such a calm reaction. Henderson's next move was even more surprising. He took the offensive for the first time in memory and did more talking than Hitler. Ordinarily this would have caused an eruption but Hitler sat calmly, occasionally staring out at the dark garden where his famed predecessor, Bismarck, had so often strolled.

In the meantime Henderson was proclaiming that England's word was her bond and she "had never and would never break it." In the old days Germany's word also had the same value and he quoted Field Marshal von Blücher's exhortation to his troops when hurrying to support Wellington at Waterloo: "Forward, my children, forward; I have given my word to my brother Wellington, and you cannot wish me to break it." Things were quite a bit different a hundred and twenty-five years ago, commented Hitler but with no asperity, and then insisted that while *he* was quite ready to settle his differences with Poland on a reasonable basis the Poles were continuing their violence against Germans. Such acts seemed to be a matter of indifference to the British.

Henderson—perhaps it was the champagne—somehow took this as a personal insult, heatedly replying that he had done everything in his power to prevent war and bloodshed. Herr Hitler, he said, must choose between friendship with England and excessive demands on Poland. The choice between war and peace was his. Still retaining his calm, Hitler replied that this was not a correct picture of the situation. His alternatives were either to defend the rights of the German people or to abandon them at the cost of an agreement with England. And there could be no choice: his duty was to defend the rights of all Germans.

At the end of this extraordinary colloquy Hitler again expressed a desire for agreement with England. It left Henderson with some optimism. He was also cheered by Schmidt's parting remark: "You were quite marvelous."

But there was pessimism at the chancellery. The Führer, Engel wrote in his diary, "is exceptionally irritated, bitter and sharp," and he made it clear to his adjutants that he would not take advice from the military on the question of peace or war. "He simply could not understand a German soldier who feared war. Frederick the Great would turn in his grave if he saw today's generals." All he wanted was liquidation of the unjust conditions of the Poles, not war with the Western Allies. "If they were stupid enough to take part that was their fault and they would have to be destroyed."

The air of depression and anxiety in the winter garden heightened as Hitler composed an answer to the British, and this turned to alarm when the noon papers reported in glaring headlines that at least six German nationals had been murdered in Poland. Whether this report was true or not, Hitler himself believed it and was incensed. And so by the time Henderson reappeared early that evening there was a feeling in the waiting rooms and corridors of the chancellery that little less than a miracle could prevent war. The ambassador was still hoping for the best and, as on the day before, wore a red carnation, his private signal to insiders that he still had hope. Once Henderson entered Hitler's study and was handed a copy of the German reply, however, he sensed an attitude more uncompromising than last night. With the Führer and Ribbentrop eying him closely, he began reading the German note. It started reasonably. Germany readily consented to the proposed mediation by the British; Hitler was pleased to receive a Polish emissary in Berlin with full powers to negotiate. But the next words were completely unacceptable: the German government calculated that "this delegate will arrive on Wednesday, 30 August, 1939."

"It sounds like an ultimatum," protested Henderson. "The Poles are given barely twenty-four hours to make their plans." Supported by Ribbentrop, the Führer heatedly denied the charge. "The time is short," he explained, "because there is the danger that fresh provocation may result in the outbreak of fighting."

Henderson was not impressed. He still could not accept such a time limit. It was the Diktat of Bad Godesberg all over again. Hitler argued that he was being pressed by his General Staff. "My soldiers," he said, "are asking me 'yes' or 'no.'" The Wehrmacht was ready to strike and its commanders were complaining that a week had been lost already. Another week might bring them into the rainy season.

But the ambassador would not budge and Hitler at last lost his temper. He angrily made a countercharge: neither Henderson nor his government cared a row of pins how many Germans were being slaughtered in Poland. Henderson shouted back that he would not listen to such language from Hitler or anybody else. It seemed the ambassador had also lost his temper, but he explained in his report that this was a trick; the time had come to play Herr Hitler at his own game. Glaring into his opponent's eyes, at the top of his voice he bellowed that if Hitler wanted war he could have it! England was every bit as resolute as Germany and would in fact "hold out a little bit longer than Germany could!"

The Führer took this new departure in British diplomacy with relative grace and, once the clamor subsided, asserted his constant desire to win Britain's friendship, his respect for the Empire, and his liking for Englishmen in general. But genuine as Hitler's expression of admiration for the English appeared to be, it was still apparent to Henderson that their two countries had reached an impasse. As he was leaving the chancellery he was "filled with the gloomiest of forebodings." In the farewell to his German escort, Henderson glumly expressed the fear that he would never again wear a red carnation in Germany.

Later that evening Göring summoned Dahlerus to his residence and revealed a secret: Hitler was working on a *grosszügiges Angebot* (magnanimous offer) to Poland. It was going to be presented the next morning and would include a lasting and just solution of the Corridor by a plebiscite. Once more Göring tore a page out of an atlas and hastily sketched with a green pencil the territory that would be settled by plebiscite; then he outlined in red the area Hitler regarded as pure Polish.

Göring urged Dahlerus to fly immediately to London so he could once more stress Germany's determination to negotiate and "hint confidentially" that Hitler was going to present the Poles with an offer so generous they would be bound to accept.

The next morning was one of reaffirmation for Chamberlain. The most pressing matter on his agenda was Hitler's invitation to the Poles. The Prime Minister's Foreign Secretary was convinced that it was "of course unreasonable to expect that we can produce a Polish representative in Berlin today" nor should the Germans expect it; and his ambassador in

Warsaw telephoned that he saw little chance of inducing the Poles to send Beck or any other representative to Berlin immediately. "They would certainly sooner fight and perish rather than submit to such humiliation especially after the examples of Czechoslovakia, Lithuania and Austria."

Chamberlain himself was now so determined to resist Hitler that he never even asked the Poles if they would submit and by the time Dahlerus was back at 10 Downing Street negotiation seemed impossible. Chamberlain, Wilson and Cadogan listened to the Swede, but their reaction to Hitler's "magnanimous offer" was that it was all talk and only a trick to gain time. Why not phone Göring and find out if the offer had actually been typed up? suggested Dahlerus. In a few minutes he was talking to the Reichsmarschall, who assured him that the note to Poland was not only finished but its terms were more generous than he had predicted.

Encouraged, Dahlerus did his utmost to allay British distrust, going over the terms of the offer with the help of the map Göring had marked up. While the terms seemed reasonable, the British were still disturbed by Hitler's insistence that a Polish delegate present himself in Berlin on the thirtieth, that very day. Beyond the time limit, Chamberlain and his colleagues opposed the place, Berlin. Look what had happened to Tiso and Hacha!

Dahlerus phoned Göring again, this time with the suggestion that the negotiations with Poland take place out of Berlin, preferably in a neutral territory. "Nonsense," was the annoyed reply, "the negotiations must take place in Berlin where Hitler had his headquarters, and anyhow I can see no reason why the Poles should find it difficult to send emissaries to Berlin." Despite the rebuff, as well as their own continuing distrust, the British decided to at least keep the door to peace open. Dahlerus was urged to fly back to Berlin and reassure Hitler that England remained willing to negotiate. Further, as evidence of good faith, Halifax telegraphed Warsaw cautioning the Poles not to fire on troublemakers from their German minority and to stop inflammatory radio propaganda.

The Polish response was to order a general mobilization. Hitler was indignant, for his Foreign Office had spent the day drafting an offer to Poland so generous that his objective interpreter, Schmidt, could scarcely believe his eyes. Besides suggesting a plebiscite in the Corridor under an international commission, it gave the Poles an international road and railway through territory which would become German. "It was a real League of Nations proposal," recalled Schmidt. "I felt I was back in Geneva." Despite his wrath at the Polish mobilization, Hitler instructed Brauchitsch and Keitel to postpone the invasion of Poland another twenty-four hours. This, he said, was the final postponement. Unless his demands were accepted by Warsaw the attack was to begin at 4:30 A.M. September 1. By nightfall there was still no word from Warsaw and the news from London was inconclusive: the British were considering Hitler's latest note "with all urgency" and would send a reply later in the day. In the meantime they advised Colonel Beck to negotiate with the Germans "without delay." It was an ironic request after their own long delay. Perhaps the British irresolution was aroused, if not occasioned, by secret revelations earlier in the day from a German civilian in close contact with the Wehrmacht. Ewald von Kleist-Schmenzin revealed to the British military attaché a number of German military secrets along with an assurance that Hitler had recently suffered a nervous breakdown and the General Staff planned to take advantage of this to stage a military coup.

It was 10 P.M. Berlin time before Henderson finally got permission to present the reply to the Germans. He phoned Ribbentrop proposing they meet at midnight. This happened to be the deadline for the Polish representative to arrive in Berlin and Ribbentrop thought it was deliberate. It was done in all innocence—more time was needed to decipher the London message—but it set an unwholesome atmosphere of suspicion for the interview. After Henderson suggested the Germans follow normal procedure by transmitting their proposals through the Polish Embassy in Berlin, Ribbentrop leaped to his feet. "That's out of the question after what has happened!" he shouted, the last vestige of self-control gone. "We demand that a negotiator empowered by his government with full authority should come here to Berlin."

Henderson's face grew red. London had warned him to keep calm this time and his hands trembled as he read the official answer to Hitler's last memorandum. Ribbentrop fumed as if listening under duress. Undoubtedly he knew its contents since most telephone calls at the British Embassy, particularly the overseas line to London, were being monitored by a German intelligence agency known as the Research Office. The note itself, while conciliatory in tone, offered little more than the previous phone messages of the day.

"That's an unheard-of suggestion!" Ribbentrop angrily interrupted at the suggestion that no aggressive military action take place during the negotiations. Crossing his arms belligerently, he glared at Henderson. "Have you anything more to say?" Perhaps he was paying the ambassador back for yesterday's shouting match with the Führer. The Englishman responded to this rudeness by remarking that His Majesty's Government had information the Germans were committing acts of sabotage in Poland.

This time Ribbentrop was truly enraged. "That's a damned lie of the Polish government!" he shouted. "I can only tell you, Herr Henderson, that the position is damned serious."

Henderson half rose in his seat and shouted in return, "You have just said 'damned!' " He wagged an admonitory finger like an outraged schoolmaster. "That's no word for a statesman to use in so grave a situation."

Ribbentrop looked as if a glass of cold water had been thrown in his face. For a split second he was the picture of shock and indignation. To be reprimanded by an arrogant Englishman! He jumped to his feet. "What did you say?" Henderson was also on his feet and the two men glared at each other like fighting cocks. "According to diplomatic convention," recalled Schmidt, "I too should have risen; but to be frank I did not quite know how an interpreter should behave when speakers passed from words to deeds—and I really feared they might do so now." He kept his seat, pretending to be writing in his notebook. When he heard heavy breathing above, he feared the German Foreign Minister was about to throw His Majesty's ambassador bodily through the doorway. Over the years as interpreter he had rather enjoyed grotesque situations but this one was extremely painful. He heard more heavy breathing to right and left but finally Ribbentrop and then Henderson sat down. Cautiously the interpreter raised his head. All clear. The storm was over.

The conversation continued in relative calm for a few minutes. Then Ribbentrop took a paper out of his pocket. It was Hitler's offer to Poland which had so surprised Schmidt. Ribbentrop began reading the sixteen points in German. Henderson had difficulty in understanding them, he later complained, because Ribbentrop "garbled through" the document at top speed and he asked for the text so he could transmit it to his government. It was such normal diplomatic procedure that Schmidt wondered why the ambassador bothered asking at all and he could scarcely believe what he heard next. "No," said Ribbentrop quietly, with an uneasy smile, "I cannot hand you those proposals." He couldn't explain that the Führer had expressly forbidden him to let the document out of his hand.

Henderson, also unable to believe his ears, repeated his request. Once more Ribbentrop refused, this time emotionally slapping the document on the table. "It is out of date, anyhow," he said, "As the Polish envoy has not appeared."

Watching in agitation, Schmidt suddenly realized that Hitler was playing a game: he feared that if the British passed on the proposals to the Poles they might accept them. It was a mortal sin for an interpreter to make a comment but he did stare fixedly and "invitingly" at Henderson, silently willing him to ask for an English translation. Ribbentrop could hardly refuse such a request and Schmidt was determined to translate with such deliberation that the ambassador could copy every word in longhand. But Henderson did not understand the signal and all the interpreter could do was make a thick red mark in his notebook, a personal notation meaning that the die was cast for war.

Thus ended the stormy interview which, according to Ribbentrop, was conducted "with discourtesy" by Henderson and "with coolness" by himself. Despite the late hour, the Foreign Minister reported immediately to Hitler at the chancellery and suggested that Henderson be given the German proposals in writing. The Führer refused.

3

Early the next morning Henderson telephoned the secretary of the Polish Embassy, warning him that he had information "from an unquestionably accurate source that there would be war if Poland did not undertake to do something within two or three hours."

Every word was taken down by Hitler's wire tappers. So was Henderson's message to London fifteen minutes later, repeating the same information with the comment that while it might be a bluff there was an equal possibility it was not. Although the Germans were still not privy to all the British ciphers, Henderson's indiscreet use of the telephone was making their task easier. (The security in the British Embassy in Rome, incidentally, was even slacker. Lord Perth's safe was regularly burgled each week by a professional thief in the employ of Italian intelligence authorities. Besides copying confidential material that revealed all British diplomatic codes and ciphers, the thief one night appropriated Lady Perth's tiara for himself. But even this loss brought no improvement in the embassy security measures. Fortunately for England, Mussolini was not yet turning over foreign codes and ciphers to his ally.)

The last day of August was a frantic one for men of good will. Dahlerus got permission from Henderson to telephone London and a little after noon was telling Sir Horace Wilson that Hitler's proposals were "extremely liberal." According to Göring, he said, the Führer had put forward such terms with the sole intention of showing the British how anxious he was to secure a friendly settlement with the English. As Dahlerus was speaking, Wilson heard a German voice repeating the words. Realizing the phone was tapped, he instructed Dahlerus to give his information to Henderson, but the amateur diplomat did not get the hint. Nor did he stop when Wilson warned that he should not "get ahead of the clock." Finally Wilson told Dahlerus in plain language to shut up and, when he did not, slammed down the receiver.

While the professional and amateur diplomats were grasping for a peaceful solution, the program for war proceeded relentlessly. That noon Hitler issued the second order for invasion, driven to this extremity (according to A. I. Berndt, his liaison man with DNB) by a gross lie. Berndt thought the reported number of German nationals killed by Poles too small and simply added a nought. At first Hitler refused to believe such a large figure but, when Berndt replied that it may have been somewhat exaggerated but something monstrous must have happened to give rise to such stories, Hitler shouted, "They'll pay for this! Now no one will stop me from teaching these fellows a lesson they'll never forget! I will not have my Germans butchered like cattle!" At this point the Führer went to the phone and, in Berndt's presence, ordered Keitel to issue "Directive No. 1 for the Conduct of the War."

Already prepared, its opening words were tailored to fit the moment: "Since the situation on Germany's eastern frontier has become intolerable and all political possibilities of peaceful settlement have been exhausted, I have decided upon a *solution by force.*" The attack on Poland was definitely set for the following day, Friday, the first of September, and no action would be taken in the West. The directive was hand-carried to all senior commanders, who transmitted, with the greatest possible secrecy, special orders to field commanders. At 4 P.M. the executive order to begin the invasion was confirmed; troops and equipment began moving up to forward positions near the frontier. Simultaneously special orders were transmitted to a secret German unit on the Polish border by the chief of the SS Security Service. Reinhard Heydrich had concocted a diabolical scheme—Operation Himmler—to give Hitler a perfect excuse for launching his attack. SD detachments disguised as Polish soldiers and guerrillas would create incidents along the border the night before the invasion. In exactly four hours they were to attack a forestry station, destroy a German customs building and, most important, briefly occupy the German radio station at Gleiwitz. After shouting anti-German slogans into the microphone the "Poles" would retreat, leaving behind a number of dead bodies as proof that a fight had taken place. The bodies presented no problem. Heydrich had already selected the victims—they were called "canned goods"—from concentration camps.

In Berlin Ambassador Lipski, after a five-and-a-half-hour delay, was finally escorted into Ribbentrop's office at 6:30 P.M. Fatigued and nervous, Lipski read a brief communication stating that his government was "favorably considering" British proposals for direct negotiations between Germany and Poland and would make "a formal reply on the subject within the next few hours." He added pointedly that he had been trying to make this declaration since 1 P.M.

Have you come as an emissary empowered to negotiate? asked Ribbentrop coolly, to which Lipski replied that he merely had instructions "for the time being" to transmit the message he had just read. Ribbentrop protested that he had expected Lipski to come as a fully empowered delegate. "Have you authority to negotiate with us now on the German proposals?" he persisted. Lipski did not. "Well, then there is no point to our continuing the conversation."

So ended one of the briefest interviews in Schmidt's experience. Lipski never asked to see Hitler's sixteen-point proposal and even if Ribbentrop had volunteered it he was not authorized to receive it. He was following his orders "not to enter into any concrete negotiations." The Poles were apparently so confident they could whip the Germans (with help from their allies) that they were not interested in discussing Hitler's offer.

Nor were England and France extending themselves to persuade the Poles to negotiate. When Lipski arrived back at his embassy he attempted to phone Warsaw. The line was dead. The Germans had cut communications. There was no more they needed to know.

At the chancellery Adolf Hitler was conversing with Italian Ambassador Attolico, who had arrived at 7 P.M. Once again Attolico urged peace. Would Hitler agree to Il Duce acting as last-minute mediator? "We must first await the course of events," said the Führer. These now marched on schedule. At exactly 8 P.M. Heydrich's fake "Polish" attack on the radio station at Gleiwitz took place. An hour later all German stations canceled regular programs so that an official statement could be read. The sixteen-point offer was repeated word for word and even unfriendly foreign correspondents were impressed by its reasonableness.

The Poles never for a moment considered accepting the German proposal. Instead of sending a hurried request to resume negotiations that might possibly have thrown Hitler's plot off balance, they retaliated aggressively with their own broadcast at 11 P.M. It charged that the German broadcast clearly exposed Hitler's aims. "Words can no longer veil the aggressive plans of the new Huns. Germany is aiming at the domination of Europe and is canceling the rights of nations with as yet unprecedented cynicism. This impudent proposal shows clearly how necessary were the military orders [mobilization] given by the Polish government."

Ribbentrop went to the chancellery to see how the Führer reacted to the Polish broadcast. Nothing else can be done, said Hitler. Things are now in motion. He was noticeably composed. After weeks of worry and doubt, the course for the future was at last set. He went to bed assured that England and France would not take action. Perhaps the greatest assurance that night to Hitler (he had recently told his military that the treaty with Stalin had been "a pact with Satan to drive out the devil") was a brief message from Moscow that the Supreme Soviet had finally ratified the treaty with Germany after a "brilliant" speech by Molotov.

To Hitler the invasion of Poland was not war, only a coup to seize what was rightfully Germany's. It was a localized action which both England and France, after making face-saving gestures, would surely accept as a fait accompli. Time and again his adjutants had heard him say at the dinner table, "The English will leave the Poles in the lurch as they did the Czechs."

Although intercepts from his own Research Office clearly indicated it was probable that both England and France would intervene in the event of a German-Polish war, Hitler could not bring himself to believe this since (according to his personal adjutant, Schaub) it "disturbed the formation of his intuition." He preferred to put more credence in a personal conviction that neither Britain nor France would act. "England is bluffing," he recently had told his court photographer, then added with a rare impish grin, "And so am I!"

Göring was in his private train when word came that Hitler had made the final decision for war. Beside himself with anger, he got Ribbentrop on the phone. "Now you've got your damned war! It's all your doing!" he shouted and slammed down the receiver. It was ironic. Perhaps no one had warned the Führer more often than Ribbentrop that England would surely fight if pushed to the limit.

4

At four forty-five Friday morning, September 1, the German cruiser *Schleswig-Holstein*, in Danzig harbor on a courtesy visit, began shelling the little peninsula where Poland maintained a military depot and eighty-eight soldiers. Simultaneously artillery fire crashed along the Polish-German border, followed by a massive surge eastward of German infantry and tanks. There was no formal declaration of war but within the hour Hitler broadcast a proclamation to his troops. He had no other choice, he said, "than to meet force with force."

In Rome Il Duce was outwardly calm. A few hours earlier, spurred by his own fear and a deluge of cautionary advice, he had come to a wise but embarrassing decision: Italy would remain neutral. He personally telephoned Attolico and urged him to beg the Führer to send him a telegram releasing him from the obligation of their alliance. Hitler quickly composed an answer that hid his anger. "I am convinced that we can carry out the task imposed upon us with the military forces of Germany," he said and thanked Mussolini for everything he could do in the future "for the common cause of Fascism and National Socialism." He signed the note at 9:40 A.M., then headed for the Kroll Opera House to address the Reichstag. The onlookers were surprised to see Hitler step briskly onto the stage in a tailored field-gray uniform. It looked like military dress but was merely the party uniform in a new color. The audience listened intently as —in a low, raucous voice—he hammered out his case against Poland, point by point, all the time working himself into a state of indignation. He also regretted that the Western powers thought their interests were involved. "I have repeatedly offered England our friendship, and if necessary closest co-operation. Love, however, is not a one-sided affair, but must be responded to by the other side." Eva Braun, in the audience, turned to her sister and whispered, "This means war, Ilse, and he'll leave—what will become of me?"

Perhaps because of its extemporaneous nature, the speech was not one of the Führer's best efforts and Helmut Sündermann, along with others in the Dietrich office, was frantically correcting the grammar and removing the redundancies so a presentable version could be submitted to the press. Hitler went on to promise that he would never wage war against women and children and then announced that Polish soldiers had fired the first shots in German territory and Wehrmacht troops were only returning the fire. "Who fights with poison," he threatened, "will be fought with poison. Who disregards the rules of human warfare can only expect us to take the same steps. I will carry on this fight, no matter against whom, until the safety of the Reich and its rights are secured! . . . From this moment, my whole life shall belong more than ever to my people. I now want to be nothing but the first soldier of the German Reich. Therefore, I have once again put on that uniform which was always so sacred to and dear to me. I shall not take it off until after the victory—or I shall not live to see the end!"

The audience cheered and in the fanatical excitement it went unnoticed that Eva Braun had covered her face and was weeping. "If something happens to him," she finally told her sister, "I will die too." Hitler was announcing that if anything *should* happen to him Göring would be his successor. If the Reichsmarschall fell Hess would take over. It was a unilateral decision, perhaps made on the spur of the moment, and indicated that there was really no longer a German government. The Führer was Germany.

In startling contrast to the wild cheers of "Sieg Heil" in the opera house, the streets outside were almost deathly quiet. The few people abroad were serious as if oppressed with concern for the future. There were no signs of the jubilation as on that August day, twenty-five years before, when the Kaiser announced his war. Today there was no eager young Adolf Hitler in the streets, eyes alight with exultation. In 1914 the majority of Europeans had found relief in war. "We must never forget," wrote D. H. Lawrence of the war which he had vigorously opposed, "that mankind lives by a two-fold motive: the motive of peace and increase, and the motive of contest and martial triumph. As soon as the appetite for martial adventure and triumph in conflict is satisfied, the appetite for peace and increase manifests itself and *vice versa*. It seems a law of life." Between the armistice and today there had been little peace or increase. This generation had no immediate past of dull daily life, no desire for adventure or escape. Aware that the last war had settled nothing, these Germans knew from experience that war was long, tragic and inglorious, that it might radically alter their lives for the worse.

As Eva Braun dejectedly left the opera house with Dr. Brandt, he tried to cheer her up. "Don't worry, Fräulein Braun," he said. "The Führer told me that there will be peace again in three weeks' time." She managed to force a smile.

Henderson telegraphed London that immediately after the speech Hitler had returned to the chancellery and told his generals that "his policy had broken down and that guns alone could now speak. Herr Hitler broke down and left the room without completing the speech." It could have been true. Early that afternoon Göring summoned Dahlerus to the chancellery. Hitler wished to see him. The Führer thanked Dahlerus for all his efforts, then blamed England that they had been in vain. There was now no longer any hope of an agreement. A moment later he interrupted a Göring irrelevancy to say he was determined to crush Polish resistance and annihilate Poland as a nation. If England still wanted to talk, however, he was willing to meet her halfway. Abruptly he began to shout and gesticulate. Göring averted his head in embarrassment. "If England wants to fight for a year, I shall fight two years. . . ." Hitler cut himself short but after a moment's pause bellowed even louder, as his arms milled about wildly. "If England wants to fight for three years, I shall fight for three years!" He clenched his fist and shouted: "And if it is necessary, I will fight ten years!" From a crouch he smashed his fist down so low it almost touched the floor.

When Hitler emerged into the anteroom a little later, however, he appeared to be in a state of "joyful excitement." He exclaimed to Ribbentrop and two of his adjutants that the progress of his troops was beyond his wildest hopes; the entire campaign would be over before the West had time to draw up notes of protest. At this point Otto Abetz, a French expert, offered his unsought opinion that France would declare war. Turning to Ribbentrop, Hitler raised his hands in mock terror. "Please spare me the verdicts of your experts," he said and heaped sarcasm on German diplomats who received the highest salaries, possessed the most modern means of communication, yet always came up with the wrong answer. They had predicted war over conscription, the Rhineland, the annexation of Austria, the Sudeten crisis and the occupation of Prague. His military attachés were just as bad. "Either their wits have been so dulled by their fatiguing breakfast duty that they are unable to get a better over-all picture of the situation in their countries than I can get from Berlin, or my policy does not suit them and they falsify the true position in their reports in order to put obstacles in my path. You must understand, Ribbentrop, that I have at last decided to do without the opinions of people who have misinformed me on a dozen occasions, or even lied to me, and I shall rely on my own judgment, which has in all these cases given me better counsel than the competent experts."

In London, Polish Ambassador Edward Raczynski had already taken it upon himself to call on Lord Halifax at 10 Downing Street and say, on his own responsibility, that his government considered the invasion a case of aggression under Article 1 of the Anglo-Polish Treaty of Mutual Assistance.

"I have very little doubt about it," said Halifax. As the two men emerged into the hall, ministers were already arriving for an emergency cabinet meeting. Sir John Simon, the Chancellor of the Exchequer, grasped Raczynski's hand. "We can shake hands now," he said. "We are all in the same boat. . . . Britain is not in the habit of deserting her friends." Minutes later Chamberlain was suggesting to his cabinet that Hitler be given a final warning: unless hostilities ceased, England would fulfill her obligations to Poland. The message, he warned, should be worded cautiously, not as an ultimatum. Otherwise the Germans might immediately attack British ships.

The world was shocked by the sudden attack even though it was expected. There was no condemnation from the Vatican, which had been secretly exerting pressure on the Polish government, through Cardinal Hlond, to negotiate with Hitler. President Roosevelt's first action was a plea that both belligerents promise not to bomb civilians or "unfortified cities." It was a vow that Hitler had already publicly made and Roosevelt's statement only annoyed him. His irritation escalated to indignation when his chargé in Washington reported that the deputy of the press chief in the U. S. State Department had told the DNB representative: "We only pity you people, your government already stands convicted; they are condemned from one end of the earth to the other; for this bloodbath, if it now comes to war between Britain, France and Germany, will have been absolutely unnecessary. The whole manner of conducting negotiations was as stupid as it could possibly be." Hitler blamed American hostility on the Jewish-controlled press and the Jews around President "Rosenfeld." He retaliated by prohibiting all German Jews, as enemies of the state, from henceforth going outdoors after 8 P.M. in the winter and 9 P.M. in the summer. Before long all Jewish radios would be confiscated.

Late that afternoon the British message to Germany was finally dispatched to Henderson, who was instructed to take it at once, in the company of his French colleague, to Ribbentrop. He should explain that it was a warning, not an ultimatum—but for his own information (and incidentally that of Hitler's wire tappers) that if the German reply was unsatisfactory the next stage would be either an ultimatum with a time limit or an immediate declaration of war.

Henderson and Coulondre arrived at the Wilhelmstrasse just before 9:30 P.M. But Ribbentrop refused to meet them together. First he saw the British ambassador, receiving him with pointed courtesy. Ribbentrop remarked that it was Poland which had provoked Germany and began arguing, though not raucously. This time they did not stand nose to nose but conducted themselves correctly. No sooner had Henderson left than Coulondre entered with an almost identical note from France. Ribbentrop repeated that it was Poland's fault, not Germany's, but promised to pass on the message to Hitler.

In London Chamberlain was telling the Commons about the note sent to Hitler. England's only quarrel with the German people, he said, was that they allowed themselves to be governed by a Nazi government.

"As long as that government exists and pursues the methods it has so persistently followed during the last two years, there will be no peace in Europe. We shall merely pass from one crisis to another, and see one country after another attacked by methods which have now become familiar to us in their sickening technique. We are resolved that these methods must come to an end." There were cheers from all benches.

5

Despite indications that Hitler would resent further attempts at mediation from Rome, Mussolini decided to make a final effort and the next morning suggested a big-power conference to settle the dispute. But the Führer was not enthusiastic while both France and England were reluctant. "There is only one chance," Fritz Hesse in London phoned Hewel of the Wilhelmstrasse, "namely that we immediately move out of Poland and offer reparation payment for damages. If Hitler does that there is probably one chance in a million of avoiding the catastrophe." Within two hours Hewel called back. A deep voice broke in, Ribbentrop's. "You know who is speaking," he said but asked not to be mentioned by name. "Please go immediately to your confidant—you know who I mean [he was referring to Sir Horace Wilson]—and tell him this: the Führer is prepared to move out of Poland and to offer reparation damages provided that we receive Danzig and a road through the Corridor, if England will act as mediator in the German-Polish conflict. You are empowered by the Führer to submit this proposal to the British cabinet and initiate negotiations immediately."

Hesse was flabbergasted. Had a specter of things to come finally dawned on the Führer at the last moment? Or was it just a charade to see how far the British would compromise with the sword of war dangling overhead? Hesse asked Ribbentrop to repeat the offer. He did, adding, "So there will be no misunderstanding, point out again that you are acting on the express instructions of Hitler and that this is no private action of mine."

Hesse phoned 10 Downing Street. He was informed that Wilson would not be available for some time. A few minutes later, at exactly 7:44 P.M., Chamberlain walked into the House of Commons to make his statement. "We waited there exactly like a court awaiting the verdict of the jury," recalled Harold Nicolson. But from the beginning the Prime Minister's speech was a letdown. "His voice betrayed some emotion as if he were sickening for a cold. He is a strange man. We expected one of his dramatic speeches. But none came." After assuring his listeners that His Majesty's Government was bound to take action unless Hitler withdrew his forces from Poland, Chamberlain astounded them by asserting an agreement to do so would return matters to pre-invasion status—"that is to say, the way would be open to discussions between the German and Polish governments of the matters at issue between them, on the understanding that the settlement arrived at was one that safeguarded the vital interests of Poland and was secured by an international guarantee."

In other words, Chamberlain still hesitated. (Later, according to Ambassador Kennedy, he said that the "Americans and the world Jews had forced him into the war.") There were indignant cries of "Speak for England, Arthur!" as acting Labour leader Arthur Greenwood sprang to his feet. "I wonder," he said, "how long we are prepared to vacillate at a time when Britain and all that Britain stands for, and human civilization, are in peril."

A mutiny of the MPs was in the air, many demanding that an ultimatum to Hitler be issued at once without the French. But Chamberlain insisted on acting in concert. At 9:50 P.M. he phoned Daladier and proposed a compromise. Daladier hedged: his cabinet insisted on giving Hitler until noon tomorrow to withdraw from Poland. Almost at the moment they hung up, Hesse arrived at 10 Downing Street to see Wilson. Sir Horace was "visibly impressed" by Hitler's new proposal to quit Poland but was reluctant to present it to the cabinet. The situation, he said, had changed drastically since their last meeting: Roosevelt had secretly promised to help Chamberlain if he declared war and Russia certainly would not fight on Germany's side.

Hesse persisted. "I see in this offer," he said, "the last and only chance to avoid war and also a sign that Hitler recognizes he has made a mistake. Otherwise I would not have this proposal in my hands."

Sir Horace could not believe that Hitler had changed his mind. Would he make a public apology for his acts of violence? If so, there might still be a chance. Such a suggestion, said Hesse, was a psychological error. In Hitler's eyes at least, the responsibility for the present crisis was not solely his. This brought an unusually loud rejoinder from Wilson. Hitler and Hitler alone was responsible for the situation!

"If this proposal fails merely because Hitler won't apologize," said Hesse in desperation, "then the world will believe that Chamberlain wanted the war, inasmuch as he had the chance of avoiding it."

Wilson thought this over. "All right," he said, "repeat your suggestion again; perhaps I can transmit it to the cabinet." After Hesse did so, Sir Horace paced up and down, hands behind his back. There was a knock at the door. A servant handed Wilson a slip of paper. After reading it twice he held it over the flame of a candle, paced anew. Finally he turned to Hesse. "I cannot forward your suggestion to the cabinet," he said. The note undoubtedly was that Chamberlain had just decided to act even if it had to be without France. At 11:30 P.M. the cabinet met once more in emergency session. Chamberlain said he wanted to make a statement to the British people the following noon. "I therefore suggest," he said, "that

Sir Nevile Henderson should be instructed to see Herr von Ribbentrop at 9 A.M. tomorrow, and to say that unless a reply is received by 12 noon a state of war will exist between England and Germany as from that hour." It was possible, he added, that this decision might spur the French to act earlier but he doubted it.

Simon protested that the noon ultimatum would not give Chamberlain time to make his statement to the people; it should be 11 A.M. There was general agreement and the meeting ended. Then came a loud clap of thunder and through the window could be seen a flash of lightning.

The Führer, according to his valet, spent that evening at the chancellery quietly discussing the Polish campaign. But upon reading Hesse's report of the futile meeting with Wilson—it arrived two hours after midnight—he purportedly lost his temper and began blaming Ribbentrop for Italy's refusal to take part in the war. Nor was the harried Foreign Minister's day yet over. At about 4 A.M. the British Embassy telephoned to say that Henderson wished to give Ribbentrop an important communication at 9 A.M. It was obviously a disagreeable message and might even contain an ultimatum. Ribbentrop didn't feel like facing this. He turned to Schmidt, who happened to be on hand, and told him to receive Henderson in his place.

6

Sunday, September 3, dawned clear and balmy. It was a lovely day and ordinarily Berliners would be streaming out to the nearby woods and lakes to enjoy the holiday. Today they were depressed and confused to find themselves at the threshold of a major war.

Of all mornings, this was the one that Schmidt, in bed only a few hours, overslept. Rushing by taxi to the Foreign Office, he saw Henderson enter the building and himself raced into a side entrance. He was standing, somewhat breathless, in Ribbentrop's office as the hour of nine struck and Henderson was announced. The ambassador shook hands but declined Schmidt's invitation to sit down. "I regret that on the instructions of my government," he said with deep emotion, "I have to hand you an ultimatum for the German government." He read out the statement, which called for war unless Germany gave assurances that all troops would be withdrawn from Poland by eleven o'clock, British Summer Time.

Henderson extended the document. "I am sincerely sorry," he said, "that I must hand such a document to you in particular as you have always been most anxious to help." While Henderson would not be remembered for astuteness, retaining as he did a naïve conception of the Führer to the end, he had succeeded in outshouting him and staring down Ribbentrop on successive evenings, feats worthy of some applause.

In a few minutes Schmidt was at the chancellery. He made his way with some difficulty through the crowd gathered outside of the Führer's office. To anxious questions on his mission, he said cryptically, "Classroom dismissed." Hitler was at his desk; Ribbentrop stood by the window. Both turned expectantly as Schmidt entered. He slowly translated the British ultimatum. At last Hitler turned to Ribbentrop and abruptly said, "What now?"

"I assume," said Ribbentrop quietly, "that the French will hand in a similar ultimatum within the hour."

Schmidt was engulfed in the anteroom by eager questions but once he revealed that England was declaring war in two hours there was complete silence. Finally Göring said, "If we lose this war, then God have mercy on us!" Everywhere Schmidt saw grave faces. Even the usually ebullient Goebbels stood in a corner, downcast and self-absorbed.

One man refused to give up hope. Dahlerus located Göring at his private train. Why didn't the Reichsmarschall fly to London and negotiate with the British? Göring was persuaded to telephone Hitler. Surprisingly, he reported, the Führer liked the idea, but first wanted British concurrence. Dahlerus telephoned the counselor at the British Embassy, who replied that the Germans must first answer the ultimatum. Undeterred, Dahlerus phoned the Foreign Office in London. He got the same answer. Still he persisted. He somehow persuaded Göring to ring up Hitler again and suggest sending a conciliatory official reply to the British. Dahlerus waited outside the train, nervously pacing up and down, while Göring talked with the Führer. Finally Göring stepped out of the train, seating himself at a large collapsible table in a stand of beech trees. He muttered that a plane was standing by to take him to England. But Dahlerus concluded from the "disappointed" look on his face that he had been refused by the Führer; but the Swede was not perspicacious (at Nuremberg he dolefully admitted that he had been misled in general by both Hitler and Göring) and could have been taken in by Göring's play-acting. The extent of Dahlerus' naïveté was revealed in his own recorded reaction to the moment: "My blood boiled as I saw the hopelessness of this powerful man. And I could not understand why, knowing what he did, he did not jump into his car, drive to the chancellery and tell them what he really thought —always supposing he really meant all the things he had been telling me for the past two months." So ended the stout, if amateurish, efforts of Dahlerus to prevent war.

At 11:15 A.M. Ambassador Henderson received a message to call upon Ribbentrop. Within fifteen minutes he was handed Germany's reply to the ultimatum—a flat refusal. Henderson looked up from the statement and remarked that it "would be left to history to judge where the blame really lay." Ribbentrop replied that "nobody had striven harder for peace and good relations with England than Herr Hitler had done," and wished Henderson well personally.

At noon loudspeakers in the streets of Berlin blared out the news of war with England to shocked listeners.

London, where it was 11 A.M., was hot and summery and Chamberlain was steeling himself for his broadcast to the people. Fifteen minutes later he announced that England was at war. The British government, he said, had done everything possible to establish peace and had a clear conscience. "Now may God bless you all and may He defend the right."

Even as he was speaking, Coulondre handed over to Ribbentrop France's ultimatum—and was told that France would therefore be the aggressor. But it was England that bore the brunt of Hitler's resentment. He who so readily perceived British weakness had completely failed to judge British strength. His localized war was turning into a general conflagration because of this miscalculation. It was an impasse born of his first crucial mistake: the decision to seize all of Czechoslovakia. If he had not done so and had waited for that country to fall in his lap, it is doubtful that the English would have reacted so positively to his demands on Poland. What Hitler had refused to accept—even though he may have guessed as much —was that an Englishman will go so far but not one inch farther. Despite information to the contrary by Hesse and intelligence reports, Hitler had been misled by his own distorted picture of British character. It was with unprecedented embarrassment, therefore, that he informed Admiral Raeder of the Western ultimatum.

There was little doubt that the occupants of the Kremlin were surprised by the British declaration. "The news of war," reported the Moscow correspondent of the London *Daily Telegraph*, "astonished the Russians. They expected a compromise." Curiously the Soviets showed so little inclination to join the attack on Poland that Ribbentrop invited them to do so in a telegram dispatched early that evening to Ambassador von der Schulenburg. "In our estimation," explained Ribbentrop, "this would be not only a relief for us, but also be in the sense of the Moscow agreements, and in the Soviet interest as well."

Hitler was already preparing to leave the chancellery with his entourage to board a special train bound for the fighting front. Nine minutes before it left Berlin, the Führer sent off a message to the ally who had failed to support him in his greatest crisis. Unlike the telegram to Moscow, this one to Mussolini was sent in the clear and was replete with dramatic phrases. He was aware, said Hitler, that this was "a struggle of life and death" but he had chosen to wage war with "deliberation," and his faith remained as "firm as a rock." As the Führer's train pulled out of the station at exactly 9 P.M. he did not show the confidence of this letter.

One secretary, Gerda Daranowsky, noticed he was very quiet, pale and thoughtful; never before had she seen him like that. And another, Christa Schröder, overheard him say to Hess: "Now, all my work crumbles. I wrote my book for nothing."

But to his valet he seemed the epitome of assurance; there was, he said, nothing to worry about in the West; Britain and France would "break their teeth" on the Westwall. As the train headed east Hitler called Linge to the dining salon and ordered an even more spartan diet from that day on. "You will see to it," he said, "that I have only what the ordinary people of Germany can have. It is my duty to set an example."

Part 7

BY FORCE OF ARMS

VICTORY IN THE WEST
SEPTEMBER 3, 1939–JUNE 25, 1940

1

The invasion of Poland proceeded rapidly. Polish cavalrymen, carrying long lances, were no match for German tanks. In a concentrated land and air attack, the defenders were overwhelmed. Harried from the air by fighter planes, bombers and screeching Stukas, the Polish ground forces were quickly dispersed by a million and a half men supported by heavy self-propelled guns and tanks. It was this incredible mass of Panzers in particular which wreaked havoc. They burst through defenses and ravaged the rear. The Blitzkrieg was almost as terrifying to foreign observers as the victims, for it presaged a frightening turning point in the art of warfare. By morning of September 5 the Polish air force was destroyed, the battle for the Corridor ended. Two days later most of Poland's thirty-five divisions were either routed or surrounded.

Hitler closely followed the action in his special train, designating it as Führer Headquarters even though Jodl's operations staff remained in Berlin. Once he had donned a uniform his way of life changed drastically. Assuming the old role of front-line soldier, he imposed on Führer Headquarters an austere simplicity. His new motto was: "Front-line troops must be assured that their leader shares their privations." Every morning, after dictating orders of the day to Fräulein Schröder, he set out for the battlefield with pistol and oxhide whip. He rode in an open vehicle, weather permitting, so the troops would recognize him while his valet and adjutant tossed out packs of cigarettes. To the wonder of his entourage, he began devoting himself tirelessly to the most minute details of operations. He spent hours, for example, personally inspecting kitchens and mess halls, tyrannically imposing the enlisted man's diet on officers. This aspect of the new regimen soon ended but in all matters of the battlefield he continued to have unflagging interest—that is, with one significant exception. When Schmundt asked him to speak to the first trainload of wounded he could not do so. The sight of their suffering, he confessed, would be intolerable.

As the one-sided campaign drew to a close an unexpected visitor appeared at Führer Headquarters. Fritz Hesse had come to report that the German official delegation in London had been given a friendly farewell not only by their high-ranking British friends but by the population. A crowd outside the embassy had shouted, "See you at Christmas!" Hesse had also come to Poland out of personal concern; he understood he was in disfavor because of his persistence in seeking peace. But Hewel, who presently enjoyed Hitler's complete confidence, assured him that the Führer had sincerely sought negotiations with the British. What provoked him into invading Poland were the reports of atrocities inflicted on German nationals. Hesse could not believe that the order to invade had come in a moment of rage. "Yes, this was without a doubt the cause," insisted Hewel. "And he soon regretted that he had given way to his temper." That was why he had permitted Hesse to negotiate with Sir Horace Wilson after the invasion. "Yes, Hitler would have just liked to say, 'Everybody about face, march, march!'"

"My God," exclaimed Hesse bitterly, "couldn't anyone make it clear to him that although a dictator can order, 'About face, march, march!' it is impossible in a parliamentary nation to cancel a decision for war made after long and thoughtful preparation? How can he imagine such a thing? I always warned that there was a war party in England and that the collapse of Chamberlain's foreign policy would certainly bring victory to this war party. Didn't anyone read this report?"

After a silence the disconcerted Hewel admitted that the Führer had a rather strange concept of the workings of a democracy. "He snorted at me when I tried to explain to him your report on the statements Chamberlain made in the House of Commons. He simply did not want to believe it. Don't be afraid though. In the meantime he has realized your report was correct. But for heaven's sake don't make use of this. Nothing irritates the Führer more than people who were right when he was wrong."

What concerned Hitler more than England—for there was no action at all on the western front—was the reluctance of the Soviet Union to join in the attack on Poland. Apparently Stalin wanted to wait until the last possible moment so as to minimize Red Army losses. It was not until 2 A.M., September 17, that the German ambassador in Moscow was personally informed by Stalin that the Red Army would cross the Polish frontier in several hours. At 4 A.M. local time the Red Army crossed the long eastern frontier of Poland. At one point men of the Polish Frontier Corps saw a horde of horse-drawn carts filled with soldiers coming through the morning mist. "Don't shoot," shouted the Red Army men, "we've come to help you against the Germans." The defenders were so confused—white flags were attached to the leading Russian vehicles—that the Soviets passed through in many places without receiving a shot. It was the end of eastern Poland.

Ribbentrop was not awakened until 8 A.M. and when he learned that Schmidt had let him sleep three hours he shouted angrily, "The German and Russian armies are rushing toward each other—there may be clashes —and all because you were too slack to waken me!" The interpreter tried to calm him by reminding him that a demarcation line had been set up. But the Foreign Minister, his face lathered, continued to rage as he brandished a razor: "You have meddled with the course of world history! You have not enough experience for that!" What really infuriated Ribbentrop, who was up front with a skeleton staff, was that the delay allowed Goebbels and not his own office to issue the news to foreign journalists in Berlin.

The only contest now was between the victors. Before the first day of Russian participation ended the two allies were wrangling over the text of the joint communiqué which would attempt to justify the conquest of Poland. Stalin objected to the German draft ("it presented the facts all too frankly"), then wrote out in his own hand a new version. No sooner had Hitler bowed to this revision than Stalin presented another far more important one: an out-and-out partition of the spoils which would deprive the Poles of even the semblance of independence. On the face of it the Russian proposal was advantageous to Germany but Hitler's suspicion was such that it was four days before Ribbentrop was empowered to endorse it.

The Foreign Minister arrived in the Russian capital at 5:50 P.M., September 27, to negotiate the new treaty. It seemed to have been timed auspiciously since Warsaw had just capitulated to German arms. That was, until Ribbentrop received a warning from Berlin of imminent Soviet attacks on Estonia and Latvia. It was, therefore, with apprehension that Ribbentrop set out for the Kremlin later that evening. He already was sure that Stalin was going to make him a tempting offer but feared the price might be too high. At 10 P.M. the conference began. As expected, Stalin formally offered all Polish territory east of the Vistula, which included most of Poland's populated areas. In return, all he wanted was the third Baltic state, Lithuania.

After the three-hour meeting ended, Ribbentrop sent off a message by telephone to the Führer. Stalin's proposal, he reported, had one very attractive feature, namely that, with control of the bulk of their population, "the Polish national problem might be dealt with as Germany saw fit."

Shrewd Stalin knew his Hitler. Beyond a need for continuing good relations with the Soviets, the Führer could not resist the opportunity of controlling this breeding ground of Jews. He authorized Ribbentrop to sign the treaty and presented Stalin with the last of the Baltic States. It was a heavy price to pay for keeping his rear in the East free while he dealt with the West. On the surface it looked like another instance of opportunism, sacrificing the future for the present. But Hitler was so convinced of the weakness of the Red Army that he must have felt he could easily take back by force what he had given away on paper. During the next day's final negotiations the Soviets insisted that Ribbentrop telephone the Führer for definite approval of all angles of the treaty. Hitler affirmed the agreement although Ribbentrop sensed that it was with some misgivings. "I want to establish quite firm and close relations," he said and when Ribbentrop reported these words Stalin replied laconically, "Hitler knows his business."

Stalin beamed upon Molotov and Ribbentrop as they signed the pact at 5 A.M. on the twenty-ninth, but Ribbentrop's remark that Russians and Germans must never again fight brought an embarrassing silence. Finally Stalin replied, "This ought to be the case." The coolness of the tone and the unusual phrasing impelled Ribbentrop to ask the interpreter for confirmation. A second Stalin remark was equally vague: when Ribbentrop wondered whether the Soviets were willing to go beyond the friendship agreement and conclude an alliance for the coming battles with the West, the answer was: "I shall never allow Germany to become weak." The words were uttered so spontaneously that Ribbentrop concluded they must have expressed Stalin's conviction.

He returned to Berlin still puzzling over the two remarks. Hitler was even more concerned, interpreting Stalin's words to mean that the chasm between their philosophies was too wide for bridging and that a dispute was bound to arise. Only then did the Führer explain that he had made the Lithuanian concession to prove to Stalin "his intention of settling questions with his Eastern neighbor for good and of establishing real confidence from the start." Taking these words at face value as he had those of Stalin, Ribbentrop remained convinced that Hitler really sought a permanent understanding with the Soviets.

While Stalin was digesting the three Baltic States and eastern Poland, Hitler was transforming the rest of that nation into a massive killing ground. He had already ordered Jews from the Reich massed in specific Polish cities having good rail connections. Object: "final solution, which will take some time," as Heydrich explained to SS commanders on September 21. He was talking of the extermination of the Jews, already an open secret among many high-ranking party officials.

These grisly preparations were augmented by a "house cleaning" of Polish intelligentsia, clergy and nobility by five murder squads known as *Einsatzgruppen* (Special Groups). Hitler's hatred of Poles was of relatively recent origin. He was convinced that during the past few years numerous atrocities had been inflicted on the German minority in Poland. "Tens of thousands were carried off, mistreated, and murdered in the most gruesome manner," he told a partisan crowd in Danzig on September 19. "Sadistic beasts vented their perverted instincts—and this democratic, religious world looked on without even a whimper." But, he added, "Almighty God has now blessed our weapons." Now he was getting his revenge. By mid-autumn 3500 intelligentsia (whom Hitler considered "carriers of Polish nationalism") were liquidated. "It is only in this manner," he explained, "that we can acquire the vital territory which we need. After all, who today remembers the extermination of the Armenians!" This terror was accompanied by the ruthless expulsion of 1,200,000 ordinary Poles from their ancestral homes so that Germans from the Baltic and outlying portions of Poland could be properly housed. In the ensuing bitter months more Poles lost their lives in the resettlement from exposure to zero weather than those on the execution list.

2

Even as the SS carried out Hitler's radical program in the East, he turned his attention to the West.* With the better part of Poland his, he sought to end the war with France and England, one way or the other. First he launched a peace offensive in press and radio. "Hitler will again reach an understanding with the English," Hewel assured Fritz Hesse, "and wants to make it as easy as possible for them." The Führer, he said, was also prepared to let Hesse resume his sub rosa negotiations with Sir Horace Wilson so long as Germany was guaranteed an absolutely free hand in the East. Hitler could not agree, for instance, to refrain from attacking Russia. Hesse was puzzled and if it had not been anyone as close to Hitler as Hewel he would have dismissed such a fantastic idea. Why then,

* Since the SS comprised a number of sections, each with different duties and characteristics, each should be judged separately. See Glossary, page 902. The Waffen (armed) SS, for instance, was purely a military aggregation of elitists, and its members' allegiance was to the Reich and Hitler, not Himmler. They fought better than army troops, being better motivated and more democratically organized. There was little differentiation between officers and enlisted men. In the Wehrmacht the men were forbidden to keep their footlockers open so as to prevent stealing; but the Waffen SS considered themselves "a band of brothers" and it was forbidden to lock them. Any stealing was punished by the men themselves; and a thief was cashiered on their recommendation. Many myths about the Waffen SS still persist. Its notorious tattoo, for example, had no sinister symbolism. It was merely a man's blood type in case he was wounded and needed a battlefield transfusion. Himmler, whom the "band of brothers" regarded as an outsider, was not tattooed.

he asked, did the Führer make a pact with Stalin if he intended to attack the Soviet Union?

Hewel explained that Hitler had made the deal for one reason: to keep the English neutral. Since it had failed to do so, he was already thinking of breaking it. Stalin's greed for territory had exasperated the Führer, who had given up the Baltic "only with a bleeding heart." Hesse protested that this completely contradicted Ribbentrop's assessment.

"In Hitler's eyes," was Hewel's surprising reply, "Ribbentrop plays no role at all." Hitler looked upon him merely as a sort of secretary. That was why the Führer had been playing the English game through unofficial channels like Hesse, Göring and Dahlerus. Later that September he encouraged the last to make another trip to London. "The British can have peace if they want it," said Hitler, "but they will have to hurry." But while he talked peace to Dahlerus he was privately determined to make war. Within hours he was telling the commanders of the army, navy and air force of his decision to launch an early attack in the West "since the Franco-British army is not yet prepared." He set the date: November 12. Colonel Warlimont noticed that everyone, including Göring, was "clearly entirely taken aback." The Führer occasionally glanced at a small piece of paper as he gave the background of his decision and outlined the broad directives for operations. He did not, for example, intend to use the Schlieffen plan of 1914 but would attack through Belgium and Luxembourg in approximately a west-northwest direction so as to gain the Channel ports. No one spoke a word in protest and as soon as Hitler finished speaking he tossed his notes into the fire.

Dahlerus, granted free transit by both sides, was back in London on September 28. He talked to Cadogan that morning for more than two hours but the latter predictably was not at all impressed. "He really hadn't much to say," Cadogan wrote in his diary. "He's like a wasp at a picnic—one can't beat him off. He's brought very little from Berlin." Dahlerus was no more successful with Chamberlain and Halifax, but Hitler was not daunted. On October 6 he made a public appeal for peace at the Kroll Opera House. "Why should this war in the West be fought? For restoration of Poland? Poland of the Versailles Treaty will never rise again." The establishment of the Polish state, he said, was a problem to be solved by Russia and Germany—not the West. What other reason was there for war? Admittedly there were numerous problems of great importance which had to be solved sooner or later. Was it not more "sensible" to do so at the conference table before millions of men were uselessly killed and billions of riches destroyed?

Courtship was followed by dire prediction. "Destiny will decide who is right. One thing only is certain. In the course of world history there have never been two victors, but very often only vanquished." He prayed that God might show the Third Reich and all other nations the correct course. "If, however, the opinions of Messrs. Churchill and followers should prevail, this statement will have been my last. Then we shall fight. . . . There will never be another November 1918 in German history!"

Almost certainly Hitler had no intention of accepting a permanent peace with two great powers capable of threatening the Reich's security. A temporary one, however, might enable him to divide France from England and so vanquish them separately. That was why he could speak so sincerely. Throughout Germany there was a feeling of widespread relief over the Führer's plea for peace and even premature celebrations of joy, only slightly dampened by Daladier's quick answer the following day. France, he declared, would never lay down arms until assured of a "real peace and general security." But as the days passed without word from London hope grew in Berlin. The Führer, however, was preparing for the worst. On October 9 he issued Directive No. 6 for the Conduct of War, which outlined an invasion through Luxembourg, Belgium and Holland.

The next morning at eleven, seven of his military commanders reported to the chancellery. Before presenting the new directive Hitler read out a memorandum of his own composition which indicated that he was a student of military and political history. Germany and the West, he said, had been enemies since the dissolution of the First German Reich in 1648 and this struggle "would have to be fought out one way or the other." But he had no objection "to ending the war immediately," so long as the gains in Poland were accepted. His listeners were not asked for comment nor did they volunteer any. They were called upon only to endorse the German war aim: "the destruction of the power and ability of the Western powers ever again to be able to oppose the state consolidation and further development of the German people in Europe."

He acknowledged the objections to haste in launching the attack. But time was on the enemy's side. Because of the Russian treaty and the great victory in Poland, Germany was at last in position—for the first time in many years—to make war on a single front. With the East secured, the Wehrmacht could throw all its forces against England and France. It was a situation that could terminate abruptly. "By no treaty or pact can a lasting neutrality of Soviet Russia be insured with certainty." The greatest safeguard against any Soviet attack lay "in a prompt demonstration of German strength."

Furthermore, hope of Italian support depended primarily on how long Mussolini remained alive. The situation in Rome could change in a flash. So could the neutrality of Belgium, Holland and the United States. Time was working against Germany in many ways. At present she enjoyed military superiority but England and France were closing the gap since their war industries could call upon the resources of most of the world. A long war presented great dangers. The Reich had limited supplies of food and raw materials, and the fount of war production, the Ruhr, was dangerously vulnerable to air attack and long-range artillery.

He proceeded to purely military matters. They must avoid the trench warfare of 1914–18. The attack, he said, would depend on the new tank and air tactics developed in Poland. Panzers would lead the breakthrough. He urged his commanders to improvise, improvise; and illustrated how they could "prevent fronts from becoming stable by massed drives through identified weakly held positions."

It was a brilliant display but almost every one of his commanders remained convinced that the Wehrmacht was not yet prepared or suitably supplied for war with the West. Yet there was not a single objection, not even after the Führer's announcement that the start of the attack could not begin "too early. It is to take place in all circumstances (if at all possible) this autumn."*

In London, Chamberlain was still pondering an answer to Hitler's latest peace offer. As he walked into the cabinet meeting on the day the Führer's invasion directive was issued, he was perturbed by the first enthusiastic American reaction to Hitler's "very attractive series of proposals." He was clear in his own mind that the Hitler speech offered no real advance toward a reasonable peace and he told the cabinet that their reply should be "stiff." The ministers agreed but it was decided to hold up the answer two days.

On the morning of October 11 it was rumored in Berlin that the Chamberlain government had fallen and an armistice was imminent. The old women in the capital's vegetable markets, reported an assistant correspondent on the New York *Herald Tribune*, threw cabbages in the air and wrecked their own stands in sheer joy. A holiday spirit spread through the city until Berlin radio denied the report.

The following afternoon, after a week's delay, Chamberlain finally answered Hitler. He announced in Commons that the German proposals were hereby rejected as "vague and uncertain." If Hitler wanted peace, "acts, not words alone must be forthcoming"; he must supply "convincing proof" that he truly sought peace. Applause from the House was moderate.

In Berlin a circular from the Press Department of the Foreign Ministry was immediately telegraphed, in the clear, to all foreign stations. It denounced the Prime Minister's reply as an outrageous affront. To Hitler the rejection was disappointing but not unexpected. He summoned Göring and the two men responsible for Luftwaffe production—Field Marshal Erhard Milch and Colonel General Ernst Udet. "My attempts to

---

* About this same time he also issued an order legalizing euthanasia for those patients deemed "incurable." Perhaps he was thinking of his mother's suffering from cancer but more likely it was an opportunity to get rid of the mentally ill, the elderly non-productive and those groups he regarded as racially harmful.

make peace with the West have failed," he said. "The war continues. Now we can and must manufacture the bombs."

3

As word spread of Hitler's decision to attack the West, various resistance groups inside Germany concocted plans for coups d'état and assassinations. Some wanted to execute the Führer; others simply to kidnap him and set up either a military junta or a democratic regime. Lists of ministers were drawn up; peace feelers were extended to the United States and other neutrals. The most serious group of conspirators came from the OKW itself and its leading spirit was an impetuous cavalry officer, Colonel Hans Oster. As chief assistant to Admiral Canaris in the *Abwehr*, the Intelligence Service, this impatient, often imprudent man could not have been in a more strategic position. Moreover, he had connections with every faction in the Wehrmacht, private individuals like Schacht, the Foreign Ministry, and even the SS.

Oster found a valuable recruit in a Munich lawyer, Josef Müller, who had detested Hitler for years. Müller—a devout Catholic—made a clandestine trip to Rome early that October with the connivance of Oster, his object to discover if the British were prepared to make peace with an anti-Nazi regime. He met Pius XII and found him willing to act as intermediary. The Pope's secretary sounded out the British minister and was informed that Great Britain was not averse to making a "soft peace" with an anti-Hitler Germany.

Müller was empowered to take this information orally back to Germany but begged for something in writing that would prove to the Abwehr and military commanders that this peace proposal was authorized by the Holy Father himself. Surprisingly, the Vatican agreed and a letter was written by the Pope's private secretary outlining the main bases for peace with England.

The Oster group was cheered. Of all their attempts to make contact with the West, this was the most promising. Perhaps the Pope's promise of participation would at last induce Brauchitsch to take an active part in the conspiracy. But the army commander-in-chief was not impressed. He was convinced that the German people were "all for Hitler." General Halder proved to be almost as timid, but under pressure from Oster and others he finally agreed to help carry out a Putsch. All at once it appeared as if the leading officers were willing to take action. The conspirators were even assured that Brauchitsch himself was prepared to join them if Hitler refused to call off the invasion.

A showdown between army chief and Führer was set for Sunday, November 5—the day the troops were scheduled to move to attack positions on the western front. Brauchitsch appeared as scheduled at the chan-

cellery. After presenting a memorandum, he elaborated on the main arguments against the invasion. It would be impossible, he said, to mount such
a massive offensive in the autumn or spring rains. "It rains on the enemy
too," replied Hitler curtly. In desperation, Brauchitsch argued that the
Polish campaign indicated that the fighting spirit of the German infantryman was far below that of the World War. There were even signs of
insubordination similar to those in 1918.

Hitler had been listening politely, if coolly. This remark enraged him.
"In what units have there been any cases of lack of discipline?" he
demanded. "What happened? Where?" Brauchitsch had deliberately exaggerated "to deter Hitler" and he shrank before such fury. "What action
has been taken by the army commander?" demanded the Führer. "How
many death sentences have been carried out?"

He turned his vitriol on the army. It had never been loyal or had
confidence in his genius and had consistently sabotaged rearmament by
deliberate slowdown methods. The army, in fact, was afraid to fight! Suddenly Hitler spun around and marched out of the room. Brauchitsch was
still in a state of shock when he staggered into army headquarters at Zossen, eighteen miles away, and stammered out an incoherent account of
what had taken place. Almost simultaneously a telephone call from the
chancellery reaffirmed November 12 as the date for invasion. An exact
hour was set—7:15 A.M. General Halder requested written confirmation
and got it immediately by messenger.

The army conspirators now had the necessary documentary evidence
to overthrow Hitler. But there was no call for revolt, no signal for assassination. Instead they furtively burned all incriminating papers. Colonel
Oster alone did not panic; through Count Albrecht von Bernstorff, whose
father had been ambassador to Washington during the Great War, he
warned the Belgian and Netherlands legations to expect an attack at dawn
on November 12.

Sunday's storm in the chancellery was followed by anticlimax. The
Luftwaffe needed five consecutive days of good weather to destroy the
French air force and the meteorological report on Tuesday the seventh
was so unpromising that Hitler postponed A-Day.

Although Hitler knew nothing of the military plot, Göring had
warned him against Brauchitsch and Halder: "My Führer, get rid of these
birds of ill omen." A more definite admonition came from the Swiss astrologer, Karl Ernst Krafft, hired by Himmler's secret intelligence service
as an astral adviser. He had recently submitted a paper indicating that
Hitler would be in danger of assassination between November 7 and 10;
but the document was hastily filed since astrological speculation concerning the Führer was *verboten*.

When Hitler came to Munich on the morning of November 8 to attend the annual reunion of the Old Fighters, Frau Troost, the architect, also sounded a note of warning. She asked why he was so lax about security measures, coming as he did to her studio with only one or two bodyguards. He replied that a man must have faith in Providence, then slapped his trouser pocket. "See, I always carry a pistol but even that would be useless. If my end is decided, only this will protect me." He put hand over heart. "One must listen to an inner voice and believe in one's fate. And I believe very deeply that destiny has selected me for the German nation. So long as I am needed by the people, so long as I am responsible for the life of the Reich, I shall live." He pictured himself as another Christ. "And when I am no longer needed, after my mission is accomplished, then I shall be called away."

Even though the talk switched to architecture, Frau Troost noticed Hitler's uneasiness. "I must change the schedule today," he suddenly said and muttered something about checking with Schaub. But he did nothing, being so occupied with other matters. He visited Unity Mitford, who had shot herself in the temple and was recuperating in a Munich clinic.* By this time she had regained consciousness and when she asked to go home Hitler promised to send her by special train to Switzerland as soon as she was strong enough to travel.

He spent much of the afternoon on a speech he had just decided to make that evening at the Bürgerbräukeller. It would be another attack on England, designed primarily for German ears. The main room of the vast beer hall was already gaily decorated with banners and flags and by late afternoon the microphones were in place and tested. At dusk a small, pale man with a high forehead and clear bright eyes entered carrying a box. He was a skilled artisan named Georg Elser and he had recently been discharged from Dachau concentration camp where he had been held as a Communist sympathizer. His goal was peace and he had come here to kill Hitler. In the box was a timing device connected to sticks of dynamite. As waiters and party officials made the final preparations for the meeting Elser inconspicuously walked up to the gallery and hid behind the pillar rising from the back of the festooned speakers' platform. Several days earlier he had cut the wooden paneling of the pillar with a special saw—he was a cabinetmaker as well as a mechanic—fixed several hinges and replaced the piece of wood as a little door.

* "If it comes to war," Unity Mitford told her sister Diana at the Bayreuth Festival, "I shall kill myself." She did not care to live, she said, if the two countries she loved took up arms against each other. After the radio blared out the news of England's declaration of war she walked into the English Gardens, and tried to kill herself with a small pistol. She was taken to a clinic in the Nussbaumstrasse where, at Hitler's orders, she was treated by a distinguished surgeon, Professor Magnus. He decided it was too dangerous to extract the bullet still lodged in her temple. News of the suicide attempt was suppressed: Unity's parents were informed discreetly through the German minister in Berne.

At last the lights of the hall were extinguished, the doors closed. Elser waited another half hour, then placed the bomb in the pillar and set it to detonate at about 11:20 P.M. The Führer would start speaking at 10 P.M. and the explosion would come midway in the speech.*

At his apartment on the Prinzregentenplatz, Hitler summoned his young ordnance officer, Max Wünsche. Would it be possible, he asked, to leave Munich earlier than planned? Wünsche assured him it would be no problem; there were always two trains at the Führer's disposal as a security precaution. The young man immediately made arrangements to use the early one.

The Führer was greeted at the Bürgerbräukeller with such wild acclaim that he did not begin speaking until ten minutes past ten. His audience reveled in the insults and jibes he heaped upon the English. It took little, in fact, to draw applause and there were so many interruptions that Wünsche, seated in the front row, feared the Führer would miss the early train.

At 11:07 P.M. Hitler unexpectedly brought his tirade to a hurried conclusion. A few yards away, inside the pillar, Elser's clock was ticking. In thirteen minutes the bomb was supposed to explode. Ordinarily Hitler spent considerable time after a speech chatting with the comrades of the Putsch but tonight, without shaking hands, he rushed out of the building accompanied by Hess and several adjutants and into the car waiting outside. Kempka headed directly for the railroad station. Before they arrived —exactly eight minutes after Hitler left the Bürgerbräukeller—Wünsche heard a distant explosion. He wondered what it was. If Hitler heard the noise he did not think it worth mentioning.

In the hubbub that followed the explosion—the shrieking of sirens from police cars and ambulances—a rumor started that the war was over. It might have been if Hitler had been standing on the platform. He surely would have died. The bomb killed seven and wounded sixty-three, including Eva Braun's father, who had gained admission thanks to a special low-numbered membership card, though he was actually party member No. 5,021,670. His daughter, accompanied by her best friend, Herta Schneider, arrived at the station just as the Führer's train was leaving. Aboard they found an air of carefree gaiety. No one knew of the explosion and almost everyone was drinking. The lone teetotaler, Hitler, was animated but it was Goebbels who enlivened the conversation with his caustic wit.

At Nuremberg the propaganda chief left the train to send several

* There had already been a number of attempts to assassinate Hitler. One he knew nothing about was plotted by a disillusioned SS guard who, about 1929, planted a bomb under the podium just before a speech in the Sportpalast. During the speech the malcontented SS man had a sudden urge to go to the toilet; by chance someone locked him in the men's room and he was unable to set off the bomb. "It was the joke of the century," recalled a friend of the would-be assassin. "The history of the world might have been changed if he hadn't had to go to the bathroom."

messages and gather the latest news. When he returned to the Führer's compartment he told of the bomb in a trembling voice. Hitler thought it was a joke until he noticed Goebbels' pale face. His own became a grim mask. Finally in a voice hoarse with emotion he exclaimed, "Now I am completely content! The fact that I left the Bürgerbräukeller earlier than usual is a corroboration of Providence's intention to let me reach my goal."

First he demanded information on the wounded and charged Schaub with the task of doing everything possible for them, then he began to hypothesize out loud on possible conspirators. He concluded that the bombing must have been planned by two known British intelligence agents. Captain S. Payne Best and Major R. Stevens were privately negotiating with one of Heydrich's secret agents who was posing as an OKW captain in the anti-Nazi conspiracy. Acting immediately on Hitler's conjecture, Himmler detrained and telephoned an order to kidnap the two Britons in Holland.

The following afternoon Stevens and Best were trapped in Venlo and brought across the border to Germany for questioning. Hours later the real bomber was arrested at the Swiss border and returned to Munich. Under glaring arc lights in an interrogation room at Gestapo headquarters Elser admitted he had planted the bomb. No, he had no accomplices. He had done it to end the war. He described in detail how he had cut the panel and come back to set the clock.

Upon reading the Gestapo report Hitler angrily scrawled on it: "What idiot conducted this interrogation?" It was ridiculous, he thought, to imagine that Elser was a lone wolf. Wasn't it obvious that this was a wide conspiracy involving his worst enemies: the English, the Jews, the Freemasons and Otto Strasser?

Himmler personally tried to beat the truth out of the prisoner. According to one witness, he cursed wildly as he drove his boots hard into the body of the handcuffed Elser. Despite the kicks and a beating "with a whip or some similar instrument," the little cabinetmaker stubbornly held to his testimony. Even under hypnosis, Elser repeated his story. This convinced Heydrich that Elser had no accomplice, but the Führer bitterly reproached Himmler for failing to find the real criminals.*

---

* Perhaps that is why Himmler saw to it that Elser was not brought to public trial and executed. Instead he was installed as a privileged prisoner in a concentration camp; Elser alone could confirm that the SD had, in fact, found the one and only criminal. Later Elser smuggled a letter to Captain Best, a fellow prisoner. In it he swore that he had been summoned to the office of the commandant of Dachau in October 1939 where two men—presumably Heydrich agents—persuaded him to plant a bomb in the Bürgerbräukeller. It was to explode as soon as Hitler left the building and kill a group of traitors who were plotting against the Führer. Elser agreed and was released from the concentration camp to install the bomb. At Berlin Gestapo headquarters he was told by the same two agents that he was going to be used as a prosecution witness at a trial of the English agents. He would testify that Otto Strasser had introduced him to Best and Stevens, who paid him to plant the bomb. But Best and Stevens were never tried and survived five years in various concentration camps.

The official version of the plot was bizarre: Elser was a Communist "deviationist" who had been persuaded by the National Socialist "deviationist," Otto Strasser, to become the tool of the British Secret Service. To this main plot propagandists added subplots. One pamphlet claimed that the English agents not only set off the bomb in Munich but were responsible for the political murders and mysterious deaths of such notable figures as Lord Kitchener, Archduke Franz Ferdinand and King Alexander of Yugoslavia.

Besides inciting hatred for England, the attempted assassination was exploited to bolster the Führer's popularity. Messages of congratulation on his narrow escape arrived from Germans on every level of society. The Catholic press throughout the Reich piously declared that it was the miraculous working of Providence which had protected the Führer. Cardinal Faulhaber sent a telegram and instructed that a Te Deum be sung in the cathedral of Munich, "to thank Divine Providence in the name of the archdiocese for the Führer's fortunate escape." The Pope, who had yet to explicitly condemn Germany's liquidation of Poland, sent his special personal congratulations. But Hitler doubted his sincerity. "He would much rather have seen the plot succeed," he told a group at dinner and, when Frank protested that Pius XII had always been a good friend of Germany, added "That's possible but he's no friend of mine."

Hitler gave thanks to his own inner voice as well as to Providence for quitting the beer hall ahead of time. He told Hoffmann: "I had the most extraordinary feeling and I don't myself know how or why—but I felt compelled to leave the cellar just as quickly as I could." Foreign observers, however, had other theories. "Most of us think it smells of another Reichstag fire," wrote Shirer in his diary.

4

Twelve days after the bombing Hitler issued War Directive No. 8. The land invasion would be conducted as planned but he forbade bombardment of centers of population in Holland, Belgium and Luxembourg "without compelling military necessity." This was more pragmatic than humanitarian and revealed Hitler's ultimate goal. His real intent in attacking the West was to secure his rear for the assault on Russia, not to conquer territory in Europe or destroy England, which might later be inveigled into condoning his drive to the East.

A few days later he called a special conference, this time inviting not only his commanders-in-chief but those who would lead the attack. The meeting took place in the chancellery at noon, November 23, and began on a low key. "The purpose of this conference," he explained, "is to give you an idea of the world of my thoughts, which governs me in the face of future events, and to tell you my decisions." Next he revealed what all his listeners should have already known: that the military with its proud tradition had degenerated into a subservient weapon of a one-man dictatorship. "I have doubted for a long time whether I should strike in the East and then in the West," he said. "Basically I did not organize the armed forces in order *not* to strike. The decision to strike was always in me. Sooner or later I wanted to solve the problem."

It was an open declaration of mastery but there was not a murmur of dissent. It would have defied understanding, so Göring testified later, if any of those present *had* protested. "The Supreme Commander had decided and therefore there was nothing left for a soldier to discuss; and that applies to a field marshal as well as to the ordinary soldier."

Hitler went on to say, "in all modesty," that he was irreplaceable. "The fate of the Reich depends only on me. I shall deal accordingly." He admitted that his entire plan was a gamble, yet somehow made his admission aggressive. "I have to choose between victory or destruction," he said. "I choose victory." It was a historical choice, to be compared with the momentous decision of Frederick the Great before the First Silesian War. "I have decided to live my life so that I can stand unashamed if I have to die." Remarkably, he ended with a grim prophecy of his own fate. "I shall stand or fall in this struggle. I shall never survive the defeat of my people." These were truthful words. For Hitler there was only black or white; only complete victory or Götterdämmerung.

That afternoon Hitler read Brauchitsch and Halder a personal lecture on the defeatism of the army high command. Stricken, the former offered his resignation. But Hitler refused to accept it, reminding him that a general had to fulfill his duty and obligation "just like every other soldier." It had been a harrowing day for the military, one described with eloquent brevity in Halder's diary: "A day of crisis!" Both he and Brauchitsch had been so thoroughly cowed by Hitler's threat to annihilate everyone who stood in his way that they made frantic efforts to disassociate themselves from the Resistance.

Exactly one week later it was Stalin's turn to startle the world. On November 30 he invaded Finland, which had repelled a Communist rebellion in 1918 with the help of German troops. It was an embarrassment for Hitler, not only because of the extremely friendly relations between Germans and Finns but also because it weakened the already tenuous bonds with Mussolini. The Italians, from the first opponents of the Russo-German pact, were as indignant over the unprovoked Soviet invasion of Finland as the West. The official organ of the papacy, *Osservatore Romano*, which had followed the Pope's lead in failing to condemn Fascist or Nazi incursions, now joined him in excoriating the Soviet attack as a calculated act of aggression. So much pressure was exerted on Mussolini from church and civilian sources that, "for the first time," wrote Ciano, "he desired German defeat." In fact, on December 26 he authorized his son-in-law to inform the representatives of Belgium and Holland that they were about to be invaded by Hitler.*

For a week Mussolini was in a turmoil, vacillating between fear that his ally might succeed and hope that he would. On New Year's Eve he considered entering the war on Hitler's side but when signs multiplied that Germany was on the point of invading the West he sat down and in the role of big brother wrote his junior partner a letter of advice. Never had Il Duce spoken out so boldly and his own frankness concerned him so that it was not until January 5, 1940, that he finally gave Ciano permission to send it off. He urged Hitler to refrain from invading the West. Both sides would lose such a war. "Now that you have secured your eastern frontiers and created the Greater Reich of ninety million inhabitants, is it worth while to risk all—including the regime—and sacrifice the flower of German generations in order to hasten the fall of a fruit which must of necessity fall and be harvested by us, who represent the new forces of Europe? The big democracies carry within themselves the seeds of their decadence."

He then criticized the treaty with Russia in a manner that he must have known would provoke the Führer. "I feel that you cannot abandon the anti-Semitic and anti-Bolshevist banner which you have been flying for twenty years and for which so many of your comrades have died; you cannot renounce your gospel, in which the German people have blindly believed." Four months ago the Soviet Union was world enemy number one; how could she now be friend number one? "The day when we shall have demolished Bolshevism we shall have kept faith with our two Revolutions."

Attolico delivered this unique letter by hand on the afternoon of January 8. The Führer, understandably, was in no mood to answer and put it aside. This was the high point of Mussolini's effort to free himself from domination by his ally but, having asserted himself, he experienced an almost immediate predictable reaction and began slipping back into his servile role.

5

Neither Hitler nor Mussolini knew that the British were seriously considering declaring war on the U.S.S.R. over the Finnish invasion, thanks in large part to the pressure exerted by church groups and the Cliveden Set, which argued that the real enemy was Red Russia, not Germany. After all, Hitler's demands on Poland were reasonable and only his manner was obnoxious. In the meantime the shooting war against Hitler

* The Belgian ambassador in Rome rashly transmitted this warning to Brussels by telegram. The message was intercepted and deciphered by the Germans.

had diminished to one in name only. On a train trip skirting the French frontier, the crew told William Shirer that not a shot had been fired on this front since the war began. Then he saw for himself that both sides seemed to be observing an unofficial armistice. "For that matter one blast from a French '75' could have liquidated our train. The Germans were hauling up guns and supplies on the railroad line, but the French did not disturb them. Queer kind of war." So queer, in fact, that when a former First Lord of the Admiralty suggested that the RAF bomb the timber areas of southwestern Germany, the British Air Minister, Sir Kingsley Wood, replied: "Oh, you can't do that. That's private property. You'll be asking me to bomb the Ruhr next."

Hitler's main offensive weapon in these unsettled days was Goebbels, brought back to full favor by the outbreak of war. The force of his propaganda campaign was directed against the French; his purpose was to divide them from the British. Goebbels visited the Westwall in the bitter rain and snow so he could determine first hand what the poilu a few hundred yards away in the Maginot Line was experiencing. He concluded that the average French soldier was so weary, miserable and bored that he would be a ready victim of his concerns and prejudices. "Goebbels knew," recalled his secretary, Werner Naumann, "that the average little French soldier only wanted a good bed, a woman, a warm room, his garden and peace of mind." He worried about the Jews, the English and, above all, this ridiculous war. The Propaganda Minister, therefore, instructed German soldiers to shout friendly greetings across no man's land and engage the French in brotherly conversation. Propaganda teams blasted information and news over loudspeakers, aimed at proving that France and Germany were really not enemies. At night sentimental French songs were broadcast to the Maginot Line and before signing off the announcer would say something like: "Good night, dear enemy, we don't like this war any more than you do. Who is responsible? Not you or I and so why shoot each other? Another day has ended and we will all have a good night's sleep." The final touch would be a recorded lullaby. In the daytime the French troops were showered with leaflets showing a shivering poilu at the front in one picture and his wife in bed with an English soldier in another.

The French civilians were approached differently. They were bombarded with broadcasts over secret transmitters illustrating the corruption of their government, the profiteering of Jews and the terrifying might of Hitler's army and air force. One particularly effective leaflet was a German version of the prophecies of Nostradamus which foretold the conquest of France by the Third Reich.

At home Goebbels ordered Germans to harden themselves for the coming battle. Their very existence was at stake since the enemy was "determined to annihilate Germany for good." In mid-December he forbade newspapers to print a word about peace. "In line with this point of view any sentimental note in connection with Christmas must be avoided in the press and on the radio." Only one day would be celebrated, December 24. To unite front and homeland, the theme of 1939's radio Christmas program would be: "Soldiers' Christmas—People's Christmas."

The British soldiers in France were not at all concerned by Goebbels' propaganda. The war, in fact, had turned into a contest of lame jokes. British civilians were as bored as their troops and referred to it as the *Sitzkrieg* or Phony War. More and more members of Parliament dozed as Chamberlain read off his weekly reports.

Hitler was waiting for a stretch of five clear days to turn a joke into grim battle. His own air chief was in a quandary. Göring had to give the impression of being eager while privately praying for a continuation of the bad weather since he feared his Luftwaffe was not yet ready for combat. He attended the daily weather conferences, pestering Chief Meteorologist Diesing for additional information. Hitler also pressed Diesing for longer-range forecasts but he stubbornly refused. "Mein Führer," he replied, "I will gladly be bold and predict weather for three days; but not foolhardy—not five days!"

In desperation Göring hired a rainmaker, Herr Schwefler, for 100,000 marks. It is not clear whether the field marshal ordered him to bring five clear days or to continue the bad weather but it would not have made any difference since Schwefler's only equipment turned out to be a defunct commercial radio set. On the other hand, Milch was hoping for good weather since he agreed with Hitler that time was on the side of the enemy. Despite its deficiencies, the Luftwaffe still enjoyed air superiority, an advantage that was steadily decreasing with the flow of planes to both England and France from the United States.

⚡ On January 10, 1940, the impatient Führer fixed another specific date for invasion: a week later at exactly fifteen minutes before sunrise. Fate intervened before the day was over. A light Luftwaffe plane strayed across the frontier, crash-landing in Belgium. Of all of the German planes in the sky that day, this was the most important. It carried an unauthorized passenger, Major Helmut Reinberger, who had a briefcase filled with the operation plans for the airborne attack on Belgium. While Reinberger was burning the papers he was seized by Belgian soldiers; but he reported optimistically to Luftwaffe headquarters through the German Embassy in Brussels that he had succeeded in burning the plans to "insignificant fragments, the size of the palm of his hand." Göring, in a state of consternation, experimented by burning a similar packet of papers. The results were so inconclusive that his wife suggested using clairvoyants, not unusual advice to a man who utilized a rainmaker. The team of clairvoyants unanimously agreed that not a scrap of the documents remained.

Their report may have relieved Göring but not Hitler. He canceled the invasion order on the assumption that the plans had been revealed to the enemy. He, not the clairvoyants, was correct. Enough fragments had remained for the Belgians to learn of the invasion. This information was passed on to London where it was received with considerable suspicion. Halifax, for instance, told the cabinet, "I doubt very much whether the documents are genuine." The General Staff agreed; obviously the papers had been planted. They were engrossed in their own offensive, the landing of an expeditionary force in Norway. The very concept of such a *coup de main* appealed to Churchill, the new First Lord of the Admiralty; and, despite his sad experience in a similar venture in the Great War, he pressed the issue until the cabinet was won over.

Hitler was also preparing to seize Norway. He had not even considered such action—after all, these were Nordic peoples who could be counted on to remain neutral as they had in 1914—until his ally, Stalin, upset calculations by invading Finland. This, Hitler feared, might give the Allies an excuse to move into Norway, thus outflanking Germany from the north. He authorized a study of a possible invasion but it was given low priority. Then, late in February, alarming reports of an imminent British landing in Scandinavia turned the Führer into an ardent advocate—out of concern that a British foothold in Norway would close off the Baltic and bottle up all his submarines. Equally foreboding was the economic threat. More than half of Germany's iron ore came from Norway and Sweden; an end to this supply would cripple her war production. On March 1, 1940, therefore, Hitler issued a directive for the simultaneous occupation of Denmark and Norway. It was to have "the character of a *peaceful* occupation, designed to protect by force of arms the neutrality of the northern countries," but resistance would be "broken by all means available."

Hitler became so concerned by the time element that within two days he decided to launch his attack—the "most daring and most important undertaking in the history of warfare"—before invading the West. It would begin on March 15.

In the meantime he had been attempting to shore up deteriorating relations with his two allies. Those with Russia, in particular, had entered a disturbing phase. Negotiations for a trade agreement had started soon after the conquest of Poland. A visit of a thirty-seven-man German economic delegation to Moscow was followed by an even larger Soviet mission to Berlin, which brought a list of industrial and military orders totaling more than one and a half billion Reichsmarks. The Germans were dismayed since most of the orders were for machinery and armaments essential to their own war production. The result was a bitter and lengthy wrangle finally brought to a head by Stalin himself. He querulously declared that if Germany did not give way "the treaty would not be concluded."

Hitler could not permit this, and early in February Ribbentrop was instructed to send a personal letter to Stalin urging him to re-examine the German position. Apparently Stalin, whose hardheaded negotiations had already wrung concessions from the Germans, realized he had pushed his ally to the limit. (Two months earlier his archenemy, Trotsky, had observed: "Before the hour of Hitler's defeat strikes, many, very many in Europe will be wiped out. Stalin does not want to be among them and so he is wary of detaching himself from Hitler too early.") In one of his lightning changes, Stalin called for an end of bickering. He agreed to accept German deliveries over a period of twenty-seven months while promising delivery of raw materials over a period of eighteen months. With all difficulties removed, the trade pact was signed three days later. The German delegation was delighted. "The agreement," reported the chairman, "means a wide-open door to the East for us."

Hitler was pleased as well as relieved. He had become even more fascinated by his counterpart in the Kremlin. Stalin was the only world leader he wanted to know intimately and he interrogated envoys from Russia at length for the most trivial details about his ally. Often, recalled Christa Schröder, he would interrupt to exclaim enthusiastically, "That Stalin is a brute, but really you must admit he's an extraordinary fellow." It was almost as if he were talking about himself.

The solution of this Russian problem was accompanied by the termination of another when the Finns were forced to accept harsh Soviet peace terms that March to end their brief, bloody war. Greatly relieved at being freed from the embarrassment of having to give moral support to such an unpopular cause, Hitler turned to more productive arenas. One of these was Italy. He had just made a step in this direction by finally answering Mussolini's letter of unwelcome advice. Hitler vindicated all his actions in minute detail, taking time out to rhapsodize about Italy, using as many italicized words as a schoolgirl writing of her latest crush.

Naturally a letter delayed so long could only be delivered by a prestigious messenger. And so the following day, March 9, Foreign Minister von Ribbentrop left Berlin with a large retinue: advisers, secretaries, barbers, a doctor, a gymnastics teacher and a masseur. At their first meeting Il Duce gave a guarded answer to Ribbentrop's question: Would Italy participate in the war? He intended, he said, "to intervene in the conflict and to fight a war parallel to that of Germany." *But* he must be free to choose the date. Ribbentrop attempted in vain to tie Mussolini down more definitely but he would merely agree to see Hitler. The following Monday, March 18, the two dictators met at the Brenner Pass in a snowstorm. The session was cordial with Hitler dominating the conversation. But he spoke quietly and made few gestures. He had come, he said, "simply to explain the situation" so Il Duce could make his own decision.

To Schmidt's surprise, Mussolini used his few minutes of talk to reassert emphatically his intention of coming into the war. It was merely a matter of choosing the best moment, he said. The two men departed in an aura of eternal trust and friendship. But Hitler instructed Schmidt not to submit a copy of the interview to the Italians. "One never knows who may read this document on the Italian side, and what Allied diplomats may be told." For his part, Il Duce seemed to belie his recent vow to join the war. On the return trip to Rome he pointed out the train window to the thick fall of snowflakes with the remark that he would need snow as far south as Etna to turn Italians into a race of warriors. Although irritated that the Führer had done almost all the talking, he was now convinced his ally was not preparing to launch any land offensive.

6

Recently the Schirachs had come upon the Führer in the chancellery library reading a book with the help of glasses.* He hurriedly put them away (Hoffmann was forbidden to take pictures when he wore them) and rubbed his eyes. "You see," he confessed, "I need glasses. I am getting old and that is why I prefer to wage war at fifty rather than sixty." He ruffled the pages of his book, a picture album containing photographs of London. "How gratifying not to find any baroque buildings," he murmured, then snapped the book shut. "I must not look at this sort of thing any more."

He was determined that Germany should be first in Norway and on April 2 ordered the invasion to begin at 5:15 A.M. a week later. The anti-Hitler conspirators were just as determined to hamstring the invasion. To do so they needed Halder. He had recently promised to help but was wavering and, to bring him to action, he was shown Müller's memorandum summarizing the Pope's participation in secret peace negotiations with the English. The chief of the army General Staff was impressed but reduced to tears. His conscience, he sobbed, would not permit him to act.

The failure of this plot failed to discourage the redoubtable Colonel Oster. He decided to stop Hitler by personal action and early in April secretly informed the Dutch military attaché that Norway was about to be invaded. But the information was forwarded to a member of the Norwegian Legation in Berlin who did not think it worth relaying to Oslo. The British also failed to believe similar reports that Hitler was doing what they themselves planned to do a day or so later. Remarkably, an aura of overconfidence had enveloped 10 Downing Street.

On Sunday morning, April 7, five German naval groups put to sea destined for six Norwegian cities. At three of these ports—Narvik, Trondheim and Stavanger—waited German merchant ships with combat troops hidden in their holds. British ships were laying mines in Norwegian

* Hitler's secretaries used a special large-print typewriter so he could read in public without glasses.

waters below Narvik in preparation for their own invasion and HMS *Glowworm* sighted two German destroyers. It was assumed in London that these ships were part of a limited force intent on capturing Narvik. Not until Monday morning did the cabinet learn that enemy warships were also approaching at least three other Norwegian ports. The ministers were aghast but it was too late to thwart Hitler.

Early Tuesday morning the Germans struck. By 8 A.M. Narvik was seized by two battalions of special mountain troops under the command of Brigadier General Eduard Dietl, an intimate of the Führer since the Beer Hall Putsch. Before noon four other important ports fell but the raiders were delayed long enough by defenders in the ancient fortress of Oskarberg to allow the royal family, the government and members of Parliament to escape from Oslo by special train while twenty-three trucks were carting off the gold of the Bank of Norway and the secret papers of the Foreign Office.

In Denmark the Germans met little resistance, their plan working as it had been laid out on paper. For some reason the Danish navy never opened fire and the land troops only managed to inflict twenty casualties on the invaders. It was all over by midmorning. The King capitulated, ordering all resistance to cease. He assured the chief of staff of the German task force that he would do everything possible to keep peace and order in the country. Then he turned complimentary. "You Germans," he said, "have done the incredible again! One must admit that it is magnificent work!"

By the end of the day it appeared as if Hitler had scored a complete triumph in Norway as well—until the British navy unexpectedly appeared. On Wednesday morning five destroyers broke into Narvik harbor to sink two destroyers and all but one cargo ship. Three days later the *Warspite* returned with a flotilla of destroyers and sank the rest of the German vessels.

This news so agitated Hitler that he told Brauchitsch it didn't look as though they could possibly hold Narvik. By April 17 his vexation was apparent. He railed at everyone in sight. While Brauchitsch, Keitel and Halder held their tongues, Chief of Operations Jodl brusquely announced that there was but one thing to do: "Concentrate, hold on and do not give up." To the consternation of the onlookers, he and Hitler began arguing as if they were equals. Finally, in a temper, the chief of operations stormed out of the room, slamming the door. Hitler said not a word. Tight-lipped, he left by another door but that night he signed an order to Dietl: "Hold on as long as possible." The nineteenth brought a new crisis. From his hide-out on the rugged northern coast of Norway, King Haakon VII, the sole monarch of the century elected to the throne by popular vote, steadfastly refused to name a government headed by Vidkun Quisling, the leader of a Norwegian Fascist party and a disciple of Rosenberg.

By this time the British had finally landed two brigades of 13,000 men near Narvik and Trondheim. As their attack gained momentum more British arrived, and by the end of the week the Germans were in desperate straits. But Milch came to the rescue by taking personal command of the Luftwaffe attack. He sent two huge seaplanes loaded with mountain troops to Narvik; then supervised dive-bombing strikes that weakened the British and Norwegian resistance in central Norway. By April 28 the British ordered evacuation of the bulk of their troops. The following day King Haakon and members of his government were transferred by British cruiser to Tromsö, a city far above the Arctic Circle, where a provisional capital was established.

Most of Norway was now under German control except for Narvik where Dietl's 6000 men still gallantly held off 20,000 Allied troops. On the last day of April Jodl informed Hitler that communications had finally been established overland between Oslo and Trondheim. At lunch Hitler, "beside himself with joy," admitted his error and thanked Jodl for his contributions to the victory. The Führer also showed his gratitude to Dietl and Milch with promotions. He was unstinting in his praise of the latter, remarking at one conference how Milch had taken over the Luftwaffe in Norway when it appeared that all was lost. "And why?" he asked rhetorically, conveniently forgetting his own argument with Jodl. "Because there was a man like me, who just did not know the word 'impossible.'"

With the northern flank secure, Hitler again devoted his energy to the invasion of the West. He had never liked the original plan of attack, an unimaginative version of that used in the World War: an attack through northern France and Belgium to the Channel ports. Its objective was not only to smash the French army but, by occupying the Channel coast, to cut the British off from their ally while establishing submarine and air bases for attacks on the British Isles.

"This is just the old Schlieffen plan," he objected to Keitel and Jodl, "with a strong right flank along the Atlantic coast; you won't get away with an operation like that twice running." Even if it succeeded, it violated his principle of Blitzkrieg warfare and he had vowed never to allow this generation to suffer what *he* had in Flanders. He envisioned a daring thrust farther south through the Ardennes with a sudden armored breakthrough at Sedan and a sweep to the Channel. The main force would then swing to the north, in a reversal of the Schlieffen plan, for a drive into the rear of the retreating Anglo-French army. Night after night his adjutants would see him poring over a specially constructed relief map to make sure that the Sedan was, after all, the correct place to penetrate.

Independently, perhaps the most brilliant strategist of the Wehrmacht, Colonel General Fritz Erich von Manstein, had devised a similar offensive. He presented it to Brauchitsch, who rejected it on the grounds that it was too risky. But the Führer heard talk of Manstein's "risky" proposal and asked him for the details. To Manstein's surprise, Hitler was delighted with what he heard. It not only reinforced his own convictions but contained a number of improvements to his own plan. The supreme command liked Hitler's revised version no more than they had Manstein's. To a man they opposed it but the Führer overrode all objections, deriding opponents as "Schlieffen worshipers," embalmed in a "petrified" strategy. "They should have read more Karl May!"

The Hitler-Manstein offensive was formally adopted in late February and by the time the battle for Norway was ended there were 136 German divisions ready for action along the western front. They waited only for a stretch of good weather. On May Day Hitler set the invasion for the fifth but forty-eight hours later, after another unfavorable meteorological report, he postponed X-Day until the seventh—and then the eighth. Göring was pleading for still more time when alarming news arrived from Holland: cancellation of furloughs, evacuations and road blocks. Agitated, Hitler agreed to another postponement until Friday, May 10, but added, "not a day longer!" The sustained effort at the front to keep two million men at the point of attack, he said, was becoming increasingly difficult.

By now he was determined to strike without waiting for the five-day favorable weather prerequisite which had already cost three months. He was gambling on the tool that had proved so valuable in the past—his "intuition," that is, a suspension of logic born of impatience. On Thursday morning a corps commander near Aachen reported heavy fog in his area. This was followed by a prediction that the fog would lift and the tenth would be a good day. Hitler ordered his special train prepared for departure from a small station outside of Berlin and went through elaborate measures to keep his own inner circle in the dark as to its destination and purpose. Outwardly calm during the tedious train trip, he was gnawed with worry that evening as the deadline for confirmation of the attack order approached. The train stopped near Hannover for a final weather report. This time Chief Meteorologist Diesing (who later got a gold watch as a reward) predicted good weather for the tenth. Hitler confirmed the order to attack at dawn, then retired earlier than usual. But he could not get to sleep. Despite the report he kept worrying about the weather.

A greater peril to success came from his own intelligence service. Of the few Hitler had entrusted with the final details of the invasion, one was Admiral Canaris and whatever he knew was passed on to his impetuous deputy, Colonel Oster. Earlier that evening Oster had reported to his old friend the Dutch military attaché, over the dinner table, that Hitler had issued the final attack order. After the meal Oster stopped off at OKW headquarters in the Bendlerstrasse and got information that there would be no last-minute postponement. "The swine has gone to the western front," he told the Dutch attaché, who first informed a Belgian colleague, then phoned The Hague in code: "Tomorrow, at dawn. Hold tight!"

At 4:25 A.M. on the tenth the Führer's train reached its destination, Euskirchen, a town near the Holland-Belgian borders. Under a canopy of stars, the party was driven to the Führer's new headquarters, *Felsennest* (Rocky Nest). Dawn was breaking as they settled into the bunker installation which had been blasted out of a wooded mountaintop. Checking his watch, Hitler got an unwelcome surprise ("I was filled with rage"). Dawn had come fifteen minutes earlier than he had been told it would.

Twenty-five miles to the west his troops were charging across the Belgian, Holland and Luxembourg borders. The air was darkened with his Luftwaffe. Twenty-five hundred aircraft had been gathered for the attack, far outnumbering those the Allies could send up. Wave after wave of German planes swept westward to devastate more than seventy enemy airfields. Airborne troops captured key points in Holland while glider forces swooped down prepared to capture Belgian fortresses by surprise. The Führer was patricularly interested in the attack on Fort Eben Emael. He had personally briefed the commanders and non-coms involved in this glider operation, using a scale model for the purpose, and he awaited reports "feverishly." By noon of the eleventh, this supposedly impregnable fortress, along with a bridge over the Meuse, was in German hands. On hearing this Hitler literally hugged himself with joy. Later came even more meaningful information: the enemy were striking back! "When the news came that the enemy was advancing along the whole front," Hitler recalled, "I could have wept for joy; they'd fallen into the trap! It had been a clever piece of work to attack Liège. We had to make them believe we were remaining faithful to the old Schlieffen plan."

7

On May 10 England and France were caught by surprise, their General Staffs not heeding the warnings from Brussels and The Hague or their own intelligence experts.* Pale and somber, Chamberlain wanted to stay on as Prime Minister but he was persuaded to step down. King George VI accepted his resignation regretfully and suggested that Halifax succeed him. But it was obvious that Winston Churchill alone had the confidence of the nation and at 6 P.M. His Majesty summmoned him to the palace. Churchill had once paid a grudging compliment to the Führer in a letter to the *Times:* "I have always said that I hoped if Great Britain were beaten

* In 1938 MI-6, the British secret intelligence service, had bought the secret of a German cipher machine (called "Enigma") from a Polish mathematician for £10,000, a British passport and a resident's permit in France for himself and his wife. He had memorized diagrams of the main parts of the machine and created a replica in an apartment on the Left Bank in Paris. A working model of Enigma was successfully completed and installed in Bletchley Park, a Victorian mansion forty miles north of London. By the time England declared war in 1939 the machine, code-named Ultra, was operational; and its first major contribution was to warn the British General Staff of Hitler's plan to invade the West.

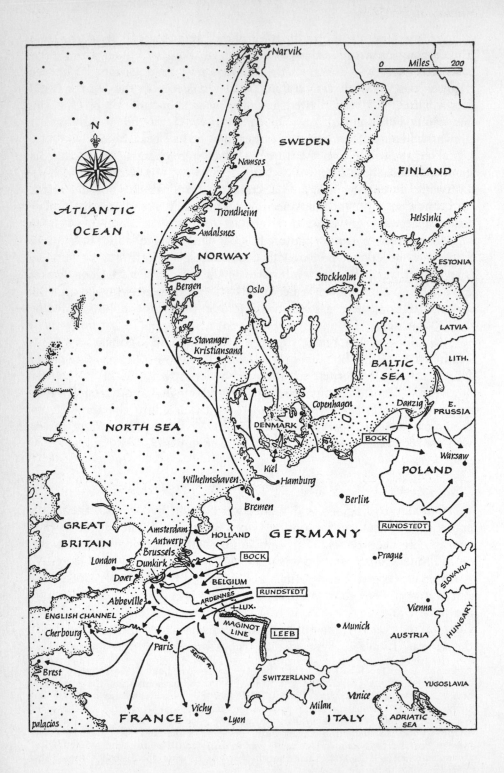

Narvik

SWEDEN

FINLAND

Helsinki

ATLANTIC
OCEAN

Namsos

Trondheim

Andalsnes

NORWAY

Bergen

Oslo

Stockholm

ESTONIA

LATVIA

LITH.

BALTIC
SEA

NORTH SEA

Stavanger
Kristiansand

DENMARK

Copenhagen

Danzig

E.
PRUSSIA

BOCK

Kiel

Wilhelmshaven

Hamburg

Warsaw

POLAND

Bremen

GREAT
BRITAIN

Amsterdam
Antwerp
Brussels
Dunkirk

London

Dover

Abbeville

ENGLISH CHANNEL

Cherbourg

Paris

Brest

palacios

FRANCE

Vichy

HOLLAND

Berlin

GERMANY

RUNDSTEDT

Prague

BOCK

BELGIUM

ARDENNES

RUNDSTEDT

LUX.

MAGINOT
LINE

LEEB

SEINE R.

SWITZERLAND

Lyon

Milan

Vienna

Munich

AUSTRIA

Venice

ITALY

SLOVAKIA

HUNGARY

YUGOSLAVIA

ADRIATIC
SEA

N

0   Miles   200

in a war we should find a Hitler who would lead us back to our rightful place among nations." These words had not mollified the Führer, who continued to look upon Churchill as his worst enemy, the tool of those English Jews who had scotched an Anglo-German alliance. It was a profound hatred contrasting strangely with his admiration for Stalin, and Churchill's elevation to Prime Minister was galling news.

As Hitler's troops and tanks advanced into Holland and Belgium, Goebbels prepared his staff for the next step in the propaganda war. "The minister," read the secret staff meeting of May 11, "formulates the principle for the immediate future that anything in enemy reports that is not correct or even anything that could be dangerous to us must immediately be denied. There is no need at all to examine whether the report is factually correct or not—the decisive point is merely whether the enemy's assertions could in any way be damaging to us." More important, the French and English must be told again and again that it was they who had declared war. "It was *their* war which was now bursting upon them. On no account must we allow ourselves to be maneuvered once more into the role of aggressor."

The drive into western Belgium gained the most impressive victories. This, of course, was part of Hitler's plan to divert attention from the main attack through the hills of the Ardennes. By May 13 these troops had crossed the Meuse at several points to approach Sedan where Hitler hoped to break through the weak link in the Maginot Line.

Despite the steady advance in the north, Hitler was disturbed by the stubborn defense put up by the outnumbered Dutch troops and, on the morning of the fourteenth, issued a directive to break this resistance "speedily." Detachments of the Luftwaffe were sent from the Belgian area "to facilitate the rapid conquest of Fortress Holland." Within hours the Luftwaffe dropped ninety-eight tons of high explosives on Rotterdam. The intent was to eliminate Dutch resistance at the bridges over the Nieuwe Maas but the bombs slammed into the center of the city, killing 814 civilians. The facts were grossly misrepresented by the democratic press, which listed the death toll as between 25,000 and 30,000. Nor did Western newspapers reveal that the tacit agreement between the two sides to limit bombing to military targets had been first violated by the British. Three days earlier, over strenuous French objections, thirty-five Royal Air Force bombers had attacked an industrial city in the Rhineland, killing four civilians, including an Englishwoman. "This raid on the night of 11th May, although in itself trivial, was an epoch-making event," commented F. J. P. Veale, an English jurist, "since it was the first deliberate breach of the fundamental rule of civilized warfare that hostilities must only be waged against the enemy combatant forces." Despite Hitler's frightful retaliation in Holland, he resisted proposals to bomb London itself. He was not willing to go that far—as yet. The tragedy of Rotterdam ended Dutch resistance, the commander-in-chief of the Dutch forces ordering his men to lay down arms a few hours later. That same day German tanks burst through the French Ninth and Second Armies at Sedan. Supported by screaming Stuka dive bombers, three long columns of Panzers rattled and rumbled toward the English Channel.

Churchill was wakened the next morning by a telephone call from Paris. "We have been defeated!" exclaimed Premier Reynaud. "We are beaten!" Churchill could not believe it, nor could his generals, who had misread the armored conquest of Poland as a simple maneuver against an inept, primitive defense.

The terror that seized France was aggravated by Goebbels. "The task of the secret transmitter, from now on," he told his staff on May 17, "is to use every means to create a mood of panic in France. . . . It must further utter an urgent warning against the dangers of a 'Fifth Column' which undoubtedly includes all German refugees. It should point out that, in the present situation, even the Jews from Germany are nothing but German agents." That morning Hitler motored forward to Bastogne in the heart of the Ardennes. "All the world hearkens!" he declared triumphantly. He had come to the headquarters of Army Group A, commanded by General Gerd von Rundstedt, to discuss progress of the main drive to the Channel and was in such an expansive mood that he stayed for lunch and later walked among the men exuding success.

Back in the homeland, it was the rare German who did not share his exultation. Most of those who had once feared Hitler was traveling too fast and too dangerously had become true believers in his infallibility. Four industrialists, including Alfried Krupp, grew so excited as they listened to the radio reports of the drive through Holland that they began poking their fingers at a map of northeastern Europe jabbering: "This one here is yours; that one there is ours; we shall have that man arrested; he has two factories. . . ." One industrialist left the hubbub to phone a subordinate to get Wehrmacht permission for two of the group to visit Holland at once.

By the morning of May 19 several armored divisions were within fifty miles of the Channel and one, the 2nd, rolled into Abbeville at the mouth of the Somme the following evening. The trap was sprung and inside the giant net were the Belgians, the entire British Expeditionary Force and three French armies. Hitler was so surprised when Brauchitsch telephoned him of the capture of Abbeville that his voice choked with emotion. He praised everyone. Jodl wrote in his diary that the Führer went into raptures. "Talks in words of appreciation of the German Army and its leadership. Busies himself with the peace treaty which shall express this theme: return of territory robbed over the last 400 years from the German people, and of other values."

Things were turning out exactly as he had dreamed. Within three days the tanks of Army Group A had wheeled north, closing on the Channel ports of Calais and Dunkirk, whose capture would cut off the British from a sea retreat to England. Göring slammed his big hand on a table when he heard the report. "This is a special job for the Luftwaffe!" he exclaimed. "I must speak to the Führer at once. Get a line through by phone!" In moments he was assuring Hitler unconditionally that the Luftwaffe by itself could annihilate the trapped remnants of the enemy. All he asked was withdrawal of German tanks and ground troops so that they wouldn't be hit by friendly bombs. Having resumed his feud with both the Wehrmacht and army high commands, Hitler might have seen this as an opportunity to strengthen his hold on the military. He gave Göring consent to finish off the enemy from the air.

Overhearing this, Jodl sarcastically remarked to an adjutant, "There goes Göring shooting off his big mouth again!" then dutifully began making the necessary arrangements over the phone with Göring's chief of staff. "We have done it!" Göring exulted to Milch on his return to air force headquarters. "The Luftwaffe is to wipe out the British on the beaches. I have managed to talk the Führer round to halting the army." Milch did not share his enthusiasm and objected that their bombs would sink too deeply into the sand before exploding. Besides, the Luftwaffe was not strong enough for such an operation. "Leave it to me, it's not your business," said Göring and returned to his boasting. "The army always wants to act like gentlemen. They round up the British as prisoners with as little harm to them as possible. But the Führer wants to teach them a lesson they won't easily forget."

The following morning, May 24, Hitler visited Rundstedt and his staff at Group A's forward headquarters. In high spirits, the Führer predicted that the war would be over in six weeks. Then the way would be free for an agreement with the English. All he wanted from them was their acknowledgment of Germany's position on the Continent. When they got down to tactics, General von Rundstedt did not oppose the use of planes to reduce the entrapped enemy at Dunkirk. He proposed that tanks be halted at the canal below the besieged city. Hitler agreed with his observation that this armor should be saved for operations against the French. At 12:45 P.M. the halt order was issued to the Fourth Army in the Führer's name.

That evening four Panzer divisions were stopped at the Aa Canal. The tank crews were astounded. No fire was coming from the opposite shore. Beyond they could make out the peaceful spires of Dunkirk. Had Operations gone crazy? The division commanders were even more amazed. They knew they could take Dunkirk with little trouble since the British were still heavily engaged near Lille. Why weren't they allowed to seize the last escape port to England?

Army Chief of Staff Halder was contemptuous. "Our left wing, consisting of armor and motorized forces," he wrote in his diary, "will thus be stopped in its tracks on the direct order of the Führer! Finishing off the encircled army is to be left to the Luftwaffe!" Halder was convinced, with some reason, that Göring was merely looking for personal glory and had won over the Führer by arguing that if the army generals got the victory Hitler's own prestige at home would be damaged beyond repair.

The ground commanders reiterated their request to move into Dunkirk with tanks and infantry, but Hitler would not listen. It was only on May 26, after reports of heavy shipping in the Channel (was it possible the British were preparing to evacuate their forces?), that he grudgingly authorized an advance on Dunkirk from the west. But that same day Göring assured him that the Luftwaffe had destroyed Dunkirk harbor. "Only fish bait will reach the other side. I hope the Tommies are good swimmers."

As the English and Allied troops fell back into the cul-de-sac, a crazy-quilt fleet of almost 900 vessels began leaving dozens of English ports. There were warships and sailboats, launches and strange-looking Dutch craft—manned by career officers, fishermen, tugboat operators, expert amateur seamen and Sunday sailors who had never before ventured beyond the three-mile limit. This was Operation Dynamo, a mission to evacuate 45,000 men in two days. But this modest estimate had not taken into consideration Hitler's low opinion of democracy in action. He was completely surprised by a sporting operation carried out gallantly and effectively by a pickup group of amateurs and professionals. By the thirtieth of May, 126,606 men were back in England—and more were coming every hour.

Hitler's commanders were no more perceptive. That day Halder wrote in his diary that the encircled enemy was disintegrating. Admittedly some were fleeing across the Channel "on anything that floats," but he described this disparagingly as another *Le Débâcle*, a reference to Zola's novel about the French rout in the Franco-Prussian War. By midday, however, the German high command finally realized the extent of the evacuation and massive bombing attacks were mounted. But fog came to the rescue of the British. Not only was Dunkirk itself enshrouded but all the Luftwaffe fields were blanketed by low clouds which grounded their three thousand bombers.

In the meantime the Stukas of the Eighth Air Corps were doing surprisingly little damage to the flotilla of small vessels; and those bombs dropped on the beaches dug so deeply before exploding that casualties were low. Equally surprising was the performance of a new British fighter plane, the Spitfire, which ravaged Göring's fighter squadrons; and once the weather cleared enough for bombers to get into the air, they too were picked off by the deadly little Spitfires.

Oddly, the continuing evacuation did not seem to perturb Hitler. It was almost as though it was no concern of his. While Brauchitsch and Halder frantically looked for ways to stop the steady flow to England, the

Führer responded haltingly, almost lackadaisically. It was the commanders who waved their arms at conferences these days, not he. In striking contrast to the Narvik crisis, he pounded no tables, made no threats, called for no frantic measure to stop the exodus to England. He let his subordinates carry the burden of decision.

The thin perimeter of the Dunkirk defense line held until June 4 but by then 338,226 British and Allied troops had been ferried to England to fight another day. Now speculation arose on both sides of the Channel regarding Hitler's strange behavior. Why had he given Göring the license to bomb the encircled army "to teach them a lesson," then apparently assisted in their escape by not acting forcefully? His own words only confused matters. He told his naval adjutant that he had expected the BEF would fight to the last man as they had done in *his* war, and hoped to contain them until they ran out of ammunition, thus gaining for himself a mass of prisoners for use in peace negotiations. Yet when this strategy failed—if it had been his strategy—and almost no British were captured, he showed no signs of rage or even petulance.

A variation on this theme was his remark to Linge as they surveyed the pock-marked beaches of Dunkirk, strewn with books, photographs, shoes, rifles, bicycles and other possessions: "It is always good to let a broken army return home to show the civilian population what a beating they have had." He also told Bormann that he had purposely spared the English. "Churchill," he complained, "was quite unable to appreciate the sporting spirit of which I had given proof by refraining from creating an irreparable breach between the British and ourselves."

The military men, including all the adjutants, smiled at those who believed the Führer had been motivated by political or humanitarian considerations. "That Hitler purposely let the British escape, belongs to the realm of fables," commented Puttkamer. Others equally close to Hitler were sure he had been moved to pity by his affection for the English. "The blood of every single Englishman is too valuable to be shed," he told Frau Troost. "Our two people belong together, racially and traditionally— this is and always has been my aim even if our generals can't grasp it." Competent foreign observers gave some credence to this theory. François-Poncet, for instance, was convinced that Hitler never really wanted to war with the English—only to neutralize them.

He had given witness to this recently by sending Unity Mitford home via Zurich in a special train. He deeply regretted her fate, he told Engel. "She lost her nerve, just when, for the first time, I could really have used her." It was a hostile England to which she returned; her brother-in-law, Sir Oswald Mosley, together with other leaders of the British Union of Fascists, were jailed without trial three days after Hitler invaded Belgium to prevent his propaganda for peace. Mosley had already admonished his Blackshirts to remain steadfast and loyal to their native land. His attitude was: "I will fight to the last day to keep England and Germany friends and prevent war, but the moment war is declared I will fight for my country." Lady Diana Mosley soon followed her husband into prison on the order of her relative, the Prime Minister, while she was still nursing her eleven-week-old son. The authorities gave her permission to take the baby into Holloway prison, but not his ninteen-month-old brother. One child to a mother was the rule, and she decided to take neither so that they would not be separated. It was fortunate since her cell, its floor swimming in water, had no bed, only a thin mattress. When Mosley became gravely ill three years later, he and his wife were finally released. Public uproar ensued which was derided by George Bernard Shaw. "I think this Mosley panic shameful," he told a girl reporter. "What sort of people are they who can be frightened out of their wits by a single man? Even if Mosley were in rude health, it was high time to release him with apologies for having let him frighten us into scrapping the Habeas Corpus Act. . . . We are still afraid to let Mosley defend himself and we have produced the ridiculous situation in which we may buy Hitler's *Mein Kampf* in any bookshop in Britain, but may not buy ten lines written by Mosley. The whole affair has become too silly for words. Good evening."

Unity Mitford arrived home, the bullet still in her head. Sad and depressed, she was unable to feed herself. She died eight years later when the bullet moved on its own.

8

Hitler left Felsennest on the eve of the fall of Dunkirk with instructions to preserve the entire area as a "national monument." Every room in the complex was to be kept intact, every name-plate to remain on its door. Führer Headquarters was moved to the small Belgian village of Brûly-de-Pesche, near the border of France. By the time Hitler arrived the place was deserted, every inhabitant evacuated. A special garden had been laid out along with gravel paths but the cement of the Führer bunker was still wet. He gave this peaceful scene a warlike name, *Wolfsschlucht* (Wolf's Gorge), after his own nickname of early party days.

By this time King Leopold had not only surrendered Belgium but refused to go into exile. "I have decided to stay," he told his Prime Minister. "The cause of the Allies is lost." This seemed certain on June 5 when 143 German divisions turned on the remnants of the French army—65 divisions. The defenders had few tanks and almost no air cover and the Wehrmacht swept forward on a 400-mile front. In Paris Reynaud made a desperate impossible plea to Roosevelt for "clouds of planes," then packed his bags.

It was an auspicious moment to enter the war on Hitler's side and Mussolini expressed his desire to join the lists. But his ally urged him to wait until the Luftwaffe wiped out the French air force. Il Duce could only restrain himself until June 10 before declaring war, and the supremely confident tone of his explanatory letter to Hitler brought this burst of sarcasm: "I have quite often in the past wondered about his naïveté," the Führer told his military staff. "The whole letter is proof that in the future I must be much more careful with the Italians in political matters. Evidently Mussolini thinks of this as a walk in *Passo romano*." The Italians would get a rude surprise. "First they were too cowardly to take part, now they are in a hurry so that they can share in the spoils."

At dawn thirty-two Italian divisions attacked six French divisions in the south, but with such a lack of drive that any advance had to be measured in feet. By this time both ends of the French line in the north had crumbled and on the morning of the fourteenth German troops began entering Paris. It was one of the few times in the history of modern warfare that the commander of an operation reached the objective before his troops. General von Bock, chief of Army Group B, had flown ahead in his liaison plane, arriving at the Arc de Triomphe just in time to take the salute of the first combat troops. It was a parade, not a battle, and Bock took time off to visit the tomb of Napoleon before having lunch at the Ritz and doing a little shopping.

At Wolf's Gorge, Göring was trying to persuade Hitler to avenge the British bombing of residential areas in Germany. As they conversed in the village square, Colonel Warlimont overheard Göring announce that he could not tolerate these British atrocities any longer and wanted to "give them back ten bombs for every one of theirs." But Hitler could not be swayed. He said, so Warlimont recalled, "he thought it quite possible that the British government was so shaken by Dunkirk that it had temporarily lost its head, alternatively that the reason for the attacks on the civilian population was that the British bombers had inaccuarate bomb sights and were flown by untrained crews. In any case he thought we should wait before taking countermeasures."

The Führer was in a negotiating mood. Capitalizing on the excitement of the fall of Paris, he made a statement to the West by means of a unique interview with Karl von Wiegand of the Hearst press. He asserted that he had had no intention of attacking "the beautiful French capital" so long as it remained an open city, then vehemently denied it had been his aim or intention to destroy the British Empire. And all he asked from the United States was a regional Monroe Doctrine: America for Americans, Europe for Europeans.

While German troops continued to advance, the Italians in the south seemed to be marching in place. Fortunately for Il Duce, events in the north soon precluded the necessity for any action at all in the south. By evening of the sixteenth Germans were pouring through the haphazard French defenses almost at will. Late the next morning, as Hitler was discussing the situation with his military advisers at Wolf's Gorge, word came that the French wanted an armistice. Throwing dignity to the winds, he slapped his thigh and jerked up a knee in a spontaneous spasm of ecstasy.* "He was literally shaken by frantic exuberance," recalled Fräulein Schröder. The staff gaped in wonder but Keitel rose to the moment. "Mein Führer," he said ponderously, "you are the greatest *Feldherr* [field commander] of all time!"

Although the British were stricken by the French capitulation, Churchill revived their courage with talk of England's "finest hour." And from the British Broadcasting Corporation came another voice of resistance, this beamed to France. "The flame of French resistance cannot go out," proclaimed General Charles de Gaulle from Studio B-2. "It will not go out." France, he said, had lost only a battle. "She has not lost the war." Neither man noted that it was June 18, the hundred and twenty-fifth anniversary of the Battle of Waterloo, a contest ultimately decided by Blücher's German troops.

At noon Hitler met with Mussolini in the Führerbau, scene of the latter's personal trimph at the historic Munich Conference of 1938. This time the Italian dictator was noticeably subdued. His own declaration of war had been a military fraud, a diplomatic gamble. Hitler had achieved victory without help and would, of course, have the last word today. Both Ciano and Mussolini were startled to find Hitler in a peace-loving, magnanimous mood. Hitler made "many reservations on the desirability of demolishing the British Empire, which he considers, even today, to be an important factor in world equilibrium," then, in the face of Mussolini's objections, stoutly supported Ribbentrop's proposal of lenient peace terms to the French. "Hitler is now the gambler who has made a big scoop and would like to get up from the table, risking nothing more," Ciano wrote in his diary. "Today he speaks with a reserve and perspicacity which, after such a victory, are really astonishing. I cannot be accused of excessive tenderness toward him, but today I truly admire him."

The two dictators took time off to autograph souvenir postcards of their meeting. On one such card Mussolini scratched in his bold, upright hand: "Men make history!" Underneath, in his much softer script, Hitler wrote: "History makes men." Mussolini left for Rome in dejection. "In truth," wrote Ciano that evening, "the Duce fears that the hour of peace is growing near and sees fading once again that unattainable dream of his life: glory on the field of battle."

Two days later, on the first day of summer, Hitler motored to the

* The Western newsreel version turned this brief moment into an extended scene. According to Laurence Stallings, the film was doctored by John Grierson, the documentary producer then serving as propagandist in the Canadian army. By "looping" the frames (a technique subsequently used in TV cat food commercials), Grierson transformed Hitler's gesture into a ludicrous series of gay pirouettes. Hitler's official cameraman, Walter Frentz, filmed the scene; he asserts that there were only eight frames, and provided them to the author.

same woods near Compiègne where the Kaiser's representative had surrendered. It was a vindictive as well as historic choice. There stood the famous wooden railroad dining car used on that occasion, hoisted from its museum through a torn-out wall to the original site. At exactly 3:15 P.M. the Führer motorcade arrived. Hitler walked toward the car with springy step, face grave, manner solemn. He stopped at a granite block which read:

HERE ON THE ELEVENTH OF NOVEMBER 1918 SUCCUMBED
THE CRIMINAL PRIDE OF THE GERMAN EMPIRE—VANQUISHED
BY THE FREE PEOPLE WHICH IT TRIED TO ENSLAVE

William Shirer was watching through binoculars to catch Hitler's expression. "I have seen that face many times at the great moments of his life. But today! It is afire with scorn, anger, hate, revenge, triumph." He was muttering, so recalled Linge, something that sounded like "We will destroy everything that can remind the world of that shameful day in 1918."

A long plain table had been set up in the old railroad car with half a dozen chairs on each side for the two delegations. At the head stood Schmidt where he would be able to hear both groups. After the Führer seated himself next to his interpreter, Göring, Raeder, Brauchitsch, Ribbentrop and Hess took their places. Several minutes later General Charles Huntziger led in the French delegation—an admiral, an air force general, and a former ambassador, their faces still showing the shock of learning at the last moment where the negotiations would take place.

Hitler and his associates rose. Not a word was spoken. Both delegations bowed and sat down. First Keitel read out the preamble to the armistice conditions, which had been composed by Hitler. The French and the Germans stared at each other, thought Schmidt, like wax figures as Keitel spoke the Führer's words: Germany did not intend that the conditions should cast any aspersion on so courageous an enemy. "The aim of the German demands is to prevent a resumption of hostilities, to give Germany security for the further conduct of the war against England which she has no choice but to continue, and also to create the conditions for a new peace which will repair the injustice inflicted by force on the German Reich." It seemed as though Hitler addressed England rather than France, offering them an honorable peace too if they chose. This became more evident in the stipulations which included German renouncement of any intent to challenge Britain's sea power. He solemnly swore he would not take over the French war fleet for his own use in the war or, indeed, use any French naval equipment (for a possible crossing of the Channel). Hitler had included this promise against advice from his own navy to make good the heavy losses in the Norway campaign with French ships; a proposal he curtly rejected out of both fear and hope. He feared seizure of the French fleet would harden English determination to fight since it would challenge their supremacy of the seas; he hoped his appeasement would lead to peace with a tacit gentlemen's agreement that Britannia should continue to rule the waves while Germania turned east for Lebensraum.

Once Schmidt finished reading the French text, Hitler got to his feet. So did the others. After more polite bows, the Führer left with most of his followers. Keitel and Schmidt stayed behind and were joined directly by Jodl and several other German officers. After the French had re-examined the terms, they insisted upon transmitting them to their government at Bordeaux. "Absolutely impossible!" said Keitel. "You must sign at once."

But the French stubbornly demanded the same courtesy extended to the German delegation in 1918 and in a few minutes Huntziger was talking to General Weygand, the French commander-in-chief. "I am telephoning from the coach"—he paused—"from the coach you know." He reported that the conditions were hard but not dishonorable. Even so, Huntziger felt they were "merciless," far worse than the conditions France had forced on Germany in the previous war, and the negotiations continued without resolution until dusk. They resumed the following morning, June 22, dragging on into late afternoon. By 6 P.M. Keitel lost all patience and sent Schmidt to the French with an ultimatum: "If we cannot reach an agreement within an hour, the negotiations will be broken off, and the delegation will be conducted back to the French lines."

There was no alternative. At 6:50 P.M., after more telephone conversations with Bordeaux, General Huntziger signed the armistice treaty. After the ceremony Keitel asked him to stay a moment. When they were alone the two generals looked at each other silently and Schmidt noticed both had tears in their eyes. Controlling his emotion, Keitel congratulated the Frenchman for having represented his country's interests with such dignity, then held out his hand. Huntziger shook it.

All these events were being radioed back to Germany as they occurred and as soon as the proud but downcast Huntziger stepped down from the old dining car, there was a brisk recorded rendition of "Then we strike, then we strike, then we strike at England!" that must have stirred German hearts. It was the Goebbels touch. He had music for all occasions; but his choice this time was provoking to his Führer, who had been trying to give the opposite impression in the treaty.

Back at Wolf's Gorge Hitler was planning a sightseeing tour of Paris. He had summoned a sculptor and his two favorite architects—Speer and Giesler—to go along as guides. "Paris has always fascinated me," he told Arno Breker, whose heroic-classical works were also admired by Stalin. Hitler admitted that it had long been one of his most ardent wishes to visit the City of Light. It was a metropolis of art and that was why he insisted on seeing it first with his artists. He was sure they would find inspiration for the rebuilding of important German cities. "I am interested in actually seeing the buildings with which I am theoretically familiar."

It was pitch-dark when the party—which included Keitel and Bormann and several adjutants—arrived at a meadow outside Brûly-de-Pesche and climbed into a plane piloted by Baur, but by the time they reached Le Bourget the sun was up. June 23 was going to be a bright, hot day. Hitler climbed into the first open car of a motor column, seating himself as usual beside the driver. Behind him sat the rest of the party. As they headed for the first stop, the Opéra, the streets of the city were deserted except for an occasional gendarme who would dutifully greet the Führer with a smart salute. Breker had spent his most decisive years in Paris and was shocked to see the almost complete absence of life.

Hitler's features slowly relaxed as he took in the architectural wonders of the Opéra, which he had admired since his early days in Vienna. He was as familiar with the building as with his own chancellery and his eyes shone with excitement. "This is the most beautiful theater in the world!" he called out to his entourage. He inspected the boxes and noted that one room was missing. The white-haired attendant who had been accompanying them with stiff pride announced coolly that it had been eliminated years ago. "There, you see how well I know my way about!" said Hitler with the pride of a schoolboy.

After a stop at the Eiffel Tower they visited Napoleon's tomb. Here Hitler placed cap over heart, bowed and gazed for some time down into the deep round crypt. He was very moved. Finally he turned to Giesler and said quietly, "You will build my tomb."* He lapsed into pensive silence, then instructed Bormann to transfer the bones of young Napoleon from Vienna to his father's side.

The three-hour tour ended on the heights of Montmartre, the mecca of art students. Perhaps it reminded Hitler of his own student days. Lost in thought for some moments, he finally turned to Giesler, Breker and Speer. "Now your work begins," he said. The rebuilding of cities and monuments was entrusted to them. "Bormann," he said, "help me with this. Take care of my artists." Hitler again surveyed the city which stretched below. "I thank Fate to have seen this city whose magic atmosphere has always fascinated me," he said. That was why he had ordered his troops to by-pass Paris and to avoid combat in its vicinity. "So that picture below us would be preserved for the future." But the few Parisians who saw him that morning were reduced to panic. As his cavalcade came upon a group of boisterous market women the fattest pointed in terror at Hitler. Her shriek of "It's him! It's him!" spread pandemonium.

The next day Hitler instructed Speer to draw up a decree in his name

* Later he gave Giesler explicit instructions. His tomb was to be extremely simple and it would be placed in Munich. "Here I was truly born," he said. "Here I started my movement and here is my heart."

to resume full-scale work on the Berlin buildings. "Wasn't Paris beautiful?" he said. "But Berlin must be made more beautiful." Hitler also took Breker aside and began rhapsodizing on what they had seen the previous morning. "I love Paris—it has been a place of artistic importance since the nineteenth century—just as you do. And like you, I would have studied here if Fate had not pushed me into politics since my ambitions before the World War were in the field of art."

The armistice was scheduled to go into effect an hour and thirty-five minutes past midnight and there was an atmosphere of jollity as they sat down to a late dinner at a table lit by candles. The sky darkened, thunder rumbled in the distance. Just before midnight an aide reported enemy planes approaching. The lights were extinguished and they sat in pitch-darkness, faces periodically lit up by flashes of lightning.

Champagne glasses were passed around. There was an unearthly silence as watches were checked. At 1:35 A.M. came the startling brassy cry of a bugle. Someone whispered to Breker that it was the traditional signal for "Weapons at rest." Someone else, overcome by emotion, blew his nose. Keitel stood and in the darkness made a short speech. He raised his glass and called for three "Hocks" to the Führer, their Supreme Commander.

Everyone rose and clinked glasses while Hitler sat somewhat uneasily —he didn't like such displays but was bowing to the tradition of the Wehrmacht. He brought glass to mouth as a courtesy but did not drink, then slumped, head bowed, a man alone in this jubilant company. At last he said almost inaudibly, "It was a great responsibility," and left the room.

Chapter Twenty-two

"EV'N VICTORS BY VICTORY ARE UNDONE" (DRYDEN) JUNE–OCTOBER 28, 1940

1

That summer Hitler made it evident he was more interested in negotiating than in fighting. In France his weapons were persuasion and the projection of himself as the magnanimous victor who offered the French a share in the fruits of a united and prosperous Fascist Europe, a hegemony designed not only for moral regeneration but as a bulwark against Godless Bolshevism. One of the first acts in this campaign was a demand that his troops act like liberators, not conquerors. "I do not wish my soldiers to behave in France the way the French behaved in the Rhineland after the first war!" He told Hoffmann that anyone found looting would be shot on the spot. "I want to come to a real understanding with France."

Consequently troops who entered Paris did not swagger around the city demanding homage and free food. They conscientiously paid for every purchase and enjoyed the late June sun outside the cafés of the Champs-Élysées side by side with Frenchmen. It was an embarrassed, often silent and indifferent companionship but fear was leaving Parisians who had expected their women to be raped and their shops and banks to be sacked. By now it was common knowledge that the Wehrmacht was actually assisting those refugees trekking back to the capital, and there was some acceptance of the placard plastered all over the city showing a child in the arms of a friendly German with the admonition: "Frenchmen! Trust the German soldier!"

Hitler would have been proud of his troops. They were neat, quiet and ingratiating; courteous to women but not too gallant, and respectful to their mates. They stood bareheaded at the tomb of the Unknown Soldier, armed only with cameras. They acted more like a horde of tourists brought in at special holiday rates than the fearsome creatures who had just humiliated the French armies. It was astute public relations, part of a program designed to turn France into a working and productive vassal.

Hitler himself was playing the tourist with a special group including his adjutants and his World War sergeant, Max Amann. For two days this lighthearted group was guided by the Führer around the old battlefields of the conflict that had helped lead to this one. It was a sentimental journey with Hitler enjoying every moment. He pointed out the fields of Flanders that had formerly been a hellish morass, the old trenches that had been kept as memorials and attractions for sightseers. Instead of surveying the scenes in quiet solemnity, the Führer talked interminably, explaining the minutest detail of what had happened here and over there. As he drove through Lille, which he had memorialized in water color, a woman looking out of the window recognized him. "The Devil!" she gasped. Amused at first, he vowed he would erase that image from the minds of the conquered.

The sentimental junket ended on June 26 and he turned his mind to the unpleasant task ahead: subjugation of the English. It was a chore not to be relished, he reiterated to his adjutants. War with England was a war of brothers and the destruction of their empire would, in truth, be cause for German distress. That was why, he confided to Hewel, he was reluctant to invade England. "I do not want to conquer her," he said, "I want to come to terms with her, I want to force her to accept my friendship and to drive out the whole Jewish rabble that is agitating against me."

Hitler still had no definite plan for the invasion of the British Isles. Victory in the West, in fact, had come so quickly that there was not a single landing craft or barge ready for launching across the Channel. He seemed to be waiting instead for England to sue for peace. But such expectations were rudely jolted on July 3 by the surprise Royal Navy bombardment of the French fleet lying at anchor in the Algerian port of Mers-el-Kebir. Within thirteen minutes the battleship *Bretagne* was sunk with the loss of 977 men, and three other vessels, including the *Dunkerque*, were badly damaged with heavy losses in life. The rest of the fleet escaped. The victors paid a heavy price for their fear that Hitler might possibly use these warships in her invasion of England. With British evacuation from Dunkirk still a bitter memory to most Frenchmen, this attack, particularly after Admiral Darlan's sincere vows to deny Hitler their ships, roused deep animosity throughout France. "Perfidious Albion" became a café phrase.

The shelling also confirmed the convictions of those who felt that collaboration with Hitler was France's only salvation. Recently the country itself had been physically divided by the armistice terms into two zones: Occupied France in the north and Vichy France in the south under a regime headed by Marshal Pétain. The bombardment made more difficult his task of preventing Deputy Premier Laval from leading France into an ever closer collaboration with Hitler while simplifying for Jean Giraudoux and other Fascist intellectuals the effort to seek new converts. Alfred Fabre-Luce in his quasi diary wrote: "In one day England killed more French sailors than Germany did during the whole war." The British blunder at Mers-el-Kebir, he predicted, was hastening Hitler's One Europe. It also wakened the Führer from his complacent dream of a quick settlement with England while emphasizing his own inability to either control the French fleet or checkmate the Royal Navy. He who was practically landbound was stunned by the shocking mobility of sea power. The explosive naval action reinforced his earlier fear that even if the British fleet did not thwart an invasion of England it would enable her rulers to set up headquarters in Canada or Australia and rule the seas from there.

He hovered in an agony of indecision between negotiation and force. "I must not give up," he told Puttkamer. "The English will eventually see it my way." But when Brauchitsch and Halder flew to the Berghof on July 13 he readily approved their plan to invade England, yet moments later protested that he had no desire to fight his English brothers. He had no desire to dismantle the Empire; bloodshed would only draw the jackals eager to share in the spoils. Why was England still so unwilling to make peace? he asked and answered, so Halder wrote in his diary, "that England still has some hopes of action on the part of Russia."

Three days after, he issued a specific invasion directive designed to eliminate the English homeland as a base for the prosecution of the war against Germany and, if necessary, to occupy it completely. The operation was given an imaginative code name: Sea Lion. No sooner had Hitler approved it than he decided to make a peace proposal of his own. "The Führer is going to make a very magnanimous peace offer to England," Ribbentrop told Schmidt. "When Lloyd George hears of it, he will probably want to fall on our necks." When it came on July 19, it began with a derisive attack on Churchill, continued with a threat that any battle between their two countries would surely end in the annihilation of England, and concluded with a vague proposal: "I can see no reason why this war should continue."

The first English reply to Hitler's bleak offer came from someone who knew him well. Sefton Delmer, now working for BBC, was on the air within the hour. "Herr Hitler," he said in his most deferential German, "you have on occasion in the past consulted me as to the mood of the British public. So permit me to render Your Excellency this little service once again tonight. Let me tell you what we here in Britain think of this appeal of yours to what you are pleased to call our reason and common sense. *Herr Führer* and *Reichskanzler*, we hurl it right back to you, right in your evil-smelling teeth." Shirer heard this at the Berlin studio while waiting to make his own broadcast to America and observed its effect on the officials there. "Can you make it out?" one shouted to Shirer. "Can you understand those British fools? To turn down peace now? They're crazy."

President Roosevelt too was unimpressed by Hitler's offer. Later that evening, in a radio address from the White House accepting the nomination for the presidency, he declared there was only one way to deal with a totalitarian country—by resistance, not appeasement. Never, reported Ambassador Dieckhoff to Berlin, had Roosevelt's "complicity" in the outbreak and prolongation of this war come out so clearly as in this speech. "England is to be prevented from changing her course, English resistance is to be strengthened and the war is to be continued."*

Still no official rejection came from London and when Hitler summoned his commanders to Berlin for a conference on Sunday, July 21, he seemed more puzzled than bellicose. "England's situation is hopeless," he said. "The war has been won by us. A reversal of the prospects of success is impossible." He speculated on the chances of a new cabinet under Lloyd George before lapsing into grim conjecture.

Suddenly the musing ended. He called for "a speedy ending of the war" and suggested that Sea Lion was the most effective way to do so. But his assurance—or show of it—almost immediately began to dissipate. He warned that invasion across the Channel commanded by the enemy was no one-way trip as in Norway. There could be no element of surprise. How could they solve the problem of logistic supply? He went on and on, pointing out grave problems that Admiral Raeder (who was taking diligent notes) silently seconded. Complete air superiority was essential and first-wave landings must be completed by mid-September before worsening weather prevented the Luftwaffe from full participation. He turned to Raeder. When could the navy give him a clear picture on technical preparations? When would they complete emplacement of coastal artillery? To what extent could they protect the bridging of the Channel?

The discomfited admiral was thinking of other problems: they would have to transport most of the troops in river and canal barges which were

---

* A few days later a press adviser of the Washington Embassy submitted the following memorandum to the German Foreign Minister after a talk with Fulton Lewis, Jr., political commentator for the Mutual Broadcasting Company: "L. who travels a good deal, and in connection with the Republican and Democratic conventions met Americans from all classes and parts of the country, stated that people did not want any war, but were rather helpless before Roosevelt's cunning tactics, especially now when by a cornucopia of enormous orders in all the states he had reduced the Congress to a rubber stamp without a will of its own."

still to be hauled from the Reich. And how could this enfeebled fleet of combat vessels hold off the Royal Navy? After the Norway losses there were only forty-eight U-boats, one heavy cruiser, four destroyers and three torpedo boats fit for action. With some embarrassment Raeder replied that he hoped to have an answer on technical details in a few days but how could he commence practical preparations until air superiority was a fact? Brauchitsch responded to his pessimism with a positive expression of faith. He liked Sea Lion. Göring's deputy said the Luftwaffe was only waiting for the word to start a massive air offensive; without comment, Hitler instructed Raeder to submit his report as soon as possible. "If preparations cannot be completed with certainty by the beginning of September, it is necessary to consider other plans." The burden of Sea Lion was on the navy.

When they were alone, Hitler told Brauchitsch, "Stalin is flirting with England to keep England at war and tie us down, to gain time for taking what he wants and what cannot be taken if peace breaks out." While admitting that there were at present no signs of Soviet activity against the Reich, he conceded that the Russians posed a problem that had to be dealt with. "We must begin thinking about them."

An Englishman gifted with foresight had recently perceived that Hitler's true goal was Lebensraum at the expense of the Soviet Union. "When one compares his utterances of a year or so ago with those made fifteen years earlier," wrote George Orwell in a review of the English edition of *Mein Kampf*, "a thing that strikes one is the rigidity of his mind, the way in which his world view *doesn't* develop. It is the fixed vision of a monomaniac and not likely to be much affected by the temporary maneuvers of power politics. Probably, in Hitler's mind, the Russo-German Pact represents no more than an alteration of time-table. The plan laid down in *Mein Kampf* was to smash Russia first, with the implied intention of smashing England afterwards. Now, as it has turned out, England has got to be dealt with first, because Russia was the more easily bribed of the two but Russia's turn will come when England is out of the picture—that, no doubt, is how Hitler sees it."

Although Hitler had achieved an astounding military victory in the West it had not brought him the political stability he needed to begin his holy war against Russia. His blows against England had merely made this stubborn nation more stubborn and his attempts to placate the Vichy French into joining his crusade were being thwarted by a reluctant compliance that stopped short of active assistance.

These failures notwithstanding, he was still confident he could prevent the conflict from becoming a world war, still so sure England was on the verge of surrender that he ordered an immediate intensification of the propaganda war against England. One of Goebbels' first acts was to broadcast over the secret transmitter system those Nostradamus prophecies which had already come to pass and ending with the one foretelling the destruction of London in 1940. Modern interpretations of Nostradamus were supplied by Krafft, the astrologer who had predicted the beer-hall bombing.

During this season of misgivings Hitler took time off for another reunion with his old friend Kubizek, to whom he had sent tickets to the 1940 Wagner festival. During the first interval of *Götterdämmerung* on July 23 the two met in the drawing room. After greeting Kubizek warmly Hitler complained that the war had checked his rebuilding program. "I still have so infinitely much to do. Who else is there to do it? And here I have to stand by and watch the war robbing me of my best years. . . . We are growing older, Kubizek. Not many more years—and it will be too late to do what remains to be done."

Today's personal encounter with Kubizek was a rare intrusion in Hitler's growing public responsibilities. Paradoxically, his relationship with Eva Braun had become more conjugal. Rather than separating them, the war brought them closer together since he could now spend much more time at the Berghof. Gone were the elaborate attempts to convince everyone that they were merely friends; the staff and servants treated her with the greatest respect, among themselves referring to her as *Chefin*, wife of the Chief. She addressed Hitler openly with the familiar *Du* and he replied in kind, sometimes calling her "Tschapperl," a Viennese diminutive meaning little thing. In front of close friends he would even occasionally stroke her hand or give some other sign of overt affection. According to intimates, their sexual relations were normal, keeping in mind that Hitler was almost fifty and completely absorbed in work. At last the accepted mistress of the Berghof, Eva had gained in self-assurance and elegance. Difficult though her life might be, the conviction that she no longer had rivals was solace enough for her.

That summer Hitler decided that the time had come for Lebensraum and to destroy Bolshevism. He instructed the military to make preparations in this direction and on July 29, 1940, Jodl journeyed to the Bad Reichenhall railroad station to discuss the matter with Colonel Warlimont, chief of OKW's planning section, in his special train. Warlimont and his three senior officers thought the unusual visit might mean promotion or some award. To their mystification, Jodl checked to see that all doors and windows of the dining car were closed and then abruptly announced in a quiet, dry voice that Hitler had decided to rid the world "once and for all" of the danger of Bolshevism. A surprise attack was to be launched on the Soviet Union as soon as possible—May 1941. "The effect of Jodl's words was electric," recalled Warlimont, who at the time grasped his chair because he could not believe his own ears.

"That's impossible!" burst out a colonel named Lossberg. How could Hitler fight Russia before England was defeated! Jodl gave a curious answer: "The Führer is afraid that the mood of the people after a victory over England would hardly permit him to embark on a new war against Russia."

A chorus of protests erupted. This was the two-front war which had defeated Germany in the First World War. And why this sudden change after the Moscow Pact? Hadn't Stalin kept his promise to deliver raw materials and food punctually and fully? Jodl tersely answered every objection: a collision with Bolshevism was inevitable; it was better to attack now at the peak of German armed strength. The answers did not convince Warlimont but Jodl, who had presented similar protests to Hitler, cut short the debate. "Gentlemen," he said, "it is not a question for discussion but a decision of the Führer!" He ordered Warlimont to prepare planning papers under the code name Build-up East.

On the last day of July the Führer summoned his commanders to the Berghof for a conference that purported to concern Sea Lion but would lead in the opposite direction. Admiral Raeder spoke first. Preparations were in full swing: matériel had been brought up according to plan and the conversion of barges would be finished by the end of August. On the other hand, the merchant shipping situation was unfavorable due to losses sustained in Norway and from mines; and while minesweeping had commenced it was hampered by Allied air superiority. Therefore, he concluded, it would be better to postpone the invasion until the following May.

Hitler protested. Waiting that long, he said, would enable England to improve her army and stockpile considerable supplies from America—and perhaps even Russia. "How can we bridge the gap until May?" he asked and set the operation for September 15. No sooner had he made this categorical decision than he diluted it. That is, he added, if a concentrated weeklong bombing attack on southern England could damage the RAF, the Royal Navy and key harbors. "Otherwise it is postponed until May 1941."

If this was a decision it was the kind of halfhearted one that pleased Raeder. It gave him top priority to prepare Sea Lion while shifting the burden of responsibility onto the Luftwaffe. More important, it gave Hitler the option of turning the war from West to East, and once the two navy men, Raeder and Puttkamer, left the room, he began belittling Sea Lion's chances. "Our little navy," he sighed, "only fifteen per cent of that of the enemy!" Moreover, the Channel was far more formidable than it appeared on a map as any voyager on that treacherous body of water in foul weather could testify.

It was almost as though he had dismissed the invasion of England. "Russia needs only to hint to England that she does not wish to see Germany too strong and the English, like a drowning man, will regain hope that things will be entirely different in six to eight months. But if Russia is smashed, England's last hope is extinguished. Then Germany will be the master of Europe and the Balkans." This time his musings came to a resolute conclusion. "Decision," he said curtly. "In view of these considerations Russia must be liquidated. Spring '41." Gone was the hesitation of the past few conferences. Again he was the old Führer, the man of destiny. "The sooner we smash Russia the better. The operation only makes sense if we smash the state to its core in one blow. Mere conquest of land areas will not suffice." The offensive, he said, must be carried out as a single, unbroken operation. He would not make Napoleon's mistake and be whipped by the Russian winter. We will wait, he said, until May. "Five months' time," he said with satisfaction, "to prepare."

He was carried away by his vision. "Object," he said with animation, "annihilation of Russia's vital energy." The war lord personified, he rapidly outlined an attack of some 120 divisions: first a drive to Kiev; second, one through the Baltic toward Moscow; finally, a convergence from north and south followed by a special operation against the Baku oil area. The dream was materializing into a reality.

2

Within twenty-four hours the man of decision was again vacillating. He issued two directives, one calling for quick conquest of Britain and the other expressing doubt of its execution. The first began in confidence: "In order to establish the conditions necessary for the final subjugation of England, I intend to intensify the air and naval war against the English homeland." The Luftwaffe was to overpower the RAF as quickly as possible, then stand by in force for Operation Sea Lion. "I reserve for myself," he pointed out, "the decision on terror attacks as a means of reprisal."

The second order, signed by Keitel in the name of the Führer, directed preparations for Sea Lion to be completed by mid-September, then stated: "Eight to fourteen days after the launching of the air offensive against Britain, scheduled to begin about August 5, the Führer will decide whether the invasion will take place this year or not; his decision will depend largely on the outcome of the air offensive."

Even as Keitel sent out this directive he sensed Hitler's ambivalence. "Although the Führer appeared to be throwing himself into all the preparations with great enthusiasm and demanded the adoption of every conceivable improvisation to speed the preparations, I could not help gaining the impression that when it came to the question of actually *executing* the operation, he was in the grip of doubts and inhibitions: he was wide awake to the enormous risk he would be running and to the responsibility he was being called upon to shoulder." Keitel also had the feeling that above all Hitler was "reluctant to countenance the inevitable loss of his last chance of settling the war with Britain by diplomatic means, something which I am convinced he was at that time hoping to achieve." It never occurred to Keitel that this might have been more than an exercise in vacillation; that Hitler might possibly be using the showy preparations for Sea Lion to mask his attack on Russia.

Nor did it occur to Hitler that the substance of his two directives on that August 1 had been decoded by Ultra. The messages assured Churchill that he truly possessed the German code and his faith was confirmed beyond doubt when Ultra shortly decoded a signal from Göring designating August 13 as the beginning of Operation Eagle, the all-out air assault on England.

The offensive began on schedule, but because of worsening weather only the Third Air Force took part. There were almost five hundred bombing sorties but, thanks primarily to radar and secondarily to the Ultra warning, damage was slight and German losses were serious: 45 Luftwaffe aircraft against 13 RAF fighters. The next day was equally disappointing to Göring. On the fifteenth he launched all three of his air fleets. This time Ultra disclosed exactly what forces Göring would use and approximately where each would strike and with this knowledge the RAF was able to assemble its few fighter squadrons at the right place and altitude, parceling them so economically that each German wave met fierce resistance. In the greatest air battle to date, the RAF shot down 75 planes while losing 34. Operation Eagle was turning sour: on the seventeenth the score was 70 to 27. That was the day the slow Stuka dive bomber, which had wreaked such havoc in France, was taken out of the campaign by Göring. It was simply no match for the Spitfires.

Bad weather began on the nineteenth and kept the Luftwaffe grounded four days. During the respite Göring summoned his commanders. The daylight attacks on aircraft factories and other such targets, he said, would have to be replaced by night raids. Göring also took the opportunity to bitterly reproach the single- and double-engine fighter pilots for their performances. "Neither type of fighter is allowed to break off its escort mission because of weather," he ordered. Any pilot who did so would be court-martialed.

When the weather lifted on August 23 the Luftwaffe came over the Channel that night en masse. One flight of a dozen bombers strayed off course and, instead of hitting aircraft factories and oil tanks outside of London, dropped their loads directly on the city. Nine civilians were killed and the RAF, assuming it had been done on purpose, retaliated the next night by bombing Berlin. Little damage was suffered but the Berliners were stunned. "They did not think it could happen," Shirer wrote in his diary. "When this war began Göring assured them it couldn't. . . . They believed him. Their disillusionment today therefore is all the greater. You have to see their faces to measure it."

The RAF returned to Berlin three nights later, this time killing ten civilians and wounding twenty-nine others. Hitler was outraged since the German attack on London had been due to a navigational error, yet still refused to let the Luftwaffe bomb the English capital. Berlin was hit twice more. Aroused to action, he finally threatened dire retaliation on the afternoon of September 4, in an unscheduled speech at the Sportpalast. His audience of women social workers and nurses cheered at his promise to surpass Churchill's bombings. "When the British air force drops two or three or four thousand kilograms of bombs," he said, "then we will in one night drop 150-, 230-, or 400,000 kilograms." The din in the auditorium forced him to pause. "When they declare that they will increase the attacks on our cities, then we will raze their cities to the ground. We will stop the handiwork of these air pirates, so help us God! The hour will come when one of us will break, and it will not be National Socialist Germany!"

The answer was a frenzied: "Never, never!"

3

Two days later Admiral Raeder reported to Hitler at the chancellery. The two discussed Sea Lion cautiously as if neither had much faith in it, the admiral concluding his comments with a question that should have drawn a hot retort: "What," he asked, "are the Führer's political and military directives in the event that Operation Sea Lion does not take place?"

But Hitler was not at all ruffled and it was with some satisfaction that Raeder reported to his colleagues, "Decision of the Führer to land in England is by no means yet firm since the Führer has the conviction that the submission of England will be achieved even without landing. Landing is, however, now as before, regarded by the Führer as the means by which, according to every prospect, an immediate crushing end can be made of the war. Yet the Führer has no thought of executing the landing if the *risk* of the operation is too high." It was obvious that Hitler could not tolerate a miscarriage of Sea Lion since that would decisively redound to the prestige of Great Britain. He wanted a triumphant blitz finale to the end of the war—but one without risks. What particularly disturbed him was Puttkamer's eyewitness report of a recent exercise near Boulogne in which landing barges drawn by tugs were thrown into complete disorder by the tide. In Puttkamer's opinion, a similar landing operation on the English coast would be equally catastrophic.

The success of invasion or capitulation depended on the air assault and Hitler sanctioned mass raids on London the day after his desultory meeting with Raeder. Wave after wave of planes took off for England. Late that afternoon the first group of 320 bombers, heavily protected by fighters, passed over the head of Göring, who was watching from the cliffs of Cape Blanc Nez. The tightly massed planes swarmed over the Channel, then flew up the Thames to blast Woolwich Arsenal, power stations and docks. As soon as Göring got the report that the last target was "a sea of flames," he hurried to a microphone and began broadcasting that London was being destroyed. His planes, he boasted, were striking "right into the enemy's heart." The devastating attack continued until dawn and was resumed the following dusk. Eight hundred and forty-two Londoners died in those two days of terror. Making good his threat to "raze their cities to the ground," Hitler authorized another massive raid for September 15. This would be the grand finale, designed not only to punish London but to destroy the RAF.

Again Ultra warned Churchill and, four days before the raid, he broadcast an exhortation to the nation. "There is no doubt that Herr Hitler is using up his fighter force at a very high rate, and that if he goes on for many more weeks he will wear down and ruin the vital part of his air force." At the same time he warned that "no one should blind himself to the fact that a heavy full-scale invasion of this island is being prepared with all the usual German thoroughness and method, and that it may be launched now—upon England, upon Scotland, or upon Ireland, or upon all three." It could come in the next few days. "Therefore, we must regard the next week or so as a very important period in our history. It ranks with the days when the Spanish Armada was approaching the Channel, and Drake was finishing his game of bowls; or when Nelson stood between us and Napoleon's Grand Army at Boulogne." His words lifted spirits in the fortress island, inspiring civilians to feel that they too were involved in the battle.

Although Hitler was putting on a public show of confidence, he revealed considerable concern at a Führer conference on September 14. After praising the Luftwaffe for the "terrific" effect of Operation Eagle, he admitted that the prerequisites for Sea Lion were "not yet on hand." Bad weather had prevented the Luftwaffe from gaining complete air command. But he still refused to call off the invasion. The air attacks were having a devastating effect on English nerves and mass hysteria would break out in ten or twelve days.

Göring's deputy seized on this to advance his scheme of bombing civilians into submission. Raeder, who seemed enthusiastic about everything but a sea invasion, gave his hearty approval but Hitler insisted that the Luftwaffe confine itself to vital military targets. "Bombing with the object of causing mass panic must be the last resort."

All the talk subsided and what had apparently been a decision to launch Sea Lion was only an agreement to make one on September 17. In the meantime the Battle of Britain intensified, with increasingly heavy German losses. On the fifteenth, for instance, 60 planes were destroyed while the British were losing 26. Consequently Hitler was forced at last to face reality on Tuesday, the seventeenth. He admitted to himself that bombing would probably never bring the English to their knees, then curtly announced his decision: due to inability to achieve air superiority, Operation Sea Lion was hereby postponed until further notice. Postponement meant cancellation; from that moment on the invasion of England existed only on paper. Ultra and a small band of British pilots, typifying the united spirit of the people, had dealt Adolf Hitler his first military defeat. "This blessed plot, this earth, this realm, this England," was saved.

"We have conquered France at the cost of 30,000 men," the Führer told Puttkamer once the decision was made. "During one night of crossing the Channel we could lose many times that—and success is not certain." He seemed happy, thought his naval adjutant, now that Sea Lion was shelved.

That same day Ultra learned that Hitler had authorized the dismantling of air-loading equipment at all Dutch airfields. Churchill summoned the chiefs of staff in the evening. "It was," F. W. Winterbotham recalled, "as if someone cut all the strings of the violins in the middle of a dreary concerto. There were controlled smiles on the faces of these men." Then the chief of the air staff said what everyone privately hoped: in his opinion Hitler had abandoned Sea Lion, at least for the year. "There was a very broad smile on Churchill's face now as he lit up his massive cigar and suggested that we should all take a little fresh air."

4

Hitler still hoped to bring England to the negotiating table, if not by air or sea assault, by the capture of the most strategic mass of rock in the world, Gibraltar. Its seizure would not only keep the Royal Navy out of the Mediterranean and thus insure German take-over of North Africa and the Mideast but drastically lengthen the Empire's life lines to the Far East. How could the British continue a war on such a basis? reasoned Hitler. Particularly since he was willing to give them an honorable peace and let them be a silent partner in the crusade against Bolshevism.

It so happened that Franco's Minister of the Interior, Ramon Serrano Suñer, was then in Berlin to discuss Spain's entry into the war in general and a possible attack on Gibraltar in particular. On the way to the chancellery on that eventful morning he was in an apprehensive mood. Yesterday's conference with Ribbentrop had left him both disturbed and irritated, for he feared Ribbentrop's arrogant behavior was merely a reflection of his master's irritation with the Franco regime.

The Spaniard was pleasantly surprised to be received by Hitler with serene politeness and it was with some confidence that he explained he had been sent as personal agent of Franco as well as a representative of the Spanish government. He was married to the former Zita Polo, sister of the Generalissimo's wife. He had come, he said, to clarify the conditions under which Spain would join Germany in the war. That would be "whenever Spain's supply of foodstuffs and war material was secure."

The Führer seemed more interested in politics than war. Europe, he said, must be united into a continental political system by establishing her own Monroe Doctrine, with Africa under her protection. His allusions to Spain's entry into the war, however, were "indirect and vague." Only when his guest stressed the need for artillery in the Gibraltar area did Hitler become specific—and then about the superiority of bombs over shells. Rattling off figures, he explained that a long-barreled cannon needed repairs after firing about 200 rounds, each containing 75 kilograms of explosives, while a Stuka squadron of 36 machines could indefinitely drop 120 bombs of 1000 kilograms at a time. How long, argued Hitler, could the enemy resist these dive bombers? At the mere sight of them, the Royal Navy would flee from Gibraltar. Therefore there was no need for artillery. Besides, he added, the Germans could not possibly supply 38-centimeter guns for the Gibraltar operation. This virtuoso verbal performance, which left his listener speechless with wonder, was followed by an assurance that Germany would do everything in her power to help Spain.

Serrano Suñer left the chancellery so relieved that his host had not once used a threatening or even pressing tone that he advised Franco to accept Hitler's suggestion that the two leaders meet at the Spanish frontier in the near future for a more definite discussion. Equally impressed by Serrano Suñer, Hitler decided to approach his brother-in-law more forthrightly. "Spain's entry into the war on the side of the Axis Powers," he wrote Franco the next morning, "must begin with the expulsion of the English fleet from Gibraltar and immediately thereafter the seizure of the fortified rock." Once Spain came over to the Axis side, he promised with the persuasiveness of a salesman, Germany would supply not only military but economic aid to the greatest extent possible. In other words, quick victory was to be followed by quick profits.

In his reply on September 22 Franco seemed to agree with almost everything Hitler proposed but a meeting between Serrano Suñer and Ribbentrop two days later foretold difficulties. The Spaniard objected politely but firmly to German claims for several strategic islands off Africa. Even the interpreter thought Serrano Suñer was being quite "niggardly" about these bases after a wholesale offer by Ribbentrop of territory in Africa. "This," Schmidt observed, "brought the first chill to the warm friendship between Franco and Hitler."

If Ribbentrop was frustrated at the difficulties of negotiating with Franco's relative, he had cause for celebration later in the month when his brain child, the Tripartite Pact with Japan and Italy, was signed in Berlin. In it Japan agreed to recognize the leadership of Germany and

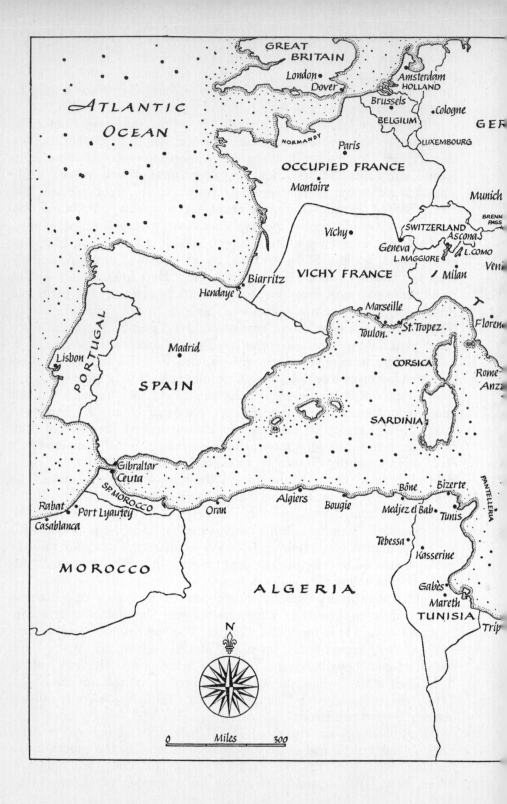

- Berlin
- NY
- Prague

- Warsaw
- OCCUPIED POLAND
- SLOVAKIA
- Vienna
- Bratislava
- Budapest
- HUNGARY

U.S.S.R.

- Kiev

- Odessa
- Trieste
- Belgrade
- YUGOSLAVIA
- ROMANIA
- Bucharest
- BULGARIA
- Sofia
- Sevastopol
- Yalta
- BLACK SEA
- Istanbul

ADRIATIC SEA

- Foggia
- Naples
- Taranto
- Salerno
- Tirana
- ALBANIA
- GREECE
- Athens
- Ankara

TURKEY

- Messina
- Gela
- Syracuse
- SICILY
- MALTA
- CRETE
- CYPRUS

MEDITERRANEAN SEA

- Derna
- El Gazala
- Benghazi
- Tobruk
- Matruh
- Salum
- El Alamein
- Alexandria
- Cairo
- SUEZ CANAL

- El Agheila

LIBYA

EGYPT

Italy in the establishment of a new order in Europe as long as they recognized her new order in Asia. The signatories also promised "to assist one another with all political, economic and military means when one of the three Contracting Parties is attacked by a power at present not involved in the European War or in the Sino-Japanese Conflict."

To the British and Americans this was further evidence that Japan was no better than Nazi Germany and Fascist Italy, and that the three "gangster" nations had joined forces to conquer the world. The Soviets were disturbed but Ribbentrop assured Molotov that the treaty was directed exclusively against the warmonger elements in America. Why not make it a quadripartite pact? he urged, and then wrote a long letter to Stalin saying that it was "the historical mission of the four powers—the Soviet Union, Japan, Italy, and Germany—to adopt a long-range policy and to direct the future development of their peoples into the right channels by delimitation of their interests for the ages."

5

Hitler devoted October to diplomacy. On the fourth he met Mussolini at the Brenner Pass. "The war is won! The rest is only a question of time," he said. While admitting that the Luftwaffe had not yet achieved air supremacy, he claimed that British planes were being knocked out of the air at a ratio of three to one. For some reason, however, England continued to hold out even though her military situation was hopeless. Her people were under inhuman strain. Why does she keep on? he complained and answered his own question: hope of American and Russian aid.

That, he said, was an illusion. The Tripartite Pact was already having a "dampening effect" on the cowardly American leaders and forty German divisions on the eastern front discouraged any Russian intervention. Therefore the time was ripe to strike a new blow at the very roots of the British Empire: to seize Gibraltar. This digressed into a diatribe against the Spaniards, who demanded 400,000 tons of grain and considerable gasoline as their price for entry into the war. And, complained Hitler, when he had brought up the matter of eventual repayment, Franco had the gall to reply that this "was a matter of confusing idealism with materialism." Almost beside himself with resentment, Hitler exclaimed that he had been practically represented "as if I were a little Jew who was haggling about the most sacred possessions of mankind!"

After the two dictators parted in a spirit of warmth and trust, the Führer made for Berchtesgaden "to think over quietly the new political scheme." He paced the rooms of the Berghof and took long walks by himself on the slopes of the Obersalzberg. He spoke out some thoughts over the dinner table, some at conferences. The result of these monologues was a decision to sound out the French during his trip to see Franco. Then, and only then, would he speak to the Russians.

His special train (it bore the curious name *Amerika*) left Germany on the twenty-second, arriving that evening at Montoire in west central France. Here Laval, Deputy Premier of Vichy France, came aboard for a brief conference. It dealt primarily with arrangements for a meeting with Marshal Pétain in two days. At this time the Führer planned to extend his program reducing France to complete vassalage. He hoped to do it with the willing help of the victims but was ready to use force and ruthless reprisals if necessary. Beyond subjecting France, as he had other conquered nations, to what Göring blandly called plunder economy (which included the outright theft of everything of value from raw materials and slave labor to national art treasures), he hoped to gain Vichy France as an active ally against England. From Laval's attitude, Hitler was assured that this could be done and he was in a confident mood as the train continued its journey through the night for the crucial meeting with Franco.

They were to meet next day at a little French border town more suitable for a holiday than a conference of world importance. Hendaye lay just below Biarritz in the resort area of southwest France, with beaches and palm trees worthy of a travel poster. The rendezvous was at the edge of town where the French narrow-gauge and Spanish wide-gauge rails met. The Führer train arrived in good time for the two o'clock meeting but there was no Spanish train on the adjoining platform. It was a sparkling, clear October day, so pleasant that the punctual Germans were not annoyed. After all, what could you expect from those lazy Spaniards with their interminable siestas?

Hitler was convinced that once he met Franco face to face he would bring him around just as he had Chamberlain, Laval and the others. Where would the Generalissimo be without the help of Germany? It was not, as devout Spaniards believed, the intervention of the Mother of God which had won the Civil War but the bombs German squadrons had "rained from the heavens that decided the issue."

While they waited, Hitler and Ribbentrop chatted on the platform. "We cannot at the moment," Schmidt overheard the Führer say, "give the Spaniards any written promises about transfers of territory from the French colonial possessions. If they get hold of anything in writing on this ticklish question with these talkative Latins, the French are sure to hear something about it sooner or later." Tomorrow he wanted to induce Pétain to start active hostilities against England and so could not give away French territory today. "Quite apart from that," he continued, "if such an agreement with the Spaniards became known, the French colonial empire would probably go over bodily to De Gaulle."

At last, an hour late, the Spanish train appeared on the International Bridge over the Bidassoa River. The tardiness had been deliberate, not due to any siesta. "This is the most important meeting of my life," Franco told one of his officers. "I'll have to use every trick I can—and this is one of them. If I make Hitler wait, he will be at a psychological disadvantage from the start." The *Caudillo* (Leader) was short and plump with dark, piercing eyes. In a nation of distinguished-looking men, he appeared to be a nonentity, a Sancho Panza, who had risen to power by luck and perseverance. His success was hard-won. Coming from Galicia, a province noted for its sober pragmatists, he brought to his high rank a grim sense of reality and shrewdness.

Although a peasant at heart, Franco was not even a man of the people. He also was too close to the Church and the monarchists and, while giving lip service to the Falangists (a Fascist-type party), it was obvious he was not one of them. The true Falangists, such as his brother-in-law, who had recently been promoted to Foreign Minister, were much more pro-German. Despite his recent unhappy experiences in Berlin, Serrano Suñer remained convinced that Germany was invincible and that Spain should go over to the winning side. Franco was skeptical. "I tell you that the English will never give in," he told his generals. "They'll fight and go on fighting: and if they are driven out of Britain, they'll carry on the fight from Canada: they'll get the Americans to come in with them. Germany has not won the war." At the same time he did not want to exhaust Hitler's patience and subject Spain to the fate of Czechoslovakia and the succeeding line of small countries which had stood in his way.

As his train drew alongside of Hitler's, Franco knew the fate of his country rested on his ability to keep it out of the European conflict. The Civil War had left Spain's economy in a shambles and with the failure of last year's harvest his people faced starvation. But would Hitler let him remain neutral? If he gave the Führer a flat refusal, what could stop a German invasion? The solution was to give the impression of joining the Axis, yet find some slight point that needed further clarification. His Galician heritage was his armor as he stepped onto the platform and started toward Hitler to the accompanying blast of military music.

Franco began with a set speech laden with compliments and vocal promises. Spain had always been "spiritually united with the German people without any reservation and in complete loyalty," and, in fact, "at every moment felt herself united with the Axis." Historically there were only forces of unity between their two nations and, in the present war, "Spain would gladly fight at Germany's side." The difficulties of doing so, he added, were well known to the Führer: in particular the food shortage and the difficulties anti-Axis elements were making for his poor country in America and Europe. "Therefore, Spain must mark time and often look kindly toward things of which she thoroughly disapproves." He said this with a tone of regret but quickly noted that despite all these problems Spain—mindful of her spiritual alliance with the Axis—was assuming "the same attitude toward the war as had Italy in the past autumn." This artful dodge was followed by a promise from Hitler. In return for Spanish co-operation in the war, he said, Germany would let Franco have Gibraltar—it would be seized on the tenth of January—as well as some colonial territories in Africa.

Franco sat huddled silently in his chair, face expressionless. Finally he began to talk, slowly and deliberately, offering up excuses while insisting on more concessions. His country, he said, needed several hundred thousand tons of wheat immediately. Fixing Hitler with "a slyly watchful expression," he asked if Germany was prepared to deliver it. And what about the large number of heavy guns Spain needed to defend the coast from attacks by the Royal Navy, not to mention anti-aircraft guns? He shifted in seemingly haphazard manner from one subject to another, from recompense for the certain loss of the Canary Islands to the impossibility of accepting Gibraltar as a present from foreign soldiers. That fortress must be taken by Spaniards! Abruptly he pragmatically assessed Hitler's chances of clearing the British out of Africa: to the edge of the desert, perhaps, but no farther. "As an old African campaigner I am quite clear about that." Similarly, he cast doubt on the Führer's ability to conquer Britain itself. At best England might fall but Churchill's government would flee to Canada and continue the war with America's aid.

Franco spoke in a monotonous singsong that reminded Schmidt of a muezzin calling the faithful to prayer. It only frustrated Hitler, who finally shot to his feet and blurted out that it was futile to continue. He immediately sat down again, as if regretting his display of nerves, and once more tried to persuade Franco to sign a treaty. Of course! said Franco. What would be more logical? As long as Germany supplied the food and armaments, of course; and as long as Spain was given the option to decide the right moment for war. Having come full circle, the meeting was adjourned.

As a disgruntled Hitler departed for his private compartment, the two Foreign Ministers walked down the platform to Ribbentrop's train for further discussions. After some sparring, Ribbentrop revealed that the Führer had come to Hendaye "to ascertain whether the Spanish claims and the French hopes were compatible with one another." Surely the Caudillo would understand Hitler's dilemma and sign a secret protocol to which Italy would later add her signature. Whereupon Ribbentrop handed over a Spanish translation of the proposal. It stated that Spain would receive territories from French colonial possessions "to the extent that France can be indemnified from British colonial possessions."

With a show of surprise, Serrano Suñer exclaimed that evidently a new course was to be followed in the African question and Germany's attitude toward France apparently had changed! This made Spain's compensation for entering the war very vague. And Franco, he concluded with a little smile, would have "to define more exactly the rewards of victory" to his people. Ribbentrop was no match for such verbal gymnastics and fought to restrain his anger as the Spaniard made a dramatic but elegantly formal exit.

That evening the Germans entertained the Spaniards at a state dinner in the dining car of the Führer's train. Franco was warm and friendly, his brother-in-law charming. Perhaps their ingratiating manner throughout the meal encouraged Hitler to draw Franco aside as the guests were rising to depart. For almost two hours the two men talked in private with the Führer becoming increasingly agitated at his inability to manipulate the imperturbable Caudillo, who stood firm on every important point. He believed, for instance, that the eastern gate of the Mediterranean, the Suez Canal, should be closed before the western gate, Gibraltar; nor was he moved by Hitler's protests. Even when his firmness drove Hitler from insistence to an outburst of temper, Franco remained impassive, insisting that if Spain did not get the ten million quintals of wheat, history (he was referring to the rising against Napoleon) might repeat itself. The Führer left the banquet car in a fume. "Franco is a little major!" he told Puttkamer. To Linge he reduced him in rank: "In Germany, that man would never rise higher than sergeant!" Another heard him bring down the Caudillo to corporal, his own World War grade. He was even more annoyed at the cunning tactics of his Foreign Minister. "Suñer has Franco in his pocket," he told Keitel and threatened to break off the talks with the Spaniards there and then.

In the meantime Ribbentrop was in his train trying to work out an agreement with Suñer, but he had become as frustrated as the Führer with the Spaniard's polite but insistent objections. Losing all patience, he dismissed Serrano Suñer and his aides as if they were schoolboys, instructing them to bring in the completed text by eight in the morning.

Serrano Suñer failed to appear in person on the twenty-fourth, entrusting the text instead to his subordinate, a former ambassador to Berlin who spoke German with a Viennese accent. Ribbentrop was so infuriated at the substitution that his rude shouts could be heard outside the train. "Unsatisfactory!" exclaimed Ribbentrop in his role as schoolmaster after reading Serrano Suñer's draft, which described the French Zone of Morocco as a territory later to belong to Spain. He demanded that the Spaniards submit a new draft, then drove off with Schmidt to the nearest airport so they could reach Montoire in time for the Hitler-Pétain meeting. Spluttering with rage all the way, the Foreign Minister cursed Suñer as a "Jesuit" and Franco as an "ungrateful coward." Secretly the interpreter was delighted by the tactics of the Spaniards. For the first time Hitler had been outwitted before he could play his own tricks.

He had already arrived in Montoire and was waiting in his train to meet Marshal Pétain, who had recently elevated himself from Premier to

Head of State, a new title disassociating him from the old republican regime. It would have made the Führer even unhappier with Franco to
know that he had already warned Pétain not to assume the burden of
leading France out of chaos. "Make your age your excuse," he had said.
"Let those who lost the war sign the peace. . . . You are the hero of Verdun. Don't let your name be mingled with the others who have been
defeated." "I know, General," Pétain had replied, "but my country calls
me, and I am hers. . . . It may be the last service I can do for her."

The aged marshal, smartly uniformed, was greeted at the entrance of
the railway station by Keitel. Pétain returned his salute and walked erectly
past the German honor guard, eyes front, with Ribbentrop and Laval at
his heels. They silently filed through the station to the Führer's train. As
Pétain emerged from the ticket hall, Hitler came forward, hand outstretched. The marshal allowed himself to be led into the private coach
but sat very straight facing Hitler, listening to Schmidt translate—he was
talking rather loudly for the old man's benefit—"with calm indolence."
He seemed confident rather than servile. Laval, next to him, was a vivid
contrast. He was dying for a cigarette and knew smoking was anathema to
both Hitler and Pétain. Laval's searching eyes darted alternately from
Hitler to Ribbentrop as the former pointed out that he was aware the
marshal did not belong among those who had favored declaring war on
Germany. "If this were not the case," he said, "this talk could not have
taken place."

After listing French sins in a moderate tone, the Führer repeated
what he had said to Franco: "We have already won the war. England is
beaten and will sooner or later have to admit it." And, he added meaning-
fully, it was obvious someone would have to pay for the lost war. "That
will be either France or England. If England bears the cost, then France
can take the place in Europe which is due her, and can fully retain her position as a colonial power." To do this, of course, France would have to
protect her colonial empire from attack as well as reconquer the central
African colonies, which had gone over to De Gaulle. At this point he indirectly suggested that France join the war against Britain by asking
Pétain what France would do if the English continued to attack her battleships as she had at Mers-el-Kebir and a few weeks later at Dakar.

While admitting that both of these attacks affronted most Frenchmen, Pétain replied that his country was in no position to wage another
war. He countered with a request for a final peace treaty "so that France
may be clear about her fate, and the two million French prisoners of war
may return to their families as soon as possible." Hitler glided over this
problem and the two Frenchmen, in turn, made no response to another
hint that France should enter the war. The two sides were at cross-purposes and although Pétain expressed his personal admiration for the
Führer and seemed to agree with many of his opinions, he expressed him-

self so curtly that Schmidt took it as an overt rebuff. "The great stake for which Hitler had played," recalled the interpreter, "had been lost as a result of the prudent reticence shown by Pétain and Laval." In his opinion France was not shamed by the actions of their two representatives at Montoire.

It was with honor, Pétain told his countrymen a few days later over the radio, that he accepted collaboration with Germany. He did so to maintain French unity. It would also lighten the weight of France's sufferings and better the lot of her prisoners. "This collaboration," he warned, "must be sincere. It must exclude all idea of aggression. It must carry with it a patient and confident effort." France had numerous obligations to the victor. Hadn't Hitler let France keep her sovereignty? "So far," continued Pétain, "I have spoken to you as a father. Today I am addressing you as a leader. Follow me. Trust in eternal France."

The mood aboard the Führer train was glum. Hitler had failed to get what he wanted at both Hendaye and Montoire. The third disappointment came before *Amerika* crossed the border of France with delivery of a letter from Mussolini dated six days earlier. In it he venomously attacked the French. In their hearts, he wrote, they hated the Axis and, despite the sweet words coming from Vichy, "one cannot think of their collaboration." Anxious lest Il Duce's vengeful attitude toward France endanger his own plan to draw Vichy into the anti-democratic crusade, Hitler instructed Ribbentrop to move up his meeting with Mussolini in Florence to October 28. Ribbentrop's telephone call to Ciano a few minutes later caused a minor panic in Rome. "This rush of the Führer to Italy so soon after his conference with Pétain," Ciano wrote in his diary, "is not at all pleasing to me. I hope he will not offer us a cup of hemlock because of our claims against France. This will be a bitter pill for the Italian people, even more so than the Versailles delusion."

Rather than return to Berlin as planned, Hitler ordered his train to Munich so he could rest and prepare for the hastily updated trip to Italy. On October 27, just before heading south late that afternoon, word came from the German military attaché in Rome that it was now "practically certain" that Mussolini would attack Greece early the next morning. According to Schmidt, the Führer "was beside himself" at this news and that evening at supper Ribbentrop reflected his master's ire. "The Italians will never get anywhere against the Greeks in the autumn rains and winter snows," he said. "Besides the consequences of war in the Balkans are quite unpredictable. The Führer intends at all costs to hold up this crazy scheme of the Duce's, so we are to go to Italy at once, to talk to Mussolini personally."

Ribbentrop could not have meant this seriously. He himself had set the meeting two days earlier. Further, he was aware that the Führer had just refused to sign a message to Rome, composed by his own staff, which criticized any such attack in straight language. "Ribbentrop," recalled Weizsäcker, who had written the message, "approved this, but Hitler said he did not want to cross Mussolini. Hitler's silence meant indirectly giving Italy the sign to go ahead with her decisive and dangerous step to the Balkans."

The next morning at 10 A.M., as *Amerika* was passing through Bologna, Hitler learned that the Italians had just marched into Greece. His first outburst of swearing and cursing, recalled Engel, was directed not at Mussolini but at the German liaison staffs and attachés who had "spoiled many a recipe for him." Only then did Hitler begin berating the Italians for their duplicity. "This is the revenge for Norway and France!" he exclaimed, then complained that "every second Italian is either a traitor or a spy." His emotions released, he turned to a more sober analysis of the situation. Il Duce, he guessed, had gone into Greece to counter Germany's growing economic influence in the Balkans. "I am greatly disturbed," he said. The Italian invasion, he feared, would have "grave consequences and give the British a welcome opportunity to set up an air base in the Balkans."

An hour later his train pulled into the gaily decorated station of Florence. An exuberant Duce rushed forward to embrace his ally. "Führer," he exclaimed, "we are on the march!" Hitler controlled himself. The damage had been done and it would be useless to complain. His greeting was aloof, a far cry from the usual warm reception he gave Mussolini, but even this coolness was momentary. In moments both dictators, being politicians, were put in good spirits by the ecstatic cries of "Führer, Heil Führer! Duce! Duce!" from the crowd outside the Palazzo Pitti where the talks would take place. Several times the two dictators had to appear at the balcony to appease the crowd. "It was a greeting such as the Romans gave their Caesars," Hitler later told his valet. "But they did not deceive me. They are trying to soften me now because of the way they have messed up my plans."

During the talk Hitler controlled himself well to Schmidt's surprise, with not "the slightest sign of his mental gnashing of teeth." Mussolini was in exceptional good humor. Any guilt he may have felt for doing what Hitler had only given reluctant consent to had been dispelled by his own resentment over Hitler's recent dispatch of troops to Romania days after they both had promised at the Brenner Pass to preserve peace in the Balkans. "Hitler always faces me with a fait accompli," he had complained to Ciano. "This time I am going to pay him back in his own coin. He will find out from the papers that I have occupied Greece. In this way the equilibrium will be re-established."

Apparently he had succeeded, for the Führer never uttered a syllable of complaint about Greece. Instead he devoted most of his time to the problem that had brought him to Florence. He told Mussolini of the meeting with Pétain and Laval in which he had been much impressed by the dignity of the former—and had not been at all deceived by the servility of the latter. He described his talks with Franco as an ordeal and rather than go through another he would "prefer to have three or four teeth out." The Caudillo, he complained, had been "very vague" about entering the war; he must have become leader of Spain by an accident.

The long meeting ended in brotherliness with Hitler repeating the promise made at the Brenner Pass that he would "on no account conclude peace with France if the claims of Italy were not completely satisfied." On his part, Mussolini observed that their two countries were, as always, completely in accord. Once aboard *Amerika*, however, Hitler began fulminating against Il Duce's new "adventure," the outcome of which could only be military catastrophe. Why on earth, he exclaimed, didn't Mussolini attack Malta or Crete? That would still make some sense in the context of their war with England in the Mediterranean. Particularly with the Italian troops in such straits in North Africa that they had just requested a German armored division!

The return trip through the snow-covered Alps was a morose one for the Führer. In little more than six months he had conquered more land than even the most optimistic German could have imagined. Norway, Denmark, Luxembourg, Belgium, Holland and France were his. He had outstripped Alexander and Napoleon. Yet nothing, it seems, fails like success; this incredible string of victories had been followed by frustration at Hendaye, Montoire and Florence. The mediocre leader of a second-rate country and the chief of a defeated nation were avoiding being led into the crusade against England and his own dependable ally was stupidly endangering the Axis position in the Mediterranean out of need for personal glory on the battlefield. As if that were not enough, the air campaign designed to bring England to the green table was now an admitted failure—at a frightful cost in planes.

Unable to hide his annoyance during the tedious voyage back to the Fatherland, he railed at "deceiving" collaborators and ungrateful, unreliable friends. What other conqueror had ever been faced with such a superfluity of frustrations! Much of his display must have been theater. Hitler could not have been as disturbed by Pétain's lack of commitment as he pretended and he surely knew he could have prevented the incursion into Greece if he had been willing to put pressure on Mussolini. But his bitterness at Franco's refusal to commit himself was sincere. The Caudillo must be forced into compliance, for he was the key to Gibraltar and seizure of this fortress could checkmate the English—and clear the way for the crusade in the East.

"THE WORLD WILL HOLD ITS BREATH"
NOVEMBER 12, 1940–JUNE 22, 1941

1

Although Hitler had given only reluctant support to the Tripartite Pact with Japan and Italy, he was persuaded by its father, Ribbentrop, to invite the Soviets to make it a four-power agreement. And so, on November 12, 1940, Foreign Commissar Molotov arrived in Berlin to talk of coalition. The meeting began without Hitler at Ribbentrop's new office in the former presidential palace and the host did his utmost to make the Soviet delegation feel at home, bestowing smiles on all sides. "Only at long intervals," recalled Schmidt, "did Molotov reciprocate, when a frosty smile glided over his intelligent, chess player's face." He listened impassively to Ribbentrop voice loud assurance that the Tripartite Pact was not aimed against the Soviet Union. In fact, Ribbentrop observed, Japan had already turned her face to the south and would be occupied for centuries in consolidating her territorial gains in Southeast Asia. "For her Lebensraum Germany, too, will seek expansion in a southerly direction, that is in central Africa, in the territories of the former German colonies." Everyone, he said reassuringly, was going south, as if talking of the latest fad. He suggested in his heavy-handed manner that the Soviets also head south and named the Persian Gulf and other areas in which Germany was disinterested. It was an obvious reference to India but Molotov just peered without expression through his old-fashioned pince-nez.

Disconcerted, Ribbentrop suggested that the Soviet Union join the Tripartite Pact. But Molotov, whose unerring logic in the presentation of arguments reminded Schmidt of his mathematics teacher, was saving his ammunition for Hitler. That afternoon Molotov listened impassively to the Führer, but when Hitler finally stopped talking complained politely that his statements had been of too general a nature. He wanted details; and began posing a succession of embarrassing questions: "Does the German-Soviet agreement of 1939 still apply to Finland? What does the New Order in Europe and Asia amount to, and what part is the U.S.S.R. to play in it? What is the position with regard to Bulgaria, Romania and Turkey; and how do matters stand with regard to the safeguarding of Russian interests in the Balkans and on the Black Sea?"

No foreigner had ever before dared to express himself quite so boldly and Schmidt wondered if Hitler would rush irately out the door as he had two years earlier when Sir Horace Wilson handed him Chamberlain's letter. But he meekly supplied reassuring answers. The Tripartite Pact, he said, would only regulate conditions in Europe; there would be no settlement without Russian collaboration—not only in Europe but in the Far East.

Molotov was skeptical. "If we are to be treated as equal partners and not mere dummies," he said, "we could, in principle, join the Tripartite Pact. But first the aim and object of the pact must be closely defined, and I must be more precisely informed about the boundaries of the Greater Asia area." Obviously disconcerted at being put on the defensive, Hitler abruptly ended the interrogation with the announcement that they would have to break off their discussion. "Otherwise we shall be caught by the air-raid warning."

He sent the Russians an invitation for luncheon on the thirteenth even though he disliked eating with foreigners. But the rare concession to cordiality did not moderate his guest's persistence. Molotov opened the second conference with continuing aggression. He brought up Finland, which Hitler was secretly planning to use as a military ally in case of war with Russia. The mere mention of Finland turned the Führer from genial luncheon host to testy litigant. "We have no political interest there," he protested.

Molotov was not convinced. "If good relations are maintained between Russia and Germany," he said with studied calm, "the Finnish question can be settled without war. But in that case there must be no German troops in Finland and no demonstrations against the Soviet government there." Hitler controlled himself, answering in a quiet but emphatic tone that the only German troops in Finland were in transit to northern Norway.

Molotov's suspicions were not allayed and Hitler became so ruffled he began to repeat himself. "We must have peace with Finland, because of their nickel and timber." But the next sentence, perhaps unwittingly, exposed his ultimate plan. "A conflict in the Baltic would put a severe strain on Russo-German relations—with unpredictable consequences." If Molotov did not see that this was a threat, he ignored it, thereby making a grave diplomatic error. "It's not a question of the Baltic but of Finland," he replied sharply.

"No war with Finland!" said Hitler obstinately.

"Then you are departing from our agreement of last year," said Molotov with equal obstinence.

This was a far grimmer, if less spectacular, contest than the debate with the British and Ribbentrop saw his cherished policy of Russian-German entente in grave danger. He intervened conciliatingly and Hitler took the cue to sound the Ribbentrop theme of Southward Ho! "After the conquest of England," he said, "the British Empire will be apportioned as a gigantic world-wide estate in bankruptcy of forty million square kilometers." Like the promoter of a new real estate development, Hitler painted a tempting picture. "In this bankrupt estate Russia will get access to the ice-free and really open seas. Thus far, a minority of 45 million Englishmen have ruled 600 million inhabitants of the British Empire. I am about to crush this minority." Germany, he said, wanted no diversion from her struggle against the heart of the Empire, the British Isles. This was why he opposed any Baltic war.

But this excursion did not mollify Molotov, who resumed his complaints. "You have given a guarantee to Romania which displeases us," he said with characteristic brusqueness. This referred to Germany's recent guarantee of Romania's new frontiers from foreign attacks. "Is this guarantee also valid against us?"

In diplomacy it is considered a blunder to pin down an opponent. "It applies to anyone who attacks Romania," Hitler said flatly and a few moments later abruptly adjourned the meeting, using the same excuse as yesterday—possible English air raid.

Hitler did not attend the banquet at the Russian Embassy that evening, an occasion marred by the appearance of British planes just as Molotov was proposing a friendly toast. Ribbentrop escorted the host to his own air shelter in the Wilhelmstrasse and while there took the opportunity to show Molotov a draft of the four-power treaty he so devoutly sought. It called for Germany, Russia, Japan and Italy to respect each other's natural spheres of influence and settle any dispute "in an amicable way." It defined the Soviet's "territorial aspirations" as south "in the direction of the Indian Ocean."

Molotov was not impressed. Russia, he said, was more interested in Europe and the Dardanelles than the Indian Ocean. "Consequently," he said, "paper agreements will not suffice for the Soviet Union; she would have to insist on effective guarantees of her security." He made an exhaustive list of other Soviet interests: Swedish neutrality, access to the Baltic Sea; and the fate of Romania, Hungary, Bulgaria, Yugoslavia and Greece.

Ribbentrop was so taken aback that, according to the minutes of that meeting, he could "only repeat again and again that the decisive question was whether the Soviet Union was prepared and in a position to co-operate with us in the liquidation of the British Empire." Molotov replied with sarcasm: if Germany was waging a life-and-death struggle against England as Hitler had remarked that afternoon, he could only assume this meant that Germany was fighting "for life" and England "for death." And when Ribbentrop persisted that England was beaten but didn't know it, the Russian replied, "If that is so, why are we sitting in this air-raid shelter? And whose bombs are those that are falling so close that their explosions are heard even here?"

Molotov won the argument but lost the case. When Hitler read the report of the air-shelter discussion he was galled. Convinced that the Russians were not serious about a four-power pact, he gave up the last scant hope of entente and resolved to do what he had vowed to do since 1928. At last he irrevocably decided to attack Russia, confiding later to Bormann that Molotov's visit had convinced him "that sooner or later Stalin would abandon us and go over to the enemy." He could not submit to Soviet blackmail regarding Finland, Romania, Bulgaria and Turkey. "The Third Reich, defender and protector of Europe, could not have sacrificed these friendly countries on the altar of Communism. Such behavior would have been dishonorable, and we should have been punished for it. From the moral as well as from the strategic point of view it would have been a miserable gambit. War with Russia had become inevitable, whatever we did; and to postpone it only meant that we should later have to fight under conditions far less favorable. I therefore decided, as soon as Molotov departed, that I would settle accounts with Russia as soon as fair weather permitted." One encouragement was the miserable performance of the Red Army against little Finland. He had also come to regard himself as a man of destiny, superior to any other human being, whose genius and will power would conquer any enemy. Mesmerized by his political and military victories, he explained to one Nazi commander that he was the first and only mortal who had emerged into a "superhuman state." His nature was "more godlike than human," and therefore as the first of the new race of supermen he was "bound by none of the conventions of human morality" and stood "above the law."

2

Hitler kept his decision to himself, however, leaving his commanders under the impression that England was still the primary target. On the day of Molotov's arrival in Berlin he had issued a directive aimed at bringing England to her knees without having to risk an invasion across the Channel. This plan called for a combination of blows to finish what the Italians had so ineptly started in Egypt and Greece. These attacks—combined with seizure of Gibraltar, the Canaries, Azores, Madeira and parts of Morocco—would assuredly cut off England from the Empire and force her to capitulate.

It was a chancy if clever plan since it involved co-operation with a dubious collaborator, an unstable ally and a reluctant neutral. No one was more aware of the difficulties of such a complex campaign than the Führer, but despite recent frustrations he was confident of bringing Pétain, Mussolini and Franco to heel. He began with the last. "I have decided to attack Gibraltar," he told the Caudillo's envoy, Serrano Suñer, on November 18. "All that is required is the signal to begin, and a beginning must be made."

But Franco's brother-in-law was as impossible to pin down as ever. He repeated Spain's dire need for grain and renewed her territorial demands. Hitler refused the latter outright, pointing out how well paid Spain would be if she joined the victorious side. Serrano Suñer observed that Spain, as Napoleon had found to his dismay, had always been ready to resist *any* invasion of its territory. This was succeeded by a final observation which somehow managed to combine another threat with the promise of compliance: Spain would have to use the remaining period of neutrality to buy wheat from the West. It was a tantalizing performance that left Hitler irritated and frustrated, and he later told intimates that Serrano Suñer was "the most evil spirit . . . the (gravedigger) of modern Spain!"

Convinced that Franco would eventually join the war, the Führer held the final briefing on the seizure of Gibraltar, Operation Felix, early in December. He told his commanders that he would undoubtedly get Franco's formal consent in the near future and then sent a personal friend of Franco's to bring him to terms. His choice, Canaris, was disastrous. The admiral, working against Hitler since 1938, formally presented Hitler's arguments, then informally advised Franco to stay out of a war that the Axis was bound to lose.*

When Canaris reported that Franco would enter the war only "when England was about ready to collapse," Hitler lost his patience; on December 10 he instructed his commanders to abandon Felix as a lost cause. But a few weeks later he made another appeal to Franco. In a long plaintive letter he promised to deliver grain immediately if the Caudillo would only approve an early assault on Gibraltar. He made a pledge never to forsake

---

* After the war the Marquis de Valdeglesias, in the presence of Franco, asked General Vigon (a close friend of Canaris) if it was true that the admiral had worked against Spanish interests. Franco lunged from his chair. "No, no," he exclaimed, "Canaris was an excellent friend of Spain!" "Perhaps," observed the marquis, "he was a closer friend of Spain than his own country." At this point, recalled Valdeglesias, "the Caudillo's extreme excitement confirmed my impression that this was true."

Franco that was followed by a final plea: "I believe, Caudillo, that we three men, the Duce, you and I, are linked to one another by the most implacable force of history, and that we should therefore, in this historic conflict, obey the supreme commandment to realize that in grave times such as these nations can be saved by stout hearts rather than by seemingly prudent caution."

Once more Franco appeared to agree with everything Hitler said, yet did nothing. It was by will power alone that he stalled Felix and saved Gibraltar for England, and by so doing he kept the Mediterranean open to the West while confining Adolf Hitler to the continent of Europe. If the Mediterranean had been closed, it is most likely that all of North Africa and the Middle East would have fallen to the Reich. The entire Arab world would have enthusiastically joined the Axis with all its resources—because of their hatred of the Jews. Apart from Spain's desperate economic situation and his fear of aligning himself with an eventual loser, there was a compelling personal motive for Franco's decision to thwart Hitler. He was part Jewish.*

3

Stalin waited almost two weeks before informing the Germans that the Soviets would join Hitler's proposed four-power pact on several conditions, such as withdrawal of troops from Finland. The demands were not excessive but, to the surprise of the Foreign Office, Hitler did not deign to haggle—or even bother to send Moscow a reply.

His mind was set on force of arms and late in the month his field commanders began a series of war games involving the attack on Russia. A day after their conclusion, on December 5, the chiefs of staff of the three army groups involved met with Hitler, Brauchitsch and Halder. While approving Halder's basic plan of attack, the Führer was averse to imitating Napoleon with a main drive on Moscow. Seizure of the capital, he said, "was not so very important." Brauchitsch protested that Moscow was of supreme importance not only as the focal point of the Soviet communications network but as an armament center. This brought forth a heated retort. "Only completely ossified brains, absorbed in the ideas of past centuries," said Hitler, "could see any worth-while objective in taking the capital." *His* interest lay in Leningrad and Stalingrad, the Bolshevik breeding grounds. With these two nests destroyed, Bolshevism would be dead. And that was the primary aim of their attack.

* This was known by the British ambassador to Spain, Sir Samuel Hoare, and others in the diplomatic community but it is extremely doubtful that Hitler—who had recently complained that Franco treated him like a little haggling Jew—had been informed of this by his own diplomats, who had also hidden from him the fact that Molotov's wife was Jewish.

Brauchitsch's protest that this was the aim of a politician led to a lecture proving that politics and military strategy were interdependent. "Hegemony over Europe," said Hitler, "will be decided in battle against *Russia*." The defeat of the Soviet Union, for example, would help bring his secondary enemy, England, to terms. Five days later Hitler began preparing his own people for the coming crusade with a ringing speech in Berlin on the inequitable distribution of the riches of the earth. It was not fair, he said, for Germans to live 360 persons per square mile while other countries were sparsely populated. "We must solve these problems," he concluded, "and, therefore, we will solve them."

At the same time Goebbels was preparing Germany for hard times ahead. The prolonged Yuletide atmosphere, he told his associates, must be confined exclusively to two days. "Even then the feast of Christmas itself should be fitted into the framework of present-day happenings. A sloppy Christmas tree atmosphere lasting several weeks is out of tune with the militant mood of the German people." There would also be a raising of Germany's moral tone—outside of the big cities. "No strip dancers are to perform in rural areas, in small towns, or in front of soldiers." Comedians were also forbidden in the future to make political jibes or "lewd erotic jokes."

The revised plan of attack was presented to Hitler on December 17. He altered it to delay the drive on Moscow until the Baltic States were cleared and Leningrad captured, then changed the name of the operation from Otto to a more meaningful title: Barbarossa (Red Beard) after Frederick I, the Holy Roman Emperor who had marched east in 1190 with his legions to take the Holy Land. The bulk of the Red Army standing on its western frontier, he directed, would be "destroyed by daring operations led by deeply penetrating armored spearheads." Those forces still capable of giving battle would be prevented from withdrawing into the depths of the U.S.S.R. "The final objective of the operation is to erect a barrier against Asiatic Russia on the general line Volga–Archangel. The last surviving area of Russia in the Urals can then, if necessary, be eliminated by the air force."

Halder suspected that Hitler was only bluffing and asked Engel if this was a genuine plan. The adjutant believed that Hitler himself did not yet know. But the die indeed was cast, the crusade set in motion. Hitler had no patience with those who, counseling moderation in triumph, wanted Germany to cease its aggression and enjoy the fruits of conquest. Most of Europe, they argued, was Hitler's and if he bided his time England too would recognize the reality of his hegemony. But to Adolf Hitler such a passive policy was unacceptable. The aim of National Socialism was the destruction of Bolshevism. How could he turn his back on his mission in life?

"I had always maintained that we ought at all costs to avoid waging war on two fronts," he later told Bormann, "and you may rest assured that I pondered long and anxiously over Napoleon, and his experiences in Russia. Why, then, you may ask, this war against Russia, and why at the time that I selected?" There was no hope of ending the war by invasion of England and hostilities would have gone on interminably with the Americans playing an increasingly active role. The one and only chance of vanquishing the Soviet Union was to take the initiative. Why attack in 1941? Because time was working in Russia's favor and against the Germans. Only when he held the territories of Russia would time be on *Germany's* side.

4

On the surface relations between the two unnatural allies prospered. Within days after setting Barbarossa into action—on January 10, 1941— Hitler authorized promulgation of two agreements with the Soviets: an economic treaty specifying reciprocal deliveries of commodities; and a secret protocol in which Germany renounced its previous claim to a strip of Lithuanian territory for 7,500,000 gold dollars.

Behind the façade of amity, however, dissension increased between the trade delegations. The flow of raw materials from the Soviet Union was steady and on schedule, while German deliveries were painfully slow and erratic. Whenever, for instance, machine tools were ready for shipment to Russia some inspector from the Air or War Ministry would appear to praise the workmanship, then hijack the tools in the name of national defense. This organized slowdown extended to warships. Hitler himself ordered work stopped on a heavy cruiser promised to Stalin so more submarines could be produced. The Germans did offer to tow the hull to Leningrad and arm it with 380-mm. Krupp guns but they wrangled so insistently over price that the ship was still in Wilhelmshaven.

Stalin became involved in the argument over German deliveries but he always restrained his own negotiators. He was determined to maintain good relations with his obstreperous ally for as long as possible. While he was striving for peace—at least until the Red Army was brought up to fighting strength—Hitler continued to prepare his people for war and the New Order. He did so in an ominously oblique manner in his annual January 30 address at the Sportpalast. After a rousing introductory speech by Goebbels, he strode rigidly to the platform, raising an arm diffidently in the party salute, amidst wild cheers. He stood silent for a moment and then began speaking. "His voice," recalled Shirer's replacement at CBS, "was first a slow, low rumble." Then, with sudden vehemence, his arms began sweeping in wide gestures.

He could have been thinking of Barbarossa and the racial cleansing that would follow when he said, "I am convinced that 1941 will be the crucial year of the great New Order in Europe," but the enemy he attacked was Britain, leader of the "pluto-democracies," which, he charged, were under the control of an international Jewish clique and supported by dissident émigrés. These words provided cover for his attack on the Soviet Union while preparing his own people for the final assault on Jewry and, upon hearing Halder's report four days later that German troop strength would be equal to Russia's and far superior in quality, Hitler exclaimed, "When Barbarossa commences the world will hold its breath and make no comment!" His vision of conquest, in fact, soared beyond the limits of his own continent; on February 17 he ordered preparation of a drive to the heart of Britain's empire, India. This would be accompanied by seizure of the Near East in a pincer movement: on the left from Russia across Iran and on the right from North Africa toward the Suez Canal. While these grandiose plans were primarily designed to force Britain onto the side of Germany, they indicated the extent of Hitler's vaulting aspirations. Russia was as good as won and his restless mind was already seeking new worlds to conquer, new enemies, America and Roosevelt in particular, to bring to heel.

For a dreamer Hitler could, quite often, be practical. No sooner had he envisaged vast fields of conquest than he began devoting himself to a relatively modest one. The defeat of Italian troops in Albania and Greece had, in his own words, indirectly "struck a blow at the belief of our invincibility, that was held by friend and foe alike." Greece, therefore, had to be occupied and order re-established throughout the area before Barbarossa could safely be launched. This was not his sole motivation. Hitler also looked upon Italian failure in the Balkans as a golden opportunity to gain more territory and economic assets.

The occupation of Greece, no simple matter, was particularly complicated by geography. Four countries lay between Hitler and his target—Hungary, Romania, Bulgaria and Yugoslavia. The first two, virtual German satellites, had been invested by his troops for some months; and the third, under considerable pressure, had joined the Tripartite Pact on the first of March. While this gave German troops a clear road to Greece, strategic Yugoslavia remained a military as well as political concern. Its leaders wanted neither German nor Russian intervention in the Balkans and, after veiled threats and vague promises failed to bring them into the Axis, Hitler invited Prince Paul, the Yugoslav Regent, to the Berghof so that he could exert his personal influence.

Tempted as he was by Hitler's promise to guarantee Yugoslavia territorial integrity, Prince Paul protested that the decision was most difficult for personal reasons: his wife's Greek ancestry, her personal sympathies for

England and his own antagonism toward Mussolini. The Prince left without giving an answer but three days later—an interminable wait for Hitler —he replied that he was willing to sign the Tripartite Pact, provided Yugoslavia was not required to lend any military assistance or allow passage of German troops through its territory. This was unsatisfactory but Hitler, controlling his feelings, sent back word that Germany accepted these conditions. This conciliatory offer unexpectedly brought a rebuff. The Yugoslavs could do nothing that might involve them in a war, "possibly with America or even Russia."

By mid-March it was evident that the Yugoslav government would not yield and the strain on the Führer was visible as he spoke on the sixteenth at the Memorial Day ceremony in the Berlin War Museum. "His face was drawn and haggard," recalled Louis Lochner, "his skin was ashy gray, his eyes devoid of their usual luster. Care and worry was stamped on him. But that was not the most striking thing. What amazed me was the matter of fact, uninterested, detached way in which he rattled off his usual platitudes appropriate to such an occasion." He read the brief speech as though it bored him, making no attempt to rouse the millions listening to him over the radio.

The next day the situation in Yugoslavia changed with dramatic suddenness. The Crown Council agreed to sign the Tripartite Pact. This brought a public outcry of indignation and, after three ministers resigned in protest, high-ranking air force officers led a revolt. By dawn of March 27 the rebels had overthrown the government and the youthful heir to the throne, Peter, was King.

In Berlin that morning, Hitler was congratulating himself on the happy conclusion of the Yugoslav problem; he had just received a message that the local population had been "universally most impressed" by Yugoslavia's acceptance of the new pact and that the government was "entirely master of the situation." Five minutes before noon, as he was preparing himself for an important conference with Japanese Foreign Minister Matsuoka, a telegram arrived from Belgrade. When Hitler read that the former members of the Yugoslav government were reportedly under arrest, he first thought it was a joke. Then he was seized with indignation. To be robbed of victory at the last moment was insupportable. This time his rage was genuine. He felt he'd been "personally insulted." He shouted an order for military commanders to report at once to the chancellery, sent an emergency call for Ribbentrop, who was talking with Matsuoka at the Wilhelmstrasse, then burst into the conference room where Jodl and Keitel were waiting for the daily briefing. Brandishing the telegram, Hitler exclaimed that he was now going to smash Yugoslavia once and for all!

Like a lover spurned moments after being accepted, the more he talked the angrier and more excited he became. He vowed he would issue orders for immediate, simultaneous attacks from north and east. Keitel protested that such an ambitious operation was impossible. The Barbarossa deadline could not be postponed since troop movements were already proceeding according to their planned maximum railway-capacity program. Furthermore, List's army in Bulgaria was too weak to pit against Yugoslavia and only a fool would rely on help from the Hungarians.

"That is the very reason why I have called in Brauchitsch and Halder," said Hitler. They would have to find some solution. "Now I intend to make a clean sweep of the Balkans—it is time people got to know me better."

By ones and twos, Brauchitsch, Halder, Göring, Ribbentrop and their adjutants joined the meeting. All listened in awe as Hitler declared in a harsh and vengeful tone that he was determined "to smash Yugoslavia militarily and as a state." To Ribbentrop's protest that they should first confront the Yugoslavs with an ultimatum, Hitler replied acidly, "Is that how you size up the situation? The Yugoslavs would swear black is white. Of course, they say they have no warlike intentions, and when we march into Greece they will stab us in the back." The attack, he exclaimed, must start as soon as possible! "Politically it is especially important that the blow against Yugoslavia be carried out with merciless harshness and that the military destruction be done in Blitzkrieg style." That would frighten the Turks as well as Greece. Göring's main task was to eliminate the Yugoslav air force ground installations before destroying the capital "in attacks by waves."

Hitler disposed of the hastily summoned Hungarian and Bulgarian ministers with dispatch. In a fifteen-minute meeting with the former his comment on the revolt in Belgrade was reduced to a quotation: "Whom the gods would destroy they first make mad." This was followed by a promise: if Hungary helped on this crisis, she would win back the long-coveted Banat area. It was a unique opportunity for Hungary to obtain revisions she might otherwise not get for years. "You can believe me that I am not pretending, for I am not saying more than I can be answerable for."

The next interview took but five minutes. Hitler told the Bulgarian minister that he was relieved by the events in Yugoslavia. "The everlasting uncertainty down there is over," he said and used Macedonia as the bait for continued Bulgarian co-operation with the Axis. The dispensing of largesse—of other people's property—was abruptly followed by rage. "The storm," he exclaimed, "will burst over Yugoslavia with a rapidity that will dumfound those gentlemen!"

With orders for attack issued and two hesitant allies bribed into line, Hitler at last found time that afternoon to see the Japanese envoy. Hitler hoped that America could be kept out of the war and suggested that the best way might be for Japan to seize Singapore. This should be done quickly since another such golden opportunity would not soon occur. And Japan, he added, need have no fear that Russia could counter with an attack in Manchuria in view of the strength of the German army.

Matsuoka, a graduate of the University of Oregon, answered slowly and deliberately in English. He was convinced, he said, that the German proposal was the right one, then added: "But I can give no firm promise on behalf of Japan at the moment." He hastily assured the visibly disappointed Hitler that he himself was for action. In truth, he was so eager for it that the Japanese army had sent Colonel Yatsugi Nagai along on this trip to see that he made no harsh promises about Singapore. Consequently Matsuoka was forced to respond evasively to every mention of the British stronghold. Even when Hermann Göring, after accepting a scroll of Mount Fuji, jokingly promised to come and see the real thing "if Japan takes Singapore," the envoy nodded toward the edgy Colonel Nagai and said, "You'll have to ask him."

Matsuoka was not at all reticent about a treaty he hoped to make with Stalin in the near future and was surprised to hear Ribbentrop, who had given him the idea of a grand four-power treaty, say, "How can you conclude such a pact at this time? Just remember, the U.S.S.R. never gives anything for nothing." Nagai took this to be a warning, but Matsuoka's enthusiasm could not be damped even when Ambassador Oshima told him in confidence that there was a strong likelihood that Germany and Russia would soon be at war.

The meeting with Matsuoka was not the end of Hitler's day. He signed Directive No. 25 calling for simultaneous attacks on Yugoslavia and Greece before sitting down at midnight to tell Mussolini about Yugoslavia. "Now I do not regard this situation as disastrous, to be sure," he wrote, "but nevertheless as one which is so difficult that we, for our part, must avoid making any mistakes if we do not want ultimately to imperil our entire position." He had, therefore, taken all necessary measures to meet any developing crisis with the necessary military means. "I now urgently request you, Duce, not to carry out any further operations in Albania for the next few days." After this polite reminder not to endanger the situation with another hopeless adventure, he called for "*absolute secrecy,*" underlining these words for emphasis.

The letter with all its punctilious courtesy emphasized the new relationship between the two men. After the misadventures in Greece and Africa, Mussolini was no longer the "senior partner." In the Führer's eyes, he was branded with the unforgivable defect of failure. The list of Hitler's grievances was formidable, if debatable: the abortive Grecian campaign had not only encouraged the British to launch a successful offensive in Libya, and discouraged Franco from supporting the Gibraltar operation, but forced Germany to deal with the dissident Yugoslavs at a most inappropriate time. Barbarossa would have to be postponed for at least a month.

5

Although Hitler blamed the delay of Barbarossa on the Yugoslav campaign, the general shortage of equipment for the Wehrmacht—his responsibility—could have been a more determining factor. In any event, he did not regard the postponement as a calamity despite a gnawing dread: "I was haunted by the obsession that the Russians might take the offensive." He did not seem perturbed when he summoned his field commanders to the chancellery to announce a definite date of attack and, more important, deliver a doctrinal lecture on the coming "struggle of two opposing ideologies." By 11 A.M. March 30 the senior commanders for Barbarossa, along with their leading staff officers, were gathered in the small cabinet chamber where a speaker's lectern had been set up. More than two hundred were seated in long rows according to rank and seniority by the time Hitler entered from the rear. With a shuffling of chairs the assemblage smartly rose, then sat down once Hitler stepped to the rostrum. His mood was grave as he spoke of the military and political situation. The United States could not reach the peak of production and military power for four years. Consequently this was the time to clean up Europe. War with Russia was inevitable, he said, and merely to sit back and wait would be disastrous. The attack would begin on June 22.

It could not be postponed, he said, since no successor would ever again exercise sufficient authority to accept responsibility for unleashing it. He and he alone could stop the Bolshevik steamroller before all Europe succumbed to it. He called for the destruction of the Bolshevik state and the annihilation of the Red Army, adding an assurance that victory would be quick and overwhelming. The only problem, he added ominously, was how to deal with the conquered Russians, how to treat prisoners of war and non-combatants.

The military sat stiff in their chairs, wondering if they would be called upon to take part in this program. As military professionals most of them had been repelled by Hitler's ruthless measures, after the conquest of Poland, against Polish Jews, intelligentsia, clergy and nobility. Their fears were quickened by Hitler's next loud threat: "The war against Russia will be such that it cannot be fought in a knightly fashion! This struggle is one of ideologies and racial differences and will have to be conducted with unprecedented, merciless and unrelenting harshness." There was no utterance of protest, any more than there had been in Poland, not even an involuntary gesture of protest.

That morning Hitler had put his military leaders to the final humiliating test with his demand that they compromise their honor as warriors.

Now they, like so many in Germany who shared his fear and hatred of Jews and Slavs, were reluctant partners in his crusade. Today Lebensraum, which they considered just recompense for the Russian territories won in battle but lost at Versailles, had been relegated to the background and Hitler's real grounds for invasion lay exposed: annihilation of Bolshevism —that is, annihilation of the Jews.

In the meantime preparations for the Yugoslav-Greek invasions were brought to a conclusion. In Belgrade there were daily patriotic demonstrations, some instigated by local Communists carrying out Soviet Balkan policy. Russia, in fact, was so eager to bolster the Yugoslavs against German incursion that she signed a pact with the new government on April 5. This did not daunt Hitler. The following dawn German troops crossed the Yugoslav border in overwhelming force. Bombers began systematically destroying Belgrade in an operation to which Hitler had given a significant code name, Punishment. The Soviet leaders, their signature hardly dry on the treaty with Yugoslavia, reacted with striking indifference, relegating the attack on Yugoslavia and Greece to the back pages of *Pravda*. Mere passing mention was made of the devastating air raids on Belgrade which were continuing around the clock.

Hitler warned Goebbels that the entire campaign would take at least two months and this information was passed on to the people. It was based on a gross overestimation of enemy strength. Within a single week German and Hungarian troops marched into a shattered Belgrade which was little more than rubble. In the process of Punishment, 17,000 civilians had died. On the seventeenth the remnants of the Yugoslav army surrendered. Ten days later the Grecian campaign was virtually concluded when German tanks rumbled into Athens. Twenty-nine German divisions had been transported into the battle zones over primitive roads and rail systems at an extravagant cost of energy, fuel and time. Of this huge force, only ten divisions saw action for more than six days. A sledge hammer had been used to kill mosquitoes. It was this shocking failure of German intelligence which was more responsible for the delay of Barbarossa than Mussolini.

Hitler's dismay at the cost of the Balkan invasion was more than mitigated by a startling development in North Africa. With only three divisions at his disposal, General Erwin Rommel burst across Cyrenaica to within a few miles of Egypt. This triumph, which surprised Hitler as much as the enemy, compromised Britain's hold on the entire eastern Mediterranean. It also damaged British prestige and persuaded Stalin to maintain good relations with the Germans despite provocations. Besides shutting his eyes to their aggressions in the Balkans, the Soviet leader persistently ignored the growing rumors that Hitler was planning to invade his own country. Warnings had already come from numerous sources, including the U. S. State Department. Foreign diplomats in Moscow talked openly of an imminent clash. "Thus, the [Jewish] wife of the American Ambassador Steinhardt," reported a German diplomat to Berlin, "remarked that she would like to be out of Moscow before the troops entered it."

For months the Soviet intelligence service itself had been predicting the attack. But Stalin did not trust his own informants and his paranoia increased with the volume of reports. Convinced that Hitler would not be stupid enough to attack Russia without first neutralizing England, he imagined these were rumors manufactured by the capitalist West, which hoped to come between him and Hitler. He wrote in red ink on one alarming report from a Czech agent: "This information is a British provocation. Find out where it comes from and punish the culprit."

Marshal Yeremenko confirmed Stalin's irrational suspicions in his memoirs: "That was why he failed to authorize all urgent or decisive defense measures along the frontier, for fear that this would serve the Hitlerites as a pretext to believe the rumors since his own hope was for the capitalists and Nazis to destroy each other. In any event, he wanted to avoid provoking Hitler into an attack before the Red Army was fully armed."

He was equally anxious to placate Japan. He treated Foreign Minister Matsuoka, fresh from Berlin, as an honored guest, making a public show of his delight when a neutrality pact was signed. At the celebration party in the Kremlin—it came on the day Belgrade fell—Stalin personally brought plates of food to the Japanese envoys, embraced them, kissed them and danced around. The treaty was a coup for his diplomacy, convincing proof that he could disregard rumors of a German attack on Russia. Certainly Hitler would never have permitted Japan to conclude this agreement if he had any such notion.

Stalin was in such a good humor that he followed the Japanese delegation to the station platform for a final tipsy good-by. He kissed General Nagai, then, encompassing the diminutive Matsuoka in a bear hug, gave him several affectionate smacks. "There is nothing to fear in Europe," he said, "now that there is a Japan-Soviet neutrality pact!"

A few minutes later, as the Japanese train moved off, he threw an arm around German Ambassador von der Schulenburg. "We must remain friends," he said, "and you must now do everything to that end!" He turned to a colonel, checked to make sure he too was a German, and roared out: "We shall remain friends with you—*in any event!*" He was probably referring to the numerous flights of German planes over Russian territory. In the past two weeks alone there had been fifty such incursions. Two days after embracing Schulenburg, however, Stalin was spurred to action by the emergency landing of a German plane almost a hundred miles inside the Soviet Union; aboard were found a camera, unexposed rolls of film and a torn topographical map of the districts of the U.S.S.R.

The Soviets lodged a formal complaint with Berlin, adding that eighty other violations of Soviet air space had occurred since the end of March. Still it was a mild protest and Stalin persisted in ignoring a new flood of warnings, the latest from British Ambassador Cripps, who predicted Hitler would attack on June 22.*

While everyone in the German Foreign Office suspected an attack on Russia might be imminent, it was not until now that Hitler told Ribbentrop of Barbarossa. The unhappy Foreign Minister "wanted to try one more diplomatic approach to Moscow but Hitler refused to allow any further démarche." He forbade Ribbentrop to discuss the matter with anyone, and then assured Ambassador von der Schulenburg in Moscow: "I do not intend a war against Russia." Two days later Hitler again confirmed the attack date, the one Cripps had mentioned, June 22.

There was no doubt that Germany was entering this contest with the most powerful armed force in the world. Yet she had no valid ally. Japan was on the other side of the world; Italy was a liability; Spain was intransigent; and Vichy France was unreliable. Hitler's alliances had been diminished by victory. His easy conquests had made all his friends—including little ones like Yugoslavia, Hungary and Romania—uneasy. His only strength was the Wehrmacht and reliance on force was fatal for any conqueror. Wars are won by politics, not by arms. Napoleon had learned this hard lesson from the British, who had a tradition of losing battles and winning wars. They had lost the battle against Hitler on the Continent but had already won the battle for their dominions and the battle for American aid.

Hitler's only chance for victory in the East was an alliance with those millions in the Soviet Union who hated Stalin but, unless he followed the advice of the Rosenberg group to treat them liberally, he would not only lose his last chance for a genuine Grand Alliance but turn potential allies into relentless enemies.

6

Although Hitler's military leaders had first been appalled by the thought of invading Russia, they now almost universally shared his conviction that victory would come quickly. The consensus was that the cam-

* For some time members of the Ultra team had been attempting to relay vital information to the Soviets without revealing the source. "For this purpose," recalled Hugh Trevor-Roper, "we had a special liaison officer in Moscow. But such was the Russian distrust that he was never able to make contact with his Russian opposite number. I remember that he once told me that the nearest he had got to him was when the Russian, a general, waved to him in the opera."

"We were luckier with the Russians in London," said Asher Lee, "and gave them the guts but not the teeth of Ultra." Lee dealt with a mixed bag: an officer in the NKVD, an air attaché, a test pilot and a member of the Supreme Soviet with the rank of colonel. But they too were suspicious and, according to Lee, "virtually ignored Ultra material, at any rate for the pre-Stalingrad period."

paign would be successfully completed within three months and Field Marshal von Brauchitsch had just drastically reduced this estimate. After "up to four weeks" of major battle, he predicted, the war would degenerate into a mopping-up operation against "minor resistance." The hardheaded Jodl concurred and curtly silenced Warlimont who questioned the categorical statement that "the Russian colossus will be proved to be a pig's bladder; prick it and it will burst."

The Führer, according to General Guderian, "had succeeded in infecting his immediate military entourage with his own baseless optimism. The OKW and OKH were so serenely confident of victory before winter set in that winter clothing had only been prepared for every fifth man in the army." There were, of course, a few dissidents in high places. From the beginning Ribbentrop and Admiral Raeder openly opposed Barbarossa. Keitel, too, had serious reservations but he had learned to keep any objections to himself. There was also opposition within Hitler's inner circle. Rudolf Hess—second in line after Göring to succeed the Führer— heartily approved the theory of Lebensraum but opposed attacking Russia so long as the war with England continued. The Bolsheviks alone, he confided to Schwerin von Krosigk, were profiting by this unfortunate conflict. Determined to resolve the question of how to neutralize Britain, he had met with Professor Karl Haushofer, the geopolitician, in the Grunewald Forest the previous summer. Until two in the morning they discussed the best means of negotiating a peace. Haushofer suggested a secret rendezvous with some prominent Englishman in a neutral city. From this modest beginning sprang an adventure that would intrigue the world.

Excited by the prospect of a secret mission, Hess took the plan to Hitler, hoping perhaps that this would restore his own waning influence. Despite Hess's lofty rank, Hitler had not taken him seriously for over a year. "I hope he never becomes my successor," he reportedly told Hanfstaengl. "I wouldn't know whom to be more sorry for, Hess or the party." But his affection for *"mein Hesserl,"* his second Kubizek, had not diminished and he gave the Deputy Führer grudging approval to make inquiries through Albrecht Haushofer, the professor's elder son, who worked in the Foreign Office.

Young Haushofer, a member of the Resistance for several years, diffidently suggested to Hess that the best possibility would be a meeting with his own closest English friend, the Duke of Hamilton, since he had ready access to Churchill and the King. Hess left the meeting with enthusiasm but Albrecht wrote his father that "the whole thing is a fool's errand." At the same time he decided to do what he could, as a patriotic German, to make peace with England. He wrote the Duke of Hamilton proposing a meeting with Hess in Lisbon. He signed the message "A" and sent it, via Hess's brother, to a Mrs. V. Roberts in Lisbon. She transmitted it to England but the letter was intercepted by the British censor. He turned it over to the Secret Service, which eventually instructed RAF intelligence to take appropriate action. So much time had passed by then that Hess decided to act on his own without the knowledge of the Haushofers or Hitler. His plan was to embark on the mission himself, doing so in a dramatic manner that would strike the English as a sporting gesture. He would fly over the estate of the Duke of Hamilton, land by parachute and secretly conduct negotiations under a false name. He was an expert flier, a flight officer in the First World War, the winner in 1934 of the hazardous air race around the Zugspitze, Germany's highest peak, near Garmisch. A solo flight over enemy lines to a remote area of Scotland would surely appeal to young Hamilton, the first to fly over Mount Everest. "I was confronted by a very hard decision," Hess later told interrogators. "I do not think I could have arrived at my final choice unless I had continually kept before my eyes the vision of an endless line of children's coffins with weeping mothers behind them, both English and German; and another line of coffins of mothers with mourning children." Hess was convinced that only by such an original stratagem could the Führer's dream of a coalition between Germany and England be effectuated. If he failed, it would not involve Hitler; if he succeeded, he would give the Führer credit for the scheme. Admittedly the chances were slim that he would even reach Scotland alive—perhaps ten to one. But the prize was worth the hazard.

Hess was sure that Hitler would welcome a novel peace venture but would never allow him to risk his life in the attempt. Hadn't he already refused to let Hess fly at the front? Therefore secrecy was essential. It was the decision of a naïve, not too bright acolyte who, according to Adjutant Wiedemann, was the Führer's "most devoted and dedicated subordinate." A painfully shy man whose greatest ambition was to further his master's career, Hess hid behind tightly stern lips, heavy jowls, fanatic eyes and a fearsome pair of eyebrows. But this was no Teutonic Oliver Cromwell. Once he smiled the severity vanished.

It was this Parsifal who conjured up the dream of flight to the enemy, this man of culture without judgment, this completely devoted servant who convinced himself that he was carrying out the *true* will of his master. If it was a woolly scheme, it was organized and prepared with exquisite efficiency. He persuaded Willy Messerschmidt, the aeronautical engineer, to let him borrow an ME-110 two-man plane for practice flights, then criticized its limited range. It should, he said, have two auxiliary tanks of 700 liters fitted on each wing. After reluctantly making this change, Messerschmidt was talked into adding special radio equipment. Then came training under the excuse of recreation, and after twenty flights Hess felt he had mastered the modified plane. In the meantime, contrary to wartime regulations, he had acquired a new leather flying suit, persuaded Baur (Hitler's personal pilot) to get him a secret map of forbidden air zones, and installed a new radio in his home on the outskirts of Munich.

It was quite possible, he later wrote his wife from prison, "that I became not quite normal. The flight and its purpose had taken hold of me with the force of a fixed idea. Anything else, I seemed to see and hear only partly . . ." He lived and moved in those early days of May in a world of instruments, piston pressures, detachable petrol containers, auxiliary air pumps, cooling temperatures and radio bearings.

His secretary, Hildegard Fath, noticed that Hess often did not listen to what she was saying. His wife was equally aware of his preoccupation. What surprised her even more was the unusual amount of time he spent with their four-year-old son, who bore Hitler's secret name, Wolf. Surprising too, in view of Hess's reluctance to pose for pictures, was his own recent suggestion that photographs of father and son be taken.

Hess rose early on the morning of May 10, a Saturday, and, upon learning that the weather forecast was good, he made arrangements for the flight. Never had he been more gallant to his wife. After tea he kissed her hand and then stood gravely at the door of the nursery "with an air of one deep in thought and almost hesitating." She asked him when he was returning and, told it would be Monday at the latest, she bluntly said, "I cannot believe it. You will not come back as soon as that!" She guessed he was bound for a meeting with someone like Pétain but he feared that she had guessed the truth. He "turned hot and cold in turns" and, before she could say anything more, he dashed into the nursery to take a last look at their slumbering son.

At 6 p.m., after giving his adjutant a letter for Hitler, Hess took off from the Augsburg airport and headed for the North Sea. Abruptly, contrary to the weather report, the cloud cover vanished and for a moment he thought of turning back. But he kept going and found England covered by a veil of mist. Seeking shelter, he dived down with full throttle, at first unaware that a Spitfire was on his tail. Outdistancing the pursuer, he hedgehopped over the dark countryside at more than 450 miles an hour, narrowly skimming trees and houses. Baur had always claimed Hess was the type of pilot who liked to fly through open hangar doors and it was in this barnstormer's spirit that he aimed at the mountain looming ahead. It was his guidepost and he literally climbed up the steep slope and slid down the other side, always keeping within a few yards of the ground. Just before 11 p.m. he turned east and picked out a railway and small lake which he remembered were just south of the duke's residence. He climbed to 6000 feet, a safe height from which to parachute, and switched off the motor. He opened the hatch—then suddenly realized he had overlooked one step in his elaborate training: "I had never asked how to jump; I thought it was too simple!" As the ME-110 plummeted, he recalled a friend mentioning that a plane should be on its back. After a half roll, he found himself upside down, held inside by centrifugal force. He began to see stars; just before passing out, he thought: "Soon the crash must come!" Regaining consciousness, he saw the speed gauge indicate zero. He flung himself out of the plane, pulled at the parachute ring. Fortunately, while unconscious, he had automatically brought the plane out of its semi-looping curve to finish almost perpendicular on its tail. And so, to his amazement, he found himself safely in mid-air.

He hit the ground, stumbled forward and blacked out a second time. He was found by a farmer, marched off to the Home Guard and brought to a barracks in Glasgow. Insisting that he was one Oberleutnant Alfred Horn, he asked to see the Duke of Hamilton.

It was not until Sunday morning that his letter was delivered to Hitler at the Berghof. While Engel was making his daily report, Martin Bormann's brother Albert broke in to announce that Hess's adjutant wanted to see the Führer on a very urgent matter. Albert was driven out with an angry "Can't you see I'm in the middle of a military report and do not wish to be disturbed!" A minute later Albert, face ashen, sidled in again. But this time he would not be put off. Insisting the matter was important and possibly dangerous, he extended the letter from Hess. Hitler put on his glasses and began to read indifferently but as soon as he saw the words "My Führer, when you receive this letter I shall be in England" he dropped into a chair and shouted so loudly he could be heard downstairs: "Oh, my God, my God! He has flown to England!" He hastily read of the technical difficulties of the flight and that Hess's goal was to further the Führer's own aim of alliance with England but he had kept the flight secret since he knew the Führer would have forbidden it.

> And if, my Führer, this project—which I admit has but very little chance of success—ends in failure and the fates decide against me, this can have no detrimental results either for you or for Germany; it will always be possible for you to deny all responsibility. Simply say I am crazy.

Chalk white, the Führer ordered Engel to get the Reichsmarschall on the phone. As soon as he was located near Nuremberg, Hitler shouted, "Göring, come here immediately!" He yelled at Albert Bormann to fetch his brother and Ribbentrop, placed Hess's hapless adjutant under arrest, and began pacing the room angrily. When Martin Bormann arrived out of breath, Hitler demanded to know if Hess could possibly reach England in an ME-110. The question was answered by the famous ace of the Great War, Luftwaffe General Udet. Never, he said, not with its limited range. And the Führer muttered, "I hope he falls into the sea!"

As the day wore on, Hitler's anger developed into a rage. Private guests, confined to the upper floor, wondered in fear what had happened, while Hitler agitatedly stalked his study trying to work out a believable explanation for the public. Would the Japanese and Italians suspect that

Germany was after a separate peace? Would his own soldiers fight less hard? Worst of all, had Hess revealed the plans for Barbarossa? After many drafts a communiqué was finally drawn up explaining that Hess had commandeered a plane against orders and disappeared. It was assumed he had crashed. A letter left behind "unfortunately showed traces of a mental disturbance which justifies the fear that Hess was a victim of hallucinations."

Fräulein Fath heard a broadcast of this announcement while dining. Its tone was so unfriendly that she thought: "Is this the thanks for his lifetime devotion?" She phoned Hess's brother, Alfred, and they mulled over the possibilities. Frau Hess was watching a movie with chauffeurs, servants and adjutants when she was called out by the most junior adjutant. Distraught, he begged her to put on her things. It was such a senseless request that swift dread crossed her mind. But upon learning that it was only a radio broadcast presuming that her husband was dead, she angrily replied: "Nonsense!" She doubted that anything tragic had occurred and put in a priority call to the Berghof, intending to speak to the Führer. But she got Bormann, who said he had absolutely no information. Knowing her husband's assistant as she did, she did not believe him. She phoned Alfred Hess in Berlin. He too could not believe Rudolf was dead.

No announcement had yet come from England even though Hess, admitting his true identify to the Duke of Hamilton, told about his mission of peace and how he and Albrecht Haushofer had tried to arrange a meeting in Lisbon. Hamilton rushed off to see Churchill, who said, "Well, Hess or no Hess, I am going to see the Marx brothers." Only after the film ended did the Prime Minister interrogate Hamilton thoroughly.

A few hours following the German announcement that Hess was missing, the British finally revealed that he had arrived in England. No details were released. German newspapers were already putting out a reprint of the radio broadcast but the news from London made it necessary to concoct a fuller official version. This one, published on Tuesday the thirteenth, acknowledged the landing of the Deputy Führer in Britain before enlarging on his mental state:

> As is well known in party circles, Hess had undergone severe physical suffering for some years. Recently he had sought relief to an increasing extent in various methods practiced by mesmerists and astrologers, etc. An attempt is also being made to determine to what extent these persons are responsible for bringing about the condition of mental distraction which led him to take this step. . . .

Such an admission caused confusion in Germany that extended to the highest levels. Goebbels told his staff, "Our job is for the moment to keep a stiff upper lip, not to react, not to explain anything, not to enter into polemics. The affair will be fully cleared up in the course of the afternoon and I shall issue detailed instructions from the Obersalzberg this afternoon." He tried to assure his people that the Hess flight, admittedly embarrassing at the moment, would be seen in the future as a mere dramatic episode. "However, there are no grounds for letting our wings droop in any way or for thinking that we shall never live this down."

From this meeting Goebbels flew to Berchtesgaden to attend an emergency convocation of Gauleiters and Reichsleiters. After Bormann had read aloud the Hess letter, the Führer appeared. Hans Frank had not seen him for some time and was shocked at his "disturbed appearance." At first he spoke about Hess "very softly, hesitatingly and with a deep sense of melancholy," but soon his tone changed to one of anger. The flight, he said, was sheer insanity. "Hess is first of all a deserter and if I ever catch him, he will pay for this as any ordinary traitor. Furthermore, it seems to me that this step was strongly influenced by astrological cliques which Hess kept around him. It is time, therefore, to put an end to all these stargazers.* Because of this insanity our position is made much more difficult though not shaken, particularly my belief that the victory in this Jewish war against National Socialism belongs to our unblemished flag." His listeners had already heard stories of Hess's pet lion, as well as his interest in homeopathic medicine and astrology, and were prepared to believe he was mentally disturbed. Yet they wondered, as ordinary citizens did, why then had Hitler retained him in high office?

It was significant that the Führer mentioned not a word to his party leaders about the coming invasion of Russia and his fear that Hess might have revealed it to the English. He need not have worried. Under the interrogation of Hamilton and Sir Ivone Kirkpatrick, Hess insisted there was "no foundation for the rumors now being spread that Hitler is contemplating an early attack on Russia." What he wanted to talk about was peace with England. He had come without Hitler's permission, he said, to "convince responsible persons that since England could not win the war, the wisest course was to make peace now."

As soon as Albrecht Haushofer learned of the flight he hurried to his father's study. "And with such fools we make politics!" he exclaimed. The English would never deal with such a man under such ridiculous circumstances! His father sadly agreed it was a "terrible sacrifice all in vain." Young Haushofer was ordered to Obersalzberg, placed under guard and given pen and paper to write a report for the Führer, who refused to see him. Entitled "English Connections and the Possibility of Utilizing Them," it revealed as much of the truth as possible without implicating friends in the Resistance. Albrecht told of his friendship with the Duke of Hamilton and of the letter he had written at Hess's behest, adding that he himself would be indispensable in case of future negotiations with the

* There were wholesale arrests of astrologers and occultists suspected of knowing Hess. Performances involving demonstrations of an occult, spiritualist, clairvoyant, telepathic or astrological nature were outlawed.

English because of his many connections. This report persuaded Hitler not to act hastily. He ordered Haushofer transported to the Gestapo prison in Berlin on the Prince Albrecht Strasse for further interrogation. His father was spared but drew Hitler's special rage. "The Jewish-tainted professor has Hess on his conscience!" he said and reproached himself for not taking steps earlier "to tear apart that whole Munich breed and silence them."

Others connected with Hess were arrested—his brother Alfred, adjutants, orderlies, secretaries and chauffeurs. Ilse Hess was not imprisoned but Martin Bormann did his utmost to humiliate her. He also put as much distance as possible between himself and his former chief. He changed the praenomina of his two children, Rudolf and Ilse, named after the Hesses, and appointed more appropriate godparents. Selected as Hess's successor, he eliminated everything that reminded him of his former employer. All photographs of Hess, books and official literature bearing his picture were destroyed. He even attempted to confiscate the Hess home but this was too much even for Hitler. He refused to sign the eviction notice.

The guests at the Berghof were released from the top floor but no one dared speak of the flight to England, not after someone innocently asked why Hess's adjutant was not at the table and Bormann replied that he was in prison—"and he will not come out again." "Typically," commented Engel in his diary, "the only one who walks around this beehive expectantly is Bormann; we all agree that he considers this *his* hour."

In England the government had decided not to make public the interrogations of Hess; it would be best to keep the Nazis guessing. Hess was transported secretly to the Tower of London during the night of May 16 to become the world's most famous prisoner of war. A few days later A. P. Herbert summarized in verse the Englishman's view of Hess:

> *He is insane. He is a Dove of Peace.*
> *He is Messiah. He is Hitler's niece.*
> *He is the one clean honest man they've got.*
> *He is the worst assassin of the lot.*
> *He has a mission to preserve mankind.*
> *He's non-alcoholic. He was a "blind."*
> *He has been dotty since the age of ten,*
> *But all the time was top of Hitler's men. . . .*

Stalin was far more perturbed by the Hess flight than Mussolini who, according to his son-in-law, was "glad of it because this will have the effect of bringing down German stock, even with the Italians." Those in the Kremlin, particularly in light of the invasion rumors, suspected the British were really intriguing with Hitler. New regulations were imposed. Travel outside of Moscow by foreigners was forbidden except in rare cases.

Irate as he was, Hitler confided to several intimates that he respected Hess for his willingness to sacrifice himself on such a dangerous mission. On reflection he realized that his deputy had made the hazardous flight for him. Hitler did not believe that Hess was mad, only foolish not to have seen what a disastrous political mistake he was making.

This more sober judgment was corroborated some months later when Hitler consoled Frau Bruckmann on the death of her husband: "We all have our graves and grow more and more lonely, but we have to overcome and go on living, my dear gracious lady! I, too, am now deprived of the only two human beings among all those around me to whom I have been truly and inwardly attached: Dr. Todt [builder of the Westwall and Autobahn] is dead and Hess has flown away from me!"

"That is what you say now and to me," reportedly replied Frau Bruckmann, who had a reputation for frankness, "but what does your official press say? Year after year we all go to Bayreuth and are deeply moved, but who understands the real meaning? When our unhappy age at last produces a man who, like the Valkyrie, fulfills the deeper meaning of Wotan's command—seeks to carry out *your* most sacred wish with heroism and self-sacrifice—then he is described as insane!" She expected the Führer would retort sharply but he remained quiet and thoughtful. "Is it not enough, what I have said to you—and to you alone—about my real feeling?" he finally said. "Is that not enough for you?"

As for Hess, it was enough that he had done his utmost. He was glad, he wrote his wife from the Tower of London, that he had been impelled to fly to England, an urge which he described as "the obstinate dragon" that would not let him go. "True, I achieved nothing. I was not able to stop the madness of the war and could not prevent what I saw coming. I could not save the people but it makes me happy to think that I tried to do it."*

7

The day after learning about Hess, Hitler issued two repressive decrees. One declared that Russian civilians taking arms against the Wehrmacht in the coming invasion should be considered outlaws and shot without trial. The other empowered Himmler to carry out "special tasks which result from the struggle which has to be carried out between two opposing political systems." He was to act independently of the Wehrmacht "under his own responsibility." There would be no interference from any source and "the highest personalities of the government and party" were to be

---

* As a reward Hess—described by Wiedemann as "the straightest character" among the Nazi leaders—has already served more than thirty years of solitary confinement. He remains the last Allied prisoner at Spandau prison. In all those years he has been separated from visitors by a wide table. Never has he been allowed to embrace or kiss a loved one.

forbidden entrance into the occupied Russian areas which would be "cleansed" of Jews and other troublemakers by special SS units of assassins known as *Einsatzgruppen* (Special Action Groups).

Both directives troubled Alfred Rosenberg, who had recently been appointed Commissioner for the Central Control of Questions Connected with the East European Region. A Balt himself, he believed the Soviet people should be treated as anti-Stalinists rather than as enemies of the Reich. He assured Hitler that they would welcome the Germans as liberators from Bolshevik-Stalinist tyranny and could be trusted with a certain amount of self-rule. Each state would have to be treated differently. The Ukraine, for instance, would be "an independent state in alliance with Germany" but Caucasia must be ruled by a German "plenipotentiary."

Convinced that a heavy-handed policy in the East would destroy the spirit of Lebensraum, Rosenberg submitted a memorandum to Hitler objecting to the two directives. How could one possibly build a civil administration in the occupied areas without using the Soviet civil commissars and officials now administering them? He recommended that "only senior and very senior officials" should be "liquidated." Hitler gave no definite answer. Characteristically, he was content to take no active part in the power struggle between Himmler and Rosenberg that would surely begin once the Wehrmacht advanced into the Soviet Union. Bormann, the rising star in the National Socialist hierarchy, would be a decisive factor in this contest. He had already joined forces with Himmler.

In the meantime, final preparations for Barbarossa continued. Admiral Raeder informed Hitler on May 22 that he would cease delivering important materials to Russia. Comparatively few shipments had, in fact, been sent to the Soviet Union, while many had come from the East. In addition to almost 1,500,000 tons of grain, the Soviets had delivered 100,000 tons of cotton, 2,000,000 tons of petroleum products, 1,500,000 tons of timber, 140,000 tons of manganese and 25,000 tons of chromium. Despite suspicions over the Hess flight, Stalin was still so eager to appease Hitler that he authorized further shipments by express trains from the Far East of other important raw materials, such as copper.

On the same day a meeting with Molotov reinforced Ambassador von der Schulenburg's earlier conjecture that the recent consolidation of power by Stalin merely meant that the foreign policy of the Soviet Union was completely in his hands. In hopes of staving off Barbarossa, Schulenburg reported that the Soviet attitude toward Germany had improved markedly in the past few weeks. But Hitler was not to be dissuaded by his diplomats any more than he was by his naval chief. On May 30, three days after German paratroopers wrested the strategic island of Crete from the British, Admiral Raeder attempted to turn Hitler's attention from the East by urging him to mount a substantial offensive against Egypt and Suez. Now, he urged, was the time to strike. With reinforcements General

Rommel could score a decisive victory. "This stroke," he said, "would be more deadly to the British Empire than the capture of London!"

Hitler was beyond such advice. Barbarossa was in motion and nothing short of catastrophe could postpone it. His greatest concern was security. Haunted by the mishap in Belgium a year earlier, he still had not informed Mussolini of the invasion. When he met his senior ally at the Brenner Pass on June 2, he talked at length of his determination to force British capitulation (this time by U-boats), of Hess, and of the situation in the Balkans. Not a word did he utter about Barbarossa, not only for the sake of secrecy but because Il Duce had already cautioned him in explicit terms not to attack Russia, which had become "a running sore" to Germany.

The roads and rail lines leading east were dense with traffic as the final phase of preparations for Barbarossa began. On June 6 Hitler summoned Japanese Ambassador Oshima to Berchtesgaden and revealed that large numbers of troops were being sent east because of Soviet border violations. "Under such circumstances," he concluded with a confidence that impressed his listener, "war might be unavoidable between us." To Oshima this was tantamount to a declaration of war and he immediately warned Tokyo that an invasion of Russia was imminent.

It was a significant day for the Führer. He legalized his threat to wage ruthless ideological warfare by instructing Field Marshal von Brauchitsch to issue a directive to liquidate captured Soviet commissars as bearers of an ideology diametrically opposed to National Socialism. His commander-in-chief objected violently until Hitler curtly said, "I cannot demand that my generals should understand my orders, but I do demand that they follow them." The terms of this directive could not be misinterpreted. "These commissars are the originators of barbarous, Asiatic methods of warfare, and they must therefore be treated with all possible severity and dispatch. . . . Whether captured during battle or while offering resistance, they must be shot at once." This ideologically motivated order was to be executed by the Wehrmacht together with Himmler's Einsatzgruppen and its issuance by OKW was more than another victory for Hitler over the military. It bound them to his political program and made them unwilling accomplices, along with the SS, in his grand plan of the future.

To achieve this goal he must first conquer the Red Army and to do this he needed the help of those states bordering the Soviet Union that could be trusted—and that, sharing his own fear and hatred of Bolshevism, had accounts of their own to settle with Stalin. The Finns, forced to accept harsh terms to end their brief, bloody war with Russia, needed little urging to join the crusade; and on June 8 the first elements of a German infantry division landed in Finland. Two days later Field Marshal Mannerheim ordered a partial mobilization. Hitler also trusted Romania and on June 11 he intimated to General Ion Antonescu that he had decided to attack Russia. He was by no means asking Antonescu for assistance in such a war, he said, and "merely expected of Romania that in her own interest she do everything to facilitate a successful conclusion of this conflict." Stirred by visions of spoils and military glory, the Romanian dictator hastily declared that he wanted to be in on the fight from the first day.

8

On June 14 Soviet secret agent Sorge dispatched a definite warning from Tokyo: "War begins June 22." But Stalin still chose not to credit this or similar alarums. He had reassured himself, despite qualms, that the war could not possibly start until 1942 and that very day ordered publication of a Tass communiqué ridiculing the numerous rumors of war: "All this is nothing but clumsy propaganda by forces hostile to the U.S.S.R. and Germany and interested in an extension of the war." This statement was so reassuring that there was an easing of tension in the forward positions of the Red Army.

In Berlin selected combat officers were arriving at the chancellery for a special briefing and luncheon. By now each one had digested his own orders and become reconciled (if grudgingly) to the inhumane methods Hitler had imposed on the enemy. At 2 P.M. there was a break for lunch and this, unlike so many other meals at the chancellery, was mellow and relaxed. Nor was the atmosphere of camaraderie dispelled when Hitler ascended to the podium and began a persuasive lecture on the need to launch Barbarossa. The collapse of Russia, he said, would lead to England's surrender.

A final signal went out on June 17 confirming 3 A.M., Sunday, June 22, as zero hour. That day a German sergeant, who had struck an officer and feared execution, crossed into Soviet lines to surrender. He revealed that the German attack would begin before dawn on the twenty-second. Front-line officers who learned of the report were disturbed but their commanding general's reaction was: "No use beating an alarm."

As zero hour approached, Hitler appeared calm and confident. On Friday the twentieth he sent for Frank—formerly his personal lawyer and now governor general of German-occupied Poland. "We are facing a war with the Soviet Union," he said and, when the other reacted with consternation, added, "Calm yourself." He promised that the German attack units would soon pass through Frank's area and then waved off his attempt to make another objection. "I understand your problem very well. But I must insist that you come to an understanding with Himmler." He was referring to their conflicting concepts of treating the occupied areas. "I can tolerate no more differences; you two must come to an understanding." That evening Hitler's proclamation to the troops was secretly distributed and, under cover of darkness, assault units began moving forward. By dawn of the twenty-first more than three million men were in attack position.

In London Cripps, home for consultations, was sounding another warning that Hitler was about to invade Russia. "Well," he told Soviet Ambassador Maisky, "we have reliable information that this attack will take place tomorrow, 22 June, or at the very latest 29 June. . . . You know that Hitler always attacks on Sundays." Maisky sent an urgent cipher message to Moscow. At last Stalin sanctioned an alert for the armed forces. He also instructed his ambassador in Berlin to present a verbal note to Ribbentrop vigorously objecting to the 180 German overflights since April, which "assumed a systematic and intentional character."

There was tension at the Bendlerstrasse as the clock neared 1:30 P.M., the final moment the attack could be called off. No word came from the chancellery. Barbarossa was on! At the chancellery Hitler was trying to explain to Mussolini why he was launching Barbarossa: "Duce!" he wrote. "I am writing this letter to you at a moment when months of anxious deliberations and continuous nerve-racking waiting are ending in the hardest decision of my life." The concentration of Soviet forces at the Reich border, he said, was tremendous, and time was on the side of the enemy. "I have therefore, after constantly racking my brains, finally reached the decision to cut the noose before it can be drawn tight."

He made no criticism of Italy's disastrous ventures in Greece and Africa nor hinted at other grievances. He maintained a tone of respect, approaching supplication, throughout and ended the letter almost as if he were in the confessional: "The partnership with the Soviet Union, in spite of the complete sincerity of the efforts to bring about a final conciliation, was nevertheless often very irksome to me, for in some way or other it seemed to me to be a break with my whole origin, my concepts, and my former obligations. I am happy now to be relieved of these mental agonies."

In Moscow Molotov had just summoned Ambassador von der Schulenburg. The Foreign Commissar wanted to add weight to the *note verbale* which his ambassador in Berlin had not yet been able to deliver to Ribbentrop. "There are a number of indications," he told Schulenburg, "that the German government is dissatisfied with the Soviet government. Rumors are even current that a war is impending between Germany and the Soviet Union." It was an embarrassing situation and all Schulenburg could do was promise to transmit the question to Berlin. He returned to his office as ignorant as Molotov that an attack was coming in a few hours.

One of the eastern front commanders was reading out Hitler's exhortation to the troops. "Weighed down for many months by grave anxieties, compelled to keep silent, I can at last speak openly to you, my soldiers." He told of the Russian build-up on the German frontier, of the numerous border violations. That was why they had been brought up to the "greatest front in world history" along with allies from Finland and Romania. "German soldiers! You are about to join battle, a hard and crucial battle. The destiny of Europe, and future of the German Reich, the existence of our nation now lie in your hands alone."

All along the tortuous 930-mile front, from the Baltic to the Black Sea, three million men listened and believed. With fear and expectation they huddled in their positions. It was the shortest night of the year, the summer solstice, but it seemed endless to those waiting in the pale light for the command to attack. Just before midnight the Moscow–Berlin express rumbled over the frontier bridge into German territory. It was followed by a long freight train filled with grain, the last delivery Stalin would make to his ally, Adolf Hitler.

In Berlin that evening there was an air of expectation. The international journalists were gathered at the Foreign Press Club in the Fasenstrasse, hoping to get some information from a group of Foreign Office officials, but as midnight approached with no official announcement the newsmen began to leave for home. At the chancellery there was such unusual activity that even those like Hitler's press chief, Dietrich, who knew nothing of Barbarossa, felt sure "that some tremendous action against Russia was in progress." Hitler was the personification of confidence. "In three months at the latest," he told one adjutant, "there will be a collapse on the part of the Russians such as the world has never before seen." But this was only a sham. He could not close his eyes that night any more than he could on the eve of the invasion of the West.

At 3 A.M., June 22—exactly a year after the surrender of France at Compiègne—German infantrymen moved forward. Fifteen minutes later flame and smoke burst out all along the eastern front. The pale night sky was turned to day by the flash of guns. Barbarossa, long a dream, was reality. But its creator was already nagged by concern. The five-week delay caused by the Yugoslav venture loomed more ominously. Being of historic bent, perhaps Hitler recalled that on that same day in June a hundred and twenty-nine years before Napoleon had crossed the Niemen River on his way to Moscow.

Fifteen minutes before zero hour Ambassador von Bismarck delivered Hitler's long letter to Ciano, who immediately telephoned Il Duce. Mussolini was incensed as much by the ungodly hour as by having been kept uninformed. "Not even I disturb my servants at night," he grumbled to his son-in-law, "but the Germans make me jump out of bed at any hour without the least consideration."

In Moscow Schulenburg was en route to the Kremlin with an accusation that the Soviet Union was about to "fall on Germany's back." Consequently the Führer had ordered the Wehrmacht "to oppose this threat with all the means at its disposal." Molotov listened silently to a solemn reading of the statement, then said bitterly, "It is war. Your aircraft have just bombarded some ten open villages. Do you believe that we deserved that?"

At the Wilhelmstrasse Ribbentrop finally sent word that he would see the Russian ambassador at 4 A.M. Never before had Schmidt seen his chief so excited. Pacing up and down the room like a caged animal, Ribbentrop kept repeating, "The Führer is absolutely right to attack Russia now." It seemed, thought Schmidt, as if he were trying to reassure himself. "The Russians would certainly themselves attack us, if we did not do so now."

At exactly 4 A.M. Soviet Ambassador Dekanozov entered, right hand innocently extended. Ribbentrop interrupted his attempt to relay the Soviet grievances. "That is not the question now," he said and announced that the Soviet government's hostility had compelled the Reich to take military countermeasures. "I regret that I can say nothing further," he said, "especially as I myself have come to the conclusion that, in spite of serious endeavors, I have not succeeded in establishing reasonable relations between our two countries."

Quickly regaining his composure, Dekanozov expressed his own regret at the course of events, laying the entire blame on the non-co-operative attitude of the Germans. He rose, bowed perfunctorily, and left the room without offering Ribbentrop another handshake.

Correspondents all over Berlin were being wakened for a 6 A.M. press conference at the Foreign Office. Several heard the news en route to the Wilhelmstrasse from outdoor loudspeakers as a message from the Führer was broadcast: "People of Germany! National Socialists! The hour has come. Oppressed by grave cares, doomed to months of silence, I can at last speak frankly." He told of the machinations of Russia and England to crush the Axis with the aid of American supplies. "I therefore decided today to lay the fate and future of the German Reich in the hands of our soldiers. May God help us above all in this fight!"

Chapter Twenty-four

"A DOOR INTO
A DARK, UNSEEN ROOM"
JUNE 22–DECEMBER 19, 1941

1

By early morning of June 22 single-sheet extra editions of Berlin newspapers were on the streets. Although confused by the abrupt attack on an ally, the public felt a sense of relief since few had been able to understand why a treaty had been made with the Reds in the first place. Hitler set Goebbels the task of explanation and that morning the propaganda chief began laying down the guidelines to his subordinates: "Now that the Führer has unmasked the treachery of the Bolshevik rulers, National Socialism, and hence the German people, are reverting to the principles which impelled them—the struggle against plutocracy and Bolshevism." The Führer, he added, had assured him the Russian campaign would end within four months. "But I tell you it will take only eight weeks."

That afternoon he was repeating his prophecy to guests at a party. Turning to film star Olga Tschechowa, the niece of Chekhov, he said, "We have a Russian expert here. Will we be in Moscow by Christmas?" Irritated by both his manner and the question, her answer was terse: "You know Russia, the endless land. Even Napoleon had to retreat." For once Goebbels was at a loss for words and could only say, "So." But within ten minutes his adjutant was telling the actress, "I imagine, madame, you are ready to leave. The car is outside."

The Soviet Union was in disarray. Within hours the Red Air Force had admittedly lost 1200 aircraft, and infantry resistance was unco-ordinated. Refusing to believe in the gravity of first reports, Stalin ordered the Red Army to keep out of German territory and the Red Air Force to restrict raids to within ninety miles of the frontier. He was so convinced that the Nazi invasion was a mistake and he could halt the war by diplomatic means that he kept open radio communications with the Wilhelmstrasse while requesting Japan to mediate any political and economic differences between Germany and the Soviet Union.

His ambassador in England was under no such illusion. Maisky called upon Foreign Secretary Eden and asked directly whether the British government was going to reduce its war effort somewhat and perhaps now listen to Hitler's "peace offensive." Eden firmly replied in the negative, and that evening Churchill (who had recently remarked: "If Hitler invaded Hell, I would make at least a favourable reference to the Devil in the House of Commons") made it official in a stirring broadcast to the nation. "We are resolved to destroy Hitler and every vestige of the Nazi regime. From this nothing will turn us—nothing. We will never parley, we will never negotiate with Hitler or any of his gang." He pledged to give the utmost help to the Russians. "We shall appeal to all our friends and allies in every part of the world to take the same course and pursue it, as we shall faithfully and steadfastly to the end."

George Kennan, assigned to the American Embassy in Berlin, had reservations which he passed on in a personal note to a friend in the State Department: "It seems to me that to welcome Russia as an associate in the defense of democracy would invite misunderstanding of our own position and would lend to the German war effort a gratuitous and sorely needed aura of morality. In following such a course I do not see how we could help but identify ourselves with the Russian destruction of the Baltic states, with the attack against Finnish independence, with the partitioning of Poland and Rumania, with the crushing of religion throughout Eastern Europe, and with the domestic policy of a regime which is widely feared and detested throughout this part of the world and the methods of which are far from democratic." At the same time this should not prohibit "the extension of material aid whenever called for by our own self-interest. It would, however, preclude anything which might identify us politically or ideologically with the Russian war effort."

Roosevelt was equally aware of Stalin's dictatorial policies, his secretiveness and greed for territory. But he feared Hitler far more and promptly approved a State Department declaration that giving assistance to Communism would benefit American security. He told reporters: "Of course we are going to give all the aid we possibly can to Russia"—but failed to add when or how this could be done.

The Pope's attitude was not at all vague. While taking no definite stand on the German invasion, he made it clear that he backed the Nazi fight against Bolshevism, describing it as "high-minded gallantry in defense of the foundations of Christian culture." A number of German bishops, predictably, openly supported the attack. One called it "a European crusade," a mission similar to that of the Teutonic Knights. He exhorted all Catholics to fight for "a victory that will allow Europe to breathe freely again and will promise all nations a new future."

Within twenty-four hours German public interest began to slacken. After the first rush for the newspapers, which contained only general reports from the front, the citizens returned to their normal life as if it were only another of Hitler's exploits. At 12:30 P.M. on June 23 he and his entourage left the capital in the Führer train: destination *Wolfsschanze* (Wolf's Lair), the new headquarters in a forest several miles from Rastenburg, East Prussia. Confidence in a quick victory ran high among the staff as they settled into the wooden huts and concrete bunkers but the Führer had mixed feelings. "We have only to kick in the door and the whole rotten structure will come crashing down," he told Jodl, yet shortly remarked to an aide, "At the beginning of each campaign one pushes a door into a dark, unseen room. One can never know what is hiding inside."

The early victories seemed to justify the highest hopes. Within two days hordes of prisoners were taken and bridges seized intact. There seemed to be no organized enemy resistance as German tanks burst through Soviet lines and roamed at will. For a week no details were given to the German public, then on Sunday, the twenty-ninth, ten special communiqués, personally prepared by Hitler, were announced over the radio at hourly intervals. Goebbels had objected to this abrupt flood of information but Hitler thought it a brilliant idea. As the day wore on, however, he received complaints that a spectacle was being made of the war, and when Otto Dietrich reported that Sunday radio listeners were extremely annoyed at having to keep to their apartments on such a fine day he retorted that he knew the mentality and emotion of the masses better than Dietrich "and all the other intellectuals put together."

There were such piercing advances, such mass surrenders—almost half a million to date—that Halder wrote in his diary on July 3, "It is no exaggeration to say that the campaign against Russia has been won in fourteen days." The Führer also told his entourage that "to all intents and purposes the Russians have lost the war." How fortunate it was, he exulted, "that we smashed the Russian armor and air force right at the beginning!" Never, he said, could the Russians replace them. Many Western military experts shared this estimate and talk in the Pentagon was that the Red Army would fold up in a month or so.

2

Following in the wake of the advancing troops were four SS Einsatzgruppen of 3000 men each, whose mission was to insure the security of the operational zone; that is, prevent resistance by civilians. These were police of a very special nature, given an additional task by their chief, Reinhard Heydrich. They were to round up and liquidate not only Bolshevik leaders but all Jews, as well as gypsies, "Asiatic inferiors" and "useless eaters," such as the deranged and incurably sick.

To supervise this mass killing, Heydrich and Himmler had been inspired to select officers who, for the most part, were professional men. They included a Protestant pastor, a physician, a professional opera singer and numerous lawyers. The majority were intellectuals in their early thirties and it might be supposed such men were unsuited for this work. On the contrary, they brought to the brutal task their considerable skills and training and became, despite qualms, efficient executioners.

The majority of the victims were Jews. They had no idea of Hitler's "racial cleansing" program since few German anti-Semitic atrocities were reported in the Soviet press. Consequently, many Jews welcomed the Germans as liberators and were easily trapped by the Special Units. "Contrary to the opinion of the National Socialists that the Jews were a highly organized group," testified Obergruppenführer von dem Bach-Zelewski, the senior SS and police commander for Central Russia, the appalling fact was that they were taken completely by surprise. It gave the lie to the old anti-Semitic myth that the Jews were conspiring to dominate the world and were thus highly organized. "Never before has a people gone as unsuspectingly to its disaster. Nothing was prepared. Absolutely nothing."

The exterminations proceeded with cool calculation. It was a tidy, businesslike operation; and the reports were couched in the arid language of bureaucracy as if the executioners were dealing with cabbages, not human beings. The methodical work of the killing units was rarely marred by resistance. "Strange is the calmness with which the delinquents allow themselves to be shot," reported one commander, "and that goes for non-Jews as well as Jews. Their fear of death appears to have been blunted by a kind of indifference which has been created in the course of twenty years of Soviet rule."

Heydrich's most awkward problem was coping with the psychological effects of the exterminators. Some enlisted men had nervous breakdowns or took to drinking, and a number of the officers suffered from serious stomach and intestinal ailments. Others took to their task with excess enthusiasm and sadistically beat the prisoners in violation of Himmler's orders to exterminate as humanely as possible.

He himself was witness to the demoralizing effect of daily murder. On a visit to Minsk that summer he asked the commander of Einsatzgruppe B to shoot a hundred prisoners so he could observe the actual liquidation. As the firing squad raised rifles, he noticed one young man was blond and blue-eyed, the hallmark of the true Teuton, and did not belong in this group. Himmler asked if he was a Jew. He was. Both parents?

Hitler with Keitel and Engel aboard the special Führer train. FRENTZ

Hitler reads latest radio dispatch. FRENTZ

Hitler and his dog Blondi inspect Flak crew. To his right, Albert Bormann (brother of Martin), valet Linge and Richard Schulze (Hitler's ordnance officer). FRENTZ

Engel, Puttkamer and Jodl outside train. PUTTKAMER

Göring's favorite trains, in his basement at Karinhall. FRENTZ

Left, on February 15, 1942, after the military reverses in Russia of November–December 1941, Hitler exhorts recent SS officer graduates to stem the Red tide and save civilization. Behind: Schaub and Schulze. The latter, recently made the Führer's personal adjutant, was so moved he wanted to join the fight. The young lieutenants, Schulze recalled, jumped onto their seats and cheered in a spontaneous demonstration.
SCHULZE

Below, a few days later Hitler loses his Minister of Armaments, the famed engineer Fritz Todt, in a mysterious plane crash on the eastern front. Todt was replaced by architect Speer.
PUTTKAMER

Mussolini flies over the Russian lines in 1942. Moments after this unusual picture was taken, he insisted on taking the controls from pilot Baur. Hitler consented, to his regret. Il Duce maneuvered the plane with boyish élan. PUTTKAMER

Mussolini's son-in-law, Count Ciano, visits Hitler at Wolf's Lair, his headquarters in Poland. Behind: Schmundt, Ribbentrop and Schulze. BIBLIO. FÜR ZEIT.

Hitler and Speer at Wolf's Lair. Behind is Otto Günsche, Hitler's SS adjutant.
GÜNSCHE

In July 1942 Hitler moves east to Werewolf, the new headquarters in the Ukraine, so he can personally direct the attack on Stalingrad. Birthday celebration that August for Bormann's secretary Fräulein Wahlmann. L. to r., Schaub, Hewel, Fräulein Wahlmann, Bormann, Engel, Fräulein Fugger (another Bormann secretary) and Heinrich Heim, instructed by Bormann to note down surreptitiously Hitler's table conversations. PUTTKAMER

A month later the inner circle celebrates Below's birthday. L. to r., Schulze, Johanna Wolf (Hitler's secretary), Below, Christa Schröder (Hitler's secretary), Dr. Brandt, Hewel, Albert Bormann, Schaub, Puttkamer, Engel. PUTTKAMER

22/Dez 1918

Die besten Weihnachtsgrüsse

lieber Heinzi,

sendet Dir und Papa und Mama

Dein Onkel Adolf.

Christmas card from Uncle Adolf to his favorite nephew, son of Alois Hitler, Jr., Heinz Hitler, who was later captured at Stalingrad. HANS HITLER

Yes. Did he have any antecedents who were not Jewish? No. Himmler stamped his foot. "Then I cannot help you."

The squad fired but Himmler, who had come to see, stared into the ground. He shuffled nervously. Then came a second volley. Again he promptly averted his eyes. Glancing up, he saw that two women still writhed. "Don't torture those women!" he shouted. "Get on with it, shoot quickly!" This was the opportunity Bach-Zelewski was hoping for. He asked Himmler to note how deeply shaken the firing squad was. "They are finished for the rest of their lives!" the SS man said. "What kind of followers are we creating by these things? Either neurotics or brutes!"

Himmler impulsively ordered everyone to gather around so he could make a speech. Theirs was a disgusting task, he said, but as good Germans they should not enjoy doing it. Their conscience, however, should be in no way affected because they were soldiers who had to carry out every order without question. He alone, before God and the Führer, bore the terrible responsibility for what had to be done. Surely they had noticed that this bloody work was as odious to him and moved him to the depths of his soul. But he too was obeying the highest law by doing his duty.

Rumors of these atrocities distressed Rosenberg, ordered by Hitler to draw up a blueprint for occupation of the conquered Eastern territories. He had envisaged a far different program with a degree of self-rule. Since the Führer had earlier agreed to establish "weak socialist states" in the conquered lands of Russia, Rosenberg optimistically assumed that Hitler approved his own plan in principle and that it would be accepted at a special conference on the subject to be held at the Wolfsschanze on July 16. "It is essential," said Hitler (according to Bormann's notes of the meeting), "that we do not proclaim our views before the whole world. There is no need for that but the main thing is that we ourselves know what we want." If this did not reveal to Rosenberg that Hitler had changed his mind about establishing "weak socialist states," what followed surely did. "This need not prevent our taking all necessary measures—shooting, resettlement, etc.—and we shall take them. . . . In principle we must now face the task of cutting up the giant cake according to our needs in order to be able: first, to dominate it; second, to administer it; third, to exploit it. The Russians have now given an order for partisan warfare behind our front. This guerrilla activity again has some advantage for us; it enables us to exterminate everyone who opposes us."

Although Rosenberg left the meeting with the title of Reich Minister of the East, it was a hollow one, for he realized his own dream of the East now had little chance to materialize. What a tragedy, he thought, that Hitler still maintained the false conception of Slavs, born during his youthful days in Vienna out of inflammatory pamphlets which described the Slavs as lazy primitives, a hopelessly second-class race. Equally disastrous was Hitler's complete misunderstanding of the structure of the Soviet Union. The Ukrainians and other tribes under the yoke of the Great Russians were potential allies of the Third Reich and could be a bulwark of defense against Bolshevism if treated properly and given a measure of self-rule. But the Führer had been persuaded by Bormann and Göring that they were enemies to be controlled by the whip. The struggle to turn Hitler from this path seemed hopeless but Rosenberg resolved to keep trying. It was a diluted resolve, for no one knew better than he that, once the Führer looked into his eyes, he would, as usual, be too frightened to speak out.

3

O what can ail thee, Knight at arms,
Alone and palely loitering?—Keats

During these early summer days of 1941 Hitler became sick. To begin with there were recurrent stomach pains which may have been of hysterical nature. His system was already undermined by an overdose of drugs— 120 to 150 anti-gas pills a week as well as ten injections of Ultraseptyl, a strong sulfonamide. Then he was struck down by dysentery—a common malady in the swampy surroundings of the Wolfsschanze. A victim of diarrhea, nausea and aching limbs, he would shiver one moment, sweat the next. A more serious threat to his health came to light during a hot argument with Ribbentrop late in July. The Foreign Minister, opposed to Barbarossa from the beginning, lost his temper and began to shout his disapproval. Hitler paled at the extraordinary attack. He tried to defend himself but halted in mid-sentence, clutched his heart and sank into a chair. There was a frightening moment of silence. "I thought I was going to have a heart attack," Hitler finally said. "You must never again oppose me in this manner!"

Dr. Morell was so perturbed he sent an electrocardiogram of the Führer's heart to Professor Dr. Karl Weber, director of the Heart Institute at Bad Nauheim and a leading authority on heart disease. He had no idea that the patient was Hitler, only that he was "a very busy diplomat." His diagnosis was: a rapidly progressive coronary sclerosis, a virtually incurable heart disease. Morell probably did not pass this information on to Hitler; at least once announcing in his presence that the Führer's heart was in good shape. Morell did add a number of other medicines to his patient's growing list of prescriptions: a heart tonic, Cardiazol (a quite harmless solution for circulatory weakness, fainting and exhaustion) and Sympathol 3, one per cent as efficacious as adrenalin.

Hitler's illness came at the height of a bitter conflict with his commanders on the conduct of the campaign in the East. He had already ordered the direct attack on Moscow halted; he stripped Army Group Cen-

ter of its most powerful armored units, one being sent north to facilitate
the capture of Leningrad, the other south to bolster the drive into the
Ukraine. Both these areas, in Hitler's opinion, superseded Moscow in importance; the first because it was a key industrial center (and was named
after Lenin), and the second because of its economic importance. Not
only was the Ukraine vital for its industry and grain but the Crimea itself
was a potential Soviet aircraft carrier for the bombing of the Ploesti
oilfields in Romania. Further, once the Crimea was occupied, the Wehrmacht would have easy access to the Caucasus.

Hitler's sick spell gave Brauchitsch and Halder the chance to sabotage
the Führer's strategy. Quietly they began trying to put their own plan into
operation, with Halder exerting his personal influence on Jodl to gain his
support. It was not until Hitler was on the road to recovery in mid-August
that he fully realized what had been going on behind his back: neither his
own strategy nor that of Halder had been put into effect but a compromise of both. To clarify the situation, Hitler composed an order on August 21 that could not possibly be misunderstood: "The most important
objective to be reached by winter is not Moscow, but the Crimea." The
attack on Moscow could not begin until Leningrad had been isolated and
the Russian Fifth Army in the south destroyed. This order was followed a
few hours later by a lengthy memorandum, dictated in anger and read
with indignation. Little better than a stern lecture on how to wage a campaign, it charged that unnamed commanders were driven by "selfish
desires" and "despotic dispositions," then characterized the army high
command as a gathering of minds "fossilized in out-of-date theories."

"A black day for the army!" Engel wrote in his diary. "Unbearable!"
scrawled Halder in his. "Unheard of! The limit!" He spent hours on the
twenty-second with Brauchitsch complaining about the Führer's "inadmis-
sible" interference with army affairs, ending with the suggestion that the
two of them resign. But the dispirited, ailing marshal refused on the
grounds that "it wouldn't be practical and would change nothing." He
even did his utmost to quell rebellion in his own staff by assuring them
that the Führer had personally promised that, once victory was certain in
the Ukraine, all available forces would be thrown into the attack on Moscow. The rebellion—if it could be dignified as such—died out in a
diminishing chorus of grumbles.

4

This minor crisis was soon overshadowed by the highly publicized
visit of Mussolini to the front. He was coming to persuade Hitler to enlarge the Italian Expeditionary Force on the Russian front and so share
some of the glory of crushing Communism. But as his special train
approached Wolfsschanze Il Duce was in poor condition to match wits

with his ally; he was still pale and grieving over the recent loss of his son Bruno in an air crash.

Hitler met Mussolini at the little railroad station near the Wolfsschanze and for the rest of the day scarcely gave him a chance to open his mouth. The Führer talked incessantly of the forthcoming victory in the East, the stupidity of France and the evil machinations of the Jewish clique that surrounded Roosevelt. When his guest finally managed to make his offer of more troops Hitler changed the subject. His almost incessant monologue continued for the next few days until Mussolini became so tired of hearing of German glory and exploits that he began a long discourse on the triumphs of ancient Rome in general and Trajan, who had fought in the region they were inspecting, in particular.

Later in the day, at Uman in the Ukraine, they inspected an Italian division and as Bersaglieri with waving feathers in their steel helmets roared past on motorcycles shouting "Duce!" Mussolini's face glowed. But Hitler soon regained the limelight once they entered the still smoking ruins of Uman and he was cheered by *his* soldiers. After lunch he left Mussolini behind and walked informally among his troops. Il Duce felt insulted but got his revenge on the return flight. He went forward to talk with Baur, Hitler's pilot, who was delighted at his enthusiasm and particularly Mussolini's request to take over the controls. Caught off guard, Hitler gave his consent but immediately regretted it, constantly fidgeting while his erstwhile idol maneuvered the craft with boyish élan.

It was only a passing triumph. On the long rail trip back home Mussolini was dejected. He had not only failed to get approval for a large Italian contingent but had gained the uneasy feeling that the war in the East would be a lengthy and bloody one. His depression changed to rage upon learning that Ribbentrop was not going to publish the agreed joint communiqué of the visit; the Foreign Minister's name, it seemed, had been mentioned *after* Keitel's.

This time Hitler bowed to Mussolini and asked Ribbentrop to get into line. His honor avenged, Il Duce's spirit rose. He summoned Dino Alfieri, his ambassador to Berlin, and gave him directives for a report on their visit to the front. "Don't forget to mention," he said, "that for a considerable part of the way I piloted the Führer's four-engined plane myself."

At the Wolfsschanze Hitler changed his mind and decided it was now time to launch the attack on Moscow. During tea in the casino with his secretaries and aides, he stared fixedly at a large map on the wall. "In several weeks we will be in Moscow," he said in a deep, rough voice. "There is no doubt of it. I will raze that damned city and I will construct in its place an artificial lake with central lighting. The name of Moscow will disappear forever." And so on the afternoon of September 5 he told Halder, "Get started on the central front within eight to ten days." His

THE
RUSSIAN FRONT

——— Line of Nov. 15, 1941

······ Deepest German Penetration

0   Miles   200

N

FALKENHORST
FROM NORWAY

WHITE SEA

FINLAND

MANNERHEIM

FINNISH

L. ONEGA

Helsinki

L. LADOGA

BALTIC
SEA

GULF OF FINLAND

Volkhov

Tallinn

Leningrad

Tikhvin

ESTONIA

Novgorod

RUSSIAN
COUNTEROFFENSIVE,
WINTER 1942

Riga

Pskov

DEC 6, '41

LATVIA

Kalinin

Yaroslavl

VOLGA R.

Gorki

LITHUANIA

KUECHLER

MAY '42

LEEB

Velikiye
Luki

Dvinsk

Moscow

U. S. S. R.

Kaunas

Vyazma

Tula

BOCK

Minsk

Smolensk

Kaluga

Penza

KLUGE

Bryansk

Saratov

Brest-Litovsk

Mogilev

Orel

POLAND

Pinsk

RUNDSTEDT

Gomel

Kursk

Voronezh

BATTLE OF
STALINGRAD,
NOV.'42-JAN.'43

DON R.

L'vov

Kiev

Belgorod

Werewolf

Vinnitsa

DNIEPER R.

Kharkov

WEICHS

VOLGA R.

Lugansk

Stalingrad

Dniepropetrovsk

DON R.

NOV. '42

ROMANIAN

Krivoy Rog

Nikolaevsk

Rostov

Odessa

SEA OF
AZOV

LIST

ROMANIA

Krasnodar

Stavropol

Bucharest

Constanza

Sevastopol

Novorossisk

BULGARIA

BLACK SEA

Grozny

palacios

mood at supper that night was light, almost frolicsome. His comments were noted down by Werner Koeppen, Rosenberg's liaison man at Führer Headquarters. Since early July that year, at Rosenberg's behest, he had been circumspectly recording the Führer's table conversations. Koeppen assumed Hitler knew what he was doing and would furtively jot down notes on his paper napkin, then immediately after the meal write out only those parts of the conversation he could distinctly remember. An original and one copy of his records were forwarded to Berlin by courier.

Unbeknown to Koeppen, there was a second Boswell at the main table. Shortly after their arrival at Wolfsschanze, Bormann had suggested almost offhandedly to Heinrich Heim, his adjutant, that he surreptitiously note down what the Chief said. So Hitler wouldn't know he was being put on record, Bormann instructed his adjutant to rely on his memory. But Heim wanted more accurate results and on his own initiative he began making copious notes on index cards which he hid on his lap. Bormann was taken aback but he gave Heim tacit approval to continue taking notes.* "So the matter went on," Heim recalled, "without Bormann giving me any instructions, expressing any wishes or anything else except to silently show his happiness that in this way much would be preserved and not forgotten."

Heim was constantly faced with two problems: to select the most meaningful reflections (sometimes what he was writing down was superseded in importance by Hitler's next words) and to keep the Führer from seeing what he was doing. At the noon meal and the evening supper he was able to mask his activities but during the late night tea sessions, which took place in the bunker, he had to rely on memory alone, except for an occasional scribbled word or two. Heimchen, as the gentle soul was affectionately called, was so unobtrusive (as was Koeppen) that Hitler continued to speak freely, spontaneously on a limitless variety of subjects in an oral stream of consciousness.

The records of Heim and Koeppen gave rare insight into the momentous events unfolding each day on the eastern front. On September 17, for instance, Hitler expounded on the spirit of decision, which consisted, he

---

* Some of these notes were later published in various editions in England, France and Germany, the last under the title *Hitler's Tischgespräche*, by Henry Picker, who deputized for Heim as court reporter from March through July 1942. Heim was never consulted by any of the publishers or given the opportunity of commenting on the notes and correcting misconceptions on their history. While the published portion of his notes sounds quite accurate, he misses many important passages. Only about one sixth of his original notes, for instance, appear in the Picker edition. Heim is positive that Hitler never knew his table talk was being recorded. After the war he was assured of this by Hitler's personal adjutant, Schaub. Heim presently lives in Munich within blocks of Koeppen but was unaware until recently that the other was also making notes. Their two accounts complement each other. Heim purposely omitted all military matters for security; Koeppen did not. The latter's notes, moreover, are valuable as corroboration of Heim's far more detailed and personalized minutes.

said, "in not hesitating when an inner conviction commands you to act. Last year I needed great spiritual strength to take the decision to attack Bolshevism. I had to foresee that Stalin might pass over to the attack in 1941. It was therefore necessary to get started without delay, in order not to be forestalled—and that wasn't possible before June. Even to make war, one must have luck on one's side. When I think of it, what luck we did have!" The tremendous military operation presently in progress, he said, had been widely criticized as impracticable. "I had to throw all my authority into the scales to force it through. I note in passing that a great part of our successes have originated in 'mistakes' we've had the audacity to commit."

He assured his fascinated listeners that the hegemony of the world would be decided by the seizure of Russian space. "Thus Europe will be an impregnable fortress, safe from all threat of blockade. All this opens up economic vistas which, one might think, will incline the most liberal of the Western democrats toward the New Order. The essential thing, for the moment, is to conquer. After that everything will be simply a question of organization." The Slavs, he said, were born slaves who felt the need of a master and Germany's role in Russia would be analogous to that of England in India. "Like the English, we shall rule this empire with a handful of men."

He talked at length of his plans to make the Ukraine the granary for all Europe and to keep its conquered people happy with scarves and glass beads, then ended in a confession: while everyone else was dreaming of a world peace conference, he preferred to wage war for another ten years rather than be cheated of the spoils of victory.

The capture of Kiev, three days later, caused elation at Wolfsschanze. It meant, predicted Hitler, the early conquest of the entire Ukraine and justified his insistence on giving priority to the southern offensive. At dinner on September 21 Hitler glowed with satisfaction as he told of the capture of 145,000 prisoners in the valley near Kiev. This battle of encirclement, he claimed, was the most confused in the entire history of warfare. The Soviet Union was on the verge of collapse.

At the noon meal on September 25 he revealed his fear of the subhuman farther east: Europe would be endangered until these Asians had been driven back behind the Urals. "They are brutes, and neither Bolshevism nor Czarism makes any difference—they are brutes in a state of nature." Late that evening he extolled the virtues of battle by comparing a soldier's first battle to a woman's first sexual encounter, as if he regarded each as an act of aggression. "In a few days a youth becomes a man. If I weren't myself hardened by this experience, I would have been incapable of undertaking this Cyclopean task which the building of an empire means for a single man." It was with feelings of pure idealism that he had set out for the front in 1914. "Then I saw men falling around me in thousands. Thus I learned that life is a struggle and has no other object but the preservation of the species."

The table talk was almost exclusively of the battle in the East, since there was little action on the only other active war front, North Africa. The British effort to throw back Rommel had failed miserably; and by the beginning of autumn there was a standoff in the desert with neither side prepared to mount another offensive. Hitler's energy and the might of the Wehrmacht were being concentrated for an all-out assault on Moscow but Field Marshal von Bock warned that it was too late in the season. Why not spend the winter in fortified positions? Hitler replied with an allegory of sorts: "Before I became Chancellor, I used to think the General Staff was like a mastiff which had to be held tight by the collar to keep it from attacking anyone in sight." But it had turned out to be anything but ferocious. It had opposed rearmament, the occupation of the Rhineland, the invasion of Austria and Czechoslovakia, and even the war in Poland. "It is I who have always had to goad on this mastiff."

He insisted upon attacking the capital in force and the operation, code-named Typhoon, was launched on the last day of September by Bock. His mission was to destroy the central Soviet forces with a fearsome aggregation of sixty-nine divisions before advancing on the capital; his basic strategy was a drive aimed at Moscow with a double tank envelopment, the pincers meeting eighty miles behind the Red Army.

The Soviet high command, unable to conceive of a major offensive started so late in the year, was caught so completely by surprise that Guderian's 2nd Panzer Group raced fifty miles in the first twenty-four hours through the Red Army ranks. German infantrymen rushed into the vacuum to mop up disintegrating pockets of resistance.

By October 2 Hitler was confident enough of victory to set off for Berlin in his special train. He had not spoken to the people for months and the next afternoon he strode into the Sportpalast purportedly to make an appeal in support of the Wartime Winter Assistance Program. But he had come to issue a major proclamation. "On the morning of June 22," he said, his words booming over loudspeakers throughout the Reich, "the greatest battle in the history of the world began." Everything had gone according to plan, he said, and then announced that the enemy was "already beaten and would never rise again!" The audience broke into wild acclaim.

He began listing the statistics of victory: 2,500,000 prisoners, 22,000 destroyed or captured artillery pieces, 18,000 destroyed or captured tanks, more than 14,500 destroyed planes. The figures rolled on: German soldiers had advanced up to 1000 kilometers ("This is as the crow flies!"), over 25,000 kilometers of Russian railway were again in operation with most of this already converted to the German narrow gauge. For a man who had just professed that Russia was beaten and would never rise again, he entertained deep concerns. The war in the East, he admitted, was one of ideologies, therefore all the best elements in Germany must now be welded into one indissoluble community. "Only when the entire German people becomes a single community of sacrifice can we hope and expect that Providence will stand by us in the future. Almighty God never helped a lazy man. Nor does He help a coward."

It was a remarkable speech, one boasting of victory while calling for further sacrifice to ward off destruction. By evening the people's thoughts were diverted solely to triumph with the news that Orel had been seized so rapidly by Guderian's tankers that passengers in streetcars waved, assuming they were Russians; and vital factory equipment destined for evacuation to the Urals was seized intact.

The following day Hitler was back at Wolfsschanze and Koeppen noted that at supper he was in a particularly good mood. The noonday meal on October 6 was devoted to Czechoslovakia where there was considerable underground activity. His solution: deport all Jews "far to the East." This reminded him that, since Jews were the source through which all enemy information is spread, they should also think of deporting Jews from Berlin and Vienna to the same destination.

During the day Bryansk was taken as Guderian completed the encirclement of three entire Soviet armies. At supper Hitler was in a light-hearted mood and there was no talk of politics. Instead he made a lame joke: Major Engel had just been bitten by a dog and that explained the epidemic of madness ravaging Führer Headquarters. Victory continued and within two days reports from the front indicated that the Red Army could "essentially be considered defeated." With conquest of Moscow in sight, Hitler ordered that not a single German soldier should enter the capital. "The city," he said, "will be destroyed and completely wiped from the earth."

As Hitler emerged from the military conference on October 9 he called out to Otto Dietrich that the public could now be informed of the latest operations. Half an hour later, as he paced his study in the bunker with vigorous strides, Hitler dictated word for word the victory statement Dietrich was to submit to the press. Dietrich did so the next day in Berlin, then raised his fist high in the air. "And on that, gentlemen," he shouted, "I stake my whole journalistic reputation!" "Axis and Balkan correspondents applauded and cheered," recalled Howard K. Smith of the New York *Times*, "then stood and raised their arms in salute to Dietrich."

That morning German newspapers told of a great victory: two Soviet army groups had been encircled. The public reaction was electric. Faces previously wan and drawn were now beaming. In beer-restaurants, people stood and saluted when the radio played "Horst Wessel" and "Deutschland über Alles." Rumors spread throughout the capital that Moscow had fallen.

Significantly, on that same day Field Marshal von Reichenau, the first general to espouse National Socialism, issued an order to the Sixth Army for sterner treatment of partisans. This was no ordinary war, he said, but a struggle to the death between German culture and the Jewish-Bolshevist system. "Therefore, the soldier must have full understanding of the necessity for harsh but just measures of atonement against Jewish subhumanity." Similar orders came from Rundstedt, Manstein and other senior commanders.

Hitler's declaration that the Soviets were defeated and total victory assured was not merely propaganda to raise morale at home. He believed what he said. But he had not quite convinced his pragmatic propaganda chief. Josef Goebbels started the briefing to his subordinates on the fourteenth with the optimism of a Dietrich: "Militarily this war has already been decided. All that remains to be done is of predominantly political character both at home and abroad." Then he contradicted himself by warning that the German people must reconcile themselves to continued fighting in the East for another ten years. Therefore it was the task of the German press to help strengthen the people's "staying power" and when that was done "the rest will follow of its own accord, so that, within a very short space of time, no one will notice that no peace has been concluded at all."

If Hitler had similar reservations they were dispelled upon learning that the Soviet diplomatic corps had fled Moscow on October 15 for Kuibyshev, six hundred miles to the east. Panic was truly sweeping the city and at the Kremlin Stalin reputedly had lost his nerve. A report that two German tanks had reached a suburb caused stampedes at railway stations. High-ranking party officials and secret police joined the pell-mell flight in cars, causing the first traffic jam in Soviet history. Pedestrians stormed the stalled cars, robbing and blackmailing the occupants, particularly those thought to be Jews.

Other bands of deserters and workers were plundering stores since no police were on hand to stop them. One rumor circulated that Lenin's body had been removed from Red Square for safekeeping, another that Stalin himself had taken to his heels. A grim minority was building barricades and preparing to die rather than let a single Nazi pass, but most Moscovites were demoralized, awaiting the Germans with a strange mixture of expectancy and apathy. Many of them bought German-Russian dictionaries so they could greet the conquerors in their own language.

In Berlin there was talk in the halls of the Wilhelmstrasse that Stalin had made an offer of peace through King Boris of Bulgaria. Fritz Hesse asked Ribbentrop whether it was true and was told in strict secrecy that Hitler had rejected the offer "clearly because he was convinced he could stand the immediate test and emerge victorious in the end." Most of Hitler's commanders shared his confidence. Jodl, for instance, had no doubt that the Soviets had used up their last reserves. At supper on the seventeenth Hitler's talk was mostly of the bright future. As far as he was concerned Lebensraum was a fact.

Two days after Hitler's euphoric monologue, the man he admired and derided had regained his aplomb. Reappearing in the Kremlin, Stalin asked the chairman of the Moscow Soviet, "Should we defend Moscow?" and without waiting for an answer proclaimed a state of siege. Breaches of law and order were to be dealt with promptly; all spies, diversionists and agents provocateurs were to be shot without trial. With firm direction from the top, morale throughout the city began to lift.

Before Moscow, the Soviet troops stiffened and the German spear-heads which had driven to within forty miles of the capital were slowed. Then came a break in the weather. The fall rains began and while the powerful German Mark IVs became mired in the muddy roads, the more maneuverable Soviet T-34 tanks rolled free. Hitler's victories of the past two years had come through the superior mobility and firepower brought about by massed Panzer attacks closely supported by tactical air forces. But the seas of mud below foundered the armor and the low visibil-ity above grounded the Luftwaffe, which had already gained air suprem-acy. With mobility went firepower—and Blitzkrieg, upon which Hitler based his hopes.

To say that Typhoon was stemmed by the mud and freezing rain and the Red Army was only partially true. The principal reason for failure, so asserted most of his commanders, was Hitler's refusal to launch it a month earlier. If he had followed their advice Moscow would have been a mass of rubble and the Soviet government and its forces defeated. But Captain von Puttkamer, for one, was convinced that it was the fault of Brauchitsch and Halder for sabotaging the Führer's basic plan during his illness.

In late October the sleet turned into snow and the mud froze. Condi-tions for the troops were almost unbearable. There were few advances along the entire line and these were modest ones. By the end of the month the situation was so desperate that Giesler, the architect, was or-dered to stop work on the reconstruction of German cities. All workers, engineers, building materials and machinery were to be transported at once to the East to construct highways, repair railroad tracks and con-struct stations and locomotive sheds.

At meals Hitler appeared as confident as ever. On the eve of his de-parture for the annual celebration of the Munich Putsch he enlivened sup-per with jokes and reminiscences. In Moscow his admired enemy was mak-ing a speech at the annual Eve-of-Revolution Day meeting in the huge hall of the Mayakovsky subway station. It was an odd mixture of dejection and confidence. First Stalin admitted that the building of socialism had been greatly impeded by the war and that casualties on the battlefield al-ready were almost 1,700,000. But the Nazi claim that the Soviet regime was collapsing had no basis in fact. "Instead," he said, "the Soviet rear is today more solid than ever. It is probable that any other country, having lost as much territory as we have, would have collapsed." Admittedly Russia faced a tremendous task since the Germans were fighting with numerous allies—Finns, Romanians, Italians and Hungarians—while not a single English or American soldier was yet in position to help the Soviet Union.

He made an impassioned appeal to Russian national pride in the name of Plekhanov and Lenin, Belinsky and Chernyshevsky, Pushkin and Tolstoy, Gorki and Chekhov, Glinka and Tschaikovsky, Sechenov and Pavlov, Suvorov and Kutuzov. "The German invaders want a war of extermination against the peoples of the Soviet Union. Very well then! If they want a war of extermination, they shall have it."

Stalin was back in command and the next morning, November 7, he spoke with equal force to troops gathered in Red Square. In the distance guns boomed and overhead came the snarl of patrolling Soviet fighter planes as he compared their position with that of twenty-three years ago. How could anyone doubt that they could and must defeat the German invaders? Again he shrewdly used names of the past—the conquerors of the Teutonic Knights, the Tartars, the Poles and Napoleon—as a rallying cry. "May you be inspired by the heroic figures of our great ancestors, Alexander Nevsky, Dimitri Donskoi, Minin and Pozharsky, Alexander Suvorov, Michael Kutuzov!"

Hitler arrived in Munich the following afternoon. He made an impassioned appeal to a convocation of Reichsleiters and Gauleiters and later delivered a speech at the Löwenbräukeller which included a warning to President Roosevelt that if an American ship shot at a German vessel "it will do so at its own risk." His threatening words did not have Stalin's forceful ring. In fact, he was depressed by the stalemate on the eastern front and the next day reminded his staff what had befallen Napoleon's army in Russia. "The recognition that neither force is capable of annihilating the other," he predicted, "will lead to a compromise peace."

But Marshal von Bock argued against such pessimism. He urged that their offensive be continued. So did Brauchitsch and Halder. On November 12 the latter was the picture of optimism as he announced that in his opinion the Russians were on the verge of collapse. Hitler was impressed and three days later the push for Moscow resumed.

At first the weather was good but soon ice, mud and snow began taking control of the battlefield. When General Oshima appeared at Wolfsschanze on one of his periodic visits Hitler explained winter had come much earlier than his weather man had predicted. Then, in the strictest confidence, he admitted that it was doubtful if they could take Moscow that year. Gone was the season of good humor. There were no jokes at mealtime and the request for seats at his table diminished.

The cold intensified, provoking bitter denunciation of Hitler's earlier edict prohibiting the preparation of winter clothing. On November 21 Guderian phoned Halder to say that his troops had reached the end of their endurance. He was going to visit Bock and request that the orders he had just received be changed since he could "see no way of carrying them out." But the marshal, under direct pressure from the Führer, would not listen to Guderian's pleas and ordered the attack on Moscow resumed. After short, spasmodic advances the drive once more faltered. Taking over personal direction from an advanced command post, Bock called for another assault on November 24 despite a brewing storm. The attack was halted by snow, ice and fanatic Soviet resistance.

Frustration in the center was compounded five days later by a crisis in the south. Field Marshal von Rundstedt was forced to evacuate Rostov, the gate to the Caucasus, captured only a week previously. Angered by this thirty-mile retreat, Hitler telegraphed Rundstedt to remain where he was. The marshal immediately wired back:

IT IS MADNESS TO ATTEMPT TO HOLD. FIRST THE TROOPS CANNOT DO IT AND SECOND IF THEY DO NOT RETREAT THEY WILL BE DESTROYED. I REPEAT THAT THIS ORDER MUST BE RESCINDED OR THAT YOU FIND SOMEONE ELSE.

The message was drafted by a subordinate, except for the last sentence, which Rundstedt added in his own hand. It was these final words that infuriated Hitler and, without consulting the commander-in-chief of the army, he replied that same night:

I AM ACCEDING TO YOUR REQUEST. PLEASE GIVE UP YOUR COMMAND.

After replacing Rundstedt with Field Marshal von Reichenau, one of the few who dared speak openly to him, the Führer flew to Mariupol for firsthand information. He sought out an old comrade, Sepp Dietrich, commander of the SS Leibstandarte, but to his chagrin learned that the officers of this elite division agreed with Rundstedt that they would have been wiped out if they had not fallen back.

After giving Reichenau orders to do what he had fired his predecessor for doing, Hitler summoned Rundstedt. He was packing to go home and thought the Führer might make some sort of apology. But their personal discussion turned into a threat; Hitler said that in the future he would not tolerate any more applications to resign. "I myself, for instance, am not in a position to go to my superior, God Almighty, and say to Him, 'I am not going on with it, because I don't want to take the responsibility.'"

Announcement of the fall of Rostov caused gloom in Berlin in both the Propaganda Ministry and the Foreign Office. But this defeat soon paled before a looming disaster on the central front. The all-out offensive against Moscow was foundering. Although an infantry reconnaissance reached the edge of Moscow early in December and sighted the Kremlin's spires, it was dispersed by several Red Army tanks and an emergency force of factory workers. Field Marshal von Bock, suffering from severe stomach cramps, admitted to Brauchitsch on the phone that the entire attack had no depth and the troops were physically exhausted. On December 3 Bock phoned Halder. This call was even more pessimistic and when Bock suggested going over to the defensive the chief of the General Staff tried to inspirit him with the kind of admonition that comes from those far from the front line; he said that "the best defense was to stick to the attack."

The following day Guderian reported that the thermometer was down to 31 degrees below zero. It took fires under the tank engines to get them started and the cold made telescopic sights useless. Worse, there were still no winter overcoats and long woolen stockings and the men suffered intensely. On the fifth it was five degrees colder. Guderian not only broke off his attack but began to withdraw his foremost units into defensive positions.

That same night the new Soviet commander of the central front, General Georgi Zhukov, launched a massive counteroffensive—one hundred divisions—on a two-hundred-mile front. This combined infantry-tank-air assault caught the Germans off guard and Hitler had not only lost Moscow but seemed destined to suffer Napoleon's fate in the winter snows of Russia. Despair and consternation swept the German Supreme Command. Commander-in-Chief of the Army von Brauchitsch, sick and discouraged, wanted to resign.

Hitler himself was confused. In the Great War the Russian infantrymen had fought poorly; now they were tigers. Why? Despondent, he admitted on December 6 to Jodl that "victory could no longer be achieved."

5

For the past two years Hitler had been sedulously avoiding confrontation with the United States. Convinced that the entire nation was in the clutches of the "Jewish clique," which not only dominated Washington but controlled the press, radio and cinema, he exercised the utmost restraint in the face of Roosevelt's increasing aid to Britain. Although he despised Americans as fighters, he did acknowledge their industrial strength and was set upon keeping them neutral—until he was prepared to deal with them properly.

Despite the steady flow of war matériel to the British Isles, Hitler was so eager to avoid incidents that he had forbidden attacks on United States naval or merchant ships. "Weapons," he ordered, "are to be used only if *U.S. ships fire the first shot.*" But Roosevelt's quick reaction to Barbarossa threatened to end Hitler's patience. On the day after the attack the President authorized Acting Secretary of State Sumner Welles to release a statement that Hitler must be stopped even if it meant giving aid to another totalitarian country. Although Roosevelt was vague as to how this was to be done, he soon made it clear, first by releasing some forty million dollars in frozen Soviet assets, and then by announcing that the provisions of the Neutrality Act did not apply to the Soviet Union, thus leaving the port of Vladivostok open to American shipping.

Two weeks later, July 7, German claims that Roosevelt was intervening in the European war were reinforced; it was revealed that American forces had arrived in Iceland to eventually replace British forces then occupying that strategic island. The German chargé d'affaires in Washington, Hans Thomsen, cabled the Wilhelmstrasse that this was a further attempt on FDR's part to provoke Hitler into attacking America through some naval incident so she could declare war on Germany.

Disturbed by these reports, Hitler made a proposition to Ambassador Oshima in mid-July that was a reversal of his former determination to limit Japan to the task of holding off England and keeping America neutral. "The United States and England will always be our enemies," he said. "This realization must be the basis of our foreign policy." It was a sacred conviction reached after lengthy deliberations. "America and England will always turn against whomever, in their eyes, is isolated. Today there are only two states whose interests cannot conflict with one another, and these are Germany and Japan." Wasn't it obvious that America under Roosevelt, bent on a new imperialism, was exerting pressure alternately on the European and Asiatic Lebensraum? "Therefore," he concluded, "I am of the opinion that we must jointly destroy them." As bait, he suggested Japan help "liquidate the assets" of the defeated Soviet Union and occupy its Far Eastern territories.

The proposition was received in Tokyo with polite reserve. The Japanese had already decided not to attack Russia from the east but instead move south to Indochina. They did so and its peaceful seizure brought a quick response from Roosevelt on the night of July 26. Taking the advice of those like Harold Ickes, who had long been urging him to act forcefully against all aggressors, the President ordered Japanese assets in America frozen, an act which deprived Japan of her major source of oil. To the New York *Times* it was "the most drastic blow short of war." To Japan's leaders it was the last step in the encirclement of the Empire by the ABCD (American, British, Chinese, Dutch) powers, denying Nippon her rightful place as leader of Asia, a challenge to her existence. In any case, it was a giant step toward war in the Far East and, to some observers, Roosevelt's backdoor entrance to war against Hitler.

A month later the President went further when he met Churchill at sea off Newfoundland and signed the Atlantic Charter, a joint declaration of British and American war aims. Its terms not only left no doubt that Roosevelt was Hitler's implacable enemy but, ironically, disillusioned the Führer's enemies inside Germany, for no difference was made between a Nazi and an anti-Nazi. Those in the Resistance regarded the charter as Roosevelt's unofficial declaration of war against all Germans. They particularly resented Point 8, which stipulated that Germans must be disarmed after the war; a demand which, Hassell wrote in his journal, "destroys every reasonable chance for peace."

Roosevelt's determination to smash Hitler was opposed to the sentiments of millions of Americans. In addition to the right-wing America Firsters of Charles Lindbergh and the German-American Bund, there was the traditional isolationist Midwest which, though sympathetic to Britain and China, wanted no part of a shooting war. Other Americans hated Communism so intensely that they resented any aid going to the Soviet Union. Roosevelt was undeterred by violent press and radio attacks. "From now on," he announced in a radio broadcast on September 11, "if German or Italian vessels of war enter these waters [i.e., Iceland and similar areas under United States protection] they do so at their peril." Although this was a ready excuse for Hitler to remove the last restrictions on U-boat warfare, he could not be provoked into a misstep. He ordered Admiral Raeder "to avoid any incidents in the war on merchant shipping before the middle of October." By then, he explained, the Russian campaign would be as good as over.

Hitler's hope of avoiding a major incident vanished on the last day of October when the United States destroyer *Reuben James*, escorting a convoy six hundred miles west of Iceland, was torpedoed. It sank with 101 Americans aboard. Roosevelt withheld comment but his Secretary of the Navy told an audience of marines that the French liner *Normandie* would be expropriated, loaded with 400 airplanes and sent to Murmansk. The San Francisco *Chronicle* demanded that the Neutrality Act be repealed immediately and the Cleveland *Plain Dealer* called for immediate "action." But isolationist Senator Nye urged restraint: "You can't walk into a barroom brawl and hope to stay out of the fight!" and another senator, who was not isolationist, advised, "Let us keep cool."

The storm of anti-German sentiment couldn't have come at a more propitious time for Roosevelt. A week later the Office of Lend-Lease Administration was directed to do everything in its power to supply military and economic aid to the Soviet Union. One billion dollars was immediately allocated to that end.

The following day, November 8, Hitler made his belligerent speech at Munich, which was, in fact, an excuse for the sinking of the *Reuben James*. "President Roosevelt has ordered his ships to shoot the moment they sight German ships!" he shouted. "I have ordered German ships not to shoot when they sight American vessels but to defend themselves as soon as attacked. I will have any German officer court-martialed who fails to defend himself." Despite the show of anger this merely indicated that the Führer still wanted to avoid war. Say what he would, he feared Franklin Roosevelt and the industrial power of America.

He revealed as much in spite of himself in an interview early that autumn at Wolfsschanze. "I will outlast your President Roosevelt," he explained to Pierre Huss of INS. "I can afford to wait and take my time to win this war in my own way." They were outdoors and Hitler, wearing his long greatcoat of rubberized field gray, stood with hands folded behind his back staring vacantly, lost in thought. Suddenly he said, "I am Führer of a Reich that will last for a thousand years to come." He slapped a glove into his left palm. "No power can shake the German Reich now. Divine Providence has willed it that I carry the fulfillment of a Germanic task." Although he talked of his own destiny, he was obsessed by resentment of Churchill and Roosevelt, whom he disparaged as minor characters on the world stage. "They are sitting over there in their plutocratic little world, surrounded and enslaved by everything proved obsolete in the last decade. The money bags and Jews run the show behind the scenes; a parliamentary circus tramples on what is left in rights and privileges of their people. I have my people behind me and they have faith in me, their Führer." As the two men continued their walk, followed by a small group of guards and subordinates, Hitler resumed his complaint about "the madmen" who had driven him to war. "I had plans and work for my people for fifty years to come, and didn't need a war to stay in office like the Daladiers and Chamberlains. And, for that matter, Herr Roosevelt of America."

Huss noted his brow pucker into a slight frown at the mention of the President. "It struck me suddenly, with unmistakable clarity," recalled Huss, "that I had stumbled on a secret locked within the Führer's breast, a secret he would never let out and which he may never admit having." Hitler by instinct *feared* Franklin D. Roosevelt. "Ja, Herr Roosevelt—and his Jews!" exclaimed Hitler. "He wants to run the world and rob us all of a place in the sun. He says he wants to save England but he means he wants to be ruler and heir of the British Empire."

Hitler's hardening attitude toward America was reflected by Ribbentrop. On the evening of November 28 he summoned General Oshima and urged Japan to declare war against both the United States and Britain. Oshima was surprised. "Is Your Excellency indicating that a state of actual war is to be established between Germany and the United States?" Ribbentrop had not meant to go that far. "Roosevelt is a fanatic," he explained, "so it is impossible to tell what he would do." He promised that if Japan should fight the United States, Germany would join her ally. "There is absolutely no possibility of Germany's entering into a separate peace with the United States under such circumstances. The Führer is determined on this point."

This information was a great relief to the Japanese high command. A carrier task force was already en route to Pearl Harbor. On the last day of November Oshima was ordered to inform Hitler and Ribbentrop immediately that the English and Americans were planning to move military forces into East Asia and this must be countered:

> . . . SAY VERY SECRETLY TO THEM THAT THERE IS EXTREME DANGER THAT WAR MAY SUDDENLY BREAK OUT BETWEEN JAPAN AND THE ANGLO-SAXON NATIONS THROUGH SOME CLASH OF ARMS AND ADD THAT THE TIME OF THE BREAKING OUT OF THAT WAR MAY COME QUICKER THAN ANYONE DREAMS.

These instructions were quickly followed by orders to obtain specific pledges from the Germans, yet when Oshima approached Ribbentrop late on the evening of December 1 the Foreign Minister was surprisingly evasive. He excused himself on the grounds that he would first have to consult with the Führer, who was still at the Wolfsschanze. Both men knew that Hitler had little time to devote to the drama brewing on the other side of the world and so Oshima was not surprised that he did not receive a draft treaty until 3 A.M. on the fifth. In it Germany promised to join Japan in any war against the United States and not to conclude a separate peace.

The first to learn of Pearl Harbor at the Wolfsschanze was Otto Dietrich. Late in the afternoon of December 7 he hurried to Hitler's bunker with word that he was bearing an extremely important message. Hitler had just received depressing reports from the Russian front and feared Dietrich was bringing more bad news, but as his press chief hastily read the message his look of surprise was unmistakable. He brightened. Extremely excited, he asked, "Is this report correct?"

Dietrich said that he had received a telephone confirmation from his office. Hitler snatched the paper and, without putting on coat or hat, strode to the military bunker. Keitel and Jodl were amazed to see him, telegram in hand, a "stunned" look on his face. It seemed to Keitel as if the war between Japan and America had suddenly relieved Hitler of "a nightmare burden." With Hewel, the Führer could barely conceal the elation in his voice. "We cannot lose the war!" he exclaimed. "Now we have a partner who has not been defeated in three thousand years."

6

The desperate reports streaming in from the Russian front on Pearl Harbor day forced Hitler to draft a new directive which he issued twenty-four hours later. "The severe winter weather," it began, "which has come surprisingly early in the East, and the consequent difficulties in bringing up supplies, compel us to abandon immediately all major offensive operations and to go over to the defensive." He set down the general principles for defense while turning over to Halder the task of issuing subsequent instructions. Then he set off for Berlin to take personal charge of the crisis raised by Pearl Harbor. By this time his initial relief at the Japanese attack had been replaced by concern. In one stroke, Pearl Harbor had freed Stalin from worry over attack from the east; he could now transfer almost all his strength in Asia against Germany. "This war against America is a tragedy," Hitler later admitted to Bormann. "It is illogical and devoid of any foundation of reality. It is one of those queer twists of history that just as I was assuming power in Germany, Roosevelt, the elect of the Jews, was taking command in the United States. Without the Jews and without this lackey of theirs, things could have been quite different. From every point of view Germany and the United States should have been able, if not to understand each other and sympathize with each other, then at least to support each other without undue strain on either of them."

One of Hitler's first visitors in Berlin on the morning of the ninth was Ribbentrop with the unwelcome information that General Oshima was requesting an immediate declaration of war against America. But the Foreign Minister didn't think Germany was obligated to do so since, according to the Tripartite Pact, she was bound to assist her ally only in case of a direct attack upon Japan.

Hitler could not accept this loophole. "If we don't stand on the side of Japan, the pact is politically dead," he said. "But that is not the main reason. The chief reason is that the United States already is shooting at our ships. They have been a forceful factor in this war and through their actions have already created a situation of war."

His decision to declare war on America was not lightly taken, nor was its motivation simple. Beyond upholding the spirit of the Tripartite Pact there were far weightier arguments: the assistance received from Japan would considerably offset the disadvantages caused by America's entry into the war; from a propaganda point of view the acquisition of a new, powerful ally would have a tremendously heartening effect after the recent setbacks in Russia. Further, an outright declaration of war was in line with his ideological world view. Why not make 1941 the year in which he declared total war upon the two major enemies of human survival—international Marxism (Russia) and international finance capitalism (America), both the creatures of international Jewry?

His Foreign Office regarded the decision as a colossal mistake. In addition to the obvious reasons it neatly solved another of Roosevelt's domestic problems. The President would not have to declare war on Germany and risk opposition from a substantial segment of the citizenry.

American national unity, so unexpectedly won by the surprise attack at Pearl Harbor, would remain intact.

On December 11 Hitler convoked the Reichstag. "We will always strike first!" he said. Roosevelt was as "mad" as Woodrow Wilson. "First he incites war, then falsifies the causes, then odiously wraps himself in a cloak of Christian hypocrisy and slowly but surely leads mankind to war, not without calling God to witness the honesty of his attack." After equating international Jewry with Bolshevik Russia and Roosevelt's regime, Hitler made his declaration of hostilities. "I have therefore arranged for passports to be handed to the American chargé d'affaires today and the following . . ." His words were drowned in a bedlam of cheers, and it was some time before he could announce that Germany was "at war with the United States, as from today." The chief of operations of OKW listened to this speech with more concern than enthusiasm and as soon as Jodl left the Kroll Opera House he telephoned his deputy, General Warlimont, in Wolfsschanze. "You have heard that the Führer has just declared war on America?"

Warlimont had just been discussing the matter with staff officers and said they couldn't be more surprised. "The staff," said Jodl, "must now examine where the United States is most likely to employ the bulk of her forces initially, the Far East or Europe. We cannot take further decisions until that has been clarified."

"Agreed; this examination is obviously necessary, but so far we have never even considered a war against the United States and so have no data on which to base this examination; we can hardly undertake this job just like that."

"See what you can do," said Jodl. "When I get back tomorrow we will talk about this in more detail."

Anxiety over America was soon overriden by new reverses in the East. The German retreat on the central front threatened to degenerate into panic flight. The area west of Moscow and the Tula area was a snow-covered graveyard of abandoned guns, trucks and tanks. German despondency was accompanied by rising Russian confidence. On December 13 the Soviets publicly announced the failure of Hitler's attempt to surround Moscow and two days later the Politburo ordered the principal organs of government to return to the capital.

The exhausted Brauchitsch wanted to continue the withdrawal but Hitler overruled him and sent out a general order that spread despair among the military hierarchy: "Stand fast, not one step back!" Marshal von Bock, commander of the central front, already suffering from a stomach ailment, reported himself physically unfit for duty. He was replaced by Kluge. The next day, the nineteenth, Brauchitsch—just recovering from a heart attack—summoned up nerve enough to face Hitler. For two hours they argued in private. Brauchitsch left the Führer, ashen and shaken. "I am going home," he told Keitel. "He has sacked me. I can't go on any longer."

"What is going to happen now, then?" asked Keitel.

"I don't know; ask him yourself."

A few hours later Keitel was summoned. The Führer read out a brief Order of the Day he had composed. He was assuming personal command of the army, inextricably binding the fate of Germany with his own. The news was to be kept secret for the moment but he felt Halder should be informed at once. Hitler did so, minimizing the difficulties of the post. "This little affair of operational command is something anybody can do," he said. "The commander-in-chief's job is to train the army in the National Socialist idea and I know of no general who could do that as I want it done. For that reason I have taken over command of the army myself."

Previously he had been de facto commander of the army, keeping himself in the background and allowing the military to take blame for all setbacks. Now he was the official commander-in-chief and would have to accept praise or blame for whatever happened.

Part 8

THE FOURTH HORSEMAN

And I looked, and behold a pale horse: and his name that sat on him was Death, and Hell followed with him. And power was given unto them over the fourth part of the earth, to kill with sword, and with hunger, and with death, and with the beasts of the earth.

REVELATION 6:8

"AND HELL FOLLOWED
WITH HIM"
1941-1943

1

Two days after the invasion of the Soviet Union the man responsible for the deportation of Jews, Reinhard Heydrich, complained in writing that this was no answer to the Jewish problem. Deporting these misfits to the French island of Madagascar, for instance, would have to be dropped in favor of a more practical solution. It was fitting, therefore, that on the last day of July Heydrich received a cryptic order (signed by Göring upon instructions from the Führer) instructing him "to make all necessary preparations regarding organizations and financial matters to bring about a complete solution of the Jewish question in the German sphere of influence in Europe."*

Behind the innocuous bureaucratic language lay sweeping authority for the SS to organize the extermination of European Jewry. As a preliminary step, Himmler—still shaken by his experience in Minsk—asked the chief physician of the SS what was the best method of mass extermination. The answer was: gas chambers. The next step was to summon Rudolf Höss, the commandant of the largest concentration camp in Poland, and give him secret oral instructions. "He told me," testified Höss,

---

* Three weeks earlier Hitler had hinted to Hewel what he intended to do. "I feel like a Robert Koch in politics," he said during a long, late night discussion in the hot bunker. "He found the bacillus and with it showed medical science a new way. I discovered the Jew as a bacillus and the ferment of all social decomposition . . . and one thing I have proven is that a state can live without Jews; that economy, art, culture, etc., can exist even better without Jews, which is the worst blow I could give the Jews."

"something to the effect—I do not remember the exact words—that the Führer had given the order for a final solution of the Jewish question. We, the SS, must carry out that order. If it is not carried out now the Jews will later on destroy the German people." Himmler said he had chosen Höss's camp since Auschwitz, strategically located near the border of Germany, afforded space for measures requiring isolation. Höss was warned that this operation was to be treated as a secret Reich matter. He was forbidden to discuss the matter with his immediate superior. And so Höss returned to Poland and, behind the back of the inspector of concentration camps, quietly began to expand his grounds with intent to turn them into the greatest killing center in man's history. He did not even tell his wife what he was doing.

Hitler's concept of concentration camps as well as the practicality of genocide owed much, so he claimed, to his studies of English and United States history. He admired the camps for Boer prisoners in South Africa and for the Indians in the wild West; and often praised to his inner circle the efficiency of America's extermination—by starvation and uneven combat—of the red savages who could not be tamed by captivity.

Until now he had scrupulously integrated his own general policy with that of Germany, since both led in the same general direction. The resurgence of German honor and military might, the seizure of lost Germanic territories, and even Lebensraum in the East were approved heartily by most of his countrymen. But at last had come the crossroads where Hitler must take his personal detour and solve, once and for all, the Jewish question. While many Germans were willing to join this racist crusade, the great majority merely wanted a continuation of the limited Jewish persecution which had already received the tacit approval of millions of Westerners.

It was Hitler's intent to start eliminating the Jews secretly before leaking out the truth a little at a time to his own people. Eventually the time would be ripe for revelations that would tie all Germans to his own fate; his destiny would become Germany's. Complicity in his crusade to cleanse Europe of Jewry would make it a national mission and rouse the people to greater efforts and sacrifices. It would also burn all bridges behind the hesitant and weak-hearted.

Until now all this was kept secret from Hitler's innermost circle—the secretaries, adjutants, servants and personal staff. But in the autumn of 1941 the Führer began making overt remarks during his table conversations, perhaps as an experiment in revelation. In mid-October, after lecturing on the necessity of bringing decency into civil life, he said, "But the first thing, above all, is to get rid of the Jews. Without that, it will be useless to clean the Augean stables." Two days later he was more explicit. "From the rostrum of the Reichstag, I prophesied to Jewry that, in the event of war's proving inevitable, the Jew would disappear from Europe.

That race of criminals has on its conscience the two million dead of the First World War, and now already hundreds and thousands more. Let nobody tell me that all the same we can't park them in the marshy parts of Russia! Who's worrying about our troops? It's not a bad idea, by the way, that public rumor attributes to us a plan to exterminate the Jews. Terror is a salutary thing." He predicted that the attempt to create a Jewish state would be a failure. "I have numerous accounts to settle, about which I cannot think today. But that doesn't mean I forget them. I write them down. The time will come to bring out the big book! Even with regard to the Jews, I've found myself remaining inactive. There's no sense in adding uselessly to the difficulties of the moment. One acts shrewdly when one bides one's time."

One reason Hitler had delayed implementing the Final Solution was hope that his implied threat to exterminate the Jews would keep Roosevelt out of the war. But Pearl Harbor ended this faint expectation and Hitler's hope turned into bitterness, with extermination becoming a form of international reprisal.

The decision taken, the Führer made it known to those entrusted with the Final Solution that the killings should be done as humanely as possible. This was in line with his conviction that he was observing God's injunction to cleanse the world of vermin. Still a member in good standing of the Church of Rome despite detestation of its hierarchy ("I am now as before a Catholic and will always remain so"), he carried within him its teaching that the Jew was the killer of God. The extermination, therefore, could be done without a twinge of conscience since he was merely acting as the avenging hand of God—so long as it was done impersonally, without cruelty. Himmler was pleased to murder with mercy. He ordered technical experts to devise gas chambers which would eliminate masses of Jews efficiently and "humanely," then crowded the victims into boxcars and sent them east to stay in ghettos until the killing centers in Poland were completed.

The time had come to establish the bureaucracy of liquidation and the man in charge, Heydrich, sent out invitations to a number of state secretaries and chiefs of the SS main offices for a "Final Solution" Conference, to take place on December 10, 1941. The recipients of his invitation, aware only that Jews were being deported to the East, had little idea of the meaning of "final solution" and awaited the conference with expectation and keen interest.

Their curiosity was whetted by a six-week postponement. Frank, head of the *Generalgouvernement* (German-occupied Poland), became so impatient that he sent Philipp Bouhler, his deputy, to Heydrich for more details, then convened a conference of his own at Cracow in mid-December. "I want to say to you quite openly," said Hitler's former lawyer, "that we shall have to finish the Jews, one way or another." He told about the im-

portant conference soon to take place in Berlin which Bouhler would attend for the Generalgouvernement. "Certainly the major migration is
about to start. But what is to happen to the Jews? Do you think they will
actually be settled in Eastern villages? We were told in Berlin, 'Why all
this fuss? We can't use them in the *Ostland* either; let the dead bury their
dead!'" He urged his listeners to arm themselves against all feelings of
sympathy. "We have to annihilate the Jews wherever we find them and
wherever it is at all possible." It was a gigantic task and could not be
carried out by legal methods. Judges and courts could not take the heavy
responsibility for such an extreme policy. He estimated—and it was a gross
overestimate—that there were 3,500,000 Jews in the Generalgouvernement
alone. "We can't shoot these 3,500,000 Jews, we can't poison them, but
we can take steps which, one way or another, will lead to an annihilation
success, and I am referring to the measures under discussion in the Reich.
The Generalgouvernement will have to become just as free of Jews as the
Reich itself. Where and how this is going to happen is the task for the
agencies which we will have to create and establish here, and I am going
to tell you how they will work when the time comes."

When Bouhler arrived in Berlin on January 20, 1942, for the
Heydrich conference he was far better prepared than most of the conferees to understand the generalities uttered. At about 11 A.M. fifteen men
gathered in a room at the Reich Security Main Office at number 56–58
Grossen Wannsee. There were representatives from Rosenberg's East
Ministry, Göring's Four-Year Plan agency, the Interior Ministry, the Justice Ministry, the Foreign Office and the party chancellery. Once they had
seated themselves informally at tables, Chairman Heydrich began to
speak. He had been given, he said, "the responsibility for working out the
final solution of the Jewish problem regardless of geographical boundaries." This euphemism was followed by a veiled and puzzling remark
which involved Hitler himself. "Instead of emigration," he said, "there is
now a further possible solution to which the Führer has already signified
his consent—namely deportation to the East."

At this point Heydrich exhibited a chart indicating which Jewish
communities were to be evacuated, and gave a hint as to their fate. Those
fit to work would be formed into labor gangs but even those who survived
the rigors would not be allowed to go free and so "form a new germ cell
from which the Jewish race would again arise. History teaches us that."
Georg Leibbrandt, of Rosenberg's office, was at a loss. Martin Luther of
the Foreign Office was also confused. He protested that mass Jewish evacuations would create grave difficulties in such countries as Denmark and
Norway. Why not confine the deportations to the Balkans and western
Europe? The conferees left Berlin with a variety of impressions. Bouhler
knew exactly what Heydrich was talking about but Luther assured Fritz
Hesse that there were no plans at all to kill the Jews. Leibbrandt and his

superior, Alfred Meyer, gave a similar report to Rosenberg. Not a word, they agreed, had been said of extermination.

Thirty copies of the conference record were distributed to the ministries and SS main offices and the term "Final Solution" became known throughout the Reich bureaucracy yet the true meaning of what Heydrich had said was fathomed only by those privy to the killing operations, and many of this select group, curiously, were convinced that Adolf Hitler himself was not totally aware that mass murder was being plotted. SS Lieutenant Colonel Adolf Eichmann, in charge of the Gestapo's Jewish Evacuation Office, for one knew this was a myth. After the Wannsee conference he sat "cozily around a fireplace" with Gestapo Chief Müller and Heydrich, drinking and singing songs. "After a while we climbed onto the chairs and drank a toast; then onto the table and traipsed round and round—on the chairs and on the table again." Eichmann joined in this celebration with no qualms. "At that moment," he later testified, "I sensed a kind of Pontius Pilate feeling, for I was free of all guilt. . . . Who was I to judge? Who was I to have my own thoughts in this matter?" He, Müller and Heydrich were only carrying out the laws of the land as prescribed by the Führer himself.

A few days later Hitler confirmed in spite of himself, that he was indeed the architect of the Final Solution. "One must act radically," he said at lunch on January 23, in the presence of Himmler. "When one pulls out a tooth, one does it with a single tug, and the pain quickly goes away. The Jew must clear out of Europe. It's the Jew who prevents everything. When I think about it, I realize that I'm extraordinarily humane. At the time of the rules of the Popes the Jews were mistreated in Rome. Until 1830, eight Jews mounted on donkeys were led once a year through the streets of Rome. For my part, I restrict myself to telling them they must go away. If they break their pipes on the journey, I can't do anything about it. But if they refuse to go voluntarily I see no other solution but extermination." Never before had he talked so openly to his inner circle and he was so absorbed by the subject that on the twenty-seventh he again demanded the disappearance of all Jews from Europe.

His obsession with Jews was publicly expressed a few days later in a speech at the Sportpalast on the ninth anniversary of National Socialism's rise to power. "I do not even want to speak of the Jews," he said, and proceeded to do so at length. "They are simply our old enemies, their plans have suffered shipwreck through us, and they rightly hate us, just as we hate them. We realize that this war can only end either in the wiping out of the Germanic nations, or by the disappearance of Jewry from Europe." He reminded the audience, which included some forty high-ranking military officers, of his 1939 prophecy that the Jews would be destroyed. "For the first time, it will not be the others who will bleed to death, but for the first time the genuine ancient Jewish law, 'an eye for an eye, a tooth for a tooth,' is being applied. The more this struggle spreads, the more anti-Semitism will spread—and world Jewry may rely on this. It will find nourishment in every prison camp, it will find nourishment in every family which is being enlightened as to why it is being called upon to make such sacrifices, and the hour will come when the worst enemy in the world will have finished his part for at least a thousand years to come."

To those presently engaged in designing gas chambers, to those constructing the killing centers in Poland, and particularly to those who were being prepared to administer the mechanics of the final solution, this statement was a clarion call for genocide. But to foreign observers, such as Arvid Fredborg, Hitler's words and appearance that afternoon seemed to foreshadow a German disaster. "His face," wrote the Swedish journalist, "now seemed ravaged and his manner uncertain."

2

To the Führer the extermination of Jews and Slavs was as important as Lebensraum. He had turned the invasion into ideological warfare and his military decisions, therefore, could only be understood in this context. What appeared irrational to his generals was no sudden mental lapse but the fruit of decisions made in 1928. Ironically, never had he shown more military acumen than after the shocking defeats at the gates of Moscow. Surrounded by demoralized military leaders pleading for general retreat, Hitler did not lose his nerve. He refused to grant any requests to withdraw. He was not swayed by the most successful tank commander, Guderian, who argued that taking up positional warfare in such unsuitable terrain would lead to the useless sacrifice of the best part of the army. He accused Guderian of being too deeply impressed by the suffering of the soldiers. "You feel too much pity for them. You should stand back more. Believe me, things appear clearer when examined at longer range."

Enforcing his order ruthlessly, Hitler managed to rally the army and stem the Russian advance. The cost was great but a number of his generals, including Jodl, were forced to agree that he had personally saved his troops from the fate of Napoleon's army. "I intervened ruthlessly," he told Milch and Speer, and explained that his top commanders were willing to retreat all the way to the German border to save their troops. "I could only tell these gentlemen, 'Mein Herren, return personally to Germany as soon as possible but leave the army to my leadership.'"

All was well on the other war fronts. In France the Resistance, still hopelessly splintered, was of little concern; and in the Mediterranean, U-boats, Italian "human torpedoes" and mines had recently sunk or crippled a carrier, three battleships and two cruisers, thus eliminating Great Britain's Eastern battle fleet as a fighting force. Moreover, Rommel was almost ready to launch another major offensive in North Africa and

Germany's Japanese allies were continuing their unbroken series of victories in the Pacific. At the same time Hitler knew the crisis in the East was by no means over and so ordered a general mobilization of the industry and economy of the Reich. The present effort, he said, was insufficient and the Blitzkrieg strategy must be abandoned. Although he couched this call for a long war in hopeful terms, he privately retained the nagging fear, so recently confided to Jodl, that victory could no longer be achieved.

Such dark doubts were never revealed in his table conversations. He continued to chat about the evils of smoking, the joys of motoring, dogs, the origin of Tristan and Isolde, the beauty of Frau Hanfstaengl and Jews. Of the grim struggle at the front he spoke little and then with optimism. At the height of the winter crisis, for instance, he declared that no cause was hopeless provided the leadership stood firm. "As long as there is one stouthearted man to hold up the banner, nothing has been lost. Faith moves mountains. In this respect, I am ice cold: if the German people are not prepared to give everything for the sake of their self-preservation, very well! Then let them disappear!"

Such imperturbable performances at mealtime were belied by his appearance. "He is not the man he was," Hewel told a friend. "He has grown gloomy and obdurate. He will shrink from no sacrifice and show no mercy or forgiveness. You would not recognize him if you saw him." His morale received a crushing blow on February 8 when Fritz Todt, builder of the Westwall and the Autobahn system, died in a plane crash. At the breakfast table there was speculation on who would take over Todt's position as Minister of Armaments and Munitions, one of the most crucial posts in the Reich. Everyone agreed that Todt was irreplaceable; and Albert Speer, who had spent most of the night talking to Hitler about the Berlin and Nuremberg building projects, was thunderstruck when the Führer appointed him next morning. The architect's protest that he knew nothing about such matters was cut short. "I have confidence in you. I know you will manage it. Besides I have no one else."

At the funeral of Todt in the Mosaic Hall of the Reich chancellery, Hitler was so shaken that during his eulogy he could hardly continue and, once the ceremony ended, he took refuge in his apartment. Somehow he managed to recover his composure enough in the next few days to address 10,000 newly appointed Wehrmacht and Waffen SS lieutenants at the Sportpalast. Grim-faced, he told of the disaster in Russia, sparing no details. You young officers, he said, are going East to save Germany and Western civilization from the Reds. It was such a stirring speech that many in the audience wept. Standing at his side, Richard Schulze, recently promoted to personal adjutant, was so moved he wanted to join in the fight. "I felt ashamed to stay home at such a time." The new lieutenants had been ordered not to applaud but when Hitler started down the aisle they could not restrain themselves. They cheered wildly, many jumping onto their chairs.

This spontaneous outburst was a tonic to Hitler but by the time he returned to the Wolfsschanze he was again depressed. He looked exhausted and sallow. The blanket of snow covering the area deepened his despondency. "I've always detested snow," he confided to his shadow. "Bormann, you know I've always hated it. Now I know why. It was a presentiment."

Hitler despaired upon reading the report of casualties in Russia up to February 20: 199,448 dead, 708,351 wounded, 44,342 missing, 112,627 cases of frostbite. Yet he soon rebounded. Confidence abruptly regained, he began to talk at the dinner table of the terrible winter as an ordeal successfully, miraculously endured. He announced to the company with a sigh of relief that Sunday would be the first of March. "Boys, you can't imagine what that means to me—how much the last three months have worn out my strength, tested my nervous resistance." He revealed that during the first two weeks of December alone a thousand tanks had been lost and two thousand locomotives put out of operation. But the worst of winter was at last over. "Now that January and February are past, our enemies can give up the hope of our suffering the fate of Napoleon. . . . Now we're about to switch over to squaring the account. What a relief!" His high spirits were no longer spurious and he began to boast. "I've noticed, on the occasion of such events, that when everybody loses his nerve, I'm the only one who keeps calm. It was the same thing at the time of the struggle for power."

In the meantime preparations for the Final Solution were maturing and Himmler's Einsatzgruppen had begun another deadly sweep. While this second roundup of Jews, commissars and partisans was carried out in a co-ordinated manner in the military areas, progress in civilian territories proceeded less smoothly. Even so the death toll was massive and Rosenberg's staff begged him once more to urge Hitler to treat the peoples of the occupied areas as allies, not enemies. Rosenberg's aides warmly supported his relatively liberal concept of setting up separate states with varying degrees of self-government, but his turn toward liberalism had not been accompanied by a strengthening of character and he still trembled at the thought of antagonizing his Führer. A stronger man might have proved as ineffective; to approach the Führer it was necessary to go through Bormann, who had solidly aligned himself with Himmler and Heydrich. Rosenberg's liaison man at Wolfsschanze, Koeppen, was finding it increasingly difficult to convey to Hitler the true story of what was going on in the East. Before the Hess flight, he had simply passed on memoranda directly to Hitler but now Bormann insisted on acting as go-between with the excuse that the Führer was too busy with military matters. And so, concluded Koeppen, Hitler only saw the problem of the occupied East through the eyes of his right-hand man. "Therein lay the fateful development which, in my opinion, cost us victory in the East."

While it was true that Hitler had little time for internal matters, it was more likely that Bormann always followed his personal instructions; and there was no doubt that Hitler always took time to oversee the Final Solution. In this matter he neither needed nor took advice. He made this clear in his message on the anniversary of the promulgation of the party program in late February. "My prophecy," he said, "shall be fulfilled that this war will not destroy Aryan humanity but it will exterminate the Jew. Whatever the battle may bring in its course or however long it may last, that will be its final course." The elimination of Jewry overrode victory itself.

Despite such open hints, few had yet been initiated into the secret. Goebbels himself still did not realize the enormity of the measures being prepared. One of his employees, Hans Fritzsche, did learn about the Einsatzgruppen killings from a letter sent by an SS man in the Ukraine. The writer complained that he had suffered a nervous breakdown after receiving an order to kill Jews and Ukrainian intelligentsia. He could not protest through official channels and asked for help. Fritzsche immediately went to Heydrich and asked point-blank, "Is the SS there for the purpose of committing mass murders?" Heydrich indignantly denied the charge, promising to start an investigation at once. He reported back the next day that the culprit was Gauleiter Koch, who had acted without the Führer's knowledge, then vowed that the killings would cease. "Believe me, Herr Fritzsche," said Heydrich, "anyone who has the reputation of being cruel does not have to be cruel; he can act humanely."

Only that March did Goebbels himself learn the exact meaning of Final Solution. Then Hitler told him flatly that Europe must be cleansed of all Jews, "if necessary by applying the most brutal methods." The Führer was so explicit that Goebbels could now write in his diary:

> . . . A judgment is being visited upon the Jews that, while barbaric, is fully deserved. . . . One must not be sentimental in these matters. If we did not fight the Jew, they would destroy us. It's a life-and-death struggle between the Aryan race and the Jewish bacillus. No other government and no other regime would have the strength for such a global solution of this question.

By spring six killing centers had been set up in Poland. There were four in Frank's Generalgouvernement: Treblinka, Sobibor, Belzec and Lublin; two in the incorporated territories: Kulmhof and Auschwitz. The first four gassed the Jews by engine-exhaust fumes but Rudolf Höss, commandant of the huge complex near Auschwitz, thought this too "inefficient" and introduced to his camp a more lethal gas, hydrogen cyanide, marketed commercially under the name of Zyklon B.

Spring revitalized the Führer. His health improved, his spirits rose. The Soviet winter counteroffensive had ground to a complete halt and a lull set in all along the front. This gave him more time to think of future policies and on April 24 he telephoned Goebbels that he wanted to deliver a major speech before the Reichstag. The following Sunday at 3 P.M. he denounced Bolshevism as "the dictatorship of Jews" and labeled the Jew "a parasitic germ" who had to be dealt with ruthlessly. But the thrust of his speech was a vocal reaffirmation of renewed faith in eventual triumph. At the same time he made no effort to conceal how close the army had come to disaster. He exaggerated the situation to make his personal role more effective. "Deputies," he exclaimed dramatically, "a world struggle was decided during the winter." He compared himself with Napoleon. "We have mastered destiny which broke another man a hundred and thirty years ago." To prevent a similar crisis he went on to demand passage of a law granting him plenary powers. Its terms were sweeping. Every German was henceforth obliged to follow his personal orders—or suffer dire punishment. He was now officially above the law with the power of life and death. He had, in essence, appointed himself God's deputy and could do the Lord's work: wipe out the vermin and create a race of supermen.

The members of the Reichstag, stirred to the roots by his manner and words, unanimously approved the measure "enthusiastically and noisily." To foreign observers there seemed little reason for such a law. Hitler already had grasped more de facto power than Stalin or Mussolini, more, in fact, than either Caesar or Napoleon had enjoyed. He had done so, he claimed, to end war profiteering and the black market, and to prune the overgrown staffs of bureaucracy for additional manpower in the battle of production. He ignored the fact that the bleeding of the German economy had been caused not only by the conservatism in the civil service and the judiciary, but by corruption within the party itself. The plundering by such men as Göring, along with the widespread venality and inefficiency on every level of National Socialism, had been draining the strength of the Reich for almost a decade.

Three days later the Führer met Mussolini at the baroque Klessheim Castle near Salzburg. The Italians, unlike the enrapt audience at the Sportpalast, had been depressed by Hitler's oratory and they entered the first conference with some foreboding. The Führer talked interminably but said little of interest, glossing over the misfortunes of the eastern front ("The German army this winter wrote the finest pages of its history"). He declared that America was a big bluff, and again favorably compared himself to Napoleon. He also expounded on India, Japan and practically every country in Europe, with categorical pronouncements in each case. On the second day, after lunch, although everything had been said, Hitler continued talking uninterrupted for another hour and forty minutes, as Mussolini kept checking his wrist watch. Hitler's own commanders were bored. "General Jodl," recalled Ciano, "after an epic struggle, finally went to sleep on the divan."

3

Within the SD it was no secret that Himmler distrusted Heydrich, who had monumental files on everyone in the party, including the Führer, and was despised in return. (One day Heydrich showed a subordinate, Günter Syrup, a picture of Himmler. Covering the upper part of his face, he said, "The top half is the teacher but the lower half is a sadist.") But Hitler had great plans for Heydrich. He was even considering him as a successor now that Göring had fallen from favor after the disappointing performance of his Luftwaffe, and made him Acting Protector of Moravia and Bohemia in addition to his other high offices. After initiating a wave of terror in Czechoslovakia that quickly crushed the resistance movement, Heydrich adopted the guise of benefactor, particularly to workers and peasants. He raised the fat ration for industrial laborers, improved the social security system and requisitioned luxury hotels for the working class. "He plays cat and mouse with the Czechs," observed his fellow intellectual, Goebbels, "and they swallow everything he places before them. He has carried out a number of extremely popular measures, particularly the almost complete conquest of the black market."

The Reich Protector's achievements in Czechoslovakia roused the Czech government-in-exile to action. Since it appeared that the population might passively accept domination by the Third Reich under such a benevolent despot, they decided to assassinate Heydrich. Two non-coms, Jan Kubis and Josef Gabcik, trained at a school for sabotage in Scotland, were parachuted into the protectorate from a British plane.

On the morning of May 27 the assassins, accompanied by two compatriots, hid at a curve on the road between Heydrich's country villa and Hradschin Castle in Prague. As the Protector's green open Mercedes was approaching, Gabcik jumped to the road and pressed the trigger of his Sten. Nothing happened. He cocked the gun. Again it jammed. Behind him, Kubis lobbed a grenade at the car, which was slowing to a halt. Heydrich shouted, "Step on it, man!" but the driver, a last-minute substitute, kept slamming on the brakes. The grenade exploded, wrecking the rear of the car. Apparently unwounded, Heydrich leaped to the road, revolver in hand, shooting and yelling as if he were "the central figure in a scene out of any Western." Kubis escaped on a bicycle; Gabcik, still unhurt, stood momentarily immobilized when his weapon jammed, then escaped. Suddenly Heydrich dropped his revolver, grasped his right hip and staggered. Fragments of leather and steel springs from the Mercedes' upholstery had penetrated his ribs and stomach. He was taken to a nearby hospital but his wound did not seem serious and he refused to be attended by any but a German doctor. One was finally found who announced that an operation was necessary since grenade fragments were lodged in the membrane between the ribs and lungs as well as the spleen.

Himmler, at temporary headquarters near Wolfsschanze, wept upon learning that his right-hand man was dying, but some SS men were convinced these were crocodile tears since he resented Heydrich's rise to favor with Hitler. As Heydrich lay dying in Prague he whispered a warning to his subordinate Syrup to beware of Himmler.

Later, while surveying the death mask of Heydrich, Himmler remarked to Walter Schellenberg, chief of the SS Foreign Intelligence Service, "Yes, as the Führer said at the funeral, he was indeed a man with an iron heart. And at the height of his power fate purposefully took him away." His voice was somber but Schellenberg could never forget "the nod of Buddha-like approval that accompanied these words, while the small cold eyes behind the pince-nez were suddenly lit with sparkle like the eyes of a basilisk."

The two assassins, along with five other members of the Czech Resistance, were finally trapped in a Budapest church by the SS and executed. But this was only the beginning of the reprisal. A reign of terror which made Heydrich's actions seem benevolent descended on Bohemia and Moravia. More than 1300 Czechs were executed out of hand, including all the male inhabitants of Lidice on the fake charge that these villagers had harbored the assassins. Lidice itself was burned, the ruins dynamited and the ground leveled. The eradication of this obscure village not only aroused the disgust and indignation of the Western world but rekindled the spirit of resistance within Czechoslovakia.*

It was the Jews who suffered most by the assassination. On the day Heydrich died 152 were executed in Berlin. Three thousand others were removed from the concentration camp of Theresienstadt and shipped to Poland where the killing centers were already receiving a steady flow of victims.

Perhaps the most diabolical innovation of the Final Solution was the establishment of Jewish Councils to administer their own deportation and destruction. This organization, comprising those leaders of the community who believed that co-operation with the Germans was the best policy, discouraged resistance. "I will not be afraid to sacrifice 50,000 of our community," reasoned a typical leader, Moses Merin, "in order to save the other 50,000."

* "This was our general idea when we flew in a party to murder Heydrich in Czechoslovakia," admitted British Labour M.P. R. T. Paget, after the war. "The main Czech Resistance movement was the direct result of the consequent SS reprisals."

By early summer the mass exterminations began under the authority of a written order from Himmler. Eichmann showed this authorization to one of his assistants, Dieter Wisliceny, with the explanation that Final Solution meant the biological extermination of the Jewish race. "May God forbid," exclaimed the appalled Wisliceny, "that our enemies should ever do anything similar to the German people!"

"Don't be sentimental," said Eichmann. "This is a Führer order." This was corroborated by Himmler in a letter to the chief of the SS Main Office at the end of July: "The occupied Eastern territories will be cleared of Jews. The implementation of this very hard order has been placed on my shoulders by the Führer. No one can release me from this responsibility in any case. So I forbid all interference."

What Kurt Gerstein learned, as head of the Technical Disinfection Service of the Waffen SS, had already driven him to despair. "He was so appalled by the satanic practices of the Nazis," recalled a friend, "that their eventual victory did not seem to him impossible." During a tour that summer of the four extermination camps in the Generalgouvernement, Gerstein saw with his own eyes what he had read about. At the first camp he and two companions—Eichmann's deputy and a professor of hygiene named Pfannenstiel—were informed that Hitler and Himmler had just ordered "all action speeded up." At Belzec, two days later, Gerstein saw these words translated into reality.

"There are not ten people alive," he was told by the man in charge, Kriminalkommissar Christian Wirth, "who have seen or will see as much as you." Gerstein witnessed the entire procedure from the arrival of 6000 Jews in boxcars, 1450 of whom were already dead. As the survivors were driven out of the cars with whips, they were ordered over a loudspeaker to remove all clothing, artificial limbs, and spectacles and turn in all valuables and money. Women and young girls were to have their hair cut off. "That's to make something special for U-boat crews," explained an SS man, "nice slippers."

Revolted, Gerstein watched the march to the death chambers. Men, women, children—all stark naked—filed past in ghastly parade as a burly SS man promised in a loud, priestlike voice that nothing terrible was going to happen to them. "All you have to do is breathe in deeply. That strengthens the lungs. Inhaling is a means of preventing infectious diseases. It's a good method of disinfection." To those who timorously asked what their fate would be, the SS man gave more reassurance: the men would build roads and houses; the women would do housework or help in the kitchen. But the odor from the death chambers was telltale and those at the head of the column had to be shoved by those behind. Most were silent, but one woman, eyes flashing, cursed her murderers. She was spurred on by whiplashes from Wirth, a former chief of criminal police in

Stuttgart. Some prayed, others asked, "Who will give us water to wash the dead?" Gerstein prayed with them.

By now the chambers were jammed with humanity. But the driver of the diesel truck, whose exhaust gases would exterminate the Jews, could not start the engine. Incensed at the delay, Wirth began lashing at the driver with his whip. Two hours and forty-nine minutes later the engine started. After another interminable twenty-five minutes Gerstein peered into one chamber. Most of the occupants were already dead. At the end of thirty-two minutes all were lifeless. They were standing erect, recalled Gerstein, "like pillars of basalt, since there had not been an inch of space for them to fall in or even lean. Families could still be seen holding hands, even in death." The horror continued as one group of workers began tearing open the mouths of the dead with iron hooks, while others searched anuses and genital organs for jewelry. Wirth was in his element. "See for yourself," he said, pointing to a large can filled with teeth. "Just look at the amount of gold there is! And we have collected as much only yesterday and the day before. You can't imagine what we find every day—dollars, diamonds, gold! You'll see!"

Gerstein forced himself to watch the final process. The bodies were flung into trenches, each some hundred yards long, conveniently located near the gas chambers. He was told that the bodies would swell from gas after a few days, raising the mound as much as six to ten feet. Once the swelling subsided, the bodies would be piled on railway ties covered with diesel oil and burned to cinders.

The following day the Gerstein party was driven to Treblinka near Warsaw where they saw almost identical installations but on a larger scale: "eight gas chambers and veritable mountains of clothing and underwear, 115 to 130 feet high." In honor of their visit, a banquet was held for employees. "When one sees the bodies of these Jews," Professor Pfannenstiel told them, "one understands the greatness of the work you are doing!" After dinner the guests were offered butter, meat and alcohol as going-away presents. Gerstein lied that he was adequately supplied from his own farm and so Pfannenstiel took the former's share as well as his own.

Upon arrival in Warsaw, Gerstein set off immediately for Berlin, resolved to tell those who would listen of the ghastly sights he had witnessed. A modern Ancient Mariner, he began spreading the truth to incredulous colleagues. As a rock thrown into a pond creates ever widening ripples, so did the tale of Kurt Gerstein.

4

The coming of spring 1942 saw almost no change in Germany's military situation. The eastern front remained stagnant and Rommel was still not quite ready for his new desert offensive. There was little of cheer to re-port except continuing Japanese victories and Hitler's enthusiasm over these was dampened by his ally's polite but stubborn refusal to conduct the war as he saw it. Ribbentrop persistently pressed the Japanese, through Ambassador Oshima, to turn their major attack toward India, but to no avail. Nor was Hitler any more successful when he invited Oshima to Wolfsschanze and repeated the request. The Wehrmacht, he said, was about to invade the Caucasus and once that oil region was seized the road to Persia would be open. Then the Germans and Japanese could catch all the British Far East forces in a giant pincers movement. It was tempting but the Japanese declined the opportunity. They were already contem-plating negotiations with the West. Prime Minister Tojo had been sum-moned to the palace and instructed by the Emperor "not to miss any opportunity to terminate the war." Tojo summoned the German ambas-sador, General Eugen Ott, and suggested that their two nations secretly approach the Allies; he would fly to Berlin as a personal representative of the Emperor if Hitler would send a long-range bomber. The Führer's reply was polite but lukewarm; he could not take the risk of Tojo crashing in a German plane.

Determined to defeat Russia even without the aid of Japan, Hitler proceeded as planned with his contemplated drive into the Caucasus. He stressed the importance of the area in words that alarmed his field com-manders. If they didn't seize the oilfields at Maikop and Grozny, he said, "I shall have to liquidate the war."

The ambitious operation, code-named Blau, was slowed for weeks by heavy spring rains and it was not launched by Marshal von Bock until June 28. Six Hungarian and seventeen German divisions drove toward Kursk. Forty-eight hours later the powerful Sixth Army, consisting of eighteen divisions, struck just to the south. The Russians made the mis-take of committing their tanks piecemeal and within forty-eight hours the two German forces met, encircling large number of prisoners. Just ahead lay the Don and the strategic city of Voronezh, but Bock was reluctant to press the attack. He finally took the city on July 6 but by this time Hitler was so disgusted with his dilatory tactics that he relieved him perma-nently.

As Bock headed west into retirement, complaining of mistreatment, Hitler moved his headquarters deep into the Ukraine, occupying a camp in the woods a few miles northeast of Vinnitsa. Christened Werewolf by himself, it was an uncamouflaged collection of wooden huts located in a dreary area. There were no hills, no trees, simply an endless expanse of nothingness. Under the cloudless July sky, the heat was stifling and this in turn markedly affected Hitler, contributing to the arguments and explo-sions which would reach unprecedented heights in the weeks to come.

Perhaps the heat also contributed to a crucial mistake. Hitler quixotically decided to mount a major attack on Stalingrad, an industrial city on the Volga, while continuing the drive to the Caucasus. Halder, for one, complained openly that it was impossible to take both Stalingrad and the Caucasus simultaneously and urged that they concentrate on the former alone. But Hitler remained convinced that the Russians were "finished."

There was deep concern within the Soviet high command itself. Stalin replaced the commander of the Stalingrad front and ordered the city to be readied for a siege. As at Moscow and Leningrad, thousands of workers began constructing three lines of defense works around the city. Home guard and worker battalions were sent west to back up retreating Red Army forces.

The arguments at Werewolf intensified. After one stormy session Hitler told his personal adjutant, "If I listen to Halder much longer, I'll become a pacifist!" Debate became outright rancor on July 30 at the daily Führer conference when Jodl solemnly stated that the fate of the Caucasus would be decided at Stalingrad, and that the Fourth Panzer Army, earlier diverted to the former, must be returned to the latter. Hitler exploded—and then agreed to do so. If this tank army had never been shifted to the south, Stalingrad would probably already have been in German hands, but by now the Soviets had gathered enough strength in front of the Volga to slow if not stem the new assault. On such apparently minor decisions do great issues often depend. With Stalingrad invested by midsummer, the entire Soviet defense system might have been irrevocably split by winter. It was another revealing example of Hitler's dangerous dispersion of forces. First had come his insistence on striking simultaneously at both Leningrad and the Ukraine, before belatedly pressing on to Moscow. All this was accompanied by a further diffusion of energy through waging political and ideological warfare while pursuing his personal goal of exterminating Jews. Similarly in the present dilemma—Stalingrad or the Caucasus?—he was insisting on taking both, at the risk of taking neither. The ancient Greeks would have called it hubris, the overweening pride that eventually overtakes all conquerors.

If Hitler had qualms over the jeopardy in which his overleaping ambition had placed the Wehrmacht, they were not apparent. A week later he was blandly assuring an Italian visitor that Stalingrad and the Caucasus would both be taken. His optimism seemed to be well founded. The over-all military situation was auspicious. Rommel had won an unexpected victory in North Africa by taking Tobruk, the linchpin to the British defenses, and then pushing on to El Alamein, only sixty-five miles from Alexandria. This triumph was followed by announcement of an even greater one at Midway. Hitler had believed the Japanese, whose communiqués had been much more accurate than those of the Americans. But this time it turned out to be his ally who grossly exaggerated; Nippon had not only lost four carriers and the cream of her naval aviators but the tide of battle in the Pacific had swung. The extent of defeat was confirmed by the news that the Americans had just landed in force on Guadalcanal, a strategic island deep inside Japan's defense perimeter.

It was a colossal setback and so unexpected that it was no wonder the arguments at Werewolf grew even more intense. A violent one erupted on August 24 following Halder's request that a unit presently under heavy Soviet attack be permitted to withdraw to a shorter line. Hitler shouted that his army chief of staff always came with the same proposal—withdrawal! "I expect my commanders to be as tough as the fighting troops."

Ordinarily Halder could restrain his resentment but today he retorted that brave Germans were falling in thousands simply because their commanders were not allowed to make reasonable decisions. Hitler recoiled. He stared fixedly, then said hoarsely, "Colonel General Halder, how dare you use language like that in front of me! Do you think you can teach me what the man at the front is thinking? What do you know about what goes on at the front? Where were you in the First World War? And you try to pretend to me that I don't understand what it's like at the front. I won't stand that! It's outrageous." The other military men sidled out of the conference room, heads bowed. It was obvious that Halder's days at Führer Headquarters were numbered.

By late August fighting began in the northern outskirts of Stalingrad. Already set afire by heavy bombings, the city was temporarily cut off when the Red Army communication networks broke down. But apparent victory did not mellow Hitler. He felt he had been lied to by commanders in the field and deceived by those at his own headquarters. His suspicion of both groups was growing pathological and he rarely listened to advice, never to criticism. Oppressed by the summer torpor, he began making hasty decisions in the grip of anger and recrimination. He was particularly incensed with Bock's replacement, Marshal List, and when he left the conference of August 31 Hitler began to insult and revile him. List's days too were numbered.

5

Hitler's conviction that he was surrounded by traitors was confirmed by the discovery late in August of a spy ring, the *Rote Kapelle* (Red Orchestra), which was comprised of prominent Germans. This group had succeeded in informing Moscow about the attack on Maikop, the fuel situation in Germany, the location of chemical warfare materials in the Reich, and Hitler's insistence on taking Stalingrad. After wholesale arrests, forty-six members of the ring, including Mildred Harnack, an American citizen, were executed. But secret information continued to flow to Moscow from another German spy, Rudolf Rössler, a publisher of leftist Catholic books in Lucerne. Rössler, whose code name was Lucy, had informants inside Germany, including General Fritz Thiele, the number two man in the OKW signal organizations; and his reports consequently were far more important than those of the Rote Kapelle; he could provide the Red Army with the German daily order of battle.

Hitler suspected there was a spy at Führer Headquarters since all his moves seemed to be anticipated. Suspicion bred irritability and his military leaders took the brunt of it. The argument on September 7 was the most tempestuous of all. That morning Hitler sent Jodl, one of the few staff officers still in his good graces, to the Caucasus to find out why List was making such slow progress in the mountain passes leading out to the Black Sea. After a long interview with List and the commander of the Mountain Corps, Jodl concluded that the situation was hopeless. He flew back to Vinnitsa and reported that List was adhering strictly to the instructions he had received.

The Führer jumped to his feet. "That's a lie!" he shouted and accused Jodl of having colluded with List. He was only supposed to transmit orders. Never had Jodl seen such an outburst of rage from a human being. Stung, he struck back. If Hitler had wanted a mere messenger, he said, why hadn't he sent a young lieutenant? Infuriated that Jodl had "wounded" him in the presence of others, Hitler stalked out of the room, casting glares at everyone. More convinced than ever that he was the victim of lies, Hitler shut himself up in his bunker.

The briefing conferences now took place in his hut. He pointedly refused to shake hands with any staff officer. The atmosphere of the meetings was glacial, with stenographers recording every word of the Führer's instructions. He was determined that never again would his orders be disputed. It was also the end of the camaraderie at mealtimes that he cherished. From now on the Führer ate alone in his room, attended only by Blondi, the Alsatian bitch which Bormann had recently given him to take his mind off escalating problems.*

The military community at Vinnitsa waited in anxious silence. No one felt secure. On September 9 Hitler summarily removed List and took personal command of Army Group A. Then came rumors that Halder, Jodl and Keitel were soon to be released. Although the latter had never been on intimate terms with General Warlimont, he now sought out his advice. Was it possible, he forced himself to ask, to keep his position and retain his self-respect? "Only you can answer that," replied Warlimont in embarrassment. He recalled how petrified Keitel had become the time Hitler angrily threw a file on the table. As it tumbled to the floor the chief of staff, forgetting his exalted position, had stood petrified as if he were a junior officer. It was a typical case, thought Warlimont, "of a man given a

---

* Heim never took another note of table conversation but Koeppen, upon Hitler's return to the communal table several months later, made notes until the following January. Thereafter a few inconsequential table conversations were recorded by Bormann or a reporter named Müller.

position for which he was unqualified." Poor Keitel had overreached himself; it was tragic since he had never wanted the job.

At conferences Hitler continued to display dogged confidence. When General von Weichs of Army Group B and General Friedrich Paulus, the field commander whose task it was to take Stalingrad, warned of the extremely long and lightly held Don front on the northern flank, the Führer made light of their concern. He assured them that the Russians were at the end of their resources and the resistance at Stalingrad was "a purely local affair." Since the Russians were no longer capable of launching a major counteroffensive, there was no real danger on the Don flank. The vital thing, he said, was "to concentrate every available man and capture as quickly as possible the whole of Stalingrad itself and the banks of the Volga." That was why he proposed to reinforce Paulus' Sixth Army with three more divisions.

This time there were some grounds for Hitler's optimism. Disorder was rampant among Soviet troops in the Stalingrad area. Numerous units between the Don and the Volga had already disintegrated as officers and troops deserted or fled to the rear. Columns of refugees, taking cattle and farm equipment with them, cluttered all roads to the east. One recently assigned commander found that his armor had vanished without orders and that leading artillery, anti-tank and engineer commanders, some holding the rank of general, had decamped. By September 14 disaster seemed imminent. Luftwaffe planes were already mining the Volga behind Stalingrad as German infantrymen ranged through the center of the city, seizing the main railroad station and driving as far as the waterfront.

Abruptly the Soviet defense stiffened. Reinforcements, ferried across the river, began challenging the Germans. On the fifteenth the main railroad station changed hands several times and Paulus felt obliged to narrow his attack. The fighting became listless and this had a marked effect on Hitler, so Warlimont noted upon his return to the briefing sessions after an absence of two weeks. As the Führer fixed him with a long, malevolent stare, Warlimont thought: "The man's confidence has gone with realization that the Soviets cannot be beaten"; that was why he could no longer abide those generals who had witnessed "his faults, his errors, his illusions and his daydreams."

"He trusts none of the generals," wrote Engel in his diary; ". . . he would promote a major to a general and make him chief of staff, if he only knew such a man. Nothing seems to suit him and he curses himself for having gone to war with such poor generals." Hitler decided to rid himself of Halder, who had annoyed him above all others as a prophet of doom, but whom he tolerated for his competence. The end came on September 24. "You and I have been suffering from nerves," said Hitler. "Half of my exhaustion is due to you. It is not worth while going on. We need National Socialist ardor now, not professional ability. I cannot expect this of an officer of the old school such as you." Tears welled in Halder's eyes, a sign of weakness to Hitler, further grounds for dismissal. Halder said not a word in his own behalf. He rose when Hitler finished his tirade. "I am leaving," he said simply, and walked out of the room with dignity. He was convinced that Hitler was dominated by feminine characteristics. "The intuition which mastered him instead of pure logic," he later wrote, "was only one of the many proofs of this fact."

As a replacement, Hitler wanted the antithesis of Halder, and chose Kurt Zeitzler. A newly appointed major general, he had none of the advantages of seniority and authority enjoyed by Halder and it seemed doubtful he could have much influence with OKW and the army group commanders. But Zeitzler's relative youth and inexperience made him all the more attractive to the Führer. He promoted Zeitzler two grades to colonel general.

In appearance he did not fit the role. An extremely short, heavy man, he seemed to be constructed of three balls. But in his first meeting with Hitler in the presence of some twenty officers Zeitzler did not fawn. He listened stolidly as the Führer excoriated the General Staff for doubts and fears. Once the scorching attack, aimed at almost everyone in the room, ended, Zeitzler said, "Mein Führer, if you have any further objections to the General Staff, please tell them to me under four eyes but not in the presence of so many other officers. Otherwise, you must seek a new chief of the General Staff." He saluted and marched out of the room. The other officers waited for the expected explosion but Hitler was impressed. "Eh," he said with a little grin, "he will be back, *ja?*"

Those expecting a new spirit of defiance at Führer Headquarters were quickly disillusioned. In his inaugural address to the officers of OKH, Zeitzler said, "I require the following from every staff officer: he must believe in the Führer and in his method of command. He must on every occasion radiate this confidence to his subordinate and those around him. I have no use for anybody on the General Staff who cannot meet these requirements."

Reassured that he had at last found the right army chief of staff, Hitler set out for Berlin to make another speech. It came on the last day of September at the Sportpalast rally for Winter Relief. Eagerly awaited by a hand-picked audience which had no idea what their Führer would say, it was a short, uninspired speech delivered without the usual sparkle. It struck many foreign listeners as pure bombast of no import, but they missed the implications of the anti-Semitic remarks that accompanied Hitler's pledge to take Stalingrad. Perhaps it was because his words about the Jews had been so oft repeated. For the third time that year he reiterated his prediction that if the Jews instigated "an international war to exterminate the Aryan peoples it would not be the Aryan peoples that would be annihilated but Jewry itself." The motivation for this repetition was obscure except to those privy to the secret of the Final Solution. Each mention was a public acknowledgment of his program of extermination; each gave reassurance and authority to the elite charged with the task of mass murder. Noteworthy too was his repetition of the false date of the original prophecy. It was made on January 30, 1939, not, as he kept saying, on the first of September. This could not have been a slip of the tongue since Hitler repeated it three times. By changing the date to that of the attack on Poland, the beginning of the Second World War, he linked his racial program to the war. He was preparing the people for the hard truth they must eventually face: the extermination of the Jews was an integral part of the war from the very first day of combat.

He was also announcing, if obscurely, that his twin program—the Final Solution and Lebensraum—was progressing as planned. His listeners left the auditorium with a generally uneasy impression. They themselves had contributed the only lift to the meeting, the unison rendition of "The Song of the Eastern Campaign," whose melody even foreign correspondents found extremely moving:

> *We have been standing guard for Germany,*
> *Keeping the eternal watch.*
> *Now at last the sun is rising in the East,*
> *Calling millions into battle.*

Their spirit was not shared by a number of officials, shocked by the repressive measures in the East. The most forceful rebukes came from Rosenberg's Ministry for the East Territories, and these despite its chief's reluctance to do battle with the formidable combine of Himmler, Bormann and Erich Koch, the Reich commissar for the Ukraine. The last, a former railroad conductor, had delusions of grandeur and rode around in a horse-drawn carriage like a little emperor. Cowed by the ruthless measures of this trio, Rosenberg had recently made them a peace offering: he fired Georg Leibbrandt, symbol of his own more liberal principles for governing occupied areas. But remaining subordinates continued to increase pressure on Rosenberg to by-pass Bormann and go directly to the Führer; they kept submitting new suggestions and reports. The most damning indictment of the Bormann-Himmler-Koch policy was a thirteen-page memorandum from Otto Bräutigam, who had spent seven years in the Soviet Union. The Germans, he said, had been greeted as liberators but the occupied peoples soon discovered that the slogan "Liberation from Bolshevism" was merely a blind for enslavement. Instead of gaining allies against Stalinism, the Germans were creating bitter enemies. "Our policy," charged Bräutigam, "has forced both Bolsheviks and Russian nationalists into a common front against us. The Russian fights today with exceptional bravery and self-sacrifice for nothing more or less than recognition of his human dignity." There was only one solution, concluded Bräutigam: "The Russian people must be told something concrete about their future." If Hitler ever read this memorandum, he never followed its advice. He was determined to win or lose on his own terms.

6

November proved to be a month of disaster for Germany with the enemy scoring victories in both East and West. Since conquest of Egypt was low among Hitler's priorities, he had made defeat in North Africa inevitable by failing to send Rommel sufficient supplies and reinforcements. With the pyramids practically in sight, the Desert Fox was forced into defensive warfare. When his southern section (held by Italians) was pierced by British General Montgomery, Rommel radioed for permission to retreat. On the evening of November 2 the Führer sent his reply: Do not fall back "one inch." The troops must "triumph or die."

Just before receiving this message Rommel radioed that he had been forced to withdraw; in fact a retreat had been under way for five hours. This information reached OKW at 3 A.M. and since the Operations Staff duty officer knew nothing of Hitler's original message, he did not think it important enough to pass on to the Führer.

Hitler, of course, was angry that he had not been awakened. He summoned Warlimont but as the deputy operations chief started down the path toward his office Keitel shouted from a distance in a highly unmilitary manner, "You, Warlimont, come here! Hitler doesn't want to ever see you again!" He was informed that he was relieved of his post.

Rommel's retreat, an augury of total defeat in the desert, was closely followed on November 7 by a disturbing report: a huge armada of Allied ships had entered the Mediterranean and was approaching the north coast of Africa. Although these ships had been sighted outside Gibraltar for several days Hitler and OKW had assumed they were bound for Sardinia or Sicily. The main reason for German surprise, explained Jodl, "probably was that we did not expect such a political false play after the upright, one can properly say, noble treatment which France had received [from Germany] since the collapse in the Forest of Compiègne. For this landing was only possible in agreement with the French and not against the will of France."

Hitler neither bothered to make excuses nor reflected the alarm of his military commanders. He cut short the midday briefing conference and, accompanied by most of the high-ranking population of Wolfsschanze, boarded his special train. Their destination was Munich; the occasion, the nineteenth anniversary of the Putsch. While the Führer slept, the first

American and British troops landed on the beaches of Morocco and Algeria. Early reports indicated the French were repelling the landings and Hitler chided his advisers for their initial panic. To their dismay he ordered reinforcements sent to Crete at the other end of the Mediterranean. Outwardly, at least, he was more concerned about the address he was to make to old comrades at the Löwenbräukeller at 6 P.M. It was a fighting speech. Defending himself against the charge that his insistence on taking the city, which "happens to bear the name of Stalin," was as costly to the German army as Verdun, he warned that he was no Wilhelm II, a weakling who had surrendered the Reich's vast Eastern conquests because of a few traitors' sudden desire for an accommodation with the West. "All our enemies may rest assured that while the Germany of that time laid down its arms at a quarter of twelve, I on principle have never finished before five minutes past twelve."

By evening the reports from Africa were too grim for Hitler to ignore. He ordered Ribbentrop to summon Mussolini for an immediate conference. Roused from bed for the second time within twenty-four hours, Ciano was persuaded to waken Mussolini. But Il Duce refused to make the trip to Bavaria. Already ill, he did not relish facing the Führer under the shadow of defeat. By the time his substitute, Ciano, arrived in Munich, Hitler had accepted the significance of the Africa landings. It was clear to him that "the God of war had now turned from Germany and gone over to the other camp." At the same time he reacted violently to Ribbentrop's suggestion that Stalin be approached through Madame Kollontai, the Soviet ambassador in Stockholm. A proposal that most of the conquered territories in the East be given up, "if need be," brought the Führer to his feet. "All I want to discuss," he said with a violence that terrorized Ribbentrop, "is Africa—nothing else!"

He also rejected another Japanese attempt to secure a peace with Russia, as well as a formal request for the Germans to go over to the defensive in the East and shift the bulk of their forces to the West. "I understand Japanese reasoning," Hitler told Ambassador Oshima. It was a good idea but impossible to execute. In such cold country it was extremely difficult to dig defensive positions. But this was merely rhetoric, designed to make refusal palatable to an ally. Any accommodation with Stalin was impossible for a man whose program stood or fell on victory over Bolshevism. And if he could not have victory in the East, Hitler was condemned by his mission to hold back the Red Army until he could rid Europe of Jews.

There were increasing rumors in Berlin that Hitler had gone mad. At one large gathering the wife of Reichsminister Funk reportedly told the wife of Reichsminister Frick, "The Führer is leading us headlong into disaster." "Yes," replied Frau Frick, "the man is insane." This opinion was echoed by Dr. Ferdinand Sauerbruch, the noted surgeon. He told friends that during a recent visit to the Führer he had heard an old and broken Hitler muttering such disjointed phrases as, "I must go to India," or "For one German who is killed ten of the enemy must die."

7

Hitler faced another defeat at Stalingrad. For weeks the Sixth Army of Paulus had made little progress. Advances were measured in yards and the cost of each yard was exorbitant. Both Paulus and Lieutenant Colonel Reinhard Gehlen, chief of intelligence in the East, warned of dangerous enemy concentrations to the north. "While it is not possible to make any over-all assessments of the enemy situation with the picture as uncertain as it is at present," reported Gehlen on November 12, "we must expect an early attack on the Romanian Third Army, with the interruption of our railroad to Stalingrad as its objective so as to endanger all German forces further to the east and to compel our forces in Stalingrad to withdraw."

Hitler was at the Berghof and did not read this ominous report. But he too was concerned about the Romanians and specifically asked if something was brewing in their area. The answer was no, repeatedly no, recalled Puttkamer, who attended every military conference that week. Since bad news notoriously travels slowly, the Führer was not informed of the gravity of the situation. There was still some doubt as to the strength of the Soviet build-up and the high command, stung by a recent Hitler criticism that it "repeatedly overestimated the enemy," was reluctant to repeat their timorous miscalculations in Poland and France.

At dawn November 19 forty Soviet divisions attacked the Romanians. The defenders fought ably and with gallantry but were crushed by overwhelming numbers. The Army Group B commander reacted quickly. First he ordered Paulus to cease attacking Stalingrad and prepare units to meet the threat to his left flank; then once it became obvious that the Romanians would collapse, he suggested immediate withdrawal of the Sixth Army.

Hitler peremptorily vetoed this. Convinced by earlier reports that the Soviets had been bled to the point of death and this counteroffensive was only a last gasp, he ordered the men at Stalingrad to stand firm. Help was on the way. The reassuring words did not reflect the state of disarray within Hitler's headquarters itself. Major Engel recorded in his diary that there was complete confusion. "Führer himself completely unsure what is to be done." During these trying hours he incessantly paced the great hall of the Berghof, inveighing against his commanders for repeating the same old mistakes.

The tanks he had sent so reluctantly into the battle had already been thrown back and by November 21 the Romanians, half of whose tanks had been disabled by mice which had gnawed through wires, were cut off. "Absolute dismay," hastily scrawled one Romanian officer in his diary. "What sins have we or our forebears committed? Why must we suffer so?" Only that day did Paulus and his chief of staff, Major General Arthur Schmidt, realize their own peril. The appearance of Soviet tanks a few miles from their battle headquarters confirmed that vital links in Sixth Army lines of communication had been captured. After hastily transferring his own headquarters, Paulus asked permission to withdraw. His superior approved the proposal and passed it on to OKW. At the evening's conference in the Berghof, Jodl proposed a general evacuation of the Sixth Army but again the Führer said no. "No matter what happens we must hold the area around Stalingrad."

The next morning, the twenty-second, the two arms of a tremendous Soviet pincer movement met, encircling the entire Sixth Army. More than 200,000 of Germany's finest troops along with 100 tanks, 1800 big guns and more than 10,000 vehicles were caught in a giant *Kessel* (cauldron). At a Sixth Army conference that morning someone suggested they break out to the southwest. "We can't," said Chief of Staff Schmidt, "because we haven't got the necessary fuel. And if we tried we should end up with a catastrophe like that of Napoleon." Sixth Army, he added, would have to go into a "hedgehog" defense. By afternoon the situation had worsened so much that Schmidt began to question his own argument. At this point Paulus received fresh orders: Stand fast and await further orders. "Well," said Paulus, turning to his chief of staff, "now we'll have time to think over what we ought to do. This we'll do separately. Meet me, please, in an hour's time and we'll compare the conclusions we have reached." They were identical: break out to the southwest.

Hitler, now en route back to Wolfsschanze, could not contemplate retreat. That evening he sent a personal message to Paulus. "Sixth Army must know," he said, "that I am doing everything to help and to relieve it. I shall issue my orders in good time." Paulus accepted the decision but one of his corps commanders began a withdrawal on his own initiative in order to force Paulus into ordering a general retreat. Paulus had authority to remove or arrest him but did neither, since the situation was so critical. Ironically, once Hitler learned a retreat was under way, he put the blame on the innocent Paulus and rewarded the guilty man, in whom he had great faith, by giving him an independent command.

His suspicion of Paulus was one reason Hitler ignored a personal plea from the Sixth Army commander, late on the night of November 23, to break out of the trap. Instead he chose to accept Göring's assurance that the Luftwaffe could keep the encircled Sixth Army supplied by air despite the Reichsmarschall's poor performance record, and he dispatched a radio signal next morning ordering Paulus to hold "at all costs" since supplies were coming by air. In a display of wishful thinking, Hitler eagerly seized upon Göring's rash promise and declared Stalingrad a fortress, thus sealing the fate of the almost 250,000 German and allied troops.

Having lost faith in Paulus' superior, Hitler turned over most of that commander's responsibility to Field Marshal von Manstein, whose ingenious invasion plan of the West had coincided so closely with his own. Manstein was to command a new force, Army Group Don, his task to halt the Soviet advance westward so as to take all pressure off the defenders of Stalingrad. Manstein sent a reassuring message to Paulus that noon: "We will do all we can to get you out of this mess." Paulus' present task, he added, was to "maintain the Volga and north front according to the Führer's order and prepare strong forces to break out to the rear." Taking this to mean that Sixth Army was to stand firm while Manstein opened up a corridor, Paulus and Schmidt abandoned their own plan to break out without Hitler's permission.

Twenty-two of the planes flying supplies to Stalingrad were shot down before the end of the day. On the twenty-fifth another nine were destroyed, and a mere seventy-five tons of food and armaments reached Paulus. Back at Wolfsschanze Army Chief of Staff Zeitzler braved Hitler's wrath on the twenty-sixth by suggesting that Paulus be given "freedom of action"; that is, to attempt to break out or, that failing, have tacit permission to capitulate. Hitler rejected this proposal out of hand, agreeing only to a relief action on the part of Manstein. To all protests the Führer referred to Göring's repeated hollow assurances of sufficient air supply. "We are horrified by so much optimism," noted Engel in his diary, "which even Luftwaffe General Staff officers do not share."

That day Paulus sent a handwritten letter to Manstein, thanking him for the recent promise to help Sixth Army. He told of his request to Hitler asking for freedom of action if it should become necessary. "I wanted to have this authority," he explained, "in order to guard against issuing the only possible order in that situation too late. I have no means of proving that I should only issue such an order in an extreme emergency and I can merely ask you to accept my word for this."

Paulus got his answer from the Führer at five minutes before midnight. In a personal message to the men of Sixth Army, Hitler ordered them to stand fast with the assurance that he would do all in his power to send them relief.

The relief operation, Winter Storm, was relatively stingy, consisting of a single thrust by two armored divisions. Scheduled to begin in early December, there were so many delays in assembling this minimal force that it was not mounted until the morning of December 12. As 230 tanks rolled northeast toward Stalingrad, some sixty miles distant, there was very little resistance. In some places there were no Russians at all and the Germans were puzzled. Even so only twelve miles were made; the frozen ground began to melt under the sun's rays and slopes were turned into slippery traps.

At the noon conference Hitler's first question was, "Has there been some disaster?" and, when told that the sole enemy attacks were at the sector held by Italian troops, began grumbling. "I've had more sleepless nights over this business in the south than anything else. One doesn't know what's going on."

For six days the men of Sixth Army anxiously waited for sight of friendly tanks but all they could see were streams of Russians plodding west to stem Winter Storm. Manstein was equally depressed and requested permission on the eighteenth for Paulus to break out so that most of his men could be saved. Zeitzler "very urgently" approved the measure, but Hitler remained adamant since the Italian Eighth Army had collapsed that day, opening a huge hole north of the relief force.

The following afternoon Manstein once more radioed Hitler for permission to break out Sixth Army. At first Hitler refused but he showed signs of relenting under Zeitzler's continued urgings. His indecision encouraged some staff officers to hope against hope that Paulus, on his own responsibility, would attempt the breakout. Paulus would have done so if he could. He was prepared to disobey the Führer's original order, but by now had less than a hundred tanks with fuel enough, at best, for twenty miles. Moreover, there was hardly enough ammunition for defense, let alone an offensive. He and Schmidt rested their hopes on the columns driving to their relief.

But the tanks coming to their aid would get no farther east. On December 23 Manstein was forced to call off the relief attack since one Panzer division of this force had to be diverted to plug up the hole left by the fleeing Italians. At 5:40 P.M. he got in touch with Paulus by teleprinter and asked, "if worst came to worst," could he break out? Did this mean, asked Paulus, that he was now authorized to initiate the move? "Once it is launched," he said, "there'll be no turning back."

"I can't give you full authority today," replied Manstein. "But I hope to get a decision tomorrow."

At his headquarters Hitler remained reluctant to make it and, on Christmas Eve, Manstein had only gloomy words and holiday wishes for the Sixth Army. That evening Manstein radioed Wolfsschanze that the stamina of the troops at Stalingrad had diminished considerably and would continue to do so at an increasing rate. "It might be possible to provide for the men a little longer but then they would be quite incapable of fighting their way out. The end of the month is, in my opinion, the last possible date." Even as Manstein signed the message he knew that Hitler would not listen. The Sixth Army was already doomed. Much as Paulus wanted to break out, he knew it would now be suicidal. He agreed with

Manstein that it was the end. But should he explain the situation to his men? Troops without hope would not fight.

Goebbels tried to give it to them in his New Year message. In an address directed specifically to front-line troops he promised that 1943 would bring the Reich closer to its "final victory," its "ultimate victory." He spoke far more frankly to his staff. Propaganda for the coming months, he said, must avoid producing a basically defensive attitude among the people. "Since the beginning of the war our propaganda has taken the following mistaken line of development. First year of the war: We have won. Second year: We will win. Third year: We must win. Fourth year: We cannot be defeated." Such a development, he said, was disastrous. "Instead, the German public must be made to realize that we are also *able* to win because the prerequisites exist as soon as work and effort in the country are fully placed at the service of the war." It was a grim picture and foreshadowed a Führer decree, a fortnight later, ordering the total mobilization of the homeland for the war effort.

8

Just before the New Year Hitler sent his personal pilot, Baur, to the Stalingrad pocket with instructions to bring back General Hans Hube, commander of the 14th Panzer Corps. At Führer Headquarters the puzzled Hube, who had lost a hand in the First World War, was asked to give an accurate report of Sixth Army's position. Hube's fearless and blunt revelation of the desperate plight of his comrades impressed Hitler, who listened in silence. "Much of this is new to me," he said and promised to send the SS Panzer Corps, presently in France, to the relief of Stalingrad. In the meantime the airlift would be increased at all costs. With deep emotion the Führer vowed that he would turn the setback at Stalingrad into victory just as he had done after last winter's crisis.

Hube flew back to the battle with orders to instill new hope in his comrades. He arrived on the eighth, the day enemy planes dropped leaflets containing a Soviet ultimatum to capitulate or die. Heartened by Hube's news, Paulus told his corps commanders that there could be no question of surrender.

Two days later the main Soviet assault began and Sixth Army's western front was slowly pushed back. Food and ammunition supplies rapidly dwindled; the daily ration of most big guns was a single round and each man got a slice of bread and a little horse meat. The amount of supplies coming into the pocket remained far below that promised by Göring and by now Hitler was disillusioned to the point of biting sarcasm, referring to him as "this fellow Göring, this fat, well-fed pig!" Perhaps the greatest insult was selecting a subordinate to reorganize the airlift and save Sixth Army. The Führer had already twice praised Field Marshal Milch as one who did not know the word "impossible." In mid-January he was brought to Wolfsschanze and instructed by Hitler to get three hundred tons of supplies daily into the cauldron. To do so he was given special powers, including authority to issue orders to any military command. Milch's energetic reforms raised the daily level of supply from sixty to eighty tons and there was a glimmer of hope inside the pocket. But it soon became obvious that even Milch could do little better and finally he himself realized his mission was impossible.

By January 20 the pocket, already reduced to half its size, showed unmistakable signs of disintegration, particularly in those areas where the fighting was fiercest. Moved by the suffering he saw with his own eyes, Paulus felt duty-bound to appeal once more to higher authority. That day he summoned Schmidt and two staff members for their opinion. Only one of the three, an operations officer, favored continuing the fight and Paulus dispatched identical messages to Manstein and Führer Headquarters requesting permission, once operations were no longer possible, "to avoid complete annihilation."

Both Manstein and Zeitzler urged Hitler to reply favorably but he continued to demand that Sixth Army "fight to the last man." In a last desperate measure to bring him around, a major named Zitzewitz was flown out of Stalingrad to make a firsthand report of the hopeless situation. Hitler gripped both Zitzewitz's hands when he was presented on January 22. "You have come from a deplorable situation," he said, then talked of another relief drive through enemy lines by a battalion of new Panther tanks.

Zitzewitz was flabbergasted. How could a battalion succeed where an entire Panzer army had failed? During a pause in Hitler's dissertation the major read off figures from a slip of paper he had prepared. He spoke movingly of the trapped men's hunger and frostbite, the dwindling supplies, the feeling that they had been written off. "My Führer," he concluded, "permit me to state that the troops at Stalingrad can no longer be ordered to fight to their last round because they are no longer physically capable of fighting and because they no longer have a last round."

Hitler turned to him in surprise, and, Zitzewitz felt, stared straight through him. "Man recovers very quickly," Hitler said. He dismissed the major and ordered this message sent to Paulus: "Surrender out of the question. Troops will resist to the end."

Hitler himself had gnawing doubts but two days later his spirits were lifted by a startling announcement that Roosevelt had just called for the unconditional surrender of the Axis at the conclusion of an Allied conference in Casablanca. (For some time the Germans believed Casablanca was the code name for the White House and that the conference had taken place in Washington.) By making any political settlement of the world conflict quite impossible, the President had handed Hitler an invaluable piece of propaganda to incite his people to resistance to the end. It was a ray of hope, for Hitler himself had been forced at last to accept the hopeless situation at Stalingrad. He had reportedly ordered Chief Adjutant Schmundt to fly to Stalingrad and give Paulus a pistol to use on himself—at the last moment.

Isolated groups of Germans were already surrendering in considerable numbers but Paulus himself stood firm. He told two divisional commanders who brought up the subject of capitulation that the general situation did not permit such action. They must obey the Führer's injunction to hold out to the last possible moment. His own decision weighed heavily on his conscience since he knew the torments his men were suffering. Until recently their fighting spirit had been remarkable. With faith in their leaders, they had taken it for granted that relief was coming. Today, the tenth anniversary of the National Socialist take-over, an air of hopelessness pervaded the air. There was no place to put the newly wounded since every cellar in Stalingrad was crowded almost to suffocation. The supply of drugs, medicines and bandages was fast disappearing. It was no longer possible to bury the dead in the frozen ground.

Forcing himself to rise to the occasion of the day, Paulus radioed Hitler:

ON THE ANNIVERSARY OF YOUR ASSUMPTION OF POWER, THE SIXTH ARMY SENDS GREETINGS TO THE FÜHRER. THE SWASTIKA STILL FLUTTERS OVER STALINGRAD. MAY OUR STRUGGLE STAND AS AN EXAMPLE TO GENERATIONS AS YET UNBORN, NEVER TO SURRENDER, HOWEVER DESPERATE THE ODDS. THEN GERMANY WILL BE VICTORIOUS.

In another personal message, Paulus informed the Führer that his nephew, Leo Raubal, was wounded. Should he be evacuated by air? The reply was negative: as a soldier he must remain with his comrades. Thus the brother of Hitler's true love, Geli, was consigned to almost certain death.*

In a final letter Paulus wrote his wife, a Romanian of noble birth, "I stand and fight—these are my orders!" On the evening of January 30 he armed himself with a rifle for his last battle. Then came word from Wolfsschanze that the Führer had promoted him to the rank of field

---

* Hitler had two other relatives on this front: Hans Hitler, whose father was the Führer's first cousin; and Heinz Hitler, son of his half brother, Alois, Jr. Hans escaped to Germany; both Leo and Heinz were captured. According to Stalin's daughter, the Germans proposed exchanging one of their prisoners (it could have been either Leo or Heinz) for her brother Yasha. But Stalin told her, "I won't do it. War is war." Reportedly young Stalin was shot by the Germans. Heinz Hitler died in captivity but Geli's brother returned home in 1955, reconciled to the fact that his uncle had done nothing to save him and more than ever convinced that Hitler was "absolutely innocent" of his sister's death.

marshal. It was an honor that every officer dreamed of, yet at this moment it seemed of little consequence. The promotion was followed, after midnight, by a message from Zeitzler, which was its price tag: "The Führer asks me to point out that each day the fortress of Stalingrad can continue to hold out is of importance."

Just before dawn of the thirty-first, Chief of Staff Schmidt peered out a window and in the glare of innumerable fires saw an incredible sight. In the market place a large group of German and Russian soldiers were standing together, smoking cigarettes, talking animatedly. Schmidt told Paulus that the end had come. Further local resistance was senseless unless they were willing to fire at their own troops. Paulus agreed that surrender was the only alternative. Within the hour the two men were in a Soviet car bound for the headquarters of General M. S. Shumilov's Sixty-fourth Army.

When Shumilov suggested they go to lunch Paulus said he could not eat a bite until the Russians promised to provide food and medicine for his men. "We are human," said Shumilov sympathetically. "Of course we will do all this." They stepped outside. It was bitter cold but the sun shone brilliantly. Shumilov spread his arms. "Ah, a wonderful spring day!" At lunch Shumilov proposed a toast to victory for the Red Army. After some hestitation Paulus held up his glass. "I drink to the victory of German arms!" Affronted, Shumilov put down his own glass, then said good-naturedly, "Forget it. Prosit!"

Early the following morning, February 1, Moscow announced the surrender of Paulus and Schmidt. At the midday conference Zeitzler could not believe this was true but Hitler had no doubts. "They have surrendered there formally and absolutely," he insisted. "Otherwise they would have closed ranks, formed a hedgehog, and shot themselves with their last bullets." Zeitzler continued to express doubt that Paulus had capitulated. Perhaps he was lying somewhere badly wounded. "No, it is true," said Hitler. "They'll be brought straight to Moscow and put into the hands of the GPU and they'll blurt out orders for the northern pocket to surrender too." He rambled on, commending those military men who, unlike Paulus, ended their problems with a shot in the head. "How easy it is to do that! A revolver—makes it easy. What cowardice to be afraid of that. Ha! Better be buried alive! And in a situation like this where he knows well enough that his death would set the example for behavior in the pocket next door. If he sets an example like this, one can hardly expect people to go on fighting."

He continued to berate Paulus. "What hurts me the most personally is that I promoted him to field marshal. I wanted to give him this final satisfaction. That's the last field marshal I shall appoint in this war. You mustn't count your chickens before they're hatched. I don't understand it at all. When a man sees so many men die—I must really say: how easy it is for our . . ." His words became incoherent. ". . . he can't have thought of that. It's ridiculous, a thing like this. So many men have to die and then a man like this besmirches the heroism of so many others. He could have got out of his vale of tears and into eternity and been immortalized by the nation, but he'd rather go to Moscow. What kind of a choice is that? It just doesn't make any sense!"

The next day the northern pocket surrendered. The Soviets claimed the capture of 91,000 prisoners including 24 generals and 2500 officers. Thanks in large part to Hitler's own brutal treatment of Soviet prisoners, these men were treated inhumanely. Reportedly more than 400,000 German, Italian and Romanian prisoners of war died between February and April 1942. Starvation was the chief cause of death and cannibalism became a common practice. The strong alone survived and these lived on excrement from which undigested corn and mullet was picked and washed. Only a few thousand of those captured at Stalingrad would ever return to Germany. One was Paulus, who pleased the Soviets by publicly condemning Hitler and Nazism.

After visiting the wreckage of Stalingrad, General Charles de Gaulle remarked to a correspondent, "Ah, Stalingrad, a remarkable people, a very great people." The correspondent assumed he was talking of the Russians. "*Mais non*, I'm not speaking of the Russians but of the Germans. To have come so far!"

THE FAMILY CIRCLE
1943

1

After the traumatic scene with Jodl, Hitler retreated to his bunker at Werewolf. Here he ate and slept in solitude, his sole companion Blondi, the Alsatian bitch. As the Battle of Stalingrad approached its climax the Führer returned to Wolfsschanze and slowly emerged from solitary confinement. Occasionally he would invite an adjutant or visitor from Berlin to share his meager repast. As the group enlarged to include the secretaries and other select members of the family circle, the meals were transferred back to the communal dining hall. The military leaders were still excluded and he still refused to shake hands with them at briefings. For their part, they felt constrained in his presence, most considering him a tyrant and more than a little mad.

Even in the depth of his depression the Führer had treated his adjutants with polite consideration and his interest in the younger ones, like Richard Schulze, a former Ribbentrop aide, was avuncular. This was the side of Hitler that the Halders never knew. They did not see the man who could be gracious to servants and at ease with chauffeurs and secretaries. Isolation from the military drove him even closer to this family circle and so his new secretary, Gertraud Humps, had a special opportunity to get to know her Führer. She was brought to the Wolfsschanze early that winter to replace the attractive and ebullient Gerda Daranowsky. "Dara" had left a job with Elizabeth Arden to work for Hitler and now was marrying his Luftwaffe liaison officer.

Traudl Humps, the granddaughter of a general, was twenty-two, naïve and impressionable. She was so nervous the first time she took dictation that Hitler soothed her as if she were a child. "You don't have to get excited," he said, "I myself will make far more mistakes during the dictation than you will." She was summoned again on January 3, 1943. This time Hitler asked if she would like the job of permanent private secretary. It was an exciting and flattering offer and, without hesitation, she accepted it. She soon became accustomed to this new, strange world. With no full office routine or fixed duty time, she had leisure to spend much of the day wandering in the snow-covered forest. She particularly enjoyed watching her new employer play with Blondi in the morning. The big dog would jump through hoops, leap over a six-foot wooden wall, climb up a ladder, then beg at the top. Whenever Hitler noticed Traudl, he would come over, shake hands and ask how she was doing.

This affable Hitler was not in evidence at the military briefings. After the fall of Stalingrad his irascibility was such that attendance at situation conferences was kept to a minimum. Guderian, who hadn't seen the Führer since the failure to take Moscow, noticed that, while he hadn't aged greatly, he "easily lost his temper and raged, and was then unpredictable in what he said and decided."

At mealtimes he managed to control his temper with the family circle but his conversation deteriorated in quality. "After Stalingrad," recalled Fräulein Schröder "Hitler would not listen to music any more, and every evening we had to listen to his monologues instead. But his table talk was by now as overplayed as his gramophone records. It was always the same: his early days in Vienna, the *Kampfzeit*, the history of man, the microcosm and the macrocosm. On every subject we all knew in advance what he would say. In the course of time these monologues bored us. But world affairs and events at the front were never mentioned: everything to do with the war was taboo."

In Berlin, Goebbels proclaimed a three-day mourning in honor of Stalingrad's dead. During that period all places of entertainment, including theaters and cinemas, were closed. He also began preparing the nation for hard times ahead. Everywhere—on trains, walls, shopwindows and billboards—was splattered the slogan: "The Wheels Must Turn Only for Victory." On February 15 he issued a decree addressed to Reichsleiters, Gauleiters and all army headquarters demanding complete mobilization for victory.

That same day in a speech at Düsseldorf, entitled, "Do You Want Total War?" he all but announced Hitler's Final Solution. Two thousand years of Western civilization, he said, were in danger from a Russian victory, one forged by international Jewry. There were cries from the audience of "Hang them!" and Goebbels promised that Germany *would* retaliate "with the total and radical extermination and elimination of Jewry!" This brought wild shouts and manic laughter.

The gravity of the military situation was underlined, next day, in a letter from Bormann to his wife, whom he addressed as his dearest Mummy-Girl. "Should the war take a turn for the worse, either now or at some later stage, it would be better for you to move to the West, because you simply must do everything in your power to keep your—our—children out of any danger. In due course they will have to carry on the work of the future."

On the eighteenth Goebbels again presented his theme of total war in a speech at the Sportpalast to a select audience of trusted party members. It was a staged affair in every detail. The crowd arrived in civilian clothes rather than uniforms for the visual effect. The songs they sang, their shouts of approval, their spoken choruses were admirably orchestrated. On the podium Goebbels was more actor than orator and what he said was not as important as how he said it. In a rhetorical tour de force, he raised his listeners to such frenzy that when he shouted, "Do you want total war? Do you want total war? Do you want it, if necessary, to be even more total and radical than can even be imagined today?" the response was a mighty chorus of Ja's. And when he asked: "Do you accept the fact that anyone who detracts from the war effort will lose his head?" there was thundering approval. "What an hour of idiocy!" he later cynically remarked to his entourage. "If I had told these people to jump from the fourth floor of the Columbus House they would have done it."

So dedicated was Goebbels to the concept of total war that he took it upon himself to organize the highest ranks of the party into an ad hoc committee of action. Early in March he drove up to Göring's home on the Obersalzberg to enlist his help. Matters, he said, would have to be taken out of the Führer's hands; Hitler had aged fifteen years since the war and it was tragic that he had become such a recluse and led such an unhealthy life. It was essential therefore that they make up for the present lack of leadership in domestic and foreign policy. "One must not bother the Führer with everything." He impressed upon Göring that war must be waged politically and that the political leadership of the Reich must be transferred to the Ministerial Council for the Defense of the Reich. Its membership should be bolstered by ruthless men, dedicated to victory at all costs.

Goebbels reassured Göring that they would be acting in Hitler's behalf. "We have no other ambition than that of supporting each other and of forming a solid phalanx around the Führer. The Führer sometimes wavers in his decisions if the same matter is brought to him from different sides. Nor does he always react to people as he should. That's where he needs help."

Göring promised to do his best to bring Himmler into their group and Goebbels revealed that he had already won over such important officials as Funk, Ley and Speer, all men of unparalleled fidelity to the Führer. "The cause is greater than any of us; that goes without saying. The men who helped the Führer win the revolution will now have to help him win the war. They were not bureaucrats then, they must not be bureaucrats today."

Göring never considered approaching Director of Air Armament Field Marshal Milch. Besides lacking qualification as a National Socialist, he made no secret of his opposition to the Reichsmarschall. A few days after the conspiratorial Göring-Goebbels conversation Milch took the opportunity, while dining alone with Hitler, to advise replacement of Göring, whom he suspected of reverting to narcotics. He also had the nerve to tell the latest Göring-Goebbels joke. When those two went to heaven, St. Peter ordered the first to run to a distant cloud and back as punishment for lying so often. St. Peter then looked around for Goebbels. "Where is the little one with the clubfoot?" he asked. "Oh," explained an angel, "he returned to earth for his motorcycle."

After supper Milch said that he had a long list of recommendations and hoped the Führer would not be offended by his frankness. First he urged Hitler to abandon the offensive designed to retake Kursk and go over to the defense. The Wehrmacht was weak, supplies were scanty and lines must be shortened. "You cannot persuade me," said Hitler mildly and made a dot on his pad. The next response was just as radical: Hitler should cancel his daily staff discussions and appoint a new chief of the General Staff—Manstein, for instance. "Give him control of all fronts, not only one area. All under your command. You remain supreme commander while he acts as your assistant." Hitler said nothing but made another pencil mark that Milch took for nervousness. For another hour the field marshal listed equally provoking suggestions. Finally he came to the last and most unpalatable one. "Mein Führer," he said, "Stalingrad has been the gravest crisis for both Reich and Wehrmacht. You simply must act decisively to bring Germany out of this war. I assure you many agree with me. There is still time. You must act at once. Do so without ceremony but, above all, act now!"

It was past midnight. Milch was sweating from exertion and apprehension. He apologized for annoying the Führer with twenty contradictions. Hitler glanced at the dots on his pad. "You have contradicted me twenty-four times, not twenty," he said. He did not seem at all angry or even upset. "I thank you for telling me this. No one else has given me such a clear picture."

2

Correspondent Louis Lochner had already made several attempts to inform Roosevelt of the resistance movement inside the Reich. In hopes of convincing Roosevelt that not all Germans were Nazis, Lochner was prepared to give him the radio code of two separate groups opposed to Hitler so that Roosevelt could inform them directly what political administration in Germany would be acceptable to the Allies. After failing to reach the President through his appointments secretary, Lochner wrote a personal note revealing the existence of these codes and emphasizing that they could be handed over to Roosevelt alone. There was no reply but several days later Lochner was informed that his insistence was viewed by official sources as "most embarrassing." Would he please desist? What Lochner did not know was that the President's refusal to see him was official American policy in line with unconditional surrender, designed not only to withhold encouragement to German resisters but to avoid any important contact. Recognition of the existence of any anti-Hitler movement within Germany was forbidden.

The Resistance was discouraged but continued to plot the overthrow of Hitler. It was agreed that seizure of power alone was not sufficient. The Führer himself must first be assassinated and General Oster and his group selected General Henning von Tresckow, Field Marshal von Kluge's chief of staff, as executioner. He decided to lure Hitler up front, then plant a bomb in his plane that would explode on the return flight. On the evening of March 13, 1943, one of Tresckow's junior officers, Fabian von Schlabrendorff, arrived at the airport with a parcel supposedly containing two bottles of brandy. It was a bomb made from British plastic explosives. Using a key, Schlabrendorff pressed down hard on the fuse, triggering the bomb. Moments later he delivered the parcel to a colonel in Hitler's party who had promised to deliver it to a friend at Wolfsschanze.

The Führer boarded the plane and it took off. The bomb was expected to explode above Minsk but two hours passed without news of any accident. Then came word that the plane had landed safely in Rastenburg. The conspirators were confounded. Now they had to retrieve the erratic bomb before it exploded or was discovered. Schlabrendorff did so and discovered that its firing pin had been released but the detonator was a dud.

A few days later the conspirators tried again. Near midnight, March 20, in a room at a Berlin hotel, the Eden, Schlabrendorff turned over plastic explosives to Colonel Rudolf Christoph Freiherr von Gerstdorff, Kluge's chief of intelligence. His mission was suicidal. He was to approach the Führer at tomorrow's celebration of Heroes' Memorial Day at the Zeughaus in Berlin and blow himself and Hitler to bits.

The next day Gerstdorff appeared at the Zeughaus, a bomb in each overcoat pocket. At 1 P.M. Hitler arrived, and after listening to a passage from Bruckner by the Berlin Symphony he gave a short speech in the inner court. As he headed for the exhibition hall where captured Russian trophies were on display, Gerstdorff reached into his left pocket and broke the acid capsule of the British fuse, which needed at least ten minutes to detonate. Hitler was accompanied by Himmler, Keitel, Göring and a dozen others but the would-be assassin had no difficulty getting to his left side.

Schmundt had assured Gerstdorff that the Führer would spend half an hour at the exhibit but he showed little interest and, to Gerstdorff's consternation, was out of the building in five minutes. There was no possibility of following and Gerstdorff knew he had only another five minutes to dispose of the fuse without being observed. He elbowed his way to the corridor. Finally he found a men's room. Fortunately it was empty. He hastily removed the fuse from his pocket and—seconds before it was due to explode—flushed it down the toilet and left the building with the bombs.

Although the Gestapo had no suspicion of these two attempts against the Führer's life, they suspected that traitors infested the Abwehr. Fifteen days later they arrested Hans von Dohnanyi at Abwehr headquarters. Oster managed to destroy most of the papers incriminating himself but before long he too was placed under arrest. The conspirators had lost not only an able leader but their best means of communicating with each other and any friends in the West.

3

Early that April Hitler and his entourage boarded the train for Berchtesgaden, which would be a welcome respite from the gloomy surroundings at the Wolfsschanze. It was a clear, mild winter night and as they left the snow-covered forest of Rastenburg, Traudl Humps was a bit saddened to leave, yet exhilarated by the promise of new experiences. There was every comfort on the train including a special car equipped with showers and bathtubs; the food was excellent and the seats could be converted into comfortable beds. As the train rolled quietly toward its destination the next morning, she thought of other trains in the Reich, without light or heat, their passengers uncomfortable and hungry. Her thoughts were interrupted by an invitation to join the Führer for lunch. The following morning she breakfasted in less exalted company. The gossip among the servants and secretaries was about Eva Braun, who was to board the train at Munich. To them she was "the lady at the Berghof," and as such was silently accepted by all guests. That is, except by the wives of Ribbentrop, Göring and Goebbels. The first ignored her regally; the other two snubbed her openly, despite Hitler's request that she be treated with respect.

Traudl was given a tour of the Berghof by one of the older secretaries. They started on the second floor where the Führer lived. The walls of the hallway were decorated with paintings by the old masters, beautiful pieces of sculpture and exotic vases. Everything, thought Traudl, was wonderful but strange and impersonal. There was deadly silence since the Führer still slept. In front of one door were two black Scotch terriers—Eva's dogs, Stasi and Negus. Next came Hitler's bedroom. The two rooms, it seemed, were connected by a large bathroom and it was apparent they lived discreetly as man and wife. Traudl was taken downstairs to the large living room which was separated from the famous picture-window room by a heavy velvet curtain. The furnishings were luxurious but despite the beautiful Gobelins and thick carpets she got the impression of coldness. The accommodations were far superior to those at Wolfsschanze but here she felt ill at ease. While she was treated as a guest, she was not there of her own free will but as an employee.

The daily schedule at the Berghof was something of a strain even though it never varied. Hitler's noon briefing rarely ended before midafternoon and it was usually 4 P.M. before the last officer left and the Führer entered the living room where his hungry guests were gathered. As if by signal, Eva would then make her appearance, accompanied by her two scampering dogs. Hitler would kiss her hand, before greeting each guest with a handshake. The transformation of man of state burdened by the tragedies of battle to jovial host eager to please guests and helpmate was unexpected and somewhat ludicrous. His private life in fact was not much different from that of a very successful businessman.

The men addressed Eva with a slight bow and a polite "Gnädiges Fräulein"; the women called her Fräulein Braun. Several seemed very intimate, particularly Herta Schneider, a school friend. The women began an animated discussion on children, fashion and personal experiences. Finally Hitler interrupted, ridiculing Eva's dogs as "hand-sweepers." She blithely retorted that Hitler's dog, Blondi, was a calf.

The banal pleasantries, enlivened by not so much as an aperitif, were ended when Hitler escorted one of the ladies to the table. They were followed by Bormann and Eva, who heartily disliked him, primarily for his flagrant philandering.* "Anything in skirts is his target," remarked one adjutant, "except, of course, Eva herself."

The guests enjoyed sauerbraten but Hitler kept to the vegetarian meals cooked under the supervision of Dr. Werner Zabel in his Berchtesgaden clinic and warmed over at the Berghof kitchen. Nothing would induce Eva to so much as taste Hitler's thick gruel, oatmeal soup or baked potato liberally soaked in raw linseed oil. The Führer teased her about her own meager diet. "When I first met you," he said, "you were pleasingly

---

* Somehow he managed to convince his wife, whom he kept almost permanently pregnant, that his infidelities were for the greater good of National Socialism. In one remarkable letter she suggested he bring his latest mistress, M., to their Berchtesgaden home and then expressed the hope that Bormann see to it that "one year M. has a child, and the next year I, so that you always have a wife who is mobile."

plump and now you are quite thin." Women underwent these sacrifices, he added sardonically, "only to make their girl friends envious."

The conversation was gay and superficial until Hitler abruptly began propagandizing for vegetarianism by describing in detail the horrors of a slaughterhouse he had recently visited in the Ukraine. The guests blanched as he described work girls in rubber boots, standing in fresh blood up to their ankles. One, Otto Dietrich, laid down knife and fork with the comment that he was no longer hungry.

After lunch Hitler set out on the daily twenty-minute walk to his tea house. It was a round stone building located below the Berghof, reminding some of the guests of a silo or power plant. Tea was served in a large round room whose six large windows provided a wide vista. From one end there was a magnificent view of the Ach River roaring down the mountainside between houses that looked like matchboxes. Beyond lay the baroque towers of Salzburg.

Hitler drank apple-peel tea while Eva talked of plays and movies. His only comment was that he could not watch a film while the people were making so many sacrifices. "Besides, I must save my eyes for studying maps and reading front-line reports." The conversation that day palled on Hitler. He closed his eyes and shortly was asleep. His guests continued to chat but in lowered voices, and when the Führer wakened he joined in as if he had just closed his eyes momentarily to think.

At 7 P.M. a parade of vehicles arrived at the Berghof, and the business of government resumed. Two hours later Hitler left the conference and led the way to the dining room where he ate mashed potatoes and a tomato salad while his guests dined on cold meat. He charmed everyone with tales of his youth, until he noticed the lipstick on Eva's napkin. Did she know what it consisted of? Eva protested that she only used French lipstick made of the finest materials. With a pitying smile Hitler said, "If you women knew that lipstick, particularly from Paris, is manufactured from the grease of waste water, you certainly wouldn't color your lips any more." Everyone laughed. He had won another argument—if no adherents.

An adjutant quietly informed Hitler that everyone had arrived for the evening military conference. Not wanting his guests, particularly the women, to come in contact with the military, he told them to remain seated. "It won't take too long," he said and left, head lowered but with a strong step. The secretaries went to an office to type air raid reports, while Eva and most of the guests descended to the basement to see a movie. Before it concluded a telephone rang: a servant reported that the conference was over and the Führer expected everyone in the main hall. Eva hurried to her room to refresh her make-up; her sister Gretl smoked a last cigarette, then chewed peppermint candy to camouflage her breath; and the

Eva Braun, right, and sister Ilse.
FR. SCHNEIDER

Eva at nineteen. Hitler's favorite photograph. FR. SCHNEIDER

The wedding of Eva's friend Marion Schönemann to Herr Theissen, at the Berghof, August 1937. Kneeling near groom, Gretl Braun, Eva's sister. Standing, l. to r., Heinrich Hoffmann, Frau Honni Morell, Erma Hoffmann, Eva Braun, Frau Dreesen (her husband owned the Hotel Dreesen), Dr. Morell, Herta Schneider (Eva's best friend), two unidentified men and Hitler. U. S. ARMY

Eva poses for photographer Hoffmann.
N. GUN

Eva in the war years.

FR. SCHNEIDER

PHOTOGRAPHER UNKNOWN

N GUN

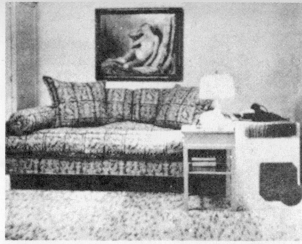

Eva's bedroom at the Berghof. N. GUN

The passageway leading to Eva's bedroom. N. GUN

Hitler's study in the Reich Chancellery. N. GUN

His favorite tea house, just below the Berghof. FRENTZ

Adolf dozes after dinner with Eva at the tea house. N. GUN

Hitler reading at the tea house. (Note glasses) N. GUN

Above, omnipresent Bormann in the Führer's car. FRENTZ

Left, Frau Gerda Bormann with one of their nine children. FATH

Above, Frau Gertraud
"Traudl" Junge
(Hitler's youngest secretary)
and her husband, Hans Junge
(Hitler's valet), dine on the
Führer's train with the oldest
secretary, Fräulein Wolf.
(Note reflection) FRENTZ

Left, the two other Hitler
secretaries waiting for the
train. Gerda Daranowsky
Christian, left, and
Christa Schröder. FRENTZ

Hitler leaves the eastern front for relaxation on the Obersalzberg. FRENTZ

Left, Hitler and SS adjutant
Günsche on the Obersalzberg.
GÜNSCHE

Below, Hitler and ordnance
officer Wünsche visit a
girls' school in Berchtesgaden.
WÜNSCHE

rest dutifully repaired to the great hall. It was almost midnight by the time Hitler came down the stairs and seated himself at the fireplace next to Eva and her two little terriers. Since they did not get along with Blondi, the latter was excluded except on the rare occasions when Hitler asked Eva to banish her two darlings so his dog could have a moment in the limelight.

Liquor was served but Hitler took tea and apple cake. The group sat silently around the fire in the semidarkness waiting for him to begin the general conversation. Finally he raised his voice for another lecture on the evils of tobacco. His dentist declared that smoking disinfected the mouth. In moderation, it was not at all dangerous. Hitler dissented. "I wouldn't offer a cigar or cigarette to anyone I admired or loved since I would be doing them a bad service. It is universally agreed that non-smokers live longer than smokers and during sickness have more resistance." He never tired of this crusade against pollution of the body, and had a standing offer of a gold watch for anyone within the circle who renounced tobacco. To Eva, however, he gave an ultimatum: "Either give up smoking or me."

The argument turned to liquor, which he thought less dangerous, and on to painting. Dr. Morell, after a single glass of port, was fighting to stay awake. He lolled back, fat hands folded over his paunch, and his eyes suddenly closed from bottom to top. Magnified by his thick glasses, it was a frightening sight. Colonel von Below nudged Morell, who wakened with a start and broke into a big smile, assuming that the Führer had told a joke.

"Are you tired, Morell?" asked Hitler.

"No, mein Führer, I was just daydreaming," he said and, to show how wide awake he was, began an oft-told anecdote about his experiences in Africa. The Führer began softly whistling a popular song. No, said Eva, and demonstrated how the tune should go. They argued amiably. She wanted to bet but Hitler complained that if he won he always had to forgive the bet in a spirit of generosity, but if she won he had to pay. Refusing to be put off, she suggested they play the music to see who was right. Albert Bormann dutifully rose and put on the record. Eva was triumphant. "The composer made the mistake," said Hitler, who had written an opera in his youth. "If he were really talented he would have written my melody." Everyone laughed as Hitler made this joke. At last at 4 A.M. Hitler summoned a servant to ask if the air raid reports had arrived; he could not go to bed until he was assured no enemy plane was over Germany.

In hopes of transfusing some of his own fighting spirit into Mussolini, the Führer requested another conference. On April 7 he went to the Salzburg railroad station to meet his ally. The two dictators greeted each other emotionally. Hitler was shocked by Il Duce's sunken cheeks and pallid face. He kept to his rooms at Klessheim Castle during most of the four-day session and rarely saw anyone but Hitler. In their talks, all private, Mussolini was dispirited. The trouble with Il Duce, concluded Hitler, was age; he was sixty and in poor health. With this in mind Hitler did his utmost to revive his ally's spirit. Mussolini had come resolved to urge peace with the Soviets and the complete withdrawal of all Italian forces abroad but was too weak to enunciate this resolve and too dispirited to be animated by Hitler's exhortations. After a final session on April 10 the two men started down the magnificent staircase of the main hall. It was the first most of the Italian delegates had seen of Mussolini since his arrival. "They seem like two invalids," whispered one. "Rather like two corpses," commented Mussolini's personal physician.

That afternoon an aide telephoned the Berghof that the Führer was just leaving Klessheim. He wanted all his guests to meet him at the tea house so he could resume his private existence as paterfamilias of the family circle. "As a general rule," one of Dostoevski's characters, old Karamazov, observed, "people, even the wicked, are much more naïve and simple-hearted than we suppose. And we ourselves are, too."

Before long a procession of cars drew up outside and the Berghof was filled with uniforms. Then the Führer himself arrived and, without ado, led another processional, this one on foot, to his tea house. Hitler was obviously pleased with the talks with Mussolini and the atmosphere was more relaxed. He had become a creature of routine and his private life continued with little variation. He laughed as usual when the adjutant assigned to reading descriptions of the soundless newsreels made the usual mistakes, such as announcing a battle only to have a group of farm girls appear.

While rarely mentioning war or politics to the family circle, one evening he expressed regret for having to wear a uniform. "But after the war, I'll hang it on the hook, retire here and let someone else run the government. Then, as an old man, I'll write my memoirs and will only have around me bright, gifted people." He blanched at the thought of the Berghof being turned into a museum after his death. "I can already see the guide from Berchtesgaden showing visitors over the various rooms of my house: 'This is where he had breakfast!'" He would much rather be cremated inside the Berghof with all its contents—it would make a "magnificent pyre!"

Traudl could not restrain herself. "Mein Führer, when will the war be over?" The affable face of Uncle Adi was transformed.* "I don't know," he said harshly. "But only after victory!" The sudden change of mood chilled the room. A similar moment came on Good Friday. Henriette von

* To Egon Hanfstaengl he had been Uncle Dolf, to Geli Uncle Alf.

Schirach, just returned from Holland, presumed on her long friendship with Hitler to describe a frightful scene she had witnessed in Amsterdam: Jewish women being rounded up in the dead of night for deportation. There was a painful silence. Hitler seemed to be baffled as she went on to criticize other restrictive measures in Holland. The guests looked away in embarrassment. Finally Hitler turned to her. His face was drawn, his skin and eyes seemed colorless. "The demons are devouring him," she thought even though the idea seemed a little odd. He stared at her for some time before slowly getting to his feet. She too rose. It was apparent he was trying to control himself but suddenly he burst out angrily: "You are a sentimentalist! What business of yours is it? The Jewesses are none of your business!" As he continued to shout, she ran up the stairs to her room. An adjutant reached her before she could close the door. "Why did you have to do this?" he asked. "You have made him very angry. Please leave at once!"

On the eve of his fifty-fourth birthday, Hitler celebrated by inviting Blondi to the tea session and putting her through her paces. She begged; she played schoolgirl. She even gave a concert and the more her master praised the more intensely she sang. Just before midnight the large doors opened dramatically and orderlies entered with trays of glasses. All were filled with champagne except Hitler's, which contained a sweet white wine. At the last stroke of twelve glasses were touched. Some of the guests voiced simple congratulations and others made little speeches.

On April 20 Hitler came downstairs earlier than usual so he could look over his presents. At lunch Traudl's escort was Himmler. She disliked him, not because he gave the impression of brutality but because of his attempt to charm her. He kissed her hand, talked in a soft voice and perpetually presented a genial, obliging countenance. Even his eyes smiled endlessly. Goebbels impressed her. "He was not good-looking at all," she remembered, "but now I could understand why the girls at the chancellery used to run to the window to see the propaganda chief leave his ministry while they scarcely took notice of the Führer." She noticed that most of the ladies at the Berghof flirted with him as much for his wit as his charm.

Shortly after the birthday celebration Hitler learned that Traudl had become engaged to Hans Junge, one of his valets. "I really have such bad luck with my people," he remarked at lunch with an exaggerated sigh. "First Christian married Dara and took my best secretary; then I found a satisfactory replacement and now Traudl Humps is going to leave me— and take with her my best servant." He suggested that they get married at once since Junge was scheduled to leave for the eastern front. Traudl wanted to postpone such a decisive step after so short an acquaintance. "But you love each other!" was Hitler's surprising reply. "Therefore it is best to get married right away. If you're married, you know, then I can protect you any time someone tries to molest you. I couldn't do that if you

were only engaged. And you can still work for me after you're married."
Traudl had to keep from laughing and was tempted to ask why *he* didn't
marry Eva Braun if love was that important.

4

On May 7 Hitler made a sad pilgrimage to the capital to attend the
funeral of another old comrade. Viktor Lutze, the successor to Röhm, had
died in an auto accident. At least that was the official story; some survivors of the Röhm Putsch suspected foul play. After the funeral Reich-
leiters and Gauleiters attended a luncheon at the chancellery. This
was followed by a detailed survey of the general situation which began
with the Führer's statement that in 1939 Germany—a revolutionary state
—had faced only bourgeois states. It was easy, he explained, to knock out
such nations since they were quite inferior in upbringing and attitude. A
country with an ideology always had the edge over a bourgeois state since
it rested upon a firm spiritual foundation. This superiority, however, had
ended with Barbarossa. There the Germans had met an opponent which
also sponsored an ideology, if a wrong one. He praised Stalin for purging
the Red Army of defeatists and installing political commissars with the
fighting forces. Stalin enjoyed the further advantage of having rid himself
of "high society" by other liquidations so that Bolshevism could devote all
its energy to fighting the enemy.

Another reason for failure in the East was the poor performance of
Germany's allies, particularly the Hungarians. Lasting resistance to the Soviets, he concluded, could be offered in Europe only by the Germans since
victory in battle was linked with ideology. Consequently the anti-
Semitism which formerly animated party members must once more become the focal point of their spiritual struggle. It should also be a rallying
cry for the troops; if they did not stand firm as a wall, the hordes of the
East would sweep into Europe. A constant, untiring effort must therefore
focus on taking the necessary measures for the security of European culture. "If it be true today that the Bolshevism of the East is mainly under
Jewish leadership and that the Jews are also the dominant influence in the
Western plutocracies, then our anti-Semitic propaganda must begin at
this point." That was why there was practically no possibility of any
compromise with the Soviets. "They must be knocked out, exactly as
we formerly had to knock out our own Communists to attain power. At
that time we never thought of a compromise either."

Despite the vigorous tenor of his talk, it was apparent that Hitler's
health was failing. Dr. Morell doubled the hormone injections as well as
adding still another drug, Prostakrin, but there was little improvement.
Another electrocardiogram indicated a worsening of his heart condition.
Fearing that the diet regime of Dr. Zabel was aggravating matters, Morell

recommended that the Führer hire a special cook. They settled on a woman from Vienna, a Frau von Exner, who would surely know how to please an Austrian palate. Neither was aware there was Jewish blood in her mother's family.

On May 12 Hitler returned to Wolfsschanze satisfied that his leadership had ended the withdrawals after the fall of Stalingrad. His complacency ended the next day upon learning that two German-Italian armies in Tunisia, some 300,000 men, had been bagged by the Allies. It was another Stalingrad. A week later there was worse news. Mussolini's regime was close to collapse. Italians in high places were using phrases such as "you never know what's going to happen" and "when the war is over." On the streets German soldiers were openly cursed as enemies.

In mid-June Hitler's youngest secretary married his valet Junge. After a short honeymoon the groom went to the eastern front while Traudl returned to her duties at Wolfsschanze. "You've become very pale and thin," was Hitler's first observation. Kindly meant, it caused Traudl embarrassment when Linge, Schaub and Bormann broke into knowing leers. No longer was she the naïve girl who first came to Führer Headquarters. The daily routine of the loftiest circle in the Reich was causing a curious depression. She tried to express some of this in her diary, then spoke to others, particularly the sympathetic Hewel, of her misgivings. She discovered that most of the others shared the vague sense of dissatisfaction and gloom. They too suffered from "cabin fever" but nobody could give a concrete reason for their common uneasiness.

That June Hitler persuaded Dara Christian to return. She arrived with many suitcases and soon filled the bunker and barracks with her effervescence. Her songs, jokes and gaiety raised everyone's spirits. By this time Traudl had lost her bashfulness and one day asked Hitler point-blank why he was so eager to get everyone else married when he hadn't done so himself. The reply was that he did not want to be a father. "I think the children of a genius have a hard time in this world. One expects such a child to be a replica of his famous father and don't forgive him for being average." Until now he had seemed quite modest and she was disturbed by the complacent announcement that he was a genius.

Despite the reverses in North Africa, Hitler was still considering the all-out attack on Kursk so vigorously opposed by Milch. Armored expert Guderian came to Berlin and added his objections: first on the grounds that the new Panther tank had a limited supply of spare parts; and second —in answer to the Führer's argument that the attack was necessary for political reasons—that few people even knew where Kursk (on the southern wing of the central front) was. Hitler confessed that the mere thought of this offensive churned his stomach, but in the ensuing days he was persuaded by both Zeitzler and Kluge to launch it while there was still time. The operation was entitled Citadel and, on the first of July, Hitler addressed his senior commanders. Germany, he said, must either tenaciously hold on to all conquered territory or fall. The German soldier had to realize he must stand and fight to the end. He admitted Citadel was a gamble yet felt sure it would succeed. Hadn't he been right, against all military advice, about Austria, Czechoslovakia, Poland and the Soviet Union? His inclusion of the last country struck a chill in the audience.

Manstein's attack force in the north consisted of eighteen divisions but less than 1000 tanks and 150 assault guns were fit for combat. In the south General Model had fifteen divisions and only 900 tanks. The assault began at an unusual hour, 3 P.M. on the fourth of July. It was hot and sultry. Thunder rumbled threateningly in the distance. At first it seemed as if the Soviets had been caught by surprise, for Red Army artillery did not respond until long after dark. But visions of a quick victory vanished once heavy rains began to fall. By dawn roads and trails were veritable quagmires. Later that morning a cloudburst transformed streams into roaring cascades, and it took sappers twelve hours to bridge them for tanks.

By July 9 the leading German tanks were still fifty-five miles from Kursk. The disappointment was followed next day by news that an Anglo-American force had landed on Sicily and were meeting a spiritless defense. This came as no surprise to Hitler and on July 13 he stopped the offensive he had so reluctantly supported so he could send reinforcements, including the SS Panzer Corps, to western Europe. Manstein argued that failure to continue the Kursk operation would endanger a long salient stretching all the way to the Black Sea. A gambler, Hitler accepted the loss of Kursk in return for more probable success in another quarter. But Citadel turned out to be more than a lost campaign. Thereafter the initiative in the East would belong to the Soviets.

5

Turning his back on the East, Hitler journeyed to northern Italy for another meeting with Il Duce, their thirteenth, on July 19. The conference, held at the imposing Villa Gaggia near Feltre, began promptly at 11 A.M. with the two men facing each other from large armchairs. Circling them was an elite group of military and diplomatic dignitaries. There were a few moments of embarrassed silence as both Mussolini and Hitler waited for the other to begin. It was a strange prelude, more like the stiff meeting of two families arranging a dowry. At last the Führer began speaking quietly of the general military and political situation. Il Duce sat cross-legged, hands clasped on knees, on the edge of a chair that was too large and too deep, listening with impassive patience. Then he began to fidget and he nervously passed a hand over the lower part of his face as Hitler abruptly assailed the Italians for their defeatism.

Occasionally Mussolini would press a spot behind his back that apparently pained him; occasionally he would heave a deep sigh as if resigned but wearied by a monologue which grew increasingly strident. Struggling to hide his distress, he mopped his brow with a handkerchief. Hitler showed no mercy, and even after an adjutant whispered something into his ear at five minutes to one, he did not pause in his reiterated assurance to the wilting Duce that the crisis could be overridden if Italy emulated Germany's fanatic determination to fight. Every German, he said, was imbued with the will to conquer. Lads of fifteen were manning AA batteries. "If anyone tells me that our task can be left for another generation, I reply that this is not the case. No one can say that the future generation will be a generation of giants. Germany took thirty years to recover; Rome never rose again. This is the voice of history."

At exactly 1 P.M. the adjutant again whispered to Hitler and the others imagined it must indeed be an urgent message. This time, after a look of annoyance, he ended his sermon. The meeting was over, he announced, and luncheon was served. The other Italians were distressed at Mussolini's silence during the harangue. Not once had he protested or even attempted to explain that within a month most Italian soldiers would no longer have the means or the will to offer effective resistance.

Five days later Il Duce was forced to listen to another diatribe, this from his own Fascist Grand Council, which was convening for the first time since 1939. After a long exhausting debate on his conduct of the war, a resolution was proposed demanding restoration of a constitutional monarchy with the King in command of the armed forces. The vote was taken and the motion passed 19 to 8. The next day, July 25, a sultry Sunday, Mussolini called on Victor Emmanuel III. He tried to control himself, but the notes in his hand rattled. The King stopped his arguments; it was useless to go on; Italy was defeated and the soldiers would no longer fight for Fascism. He requested Mussolini's resignation, then revealed he had already appointed Marshal Pietro Badoglio as head of government. "I am sorry, I am sorry," he was heard to say through the door. "But the solution could not have been otherwise." The little King accompanied Il Duce to the front door where he shook his hand warmly. As Mussolini stepped out of the villa he was approached by a Carabinieri officer who said His Majesty had charged him with the protection of Il Duce's person. Mussolini, protesting that it was not necessary, was led into an ambulance. He was under arrest.

At nine-thirty that night Hitler shocked his military advisers by announcing, "The Duce has resigned." The government had been taken over by Badoglio, their bitterest enemy. He quelled the rising panic and when

Jodl suggested they do nothing until receiving a complete report from Rome Hitler curtly replied: "Certainly, but we have to plan ahead. Undoubtedly, in their treachery, they will proclaim that they will remain loyal to us; but this is treachery. Of course, they won't remain loyal. . . . Anyway what's-his-name [Badoglio] said straightaway that the war would be continued but that doesn't mean a thing. They have to say that. But we can play the same game; we'll get ready to grab the whole mess, all that rabble. I'll send a man down tomorrow with orders to the commandant of the 3rd Panzer Grenadier Division to take a special detachment into Rome and arrest the whole government, the King—all that scum but most of all the Crown Prince—to grab all that riffraff, particularly Badoglio and the entire gang. And then you watch them creep and crawl and in two or three days there'll be another coup."

At a midnight conference Hitler issued more instructions. The 2nd Parachute Division was to prepare a jump in the capital area. "Rome must be occupied. Nobody is to leave Rome and then the 3rd Panzer Grenadier Division moves in." Someone wanted to know if the exits to the Vatican should be occupied. "That doesn't matter," said Hitler, "I'll go right into the Vatican. Do you think I worry about the Vatican? We'll take that right off. All the diplomatic corps will be hiding in there. I don't give a damn; if the entire crew's in there, we'll get the whole lot of swine out. Afterward, we can say we're sorry. We can easily do that. We've got a war on."

In the presence of his secretaries he managed to gain control of himself. "Mussolini is much weaker than I thought," he muttered, as if talking to himself. "I personally protected his rear and he has given way. Well, we never could depend on our Italian allies and I believe we'll be better off without such an irresponsible nation."

He sent for the two men he felt he could depend on most in a crisis —Goebbels and Göring. (Of the latter, he told his military leaders, "At such a time one can't have a better adviser than the Reichsmarschall. In time of crisis the Reichsmarschall is brutal and ice cold. I've always noticed that when it comes to the breaking point he is a man of iron without scruples." The three met at ten in the morning and half an hour later were joined by Ribbentrop, who was recovering from an attack of pneumonia. With quiet "self-assurance" Hitler expressed a suspicion that Mussolini had not resigned voluntarily. He had been arrested. That meant Fascism was in mortal danger and they must seize any possibility of averting its collapse. He told of his plan to drop a parachute division around Rome and arrest the King and his family along with Badoglio and his henchmen.

The catastrophe in Italy was almost immediately followed by the carpet bombing of Hamburg. By the morning of August 3 the city was a blazing mass of ruins. More than 6000 acres of homes, factories and office buildings were gutted. Seventy thousand people were dead. Hitler was enraged, convinced as he was that such terror raids were a product of the Jews; he accused the leading British air commanders, including Portal and Harris, of being Jews or part Jewish. Psychologically Hamburg's destruction was as devastating as Stalingrad, not only to ordinary citizens but to Hitler's paladins. Goebbels was in a "blue funk" after inspecting the ruins of Hamburg, according to the diary of his own press officer, and for the first time posed the question: "What if we lose?" to his subordinates. He armed himself with a pistol.

The chief of the Luftwaffe, so recently characterized as "ice cold," was even more crushed by the bombings. "We were met with a shattering picture," recalled Adolf Galland, one of those hastily summoned to his office. "Göring had completely broken down. His head buried in his arm on the table, he moaned some indistinguishable words. We stood there for some time in embarrassment. At last Göring pulled himself together and said we were witnessing his deepest moments of despair. The Führer had lost faith in him."

6

Negotiation with the enemy had become a common, if covert, topic at the Foreign Office ever since receipt of another peace feeler from Stalin soon after the Battle of Stalingrad. Admiral Canaris (who himself had tried in vain to deal secretly with Roosevelt, through former Governor of Pennsylvania George Earle) was so convinced this was a serious offer that he persuaded Ribbentrop to present it to the Führer. He did so in the form of a memorandum which Hitler angrily tore up with a threat to execute anyone attempting to mediate on his own. There would be no negotiations, he said, until the Wehrmacht regained the initiative. He forbade Ribbentrop even to mention the matter again, and when his Foreign Minister timidly proposed they reduce the program of conquest in Europe so as to make it more acceptable to the Allies, Hitler was incensed. "Believe me, we shall win," he said. "The blow that has fallen is a sign telling me to grow harder and harder and risk all we have. If we do, we shall win in the end."

In the strictest confidence, Ribbentrop revealed all this to Fritz Hesse. For safety's sake, their conversation took place on a walk through a wood near Wolfsschanze in a March snow flurry. "All we can hope for now," he said, "is that at least one of our opponents will grow sensible. Surely the English must realize that it would be madness to deliver us into the hands of the Russians." Tears came to his eyes but he pulled himself together. He pledged Hesse to secrecy.

A few days later they went for another walk in the snow. "There must be some way," said Ribbentrop, "of persuading the British and

Americans of the insanity of the war they are waging against us." Didn't they understand that the defeat of Germany would only help Stalin and upset the balance of power in Europe? Wasn't it possible to make them see that their own position throughout the world would be compromised? The Soviet military potential was already superior to that of the Western Allies. "Can't we somehow make the British and Americans see that the victory of the Soviets is the opposite of what they want?" Having spent years in England, Hesse did not think this was possible. The two Allies were not unduly worried about a Russian victory. Unlike the Germans, neither had experienced the firsthand terrors of Bolshevism.

One of Ribbentrop's men, Peter Kleist, was already resuming his personal efforts to seek peace with Russia despite Hitler's definite injunction to cease further contact with Madame Kollontai, the Soviet ambassador to Sweden. His middleman was Edgar Clauss, a nondescript businessman who came from East Europe, spoke Russian and German with equal ineptitude and lived in Sweden with a Swedish wife of Russian extraction. Clauss had met Stalin and Trotsky before the Revolution and had connections with the Soviet Embassy in Stockholm; local Germans regarded him as "either a braggart or a spy." After two long talks with members of the embassy, Clauss reported to Kleist on June 18, 1943, that the Soviets were determined "not to fight for a day or even a minute—'*ni odnu minitu*'— longer than necessary on behalf of British and American interests." They felt that Hitler, blinded by ideology, had allowed himself to be pushed into the war by the intrigues of the capitalist powers. While confident that the Red Army could stand off the Wehrmacht, they feared it would be in an extremely weakened position after victory when it would have to "confront the cold steel" of the Western Powers. The Soviets distrusted the Americans and British since they had not yet come forward with any definite statements about war aims and territorial boundaries; nor had they promised anything definite on the so-called Second Front in Europe. The Anglo-American landing in Africa seemed more like an attempt to protect their own flank from the Soviet Union than an attack on the Axis. Stalin therefore could not attach any real value to the promises of Roosevelt and Churchill, said Clauss. On the other hand, the vast Soviet areas held by Hitler were a negotiable object, and a concrete deal could be concluded immediately.

Stalin wanted only two things: a guarantee that peace would be preserved and economic aid. It was a tempting proposal since it seemed clear that Clauss had received his information directly from the Soviets but there was always the chance that Kleist himself might be the victim of a Soviet trick. For hours that night he wandered the streets of Stockholm, debating with himself. Finally he decided that if there was the slightest possibility of ending the war and saving Europe from a Soviet invasion he had no choice. The next morning he flew to Berlin intending to "confess" his forbidden conversation but as he stepped out of the plane at Tempelhof he was arrested on the charge that he had been conniving with "the Jew Clauss."

Kleist was interrogated by Heydrich's successor, Ernst Kaltenbrunner, a burly man six foot seven with a lantern jaw, a saber cut across one cadaverous cheek and dangling, simian arms. He was impressed by Kleist's straightforward account. It rang true, he said. Kaltenbrunner also believed his denial that Clauss was a Jew and so only placed Kleist under house arrest. A fortnight later this was canceled and he turned to the less dangerous operation of resettling Estonian Swedes. To his surprise, the question of peace was soon raised again, this time by Ribbentrop. The defeat at Kursk that summer had convinced him that German defeat was now irreversible and he should brave the Führer's wrath. He summoned Kleist to Wolfsschanze on August 16 and said, "I have asked you here because I want to hear that absurd story again of what went on up north. I mean your meeting with the Jew in Stockholm—before it's finally filed and put away." For the next few hours the two men thoroughly analyzed every detail about the possible motives of the Kremlin.

Ignoring Hitler's order never to bring up negotiations again, Ribbentrop told him about the conversation with Kleist. The Führer did not explode but repeated that there could never be any question of negotiating with Moscow; the war was to be fought relentlessly until victory. At the same time he would allow Kleist to keep in touch with Clauss and if the Kremlin had any kind of offer it was to be transmitted at once to Berlin.

Kleist did not see Clauss again for almost three weeks. At their meeting in early September the go-between (who may very well have been misleading both the Russians and Germans about the extent of his intimacy with each of them) showed his displeasure. He was sick, he said, of playing at politics with people who didn't know what they wanted. A Soviet contact, it seemed, had stayed in Stockholm for nine days waiting in vain for Kleist. Not even a refusal had come from Berlin! Kleist managed to pacify Clauss, then persuaded him to pay his respects to Madame Kollontai and resume the contact.

Clauss returned with bad news. The Soviets, bolstered by continuing success in battle, would not negotiate unless the Germans gave a sign they were serious: for example, dismissing Rosenberg and Ribbentrop. Kleist could barely restrain a grin; that was going to be a delightful point to put into his report to the Foreign Minister; but he respectfully pointed out that Hitler had no intention of negotiating. Clauss was not at all surprised. He sighed. The Germans didn't understand anything about negotiating. To do so one needed patience and knowledge of one's partner. The Führer failed on both counts.

Surprisingly, four days later Kleist found Clauss extraordinarily excited. His source at the Soviet Embassy had just informed him that Moscow was about to take another dramatic step! Vice-Commissar for Foreign Affairs Dekanozov, former ambassador in Berlin, would arrive in a week or so with authorization to speak directly to Kleist. There were conditions: Kleist must return to Stockholm *before* Dekanozov's arrival; and the Germans must release a previously agreed-upon sign—the resignation of Ribbentrop and Rosenberg—which would confirm that Kleist was authorized to take part in the talks. "What do you say now?" asked Clauss, his face flushed with eagerness and impatience. "We have managed to refloat the wreck! Now all Hitler has to do is to get on board and set sail, and he'll be out of his dilemma. Will he do it?"

On September 10 Kleist reported all this to Ribbentrop. Predictably, the Foreign Minister was hurt and angry that, after all he had done to bring about Soviet-German rapport, his own resignation was a prerequisite for negotiations! He was also dubious that a man of Dekanozov's standing would be used in this kind of game. The next moment his press officer interrupted with an announcement from Radio Moscow: Dekanozov was about to leave for Sofia to become ambassador. That, exclaimed Ribbentrop, proved his point. On the contrary, said Kleist, who knew more about Soviet tactics, this was confirmation from the Kremlin that Dekanozov *was* involved and would appear on neutral soil for talks. He suggested they reply with an announcement that Schulenburg had just been appointed Germany's ambassador to Sofia. Ribbentrop shook his head vigorously. The Führer would never send Schulenburg to Sofia! Kleist patiently explained that Stalin hadn't really intended to send Dekanozov there either. "Both announcements would merely act as a sign understood only by the 'augurs' and by nobody else in the world."

Ribbentrop saw the light and, with renewed enthusiasm, left immediately for the Wolfsschanze. He returned late at night somewhat sheepishly with inhibiting instructions from Hitler: Kleist was to tell Clauss privately that he was unable to get back to Sweden for the time being. "Try to hold on to the thread," said Ribbentrop. "The Führer is interested to find out how far the Russians will go." The next day Kleist was recalled for another interview, this one completely discouraging. The Führer had decided to avoid *any* direct contact with the Soviets however fleeting. Kleist left the room utterly dejected. They had come so close—to no avail.

7

Hitler's categorical refusal to negotiate with Stalin came at a curious time. Forty-eight hours earlier, on September 8, shortly after Allied troops breached the narrow channel between Sicily and the toe of Italy, it had been announced that the new Italian regime under Marshal Badoglio had signed an armistice with the West. Hitler was badly shaken even though he himself had predicted Badoglio would betray Germany. But he hadn't thought it possible (so he told the hastily summoned Goebbels) that this treachery would be committed so dishonorably.

Hitler's concern over the fate of 54,000 German troops in Sardinia and Corsica was succeeded by fear that the Allies might take the opportunity to launch their second front; the recent heavy English bombings were certainly suspicious. He was similarly haunted by another critical situation on the eastern front: the Wehrmacht, under heavy Soviet pressure, was withdrawing to the Dnieper.

At this point Goebbels wondered whether anything might be done with Stalin. "Not for a moment," said Hitler. It would be easier to make a deal with the English. At a given moment they would come to their senses. Goebbels disagreed. Stalin was more approachable, being a practical politician. Churchill was a romantic adventurer with whom one could not even talk sensibly. "Sooner or later," predicted Goebbels, "we shall have to face the question of inclining toward one enemy side or the other. Germany has never yet had luck with a two-front war; it won't be able to stand this one in the long run either." Concessions would have to be made, he said, pointing out how they had not come to power in 1933 by making unqualified demands. "We did present absolute demands on August 13, 1932, but failed because of them." The first thing to do was admit that Italy was lost, and he urged Hitler to address the nation on this subject without delay. The people were entitled to frankness, as well as a word of encouragement and solace from the Führer.

With reluctance Hitler agreed and on the night of September 10, from his bunker at Wolf's Lair, delivered a twenty-page speech which was taped in Berlin and broadcast to the nation. "My right to believe unconditionally in success," he said, "is founded not only on my own life but also on the destiny of our people." Neither time nor force of arms would ever bring the German people down.

Those who joined Hitler at tea after the speech were revivified by his own display of good spirits. "I must admit," wrote Goebbels' press officer in his diary, "that for a while I was completely captivated. What secret strength comes from this man who can, with a look and a handshake, totally confuse a sober, realistic man such as myself!" Even so, the rather stilted words he broadcast must have sounded hollow to civilians undergoing devastating air raids and to troops on the eastern front who were falling back with frightening losses.

Hitler, too, realized that words alone could not bolster his people's morale and decided to act drastically, dramatically. He would rescue Mussolini, now held prisoner in a hotel near the top of Gran Sasso, the loftiest peak in the Apennines range of mountains a hundred miles from Rome. An attack up the steep, rocky slope would not only cost many casualties but give guards time to kill Mussolini. Parachuting into such terrain was about as risky and so it was decided to use gliders. To carry off this piece of derring-do, Hitler chose a fellow Austrian. SS Captain Otto Skorzeny, a Viennese who stood six foot four, was, apart from his size, an imposing figure. He bore deep scars on his face from the fourteen duels he had fought as a student and carried himself with the air of a fourteenth-century condottiere. Skorzeny was not only a bold man of action but a canny one who believed commando operations should be carried out with a minimum force and as few casualties to both sides as possible. At 1 P.M. on Sunday, September 12, he and 107 men boarded gliders which, once airborne, began jerking erratically on their tow lines. The plan was to land on what appeared in photographs to be flat grassy meadow near Il Duce's hotel.

Mussolini, who had been threatening to commit suicide, was sitting by an open window with arms folded when a glider suddenly loomed and a parachute, acting as a brake, blossomed behind just before it crashed with a shattering noise a hundred yards away. Four or five men in khaki piled out and began assembling a machine gun. Mussolini had no idea who they were, only that they were not English. An alarm rang and Carabinieri guards and police excitedly rushed from their barracks, as other gliders began landing. One skidded to rest less than twenty yards from the hotel. It was Skorzeny's. Looking up, he saw Il Duce staring out at him. "Away from the window!" he shouted and lunged into the lobby.

Skorzeny and his band literally bowled over the detachment of soldiers trying to stop them; then he bolted up a staircase, three steps at a time, to the next floor and flung open a door. Mussolini stood in the middle of the room. "Duce," he said, "the Führer has sent me. You are free!" Mussolini embraced him. "I knew my friend Adolf Hitler would not abandon me," he said and profusely thanked his rescuer. Skorzeny was surprised at Il Duce's appearance. He looked sick and unkempt in ill-fitting civilian clothes. He was unshaven; his usually smooth head was covered with short, stubbly hair.

By 3 P.M. they were in a small Fieseler-Storch which had managed to land safely on the sloping meadow. While happy to be free, Mussolini was apprehensive. Being a pilot, he knew how risky the take-off from this unlikely strip would be. As the plane gathered speed it bumped erratically over rocks toward a yawning gully. The Storch finally lifted but its left wheel almost immediately struck the ground. The little plane bounced into space, then plunged straight into the gully. Skorzeny closed his eyes and held his breath, awaiting the inevitable crash. Somehow the pilot managed to pull the plane out of its dive and, to the shouts and waves of Germans and Italians on the meadow, guided it safely down into the valley.*

---

* Skorzeny's men escaped by cable car with their only casualties, ten men injured in a glider crash.

Nobody uttered a word. Only now, in "most unsoldierly fashion," did Skorzeny lay a reassuring hand on Il Duce's shoulder. Within the hour they landed in Rome, transferred to a trimotor Heinkel and were bound for Vienna. They arrived late at night and were driven to the Hotel Imperial. When Skorzeny brought Il Duce a pair of pajamas he rejected them. "I never wear anything at night," he said, "and I would advise you to do the same, Captain Skorzeny." He grinned roguishly. "Especially if you sleep with a woman."

As midnight struck Skorzeny's telephone rang. It was Hitler, who until he received word of the rescue had been "like a caged lion, pacing to and fro, listening for every ring of the telephone." His voice was husky with emotion. "You have performed a military feat which will become part of history," he said. "You have given me back my friend Mussolini."

After a stopover in Munich, where Mussolini was reunited with his family, he and Skorzeny set off for East Prussia early on the morning of September 14. The Führer was waiting at the Wolfsschanze airstrip. He warmly embraced his ally and for some time the two stood hand in hand. Finally Hitler turned to Skorzeny, who had discreetly waited before disembarking, and thanked him effusively. This one daring feat had forever endeared him to Hitler. It had also captured the imagination and admiration of foes as well as friends. More important, the spirits of Germans were uplifted not only by the rescue of Mussolini but by the manner in which it was done.

The Führer expected Mussolini to wreak vengeance on Badoglio and the regime in power. But Il Duce's only ambition was retirement to the Romagna. Privately he knew that his political life was over. His only future was as Hitler's pawn and the latter reacted with sarcasm and resentment. "What is this sort of Fascism which melts like snow before the sun!" he said. "For years I have explained to my generals that Fascism was the soundest alliance for the German people. I have never concealed my distrust of the Italian monarchy; at your insistence, however, I did nothing to obstruct the work which you carried out to the advantage of your King. But I must confess to you that we Germans have never understood your attitude in this respect." These words of intimidation were followed by a promise—even more ominous—to treat Italy well despite Badoglio's treachery *if* Il Duce would assume his role in a new republic. "The war must be won and once it is won Italy will be restored to her rights. The fundamental condition is that Fascism be reborn and that the traitors be brought to justice." Otherwise Hitler would be forced to treat Italy as an enemy. The country would be occupied and governed by Germans.

Mussolini wilted. If Hitler did not have his way the Italian people would undoubtedly suffer. Renouncing his plans to retire, he issued an official communiqué announcing that he had today assumed the supreme direction of Fascism in Italy. This was accompanied by four orders of the day which reinstated those authorities dismissed by Badoglio, reconstituted the Fascist militia, instructed the party to support the Wehrmacht and investigate the conduct of members relative to the July 25 coup d'état. By sheer force of will, Hitler had turned things around in Italy. But he no longer had any illusions about his partner. "I admit that I was deceived," he told his family circle. "It has turned out that Mussolini is only a little man."

During his guest's brief stay Hitler remarked that he wanted to settle with Russia. It was only said to impress Mussolini but Ribbentrop, who happened to be present, took it seriously and promptly asked for instructions. Hitler put him off but, once they were alone, again forbade Ribbentrop to make any overtures. He must have noticed his Foreign Minister's dejection, for he later took the trouble to call at his quarters. "You know, Ribbentrop," he said, "if I settled with Russia today I would only come to grips with her again tomorrow—I just can't help it."

Ever the wishful thinker, Ribbentrop still felt Hitler might relent. Late in the evening of September 22 he telephoned Kleist and asked if he could fly to Stockholm the next day. Kleist was astonished. It would be pointless to take such a trip, he said, without definite instructions. Ribbentrop admitted he had none to give but ordered Kleist to go anyway as soon as possible!

The following day it was Goebbels, taking advantage of a seat near Hitler at dinner, who urged him to seek some sort of peace. With either England or Russia. But Hitler said that negotiating with Churchill would be useless since he was "guided by hatred and not by reason," and Stalin could not possibly accede to German demands in the East.

And so, against this background, Kleist set off again for Sweden, this time with a feeling ranging between annoyance and despair. It seemed obvious that Hitler was only flirting with peace. In Stockholm Kleist was informed by a depressed Clauss that the recent German refusal to accept terms for the talks had made him persona non grata at the Soviet Embassy. Germany, he said, had lost her last chance in the East. He was right. Ten days earlier Stalin had rejected another peace bid by the Japanese and promptly reported it to Washington. Then, following months of excuses, he agreed to a conference with Churchill and Roosevelt at Teheran. It took place late that November and bound the Grand Alliance, so it seemed, inextricably together.

"AND WITH THE BEASTS OF THE EARTH" APRIL 1943–APRIL 1944

1

To most Germans, Hitler's treatment of the Jews was a matter of minor importance. They had been indifferent to the lot of Jewish neighbors forced to wear the Star of David—after all, didn't they deserve it? And even after the same neighbors began to disappear it was assumed they had been deported. It was only wise to discount unspeakable rumors in a land where listening to a foreign broadcast was punishable by death.

Not many knew about the killing centers. These were all in Poland and each was surrounded by a barren stretch several miles wide posted with notices that trespassers would be shot on sight. To ensure secrecy, the process from deportation to murder was not only executed speedily but done so under a smoke screen of euphemism: the over-all operation was referred to as "special treatment"; collectively the centers were described as the "East"; individual installations were called labor, concentration, transit or PW camps; and gas chambers and crematorium units were "bathhouses" and "corpse cellars."

Rumors of atrocities were answered by lies. When an important Nazi official, Hans Lammers, brought Himmler several reports that Jews were being executed in large numbers, the Reichsführer was vehement in denial. He explained that the so-called Final Solution order, received from the Führer through Heydrich, merely entailed evacuation of Jews from the homeland. During these movements there had unfortunately been some deaths from sickness and attacks by enemy aircraft—and a number of Jews, he admitted, had to be killed during revolts as examples. Himmler assured Lammers that the majority of Jews were being "accommodated" in camps in the East and brought out photo albums to show how they were working for the war effort as shoemakers, tailors and such. "This is the order of the Führer," emphasized Himmler. "If you believe you have to take action, then tell the Führer and tell me the names of the people who made these reports to you." Lammers refused to divulge any information and sought more information from Hitler himself. He gave almost identical information. "I shall later on decide where these Jews will be taken," he said, then added reassuringly—"and in the meantime they are being cared for there."

While some of those closest to Hitler truly did not know what was going on in the East, many others, victims of self-deception, guessed if they did not know the terrifying facts. "Don't let anyone tell you he had no idea," Hans Frank later wrote, including himself in the accusation. "Everyone sensed that there was something horribly wrong with this system, even if we didn't know all the details. We didn't *want* to know! It was too comfortable to live on the system, to support our families in royal style, and to believe that it was all right."

This was the man who had recently told his subordinates that they were all accomplices in the elimination of the Jews which, disagreeable as it might be, "was necessary in the interests of Europe." In his role as head of the Generalgouvernement in Poland, Frank knew the order had come directly from the Führer. But the average German still was convinced that Hitler had no part in any brutality. "People are now clinging to the hope that the Führer doesn't know about such things, can't know, otherwise he would take some steps," wrote an ardent Nazi woman to a friend in reference to the Euthanasia Program, the overture to the Final Solution. "Anyway, they think he can't know how this is being done or on what scale. I feel, however, that this can't go on much longer without even this hope being lost."

Those in Hitler's family circle could not imagine Uncle Adi authorizing the murder of Jews. It was unthinkable. Hadn't both Schmundt and Engel successfully persuaded the Führer to let a number of part Jewish Wehrmacht officers keep their commissions? The villain had to be either Bormann or Himmler, acting behind his back. But these two were only Hitler's faithful agents. He alone conceived the Final Solution and he alone could have ordered its execution. Without him there would have been no Final Solution, and he was confident he could get away with it if it were presented to the world as a fait accompli. There would be threats of retribution but the memories of men are short. Who today recalled the bitter condemnation of Turks for massacring a million Armenians during the Great War?

In a secret conversation on June 19, 1943, the Führer instructed Himmler to proceed with the deportation of Jews to the East "regardless of any unrest it might cause during the next three or four months." It must be carried out, he added, "in an all-embracing way." While these words would certainly not have convinced the family circle that Hitler was a mass murderer, those he uttered some time later to Bormann would have. "For us," he said after proudly admitting that he had purged the German world of the Jewish poison, "this has been an essential process of disinfection, which we have prosecuted to its ultimate limit and without which we should ourselves have been asphyxiated and destroyed." Hadn't he always been absolutely fair in his dealings with the Jews? "On the eve of the war, I gave them one final warning. I told them that, if they precipitated another war, they would not be spared and that I would exterminate the vermin throughout Europe, and this time once and for all. To this warning they retorted with a declaration of war and affirmed that wherever in the world there was a Jew, there, too, was an implacable enemy of National Socialist Germany. Well, we have lanced the Jewish abscess; and the world of the future will be eternally grateful to us."

One particularly horrifying aspect of Hitler's Final Solution had recently come to an apocalyptical ending. Of the 380,000 Jews crowded into the Warsaw ghetto, all but 70,000 had been deported to the killing centers in an operation devoid of resistance. By this time, however, those left behind had come to the realization that deportation meant death. With this in mind, Jewish political parties within the ghetto finally resolved their differences and banded together to resist further shipments with force. They did so to Himmler's amazement and he thereupon ordered the total dissolution of the Warsaw ghetto. At three in the morning of April 9, 1943, more than 2000 Waffen SS infantrymen—accompanied by tanks, flame throwers and dynamite squads—invaded the ghetto, expecting an easy conquest, only to be met by determined fire from 1500 fighters armed with weapons smuggled into the ghetto over a long period: several light machine guns, hand grenades, a hundred or so rifles and carbines, several hundred pistols and revolvers, and Molotov cocktails. Himmler had expected the action to take three days but by nightfall his forces had to withdraw. The one-sided battle continued day after day to the bewilderment of the SS commander, General Jürgen Stroop, who could not understand why "this trash and subhumanity" refused to abandon a hopeless cause. He reported that, although his men had initially captured "considerable numbers of Jews, who are cowards by nature," it was becoming more and more difficult. "Over and over again new battle groups consisting of twenty to thirty Jewish men, accompanied by a corresponding number of women, kindled new resistance." The women, he noted, had the disconcerting habit of suddenly hurling grenades they had hidden in their bloomers.

On the fifth day of frustration Himmler ordered the ghetto combed out "with the greatest severity and relentless tenacity." Stroop decided to do this by setting fire to the entire Jewish area, block by block. The Jews, he reported, remained in the burning buildings until the last possible moment before jumping from the upper stories to the street. "With their bones broken, they still tried to crawl across the street into buildings which had not yet been set on fire. . . . Despite the danger of being burned alive the Jews and bandits often preferred to return into the flames rather than risk being caught by us."

The defenders fought two, three weeks with reckless heroism, taking refuge, as a last resort, in the sewers. Finally, on May 15, firing from the few remaining Jewish nests of resistance became sporadic and the following day General Stroop blew up the Tlomacki Synagogue, in the "Aryan" section of Warsaw, to celebrate the end of the battle. For exactly four weeks the little Jewish army had held off superior, well-armed forces until almost the last man was killed or wounded. Of the 56,065 who were rounded up, 7000 were shot out of hand; 22,000 were sent to Treblinka and Lublin; the remainder to labor camps. The German losses were 16 dead and 85 wounded. Of far more significance was the blow dealt to Hitler's concept of Jewish cowardice.

2

Early that June Pius XII secretly addressed the Sacred College of Cardinals on the extermination of the Jews. "Every word We address to the competent authority on this subject, and all Our public utterances," he said in explanation of his reluctance to express more open condemnation, "have to be carefully weighed and measured by Us in the interests of the victims themselves, lest, contrary to Our intentions, We make their situation worse and harder to bear." He did not add that another reason for proceeding cautiously was that he regarded Bolshevism as a far greater danger than Nazism.

The position of the Holy See was deplorable but it was an offense of omission rather than commission. The Church, under the Pope's guidance, had already saved the lives of more Jews than all other churches, religious institutions and rescue organizations combined, and was presently hiding thousands of Jews in monasteries, convents and Vatican City itself. The record of the Allies was far more shameful. The British and Americans, despite lofty pronouncements, had not only avoided taking any meaningful action but gave sanctuary to few persecuted Jews. The Moscow Declaration of that year—signed by Roosevelt, Churchill and Stalin—methodically listed Hitler's victims as Polish, Italian, French, Dutch, Belgian, Norwegian, Soviet and Cretan. The curious omission of Jews (a policy emulated by the U. S. Office of War Information) was protested vehemently but uselessly by the World Jewish Congress. By the simple expedient of converting the Jews of Poland into Poles, and so on, the Final Solution was lost in the Big Three's general classification of Nazi terrorism.

Contrasting with their reluctance to face the issue of systematic Jewish extermination was the forthrightness and courage of the Danes, who defied German occupation by transporting to Sweden almost every one of their 6500 Jews; of the Finns, allies of Hitler, who saved all but four of their 4000 Jews; and of the Japanese, another ally, who provided refuge in Manchuria for some 5000 wandering European Jews in recognition of financial aid given by the Jewish firm of Kuhn, Loeb & Company during the Russo-Japanese War of 1904–5.

But the man who did most to hinder the atrocities in the East was a thirty-four-year-old German lawyer who worked for Himmler. Konrad Morgen, son of a railroad conductor, had become imbued with the ethics of law from his student days and even as an assistant SS judge was outspoken in his disapproval of illegality whoever committed it. His judgments, based strictly on the evidence, so exasperated his superiors that Morgen was posted to a front-line SS division as punishment. Because of his outstanding reputation he was transferred in 1943 to the SD's Financial Crimes Office with the understanding that he was not to deal with political cases. Early that summer he was given a routine investigative mission to clear up a long-standing corruption case at Buchenwald concentration camp. The commandant, Karl Koch, had been suspected of hiring out camp laborers to civilian employers, racketeering in food supplies and, in general, running the camp for his own personal profit. The initial investigation had failed to bring conviction when a parade of witnesses categorically supported Koch's plea of innocence.

Morgen journeyed in July to Weimar where he installed himself in Hitler's favorite local hostelry, the Elephant Hotel, and quietly began his research. To his surprise he found the concentration camp, located on a hill above Weimar, a prospect pleasing to the eye. The installations were clean and freshly painted; the grounds covered with grass and flowers. The prisoners appeared to be healthy, sun-tanned, normally fed. They enjoyed regular mail service and a large camp library which boasted books in foreign languages. There were variety shows, movies, sporting contests and even a brothel. As Morgen began to dig deeper he learned that the corruption at Buchenwald had started with the influx of Jews after Crystal Night. Unfortunately, the closer he got to the truth about Koch, the further he was from proof. Too often for coincidence he found that prisoners said to have information of corruption were now dead. From their files he discovered that the dates of death were years apart and in each case a different cause was given. Suspecting murder, he ordered an investigation but his own special agent could not find a single clue and refused to continue his search.

An ordinary man would have abandoned the investigation, but Morgen was so convinced that crime had been committed that he turned detective himself. He went to local banks where he briefly displayed official-looking papers and pretended that he had been authorized by Himmler to examine Koch's accounts. His persistence was rewarded. At one bank he found undeniable evidence that Koch had embezzled 100,000 marks. Finally proof of murder came when Morgen burrowed deep into the prison records to discover that witnesses were taken to a secret cell and eliminated.

Armed with a bulging briefcase of records and affidavits, Morgen set out for Berlin. His superior, the chief of criminal police, blanched at the evidence. He had not expected Morgen to take his assignment so seriously and hurriedly passed him on to Kaltenbrunner. Heydrich's successor was equally aghast—or pretended to be—and said, "That's not my business. Take it to your own boss in Munich." Morgen dutifully took the evidence to the head of the SS Legal Department, who was just as unwilling to take any responsibility. "You'll have to tell all that to Himmler," he said. Morgen proceeded to the Reichsführer's field headquarters where he was refused an interview. With the help of a sympathetic member of Himmler's personal staff, Morgen proceeded to draft a cautiously worded telegram outlining the case. The problem was to get it delivered personally. Somehow it was slipped through the bureaucratic barrier and came to Himmler's attention. To the amazement of almost everyone, he gave Morgen complete authority to proceed against Koch, his wife and anyone else connected with the sordid case. Some thought it was because of Himmler's mistrust of Oswald Pohl, the administrator of all concentration camps; others believed that he did not realize the case was a potential Pandora's box; but those who knew Himmler most intimately felt it was another instance of his peculiar sense of honor.

3

"Cruelty has a human heart."

WILLIAM BLAKE

There was no more paradoxical figure in the higher reaches of National Socialism than Heinrich Himmler. He impressed many by his charm and politeness, his modesty at meetings, his reasonableness. Diplomats described him as a man of sober judgment and the resistance movement regarded him as the sole leading Nazi who could be utilized in ending Hitler's rule. To General Hossbach he was the Führer's evil spirit, cold and calculating, the "most unscrupulous figure in the Third Reich." To Max Amann he was "a kind of Robespierre or witch-burning Jesuit." What made him sinister to Carl Burckhardt, the former League of Nations High Commissioner of Danzig, was "his capacity to concentrate upon little things, his pettifogging conscientiousness and his inhuman methodology; he had a touch of the robot." To his young daughter Gudrun he was a loving father. "Whatever is said about my *Papi*," she recently said, "what has been written or shall be written in the future about him—he was my father, the best father I could have and I loved him and still love him."

Most of his subordinates regarded Himmler as a warm, thoughtful employer with a deep sense of democracy. He played skat with secretaries and soccer with aides and adjutants. Once he invited a dozen young charwomen to his birthday dinner and ordered his reluctant officers to choose them as table companions, then himself led off the head charwoman.

The key to this enigmatic character did not lie in his youth. He came from a well-to-do Bavarian middle-class family and was named after his father's most famous pupil, Prince Heinrich von Wittelsbach. Young Himmler was neither more nor less anti-Semitic than the average young Bavarian of his class and the remarks about Jews in his diary were those of a bigot trying to be fair rather than of a racist. He had rigid convictions concerning sex and these were not unusual for his day. In short, he seemed to be the predictable product of Bavarian education and training—a promising young bureaucrat, meticulous and regulated.

By 1922, at age twenty-two, Himmler was a typical young nationalist with anti-Semitic leanings and a romantic vision of military life. That year he wrote a poem on the flyleaf of his diary, which revealed his dream of dying for a cause:

> *Although they may pierce you,*
> *Fight, resist, stand by.*
> *You yourself may perish*
> *But keep the banner high.*

It was not strange that a young man of such bent should be attracted by the theories of National Socialism and its charismatic leader; a bureaucrat by training and loyal by nature, he was a perfect Nazi career man. As he rose in the party he became the victim of a battle raging within himself. He was a Bavarian, yet fervently admired Prussian kings like Frederick the Great and constantly praised Prussian austerity and hardness. Himself dark, of average size and somewhat oriental features, he believed fanatically that the ideal German was Nordic and, like his master, preferred to surround himself with tall, blond, blue-eyed subordinates.* He admired physical perfection as well as athletic skill, yet was constantly suffering from stomach cramps. He presented a ridiculous figure on skis or in the water and once collapsed trying to win a lowly bronze medal in the mile run.

With more personal power than anyone in the Reich except Hitler, he remained unpretentious and conscientious. Born and bred a Catholic, he now relentlessly attacked the Church and yet, according to a close associate, conscientiously rebuilt his SS on Jesuit principles by assiduously copying "the service statutes and spiritual exercises presented by Ignatius Loyola."

Dreaded by millions, he trembled before the Führer who, he confessed to a subordinate, made him feel like a schoolboy who hadn't done his homework. Like his Führer, Himmler was indifferent to things material and, unlike Göring and others, never profited from his position. He lived in frugal simplicity, eating moderately, drinking sparingly and restricting himself to two cigars a day. He maintained one household on the Tegernsee for his wife and daughter, another near the Königsee for his personal secretary, Hedwig Potthast, who bore him a son and a daughter. And as a man of responsibility, he provided for each family in a style which left him very little for his personal use.

Some of his tenets were so eccentric that even his faithful followers found them difficult to accept: glacial cosmogony, magnetism, homeopathy, mesmerism, natural eugenics, clairvoyance, faith healing and sorcery. He sponsored experiments in obtaining gasoline by having water run over coal and in producing gold out of base metals.

While his power had all come from Hitler, the Führer wanted nothing to do with him personally. "I need such policemen," he told Schaub, who had been entreated by Himmler to get him an invitation to the Berghof, "but I don't like them." Hitler went so far as to order his per-

---

* Himmler was determined to breed out, within a hundred years, the dark German types (like himself and Hitler) by mating them exclusively with blonde women. To promote this racial policy he established *Lebensborn* (Spring of Life), an SS maternity organization whose main function was to adopt racially suitable children for childless SS families and to assist racially sound unwed mothers and their children. Thousands of children in the occupied territories were kidnaped and raised in special SS installations. "All good blood in the world," Himmler told his SS generals, "all Germanic blood which is not on the side of the Reich can one day be our destruction. Therefore . . . every German of the best blood whom we can bring to Germany and make into a self-aware German is a fighter for us, and one less on the other side. I really have the intention of fetching German blood from all over the world; to rob and steal where I can." Lurid postwar accounts describe Lebensborn as "stud farms" where SS men and suitable young women were mated to breed a master race. While Himmler's program did nothing to discourage illegitimacy, there is no evidence that he sponsored illicit sexual liaisons, nor is there proof that the kidnaping of children was done on a large scale. The fact that there were only 700 employees in all the Lebensborn homes casts doubts on such claims. Certainly Himmler envisaged a huge operation but Lebensborn never realized anywhere near its full potential because of the overriding needs of the resettlement and extermination operations.

sonal adjutant, Schulze, an SS captain, not to keep his nominal chief informed about the daily military discussions.

At the same time, he put the Reichsführer in full charge of the operation closest to his heart, the Final Solution. In some respects it was an appropriate appointment. From the beginning Himmler had been under Hitler's spell and he remained totally Hitler's man, his disciple and subject. Furthermore, Himmler was the epitome of National Socialism, for it was as a diligent professional party worker that Himmler had overcome his own problems of identity. He was the Führer's faithful right hand who, despite squeamishness in the face of blood or beatings, had become a mass killer by remote control, an efficient businessman murderer.

He had done so while retaining his sentimentality. "I've often bagged a deer," he confided to his personal physician, "but I must tell you I've had a bad conscience each time I've looked into its dead eyes." Recently, at some personal risk, he had connived with Field Marshal Milch to save the lives of 14,000 Jewish skilled laborers in Holland. He had also released from Ravensbrück concentration camp the mother of a Luftwaffe colonel who refused to renounce her belief as a Jehovah's Witness.* He did so under Milch's threat never to speak to him again; he so wanted to be considered a "good fellow."

If approached diplomatically he found it difficult to resist a reasonable plea for mercy. In one case he freed a deserter; in another, forgave an official for writing a biting critique of SS treatment of the Poles. But his sense of honor forbade him to show mercy to his own flesh and blood. When a nephew, an SS officer, was brought up on charges of homosexuality he immediately signed the order sending him to a punishment camp. During imprisonment, the young man committed other homosexual acts and the uncle ordered his execution. Rolf Wehser, an SS judge, urged leniency but Himmler refused. "I do not want anyone to say that I was more lenient because it was my own nephew." It was Hitler himself who had to revoke the judgment of death.

Under Himmler's supervision the work of the killing centers reached the peak of efficiency by the fall of 1943. At Auschwitz those selected for death marched to the gas chambers, unaware of their fate, past an inmate symphony orchestra conducted by the Jewish violinist Alma Rose. At Treblinka, however, the Jews almost always knew they were about to die and would cry and laugh from shock. Annoyed guards lashed away at them; babies, who hindered attendants while shaving their mothers' hair, would be smashed against a wall. If there was any resistance, guards and *Kapos* (trusties) would use whips to drive the naked victims into trucks bound for the gas chamber.

The thought of refusing the order to murder never entered the heads

---

* These were among the most indomitable of Hitler's victims and most of those imprisoned refused a standing offer of freedom if they would but renounce their faith.

of the executioners. "I could only say *Jawohl*," Höss, the commandant of Auschwitz, later confessed. "It didn't occur to me at all that I would be held responsible. You see, in Germany it was understood that if something went wrong, then the man who gave the orders was responsible." Nor did these executioners ever question whether the Jews deserved their fate. "Don't you see, we SS men were not supposed to think about these things; it never even occurred to us. . . . We were all so trained to obey orders, without even thinking, that the thought of disobeying an order would simply never have occurred to anybody, and somebody else would have done it just as well if I hadn't." Besides, those who participated in the exterminations had been trained so rigorously "that one would shoot his own brother if ordered to. Orders were everything."*

Some of the executioners thoroughly enjoyed their work but these were sadistic at the peril of punishment from their chief. Years earlier Himmler had forbidden independent action against the Jews by any member of his organization. "The SS commander must be hard but not hardened," he instructed one Sturmbannführer. "If, during your work, you come across cases in which some commander exceeds his duty or shows signs that his restraint is becoming blurred, intervene at once." Recently he had passed down a similar judgment to the SS Legal Department in regard to unauthorized shootings of Jews. "If the motive is selfish, sadistic or sexual, judicial punishment should be imposed for murder or manslaughter as the case may be." That was undoubtedly why he had authorized Morgen to bring the commandant of Buchenwald to trial.

Training his men to become hard but not hardened was a difficult task for Himmler and he attempted to do so by transforming the SS into an order of knights with the motto: "Loyalty is my honor." He imbued the SS, therefore, not only with a sense of racial superiority but with the hard virtues of loyalty, comradeship, duty, truth, diligence, honesty and knighthood. His SS, as the elite of the party, was the elite of the German Volk, and therefore the elite of the entire world. By establishing castles of the order to indoctrinate SS members in his ideals, he hoped to breed a New Man, "far finer and more valuable than the world had yet seen." He also lectured his men on good manners and good breeding. "Whether it is a dinner you are giving or the organization of a march, wherever there are guests, I insist that you attend to the slightest details, for I want the SS to set an example of propriety everywhere, and show the utmost courtesy and consideration to all fellow Germans." His SS men were to be models of

* The experiments made by Stanley Milgram in the United States as described in his book, *Obedience to Authority*, indicate that blind obedience is not limited to Germans. During the Milgram experiments only thirty-five per cent of those tested refused an order to inflict pain on fellow human beings. The majority simply obeyed the voice of authority. These tests made in 1960 were corroborated by Vietnam and, to an extent, by Watergate.

neatness. "I do not want to see a single white vest with the slightest spot of dirt." Furthermore they must drink like gentlemen "or you will be sent a pistol and asked to put an end to it."

They were to be gentlemen, in fact, no matter how atrocious their mission. And with this in mind, Himmler summoned his SS generals to Posen on October 4, 1943. His primary purpose was to enlarge the circle of those privy to the extermination of the Jews. The recent revelations by Morgen, combined with persistent rumors of terrors in the concentration camps, were causing apprehension and some revulsion among the most loyal adherents of the Führer. Now that the truth was leaking out, he had decided to involve the party and the military in his Final Solution. By making them, in effect, co-conspirators, he would force them to fight on to the end. The war was probably lost, but this would give him time to fulfill his main ambition. If worse came to worst he would take millions of Jews to death with him.

The speech to the SS officers was only the first in a series of information lectures by Himmler that were to include many civilian leaders and Wehrmacht officers. In a sense, the first was the most important of the scheduled speeches since he must convince the SS that the execution of this distasteful deed was not at variance with the highest principles of their order. He said he wanted to talk to them quite frankly, on a very grave matter. "Among ourselves it should be mentioned once, quite openly, but we will never speak of it publicly." His reluctance to proceed was obvious but finally he said, "I mean the evacuation of the Jews, the extermination of the Jewish race. It's one of those things it is easy to talk about—'The Jewish race is being exterminated,' says one party member, 'that's quite clear, it's in our program—elimination of the Jews, and we're doing it, exterminating them.'"

These plain words, after years of rhetoric and sloganeering, were shocking despite the unwelcome suspicions raised by Morgen and Kurt Gerstein. More so was Himmler's condemnation of those who had been profiting by the Final Solution. "A number of SS men—there are not very many of them—have fallen short, and they will die without mercy. We had the moral right, we had the duty of our people, to destroy this race which wanted to destroy us. But we have not the right to enrich ourselves with so much as a fur, a watch, a mark, or a cigarette or anything else. Because we have exterminated a bacterium we do not want to be eventually infected by the bacterium or die of it. I will not allow so much as a sepsis to appear here or gain a hold. Wherever it may form, we must cauterize it. In the final analysis, however, we can say that we have fulfilled this most difficult duty for the love of our people. And our spirit, our soul, our character have not suffered injury from it."

Two days later Himmler spoke in the same vein to a group of

Gauleiters and Reichsleiters. "The sentence 'The Jews must be exterminated,' with its few words, gentlemen, can be uttered easily. But what that sentence demands of the man who must execute it is the hardest and toughest thing in existence." It was apparent to his listeners that they were about to hear what they had been closing their ears to for months. "I ask you really only to hear and never to talk about what I tell you in this circle. When the question arose, 'What should be done with the women and children?' I decided here also to adopt a clear solution. I did not deem myself justified in exterminating the men, that is to say, to kill them or let them be killed, while allowing their children to grow up to avenge themselves on our sons and grandchildren. The hard decision had to be taken— *this people must disappear from the face of the earth.*"

This was, he said, the most onerous assignment the SS ever had. "It was carried out—I think I can say—without our men and our leaders suffering the slightest damage to spirit or soul." They had remained knights despite mass extermination. A leaden silence fell over the hall. "He spoke," recalled Baldur von Schirach, "with such icy coldness of the extermination of men, women and children, as a businessman speaks of his balance sheet. There was nothing emotional in his speech, nothing that suggested an inner involvement."

After enlarging on the difficulties of this awesome task, Himmler brought the subject to a close. "You now know what is what and you must keep it to yourself. Perhaps at a much later time we shall consider whether something about it can be told to the German people. But it is probably better to bear the responsibility on behalf of our people (a responsibility for the deed as well as for the idea) and take the secret with us into our graves." He was like Brutus, forcing his colleagues to dip their hands in Caesar's blood. The Final Solution was no longer the burden only of Hitler and Himmler but theirs, a burden they must carry in silence.

Bormann closed the meeting with an invitation to lunch in the adjoining hall. During the meal Schirach and the other Gauleiters and Reichsleiters wordlessly avoided each other's eyes. Most guessed that Himmler had only revealed the truth so as to make them accomplices and that evening they drank so much that a good number had to be helped into the train that was taking them to the Wolfsschanze. Albert Speer, who had addressed the same audience just before Himmler, was so disgusted by the drunken spectacle that the next day he urged Hitler to read his party leaders a lecture on temperance.*

* Speer claims to this day that he knew nothing of the Final Solution. Some scholars have accused him of attending Himmler's speech since during it the Reichsführer specifically addressed him. Speer insists he left for Rastenburg immediately after his own speech. Field Marshal Milch confirmed this. Granted that Speer was not present, it is difficult to believe he did not know of the extermination camps. From the text of Himmler's speech it is clear that he *thought* he was talking directly to Speer—and assuming that he was one of the high-ranking conspirators.

4

The Jews were not the only victims of Hitler's New Order. Millions of others, particularly in occupied Russia, had been shot, gassed and beaten to death. During a recent visit to Wolfsschanze Peter Kleist had voiced opposition to this policy to the Führer himself in a long detailed memorandum. "You've given me a very unpleasant picture of conditions in occupied Russia," said Hitler after reading it. "Isn't this idea of improving conditions by giving in to the ambitious demands of any nationalist politician that comes along nothing but an illusion? These nationalists will just think we are weak, and their ambition will spur them on to make more and more demands." Kleist spoke out boldly, explaining that he did not mean they should give in to demands, rather create conditions that would make the peoples of the East choose Germany instead of the Soviet Union. As he continued, Hitler listened thoughtfully, eyes on the floor. This gave Kleist the rare opportunity of observing his face at leisure. "I had always been struck by the way in which his expression was split up into many different units. It seemed to be composed of single elements that did not combine to form any real unity."

Finally Hitler interrupted. He was not at all angry but completely cool, calm and thoughtful as if talking to himself. "I cannot turn back now," he said, gazing into space. "Any change in my attitude would certainly be misunderstood as giving in, the military situation being what it is, and would bring a landslide." He did promise to consider a more liberal course once he had gained the military initiative, but Kleist felt this was only rhetoric. How could you change such a mind?

Abruptly Hitler looked up at Kleist. Gone was the calm, contemplative mood. "It's an illusion," he exclaimed with some violence. "You have a right to think only of the moment and of the situation weighing upon us at the present time, but that is also where you fall short. I have a duty to think of tomorrow, and the day after tomorrow. I cannot forget the future for the sake of a few momentary successes." In a hundred years Germany would be a nation of 120,000,000. "For that population I need empty space. I cannot grant the Eastern peoples any sovereign rights of independence and replace Soviet Russia with a new national Russia which is, for that very reason, much more firmly knit together. Policy is made not with illusions but with facts. Space is the deciding question for me in the East!"

And so his policy of oppression continued, accompanied by the ruthless starvation of Soviet prisoners of war. Alfred Rosenberg himself bore witness to this inhumanity in a scorching letter to Keitel that must have been prepared and thrust upon the Minister for the Occupied Eastern Territories by more forceful subordinates. It charged that of the 3,600,000

Soviet prisoners of war only a few hundred thousand were in good health. The great majority had been starved or shot out of hand in a series of atrocities that ignored "potential understanding."

Countless other Soviet prisoners, along with non-Jewish inmates of concentration camps, were dying in a series of medical experiments: some after lying naked in snow or icy water; some during high-altitude tests; some as guinea pigs for mustard gas and poison bullets. Polish women at the Ravensbrück camp were inflicted with gas gangrene wounds; gypsies at Dachau and Buchenwald satisfied the curiosity of a group of doctors who wanted to know how long human beings could live on salt water.

The administration of occupied territories throughout Europe had also resulted in manifold executions as reprisals for acts of sabotage and rebellion. These were legalized by an order issued by the Führer on Pearl Harbor Day, once he realized all hope of taking Moscow was gone and eventual victory was dubious. Bearing the odd but apt title, "Night and Fog Decree," it ordered that all persons endangering German security, except those to be executed immediately, were to "vanish" without leaving a trace. Their families were to be told nothing of their fate.

By the fall of 1943 Hitler's New Order in Western Europe, which purported to be an amalgamation of states for the common good, was exposed for what it was: a plunder economy. Faced with millions reluctant to become mere vassals, Hitler turned from persuasion to sheer force. Acts of work stoppage and sabotage were answered by enforced labor and the execution of hostages. In Holland and France the death toll was more than 20,000. Legalized pillage had become the order of the day with boxcars of loot (including food, clothing and art treasures) converging on the homeland from Norway, Holland, Belgium, Luxembourg, France and Denmark. This did not include enormous occupation assessments. France alone was paying seven billion marks a year for membership in the New Order.

Hitler revealed the truth to the entire party leadership at a meeting in Berlin. "All that rubbish of small states still existing in Europe must be liquidated as fast as possible. The aim of our struggle must be to create a unified Europe: the Germans alone can really organize Europe."

A unified Europe, of course, meant one completely dominated by Germany; one kept orderly by the Gestapo and collaboration police. Yet with all its oppressions and brutal reprisals, Hitler's New Order had not aroused the spirit of rebellion among the masses. Most of the occupied peoples still co-operated with Nazi authorities so that they could lead comparatively normal lives, convinced that general strikes, attacks on German overseers or attempts to disrupt the administration and economy of their nation would inevitably lead to massive reprisals at worst or a lowering of their own standard of living at best. It was easier and more prudent to make common cause with an occupation that probably would last indefinitely. It was this will to survive that reduced resistance activities to a mini-mum. Few, indeed, belonged to the underground and too often, as in France, there was bloody, debilitating rivalry between Communist and non-Communist partisan units. The only substantial resistance movement was in Yugoslavia and this too was blunted by the internecine quarrel be-tween Tito, a Communist, who strove to unite all anti-Hitler elements, and Mihailovic, the Serbian nationalist.

Although Hitler's ultimate aim to transform most of Europe into a Germanic empire was now in the open, the extent of his ambitions was not. Even many of his enemies surmised he would restrict himself to Europe; they would have been confounded to read his secret handwritten notes on the subject.*

> England for the good of the world must remain unchanged in its pres-ent form.
> Consequently, after final victory, we must effect a reconciliation.
> Only the King must go—in his place the Duke of Windsor. With him we will make a permanent treaty of friendship instead of a peace treaty.

Scandinavia and the Iberian Peninsula, he continued, would be joined under the New Order, thus materializing that United Europe en-visaged by Charles the Great, Prince Eugene and Napoleon.

> The most important point of final victory will be the exclusion of the United States from world politics for all time and the destruction of their Jewish community.
> For this purpose Dr. Goebbels will have dictatorial authority as Gover-nor to accomplish the total re-education of the racially mixed and inferior population. Göring will also help in this respect, above all by mobilizing all those with German blood, at least fifty per cent of the inhabitants, so they can be educated militarily and regenerated nationalistically.

5

While Hitler envisaged grandiose plans of conquest that en-compassed five continents, his armies in the East were being steadily driven back toward the homeland. Inspired by success in repelling Opera-tion Citadel, the Soviet high command had gone over to the attack with confidence and daring. In the last six months of 1943 the Red Army had advanced in some places as much as two hundred and fifty miles, throwing the Germans in the south and center back across the Dnieper River.

This only spurred Hitler to accelerate the Final Solution and early in 1944 he allowed the secret to be revealed to a large non-party, non-SS group. On January 26, 1944, Himmler made his third address, this to some 260 high-ranking army and navy officers in a theater at Posen. In his cool,

* These documents are presently in the Müllern-Schönhausen Collection.

antiseptic manner he told how Hitler had given him the mission of extermination. "I can assure you that the Jewish question has been solved. Six
million have been killed." A wave of applause swept the auditorium. One
Wehrmacht officer near Colonel von Gerstdorff (who had tried in vain to
bomb Hitler and himself to bits) stood up on a chair in his enthusiasm.
From the rear of the hall an aghast general checked to see how many of
his colleagues were *not* applauding. He could count but five.

Himmler continued this campaign of enlightenment in the next
weeks. He admitted to a group of navy leaders that he had ordered women
and children killed. "I would be a weakling, a criminal to our descendants
if I allowed hate-filled sons to grow to manhood in this battle of humans
against subhumans . . . but we must recognize more and more that we are
engaged in a primitive, original, natural racial battle." He told much the
same story to another group of generals at Sonthofen. "The Jewish question in Germany and in general throughout the occupied territories is
solved," he said. And when he added that it had been done "without
compromise," there was applause. In all, Himmler made some fifteen
speeches on the Final Solution, covering a wide range of audiences but,
significantly, never one of Foreign Office personnel.

The last days of 1943 were oppressive ones for Hitler. Not only did
his troops face new setbacks at Leningrad and throughout the Ukraine,
but his extermination program was threatened when SS Judge Morgen
finally uncovered the network of corruption at Buchenwald. An accomplice of Camp Commandant Koch's, named Köhler, lost his nerve and
agreed to testify. He was jailed as a material witness but within days was
found dead in his cell. In the light of such damning evidence, Koch
wilted under Morgen's relentless interrogation. He confessed that, besides
enriching himself at the expense of the inmates, he had executed a number of them to cover up his secret.

The successful prosecution of Koch by no means satisfied Morgen's
sense of justice. He pursued the trail of corruption to Poland. In Lublin
Morgen was warmly greeted by the camp's commandant, Kriminalkommissar Wirth, who had acted as Gerstein's guide in Belzec. He revealed
with pride that it was he who had not only built the four extermination
camps in the Lublin area but organized the system of extermination.
Each establishment, he said, had been built up like a Potemkin village.
As trains pulled into a dummy railroad station, the occupants imagined
they were entering a city or town. With relish, Wirth described how he
or one of his representatives would greet the newcomers with a set speech:
"Jews, you were brought here to be resettled but before we organize the
future Jewish state, you must of course learn how to work. You must learn
a new trade." After these calming words the victims would innocently
start off on their march to death.

Wirth's description of the entire process seemed "completely fantastic" to Morgen but not after he toured the buildings which housed the loot. From the massive piles—including one incredible heap of watches—he realized that "something frightful was going on here." Never had he seen so much money at one time, particularly foreign currency. There were coins from all over the world. He gaped in wonder at the gold-smelting furnace and its prodigious stack of gold bars.

Morgen inspected all four camps built by Wirth—Maidanek, Treblinka, Sobibor and Belzec. In each one he saw evidence of execution —the gas chambers, the ovens, the mass graves. Here was crime on a ghastly scale, yet he was helpless to act since the order had come directly from the Führer's chancellery. Morgen's only recourse was to prosecute the "arbitrary killings" of prisoners; these could be brought before the SS judicial system. He set out to get evidence and persevered, despite continued hindrances, until he found sufficient proof to bring charges of murder against the two top officials at Maidanek.

The guiding spirit of all four camps, the helpful Christian Wirth, continued to talk freely to Morgen. One day he remarked casually that a man named Höss ran another large extermination complex near Auschwitz. This sounded like fertile ground for Morgen, but his authority was limited and he had to find some good reason to go so far afield. He soon found his excuse: an unsolved case of gold smuggling involving several men on Höss's staff. And so by early 1944 the doughty Morgen was investigating the death camps near Auschwitz. He had no trouble locating numerous sheds loaded with loot, gas chambers and crematories. But investigations of "illegal" killings and corruption were blocked every time one of his men got too close to the truth and Morgen decided to return to Germany so he could attend to a more important matter—the mass official killing themselves. Morgen decided to approach Himmler personally and make it clear that the extermination system was leading Germany "straight into the abyss." To reach the Reichsführer he again had to go through channels. First on the list was his immediate superior, the chief of the criminal police. Nebe listened in shocked silence ("I could see his hair stand on end when I made my report") and when he found tongue he told Morgen to report the matter immediately to Kaltenbrunner. He too was appalled and promised to take his protest to both Himmler and Hitler. Next came Chief Justice of the SS Court Breithaupt. He was so incensed that he promised to arrange a meeting between Himmler and Morgen. But this time the machinery of bureaucracy prevented Morgen from getting beyond the Reichsführer's anteroom. This convinced Morgen that he would have to take a more practical route to justice: "that is, by removing from this system of destruction the leaders and important elements through the means offered by the system itself. I could not do this with regard to the killings ordered by the head of the state, but I could do it for killings outside of this order, or against this order, or for other serious charges."

He returned to his task with spirit, determined to institute proceedings against as many leaders as possible in hopes of undermining the entire system of mass murder. He expanded the scope of investigation to concentration camps despite threats and attempted reprisals. At Oranienburg one of his informers—a prisoner named Rothe—was saved at the last moment from a public execution designed to warn other inmates not to collaborate with Morgen. Even so he won the nickname, "The Bloodhound Judge," bringing some 800 cases of corruption and murder to trial, 200 of which resulted in sentences. Karl Koch of Buchenwald was shot. The commandant of Maidanek was also executed, his chief assistant condemned to death. The commandant of 's Hertogenbosch was posted to a penal unit for maltreatment of prisoners and the head of Flossenburg was fired for drunkenness and debauchery.

These trials caused such reverberations in the hierarchy by the early spring of 1944 that Himmler, undoubtedly at Hitler's order, instructed Morgen to cease further investigations. "The Bloodhound Judge" was going too far, too successfully and was about to launch a full-scale inquiry into Rudolf Höss and the Auschwitz constellation of camps. The shock wave of Morgen's one-man house cleaning had already compromised the Lublin killing complex. Kriminalkommissar Wirth was instructed to destroy three of the four camps he had built—Treblinka, Sobibor and Belzec —without leaving a trace. That task completed, Wirth was dispatched to Italy to defend roads against partisans. Here the man who had escaped Morgen's justice was soon brought down by a ruder one—a partisan bullet in the back. In the meantime, despite the Himmler-Hitler order, Konrad Morgen was surreptitiously continuing his lonesome attempt to end the Final Solution.* He was particularly interested in a rather low-ranking SD officer named Eichmann.

* Morgen also did his best to convict Ilse Koch, the wife of the Buchenwald commandant. He was convinced that she was guilty of sadistic crimes, but the charges against her could not be proven. After the war Morgen was asked by an American official to testify that Frau Koch made lampshades from the skin of inmates. Morgen replied that, while she undoubtedly was guilty of many crimes, she was truly innocent of this charge. After personally investigating the matter, he had thrown it out of his own case. Even so, the American insisted that Morgen sign an affidavit that Frau Koch had made the lampshades. Anyone undaunted by Nazi threats was not likely to submit to those of a representative of the democracies. His refusal to lie was followed by a threat to turn him over to the Russians, who would surely beat him to death. Morgen's second and third refusals were followed by severe beatings. Though he detested Frau Koch, nothing could induce him to bear false witness. Fortunately, Morgen survived and is presently practicing law in West Germany.

Part 9

INTO THE ABYSS

Chapter Twenty-eight

THE ARMY BOMB PLOT
NOVEMBER 1943–JULY 21, 1944

1

On the eve of the twentieth anniversary of the Beer Hall Putsch Germany's strategic position was frankly revealed to a hundred or so Reichsleiters and Gauleiters by General Jodl. In a top secret lecture at Munich he told of the bitter defeats in Russia, of the failure to draw Spain into the war and thus seize Gibraltar (because of that "Jesuit Foreign Minister Serrano Suñer"), and of the "most monstrous of all betrayals in history"—that of the Italians. Jodl spoke extemporaneously of the future, alarming his listeners with the admission that the Western Allies enjoyed such tremendous air superiority that a mass landing could not possibly be contained by the present defense forces. There was, he concluded, only one solution: to mobilize every German able to bear arms. It would not be possible to drain troops and supplies from the East, he said, since things were indeed "getting warm" there. New ways had to be found to solve the dilemma of manpower shortage in the West. "In my opinion, the time has come to take steps with remorseless vigor and resolution in Denmark, Holland, France and Belgium, to compel thousands of idle ones to carry out the fortification work, which is more important than any other work. The necessary orders for this have already been given."

The glum picture of the present ended with the acknowledgment that the terror air raids by the West "weighed most heavily on the home front" and that U-boat reprisals were declining drastically because of enemy air superiority over the Atlantic. At the same time, he said, there were considerable grounds for confidence in final victory. They were blessed with a leader who was "the soul not only of the political but also of the military conduct of the war," and it was his will power alone that was animating "the whole of the German armed forces, with respect to strategy, organization, and munitions of war. Similarly the unity of political and military command, which is so important, is personified by him in a way such as has never been known since the days of Frederick the Great." He ended with a burst of hyperbole worthy of Hitler. No one could predict what troubles lay hidden in the darkness of the future. One thing alone was certain: Germany would never cease the fight for the culture and freedom of the Continent. "A Europe under the whip of American Jews or Bolshevik commissars is unthinkable."

The politicians cheered. Jodl's talk was a tour-de-force mixture of candor and hope that was followed two days later by a purely inspirational performance on the part of Hitler. In a speech from the Löwenbräu cellar, he spoke with such confidence and fire that many of those listening on the radio were as uplifted as those present.

These attempts to inspire the party and the people were undermined within weeks by deterioration in both the political and the military situation. Hungarians were eying Italy's desertion with envy and Romanians were bitter at the destruction of eighteen divisions on the Don and Volga. The Wehrmacht itself had suffered 1,686,000 casualties in the past twelve months and it was so difficult to find replacements that the conscription law exempting the youngest or only son of a family was suspended, and fifty-year-old men, veterans of the First World War, were deemed eligible for service.

With prospects of another disastrous winter on the eastern front, the atmosphere at Wolfsschanze was glum. The Führer completely ignored the holiday season. There was no Christmas tree, not a single candle to celebrate the festival of love and peace. Early in 1944, on January 26, he summoned several hundred generals and admirals to Rastenburg. After explaining the ideological basis of the war, he made it clear that his officers must take an unequivocal stand in regard to National Socialism. They must support its principles from inner conviction. He said all this in a calm, matter-of-fact manner and so his next words, uttered with an intense sincerity, caught his listeners off balance. "My generals and admirals," he said, "if Providence should actually deny us victory in this battle of life and death, and if it is the will of the Almighty that this should end in catastrophe for the German people, then you, my generals and admirals, must gather around me with upraised swords to fight to the last drop of blood for the honor of Germany—I say, gentlemen, that is the way it actually *must* be!"

There was deathly silence in the room. Everyone, it seemed, was holding his breath. Finally the silence was broken by an officer in the first row who felt insulted. In an ironic voice Field Marshal von Manstein said, "My Führer, it shall be so!" There followed another silence, this one fearful, as Hitler waited for his military leaders to rise as one man and cheer these words—even though they had been uttered sarcastically. But there was not a sound, not a movement. On the rostrum, Hitler paled. He scanned the room, his eyes like searchlights, finally stopping at Manstein in the front row. "Field Marshal," he said harshly, "I have good reason to doubt the faith which your response implies." There was another long, embarrassing pause. Finally he said he knew all about the anti-Hitler movement in the Wehrmacht, the strong negative attitude of numerous officers. He had proof positive that some of these gentlemen were refusing to execute certain Führer orders. Yes, and he knew all about the Free Germany movement among certain officers captured by the Soviets!

These impromptu accusations broke his concentration and he was unable to finish his speech as planned. Instead he brought it to an abrupt close and stalked out of the room. Moments later Manstein was ordered to report at once to the Führer's study. Hitler glared at him. "Field Marshal," he said, "I must forbid you ever to interrupt me again during a speech. How would you like it if someone broke in while *you* were addressing your subordinates?"

One of the few pleasures of Hitler's life in those dreary winter days was the excellent cuisine of his new diet cook. Marlene von Exner was also young, attractive and Viennese. He enjoyed her company and the two would talk at length about Austria and her family, which had supported the National Socialist movement when it was illegal. Her only complaint was Hitler's limited menu. How monotonous, she confided to Traudl Junge, to live on vegetarian soup, carrots, potatoes and soft-boiled eggs! She feared he might get so bored with her meals that he would send her away—and she had fallen in love with a young SS adjutant. She was destined to leave for quite another reason. Bormann, whose advances had been repelled by Frau von Exner, discovered there was Jewish blood on her mother's side and got his revenge by pressing the matter until Hitler, who wished it had never been raised, felt obliged to dismiss her. But he gave her six months' salary and made the entire Exner family honorary Aryans.

Late that February Hitler returned to the Obersalzberg so that the Wolfsschanze buildings could be reinforced against Russian air raids. But life at the Berghof was scarcely more cheerful. "The forced gaiety, the light conversations and the variety of guests," recalled Traudl Junge, "could not hide the disquiet which we all felt in our hearts." Eva had not seen her lover for some time and was shocked by his appearance. "He has become so old and somber," she confided to Traudl. "Do you know what is troubling him?"

The secretary was embarrassed. "You know the Führer much better than I do and you must be able to guess about those things he doesn't speak of." The military situation alone, she said, must be sufficient cause for deep concern. Later in the day, at the tea house, Eva scolded Hitler for his stoop but he turned it into a joke. "That's because I have heavy keys in my pocket. Besides I tote along a full pack of troubles." He grinned facetiously. "Now you and I will go better together. You are always wearing high heels to be taller so if I bend down a little we will harmonize well."

On the last day of February an unusual guest arrived at the Berghof. Hanna Reitsch, the aviator and glider pilot, had come to tell the Führer how to win the war. The new V-1 rocket, she argued, was too inaccurate. A piloted rocket was the answer and she offered to be the first volunteer. Hitler rejected the project out of hand. This was not the right psychological moment for such a suicidal idea to be accepted by the German people. He changed the subject to the jet plane, one of his secret weapons. Hanna knew that jet propulsion was only in its early stages of development and could not resist interrupting him in mid-sentence. "Mein Führer, you are speaking of the grandchild of an embryo." He was poorly informed about the German jet program, she said, and again brought up the subject of suicide pilots. Surprisingly, he gave peevish permission to begin experimental work on the project so long as he was not pestered during the development stage.

It snowed almost continuously at the Obersalzberg, but the isolation seemed to improve the Führer's spirits. At lunch he began deriding the water colors he had painted in Vienna and which now commanded high prices. It would be crazy, he said, to pay more than two hundred marks for such amateurish efforts. "I did not really want to be a painter," he confessed. "I only painted these things to live and study." He had disposed of them but kept his architectural sketches—"my most treasured possessions, my mental property, which I could never part with. One must not forget that all my present ideas, my architectural plans, go back to those years when I worked all night long."

Life at the Berghof seemed to give him renewed confidence and by the time Goebbels arrived in March, deeply depressed over the first daylight American bombings, Hitler had to instill him with hope for the future. Yet the next day it was the Führer who suffered an attack of nerves. In a conference on March 17 at nearby Klessheim Castle he lost his temper with Admiral Horthy, Regent of Hungary, and accused the Hungarians of planning an Italian-style betrayal. Schmidt, waiting outside, was astounded to see the aged Horthy rush out, red in the face, with Hitler at his heels, looking angry and embarrassed, calling out to come back.

The affronted Horthy sent for his special train but, before it could move, Ribbentrop faked a convincing air raid, including a smoke screen over the castle, which successfully kept the Regent a prisoner. When he had cooled down Ribbentrop informed him that he could leave and read the draft of a joint communiqué stating that the entry of German troops into Hungary had been arranged by mutual consent. "You may as well have added," protested the admiral, "that I begged Hitler to have Hungary occupied by Slovak and Romanian troops, which is another of the threats he made!" This sentence was deleted but by the time Horthy arrived in Budapest he found his country occupied by eleven German divisions.

Hitler's nerves had led to a petty triumph that was a military as well as a political blunder. It took divisions away from the West, where there were increasing indications of an impending invasion, and from the East where, reported intelligence expert Gehlen, the enemy was about to launch a massive offensive in the Ukraine which could have imminent and "far-reaching political, military and economic repercussions on the rest of the war in Europe." The only prospect of regaining the initiative, Gehlen added, was to make bold strategic withdrawals. In line with his policy of hanging tenaciously to every bit of conquered territory, the Führer turned down the recommendation.

This decision may have been influenced by bad health. Others besides Eva noticed how his knees would tremble if he stood too long; and his left hand would shake enough to rattle a cup in its saucer. Early in May he was again plagued by agonizing stomach spasms. While ignoring Dr. Morell's advice to submit to gentle massage and go on long walks, he did agree to take Cardizol and subject himself to intravenous injections of two other drugs (Glucad and Testoviron) to combat increasing fatigue. Morell also urged Hitler to get to bed earlier, but he said that was impossible. He could not sleep until the last British bomber had left the Reich.

That spring enemy planes ravaged Bavaria. Almost every day the warning sirens screeched and Hitler would climb down the sixty-five steps to the deep bunker under the Berghof. But no bombs dropped on the Obersalzberg; the raiders were bound for Vienna, Hungary or other populated targets. In clear weather one could see the red of the fires in Munich and Eva begged permission to drive there to see if her house on the Wasserburgerstrasse was safe. She persisted until the Führer finally let her go. She returned so shocked by the havoc that Hitler vowed vengeance. "Panic will break out in England!" he promised and told her about the new rocket. "The effect of this weapon will be too much for anyone's nerves. I shall pay back those barbarians who are now massacring women and children and destroying German culture."

The air raid alerts became so common that some of the guests at the Berghof began to ignore them. One early morning Traudl rushed from her bed to safety but found no one in the bunker. When she came up to see why, there was Hitler standing at the entrance like Cerberus, scanning the skies anxiously. He wagged an admonishing finger at her. "Don't be so careless, young lady. Get back to the bunker; the alarm is not yet over." She didn't tell him that the other guests were still in their beds but obediently descended the long flight of steps. During lunch Hitler delivered a lecture on the stupidity of not taking shelter. "My co-workers, some of whom are irreplaceable, simply have an obligation to go to the bunker," he scolded. "It is idiotic to prove your courage by placing yourself in danger of being struck by a bomb."

He was placing his own body in jeopardy by steadfastly refusing to exercise, rest or undergo massage, while depending more and more on medication. In addition to the other pills and injections, he allowed himself to be dosed with a heart and liver extract and four to six multivitamin tablets a day. It was almost as though his health was no longer important and he was only keeping himself alive until he had accomplished his mission in life. He did succeed in lifting himself out of depression and resumed preaching his message of hope. One fine day, he assured the family circle, something would change the entire situation. The Anglo-Saxons would eventually realize their best interests lay with his anti-Bolshevist crusade. *It had to happen.*

The Allies responded with a new strategic bombing campaign of coordinated and concentrated raids. By early May attacks by American daylight bombers on fuel plants in central and eastern Germany seriously endangered Hitler's entire armament program. The daily output of 5850 metric tons abruptly fell to 4820 tons. "The enemy has struck us at one of our weakest points," Albert Speer reported to Hitler. "If they persist this time, we will soon no longer have any fuel production worth mentioning. Our one hope is that the other side has an air force General Staff as scatterbrained as ours!"

Keitel hastily protested that there was still a huge reserve of fuel but Hitler was more realistic and called a meeting, a few days later, to discuss the problem. Four industrialists agreed that the situation was hopeless if the air raids continued systematically.* At first Hitler replied with the usual argument that they had survived worse crises—with Keitel and Göring nodding in unison—but when the industrialists supported their conclusions with data and comparative figures, Hitler made an abrupt

* In a similar meeting the previous fall, industrialist Paul Pleiger had asserted that there simply was not sufficient coal and coke to expand steel production. "To my boundless surprise," recalled one witness, "Hitler in the course of the conversation quite dryly said, 'Pleiger, if we cannot produce more coal and steel, the war is lost.'"

about-face. He seemed, thought Speer, eager at last "to hear the unpleasant truth"; the Führer, he hoped, had finally realized that this was the beginning of the collapse of German economy.

2

The war of mobility which the Germans had so successfully employed in the early stages of the war was now turned against them. In the First World War the protracted stalemate had enabled German propaganda to argue plausibly almost to the end that the war could still be won. No such assertions were possible amid the military realities of World War II. There could no longer be any question of another German summer offensive. Last year's defeat at Kursk had ended all hopes for success and it was now only a question of how long the Wehrmacht could hold back the resurgent Red Army. Notwithstanding the staggering losses of manpower in the past three years, Russia still had some 300 divisions of over 5,000,000 men in the field, opposing 20 undermanned German divisions totaling 2,000,000 men. The most painful surprise to the Germans was not the astounding reserve strength of the Red Army but its tenacious fighting spirit. During the siege of Stalingrad Hitler had captiously explained the inability of Paulus to take the city with the fact that the Russians fought like "swamp animals." Whatever the designation, the vigor and valor of these *Untermenschen* of the East had proved more than a match for the Teutonic race. So much for the underlying premise of Hitler's *Ostpolitik*. He had no thought of even a token victory in 1944. His concern, in fact, was invasion from the West. "It will decide the issue not only of the year but of the whole war," he told his military advisers one day in early June as he gazed absently out the window. "If we succeed in throwing back the invasion, such an attempt cannot and will not be repeated within a short time. It will mean that our reserves will be set free to use in Italy and the East." Then the latter front could at least be stabilized. But if they could not throw back the Western invaders it meant final defeat. "We cannot win a static war in the West for the additional reason that each step backward means a broadening of the front lines across more of France. With no strategic reserves of any importance it will be impossible to build up sufficient strength along such a line. Therefore," he concluded, "the invader *must* be thrown back on his first attempt." He did not add something he told General Heusinger in private: "If the invasion succeeds, then I must try to bring the war to an end by political means."

Hitler had turned over the task of repelling the West to Rommel, who had already presided over one catastrophe, the loss of North Africa, through no fault of his own. Rommel was convinced that the invasion could best be stopped at the beaches where the enemy was at his weakest.

"The troops are unsure and possibly even seasick," he argued. "They are unfamiliar with the terrain. Heavy weapons are not yet available in sufficient quantity. That is the moment to strike and defeat them." His elderly superior, Gerd von Rundstedt, Commander-in-Chief West, held the opposite view. The decisive battle should be fought far behind the coast. All armor and tactical reserves, therefore, should be well inside France so they could encircle and destroy the oncoming enemy. Hitler settled the dispute by a compromise that pleased neither. He took all armored units from Rommel but placed them much closer to the coast than Rundstedt wanted.

On the morning of June 4 Rommel set out for Germany by car, ostensibly to visit his wife, whose birthday fell on the sixth, but his main purpose was to drive on to Berchtesgaden and persuade Hitler to transfer two additional armored divisions and one mortar brigade to Normandy. "The most urgent problem," he wrote in his diary, "is to win the Führer over by personal conversation." It was an appropriate time for a brief holiday. The Luftwaffe meteorologist in Paris had just reported that no Allied invasion could be expected for two weeks because of stormy conditions.

Across the Channel General Dwight Eisenhower, the Allied commander-in-chief, was faced with his own dilemma. The invasion, Operation Overlord, was scheduled to start the next day but the unfavorable weather reports induced him to postpone the great venture for at least another twenty-four hours. He spent most of the day alone in his cramped house trailer in a woods near Portsmouth, mulling over the pros and cons of risking an attack under bad conditions or waiting until July. More than 200,000 men had already been briefed on the operation and it seemed inevitable that the secret would leak out by that time. That evening a new weather front was reported: there would be relatively good conditions until the morning of June 6, when the weather would deteriorate. Eisenhower polled his commanders. Air Chief Marshal Sir Arthur Tedder feared the cloud cover would hinder his plans but Montgomery's reply was, "I would say go." Eisenhower made the decision: On June 6 the Allies would hit the beaches of Normandy.

June 6 was barely fifteen minutes old, British Double Summer Time, when an eighteen-year-old paratrooper named Murphy dropped into the garden of a schoolmistress in Ste. Mère Église. It was the beginning of D-Day. Within an hour vague and contradictory reports began flooding German Seventh Army command posts. It was 3 A.M., German time, before Rundstedt informed Supreme Headquarters, presently located on the Obersalzberg, that major paratroop and glider landings had been made in Normandy. Three hours later Rundstedt's chief of staff informed Warlimont that this, in all probability, was the invasion. He urged that the four motorized-armored divisions of OKW reserves be sent nearer the landing area.

But Jodl was positive it was merely a diversionary attack. He had been tricked by a secret Allied operation known as Bodyguard: a fake war plan was cleverly leaked to Führer Headquarters indicating the main landings would be farther north near Calais where the Channel was narrowest. In consequence, Jodl refused to wake up Hitler for consultation.

This caused consternation at Rundstedt's headquarters. The elderly field marshal, according to his chief of operations, "was fuming with rage, red in the face, and his anger made his speech unintelligible." Another commander might have telephoned Hitler directly but the aristocratic Rundstedt, who openly referred to his Führer as "that Bohemian corporal," would not stoop to petition. He left the entreaties to his subordinates, who kept pestering OKW with phone calls in an effort to change Jodl's mind.

It was not until 9 A.M. that the Führer was finally wakened. This, in fact, was earlier than usual but he was scheduled to receive Horthy, Tiso and Antonescu—the dictators of Hungary, Slovakia and Romania—at Klessheim Castle. Emerging from his bedroom in dressing gown, Hitler listened placidly to the latest reports before sending for Keitel and Jodl. He was not so calm by the time they arrived. "Well, is it or isn't it the invasion?" he shouted, then spun on his heel and left. But before long his mood abruptly changed. He clapped people on the back with unaccustomed familiarity as if revitalized by at last coming to grips with the West. "Now, we can give them a nice little packet!" he exclaimed with a slap on his own thigh. He was jubilant throughout the hourlong scenic auto trip to Klessheim. "I can hold the Russians as long as I like," he told his companions and then boasted how he would destroy the Anglo-Saxon powers in front of the Atlantic Wall.

Events in the West dominated the midday situation conference, which was held just before the meeting with the three dictators. As Hitler entered the conference room his military advisers, anxiously clustered around maps and charts, turned with some excitement and apprehension. To their amazement he strode in confidently, face beaming. In exceptionally broad Austrian he said, "So, we're off!" and began chuckling in a carefree manner. What he had wanted all the time had finally come true, he told them. "I am face to face with my real enemies!"

In Berlin DNB, on the authority of a minor official, announced that the invasion had begun but apparently Goebbels himself did not take it too seriously. The most important event of the day, according to Press Officer Wilfred von Oven's diary, was a party at which Goebbels played a piano duet with a countess: "Sounds off on culture at length then disappears with countess behind bar at piano," he recorded. "She sings chansons. Everybody drunk."

At 4 P.M. Hitler was back at the Berghof in time for a late lunch with Eva and a number of party dignitaries and their wives. The highlight of the meal was his comment on vegetarianism: "The elephant is the strongest animal; he also cannot stand meat." The party adjourned as usual to the tea house where the Führer treated himself to lime-blossom tea. This was followed by an hour's nap and another military conference at 11 P.M. He doubted, he said, that this was the real invasion. It was only a feint to trick him into deploying his forces to the wrong place. The main invasion would surely come at Calais since it was the shortest route across the Channel. He could not be shaken from the lie so assiduously planted by Bodyguard—perhaps because that was the route in reverse he had selected when he was planning to invade England.

By midnight the Allies had broken into Hitler's western *Festung* on a front of thirty miles. The Germans had been completely taken by surprise, their air force and navy rendered powerless and their coast defenses shattered. The enemy had achieved a great victory at the cost of fewer than 2500 lives but there was still time to throw them back into the Channel— if the right decisions were made without delay.

3

On June 3 Goebbels had given up smoking. Three days later he got drunk. On the seventh he assured his press officer that it was a genuine invasion and that same noon astonished a select audience of high officials and industrialists by remarking, according to the diary of former Ambassador von Hassell, "that one day the 'Great Powers' would certainly sit down again at the same table and 'shake hands,' and ask one another: 'Now, how did all this come about?' The last word in wisdom!" Goebbels was merely mouthing the views of his master but on the tenth he did his best to persuade Hitler that Germany's only hope was "bloody rejection of the invasion." Then the West would eagerly seek an understanding.

Hitler was still so convinced that the Normandy landing was a trick that he had not yet taken resolute action against this bridgehead, and by refusing to give his field commanders a free hand he had deprived them of their last chance to seize the initiative. The battle was already lost. By now it was obvious that the Allies had won complete air supremacy over France, and Hitler turned to Göring, whom he had praised a few days earlier. He sarcastically asked whether it was true that his vaunted Luftwaffe had taken out a "knock-for-knock" insurance policy with the West.

In desperation the Führer inaugurated the V-1 rocket campaign against London on June 12, two days ahead of schedule. The harassed catapult crews could launch only ten flying bombs. Four crashed immediately, two disappeared, and the others destroyed a single railway bridge.

After this fiasco Göring hastily reminded Hitler that this was Milch's program, not his, but when the second launching of 244 rockets two days later set disastrous fires in London the Reichsmarschall was quick to claim the credit.

All this had no effect on the situation in Normandy. Within ten days the Allies had managed to land almost a million men and 500,000 tons of matériel. The situation was so desperate that on June 17 Hitler motored west to a village north of Soissons. Here, for the first time since D-Day, he met Rundstedt and Rommel. "He looked pale and sleepless," recalled General Hans Speidel, "playing nervously with his glasses and an array of colored pencils which he held between his fingers . . . then in a loud voice he spoke bitterly of his displeasure at the success of the Allied landings, for which he tried to hold the field commanders responsible."

It was Rommel, not Rundstedt, who carried the burden of rebuttal. He pointed out, "with merciless frankness," that the struggle was hopeless against the Allies' overwhelming superiority in the air, at sea and on land. There was but one chance: to abandon the suicidal policy of holding onto every meter of ground and abruptly withdraw German forces so that all armored forces could be reorganized for a decisive battle to be fought outside the range of the withering enemy naval fire. Hitler answered by assuring his commanders that his new rocket bombs "would make the British willing to make peace." This was a sore subject to Rundstedt and Rommel, whose request to use these bombs against English south coast ports supplying the invasion had been declined by Hitler on the grounds that all rockets must be concentrated on a political target. The two field marshals confined themselves to criticism of the Luftwaffe: how could one win on the ground without a minimum of help from the air? Hitler's answer was that "masses of jet fighters" would soon sweep the skies clear of American and British planes. He neglected to explain that, against the vigorous opposition of Milch, the jet plane in production was a hybrid fighter-bomber which was efficient at neither task.

The distant drone of approaching enemy planes forced adjournment to an elaborate underground concrete bunker. The change of venue encouraged Rommel to become even more forceful. The West, he said, would inevitably smash through the Normandy front and break into the homeland. Hitler listened with compressed lips as Rommel further predicted that the eastern front would also collapse and the Reich would become politically isolated. He urgently requested, therefore, that the war be brought to an end. "Don't you worry about the future course of the war," Hitler interrupted sharply. "Look to your own invasion front."

During a break for a one-dish lunch, two SS men standing guard behind the Führer's chair tested his plate of rice and vegetables before he would take a bite. It was, concluded Speidel, visible proof of his distrust of the military. Moments after the meeting ended a V-1 bound for London erratically reversed itself and exploded on top of their bunker. Uninjured, Hitler set off at once for his refuge on the Obersalzberg, arriving in a bad temper to announce: "Rommel has lost his nerve; he's become a pessimist. In these times only optimists can achieve anything."

Within two days he received a despairing phone call from another pessimist. Rundstedt explained that the Americans had broken through and were pushing across the Cotentin Peninsula. Unless German forces hastily pulled out of Cherbourg they would be cut off. "The fortress of Cherbourg is to be held at all cost," replied the Führer, then gave sensible permission for the defenders to withdraw at the last possible moment to avoid capture.

His compromise did not mean that Hitler was weakening in his own resolve, despite disheartening news from his one strong ally. The Japanese had just been dealt a crushing blow in the Battle of the Philippine Sea, losing 3 heavy cruisers and 475 planes. Hitler's nerves remained steady in the face of defeat on all sides, exhibiting composure that amazed his family circle. Nor was it true that he no longer listened to any voice of criticism. During the late evening conference of June 23 General Dietl, incensed at the Führer's derisive comments about the Finns surrendering to Russia, smashed a fist on the table. "Mein Führer, now I must talk to you like a Bavarian!" he exclaimed in dialect and accused Hitler of speaking unjustly. To everyone's amazement, Hitler told Dietl he was absolutely correct, bade him a warm farewell, then turned to the others and said, "Gentlemen, I wish all my generals were like that."

He had shown similar respect for Admiral Dönitz from the first day of his appointment as navy chief when he, with equal frankness, had vigorously opposed a Hitler proposal. From that moment Hitler treated him with marked civility and heard him out with unlimited confidence. During this season of anxiety the Führer would even take criticism from his youngest secretary. One day while watching him examine photographs of air raids Traudl Junge could not help saying that pictures could never portray the true misery of reality. He should go out just once and see the people "warm their hands on the charred rafters as all their possessions go up in smoke." Hitler was not at all angry. "I know how it is," he said with a sigh. "But I'm going to change everything. We have built new planes and soon this whole nightmare will come to an end!"

One group he stubbornly refused to hear out were his field commanders in Normandy and as a result the situation there was beyond repair. On June 26 Cherbourg fell to American troops. Largely because of Hitler's abiding fear of a main invasion at Calais and Ultra intercepts, which were often read in London within minutes of their origin, Germany had no hope of regaining the initiative. With her armies now dedicated to a dreary, enervating period of purely passive resistance, the Third Reich faced catastrophe.

In the coffee room of the Hotel Platterhof, just above the Berghof, a disconcerted, somewhat absent-minded Führer was assuring a hundred representatives of the armaments industry of the inviolability of private property and the retention of free enterprise. Near the close of his uneasy speech, Hitler promised to show his gratitude to businessmen "again and again" once peace returned but there was so little applause that he concluded with a threat: "There is no doubt that if we were to lose this war, German private business would not survive." If defeat came, he said derisively, his listeners would not have to worry about shifting to a peacetime economy. "Then all anyone will have to think about is how he himself will accomplish his shift from this world to the hereafter. Whether he wants to take care of it himself, or let himself be hanged, or whether he prefers to starve or to labor in Siberia—these are some of the questions which the individual will have to face."

Three days later Hitler summoned Rundstedt and Rommel to the Berghof. He refused to consider the latter's suggestion that he fight a rearguard action back to the Seine so that the armies in southern France could be withdrawn and help create a new line along the river all the way to Switzerland. Instead he spoke optimistically of another offensive. There would be no general withdrawals, nor even tactical adjustments of the line.

The war would be won by new miracle weapons, he said, in a monologue that struck Rundstedt's chief of staff as one "lost in fantastic digressions." The two field marshals, committed to a futile policy of aggressive and obstinate defense, left the meeting disgruntled. Keitel shared their dejection and admitted resignedly to Rommel, "I, too, know there is nothing to be done."

Within two days Hitler's counterattack failed miserably and inspired Rundstedt to warn Keitel that this was the writing on the wall. "Then what shall we do?" asked Keitel. "What shall we do?" "Make peace, you fools!" exploded Rundstedt. "What else can you do?" Keitel reported this to Hitler, who chanced to be talking to Field Marshal Günther von Kluge. On the spur of the moment he put Kluge in charge of the western front and wrote Rundstedt a polite and proper letter of dismissal.

4

"Nothing works against the success of a conspiracy so much as the wish to make it wholly secure and certain to succeed. Such an attempt requires many men, much time and very favorable conditions. And all these in turn heighten the risk of being discovered You see, therefore, how dangerous conspiracies are!"

FRANCESCO GUICCIARDINI
Ricordi (1528–30)

The men who had already tried in vain to destroy Hitler's plane with brandy bottles filled with explosives or to blow him up with bombs concealed in an overcoat were not at all deterred by failure. They made four more attempts between September 1943 and February 11, 1944. First a general, Helmuth Stieff by name, attempted to plant a time bomb to go off during a noon conference at Wolfsschanze but lost his nerve at the last moment. A month later an infantry captain, Bussche, agreed to blow up himself and Hitler while demonstrating a new army coat, but fate in the form of an enemy aerial bomb intervened. The day before the demonstration the model coats were destroyed in a British air raid and Bussche was returned to the front.

The day after Christmas, 1944, another young front-line officer entered the noon conference with a briefcase containing a bomb. For some reason the meeting was canceled at the last moment. A few weeks later another "overcoat" attempt was made. This time the volunteer model was Ewald Heinrich von Kleist, son of one of the original conspirators. Again the RAF saved Hitler, an air raid just before the demonstration forcing its cancellation.

This last failure was followed a fortnight later by a crippling blow to the Resistance. Hitler ordered Himmler to amalgamate the Abwehr and the SD. This meant the virtual destruction of the heart of the conspiracy. General Oster had already been dismissed on suspicion. Although he was at liberty he was too closely watched to be of use. It seemed as though fate indeed was protecting Hitler and a sense of hopelessness permeated the ranks of the conspirators. This might have been the end of their secret war against Hitler but for the inspiration of a new leader, Count Claus Schenk von Stauffenberg, a staff officer with the rank of lieutenant colonel. A great-grandson of Gneisenau, a military hero in the war of liberation against Napoleon, Stauffenberg had abandoned plans to become an architect and entered the Reichswehr in 1926. Like so many other German officers, he applauded Hitler's introduction of conscription, approved the Anschluss with Austria as well as the occupation of Czechoslovakia, and was caught up in the glory of victory in Holland and France. It was Barbarossa that destroyed his illusions. He heartily approved Rosenberg's attempt to free the non-Russian peoples of the Soviet Union and, after this policy was superseded by oppression and murder, he told a fellow officer that the only solution for Germany now was to kill the Führer. By chance he met resistance leaders who had no trouble enlisting him in their cause. His role, however, seemed short-lived; his car ran over a mine and he lost an eye, his right hand and two fingers of the other hand. Almost any other man would have retired, but Stauffenberg was convinced that he alone could assassinate Hitler and was back on duty late in 1943. It was he who had brought the bomb in the briefcase to the Führer conference the day after Christmas. The failure spurred him to a similar but more ambitious plan. This time assassination would be followed by a well-planned military take-over in Berlin, Paris and Vienna.

His new position as chief of staff to the commander of the General Army Office in Berlin made it possible for him to rebuild the weakened ranks of the conspiracy. He seized the reins from the tired, older leaders and, by the dynamism of his personality, got definite commitments from a powerful group in the Wehrmacht: his own chief, the first quarter-master general of the army, the chief of signals at OKW, the general whose troops would take over Berlin after the assassination, and other key officers of middle rank.

As yet, however, not a single field marshal wholeheartedly supported the plot. Kluge was a dubious factor and Manstein refused to commit himself prematurely since he felt "any such coup d'état would collapse the eastern front." The most promising candidate was Rommel but even he had reservations. "I believe it is my duty to come to the rescue of Germany," he said—but opposed assassination. It would only make Hitler a martyr. The Führer should be arrested by the army and brought before a German court to answer for his crimes.

Rommel was brought deeper into the plot during the spring of 1944 by his new chief of staff, Lieutenant General Dr. Hans Speidel, a soldier-philosopher who had received his doctorate in philosophy summa cum laude from the University of Tübingen. Speidel persuaded Rommel to meet secretly with General Karl Stülpnagel, military governor of France, in a country home near Paris. Here the two men, with the help of their energetic chiefs of staff, worked out a plan to end war in the West by an armistice. All German troops would retire into Germany and the Allies would cease bombing the homeland. Hitler would be arrested, with the re-sistance forces temporarily taking over the country. In the meantime the war in the East would continue, the assumption being that American and British troops would join the crusade against Bolshevism. Rommel was now so enthusiastic, he tried to involve Rundstedt in the plot but, while approving it, he refused to be personally involved. "You are young," Rundstedt said. "You know and love the people. *You* do it."

Stauffenberg and his group were not too pleased with the entrance of Rommel into the conspiracy, for they considered him a Nazi who was only deserting Hitler because the war was lost. They also disapproved of the plan to continue fighting Russia, and felt it was unrealistic to expect the West would make a separate peace. Further, the Stauffenberg circle was dedicated to assassination rather than arrest and by the first of June 1944 they felt it had to be done before the Allied invasion. Once enemy forces overran the homeland there would be no possibility for any decent kind of peace. By now they had a definite scenario for a coup d'état based, ironi-cally, on a measure approved by the Führer himself. The official operation was entitled Walküre and was Hitler's plan to put down any unrest among the millions of war and foreign slave workers employed in Germany. It called for a proclamation of a state of emergency and instant mobilization of adequate forces to quell any uprising. Stauffenberg's scheme was to use the Walküre alert as the signal to start their own coup throughout the Reich and on every battle front. Hitler had specified that the orders to issue the Walküre alert be issued by the commander of the Reserve Army, General Friedrich Fromm—who was flirting halfheartedly with the idea of joining the Resistance.

D-Day caused consternation among the conspirators. The older ones argued that even a successful coup would not save Germany from enemy occupation. It was best to rely on the West to treat Germany decently and prevent Russia from ravaging the homeland. But Stauffenberg was resolved to make one final assassination attempt and chance almost immediately took a hand. He was promoted to full colonel and made Fromm's chief of staff. Now the coup did not depend on such a dubious factor. Stauffenberg himself could issue orders directly to the Reserve Army and thus seize Berlin. The new post also gave him frequent access to the Führer. He made plans to act early in July: he would report to the Führer at the daily conference, plant a time bomb which would blow up Göring and Himmler as well as the Führer, then fly back to Berlin and personally direct the military take-over of the capital.

His confederates at General Staff headquarters were inspired by the assured way he organized the complicated plan. "It was a pleasure," recalled one young lieutenant, Urban Thiersch, a sculptor, "to watch him conduct the telephone conversations—giving brief and definite orders, behaving with natural courtesy toward important people, and always in command of the situation."

Stauffenberg's chance came at last on July 11 when Hitler summoned him to report on replacements. He arrived at the Berghof with a briefcase carrying official papers and an English bomb but, to his dismay, Himmler was not in the conference room. He excused himself to phone the huge General Staff building on the Bendlerstrasse near Berlin's Tiergarten. "Shouldn't we do it anyhow?" he asked the chief of the General Army Office, General Olbricht. The bomb could still kill both Hitler and Göring. Olbricht advised him to wait until he could kill all three at once.

The opportunity came in four days; Stauffenberg was again ordered to see Hitler, who had moved his headquarters to Wolfsschanze. He arrived with bomb in briefcase and this time the conspirators were so sure of success that General Olbricht issued the orders for Operation Walküre at 11 A.M., two hours before the scheduled conference. This would give the troops of the Reserve Army and the tanks from the nearby Panzer school time to move into the capital by early afternoon.

At exactly 1:10 P.M. the conference began. Stauffenberg briefly reported to the Führer, then left the room to telephone the Bendlerstrasse that Hitler was in the room and he was going back to plant the bomb. But on his return he discovered that Hitler had left for some reason and would not be back. It took Stauffenberg another quarter of an hour to excuse himself again and warn Berlin. By this time it was 1:30 P.M. and troops were already converging on Berlin. Olbricht hurriedly canceled the Walküre alarm and the units on march were returned to their barracks as inconspicuously as possible.

Some of the conspirators were discouraged and shaken by this latest fiasco but not Stauffenberg. He met with younger colleagues at his home in Wannsee and they heard an encouraging report from a cousin of Stauffenberg, who was their liaison with the Rommel-Speidel group in France. An imminent Allied breakthrough was expected, he said, and Rommel was determined to support the conspiracy no matter what Rundstedt's replacement, Marshal von Kluge, did. But again fate intervened on behalf of Hitler. The very next day Rommel was badly injured when his car was strafed by Allied planes.

The staff returning to the Wolfsschanze could hardly recognize the area. In place of small, low bunkers were colossal concrete and iron structures, their roofs cleverly camouflaged by transplanted grass and trees. It was so hot that Hitler spent most of his time in the new bunkers, which were much cooler than the wooden barracks. "He was in a bad mood," recalled Traudl Junge, "and complained about sleeplessness and headache." The adjutants did their best to divert him with amusing guests. Hoffmann, who drank more than ever, had become a bore but Professor Giesler, the architect, never failed to bring a smile with his clever imitations. Hitler may have been short-tempered during these sultry days, but he gave the appearance of optimism. He assured Goebbels (who had resumed smoking and was resorting to sleeping pills) that the pendulum of history was about to swing back in favor of Germany.

5

On the afternoon of July 18 Stauffenberg received a summons from Wolfsschanze to report in two days. He was to brief Hitler on replacements that might be thrown into the battle in the East, where the central front was in peril of imminent collapse following recent defeats on both flanks. Stauffenberg spent the nineteenth at the Bendlerstrasse making lastminute preparations and that afternoon presided over a final conference of conspirators. The signals for the following day were hastly arranged; it was agreed that most of the messages would be passed orally in a prearranged sequence. Code words would be used on telephone and teleprinter and would be reserved for important matters since the entire system of communications was tapped by the Gestapo.

The conspirators knew this since their number included several Gestapo officials, including the SS general who had taken over the Gestapo main office in Berlin. There was, in fact, considerable anti-Hitler feeling throughout the SS. General Felix Steiner, for instance, had already evolved a vague plan of his own to kidnap the Führer, then "declare him mentally deranged," and with other Waffen SS commanders had recently assured Rommel of support in any revolt against Hitler. The hierarchy of the SD itself was infected with rebellion. Secretly the head of the Foreign Intelligence Service, Schellenberg, was as eager as the army conspirators to get rid of Hitler in the interest of German survival. In late 1942 he had inveigled Himmler into endorsing a secret plan to bring about a separate peace with the West at the price, if need be, of betraying Hitler. With Himmler's approval Carl Langbehn, a civilian member of the Resistance, met with British and American representatives in Stockholm to explore the chances of peace negotiations; then journeyed to Bern so he could personally confer with the German-born assistant of Allen Dulles, the OSS representative in Switzerland. At this point everything went wrong. The Gestapo chanced to intercept and decode a radio message which revealed that "Himmler's lawyer" had arrived in Switzerland to talk peace, and sent it directly to Hitler. Face to face with the Führer, Himmler swore eternal loyalty—and complete innocence. Hitler chose to believe him, probably because his services were so vital. The Reichsführer, on his part, arrested Langbehn, sent him to a concentration camp and promptly broke off all relations with members of the Resistance lest his master investigate further. Schellenberg, on the other hand, continued to plot, becoming involved with American military men in Spain, in an elaborate operation worthy of a spy novel to kidnap Hitler and turn him over to the Allies.

Incredibly, neither Schellenberg nor Himmler was aware on July 19 that the underground army plot was about to materialize. They knew about the resistance efforts of the conservative officials, retired officers, right-wing Christian intellectuals and socialist politicians but never even suspected Stauffenberg and his circle of younger officers. Several months earlier Schellenberg had consulted Wilhelm Wulff, one of the astrologers on the SS payroll, about a possible removal of Hitler. Wulff said that a mere deposition from office would not change the course of events. "Far too much has happened for that. I have been studying Hitler's horoscope for twenty years now. I have a pretty clear idea of what is ultimately in store for him. He will probably die under the hand of an assassin, certainly in 'Neptunian'—that is enigmatic—circumstances, in which a woman will play a part. The world will probably never know the precise details of his death, for in Hitler's horoscope Neptune has long been in bad aspect to other planets. Moreover, Neptune is extremely strong in his horoscope, and it was always to be expected that his great military projects would have a dubious outcome."

At the Bendlerstrasse late on the afternoon of the nineteenth Stauffenberg completed arrangements for the next day's operation. He instructed his driver, who knew nothing at all about the plot, to collect a briefcase from a certain colonel in Potsdam. It contained, Stauffenberg explained, two very important and confidential packages and was not to be left out of sight. As instructed, the chauffeur kept the case next to his bed that night. It held two bombs.

During evening tea at Wolfsschanze, Hitler was so nervous and uneasy that Fräulein Schröder asked why he was so preoccupied. "I hope nothing is going to happen to me," he replied cryptically. After an awkward silence, he said, "It would be too much if something troublesome happened now. I cannot allow myself to fall ill, since there is no one who can replace me in the difficult situation Germany finds herself in."

July 20, 1944

Shortly after 6 A.M. Stauffenberg was driven from his home to the city. Here he was joined by his adjutant, a lieutenant. At Rangsdorf airfield they met General Stieff and all boarded a plane provided by the quartermaster general. It touched down at the air base near Rastenburg at 10:15 A.M. The pilot was instructed to stand by until noon to take the passengers back to Berlin.

After half an hour's drive through woods, the three conspirators were passed through the first gate of Führer Headquarters. They proceeded through minefields and a ring of fortifications for almost two miles to a second gate. This opened into a large compound surrounded by electrified barbed wire. After another mile they reached the officers' checkpoint. As usual their passes were examined but not their briefcases. In two hundred yards they arrived at a third enclosure. This was Security Ring A, where Hitler and his staff lived and worked. This innermost compound, surrounded by a barbed-wire fence, was constantly patrolled by SS guards and Secret Service personnel. To enter, a field marshal himself needed a special pass issued by Himmler's chief of security, but again the shiny briefcase containing the bombs was not inspected.

While his adjutant took charge of this case, Stauffenberg carried another containing official papers. He proceeded nonchalantly to a mess hall where he had a leisurely breakfast with the camp commander's adjutant. Outwardly unperturbed and casual in bearing, he later sought out General Fellgiebel, OKW chief of signals, the key to success once the bomb exploded. It was his task to inform the Berlin conspirators that it was time to act, then to isolate Wolfsschanze by cutting all telephone, telegraph and radio communications.

Assured that Fellgiebel was ready to do his part, Stauffenberg chatted briefly with another OKW officer and at noon strolled over to the office of Keitel. The field marshal greeted him with slightly disconcerting news: since Mussolini was due to arrive that afternoon, the midday situation conference would start half an hour earlier—in just thirty minutes. Keitel urged Stauffenberg to keep his report brief since the Führer wanted to leave as soon as possible. Keitel kept glancing impatiently at the clock and, just before 12:30 P.M., said it was time to walk over to the conference barracks. In the hallway Stauffenberg approached Keitel's adjutant, Ernst John von Freyend, and asked where he could clean up. He was directed to a nearby lavatory. His own adjutant was waiting here with the brown briefcase. It was not a suitable place to arm the bombs so they returned to the hall and asked Freyend where the colonel could change his shirt. Freyend took them to his own bedroom and left them alone. Stauffenberg grasped a pair of tongs in the three fingers of his only hand and began shoving in the fuse of one bomb. This crushed a glass capsule containing acid which would eat through a thin wire within fifteen minutes and set off the bomb. His adjutant was entrusted with the second "back-up" bomb.

No sooner was the armed bomb carefully packed in the brown brief-case than a sergeant entered to hurry them up and from the hall Freyend shouted, 'Come on, Stauffenberg! The Chief is waiting." As Stauffenberg left the room Freyend suggested he carry the brown briefcase tucked under the colonel's one good arm. Stauffenberg declined the offer and they set out on the short walk along a path to the conference barracks. The two talked casually as they passed through the checkpoint to the Security Ring. Upon nearing their destination, Freyend once more offered to relieve Stauffenberg of his burden and this time he accepted with a request: "Could you place me as closely as possible to the Führer so I can understand everything?" His hearing was impaired.

Keitel was waiting impatiently at the doorway. The conference was already under way. He led the way down the central corridor of the building past the telephone room and into the conference room through a double-winged door. There were ten or so windows and all were open against the sultry midday heat. The conferees gathered around a long, narrow oak map table, notable for its thick top and two massive supports. Only Hitler was sitting, his back to the door, at the middle of the table. A pair of spectacles rested on the map. He toyed with a magnifying glass as General Adolf Heusinger, standing to his immediate right, read out a glum report on the eastern front. Hitler looked at the newcomers, acknowledged their salutes. Stauffenberg moved to the other side of Heusinger, then casually shoved the brown briefcase under the table as close to Hitler as possible. The case leaned against the inside of the heavy oaken support

only six feet from the Führer. It was twelve thirty-seven and in five minutes the bomb would explode. The others were so engrossed by Heusinger's
tale of doom that Stauffenberg managed to sidle out of the room without
being noticed. He hurried down the long corridor and out of the building.

Heusinger was also on the periphery of the anti-Hitler conspiracy but
knew none of the details of the plot. When he saw Stauffenberg enter it
hadn't occurred to him that anything was awry since the conspirators had
promised to warn him when the next assassination attempt would take
place. But he happened to glance down just as Stauffenberg shoved the
brown briefcase under the table and thought fleetingly: "Something might
happen!" But under Hitler's absorbed attention, Heusinger's suspicion
evaporated almost as soon as it was aroused. His aide leaned over the conference table to get a better look at the map but was impeded by the
brown briefcase. He couldn't budge it with his foot so leaned down and
transferred it to the *outside* of the heavy table support. It was a trivial
move which would alter the course of history.

Admiral von Puttkamer had moved to a window to get some air and
was perched on the sill debating whether he should quietly leave and
change to his best trousers for the Mussolini visit. It was twelve forty-one.
The Führer was intently leaning far over the table to check the map.
Heusinger was saying, "Unless at long last the army group is withdrawn
from Peipus, a catastrophe . . ."

At exactly 12:42 P.M. his words were obliterated by a deafening roar.
Flames shot up and a hail of glass splinters, timber and plaster rained
down. Smoke erupted in the room. Puttkamer had felt a strange jerk a
split second before the explosion. Falling down, he saw the heater under
the window and thought, "My God, it exploded!" then realized this was
nonsense; it was summer. Maybe it was a plot by the foreign laborers who
were working on the construction. Dazed as he was, he realized the best
thing was to remain on the floor. Then he heard someone shout, "Fire!"
and scrambled for the door. It was lying flat on the floor and he leaped
over it. Suddenly he wondered where everyone else was and turned to
locate the Führer. Just then Hitler, trousers in tatters, face blackened by
soot, came toward him with Keitel. Both men were covered with dust and
wood fiber. They passed him as if sleepwalking and he realized he could
hardly breathe the acid air. He followed Hitler and Keitel down the long
corridor. Outside a knee gave way and he collapsed on the ground. He
gulped air greedily and saw Hitler and Keitel heading toward the Führer
bunker, followed by some third person.

SS Adjutant Günsche didn't even hear the explosion. His eardrums
had burst. His forehead bled, his eyebrows were burned off. The room was
black with smoke; the floor had buckled up at least three feet. "Where is
the Führer?" he wondered. With the instinct of a soldier, he scrambled

out a shattered window and hurried to the other side of the building just as Keitel and Hitler were emerging. The Führer's trousers were in tatters, his hair tousled, but there was no blood in sight. *"Was ist los?"* asked Hitler as Günsche helped guide him down the path. A bomb from a Russian plane?

Upon leaving the conference room, Stauffenberg had hurried to the OKW Signals Office in Bunker 88. He and General Fellgiebel stood outside waiting for the bomb to explode. They were talking as unconcernedly as possible when the headquarters signal officer reported that Stauffenberg's car was ready, then reminded him that the headquarters commandant was expecting him for lunch. Stauffenberg confirmed the invitation but said he would first have to return to the conference. Just then came an explosion.

"What's happening?" exclaimed Fellgiebel and the signals officer nonchalantly explained that some animal must have set off another land mine. Stauffenberg now contradicted himself. He said he was *not* going back to the conference but would drive directly to the commandant's for lunch. He bade Fellgiebel a knowing farewell and set off with his adjutant in the car. Moments later their driver, wondering why Stauffenberg wore neither hat nor belt, pulled to a stop at the first checkpoint. The guard there had closed the gates upon hearing the explosion and refused to open them. Without a word, Stauffenberg hurried to the guard room and asked the lieutenant on duty, an acquaintance, for use of the telephone. He dialed, said a few quiet words, replaced the receiver and said calmly, "Lieutenant, I am allowed to pass." The barrier was opened without question and at 12:44 P.M. the Stauffenberg party was through the gate.

Ninety seconds later an alarm was sounded and Stauffenberg could not talk his way through the next barrier. A sergeant major of the guard battalion refused flatly to let any car pass. Once more Stauffenberg used the phone, this time calling the camp commandant's aide. "Colonel Count von Stauffenberg speaking," he said, "from outer Checkpoint South. Captain, you'll remember we had breakfast together this morning. Because of the explosion the guard refused to let me pass. I'm in a hurry." Then he told a lie. "Colonel General Fromm is waiting for me at the airfield." He hastily hung up. "You heard, Sergeant Major, I'm allowed through." But the sergeant major could not be bluffed. He telephoned for confirmation and, to Stauffenberg's relief, got it.

It was almost 1 P.M. by the time Stauffenberg and his adjutant drove up to their Heinkel 111. Moments later they were in the air. Ahead lay a three-hour flight. There was nothing to do but worry since the plane's radio did not have the range to hear any announcements from Berlin. Had Fellgiebel gotten the word through to the conspirators in the Bendlerstrasse? If so, would they have the resolve to seize the capital and send out the prepared messages to the military commanders on the western front?

Hitler would probably have been killed had not the brown briefcase been shifted to the outer side of the table support. It was also fortunate for the Führer that the door behind him led to a long narrow hallway through which the main force of the explosion escaped. Again, luck, incredible luck, had saved Adolf Hitler.

Doctors and rescue workers were in action minutes after the explosion. Ambulances took the seriously wounded to the field hospital at Rastenburg. Dr. Hanskarl von Hasselbach, the Führer's personal physician, was the first to treat him. He bandaged Hitler's wounds, then put his right arm—the elbow was rather badly sprained—in a sling. "Now I have those fellows!" he exclaimed with more glee than anger. "Now I can take steps!"

Dr. Morell arrived, examined Hitler's heart and administered an injection. The patient was in a state of ecstasy, repeating over and over, "Think of it. Nothing has happened to me. Just think of it." To Morell's amazement his pulse was normal. The three secretaries rushed in to see with their own eyes that the Führer still lived. Traudl Junge almost burst into laughter at the sight of his hair, which stood on end like a porcupine's. He greeted them with his left hand. "Well, my ladies," he said with a smile, "once again everything turned out well for me. More proof that Fate has selected me for my mission. Otherwise I wouldn't be alive." He was talkative, blaming the plot on a "coward," undoubtedly one of the construction workers. "I don't believe *in any other possibility*," he emphasized, turning to Bormann for confirmation. As usual Bormann nodded.

The next to arrive with congratulations was Himmler. He too thought laborers had built the bomb into the barracks. It took an amateur to set the trail straight. Valet Linge went to the conference barracks and learned from the sergeant in charge of the telephone room that Stauffenberg had been expecting an urgent call from Berlin. Then someone recalled that the colonel had left a briefcase under the table. A telephone call to the airstrip revealed that Stauffenberg had left hastily for Berlin a little after 1 P.M. Hitler now had no doubts that Stauffenberg alone was responsible. He ordered his arrest.

This order never was transmitted to Berlin because of a curious set of circumstances. Moments after the explosion one of Hitler's adjutants ordered the headquarters signals officer Colonel Sander, to cut all telephone and teleprinter communications. He did so, then told Chief Signals Officer Fellgiebel what he had done. Fellgiebel, whose assignment as a conspirator was to isolate Führer Headquarters, solemnly agreed that proper action had been taken by Sander but upon discovering, moments later, that Hitler was not dead, the general called his own office. "Something frightful has happened," he told his chief of staff. "The Führer is *alive.* Block *everything!*" The chief of staff understood the odd message, for he too was a conspirator. Within minutes the major switch centers at *both* Führer and army headquarters went dead.

This communication blackout gave the conspirators in Berlin time to seize the capital, but they failed to act since confusion was the order of the day at the Bendlerstrasse. The plotters, uncertain whether Hitler had been killed or not, were reluctant to activate Operation Walküre. The information from Wolfsschanze was too vague to risk a repetition of the false alarm of July 15.

And so everyone stood about nervously at the general staff building, waiting for Stauffenberg, who was still half an hour's flight away. The two titular leaders of the conspiracy, General Beck and Field Marshal von Witzleben, should have been issuing the prepared proclamation and commands. They should have been broadcasting to the nation that the end of Hitler's tyranny had come at last. But neither man had yet arrived at the Bendlerstrasse.

Perhaps it was the weather. The sky was murky, the air heavy. One conspirator noted glumly that it was no weather for a revolution but someone pointed out that the French had stormed the Bastille on an equally oppressive day in July. Precious time passed as the conspirators waited for further word from Fellgiebel at Wolfsschanze. None came.

Hitler refused to rest before the midday meal. He insisted on taking a walk all by himself and made a point of chatting with the construction workers he had first suspected. Watching from a distance, his SS adjutant guessed he wanted to show that he was still alive and let everyone know he no longer thought the workers were involved. At lunch Fräulein Schröder was surprised to find his countenance youthful and calm even under the dazzling light of bare electric bulbs in the spartan dining room. Without prompting he told in detail what had happened. "I had incredible luck," he said and explained how he had been protected by the heavy table support. He proudly exhibited his shredded trousers. If the explosion had occurred in the large conference room of the bunker and not in a wooden barracks, he was sure all would have been killed. "A curious thing. For some time I had a presentiment that something extraordinary was going to happen."

After the meal he was driven to the small railroad platform adjoining the Wolfsschanze. The sky was overcast and the few scattered raindrops failed to bring any relief to the sultry afternoon. He paced the platform, cap pulled down over face, black cape swirling behind him, until Mussolini's train pulled in. His guest seemed a ghost of himself; he had managed to form a new Fascist regime, but in so doing he had been forced by Hitler to execute a number of "traitors," including his own son-in-law, Ciano. The Führer was thinking only of the events of the day. "Duce," he said excitedly, extending his left hand, "a few hours ago I experienced the greatest piece of good fortune I have ever known!" He insisted on taking his guest immediately to the scene of the crime. On the three-minute drive Hitler told him what had happened "almost in a monotone as though he had no part in it."

The two men silently surveyed the wrecked conference room. As Mussolini took a chair Hitler seated himself on a box and, with the expertise of a guide at the ruins of Rome, explained exactly what had happened. Mussolini's eyes rolled in wonderment. Then Hitler displayed his tattered trousers and rather lightheartedly remarked he was saddened by the damage to a new pair of pants. Mussolini forced a laugh. Hitler then showed the back of his head where the hair was singed.

Mussolini was horrified. How could such a thing happen at Führer Headquarters? Hitler was exhilarated. He told again how other conferces were badly injured and one was blown out of the window. "Look at my uniform! Look at my burns!" He told of his other narrow escapes from assassination attempts. "What happened here today is the climax!" he exclaimed. This last miraculous escape from death was surely a sign that the great cause he served would survive its present peril. Infected by such enthusiasm, Mussolini brightened. "Our position is bad," he said, "one might almost say desperate, but what has happened here today gives me new courage."

They walked out of the wreckage down the path to resume discussion at tea. On the way Hitler walked over to a wire fence and once more began talking with the workers. He told them his first suspicions were unfounded and his investigators had found the real culprit. At the tea house his mood abruptly changed. He was restless, distracted, and—communications having been partially reopened—his conversation with Il Duce was frequently interrupted by telephone calls from generals who wanted to know if the report of his death was true. Hitler lapsed into moody suspicious silence. He sat staring ahead, sucking brightly colored pills, ignoring an angry argument among Göring, Keitel and Ribbentrop, each claiming the other's mistakes had led to Germany's desperate situation. The wrangle took a new twist once Admiral Dönitz, just arrived from his command post north of Berlin, accused the army of treason. When Göring chorused agreement, Dönitz turned his wrath on the miserable performance of the Luftwaffe. Ribbentrop chimed in but the Reichsmarschall raised his baton as if to thrash him. "Shut up, Ribbentrop, you champagne salesman!" "I'm still Foreign Minister," he retorted, "and my name is *von* Ribbentrop!"

Light rain pattered unceasingly on the windowpanes. Only mention of the Röhm Putsch brought Hitler to life. He leaned forward and began to repeat that he was the child of Fate. He got to his feet in a burst of anger. "Traitors in the bosom of their own people deserve the most ignominous of deaths—and they shall have it!" His voice rasped menacingly. "Exterminate them, yes, exterminate them!" His rage disappeared as rapidly as it had come. He was suddenly empty as the vision of vengeance faded. His eyes were drained, his face ashen.

Mussolini must have felt with his Italian flair that it was up to him to save the situation. He laid a hand on Hitler's and looked at him with a gentle smile. This brought the Führer out of his reverie. Someone had opened the outside door. Hitler sent for Il Duce's coat, explaining that a fresh east wind usually sprang up in the afternoon. He did not want his guest to catch cold. Mussolini replied in Italian, "At a time like this, a Duce does not catch cold!" But he put on his heavy army overcoat.

At 3:42 P.M. Stauffenberg finally landed at an airport outside Berlin. To his surprise, no one was waiting, friend or foe. His aide telephoned the Bendlerstrasse, got General Olbricht and gave the code word signifying that the assassination attempt had succeeded. Olbricht's vague reply made it clear that Walküre had not even been activated. Stauffenberg seized the phone, demanded they do so without waiting for his arrival. He commandeered a Luftwaffe car to take him to Berlin.

Only at 3:50 P.M. did Olbricht act. The Wehrmacht commandant of Berlin, General Kortzfleisch, was ordered to alert all units of the guard battalion, the Spandau garrison and two army weapons training schools. Kortzfleisch, who was not in the plot, did so.

To speed matters, General Olbricht personally alerted General von Hase, the Berlin garrison commander, another conspirator. By 4:10 P.M. his troops were ready to march. So were those outside Berlin. At the Bendlerstrasse itself the guards were alerted and their commander orally instructed by Olbricht to use force if any SS units tried to enter. Within minutes transit traffic was stopped, all exits blocked.

Olbricht was now doing what he should have been doing three hours earlier. He burst in on General Fromm, who was neither all the way in nor all the way out of the conspiracy, and explained that Hitler was really dead. He urged Fromm, as commander of the Replacement Army, to issue the Walküre alert to the military district commanders. Fromm, an ambitious man with a grand manner, hesitated as he had been doing for months. He insisted on telephoning Keitel for assurance that Hitler was dead.

"Everything is as usual here," said Keitel from the tea house, and when Fromm said that he had just received a report that the Führer had been assassinated, he exploded. "That's all nonsense." The Führer was alive and only slightly injured. "Where, by the way, is your chief of staff,

Colonel von Stauffenberg?" The agitated Fromm replied that the colonel had not yet reported to him—and silently resigned from the conspiracy.

A few minutes later most of the conspirators were congregated in Olbricht's large office waiting anxiously for Stauffenberg. Someone announced excitedly that he had just driven into the courtyard! In moments the colonel bounded energetically into the room, bringing with him a spirit of enthusiasm and confidence. Stauffenberg told what he had seen —a great explosion, flames and smoke. "As far as one can judge," he said, "Hitler is dead." They must act decisively without wasting another moment! Even if Hitler was alive they should do their utmost to overthrow the regime. Beck agreed.

Stauffenberg put through a call to his cousin at General von Stülpnagel's headquarters in Paris. He told about the explosion. "The way to action is open!" he said. The good news sent Stülpnagel into motion. He ordered senior signals officers in France to cut all radio and telephone communications between France and Germany except those lines needed for their own traffic with Berlin.

Back at the Bendlerstrasse, Stauffenberg was doing his utmost to bring General Fromm back into the conspiracy. He assured him that Hitler was truly dead, but Fromm repeated what Keitel had said. "Field Marshal Keitel is lying as usual," said Stauffenberg and proceeded to lie. "I myself saw Hitler being carried out dead."

"In view of this," cut in Olbricht, "we have sent out the code signal for internal unrest to the military district commanders." Fromm leaped from his chair, a startling act for such a huge, ponderous man. He banged the table and shouted in his best parade ground manner. "This is rank insubordination. What do you mean by 'we'?" He ordered the Walküre alert canceled.

Stauffenberg made another attempt to convince Fromm that Hitler was dead. "No one in that room can still be alive," he argued but Fromm was not impressed. "Count von Stauffenberg," he said, "the attempt has failed. You must shoot yourself at once." Stauffenberg refused and Olbricht added his plea to strike now. Otherwise the Fatherland would be ruined forever. Fromm turned on him. "Olbricht, does this mean that you, too, are taking part in the coup d'état?" "Yes, sir. But I am only on the fringe of the circle."

Fromm glared down from his height at Olbricht. "Then I formally put all three of you under arrest." Olbricht was not cowed. He returned the glare. "You can't arrest us. You don't realize who's in power. It's we who are arresting you." The two generals went from words to blows. Stauffenberg intervened and in the scuffle was struck in the face. Big Fromm was subdued only under threat of a drawn pistol. He was placed under arrest and locked in the next room. By 5 P.M. guards were posted at all entrances to the huge building, as well as the bombed area in the rear. Everyone entering now needed an orange pass signed by Stauffenberg; no one could leave without a similar pass or signed orders.

6

Although the Bendlerstrasse was at last under the complete control of the conspirators, their comrade, General von Hase, was in deep trouble at his office on Unter den Linden. An hour earlier, as commandant of the Berlin Garrison, he had ordered the guard battalion to seal off the government quarter; not a general or minister was to cross the barrier. Major Otto Remer, commander of the battalion, was a former Hitler Youth Leader and he first wanted assurance that his Führer was really dead. Hase gave it, adding that he had been murdered by the SS. Who was his successor? asked Remer, who felt "something was fishy." Hase told him to stop asking stupid questions and get his battalion on the move.

Remer's companion, Lieutenant Hans Hagen (in Berlin to lecture the guard battalion on National Socialism), was equally suspicious and once they were alone he convinced Remer that this looked like a military Putsch. He asked for permission to clarify the matter with Goebbels, his prewar employer. Remer put a motorcycle at his disposal with instructions to report back immediately. As the major set out to supervise the blockade of the inner city, Hagen (an author in civilian life) was bouncing in the sidecar of a motorcycle bound for the official residence of the Minister of Propaganda. He was heard to shout out periodically, like a Teutonic Paul Revere: "Military Putsch!"

The Goebbels establishment was already a center of confusion. The burgomeister of Berlin was there, along with a city councilor, and both were bewildered by the conflicting rumors. So was Speer, who had just noticed a group of Remer's men trotting toward Brandenburg Gate with machine guns; others stood guard outside the ministry. Sweating profusely, Goebbels was on the telephone querying party officials and regional military commanders. Troops from Potsdam and provincial garrisons, it seemed, were already marching toward the city. The situation was desperate but Goebbels saw a ray of hope in the fact that the rebels hadn't yet broadcast their success over the radio. He now busied himself making arrangements for his own broadcast, a tricky matter since a simple account of the facts might cause panic.

Just then Hagen, rumpled from his motorcycle ride, pushed his way into Goebbels' presence. After listening impatiently to the soldier-author's breathless account, Goebbels demanded to know if Remer could be trusted. Absolutely! Hadn't he been wounded eight times in action? Still somewhat suspicious, Goebbels instructed Hagen to fetch Remer. If the two were not back within half an hour, Goebbels would assume the major was either a traitor or held by force—and he would order SS troops to seize the headquarters of the Berlin Garrison at Unter den Linden.

Moments later, at 5:30 P.M., Goebbels was again called to the telephone. It was Hitler, who urged an immediate broadcast to let the people know that his life had been spared. Goebbels promptly phoned the text of a broadcast to the Rundfunkhaus. It was already occupied by rebellious troops of the infantry school but their commanding officer was so confused—or terrified—by Goebbels' voice that he readily agreed not to interfere with transmission of the announcement.

In the meantime Hitler, swayed by agitated advisers, had come to suspect his Propaganda Minister was a traitor. He again phoned Goebbels, this time bitterly reproaching him for delaying the newscast so long. Goebbels gave vehement assurance that he was not to blame; it was someone in the Radio Division. Hitler believed him—at least he said he did—and hung up.

The early rumor of Hitler's death brought hysteria and tears to scores of girl telephonists. The story spread and caused consternation until the reassuring newscast brought new tears, these of joy. Messages of congratulation descended on the Wolfsschanze. Field Marshal Milch for one telegraphed his "HEARTFELT JOY THAT A MERCIFUL PROVIDENCE HAS SHIELDED YOU FROM THIS BASE MURDER ATTEMPT AND PRESERVED YOU FOR THE GERMAN PEOPLE AND ITS WEHRMACHT." These expressions of relief were not completely self-serving. The great majority of Germans felt that the nation's future depended on the Führer.

In Berlin, Major Remer had just finished sealing off the government area. He was glum, for he had not yet heard that the Führer was alive. Remer had carried out his mission with misgivings, reinforced when he reported back to Hase only to be given vague answers to every question. Dissatisfied, Remer was in a rebellious mood by the time Hagen accosted him outside with the news that Minister Goebbels demanded his immediate presence! This was civil war, Remer thought, and brought Hagen upstairs to repeat Goebbels' message to Hase. The general pretended to be alarmed and, when Remer said he must report at once to the Propaganda Minister, ordered him to remain in the anteroom. But another conspirator, also a major, intervened, with a knowing wink at Hase; he suggested that it *was* Remer's duty to see Goebbels—and place him under arrest. Remer left the building in a state of confusion. "Well, I've got to gamble for my life," he finally told his adjutant and set off for the Propaganda Ministry with twenty men.

Goebbels was checking the time. He had been unsuccessful in attempts to reach Remer by phone and it was only two minutes before the deadline—7 P.M. Then Remer marched in. He did not tell Goebbels he had orders to arrest him nor did he believe the Minister's claim that he had just spoken to the Führer. He would believe Hitler was alive only, he said, if he heard it from his own mouth.

"As you wish, Major," said Goebbels and put in a call to Rastenburg. In less than a minute he was telling Hitler, "Here is Major Remer, commander of the guard battalion." Remer took the receiver warily. It could be a recording or someone imitating the Führer. "Are you on the line, Major Remer?" he heard. "What are you doing now?" The voice certainly sounded like the Führer's and Remer told what he had done to date. But he must have sounded doubtful. "Do you believe that I am alive?" The answer was Jawohl even though Remer was not entirely convinced.

Hitler said that he was giving Remer complete authorization to insure the security of the government. "Do whatever you think necessary. Every officer, regardless of rank, is now under your command." He ordered Remer to restore full order immediately. "If necessary by *brachial* (brutal) armed force." The *"brachial"* completely convinced Remer this really was Hitler. He snapped to attention. "You are responsible only to me," repeated Hitler and promoted him to the rank of colonel.

Remer turned the ministry into a command post. First he telephoned General von Hase and said he had just spoken to the Führer, who had put him in complete command. He ordered Hase to reported to him at once. Hase refused indignantly. "Since when does a general come trotting to a little major?"

"General, if you don't want to come, I will have you arrested," said Remer and sent troops to occupy Hase's headquarters. He then informed all military units in the Berlin area that they were now under his personal command, and was not surprised that their commanders, regardless of rank, accepted his authority without protest. As a finishing touch, Colonel Remer assembled his own battalion in the ministry garden so they could hear about the *Attentat* (assassination attempt) from the lips of Goebbels himself.

By this time a subdued General von Hase had arrived. He was no longer angry and, in fact, seemed at the point of embracing Remer. He was so full of compliments and questions that Remer had to politely put him off so he could get on with the job of restoring order. Goebbels was somewhat condescending to Hase, who began to stammer slightly under his curt questioning. Would the Minister mind if he telephoned his wife and had something to eat? "There go our revolutionaries," jibed Goebbels after the general left to enjoy his snack. "All they think about is eating, drinking and calling up Mamma."

The switchboard at the Bendlerstrasse was jammed with calls from officers seeking fuller details on the newscast. The recipients of the Walküre alert were also asking for direct confirmation from Fromm of the earlier report of Hitler's death. They were answered by Stauffenberg, who insisted that Hitler *was* dead and, if they were conspirators, he gave assurance that the plot was still operative. He told them the newscast was a trick. The army was in control and all was well.

At last one of the titular leaders of the revolt, Field Marshal von Witzleben, appeared in full uniform to take charge. He had held himself aloof all day but made up for his tardiness, just before 7:30 P.M., by sending out a strong directive, as new head of the Wehrmacht:

> The Führer, Adolf Hitler, is dead. An unscrupulous clique of non-combatant party leaders utilizing this situation, has attempted to stab our fighting forces in the back and seize power for their own purpose.
>
> In this hour of extreme danger the Government of the Reich, to maintain law and order, has decreed a military state of emergency and placed me in supreme command of the German Armed Forces. . . .

This message put new life into another field marshal. Kluge, on the point of abandoning the Paris conspirators, exclaimed: "An historical hour has struck!" He proposed they seek an immediate armistice in the West. The new German regime would agree to cease the rocket attacks on London if, in return, the Allies stopped their bombing. Kluge's enthusiasm was interrupted by a telegram from Keitel: the Führer was alive and orders from the traitorous Witzleben-Beck group in the Bendlerstrasse were to be ignored.

Kluge's resolve crumbled. He asked his chief of staff to find out what was really going on at Führer Headquarters. But Warlimont could not be reached by telephone, nor could Jodl or Keitel. Their absence was so curious that Kluge's hope revived. Perhaps Beck had told the truth after all and Hitler *was* dead! A call was put in to a fellow conspirator at Wolfsschanze. But he could only confirm the worst possible news: the Führer *was* alive! Kluge put down the telephone despondently. "Well," he said, "the attempt on his life has failed." That ended the matter for the marshal. "Gentlemen," he said, "leave me out of the question!"

In Berlin the man who had signed the order to seize power had also just abandoned the conspiracy. Field Marshal von Witzleben, expressing disgust at the confusion in the Bendlerstrasse, marched out of the building and drove to army headquarters in Zossen. Here he told Quartermaster General Wagner that all was lost and proceeded toward his country estate.

At Wolfsschanze Keitel had just succeeded in dispatching an order putting Himmler in command of the Replacement Army. Keitel added that "only orders from him and myself are to be obeyed." This teleprint went out at 8:20 P.M. Ten minutes later Party Chancellor Bormann dispatched an urgent message informing all his Gauleiters of the "murderous attempt on the Führer's life by certain generals." He ordered his people to honor only orders from the Führer himself.

At 9 P.M. the people were informed by radio that the Führer would soon speak to them in person. There would be a long delay, however, since there were no facilities at Wolfsschanze to broadcast directly. The nearest recording van was in Königsberg, the capital of East Prussia, and it would take several hours to fetch it.

By chance Hitler's favorite commando, Otto Skorzeny, was in Berlin, but once he heard that the Führer was alive he saw no reason to delay a trip to Vienna to inspect his school of frogmen saboteurs. As he was boarding the train at Anhalt Station at dusk an officer raced down the platform shouting that there was a military revolt in the city and Skorzeny had been commanded to establish order.

He hurried to SD headquarters where he was told that some traitorous military leaders were seizing control of the capital. "The situation is obscure and dangerous," said Schellenberg. His face was pale; a revolver lay in front of him on the table. He made a dramatic gesture. "I'll defend myself here if they come this way!" It was a ridiculous picture and Skorzeny could not resist laughing. He advised Schellenberg to put his weapon away before he shot himself.

Skorzeny alerted a company from another of his sabotage schools located in the Berlin suburbs before setting out on a personal reconnaissance of the city. Everything was quiet in the government compound. Checking a report that the Waffen SS was in the conspiracy, he hastily inspected their barracks at Lichterfeld. All was serene. He drove to the headquarters of the SS Leibstandarte Division for information but learned very little and continued at top speed to paratroop headquarters near the Wannsee. He found General Student on the terrace of his villa poring over a mass of papers. The general was wearing a long dressing gown; his wife sat beside him, sewing. It was comic, in a way, to see one of Germany's most important commanders presiding over such a placid scene during a revolt. Student refused to take the matter seriously until a phone call from Göring confirmed Skorzeny's alarm: all orders except those issued from Wehrmacht headquarters were to be ignored. While Student began relaying these orders, Skorzeny raced back to Schellenberg's office. No sooner had he arrived than he was called to the phone. "How many men have you?" asked Jodl. Only one company. "Good. Take them to the Bendlerstrasse and support Major Remer and his guard battalion who have just been ordered to surround the building."

There was a feeling of growing desperation at the Bendlerstrasse. The guard battalion units which had been protecting the high command headquarters were withdrawing, on orders from their commander to assemble in the garden behind Goebbels' official residence. This left only about thirty-five soldiers at the main gate. Inside, General Olbricht collected his officers at 10:30 P.M. for the third time that evening and said they would now have to take over the protection of the building since the guards had left. Each of the six exits, he said, would have to be manned by a General Staff officer.

No one objected but one armed group of loyalists was secretly determined to stand by their oath to the Führer. At about 10:50 P.M. these men, eight in all, burst into Olbricht's office, grenades fastened to their belts and armed with submachine guns and pistols. As Olbricht was trying to calm them, Stauffenberg entered. He spun around and escaped in a fusillade through the anteroom. He staggered as if hit, then darted into an adjoining office. But in short order he was captured along with Beck, Olbricht and other conspirators. Soon they were faced by Fromm, who had been released from captivity. "Well, gentlemen," said the big general, brandishing a pistol, "I am now going to treat you as you treated me." He told them to lay down their weapons.

"You wouldn't demand that of me, your former commanding officer," said Beck quietly. "I will draw the consequences from this unhappy situation myself." He reached for a revolver on a suitcase.

Fromm warned him to keep the gun pointed at himself. The elderly Beck began to reminisce. "At a time like this I think of the old days . . ." "We don't want to hear about that now," interrupted Fromm. "I ask you to stop talking and do something." Beck mumbled something and fired. The bullet grazed his head; he reeled back, slumped in a chair. "Help the old gentleman," Fromm told two junior officers. They approached Beck and tried to take his gun. He resisted so he could try again but dropped back in a daze. Fromm turned to the other conspirators. "Now, you gentlemen, if you have any letters to write you may have a few minutes to do so." He returned in five minutes and informed them that a court-martial "in the name of the Führer" had just pronounced death sentences on Olbricht, Stauffenberg and their two adjutants. Stauffenberg, his left sleeve soaked in blood, stood stiffly as he and his three colleagues were led into the courtyard.

Beck's face was splotched with blood. He asked for and was given a pistol. He was left in the anteroom but those outside heard him say: "If it doesn't work this time, please help me." There was a shot. Fromm looked in and saw that the former chief of the General Staff had failed again. "Help the old gentleman," he told an officer, who refused. A sergeant dragged the unconscious Beck from the room and shot him in the neck.

Outside, the courtyard was dimly lit by the hooded lights of an army vehicle. It was midnight. The four condemned men were lined up in front of a sand pile for use in air raids. Olbricht was calm. At the order to fire, Stauffenberg shouted, "Long live our sacred Germany!" and died.*

The huge form of Fromm appeared at the doorway of the building.

* Bendlerstrasse presently is named the Stauffenbergstrasse.

He marched across the yard to review the firing squad. He talked briefly, ending with a resounding "Heil Hitler!" then somewhat pompously made for the gate. He called for his car and disappeared in the darkness. At the message center in the Bendlerstrasse a teleprint message was being transmitted: "Attempted Putsch by irresponsible generals bloodily crushed. All ringleaders shot. . . ."

Just as Fromm was walking through the gate a white sports car arrived with a screech of brakes. The driver was Speer, his passenger Colonel Remer. "Finally an honest German!" said Fromm as if he himself were innocent. "I've just had some criminals executed." And when Remer said he wouldn't have done that, Fromm blustered. "Do you intend to give me orders?"

"No, but you'll have to be responsible for your actions." Remer suggested the general report at once to Goebbels. As Fromm drove off with Speer, Otto Skorzeny arrived with his men. He wondered why such an important general was leaving at such a time, then asked Remer, "What's going on?" Remer had no idea either, he only had orders to surround the building.

Skorzeny said that he was going inside and, after posting his company in the courtyard, bounded up the stairs toward the chief of staff's office. In the corridor he passed several officers, all armed with machine pistols. They glared at him with hostility. In Olbricht's anteroom he found several staff officers of his acquaintance who gave a brief account of what had happened. It all sounded very wild but confirmed what he had guessed. After trying in vain to telephone Führer Headquarters, he realized he must act on his own to restore peace and order "to this disturbed hive." Resumption of work was the best cure and, after gathering those officers he knew personally, he suggested they get on with their jobs; the battle fronts were still in dire need of reinforcements and supplies.

The staff officers agreed, but who would sign orders? Those in command were either dead or vanished. Skorzeny said he would sign and take all responsibility. As the machinery of the high command began to move again, Skorzeny finally was connected to Jodl, who told him to stay in charge. "Send some general," suggested Skorzeny, but Jodl insisted he take over in the name of the Führer. Skorzeny began by sending out orders countermanding the Walküre alert and ordering all commanders to stand by for new instructions.

Speer chauffeured Fromm back to the Propaganda Ministry where Goebbels disregarded the latter's demand to speak privately with Hitler. Instead he put him in another room, asked Speer to leave, and telephoned the Führer in private. After some time Goebbels came to the door of his office and ordered a guard posted in front of Fromm's room.

Himmler was among those present at the ministry. He had recently arrived from Rastenburg with express orders and full powers from the

Führer to crush the rebellion. "Shoot anyone who resists, no matter who it is," Hitler had told him. Despite such credentials—including a temporary assignment as commander-in-chief of the Reserve Army—he let Goebbels take over the visual command, remaining his usual quiet, contained self. To Goebbels' assistant, Naumann, he even seemed to be indifferent, whereas Goebbels was exhilarated. His version of the day gave the impression that he had crushed the rebellion in Berlin practically singlehanded. "If they hadn't been so clumsy!" he boasted to Himmler. "They had an enormous chance. What dolts! What childishness! When I think how I would have handled such a thing. Why didn't they seize the radio station and spread the wildest lies?"

The placid Himmler nodded politely without revealing that before coming to Goebbels' he had already unleashed the terror of a counter-Putsch and set up the machinery for a special investigation of the uprising.

At Wolfsschanze General Fellgiebel knew his fate was decided but he did not attempt to kill himself since he wanted to testify to his motives at an official trial. "If you believe in a Beyond," he told his youthful aide in farewell, "we could say *auf Wiedersehen!*"

Hitler was in his tea house impatiently waiting for the recording van from Königsberg so that he could make his speech to the nation. In anticipation of its imminent arrival, he summoned his family circle to hear him read a hastily drafted message. The secretaries and adjutants arrived along with Keitel and the bandaged Jodl, but there was still no van and Hitler used the time to enlarge on the Attentat. "These cowards!" he shouted. "That's exactly what they are! If they had had the courage at least to shoot me I'd have some respect! But they didn't want to risk their lives!"

At last the van arrived and just before 1 A.M., July 21, there was a fanfare of military music over every German radio station. After a brief pause Hitler began telling of the plot, and of the death and injury to colleagues very dear to him. He repeated his mistaken conviction that the circle of conspirators was extremely small and had nothing in common with the spirit of the Wehrmacht or the German people. It was a tiny band of criminal elements which would be promptly and ruthlessly exterminated. "I was spared a fate which held no horror for me, but would have had terrible consequences for the German people. I see in it a sign from Providence that I must, and therefore shall, continue my work."

He was followed briefly by Göring, who pledged the loyalty and deep affection of the Luftwaffe, and Dönitz, who declared that the navy was "consumed with holy wrath and boundless fury at the criminal attempt on our Führer's life." Then came the official announcement that the ringleaders of the criminal officer plot had either committed suicide or been shot by the army. "There have been no incidents, anywhere. Others who are implicated in the crime will be brought to account."

These words chilled the chief conspirators in Paris, who were gathered around a radio at the staff club in the Hotel Raphael. They had just succeeded in occupying every SS barracks in the area and arresting the two senior SS men in France, Karl Oberg and Helmut Knochen. As he listened, General von Stülpnagel was almost sure this was their own death sentence. But there was one last desperate hope. Perhaps Oberg and Knochen would have the decency to shield them. These two were released and brought to the Hotel Raphael. When Stülpnagel rose in greeting Oberg lunged at him. Ambassador Otto Abetz intervened. "What happens in Berlin is one thing," he said. "Here what matters is that the Normandy battle is raging and so here we Germans must show a united front." Oberg calmed down and agreed that he and Knochen would secretly join forces with the Wehrmacht against Himmler's RSHA. They would pretend that the SS and SD arrests had simply been staged by Oberg and Stülpnagel as a trick to deceive the Putschists.

Once his speech was finished, Hitler retired to his bunker where he was again examined by Dr. Morell. The Führer wanted confirmation that he had sustained no serious injuries. His inner circle waited in the tea house until Morell returned to announce that Hitler's pulse was normal. All was well. The Führer himself, shaken by the events of the day, had not yet realized the extent of the plot against him and still felt some exhilaration at his miraculous escape. He decided to send his tattered uniform to Eva Braun in Berchtesgaden for safekeeping. It would be a historical relic, proof that Providence really did intend him to complete his mission.

7

Soon after midnight, July 21, Otto Skorzeny was in complete command of the Bendlerstrasse, and the affairs of the high command were again on course. He also found details of the Putsch in Stauffenberg's safe and placed a number of officers under arrest.

At the Propaganda Ministry, Goebbels and Himmler were interrogating a number of generals including Fromm. They were treated courteously, given wine and cigars, and some, like Kortzfleisch, were allowed to go home when their innocence was established. At 4 A.M. the investigations ended. Goebbels emerged from his office with a radiant smile. "Gentlemen," he announced, "the Putsch is over." He escorted Himmler to his car, taking leave of his old rival with a long handshake, then returned upstairs to regale his closest associates with his own exploits. Utterly pleased, he spryly perched himself on a table next to a bronze bust of the Führer. "This was a purifying thunderstorm," he said. "Who would have dared to hope when the horrible news arrived early this afternoon that all this would end so quickly and so well." It was nothing short of a miracle. If Hitler had died the people would have believed it was God's judgment. "The consequences would have been incalculable. For in history only facts speak as evidence. And they are this time on our side." The press consequently should be instructed to belittle the conspiracy.

At Wolfsschanze Bormann was still sending out instructions to his Gauleiters. At 3:40 A.M. he informed them that the Putsch "may now be considered closed," and at 11:35 A.M. he passed on an urgent request from Himmler "that you should stop any further independent action against officers whose attitude was ambiguous or even against those who have to be classified as open adversaries." In other words, the Reichsführer himself was in full charge of restoring order and implementing a thorough investigation. In his methodical way he had already set up machinery staffed by four hundred officials in eleven sections.

In Paris Kluge's chief of staff—with the continued co-operation of the two most powerful SS officials in France, Oberg and Knochen—was doing his utmost to cover up the tracks of Kluge and Stülpnagel. But the latter, so recently the most powerful man in the City of Light, assumed all hope was gone upon receiving an order to report to Berlin. Instead of going by plane Stülpnagel set off later that morning in the rain by car. He ordered his chauffeur to drive past the battlefields of the First World War, Château-Thierry and the Argonne Forest, then to Sedan where so many old comrades of the Darmstadt Grenadiers had fallen in 1916. He continued the sentimental journey throughout the afternoon, finally disembarking for "a little walk." Soon after he disappeared over a rise near the Meuse Canal the driver heard a shot, perhaps two. He found the general floating in the canal, face upturned. Stülpnagel was barely alive but by wounding himself he had established his guilt beyond doubt. He was destined to be hanged.

At the Wolfsschanze it was apparent that Hitler's head injury was not superficial. He could hear nothing with his right ear and his eyes constantly flickered to the right. That evening while strolling outside he twice wandered off the path. Dr. Karl Brandt urged him to rest in bed for several days, but the Führer would not listen. "That's impossible." He had too much work to do. Besides it would certainly look ridiculous to foreign guests to see such a healthy man lying in bed.

The next day, despite a persistent earache, he insisted on visiting his wounded officers at the nearby field hospital. Two were at the point of death. General Schmundt was in critical condition. Deeply disturbed, Hitler unburdened himself to the two injured navy men, Puttkamer and Assmann, who shared a room. Sitting on the latter's bed, he expressed sorrow that they were victims of the plot. "These gentlemen had me, and only me, in mind." Yet miraculously he had escaped assassination once more. "Don't you agree that I should consider it a sign of Fate that it intends to preserve me for my assigned task?" The twentieth of July, he said, "only confirmed the conviction that Almighty God has called me to lead the German people—not to final defeat but to victory."

As the day progressed the pain in his ear became so intense that Morell sent for Professor van Eicken, the eminent Berlin eye-ear-nose-throat specialist who had operated on the Führer's throat in 1935. He was unavailable and the EENT specialist at a nearby field hospital was summoned. Dr. Erwin Giesing was well qualified, having worked two years in Professor van Eicken's clinic before opening his own office. Giesing found that the eardrum was badly ruptured and the inner ear was damaged. But, he said, it was not serious provided no infection of the middle ear set in.

At this point Dr. Morell appeared, breathing heavily. He sharply reprimanded Giesing for not reporting to him first and was told stiffly that "an officer was required to report only to his superior and not to any civilian." Although Hitler could hear little of this exchange, he noticed Morell's look of indignation. "Come now, end this quarrel, my dear Professor," he placated. "Dr. Giesing was van Eicken's assistant and he has told me that tomorrow he will have to do a small drum cauterization if the bleeding does not stop." Morell wanted to inject a hemostat but grudgingly agreed to send to Berlin for the medication prescribed by his rival.

Although Hitler was convinced he would never hear with his right ear, he remained in relatively good spirits. He took the time to peck out a letter on a typewriter to "My dear Tschapperl," the Viennese diminutive which he often used affectionately for Eva Braun. Illustrated by a sketch of the bombed barracks, it assured her that he was fine, just somewhat tired. "I hope to come back soon and so be able to rest, putting myself in your hands. I greatly need tranquillity."

She replied at once on her blue monogrammed stationery that she was deeply unhappy. "I am half dead now that I know that you are in danger." She asserted she could not go on living if anything happened to him. "From the time of our first meetings, I promised myself to follow you everywhere even in death. You know that my whole life is in loving you."

On July 23 Gestapo investigators by accident found incriminating diaries in the ruins of a bombed house which implicated Canaris and other important officials in the coup. The admiral was arrested, as was former Minister of Economics Schacht. At first Hitler could not believe that such high-ranking people—and so many of them!—were involved. It was a blow to his convictions that only a small clique of traitors existed and he was hurt. "My life is so full of sorrow, so heavily leaden," he told Traudl Junge, "that death itself would be salvation." And another secretary heard him chide his dog for disobeying him: "Look me in the eyes, Blondi. Are you also a traitor like the generals of my staff?"

At the situation meeting the next morning he declared that the English had backed Stauffenberg, then tried to convince his listeners that the plot was *not* really so widespread. "The important thing is to explain to the whole world that the overwhelming multitude of the officers' corps had nothing to do with those swine." It should be emphasized in the press that the commanders in the Bendlerstrasse had refused to go along with the handful of traitors and, in fact, executed four of them out of hand. "I am too much of a psychologist," he concluded, "not to see that a divine hand led this man with the bomb here at precisely the most favorable time for us. If I and the entire staff had been killed, it would have been a real catastrophe."

Goebbels followed Hitler's instructions in an address broadcast over all German radio stations. It was a clever speech replete with dramatic moralizing and appeal to the emotions. He pictured Stauffenberg as the satanic leader of a relatively small officers' clique that did not represent the Wehrmacht as a whole. He charged that Stauffenberg had been conspiring with the Western Allies and listed four evidences of proof: constant reference in their press to a group of German generals opposed to Hitler; use of an English bomb; relationship of Stauffenberg to the English aristocracy; and the hope expressed in London papers, after first news of the bombing, that the collapse of Germany was at hand.

Reports to the Gauleiters indicated that Goebbels' propaganda effectively aroused the people. At a hospital in Braunschweig, for example, the patients spontaneously decorated every picture of the Führer with flowers. Loyalty demonstrations were organized in numerous cities. High school teachers told their pupils that the conspiracy now explained the military defeats in Africa and Russia; traitors had prevented the Führer's orders from filtering down to the divisions.

On July 25 Dr. van Eicken arrived from Berlin to be greeted warmly by the Führer, who predicted that with all his worries he would "only last another two or three years." There was one consolation: by then he would have accomplished his task and others could continue the work. He eased himself painfully into a chair and described his symptoms in detail.

Dr. Giesing, who prided himself on his memory, was unobtrusively jotting down everything Hitler said in a yellow pocket almanac. So that no one else could decipher his notes he wrote in code, using Latin and a combination of personal symbols. Professor van Eicken confirmed Giesing's diagnosis and treatment but the Führer refused his advice to rest in bed for at least a week. "You have all conspired among you to make a sick man out of me!"

The following day Hitler complained to Giesing that his left ear still bled internally and he wanted it cauterized again, no matter how painful. "I don't feel any more pain," he said, adding as an afterthought, "Pain is meant to make a man *hard*." He proved it a minute later when an adjutant brought in reports on the assassination attempt. "Ja," he said, ruffling through the pages, "I would not have thought this Helldorf was such a scoundrel." He vowed "to tear out those traitors by the roots," then reviled Stauffenberg for his cowardice. "He at least should have had the courage to stand next to me with his briefcase. The bullet that killed him was too good for him."

Two days later Hitler complained of insomnia and when Giesing recommended cancellation of the nightly tea session Hitler said he had already tried that but it only made sleep more difficult. "I have to relax beforehand and talk about other things. If not, I see before me in the dark the General Staff maps and my brain keeps working. It takes hours before I can get rid of such visions. If I put on the light I can draw an exact map of each army group position. I know where every single division stands— and so it goes on and on for hours until I fall asleep around five or six. I know this is not good for my health but I can't change my habits."

8

The day after the bombing Hitler replaced his ailing chief of staff, Zeitzler, with a man he had previously banished from a front-line command for differing with him. By the time Heinz Guderian, perhaps the most respected Panzer expert in the Wehrmacht, arrived in Rastenburg to take charge, he found the offices of OKH practically deserted. Zeitzler had already departed in semi-disgrace. Heusinger was gone and many department heads had been removed by the Gestapo.

One of Guderian's first tasks was to issue a loyalty order of the day, pledging to Hitler "the unity of the generals, of the officer corps and of the men of the army." By the end of the week Guderian went further; he ordered every General Staff officer to be a National Socialist officer-leader "by actively co-operating in the political indoctrination of younger commanders in accordance with the tenets of the Führer." Any officer who could not conform was ordered to apply at once for transfer. None did and the subjugation of this elite band, begun in 1933, came to a degrading finale.

By now the western front was collapsing in the face of a savage American attack on the western flank of the Normandy beachhead. At dusk of July 30 a fierce tank battle raged for the Avranches defile, the last barrier to an American breakthrough into the open spaces of France. Warlimont and others pressed for an immediate withdrawal from France while there was still time but Jodl contented himself with presenting to the Führer a draft of an order "for possible withdrawal from the coastal sector."

By the next evening American tanks were storming into Avranches.

Hitler wanted to rush west and take personal charge, but both Giesing and Eicken forbade him to fly. Restricted to Wolfsschanze, he was forced to do nothing while six of George Patton's divisions poured through the gap at Avranches and sealed the fate of France. This was but one of many concerns. On August 1, 35,000 ill-armed Poles of all ages assaulted the German garrison in Warsaw and the next day Turkey broke off diplomatic relations with the Reich.

Somehow he managed to put all these cares behind him and on that second of August play the role of budding medical student. He inundated Giesing with questions on the inner ear, then donned a surgeon's white coat and, with mirror strapped to head, began peering intently into Linge's right ear. He could see nothing. When he tried again in vain, Giesing suggested he use an electric mirror. "Ja!" he exclaimed in wonder. "Now I can see something. . . . I see clearly a small light yellow line; that will probably be the well-known eardrum." He told Linge to turn around and inserted the orthoscope into his left ear, and became so enthralled that he had to test Linge's hearing with tuning fork and stop watch. "You know, Doctor," he said somewhat shyly, "when I was young I always wanted to be a doctor. But my other career came along and I realized what my true mission was." No sooner had Giesing left than Dr. Hitler resumed his research. He summoned Linge and two SS orderlies, examining them all until he had mastered the electric mirror; then he requested a copy of Professor Knick's book on the treatment of eye, ear and throat.

If Hitler's spirits had improved, he was still so dizzy he had to walk with legs astride like a sailor on a pitching ship. Even so he insisted on talking to his Gauleiters on August 4. He went from man to man shaking hands. Many, like Friedrich Karl Florian of Düsseldorf, could not restrain their tears at the sight of his condition. "You won't misunderstand me," said Hitler, "when I assure you that for the past eighteen months I was firmly convinced I would one day be shot by someone in my own close circle." He asked them to try and imagine how terrible it was to realize that certain violent death could come at any moment. "How much inner energy I had to summon to do all that was necessary for the maintenance and protection of our people! To contemplate, cogitate, and work out these problems. And I had to do all this by myself, without the support of others and with a feeling of depression hanging over me." After the lugubrious speech, a one-pot meal was served. Finally Hitler slowly got to his feet. "Now I will retire," he said, "and you gentlemen . . ." He put two fingers to his mouth and they took out cigarettes as he walked off trying to hide his stagger.

Himmler had recently assured this same group that he would ruthlessly bring to justice not only the criminals in the conspiracy but their families. "The Stauffenberg family," he said, "will be exterminated root and branch!" Enthusiastic applause. "That will be a warning example, once and for all." He pressed the investigation in this spirit. Next of kin and other relatives of the chief conspirators were arrested, including at least a dozen women over seventy. Scores of detectives covered every angle of the conspiracy—with such dispatch and thoroughness that the first trial got under way on August 7. Eight officers were brought before a People's Court presided over by Roland Friesler, an expert on Soviet law and methods of punishment. Characterized by Hitler as "our Vishinsky," he had been instructed by the Führer to proceed harshly and "with lightning speed."

The defendants entered the great courtroom of the Kammergericht in Berlin wearing old clothes. They looked haggard and unkempt, as movie cameras recorded the event so the German people could see what happened to traitors. Field Marshal von Witzleben, deprived of his false teeth, looked like a tramp in a comedy as he kept hitching up his oversized beltless pants. Friesler, dramatically clothed in red, began shouting like one of the Soviet judges he so admired: "You dirty old man, why do you keep fiddling with your trousers?"

This was the tone and level of the show trial. "Never before in the history of German justice," recalled one shorthand secretary, "have defendants been treated with such brutality, such fanatic ruthlessness as at these proceedings." The judgment was foreordained and, in a trumpet voice, Friesler pronounced all eight men guilty of treason against the Führer (which, in fact, they were) and against German history (which they were not). In line with Hitler's specific instructions, the eight men were trucked to Plötenzee prison, then into a small room where eight meathooks dangled from the ceiling. Here the condemned were stripped to the waist and hung by nooses of piano wire. Their agonized jerking was recorded by a movie camera, and that same evening was reproduced on a screen at the Wolfsschanze. According to Speer, "Hitler loved the film and had it shown over and over again," but Adjutant von Below and others in the family circle still assert he never saw it.

There were further investigations and other trials but only the execution of the first eight victims was publicized. Almost 5000 other men and women, most of them not even directly involved in the uprising of July 20, were also executed.

9

On August 15 the Allies landed in southern France and Guderian's comment that the bravery of the Panzer forces was not enough to make up for the failure of the air force and navy infuriated Hitler. In an effort to contain himself, he adjourned to another room for a tête-à-tête with

Guderian, but their voices became so loud that an adjutant had to caution the Führer that every word was clearly audible outside. Could he please close the window?

This exhibition was mild compared to one later in the evening when Hitler learned that Field Marshal von Kluge had mysteriously disappeared. It seemed that the Commander-in-Chief West had driven up to the front that morning to confer with his armored commander but never arrived at the rendezvous. Hitler shouted that Kluge must have been involved in the bombing plot and had now sneaked off for secret surrender talks with the enemy!

Kluge, in fact, had been delayed up front by an enemy fighter-bomber attack, his car destroyed along with two transmitters. He was not only trapped, incommunicado, on congested roads but caught in a personal dilemma. While doing his best to stem the Allied breakthrough, he was convinced his was a hopeless task. Depressed ever since a serious auto accident in Russia, he would pace his office like a caged beast, torn between the oath he had sworn to Hitler and "his responsibility before God, before his nation, before his conscience."

Kluge finally reached his destination late that night but by then Hitler had already decided to replace him with Field Marshal Model. On August 17 Model arrived in France with a handwritten note from the Führer and took over command of the western front. Kluge sat at his desk dazed by the dismissal. "Here at Avranches all my reputation went," he told his chief of staff, pointing to a map. "It's all up with me." The following day he headed east, like Stülpnagel, on a leisurely motor trip across the old battlefields of France. Like Stülpnagel, he intended to take his own life. But Kluge was successful. Near Clermont-en-Argonne, after lunching under the shade of a tree, he gave his aide a letter for his brother —then swallowed cyanide.

Another letter was already on its way to the Führer. After outlining the reasons for his failure to stem the Allies, he implored Hitler to end the war and put an end to the people's unspeakable sufferings. At Wolfsschanze Hitler read the letter, then, without comment, handed it to Jodl, who was surprised by the last lines wherein Kluge praised Hitler for his iron will and genius and the "great and honorable fight" he had fought. "Prove yourself now to be so great as to put an end, if need be, to the hopeless struggle." It seemed to epitomize the final humiliation of the Wehrmacht but was not at all self-serving. Kluge stood to gain nothing. He had only made a last effort to serve his country by sounding a warning.

It was a futile one; Hitler was still bound by his ultimate mission: to rid the world of Jews, a task, so Eichmann reported in August, that was nearing its end. He told Himmler that six million Jews had already been eliminated—four million in the killing camps and the rest in mobile operations. Spurred by the rapid advance of the Red Army and the continuing investigations of the inexorable Konrad Morgen, who also calculated a figure of at least six million dead Jews, Hitler instructed Himmler to prepare the dismantling of all the killing camps except Auschwitz.* There were still Jews from Hungary, Lodz, Slovakia and Theresienstadt to be gassed but Commandant Höss had the facilities to wind up the entire job, provided the troops in the East did not allow a Soviet breakthrough.

10

The military situation was so desperate that only a man with such motivation would have banished all thoughts of surrender. From the Baltic to the Ukraine, Red Army offensives had routed or surrounded the Wehrmacht along the entire eastern front. In the south Soviet troops were seizing the oilfields of Romania; in the north they had just surrounded fifty German divisions; and in the center they were closing in on Warsaw. On Hitler's personal orders, preparations were made to remove the coffin of President von Hindenburg from the tomb at Tannenberg, scene of his great victory in the First World War.

In the emergency, Goebbels proclaimed a new Draconian policy on August 24: all theaters, music halls, drama schools and cabarets were to be closed within a week. Soon, he warned, all orchestras, music schools and conservatories (except a few leading ones) would be shut down and the artists put either in uniform or in armaments factories. There would be an end to publication of fiction or belles-lettres and of all but two illustrated papers.

On the following day Paris was liberated after four years of occupation; both Romania and Finland sued for an armistice. Twenty-four hours later the Romanians, who had thrown out Marshal Antonescu by a coup, declared war on Germany. With defeat imminent on all fronts, Hitler did not waver. His answer to signs of disintegration within the Wehrmacht was a threat to arrest the kin of any deserter.

He told Keitel and two other generals on the last day of August that the time was not yet ripe for a political decision. "Such moments come only when you are victorious." There was still hope of success, he said. The tension between the Allies would soon become so great that a major break would occur. "The only thing is to wait, no matter how hard it is, for the right moment." He mused glumly on the problems facing him in both East and West, then began feeling sorry for himself. "I think it's pretty obvious that this war is no fun for me. I've been cut off from the world for five years. I haven't been to the theater, I haven't heard a concert, and I haven't seen a film." His voice rose in wrath. "I accuse the

* The order to close the killing centers was issued by Himmler on November 24, 1944.

General Staff of failing to give the impression of iron determination and so of affecting the morale of combat officers—and when General Staff officers go up front I accuse them of spreading pessimism!" He would fight until Germany got a peace which secured the life of the nation for the next hundred years "and which, above all, does not besmirch our honor a second time, as happened in 1918." His thoughts reverted momentarily to the bomb plot. Death, he said, "would only have been a release from sorry, sleepless nights and great nervous suffering. It is only a fraction of a second and then a man is freed from everything and has quiet and eternal peace."

This mood of fatalism might have been the result of deteriorating health. Although he joked with his secretaries about his right hand, which trembled so much he could no longer shave himself, he was seriously affected by a head cold which was aggravated in turn by an incessant earache. His condition was complicated a few days later by a slight feeling of pressure in his head, particularly in the brow area. His voice grew hoarse. He began complaining of stomach pains but disregarded Dr. Giesing's warning that this might be the result of the numerous pills prescribed by Dr. Morell. By the beginning of September, however, Hitler had come to accept Dr. Giesing's prescription of a ten per cent cocaine solution to relieve the sinus pain and would faithfully crouch for hours each morning and evening over an inhalator.

Giesing's visits indeed became so pleasurable that Hitler began to show the same gratitude he had bestowed on Morell. Gratitude ripened into trust and before long the new doctor enjoyed a rare personal relationship with the Führer. The treatments were invariably followed by long discussions on a variety of subjects, ranging from the future of the Reich to the evils of smoking. During all these conversations Giesing continued to take detailed notes. He also undertook something even more dangerous: secret psychological tests. This was done so subtly and over such a long period that Hitler never guessed he had been the object of, in Giesing's terms, "rather primitive psychological tests," and had been diagnosed as "a neurotic with Caesar-mania."

Touchy as he was in these days of pain and depression, Hitler never lost his temper with his youngest secretary, Traudl Junge, or failed to show keen interest in her personal welfare. But at one noonday meal she noticed he acted strangely. He said not a word to her and when their eyes met his were serious and probing. She wondered if anyone had spread gossip about her. Later in the day SS General Otto Hermann Fegelein phoned and asked if she could come to his barracks. Putting an arm around her in a fatherly manner, he revealed that her husband had been killed in action. The Chief, he explained, had known about it since yesterday but was unable to tell her the bad news. Later she was summoned to the Führer's study. He took both her hands and said softly, "Oh, child, I am so sorry. Your husband was such a fine fellow." He asked her to remain on the job and promised to "always help" her.

In early September Professor van Eicken returned for another examination and, upon learning of Morell's injections and pills, became as concerned as Giesing and Hitler's two surgeons, Brandt and Hasselbach. The four doctors met secretly but Eicken doubted that their patient would heed his warnings any more than those of his three colleagues since Morell enjoyed Hitler's complete confidence.

A week later Hitler reported that he was getting almost no sleep. He would lie awake all night long from the agony of stomach spasms. Nor was there any relief from the sinus inflammation; the left side of his head continued to ache constantly. This was aggravated by the rattle and grind of pneumatic drills used around the clock by construction workers in an effort to strengthen his bunker from expected Soviet air attacks. A side effect of his bad health was deterioration of his remarkable memory. He had always been able to glance at a long document and repeat it word for word; now he had difficulty remembering names. It was fortunate, he wryly observed, that he only had to deal with a few people these days.

On September 12 Hitler suddenly became dizzy immediately after Giesing had administered the cocaine treatment. He complained that everything was going black and grabbed a table to keep from falling. His pulse was rapid and weak but in ninety seconds the attack—it might have been a mild coronary—passed and the pulse returned to normal. Hitler suffered a similar attack on the fourteenth. This time he broke out into a cold sweat. He summoned Morell, who gave him three injections which gave him temporary relief, but on September 16 there was a third mild attack. This time he agreed to do what Giesing had been urging for a month: undergo head X rays.

Chapter Twenty-nine

THE BATTLE OF THE BULGE
JULY 21, 1944–JANUARY 17, 1945

1

That same day Hitler issued an order demanding "fanatical determination" from every able-bodied combat man in the West. The Americans had just reached the German frontier and at one point, south of Aachen, pierced it. "There can be no large-scale operations on our part. All we can do is to hold our position or die." Hitler seemed to be calling only for a last-ditch defense of the Fatherland but it was a ruse to fool the enemy who, he feared, had a spy at Führer Headquarters privy to all directives. (The spy, of course, was Ultra.) No sooner had the regular Führer conference ended than Hitler invited four men to an inner chamber. Keitel and Jodl were followed into the new conference room by Chief of Staff Guderian and General Kreipe, representing Göring. As they were conjecturing in undertones on what surprise the Führer had in store for them, he entered, stooped, still wan and wary from the third attack. His blue eyes were watery and distant, his mouth slack.

He nodded to Jodl, who succinctly summed up their position: their allies were either finished, switching sides or attempting to do so. While the Wehrmacht listed more than 9,000,000 men under arms, there had been 1,200,000 casualties in the last three months—almost half of them on the western front. There was a respite in the East where the Soviet summer offensive seemed to have run its course. "But in the West we are getting a real test in the Ardennes." This was the last hilly area in Belgium and Luxembourg that had been the highway to German victory in the Great War and again in 1940.

At the word "Ardennes" Hitler abruptly came to life. Raising his hand, he exclaimed: "Stop!" There was a dead pause. Finally Hitler spoke: "I have made a momentous decision. I am taking the offensive. Here—out of the Ardennes!" He smashed his left fist on the unrolled map before him. "Across the Meuse and on to Antwerp!" The others stared in wonder. His shoulders were squared, his eyes luminous, the signs of care and sickness gone. This was the dynamic Hitler of 1940. In the next few days he was a model of his former vigor as he pressed preparations for the ambitious counteroffensive: he issued orders for the establishment of a new Panzer army and envisaged ways of bringing 250,000 men and thousands of machines up to the Ardennes in absolute secrecy.

Only then did he keep his promise to get X rays taken of his head. Late in the afternoon of September 19 he was driven to the field hospital at Rastenburg and escorted to the X-ray room, which had been searched carefully for hidden explosives. Afterward he again visited his wounded officers but this time the sight of the dying Schmundt brought tears.* Outside Hitler was greeted by loud shouts of "Sieg heil!" from a crowd of civilians from the town and recuperating soldiers. Their excitement at the sight of their Führer—probably for the first time—was understandable but what impressed Giesing most was the ardent enthusiasm in the eyes of the amputees and other badly wounded men.

The following morning Giesing checked the three X rays with Morell and was amazed that his colleague identified the cheekbones as the sinuses. There followed the daily examination of the patient in his bunker and Giesing noticed Hitler's face had an odd reddish tinge in the artificial light. Afterward Hitler was stricken with stomach pains and insisted on taking more than half a dozen of the "little black pills" prescribed by Morell. Concerned by the continuing dosage, Giesing began to make cautious inquiries. Linge showed him the pill container. Its label read: Antigas Pills, Dr. Koster, Berlin, Extract nux vomica 0.04; Extract belladonna 0.04.

Giesing was appalled. Hitler had been heavily dosing himself with two poisons—strychnine and atropine. Perhaps that explained his attacks, his growing debility; his irritability and aversion to light; his hoarse throat and the strange reddish tinge of his skin. Two cardiograms revealed clearly abnormal T waves. It could be hardening of the arteries or high blood pressure, but in any case it was an alarming development in the light of his other disabilities. At their regular session Hitler again complained to Giesing of intestinal discomfort. "The cramps are so severe that sometimes I could scream out loud."

* After Schmundt's death, Hitler again wept. "Don't expect me to console you," he told Frau Schmundt. "You must console me for my great loss."

After their next meeting on September 25 Dr. Giesing chanced to see his patient outside the bunker. To his surprise the tinge of Hitler's skin was not red in sunlight but yellow. His eyes were starting to turn yellow. He obviously had jaundice. After a night of agonizing pain, Hitler could not get out of bed the following morning. His secretaries, adjutants and servants were in a state of alarm; no one could remember the Führer staying in bed no matter how sick. He would see no one, wanted no food. In great excitement, Günsche told Traudl Junge that he had never seen the Chief so listless, so indifferent. Even the critical situation on the eastern front failed to interest him.

Morell advised Hitler to remain in bed all day but he insisted on getting up for his regular examination by Giesing. He, in turn, advised discontinuance of the cocaine treatment but Hitler wearily shook his head. "No, dear Doctor," he said. "I think that my physical weakness the past few days is due to the poor functioning of my intestines and cramps." Giesing hesitated, then warned his patient to take care lest he suffer another collapse. On his way out he confiscated a box of Morell's black pills and showed them to Dr. von Hasselbach. He too was horrified to learn they contained strychnine and atropine but warned Giesing to say nothing until they could confer with Dr. Brandt.

In the meantime Morell gave orders that no other doctor was to see the Führer and when Giesing reported on the twenty-seventh he was turned away by Linge. Even Dr. van Eicken, who came from Berlin to irrigate the patient's swollen sinuses, was refused admittance. For the rest of the month Morell did his utmost to isolate the patient from the other doctors. He insisted that the Führer was *not* suffering from jaundice. It was more likely a temporary gall bladder inflammation. During this time Hitler lost six pounds and lay in bed, racked with pain. He ate nothing and showed little interest in the battle fronts. Occasionally he would see his secretaries but then he would almost immediately dismiss them. "It gave me a feeling of despair," recalled Traudl Junge, "to see the one man who could have stopped this tragedy with a single stroke of a pen lying disinterested in his bed, looking around with tired eyes—while around him all hell had broken out. It seemed to me that his body had suddenly realized how senseless had been all the efforts of brain and will and gone on strike. He had just laid down and said, 'I will not do anything any more.'"

Physical pain was not the only cause of Hitler's deep depression. Another cache of incriminating documents was unexpectedly discovered in a safe at army headquarters in Zossen. They implicated a considerable segment of the army leadership in the assassination plot. The Führer was shattered and some of those in the family circle felt that this, more than the jaundice or the stomach pains, which he had endured for years, had broken his spirit.

Dr. Brandt returned to the Wolfsschanze on the twenty-ninth. Enthusiastic at the chance to finally unmask Morell as a charlatan, he managed to get into Hitler's room that afternoon. At first the patient took Brandt's denunciation seriously; but Morell convinced the Führer that he was absolutely innocent of any wrongdoing. If Hitler suffered aftereffects from the anti-gas pills it was because he himself increased the daily dosage. Disconsolate, Brandt now left it up to his colleagues to discredit Morell. Hasselbach went to Bormann. He was the last one the doctors should have sought as an ally since he had been doing his best for months to get Brandt dismissed. Bormann's ulterior motive was Byzantine; he looked on Brandt as the accomplice of Speer, whose "dangerous" influence on the Führer had to be diminished at all costs. After listening politely to Hasselbach and expressing shock at the pill stories, Bormann promptly went to Hitler and warned him that Brandt had been joined by Hasselbach and Giesing in an effort to ruin poor Dr. Morell for their own personal gains.

No doctor but Morell was allowed to see Hitler and it appeared that Bormann had won. Then, late in the afternoon on October 1, Linge telephoned Giesing. The Führer was suffering from a bad headache and insisted on seeing Giesing at once. He was lying on his spartan bed in a nightgown. He lifted his head slightly to greet Giesing but immediately dropped back to the pillow. His eyes were empty, expressionless. He complained of pressure in his head. He also could not breathe through his left nostril. As Giesing seated himself next to the bed, Hitler abruptly changed the subject. "Doctor," he asked, "how did you come upon the story of the anti-gas pills?"

Giesing explained. Hitler frowned. "Why didn't you come directly to me? Didn't you know that I have great confidence in you?" The doctor felt chills—not from the excessive air conditioning in the little cell. He explained that he had been prevented from coming. Hitler shrugged this off as well as Giesing's conviction that his intestinal problems were due to strychnine. He had suffered similar attacks frequently, if not as severely. "It is the constant worry and irritation that give me no rest; and I must work and think only of the German people day and night." He was already feeling much better and should be out of bed in a few days. "You gave Morell a great fright," he said. "He looked quite pale and disturbed and reproaches himself. But I have assured him. I myself always have believed they were simple pills to absorb my intestinal gases and I always felt very well after taking them." Giesing explained that the feeling of well-being was an illusion. "What you say is probably right," interrupted Hitler, "but the stuff did me no harm. I'd have had intestinal cramps anyway because of the continuous nervous strain of the last month and, after all, at some time the twentieth of July would have reacted on me. Up to now I'd had the will power to keep all this inside me—but now it has broken out."

Giesing diagnosed his problems as jaundice but Hitler protested. "No, you want to make a gall bladder patient out of me! Go ahead, examine my gall bladder." He folded back the bedclothes so Giesing could make his own examination. It was Giesing's first chance to give his patient a complete physical. He examined Hitler's neurological reflexes, his glands, every part of his body. Giesing satisfied himself, for instance, that the malicious rumor about the Führer's deficient sex organs was a canard; in this respect he was intact and normal.*

Hitler was once more the medical student, absorbed by each detail of the process. "You see, Doctor," he said as Linge and Giesing helped him into the nightgown, "aside from this nervous hyperactivity, I have a very healthy nervous system and I hope that soon all will be well again." He was talking himself into a state of euphoria. He thanked Giesing for everything he had done to relieve his discomfort. "And now Fate has sent you again to ferret out this anti-gas story and you have saved me further damage because I would have kept on taking these pills after I recovered." This paradoxical conclusion was followed by a perplexing outburst of gratitude and praise. "My dear Doctor, it was Providence that led you to make this examination and discover what no other doctor would ever have noticed. I am in any event very grateful to you for everything and will remain loyal to you—even if you did attack Morell—and I thank you again for everything." He took both of Giesing's hands, pressed them tightly, then requested another dose of "that cocaine stuff." The Führer instantly luxuriated under the treatment. His head was clearing up, he said, and he would soon be well enough to get up. But his words began to fade and his eyes fluttered. His face turned a deathly white. Giesing grasped Hitler's pulse. It was rapid and weak. "My Führer, are you all right?" he asked but got no answer. Hitler had passed out.

The doctor looked around but Linge had left to answer a knock on the door. It suddenly occurred to Giesing that Hitler was entirely at his mercy. He saw before him a tyrant whose knowledge of people seemed very inadequate. "At that moment," so he claimed in his diary, "I did not want such a man to exist and exercise the power of life and death in his purely subjective manner." Some inner command drove him to plunge a swab stick into the cocaine bottle—a second dose could be lethal—and he rapidly began brushing the interior of Hitler's nose with the substance that had just knocked him out. As Giesing finished the left nostril he was startled by a voice: "How much longer will the treatment take?" It was Linge.

Giesing forced himself to say he was about finished. Just then Hitler's face, paler than before, twitched and he drew up his legs as if in pain.

---

* At least two other doctors gave Hitler a complete physical. Dr. Morell found his sexual organs "completely normal." So did a physician at Berlin's Westend Hospital soon after the Führer's accession to power; this man, having heard of Hitler's "alleged homosexual tendencies, paid special attention to his penis and testicles."

"The Führer is having another one of his intestinal cramps," observed Linge. "Let him rest." Outwardly composed, Giesing bade farewell to Linge and quickly bicycled back to the field hospital, still wondering if he had killed Hitler. In a state of terror, he telephoned Hasselbach, telling what had happened and that he was taking a day off, ostensibly to check on his Berlin office, which had been bombed.

The next day Giesing phoned from the capital to learn that Hitler was alive and no one suspected the double cocaine treatment. It was safe to return to Wolfsschanze. He arrived in an atmosphere of suspicion but not from the Führer, who was as friendly as ever. Still he made it clear that he wanted the whole anti-gas pill episode relegated to the past since he had "total faith" in Morell. He was personally going to clear up the matter and had asked Brandt to see him that afternoon.

Hitler settled the question by dismissing both Brandt and Hasselbach. Early that evening Giesing was summoned to Bormann's quarters. "But, my dear Doctor," Bormann said, upon observing that the doctor had come in full uniform, "why do you come in such official style? I only wanted to discuss something with you." He seemed amused at Giesing's apprehension. "There's no need to take the whole matter so tragically. We have nothing against you. On the contrary, the Führer is full of praise and asked me to give you this letter." It thanked him for his excellent treatment. Enclosed was a check for 10,000 marks. The doctor laid the check on the table. But Bormann forced it upon him with the warning that a refusal would be an insult to Hitler.

After packing, Giesing reported to the Führer bunker. Hitler extended his hand. "You will understand," he said, "that this anti-gas pill business has to be cleared up once and for all. I know that you yourself acted only out of idealism and purely professional motives." He again thanked Giesing for his excellent treatment and promoted him on the spot.

So ended the affair of the little black pills—with the dismissal of three doctors of good reputation. Few in the family circle gave any credence to the growing rumor that Dr. Morell had willfully attempted to poison the Führer. Most of them shared Gerda Christian's opinion that Morell was a good doctor despite his slovenly appearance. Even the trio who denounced Morell for incompetence did not believe he was trying to poison Hitler. They remembered the truly shocked look on his face when Brandt pointed out that these pills—though harmless if taken in moderation—contained some strychnine. Morell, it seemed, had never checked the analysis on the label, only the name, nux vomica. And it came as a blow to discover that this was a strychnine-containing seed.

By the time Hitler left his sickbed there was considerable evidence of Rommel's implication in the bomb plot and the Führer assigned two generals the unpleasant task of offering him a deadly proposition. On October 14 they visited Rommel, who was recuperating at his castle near Ulm from the auto accident. When they left an hour later an ashen Rommel told his wife, "In a quarter of an hour I shall be dead." He explained that he had been accused of complicity in the plot and Hitler offered him the choice of taking poison or facing the People's Court.

After bidding his wife and son farewell, he took his aide aside. "Aldinger," he said, "this is it." He repeated Hitler's proposition and plan: he was supposed to drive to Ulm with the two generals and, en route, take poison. Half an hour later his death by accident would be reported. He would be given a state funeral and his family would not be persecuted. Aldinger begged him to resist but Rommel said that was impossible. The village was surrounded by SS men and the lines of communication to his own troops had been cut. "I have therefore decided to do what, obviously, I must do."

At 1:05 P.M., wearing his Afrika Korps leather jacket and carrying his field marshal's baton, Rommel was driven off. In transit to the Ulm Hospital he committed suicide. His death, according to the medical report, was caused by an embolism due to previous skull fractures. The field marshal's face, recalled his relatives, was marked by an "expression of colossal contempt."

2

By the end of September 1944 Hitler had lost three allies: Finland, Romania and Bulgaria. October brought a further defection. Horthy, the Hungarian admiral without a navy, who was nominally ruler of a kingdom without a king, sent envoys to Moscow to beg for an armistice. After all, the fiction of his independence had ended with the Nazi occupation of Hungary earlier that year—and Soviet troops were less than a hundred miles from the capital. Since a secret in Budapest was usually discussed loudly in cafés, Hitler knew all about the negotiations. While the Hungarian deputies were arguing fruitlessly in Moscow for better conditions, Hitler sent his favorite commando, Otto Skorzeny, to Hungary to bring her leaders back in line. He did so with a minimum of bloodshed in probably the most imaginative operation of the war, aptly titled Mickey Mouse. He simply kidnaped Horthy's son Miki, wrapped him in a carpet (Skorzeny got the idea from Shaw's play, *Caesar and Cleopatra*) and delivered him to the airport. He then proceeded to capture the citadel where Admiral Horthy lived and ruled with a single parachute battalion. It took half an hour and cost seven lives.

Six days later he was greeted at Wolfsschanze by Hitler with a warm "Well done!" His description of the kidnaping of young Horthy greatly amused Hitler. As Skorzeny rose to go, Hitler stayed him. "I am now go-

ing to give you the most important job of your life." He told of the surprise attack in the Ardennes. Skorzeny, he said, would play a leading role
by training men to masquerade as Americans. They would work behind
American lines—in American uniforms, with American vehicles. They
would seize bridges over the Meuse, spread rumors, issue false orders, breed
confusion and panic.

By this time Jodl had presented Hitler with the draft of his plan for
the offensive. First it was given the symbolic name of Christrose but that
morning the Führer himself changed it to Watch on the Rhine to deceive
any spy. It called for the use of three armies with a combined strength of
twelve Panzer and eighteen infantry divisions. Watch on the Rhine was
based on two premises: complete surprise, and weather that would ground
Allied planes. It was designed to break through on a wide front, cross the
Meuse on the second day and reach Antwerp on the seventh day. It would
not only destroy more than thirty American and British divisions but drive
a great wedge—psychological as well as physical—between the Americans
and British. The defeat would be so smashing that the West would sue
for a separate peace. Then all German troops would be thrown against the
Red Army.

To insure absolute secrecy only a select few were told of the offensive;
a different code name for the offensive was to be used at every command
level and changed every two weeks; nothing of the offensive was to be
trusted to telephone or teletype; officers, sworn to silence, would be used
as couriers. Only with such precautions, reasoned Hitler, could the spy at
his headquarters be foiled.

Field Marshal Model, the Führer's personal choice to command the
offensive, read the plan with dismay. "This damned thing hasn't got a leg
to stand on!" he complained. Rundstedt shared his concern and offered a
counterplan, a more modest attack of twenty divisions on a forty-mile
front. "Apparently you don't remember Frederick the Great," Hitler
remarked sarcastically. "At Rossbach and Leuten he defeated enemies
twice his strength. How? By a bold attack." It was the same old story. His
generals lacked imagination for the Big Solution. "Why don't you people
study history?"

He patiently explained how Frederick had taken his great risk and
then, as if in reward for daring, a bolt from the blue had come—*an
unpredictable historical accident*: the alliance against Prussia suddenly
split apart. And Frederick, doomed to defeat by every expert in Europe,
went on to win the Fatherland's greatest victory.

"History will repeat itself," he said. His eyes shone. This was the
Hitler of old, full of confidence and visions. "The Ardennes will by *my*
Rossbach and Leuten. And as a result another unpredictable historical accident will take place: the alliance against the Reich will suddenly split
apart!"

His own alliance with Japan, incidentally, was of little value. The Nipponese had just suffered another catastrophic loss. MacArthur had not only successfully landed in force on the Philippine island of Leyte but in the ensuing naval battle of Leyte Gulf the imperial navy had lost 300,000 tons of combat shipping: four carriers, three battleships, six heavy cruisers, three light cruisers and ten destroyers. Never again would the Japanese navy play more than a minor role in the hopeless defense of the homeland. And Japanese troops in Manchuria were no longer any threat to Hitler's nemesis, the Red Army, for they were being shipped out in force to stem the Americans.

On November 10 Hitler signed an order to prepare for the Ardennes offensive. He made it clear that this was a do-or-die proposition, a last gamble. The tone of his directiveness incurred the protests of the senior commanders in the West and Hitler decided to leave Wolfsschanze so he could explain his purpose in person despite a sudden relapse in spirit and body. His hoarseness had increased and the examination of Professor van Eicken revealed a small polyp on his right vocal cord. He was cranky and depressed; visitors were shaken to see him propped up on his spare cot, pale and drawn. Ignoring Morell's orders, he would drag himself out of bed to the map room, feeling his way like an old man. Breathing heavily, he would finally flop into a chair and wipe his brow. To keep him going during the ensuing briefings Dr. Morell had to administer numerous injections.

Hitler was advised to take a brief vacation before undertaking a trip to the western front that would be arduous, if not dangerous, in his present condition. But he was obsessed by the need to inspire those who must lead the offensive. On November 20 he entrained with his entourage. He must have known it was the last time he would ever see the Wolfsschanze, but he kept up the fiction of returning by allowing the reconstruction work to continue. His train did not leave until dawn since Hitler wanted to arrive in Berlin after dark. He sat in his compartment with all the shades drawn until lunch, then joined the others in the dining car. Traudl had never seen him so downcast and absent-minded. "His voice was only a soft whisper; his eyes were either glued to his plate or staring at a spot on the white tablecloth. It was such a depressing atmosphere that all of us had a strange ominous feeling."

Without preamble Hitler announced that Professor van Eicken would perform another operation on his throat. It was not dangerous, he said, as if assuring himself. "But it is quite possible that I am losing my voice and . . ." He never finished the sentence. He remained in seclusion for the next few days and the family circle knew only that Eicken had removed a polyp the size of a millet seed. Finally he appeared unexpectedly for breakfast; he was obviously looking for company. Everyone extinguished cigarettes; windows were opened to clear the air. He could only whisper. Doctor's orders, he said, and before long everyone was unconsciously imitating him. "My ears are fine and there is no need to spare them," he murmured softly, and everyone laughed, more in relief that he was again in good spirits than at the joke.

He returned to work with a resilience that astonished his entourage, vigorously applying himself to the Ardennes offensive that would turn around the course of the war. On December 7 he approved the final draft. It was almost exactly the same plan he had first proposed. To guarantee security radio operators dispatched coded messages to fictitious headquarters, fictitious messages to genuine headquarters, genuine messages to headquarters a hundred miles from their advertised location. False rumors were spread in lower echelons, in beer halls, in restaurants for the ears of Allied agents.

By now Otto Skorzeny, wielding more power as lieutenant colonel than some colonel generals, had reached mid-term of his "School for Americans." Though he had never been to the United States, his volunteers were doing well. The course: American slang, habits, folkways, and how to spread panic as pseudo GIs behind enemy lines. On December 11 the build-up was nearly complete. The Reichsbahn, achieving a miracle in railroading, had delivered the first wave to the Zone of the Offensive—without being observed by the enemy. Early that morning Hitler moved into his new headquarters near the medieval castle of Ziegenberg. This was Eagle's Eyrie, his headquarters for the 1940 invasion of the West, but now he and his entourage were housed in deep underground shelters.

Later in the day he met with half of his division commanders; the rest would come tomorrow. Upon arrival the first group of generals and their staffs were stripped of revolvers and briefcases by the Gestapo. Each man was forced to swear on his life that he would reveal nothing of what he was about to hear. Not one knew why he had been summoned; only that every division had been going in circles for weeks.

The meeting took place in a large underground room. The Führer sat at a narrow table flanked by Keitel and Jodl. Across were Rundstedt, Model and Lieutenant General Hasso von Manteuffel, who would command the most powerful of the three armies in the offensive. A descendant of a famous family of Prussian generals, Baron von Manteuffel was an ex-gentleman jockey and German pentathlon champion. Standing little more than five feet tall, he was tough-minded, possessed formidable energy and was one of the few who dared to disagree openly with Hitler.

For over an hour Hitler lectured to the sixty or so officers on Frederick the Great, the history of Germany and National Socialism. His voice was strong, his eyes flashed excitedly as he explained the political motives for deciding upon an all-out offensive. Then Autumn Fog—its final code name—was explained in detail. It would start at 5:30 A.M. on

December 15. The divisional commanders listened in awe, impressed not only by the grandiosity of the plan but by the Führer's vigor and good health. But Manteuffel was almost close enough to touch him and saw he was actually "a broken man, with an unhealthy color, a caved-in appearance in his manner, with trembling hands; sitting as if the burden of responsibility seemed to oppress him, and compared to his looks at the last conference in the beginning of December, his body seemed still more decrepit; he was a man grown old." Manteuffel also caught the Führer surreptitiously maneuvering his hands under the table so one could move the other which was almost completely limp.

Those out front could see none of this and remained impressed to the end, which came with a ringing pronouncement: "The battle must be fought with brutality and all resistance must be broken. In this most serious hour of the Fatherland, I expect every one of my soldiers to be courageous and again courageous. The enemy must be beaten—now or never! Thus lives Germany!"

The next day, December 12, the second group heard the same exhortations. There was one difference: the offensive was once more postponed (as in 1940). *Null*-Day was now set for December 16. This, said Hitler, was a definite date. Definite, that is, if the weather was bad enough to ground Allied aircraft.

3

The night of December 15 was cold and quiet along the Ardennes front. Twisting eighty-five miles through terrain similar to New England's Berkshires, it was held by six American divisions. Of these, three were new, the other three exhausted and bled white in battle. This was known as the Ghost Front—a cold quiet place where for over two months both sides had rested and watched and avoided irritating each other.

That night no Allied commander seriously feared a German attack. Hours earlier Montgomery had stated flatly that the Germans "cannot stage major offensive operations." In fact things were so dull he asked Eisenhower if there was any objection to his going off to England the next week.

Three German armies—250,000 men and thousands of machines—had been moved secretly to the line of departure, the noise of half-tracks drowned out by low-flying planes. By midnight of the fifteenth the troops were assembled at their assault posts. They stood shivering but listened with genuine enthusiasm as officers read a message from Field Marshal von Rundstedt:

> *We gamble everything!* You carry with you the holy obligation to give all to achieve superhuman objectives for our Fatherland and our Führer!

The excitement of old victories rose in the men. Once more they were on the attack. Deutschland über Alles!

At 5:30 A.M. an eruption of flame and smoke burst all along the Ghost Front. For eighty-five miles mortars coughed, rockets hissed up their launching platforms, 88s roared. The ground shook. Hundreds of tanks rumbled and clanked, and from the rear came the hollow boom of railroad guns hurling their fourteen-inch shells at targets miles behind the American lines.

After an hour the barrage stopped. There was a stunned, momentary silence. Ghostly white-sheeted forms, almost invisible against the new-fallen snow, came out of the haze toward GIs advancing in a slow ominous walk twelve and fourteen abreast. As Hitler's infantrymen filtered into the American forward position, planes of a new design came out of the east with a strange crackling roar, streaking by at unbelievable speed. The Germans looked up at their new jets and many cheered, wild with excitement. Hitler's "miracle weapons" were not talk but fact.

The power, fervor and surprise of their attack were met with a stubborn, if makeshift, defense by the green or worn-out American troops. Cooks and bakers, clerks and musicians, loggers and truck drivers were thrown pell-mell into the line to stem the tide. Some turned in terror and ran; many stood and fought. In some places the Americans held; in others the Germans burst through almost unopposed. In the north a narrow valley called the Losheim Gap was lightly defended even though this had been the classic gateway from east to west. Through this seven-mile corridor invading German armies had poured in 1870, in 1914 and in 1940. Once more German troops—this time accompanied by tanks, armored cars and assault guns—advanced unimpeded into the Gap.

By dusk the northern part of the United States lines was in a shambles but General Omar Bradley, leader of more combat troops than any American field commander in history, had received such fragmentary reports that he assured Eisenhower it was merely a "spoiling attack." Eisenhower disagreed. "This is no local attack, Brad," he said. "It isn't logical for the Germans to launch a local attack at our weakest point." He didn't think they could afford "to sit on their hands" until they found out, and told Bradley to send two armored divisions to the rescue.

Hitler was elated at the reports of breakthrough in the north. Late that night he telephoned the commander of Army Group B far south of the Ardennes. "From this day on, Balck," Hitler said, "not a foot of ground is to be given up. Today we march!" He told how his tanks were already poised on the heights above the road to Bastogne. And the weather was still "Hitler weather." Fog, drizzle and haze, it was forecast, would continue to ground Allied planes. "Balck, Balck," he exclaimed, "everything has changed in the West! Success—complete success—is now in our grasp!"

Success continued and at noon, December 18, German broadcasters raised the hopes of the people. "Our troops are again on the march," said one announcer. "We shall present the Führer with Antwerp by Christmas." At Eagle's Eyrie Hitler was learning that a Manteuffel column had opened up the road to Bastogne. Major penetrations had been achieved just as predicted and he talked confidently of a victory that would turn the tide. He felt so good he took a short walk in the countryside and was so refreshed he decided to do it every day.

In Paris there was near panic in many French government offices. The Blitzkrieg of 1940 was still a fresh, bitter memory. At SHAEF headquarters in Versailles an excited delegation of high-ranking French officers headed by General Juin had arrived to find out what was happening in the Ardennes. The Frenchmen were amazed at the succession of calm orderly offices. "I don't understand," exclaimed one agitated general. "You're not packing!"

By midnight the Ardennes battlefield was in turmoil, a scene of indescribable confusion to those involved in the hundreds of struggles. No one —German or American, private or general—knew what was really happening. In the next two days a series of disasters struck the defenders. On the snowy heights of the Schnee Eiffel at least 8000 Americans—perhaps 9000 for the battle was too confused for accuracy—were bagged by Hitler's troops. Next to Bataan, it was the greatest mass surrender of Americans in history.

Only seven jeeploads of Skorzeny men in American uniforms managed to break through the lines but these were raising havoc beyond his initial hopes. The leader of one team was directing an American regiment down the wrong road while his men were changing signposts and snipping telephone wires. Another jeepload, stopped by a United States column for information, feigned fear so convincingly that the Americans caught their panic and turned tail. A third group severed the main telephone cables connecting the headquarters of Bradley and his commander in the north, General Courtney Hodges.

But the greatest damage was done by a team that had been captured. When the four confessed their mission to an American intelligence officer the news was immediately broadcast that thousands of Germans in American uniforms were operating as saboteurs behind the lines. At once this information was associated with a verified report of widely dispersed parachutists north of Malmédy—an abortive paradrop which had failed even more dismally than Skorzeny's operation. Out of two fiascos was developing a formidable success.

By December 20 half a million Americans throughout the Ardennes were quizzing each other on lonely roads, in dense pine forests and in deserted villages. Passwords and dog tags no longer proved identity. You were an American only if you knew the capital of Pennsylvania, the identity of "Pruneface" or how many homers Babe Ruth had hit.

In Paris terror of Skorzeny and his men had reached panic peak. According to one hysterical report, Skorzeny men dressed as nuns and priests had just floated to earth. Their destination, according to the confession of a captured Skorzenyite, was the Café de la Paix. There they would join forces and kidnap Eisenhower. American security officers firmly believed this fabrication. SHAEF headquarters was surrounded with barbed wire and the guard quadrupled. Tanks stood at the gates, passes were examined and re-examined. If a door slammed, Eisenhower's office was pestered with calls asking if he was still alive. Skorzeny's twenty-eight men had done their work well.

By the following morning, the twenty-first, the battle had assumed a recognizable shape. It was a giant bulge. In the middle, at Bastogne, completely surrounded, was a collection of Americans under an acting commander of the 101st Airborne Division, Brigadier General Anthony McAuliffe, the division artillery officer. Called upon to surrender by a German *parlementaire*, he offhandedly replied, "Nuts." The one-word message spread throughout the Ardennes and helped raise the flagging spirits of the defenders. The time for running had stopped. The spirit of resistance was followed by an abrupt end of "Hitler weather." A bright sun shone next morning on the Ardennes for the first time and before noon sixteen big C-47s were dropping supplies to the encircled men at Bastogne.

The tide of battle was threatening to turn but Hitler did not yet know it. Manteuffel's tanks were already far beyond the American enclave of Bastogne and approaching the Meuse. But Manteuffel himself was deeply concerned; the German infantry army on his left was far behind. On December 24 he phoned Führer Headquarters from a château near La Roche. "Time is running short," he told Jodl. His left flank was exposed and the time had come for a complete new plan. He could not keep driving toward the Meuse and still take Bastogne. When Jodl protested that the Führer would never abandon the drive to Antwerp, Manteuffel argued that there was still a chance for a great victory *if* they followed his plan. "I'll wheel north on this side of the Meuse. We'll trap the Allies east of the river." The proposal shocked Jodl but he promised to pass it on to the Führer.

But Hitler would not believe that full success could not be achieved. His confidence carried over to Christmas, which he celebrated, to the amazement of his circle, with a glass of wine. It was the first time Fräulein Schröder had ever seen him take wine with any pleasure. Later in the day

Recently rescued by the famous commando Otto Skorzeny (September 1943),
Mussolini is about to face Hitler. From rare movie film. TIEFENTHALER

Hitler's trousers after the blast.
BUNDESARCHIV

Shortly after the explosion, Hitler has changed
his uniform and had a bandage put on his left
hand, which is supporting his injured right arm.
L. to r., Keitel, Göring (Günsche and Jodl in
background), Hitler, Below. To the right,
Himmler jabs finger at General Lörzer. BIBLIO.
FÜR ZEIT.

Hitler marveling at his miraculous
escape from death earlier that day.
L. to r., Mussolini (who had just ar-
rived for a visit), Bormann, Admiral
Dönitz, Hitler, Göring, SS General
Fegelein (husband of Eva's sister
Gretl), General Lörzer. BIBLIO.
FÜR ZEIT.

Major Otto Remer, promoted to major general
by Hitler for his part in squashing the army
bomb plot, is congratulated by Goebbels. On
left, Hans Hagen, an author in uniform, who
helped Remer. REMER

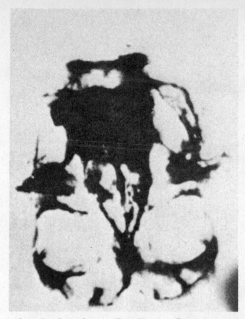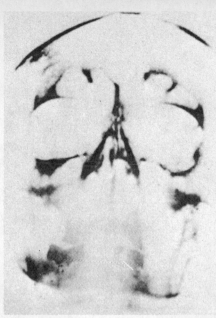

After the bombing, Dr. Erwin Giesing persuaded Hitler to allow X rays of his skull taken. NATIONAL ARCHIVES

Field Marshal Rommel was forced to take poison for participating in the plot. Here, two years earlier, he is being honored for his victories in the desert. Behind. l. to r., Engel, Keitel and Schulze. U. S. ARMY

Right, Field Marshal Walther Model, Hitler's personal choice to command his last gamble, the Battle of the Bulge, December 1944. Left, Bodenschatz; center, Luftwaffe General von Richthofen. U. S. ARMY

General Hasso von Manteuffel, German pentathlon champion, whose tanks almost reached the Meuse River. MANTEUFFEL

Left, the Reich Chancellery, March 1945. FRENTZ. Right, Hitler driven underground by Allied bombs. The waiting room of the Führer bunker. Extreme left, Dr. Morell. Center, Hitler's former valet Krause and Admiral von Puttkamer. PUTTKAMER

Cologne. AMERICAN COMMISSION FOR THE PROTECTION AND SALVAGE OF HISTORICAL MONUMENTS

Nuremberg, home of the Nazi Party Day.
AMERICAN COMMISSION FOR THE PROTECTION AND SALVAGE OF HISTORICAL MONUMENTS

In the midst of destruction, Hitler dreams of a new Munich, above, and a new Linz, below. Both cities were designed by Professor Hermann Giesler with Hitler's help. Behind, as usual, is Bormann.

One of the last pictures of Hitler. He visits Oder front, March 1945. BIBLIO. FÜR ZEIT.

On October 10, 1943, Hitler congratulates Himmler, who has just revealed that six million Jews have been exterminated. U. S. ARMY

Millions more Jews and non-Jews died in concentration camps in the spring of 1945. Belsen. U. S. OFFICE OF WAR INFORMATION

The wedding certificate of Eva and Adolf Hitler, dated April 29, 1945. Note blurred date—it was originally April 28 and then mistakenly altered—and Eva's writing mistake. EISENHOWER LIBRARY

The End. After twelve years of imprisonment in the East, SS adjutant Günsche views the ruins of the Berghof. Left, personal adjutant Schulze. MONIKA SCHULZE-KOSSENS

he refused another request by Manteuffel to abandon the attack on Bastogne even though his most advanced Panzer division had just been cut off by an American armored division and was being smashed to pieces. December 26 was a day of Allied might. The snows that now blanketed the entire Ardennes were red with blood but nowhere was the carnage greater than in the pocket a few miles from the Meuse River where General Ernest "Gravel Voice" Harmon's 2nd Armored Division was savaging Manteuffel's 2nd Panzer Division in a hundred small engagements.

At Eagle's Eyrie an argument over Autumn Fog had continued since morning. Jodl was now saying, "Mein Führer, we must face the facts squarely. We cannot force the Meuse." The 2nd Panzer was close to disaster and Patton had just opened up a narrow corridor from the south to besieged Bastogne. Throughout the Ardennes it was the same story. For the moment it was a static struggle; the great offensive had been temporarily stalled.

Everyone had a plan and Hitler listened to them all. Finally he spoke. "We have had unexpected setbacks—because my plan was not followed to the letter." He frowned. Then his face lightened with a new hope. "But all is not yet lost." He issued new orders: Manteuffel was to turn to the northeast, thus outflanking most of the Americans in the top half of the bulge. "I want three new divisions and at least 25,000 fresh replacements rushed to the Ardennes," he announced to a semicircle of somber faces. Granted the Allies could not be wiped out in a single dramatic blow as planned, Autumn Fog could still be turned into a successful battle of attrition. And this would surely bring Germany a substantial political victory.

These orders were intercepted by the Ultra team and passed on to Eisenhower—and he was assured that Hitler's attack had shot its bolt. What Ultra did not learn was that the Führer and his chosen successor had just engaged in a violent quarrel. At least the violence was on Hitler's side when Göring proposed they seek a truce. "The war is lost," he said. "Now we must get in touch with Count Bernadotte." Folke Bernadotte, whose father was Swedish King Gustavus V's brother, would surely act as mediator for any armistice negotiations.

Hitler, so a pale-faced Göring reported shortly to his wife, had raged and screamed about betrayal and cowardice but he himself had replied in an earnest and composed manner: "Mein Führer, I could never do anything behind your back." He assured Hitler that he would remain faithful in bad times as well as good, then repeated his conviction that an immediate armistice was essential. Hitler, he said, calmed down a bit but then sharply replied: "I forbid you to take any step in this matter. If you go against my orders I will have you shot." Never had Frau Göring seen her husband so shaken as he told her all this. "This is the final break," he said glumly. "There is no sense my attending any more daily briefings. He does not believe me any more. He does not listen to me."

4

To the Germans the classic struggle was known as the Ardennes Offensive but to the Americans it was the Battle of the Bulge. By December 28 its third and final phase was fast approaching. At a special meeting of his top military leaders that day Hitler admitted the situation was desperate, but he had never learned the word "capitulation" and would pursue his aim with fanaticism. "As much as I may be tormented by worries and even physically shaken by them, nothing will make the slightest change in my decision to fight on till at last the scales tip to our side." He was, therefore, launching a new offensive, North Wind, on New Year's Day south of the Ardennes. Chances of victory were bright. The final assembly of troops had been completely camouflaged from the Allies, who had failed even to send up any air reconnaissance in the area. "These people did not think it necessary to look around. They did not believe it at all likely that we could take the initiative. Perhaps they were even influenced by the conviction that I am already dead or that, at any rate, I suffer from cancer . . ." The irrelevant allusion to cancer near the anniversary of his mother's death from that disease was revealing.

He went on to say that their first aim was to clear up the situation in the West by offensive action. "We must be fanatical in this aim," he said and resorted to sarcasm. "Perhaps there are still some who will secretly object, saying: 'All right, but will it succeed?' Gentlemen, the same objection was raised in the year 1939. I was told in writing and vocally that the thing could not be done; that it was impossible. Even in the winter of 1940 I was told: 'You cannot do that. Why don't we stay behind the Westwall?'" His voice hardened. "What would have happened to us if we had not attacked them? You have exactly the same situation today."

During the military conference that same day Rundstedt made the mistake of urging Hitler to abandon Autumn Fog and retreat before an Allied counteroffensive started. Hitler flared up. They would renew the drive to the Meuse, he said, just as soon as North Wind got under way. He jabbed a finger at a point on the large wall map a hundred miles south of the Bulge. Throughout German history New Year's Eve had always been a night of good omen for German arms and this year's would be an unpleasant surprise for an enemy who always celebrated New Year rather than Christmas. The certain success of North Wind, he said, would "automatically bring about the collapse of the threat to the left of the main offensive in the Ardennes"—he stressed the next few words—"*which will then be resumed* with a fresh promise of success." His listeners were impressed by his ardor, belied as it was by a trembling left hand and wan appearance. "In the meantime," he continued, "Model will consolidate his holdings and reorganize for a new attempt on the Meuse. And he will also make another powerful assault on Bastogne. Above all, we must have Bastogne!" By midnight nine Panzer and Volksgrenadier divisions began to converge on the town Hitler wanted at all costs.

"Military qualities don't show themselves in an exercise on a sand model," he told General Thomale, inspector general of the armored forces, the following night. "In the last analysis they show themselves in the capacity to hold on, in perseverance and determination. That's the decisive factor in any victory. Genius is a will-o'-the-wisp unless it is founded on perseverance and fanatical determination. That's the most important thing in human existence." World history, he said, could only be made by a man with fanatical determination who had the courage of his convictions. "No one can last forever. We can't, the other side can't. It's merely a question of who can stand it longer. The one who must hold out longer is the one who's got everything at stake." If America gave up nothing would happen to her; New York would still be New York. "But if we were to say today, 'We've had enough,' Germany would cease to exist." That was why Hitler doggedly continued a war that seemed lost. To a gambler like him a thousand-to-one chance was worth taking. What would be sheer madness to another was only logical for one with his obsession.

His chief propagandist was not as sanguine—at least in private. At an intimate New Year's Eve supper, which included Hans Ulrich Rudel, the famous Stuka pilot, Josef Goebbels remarked sardonically that his title as Reich Plenipotentiary for the Total War Effort was quite hollow. "Now there is nothing left to put into effect," he said. "Everything, including all the flower shops, have been closed by British bombers."

At this point Frau Goebbels interrupted with a remark that the guests found hard to believe. "Why don't you tell these old soldiers that for the past three and a half years you have seldom managed to see the Führer alone." Goebbels was embarrassed and tried to stop her, but she would not be quieted: "These people have the right to know about this." Goebbels turned to Hein Ruck, who had warned him in the first days of Hitler's chancellorship that many SA men like himself were not at all happy with Hitler's compromise with the German nationalists. Such a compromise, according to Ruck, would lead eventually to the death of National Socialism. At that time Goebbels had angrily accused Ruck of being an opportunist but now the Propaganda Minister said ruefully, "I should have taken your words more seriously back in 1933." The talk switched to the political and military blunders made in the past few years and there was almost general agreement that the end was at hand. All except Rudel, who exclaimed that the Führer's new secret weapons would bring a surprise victory.

Just before midnight Operation North Wind, designed to take Allied pressure from the Bulge, was launched and eight German divisions rushed from their Westwall position with great élan to assault the Seventh U. S. Army near the boundary of northern Alsace. To the north in the Ardennes, a tremendous artillery barrage erupted at the stroke of midnight. The irrepressible George Patton had ordered every available gun in his command to fire a New Year's salute.

Five minutes later Adolf Hitler's voice, somewhat raspy but confident, was broadcast throughout the Reich. Germany, he said, would rise like a phoenix from its ruined cities and go to ultimate victory. Afterward he entertained the family circle in his private bunker. Everyone was relaxed by champagne but there was a subdued atmosphere. The most enthusiastic was Hitler, who needed no alcohol. The others listened in silence to his prophecies of great success for Germany in 1945. At first Bormann alone seconded them but as Hitler went on for more than an hour the others became infected by his enthusiasm in spite of themselves.

At 4:35 A.M. the Führer left the gathering so he could hear the first reports of North Wind. It started auspiciously but the Ultra team had succeeded in passing on his battle directives to Eisenhower, who quickly reduced the U. S. Seventh Army front and prevented the Germans from cutting off a salient. Thanks to the warning, the Americans were able to hold off the German attack, which came to a standstill after a fifteen-mile advance.

In the Ardennes the Allies went over to the offensive on January 3, 1945, with massive attacks on the center of the Bulge from north and south designed to cut the huge salient in two. The Germans fought tenaciously, yielding every yard of snow at heavy cost to both sides. They were dug in with their usual efficient use of terrain. American troops moved slowly since the dense fog eliminated air support and cut down the use of artillery. Tanks and self-propelled guns slipped and skidded on the iced trails and roads, often crashing into each other.

Churchill flew over from England to observe the counteroffensive, which was being supported by a considerable British assault on the western tip of the Bulge. On January 6 he met with Eisenhower, who was vexed by the slow, arduous progress of the British and American troops. Was it possible, he asked, to get help from the Russians to take pressure from the Ardennes? Churchill knew that Stalin was mounting a new offensive but not when it would start. "You may find many delays on the staff level," he told Eisenhower. "But I expect Stalin would tell me if I asked him. Shall I try?" The answer was a relieved yes, and that same day Churchill cabled a request for a major Russian offensive during January. The response from Moscow was immediate. A large-scale attack, said Stalin, would be launched not later than the second half of January.

Simultaneously Allied drives from north and south, designed to pinch the Bulge in its midriff, began to gain ground on the morning of January 7 and by the following day had drawn so close together that Hitler was forced to authorize a withdrawal of those units in the western half of the salient. Within an hour those Panzers which had almost crossed the Meuse did an about-face and hastened to get east of the Bastogne–Liège highway.

It was the end of Hitler's great dream. Now the question was: would the hundreds of thousands of German tanks and self-propelled guns lumbering eastward cross the highway in time or be caught in a sack? Would the attempted retreat be another Stalingrad?

On the ninth of January Guderian once more journeyed to Eagle's Eyrie and warned Hitler for the third time that the Red Army was about to launch a massive offensive. Today he brought maps and charts made up by Gehlen, his chief of intelligence, showing the relative distributions of strength—and Gehlen's recommendation that East Prussia be evacuated immediately if Berlin itself were to be held.

When Guderian displayed the maps and charts, Hitler angrily labeled them "completely idiotic" and ordered his chief of staff to have the man who had made them shut up in a lunatic asylum. Guderian lost his temper. "The man who made these," he said, "is General Gehlen, one of my best General Staff officers. I should not have shown them to you were I in disagreement with them. If you want Gehlen sent to a lunatic asylum, then you had better have me certified as well!" Hitler's flare-up subsided and he mixed reassurances with praise. "The eastern front," he said, "has never before possessed such a strong reserve as now. That is your doing. I thank you for it."

Guderian was not placated. "The eastern front," he said, "is like a house of cards. If the front is broken through at one point all the rest will collapse, since twelve and a half divisions are far too small a reserve for so extended a front." Hitler, as usual, had the last word. He refused to deprive the Ardennes of any of its reserves on the ground that there was still hope of limited success there. "The eastern front," he concluded, "must help itself and make do with what it's got." As Guderian drove back to his headquarters at Zossen he was glum. He knew that both Hitler and Jodl were as aware as he that any major Soviet offensive could easily break through the unreinforced lines. Had they blinded themselves to the catastrophe that was imminent in the East because neither had been born in that region? To Prussians like himself, it was a homeland won at great cost—to be defended at all cost.

Three days later Stalin kept his word to Churchill. Almost 3,000,000 Red Army troops—more than a dozen times those landed by the Allies on D-Day—attacked some 750,000 poorly armed Germans on a four-hundred-mile front extending from the Baltic Sea right down the middle of Poland. Supported by massed artillery and led by seemingly inexhaustible streams of "Stalin" and T-34 tanks, hordes of Red infantrymen began storming the pitifully inadequate defense system devised by Guderian. Although weather grounded most of the Red Air Force tactical support, by dusk the first echelon of attackers had pushed forward as much as twelve miles.

Germany was now caught between powerful forces on east and west, for that day also saw substantial victory in the Ardennes. American infantry divisions—including Vice-President Truman's old outfit, the 35th—joined with the 6th Armored Division to trap thousands of first-rate German troops east of Bastogne.

At Eagle's Eyrie Hitler appeared serene to Traudl Junge, who was just returning from Christmas holidays in Munich. At dinner he answered her grim stories of the heavy air raids on Munich with a promise. "This nightmare will abruptly stop in a few weeks," he said. "Our new jets are coming out in quantity now, and then the Allies will be leery of flying over Germany." In mid-January Hitler and his entourage left Eagle's Eyrie for new headquarters in Berlin. Outwardly Hitler did not appear at all depressed, and in fact laughed with the others when someone joked that Berlin was now the only practical place for headquarters since one could travel between the west and east fronts by subway.

A fresh pincer attack had just been launched on the evaporating Bulge from north and south. On January 16 the two forces met a few miles north of Bastogne. In one great bite, half of the Bulge had been eliminated and about 20,000 Germans cut off. The feat was marred by bitterness between Americans and Britons. It had started a few days earlier when Montgomery, in charge of the northern half of the Battle of the Bulge, gave correspondents the impression that he had personally saved the day and that British troops in large numbers were helping extricate the Americans from their hole. Most American correspondents were irritated at what they considered a patronizing tone in the announcement since it was well known that relatively few British troops were involved and that American generals, for the most part, felt impeded by Montgomery's deliberate tactics. For a few days it appeared as if Hitler's dream of driving a wedge between the two Allies had, thanks to human nature, succeeded. But Eisenhower, as much diplomat as soldier, effectively smoothed out ruffled feathers in both camps.

By January 17 there was no consolation at all for Hitler. Manteuffel's army had joined the full retreat. A few picked infantrymen were left behind—the very young, old and useless. These men fought a gallant rearguard battle in lonely hopelessness. Boys of fourteen and fifteen died, rifles frozen to their hands; men in their fifties were found in cellars, feet black with putrefaction. The retreating columns were harassed by planes and big guns. None who survived would ever forget the overpowering American artillery. Winding lines of trucks, tanks and self-propelled guns rumbled toward the Fatherland over icy roads and trails clogged with snowdrifts. Long columns of infantrymen tramped in the snow, tormented as much by the bitter weather as by the retreating enemy.

The Battle of the Bulge was over. Left behind were two tiny ravaged countries, destroyed homes and farms, dead cattle, dead souls, dead minds —and more than 75,000 bodies.

Autumn Fog was creeping back to the Führer like some huge wounded beast. It reminded many of Napoleon's retreat from Moscow. Men shuffled painfully through the snow, feet encased in burlap bags, with shawls wound around their heads like careless turbans. They plodded on frozen feet, bedeviled by biting winds, bombs and shells. The wounded and sick crept back to the homeland with rotting insides, ulcers oozing, pus running from destroyed ears. They staggered east on numb feet with despair in their hearts, stricken by dysentery, which left its bloody trail of filth in the snow.

Their will was broken. Few who survived the retreat believed there was now any chance of German victory. Almost every man brought back a story of doom, of Allied might and of the terrifying weapon forged in the Ardennes: the American fighter. The GI who came out of the battle was the quintessential American, the man Hitler did not believe existed.

Chapter Thirty

"THIS TIME
WE MUST NOT SURRENDER
FIVE MINUTES BEFORE
MIDNIGHT"
JANUARY 17–APRIL 20, 1945

1

By January 17, 1945, the Red Army had overrun or by-passed German troops in the Baltic and crossed the Vistula River from Warsaw to Lower Silesia. The Soviets were so close to Auschwitz that inmates could hear the rumble of their artillery. For the past weeks SS guards had been burning storehousefuls of shoes, clothing and hair to hide traces of mass exterminations. Within two days most German officials in the area were in flight and the over-age *Volkssturm* (People's Militia) had disintegrated. That afternoon guards lined up 58,000 ill-clothed, hungry inmates in a freezing wind and marched them to the west for possible use as hostages. Some 6000 others, too ill to struggle to their feet, were left behind, it was hoped, to be disposed of by bombs and shells in the Soviet advance, but when the Red Army troops finally, on January 27, streamed through the front gate with its slogan Work Brings Freedom, there were still almost 5000 emaciated survivors, so weak they could barely cheer. Efforts to obliterate all traces of the murders at the vast complex had continued until that morning with the final blasting of the gas chambers and five crematoria, but even this could not wipe out the grisly proof of what had gone on in Hitler's death factory. Despite fires and detonations, Red Cross officials found 368,820 men's suits, 836,255 women's coats, 13,964 carpets and seven tons of hair. They came upon mountains of toothbrushes, eyeglasses, shoes, artificial limbs—and the mass graves of hundreds of thousands of human beings.

In Berlin that afternoon General Guderian and his aide climbed the dozen steps up to the main door of the chancellery to attend the Führer military conference. Once inside they took a long detour to Hitler's office; direct passage was closed off by damage from Allied bombs. They passed windows covered by cardboard, through corridors and rooms barren of pictures, carpets and tapestries, finally reaching an anteroom where guards stood poised with machine pistols. An SS officer politely requested them to hand over their side arms and carefully examined their briefcases. This, a regulation since July 20, applied even to the army chief of staff.

By four o'clock the room was filled with military leaders, including Göring, Keitel and Jodl. Moments later the doors to the Führer's office were opened, revealing a spacious room sparingly decorated. In the middle of one wall was a massive desk, behind it a black-upholstered chair facing the garden. The high-ranking conferees seated themselves in heavy leather chairs while their aides and the lesser members either stood or found straight chairs.

At 4:20 P.M. Adolf Hitler shuffled in, shoulders stooped, left arm hanging loose. He greeted a few with a limp shake from his incapacitated right hand, then heavily sank into a chair pushed forward by an aide. The conference opened with Guderian reporting realistically on the growing disaster in the East. Hitler made remarkably few suggestions, almost as if it were beyond his scope, but once the western front came up for discussion he showed lively interest, interspersing criticism with nostalgic reminiscences from his war ("Usually, in the First World War, in 1915 and 1916—we really had an ammunition allowance that would make your hair stand on end"), then engaging in a lengthy argument with Göring about the reduced rank given officers called out of retirement to active duty. The conference ended at 6:50 P.M. and Guderian started back to Zossen. He was disgusted. They had talked for two and a half hours without reaching a single important decision on the problems of the critical eastern front.

One of those problems was Himmler, who had just been placed in command of an emergency army group designed to stop the main thrust of Marshal G. K. Zhukov. To Guderian his selection was plain idiocy but Hitler had argued that the Reichsführer was the only man capable of forming a major force overnight; his name alone would inspire a fight to the end. Bormann had encouraged this appointment but those close to Himmler were convinced it was a plot to ruin their chief. Sending him to the East would not only keep him away from Führer Headquarters and allow Bormann to strengthen his growing hold on Hitler, but would inevitably give convincing proof of Himmler's military incompetence.

Himmler, an ex-army cadet who secretly longed to lead troops into battle, took the bait, if a bit reluctantly. While he feared Bormann, it never occurred to him that his rival was preparing his downfall. He started east in his special train determined to halt the Russians at the Vistula River. To do so he had a few staff officers, one outdated map and a name for his unit, Army Group Vistula. Except for several scattered units, his command existed only on paper. As new divisions arrived, Himmler foolishly began forming an east-west defense line running from the Vistula to the Oder, which merely served as protection for Pomerania to the north. In other words, he barricaded the side door while leaving the front gate wide open.

Zhukov, consequently, simply by-passed this lateral line and kept moving due west, impeded only by isolated groups, and, as the Führer conference ended on January 27, his troops were a hundred miles from Berlin. Ahead lay the Oder, the last major geographical obstacle they would have to hurdle before reaching the Reich chancellery.

Three days later Hitler spoke to the people. He raised the specter of international Jewry and Asiatic Bolshevism before calling on every German to do his duty to the last. "However grave the crisis may be at the moment," he concluded, "it will, despite everything, finally be mastered by our unalterable will, by our readiness for sacrifice and by our abilities. We shall overcome this calamity, too, and this fight, too, will not be won by central Asia but by Europe; and at its head will be the nation that has represented Europe against the East for 1500 years and shall represent it for all times: our Greater German Reich, the German nation."

During the afternoon Bormann found time to advise his "beloved Mummy-Girl" to lay in a supply of dried vegetables and, "say, fifty pounds of honey"; he also wrote her of the atrocities in the East where the Bolsheviks were ravaging every village. "You and the children must never fall into the hands of these wild beasts!"

Despite such news, the Führer was in good spirits. After the evening's briefing, some of the conferees stayed while he talked informally of the political situation. Relaxed, he spoke like a professor to a group of favorite students, first explaining that he had launched Autumn Fog to split the Allies. Although the battle had been lost, he said, the Americans and British were publicly wrangling over its conduct, a split between these Allies was imminent.

Guderian kept looking impatiently at his watch but the younger officers seemed mesmerized as the Führer predicted that the West was bound to realize before long that Bolshevism was their real enemy and then would join Germany in the common crusade. Churchill knew as well as he that if the Red Army conquered Berlin half of Europe would immediately become Communist and in a few years the other half would be digested. "I never did want to fight the West," he said bitterly. "They forced it on me." But Russia's program was becoming more and more obvious and Roosevelt himself must have had his eyes opened when Stalin recognized the Communist-backed Lublin Government in Poland. "Time is our ally," he said. That was why he demanded last-ditch defenses in the East. Wasn't it obvious that every Festung they hung onto would eventually be a springboard in the German-American-British crusade to wipe out Jewish Bolshevism? His voice rose as he reminded his listeners that in 1918 the Fatherland had been stabbed in the back by the General Staff. But for its premature surrender, Germany would have gained an honorable peace and there would have been no postwar chaos, no Communist attempts to seize the country, no inflation, no depression. "This time," he said, repeating an earlier vow, "we must not surrender five minutes before midnight!"

On the last day of January Hitler was wakened with alarming news: enemy tanks had just crossed the Oder River! No natural barrier of any consequence lay between them and Berlin. The panic in the capital was heightened three days later when the city was subjected to the heaviest bombing of the war. Almost a thousand American bombers leveled much of the center of the city and among the victims was Roland Friesler, president of the People's Court, who was trying Fabian von Schlabrendorff for the July 20 plot. Now Friesler lay pinned in death by a huge beam, still clutching the folder containing Schlabrendorff's evidence of guilt. "The way of God is miraculous," thought Schlabrendorff. "I was the accused; he was the judge. Now he is dead and I am alive."

He and two other defendants were hurriedly transferred by small car to the Gestapo prison. It was still early afternoon but the sky was dark from the smoke and falling ashes. Flames were everywhere. The Gestapo building at 9 Prinz Albrechtstrasse was burning yet its bomb shelter was only slightly damaged and as Schlabrendorff passed another prisoner, Admiral Canaris, he called out, "Friesler is dead!" The good news was passed along to other prisoners. With luck, the Allies would free them before the next trials.

Hitler's headquarters was also badly damaged in the raid and the next day Bormann described its woeful state to his wife. There was no communication with the outside, not even any light, power or water. "We have a water cart standing before the Reich chancellery, and that is our only supply for cooking and washing up! And the worst thing of all, so Müller tells me, is the toilets. These Kommando pigs use them constantly, and not one of them ever thinks of taking a bucket of water with him to flush the place." By this time Bormann, who now attended the daily military discussions, had insinuated himself into an impregnable position with the Führer. No longer were Göring, Speer and Himmler rivals for his trust and affection, and Goebbels had come to realize his own influence depended on a continuation of the uneasy alliance with the Reichsleiter.

A final mark of honor came to Bormann early in February. The Führer began dictating to him a political testament. If the Reich *did* fall— and Hitler still entertained the faint hope of some miracle—he wanted to record for history how closely he had come to achieving his magnificent dream. It was typical that he wanted the last word. And so on February 4, with the Bolsheviks at the gates of Berlin, the indefatigable Bormann began jotting down the Führer's final explanation to history of what went wrong. The British, he said, could have put an end to the war at the beginning of 1941. "But the Jews would have none of it. And their lackeys, Churchill and Roosevelt, were there to prevent it." Such a peace would have kept America from meddling in European affairs and, under German guidance, Europe would have speedily become unified. With the Jewish poison eliminated, unification would have been simple. And Germany, her rear secure, could have achieved "the ambition of my life and the raison d'étre of National Socialism—the destruction of Bolshevism." How simple it all would have been if only the English had been logical and reasonable! But they were neither and so he had been forced, as custodian of the fundamental interests of Germany, to wage total war.

Two days later there was another session. "Our enemies," dictated Hitler, "are gathering all their forces for the final assault." It was the final quarter of an hour. The situation was desperate. "We have facing us an incongruous coalition, drawn together by hatred and jealousy and cemented by the panic with which the National Socialist doctrine fills this Jew-ridden motley." This will to exterminate the Third Reich left but one alternative: a fight to the end. "No game is lost until the final whistle." If Churchill were suddenly to disappear, everything could change in a flash! He began to daydream out loud of the possibility of an about-face by the British aristocracy. "We can still snatch victory in the final sprint!"

Next to Bormann, the man he saw most in these days was his favorite architect, Paul Giesler. They would spend many hours poring over an illuminated wooden model of the new Linz, which would outrank Vienna as the jewel of Austria, or talk until early morning of architecture and Bolshevism, of art and the Western Allies, of his dream of saving Europe and uniting it into one grand unity. It was the large model city that was an unfailing inspiration to him and sometimes Goebbels would be dragged out of bed so Hitler could demonstrate with lights how Linz would look in morning, noon and night. He could have been the young Hitler lecturing to Kubizek on the wonders of their rebuilt city.

2

On February 12 the Big Three announced that a meeting at Yalta had just concluded with unanimity on the defeat of the Axis and the world of the future. The communiqué was widely acclaimed in the United States, England and the Soviet Union. It also delighted Goebbels, for it gave him an opportunity to resurrect the bogey of unconditional surrender. The decision of Roosevelt, Churchill and Stalin at Yalta to dismember Germany and force her to pay crushing reparations, he argued, proved that Germany must fight with renewed vigor—or be obliterated.

Hitler's satisfaction at the propaganda windfall was tempered by an irritating conflict with Guderian at the next day's noon conference. The general bluntly declared that Himmler had neither the experience nor the proper staff to lead the proposed counterattack against the Zhukov spearhead at the Oder. "How dare you criticize the Reichsführer!" exclaimed Hitler. Guderian had gone too far to back down and insisted that his own deputy, Walter Wenck, take command of the operation. Hitler was incensed and the two men began to argue so strenuously that one by one the conferees unobtrusively left the room until only Himmler, Wenck and a few blank-faced adjutants remained. For about two hours their argument continued. Each time Hitler shouted, "How dare you!" and took a deep breath, Guderian would stolidly reiterate his demand that Wenck be made Himmler's assistant. And each time the demand was made, Himmler seemed to get a shade paler.

At last Hitler broke off his awkward pacing, stopped in front of the Reichsführer's chair and said, with a sigh of resignation, "Well, Himmler, General Wenck is going to Army Group Vistula tonight to take over as chief of staff." He sat down, exhausted. "Let us please resume the conference," he murmured and smiled wryly. "Herr Generaloberst, today the army General Staff won a battle."

Hitler found the time for more dictation the following day. The National Socialists, he told Bormann, had purged the German world of the Jewish poison by *action*, not words. "For us, this has been an essential process of disinfection, which we have prosecuted *to its ultimate limit* and without which we should have ourselves been asphyxiated and destroyed." He revealed that his elimination of Jews had become the most important aim of the war. On the eve of the attack on Poland he had warned them that "they would not be spared if they precipitated another war, and that I would exterminate the vermin throughout Europe, and this time once and for all." This was not a threat, he said, but his chief historical mission. "Well, we have lanced the Jewish abscess; and the world of the future will be eternally grateful to us."

The following evening Dr. Giesing chanced to meet Hitler in the chancellery air raid shelter. The Führer was pale, his right arm trembled; he could not walk any distance without grasping something for support. Hitler seemed quite absent-minded and several times asked the same question almost as if a needle was stuck on a record. "Where are you from, Doctor? Oh yes, Krefeld, Krefeld, yes, Krefeld . . ." He rambled on, first assuring Giesing that the Americans would never break through the Westwall, then declaring that if Germany *should* lose the war he would die with his troops, and finally boasting about a new weapon called an atom bomb, which he would use "even if the white cliffs of England disappear into the water." So saying, he walked off without a word of farewell.

Others noted this occasional absent-mindedness; and his growing shortness of temper was aggravated by the Allied bombing of Dresden on February 13. The old town was almost completely destroyed in a terrifying fire storm which lay waste 1600 acres—almost three times the damage done to London during the entire war. The preliminary report stated that at least 100,000 people, probably more, had been killed in two successive raids. The final report by the area police chief listed a probable death toll, "primarily women and children," of 25,000 with 35,000 listed as missing.

At first Goebbels refused to believe that Dresden had been destroyed, then wept. When at last he found voice it was to castigate Göring. "What a burden of guilt this parasite has brought on his head for his slackness and interest in his own comfort. Why didn't the Führer listen to my earlier warnings?" Hitler reserved his ire for the British and American fliers who had dropped the bombs, yet rejected Goebbels' suggestion that the Allied air force prisoners be executed in retaliation. He agreed in principle, he said, but wanted to wait before making the final decision. Ribbentrop and others were able to dissuade him.

That February rumors of peace negotiations appeared in newspapers of neutral European countries. They had been inspired largely by the latest efforts of Peter Kleist, who had been ordered explicitly by Hitler to cease all dealings with the Russians. He did so but then, on his own initiative, embarked on a new adventure in Sweden which led eventually to another attempt for peace, this time with the West. He had begun by agreeing to talk with Gilel Storch, an important representative of the World Jewish Congress. At their first conference in a Stockholm hotel Storch proposed that they negotiate for the release of some 4300 Jews from various concentration camps.

Kleist said it was impossible to solve the Jewish problem by such individual operations. It could only be done politically. "If the preservation of Jewry can be traded for the preservation of Europe," said Kleist, "then we will have a genuine 'deal' that's worth risking my life."

Storch was enthusiastic. He suggested Kleist speak with an American diplomat in the Stockholm Embassy, Ivor Olson, the personal adviser to

Roosevelt for the War Refugee Committee of Northern and Western Europe. Storch made the contact, reporting back excitedly that President Roosevelt was willing to redeem the lives of the 1,500,000 Jews in concentration camps "with politics." This was exactly what Kleist wanted and he repeated Storch's words to Werner Best, the Nazi commissioner of Denmark, whose advice was to approach Himmler's assistant, Kaltenbrunner.

Upon return to Berlin Kleist did so and was placed under house arrest, just as he had been for dealing with Clauss. But after a few days Kaltenbrunner informed him that Himmler was "willing to take up this Swedish possibility." Kleist was to go to Stockholm to start negotiations and, as a token of good faith, bring a gift of 2000 Jews with him. Interest in trading with Jews was not new to Himmler. He had been tentatively negotiating on this line in other quarters, using them as blackmail for a negotiated peace. He was being encouraged by two men of dubious character. One was his masseur, a doctor without a medical degree, Felix Kersten, a Balt, born in Estonia. The second self-seeker was Himmler's chief of espionage, Schellenberg. He too was attempting to convince Himmler that a show of humanity to political and war prisoners would prove to the world that he was no monster. Convinced that Hitler was leading Germany and himself to destruction, Schellenberg had been tirelessly urging Himmler to explore every possible avenue to peace.

This was no easy task since these negotiations had to be conducted without Hitler's knowledge; nor did it help that Kaltenbrunner was faithful to his Führer and, moreover, disliked and distrusted Schellenberg. Kaltenbrunner had continuously urged Himmler not to get into schemes that might result in Hitler's displeasure—or worse. That is, until he heard Kleist's latest proposition. He did trust Kleist, and that was undoubtedly one reason Himmler had been persuaded to send him back to Sweden.

But the machinations within the SS were such that no sooner did Kleist begin preparing for his trip than he was recalled to Kaltenbrunner's office and told that the case no longer concerned him. Kaltenbrunner could not explain that Schellenberg, his enemy, had just persuaded Himmler not to share any credit with the Foreign Office—and so was sending Dr. Kersten instead of Kleist to handle the transaction. Kersten promptly began negotiations with the Swedish Minister of Foreign Affairs for the freedom of Scandinavian prisoners in concentration camps, and these went so smoothly it was agreed that Count Folke Bernadotte should come to Berlin to make final arrangements with Himmler personally.

Since Kleist had been warned to keep quiet, his own chief, Ribbentrop knew nothing of all this until the Swedish ambassador in Berlin innocently sent an official message to Himmler requesting that Bernadotte be granted an interview with the Reichsführer—and being official, of course, it had to go through the Foreign Office. For the first time Ribbentrop realized that negotiations were being carried on by his rival behind his back. He sent for Fritz Hesse, who had so tirelessly worked for peace with England before the war. Did Hesse think that Count Bernadotte would be a suitable person to transmit "peace feelers"? Hesse responded with a question of his own: had the Führer given his consent for such negotiations? No, Ribbentrop admitted, but perhaps he could be persuaded. Together they prepared a memorandum on the subject which was presented to Hitler. While it did not contain the key word "capitulation," Hesse was not deceived. It was, he observed, little better than an offer to capitulate. He doubted that the West would consider such proposals but said, "Very well, you can try but I don't think anything will come of it."

Ribbentrop began by negotiating with a personal enemy, Himmler. To his surprise, the Reichsführer was more than willing to co-operate; he was terrified that the Führer might find out that Bernadotte was coming to Berlin to discuss other than humanitarian matters. First he gave assurance that the Foreign Office would have his full personal support in the future, then promised to issue an order canceling Hitler's instructions to destroy prisoners of war and inmates of concentration camps rather than abandon them alive to the enemy. Ribbentrop struggled to hold back tears of joy as he revealed all this to Hesse. "Yes, now we can at least try to save the German people," he said, and so dispatched Hesse to Stockholm on February 17.

Himmler must have regretted his rash promises to Ribbentrop almost immediately. He became terrified that the Führer might discover—and misinterpret—his actions and, once informed of Bernadotte's arrival in Berlin, he refused to see him unless two of his own antagonists—Kaltenbrunner and Ribbentrop—first met with the count. That, he figured, would prevent them from carrying tales to Hitler. Both were happy to oblige. Kaltenbrunner was first in line but Bernadotte wanted to deal directly with Himmler and decided to tell as little as possible to his assistant. Bernadotte merely proposed that the Swedish Red Cross be allowed to work in the concentration camps and was surprised that Kaltenbrunner not only nodded but said he "quite agreed" that Bernadotte should see Himmler personally.

Within the hour the count was talking to Ribbentrop at the Foreign Office, or rather, was listening. Curious as to how long this would go on, Bernadotte surreptitiously set his stop watch. Ribbentrop went from one subject to another, parroting Nazi platitudes without pause, and finally declared that the living man who contributed most to humanity was "Adolf Hitler, unquestionably Adolf Hitler!" He fell silent and Bernadotte snapped the stop watch at sixty-seven minutes.

The next day Bernadotte was driven to Dr. Gebhardt's sanatorium at Hohenlychen, seventy-five miles north of Berlin, Himmler's unofficial headquarters. Bernadotte found him disconcertingly affable. There was nothing at all diabolic in his appearance; he was quiet and polite, his small hands were meticulously manicured. Bernadotte told him that what had aroused indignation in Sweden was the seizure of hostages and the murder of innocent people. The count, Himmler replied earnestly, obviously was misinformed, and he asked if his guest had any concrete proposals.

Bernadotte proposed that Himmler release Norwegians and Danes from concentration camps for custody in Sweden. This modest request touched off a stream of vehement accusations against the Swedes that made no sense at all to Bernadotte but had probably been inspired by one of Himmler's sudden flashes of fear. "If I were to agree to your proposal," he said, his eyes blinking spasmodically, "the Swedish papers would announce with big headlines that the war criminal Himmler, in terror of punishment for his crimes, is trying to buy his freedom." Then he tacked and said he might just do what Bernadotte asked—if Sweden and the Allies assured him that sabotage would stop in Norway.

"That's unthinkable," replied the count and asked for several other small concessions, which were granted. Encouraged, Bernadotte wondered if Swedish women married to Germans could return to their homeland. This brought a blunt refusal. Himmler had been pushed to the limit, and his mood changed. "You may think it sentimental, even absurd, but I have sworn loyalty to Adolf Hitler, and as a soldier and as a German I cannot go back on my oath. For that reason I cannot do anything in opposition to the Führer's plans and wishes." Only a moment before he had granted concessions that would have infuriated Hitler, but now he began to echo him on the "Bolshevik menace" by prophesying the end of Europe if the eastern front collapsed. This was succeeded by sentimental reminiscences of the "glorious" early days of the Nazi movement—"the most wonderful years of my life."

Bernadotte managed to break in with a polite question on German treatment of the Jews. "Won't you admit there are decent people among the Jews, just as there are among all races? I have many Jewish friends." "You're right," was the reply, "but you in Sweden have no Jewish problem and therefore can't understand the German point of view." At the end of the two-and-a-half-hour conference Himmler promised to give definite answers to all of Bernadotte's requests before he returned to Sweden, and Bernadotte presented his host, who was extremely interested in Scandinavian folklore, with a seventeenth-century work on troll-drums.

Bernadotte returned to Ribbentrop's office. The Foreign Minister seemed more eager to help than before, but his overbearing good humor only irritated Bernadotte, who excused himself as soon as he could do so politely. Ribbentrop immediately called Kleist and asked who was backing Bernadotte. What did he *really* want besides saving the Scandinavians? Kleist noticed a large leather billfold bulging with papers in a chair. It was Bernadotte's. Kleist handed it over, assuming that Ribbentrop would examine the papers inside, but he put the billfold in a large plain envelope and asked that it be returned to the owner. Kleist was impressed. It seemed a unique "gesture of chivalry amidst the dissolution of a total war."

Ribbentrop's agent in Stockholm, Hesse, was receiving little encouragement from the Swedish banker, Wallenberg, who maintained that both Roosevelt and Churchill were determined to destroy Germany. He suggested that the Germans try the East. A clearly defined proposal to Stalin might succeed. "Stalin," he said, "is not committed to the West."

A few days later Hesse saw a photograph in the Swedish papers which raised his hopes. It showed Wallenberg's brother on the steps of the Russian Embassy, arm in arm with Madame Kollontai, the Russian ambassador. This could be a signal that the Kremlin was dissatisfied with the West and ready to talk with Hitler. Encouraged, Hesse returned to Berlin but found his chief completely disinterested in any tidings from Sweden. Ribbentrop lay in bed, ill and depressed. It was all in vain, he said wanly. There was no chance whatever of starting any conversations with the West. "Our enemies want to destroy Germany altogether. That is why they reject every chance of negotiation that might save German lives."

When Hesse insisted that there still were two genuine possibilities of opening conversations, one with the West (he had been assured by Olson, Roosevelt's personal adviser, that the President was willing to negotiate) and another with the East, Ribbentrop came to life. He kept Hesse at his bedside until late that night and sent for him again in the morning. March 16 was a clear sunny day and this time Ribbentrop was out of bed, pacing impatiently. "I have given your reports and comments the most careful thought," he said and confounded Hesse by ordering him to return to Stockholm and start conversations with Madame Kollontai. His instructions would be ready in a few hours. "I am sending them to the Führer for final approval. Your airplane is ready. You can leave for Stockholm tonight."

All that afternoon and late into the night Ribbentrop and his staff gave Hesse advice on how to deal with the Russians. Just after midnight they were interrupted by the telephone. It was Hewel of the Foreign Office, still one of the Führer's most trusted advisers. As Ribbentrop listened, his face turned chalk white. "Please repeat," he said tersely, then, moments later, put down the receiver. He seemed composed but his voice was not. "Gentlemen," he said, "the Führer has prohibited any further conversation with any foreign power! I thank you. You can go now!"

Later Hewel told Hesse what had happened at the chancellery. Hitler had first agreed to a contact with the Russians but, upon reading over the instructions, hesitated. He paced around his room while a phonograph ground out music from *Götterdämmerung*, then tore up the instructions, page by page. "I forbid any further contact with the enemy," he told

Hewel. "It is all senseless. Whoever talks to the enemy is a traitor to the Idea. We may fall in the fight against Bolshevism but we shall not negotiate with it. Good night!"

3

A month earlier Hitler had complained to Fräulein Schröder, "I am lied to on all sides." He could rely on no one, and if anything happened to him Germany would be without a Führer. His successor, Göring, had lost the sympathy of the people, and Reichsführer Himmler would be rejected by the party. He apologized for talking politics during lunch, then said: "Rack your brains again and tell me who my successor is to be. This is a question that I keep on asking myself, without ever getting an answer."

His spirits were raised a week later by Eva Braun's return to Berlin. She had been ordered out of the capital earlier in the month for the relative safety of Munich but after two weeks announced to her friends that she had to return to her man's side no matter what happened. She told them that death no longer mattered and she had to share the fate of the one she loved. Hitler pretended to be angry at her sudden reappearance and made a show of scolding her, but all that evening he repeated how proud he was of Fräulein Braun's devotion.

Several days later, near the end of February, Hitler convened his Gauleiters for a final meeting. They were alarmed by his appearance. He had to be supported by Schaub. His voice was low, his left hand shook badly. Everyone expected a sensational announcement, but instead he delivered a paradoxical sermon that was both inspiring and depressing. First he assured the Gauleiters that, although no wonder weapon was going to rescue the Reich at the last moment, the war could still be won so long as they inspired a "Teutonic fury" in the German people. If the nation failed to respond it had no moral worth and deserved destruction.

He thanked the Gauleiters for their co-operation and loyalty before doing something totally unexpected: he told them frankly of his failing health. He confessed that the trembling in his leg had traveled to his left arm, and made a joke: hopefully it would not move to his head. His last words were vague but ominous: in the future he would be forced to take harsh measures. He hoped they would not feel betrayed should he take steps they did not understand.

Faced as he was by almost certain disaster, Hitler's dominant mood in the days to follow became one of defiance and ire. He railed at Allied airmen who had already killed half a million civilians, and reviled those Germans who were greeting the advancing Americans almost as though they were liberators. His fury knew no bounds on March 7. The railroad bridge over the Rhine at Remagen was seized intact by Hodges' First Army before the defenders could blow it up. To Hitler this was another betrayal and he was determined to punish those responsible. It also gave him an excuse to get rid of the aging Rundstedt, who seemed only bent on retreat. In the emergency he ordered his most trusted trouble-shooter, Otto Skorzeny, to destroy the bridge. One group of Skorzeny frogmen managed to approach it with packages of "Plastit," a plastic explosive, but were discovered in time by an Allied secret weapon, Canal Defense Lights, a powerful beam whose source was undetectable.

By this time the entire German defense system in the West was in jeopardy. Model's Army Group B had been smashed, its remnants shoved back across the Rhine. To the south Hausser's Army Group G had been backed up against the river's west bank and was about to be surrounded. The situation in the East was no better and during these desperate days of mid-March Hitler decided to visit this front. His generals warned him that the situation was so fluid he might be captured or killed but he would not listen. As a concession he had Kempka drive him forward in a Völkswagen rather than the famous Mercedes. Their destination was a castle near the Oder where he pleaded with the commanders of the Ninth Army to contain the Russian drive on Berlin. Every day, every hour was precious, he said, since new secret weapons would be ready momentarily. On the trip back to Berlin, Hitler sat silently beside Kempka, deep in thought. He knew that his talk of secret weapons was visionary and had recently confessed so to his Gauleiters. His atom bomb was many months from completion and his other secret weapons were unrealistic political ones, such as the hope that the West would join in the crusade against Bolshevism. By the time he returned to the city he had seen enough out front. Never again would he venture beyond the chancellery grounds. His only hope was a last-minute political miracle.

Hitler was aware that plots were being woven around him. He knew, for example, of Ribbentrop's negotiations in Sweden and that Himmler was dickering with the Jews but he continued to allow these men to negotiate as if in his own name, even while declaring that all negotiations were futile. If a negotiation failed, he would deny any knowledge of it; if it succeeded, he could take the credit.

It is doubtful, however, that Hitler knew his trusted Speer was urging commanders such as Manteuffel to disobey orders to destroy bridges, dams and factories rather than leave them to the enemy. On March 18 Speer brought his protest against this "scorched earth" policy directly to the Führer. "At this stage of the war," he wrote in a memorandum, "it makes no sense for us to undertake demolitions which may strike at the very life of the nation." If Hitler had ever wavered in determination to scorch German earth, Speer's words spurred him to action. He summoned his quondam architect moments after reading his memorandum and said icily, "If the war is lost, the people will be lost also. It is not necessary to worry about what the German people will need for elemental survival. On the contrary, it is best for us to destroy even these things. For the nation has proved to be the weaker, and the future belongs to the stronger Eastern nation [the Soviet Union]. In any case only those who are inferior will remain after this struggle, for the good have already been killed."

4

In the year 900 Germany's borders were the Oder and the Rhine. By the beginning of March 1945 Hitler's Grossdeutschland was compressed between the same rivers. And his thousand-year Reich was coming to an end. From both east and west his enemies were poised for massive attacks which they were certain would bring quick final victory. On the morning of the third, Montgomery launched his assault across the Rhine. Two airborne divisions—one British and one American—dropped across the river to support the infantrymen, and by nightfall the Germans were in full retreat. A hundred and fifty miles upriver, the unpredictable George Patton had also crossed the Rhine, surprising Montgomery as much as the Germans. It was a brilliant, improvised maneuver done in secret, without a round of artillery preparation and at a cost of only twenty-eight men killed or wounded. A pontoon bridge was thrown across the Rhine and as Patton crossed it he stopped in the middle. "I've been looking forward to this for a long time," he said and urinated into the river.

The rapid advance east of both Montgomery and Patton in the next few weeks caused consternation at Führer Headquarters. Hitler was particularly aroused by the action of Cardinal Galen, who drove out from Münster to surrender the city to an American unit. "If I ever lay hands on that swine," exclaimed Hitler, "I'll have him hanged!" He had also reached the limit of tolerance for his outspoken and feisty army chief of staff. Guderian knew it and, on the morning of March 28, drove up to Berlin determined to have a showdown. He was particularly upset by the fate of 200,000 German soldiers needlessly trapped hundreds of miles behind Russian lines in Kurland. Once inside the partially destroyed chancellery, Guderian and his aide were escorted by a guard down a flight of stairs to a steel-reinforced door guarded by two SS men. This was the entrance to Hitler's new home: a huge bunker buried far below the chancellery garden.

They descended more stairs to a narrow corridor, which was covered with a foot of water. They balanced their way across duckboards to a door, then went down another short flight of stairs to the upper level of the bunker. Twelve small rooms opened on a central vestibule which also served as the general mess hall. Guderian and his aide traversed this passageway, then proceeded down a curving stairway and a final dozen steps to the lower level. Here, in the Führer bunker, were eighteen cubicles, separated by an entrance hall which was divided into a waiting room and the conference room. Beyond these, in a small vestibule, was the emergency exit to four steep flights of concrete steps leading up to the chancellery garden. On the left of the conference room was a small map room, a rest room for the Führer's bodyguard and the six-room suite of Hitler and Eva Braun. The air was stuffy despite a ventilating system whose shrill, monotonous whine penetrated every room of the bunker. The whole structure was protected by a twelve-foot-thick reinforced ceiling, topped by thirty feet of concrete. This would be Hitler's tomb or his bastion of miraculous victory. Perhaps it reminded him of the terrible but heroic trench life of the Great War.

Hitler shuffled in from his adjoining apartment and the noon conference opened with a report by General Theodor Busse on his unsuccessful attempts to relieve a town on the east bank of the Oder. Hitler's criticism of Busse was interrupted by a spirited defense from Guderian. Stung, Hitler suddenly got to his feet with an agility which amazed the conferees. But Guderian was not intimidated. He boldly brought up the subject he and Hitler had fought over for weeks. "Is the Führer going to evacuate the Kurland army?" he asked. "Never!" exclaimed Hitler with a wave of an arm. Large red blotches appeared on his deathly white face. Guderian stood rooted to the spot, then started toward Hitler. Jodl and his deputy shepherded Guderian away, but he kept talking in a loud voice. Finally his aide inveigled him into the anteroom "to answer a phone call" and by the time Guderian returned to the conference room he had control of himself.

Hitler was back in his chair, face pinched, and though his hands trembled, he too had regained his poise. He quietly asked all to leave the room except Guderian and Keitel, then said, "General Guderian, the state of your health requires that you immediately take six weeks' sick leave." As Guderian started to leave Hitler told him to remain until the end of the conference. It continued as if nothing had happened. After several hours, which seemed interminable to Guderian, the session was over. But he was not yet free to go. "Please take good care of yourself," the Führer said solicitously. "In six weeks the situation will be very critical. Then I shall need you urgently." Guderian said he would pick a place to rest that wouldn't be overrun before the weekend, raised his arm in salute and walked away.

On Easter Sunday all resistance in the Ruhr collapsed and Hitler was forced to face the reality of total defeat—a Reich hacked to pieces by the victors, his people exposed to the savage excesses of the Soviets and Americans. But he prophesied, in dictation to Bormann, "The laws of both history and geography will compel these two powers to a trial of strength, either military or in the field of economics and ideology. These same laws make it inevitable that both powers should become enemies of Europe. And it is equally certain that both powers will sooner or later find it desirable to seek the support of the sole surviving nation in Europe, the German people. I say with all the emphasis at my command that the Germans must at all costs avoid playing the role of pawn in either camp."

Bormann wrote his wife that same day, April 2, describing the latest raid on Berlin and the pall of desperation that hung over the city. He warned her to expect the worst at Vienna; if the Russians overpowered that citadel she should flee the Obersalzberg. A few days later Red Army troops were streaming into Vienna almost at will while resistance men carrying stolen passes and wearing Volkstürm armbands moved openly through the streets, sniping at anyone in German uniform. By evening the already frantic exodus from the city grew as fire brigades, air raid wardens and even police joined the disorderly mob fleeing the city.

5

Even as fronts everywhere were collapsing, Hitler did his utmost to instill hope of a last-minute miracle. He pointed out that the foundation for the Brave New Europe set up by his enemies at Yalta was already beginning to crack. This was not wishful thinking. The Big Three had drawn up the plan in relative harmony but were indeed already deeply embroiled in its implementation. Their representatives, meeting in Moscow to form a new Polish government, had reached an impasse, with Molotov proclaiming that the Lublin Government truly represented the people of Poland, whereas Averell Harriman and the British ambassador contended that a more representative government must be set up to include émigré Poles.

This conflict was but a preamble to a more disruptive one. For several months General Karl Wolff—formerly Himmler's personal adjutant and presently SS chief in Italy—had been negotiating with the Americans through an agent of Allen Dulles, the OSS representative in Switzerland. Wolff had the Führer's vague approval to explore the matter but on his own initiative proposed surrendering all German troops in Italy, then secretly met with two Allied generals in Ascona, Switzerland, to discuss how this could be done without Hitler's knowledge.

From the beginning the Allies had kept Stalin informed about Operation Sunrise, as this venture was named, and from the beginning he had adamantly demanded that a Soviet officer take active part in the negotiations. The Allies explained, with reason, that Wolff would never come to a meeting under such circumstances but this merely raised Stalin's suspicions. When he learned of the rendezvous at Ascona his reaction was violent. He accused the Allies of conniving with Germany, "behind the backs of the Soviet Union, which is bearing the brunt of the war against Germany," and labeled the whole affair "not a misunderstanding but something worse."

By the end of March Stalin was charging that, because of the talks at Ascona, the Germans had felt free to send three divisions from Italy to the eastern front. He further complained that the agreement at Yalta to attack Hitler simultaneously from the east, west and south was not being observed in Italy by the Allies. An explanation by Roosevelt resulted in an irate cable from Stalin openly accusing the Allies of playing a deceitful game. This so irritated the President that on April 5 he sent off the most aggressive and indignant message he had ever addressed to an ally: "Frankly I cannot avoid the feeling of bitter resentment toward your informers, whoever they are, for such vile misrepresentations of my actions or those of my trusted subordinates." Stalin hastily replied that he had never doubted Roosevelt's integrity or trustworthiness. But it was an aggressive apology; he added that a Russian should have been invited to the Ascona meeting and described his own point of view as "the only correct one."

Hitler did not know the details of the discord in the enemy camp, only that there was one and he had predicted it. It fanned the faint hope of a miracle and he was in a receptive mood when Goebbels read to him Carlyle's description of the desperate days of the Seven Years' War: Frederick the Great, dejected by apparent defeat in Prussia, declared that if there was no change before February 15 he would take poison. "Brave King," wrote Carlyle, "wait yet a little while, and the days of your suffering will be over. Already the sun of your good fortune stands behind the clouds, and soon will rise upon you." On February 12 the Czarina died and brought about the incredible change in Frederick's fortunes.

"At this touching tale," Goebbels later told Schwerin von Krosigk, "tears stood in the Führer's eyes." It also whetted Hitler's interest in his own horoscope and he sent for two that were kept in Himmler's research departments. Both predicted victories until 1941, and then a series of reversals culminating in disaster during the first half of April 1945. But there would be a temporary success in the second half of that month, followed by a lull until peace in August. Germany would endure hard times until 1948 when she would rise once more to greatness.

A skeptic by nature, Goebbels was not averse to grabbing at a straw. He was so impressed by the historical parallel that he repeated the story during a visit to General Busse's headquarters near the Oder on April 12. One officer asked caustically, "Well, what Czarina is going to die this time?" "I don't know, but Fate holds all kinds of possibilities," replied Goebbels and headed back for Berlin in the gathering dusk.

Across the Atlantic, in Warm Springs, Georgia, Franklin Roosevelt was murmuring, "I have a terrific headache," before losing consciousness. He died two hours and twenty minutes later. Goebbels received the news upon arrival at his office. "This is the turning point!" he exclaimed and then asked incredulously, "Is it really true?" Some ten people hung over him as he telephoned Hitler. "My Führer," he said, "I congratulate you!

Roosevelt is dead. It is written in the stars that the second half of April will be the turning point for us." It was a miracle! He listened to Hitler a moment before mentioning the possibility that Truman would be more moderate than Roosevelt. Anything could happen now. Goebbels hung up, eyes shining, and launched into an impassioned speech. It was as if the war was nearly over.

Ribbentrop did not share his enthusiasm. Next morning, April 13, he returned from a short visit with Hitler in a black mood. "The Führer," he told his staff, "is in seventh heaven!" That scoundrel Goebbels had convinced him that Roosevelt's death was the turn of the tide. "How nonsensical, and how criminal! How could Roosevelt's death change anything to our advantage?"

Goebbels counseled the press to write objectively and non-committally about Truman; to say nothing to irritate the new President; and to hide any rejoicing at Roosevelt's death. But by afternoon the Propaganda Minister's elation had begun to wane. When General Busse called to ask if Roosevelt's death was the situation he had alluded to the day before, Goebbels replied halfheartedly, "Oh, we don't know. We'll have to see." The reports from the fronts indicated that the change of Presidents had not at all affected the enemy's military operations, and late in the day Goebbels confessed to his staff, "Perhaps Fate has again been cruel and made fools of us. Perhaps we counted our chickens before they were hatched."

If Hitler suffered a similar letdown, he gave the opposite impression. He called a special meeting and revealed a bizarre strategy to save Berlin: German troops falling back toward the capital would create a hard nucleus of defense which would irresistibly draw Russian troops toward it. This would relieve other German forces from pressure and enable them to attack the Bolsheviks from the outside. The decisive battle would be won in Berlin, he assured a dubious audience; and he himself would remain in the city to inspire the defenders. Several urged him to go to Berchtesgaden but he would not consider it. As commander-in-chief of the Wehrmacht and as leader of the people, it was his obligation to stay in the capital. He drafted an eight-page proclamation—the last he would write to the troops —and sent it to Goebbels. Even the Propaganda Minister thought its bombast too ridiculous. He began revisions with a green pencil but had to give up and threw the statement in the wastebasket. Then he pulled it out and changed a few sentences. Without bothering to clear the final version, Goebbels had copies distributed along the front on the fifteenth. If every soldier on the eastern front did his duty, it said, Asia's last assault would fail. For Fate had removed Roosevelt, the greatest war criminal of all times, from the world, and the war would take a decisive turn.

Incredibly, many of the soldiers were heartened by Hitler's words. Even the majority of citizens still kept faith with him, despite the relentless bombings from the West and the rapidly shrinking borders of the Reich. To the average German the Führer was more than a man, he was a supernatural phenomenon. They held positive belief in his invulnerability, many clinging to the popular myth that a house wall bearing his picture could withstand any bomb. His miraculous escape on the twentieth of July bore witness to his indestructibility, making it that much easier to raise their spirits and hopes with such slogans as "Hitler Is Victory Itself."

In private, the creator of this slogan had lost his own faith. Goebbels disconsolately began preparing for the end, and started by burning his papers and personal mementos. He hesitated before destroying a large autographed photograph of his great love, Lida Baarova. "Now, there's a beautiful woman!" he remarked. After staring at the picture a long moment, he ripped it into pieces then threw them into the fire.

The following day Germany received two great blows: one from the West where all German troops within the Ruhr pocket surrendered; another from the East where Zhukov's all-out attack on Berlin breached the ridge defense lines west of the Oder, thus opening the road to the Führer bunker forty-five miles away. Though he still talked of victory, Hitler prepared for the worst. He entrusted a visiting party official with two assignments: he was to remove the German gold reserves to a salt mine in Thuringia and convey to safety a sealed package that Bormann would give him. The package contained Hitler's dictations to Bormann, his testament to Germany and the world.*

It was a time for supermen and later in the day Hitler gave orders to place one in command of all jet fighter planes. Hans Ulrich Rudel was already a legend. With his Stuka dive bomber he had sunk a Soviet battleship and knocked out 500 Red tanks. Several months earlier he had lost a leg in a crash but was already ambulatory and ready for more action. Göring's chief of staff was appalled at the choice, since Rudel knew nothing about jets, but Hitler would not listen. "Rudel is a fine fellow," he said. All the others in the Luftwaffe were actors and clowns.

Rudel himself violently opposed the assignment since he preferred to fly. He refused point-blank to take the job and began making excuses. It was only a question of time before the Russians and Allies met, he told Hitler. This would split Germany into two pockets and make jet operations impossible. Why didn't Hitler seek an armistice in the West, so a victory could be achieved in the East? "It is easy for you to talk," said Hitler with a tired smile. He had tried ever since 1943 to conclude a

* The document was deposited in the vault of a bank in Bad Gastein by the party official, who was later arrested for war crimes and imprisoned. Fearing the testament would incriminate him further, the official asked a legal friend to destroy it. The lawyer did so, but not before making a photostatic copy. In 1959 these revealing statements, each page authenticated by Bormann's signature, were finally published under the title *The Political Testament of Adolf Hitler, the Hitler-Bormann Documents.*

peace, but the Allies persisted in demanding unconditional surrender. "Therefore we must do everything to surmount this crisis so that decisive weapons may yet bring us victory."

It was late—after midnight—by the time Rudel was dismissed. As he limped into the waiting room, he noticed it was already filled with those eager to be the first to congratulate the Führer on his fifty-sixth birthday.

At Dr. Gebhardt's sanatorium Himmler was preparing to celebrate the birthday. But it was far from a happy occasion. The Reichsführer's face was lined with worry and he kept nervously twisting his snake ring around and around. Like Hitler, he too seemed on the brink of physical collapse. There was good reason. His office was an incredible nest of plots. Some of his people were secretly negotiating in Sweden with his reluctant approval, while SS General Wolff was still dealing with the Allies in Switzerland despite Himmler's flat order to desist.

Himmler was not sure just how much Hitler knew and consequently lived in terror. For the past months he had been endlessly urged to make momentous decisions. Everyone, it seemed, wanted him to do something. Kersten and Schellenberg wanted him to overthrow Hitler by a coup d'état, and earlier that day Count Schwerin von Krosigk had entreated him to persuade Hitler to seek a negotiated peace through the Pope. Himmler would only say that the Führer had a different notion. "But he won't reveal what the notion is."

The count was exasperated. "Then you must do away with the Führer whichever way you can."

"Everything is lost! And as long as the Führer lives there is no possibility of bringing the war to a proper end!" Himmler looked around in such terror that Schwerin von Krosigk wondered if he had "gone mad all at once." Himmler became hysterical, repeating several times that he couldn't promise to do a thing. Instead he fled to the sanatorium where more problems awaited him. Kersten had just landed at Tempelhof with a representative of the World Jewish Congress, Norbert Masur, a last-minute substitute for Storch. That was not all. Count Bernadotte was expected shortly in Berlin and wanted another meeting with the Reichsführer. All of Himmler's problems seemed to have come to a head.

Completely unnerved, he began to make feeble excuses. How could he meet two people at once? Couldn't both meetings be postponed? Finally, in desperation, he asked Schellenberg to "have a preliminary talk" with Masur. Schellenberg agreed and, since it was just past midnight, they toasted the Führer's birthday with champagne.

Chapter Thirty-one

FIVE MINUTES
PAST MIDNIGHT, OR,
"THE CAPTAIN ALSO GOES
DOWN WITH THIS SHIP"
APRIL 20–30, 1945

1

The Allies celebrated the occasion with another thousand-bomber raid on the capital. But nothing seemed to dampen Hitler's confidence. Throughout the twentieth of April he told birthday visitors that he still believed the Russians would suffer defeat in Berlin. In the afternoon he met a group of Hitler Youth in the chancellery garden and thanked them for their gallantry in the battle for the capital. Then he climbed down into the bunker and received Grossadmiral Karl Dönitz, who thought he looked like a man carrying an intolerable burden. Afterward he greeted Keitel with warmth. "I will never forget that you saved me at the time of the Attentat and that you got me out of Rastenburg—you made the right decisions and took the right actions."

Keitel blurted out that negotiations for peace should be initiated at once before Berlin became a battlefield. Hitler interrupted. "Keitel, I know what I want. I am going to go down fighting, either in or outside Berlin." After a tête-à-tête with Jodl, he slowly passed down a line of military and civilian leaders—including Bormann, Ribbentrop and Speer—shaking

uch an enemy in our
were infected by ty-
emics," he explained,
corpses of the large
And now they'll get

Masur said. "But if
he future, then all
many must remain
turning over the
so with Bergen-
n: faked atrocity
hen he let 2700
ad done so only
ys done what I
nsibility. It cer-

sked his mas-
d discuss im-
to convince
nd that only
le victory to
ack Russia.

aith by re-
lated that
esignated
asur fare
otte wa
did n
is fr
do
nt

eryone urged Hitler
en road but he was
be divided into two
northern sector. Field
western front, was the
considering Göring—per-
l leave it to Providence to
hand staffs split in two, and
evening for Berchtesgaden.
is chief of staff, Koller. "You
es, once so close, parted with
ll where his butler was waiting
treasures.

s secretaries. Again he was urged
e like a Tibetan lama turning an
decision here in Berlin—or perish!"
older secretaries to his private room
in half an hour or so by car for the
on Puttkamer and eighty others.* The
astonishment. His explanation was that
est. Besides, Fräulein Wolf supported her
as possible." He spoke in a whisper, vainly
of his left hand. A sigh escaped him; one,
which seemed to come from a man without
hed her to say that Berlin was surrounded. She
t light. A second call followed in minutes. The
s soon as the air raid all-clear was sounded. She
d, since his voice gurgled imperceptibly, and asked
lf. He said nothing. His last words to her colleague
: "It is all over."

evening Himmler, after paying respects to the Führer on
ft the bunker and drove through the beating rain for sev-
o meet Masur, the representative of the World Jewish
Himmler explained that he had been empowered to solve the
blem and had first planned a humane solution through emigra-
even those countries which boasted of their friendliness toward
s refused to take them. "Through the war," Himmler said, "we
into contact with the masses of the Eastern Jewish proletariat, and

* Among those sent south was Dr. Morell. He was banished in anger for suggesting that Hitler take an injection of caffeine for his fatigue. "You will probably give me morphine!" shouted Hitler and ordered him to remove his uniform as the Führer's private physician. "And act as if you've never seen me." Morell collapsed at Hitler's feet and had to be led away. He died, a broken man, soon after the war.

this created new problems. We could not have s
back." These Jews not only helped the partisans bu
phus and other diseases. "In order to curtail the epid
"we had to build crematoria where we could burn th
number of people who died because of these diseases.
us just for doing that!"

"Much has happened which cannot be undone,"
we are ever to build a bridge between our peoples for
Jews who are today alive in the areas dominated by Ger
alive." Himmler protested that he had always intended
camps to the Allies without resistance. Hadn't he done
Belsen and Buchenwald? And look what he got in retur
pictures were being circulated by the Americans! And w
Jews go to Switzerland, the foreign press claimed that he h
to get himself an alibi. "I don't need an alibi. I have alwa
felt would fill the needs of my people, and I take full respor
tainly didn't make me a rich man."

While Masur was out of the room Himmler suddenly
seur, Kersten, if he would fly to Eisenhower's headquarters ar
mediate cessation of hostilities. "Make every effort
Eisenhower that the real enemy of mankind is Soviet Russia a
we Germans are in a position to fight against her. I will concec
the Western Allies. They have only to give me time to throw b
If they let me have the equipment, I can still do it."

On Masur's return Himmler said he would show his good f
leasing 1000 Jewish women from Ravensbrück at once. He stipu
their arrival in Sweden be kept secret, suggesting that they be c
"Polish" instead of "Jewish." Just before dawn Himmler bade M
well and drove to the Gebhardt sanatorium where Count Bernad
waiting. The two sat down to breakfast. Himmler's exhaustion
seem to affect his appetite, though he compulsively kept tapping h
teeth with his fingernails. Unaccountably, he objected to Bern
modest request that the Scandinavian prisoners be allowed to co
from Denmark to Sweden, then spontaneously offered to let the S
Red Cross have *all* the women at Ravensbrück and retired to get
sleep. Early that afternoon Himmler summoned Schellenberg to his
room and said he felt ill; and as their car crept along the jammed high
toward their nearby headquarters the Reichsführer said, "Schellenber
dread what is to come."

"That should give you courage to take action."

Himmler was silent, and once Schellenberg began criticizing the unrealistic policy of evacuating all the concentration camps, he pouted like a
scolded child. "Schellenberg, don't you start too," he said. "Hitler has

been raging for days because Buchenwald and Bergen-Belsen were not completely evacuated."

At the moment Himmler assured Masur that all evacuations had ceased, the inmates of Sachsenhausen, which lay directly athwart the path of Zhukov's advance on Berlin, were being herded out of the barracks into the rain and lined up for departure; ten miles to the east Zhukov's guns roared ominously. The Red Cross delegate requested the camp commandant to turn over Sachsenhausen to his organization, but he refused, on the grounds that he had standing orders from Himmler to evacuate everything except the hospital at the approach of the Russians. And so almost 40,000 prisoners—starved, sick, poorly clothed—were shoved into two surging columns. The guards harried them through the pummeling rain in a northwesterly direction, and those who couldn't keep up the pace were shot and left in the ditches.

"What can you do with a people whose men don't even fight when their women are raped!" It was Goebbels, bitterly admitting to his aides later in the day that the war was irrevocably lost—not because of Hitler but because the people had failed him. "All the plans, all the ideas of National Socialism are too high, too noble for such a people. . . . They deserve the fate that will now descend upon them." He even turned on his own aides. "And you—why have you worked with me? Now you'll have your little throats cut! But when we step down, let the whole earth tremble!" Throughout the day Goebbels went from despair to resentment. Upon learning that two secretaries had fled to the country on bicycles, he complained, "Now I ask you, how could that ever have happened? How can there be any guarantee now of keeping regular office hours?"

On the eastern front there were rumors that the leaders in Berlin had given up all hope and that OKW was fleeing to Berchtesgaden. The Russians had broken through the lines of Army Group Vistula at half a dozen points and one Red Army task force was but twenty miles from Berlin and the Führer's bunker. By noon of April 21 it had closed to artillery range, and the explosions of its shells could be heard faintly in the bunker as Jodl reported that a Zhukov column was threatening to encircle Manteuffel's army. To counter this, the last small reserve under SS General Felix Steiner had just been positioned twenty-five miles north of Berlin.

Hitler jerked upright from a slump. Like Skorzeny and Rudel, Steiner was a magic name; it was his desperate attack from Pomerania that had slowed Zhukov's advance in February. Hitler began poring over a map. Finally he looked up. His eyes glistened. Counterattack! he said with rising excitement. Steiner was to drive to the southeast and cut straight through the Zhukov spearhead: this would, with one bold blow, save Berlin and prevent Manteuffel from being encircled. He dispatched a personal order to Steiner expressly forbidding any retreat to the west. "Officers who do not comply unconditionally with this order are to be arrested and shot immediately. You, Steiner, are answerable with your head for execution of this order." Of all the impossible orders Steiner had received from the Führer, this was the most fantastic. His Panzer corps was one in name only. He had no intention of sacrificing his troops in such a hopeless cause and would only make a show of compliance—an easy decision for a man who had once considered kidnaping the Führer.

Bormann also knew there was no hope. He telephoned his wife at Berchtesgaden and told her he'd found a "wonderful hiding place" for their children in the Tyrol. She was to pose as a director of bombed-out children seeking refuge. He had kidnaped six youngsters from the party kindergarten in Garmisch to make the group look more plausible.

2

In the bunker, on the morning of April 22, Steiner was the main topic of conversation. Had his attack from the north been launched to relieve Berlin? If so, how far had it gone? With each passing hour Hitler became increasingly upset every time General Hans Krebs, Guderian's replacement as OKH chief of staff, told him there was nothing definite to report. At the afternoon Führer conference, after learning that Berlin was three fourths surrounded, Hitler demanded to know once and for all how far Steiner had progressed in his attack. At last Krebs was forced to admit that the Steiner corps was still being organized and there just wasn't anything to report.

Hitler's head jerked and he began breathing heavily. Harshly he ordered everyone out of the room except his generals and Bormann. The rest stumbled over one another in their eagerness to escape. In the waiting room they stood in silent apprehension. Once the door closed Hitler lunged to his feet. As he lurched back and forth, swinging his right arm wildly, he shouted that he was surrounded by traitors and liars. All were too low, too mean to understand his great purpose, he shouted. He was the victim of corruption and cowardice and now everyone had deserted him. His listeners had never before seen him lose control so completely. He flung an accusing finger at the generals and blamed their ilk for the disasters of the war. The only protest came from Bormann. The officers were surprised, but Bormann's words were undoubtedly meant not so much as a defense of the military as to calm the Führer.

Hitler shouted something about Steiner and abruptly flopped into his chair. In anguish he said, "The war is lost!" Then with a trembling voice he added that the Third Reich had ended in failure and all he could do now was die. His face turned white and his body shook spasmodically, as if torn by a violent stroke. Suddenly he was still. His jaw slackened and he sat staring ahead with blank eyes. This alarmed the onlookers more than his fury. Minute after minute passed—afterward no one could remember how many. Finally a patch of color came to the Führer's cheeks and he twitched—perhaps he had suffered a coronary attack or fibrillation. Bormann, Keitel and Burgdorf, chief of army personnel, begged him to have faith. If *he* lost it, then all indeed was lost. They urged him to leave for Berchtesgaden immediately, but he slowly shook his head and in a dead, tired voice said that if they wanted to go they were free to do so, but he was meeting his end in the capital. He asked for Goebbels.

Those in the outer room had heard almost everything. Fegelein grabbed a phone and told Himmler what had happened. The shaken Reichsführer phoned Hitler and begged him not to lose hope. He promised to send SS troops at once. In the meantime Hitler sent for Traudl Junge, Gerda Christian and his new cook, Konstanze Manzialy. They came to his anteroom where he was waiting with Eva Braun. His face was expressionless, his eyes dead. In an impersonal yet imperious manner he told the four women to prepare to leave for the south by plane within the hour. "All is lost, hopelessly lost," he said.

The women stood rigid with shock. Eva was the first to move. She went up to Hitler, took both his hands in hers. She smiled softly as if to a sad child. "But you surely know that I shall stay with you. I won't let you send me away." This brought life back to his eyes and he did something no one in the family circle had ever before seen: he kissed Eva on the lips.

In spite of herself, Traudl found herself saying, "I also am staying." Gerda and the cook joined the chorus. Hitler again ordered them to leave but they stood firm. He seized their hands in turn and said with emotion, "If only my generals were as brave as you are!" As if totally exhausted, he dragged himself to the next room where a group of officers was waiting. "Gentlemen," he said, "this is the end. I shall remain here in Berlin and shoot myself when the time comes. Each of you must make his own decision on when to leave."

Goebbels was still at home when he learned that the Führer wanted him immediately. As he was preparing to leave the ministry word came that Hitler also wanted to see Magda and the children. At five o'clock Frau Goebbels calmly told the nurse to get the children ready for a visit to the Führer. They were delighted. Would Uncle Adi give them chocolate and cake as usual? The mother, guessing they might all be going to their death, put on a smile and said, "Each of you may take one toy, but no more than that."

Keitel finally cleared the conference room so that he could talk alone with Hitler. He wanted to convince him to go to Berchtesgaden directly and initiate surrender negotiations from there. But Hitler interrupted. "I already know exactly what you're going to say: 'The decision must be made at once!'" His voice was rasping. "I have already made a decision. I will never leave Berlin; I'll defend the city to my last breath!" Jodl appeared and Hitler repeated his decision to die. "I should already have made this decision, the most important in my life, in November 1944, and should never have left the headquarters in East Prussia."

Hitler summoned Bormann and ordered him to fly to Berchtesgaden with Jodl and Keitel. The latter would take command, with Göring as the Führer's personal representative. When Keitel protested, Hitler said, "Everything is falling to pieces anyway and I can do no more." The rest, he added, should be left to Göring. "There's mighty little fighting to be done, and if it comes to negotiating, the Reichsmarschall can do it better than I can. I will either fight and win the Battle of Berlin, or die in Berlin." He could not run the risk of falling into enemy hands, he said, and would shoot himself at the very last moment. "That is my final, irrevocable decision!"

The generals swore that the situation was not completely lost. Wenck's Twelfth Army could be turned around and brought to the relief of Berlin. All at once Hitler's eyes brightened. Incredibly, hope returned and with it determination. He began by asking questions, then outlining in detail exactly how Berlin could be saved. No sooner had Keitel left to give orders to Wenck in person than the Führer sank into another depression. He told his family circle that there was no hope. When someone pointed to the painting of Frederick the Great and asked if he no longer believed in a similar miracle of history, the Führer tiredly shook his head. "The army has betrayed me, my generals are good for nothing," he said. "My orders were not carried out. It is all finished. National Socialism is dead and will never rise again!" Perhaps in a hundred years a similar idea would arise with the power of a religion and spread throughout the world. "But Germany is lost. It actually was not quite ready or quite strong enough for the mission I set for the nation."

3

That evening General Eckard Christian, the Luftwaffe chief of operations, burst into Koller's headquarters just outside Berlin. "The Führer is in a state of collapse!" He gave a frightening account of what had happened. Koller drove to the new OKW headquarters and asked Jodl for confirmation of Christian's incredible story. Jodl calmly replied that it was true. Koller asked if the Führer would carry out his threat to commit suicide. Yes, he was stubborn on that point. Koller was indignant. He said he must leave at once to tell Göring in person that the Führer had said: "If it comes to negotiating, the Reichsmarschall can do it better than I can."

Just before dawn on April 23 Koller and his staff left for Munich in fifteen JU-52s. At Berchtesgaden Göring had already learned much of what had happened from an unlikely source. That morning he had told his caretaker—and no one else—of a secret radio message from Bormann informing him that the Führer had suffered a nervous breakdown and that Göring was to take over command. Göring was torn between suspicion and credulity. What should he do? Act at once or wait?

Koller did not reach Göring's comfortable, unostentatious house on the Obersalzberg until noon. Excitedly he told about Hitler's collapse. Göring, of course, knew most of this and to Koller's surprise showed little reaction. He asked if Hitler was still alive. Had he appointed Bormann as his successor? Koller replied that the Führer was alive when he left Berlin and that there were still one or two escape routes. The city would probably hold out for a week. "Anyway," he concluded, "it is now up to you to act, Herr Reichsmarschall!"

Göring was hesitant. Might not Hitler have appointed Bormann as his successor? he asked again. Bormann, an old enemy, could have sent the telegram to make him usurp power prematurely. "If I act, he will call me a traitor; if I don't, he will accuse me of having failed at a most critical time!" He sent for Hans Lammers, the legal expert and custodian of the two official documents establishing a successor, drafted by Hitler himself in 1941. In these directives Göring was appointed Hitler's deputy upon his death. He would also be Hitler's successor in case the Führer was prevented—permanently or temporarily—from performing his office.

Göring wanted to know if the military situation in Berlin warranted his taking over, but Lammers could make no decision. Well aware that his influence with the Führer had waned as Bormann's waxed, Göring asked if Hitler had issued any orders since 1941 which might have invalidated his own succession. No, said Lammers, he had made sure from time to time that the documents had not been rescinded. The decree, he declared, had the force of law and didn't even need to be promulgated again.

Someone suggested that a radio message be sent asking the Führer if he still wanted Göring to be his deputy. One was drafted: "My Führer, is it your wish, in view of your decision to stay in Berlin, that I take over complete control of the Reich, in accordance with the decree of June 29, 1941?" Göring read it and added: ". . . with full powers in domestic and foreign affairs," so that he might negotiate a peace with the Allies. Still concerned, he said, "Suppose I don't get any answer? We must give a time limit, a time by which I must receive an answer."

Koller suggested that they make it eight hours and Göring scribbled down a deadline, then added hastily, "You must realize that I feel for you in this most difficult hour of my life and I can find no words to express myself. God bless you and speed you here as soon as possible. Your most loyal, Hermann Göring." Leaning back heavily, he said, "It's frightful." If no answer came by 10 P.M. he had to do something drastic. "I'll stop the war at once."

At the bunker his telegram—the last from Göring to be intercepted in England by Ultra—seemed to outrage Bormann more than anyone else. He demanded Göring's execution. Hitler refused to go that far and sent his Reichsmarschall three conflicting messages. The first offered to disregard the death penalty for high treason if Göring resigned all his offices; the second rescinded the decree establishing Göring as his successor; and the third, perhaps more accurately reflecting Hitler's confused feelings, was couched in such vague terms ("Your assumption that I am prevented from carrying out my own wishes is an absolutely erroneous idea whose ridiculous origin I do not know") that Bormann must have feared it was a prelude to forgiveness. On his own he radioed the SS commandant at the Obersalzberg to arrest Göring for treason.

Krebs phoned Keitel from the bunker and told him in detail about Göring's dismissal. Horrified, Keitel kept insisting there must be some misunderstanding. Suddenly Bormann's voice broke into the conversation. He shouted that Göring had been fired "even from his job as Reich Chief Hunter." Keitel did not deign to reply. The situation, he thought, was "too serious for such sarcastic remarks." After a brief, frustrating meeting with Hitler that afternoon, Keitel drove back to his headquarters with Jodl. "On the way we frankly agreed that we could not leave things as they were—we discussed the possibility of abducting the Führer from his bunker, possibly even by *force*." But they gave up the idea; it would be impossible to get the collaboration of the Führer's SS guards and Security Service bodyguard.

4

With the Russians closing in on the capital, Eva Braun's normal cheerful nature had changed to one of controlled terror. Once she seized Traudl Junge's hands and in a trembling voice confessed how frightened she was. "If only everything would finally be over!" She penned a farewell letter to her best friend, Herta: "These are my last lines, and therefore the last sign of life from me," she began and explained that she was sending her jewelry to be distributed according to her will. She apologized for the letter's incoherence; the Goebbelses' six children were in the next room making an infernal racket. "I can't understand how all this can have happened, it's enough to make one lose one's faith in God!" In a postscript she added that Hitler himself had lost hope. But the next day, Monday, April 23, Eva wrote her sister that there was still a chance. "It goes without saying, however, that we will not let ourselves be captured alive." She asked Gretl to destroy all her business papers but to pack the Führer's letters and her replies in a watertight package and bury them. The message ended with a pitifully hopeful postscript: "I just spoke to the Führer. I think he is also more optimistic about the future than he was yesterday."

Himmler was making last-minute preparations. Just before midnight he again met Folke Bernadotte, this time in the Swedish Consulate at Lübeck, the German port on the Baltic. "The war must end," he unexpectedly said with a resigned sigh. "I admit that Germany is defeated." The Führer might be dead and so he was no longer bound by his personal oath. He was willing to capitulate on the western front, he said, but not in the East. "I have always been, and I shall always remain, a sworn enemy of Bolshevism." He asked if the count was willing to forward this proposal to the Swedish Minister of Foreign Affairs for transmittal to the West.

Bernadotte did not like the idea but agreed to pass it on to his government. What would Himmler do if his offer was turned down? "In that event," was the answer, "I shall take over command on the eastern front and be killed in battle." Himmler added that he hoped to meet Eisenhower and was willing to surrender unconditionally to him without delay. "Between men of the world, should I offer my hand to Eisenhower?" he asked.

After remarking that it was the bitterest day of his life, Himmler strode purposefully into the darkness and got behind the wheel of his car. He stepped on the accelerator and the vehicle lunged through a hedge into a barbed-wire fence. The Swedes and the Germans managed to push the car clear and Himmler lurched off. There was, commented the count, something symbolic about it all.

At the military conference next morning, April 24, Hitler learned that Manteuffel's army had been completely cut off by a deep Soviet tank thrust. "In view of the broad natural barrier formed by the Oder," he said after a tense silence, "the Russian success against the Third Tank Army can only be attributed to the incompetence of the German military leaders there!" Krebs tried to defend the front-line commander but this only reminded Hitler of Steiner's abortive attack. He pointed shakily at a map and said that another drive from north of Berlin must be started within twenty-four hours. "The Third Army will make use of all available forces for this assault, ruthlessly depleting those sections of our front line which are not under attack. It is imperative that the link to Berlin from the north be restored by tomorrow evening. Have that passed on at once." A suggestion that Steiner lead the attack incensed him. "Those arrogant, tedious, indecisive SS leaders are no good to me any more!"

Goebbels left the meeting to issue his last proclamation to the citizens of Berlin. He hoped that by telling the truth he could frighten them into continuing the holy crusade against the Reds to the end. "Our hearts must not waver and not tremble. It must be our pride and our ambition to break the Bolshevist mass onslaught which is surging from the East against the heartland of Europe at the walls of the Reich capital." Even as these last words were disseminated, Julius Schaub was burning the last of the Führer's private correspondence. This done, Hitler's personal adjutant enplaned for the south with orders to destroy other private documents in the Munich apartment and at the Berghof.

5

The SS commandant at Berchtesgaden had acted immediately upon receipt of Bormann's telegram by placing Göring and his family under house arrest. The past two days had been the most tempestuous in the Reichsmarschall's dramatic career: his Führer had collapsed; he thought he himself had been called upon to inherit the Third Reich; then came Hitler's three telegrams; and now he feared he was going to be executed. That morning—April 25—several SS officers tried to persuade Göring, in the presence of his wife and his butler, to sign a document stating that he was resigning all positions because of poor health. Göring refused; in spite of the telegrams he could not bring himself to believe Hitler really meant what he said. But once the SS men drew their guns Göring quickly signed. The ceremony was interrupted by the drone of approaching aircraft.

Allied planes had often passed over Berchtesgaden on their way to Salzburg, Linz and other targets, but as yet Hitler's retreat was undamaged. Today, however, 318 Lancaster bombers were bent on wiping it out. At 10 A.M., the first wave swept over the mountain, dumping high explosives on the edge of the Führer area. Half an hour later came a larger wave. For almost an hour plane after plane unloaded blockbusters directly onto the Obersalzberg. After the last bomber had disappeared Air Force General Robert Ritter von Greim, commander of Luftflotte 6 in Munich, drove up to the Berghof. It was a mass of twisted wreckage. Greim looked around in dismay. The Führer's home had been hit directly; one side was demolished and the blasted tin roof hung in mid-air.

A dedicated Nazi (he gave Hitler his first plane ride in 1920), Greim had received a telegram from Berlin to report to the bunker, and he now sought out Koller, who, he had been told, had a similar order. Greim began berating Göring for leaving the capital and performing "treasonable" acts. Koller apologized for his chief. But Greim was not at all impressed. Göring's actions should not be defended, he declared, and headed for Berlin.

By midmorning the Red Army pincers around Berlin were about to close and the conferees at the 10:30 A.M. meeting waited in an atmosphere of gloom for Hitler's arrival. He too was despondent until Heinz Lorenz of the official German news agency reported that he had just monitored an announcement from a neutral country that an argument had broken out between Russians and Americans at the first meeting of their troops on the Mulde River. There were disagreements regarding the sectors to be occupied, with the Russians accusing the Americans of infringing on area agreements made at Yalta.

Hitler sat upright, eyes gleaming. "Gentlemen," he said, "here again is striking evidence of the disunity of our enemies. The German people and history would surely brand me as a criminal if I made peace today while there is still the possibility that tomorrow our enemies might have a falling out!" He seemed to gather strength as he spoke. "Isn't it possible that at any day—yes, at any hour—war could break out between the Bolsheviks and the Anglo-Saxons over their prize, Germany?" He turned to Krebs, signaling him with a slight nod to begin the conference. The army chief of staff launched into his report only to be interrupted twice by Hitler: where was Wenck? The answer was a sheepish "No report."

The intercepted news report preoccupied Hitler, and he spent the next hour daydreaming out loud of another last-minute miracle. The time had come, he said, when the Anglo-Saxons must oppose the Reds out of a sense of self-preservation. "If it is really true that differences among the Allies are arising in San Francisco [delegates were gathering there for the first United Nations conference]—and they will occur—a turning point can be achieved if I can administer a beating to the Bolshevik colossus at some point. This might convince the others that only one person is able to contain the Bolshevik colossus, and that person is represented by me, the party and the present German state." The DNB report was incorrect. There was no disagreement between Russian and American advance troops. They did not meet, in fact, until the next day, the twenty-sixth, when two separate American patrols made contact with the Red Army at Strehla and Torgau on the Elbe. This junction cut Hitler's diminishing Reich in two.

By late morning it appeared that General Wenck's army was driving to the rescue of Hitler. Radio reports of his steady progress heartened Berliners. No one waited more eagerly than Hitler. He was counting on Wenck to prolong the battle at least until May 5 so he could die on the same day as Napoleon. It was a vain hope. Only a single corps of Wenck's army, the XX, was attacking toward the capital, and its limited mission was to reach Potsdam and provide a corridor of retreat for the Berlin garrison. The bulk of Wenck's army was driving east—against the Führer's orders—to save comrades of the entrapped Ninth Army.

Early that evening another general, the epitome of loyalty, was risking death to report to his Führer. Ritter von Greim was at the controls of a small observation plane flying at treetop level toward embattled Berlin. Overhead the sky raged with dogfights. Suddenly a gaping hole appeared in the flooring of the cockpit and Greim slumped over. As the plane plunged down out of control his passenger, Hanna Reitsch, reached over and seized the stick. Somehow she managed to right the Storch and make a safe landing on the broad avenue running through the Brandenburg Gate. She commandeered a car and helped Greim aboard.

After his injured right foot was treated, Greim was carried on a stretcher down to the Führer bunker. The little party encountered Magda Goebbels, who stared wide-eyed, marveling that any living soul could have found his way there. She had never met Hanna Reitsch but embraced her and began sobbing. In a moment they came upon Hitler in the narrow passageway. His head drooped heavily, his arms twitched continually, his eyes were glassy. But Greim's report gave Hitler new life. He seized both Greim's hands, then turned to Reitsch. "Brave woman! So there is still some loyalty and courage left in the world!"

Hitler told them about the treacherous telegram Göring had sent. "An ultimatum, a blatant ultimatum! Now there's nothing left. Look what I have to go through: no allegiances were kept, no honor lived up to; there are no disappointments or betrayals I have not experienced—and now this above all." He stopped as if unable to go on. Then, looking at Greim with half-closed eyes, said in little more than a whisper, "I hereby declare you Göring's successor as Oberbefehlshaber der Luftwaffe. In the name of the German people I give you my hand." Deeply moved, both newcomers asked to be allowed to remain in the bunker to atone for Göring's deceit. Equally moved, Hitler assented. Their decision, he said, would long be remembered in the history of the Luftwaffe.

By dawn April 27 Berlin was completely encircled and the last two airports overrun by the Red Army. Still a flurry of optimism swept through the bunker with arrival of a radiogram from Wenck, announcing that XX Corps had come to within a few miles of Potsdam. Goebbels' office immediately proclaimed over the radio that Wenck had reached Potsdam itself and predicted that he would soon be in the capital. And if Wenck made it, why not others? "The situation has changed decisively in our favor," Berliners were told. "The Americans are marching toward Berlin. The great change of the war is at hand. Berlin must be held till Army Wenck arrives, no matter at what costs!"

The daily army communiqué, also broadcast in the clear, divulged Wenck's exact position. He was appalled. "We won't be able to move a single step farther tomorrow!" Wenck exclaimed to his chief of staff. The Russians surely had heard the same broadcast and would concentrate everything available at his position. It was, he said, almost a betrayal.

At the noon military conference Hitler expressed his utmost faith in Wenck, whom he called "a real man," but a moment later, as if realizing how empty hopes of rescue were, he said, "I shall lie down today some-what calmer and do not wish to be awakened unless a Russian tank is just outside my bedroom, so that I can make my preparations." In the next breath he expressed the hope that the Russians would bleed themselves to death in Berlin; then immediately closed the meeting with a philosophic quotation from Richelieu: "What have I lost! The dearest remembrances! What does all this mean? Sooner or later the entire beastly mess must be left behind."

After the conference Hitler pinned an Iron Cross on a small, bleary-eyed boy who had just blown up a Russian tank. The youngster silently turned and walked to the corridor, where he crumpled to the floor, fast asleep. Krebs's two aides were so affected that they began to complain loudly of the unbearable situation. Bormann came up behind them, drap-ing his arms familiarly around their shoulders. There was still hope. Wenck was on the way and would soon relieve Berlin. "You, who stayed here and kept faith with our Führer through his darkest hours," he said unctuously, would be rewarded with great estates. The two aides gaped in-credulously. As professional soldiers they had always been treated with the greatest suspicion by Bormann and his people.

Hanna Reitsch spent much of the day in Goebbels' suite. He seemed unable to forget Göring's treachery. The Reichsmarschall, he said, with ex-travagant gesticulation, was an incompetent; he had destroyed the Father-land with his stupidity and now he wanted to lead the entire nation. This itself proved that "at heart he was always weak and a traitor." Goebbels gripped the back of a chair as a lectern and proclaimed that those in the bunker were making history and dying for the glory of the Reich so that the name of Germany could live forever.

Reitsch thought Goebbels was too theatrical, but she had only admi-ration for his wife. In the presence of her six children Magda was always cheerful; and when she felt self-control slipping she left the room. "My dear Hanna," she said, "you must help me to help the children out of this life. They belong to the Third Reich and the Führer, and if those two things cease to exist, there will be no place for them." Her greatest fear was that at the last moment she would weaken. Reitsch told the children stories of her flying experiences and taught them songs which they later sang to Uncle Adi. She also visited Eva Braun, and thought she was a shallow woman who spent most of her time polishing her fingernails, changing her clothes and combing her hair. It must have been a shock to Reitsch, who adored the Führer, to find him living openly with a woman.

In the second conference of the day, Hitler reverted to reminiscences. He talked of compromises he had been forced to make upon assuming power in 1933 and how this situation had lasted until Hindenburg's death. This led to another pledge to remain in Berlin. He did so, he said, so he could proceed harshly against weakness. "I would otherwise not have this moral right. I cannot constantly threaten others if I run away from the German capital in a critical hour. I must now obey the dictates of Fate. Even if I could save myself, I would not do so. The captain also goes down with this ship."

At the evening briefing the military commandant of Berlin, General Helmuth Weidling, tried to get Hitler to realize that the city was completely surrounded and that the circle of defense was fast shrinking. It was no longer possible, he said, to get supplies by air. He enlarged on the misery of the civilians and the wounded, but Hitler was more interested in complaining about those who had betrayed him. "Many cannot understand my bitterness. I cannot imagine that a party leader, to whom I have given an order, could possibly conceive of not carrying it out. This damages the total result, and the individual suffers. The greater the area of responsibility of the individual, the greater the necessity for obedience." He recalled how Field Marshal von Blomberg had told him that obedience only went up to the rank of general. "It was a mechanism," he commented sarcastically, "which allowed situations to be avoided by false reports, etc., when difficulties arose."

He began to worry about his own fate. He had no intention of allowing Stalin to exhibit him in a cage. "I must have absolute certainty," he said, "that I will not be captured by a Russian tank due to some clever trick by the enemy." At the same time he could not possibly leave Berlin. How could he ask anybody to die for the Fatherland when he himself refused to direct the battle from the heart of the nation?

During one of these reveries Goebbels' assistant, Werner Naumann, was called to a phone outside the room and informed of reports in American newspapers that "a group of highly placed Nazis acting without authority of Hitler but with the backing of the high command" had just offered to surrender to the West. Himmler's offer, submitted through the Swedish government, had somehow leaked out but his name was not mentioned nor was the source of the story revealed.

Naumann returned to the conference and whispered the news to Hitler, who then exchanged a few urgent but subdued words with Goebbels. The Berlin commandant, Weidling, was dismissed and he went to the anteroom where he found Bormann, the Führer's adjutants and the two women secretaries chatting. Frustrated in the conference room, Weidling ("Bony Karl" to his troops) poured out all the things that Hitler had refused to hear. Their only hope, he said, was to leave Berlin before it was too late. Everyone agreed, even Bormann. This encouraged Weidling to repeat the suggestion to Krebs as soon as he emerged from the conference room. Krebs too was receptive and promised to present the breakout plan in detail at the next conference.

Fifty-five miles away at Wenck's Twelfth Army headquarters a radio operator was tapping out a message to Weidling:

COUNTERATTACK OF THE TWELFTH ARMY IS STALLED SOUTH OF POTSDAM. TROOPS ARE ENGAGED IN VERY HEAVY DEFENSIVE FIGHTING. SUGGEST BREAKTHROUGH TO US. WENCK.

The operator waited for acknowledgment. None came.

6

Hitler's closest ally was also facing his last days. Ever since his rescue by Skorzeny, Mussolini had hoped to bring about some sort of "Italian political solution" to the disastrous war. He sent his son Vittorio to the Archbishop of Milan with a verbal proposition to open negotiations with the West. The proposal was duly forwarded to the Allies by the Vatican— but was summarily rejected.

Il Duce never reported this to Hitler, with whom he'd had little communication lately, nor did he withhold from journalists his disapproval of the Führer's "megalomaniacal" attack on Russia. He confessed that he was little more than a prisoner of the Germans and that his own star had set. On April 25 Mussolini left Milan in a ten-car caravan for a last stand in the north with his most faithful Blackshirts. In one of the cars, an Alfa-Romeo with Spanish license plates, was Clara Petacci, his mistress. "I am following my destiny," she wrote a friend. "I don't know what will become of me, but I cannot question my fate." Mussolini left his wife behind, giving her documents, including letters from Churchill, which he hoped would get her safely across the frontier with their children. "If they try and stop you or harm you," he said, "ask to be handed over to the English."

Before dawn of the twenty-sixth, the Mussolini party started up the winding west shore of Lake Como, beautiful even in the heavy drizzle. Twenty-five miles later the party stopped at a hotel to wait for the 3000 Blackshirts who were supposed to join them. But none appeared and the next day the caravan continued north. Near Dongo they were captured by partisans; an argument broke out between those who wanted to kill the Fascists immediately and those who wanted to turn Mussolini over to the Allies. The issue was resolved on April 28 by a three-man execution squad from Milan which gunned down Mussolini and Clara Petacci with their machine pistols.

By that morning the German forces in the East were almost completely disjointed, their leadership on the verge of open rebellion. Manteuffel's Third Panzer Army, for instance, was making a fighting withdrawal to the west in defiance of Hitler's order to stand fast. Its goal was surrender to the Anglo-Americans.

The disintegration of the military hierarchy was evident in the bunker itself. Just before dawn Bormann, Krebs and Burgdorf had been embroiled in a drunken argument. "Nine months ago I approached my present task with all my strength and idealism!" railed Burgdorf. "I tried again and again to co-ordinate the party and the Wehrmacht." And because of this, he said, his fellow officers came to despise him and even called him a traitor to the officers' caste. "Today it is clear that these accusations were justified, and my labors were for nothing. My idealism was misplaced, and not only that, I was naïve and stupid!"

Krebs tried to quiet him but the noise had already wakened his two aides in the next room. They could hear Burgdorf shout down the conciliatory Krebs: "Let me alone, Hans—all this has to be said! Perhaps it will be too late to do so in another forty-eight hours. . . . Young officers with faith and idealism have gone to their death by the thousands. For what? The Fatherland? No! They have died for you!" Burgdorf turned his attack on Bormann. Millions, he shouted, had been sacrificed so that party members could further themselves. "For your life of luxury, for your thirst for power. You've annihilated our centuries-old culture, annihilated the German nation. That is your terrible guilt!"

"My dear fellow," soothed Bormann, "you shouldn't be so personal about it. Even if all the others have enriched themselves, I at least am blameless. That much I swear on everything I hold sacred. Your health, my friend!" In the next room the two eavesdroppers heard a clink of glasses, then there was silence.

All that morning General Weidling worked on his plan to break out of Berlin in three echelons. It was obvious that the Russians would soon reach the chancellery and "Bony Karl" was so sure that he could get approval from the Führer at the evening conference that he ordered all his commanders to report at the bunker by midnight.

In her quarters Frau Goebbels was writing her son by a previous marriage, now an Allied prisoner of war. She told him that the "glorious ideas" of Nazism were coming to an end "and with them everything beautiful and noble and good I have known in my life." A world without Hitler and National Socialism was not worth living in. That was why she had brought the six children to the bunker. They were too good for the life that was coming after defeat "and a merciful God will understand my reason for sparing them that sort of life. . . . May God give me strength for my last and most difficult duty." Bormann was sending his wife a radiogram that "all was lost" and there was no hope for him. She was to leave Berchtesgaden at once for the Tyrol with their children and the half dozen kidnaped youngsters.

7

In San Francisco, where the conference to set up a United Nations Organization was in session, a Reuters reporter was told that Himmler had just offered to surrender Germany unconditionally. His telegram got through to Reuters without censorship and a bulletin was dispatched throughout the world. A DNB man on the upper level of the bunker heard a BBC version of this story just before 9 P.M. on the twenty-eighth and brought it to Hitler. He read the message without emotion, as if resigned that the end had come, then summoned Goebbels and Bormann. The three conferred behind locked doors.

All day long Bormann had been making wholesale charges of treason and only an hour earlier had radioed Dönitz: TREACHERY SEEMS TO HAVE REPLACED LOYALTY. The brother-in-law of Eva Braun was one of those under grave suspicion. Otto Hermann Fegelein, Himmler's liaison officer at the bunker, had been arrested by the Gestapo at his city apartment. Since he was wearing civilian clothes and carried jewelry and considerable money, including Swiss francs, the Gestapo agents concluded he was planning to escape to a neutral country. Brought back to the bunker in disgrace, he was saved by Eva's intercession; she pleaded for mercy on the grounds that his wife, her sister, was having a baby. Hitler had merely dressed him down for cowardice, ripped off his epaulets and Knight's Cross, and locked him in a nearby room for punishment. But the BBC news report convinced the Führer that Fegelein's flight was connected with the betrayal of his chief, Himmler. Fegelein must be bound for Switzerland to start peace talks. In the space of an hour he was court-martialed, found guilty of treason and condemned to death. This time Eva, though her eyes were red from crying, did not defend him. She had since learned that some of the jewelry in his suitcase was hers—and that he was betraying her sister. Fegelein, it seemed, was leaving Berlin with the attractive wife of a Hungarian diplomat.

The bunker was in a turmoil by the time Weidling arrived for the evening conference. He informed Hitler of the latest Russian advances. All ammunition, food and supply dumps were either in enemy hands or under heavy artillery fire. In two days his troops would be out of ammunition and no longer able to resist. "As a soldier, I suggest therefore that we risk the breakout at once." He immediately launched into the details of his plan before Hitler could comment. Pure hysteria! Goebbels exclaimed. But Krebs said it was feasible from a military viewpoint. "Naturally," he added quickly, "I must leave the decision to the Führer." Hitler was silent. What if the breakout did succeed? he finally asked. "We would merely flee from one frying pan to another. Am I, the Führer, supposed to sleep in an open field or in a farmhouse, and just wait for the end?"

He left the conference to visit the wounded Greim; Hanna Reitsch was already there. He slumped down on the edge of Greim's bed, his face ashen, and told them of Himmler's betrayal. "Our only hope is Wenck," he said, "and to make his entry possible we must call up every available aircraft to cover his approach." He ordered Reitsch to fly Greim to the Rechlin airport so he could muster his aircraft from there. Only with Luftwaffe support could Wenck get through. "That's the first reason you must leave the shelter. The second is that Himmler must be stopped." His lips and hands trembled, his voice quavered. "A traitor must never succeed me as Führer. You must get out to make sure he will not." Painfully Greim began to dress. In tears, Reitsch asked Hitler for permission to stay. Hitler refused. "God protect you."

Frau Goebbels gave Reitsch two letters to her son. She took off a diamond ring and asked her to wear it in her memory. Eva Braun also gave Hanna a letter for her sister, Frau Fegelein. Later Reitsch couldn't resist reading it; she thought it was "so vulgar, so theatrical and in such poor, adolescent taste" that she tore it up.

The dark night was lit up by flaming buildings, and Greim and Reitsch could hear intense small-arms fire as an armored car brought them to an Arado 96 trainer, hidden near the Brandenburg Gate. She taxied the little plane down the east-west axis, taking off in a hail of fire. At rooftop level Russian searchlights picked up the Arado and flak explosions began tossing it about like a feather. With full power she climbed out of the maelstrom—below lay Berlin, a sea of flames. She headed north.

8

"Better to reign in hell than serve in heaven."

Lucifer in MILTON's *Paradise Lost*

Himmler's betrayal brought an end to Hitler's last hesitation and flickering hope. Despite his show of confidence to Greim, he admitted to himself that Wenck too was a lost cause and that the time had come to prepare for the end. He sent for Traudl Junge. She wondered what he had to dictate, then noticed a table elaborately decorated for some festivity: a tablecloth with the initials A.H., the silver service, champagne glasses. Was he intending to celebrate his final farewell?

He winked. "Perhaps we can begin now," he said and led the way to the conference room. He stood at his usual place before the map table— today it was barren—and stared at the polished surface. "My last political will," he said. As she took down his words her hand trembled. This was history in the making! She was sure it was going to be a confession, a justification. Who would lie at the brink of death? But the words she jotted down were only recriminations, accusations. Usually he made numerous corrections, rephrasing every sentence. Tonight he spoke almost without pause, his eyes glued on the table. He charged that neither he nor anyone else in Germany wanted war and that it had been "provoked exclusively by those international statesmen who either were of Jewish origin or worked for Jewish interests."

He declared that he would die "with a joyful heart" but had ordered his military commanders "to continue to take part in the nation's continuing struggle." To Traudl's wonder he began to name a new government. As his successor—both as President of the Reich and Supreme Commander of the Armed Forces—Hitler appointed Admiral Dönitz. Goebbels was made Chancellor and Bormann Party Minister. Traudl could not understand, if everything was lost, if Germany was destroyed, and National Socialism dead forever, what would these new officials do?

He was still staring at the table when he finished. For a moment he said nothing; then he began to dictate his personal will. "Since I did not feel that I could accept the responsibility of marriage during the years of struggle, I have decided now, before the end of my earthly career, to take as my wife . . ." Traudl looked up, startled, at last realizing why the table had been set for a celebration. She recalled Eva's cryptic words an hour earlier to Gerda Christian and herself: "This evening I bet you I shall cry!" But Traudl could find no tears. ". . . as my wife," continued Hitler, "the girl who, after many years of loyal friendship, came of her own free will to this city, already almost besieged, in order to share my fate. At her own request she goes to her death with me as my wife. Death will compensate us for what we were both deprived of by my labors in the service of my people." He left his possessions to the party, "or if this no longer exists, to the state," and appointed his most faithful party comrade, Martin Bormann, executor of his will. He ended with words that might have been inspired by Wagner and the opera libretto he himself composed as a young man in Vienna: "My wife and I choose to die in order to escape the shame of overthrow or capitulation. It is our wish that our bodies be burned immediately, here where I have performed the greater part of my daily work during the twelve years I served my people."

While Traudl retreated to a small room to type out the two documents, Hitler joined the wedding party in the map room. He had often told his friends he could not undertake "the responsibility of marriage." Perhaps he had also feared that it might diminish his uniqueness as Führer; to most Germans he was almost a Christlike figure. But now all that was over and the bourgeois side of his nature impelled him to reward his faithful mistress with the sanctity of matrimony.

There were eight guests: Bormann, the Goebbelses, Gerda Christian, Chief Adjutant Burgdorf, Krebs, Arthur Axmann, head of the Hitler Youth, and Fräulein Manzialy, the cook. A minor official was found in a nearby Volkssturm unit and brought into the bunker to officiate—appropriately, his name was Wagner. Eva wore a long gown of black silk taffeta; Hitler was in uniform. The ceremony was brief and notable only for two slight mishaps and a minor embarrassment. The rings were too big; they had been hastily located in the Gestapo treasury. Then Eva signed the marriage certificate and, like many nervous brides, made a mistake. She started to sign it "Eva B . . . ," then hastily crossed out the "B" and wrote, Eva Hitler, née Braun. Wagner also was so nervous he signed his name wrong—with a double "a"—then Goebbels and Bormann added their signatures as witnesses. It was just before midnight, April 28.*

Arm in arm with his bride, Hitler led the way into the study for the wedding feast. He joked and drank a little Tokay. Eva was radiant. She sent for the phonograph with its single record, "Red Roses," and went out into the corridor to receive congratulations from the staff. The word spread and smaller parties began celebrating the event throughout the bunker. Hitler was jovial but distracted and kept leaving the festivities to find out how Traudl was progressing with the two testaments. Just as she was finishing, Goebbels rushed in, pale and excited. He exclaimed that the Führer had ordered him to quit Berlin so as to take over a leading position in the new government. But how could he leave his side? He stopped abruptly, oblivious of the tears rolling down his cheeks. "The Führer has made so many decisions too late! Why this one, the last one, too early?" He made her leave the typewriter so she could take down *his* last will, one to be attached to Hitler's. "For the first time in my life," he dictated, "I must categorically refuse to obey an order of the Führer. My wife and children join me in this refusal." In the nightmare of treachery surrounding Hitler, he continued, there must be at least one willing to stay unconditionally with him until death.

It was almost 4 A.M. by the time Traudl finished all three documents. By then Bormann, Goebbels and Hitler were hovering over her and one of them ripped the last page from her typewriter. The three returned to the conference room where Hitler scratched his signature at the bottom of his official political testament. Goebbels, Bormann, Burgdorf and Krebs signed as witnesses. It reaffirmed the obsession of his life and career by taking credit for the annihilation of the Jews. They had started the war, he said, and he had made them pay, "even if by more humane means, for their guilt." He had no remorse for what he had done. He was proud that he had never weakened. "Above all," he concluded, "I enjoin the leaders of the nation and those under them to uphold the racial laws to their full extent and to oppose mercilessly the universal poisoner of all peoples, In-

* It is generally believed the marriage took place in the early hours of April 29 since this is the date that appears on the document. In his nervousness Wagner had placed one paper on top of the other when the ink was wet. Half an hour or so later he noticed the original date was obliterated by a blot and began to retrace the figures. Before doing so, he checked his watch; it was thirty-five minutes past midnight and so, thoughtlessly, he wrote down April 29. This revision is evident in the original document at the Eisenhower Library, if not in photostatic copies.

ternational Jewry." He was proud for having accomplished his mission of extermination and his words reaffirmed that, though he had many accomplices, without him there would have been no Final Solution.

9

By mid-morning of April 29 Russian ground forces were driving toward the bunker in three main attacks: from the east, south and north. The circle around the dying city tightened as advance Soviet units infiltrated the zoo. A mile away in the bunker Martin Bormann was making preparations to send Hitler's testament as well as his personal will to his successor, Admiral Dönitz. To help guarantee their delivery, Bormann decided to dispatch two separate emissaries: his own personal adviser and Heinz Lorenz. Goebbels also wanted his testament to reach the outside world and gave a copy to Lorenz.

A third copy of Hitler's political testament was entrusted to the Führer's army adjutant by General Burgdorf, who ordered it delivered to the newly appointed commander-in-chief of the army, Field Marshal Schörner. The messenger was also given a handwritten covering note, explaining that the will had been written "'under the shattering news of Himmler's treason," and was the Führer's "unalterable decision." It was to be published "as soon as the Führer orders it, or as soon as his death is confirmed."

Eva did not get up until midday. She was greeted by an orderly with an embarrassed "Gnädiges Fräulein." With a smile she told him it was all right to call her Frau Hitler. She asked her maid, Liesel, to take her wedding ring and nightgown to her best friend, Herta Schneider, then gave Liesel a ring as a keepsake. A little later she turned over to Traudl Junge another cherished possession, her silver fox coat. "I always like to have well-dressed people around me," she said. "Take it, and I hope it will give you much pleasure." Traudl was too overwhelmed by the gift to foresee how absurd it would be to escape Berlin in such style.

The day dragged on for those in the bunker. There was little to do but gossip and smoke. By now everyone—even Eva—was smoking openly. The fumes did not seem to bother the Führer. Finally, at 6 P.M., he assembled the family circle in his study, which was screened from the anteroom by a red velvet curtain with gold fringes. After announcing that Wenck was not coming, he said that he and his wife were going to die unless some miracle intervened. He passed out phials containing cyanamide. It was a poor parting gift, he told the two secretaries, and again praised their courage. Goebbels wondered if the phials had lost their deadly effect with time. Hitler was seized with doubts of a different nature: they had been supplied by that traitor Himmler. He sent for his new surgeon, Dr.

Ludwig Stumpfegger—who proposed one phial be tested on Blondi. Hitler agreed, then, recalling that Stumpfegger himself belonged to the SS, sent for a doctor in the hospital bunker. This man dutifully forced the liquid down the throat of the dog Hitler adored. It killed her.

Early that evening word arrived that Mussolini and his mistress had been assassinated by Italian partisans, their bodies strung up by the feet in a Milan gas station. "I will not fall into the hands of the enemy dead or alive!" said Hitler. "After I die, my body shall be burned and so remain undiscovered forever!" The news from Italy depressed Hitler and he would have suffered additional anguish had he known that SS General Wolff had just succeeded in secretly surrendering to the Allies all German forces in Italy.

At the final briefing of the day General Weidling told of the bitter, hopeless battles in the streets. His divisions, he said with heavy heart, were little more than battalions. Morale was poor, ammunition almost exhausted. He brandished an army field newspaper filled with optimistic stories of the imminent relief of Berlin by Wenck. The troops knew better, he charged, and such deceptions only embittered them. Goebbels sharply accused Weidling of defeatism; and another argument erupted. It took Bormann to calm them down so that Weidling could continue. He concluded his report with the devastating prediction that the battle would be over within twenty-four hours.

There was a shocked silence. In a tired voice Hitler asked the commandant of the chancellery area, an SS general, if he had observed the same conditions. He had. Weidling again pleaded for a breakout. Hitler pointed to a map and, in a resigned but sarcastic tone, said he had marked down the positions of the troops according to information from foreign radio announcements, since his own troop staffs were not even bothering to report to him any longer; his orders were not executed any more and so it was useless to expect anything.

As he rose painfully from his chair to say good-by, Weidling once more begged him to change his mind before ammunition ran out. Hitler murmured something to Krebs, then turned to Weidling: "I will permit a breakout of small groups," he said, but added that capitulation was out of the question. Weidling walked down the passageway wondering what Hitler meant. Wasn't the breakout of small groups a capitulation? He radioed all his commanders to congregate at his headquarters in the Bendlerstrasse the next morning.

After midnight Hitler bade farewell to a group of twenty officers and women secretaries in the main dining room. His eyes were covered with a film of moisture and, to Frau Junge, he seemed to be looking far away. He passed down the line shaking hands, then descended the curving staircase to his suite.

Throughout the bunker barriers dropped and high-ranking officers chatted familiarly with their juniors. In the canteen where soldiers and orderlies ate, a dance began spontaneously. It became so boisterous that a messenger from Bormann brought a warning to hold the noise down. He was trying to concentrate on a telegram he was writing to Dönitz. In it Bormann complained that all incoming reports were "controlled, suppressed or distorted" by Keitel, and ordered Dönitz "to proceed at once, and mercilessly, against all traitors."

10

By late morning of April 30 the Tiergarten was overrun by the Soviets and one advance unit was reported in the street next to the bunker. It was difficult to see that this news had any effect on Hitler. During lunch with the two secretaries and the cook, he chatted as if it were merely another family circle gathering. He was self-possessed and, if anything, quieter than usual. To Traudl it seemed to be "a banquet of death under the cheerful mask of resignation and composure."

But it was no ordinary day and no sooner had the three ladies left than Hitler summoned them back, along with Bormann, the Goebbelses and several others. More stooped than ever, he slowly came out of his room with Eva, who was wearing the black dress that was his favorite; her hair was neatly combed. Hitler began shaking hands with everyone. He was pale and there were tears in his eyes. He looked directly at Traudl as he held her hand but did not seem to see her, and mumbled something she could not understand. She stood motionless in a trance, oblivious of everything in the room. The spell was broken somewhat when Eva Hitler, with a sad smile, put an arm around her. "Please, at least try to get out of here," she said. Her voice broke into a sob. "Then please greet Munich for me."

Hitler took Günsche aside and said that he and his wife were going to commit suicide. He wanted their bodies burned. "After my death," he explained, "I don't want to be put on exhibition in a Russian wax museum." Günsche phoned Kempka's quarters at the bunker, asked for something to drink and said he was coming over. Kempka knew something was wrong. In the last days no one had thought of alcohol. He found a bottle of cognac and waited. The phone rang. It was Günsche again. "I need two hundred liters of gasoline immediately," he said huskily. Kempka thought it was some kind of joke and wanted to know why he needed so much fuel.

Günsche could not tell him on the phone. "I want it at the entrance of the Führer bunker without fail." Kempka said the only gasoline left—about 40,000 liters—was buried in the Tiergarten, which was under deadly fire. They would have to wait until five o'clock when the barrage let up.

"I can't wait a single hour. See what you can siphon out of the wrecked cars."

Hitler was bidding his personal pilot for so many years an emotional farewell. As they clasped hands, Baur begged him to escape by plane to Argentina, to Japan, or to one of the Arab countries where his anti-Semitism had made him such staunch friends. But the Führer would not listen. "One must have the courage to face the consequences—I am ending it all here! I know that by tomorrow millions of people will curse me —Fate wanted it that way." He thanked Baur for his long service and offered his cherished portrait of Frederick the Great as a present. "I don't want this picture to get lost. I want it to remain for the future. It has great historical value."

Baur said he would take it only if he were allowed to turn it over, later, to a museum or gallery. Hitler insisted it was for him personally, then with a small smile recalled how often Baur had grumbled about transporting the large portrait from headquarters to headquarters. He grasped the pilot's hands. "Baur," he said bitterly, "I want them to write on my tombstone: 'He was the victim of his generals!'"

The Hitlers sat together on a couch in their suite. Behind them was the bare space where the portrait of Frederick had hung. Eva was the first to die—by poison. At about 3:30 P.M. Hitler picked up his 7.65-caliber Walther pistol (Geli killed herself with a Walther and Eva had tried to but failed). It had been his companion for years: a defense against the Reds in the early days of the party; the means of gaining attention at the Bürgerbräukeller in 1923. He had threatened to kill himself with it during several fits of depression. This time his intention was genuine. On a console was a picture of his mother as a young woman. He put the pistol barrel to his right temple and pulled the trigger.

On the upper floor, Traudl Junge was telling the Goebbels children a fairy story to keep them from going downstairs, when a shot echoed along the damp concrete. Young Helmut thought it was an enemy bomb and said, "Bull's-eye!" In the conference room Goebbels, Bormann, Axmann and Günsche hesitated momentarily after hearing the shot, then broke into Hitler's anteroom with Goebbels in the lead. Günsche saw the Führer on the couch sprawled face down across a low table. To his left lay Eva, slumped over the armrest, her lips tightly closed in death, her nostrils discolored by cyanamide. Her dress was wet, but not with blood. A jug lying on the table must have been knocked over as the Führer pitched forward. Unnerved, Günsche stumbled back into the conference room where he was accosted by Kempka.

"For God's sake, Otto," the chauffeur said, "what's going on? You must be crazy to have me send men to almost certain death just for two hundred liters of gasoline." Günsche brushed past him, slamming the door to the cloakroom so that no one else could wander in. Then he closed the door to the Führer's suite and turned, eyes wide. "The Chief is dead!"

The only thing Kempka could think of was that Hitler had had a heart attack. Günsche lost his voice. Though he had seen the bullet hole in Hitler's right temple, he pointed a finger like a pistol and put it in his mouth, his shocked gesture inspiring the widely believed story that Hitler had shot himself in the mouth.

"Where is Eva?"

Günsche indicated Hitler's anteroom and was finally able to say, "She's with him." It took Günsche several minutes to stammer out the whole story.

Linge peered out of Hitler's anteroom and asked for the gasoline. Kempka said he had about a hundred and seventy liters in jerricans at the garden entrance. Linge and Dr. Stumpfegger carried out Hitler's body in a dark brown army blanket. The Führer's face was half covered, his left arm dangled down. Bormann followed, carrying Eva. Her hair was hanging loose. The sight of her in Bormann's arms was too much for Kempka. She had always hated Bormann and the chauffeur thought, "Not one more step." He called to Günsche, "I'll carry Eva," then took her away from Bormann. Halfway up the four flights of stairs to the garden, her body almost slipped from his grasp. Kempka stopped, unable to continue until Günsche moved to his aid, and together they carried Eva into the garden.

Another Russian barrage had begun, with shells smashing into the rubble. Only the jagged walls of the chancellery remained and these trembled with every shattering explosion. Through a cloud of dust Kempka saw Hitler's body not ten feet from the bunker entrance. His trousers were pulled up; his right foot was turned in—the characteristic position he always assumed on a long auto trip.

Kempka and Günsche stretched Eva's body out on Hitler's right. All at once the artillery barrage increased in tempo, forcing them to take cover in the bunker entrance. Kempka waited a few minutes, then seized a jerrican of gasoline and ran back to the bodies. He placed Hitler's left arm closer to his side. It was done only to delay a repellent duty; he could not bring himself to drench the body with gasoline. A gust of wind moved Hitler's hair. Kempka opened the jerrican. A shell exploded, showering him with debris; shrapnel whizzed past his head. Again he scrambled back for refuge.

Günsche, Kempka and Linge waited in the entrance for a lull in the shelling. When it came they returned to the bodies. Shivering with revulsion, Kempka sprinkled them with gasoline. He thought, "I can't do it but I'm doing it." He saw the same reaction in the faces of Linge and

Günsche, who were also pouring gasoline. From the entrance Goebbels, Bormann and Dr. Stumpfegger peered out with morbid concern.

The clothing of the corpses became so soaked that even the strongest gust of wind brought no stirring. The bombardment resumed, but the three men emptied can after can until the shallow depression in which the Hitlers lay was filled with gasoline. Günsche suggested igniting it with a hand grenade but Kempka said no. The idea of blowing up the bodies was too repugnant. He saw a large rag lying near a fire hose at the entrance. He pointed it out to Günsche, who doused it with gasoline.

Goebbels handed Kempka a pack of matches. He set fire to the rag and tossed it onto the bodies. A boiling ball of fire mushroomed, followed by dark clouds of smoke. It was a small blaze in a burning city, but horrifying. The men watched, hypnotized, as the fire slowly began to consume Adolf and Eva Hitler. Shaken, Günsche and Kempka stumbled back to the entrance. More jerricans of gasoline were delivered, and for the next three hours they kept pouring the liquid on the smoldering corpses.

In a daze, Günsche finally climbed back into the bunker. On the upper level he noticed Traudl sitting on a small bench, a bottle of Steinhäger beside her. He took a drink, his big hands trembling. "I executed the Führer's last order," he said very softly. "His body is burned." She said nothing but when he left to make another inspection of the bodies she was impelled to see Hitler's apartment. The door was open. On the floor next to the couch was the brass hull of a poison capsule. It looked like an empty lipstick. On the right cushion of the couch she saw blood—Hitler's blood. On an iron clothes rack hung the dog leash and his plain gray overcoat; above it his cap with the golden party emblem and his light deerskin gloves. She decided to take the gloves as a souvenir—at least one of them, but something stayed her hand. She noticed a silver fox coat in the wardrobe. It was the one Eva had bequeathed her but Traudl could not take it. What use would it be? All she needed was a poison capsule.

That evening the charred remains of Hitler and Eva were swept into a canvas and, so Günsche recalled, "let down into a shell hole outside the exit from the bunker, covered over with earth, and the earth pounded firm with a wooden rammer."

He was buried in the rubble of defeat; not, as he had instructed architect Giesler, in Munich ("Here I was born, here I started this movement, and here is my heart"). There should have been someone present to recite the poem Baldur von Schirach had made from the Führer's own words:

> *Could be that the columns which halt here,*
> *That these endless brown rows of men,*
> *Are scattered in the wind, split up and dispersed*
> *And will desert me. Could be, could be . . .*

I shall remain faithful, even though deserted by all—
I shall carry the flag, staggering and alone.
My smiling lips may stammer mad words,
But the flag will only fall when I fall
And will be a proud shroud covering my corpse.

The flag fell where he fell and when he died so did National Socialism and the Thousand-Year Third Reich. Because of him, his beloved Germany lay in ruins.

The greatest irony of all was that the driving force of his life—his hatred and fear of Jews—was thwarted. He had intended the elimination of six million Jews to be his great gift to the world. It would lead, instead, to the formation of a Jewish state.

Epilogue

1

To the surprise of the world, Hitler's death brought an abrupt, absolute end to National Socialism. Without its only true leader, it burst like a bubble. There were no enclaves of fanatic followers bent on continuing Hitler's crusade; the feared Alpine Redoubt proved to be a chimera. What had appeared to be the most powerful and fearsome political force of the twentieth century vanished overnight. No other leader's death since Napoleon had so completely obliterated a regime.

In death the Führer remained controversial and mysterious. Even as his body smoldered, a rumor spread in the bunker that Axmann, the Youth leader, had put some of Hitler's ashes in a box with instructions to secrete it outside of Berlin. News of his suicide was received with disbelief by some Germans. The parents of Fegelein, for instance, assured an American counterintelligence agent that a courier had brought a message from their son that he and Hitler were "safe and well in Argentina." Stalin also professed doubt. He told Harry Hopkins that Hitler's end struck him as "dubious." Hitler had surely escaped and was in hiding along with Bormann. This version became U.S.S.R. history until 1968 when a Soviet journalist, Lev Bezymenski, published a book revealing that the Russians *had* found the bodies of Adolf and Eva Hitler outside the bunker on May 4, 1945. As evidence, Bezymenski included an autopsy report of the Forensic Medical Commission of the Red Army, which stated that splinters of a poison ampule had been found in the Führer's mouth—and there was no bullet hole in the skull. In other words, the Soviets implied that Hitler had taken a cowardly route to death. Moreover, added the report, he had but one testicle—a conclusion made much of by some psychohistorians despite reports from three doctors who had examined

Hitler indicating he was normal. The long-delayed Soviet revelation was received with some suspicion. Although the detailed report was authenticated by five pathologists and experts in forensic medicine, it was supported only by photographic evidence of Hitler's corpse. The remains themselves, Bezymenski admitted, had been "completely burned and their ashes strewn to the wind."

Skeptics wondered why Stalin had spread the story in 1945 that Hitler had escaped when he knew the body had been found. They were not at all convinced by Bezymenski's explanation: "First, it was resolved not to publish the results of the forensic medical report but to 'hold it in reserve' in case someone might try to slip into the role of 'the Führer saved by a miracle.' Secondly, it was resolved to continue the investigations in order to exclude any possibility of error or deliberate deception." Neither reason accounts for the wait of twenty-three years, nor was any explanation given for the destruction of the remains. Pictures of the corpse's dentures had been kept on file and in 1972 Dr. Reidar Soggnaes, a dental forensic expert from U.C.L.A., discovered that these teeth exactly matched those in the X-ray head plates of Hitler taken in 1943. This hard evidence, Dr. Soggnaes told the 6th International Meeting of Forensic Sciences at Edinburgh, proved beyond doubt that Hitler was dead and that the Soviets had autopsied the right body. But where was the proof that Hitler had not shot himself? The skull "proving" that there was no bullet hole had been conveniently destroyed. Moreover, none of the eyewitnesses in the bunker had noticed the telltale discolorations of cyanamide on Hitler's lips; and only one empty poison capsule had been found.

No mystery clouded Goebbels' death. On the first of May, after a futile attempt to negotiate with the Soviets, he told his adjutant, Günther Schwägermann, "Everything is lost." He handed Schwägermann a silver-framed photograph of Hitler and bade him farewell. Frau Goebbels roused their six children from bed. "Children, don't be afraid," she said, "the doctor is going to give you an injection, a kind that is now given to all children and soldiers." After a dentist named Kunz injected morphine to make the children sleepy, Frau Goebbels herself placed a crushed ampule containing potassium cyanide in the mouth of each child.

Others in the bunker were getting last-minute instructions for escape. They were divided into six separate groups. At 9 P.M. the first section would make a run for the nearest subway entrance and walk along the tracks to the Friedrichstrasse station. Here they would emerge, cross the Spree River and head west or northwest until they reached the Western Allies or Dönitz. The other five groups would follow the same course, at intervals. Some were captured but, miraculously, few died.

At 8:45 P.M. Kempka went to the Goebbels suite to say good-by. The children were already dead. Frau Goebbels asked Kempka in a calm voice to send greetings to her son Harald and tell him how she had died. The Goebbelses left their room arm in arm. Utterly calm, he thanked Naumann for his loyalty and understanding; Magda could only hold out her hand. Naumann kissed it. Goebbels wryly remarked that they were going to walk up the steps to the garden so that their friends wouldn't have to carry them. After shaking hands with Naumann, he escorted his silent, pale wife toward the exit. They disappeared up the steep concrete stairway. Then came a shot, followed by a second. Schwägermann and the Goebbelses' chauffeur hurried up the stairs to find the Goebbelses sprawled on the ground. An SS orderly was staring at them—he had shot them. He and the two newcomers poured four jerricans of gasoline on the bodies and set them afire. Without waiting to see the effect of the blaze, they returned to the bunker, which they had been ordered to destroy. They dumped the last can of gas in the conference room and ignited it.

The fate of Martin Bormann was more controversial than his master's. It was generally assumed that he had died while attempting to escape from Berlin but declassified United States and British intelligence documents indicated that he might have escaped to Bolzano, Italy, where his wife had already fled from Berchtesgaden with their nine children. For the next twenty-seven years there were recurring reports of Bormann's reappearance, particularly in Argentina. Then, late in 1972, an American author, Ladislas Farago, claimed he had positive proof Bormann was alive in South America. This sensational announcement was followed a few days later by another. The German authorities declared that they had just found Bormann's body near the Führer bunker. Dr. Soggnaes, who had authenticated the Hitler corpse, asked permission to examine the skull so he could corroborate the dental identification. At first permission was withheld, adding suspicion that the corpse might be a hoax. Finally in the summer of 1973 Dr. Soggnaes was allowed to examine the skeletal remains as well as the maxillary incisor bridge which had been found three months after the skull was unearthed. Dr. Soggnaes returned to U.C.L.A. to prepare a forensic analysis of the data. In September 1974 he presented his material to the World Congress of the Federation of Dentaire Internationale in London. The skull, he concluded, was indeed that of Bormann. And the mystery of Hitler's most faithful servant was finally solved.

2

To the very end, Heinrich Himmler hoped for some arrangement with the Allies while fearing that something would go wrong. After Hitler's death he fled to the north and requested the Führer's successor to appoint him the second man in his new German state. But Admiral Dönitz said, "That is impossible. I have no job for you." In desperation

Himmler turned to Schwerin von Krosigk for advice. "Please tell me what is going to become of me?" he asked the new Foreign Minister. "I am not interested in the least what will happen to you or any other man," was the exasperated answer. "Only our mission interests me, not our personal destinies." Krosigk gave Himmler two choices: either commit suicide or disappear with a false beard. "But if I were you I would drive up to Montgomery and say, 'Here I am, Himmler the SS general, and ready to take responsibility for my men.'"

That evening Himmler cryptically told his closest friends that an important new task remained. A few could accompany him. He shaved off his mustache, put a patch over one eye, changed his name and—with some nine followers, including his chief Waffen SS adjutant, Werner Grothmann—went into hiding. When Grothmann discovered his chief had a cyanide capsule and intended to use it if necessary, he accused Himmler of taking an easy way out that was not open to his followers. It was the Reichsführer's duty, he said, not only to assume responsibility for his men's actions but to make clear that the Waffen SS, the SD and the concentration camp guards were from distinctly different organizations. Himmler demurred. "After I take the poison," he said, "then you young officers must tell the world what happened here in Germany—what I did and what I did not do." Within two weeks Himmler was captured by the British. A doctor conducting a routine examination noticed something in his mouth, but when he reached in to pull out the object Himmler bit down on the cyanide capsule and died instantly. There were other suicides but their number were fewer than expected, particularly among the hierarchy, one of whom—Robert Ley—did commit suicide while awaiting trial at Nuremberg.

Göring was by far the most defiant prisoner at Nuremberg. He arrived at the prison with an incredibly large cache of Paradocin pills and was taking forty daily. By the time he testified, however, he was completely free of the drug habit and had cut his weight down more than forty per cent to 153 pounds. In the courtroom he, almost alone, defended his Führer. Unlike so many of the other defendants, he never put blame on others or hid behind the figure of Hitler. He took charge of the prisoners' dock, aggressively dictating a concerted strategy of defense. Back in the cell block, he would rub his hands enthusiastically and call himself the captain of the first-string team, boasting that he would give the prosecutors and the audience a run for their money. If any fellow defendant protested or weakened, the revivified Göring would bully and insult him into silence. "It makes me sick to see Germans selling their souls to the enemy!" he said during one lunch, then banged a fist on the table. "Damn it," he added, "I just wish we could all have the courage to confine our defense to three simple words: *Lick my ass!*"

Of the twenty-two major defendants only three (Schacht, Papen and Fritzsche) were acquitted. Eight received long terms of imprisonment; the rest were sentenced to death. At 10:45 P.M. October 15, 1946, Göring cheated the hangman with a cyanide capsule. Two hours later the executions began. The first to climb the thirteen steps of the gallows was Ribbentrop. "God protect Germany," he said loudly. "My last wish is that Germany's unity shall be preserved and that an understanding be reached between East and West." It had taken the incontrovertible evidence at Nuremberg to convince him that masses of Jews had been killed, for Hitler had assured him time and again that the Jewish problem would be solved by deportation. "I never dreamed," he told G. M. Gilbert, an American psychologist, "it would end like this!"

Next came Keitel. Minutes earlier he had sobbed while the chaplain gave him a last benediction. Now his chin was thrust out. "I call on the Almighty God to have mercy on the German people. For Germany— everything. Thank you!" He turned to the chaplain, an American. "I thank you and those who sent you with all my heart." The hangman, Master Sergeant John Woods, had looked forward with relish to these executions. He adjusted the rope around Keitel's neck, then placed a black hood over his head. At the very last moment the field marshal shouted, "Deutschland über Alles!" During the trial Keitel had confided to Gilbert that Hitler had betrayed him. "If he did not deceive us by deliberate lies, then he did it by deliberately keeping us in the dark and letting us fight under a false impression!"

3

A surprising number of Hitler's family circle survived the last cataclysmic days: the four secretaries; his two favorite architects, Speer and Giesler; his pilot, Baur; his chauffeur, Kempka; his valet, Linge; Heim and Koeppen, who copied down his table conversations; the best friend of his wife, Frau Schneider; his two favorite fighters, Skorzeny and Rudel; the three women he particularly admired: Leni Riefenstahl, Gerdy Troost and Helene Hanfstaengl.

A number of his adjutants and ordnance officers not only survived but were willing to talk freely of their experiences: Puttkamer, Engel, Below, Wünsche, Schulze and Günsche. When the last returned to West Germany after twelve years of imprisonment in the Soviet Union and East Germany, he was bewildered by the sight of young men with beards and long hair. "Dear friend," Schulze told him, "we have lost the war and all is now changed. The young people don't live as we did." To shock Günsche back to reality, Schulze took him to the Berghof. The building had been set afire by the SS on May 4, 1945, and its remains had been gradually destroyed by the Americans. Everything looked different and it was very difficult even to figure out where the long flight of steps leading up to the house had been. As the two men surveyed the scene, Schulze's wife took their picture, capturing in their stunned faces, as no words could, the definitive end of the man they had worshiped. (See page 892). The most extraordinary figure in the history of the twentieth century had vanished—unlamented except by a faithful few.

Acknowledgments

Without the co-operation of numerous people in Germany, Austria, England and the United States this book could not have been written. Archives and libraries contributed immeasurably: the National Archives (John E. Taylor, John Mendelsohn, Robert Wolfe, George Wagner); the Library of Congress; the main branch of the New York Public Library; the Danbury, Ct., Public Library; the Yale University Library; the Franklin D. Roosevelt Library (Bettie Sprigg, Robert Parks); the Wiener Library, London; the Imperial War Museum, London (Rose Coombs); the Institut für Zeitgeschichte, Munich (Frl. Danyl); the Bayerisches Hauptstaatarchiv, Munich; the Forschungstelle für die Geschichte des Nationalsozialismus, Hamburg (Werner Jochmann); the Bibliothek für Zeitgeschichte, Stuttgart (Werner Haupt, Gerhard Buck, Dr. Jurgen Röhwer); the Bundesarchiv, Koblenz; the Institut für Zeitgeschichte, Vienna (Dr. Ludwig Jedlicka); and the Landesarchiv, Linz (Dr. Hans Sturmberger).

Numerous agencies, organizations and individuals made substantial contributions to this book:

United States: Charles MacDonald and Hannah Zeidlik of the Office of the Chief of Military History, Department of the Army; U. S. Army Intelligence Command, Fort Holabird, Md. (Elaine M. Pospishil); fellow authors and historians: Richard Hanser, Telford Taylor, Richard Walton, Dr. John Lukacs, Dr. Harold J. Gordon, Jr., Dr. Eberhard Jäckel, Dr. Ernst Deuerlein, Dr. Dietrich Orlow, Dr. Reginald Phelps, Dr. Oron Hale, Dr. Bradley F. Smith; contributors of documents: Edward Whalen, Dave Stanton, Peter Thayer and Ben E. Swearingen; psychiatrists and physicians: Drs. R. Walzar, Richmond Hubbard, Jason Weiner and Warren Sherman; Edward Weiss; Raymond Garthoff; Michael Erlanger; Arthur Shilstone; Sig Muller; Otto Zundricht; Peter Repetti; John Stillman and Stewart Richardson of Doubleday & Company.

Austria: Alfred Janicek, Heimleiter, Männerheim, Vienna; Josef Adler, Asylum, Vienna; Dr. Wilfried Daim; and Dr. Eleonore (Kandl) Weber.

England: Ellic Howe, Walter Henry Nelson and Hugh Trevor-Roper.

Spain: Otto Skorzeny.

Germany: Bavaria Atelier Fernsik-Productions (Dr. Helmut Pigge); Bayerischer Rundfunk and Fernseher (Thilo Schneider and Dietmar Ebert);

Prof. Gerdy Troost; Nerin Gun; Egon Hanfstaengl; Harry Schulze-Wilde (H. S. Hegner); Günter Syrup; Klaus Wiedemann; Major General Gustav Lombard; Erich Kempka; Dr. Werner Koeppen; Heinrich Heim; Erich Kempmayer; Helmut Sündermann; Admiral Karl Jesko von Puttkamer; General Hasso von Manteuffel; Frau Luise Jodl; Dr. H. D. Röhrs; Hein Ruck; Richard Schulze-Kossens; Max Wünsche; Hans Ulrich Rudel; Frau Ilse (Braun) Fucke-Michels; and two research assistants and interpreters: Inge Gehrich and Wolfgang Glaser.

Finally I would like to thank eleven people who contributed outstandingly to the book: Roger Bell, The Society for the Studies of the E.T.O. 1944–45, London, for supplying numerous books; Dr. Rudolph Binion, John Jamieson, Dr. George Breitbart and Dr. Eric Roman, all of whom read the entire manuscript and made valuable suggestions; my chief research assistant and interpreter in Germany, Karola Gillich, an indefatigible aide since 1957; my secretary-translator-typist, Ann Thomas, whose suggestions and corrections have been of inestimable value; my two editors at Doubleday, Carolyn Blakemore and Ken McCormick, who somehow managed to make the revisions a pleasure; and my wife, Toshiko, for putting up with Adolf Hitler more than five years.

Glossary

ABWEHR Espionage, counterespionage and sabotage service of the German high command.

ANSCHLUSS Union. Especially the political union of Austria and Germany in 1938.

BLITZKRIEG Lightning warfare.

BLUE POLICE Municipal police, so called for color of their uniform.

EINSATZGRUPPE An operational task force of the SD and Sipo for special missions in occupied Eastern territory. Its task was to maintain law and order but its primary occupation was liquidation of partisans, Jews and other "dangerous elements." There were four Einsatzgruppen and, although they were administratively subordinated to the military command, the RSHA retained functional control over them.

ENDLÖSUNG The Final Solution, extermination of Jews.

FESTUNG Fortress.

GAU Territorial division of the NSDAP.

GAULEITER High-ranking, Nazi Party official in a Gau. Responsible for political and economic activity as well as mobilization of labor and civil defense.

GENERALGOUVERNEMENT German-occupied Poland. Administered by a German civilian, Hans Frank.

GESTAPO Abbreviation for Geheime Staatspolizei. Secret state police. (See SS.)

GLEICHSCHALTUNG Unification. Nazi program begun in 1933.

GREEN POLICE State police, so called for the color of their uniforms.

HEER German army.

HITLERJUGEND (HJ) Hitler Youth.

KREIS Administrative district in a Gau.

KREISLEITER Head of Kreis.

KRIPO Kriminalpolizei. Criminal police which, with the Gestapo, formed the Sipo, secret police.

LEBENSBORN Spring of Life. SS maternity organization to promote Himmler's racial policy.

LEBENSRAUM Living room. Living space. Additional territory desired by a nation for expansion.

LEIBSTANDARTE SS ADOLF HITLER Adolf Hitler Bodyguard Regiment.

LUFTWAFFE German air force.

NSDAP Nationalsozialistische Deutsche Arbeiter Partei, National Socialist German Worker's Party. Nazi Party.

OBERKOMMANDO DES HEERES (OKH) High command of the German army.

OBERKOMMANDO DER WEHRMACHT (OKW) High command of the German armed forces.

OSTMINISTERIUM Ministry of the East.

REICHSFÜHRER Highest rank in SS.

REICHSLEITER Highest-ranking Nazi official.

REICHSSICHERHEITSHAUPTAMT (RSHA) Reich Central Security Department. Under Heydrich, then Kaltenbrunner. (*See* SS.)

REICHSWEHR The 100,000-man army Germany was restricted to under the Treaty of Versailles.

SCHUTZSTAFFEL (SS) Guard Detachment. It contained the following sections:
1. *Allgemeine* (General) SS. Strictly civilian. Most diplomats, top-level state employees, industrialists, lawyers, doctors, etc., held high ranks in the *Allgemeine* SS.
2. RSHA (*Reichssicherheitshauptampt*, National Central Security Office). Civilian and paramilitary. Of its seven departments, the most important were: Bureau III, the SD (*Sicherheitsdienst*, Security Service inside the Reich); Bureau IV, the Gestapo (State Security Police); Bureau V, Criminal Police; and Bureau VI, Foreign Intelligence.
3. *Waffen* (Armed) SS. Strictly elitist military organization with recruitment open not only to Germans but to qualified Aryans of other nations. Its divisions included volunteers from Belgium, France, Holland, Norway, Lithuania, Denmark, Sweden, Hungary, Romania, etc., who had joined primarily to fight Bolshevism.
4. *Totenkopfverbände* (Death's Head units). Paramilitary. Concentration and death camp guards. By 1943 the majority were elderly or wounded soldiers unfit for front-line duty. In 1940 the youngest and healthiest were formed into an elite battle unit, the *Totenkopf* Division, and thus became a genuine part of the Waffen SS. Those who remained as concentration and death camp guards also ranked as members of the Waffen SS, carrying the same pay-books and wearing the same uniforms. It was an insult to those Waffen SS troops who had fought gallantly at the front and were not at all involved in the terrorism of the camps. But their commanders did not protest and, besides providing the bulk of the troops for the annihilation of the Warsaw ghetto, contributed some 1500 men to the notorious Einsatzgruppen squads.

SICHERHEITSDIENST RFSS (SD) SS Security Service. (*See* RSHA and SS.)

SICHERHEITSPOLIZEI (Sipo) Security police consisting of Gestapo and Kripo.

STAHLHELM Steel Helmet. Nationalist ex-servicemen's organization founded in 1918. Absorbed into SA in 1933.

STURMABTEILUNG (SA) Storm Detachment. The Brownshirts, storm troopers.

TOTENKOPFVERBÄNDE Death's Head Detachments. (*See* SS.)

VERTRAUENSMANN (V-mann) An intelligence agent or informer. Hitler was a V-mann in 1919.

VOLKSSTURM Home Guard.

WAFFEN SS Armed SS. Militarized SS units. Almost 40 divisions were fielded in World War II. (*See* SS.)

WEHRMACHT The German armed forces—army, navy and air force.

Table of Ranks

SS	GERMAN ARMY	BRITISH ARMY	U.S. ARMY	RED ARMY (Soviet ranks compiled by Raymond Garthoff)	NSDAP (The first entry in each section represents a function, the second denotes the appropriate rank)
Reichsführer	Generalfeldmarschall	Field Marshal	General of the Army	Marshal of the Soviet Union [Marshal Sovetskogo Soiuza] Chief Marshal of (an Arm: i.e., Artillery, Armor, Aviation, Signals, Engineers) [Glavnyi Marshal—(Artillerii)]	Reichsleiter / Hauptbefehlsleiter
Oberstgruppenführer (from 1942 only)	Generaloberst	General	General	Marshal of an Arm (as above) [Marshal (Artillerii)] General of the Army [General armii]	Gauleiter / Oberbefehlsleiter
Obergruppenführer	General (der Infanterie etc.)	Lieutenant-General	Lieutenant General	Colonel General [also, Col. Gen. of an Arm) [General polkovnik]	Gauleiter (or deputy) / Befehlsleiter
Gruppenführer	Generalleutnant	Major-General	Major General	Lieutenant General [also, Lt. Gen. of an Arm] [General leytenant]	Gauleiter (or deputy) / Hauptdienstleiter
Brigadeführer	Generalmajor	Brigadier	Brigadier General	Major General [also, Maj. Gen. of an Arm] [General Mayor]	Gauleiter (or deputy) / Oberdienstleiter
Oberführer	· · · · · · · ·	· · · · · · · · · · no such rank · · · · · · · · · ·			Gauleiter (or deputy) / Oberdienstleiter
Standartenführer	Oberst	Colonel	Colonel	Colonel [Polkovnik]	Kreisleiter / Dienstleiter or Hauptbereichsleiter
Obersturmbannführer	Oberstleutnant	Lieutenant-Colonel	Lieutenant Colonel	Lieutenant Colonel [Podpolkovnik]	
Sturmbannführer	Major	Major	Major	Major [Mayor]	(a) Kreisleiter / Oberbereichsleiter or Bereichsleiter / Hauptabschnittsleiter (b) Ortsgruppenleiter / Oberabschnittsleiter.

SS	GERMAN ARMY	BRITISH ARMY	U.S. ARMY	RED ARMY	NSDAP
Hauptsturmführer	Hauptmann or Rittmeister (Cav.)	Captain	Captain	Captain [Kapitan]	(a) Ortsgruppenleiter Abschnittsleiter; (b) Zellenleiter Hauptgemeinschafts-leiter or Obergemeinschafts-leiter
Obersturmführer	Oberleutnant	Lieutenant	First Lieutenant	Senior Lieutenant [Starshiy leytenant] Lieutenant [Leytenant]	(a) Zellenleiter Gemeinschaftsleiter; (b) Blockleiter Haupteinsatzleiter
Untersturmführer	Leutnant	Second Lieutenant	Second Lieutenant	Junior Lieutenant [Mladshiy leytenant]	Blockleiter Obereinsatzleiter Einsatzleiter
Sturmscharführer	Stabsfeldwebel Stabswachtmeister	Regimental Sergeant-Major	Sergeant Major	Sergeant Major [Starshina]	Hauptbereitschafts-leiter
Stabsscharführer	Hauptfeldwebel	....	....	no such rank	
Hauptscharführer	Oberfeldwebel Oberwachtmeister	Sergeant-Major	Master Sergeant	Sergeant Major [Starshina]	Oberbereitschaftsleiter
Oberscharführer	Feldwebel Wachtmeister	Quartermaster-Sergeant	Technical Sergeant	............no such rank	............no such rank
Scharführer	Unterfeldwebel	Staff Sergeant	Staff Sergeant	Senior Sergeant [Starshiy serzhant]	Bereitschaftsleiter
Unterscharführer	Unteroffizier	Sergeant	Sergeant	Sergeant [Serzhant]	Hauptarbeitsleiter
Rottenführer	Stabsgefreiter Obergefreiter Gefreiter	Corporal	Corporal	Junior Sergeant [Mladshiy serzhant]	Oberarbeitsleiter
Sturmmann	Oberschütze Obergrenadier etc.	Lance-Corporal	Private 1st Class	Private First Class [Yefreitor]	Arbeitsleiter Oberhelfer
SS-Mann	Schütze Grenadier etc.	Private	Private	Private [Ryadovoi]	Helfer

Sources

A. INTERVIEWS (partial list)

Dieter Allers (SA), 1971, taped
Countess Haiga von Arco auf Valley, 1971
Stephen Bauchner (Leonding), 1971, taped
Flugkapitan Hans Baur, 1970, taped
Oberst Nicolaus von Below, 1971, taped
Werner Benecke (SA), 1971, taped
Countess Estelle Manville Bernadotte, 1963
Generalleutnant Günther Blumentritt (2 interviews), 1957 **
Wolfgang Boigs (DNB), 1963
Otto Bräutigam (Rosenberg office), 1971, taped
Carl J. Burckhardt, 1963
General Theodor Busse, 1963
Gerda Daranowsky Christian (2), 1971, taped
Wilfried Daim (3) (author), 1971, taped
Léon Degrelle (2), 1963, 1971, taped
General Erich Dethleffson, 1971, taped
Wallace Deuel (Chicago *Daily News*), 1972
Prof. Ernst Deuerlein, 1971, taped **
SS Oberstgruppenführer Josef (Sepp) Dietrich, 1963 **
Eugen Dollmann (3), 1971, taped
Grossadmiral Karl Dönitz (2), 1963; 1971, taped
Allen Dulles, 1963
Hans Ehard, 1971, taped
General Gerhard Engel (2), 1971, taped
Hermann Esser (2), 1971, taped
Hildegard Fath (3), 1971, taped
Werner Fink, 1971, taped **
F. K. Florian (Gauleiter), 1971, taped
André François-Poncet, 1971, taped
Albert Frauenfeld (2), 1971, taped
Walter Frentz, 1971, taped

** Deceased

Helmuth Fuchs (SS), 1971, taped
Gero von Gaevernitz (4), 1963–64
General Adolf Galland, 1971, taped
General R. Chr. von Gerstdorff, 1971, taped
Dr. Erwin Giesing (3), 1971, taped
Paul Giesler (2), 1971, taped
G. M. Gilbert, 1972, taped
Walter Görlitz (historian), 1971
SS Lieutenant Colonel Werner Grothmann (2), 1971, taped
Nerin Gun (4), 1970–71, taped
SS Major Otto Günsche (2), 1963, 1971
Dolly Haas, 1971, taped
Otto von Habsburg, 1971, taped
General Franz Halder, 1963 **
Egon Hanfstaengl (4), 1971, taped
Ernst Hanfstaengl (15), 1970–71, taped **
Helene Hanfstaengl, 1971, taped **
Heinrich Härtle (2) (Rosenberg office), 1970–71, taped
Dr. Hanskarl von Hasselbach, 1971, taped
Heinz Haushofer, 1971, taped
SS General Paul Hausser, 1963
Heinrich Heim (6), 1971, 1974–75, taped
Richard Helms (2), 1971–72, taped
Ilse Hess, 1971, taped
Fritz Hesse (2), 1971, taped
General Adolf Heusinger, 1971, taped
Hans Hitler, 1971, taped
Wilhelm Hoegner, 1971, taped
Ellic Howe (author), 1971
Werner Huppenkothen (SS), 1971
Werner Jochman, 1971
Frau Luise Jodl (5), 1970–71, taped
Rudolf Jordan (Gauleiter), 1970, taped
Traudl Junge (2), 1971
Erich Kempka (3), 1963, 1971, taped **
Robert M. W. Kempner, 1970
Josef Keplinger (Linz), 1971, taped
Erich Kernmayr (historian), 1970
General H. Kissel, 1971, taped
August Klapprott (German-American Bund) (2), 1971–72, taped
Ewalt Heinrich von Kleist (2), 1971, taped
Peter Kleist (4), 1963, 1970–71, taped **
Werner Koeppen (4), 1971, taped
Admiral Theodor Krancke, 1971, taped
Carl-Vincent Krogmann (Bürgermeister of Hamburg), 1971, taped
Robert Kropp (Göring's butler), 1963
G. Wilhelm Kunze (German-American Bund), 1972, taped
Helmut Kurth (Göring's photographer), 1971, taped **
Hermann Lauterbacher (Gauleiter) (2), 1971, taped
Georg Leibbrandt (2) (Rosenberg office), 1971, taped
General Gustav Lombard (2), 1970–71, taped

** Deceased

Major Bernd Freytag von Loringhoven (Krebs adjutant), 1963
SS Major Heinz Macher (Himmler adjutant), 1971, taped
Field Marshal Erich von Manstein, 1971, taped **
General Hasso von Manteuffel (5) 1956, 1963, 1970, 1971, taped
Fräulein Johanna Mayrhofer (Leonding), 1971, taped
Dennis McEvoy, 1971
Hubert Meyer (SS), 1971, taped
General W. Meyer-Detring, 1971, taped
Field Marshal Erhard Milch (4), 1971, taped **
Konrad Morgen, 1971, taped
Lady Diana Mosley, 1972
Sir Oswald Mosley (3) 1971–72, taped
Josef (Oxensepp) Müller (2), 1963
Johannes von Müllern-Schönhausen, 1971
Werner Naumann (2), 1971, taped
Theodor Oberlaender (2), 1971, taped
Piotr Olender (Auschwitz), 1971, taped
Dr. Raimund von Ondarza (Göring's doctor), 1971, taped
Ambassador Hiroshi Oshima (4), 1966–67, 1971
General Eugen Ott (German ambassador to Japan), 1963
General Albert Praun, 1971, taped
Admiral Karl Jesko von Puttkamer (7), 1970–71, taped
Ambassador Count Edward Raczynski, 1963
General Otto Remer (3), 1971, taped
Annelies von Ribbentrop, 1971, taped **
Leni Riefenstahl (6), 1971, taped
Ambassador Emil von Rinteln, 1971, taped
Frau Annalies Röhm (Ernst Röhm's sister-in-law), 1971, taped
Robert Röhm (Ernst Röhm's brother), 1971, taped
Dr. H. D. Röhrs, 1971, taped
Hein Ruck (3), 1971, taped
Colonel Hans Ulrich Rudel (2), 1963, 1971
Admiral Friedrich Ruge, 1971, taped
Hjalmar Schacht (2), 1963 **
Prince Schaumberg-Lippe, 1971, taped
Gustav Scheel (Gauleiter), 1971, taped
Dr. Ernst Schenck (doctor in Führer bunker), 1971, taped
Fabian von Schlabrendorff, 1963
Dr. Gustav Schlotterer (2) (Funk office), 1971, taped
General Arthur Schmidt (2), 1971, taped
Frau Anneliese Schmundt (wife of Hitler's chief adjutant), 1971, taped
Frau Herta Schneider (4), 1971, taped
Field Marshal Ferdinand Schörner (2), 1963 **
Professor Percy Ernst Schramm (OKW diarist) (2), 1963 **
General Wilhelm Ritter von Schramm, 1971, taped
Frau Ada Schultze (3), 1974, taped
Dr. Walter Schultze (4), 1974, taped
Sigrid Schulz (3), 1971–72, taped
Harry Schulz-Wilde (2) (author), 1971, taped
Richard Schulze (Schulze-Kossens) (6), 1971, 1973–74, taped

** Deceased

Kurt von Schuschnigg, 1971, taped
Martin Schwaebe, 1971, taped
Count Lutz Schwerin von Krosigk (2), 1963; 1971, taped
Vera Semper (Lambach), 1971, taped
Ramon Serrano Suñer, 1963
SS Colonel Otto Skorzeny (7), 1956, 1963; 1971, taped **
Albert Speer (2), 1970–71, taped
SS General Felix Steiner, 1963 **
Otto Strasser (2), 1971, taped **
Johann Stütz (Spital), 1970–71, taped
Helmut Sündermann (3), 1970–71, taped **
Günter Syrup (5), 1971, taped
General Wolfgang Thomale, 1963
Professor Gerdy Troost (4), 1971, taped
Olga Tschechowa, 1971, taped
Ignacio, Marquis de Valdeglesias, 1971, taped
Admiral Gerhard Wagner, 1971, taped
General Walter Warlimont, 1971, taped
Rolf Wehser, 1971, taped
General Walter Wenck, 1963
Klaus Wiedemann (son of Fritz Wiedemann), 1971
Colonel Otto Wien (2) (Luftwaffe), 1971, taped
Johann Wiesinger (Leonding), 1971, taped
SS General Karl Wolff, 1963
Lieutenant Max Wünsche (2), 1971, taped
Dr. Werner Zabel, 1971, taped
Hans Severus Ziegler (author), 1971, taped

B. DOCUMENTS, RECORDS AND REPORTS

British Government Archives:
    The Cabinet Minutes and Memoranda, 1937–39
    Foreign Office, 1937–39
    Minutes of the Foreign Policy Committee of the Cabinet and Memoranda, 1937–39
    Papers of the Prime Minister's Office, 1937–39
    Records of the Committee of Imperial Defense. London: Her Majesty's Stationery Office.

Correspondence Between the Chairman of the Council of Ministers of the U.S.S.R. and the Presidents of the U.S.A. and the Prime Ministers of Great Britain during the Great Patriotic War of 1941–1945, 2 vols. Moscow: Foreign Language Publishing House, 1957.

Correspondence between Göring and Negrelli 1924–25. Ben E. Swearingen collection.

Der Hitler-Prozess. Munich: Deutscher Volksverlag, 1924.

Documents and Materials relating to the Eve of the Second World War, 1937–39, 2 vols. Moscow: Foreign Language Publishing House, 1948.

Documents at the Bibliothek für Zeitgeschichte, Stuttgart; Institut für Zeitgeschichte, Munich; Institut für Zeitgeschichte, Vienna; Imperial

** Deceased

War Museum, London; the National Archives, Washington; the Library of Congress, Washington; U. S. Army Military History Research Collection, Carlisle Barracks, Pa. (including dossiers of U. S. Army Intelligence); Bayerisches Hauptstaatarchiv, Munich; Bundesarchiv, Koblenz.

Documents on British Foreign Policy 1919–1939, 7 vols. London: Her Majesty's Stationery Office

Documents on German Foreign Policy, Series C, The Third Reich: Vols. I–IV. Washington: U. S. Dept. of State.

Documents on German Foreign Policy, Series D, Vols. V–XII. Washington: U. S. Dept. of State.

The French Yellow Book, diplomatic documents, 1938–39, London: Hutchinson, 1940.

Halder, General Franz. *Kriegstagebuch.* Stuttgart: Jacobsen, 1962.

Hitler Diary (January 1, 1934–June 12, 1943). *Sekretar des Führers. Führers Tagebuch.* Washington, Library of Congress, Appendix 5, Safe 5,5.

Hitler e Mussolini–Lettere e documenti. Milan: Rissoli, 1946.

Hitler's speeches:
Baynes, Norman H. ed. *The Speeches of Adolf Hitler,* April 1922–August 1939, 2 vols. New York, 1942. Prange, Gordon W., ed. *Hitler's Words,* Washington, 1944.

Hitler War Directives 1939–1945. London: Sidgwick and Jackson, 1964.

International Military Tribunal, *Trial of the Major War Criminals before the International Military Tribunal,* 14 November 1945 to 1 October 1946, 42 vols.

Koeppen, Werner. Hitler's Tabletalk. 28 surviving reports. National Archives.

Linge, Heinz. *Diaries,* March 1943 to February 1945, National Archives.

Lochner, Louis. Letters and Papers. State Historical Society of Wisconsin, Madison, Wisc.

Milch, Field Marshal Erhard. Papers and Memoirs. Unpublished.

Nazi Conspiracy and Aggression, 10 vols. Washington: U. S. Government Printing Office, 1946.

Nazi-Soviet Relations, 1939–1941. Documents from the Archives of the German Foreign Office. Washington: U. S. Dept. of State, 1948.

OSS *Hitler Source Book.* 1943. For the Langer Report.

Smith, Captain Truman. *Notebook and Report* (on trip to Munich, November 15–22, 1922). Yale University Library.

Trials of War Criminals before the Nuremberg Military Tribunals, 15 vols. Washington: U. S. Government Printing Office, 1951–52.

U. S. Embassy, Berlin Reports 1930–1939. National Archives.

Wehrmacht, Oberkommando des. *Kriegstagebuch des Oberkommandos der Wehrmacht 1940–1945.* Frankfurt am Main, 1961–65.

C. NEWSPAPERS AND MAGAZINES

Assmann, Heinz. "Adolf Hitler." *U. S. Naval Institute Proceedings,* Vol. 79, No. 12.

Bach-Zelewski, Erich von dem. "Life of an SS-General," New York *Aufbau*, August 23, 1946.

Binion, Rudolph. "Hitler's Concept of *Lebensraum:* The Psychological Basis," *History of Childhood Quarterly*, Fall 1973.

Bloch, Dr. Edward. "My Patient Hitler," *Collier's*, March 15 and 22, 1941.

Deuerlein, Ernst. "Hitlers Eintritt in die Politik und die Reichswehr." *Vierteljahreshefte für Zeitgeschichte*, April 1959.

Earle, George H. "F.D.R.'s Tragic Mistake," *Confidential*, 1958.

Eastman, Lloyd E. "Fascism in Kuomintang China: The Blue Shirts," *China Quarterly*, January/March 1972.

Elstein, David. "Operation Sea Lion," *History of the Second World War*, Part 8.

Glaser, Kurt. "World War II and the War Guilt Question," *Modern Age*, Winter 1971.

Goldhagen, Erich. "Albert Speer, Himmler, and the Secrecy of the Final Solution," *Midstream*, October 1971.

Hale, Oron James. "Gottfried Feder Calls Hitler to Order," *Journal of Modern History*, December 1958.

Hanisch, Reinhold. "I Was Hitler's Buddy," *New Republic*, April 5, 12 and 19, 1939.

Hoffmann, Peter C. "The Attempt to Assassinate Hitler on March 21, 1943." *Canadian Journal of History*, No. 1, 1967.

Kempner, Robert M. W. "Blueprint of the Nazi Underground," *Research Studies of the State College of Washington*, June 1945.

Linge, Heinz. "The Hitler I Knew," Chicago *Daily News*, October–December 1955.

Loewenberg, Peter. "The Unsuccessful Adolescence of Heinrich Himmler," *Journal of Modern History*, September 1959.

Mayr, Captain Karl. "I Was Hitler's Boss," *Current History*, November 1941.

Morell, Dr. Theodor. Interview, New York *Times*, May 22, 1945, p. 5.

Nyomarkay, Joseph L. "Factionalism in the National Socialist German Workers' Party, 1925–26," *Political Science Quarterly*, March 1965.

Orlow, Dietrich. "The Conversion of Myths into Political Power," *American Historical Review*, April 1967.

Phelps, Reginald H. "Hitler als Parteiredner im Jahre 1920," *Vierteljahreshefte für Zeitgeschichte*, 1963: 3.

——. "Hitlers Grundlegende—Rede über den Antisemitismus," op. cit., 1968: 4.

——. "Hitler und die Deutsche Arbeiter Partei," *American Historical Review*, July 1963.

Sauer, Wolfgang. "National Socialism: Totalitarianism or Fascism?" *American Historical Review*, December 1967.

Speer, Albert. Interview, *Playboy*, by Eric Norden, June 1971.

Thompson, Larry V. "*Lebensborn* and the Eugenics Policy of the Reichsführer-SS," *Central European History*, March 1971.

D. BIOGRAPHIES, DIARIES, MEMOIRS,
STUDIES OF HISTORY

Absagen, K. H. *Canaris*. London: Hutchinson, 1956.

Alfieri, Dino. *Dictators Face to Face*. New York: New York University Press, 1955.

Allen, William Sheridan. *The Nazi Seizure of Power*. Chicago: Quadrangle Books, 1965.

Andrus, Burton. *I Was the Nuremberg Jailer*. New York: Coward, McCann & Geoghegan, 1969.

Ansel, Walter. *Hitler Confronts England*. Durham, N.C.: Duke University Press, 1960.

————. *Hitler and the Middle Sea*. Durham, N.C.: Duke University Press, 1972.

Ausubel, Nathan. *Voices of History*. New York: Gramercy, 1946.

Barnett, Corelli. *The Collapse of British Power*. London: Eyre Methuen, 1972.

Baur, Hans. *Ich flog die Mächtige der Erde*. Kempten: Pröpster, 1960.

Berndt, A. I. *Der Marsch ins Grossdeutsche Reich*. Munich: Eher, 1939.

Best, S. Payne. *The Venlo Incident*. London: Hutchinson, 1950.

Bewley, Charles. *Hermann Göring and the Third Reich*. Devin-Adair 1962.

Bezymenski, Lev. *The Death of Adolf Hitler*. New York: Harcourt, Brace & World, 1968.

Blackstock, Paul W. *The Secret Road to World War II*. Chicago: Quadrangle Books, 1969.

Boelcke, Willi A., ed. *The Secret Conferences of Dr. Goebbels*. New York: E. P. Dutton, 1970.

Boldt, Gerhard. *Hitler: The Last Ten Days*. New York: Coward, McCann & Geoghegan, 1973.

Bormann, Martin and Gerda. H. R. Trevor-Roper, ed. *The Bormann Letters*. London: Weidenfeld and Nicolson, 1954.

Bracher, Karl. *The German Dictatorship*. New York and Washington: Praeger, 1970.

Bramsted, Ernest K. *Goebbels and National Socialist Propaganda, 1925–1945*. East Lansing: Michigan State University Press, The Cresset Press, 1965.

Bräutigam, Otto. *So Hat Es Sich Zugetragen* . . . Würzburg: Holzner Verlag, 1968.

Breker, Arno. *Im Strahlungsfeld der Ereignisse*. Preussisch Oldendorf: K. W. Schutz, 1972.

Brook-Shepherd, Gordon. *The Anschluss*. Philadelphia and New York: J. B. Lippincott, 1963.

Broszat, Martin. *German National Socialism 1919–1945*. Santa Barbara, Calif.: Clio Press, 1966.

Brown, Anthony Cave. *Bodyguard of Lies*. New York: Harper & Row, 1975.

Bullitt, Orville, ed. *For the President, Personal and Secret.* Correspondence between Franklin D. Roosevelt and William C. Bullitt. Boston: Houghton Mifflin, 1972.

Bullock, Alan. *Hitler, A Study in Tyranny.* New York: Bantam, 1961.

Burckhardt, Carl. *Ma mission à Dantzig.* Paris: Arthème Fayard, 1961.

Burdick, Charles B., and Lutz, Ralph H., eds. *The Political Institutions of the German Revolution 1918–1919.* New York and Washington: Praeger, 1966.

Cadogan, Sir Alexander. *The Diaries of Sir Alexander Cadogan 1938–1945.* New York: Putnam, 1972.

Carell, Paul. *Invasion—They're Coming!* New York: E. P. Dutton, 1963.

———. *Hitler Moves East: 1941–1942.* New York: Bantam Books, 1966.

———. *Scorched Earth.* Boston: Little, Brown, 1970.

Carr, William. *A History of Germany 1815–1945.* New York: St. Martin's, 1969.

———. *Arms, Autarky and Aggression.* London: Arnold, 1972.

Cecil, Robert. *The Myth of the Master Race.* New York: Dodd, Mead, 1972.

Cervi, Mario. *The Hollow Legions.* Garden City: Doubleday, 1971.

Chambers, Frank. *This Age of Conflict.* New York: Harcourt, Brace & World, 1962 (1943).

Ciano, Galeazzo. *The Ciano Diaries 1939–1943.* Garden City: Doubleday, 1946.

Colvin, Ian. *The Chamberlain Cabinet.* London: Gollancz, 1971.

———. *Hitler's Secret Enemy.* London: Pan Books, 1957.

Compton, James V. *The Swastika and the Eagle.* Boston: Houghton Mifflin, 1967.

Craig, Gordon. *The Politics of the Prussian Army: 1650–1945.* London, Oxford, New York: Oxford University Press, 1968.

Creveld, Martin van. *Hitler's Strategy 1940–1941.* Cambridge: Cambridge University Press, 1973.

Dahlerus, Birger. *The Last Attempt.* London: Hutchinson, 1948.

Dahrendorf, Ralf. *Society and Democracy in Germany.* New York: Doubleday-Anchor, 1969.

Daim, Dr. Wilfried. *Der Mann, der Hitler die Ideen gab.* Munich: Isar, 1958.

Dallin, Alexander. *German Rule in Russia, 1941–1944.* London: 1957.

Dallin, David. *Soviet Russia's Foreign Policy, 1939–1942.* New Haven: Yale University Press, 1942.

Davidson Eugene. *The Trial of the Germans.* New York: Macmillan, 1966.

Dawson, Raymond. *The Decision to Aid Russia 1941.* Chapel Hill: University of North Carolina Press, 1959.

Deakin, F. W. *The Brutal Friendship.* New York: Harper & Row, 1962.

Delarue, Jacques. *The Gestapo.* New York: William Morrow, 1964.

Delmer, Sefton. *Trail Sinister.* London: Secker & Warburg, 1961.

———. *Black Boomerang.* New York: Viking, 1962.

Dennis, Peter. *Decision by Default.* London: Routledge and Kegan Paul, 1972.

Deuerlein, Ernst. *Der Aufsteig der NSDAP 1919–1933 in Augenzeugen Berichtet.* Düsseldorf: Rauch, 1968.

——. *Der Hitler Putsch.* Stuttgart: Deutsches Verlags-Anstalt, 1962.

——. *Hitler.* Munich: List, 1969.

Dickinson, John K. *German and Jew.* Chicago: Quadrangle Books, 1967.

Dietrich, Otto. *Hitler.* Chicago: Henry Regnery, 1955.

——. *Mit Hitler in die Macht.* Munich: Franz Eher Verlag, 1934.

Dirksen, Herbert von. *Moscow, Tokyo, London.* Norman: University of Oklahoma Press, 1952.

Dodd, Martha. *My Years in Germany.* London: Gollancz, 1939.

Dodd, William. *Ambassador Dodd's Diary, 1933–1938.* London: Gollancz, 1941.

Dollmann, Eugen. *The Interpreter.* London: Hutchinson, 1967.

Dönitz, Admiral Karl. *Memoirs.* London: Weidenfeld and Nicolson, 1958.

Dorpalen, Andreas. *Hindenburg and the Weimar Republic.* Princeton: Princeton University Press, 1964.

Douglas-Hamilton, James. *Motive for a Mission.* London: Macmillan, 1971.

Eden, Anthony. *Facing the Dictators.* London: Cassell, 1962.

——. *The Reckoning.* Boston: Houghton Mifflin, 1965.

Eich, Hermann. *The Unloved Germans.* New York: Stein & Day, 1965.

Engel, Gerhard. *Heeresadjutant bei Hitler 1938–1943.* Stuttgart: Deutsche Verlags-Anstalt, 1974.

Falls, Cyril. *The Great War.* New York: Putnam, 1959.

Feiling, Keith, *The Life of Neville Chamberlain.* London: Macmillan, 1946.

Fest, Joachim. *The Face of the Third Reich.* New York: Pantheon Books, 1970.

——. *Hitler.* New York: Harcourt Brace Jovanovich, 1974.

Fischer, Fritz. *Germany's Aims in the First World War.* New York: W. W. Norton, 1967.

Fischer, Louis. *Russia's Road from Peace to War.* New York: Harper & Row, 1969.

Flannery, Harry. *Assignment to Berlin.* London: The Right Book Club, 1943.

François-Poncet, André. *The Fateful Years.* London: Gollancz, 1949.

Frank, Hans. *Im Angesicht des Galgens: Deutung Hitlers und seiner Zeit auf Grund eigener Erlebnisse und Erkenntnisse.* Munich: Beck, 1953.

Franz-Willing, Georg. *Die Hitlerbewegung: Der Ursprung, 1919–22.* Hamburg: Decker, 1962.

Fredborg, Arvid. *Behind the Steel Wall.* New York: Viking, 1944.

Freund, Gerald. *Unholy Alliance.* New York: Harcourt, Brace, 1957.

Friedländer, Saul. *Prelude to Downfall: Hitler and the United States, 1939–1941.* New York: Alfred A. Knopf, 1967.

————. *Pius XII and the Third Reich*. New York: Alfred A. Knopf, 1966.

————. *Kurt Gerstein: The Ambiguity of Good*. New York: Alfred A. Knopf, 1969.

Frischauer, Willi. *Hermann Goering*. New York: Ballantine Books, 1951.

————. *Himmler*. New York: Belmont Tower Books. 1962.

Fromm, Bella. *Blood and Banquets*. London: Bles, 1943.

Gallagher, Matthew. *Soviet History of World War II*. New York: Praeger, 1963.

Galland, Adolf. *The First and the Last*. New York: Ballantine Books, 1957.

Gallo, Max. *The Night of Long Knives*. New York: Harper & Row, 1972.

Gasman, Daniel. *Scientific Origins of National Socialism*. New York: American Elsevier, 1971.

Gatzke, Hans, ed. *European Diplomacy Between Two Wars, 1919–1939*. Chicago: Quadrangle Books, 1972.

Gedye, G. E. R. *Betrayal in Central Europe*. New York: Harper, 1939.

Gehlen, Reinhard. *The Service*. New York: World, 1972.

Giesing, Dr. Erwin. *Diary*. Unpublished.

Gilbert, Felix. *Hitler Directs His War*. New York: Oxford, 1950.

Gilbert, G. M. *Nuremberg Diary*. New York: Signet, 1961.

————. *The Psychology of Dictatorship*. New York: Ronald Press, 1950.

Gisevius, Hans B. *To the Bitter End*. Boston: Houghton Mifflin, 1947.

Goebbels, Josef. *The Early Goebbels Diaries*. London: Weidenfeld and Nicolson, 1962.

————. Louis P. Lochner, ed. *The Goebbels Diaries*. Garden City: Doubleday, 1948.

Goerlitz, Walter. *The German General Staff*. New York: Praeger, 1959.

————. *Paulus and Stalingrad*. New York: Citadel Press, 1963.

Goodspeed, D. J. *Ludendorff*. London: Hart-Davis, 1966.

Gordon, Harold J., Jr. *Hitler and the Beer Hall Putsch*. Princeton: Princeton University Press, 1972.

Greiner, Joseph. *Das Ende des Hitler-Mythos*. Vienna: Amalthea, 1947.

Griffiths, Richard. *Marshal Pétain*. London: Constable, 1970.

Grunberger, Richard. *The 12-Year Reich*. New York: Holt, Rinehart and Winston, 1971.

Guderian, Heinz. *Panzer Leader*. New York: Ballantine Books.

Gun, Nerin. *Eva Braun*, New York: Bantam Books, 1969.

————. *The Day of the Americans*. New York: Fleet, 1966.

Halder, General Franz. *Hitler as Warlord*. London: Putnam, 1950.

Hale, Oron J. *The Captive Press in the Third Reich*. Princeton: Princeton University Press, 1964.

Hamilton, Alistair. *The Appeal of Fascism*. London: Blond, 1971.

Hanfstaengl, Egon. *Memoirs*. Unpublished.

Hanfstaengl, Ernst. *Biographical Sketch of Hitler and Himmler*. OSS report, Dec. 3, 1943.

———. *The Missing Years*. London: Eyre and Spottiswoode, 1957.

———. *Zwischen Weissem und Braunen Haus*. Munich: R. Piper & Co. Verlag, 1970.

———. *Out of the Strong*. 1974. Unpublished.

Hanfstaengl, Helene. *Notes*. Unpublished.

Hanser, Richard. *Putsch!* New York: Peter H. Wyden, 1970.

Hassell, Ulrich von. *The Von Hassell Diaries, 1938–1944*. Garden City: Doubleday, 1947.

Hegner, H. S. (Harry Schulz-Wilde). *Die Reichskanzlei*. Frankfurter Societats, 1959.

Heiber, Helmut. *Goebbels*. New York: Hawthorn Books, 1972

Heiden, Konrad. *Der Führer*. Boston: Houghton Mifflin, 1944.

Hedin, Sven. *Germany and World Peace*. London: Hutchinson, 1937.

Heinz, Heinz A. *Germany's Hitler*. London: Hurst and Blackett, 1934.

Henderson, Archibald. *GBS: Man of the Century*. New York: Appleton-Century-Crofts, 1956.

Henderson, Nevile. *Failure of a Mission*. New York: Putnam, 1940.

Herzstein, Robert. *Adolf Hitler and the Third Reich*. Boston: Houghton Mifflin, 1971.

Hess, Rudolf and Ilse. *Prisoner of Peace*. London: Britons, 1954.

Hesse, Fritz. *Hitler and the English*. London: Wingate, 1954.

———. *Das Spiel um Deutschland*. Munich: List, 1953.

Higgins, Trumbull. *Hitler and Russia*. New York: Macmillan, 1966.

Hilberg, Raul. *The Destruction of the European Jews*. Chicago: Quadrangle Books, 1967.

Hildebrand, Klaus. *The Foreign Policy of the Third Reich*. Berkeley: University of California Press, 1973.

Hillgruber, Andreas. *Staatsmänner und Diplomaten bei Hitler*. 2 vols. Frankfurt am Main: Bernard und Graefe, 1967–70.

———. *Hitlers Strategie*. Frankfurt am Main: Bernard und Graefe, 1965.

———. *Die Weltpolitische Lage: 1936–1938: Deutschland in Weltpolitik 1933–1939*. Oswald Hauser, ed. 1965.

Hills, George. *Franco*. New York: Macmillan, 1967.

Hirszowicz, Lukasz. *The Third Reich and the Arab East*. London: Routledge and Kegan Paul, 1966.

Hitler, Adolf. *Hitler's Secret Conversations*. New York: Signet, 1961.

———. *Hitler's Secret Book*. New York: Grove Press, 1961.

———. *Mein Kampf*. Boston: Houghton Mifflin Company, 1943.

———. *Mein Kampf*. Munich: Eher, 1925–26.

———. *The Testament of Adolf Hitler*. The Hitler-Bormann Documents. London: Cassell, 1961.

Hitler, Brigid. *My Brother-in-law Adolf.* Unpublished. Main Branch NYPL Manuscript and Archives Room.

Hoare, Samuel. *Complacent Dictator.* New York: Alfred A. Knopf, 1947.

Hoffmann, Hans Hubert. *Der Hitlerputsch;* Munich: Nymphenburger Verlag, 1961.

Hoffmann, Heinrich. *Hitler Was My Friend.* London: Burke, 1955.

Höhne, Heinz. *The Order of the Death's Head.* New York: Coward, McCann & Geoghegan, 1970.

————. *Codeword Direktor.* New York: Coward, McCann & Geoghegan, 1971.

Holborn, Hajo, ed. *Republic to Reich.* New York: Pantheon Books, 1972.

————. *Germany and Europe.* Garden City: Doubleday, 1970.

Horthy, Admiral Nicholas. *Memoirs.* London: Hutchinson, 1956.

Howe, Ellic. *Rudolph von Sebottendorf.* Unpublished.

————. *Urania's Children.* London, Kimber, 1967.

Howe, Quincy. *Ashes of Victory.* New York: Simon & Schuster, 1972.

Hull, David. *Film in the Third Reich.* Berkeley: University of California Press, 1969.

Huss, Pierre. *Heil and Farewell.* London: Jenkins, 1943.

Irving, David. *Breach of Security.* London: Kimber, 1968.

————. *Hitler und seine Feldherren.* Berlin: Ullstein, 1975.

————. *The Rise and Fall of the Luftwaffe.* Boston: Little, Brown, 1973.

Isherwood, Christopher. *The Berlin Stories.* New York: New Directions, 1963.

Jäckel, Eberhard. *Hitler's Weltanschauung, A Blueprint for Power.* Middletown: Wesleyan University Press, 1972.

Jenks, William A. *Vienna and the Young Hitler.* New York: Columbia University Press, 1972.

Jetzinger, Franz. *Hitler's Youth.* London: Hutchinson, 1958

John, Otto. *Twice Through the Lines.* London: Macmillan, 1972.

Jones, Ernest. *The Life and Work of Sigmund Freud.* Vols. I and II. New York: Basic Books, 1953.

Jones, Thomas. *A Diary with Letters, 1931–1950.* London: Oxford University Press, 1954.

Junge, Gertraud. *Memoirs.* Unpublished.

Kallenbach, Hans. *Mit Adolf Hitler auf Festung Landsberg.* Munich: Kress and Horning, 1943.

Keitel, Wilhelm, *Memoirs.* London: Kimber, 1965.

Kele, Max H. *Nazis and Workers.* Chapel Hill: University of North Carolina Press, 1972.

Kelem, Emery. *Peace in Their Time.* New York: Alfred A. Knopf, 1963.

Kelley, Douglas M. *22 Cells in Nuremberg.* New York: Greenberg, 1947.

Kempka, Erich. *Ich habe Adolf Hitler Verbrannt.* Munich: Kyburg, 1952.

Kennan, George. *From Prague After Munich.* Princeton: Princeton University Press, 1968.

———. *Memoirs 1925–1950.* Boston: Little, Brown, 1967.

Kirkpatrick, Clifford. *Nazi Germany, Its Women and Family Life.* Indianapolis and New York: Bobbs-Merrill, 1938.

Kirkpatrick, Ivone. *Mussolini.* New York: Hawthorn, 1964.

Klein, Burton. *Germany's Economic Preparations for War.* Cambridge: Harvard University Press, 1959.

Kleist, Peter. *European Tragedy.* London: Antony Gibbs & Phillips, 1965.

Knickerbocker, H. R. *Is Tomorrow Hitler's?* New York: Reynal & Hitchcock, 1941.

Koehl, Robert L. *RKFDV, German Resettlement and Population Policy 1939–1945.* Cambridge: Harvard University Press, 1957.

Koehler, Hans Jürgen. *Inside Information.* London: Pallas, 1940.

Koller, General Karl. *Der letzte Monat.* Mannheim: Wohlgemuth, 1949.

Kramary, Joachim. *Stauffenberg.* New York: Macmillan, 1967.

Krause, Karl. *Zehn Jahre Kammerdiener bei Hitler.* Hamburg: Laatzen, 1949.

Krausnick, Helmut etc. *Anatomy of the SS State.* New York: Walker, 1968.

Kubizek, August. *The Young Hitler I Knew.* Boston: Houghton Mifflin, 1955.

Kuby, Erich. *The Russians and Berlin 1945.* New York: Hill & Wang, 1968.

Kühnl, Reinhard. *Die Nationalsozialistische Linke, 1925–1930.* Meisenheim am Glan: Hain, 1966.

Lammers, Donald. *Explaining Munich.* Stanford: Hoover Institution Press, Stanford University, 1966.

Lane, Barbara Miller. *Architecture and Politics in Germany 1918–1945.* Cambridge: Harvard University Press, 1968.

Langer, Walter C. *The Mind of Adolf Hitler.* New York: Basic Books, 1972.

Laqueur, Walter. *Russia and Germany.* Boston: Little, Brown, 1965.

Levin, Nora. *The Holocaust.* New York: Schocken Books, 1973.

Lewy, Guenter. *The Catholic Church and Nazi Germany.* New York: McGraw-Hill, 1964.

Lochner, Louis. *Always the Unexpected.* New York: Macmillan, 1946.

———. *What About Germany?* New York: Dodd, Mead, 1942.

Lüdecke, Kurt G. W. *I Knew Hitler.* London: Jarrolds, 1938.

Ludendorff, Erich. *Auf dem Weg zur Feldherrnhalle.* Munich: Ludendorffs, 1938.

Lukacs, John. *The Last European War.* Garden City: Anchor Press/Doubleday, 1976.

———. *The Passing of the Modern Age.* New York: Harper & Row, 1970.

Maass, Walter. *Assassination in Vienna.* New York: Scribner's, 1972.

MacLeod, Iain. *Neville Chamberlain.* New York: Atheneum, 1962.

Macmillan, Harold. *Winds of Change.* New York: Harper & Row, 1966.

———. *The Blast of War.* New York: Harper & Row, 1968.

Maisky, Ivan. *Memoirs of a Soviet Ambassador.* New York: Scribner's, 1968.

Manchester, William. *The Arms of Krupp.* New York: Bantam Books, 1970.

Mandell, Richard D. *The Nazi Olympics.* New York: Macmillan, 1971.

Manvell, Roger, and Fraenkel, Heinrich. *Dr. Goebbels.* New York: Simon & Schuster, 1960.

————. *Hess.* London: MacGibbon and Kee, 1971.

————. *Himmler.* New York: Putnam, 1965.

Maschmann, Melita. *Account Rendered.* London: Abelard-Schuman, 1964.

Maser, Werner. *Die Frühgeschichte der NSDAP.* Frankfurt am Main: Athenäum, 1965.

————. *Adolf Hitler.* Munich: Bechtle, 1971.

————. *Hitler.* New York: Harper & Row, 1975.

————. *Hitlers Briefe und Notizen.* Düsseldorf: Econ, 1973.

McRandle, James. *The Track of the Wolf.* Evanston: Northwestern University Press, 1965.

McSherry, James. *Stalin, Hitler and Europe, 1933–1939.* Cleveland: World, 1968.

————. *Stalin, Hitler and Europe, 1939–1941.* Cleveland: World, 1970.

Mellow, James R. *Charmed Circle.* Washington: Praeger, 1974.

Mend, Hans. *Adolf Hitler im Felde.* Munich: Eher, 1931.

Meskill, Johanna. *Hitler and Japan.* New York: Atherton, 1966.

Milward, Alan S. *The German Economy at War.* London: Athlone Press of University of London, 1965.

Mitchell, Allan. *Revolution in Bavaria.* Princeton: Princeton University Press, 1965.

Mitchell, David. *1919 Red Mirage.* New York: Macmillan, 1970.

Mosley, Philip. *The Kremlin and World Politics.* New York: Vintage, 1960.

Mosley, Sir Oswald. *My Life.* London: Nelson, 1970.

Mosse, George. *Nazi Culture.* New York: Grosset & Dunlap, 1966.

Müllern-Schönhausen, Dr. Johannes von. *Die Lösung des Rätsels Adolf Hitler.* Vienna: Verlag zur Förderung wissenschaftlicher Forschung.

Murphy, Robert. *Diplomat Among Warriors.* Garden City: Doubleday, 1964.

Mussolini, Benito. *Memoirs 1942–1943.* London: Weidenfeld & Jacobson, 1949.

Nelson, Walter. *The Soldier Kings.* New York, Putnam, 1970.

Nicolson, Harold. *The War Years 1939–1945.* New York: Atheneum, 1967.

Nogueres, Henri. *Munich.* New York: McGraw-Hill, 1965.

Nolte, Ernst. *Three Faces of Fascism.* New York: Holt, Rinehart and Winston, 1966.

Nyomarkay, Joseph. *Charisma and Factionalism in the Nazi Party.* Minneapolis: University of Minnesota Press, 1967.

Oechsner, Frederick. *This Is the Enemy.* Boston: Little, Brown, 1942.

Offner, Arnold A. *America and the Origins of World War II.* Boston: Houghton Mifflin, 1971.

O'Neill, Robert. *The German Army and the Nazi Party*. New York: Heineman, 1966.

Orlow, Dietrich. *The History of the Nazi Party, 1919–1933*. Newton Abbot: David and Charles, 1971.

————. *The History of the Nazi Party, 1933–1945*. Pittsburgh: University of Pittsburgh Press, 1973.

Oven, Wilfred von. *Mit Goebbels bis zum Ende*. 2 vols. Buenos Aires: Dürer-Verlag, 1949–50.

Papen, Franz von. *Memoirs*. London: Deutsch, 1952.

Parkinson, Roger. *Peace for Our Time*. New York: McKay, 1971.

Peterson Edward. *Limits of Hitler's Power*. Princeton: Princeton University Press, 1966.

Phillips, Peter. *The Tragedy of Nazi Germany*. New York: Praeger, 1969.

Piotrowski, Stanislaw. *Hans Frank's Diary*. Warsaw: Panstwowe Wydawnictwo Naukowe, 1961.

Pope, Ernest. *Munich Playground*. New York: Putnam, 1941.

Price, G. Ward. *I Know These Dictators*. London: Harrap, 1937.

Pridham, Geoffrey. *Hitler's Rise to Power*. New York: Harper & Row, 1973.

Raczynski, Count Edward. *In Allied London*. London: Weidenfeld and Nicolson, 1962.

Reitsch, Hanna. *Flying Is My Life*. New York: Putnam, 1954.

Remak, Joachim. *Nazi Years*. Englewood Cliffs, N.J.: Prentice-Hall, 1969.

Ribbentrop, Annelies von. *Die Kriegesschuld des Widerstandes*. Leoni: am Starnberger See Druffel, 1974.

Ribbentrop, Joachim von. *Ribbentrop Memoirs*. London: Weidenfeld and Nicolson, 1962.

Rich, Norman. *Hitler's War Aims*. 2 vols. New York: Norton, 1973, 1974.

Riess, Curt. *Joseph Goebbels*. New York: Ballantine Books, 1948.

Ringelblum, Emmanuel. *Notes from the Warsaw Ghetto*. New York: McGraw-Hill, 1958.

Roberts, Stephen. *The House That Hitler Built*. London: Methuen, 1937.

Röhl, J. C. G. *From Bismarck to Hitler*. New York: Barnes & Noble, 1970.

Rosenberg, Alfred. With commentary by Serge Land and Ernst von Schenck. *Memoirs*. Chicago: Ziff-Davis, 1949.

————. *Das politische Tagebuch Alfred Rosenbergs*. Fragmentary diaries. Göttingen: Hans-Günther Seraphim, 1956.

————. *Alfred Rosenberg, Selected Writings*. London: Cape, 1970.

Rothenbücher, Karl. *Der Fall Kahr*. Tübingen: Mohr, 1924.

Rudel, Hans Ulrich. *Stuka Pilot*. New York: Ballantine Books, 1958.

Rumpf, Hans. *The Bombing of Germany*. New York: Holt, Rinehart and Winston, 1963.

Ryder, A. J. *The German Revolution of 1918*. Cambridge: Cambridge University Press, 1967.

Santoro, Cesare. *Hitler Germany*. Berlin: Internationaler Verlag, 1938.

Sayers, Michael, and Kahn, Albert. *The Plot Against the Peace*. New York: Dial, 1945.

Schacht, Hjalmar. *Account Settled*. London: Weidenfeld and Nicolson, 1948.

———. *Confessions of the "Old Wizard."* Cambridge: Houghton Mifflin, 1956.

Schellenberg, Walter. *Hitler's Secret Service*. New York: Pyramid, 1958.

Schirach, Henriette von. *The Price of Glory*. London: Muller, 1960.

———. *Der Preis der Herrlichkeit*. Wiesbaden: Limes, 1956.

Schlabrendorff, Fabian von. *The Secret War against Hitler*. New York, Putnam, 1965.

Schmidt, Paul. *Hitler's Interpreter*. London: Heinemann, 1951.

Schramm, Percy. *Hitler: The Man and the Military Leader*. Chicago: Quadrangle Books, 1971.

Schramm, Wilhelm Ritter von. *Conspiracy Among Generals*. New York: Scribner, 1957.

Schuschnigg, Kurt von. *Brutal Takeover*. New York: Atheneum, 1971.

———. *Austrian Requiem*. London: Gollancz, 1947.

Schweitzer, Arthur. *Big Business in the Third Reich*. Bloomington: Indiana University Press, 1964.

Seaburg, Paul. *The Wilhelmstrasse*. Berkeley: University of California Press, 1954.

Seaton, Albert. *The Russo-German War, 1941–45*. London: Barker, 1971.

Sender, Toni. *Autobiography of a German Rebel*. New York: Vanguard, 1939.

Serrano Suñer, Ramon. *Entre les Pyrénées et Gibraltar*. Geneva: Cheval Ailé, 1947.

Shirer, William L. *Berlin Diary*. New York: Alfred A. Knopf, 1941.

———. *End of a Berlin Diary*. New York: Alfred A. Knopf, 1947.

———. *The Rise and Fall of the Third Reich*. New York: Simon & Schuster, 1960.

Siemsen, Hans. *Hitler Youth*. London: Lindsay Drummond, 1940.

Simpson, Amos. *Why Hitler?* Boston: Houghton Mifflin, 1971.

Skorzeny, Otto. *Skorzeny's Special Missions*. London: Hale, 1957.

———. *Lebe gefährlich*. Siegburg-Niederpleis: Ring, 1962.

———. *Wir kämpften—wir verloren*. Siegburg-Niederpleis: Ring, 1962.

Smith, Bradley. *Adolf Hitler*. Stanford: Hoover Institution Press, Stanford University, 1967.

———. *Heinrich Himmler*, Stanford: Stanford University Press, 1971.

——— and Peterson, Agnes F. *Heinrich Himmler Geheimreden 1933 bis 1945*. Frankfurt am Main: Propyläen, 1974.

Smith, Howard K. *Last Train from Berlin*. New York: Alfred A. Knopf, 1942.

Sontag, Raymond James, and Beddie, James Stuart, eds. *Nazi-Soviet Relations 1939–1941*. New York: Didier, 1948. (Selections from U. S. Department of State publications.)

Speer, Albert. *Inside the Third Reich.* New York: Macmillan, 1970.

Spengler, Oswald. *Spengler Letters.* London: Allen & Unwin, 1966.

Starhemberg, E. R. von. *Between Hitler and Mussolini.* London: Hodder and Stoughton, 1942.

Stein, George. *Hitler.* Englewood Cliffs, N.J.: Prentice-Hall International, 1968.

Stern, Fritz. *The Failure of Illiberalism.* New York: Alfred A. Knopf, 1972.

Strasser, Otto. *Hitler and I.* London: Cape, 1940.

————. *Mein Kampf.* Frankfurt am Main: Heinrich Heine, 1969.

————. *Ministersessel oder Revolution?* Berlin: Kampf Verlag, 1930.

Tobias, Fritz. *The Reichstag Fire.* New York: Putnam, 1964.

Toland, John. *Battle: The Story of the Bulge.* New York: Random House, 1959.

————. *The Last 100 Days.* New York: Random House, 1966.

————. *The Rising Sun.* New York: Random House, 1970.

Trevor-Roper, H. R. *The Last Days of Hitler.* New York: Macmillan, 1947.

Trunk, Isaiah. *Judenrat.* New York: Macmillan, 1972.

Wagner, Dieter. *Anschluss.* New York: St. Martin's, 1971.

Wagner, Friedelind. *The Royal Family of Bayreuth.* London: Eyre and Spottiswoode, 1948.

Waite, Robert G. L. *Vanguard of Nazism.* New York: W. W. Norton, 1952.

Warlimont, Walter. *Inside Hitler's Headquarters.* Washington: Praeger, 1964.

Watt, Richard. *The Kings Depart.* London: Weidenfeld and Nicolson, 1968.

Weinberg, Gerhard L. *The Foreign Policy of Hitler's Germany.* Chicago: University of Chicago Press, 1970.

Weiner, Jan. *The Assassination of Heydrich.* New York: Grossman Publishers, 1969.

Weiss, John. *Nazis and Fascists in Europe, 1918–1945.* New York: Harper & Row, 1967.

Weizsäcker, Ernst von. *Memoirs.* London: Gollancz, 1951.

Werth, Alexander. *France—1940–1955.* New York: Holt, Rinehart and Winston, 1956.

————. *Russia at War 1941–1945.* New York: E. P. Dutton, 1964.

Wheeler-Bennett, John. *Munich, Prologue to Tragedy.* London: Macmillan, 1966.

————. *The Nemesis of Power.* New York: Viking, 1967.

Wiedemann, Fritz. *Der Mann, der Feldherr werden wollte.* Velbert, 1964.

Williams, Robert C. *Culture in Exile.* Ithaca: Cornell University Press, 1972.

Windsor, Duke of. *A King's Story.* London: Cassell, 1951.

Winterbotham, F. A. *The Ultra Secret.* London: Weidenfeld and Nicolson, 1974.

Wiskemann, Elizabeth. *The Rome-Berlin Axis.* London: Collins, 1966.

Wulff, Wilhelm. *Zodiac and Swastika.* New York: Coward, McCann & Geoghegan, 1973.

Zeller, Eberhard. *The Flame of Freedom.* Coral Gables: The University of Miami Press, 1969.

Ziegler, Hans Severus. *Wer war Hitler?* Tübingen: Grabert, 1970.

Zoller, Albert. *Douze ans auprès d'Hitler.* (Memoirs of Christa Schröder.) Paris: Julliard, 1949.

Notes

Prologue STAB IN THE BACK

page xvi
"It caught him by the throat . . ." Heinz 83.
page xvi
"It was still stinking of the stuff . . ." Heinz 83.

page xvi

"with pride I can say our regiment . . ." Letter to Josef Popp, Dec. 4, 1914.

page xvii

"the poison of the hinterland . . ." Interview with Ignaz Westenkirchner by Julius Hagemann in Harry Schulze-Wilde Collection.

page xvii

"If my attack on Rheims succeeds . . ." Chambers 84.

page xviii

"the piercing in my sockets . . ." MK 203.

page xviii

Information on Dr. Forster comes from a Restricted U. S. Navy Intelligence Report, declassified for the author in 1972, from the OSS files at the National Archives. Entitled "A Psychiatric Study of Hitler," it was written in 1943 by Dr. Karl Kronor, a former Viennese nerve specialist. Apparently present at the original medical examination of Hitler at Pasewalk, he reported Dr. Forster's findings along with a definition of a psychopath as "mental inferiority usually conditioned by hereditary disposition, and distinguished especially by weakness of will and inability to adapt oneself to society. It produces in consequence a tendency to misdemeanor and crime." Further information on Dr. Forster from Dr. Rudolph Binion: Letters and article in *History of Childhood Quarterly* 203–6.

page xix

"Now they raised the red rag in the homeland." MK 203.

page xix

"I lay there broken with great pain . . ." Record of Hitler's trial in Munich, Feb. 16, 1924. PHP.

page xix

"seemed all a-tremble . . ." MK 203–4

page xix

"But now I could not help it . . ." Ibid. 204.

page xix

"The great vacillation of my life . . ." PHP, Feb. 16, 1924.

page xix

"a psychopath with hysterical symptoms." U. S. Navy Intelligence Report 31963, NA.

page xix

Hitler's "supernatural vision." HSB 901; Karl H. von Wiegand, "Hitler Foresees His End," *Cosmopolitan*, Apr. 1939, 152; *Frankfurter Zeitung*, Jan. 27, 1923, 1; Ludwell Denny, "France and the German Counter-Revolution," *The Nation*, Mar. 14, 1923, 295; Adolf-Viktor von Koerber, *Adolf Hitler. Sein Leben und seine Reden* (Munich, 1923), p. 6–7.

Chapter One. DEEP ARE THE ROOTS

page 4

"laced his tiny knapsack." MK 5.

pages 3–5

Information on Schicklgruber birth register from documents in Ph. D. dissertations, University of Vienna, at Institut für Zeitgeschichte, Vienna.

page 6

"my husband was already on duty again." Jetzinger 41.

page 7

"He was very strict . . ." from interview with Fräulein Schichtl in NA, HA, File 17, Reel 1.

page 8
"shabby and primitive . . . in exemplary order." Jetzinger 57.
page 8
"It was at this time . . . a little ringleader." MK 5–6.
page 9
"unmercifully with a hippopotamus whip . . . dog would cringe and wet the
    floor." HSB 924 and 913.
page 9
"He was imperious . . . over any triviality." Gilbert, *Psychology*, 18.
page 9
"solemn splendor of brilliant church festivals," MK 6.
page 12
"as a small boy it was his most ardent wish . . ." Interview with Helene Hanf-
    staengl, 1971.
page 12
"who challenged my father to extreme harshness . . ." CIC-PH.
page 12
"Toga boy" incident: Interview with Helene Hanfstaengl, 1971.
pages 12–13
"I then resolved never again to cry . . ." Zoller 55.
page 13
"It was not long before . . ." MK 6.
page 13
"Woods and meadows were the battlefields . . ." Ibid. 9.
page 14
"I thought that once my father saw . . ." Ibid. 10.
page 14
"We all liked him . . ." Heinz 25.
page 15
"Bismarck was for us a national hero . . ." Ibid. 26.
page 15
"You are not German . . ." Interview with Josef Keplinger, 1971.
page 15
"Let the Reich's enemy now appear . . ." Remak 14.
page 16
"The sharp words that fell . . ." Jetzinger 53.
page 16
"a great artist," Bradley Smith, *Adolf Hitler*, 100.
page 16
"Why, Adolf, what on earth do you suppose you are doing?" Heinz 26–27.
pages 16–17
Hitler's play with the Schmidt children, including all quotes: Interviews with
    Maria Schmidt Koppensteiner and Johann Schmidt in Oct. 1938, HA, File
    17, Reel 1.
page 17
"complete waste of time." HSC 625.
page 17
"He had definite talent . . . not uncommon amongst immature youths." Jet-
    zinger 68–69.
pages 17–18
"Even today I think back with gentle emotion . . ." MK 14.
page 18
"none was so sulky and surly . . . a fearful row!" Jetzinger 74–75.

page 18
"I often used to practice shooting rats from the window." HSC 201.
page 18
Footnote: Poem in BA, R43 II/957 p. 71, courtesy of Dr. Eberhard Jäckel.
page 19
"I've completely forgotten what happened . . ." HSC 202.
page 19
Hitler's health: CIC-PH
page 19
"What a horror of a film!" HSC 202.
pages 20–21
Kubizek-Hitler quotes: Kubizek 11–13, 26–27.
page 21
Life at the Humboldtstrasse: CIC-PH.
page 21
Hitler postcards: Kubizek's *Erinnerungen* as quoted in Jetzinger 98–99.
page 22
"sitting for hours at the beautiful Heitzmann grand piano . . ." CIC-PH.
page 22
"a strange almost hostile glance . . . a special mission one day would be entrusted to him." Kubizek 99–100.
page 22
"Very often he used to give lectures . . ." CIC-PH
page 22
"those dull, monotonous finger exercises . . ." Jetzinger 94.
page 22
"poor people's doctor." Kubizek 119.
pages 22–23
Frau Hitler examination: Dr. Bloch article in *Collier's*, 1941.
pages 23–24
Hitler's romance with Stephanie. Kubizek 59–60.
page 24
"Adolf never took painting seriously . . . was completely carried away by it." Ibid. 84.
pages 24–25
"When it was pointed out that he lacked . . ." HA, File 17, Reel 1, "Adolf Hitler in Urfahr."
page 25
Hitler as baker's apprentice: Interview with Fräulein Johanna Mayrhofer, 1971.
page 25
"Have you heard from Adolf? . . . this crazy trip to Vienna?" Kubizek 114.
page 25
"showed my unfitness for painting . . ." MK 20.
page 26
"there were already metastases in the pleura." OSS interview with Dr. Bloch. HSB 21.
page 26
"so deeply engrossed." Kubizek 122.
page 26
Many historians believe that Hitler did not arrive until after his mother's death. Franz Jetzinger, for example, bases his conclusions on testimony from people who interviewed Frau Presenmayer, the postmaster's wife,

after 1938. According to Jetzinger: "she told them all she could remember: how she and Frau Klara's sister, Johanna, had nursed her together and how—the old woman stressed this particularly—it was only after Frau Klara's death that her son, Adolf, had arrived from Vienna, and how sorry she had been for him that he was too late to see his mother alive." In the article, "Adolf Hitler in Urfahr!" HA, File 17, Reel 1, the same woman testified that it was she who informed Hitler of his mother's condition and that he "interrupted his studies and rushed to the sickbed of his mother." She also corroborated Dr. Bloch's statement about the sketch—"He drew a picture of his mother on her deathbed." Moreover, in 1938 she told a reporter that Hitler had come home before his mother died and nursed her with the solicitude of a loving son. (HA, Folder 17A.) Jetzinger has chosen to discount completely the accounts of both Dr. Bloch and Kubizek. It is true that Dr. Bloch's story in *Collier's* is filled with mistakes, particularly about those events where he was not present. It is also true that Kubizek's account of Hitler, both in his *Memoirs* and *The Young Hitler I Knew*, contains a number of errors, particularly in dates. Kubizek should be read with care; he has a tendency toward exaggeration, overemphasis and occasional flights of imagination. Most of Jetzinger's criticisms of Kubizek, I believe, are justified, but he himself has a tendency to accent events that make Hitler look bad. (He had been imprisoned in Vienna by the Hitler regime.) His own well-documented book borrows extensively from Kubizek's account, which is admittedly the best firsthand source on Hitler as a young man.

A new piece of evidence, which corroborates the accounts of Dr. Bloch and Kubizek regarding Hitler's ministrations to his mother at the end, is from Paula Hitler's interview with a CIC agent in 1946: "Assisting me, my brother Adolf spoiled my mother during this last time of her life with overflowing tenderness. He was indefatigable in his care for her, wanted to comply with any desire she could possibly have and did all to demonstrate his great love for her." Further corroboration comes from Dr. Rudolph Binion, who recently deciphered Dr. Bloch's casebook for 1907 and thereby reconstructed the case history it contains. The casebook indicates that on October 22, 1907, Dr. Bloch consulted Hitler in Linz.

page 26
Klara's iodoform treatment: Article by Binion, *History of Childhood Quarterly*, 197–201.
page 26–27
"The pleasure of having her son back . . . meanwhile realized his own faults," Kubizek 124–25.
page 27
"She bore her burden well . . ." Bloch, *Collier's*.
page 27
"Gustl, go on being a good friend to my son . . ." Kubizek 126.
page 27
"In all my career I never saw anyone so prostrate . . ." Bloch, *Collier's*.

Chapter Two. "THE SCHOOL OF MY LIFE"

page 28
"stern and composed." Kubizek 127.
page 29
"a young man who had failed at school . . ." Kubizek 139.

page 29
"turn their part of the inheritance over to the girls." OSS interview with William Patrick Hitler. HSB 925–26.

pages 30–31
"In his dark, good-quality overcoat . . . something else special." Kubizek 143–45.

page 31
"I had no idea I had such a clever friend . . . Never mind." Kubizek 149, 152–53, 157–58.

page 31
"so he would not be tempted again": Interview with Albert Frauenfeld, 1971.

page 32
"For days on end he could live on milk . . . Isn't this a dog's life!" Kubizek 150–51.

page 32
"And still I don't succeed." Kubizek 189.

page 32
"What would these Italians do . . . Can you imagine Lohengrin's narration on a barrel organ?" Ibid. 191.

page 32
"developing a taste for symphonic music." Ibid. 204.

page 33
"Swamped for long centuries by the Slavs . . ." Arthur J. May, *The Hapsburg Monarchy* (Cambridge, Mass., 1951), 308.

page 33
"the dubious magic of the national melting pot . . ." MK 23–24.

page 34
Hitler's lectures on "conscientious planning": Kubizek 166–68.

page 34
"Holy Mountain in the background, before it the mighty sacrificial block . . ." Kubizek 154.

page 35
"I'm going to work up Wieland . . ." Jetzinger 121. On writing the opera: Kubizek 193–202.

page 35
Hitler letter to Kubizek, Apr. 18 or 19, 1908: Maser, HBN, 20–22.

page 36
"depraved (sexual) customs": Kubizek to Jetzinger, May 6, 1949, Oberösterreichisches Landesarchiv, Folder 64.

page 36
"We must see the Sink of Iniquity once." Kubizek 235–36.

page 36
"The more anything touched him . . ." Ibid. 255.

page 37
Postcard Hitler to Kubizek about July 15, 1908: Jetzinger 125–26.

page 37
Letter Hitler to Kubizek, July 17, 1908: Jetzinger 126–27.

pages 37–38
Letter Hitler to Kubizek about Aug. 17, 1908: Jetzinger 127–28; Kubizek 260–62.

page 38
"last attempt to persuade him . . . and yet each spoiled each other's pleasure of living together." CIC-PH.

page 40
"Even now I shudder . . ." MK 28.
page 40
"an enchantment out of *The Thousand-and-One Nights*" Ibid. 19.
page 40
"I am sorry to say, merely the living memory . . ." Ibid. 21.
page 41
"We met every night and kept up our spirits . . ." Hanisch 240.
page 45
Hitler by no means anti-Semitic in Vienna: Ibid. 297, 272.
page 45
"the practical application of anthropological research . . ." Hanser 31.
page 46
Footnote: Freud castration theory: Ernest Jones, I, 292–93, 330; II, 261.
page 46
Hitler's hatred of Jews a "personal thing": Interview with Helene Hanfstaengl, 1971.
page 46
Hitler's "failure in painting" caused by Jews: CIC-PH.
page 47
Footnote: The Hitler letter appears on p. 195 of Müllern-Schönhausen's book, *Die Lösung des Rätsels Adolf Hitler,* a confusing hodgepodge of fact and fantasy. At the same time I am convinced that his collection of original Hitler documents, artifacts and paintings is, for the most part, genuine. Although he took me to the Vienna bank where the documents are stored and made photo copies of a number of them, he did not show the originals. He said he was given the items by Hans Bleyer-Härtl, an Austrian Nazi who was the lawyer for the Dollfuss murderers. After the Anschluss, Bleyer-Härtl became disenchanted with the Nazis and volunteered in the army "as a form of suicide." After turning over the collection to Müllern-Schönhausen, he died in battle. Professor Ernst Deuerlein of the University of Munich, shortly before his death, told me he had authenticated a number of the documents and urged me to see Müllern-Schönhausen. The interview was set up by Dr. Wilfried Daim of Vienna, who had seen some of the items.
pages 47–48
An orphan's pension: Jetzinger 1938; interview with Johanna Mayrhofer.
pages 48–49
"I, Anna Csillag, with the very long Lorelei-hair . . . There is no end of stupid people." Greiner 41–42.
page 49
"in a disdainful way that he was only a dilettante . . ." Statement by Karl Honisch, HA, File 17, Reel 1.
page 49
"an honor seldom granted to an inmate." Ibid.
page 49
"I learned to orate less . . ." MK 68.
page 50
"This place is occupied . . . a pity for every word wasted on you, you won't ever understand." Honisch, op. cit.
page 51
"I had set foot in this town . . ." MK 125.

Chapter Three. "OVERCOME WITH RAPTUROUS ENTHUSIASM"

page 52
"The city itself was as familiar . . ." MK 126.
page 52
"for this city more than any other place . . ." Ibid. 126.
page 53
"The young man and I soon came to terms," Heinz 50.
page 53
"achieve the goal I had set myself." MK 126.
page 53
"The nomads, which was how the Munich citizens . . ." Richard Seewald,
   Der Mann von Gegenüber (Munich, 1963).
page 54
"this doctrine of destruction . . ." MK 154.
page 54
"an Austrian charmer . . . You couldn't tell what he was thinking," Maser,
   Hitler, 74.
pages 54–55
"He just camped in his room . . . what isn't likely to be of use to him in life?"
   Heinz 51–52.
page 55
"the happiest and by far the most contented . . ." MK 126.
page 55
"If today I am more attached to this city . . ." Ibid. 127.
pages 55–56
Hitler letter to Linz: Deuerlein, *Der Aufstieg* 76–77; Jetzinger 149–56; Maser,
   HBN, 40–42.
page 56
"unfit for combatant duties, too weak . . ." Jetzinger 155.
page 57
"a state of imminent threat of war." Fritz Fischer 86.
page 57
"Heil the Kaiser! Heil the Army!" Sayers 91.
page 58
"If only the King has already read my application . . ." Julius Hagemann interview with Ignaz Westenkirchner in Schulz-Wilde Collection.
page 58
"looked at it with the delight that a woman . . ." Mend 15.
page 58
"turned tail and ran," Heinz 53.
page 59
"I was put up in a stable . . . I hope we get to England." Maser, HBN,
   55–57.
page 60
Hitler letter to Hepp, Feb. 5, 1915, BA, NS 26/4.
page 61
"What I noticed first was his unmilitary manner . . ." Wiedemann 13 (translation).
page 61
Hitler letter to Popp: Maser, *Hitler*, 83–84

page 61
"He is just an odd character . . ." Mend 24–25.
page 62
Postcard Hitler to Popp, Jan. 22, 1915: Maser, HBN, 68.
page 62
"With exemplary patience (he didn't understand a word of German), I
    gradually . . ." HSC 236.
page 62
Letter Hitler to Popp, Jan. 26, 1915: Maser, HBN, 73.
pages 62–63
Letter Hitler to Hepp, Feb. 5, 1915: BA, NS 26/4.
page 63
"Amen in the prayer," Westenkirchner interview, op. cit.
page 63
"I learned a great deal from him," HSC 662.
page 63
Footnote: "I never really caught him lying . . ." Wiedemann 40 (tr.).
page 63
"It's more important to bring our messages . . ." Julius Hagemann interview
    with Ernst Schmidt in Schulze-Wilde Collection.
page 63
"like a race horse at the starting gate." Mend 124.
page 64
"I was eating my dinner in a trench . . ." Price 40.
page 64
"I often go on bitter nights . . ." Müllern-Schönhausen 210.
page 64
"quietly spent holidays." Mend 165–66.
page 65
"in the face of almost certain death . . ." Heinz 70, 71.
page 65
"How many times at Fromelles . . ." HSC 235.
page 65
"It isn't so bad, Lieutenant, right?" Wiedemann 13 (tr.).
page 65
"for the first time in two years . . ." MK 191.
page 66
"Nearly every clerk was a Jew . . ." Ibid. 193.
page 66
"If all Jews were no more intelligent . . ." Westenkirchner interview, op. cit.
page 66
"It really seems impossible for me to believe . . ." Schmidt interview, op. cit.
page 66
One of the most quoted incidents of Hitler's wartime anti-Semitism appears on
    p. 161 of Mend's book, *Adolf Hitler im Felde:* Hitler refuses to salute a
    Jewish officer, Hugo Gutmann, and, after Gutmann angrily leaves, says,
    "I'll only acknowledge this Jew on the battlefield. Here he struts with Jew-
    ish arrogance but at the front he'd hide in a mouse hole and wouldn't con-
    cern himself with a salute." The veracity of this incident is lessened by
    later issuance of a "Mend Protocol," in which the author contradicted ma-
    terial in his own book. In the case of Gutmann, Westenkirchner testified
    that the lieutenant was generally disliked by the men. "Our dislike, how-

ever, had nothing to do with anti-Semitism." Once he heard Hitler say, "Gutmann is an ass-crawler and a coward." Westenkirchner interview, op. cit. Lieutenant Gutmann later initiated the award to Hitler of the Iron Cross, First Class.

The 16th Regiment, in fact, was known for its courageous Jewish officers. Two are commended in Wiedemann's book. Reserve Lieutenant Kuh, an assault leader, a painter like Hitler, had a reputation for fearlessness. "The most beautiful thing to me," Kuh told Wiedemann, "is the night before an assault!" One of the battalion physicians, Dr. Georg Kohn, was decorated with the Bavarian Military Medical Order, the highest decoration awarded doctors for extreme bravery in the performance of their duties. The Great War was the first major opportunity which had been given German Jews to demonstrate their patriotism to a nation which had given them legal if not social equality. Almost unanimously they supported the Fatherland in its hour of peril. The Jewish soldier consequently often did more than his duty as a retort to anti-Semitic propaganda that the Jew was a coward by nature. (Perhaps Hitler's own eager attitude was also to prove that he was a better German than his German-born comrades.)

page 66
Letter Hitler to Wiedemann: Wiedemann 30 (tr.).
page 66
"he hurled himself on me in frenzy." HSC 236.
page 66
"turned out an extra special mess . . ." Heinz 75.
page 67
Footnote: On Dec. 31, 1940, Sylvia Beach, of Shakespeare and Company, wrote Heinrich Heim, who took down Hitler's table conversations and occasionally bought paintings and sketches for him, the following letter: "Gordon Craig is going to thank you himself for your kindness to him and his family. You have not only saved his life, as in his present feeble health he would not have lived many weeks in those circumstances I am told, but the tribute you paid to his art has given him an immense joy. It is indeed a miracle that you have performed!"
page 67
"You could give me 200,000." HSC 236.
pages 67–68
The theft of the art case was the virtual end of Hitler as an artist although he did several other pictures after the war. One, a woodland scene in the Müllern-Schönhausen Collection, dated "about 1919," has an artistic quality not seen in previous pictures. Years later the stolen art items were discovered in a Munich curiosity shop and presented to the Führer.
page 68
"This has nothing to do with art . . ." Schmidt interview, op. cit.
page 68
Postcard to Schmidt: Maser, HBN, 106–7.
page 68
"War forces one to think deeply . . ." Frank 45–46.
page 69
"the biggest piece of chicanery . . ." MK 194-95.
page 70
"We must draw only one conclusion . . ." Goodspeed 207.

page 70
"more vigorous conscription of the young Jews . . ." Ibid. 209.
page 70
"became furious and shouted . . ." Schmidt interview, op. cit.
page 71
Dr. Rudolph Binion of Brandeis University believes that Hitler's vision at
Pasewalk released his unconscious resentment against Dr. Bloch, a Jew.
"Hitler was then nearly nineteen, and intellectually and emotionally re-
tarded after having lived idly with his widowed mother for some years past
at suffocatingly close quarters. Consciously, he loved Bloch like a kind father; unconsciously, he blamed Bloch for his mother's cancer, for the toxic
treatment, for the huge terminal bill paid on Christmas Eve. This blame
surfaced after 1918 as a burning rage against the Jewish profiteer, the Jewish poison, the Jewish cancer. On balance, the evidence that he was not an
anti-Semite until after World War I, despite his own account in *Mein
Kampf*, is compelling. At all odds, his deadly hate for 'the Jew' along with
his political vocation itself can be dated quite precisely from his hospi-
talization of October–November 1918 for a gas poisoning that blinded
him temporarily. The gas—mustard gas—was actually a liquid spray that
burned through the skin just like iodoform. Hitler associated his gas
poisoning with his mother's iodoform poisoning as he felt himself succumbing. By the time he was hospitalized at Pasewalk (north of Berlin)
he must have been raving, as he was assigned to psychiatric care. The chief
psychiatrist took his blindness to be hysterical—wrongly. But just when he
was recovering his vision in the normal course, he relapsed at the news of
the Revolution and Armistice. This relapse *was* hysterical. It may have
been prompted by the false diagnosis that governed his treatment. . . .
In that hallucination Hitler was summoned from on high to undo, and
reverse, Germany's defeat. The Germany that he was to restore and
avenge was transparently his mother: this is graphic in one of the accounts
of the hallucination that Hitler himself gave in the early 1920s and especially in an official party version of it that he must have approved. In his
trance he was not expressly called upon to kill the Jews; nonetheless he
emerged from his trance resolved on entering politics in order to kill the
Jews by way of discharging his mission to undo, and reverse, Germany's
defeat." Binion, unpublished article, "Hitler's Concept of *Lebensraum:*
The Psychological Basis."
page 73
"no longer complained of anything . . ." Ibid.
page 73
"The medical records at the hospital . . ." Deuerlein, *Hitler*, 68.
page 74
"Their whole activity was so repellent . . ." MK 207.
page 74
"The laziest and most impudent . . ." Heinz 89.
page 75
"parental religion was largely sham . . . shot through with hypocrisy." Howard
    Becker, *German Youth: Bond or Free* (London, 1946), 51.
page 75
"messages from the forest . . . and do the deed." Peter Viereck, "Stefan
    George's Cosmic Circle," in *Decision*, Oct. 1941.

page 75
"To them he was not their commanding officer . . ." W. Hoeppener-Flatow, *Strosstrupp Markmann Greift an!* (Berlin, 1939), 95.

page 75
"monastery with walls of flame," McRandle 63.

page 77
"Like the French in 1793 . . ." Spengler 69–70.

page 77
"to gain a fatherland for myself," Rosenberg, *Memoirs*, 29.

page 77
"Can you use a fighter against Jerusalem?" Alfred Rosenberg, *Dietrich Eckart: Ein Vermächtnis* (Munich, 1927), 45.

page 79
"who bears arms against government troops . . ." *Vorwärts*, Mar. 10, 1919.

page 79
Ben Hecht cable: Hanser 182.

page 79
"The Jewish Mafia." David Mitchell 119.

page 80
"because those dogs have not at once loaned me sixty locomotives," Gustav Noske, *Von Kiel bis Kapp* (Berlin, 1920), 136.

page 80
"Those who say we should remain neutral . . ." Thor Goote in *Aus der Geschichte der Bewegung*, Deutsche Arbeitsfront, Nov. 1934; also letter from Ernst Schmidt to Werner Maser, Aug. 16, 1962.

page 80
"even when a local or momentary success might be possible." Allan Mitchell 319.

page 81
"The liberated working class is celebrating . . ." Ibid. 329.

page 82
"It would require a volume . . ." Ambroise Got, *La Terreur en Bavière* (Paris, 1922), 269–86.

page 82
"The result of the Soviet episode in Munich . . ." David Mitchell 190.

page 82
"This is the New Man, the storm soldier . . ." Ernst Jünger, *Der Kampf als inneres Erlebnis* (Berlin, 1933), 76–77.

page 83
"When I first met him he was like a tired stray dog . . ." Mayr 194.

page 83
"Involuntarily I saw thus my own development . . ." MK, Eher edition, 296.

page 83
Throughout the whole world others besides Hitler saw Jews as the fountainhead of revolution and Communism. That July, at a meeting of the Anglo-Russian Club in London, Winston Churchill had called for support of White General Denikin against Lenin, Trotsky "and the sinister gang of Jewish anarchists around them," and a few months later told the House of Commons, "No sooner did Lenin arrive than he began beckoning a finger there to obscure persons in sheltered retreats in New York, in Glasgow, in Bern, and other countries, and he gathered together the leading spirits of a most formidable sect, the most formidable sect in the world." (Lacquer 313–14.) Churchill called for a fourteen-nation anti-Bolshevik

crusade to support the White forces in Russia battling the Soviets, and declared it was a delusion "to suppose that all this year we have been fighting the battles of the anti-Bolshevik Russians. On the contrary, they have been fighting ours: and this truth will become painfully apparent from the moment they are exterminated and the Bolshevik armies are supreme over the whole vast territories of the Russian empire." D. Mitchell 236–37.

The anti-Bolshevik crusade had also crossed the Atlantic with the U. S. Attorney General, A. Mitchell Palmer, persuading Congress to finance a Red hunt to be directed by J. Edgar Hoover. Throughout the Western world a whispering campaign spread to the effect that it was Jewish money which had started the Russian Revolution: one German primarily responsible for financing Lenin was Max Warburg, whose brother was Paul Warburg, a director of the U. S. Federal Reserve System; and wasn't the father-in-law of brother Felix Warburg the same Jacob Schiff of Kuhn, Loeb and Company who had financed the Bolshevik revolution? This charge was repeated years later on Feb. 3, 1939, in the New York *Journal-American:* "Today it is estimated by Jacob's grandson, John Schiff, that the old man sank about 20,000,000 dollars for the final triumph of Bolshevism in Russia."

page 83
"For me the value of the whole affair . . ." MK 208.
pages 83–84
"Right after listening to Feder's first lecture . . ." MK 120.
page 84
"and now for the first time . . ." Ibid. 215.
page 84
"The men seemed spellbound by one of their number . . ." Karl Alexander von Müller, *Mars und Venus* (Stuttgart, 1954), 338.
page 84
"I started out with the greatest enthusiasm . . ." MK 215–16.
page 84
"Tell me, did they shit in your brain . . ." Oskar Maria Graf, *Wir sind Gefangene* (Munich, 1927), 114.
page 84
"talked and walked in his sleep . . ." Mayr 194.
page 85
"Herr Hitler, if I may put it this way . . ." Remak 25.
page 85
"spoke very well." Heinz Zarnke, in letter to his parents, BA, NS 26/107. "I came to a meeting once by choice," he continued. "23 people were present and just think: Herr Gottfried Feder, whose wife is a Richter, was there too. A Herr Hitler also spoke very well, he is said to be a 'construction worker,' but he is probably a colleague of Herr Feder's, for only an educated man can speak like that. Herr Hitler served through the whole war and was badly wounded. He was even blinded for a short time and took a lively interest in my eye ailment."
page 85
"an artist rather than a pedant." Ellic Howe, *Rudolph von Sebottendorff*, 38.
page 86
"Our meetings were private . . ." Heinz 106–7.
page 86
"sprang out of the ground . . ." MK 218.

page 87
"left the hall like a wet poodle . . ." Ibid. 219.
page 87
"watching the droll little beasts . . ." Ibid. 219–20.
page 87
"Involuntarily I saw my own development . . ." Ibid. 220.
page 87
"Now we have an Austrian with a big mouth!" Lotter interview, HA, Feb. 17, Reel 1.
page 88
"Terrible, terrible! This was club life . . ." MK 222.
page 88
"frozen into an 'organization,' but left the individual . . ." Ibid. 222.
page 88
"to please Ludendorff, whose wishes were . . ." Mayr 195.
page 88
"He burrows into the democracies . . ." Deuerlein, *Der Aufsteig*, 91–93.

Chapter Four. BIRTH OF A PARTY

page 93
"Our small committee which in reality . . ." *Illustrierter Beobachter* ※31, Aug. 3, 1929.
page 93
"When we were assembled . . . in our hands as a 'walking stick.'" Ibid.
page 94
"We were again seven men . . ." MK 354.
page 94
"and what before I had simply felt . . ." MK 355.
page 94
"flew down the stairs with gashed heads." Ibid. 358.
page 94
"The misery of Germany . . ." Deuerlein, "Hitlers Eintritt," 207.
page 95
Police report: Deuerlein, *Der Aufsteig*, 99.
page 95
"a funeral vault than an office." MK 390.
page 96
"My little girl used to climb on Hitler's knee . . ." Heinz 140.
page 96
"We cracked our brains over it . . ." Heinz 141.
page 96
"swift as greyhounds, tough as leather . . ." MK 356.
page 97
"The first thing you felt was that there was a man . . ." Frank 39.
page 97
"made things understandable even to the foggiest brain . . ." Ibid. 41.
page 98
"if anyone could master the fate of Germany . . ." Ibid. 52.
page 98
"When I closed the meeting . . ." VB, Feb. 22, 1922.
page 98
"Since I am a wicked and immature man . . ." Ernst Röhm, *Die Geschichte eines Hochverräters* (Munich, 1928).

page 99
"I prefer a vain monkey . . ." Eckart quoted in MK 687.
page 99
"This is the man who will one day . . ." Dietrich, *Hitler*, 163.
page 100
"C'mon, boys, let's all go . . ." This very free translation of the "largely un-translatable" verse comes from Richard Hanser, who queried Mehring on his accurate prophecy. "At those times, and under the circumstances I wrote," replied the poet, "I could not help being aware of coming turmoil and terrors." Hanser's conclusion to this vague explanation was that "poets are often prophets without knowing how they do it." Hanser 338–39.
page 101
"Germany must become a Republic of Soviets . . ." Hans Spethmann, *Zwölf Jahre Ruhrbergban*, II (Berlin, 1928), 133–34.
page 101
"If I were to tell you everything . . ." Maximilian Scheer, ed., *Blut und Ehre* (Paris, 1937), 43.
page 101
"Come on, Adolf, we have no further business here." Dietrich 164.
page 101
"Some lodgers who've rented it since . . ." Heinz 240.
page 102
"I would be lying if I said . . ." BA, NS8–177.
page 103
Footnote: "I often encountered him on the stairway . . ." Heinz 240.
page 103
On speech in general: Phelps, "Hitlers Grundlegende"; Franz-Willing 150, 152.
page 104
"The Jewish race is the source of all dangers," Sayers 91.
page 104
"The bloody Jew. Butchering of spiritual leadership . . ." Maser, HBN, 229–353.
page 104
"We are tied and gagged . . ." Phelps, "Hitler als Parteiredner," 314.
page 104
"For us the enemy sits on the other side of the Rhine . . ." Maser, HBN, 305.
page 105
"We wanted something red enough . . ." Heinz 143.
pages 106–7
Quotes from Strasser-Hitler meeting: Otto Strasser, *Mein Kampf*, 16–19.
page 107
Ulrich Graf quote: Egon Hanfstaengl's unpublished memoirs, 101.
page 107
"in the style of a witty newspaper article . . ." MK 481.
page 108
Drexler quote: Deuerlein, *Der Aufsteig*, 128.
page 109
"With this the cord of my patience . . ." MK 498.
page 109
"Like a giant shell this hall . . ." Ibid. 500.

page 110
"Then you could hardly hear . . ." Ibid. 501.

page 110
"We recognized that this movement . . ." Hanser 285.

page 110
Footnote: E. J. Gumbel, *Vier Jahre politischer Mord* (Berlin, 1923).

page 111
"I make these demands not because . . ." Franz-Willing 110.

page 111
"The King of Munich." Deuerlein, *Der Aufstieg*, 138–40.

page 111
"your exceptional knowledge . . ." Maser, *Die Frühgeschichte*, 270.

page 112
"We do not wish to unite . . ." Ibid. 273.

page 112
"intended to serve as a means . . ." Konrad Heiden, A *History of National Socialism* (London, 1936), 73.

page 113
"It's all right. We got what we wanted." Ibid. 31 Ballerstedt incident in general: Deuerlein, *Der Aufstieg*, 46.

page 114
"One heard nothing but yells . . ." Heinz 119.

page 115
"Two thousand years ago the mob of Jerusalem . . ." Heiden 117.

page 116
"to blind the driver." HSC 428.

pages 116–17
Hitler speech, July 28, 1922: Baynes 28–41.

page 116
Footnote: Hell's notes for 1922 at Institut für Zeitgeschichte, Munich, ZS 640, Folio 6, Josef Hell.

page 117
Lüdecke quotes: Lüdecke 22–25.

pages 117–18
Lüdecke quotes. Ibid. 60–61.

page 118
"You have everything I lack . . ." Hamilton 125.

page 119
"We shall *be* the State . . ." Lüdecke 74.

page 119
"His eyes grew thoughtful . . ." Ibid. 81.

page 120
"Seeing that one brawls as well in an English suit . . ." Ibid. 90.

page 121
"That's typical of your bourgeois world . . ." Hitler to Jurgen von Ramin.

page 121
Indicative of the wave of approval in western Europe and the United States for the Mussolini coup d'état was a poem which appeared in Jan. 1923 in the *Wall Street Journal*:

> On constitutional technique
> And precedents he's lame,
> On grace and glamor rather weak.

Such lacks don't cramp his game!
Instead they're assets for his job,
Rough, rude, plain word and act,
To mold a nation through a mob,
To make a dream a fact!
Red nonsense had its mischief proved:
His black-shirts curbed and quelled,
Perhaps in ways not graced or grooved,
How the reins be held?
A blacksmith's son to purple Rome
A brusque command he brought;
Italia, cleansed and rescued home
But more than her he's taught!
Word-froth and demagogues and drones
Banned; sweat and service praised;
Desks manned when A.M. intones,
Languorous Italy dazed!

Chapter Five. "SUCH A LOGICAL AND FANATICAL MAN"

page 123
"wipe out the disgrace of Versailles . . ." Gilbert, *Psychology*, 93.

page 123
"I remember a meeting at which they were discussing . . . I'll tell the world it
    was military!" Ibid. 91–92. Unpublished entry in Gilbert's Nuremberg
    diary, dated Feb. 3, 1946.

pages 123–24
"precisely because it was revolutionary . . ." Ibid. 93.

page 124
Quotes from the Hess essay: Heiden 98–99.

page 125
"restlessly wandered from place to place . . ." Philipp Bouhler, *Kampf um
    Deutschland* (Munich, 1938), 83.

page 125
"More than once Dietrich Eckart told me . . ." HSC 168.

page 126
"Today, when I happen to meet . . ." Ibid. 223–24.

page 126
"In the wintertime the anteroom . . ." Bouhler, op. cit., 78.

pages 126–28
Captain Smith's trip to Munich: Truman Smith report.

page 129
"the unmistakable soldier in mufti . . ." MY 33.

page 129
"There was honesty, there was sincerity . . ." HSB 891.

page 129
"His technique resembled the thrusts . . ." MY 35.

page 129
"Our motto shall be . . ." Prange 122.

page 129
"The muffled restlessness of the masses . . ." Hanfstaengl, *Out of the Strong*,
    unpublished.

pages 129–30
"as though in some devotional . . ." MY 35.

page 130
"Whenever I make a speech . . ." HSC 534.

page 130
"Captain Truman Smith asked me . . . we will have to talk about that." HSB 892.

page 130
"I am sure we shall not have to quarrel . . ." HSB 892.

page 130
"My prognostication on the general . . ." NA, U. S. Embassy, Berlin report, State Dept. file.

page 132
"neither during the war nor during the revolution . . ." Karl Alexander von Müller, *Im Wandel einer Welt* (Munich 1966), 144.

page 132
"He is an extraordinary person . . ." Denny, *The Nation,* 295.

page 133
"Sometimes weeks go by . . ." MY 48.

page 133
"There are stupid dogs . . ." HSC 249.

page 133
"When your mother has grown older . . ." Rehse Collection, 791, Library of Congress.

page 134
"What a wonderful atmosphere . . ." HSC 22.

page 134
"And you should have seen the bathroom . . ." MY 43.

page 134
"This music affected him physically . . ." Ibid. 49.

page 135
"absolutely by heart and could whistle . . ." Ibid. 49.

page 135
"Whereas he otherwise kept the different groups . . ." Hanfstaengl, *Out of the Strong.*

page 135
"He was respectful, even diffident . . ." MY 39.

pages 135–36
"He was at the time a slim, shy young man . . . 'Please, Uncle Dolf, spank the naughty chair.'" Helene Hanfstaengl, *Notes,* 281–83. Helene Niemeyer (the former Frau Helene Hanfstaengl) agreed to write a book for Lippincott in 1940. "Got to the end of the Putsch story," explained her son Egon, "and told Lippincott she didn't want to go on. She never showed them what she'd written. . . . Today said that, in 1940, she was sick of the whole Nazi business and it also occurred to her that if she published the story, the Nazis might take it out on her relations." Letter to author, Feb. 16, 1973.

page 136
"It is imposing to think . . ." CIA files: Hanfstaengl, OSS Biography, 48.

page 136
"Someone who does not understand . . . bite off your head." Ibid. 31–32.

page 136
"Putzi, I tell you he is a neuter." MY 52.

page 137
"We chased girls together . . . and admire the ballet dancers." Gun, *Eva Braun*, 8, 59.

page 137
"If it is not the fashion now . . ." Hanfstaengl, OSS Biography, op. cit., 12.

page 138
"They would have had my head . . ." MY 57.

page 138
"in spite of the many pictures . . ." Ibid. 60.

page 138
"at least it was better than this duelling . . ." Ibid. 61.

page 138
"When he was in a good mood . . ." Ibid. 65.

page 138
"The most important thing . . ." Ibid. 64.

pages 138–39
Hitler's speech: Baynes 51–53.

page 139
"It had something of the quality of . . . annihilating his supposed adversary." MY 68–69.

page 140
"When I talk to people . . ." Ibid. 267–68.

page 140
"I'd read the description . . ." HSC 183.

page 141
"Don't forget, this building belongs to a Jew . . ." Hanfstaengl, *Out of the Strong.*

page 141
"At six o'clock gangs of Reds . . ." HSC 270.

page 142
"I reject Hitler completely!" F. W. Heinz, *Sprengstoff* (Berlin, 1930), 222.

page 142
Murphy report: NA. U. S. State Dept. file.

page 142
"I have fallen in love with the landscape." HSC 218.

pages 142–43
Eckart story: Hanfstaengl OSS Biography, op. cit., 35–37.

page 143
"such enthusiasm as had not been seen . . . so overcome were they by emotion." Deuerlein, *Der Aufsteig*, 181–82.

page 143
"In a few weeks the dice will roll . . ." Hanser 321–22.

page 144
"The task of our movement . . ." VB, Sept. 7, 1923.

page 144
Hitler trip to Switzerland: According to Wilhelm Hoegner, who conducted an extensive investigation of the NSDAP's financial sources from 1924 to 1928, Hitler went to Switzerland in 1921 and 1922 to collect money so he could lead the fight against the Catholic Church in Germany. (Hoegner interview, 1971.) Nov. 25, 1924, two Geneva newspapers claimed that the previous September Hitler had stayed at the Hotel St. Gotthard in Zurich where he received donations of 33,000 Swiss francs, some of it from French sources. Other money came from Frau Gertrud von Seidlitz, who

owned shares in Finnish paper mills, the Bechsteins, a locomotive manufacturer named Borsig, and a Munich industrialist, Hermann Aust. Reputedly, the largest single contribution, 100,000 gold marks, came from Fritz Thyssen of the United Steelworks. At this time there were approximately 170,000 gold marks in the NSDAP treasury.

page 144
"If nothing happens now the men . . ." BH, MA 103476, 1020.

page 144
"We must compromise these people . . ." MY 88.

pages 144–45
"Absolutely no one could ever persuade . . ." Helene Hanfstaengl, *Notes*.

page 145
"Hitler now had definite Napoleonic . . ." BH, MA 103476, 1151.

Chapter Six. THE BEER HALL PUTSCH

For information on the Putsch I am particularly indebted to Prof. Ernst Deuerlein, Richard Hanser, and Dr. Harold J. Gordon, Jr.

page 146
"an old member and fanatic member . . ." Letter from Maria Heiden, Munich, Sept. 30, 1923.

page 146
"A man of action born on April 20 . . ." Ellic Howe, *Urania's*, 90–91.

page 146
"violence with a disastrous outcome . . ." Wulff 39.

page 146
"psychological astrology . . ." Howe, *Urania's*, 98.

page 147
"His sharp cheekbones . . ." F. Wagner 8.

page 147
"his voice took on a tone . . ." Ibid. 9.

page 147
"Don't you feel that he is destined . . ." HSB 933.

page 147
"With one blow you have transformed . . ." Röhl 52–53.

pages 147–48
"I noticed you were not at all frightened . . ." Helene Hanfstaengl, *Notes*, 301.

page 148
Hemingway story: New York *Times*, Oct. 4, 1974.

page 149
"I can only take action . . ." Stein 97–98.

page 149
"For us this man was a whirling dervish . . ." Carl Suckmayer, *Als wär's ein Stück von mir* (Frankfurt am Main, 1966), 384.

page 149
"There are decent emotions . . ." Eduard Hamm to Theodor Wolff, Jan. 3, 1922, BA, R431, 2681.

page 150
"until an adjustment between Bavaria . . . and is Bavaria's duty to right it." NA, U. S. Embassy, Berlin, report, Oct. 22, 1923.

page 150
"as a result domestic politics are purely . . ." *Münchener Zeitung*, Oct. 22, 1923, BA, R431, 2264.

pages 150–51
Footnotes: From TV tapes, "Der Frühe Hitler," Bayerische Rundfunk.
page 151
"We must think first of a march . . ." MY 90.
page 151
Footnote for 10: "he never confided a single plan . . ." Helene Hanfstaengl,
    Notes, 295.
page 151
"The German problem will be solved . . ." E. Röhm, *Die Geschichte eines
    Hochverräters*, 229.
page 152
"Our people are under such economic . . ." BH, MA 103476, 691.
page 152
"The atypical way must be prepared . . ." PHP.
page 152
"I am ready to support a rightist . . ." Gordon 256.
page 153
Hitler toothache: Egon Hanfstaengl, *Memoirs*, 101.
page 154
"Where is Captain Göring? . . . Tonight we act!" MY 91.
page 154
Hitler-Esser meeting: Interview with Esser, 1971.
page 155
"Hansl, if things don't go right . . ." BH, MA 1042221, Aigner Bericht.
page 156
"out of the way—you there!" Heinz 154.
page 156
"Take your hand out." NA, EAP, 10517, I, 97.
page 157
"Komödie spielen . . . but I had no other means." Ibid. 98.
page 157
"There are five rounds . . ." Idem.
page 157
"What followed then was an oratorical . . ." Müller, *Im Wandel*, 162–63.
page 157
"The task of the provisional . . ." Bullock 80.
page 157
"provincial bridegroom . . ." MY 100.
page 158
"such a change of attitude in a few minutes . . . dead by dawn!" Müller, op.
    cit., 163.
page 158
One listener not converted by Hitler's speech was the man next to Müller,
    Dr. Max von Gruber, professor of "racial hygiene" at Munich University.
    Himself an ardent nationalist, he was not impressed by this first close look
    at Hitler: "Face and head: bad race, mongrel. Low, receding forehead,
    ugly nose, broad cheekbones, small eyes, dark hair; facial expression, not of
    a man commanding with full self-control, but betraying insane excitement.
    Finally, an expression of blissful egotism." Heiden 190.
page 158
"amazed and far from pleased." Goodspeed 239.
page 158
"I am going to fulfill the vow . . ." Bullock 81.

page 159
"the only thing missing is the psychiatrist . . ." Bavarian State Document ⌗72 from Allgemeine Staatsarchiv, Munich.
pages 161–62
Schwander story: Gordon 293–94.
page 162
Murphy telegram: NA, State Department documents.
page 162
Footnote: Murphy 22.
page 163
"Crush this movement at any cost . . ." Hanser 356.
page 163
"What? Still negotiating here? . . ." BH, MA 104221, Wilde Bericht.
page 164
Message "to all German wireless stations": Hanser 356.
page 164
"It came like a blow from a club," Hanser 359.
pages 164–65
"If we get through, very well . . ." Heiden 193.
page 165
"March to Berlin! . . ." Frank 61–62.
page 166
"This is no revolution . . ." BH, MA 104221, Goebel Bericht.
page 166
"We're going to try the whole thing over again." Hanser 362.
page 166
"Greeted the appearance of the councillors . . ." Heinz 159.
page 167
"We march!" Ludendorff 65.
page 167
"We would go to the city to win the people . . ." PHP.
page 167
"the most desperately daring decision in my life . . ." Hitler speech, Nov. 11, 1935.
page 168
Eckart story: BH, MA 104221, Eckart Bericht.
page 169
Eckart story: BH, MA 104221, Eckart Bericht.
page 169
"If Ludendorff is marching that way . . ." Ludendorff 67.
pages 169–70
Godin account: BH, MA 104221, Godin Bericht.
page 170
Footnote: "both Ludendorff and Hitler behaved . . ." Murphy 22.
page 170
Dr. Schultze account: Interviews with Dr. Schultze, 1974–75.
pages 170–71
Frankel account: Memorandum, undated, by Frankel, BA, NS 26/115.
page 171
"Pfui! Jew defenders! . . ." BH, MA 104221, Salbey Bericht.
page 172
Aigner account: BH, Aigner Bericht.
pages 172–73
Dr. Schultze account: Interviews, 1974–75.

page 173
Ilse Pröhl account: Interview with Ilse Hess, 1971; letter to author, 1975.
page 173
Haushofer account: Karl Haushofer testimony, Nuremberg, Oct. 7, 1945.
pages 174–76
Helene Hanfstaengl account: *Notes* 322–27.
page 174
Dr. Schultze account: Interviews, 1974–75.
page 176
"He refused a bite or soup . . ." Heinz 170.
page 176
"There are many things that can be said . . ." Fritz Stern, *The Politics of
    Cultural Despair* (Univ. of Calif., 1961), 237–38.
page 176
"our history has gone astray . . ." Möller, *Das Dritte Riech* (Hamburg, 1931),
    3, 7–8.
pages 176–77
"The first period of the national . . ." BH, Generalstaatskommissariat, 575.

Chapter Seven. IN LANDSBERG PRISON

page 181
"She loves, and always has loved . . ." Helene Hanfstaengl, *Notes*, 333.
page 181
"These are the papers . . ." Helene Hanfstaengl interview, 1971.
page 182
Dr. Brinsteiner report, Jan. 8, 1924: Otto Lurker, *Hitler hinter Festungs-
    mauern, ein Bild aus trüben Tagen* (Berlin, 1933), 9–11, 68. Dr. Walter
    Schultze, who treated Hitler on Nov. 9–11, stated in 1974 that a break
    such as Dr. Brinsteiner described was impossible; and that Dr. Brinsteiner
    was either incompetent or a liar. Interview with Dr. Schultze, 1974.
page 182
Drexler account: BH, MA 104221, Drexler Bericht.
page 183
Knirsch account: Schlabrendorff 345–46.
page 183
"Her advice turned the scale . . ." MY 113.
pages 183–84
Ehard account: Interview with Ehard, 1971.
page 184
Angela Letter: Hans Hitler Collection.
page 184
Wagner letter: Edward Whalen Collection.
page 185
Rosenberg account: *Memoirs* 74.
page 185
"I was howled down in derision," Lüdecke 186.
page 185
"Adolf Hitler in Prison," Hoffmann 57.
pages 185–86
Schacht account: *Old Wizard*, 181–83.
page 186
"Hitler was at all times . . ." Brinsteiner report, op. cit.

page 186
"From its failure I learned . . ." Hitler speech, Prange 160.
pages 186–87
"It was the greatest good fortune . . ." Gordon 408–9.
page 187
"Landsberg was my college education . . ." Frank 47.
page 187
Hitler-Hanfstaengl meeting: Interview with Hanfstaengl, 1971.
page 187
Frau Ebertin account: Howe, *Urania's*, 92–93.
page 188
Carin Göring letter: Bewley 56–57.
page 188
"These things undoubtedly satisfy . . ." Spengler, *Politische Schriften*
(Munich, 1932), 148.
pages 188–89
"You have one classic example . . ." PHP.
page 189
Ludendorff quote: Frank 52.
pages 189–90
Rosenberg quote: Rosenberg 77.
pages 189–90
Hanfstaengl's visit: Egon Hanfstaengl *Memoirs* and interviews, 1971; MY 113.
pages 190–91
Quotes from trial: PHP.
page 191
"I can never think without melancholy . . ." Hans von Hülsen, *Zwillings-Seele*
(Munich, 1947), I, 207ff.
pages 191–92
Trial quotes: PHP.
page 192
"on the evidence of my defense . . ." HSC 282.
pages 192–93
The sentence: BA, NS 26/114.
page 193
Hemmrich quote: Heinz 171.
page 193
Hitler's diary: Müllern-Schönhausen 117.
page 194
Hemmrich quotes: Heinz 182, 174. The prison routine as described in following pages by Heinz was corroborated by Hans Kallenbach, *Mit Adolf
Hitler auf Festung Landsberg.*
page 194
"Upstairs with him were the elite . . ." Interview with Dr. Weber, Schulze-
Wilde Collection.
pages 194–95
Hemmrich quotes: Heinz 183–84.
page 195
Carin Göring letter: Bewley 58; Countess von Wilamowitz-Moellendorff, *Carin
Göring* (Stockholm, 1933).
page 196
"pioneers and forerunners . . ." NA, Microcopy T-81, Reel 116, Frame
136437.

page 196
Drexler quote: Frank 48–49.
page 196
"The various groups quarreled . . ." Lüdecke 210.
page 197
Hemmrich account: Heinz 185, 188, 189.
page 197
Hitler quotes: HSC 46.
page 198
Hemmrich account: Heinz 179, 181–82.
page 198
Hitler quotes: MY 114–15.
page 199
Ilse Pröhl account: Interview with Ilse Hess, 1971.
page 199
Haushofer statement; Karl Haushofer testimony at Nuremberg, Oct. 7, 1945, p. 7.
page 199
Hess letter to Heinrich Heim, who would later become Bormann's secretary and, in that capacity, copy down Hitler's table conversations.
page 200
Kugler-Hitler meeting: *Der Nationalsozialist*, a Leipzig news magazine, Aug. 17, 1924. Bibliothek für Zeitgeschichte, Stuttgart, Flugblattsammlung, Karton: Deutschland IV.
pages 200–1
Leybold report, Sept. 22, 1924: BH, State Ministry of Interior file.
page 201
Hemmrich account: Heinz 185, 192.
pages 201–2
Göring-Negrelli correspondence: Ben E. Swearingen Collection.
page 202
Hitler account: HSC 282.
page 202
Hoffmann account: Hoffmann 61.
page 202
Hitler-Müller quotes: HSC 282–83.
page 203
Hitler quote: HSC 284.
page 203
Hitler quote: HSC 284.
page 204
Hitler at the Hanfstaengls': MY 119–22; HSB 893; interviews with Helene and Egon Hanfstaengl, 1971.

Chapter Eight. HITLER'S SECRET BOOK

page 205
Hoffmann account: Hoffmann 145.
page 206
"This wild beast is checked . . ." Strasser, *Hitler and I*, 71.
page 206
Lüdecke article: Lüdecke 249–50.

page 206
Rosenberg quote: Lüdecke 257.

page 207
Feb. 27, 1924 meeting: Müller, *Im Wandel*, 301.

page 209
"Fight Marxism and Judaism . . . reports will be circulated . . ." BH, Munich police report, Nov. 1929.

page 209
Haushofer account: Interview with Heinz Haushofer, 1971; correspondence, 1975.

page 211
Röhm letter to Hitler: Ernst Röhm, *Die Memoiren des Stabschefs* (Saarbrücken, 1934), 160.

page 211
Röhm to Lüdecke: Lüdecke 265.

page 211
Hitler quote: HSC 586.

page 212
Hanfstaengl to Hitler: MY 133, 134, 129.

page 212
Mitzi Reiter story: Gun, *Eva Braun*, 61.

page 213
Hitler at Wahnfried: F. Wagner 30, 41.

page 213
Hitler quote: *Mein Kampf*, Eher, 69.

page 215
"the bridge from left to right . . ." Richard Hunt, *Joseph Goebbels*, Ph.D. thesis, Harvard Univ. 1960, 101.

pages 215–16
Diary entries: EGD 47, 50. The Goebbels diaries of 1925–26, for all their self-dramatization and exaggeration, present a revealing self-portrait of the author. They were discovered only after the war and turned over to ex-President Hoover. They were much more valuable testimonials than Goebbels' *Struggle for Berlin*, which was probably based on his journals.

page 215
"the servant of capital and interest . . ." EGD 62.

page 216
"was the foundation of our religion . . ." Orlow I, 70.

page 217
Goebbels quotes: EGD 78.

page 218
Hanussen story: Müllern-Schönhausen, 118.

pages 218–19
Goebbels quotes: EGD 91, 95, 100–1.

page 220
Hitler letter: Deuerlein, *Der Aufsteig*, 264–65.

page 221
Freud quotes: Tell 136.

page 221
Hitler quotes: MK 652, 651.

pages 221–22
Haushofer quote: E. A. Walsh, *Total Power* (Garden City, Garden City Publishing Co., 1948).

page 222
Hitler to Frank: Frank 46.
pages 222–23
Hitler speech, Dec. 18, 1926. BH, Sonderabgabe I, ⌗1762.
page 222
Footnote: Interview with Erich Kempka, 1971.
page 223
"There is complete confusion . . ." Riess 32.
pages 223–24
Goebbels quotes: Bramsted 20.
page 224
"What record must I use . . ." Strasser, *Mein Kampf*, 31.
page 224
Pharus Hall meeting: Heiber 51–52; Riess 33–36.
page 225
Goldschmidt story: Riess 36.
page 226
"What a miserable provincial sheet . . ." Ibid. 40.
page 227
Krebs account: Albert Krebs, *Tendenzen und Gestalten der NSDAP* (Stuttgart, 1959), 131ff.
pages 227–28
Strasser account: Strasser, *Mein Kampf*, 39–41.
page 228
"Socialism and nationalism . . ." *Der Angriff*, Apr. 2, 1928.
page 229
"I immediately rang up my sister . . ." HSC 221.
page 229
On Geli: Interviews with Ilse Hess, Ernst and Helene Hanfstaengl, 1971; Hoffmann 48; Schirach 178–79.
page 229
It was Hitler who suggested that Hess and Ilse Pröhl get married. At first Hess had not appreciated the Führer's intervention. But then he was amused. "Hitler took a personal interest in all of us who were with him in the beginning," Frau Hess revealed in a 1971 interview. "We were a very close circle. We were also intimate friends of Geli. As far as my husband and I were concerned, we were too busy to get married; he was always away and I was working. He devoted his time more to political matters, and he didn't have much of a private life."
pages 229–30
Ilse Hess account: Interview 1971.
page 230
"The compulsion to engage . . ." *Hitler's Secret Book*, 6.
page 230
"Then the Jew can make . . ." Ibid. 29.
page 230
"It is not my task . . . exactly so with Jewry too," Ibid. 211–12.
page 230
"Never before had Hitler gone quite that far in his equation of the Jews with other peoples. But what, then, was the difference? Was it only the absence of a territorial state? No, the difference was found in the struggle for life." Jäckel 103. The author is indebted to Professor Jäckel for information on this subject.

pages 230–31
"His ultimate goal . . ." *Hitler's Secret Book*, 213.
pages 231–32
Hitler quotes: Ibid. 29, 79, 23, 76, 41.
page 232
Dr. Schwenninger story: Interview with Prof. Ernst Deuerlein, 1971.

Chapter Nine. A DEATH IN THE FAMILY

page 233
Goebbels quote: *Der Angriff*, Nov. 19, 1928.
page 234
Hitler speech: Prange 40–41.
page 234
Goebbels quote: *Der Angriff*, Nov. 19, 1928.
page 234
Lochner account: Lochner, *What About Germany?*, 102–3.
page 235
Speer account: Speer 15–16.
page 236
"he hovered at her elbow . . ." MY 162.
page 236
Hoffmann account of Geli: Hoffmann, 148, 150.
page 236
Henriette Hoffmann account: Schirach 73.
page 237
"She was a terror . . ." Gun, *Eva Braun*, 21.
page 237
First meeting Hitler-Eva Braun: Ibid. 42–43.
page 238
"fading into oblivion . . ." G. M. Gathorne-Hardy, A *Short History of International Affairs* (London, 1950), 357.
page 238
Wessel story: Heiber 68–69.
page 238
Footnote: MY 149.
page 238
"His spirit has risen . . ." *Der Angriff*, Feb. 27, 1930.
page 239
"If anything goes wrong . . ." MY 149.
page 239
Burial of Wessel: Heiber 70.
pages 239–40
Hitler-Strasser meeting: Strasser, *Ministersessel*.
page 240
Hitler letter to Goebbels: Kühnl 374.
page 240
"they were united behind . . ." Ibid. 253.
page 240
"The departure of my brother . . ." BA, Slg. Ach. folder 313: Letter, Gregor Strasser to Rudolf Jung, July 22, 1930.
page 241
August Wilhelm letter: unpublished letter, dated Apr. 7, 1930, from Ben E. Swearingen Collection.

page 242
"Do it jokingly, do it seriously . . ." *Der Angriff*, Sept. 14, 1930.

page 243
Hitler-Müller conversation: HSC 179.

page 243
"Great things are before us . . ." MY 151.

page 244
"Then the November 1918 revolution . . ." *Frankfurter Zeitung*, Sept. 26, 1930.

page 244
Hitler article in London *Sunday Express*: Baynes 994–95.

page 244
Hitler in London *Times*: Baynes 192.

page 244
"This was the élite of the 'Aryan' race . . ." Sender 276.

pages 245–46
On William Patrick Hitler and his mother: Interview with Hans Hitler, 1971; OSS interview with W. P. Hitler, HSB 926–27; *Paris-Soir*, Aug. 5, 1939.

pages 246–47
Frank investigation: Frank 330–31.

page 247
"suffered all his life . . ." Correspondence between Dr. Hans Dietrich Röhrs and Rittmeister von Schuh; correspondence between Dr. Röhrs and the author, 1972.

page 247
"Hitler was not often there . . ." Frank 93–94.

page 249
"I understand your distress . . ." Heiden 409.

page 249
Stennes Putsch: Höhne, *Order of Death's Head*, 67–68; interviews with Hein Ruck, 1971.

page 250
"I found him a very decent fellow . . ." MY 157–58.

page 250
"When a mother has many children . . ." Interview with F. K. Florian, 1970.

page 250
"We were not loved everywhere . . ." Leaders' Conference, June 13–14, SS HQ Report, Berlin Documentary Center, Microfilm 87.

page 250
"I am the SA and SS . . ." *Münchener Post*, Apr. 11/12, 1931.

page 250
"The SA is a collection . . ." Feb. 3, 1931; NA, German Documents, Reel 85.

page 251
Delmer account: *Trail*, 106–7, 115–17.

page 252
Maurice account: Gun, *Eva Braun*, 8

page 252
Winter account: Ibid. 9.

page 252
"her life was very hard . . ." OSS interview with William Patrick Hitler, HSB 929–30.

page 252
Hanfstaengl's quotes: Interviews with Ernst and Helene Hanfstaengl, 1970, 1971.
page 252
Winter quote: Gun, *Eva Braun*, 10.
page 253
Geli to Frau Hoffmann: Hoffmann 151.
page 253
Hoffmann account: Hoffmann 154.
pages 253–54
Frau Reichert account: Interview with Frau Reichert, Schulze-Wilde Collection.
page 254
Eva letter to Hitler: Gun, *Eva Braun*, 13.
page 254
Hoffmann account: Hoffmann 153.
page 254
There are conflicting versions of the discovery of the body. According to Frau Winter, she knocked on the door and when Geli didn't respond she summoned her husband and together they forced their way in. Frau Hess informed the author that her husband was summoned by Frau Winter and *he* broke down the door.
 Eva Braun told her two sisters that Hitler himself had said Geli had wrapped the gun in a face cloth to muffle the explosion, then fired it in her mouth. There was also a report of an unfinished letter from Geli to a professor of music in Vienna stating that she wanted to take lessons from him. A fortuneteller (so Hitler told Friedelind Wagner) had once prophesied that a revolver bullet would end Geli's life, and since then she had a "hysterical fear" of guns. Wagner OSS 938.
page 255
Frank account: Frank 98.
pages 255–56
Frauenfeld account: Interviews with Frauenfeld, 1971; correspondence with Frauenfeld, 1975.
page 256
"So. Now let the struggle begin . . ." Hoffmann 159.
page 256
"It is like eating a corpse!" Gilbert, *Psychology*, 62.
page 256
Footnote: Interview with Frau Hess, 1971.

Chapter Ten. "IT IS ALMOST LIKE A DREAM"

page 259
"The movement is today so united . . ." VB, Oct. 31, 1931.
pages 259–60
"An interesting man with exceptional . . ." Werner Conze, in *Vierteljahreshefte für Zeitgeschichte*, 1 Jahrg. (1953) 261ff.
page 260
"the chess game for power . . ." Goebbels, *Vom Kaiserhof zur Reichskanzlei* (Munich, 1936), 19–20.
pages 260–61
Hitler speech in Düsseldorf: Schweitzer 100, Prange 253.

page 261
"I know that I shall come to power . . ." Frank 101.
pages 261–62
"Berlin was in a state of war . . ." Isherwood 86.
page 263
"dream of power was temporarily over . . ." Goebbels, *Vom Kaiserhof,* 55–56, 62.
page 263
"The first election is over . . ." Dietrich 15.
pages 263–64
Frank account of Röhm's homosexuality: Frank 88–89.
page 264
Delmer account: *Trail,* 155–56.
pages 264–65
Krebs account: Krebs, *Tendenzen,* 136–37.
page 265
"Hitler is a fool . . ." A. M. Koktanek, *Oswald Spengler in seiner Zeit* (Munich, 1968), 246.
page 265
"When one has a chance . . ." Hamilton 142–43.
page 265
"I very much doubt if I'm the right man." Papen 152.
pages 265–66
"Well, my dear Papen, I hope . . ." Dorpalen 333–34.
page 267
"Just look, Baur, there is a beautiful . . ." Baur section in Ziegler; interview with Baur, 1970.
pages 267–68
Egon Hanfstaengl account: *Memoirs,* 95.
page 269
"The President is not prepared . . ." Papen 196.
page 270
Hitler-Hindenburg meeting: Memorandum by Meissner in Walther Hubatsch, *Hindenburg und der Staat* (Göttingen, 1966), 338–39.
page 270
Hanfstaengl account: HSB 911.
page 271
"Mind you, if it amuses you . . ." MY 188.
page 271
"Now that the National Socialists . . ." Rudolf Olden, *Hitler* (New York, 1936).
page 271
"The decision was right . . ." Dorpalen 356.
page 271
Hanfstaengl account: HSB 911.
page 271
"Only we ourselves can finish . . ." Dietrich 31.
page 272
Ribbentrop quote: Stein 111.
pages 272–73
Lochner-Kaltenborn—Wiegand interview with Hitler: *Wisconsin Magazine of History,* Summer 1967, 286–90.

page 273
Habsburg account: Interview with Otto von Habsburg, 1971.
pages 273–74
Eva's attempted suicide: Hoffmann 161–62.
page 274
"If we held ourselves aloof . . ." Goebbels, *Vom Kaiserhof*, 181.
page 275
Delmer-Hitler meeting. *Trail*, 173–74.
page 275
"Open the windows quickly . . ." Interrogation of Crown Prince Frederick Wilhelm of Prussia at Nuremberg. This sentence was deleted from the stenographic text at his request, but noted in prefatory remarks.
page 275
"We must endeavor to put aside . . ." Papen 213.
page 276
"His entire manner of handling . . ." Hegner 16.
page 276
"Not long ago at Tannenberg . . ." HSC 226–27.
pages 276–77
Hitler-Hindenburg meeting: Dorpalen 379–81; Hegner 18–19.
page 277
Footnote: H. A. Turner, "Fritz Thyssen and 'I Paid Hitler'" in *Faschismus und Kapitalismus in Deutschland,* 25.
pages 277–78
"I am ready to leave at any time . . ." Dorpalen 386.
page 278
Hindenburg meeting with Papen and Schleicher: Meissner memo, Dec. 2, 1932, in *Vierteljahreshefte,* VI, 1958, 105–7. Papen 217–18.
page 279
Papen-Hindenburg meeting: Dorpalen 395–406.
page 279
"Along comes Hindenburg, a man of honor . . ." Frank 108.
page 280
"It is difficult to be cheerful," Goebbels, *Vom Kaiserhof,* 206.
page 281
"stabbed him in the back . . ." Orlow I, 293.
page 281
"Such contemptible behavior . . ." Goebbels, *Vom Kaiserhof,* 206.
page 281
Strasser quote: MY 190–91; Heiber 104.
page 281
Strasser to Rosenberg: Rosenberg, *Memoirs,* 148.
page 281
"burst into a spontaneous ovation . . ." Goebbels, *Vom Kaiserhof,* 209.
page 281
"most familiar with [Hitler's] basic ideas . . ." VB, Dec. 18–19, 1932.
page 282
On Hitler and Christmas decorations: Krause 52.

page 282
Hitler letter to Frau Wagner: Wagner 73.
page 282
Bullitt report: Bullitt 23.
pages 282–83
Hanussen prediction: Müllern-Schönhausen 155–56.
page 283
Hanfstaengl account: MY 195.
page 284
"success whose importance . . ." HSC 467.
page 284
"break the necks of all . . ." Dorpalen 416.
page 285
Hitler at Ribbentrop's: Ribbentrop, *Memoirs*, 23.
pages 285–86
Oskar Hindenburg-Hitler meeting: Meissner, IMT, XXXII, 152; same, Case
     No. 11 transcript, 4494; Hans Otto Meissner and Harry Wilde, *Die Mach-
     tergreifung* (Stuttgart, 1958), 161–64. Papen's account of the Janu-
     ary negotiations in his memoirs is inaccurate. He states, for example, that
     he "had no contact whatever with Hitler between January 4 and 22," a
     palpable lie; nor does he mention his abrupt switch to Hitler on the eve-
     ning of January 22.
page 287
"Joachim proposes link-up with Hugenberg . . ." Ribbentrop, *Memoirs*, 24.
page 287
"Whether what I am going to do . . ." Unsigned memorandum on Hinden-
     burg-Schleicher conference, Jan. 28, 1933, in Thilo Vogelsang, *Reichs-
     wehr, Staat und NSDAP* (Stuttgart, 1962), 490–91.
page 287
"After this breach of trust . . ." Hammerstein Memorandum in John
     Wheeler-Bennett, *Nemesis*, 280.
page 288
"It is my unpleasant duty . . ." Papen 239.
page 289
"If the new government . . ." Dorpalen 440.
pages 289–90
"Gentlemen, it is five minutes past . . . And now, gentlemen, forward with
     God!" Dorpalen 441–42.
page 290
Hoffmann account: Hoffmann 68.
page 290
Egon Hanfstaengl account: *Memoirs*, 191.
page 291
"How on earth did he conjure . . ." Hoffmann 69.
page 291
Hitler-Papen: Papen 264.
page 291
Frank quote: Frank 111.
page 291
"Everyone felt the same . . ." Interview with H. Ruck, 1971.
page 291
Maschmann quote: Maschmann 10–13.

page 291
"The river of fire . . ." François-Poncet 48.

pages 291–92
Frank account: Frank 129–30.

page 292
Heine quote, 1834. From Louis Untermeyer, *Heinrich Heine, Paradox and Poet* (New York, 1937), I, 230.

Chapter Eleven. AN UNGUARDED HOUR

page 293
Frau Goebbels story: Frau Goebbels section in Ziegler.

page 293
Papen quote: Ewald von Kleist-Schmenzin, *"Die Letzte Möglichkeit,"* *Politische Studien*, X, 1939, 92.

page 294
New York *Times*, Jan. 31, 1933.

page 294
Schacht quote: NA, U. S. Dept. of State file, Berlin Embassy Report, Feb. 2, 1933.

page 295
Party at Hammerstein's: Institut für Zeitgeschichte, ZS 105–5, Horstom Mellenthin; O'Neill 125–26.

page 297
"to avoid at all costs . . ." Heiden, *A History of National Socialism*, 216.

page 297
"Every comrade a commander . . ." Bewley 97–98.

page 298
Hanfstaengl account: Interview, 1970.

pages 298–99
Hitler at Reichstag fire: Delmer, *Trail*, 187–88; Papen 268–69; Tobias 84.

pages 299–300
Conference after fire: Tobias 84–87; Holborn, *Republic*, 168.

page 300
"It took half an hour before I could find . . ." HSC 604.

page 300
"That's sheer rubbish! . . . if you sign it officially," Tobias 89–91.

page 301
"a ruthless settling of accounts . . . documents of the German people," Holborn, *Republic*, 183.

page 302
"I may say to the Communists . . ." Bewley 100–1.

page 302
Delmer–Hitler: *Trail*, 192–94.

page 303
Göring speech: Bullock 223–24.

page 303
"pragmatic, decent men . . ." Interview in 1971 with Kurt Schuschnigg, who was the visiting Austrian.

page 303
Göring quote: Bullock 219.

page 304
Schacht quote: Interview with Schacht, 1963; Manchester 407.
page 304
"He rants much less . . ." Eich 92.
page 305
"Munich is *the* city of Germany . . ." Frank 137–38.
page 305
Hitler to Ehard: Interview with Ehard, 1971.
page 305
"Authority is only a springboard . . ." Frank 156.
page 306
"like a timid newcomer . . ." François-Poncet 62.
page 306
"We consider it a blessing . . ." Dorpalen 466.
pages 306–7
Hitler speech: Baynes 426.
page 307
"We want the bill . . . your death knell has sounded," Bullock 229.
page 307
"I wish to assure you . . ." John Wheeler-Bennett, *Wooden Titan* (New York, 1936), 449.
page 308
"He stretched the truth . . ." Interview with Schwerin von Krosigk, 1971.
page 308
Binding quote: R. Binding, *Die Briefe* (Hamburg, 1957), 182.
page 309
Isherwood account: Isherwood 180–81.
page 310
Hitler quote: E. De Felice, *Storia degli ebrei italiani sotto il fascismo* (Turin, 1961), 113.
page 310
"Little knots of passers-by . . ." Isherwood 183.
page 310
Hindenburg-Hitler correspondence: Walther Hubatsch, *Hindenburg und der Staat*, op. cit., 375–78.
page 311
"It is precisely for these young Germans . . ." Baynes 729.
page 311
"nothing but pernicious enemies . . ." GFP, C, I, 347.
pages 311–12
François-Poncet account: François-Poncet 69–70.
page 312
"The German government wishes . . ." Prange 349.
page 312
State Historical Society of Wisconsin: Lochner letter, May 28, 1933.
page 312
Footnote: New York *Times*, July 10, 1933.
page 313
"Within three weeks we had progressed . . ." HSC 470.
page 313
"We must now eliminate . . ." VB, July 6, 1933.
page 313
"When we discussed the measure . . ." Papen 304.

page 314
"The revolution is not a permanent . . ." Speech, July 6, 1933, in Baynes 865–66.

page 314
"To gain political power . . ." Speech, July 13, 1933 in Baynes 848–85, 867–68.

page 315
"German socialism is directed by Germans . . ." Heinz 232.

page 315
Hitler to Spengler: *Spengler Letters* 290.

page 315
Richard Strauss received by Hitler: Koehler 67–68.

page 315
Pope welcomes Papen: Papen 279.

page 316
"It was like a country fair . . ." Interview, Stütz, 1971.

page 316
Hitler quote: F. Wagner 89.

pages 316–18
Hanfstaengls' trip to Obersalzberg: Egon Hanfstaengl, *Memoirs*, 216–29.

page 318
Literary Digest, Aug. 26, 1933, 13.

page 318
Lord Lothian quote: J. R. M. Butler, *Lord Lothian* (London, 1960), 206.

page 319
Dirksen quote: Herzstein 24.

page 319
"We must make a break . . ." Papen 297–98.

pages 319–20
Lord Allen quote: Martin Gilbert, *Plough My Own Furrow* (London, 1965), 340–41.

page 320
Heidegger quote: *Freiburger Studentenzeitung*, Nov. 10, 1933.

page 320
"very much upset over our step . . ." GFP, C, II, 28–29.

page 320
Cardinal Faulhaber quote: Amtsblatt Passau, #25, Nov. 10, 1933.

pages 320–21
Hitler speech at Siemens plant: Berlin, Nov. 10, 1933.

page 321
"Tomorrow show your national . . ." Dorpalen, 474.

page 321
"the representative of the German state idea . . ." Bracher 231.

pages 321–22
"We wish thus to conform to the spirit . . ." *Jahresbericht der Deutschen Mathematiker-Vereinigung* (Leipzig, 1934), XLIII, 81–82.

page 322
Shaw quote: Tobias 124.

page 322
"grave grounds exist for suspecting . . ." Ibid. 126–27.

page 322
Göring-Dimitrov exchange: *Neue Züricher Zeitung*, Nov. 6, 1933.

page 323
Hitler quote: MY 203.
page 323
Hanfstaengl quote: Martha Dodd 58.
page 323
Dodd account: Ibid. 58–60.
pages 323–24
Eden account: Eden, *Facing,* 61–65.
page 324
Neurath cable: GFP, II, 611.
page 325
"The British were eager to get . . ." François-Poncet 122–23.
page 325
Hitler letter to Mussolini, Nov. 2, 1933; GFP, II, 63–64.
pages 325–26
Hanfstaengl to Mussolini: Hanfstaengl, *Out of the Strong.*
page 326
Mussolini quote: Bojano 30–31.
page 326
"They were not over three yards from me . . ." Knickerbocker, 5–6.
page 327
"Mussolini stepped forth superbly . . ." Sisley Huddleston, *In My Time* (London: 1938), 309.
page 327
Wiedemann account: Wiedemann 32 (tr.).
page 327
Bojano account: Bojano 31.
pages 327–28
Neurath's circular: GFP, C, III, 18.
page 328
"could not foresee any closer . . ." Weizsäcker 101.

Chapter Twelve. THE SECOND REVOLUTION—
"ALL REVOLUTIONS DEVOUR THEIR OWN CHILDREN"

page 329
"The Reichswehr is the sole bearer . . ." Schweitzer 244.
pages 329–30
"Anyone who thinks that the tasks . . ." Heiden, *Der Führer,* 724.
pages 330–31
Conference, Feb. 28, 1934: Unpublished memoirs of Field Marshal von Weichs in O'Neill 39–41; Höhne, *Order,* 96. "What that ridiculous corporal . . ." Helmut Krausnick, "Der 30 Juni 1934," in *Das Parlament 30 Juni,* 1954, 320.
page 331
"The SA is the heroic incarnation . . ." Röhm speech, Apr. 18, 1934.
page 332
"I implored him for the last time . . ." Baynes 315–16.
page 332
"He had some feeling that there was . . ." Interview with Röhm's sister-in-law, 1971.
pages 332–33
Papen speech: Papen 305–7.

page 334
"If during these months I hesitated . . ." Baynes 309.

page 334
"He led me to his study . . ." The Lutze diary, in *Frankfurter Rundschau*, May 14, 1957.

page 334
"square accounts," Höhne, *Order*, 109.

page 335
"Woe to him who breaks faith . . ." VB, June 26, 1934.

page 335
"Now we are in the middle . . ." Delmer, *Trail*, 231–33.

page 335
"I had a feeling . . . would now have to take action . . ." Lutze diary, op. cit.

page 336
Hitler phone call to Röhm: Holborn, *Republic*, 235.

page 336
"That may be true . . ." Unpublished affidavit of Field Marshal Ewald von Kleist at Nuremberg, 1946. Institut für Zeitgeschichte, Munich.

page 337
"making a fatal error." *The Answers of Ernst von Salomon* (London, 1954), 273–74.

page 337
"The Reichswehr is against us!" Höhne, *Order*, 112; Case against Josef Dietrich, Munich Provisional Court I, July 4, 1956, 58, 80.

page 337
"It was at last clear to me . . ." Baynes 321.

page 338
"*Red of the morning . . .*" Lutze diary, op. cit.

page 338
"This is the blackest day . . ." Case against Dietrich, op. cit., 77.

page 338
"Lock him up!" Gallo 207.

page 338
"You are under arrest . . ." Lutze diary, op. cit.

pages 338–40
Kempka account: Interviews with Kempka, 1971.

page 339
"somewhat tense but not visibly excited." CIC interview of Wilhelm Brückner.

page 339
Lutze account: Lutze diary, op. cit.

page 340
Brückner account: CIC interview, op. cit.; Kempka interview, 1971.

page 340
"I gave the order . . ." Baynes 321–22.

page 340
Epp account: Judgment on Josef Dietrich, Munich, May 14, 1957, 60.

page 341
"In a voice frequently . . ." Letter from Gruppenführer Karl Schreyer to Munich Police HQ, 4; Höhne, *Order*, 116.

page 341
Papen account: Papen 315.

page 341
Delmer account: *Trail,* 234.
page 342
Dietrich account: Interview with Dietrich, 1963.
page 342
"Select an officer and six men . . ." Höhne, *Order,* 117.
pages 342–43
Frank account: Frank 149–51.
page 343
Execution of the six men: Judgment on Dietrich, op. cit., 15–16; Case against
     Dietrich, op. cit., 69–70, 72.
page 343
"I have pardoned Röhm . . ." Judgment on Dietrich, op. cit., 61.
page 343
"Göring arrived in one of his . . ." Gisevius 156.
page 343
"He was foolish enough . . ." Wheeler-Bennett, *Nemesis,* 323.
page 344
DNB report: NA, Report, U. S. Embassy, Berlin, July 2, 1934.
page 344
Reference Karl Ernst: He was rumored to be involved in the mysterious
     murder of Hanussen, the astrologer, whose body was found in a forest near
     Stahnsdorf several weeks after his prediction of the Reichstag fire. There
     was some speculation that Hitler, reportedly incensed at the murder, took
     vengeance on Ernst. Hegner 21.
     Curiously, another well-known astrologer was a victim of the Röhm
     purge: Dr. Karl-Günther Heimsoth, a close friend of Gregor Strasser, whose
     correspondence with Röhm about homosexuality and astrology was given
     wide publicity in the 1932 attempt to discredit the SA and the party. Dr.
     Heimsoth's death could also have been related to the recent ban on all
     forms of professional fortunetelling in the Berlin area. The predictions of
     Hanussen and his successors were becoming an embarrassment to the
     Third Reich. In the horoscope published by Frank Glahn in February
     1933, for instance, it was predicted that the Führer would not be able to
     form a viable government.
     Hitler's horoscope, however, continued to fascinate many Germans and a
     number were circulated surreptitiously. Soon after the Röhm purge, Hans
     Blüher, a founder of the *Wandervögel* movement, met an astrologer
     friend, Count Finckenstein, in a Berlin restaurant to discuss a horoscope
     of the Führer. "My friend Ulrich looked cautiously around to see if any-
     one was listening to us," wrote Blüher in his diary. "Then he leaned to-
     wards me and whispered in my ear through a cupped hand: 'He's a
     homocidal maniac!' Ever since then I knew that Germany had sold herself
     into the hands of a murderer." Howe, *Urania's,* 109.
pages 344–45
"He wore no hat . . ." Gisevius 160–61.
page 345
"For months I have been telling . . ." Dorpalen 479.
page 345
Death of Röhm: Statement by Lippert, *Stuttgarter Zeitung,* May 7, 1957; VB,
     July 1, 1934; *Süddeutsche Zeitung,* Mar. 30–31, May 11, May 14, 1947;
     Frankfurter Rundschau, May 8, 1957; Höhne, *Order,* 126–27.
page 346
"I hope we may call . . ." Martha Dodd 136.

page 346
Göring statement: NA, U. S. Embassy, Berlin, report, July 9, 1934.
page 346
Blomberg statement: Ibid.
page 346
Schreyer account: Höhne, *Order*, 127.
pages 346–47
Delmer statement: *Trail*, 235.
page 347
Hindenburg telegram: Wheeler-Bennett, *Nemesis*, 325–26.
pages 347–48
Papen account: Papen 318.
page 348
"When a mutiny takes place . . ." Interview with Schwerin von Krosigk, 1971.
pages 348–49
Frank–Hitler: Frank 152–54.
page 349
"I have often seen governments . . . among the men who wield power."
   Anonymous source from *Das Neue Tage-Buch* in Paris.
pages 349–50
Hitler speech: Baynes 290–328.
page 350
"emergency defense measures of the state," Orlow II, 115.
page 350
"Our verdict on the affair . . ." Dönitz 304.
page 350
"This type of spontaneous . . ." Gallo 289.
page 350
"It may be as you say . . ." Heinz Assmann 289ff.; also Assmann article,
   "Adolf Hitler—Genius and Demon."
pages 350–51
Mackensen Memorandum: Wheeler-Bennett, *Nemesis*, 329–31.
page 351
Ruck statement: Interview with Ruck, 1971.
pages 351–52
Naumann statement: Interview, 1971.
page 352
Lutze story: Report by Robert Schulz, Aug. 21, 1935, RFSS microfilm 33 at
   NA (Group T-175).
page 353
"The inevitable has happened . . ." Ivone Kirkpatrick 297.
page 353
Friedelind Wagner account: OSS interview, HSB 934.
pages 353–54
Bülow account: GFP, C, III, 235–41.
page 354
Papen account: Papen 337–41.
page 354
Schacht account: *Old Wizard*, 292.
pages 354–55
Mussolini quote: Starhemberg 164–68.
pages 355–56
Hitler at Hindenburg's: MY 262.

page 356
"We were in his study . . ." Raeder testimony at Nuremberg, 1946.
page 356
Oath: Wheeler-Bennett, *Nemesis*, 339.
page 357
Lochner account: *What About Germany?*, 120.
page 357
Papen account: Papen 333.
page 357
Hitler to Hanfstaengl: MY 263–64.

Chapter Thirteen. TRIUMPH OF THE WILL

page 359
Thompson account: *Harper's Bazaar*, Dec. 1934.
pages 359–60
Dodd account: William Dodd 154.
page 360
Jüttner account: Interrogation of Max Jüttner, Provincial Court I, Munich, Apr. 8, 1949.
page 360
Speer account: Speer 58–59.
pages 360–61
Leni Riefenstahl account: Interviews, 1971.
page 361
"The German form of life . . ." Shirer, *Berlin Diary*, 19.
pages 361–62
Frank account: Frank 154–55.
page 362
"The floodlit stadium gave the impression . . ." Speer in *Playboy* 78.
page 362
Shirer account: *Berlin Diary*, 22.
page 363
Hitler to generals: Unpublished memoirs of Field Marshal von Weichs; BA, H 07-19/1, 19/14.
page 363
Dodd comment: William Dodd 164.
pages 363–64
Riefenstahl account: Interviews, 1971.
page 364
"During these violent scoldings . . ." OSS interview of Friedelind Wagner: HSB 939.
page 365
Hitler to Wiedemann: Wiedemann 35 (tr.).
page 365
Hitler to Schröder: Zoller 101.
page 365
Brigid Hitler and son account: HSB 927; Brigid Hitler manuscript.
page 365
Footnote: Interview with Hans Hitler, 1971.
page 365
"No country, and especially not England . . ." Weinberg 202.

page 366
"It is ten years today . . ." Price 31.
page 366
"Something has gone wrong . . ." Shirer, *Berlin Diary,* 27.
page 367
"looking very important and grave," Ibid. 29.
pages 367–68
François-Poncet account: Interview, 1971.
page 368
"withdrawal from the League of Nations . . ." GFP, III, 1043–44.
page 368
Eden account: *Facing,* 134, 133, 135.
pages 368–69
"We will have nothing whatever . . ." Schmidt 19–20. The quotes from
    Schmidt throughout this book have been illuminated by two interviews
    with Dr. Schmidt in 1963.
page 369
Eden account: *Facing,* 138–39.
pages 369–70
"Only two years ago the skies . . . atmosphere of the great house." Schmidt
    25.
page 370
"Great fellows, the English . . ." F. Wagner 129.
page 370
Mosley account: Mosley, 365; interviews, 1971–72.
page 370
"once again showed his complete . . ." GFP, C, IV, 49.
page 371
Lochner account: Letter to his daughter, Apr. 1935. State Historical Society
    of Wisconsin.
page 372
Oka's account: Robert Ingrim, *Hitlers glücklichster Tag* (Stuttgart, 1962).
pages 372–73
"If the British government . . ." Schmidt 32–33.
pages 373–74
"How often have I told you . . ." Windsor 254.
page 374
"the timidity and hesitation . . ." GFP, IV, 331.
page 375
"He was of the opinion . . ." Wiedemann 35 (tr.).
page 375
"For me marriage would have been . . ." HSC 247–48.
page 377
Speer on Hitler's fear of cancer: Speer 104.
page 379
Hitler to Reichstag: Baynes 732.
page 380
"formed a single community . . ." Orlow II, 138.
pages 380–81
Luther cable: GFP, IV, 1017.
page 381
Coburg report: Ibid. 1063. Hassell's memorandum: Ibid. 1142–43.

pages 381–82
Hitler to Jouvenel: Maser, *Hitlers "Mein Kampf"* (Munich, 1966), 47–48.
page 382
"To the British people . . ." Eden, *Facing*, 337–38.
page 382
Hitler to Hoffmann: Hoffmann 84.
pages 382–83
Hitler to Wiedemann: Wiedemann 111 (tr.).
page 383
Hoesch to Eden: *Facing*, 338–39.
page 383
Eden to Baldwin: Ibid. 343.
page 384
Helms account: Interviews, 1971.

Chapter Fourteen. "WITH THE ASSURANCE OF A SLEEPWALKER"

page 388
Hitler to Schmidt: Schmidt 41.
page 388
"Good Lord, am I relieved how smoothly . . ." Frank 204ff.
page 388
"The Germans, after all, are only . . ." Shirer, *Rise*, 293.
page 388
"His view is that, if a firm front . . ." Feiling 279.
page 388
"I go the way that Providence . . ." Hitler speech, Munich, Mar. 14, 1936.
pages 388–89
Hitler quote: HSC 259.
page 389
Hitler speech: Prange 110.
pages 389–90
Ribbentrop-Jones meeting: Thomas Jones 197–98.
page 390
Hitler-Jones meeting: Ibid. 198–201.
page 391
Kirkpatrick comment: Ivone Kirkpatrick, *The Inner Circle* (London, 1959), 97–98.
page 391
Hitler to Frau Wagner: F. Wagner 127.
page 392
"Wedged between the powerful Soviet bloc . . ." *Ribbentrop Memoirs*, 59–60.
page 393
Owens quote: Mandell 227.
page 394
Dietrich comment: Dietrich, *Hitler*, 30–31.
page 394
Phayre article: *Current History*, July 1936.
page 394
"Look, Adolf, it is not that bad . . ." Section on Ilse Hess in Ziegler.
page 395
Footnote: Interview with Hans Hitler; CIC-PH.

page 395
Maggi story: Interview with Dieter Allers, 1971.

page 395
Bormann-Fath: Interview with Hildegard Fath, 1971.

page 395
Helene Hanfstaengl divorce: Interview, 1971; correspondence with Egon Hanfstaengl, 1973.

pages 395–96
Lake Starnberg incident: Egon Hanfstaengl, *Memoirs*, 362ff.

page 397
"It is better to consider and solve . . ." Gerhard Meinck, *Hitler und die Deutache Aufrüstung* (Wiesbaden, 1959), 234.

pages 397–98
Lloyd George-Hitler meeting: Thomas Jones 245–46.

page 398
Lloyd George-Linge: Linge, Installment ℀12.

page 398
Lloyd George-Schmidt: Schmidt 59.

page 398
Helms account: Interview with Helms, 1971.

page 399
"Mussolini is the first statesman of the world . . ." Wiskemann 90.

page 400
"According to the English there are . . ." *Ciano's Diplomatic Papers* (London, 1948), 60.

page 400
"this Berlin-Rome line is not a diaphragm . . ." Ivone Kirkpatrick 347.

page 400
"We are already in a state of war . . ." IMT, IX, 40.

page 400
"The battle we are now approaching . . ." Shirer, *Rise*, 300.

page 401
"If I can marry her as King . . ." Windsor 332.

pages 401–2
Ribbentrop to Hesse: HH 31–32.

page 402
"carry the heavy burden of responsibility . . ." Windsor 411.

page 402
Hitler to Ribbentrop: HH 33.

page 403
"Both Grawitz and Bergmann . . ." Interview with Dr. Giesing, 1971.

page 403
Hitler speech: Baynes 1334–47.

page 403
Footnote: New York *Times* Book Review, Apr. 22, 1973.

page 404
Hitler quote: HSC 425.

page 404
"The goal of our education . . ." *Hans Schemm spricht: Seine Reden und sein Werk* (Gauverlag Bayerische Ostmark, 1935), 175–78.
page 404
Phipps report: CAB 27/599.
pages 404–5
Hitler Youth: Siemsen 145, 154; interview with Lauterbacher, 1971; Lauterbacher testimony at Nuremberg, May 27, 1936, 534.
page 405
Wilson quote: Santoro 416.
page 406
Ley quote: David Schoenbaum, *Hitler's Social Revolution* (Garden City, 1966), 105.
page 406
"The bourgeois must no longer feel . . ." Ibid. 58.
pages 406–7
G. S. Cox article in New York *Times Magazine*, Oct. 28, 1934.
page 407
Kennan comment: *Memoirs*, 118.
page 408
On autarchy: Carr 52–61.
page 408
Göring quote: Speech, Oct. 28, 1936, reprinted in *Der Vierjahresplan*, Jan. 1937, 33–35.
page 408
Hitler quote: Santoro 423.
pages 408–9
Schacht comment: *Account*, 98–99.
page 409
On Shaw: "His defense of 'Bosses' in the Preface of *The Millionairess* and in numerous magazine and newspaper articles, included Hitler . . . Mussolini . . . Lenin . . . and Trotsky . . . and, above all, Stalin, whom he regarded as the world's greatest man." Archibald Henderson, *GBS*, 311.
page 409
Hedin quotes: Hedin 71, 99.
page 410
Degrelle comment: Interview, 1971.
page 410
Chiang Kai-shek quote: Eastman 4–5. The philosophy from Europe was accompanied by military assistance from Germany and, significantly, the adviser sent by the Weimar Republic to Chiang in 1929 was Colonel Hermann Kriebel, who had served time with Adolf Hitler in Landsberg for his involvement in the Beer Hall Putsch. See "The Development of German-Chinese Military Relations, 1928–1936," by Thomas M. Williamson, thesis for Department of History in the Graduate School of Arts and Sciences, Duke University, 1967.

Chapter Fifteen. "SUCH A LITTLE HUMAN WORM"

pages 412–13
Hitler speech to the Kreisleiters: *Es spricht der Führer*, edited by Hildegard von Kotze and Helmuth Krausnick (Gütersloh, 1966), 123–77. A German

farmer found the tapes in a ditch where they had been dumped in the last days of the Third Reich. Now at the Bundesarchiv.

page 414
Hitler to Speer: Speer, *Inside*, 41.

pages 414–15
Frau Troost account: Interviews, 1971; correspondence, 1975.

pages 415–16
Hitler speech: Baynes 584–92.

page 416
"Thus did sick minds view Nature . . ." Grunberger 426.

page 416
"The artists ought to be tied to their pictures . . ." Ibid. 425.

page 417
Schmidt comments on Mussolini and Hitler: Schmidt 71.

pages 418–19
Hitler and Mussolini speech: Schmidt 73.

page 419
Jung on Hitler: Knickerbocker 49–50.

pages 419–20
"Now I feel as fresh as a foal . . ." Fest, *Face*, 48.

page 420
Hitler to Göring: IMT, IX, 307.

pages 420–21
Hossbach Minutes: GFP, D, I, 29ff.; Hossbach, *Zwischen Wehrmacht und Hitler* (Hannover, 1949), 207–20.

page 422
Raeder comment: Testimony at Nuremberg, May 16, 1946, 35.

page 422
"Again and again difficult matters . . ." Adolf von Kielmansegg, *Der Fritsch Prozess 1938* (Hamburg, 1949), 586.

page 423
"Our objective should be set out . . ." CAB 27-626, FP (36) 23.

page 423
"I believe the double policy . . ." Feiling 319.

page 423
Halifax comment on Göring: London *Times*, May 28, 1973.

page 423
Halifax on Goebbels: Lord Birkenhead, *Halifax* (London, 1965), 373.

page 424
Halifax-Hitler meeting: Schmidt 76–77.

pages 424–25
Kirkpatrick account: Kirkpatrick, *Inner Circle*, op. cit., 94–98.

page 425
"Under no circumstances shall we use force." Schmidt 78.

page 425
Halifax to cabinet: CAB 43 (37).

page 425
"I am amazed that Halifax . . ." London *Times*, op. cit.

page 425
"I have always said that the English . . ." Günsche testimony to Russians Bezymenski 16.

pages 425–26
Krause account: Krause 53–55.
page 426
Eden recommendations: CAB 237, 626, FP (36) 41.
page 427
Wiedemann account: Wiedemann 58 (tr.).
page 428
Wiedemann account, Wiedemann, idem.
pages 428–29
Keitel account: Keitel, 45–47.
pages 429–30
Wiedemann account: Wiedemann 62 (tr.).
pages 430–31
Guderian comment: Guderian 28.
page 431
"On that point they will fight," Annelies von Ribbentrop, 80.

Chapter Sixteen. THE RETURN OF THE NATIVE

page 432
Papen account: Papen 406–8.
page 433
"to forestall a coup . . ." Guido Schmidt interrogation, IMT, XVI, 152.
pages 433–35
Schuschnigg-Hitler first interview: Schuschnigg, *Austrian*, 12–19; interview
    with Schuschnigg, 1971.
page 435
Second interview: Ibid. 24–26; Keitel 57; IMT, X, 505.
pages 435–36
Third interview: Schuschnigg, *Austrian*, 25–27.
page 436
"Now you have some idea . . ." Papen 420; Schuschnigg, *Austrian*, 27.
page 436
Hitler notation: Müllern-Schönhausen 162.
pages 436–37
"The Jews were attacking . . ." Schuschnigg, *Brutal*, 225.
page 437
Hitler speech: Gedye 232.
pages 437–38
Yeats-Brown comment: *Living Age*, August 1938, 512–14.
page 438
Gedye account: Gedye 233.
page 438
"should continue to use this method." Schuschnigg, *Brutal*, 230.
pages 438–39
Schuschnigg speech: Gedye 238–39; interview with Schuschnigg, 1971.
page 439
"an indispensable element . . ." Brook-Shepherd 103.
page 439
"Fundamentally, a close understanding . . ." Ibid. 85.

pages 439–40
Ingersoll incident: Toland, *Rising Sun*, 49.

page 440
Schmidt on Henderson: Schmidt 86.

page 440
Henderson-Hitler meeting: N. Henderson 115–16.

page 441
Schuschnigg-Keppler meeting: Schuschnigg, *Brutal*, 250.

page 441
Keppler report: Ibid. 249.

page 442
Starhemberg comment: Starhemberg 272.

page 442
"We have prepared nothing . . ." Shirer, *Rise*, 335.

pages 442–43
Hitler letter to Mussolini: GFP, D., I, #352.

page 443
Schuschnigg letter to Seyss-Inquart: Schuschnigg, *Brutal*, 264.

pages 444–45
Glaise-Horstenau account: IMT, XIV, 131–32.

page 444ff.
Telephone conversations between Berlin and other cities throughout the chapter: Schuschnigg, *Austrian*, Appendix 290ff.

page 446
"professed to be ignorant . . ." Cadogan 60.

page 446
Halifax to Schuschnigg: BFP, 3rd, I, 13.

page 446
"directly or indirectly—in the preparations . . ." Schuschnigg, *Austrian*, 48–49.

pages 446–47
Schuschnigg account: *Austrian*, 48–52; interview with Schuschnigg, 1971.

pages 447–48
Schuschnigg speech: Shirer, *Berlin Diary*, 99; Guido Schmidt Trial Protocols, Nuremberg, 290.

page 448
"Now, get moving!" Grolmann affidavit, quoted in Eichstaedt, *Von Dollfuss zu Hitler* (Wiesbaden, 1955), 411.

page 449
Ems telegram: Papen 429. Papen-Wiedemann: Wiedemann 64 (tr.).

pages 449–50
"Or would you like to go . . ." Schuschnigg, *Austrian*, 54–55.

page 450
Viebahn incident: Keitel 58–59; W. Görlitz, *Keitel* (Göttingen, 1961), 179.

page 450
Hitler proclamation: Santoro 102.

page 451
Guderian comment: Guderian 32.

page 451
Keitel comment: Keitel 59.

page 451
Guderian comment: Guderian 37.
page 452
Hitler to Linge: Linge ⚔21.
page 452
Guderian account: Guderian 33.
pages 452–53
"If the enthusiasm is so great . . ." Brook-Shepherd 193.
page 453
Mussolini telegram: Mussolini 190.
page 453
"Yes, a good political action . . ." Memorandum by Seyss-Inquart, Sept. 9, 1945; ND, 3254-PS.
pages 453–54
Freud story: Ernest Jones 294.
page 454
Gedye account: Gedye 299.
page 454
Telegram to Halifax: BFP, I, 44.
page 455
Huss account: Huss 19–20. IMT, XV, 633.
pages 455–56
On Cardinal Innitzer: Papen 432–33; Schmidt Trial Protocols, op. cit., 383.
page 456
Eva Braun account: Gun, *Eva Braun*, 127–28.
page 456
Lochner letter, Mar. 15, 1938.
page 456
Hitler speech: Baynes 1427.
page 456
Hitler to Reichstag: Santoro 108–10.
page 456
Footnote: Interview with Schuschnigg, 1971.
page 457
Innitzer proclamation: Brook-Shepherd 202.
page 457
Kubizek-Hitler: Kubizek 277–81.
page 458
"For me, this is the proudest . . ." Baynes 1459.

Chapter Seventeen. "ON THE RAZOR'S EDGE"

page 460
Linge account: Linge ⚔22.
page 461
Baur account: Section on Baur in Ziegler; interview with Baur, 1970.
page 461
Ciano account; Ciano diary, May 7, 1938; interview with Dollmann, 1971.
page 461
Lochner account: *What About Germany?*, II.
page 462
"was extremely successful in melting . . ." Dollmann 110.

page 462
Ciano account: Ciano diary, May 5, 1938.
pages 462–63
Chamberlain letter, Mar. 20, 1938; Private Collection to be available at Birmingham University Library.
page 463
"even if France does not do so . . ." Louis Fischer 311.
pages 463–64
"It depends upon you, Excellency . . ." Wheeler-Bennett, *Munich*, 57.
page 464
Henderson-Ribbentrop: GFP, D. 11, 317.
page 464
Weizsäcker comment: Weizsäcker 135–36.
pages 464–65
May 28 conference: *Nazi Conspiracy and Aggression*, V, 3037-PS, 743–44; Wiedemann Testimony, Nuremberg, Oct. 24, 1945, 3; Braddick 22.
page 465
Beck memorandum: O'Neill 155–56.
page 465
Keitel comment: Keitel 63–64.
page 465
"to intimidate the Czechs by means . . ." GFP, II, 359.
pages 465–66
"Here the view prevails . . ." Ibid. 363.
pages 466–67
Wiedemann account: Wiedemann 94 (tr.).
page 467
Hesse account: HH 40–51; letter, Hesse, 1974.
page 467
Beck memorandum: O'Neill 157–58; Wolfgang Förster, *Ein General Kämpft gegen den Krieg* (Munich, 1949), 98–102.
page 468
Maisky to Halifax: McSherry I, 63.
pages 468–69
Kleist-Schmenzin-Vansittart meeting: BFP, 3 II-683–86.
page 469
Henderson telegram: Ibid. 118.
pages 469–70
Schwerin von Krosigk letter to Hitler: SvK to author.
page 470
"Every generation must experience . . ." Wiedemann testimony at Nuremberg, Sept. 28, 1945, 23; Wiedemann 97 (tr.).
pages 470–71
Henderson letter: BFP, II, 257.
page 471
"You know I am like a wanderer . . ." Frank 320.
page 471
"But its success is nevertheless . . ." GFP, II, 729.
pages 471–72
Keitel-Brauchitsch: Keitel 69–70.
page 472
Jodl comment: Jodl's diary, Sept. 10, 12, 13, 1938; Warlimont 116.

page 472
Göring speech: Nogueres 107.
page 472
Shirer account: *Berlin Diary*, 125.
page 472
Chamberlain to journalists: BFP, II, 680–82.
page 472
Chamberlain letter: Feiling 360.
page 473
Mussolini quote: Nogueres 116.
page 473
Chamberlain to Daladier: BFP, II, 314.
page 473
"I fell from Heaven!" L. B. Namier, *Diplomatique prelude* (London, 1948),
    35.
page 474
Mussolini quote: Ciano diary, Sept. 14, 1938.
page 474
Chamberlain on BBC: Nogueres 124.
pages 474–76
Hitler-Chamberlain meeting: Schmidt 92–93; Feiling 366–67.
page 476
Masefield poem: London *Times*, Sept. 16, 1938.
page 476
Roosevelt quote: Ickes diary, Sept. 18, 1938.
page 476
Chamberlain-Daladier: BFP, II, 387–96.
pages 476–77
Chamberlain letter: Feiling 368.
page 477
Newton report: BFP, II, 416–17.
page 477
Hodža to Lacroix: Nogueres 148.
pages 477–78
Newton report: BFP, II, 425.
page 478
Czech communiqué: Nogueres 155.
page 478
Chamberlain to journalists: MacLeod 242.
pages 478–79
First Chamberlain-Hitler meeting: Schmidt 96–97; GFP, II, 876; BFP, II,
    472.
page 480
On Hitler's outbursts: Wiedemann 126 (tr.).
pages 480–81
Schmidt account: Schmidt 99–100.
pages 481–82
Second Chamberlain-Hitler meeting: Schmidt 100–3; BFP, II, 502; MacLeod
    246; GFP, II, 907–8.
page 482
Chamberlain to cabinet: CAB 23/95, 42 (38); BFP, II, 510; Parkinson
    41–42.

page 483
Sunday cabinet meeting: Parkinson 43; CAB 23/95, 43 (38); Barnett 540.
page 483
Daladier quote: Parkinson 47.
page 483
Chamberlain to cabinet: Parkinson 48.
page 483
Footnote: Colin Cross, *Adolf Hitler* (London, 1973), 268.
pages 483–84
Hitler-Wilson meeting: Schmidt 103; GFP, II, 555–57.
page 484
Hitler speech: Prange 114–15; Parkinson 52.
page 484
Bullitt phone call: Bullitt 296.
page 485
Wilson-Hitler meeting: BFP, II, 565; Schmidt 104–5; Bullock 410; GFP, II, 965.
page 485
Shirer comments: *Berlin Diary*, 141, 143.
page 485
Wiedemann-Schaub: Wiedemann 101 (tr.).
page 485
"I can't wage war . . ." Fest, *Face*, 43.
pages 485–86
Chamberlain broadcast: Feiling 372; Nogueres 212–13.
page 486
Hitler letter: BFP, II, 578.
page 486
Chamberlain reply: Feiling 373.
page 486
Chamberlain letter to Mussolini: Feiling 373.
page 486
Weizsäcker-Ribbentrop: Weizsäcker 153–54.
page 487
"You need not say a word more . . ." N. Henderson 167.
page 487
Schmidt account: Schmidt 105–7.
page 487
Wiedemann account: Wiedemann 104 (tr.).
page 488
Henderson account: N. Henderson 168–69.
page 488
House of Commons scene: MacLeod 249–50.
pages 488–89
Bullitt letter: Bullitt 297.
page 489
Beneš message: BFP, II, 604.
page 489
Mussolini quote: Ciano diary, Sept. 29–30, 1938.

page 489
"I have no need to mobilize . . ." I. Kirkpatrick, *Mussolini*, 383.
page 489
Chamberlain to journalists: Nogueres 250–51.
page 490
"Our time is too valuable . . ." Schmidt 110.
page 491
"That was my great day . . ." Interview with Dollmann, 1971.
page 491
Dollmann account: Dollmann 131–32; interview with Dollmann, 1971.
page 492
Göring comment: G. M. Gilbert, *Nuremberg*, 88.
page 492
Shirer comment: Shirer, *Rise*, 418.
page 492
François-Poncet account: *Fateful*, 273.
pages 492–93
Chamberlain-Hitler: Schmidt 112–13; Feiling 376–77.
page 493
"I gave him a noseful . . ." Linge ⚡13.
page 493
Hitler to Engel: Engel 40–41.
page 493
Letter from King to Chamberlain: Feiling 378–79.
page 493
Chamberlain letter: Feiling 377.
page 493
London *Times* comment: Oct. 1, 1938.
page 493
Chamberlain at 10 Downing St.: Feiling 381.
page 494
Syrovy announcement: Gatzke 214.
page 494
Kaiser letter: Nelson 447.
page 494
Wiedemann account: Wiedemann 108 (tr.).
page 494
Chamberlain letter: Feiling 377.
page 495
Duff Cooper quote: Parkinson 69.
page 495
Churchill quote: Ibid. 70.
page 495
Chamberlain to Hitler: Irving, *Breach*, 50.
page 496
François-Poncet comment: *Fateful*, 275.
pages 496–97
François-Poncet report: *French Yellow Book*, 22–26.
page 497
Freud quote: Blanton 101–2.
pages 497–98
Jung quotes: Knickerbocker 45–56.

Chapter Eighteen. CRYSTAL NIGHT

pages 501–2
Schacht conference, Aug. 20, 1935: ND, NG-4067.
page 502
Streicher quote: speech before German Labor Front mass meeting, Oct. 4, 1935; ND, M-35.
page 502
Fromm quote: Fromm 235–36.
page 502
Grynszpan quote: Arthur Morse, *While Six Million Died* (New York, 1967), 222.
page 503
Himmler memorandum: Affidavit by Schallermeier, July 5, 1946, ND, SS(A) 5.
page 503
Himmler speech: Bradley Smith and Agnes Peterson 24–49.
page 503
Heydrich teletyped orders: ND, PS-3051.
page 503
"must have been exceeded considerably." Levin 80.
pages 503–4
Tolischus story: New York *Times,* Nov. 11, 1938.
page 504
Frau Funk account: Affidavit by Louise Funk, Nov. 5, 1945, Funk-3.
page 504
Göring testimony: IMT, IX, 277.
page 504
Hitler to Frau Troost: Interview with Gerdy Troost, 1971.
pages 504–5
Hesse account: HH 59–61.
page 505
Footnote: Hassell 123.
page 505
Footnote: Gutterer affidavit, signed in Neuengamme, Oct. 19, 1947; notarized by Moritz Augustus von Schirrmeister.
pages 505–6
Göring quote: Levin 87.
page 506
Hauptmann quote: *Die Welt,* Nov. 10, 1962.
page 506
Dieckhoff report: GFP, D, IV, ⋕501.
page 506
Roosevelt news conference: Morse, op. cit., 231.
page 507
Hitler at the Bruckmanns': Hassell 28.
pages 507–8
Ilse Braun account: Gun, *Eva Braun,* 104–5.
pages 508–9
Schacht account: *Account,* 134–37.
page 509
Hitler-Wiedemann; Wiedemann 146–47 (tr.).

pages 509–10
Piechler story: Interview with Gerdy Troost, 1971.
page 510
Hitler to Chvalkovsky: *French Yellow Book*, 210; Krausnick 44.
pages 510–11
Foreign Ministry circular: GFP, IV, 932–33.
page 511
Hitler speech: Baynes 740–41.
page 511
"During this month he plans . . ." Ciano 3.
page 512
Cadogan comment: Cadogan 151–52.
page 512
Henderson report: BFP, 3rd, IV, 165.
page 512
Henderson on Hitler: N. Henderson 209.
pages 512–13
Newton report: BFP, IV, 183–84.
page 513
Henderson letter: Ibid. 210–11.
page 513
Henderson telephone call: Ibid. 223.
page 514
"When I get worked up . . ." Schmidt 236.
page 514
Tiso-Hitler: BFP, IV, 439; GFP, D, IV, 243–45.
pages 514–15
Chamberlain quote: BFP, IV, 250.
pages 515–17
Hacha-Hitler: Schmidt 122; GFP, IV, 263–69; HSC 211; *French Yellow Book*, 96.
page 517
Footnote: IMT, IX, 303–4.
page 517
Hitler to secretaries: Zoller 91–92.
page 517
Hitler to Hoffmann: Hoffmann 95.
page 518
Kennan account: *Memoirs*, 98.
page 518
Henderson phone calls: BFP, IV, 255, 257.
page 518
Henderson letter: Ibid. 595.
page 518
Hitler to Linge: Linge #14.
pages 518–19
Kempka account: Interview, 1971.
page 519
"The Italians will laugh at me," Ciano 44: Bullock 433.
page 519
"I knew it. In fourteen days . . ." Erich Kordt, *Nicht aus den Akten* (Stuttgart, 1950), 298.

page 520
Halifax quote: BFP, IV, 271.
page 520
"has so lost its fibre . . ." *British Blue Book*, 5.

Chapter Nineteen. THE FOX AND THE BEAR

page 521
Phipps note: BFP, IV, 596.
page 523
"You want to negotiate . . ." *Polish White Book*, No. 64.
page 523
Chamberlain statement: Bullock 444.
pages 523–24
Hitler speech: Prange 303–4.
page 524
Canaris-Hitler: Gisevius 363
page 524
Hitler to Keitel: Keitel 84.
page 525
Footnote: Höhne, *Order*, 232.
page 526
Kleist account: Kleist 15.
pages 526–27
Merekalov-Weizsäcker: NSR 2.
page 527
Hitler to Gafencu: Grégoire Gafencu, *Derniers jours de l'Europe* (Paris, 1946), 89.
page 528
Song: Gregor Ziemer, *Education for Death* (London and New York, 1941), 120
page 528
Talking dog: *Schwarzes Korps*, July 31, 1935; Grunberger 86.
page 528
Bishop of Mainz quote: *Amtsblatt Mainz*, No. 7, Apr. 17, 1939.
page 528
Footnote: New York *Post*, 1974; correspondence with Senator Cranston, 1975.
page 529
Hitler speech: Prange 306; Shirer, *Rise*, 471–75.
page 530
"like a cannon ball." A. Rossi, *Deux ans d'alliance germano-soviétique* (Paris, 1949), 27.
page 530
Hitler-Hilger: Kleist 21–22; Gustav Hilger and Alfred Meyer, *The Incompatible Allies* (New York, 1953), 293–97; McSherry I, 149–50.
page 531
Hitler conference: GFP, D, VI, 574–80; Shirer, *End*, 233.

page 532
"sell more dearly its own goods." McSherry I, 153.

page 533
Ribbentrop instructions, May 26, 1939: Louis Fischer 337–38. This watershed message, not published in any collection of official documents, was discovered in 1966 by Fischer in the German Foreign Office archives in Bonn.

page 533
Message to Schulenburg: NSR 5.

page 533
Halifax to Maisky: CAB 23/100, Cabinet 33 (39).

page 533
Mussolini letter to Hitler, May 30, 1939: Deakin 8.

page 534
Hitler-Kubizek meeting: Kubizek 287–89.

page 535
Molotov-Schulenburg meeting, Aug. 3, 1939; NSR 41.

page 536
Schnurre to Astakhov: NSR 45.

page 536
Hitler to Speer: Speer, *Inside*, 161.

pages 536–37
Hitler-Burckhardt meeting: Burckhardt 378–88.

pages 537–38
Hesse account: HH 71–74; interview with Hesse, 1971.

page 538
Ribbentrop-Ciano meeting: Wiskemann 191–92.

pages 538–39
Ciano-Hitler meetings: Dollmann 168; Schmidt 132–33; Wiskemann 194–98; Ciano 119–20.

page 539
Hesse-Ribbentrop meeting: HH 75.

page 540
Ribbentrop to Schulenburg: NSR 63.

pages 540–41
Trade agreement: NSR 83.

page 541
"I have them!" Speer, *Playboy*, 88.

pages 541–42
Hoffmann account: Hoffmann 102–3.

page 542
"one of the extraordinary figures . . ." HSC 38.

page 542
"If Stalin did commit a bank robbery . . ." Hitler to Baur: Baur section in Ziegler; interview with Baur, 1970.

page 542
"In actual fact, he identifies himself . . ." HSC 190–91.

page 543
This is not a verbatim account of the August 22 conference but based on notes taken by several officers present. GFP, D, VII, 200–6, 557–59; Shirer, *End*, 252–55.

page 543
Göring leads applause: IMT, IX, 492.

pages 544–45
Kleist quote: Kleist 35.

page 545
Chamberlain letter to Hitler: BFP, 3rd, VII, 171.

pages 545–46
Hitler-Henderson meeting: GFP, VII, 210–13; Weizsäcker 203.

page 546
Second Hitler-Henderson meeting: BFP, VII, 201–2; GFP, VII, 214.

page 546
"Odd Moscow customs." J. von Ribbentrop, *Memoirs*, 111.

pages 546–47
Ribbentrop-Stalin meeting: Ibid. 111–13; J. von Ribbentrop, *De Londres à Moscou* (Paris, 1954), 147; NSR 72; Schmidt 137; interview with Richard Schulze, 1971; GFP, VII, 228.

page 548
Hitler to Bormann: TAH 99–100.

page 548
"We've won!" Dietrich 64.

pages 548–49
Speer comment; Hitler quote: Speer, *Inside*, 161

Chapter Twenty. "A CALAMITY WITHOUT PARALLEL IN HISTORY"

page 550
Henderson report: BFP, VII, 212–13.

page 551
Hiranuma announcement: Toland, *Rising*, 59.

page 551
"ingrown and Jewish . . ." Delmer, *Trail*, 386.

page 551
"The signing of the pact . . ." Hoffmann 113.

page 551
"My servants and *my* house . . ." Zoller 141.

page 552
Schmidt account: Schmidt 142.

page 552
"to make a move toward England . . ." GFP, VII, 279.

page 552
Henderson-Hitler meeting: Ibid. 280–81; Schmidt 143.

pages 552–53
Mackensen report: GFP, VII, 293.

page 553
"military supplies and raw materials . . ." Ibid. 285–86.

pages 553–54
Schmidt account: Schmidt 145–46.

page 554
Hitler-Attolico: GFP, VII, 286.

page 554
Hitler to Keitel: IMT, X, 514.

page 554
Engel comments: Engel 59–61.

page 554
Schmundt to Warlimont: Warlimont 3.
page 555
Dahlerus phone call to Göring: Dahlerus 53.
page 555
"Why, at once, before hostilities begin." Wiskemann 206.
page 556
Hitler to Mussolini: GFP, VII, 314.
page 556
Hitler to Mussolini, Ibid. 232.
pages 556–57
Dahlerus-Hitler: Dahlerus 60–62.
page 558
Hitler to Daladier: GFP, VII, 357–59.
page 559
Dahlerus-Chamberlain: Dahlerus 72–73.
pages 560–61
Henderson-Hitler: GFP, VII, 332; N. Henderson 276; BFP, VII, 351, 381–82, 388.
page 561
Engel comments: Engel 61.
pages 561–62
Henderson-Hitler: N. Henderson 280; Schmidt 149; BFP, VII, 393.
page 562
Dahlerus-Göring: Dahlerus 90–94.
page 563
"They would sooner fight . . ." BFP, VII, 395.
page 563
Dahlerus-Chamberlain: Dahlerus 98–99.
page 563
Schmidt comment: Schmidt 150.
page 564
Kleist-Schmenzin story: BFP, VII, 415–17.
pages 564–65
Henderson-Ribbentrop: Schmidt 151–53; J. von Ribbentrop, *Memoirs*, 124.
page 566
Wiretap: Irving, *Breach*, 113, 32.
page 566
"get ahead of the clock . . ." BFP, VII, 442.
pages 566–67
Berndt story: HH 82–83.
page 567
Directive #1: HWD 3–4.
page 567
Operation Himmler: Naujocks affidavit, ND 2751-PS; Höhne, *Order*, 264–65.
page 567
Lipski-Ribbentrop: Schmidt 154; GFP, VII, 463.
page 568
Hitler-Attolico: Ibid. 465.

page 568
Polish broadcast: *German White Book* (German Library of Information, New York, 1939), 35–36.
page 568
"a pact with Satan . . ." Fest, *Hitler*, 585.
page 568
"The English will leave the Poles in the lurch . . ." Interviews with Engel, Below, Puttkamer, 1970–71.
page 568
"it disturbed the formation of his intuition." Irving, *Breach*, 39.
pages 568–69
"England is bluffing . . ." Hoffmann 115.
page 569
"Now you've got your damned war!" Albert Kesselring, A *Soldier's Record* (New York, 1954), 37.
page 569
Hitler to Mussolini: GFP, VII, 483.
pages 569–70
Eva Braun quote: Gun, *Eva Braun*, 151–52.
page 570
Lawrence quote: D. H. Lawrence, *Movements in European History* (London, 1922), 306.
pages 570–71
"his policy has broken down . . ." BFP, VII, 517.
page 571
Dahlerus-Göring: Dahlerus 119.
page 571
Ribbentrop-Hitler-Abetz: Kleist 70.
pages 571–72
Raczynski account: Raczynski 25–26.
page 572
"We only pity you people . . ." GFP, VII, 521.
page 573
Chamberlain speech: Feiling 415.
page 573
Hesse-Hewel: HH 84–85; Hesse, *Das Spiel*, Chap. 4; interview with Hesse, 1970.
On Hitler offer: Annelies von Ribbentrop 380; interview with Frau von Ribbentrop, 1971.
page 573
Nicolson account: Nicolson, *Diaries and Letters*, 1930–1939 (London, 1969), 412.
pages 573–74
Chamberlain speech: BFP, VII, 521.
page 574
Greenwood quote: Parkinson 215.
page 574
Hesse-Wilson: HH 85–88; interview with Hesse, 1971.
pages 574–75
"I therefore suggest that Sir Nevile Henderson . . ." CAB 23/100, Cabinet 49 (39); Parkinson 216.

page 575
Henderson-Schmidt meeting: Schmidt 157.
page 576
Schmidt at Chancellery: Schmidt 158.
page 576
Dahlerus-Göring: Dahlerus 129–30.
pages 576–77
Henderson-Ribbentrop meeting: N. Henderson 300.
page 577
Chamberlain broadcast: Feiling 415–16; Colvin, *Chamberlain Cabinet,* 253–54.
page 577
Ribbentrop to Schulenburg: GFP, VII, 541.
page 577
Hitler to Mussolini: Ibid. 538–39.
page 578
"Now, all my work crumbles . . ." Zoller 175.
page 578
Hitler to Linge: Linge #15.

Chapter Twenty-one. VICTORY IN THE WEST

page 581
Hitler motto: Zoller 156–57.
page 582
Hesse-Hewel: Hesse, *Das Spiel,* Chap. 5; interview with Hesse, 1971.
page 583
Ribbentrop to Schmidt: Schmidt 162.
page 584
"the Polish national problem . . ." GFP, D, VIII, 161.
page 584
Ribbentrop-Stalin meeting: J. von Ribbentrop, *Memoirs,* 129–31; GFP, VIII, 943.
page 584
"his intention of settling questions . . ." J. von Ribbentrop, *Memoirs,* 129.
page 584
Heydrich to SS commanders, Sept. 21, 1939: ND, EC-307, PS-3362.
page 585
Hitler speech at Danzig: Irving, *Hitler,* 28.
page 585
Footnote: Interviews with Richard Schulze, Helmuth Fuchs, and Herbert Meyer, 1971.
pages 585–86
Hewel to Hesse: Hesse, *Das Spiel,* Chap. 5.
page 586
"The British can have peace . . ." GFP, VIII, 140–45.
page 586
"clearly taken aback." Warlimont 37.
page 586
Cadogan on Dahlerus: Cadogan 220.

pages 586–87
Hitler speech: Prange 173; Shirer, *Rise,* 641–42.
pages 587–88
Hitler memorandum: *Nazi Conspiracy and Aggression,* VII, 800–14.
page 588
Footnote: Remak 113–14.
pages 588–89
"My attempts to make peace . . ." IMT, IX, 50; interview with Milch, 1971.
page 589
Müller account: Interview with Müller, 1963.
page 590
Brauchitsch-Hitler meeting: Halder Diary, Nov. 4–5, 1939; Brauchitsch testimony, IMT, XX, 575; Wheeler-Bennett, *Nemesis,* 471.
page 590
Krafft warning: E. Howe, *Urania's,* 169.
page 591
Hitler-Frau Troost meeting: Interview with Gerdy Troost, 1971.
page 591
Footnote: Interviews with Sir Oswald Mosley and Lady Diana Mosley,
   1971–72.
pages 591–92
Elser account: Record of interrogation, *Der Stern,* May 10, 1966.
page 592
Hitler at Bürgerbräukeller: interviews with Kempka and Wünsche, 1971.
page 592
Footnote: Interview with Hein Ruck, 1971.
page 593
"Now I am completely content!" Zoller 204. There is conflicting evidence on
   when Hitler learned of the bombing. Höhne wrote it was at the Munich
   railroad station (*Order,* 286). Herta Schneider and Kempka agreed it was
   near Augsburg (Interviews, 1971).
page 593
"What idiot conducted this interrogation?" *Schellenberg Memoirs* (London,
   1961), 110.
page 594
Official version: Wheeler-Bennett, *Nemesis,* 481.
page 594
Cardinal Faulhaber story: Lewy 311.
page 594
Hitler comment on Pope: Frank 408.
page 594
Hitler to Hoffmann: Hoffmann 119.
pages 594–95
Nov. 23 conference: Shirer, *End,* 256–62; GFP, VIII, 439–46; IMT, IX, 311;
   Warlimont 58–59; interview with Warlimont, 1971.
pages 595–96
"for the first time he desired German defeat." Ciano 183.
page 596
Footnote: GFP, VIII, 683.
page 596
Mussolini letter to Hitler: Ibid. 607–9.
page 597
Shirer comment: *Berlin,* 234.

page 597
Sir Kingsley Wood quote: John Lukacs, *The Last European War* (Garden City, 1975).
page 597
Goebbels' propaganda methods: Interview with Naumann, 1971.
pages 597–98
Goebbels' instructions: Boelcke 8.
page 598
Diesing story: Irving, *Rise*, 83.
page 599
"I doubt very much . . ." CAB 65/5, War Cabinet 30 (40).
page 599
War Directive: HWD 23–24.
page 599
"most daring and most important . . ." Rich I, 142.
page 599
Soviet mission to Berlin: Interview with Schlotterer, 1971; GFP, VIII, 722.
page 600
Trotsky quote: Higgins 34.
page 600
"The agreement means a wide-open door . . ." GFP, VIII, 817.
page 600
Hitler on Stalin: Zoller 178.
pages 600–1
Hitler-Mussolini meeting: Schmidt 173; Ciano 223–24; Dollmann 183.
page 601
Hitler-Schirach: Schirach 171–72.
page 602
"You Germans have done the incredible again!" ND, 3596-PS; Shirer, *Rise*, 700.
page 602
Hitler-Brauchitsch: Assmann; Warlimont 77–78.
page 603
"beside himself with joy." Warlimont 79; interview with Warlimont, 1971.
page 603
Hitler on Milch: Irving, *Breach*, 88.
pages 603–4
Hitler's plan: Interviews with Wünsche, Below, Puttkamer, Manstein, 1970–71; Dietrich, *Hitler*, 81; Keitel 102–3.
page 604
"The swine has gone . . ." Allen Dulles, *Germany's Underground* (New York, 1947), 58–61; interview with Dulles, 1963.
page 605
"I was filled with rage." HSC 93.
page 605
"When the news came that the enemy . . ." Ibid. 94.
page 605, 607
"I have always said . . ." London *Times*, Nov. 7, 1938.
page 607
Goebbels conference: Boelcke 40.
page 607
"This raid on the night of the 11th May . . ." F. J. P. Veale, *Advance Towards Barbarism* (Appleton, Wisc., 1953), 120.

page 608
Goebbels conference: Boelcke 42.
page 608
"This one here is yours . . ." Gerd von Klaus, *Krupps, the Story of an Industrial Empire* (London, 1954), 415.
page 608
"Talks in words of appreciation . . ." Jodl diary, May 20, 1940.
page 609
Göring incident: Engel 80; Irving, *Rise*, 89–90.
pages 609–10
"Our left wing, consisting of armor . . ." Halder diary, May 24, 1940.
page 610
"Only fish bait will reach . . ." Engel 81.
page 611
"It is always good to let . . ." Ansel, *Hitler Confronts*, 87.
page 611
"Churchill was quite unable to appreciate . . ." TAH 96.
page 611
Puttkamer on Hitler: Interview, 1971.
page 611
Hitler to Frau Troost: Interview with Gerdy Troost, 1971; correspondence, 1975.
page 611
François-Poncet on Hitler: Interview, 1971.
page 611
"She lost her nerve . . ." Engel 85.
pages 611–12
On Unity Mitford: Interviews with Sir Oswald Mosley and Lady Diana Mosley, 1971–72; Oswald Mosley 411–12.
page 612
"I have decided to stay . . ." *Belgian Rapport*, Annexes, 69–75.
page 613
"I have quite often in the past . . ." Engel 82.
page 613
Warlimont account: Warlimont 102; interview, 1971.
page 614
Hitler's "jig": Interview with Walter Frentz, 1971; correspondence, 1975; Ansel, *Hitler Confronts*, 92; Hoffmann 121; Zoller 92; *Esquire*, Oct. 1958.
page 614
Mussolini-Hitler meeting: Ciano 265–66.
page 614
Mussolini-Hitler autographs on postcard: Müllern-Schönhausen 159.
page 614
"In truth the Duce fears that . . ." Ciano 266.
page 615
Shirer account: *Berlin*, 422.
page 615
"We will destroy everything . . ." Linge #17.
pages 615–16
French surrender: Schmidt 181–83.
pages 616–17
Breker account: Breker 151–67; correspondence, 1975.

page 617
"Now your work begins . . ." Interview with Giesler, 1971; correspondence,
    1975.
page 617
Footnote: Interview with Giesler, 1971.
page 618
Hitler to Speer: Speer, *Inside*, 172.
page 618
"It was a great responsibility," Breker 167; Speer, *Inside*, 170–71.

Chapter Twenty-two. "EV'N VICTORS BY VICTORY ARE UNDONE"

page 619
Hitler to Hoffmann: Hoffmann 122.
page 620
Hitler to Hewel: HH 114.
page 621
Halder diary: July 13, 1940.
page 621
Ribbentrop to Schmidt: Schmidt 185.
pages 621–22
Delmer account: *Black Boomerang*, 10–11.
page 622
Shirer account: *Berlin Diary*, 453
page 622
Dieckhoff report: GFP, D, X, 260.
page 622
Footnote: Ibid. 298.
pages 622–23
Conference, July 21: Ansel, *Hitler Confronts*, 163–65. Halder diary, July 22,
    1940.
page 623
Orwell review: *New English Weekly*, Mar. 21, 1940.
page 624
Kubizek account: Kubizek 292.
pages 624–25
Jodl-Warlimont: Warlimont 111–12; interview, 1971; Ansel, op. cit., 181.
pages 625–26
Conference, July 31: GFP, X, 370–74; Ansel, op. cit., 184–89; Shirer, *Rise*,
    764–66.
page 626
Directives: HWD 37–38; *Führer Conferences on Naval Affairs*, 82–83.
page 627
"Neither type of fighter . . ." Irving, *Rise*, 101.
pages 627–28
Shirer comment: *Berlin Diary*, 486.
page 628
Hitler speech: Ibid. 496; Ansel, op. cit., 283.
page 628
Raeder-Hitler conference: Report of CIC Navy to Führer, dated Sept. 7, 1940;
    Ansel, op. cit., 284–86.

page 629
Göring broadcast: Ibid. 250.
page 629
Churchill speech: Churchill, *Their Finest Hour* (New York, Bantam), 1962, 282.
page 630
Hitler to Puttkamer: Interview with Puttkamer, 1971.
page 630
Churchill conference: Brown 41.
page 631
Hitler-Serrano Suñer meeting: GFP, D, XI, 93–98.
page 631
Hitler letter to Franco: Ibid. 106–8.
page 634
Ribbentrop letter to Stalin: Ibid. 296–97; Toland, *Rising*, 64.
page 634
Hitler-Mussolini meeting: Ansel, *Hitler and Middle Sea*, 33; GFP, XI, 250–51.
pages 635–38
Hitler-Franco meeting: HSC 532; Schmidt 193–97; Hills 345, 342; GFP, XI, 371–79; interviews with Puttkamer, Schulze (1971) and Serrano Suñer (1963); Linge ⚡19; Keitel 126.
page 639
Franco to Pétain: Francisco Franco, *Discursos y mensajes del Jefe del Estado, 1951–54* (Madrid, 1955), 41.
pages 639–40
Hitler-Pétain meeting: Hamilton 231–32; Griffiths 271.
page 640
Ciano comment: Ciano 305; Martin van Creveld, *Hitler's Strategy 1940–1941: The Balkan Clue* (London, 1973), 43–47.
page 640
Ribbentrop quote: Schmidt 199.
page 641
"Ribbentrop approved this . . ." Weizsäcker 244.
page 641
Engel account: Engel 88.
pages 641–42
Mussolini meeting: Keitel 126–27; Linge ⚡19; Ciano 300; Ciano Minute, Oct. 28, 1940; Wiskemann 283; GFP, XI, 411–22.

Chapter Twenty-three. "THE WORLD WILL HOLD ITS BREATH"

pages 643–44
Ribbentrop-Molotov meeting: Schmidt 210–13; GFP, XI, 537–38.
pages 644–45
Hitler-Molotov meeting: Ibid. 542–61; Schmidt 213–19.
pages 645–46
Molotov-Ribbentrop meeting: GFP, XI, 562–70; Louis Fischer 431–32.
page 646
Hitler to Bormann: TAH 65–66.
page 646
"more godlike than human." Public Record Office, London, FO 800/316, H/XV/212.

page 647
Hitler-Serrano Suñer meeting: GFP, XI, 598–606; Hills 348; HSC 567.
page 647
Footnote: Interview with Marquis de Valdeglesias, 1971.
page 648
Franco part Jewish: Interview with Otto Skorzeny, 1971; Hoare 31.
page 648
"Only completely ossified . . ." Halder 41.
page 649
"Hegemony over Europe . . ." McSherry II, 191.
page 649
Hitler speech: Prange 32–33.
page 649
Goebbels conference: Boelcke 110, 112.
page 649
Directive: HWD 49–50.
page 650
Hitler to Bormann: TAH 17.
paages 650–51
Hitler speech: Flannery 107–9; Hitler, *My New Order* (New York, 1941), 901–24.
page 651
"When Barbarossa commences . . ." ND, 872-PS; Shirer, *Rise*, 822.
page 651
"struck a blow at the belief . . ." TAH 97–98.
page 652
Lochner account: *What About Germany?*, 122.
pages 652–53
Hitler and Yugoslavia: GFP, D, XII, 364, 369–75; Weizsäcker 25; Keitel 138–39; Jodl testimony at Nuremberg, June 5, 1946, 422.
page 654
Matsuoka to Hitler: Schmidt 227.
page 654
Matsuoka to Göring and Ribbentrop: Toland, *Rising*, 65–66, GFP, XII, 376–83, 386–94.
page 654
Hitler letter to Mussolini: Ibid. 397–98.
page 655
"I was haunted . . ." TAH 97.
page 655
Hitler lecture: Keitel 134–36. Halder affidavit at Nuremberg, Nov. 22, 1945; Warlimont 160–61; Halder diary, Mar. 30, 1941.
page 657
"Thus, the (Jewish) wife . . ." GFP, XII, 446.
page 657
Stalin notation: David Dallin, *Die Sowjetspionage* (Cologne, 1956); Carell, *Hitler Moves*, 59.
page 657
Matsuoka-Stalin: Toland, *Rising*, 66–67.
page 657
Stalin to Schulenburg: GFP, XII, 537.

page 658
"wanted to try one more . . ." J. von Ribbentrop, *Memoirs*, 152.
page 658
"I do not intend a war . . ." GFP, XII, 66–69.
page 658
Footnote: Letters from Trevor-Roper and Lee, 1975.
page 659
Jodl to Warlimont: Warlimont 140.
page 659
"had succeeded in infecting . . ." Guderian, 125.
page 659
Hitler to Hanfstaengl: *Out of the Strong*, 34.
page 660
"I was confronted by a very hard . . ." Hess 14.
pages 660–61
Background information on Hess: Interview with Hildegard Fath, 1971.
page 661
Hess letter to wife: Hess 138.
pages 661–62
Events of May 10: Hess 19–21, 31–37; correspondence with Frau Hess, 1975.
page 662
Engel account: Engel 103–4.
page 662
"Oh, my God, my God!" Speer interrogation, June–July 1945, Field Intelligence Agency; Bodenschatz interrogation, May 30, 1945.
page 662
Hess letter: Hess 27; Dietrich, *Hitler*, 62–63.
page 662
"I hope he falls into the sea!" Schmidt 233.
page 663
Fath account: Interview, 1971.
page 663
Frau Hess account: Hess 21–22; correspondence with Frau Hess, 1975.
page 663
"well, Hess or no Hess . . ." Douglas-Hamilton 163.
page 663
"As is well known in party . . ." Ibid. 197–98.
pages 663–64
Goebbels conference: Boelcke 162.
page 664
Frank account: Frank 411.
page 664
Hess interrogation: Douglas-Hamilton 167.
pages 664–65
Haushofer story: Interview with Heinz Haushofer, 1971; correspondence, 1975.
page 665
"The Jewish tainted professor . . ." Engel 105.
page 665
Engel quote: Idem.
page 665
Herbert poem: "Let Us Be Glum."

page 665
Ciano comment: Ciano 451.
page 666
Hitler did not think Hess mad: Interview with Schwaebe and Florian, 1971.
page 666
Hitler to Frau Bruckmann: Hess 26–27.
page 666
"True, I achieved nothing . . ." Ibid. 138.
page 667
Molotov-Schulenburg meeting: GFP, XII, 870.
page 668
"This stroke would be more deadly . . ." Shirer, *Rise,* 829.
page 668
Hitler-Oshima meeting: Interview with Oshima, 1966.
page 668
"I cannot demand that my generals . . ." Jodl testimony at Nuremberg, June
    3, 1946, 308.
page 668
"These commissars are the originators . . ." Krausnick 519–20.
page 669
Tass communiqué: Werth, *Russia,* 125–26.
page 669
"No use beating an alarm." A. M. Nekrich, *June 22, 1941* (Moscow, 1965),
    144–45.
page 669
Hitler-Frank meeting: Frank 408, 414.
page 670
Cripps to Maisky: Maisky 156.
page 670
Hitler letter to Mussolini: GFP, XII, 1066–69.
page 670
Molotov to Schulenburg: GFP, XII, 1072.
pages 670–71
Hitler to troops: Carell, *Hitler Moves,* 4–5.
page 671
"that some tremendous action . . ." Dietrich, *Hitler,* 66.
page 671
"In three months at the latest." Interview with Puttkamer, 1971.
page 671
Mussolini to Ciano: Ciano 372.
pages 671–72
Molotov-Schulenburg meeting: Winston Churchill, *The Grand Alliance*
    (Boston, 1950), 366–67.
page 672
Ribbentrop-Dekanozov meeting: Schmidt 234.
page 672
Hitler's message: Ansel, *Hitler and Middle Sea,* 441.

Chapter Twenty-four. "A DOOR INTO A DARK, UNSEEN ROOM"

page 673
Goebbels conference: Boelcke 176.

page 673
Olga Tschechowa account: Interview, 1971.
page 674
Churchill quotes: *Grand Alliance*, 370–72.
page 674
Kennan note: *Memoirs*, 133.
page 674
Roosevelt quotes: James M. Burns, *Roosevelt: the Soldier of Freedom* (New York, 1970), 103.
pages 674–75
"high-handed gallantry . . ." Friedländer, *Pius*, 78.
page 675
"We have only to kick . . ." Bullock 587.
page 675
"At the beginning of each campaign . . ." Zoller 160.
page 675
Hitler to Dietrich: Dietrich, *Hitler*, 89.
page 675
"to all intents and purposes . . ." Warlimont 180.
page 676
"Contrary to the opinions . . ." Leo Alexander, *Journal of Criminal Law and Criminology*, Sept.–Oct. 1948, 315.
page 676
"Stange is the calmness . . ." ND, RSHA IV-A-1, Operational Report, Sept. 12, 1941, No. 3154.
pages 676–77
Himmler in Minsk: Bach-Zelewski, *Aufbau*, Aug. 23, 1946.
page 677
Conference, July 16: GFP, D, XIII, 149–56; 606–8. Interviews with Koeppen, Bräutigam and Leibbrandt, 1971.
page 678
Hitler-Ribbentrop meeting: U. S. State Dept. interrogation of Steengracht, Sept. 4, 1945.
page 679
"A black day for the army!" Engel 110.
pages 679–80
Hitler-Mussolini meetings: Dollmann 191–92; Alfieri 159.
page 680
"In several weeks we will . . ." Zoller 160.
page 682
Table conversations: Interviews with Koeppen and Heim, 1971, 1974–75.
page 683
Sept. 17 conversation: HSC 58–60.
page 683
"They are brutes . . ." HSC 66.
pages 683–84
"In a few days a youth . . . preservation of the species," Ibid. 69–70.
page 684
"Before I became Chancellor . . ." Fabian von Schlabrendorff, *Offiziere gegen Hitler* (Zurich, 1946), 47–48; Halder diary, Aug. 4, 1941.
pages 684–85
Hitler speech: VB, Oct. 5, 1941; Stein 78–82.

page 685
"The city will be destroyed . . ." Koeppen notes, Oct. 9, 1941.
page 685
Smith account: Smith 86–88.
page 686
Goebbels conference: Boelcke 186.
page 686
Ribbentrop to Hesse: HH 145–46.
page 687
Supper conversation, Oct. 17: Koeppen notes; interview with Koeppen, 1975;
    HSC 91–93.
pages 687–88
Stalin speeches: Werth, *Russia,* 246, 248–49.
page 688
Oshima-Hitler meeting: Interview with Oshima, 1966.
page 689
Guderian account: Guderian 191–92.
page 689
Rundstedt-Hitler telegrams: U.S. interrogation of Rundstedt, 1945; Shirer,
    Rise, 861.
page 689
"I myself, for instance, am not . . ." Testimony of General August Winter at
    Nuremberg, June 8, 1946, 604.
page 690
"victory could no longer be achieved . . ." Percy Schramm 26–27.
page 691
"The United States and England will always . . ." Hillgruber, *Staatsmänner,*
    300ff.
page 692
Hassell comment: Hassell 208.
page 692
Hitler to Raeder: *Brassey's Naval Annual,* 232–33.
pages 692–93
Hitler speech: Prange 366.
page 693
Hitler to Huss: Huss 208–22.
pages 693–94
Ribbentrop-Oshima meeting: Interview with Oshima, 1966; intercepted mes-
    sage, Oshima to Tokyo, Nov. 29, 1941, ND, D-656.
page 694
Message to Oshima, Nov. 30, 1941: ND, 3598-PS.
page 694
Dietrich account: Dietrich, *Hitler,* 70–71.
page 694
Keitel account: Keitel 162.
page 694
Hitler to Hewel: Irving, *Hitler,* 354.
pages 694–95
Directive: HWD 107.
page 695
Hitler to Bormann: TAH 87–88.
page 695
Hitler-Ribbentrop meeting: TMWC 297–98; Shirer, *Rise,* 894.

page 696
Hitler to Reichstag: Prange 97, 367–77.
page 696
Warlimont-Jodl: Warlimont 208.
page 696
"Stand fast, not one step back!" Keitel 166.
pages 696–97
Brauchitsch-Keitel: Keitel 164.
page 697
Hitler-Halder: Halder 49.

Chapter Twenty-five. "AND HELL FOLLOWED WITH HIM"

page 701
"to make all necessary . . ." Göring to Heydrich, July 31, 1941, ND, PS 710.
pages 701–2
Höss account: IMT, XI, 398.
page 702
"but the first thing, above all . . ." HSC 91.
pages 702–3
"From the rostrum . . ." Ibid. 108–9, 111.
page 703
"I am now as before a Catholic . . ." Engel 31.
pages 703–4
Frank account: ND, PS-2233; IMT, XXIX, 498ff.
pages 704–5
Wannsee conference: Eichmann minutes, ND, NG 2586; Hilberg 264–65; ND, PS-709; Krausnick 82–87; Röhl 163; interviews with Leibbrandt and Hesse.
page 705
After conference: *Life*, Nov. 28, 1960, pp. 24, 101.
page 705
"One must act radically . . ." HSC 238.
pages 705–6
Hitler speech: Prange 83.
page 706
Fredborg comment: Fredborg 69.
page 706
Guderian-Hitler: Guderian 205–6.
page 706
Hitler to Speer and Milch: Irving, *Hitler*, 357; interview with Milch, 1971.
page 707
"As long as there . . ." HSC 257; Percy Schramm 28.
page 707
Hewel quote: HH 148.
page 707
Hitler to Speer: Speer, *Inside*, 195.
pages 707–8
Hitler to lieutenants: Interview with Richard Schulze, 1973; correspondence, 1975.

page 708
"I've always detested snow." HSC 309.
page 708
"Boys, you can't imagine . . ." Ibid. 327.
pages 708–9
Koeppen account: Interviews with Koeppen, 1971, 1975.
page 709
"My prophecy shall be fulfilled . . ." *Keesings Archiv der Gegenwart*, 1940, 5409.
page 709
Fritzsche account: IMT, XVII, 172–73.
page 709
Goebbels comment: *Goebbels Diaries*, 138.
page 710
Hitler speech: BBC Monitoring Report; ND, 1961-PS.
pages 710–11
Mussolini-Hitler meeting: Ciano 478–79.
page 711
Heydrich to Syrup: Interview with Syrup, 1971.
page 711
"He plays cat and mouse . . ." *Goebbels Diaries*, 88.
pages 711–12
Heydrich assassination: Jan Wiener, *The Assassination of Heydrich* (New York, 1969), 82–90; Höhne, *Order*, 494–95.
page 712
Schellenberg account: Schellenberg 294.
page 712
Merin quote: *Commentary*, Dec. 1958, 481–83.
page 712
Footnote: Charles Wighton, *Heydrich* (London, 1962), 270; Höhne, *Order*, 496.
page 713
Eichmann-Wisliceny: Wisliceny affidavit, Nov. 18, 1946; Levin 300.
page 713
"The occupied Eastern territories . . ." Himmler to Berger, July 28, 1942; ND, NO-626.
pages 713–14
Gerstein account: Friedländer, *Kurt Gerstein*, 104–13.
page 715
Tojo-Emperor: Toland, *Rising*, 476.
page 716
"If I listen to Halder . . ." Interview with Richard Schulze, 1972.
page 717
Hitler-Halder: Halder diary, Aug. 24, 1942; A. Heusinger, *Befehl im Widerstreit* (Tübingen, 1950), 200–1.
page 718
Hitler-Jodl: Jodl testimony at Nuremberg, June 3, 1946, 300–1; Warlimont 256–57; interviews with Warlimont, Heusinger and Wien, 1971.
pages 718–19
Keitel-Warlimont: Interview with Warlimont, 1971.
page 719
Hitler-Paulus: Goerlitz, *Paulus*, 159–60.

page 719
Hitler-Warlimont: Warlimont 258.
page 719
"He trusts none of his generals . . ." Engel 127–28.
pages 719–20
Hitler-Halder: Halder diary, Sept. 24, 1942; Keitel 184; correspondence with Halder, 1971; Shirer, *Rise*, 917–18.
page 720
Hitler-Zeitzler: Interview with Heusinger, 1971.
page 720
Zeitzler to officers: Warlimont 260.
pages 720–21
Sportpalast speech: *Keesings Archiv*, op. cit., 5657.
page 721
Song: Fredborg 129.
pages 721–22
Bräutigam memorandum: TMWC, XXV, 331–42, ND 294-PS; interview with Bräutigam, 1971.
page 722
Warlimont-Keitel: Interview with Warlimont, 1971; correspondence, 1975.
page 722
Jodl comment: "Answers to Questions Put to General Jodl," OCHM, MS ⅍A-914.
page 723
Hitler speech: BBC Monitoring Report.
page 723
"the God of war had now turned . . ." Percy Schramm 27.
page 723
"All I want to discuss . . ." J. von Ribbentrop, *Memoirs*, 169.
page 723
Hitler-Oshima: Interview with Oshima, 1966.
page 724
Gehlen report: Gehlen 59.
page 724
"repeatedly overestimated the enemy . . ." Percy Schramm 109.
page 724
"Führer himself completely unsure . . ." Ibid. 113.
page 725
"Absolute dismay . . ." G. K. Zhukov, *Memoirs of Marshal Zhukov* (New York, 1971), 409.
page 725
Paulus to Schmidt: Goerlitz, *Paulus*, 210.
page 725
Hitler to Paulus: Carell, *Hitler Moves*, 635.
page 726
Manstein to Paulus: Goerlitz, op. cit., 234; interview with Schmidt, 1971.
page 726
Paulus to Manstein: Goerlitz, op. cit., 236.
page 727
Conference, Dec. 12: Warlimont 292.
page 727
On breakout: Interview with Schmidt, 1971; correspondence, 1975.

page 727
Manstein-Paulus: Interview with Manstein, 1971; Goerlitz, op. cit., 277.
page 727
Manstein-Führer HQ: Ibid. 280.
page 728
Goebbels message and conference: Boelcke 312, 314–15.
page 728
Hube story: Carell, op. cit., 664; Goerlitz, op. cit., 260–61: interview with
    Schmidt, 1971.
page 728
"this fellow Göring, this fat . . ." HH 152.
page 729
Hitler-Zitzewitz: Carell, op. cit., 669; Goerlitz, op. cit., 264.
page 730
Paulus to Hitler: Jan. 29, 1943.
page 730
Paulus letter: Goerlitz, op. cit., 250.
page 730
Footnote: Interview with Hans Hitler, 1971; Maser, *Adolf Hitler,* 479;
    Svetlana Alliluyeva, *Twenty Letters to a Friend* (New York, 1967),
    161–63.
page 731
Zeitzler to Paulus: Carell, op. cit., 670.
page 731
Schmidt account: Interviews with Schmidt, 1971.
pages 731–32
Conference Feb. 1, 1943: Warlimont 300–6; Felix Gilbert 17–22.
page 732
De Gaulle quote: William Craig, *Enemy at the Gates* (New York, 1973)
    XV.

Chapter Twenty-six. THE FAMILY CIRCLE

page 734
"You don't have to get excited . . ." Unpublished memoirs of Gertraud
    (Humps) Junge; interview, 1971.
page 734
"After Stalingrad Hitler would not . . ." A. Zoller, *Hitler Privat* (Düsseldorf,
    1949), 44–45.
pages 734–35
Goebbels speech: *Josef Goebbels Reden,* II, 1939–45 (Düsseldorf, 1971),
    177–83.
page 735
Bormann letter: Bormann 6–7.
page 735
Goebbels speech: Holborn, *Republic,* 316.
pages 735–36
Göring-Goebbels: *Goebbels Diaries,* 266–69.
page 736
Milch-Hitler: Interviews with Milch, 1971; Irving, *Rise,* 202.
pages 736–37
Lochner account: *Always the Unexpected,* 294–95.
page 737
Schlabrendorff account: Interview with Schlabrendorff, 1963.

pages 737–38
Gerstdorff account: Interview with Gerstdorff, 1971; Gerstdorff correspondence, 1975; Peter Hoffmann, *Canadian Journal of History*, 1967.

pages 738–41
Gertraud Humps (Junge) account: Junge, *Memoirs*.

page 739
Footnote: Bormann 42–43.

page 741
"Either give up smoking or me." Interview with Herta Schneider, 1971.

page 742
"They seem like two invalids." A. Pozzi, *Come li ho visto Io* (Mondadori, 1947), 147–48.

page 742
"As a general rule . . ." Dostoevski, *The Brothers Karamazov* (Modern Library, New York), 5.

page 742
"But after the war . . ." HSC 306.

page 742
Traudl-Hitler: Junge, *Memoirs*; correspondence, 1975.

pages 742–43
Hitler-Henriette von Schirach: Schirach 187–88.

pages 743–44
Traudl account: Junge, *Memoirs*.

page 744
"If it be true today . . ." *Goebbels Diaries* 354–59.

pages 744–45
Hitler diet: Interview with Zabel, 1971.

page 745
Traudl account: Junge, *Memoirs*; correspondence, 1975.

page 746
On Citadel: Interviews with Manstein and Puttkamer, 1971; Guderian 246–47; Seaton 356; Gehlen 64–65.

pages 746–47
Hitler-Mussolini: *Hitler e Mussolini* 165–90; Alfieri 237–48.

pages 747–48
Two conferences: Warlimont 342–586; Felix Gilbert 39ff.

page 748
"Mussolini is much weaker . . ." Junge, *Memoirs*.

page 748
"At such a time one can't have a better adviser . . ." Felix Gilbert 44.

page 749
Goebbels in "blue funk": Diary of Wilfred von Oven, Aug. 4, 1943.

page 749
Galland account: Galland 163.

page 749
Hitler to Ribbentrop: HH 154–55; interview with Hesse, 1971.

pages 749–50
Hesse-Ribbentrop: HH 155–56.

pages 750–52
Kleist-Clauss negotiations: Kleist 145–52, 162–68; interviews, 1963, 1970–71; Vojtech Mastny, "Stalin and the Prospects of a Separate Peace," Dec. 1942, 1371, 1387.

pages 752–53
Hitler-Goebbels: *Goebbels Diaries* 435–37.
page 753
Hitler speech: Prange 384.
page 753
"I must admit that for a while . . ." Oven diary, Sept. 10, 1943.
pages 753–55
Skorzeny-Mussolini: Skorzeny, *Special Missions,* 70–90; interviews with Skor-
    zeny, 1956, 1963, 1971; correspondence, 1975.
pages 755–56
Hitler-Mussolini: F. Anfuso, *Da Palazzo Venezie al Lago di Garda* (Cappelli,
    1957), 326–27; Zoller 180; J. von Ribbentrop, *Memoirs,* 170–71.
page 756
Goebbels-Hitler: *Goebbels Diaries,* 477.
page 756
Kleist to Sweden: Kleist 169–70.
page 756
Japanese peace bid: Mastny, op. cit., 1384, 1388.

Chapter Twenty-seven. "AND WITH THE BEASTS OF THE EARTH"
pages 757–58
Lammers account: IMT, XI, 52–53.
page 758
Frank comment: Interview with G. M. Gilbert, 1972; Gilbert, *Nuremberg.*
page 758
"was necessary in the interests of Europe." Piotrowski 281–82.
page 758
"People are now clinging." Krausnick 371.
page 759
Hitler to Himmler: Ibid. 123.
page 759
Hitler to Bormann: TAH 57.
pages 759–60
Warsaw ghetto: Hilberg 320–26; Ringelblum 310, 326; Stroop Report, ND
    1061-PS.
page 760
Pius XII quote: Alexis Curvers, *Pie XII, Le Pape outragé* (Paris, 1964), 139.
pages 761–62
Morgen story: Interview, 1971.
page 762
Comments on Himmler: Höhne, *Order,* 30; interviews, Gudrun Himmler
    (1974), Wehser (1971).
page 763
Poem: Werner Angress and Bradley Smith, "Diaries of Heinrich Himmler's
    Early Years," *Journal of Modern History,* Sept. 1949, 223–24.
page 764
Footnote: Larry V. Thompson 54ff.
pages 763–66
On Himmler: Toland, *Last,* 132–33; interviews with Hausser, 1963, Sünder-
    mann (1970), Richard Schulze, Milch, Wehser, Grothmann (1971).
page 766
Höss quotes: Gilbert, *Nuremberg,* 230; Gilbert, *Psychology,* 255.

page 766
"The SS commander must be hard . . ." *Die Zeit,* June 25, 1965.
page 766
"If the motive is selfish . . ." Krausnick 315.
page 767
"I do not want to see . . . put an end to it," Smith and Peterson, 38, 89.
page 767
Himmler speech, Oct. 4, 1943: ND, 1919-PS.
page 768
Himmler speech, Oct. 6, 1943: Smith and Peterson 162ff.; Goldhagen 44–48.
page 769
Kleist account: Kleist 126–28; interview, 1971.
page 770
"All that rubbish . . ." *Goebbels Diaries,* 279.
page 771
Hitler's handwritten notes: Müllern-Schönhausen 220–24.
pages 771–72
Himmler speech, Jan. 26, 1934: Interview with Gerstdorff, 1971; Kunrat von
    Hammerstein, *Spaehtrupp* (Stuttgart, 1963), 192–93; Smith and Peterson
    201.
page 772
Himmler speech to Navy at Weimar, Dec. 16, 1943: Ibid. 201.
page 772
Himmler speech to generals at Sonthofen, May 24, 1944: Ibid. 202.
pages 772–74
Morgen story: Interview, 1971; Morgen testimony at Nuremberg, Aug. 7–8,
    1946, 488–515.

Chapter Twenty-eight. THE ARMY BOMB PLOT

pages 777–78
Jodl speech: Shirer, *End,* 279–86.
pages 778–79
Hitler to military leaders: Assmann, op. cit.; interview with Manstein, 1971.
pages 779–80
Junge account: Junge, *Memoirs.*
page 780
Reitsch account: Reitsch 212.
page 780
Hitler on painting: Hoffmann transcript for Mar. 3, 1944, from Heinrich
    Heim.
pages 780–81
Horthy story: Horthy 213–16; Warlimont 412–13.
page 781
Gehlen report: Gehlen 96.
pages 781–82
On air raids: Junge, *Memoirs.*
page 782
It had to happen: Interview with Günsche, 1971.
pages 782–83
Speer account: Speer, *Inside,* 346–47.

page 782
Footnote: Percy Schramm 27.
page 783
"It will decide the issue . . . an end by political means." Interview of
    Warlimont by Major Kenneth Hechler, July 19, 1945, 5.
page 783
"If the invasion succeeds . . ." Interview with Heusinger, 1971.
pages 783–84
Rommel account: Carell, *Invasion*, 14–16.
page 785
"Now we can give them . . ." Linge ✳34; interview with Günsche, 1971.
page 785
Hitler conference: Interview with Warlimont, 1971; Warlimont 427.
page 785
"Sounds off on culture . . ." Oven diary, June 6, 1944.
page 786
Hassell comment: Hassell 349–50.
page 786
Hitler to Göring: Irving, *Rise*, 285.
page 787
Hitler near Soissons: Hans Speidel, *Invasion* (Chicago, 1950), 93; Shirer, *Rise*,
    1039–41: Speer, *Inside*, 356; OCMH, Speidel monograph.
page 788
Dietl story: Assmann, op. cit.
page 788
Junge-Hitler: Junge, *Memoirs*.
page 789
Hitler at Platterhof: Speer, *Inside*, 359–61.
page 789
"I, too, know . . ." Speidel monograph, op. cit.
page 789
Keitel-Rundstedt: Chester Wilmot, *The Struggle for Europe* (London, 1952),
    347.
page 791
"any such coup d'état . . ." Interview with Manstein, 1971.
page 791
"I believe it is my duty . . ." Desmond Young, *Rommel—The Desert Fox*
    (New York, 1950), 223–24.
page 791
"You are young . . ." Speidel, *Invasion*, op. cit., 71.
page 792
Thiersch account: Zeller 286.
page 794
Steiner account: Interview with Steiner, 1963; Höhne, *Order*, 513.
page 794
Langbehn story: Rainer Hildebrandt, *Wir sind die Letzten* (Berlin, 1950),
    135–37; Allen Dulles, *Germany's Underground*, 153–63; Douglas-Hamil-
    ton 219–23.
pages 794–95
Wulff account: Wulff 97.
page 795
Hitler to Schröder: Zoller 207–8.

page 796
Freyend account: *Walküre*, a TV special produced by Bavaria Atelier, Munich, and based on interviews with survivors; Zeller 302–3.

pages 796–97
Heusinger account: Interview, 1971.

page 797
Puttkamer account: Interview, 1973. Günsche account: Interview, 1971.

page 798
Fellgiebel account: Zeller 345–48; *Walküre*, op. cit.

pages 798–99
Stauffenberg escape: Ibid.; Zeller 304, 344.

page 799
Hitler-Hasselbach: Interview with Hasselbach, 1971.

page 799
Hitler-secretaries: Junge, *Memoirs*.

page 799
Fellgiebel account: Zeller 346–48; Peter Hoffmann article on July 20 plot.

page 800
Hitler-Schröder: Zoller 206–7.

pages 800–1
Hitler-Mussolini: Dollmann 324; interview with Dollmann, 1971; Schmidt 275–77; *Walküre*, op. cit.; Zeller 337–38.

pages 802–3
Keitel-Fromm: Zeller 306; Fabian von Schlabrendorff, *They Almost Killed Hitler* (New York, 1947).

pages 803–4
Stauffenberg at the Bendlerstrasse: Zeller 307–9; *Walküre*, op. cit.

page 804
Remer account: Interview, 1971.

pages 804–5
Hagen story: *Walküre*, op. cit.; Zeller 355; Bramsted 338–39.

pages 805–6
Remer story: Interviews with Remer, 1971; Zeller 339–41, 355–56; Bramsted 339–40; *Walküre*, op. cit.; Speer, *Playboy*, 193; Oven diary, July 20, 1944.

page 807
Witzleben message: *Brassey* 408

page 807
Kluge story: OCMH, MS#B-272, monograph by Günther Blumentritt, "20 July 1944,"; interview with Blumentritt, 1957.

page 807
Bormann message: Bormann 61–62.

page 808
Skorzeny account: Interview, 1971.

page 809
Fromm-Beck: Zeller 315–18; Höpner testimony, TMWC XXXIII, 299–530.

page 810
Teleprint message: Zeller 319.

page 810
Fromm-Remer: Interview with Remer, 1971.

page 810
Skorzeny account: *Special Missions*, 117–18; interview, 1971.

pages 810–11
Himmler at Goebbels': Zeller 339; interviews with Remer, 1971.
page 811
Fellgiebel to aide: Zeller 349.
page 811
Hitler quotes: Junge, *Memoirs*; interview with Christian, 1971.
page 811
Hitler and Göring speeches: Zeller 342–43.
page 812
Stülpnagel-Abetz: Wilhelm von Schramm, *Der 20 July in Paris* (Bad Wörishofen, 1953), 105; interview with Schramm, 1971.
page 812
Goebbels quotes: Oven diary, July 21, 1944.
page 813
Bormann instructions: Bormann 64–65.
pages 813–14
Hitler-Assmann-Puttkamer: Interview with Puttkamer; Assmann, op. cit.
page 814
Giesing account: Interview, 1971; Giesing unpublished *Diary*.
page 814
Hitler-Eva Braun correspondence: Gun, *Eva Braun*, 179–80.
page 814
Hitler quotes: Junge, *Memoirs*; Zoller 193; *Walküre*, op. cit.
page 815
Hitler-Eicken: NA Film, ML/125, 131; U.S. interrogation of Eicken, Sept. 30, 1945.
page 816
Guderian order of the day: Shirer, *Rise*, 1080–81.
page 817
Hitler-Giesing: Giesing *Diary*; interview with Giesing, 1971.
page 817
Hitler to Gauleiters: Interview with Florian, 1971.
pages 817–18
"The Stauffenberg family will be exterminated . . ." *Vierteljahreshefte für Zeitgeschichte*, Vol. 4, 1953, 363–94.
page 818
Trial and executions: Zeller 371–75; IMT, XXXIII, 2999, for testimony of Peter Vossen, shorthand secretary at trial; Shirer, *Rise*, 1070.
page 818
On film of executions: Speer, *Playboy*, 193; interview with Below, 1971; correspondence with Hasselbach, 1975.
pages 818–19
Guderian-Hitler argument: Guderian 296.
page 819
Kluge story: Wilhelm Schramm 189–90, 207–8; Carell, *Invasion*, 260; Percy Schramm 167–68.
page 820
Morgen account: Interview with Morgen, 1971.
pages 820–21
Hitler to Keitel: Felix Gilbert 105–6; Warlimont 450–55.
pages 821–22
Junge account: *Memoirs*.

page 822
Giesing account: *Diary.*

Chapter Twenty-nine. THE BATTLE OF THE BULGE

page 823
Directive: HWD 197.
pages 823–24
Hitler special conference: OCMH, A-862, "The Preparations for the German Offensive in the Ardennes" by Percy Schramm; interview with Schramm, 1957.
page 824
Footnote: Interview with Frau Schmundt, 1971.
pages 824–25
Giesing account: *Diary*; cardiograms in "Hitler as Seen by His Doctors," NA USFET, OI/CIR/4.
page 825
Junge comment: *Memoirs.*
page 826
Bormann-Brandt rivalry: Bormann 79–80; Giesing *Diary.*
pages 826–27
Giesing-Hitler: Giesing *Diary*; interview, 1971.
page 827
Dr. von Hasselbach does not believe that Giesing gave Hitler the double cocaine dose (correspondence, 1975).
pages 827–28
Giesing account: *Diary*; interview, 1971.
pages 828–29
Rommel story: Speidel, op. cit., 152; Desmond Young, op. cit., 251–52; Milton Schulman, *Defeat in the West* (New York, 1948), 138–39; Zeller 378–79; Shirer, *Rise*, 1077–79.
pages 829–30
Skorzeny account: Interviews with Skorzeny, 1957, 1963, 1971.
page 830
Model quote: Interview with Percy Schramm, 1957. Hitler-Rundstedt: Schramm, "Preparations," op. cit.
pages 831–32
Hitler-Junge: Junge, *Memoirs.*
pages 832–33
Dec. 11 conference: Interviews with Manteuffel, Blumentritt and Percy Schramm, 1957; OCMH, MS﹟B-151, Manteuffel; Percy Schramm, op. cit.
page 834
Bradley-Eisenhower: Dwight Eisenhower, *Crusade in Europe* (Garden City, 1948), 350; interview with Bradley, 1957.
pages 834–35
Balck-Hitler: Toland, *Battle*, 51; interview with Balck, 1963.
page 836
Manteuffel-Jodl: Interview with Manteuffel, 1957.
page 837
Jodl-Hitler: OCMH, A858, "The Course of Events of the German Offensive in the Ardennes" by Percy Schramm.

page 837
Hitler-Göring: Frau Göring account in Ziegler.
page 838
Special meeting: Felix Gilbert 158–74.
pages 838–39
Military conference: Percy Schramm, op. cit.; interview with Blumentritt, 1957.
page 839
Hitler-Thomale: Warlimont 495–96.
page 839
At the Goebbels': Interview with Ruck, 1971.
page 840
Churchill-Eisenhower: Churchill, *Triumph and Tragedy* (Bantam, New York, 1962), 240–41.
page 841
Hitler-Guderian; Guderian 315; interview with Praun, 1971.
page 842
Hitler-Junge: Junge, *Memoirs.*

Chapter Thirty. "THIS TIME WE MUST NOT SURRENDER FIVE
                                    MINUTES BEFORE MIDNIGHT"

page 846
Hitler speech: Ausubel 46.
page 846
Bormann letter: Bormann 164.
pages 846–47
Hitler lecture: Guderian 337; interviews in 1963 with two SS officers who were present but wish to remain anonymous.
page 847
Schlabrendorff account: Interview, 1963.
pages 847–48
Bormann letter: Bormann 168–69.
page 848
Hitler to Bormann: TAH 33–34; 38–41.
page 848
Hitler-Giesler: Interview with Giesler, 1971.
page 849
Feb. 13 conference: Interviews with Generals Wenck and Thomale, and Major Bernd Freytag von Loringhoven, 1963; Guderian 342–44.
page 849
Hitler to Bormann: TAH 50–57.
pages 849–50
Giesing-Hitler: Giesing *Diary;* interview with Giesing, 1971.
page 850
Goebbels comment: Rudolf Semmler, *Goebbels: The Man Next to Hitler* (London, 1947).
pages 850–51
Kleist account: Kleist, 184–90; interviews with Kleist, 1963, 1970.
page 851
The account of Kersten's achievements in his own book is unreliable. For instance, his claim to have persuaded Himmler to rescind Hitler's orders to deport masses of Dutch civilians was disproved in 1972 by the eminent

Dutch historian, Professor Lou de Jong. He discovered that Kersten had forged four documents purporting to authenticate the act that won him Holland's highest award and a place in Dutch schoolbooks as a national hero.

pages 851–52
Hesse-Ribbentrop: HH 194–303; interview with Hesse, 1971.

pages 852–53
Bernadotte account: Folke Bernadotte, *The Curtain Falls* (New York, 1945), 25–61; interview with Estelle Bernadotte, 1963.

pages 853–54
Kleist-Ribbentrop: Kleist 191–92; interview with Kleist, 1970.

pages 854–55
Hesse account: HH 202–15; interview with Hesse, 1971. After checking this section of his story, Dr. Hesse wrote in March 1975: "I was forced to give up my 'Stockholm Mission' in consequence of an indiscretion in the Swedish press. . . . It pretended that I had sought out the British Embassy in Stockholm but that the British envoy had refused to even speak to me. This was entirely untrue. I spoke to no British person in Stockholm. The indiscretion, in fact, was initiated by no other person than Schellenberg. But I found this out only years after the publication of my book through Dr. Kleist. Schellenberg told Kleist that he and Himmler could not allow Ribbentrop to conduct negotiations in behalf of the Jews, nor peace feelers; he felt it therefore necessary to torpedo my negotiations in Stockholm by a calculated indiscretion. But they never intended to harm me personally. This explains why Schellenberg tried to take up the negotiations at the very end of the war—unsuccessfully, of course—and, what is more important—why Himmler *did not rescind* the order to stop the killing of the Jews. Thus it came that approximately 3 million Jews fell *alive* (*still alive*) into the hands of the victorious Russians and why later on approximately 2 millions of Jews managed to emigrate to Israel."

page 855
Hitler to Schröder: Zoller 230–31.

page 855
Hitler to Gauleiters: Interviews with Florian, Jordan and Scheel, 1971.

page 856
Kempka-Hitler: Interview with Kempka, 1971.

pages 856–57
Speer account: Speer, *Inside*, 436–37, 440.

page 857
"If I ever lay hands . . ." Boldt 84.

pages 857–58
March 28 conference: Guderian 356–57; interviews with Puttkamer (1971), Freytag von Loringhoven, and Generals Thomale and Busse (1963).

pages 858–59
Hitler to Bormann: TAH 104–8.

page 859
Operation Sunrise: Interviews with Generals Wolff, Airey and Lemnitzer, Allen Dulles, Gero von Gaevernitz, 1963–64.

page 860
Stalin and Roosevelt messages: *Correspondence Between the Chairman of the Council of Ministers of the U.S.S.R. and the Presidents of the U.S.A. and the Prime Ministers of Great Britain during the Great Patriotic War of 1941–45*, II, 206–10.

page 860
Hitler-Carlyle story: Schwerin von Krosigk's diary (Shirer, *End*, 193). Carlyle
    is misquoted; the Czarina died on Jan. 5, 1762.
page 860
Hanussen's horoscope of Jan. 1, 1933, it will be recalled, predicted that Hitler
    would rise to power in thirty days and enjoy tremendous successes until
    the "union of the three" was broken. At this point his work would disap-
    pear during the spring of 1945 "in smoke and flames." Although Hitler
    often ridiculed astrology to his family circle, he had shown a genuine inter-
    est not only in Hanussen's horoscope but in that of Frau Ebertin in 1923.
page 860
Goebbels-Busse: Interview with Busse, 1963.
pages 860–61
Goebbels quotes: Semmler, op. cit., 192ff.
page 861
Ribbentrop quote: HH 218–19.
page 861
Goebbels to Busse: Busse interview, 1963.
page 861
Hitler proclamation: Max Domarus, *Hitler: Reden und Proklamationen*
    (Würzberg, 1962–63), 2223–24.
page 862
"Now, there's a beautiful woman!" Oven diary, Apr. 18, 1945.
pages 862–63
Rudel-Hitler: Rudel 217–20; interview, 1963.
page 863
Masur as substitute: "I was prevented from leaving Sweden for several
    reasons," Storch wrote the author in 1965. "Firstly I did not receive in the
    last minute the Swedish passport, but this was not the main reason.
    Secondly, Kleist had learnt that I was to go and, therefore, I did not want
    to leave Stockholm. Thirdly, we had, in fact, already carried through our
    aims of delivering concentration camps and transferring 10,000 Jews to
    Sweden. The only motive was to prevent Kaltenbrunner from counter-
    acting, as he had done in Buchenwald. . . . As I was prevented from
    going, I chose Masur in the last minute. I preferred him to the others be-
    cause he had a moustache and looked older than the others. But, unfortu-
    nately, Masur was not familiar with our negotiations and, in view of the
    short notice (2 hours), I could not tell him about them."
page 863
Himmler-Schwerin von Krosigk: Interview with Schwerin von Krosigk, 1963.

Chapter Thirty-one. FIVE MINUTES PAST MIDNIGHT

page 864
Hitler-Keitel: Keitel 197.
page 865
"I must force a decision . . ." Junge, *Memoirs*.
page 865
Hitler to secretaries: Zoller 247–48.
page 865
Footnote: New York *Times*, Apr. 21, 1945.

pages 865–66
Himmler-Masur: Norbert Masur, *En Jood talar med Himmler* (Stockholm, 1946); *The Memoirs of Doctor Felix Kersten* (Garden City, 1947), 284–86; Schellenberg 385–86.
pages 866–67
Himmler-Schellenberg: Schellenberg 387.
page 867
Goebbels to aides: Oven diary, Apr. 21, 1945; Semmler, op. cit.
page 868
Hitler to Steiner: Interview with Steiner, 1963; Cornelius Ryan, *The Last Battle* (New York, 1966), 426.
page 868
Bormann story: CIC Document 03649, 12 Oct. 1945, Carlisle Barracks.
pages 868–69
Hitler collapse: Trevor-Roper 117–19; interview with Freytag von Loringhoven, 1963; Junge, *Memoirs.*
page 869
Goebbels family: Semmler, op. cit.; Trevor-Roper 120.
pages 869–70
Hitler to Keitel: Keitel 201.
page 870
"I should already . . ." Memorandum dictated by Jodl to his defense counsel's wife in 1946; quoted in Percy Schramm 204.
page 870
Hitler to Keitel: Keitel 202; *Generalfeldmarschall Keitel, Verbrecher oder Offizier?* edited by Walter Görlitz (Göttingen, 1961).
page 870
"The Army has betrayed me . . ." Junge, *Memoirs.*
pages 870–72
Koller story: Koller diary, *Die Letze Monate* (Mannheim, 1949); Trevor-Roper 128–31.
page 872
Hitler's dismissal of Göring: Trevor-Roper 138–39; Toland, *Last,* 431–32.
page 872
Keitel account: Keitel 206; *Generalfeldmarschall Keitel,* op. cit.; Toland, *Last,* 432.
page 872
Eva to Traudl: Junge, *Memoirs.*
page 872
Eva letter to Herta: Gun, *Eva Braun,* 209–10; interview with Herta Schneider, 1971.
pages 872–73
Eva letter to sister: CIC, Fegelein File, inclosure 18, Carlisle Barracks.
page 873
Himmler-Bernadotte: Bernadotte 106–14.
page 873
Apr. 24 conference: Interview with Freytag von Loringhoven, 1963; Boldt 166–67.
pages 873–74
Goebbels proclamation: *Drahtloser Dienst* (Nord), Apr. 24, 1945, BBC monitoring.

page 875
Hitler quotes: *Der Spiegel*, Jan. 1966.
pages 875–76
Reitsch-Greim story: Reitsch 229; U.S. interrogation of Reitsch, Oct. 8, 1945, "The Last Days in Hitler's Air Raid Shelter," Ref. AIU/IS/1.
page 876
Wenck account: Interview with Wenck, 1963.
pages 876–77
Noon conference: *Der Spiegel*, op. cit.
page 877
"You, who stayed here . . ." Interview with Freytag von Loringhoven, 1963; Boldt 183–84.
page 877
Reitsch account: Reitsch 229; Reitsch interrogation, op. cit.
page 878
Hitler quotes: *Der Spiegel*, op. cit.
page 878
Naumann account: Interview, 1971.
page 879
Wenck message: Interview, 1963.
page 879
Mussolini story: F. Bandini, *Le Ultime Ore di Mussolini* 95 (Suger ed., 1959); Deakin 814–17; Toland, *Last*, 475–513.
page 880
"Nine months ago . . . Your health, my friend!" Interview with Freytag von Loringhoven, 1963.
page 880
Frau Goebbels letter: Manvell, *Dr. Goebbels*, 272–73.
page 881
Bormann radiogram: CIC, Bormann file ✗03649, Carlisle Barracks.
page 881
Evening conference: Weidling Diary.
page 882
Reitsch account: Reitsch interrogation, op. cit.
pages 882–83
Hitler-Junge: Junge, *Memoirs*. Text of Hitler's two wills: ND 3569-PS; English translation, Stein 83–87.
page 884
Junge-Goebbels: Junge, *Memoirs*.
page 885
Frau Hitler-Junge: Junge, *Memoirs*.
page 886
"I will not fall into the hands . . ." Ibid.
page 886
Weidling-Hitler: Weidling diary.
page 887
Junge account: Junge, *Memoirs*.
page 887
Hitler-Günsche: Interview with Günsche, 1963.
pages 887–88
Günsche-Kempka: Interviews with Günsche and Kempka, 1963.
page 888
Baur-Hitler: Baur chapter in Ziegler; interview with Baur, 1970.

pages 888–90
Death of Hitler and Eva: Junge, *Memoirs*; interviews with Kempka and Günsche, 1963, 1971.
pages 890–91
Poem: Schirach 192.

Epilogue

page 892
"safe and well in Argentina," CIC, Fegelein File, interrogation, Carlisle Barracks.
page 893
Bezymenski quotes: Bezymenski 66.
page 893
Dr. Soggnaes account: Correspondence, 1973.
page 893
"Children, don't be afraid . . ." Bezymenski 63.
pages 893–94
Kempka account: Interview, 1971.
page 894
Naumann account: Interview, 1971.
page 894
Dr. Soggnaes account: Correspondence, 1975.
page 894
Dönitz to Himmler: Interview with Dönitz, 1963.
page 895
Schwerin von Krosigk to Himmler: Interview with Schwerin von Krosigk, 1963.
page 895
Grothmann account: Interview with Grothmann, 1971.
page 895
Göring quote: Gilbert, *Psychology*, 109–10.
page 896
Ribbentrop quote: Gilbert, *Nuremberg*, 260.
page 896
Keitel quotes: Andrus 195–96; Gilbert, *Nuremberg*, 300.
pages 896–97
Günsche-Schulze: Interviews with Richard and Monika Schulze-Kossens, 1973.

Index

ABOUT THE AUTHOR

JOHN TOLAND was born in La Crosse, Wisconsin, in 1912 and educated at Exeter and Williams College. He served in the Army during World War II. He is the author of two novels and ten works of nonfiction including *Infamy: Pearl Harbor and Its Aftermath*, the 1971 Pulitzer-prize winner *The Rising Sun: The Decline and Fall of the Japanese Empire, 1936–1945*, and, most recently, *In Mortal Combat: Korea 1950–1953*. Toland lives with his wife in Danbury, Connecticut.